D1032850

ELECTORAL COLLEGE VOTES IN THE 2008 ELECTION

THE UNITED STATES
A political map showing the number of electoral votes per state

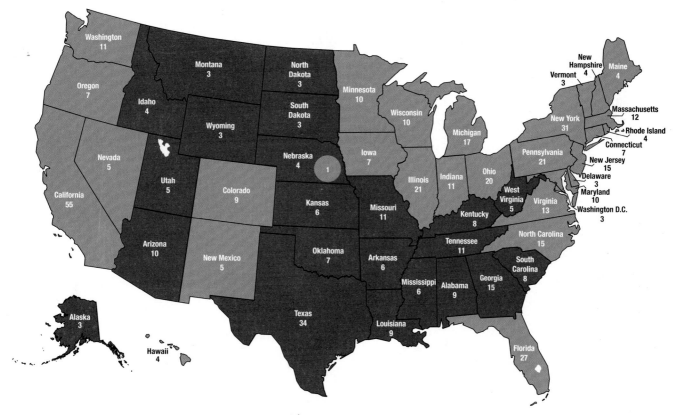

A political map with states drawn in proportion to the number of electoral votes

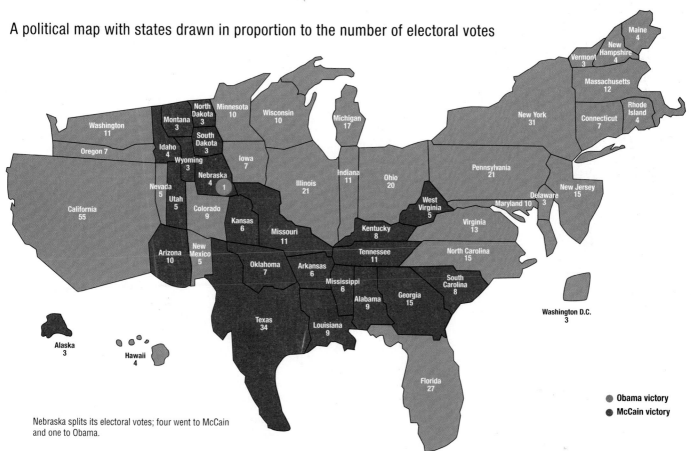

Nebraska splits its electoral votes; four went to McCain and one to Obama.

Obama victory
McCain victory

American GOVERNMENT

ROOTS AND REFORM

Tenth Edition

AP* Edition

Karen O'Connor

Jonathan N. Helfat Distinguished Professor of Political Science
American University

Larry J. Sabato

University Professor and Robert Kent Gooch Professor of Politics
University of Virginia

Longman
New York San Francisco Boston
London Toronto Sydney Tokyo Singapore Madrid
Mexico City Munich Paris Cape Town Hong Kong Montreal

Editor-in-Chief: Eric Stano
Assistant Development Manager: David B. Kear
Development Editor: Melissa Mashburn
Associate Development Editor: Donna Garnier
Marketing Manager: Lindsey Prudhomme
Production Manager: Eric Jorgensen
Project Coordination, Text Design, and Electronic Page Makeup: Electronic Publishing Services Inc., NYC
Senior Cover Design Manager: Nancy Danahy
Cover Designer: Bernadette Skok
Cover Photo: Eric L. Wheater/Lonely Planet Images
Photo Researcher: Jody Potter
Image Permission Coordination: Frances Toepfer
Senior Manufacturing Buyer: Alfred C. Dorsey
Printer and Binder: RR Donnelley & Sons Company
Cover Printer: Lehigh/Phoenix Color Corporation

For permission to use copyrighted material, grateful acknowledgment is made to the copyright holders acknowledged throughout the book, which are hereby made part of this copyright page.

Chapter opening image credits: p. 2, The Granger Collection; p. 3, Eric L. Wheater/Lonely Planet Images; p. 30, Joseph Sohm/Visions of America/Corbis; p. 31, Michael Ventura/Alamy; p. 94, Bettmann/Corbis; p. 95, Susan Walsh/AP/Wide World Photos; p. 122, AP/Wide World Photos; p. 123, Elaine Thompson/AP/Wide World Photos; p. 152, The Advertising Archives; p. 153, Kevin Clark/The Washington Post; p. 192, Flip Schulke/Corbis; p 193, Chip Somedevilla/Getty Images; p. 234, The Granger Collection; p. 235, Doug Mills/The New York Times/Redux Pictures; p. 272, George Eastman House/Getty Images; p. 273, Dennis Brack; p. 306, Hulton Archive/Getty Images; p. 307, Ron Edmonds/AP/Wide World Photos; p. 376, W. Eugene Smith/Time Life Pictures/Getty Images; p. 377, Jeff Haynes/Reuters/Landov; p. 404, Bettmann/Corbis; p. 405, Jae C. Hong/AP/Wide World Photos; p. 444, The Granger Collection; p. 445, Win McNamee/Getty Images; p. 492, Bettmann/Corbis; p. 493, Jae C. Hong/AP/Wide World Photos; p. 530, Bettmann/Corbis; p. 531, Damir Sagolj/Reuters/Landov; p. 566, U.S. District Court/AP Wide World Photos; p. 596, Bettmann/Corbis; p. 597, Purdy/Sipa Press; p. 636, Richard B. Levine/Newscom; p. 637, Joshua Roberts/Bloomberg News/Landov; p. 670, K.J. Historical/Corbis; p. 671, Chip Somodevilla/Getty Images.

Library of Congress Cataloging-in-Publication Data
O'Connor, Karen, 1952–
American government AP edition / Karen O'Connor, Larry Sabato. —10th ed.
    p. cm.
Includes bibliographical references and index.
ISBN 978-0-13-715162-2 (hardcover: alk. paper) 1. United States—
Politics and government. I. Sabato, Larry. II. Title.
JK276.022 2010
320.473--dc22
                                                              2008052696

Copyright © 2009 by Pearson Education, Inc.

All rights reserved. No part of this publication may be reproduced, stored in a retrieval system, or transmitted, in any form or by any means, electronic, mechanical, photocopying, recording, or otherwise, without the prior written permission of the publisher. Printed in the United States.

*AP and Advanced Placement Program are registered trademarks of the College Board, which was not included in the production of, and does not endorse, this product.

1 2 3 4 5 6 7 8 9 10—DOW—12 11 10 09

**Longman
is an imprint of**

www.PearsonSchool.com/Advanced

ISBN-13: 978-0-13-715162-2 (AP* edition)
ISBN-10: 0-13-715162-4
ISBN-13: 978-0-205-65222-8 (college edition)
ISBN-10: 0-205-65222-0

To Meghan,
who grew up with this book

Karen O'Connor

To my Government 101 students
over the years, who all know that
"politics is a good thing"

Larry J. Sabato

Brief Contents

Detailed Contents

PART 2

INSTITUTIONS OF GOVERNMENT

CHAPTER 7   Congress   234

Roots of the Legislative Branch of Government   236

CHAPTER 8   The Presidency   272

Roots of the Office of President of the United States   275

PART 3

POLITICAL BEHAVIOR

CHAPTER 11   Political Socialization and Public Opinion   376

CHAPTER 12   Political Parties   404

PART 4
PUBLIC POLICY

Preface

We believe that one cannot fully understand the actions, issues, and policy decisions facing the U.S. government, its constituent states, or "the people" unless these issues are examined from the perspective of how they have evolved over time. Consequently, in *American Government* we try to examine how the United States is governed today by looking not just at present structures and behavior but also at the *Framers' intentions and how they have been implemented and adapted over the years*. For example, we believe that it is critical to an understanding of the role of political parties in the United States to understand the Framers' fears of factionalism, how parties evolved, and when and why realignments in party identification occurred.

To understand all levels of American government, AP* students must appreciate its constitutional underpinnings. Our text includes a full, *annotated* Constitution of the United States and a boxed feature, "The Living Constitution," to ensure that AP* students understand and appreciate the role of the Constitution in American government and their everyday lives.

In addition to the constitutional and historical origins of American government, we explore issues that the Framers could never have envisioned, and how the basic institutions of government have changed in responding to these new demands. For instance, no one more than two centuries ago could have foreseen election campaigns in an age when nearly all American homes contain television sets, and the Internet allows instant access to information from across the nation and around the globe. Moreover, citizen demands and expectations routinely force government reforms, making an understanding of the dynamics of change essential for introductory students.

Our overriding concern is that AP* students understand their government as it exists today, so that they may become better citizens and make better choices. Careful updating in every edition to reflect the significant events that affect government and citizens alike is crucial to insuring a book that accurately communicates where the United States is as a nation. We believe that by providing AP* students with information about government, and by explaining why it is important and why their participation counts, AP* students will come to see that politics can be a good thing.

What's Changed in This Edition?

Chapter 1 of *American Government,* Tenth Edition, AP* Edition, provides updated demographic data, an expanded section on religious faith and religious freedom, an expanded discussion of the immigration policy debate, and expanded coverage of symbolic expressions of American political culture. **Chapter 2** includes a new "Key Events Leading to American Independence" timeline and a new table comparing the Articles of Confederation to the Constitution. **Chapter 3** includes an expanded discussion of federalism and the Roberts Court. A new "Living Constitution" box on the full faith and credit clause references the legalization of same-sex marriage in Connecticut and Massachusetts. **Chapter 4**'s new opening vignette is devoted to state-level outcomes in the 2008 elections with an emphasis on gubernatorial races and it discusses how party control of state government can have national ramifications. The "Toward Reform" section discusses tightening state and local budgets in the wake of foreclosures and a foundering economy. **Chapter 5**'s new opening vignette discusses the Supreme Court's ruling in *District of Columbia* v. *Heller*. This chapter also features expanded coverage of the debate over the death penalty, including a new "Join the Debate" box devoted to this topic. **Chapter 6** features expanded and updated coverage of civil rights issues affecting Hispanic Americans, including a new timeline of important moments in Latino/a and Hispanic American rights. The chapter also includes a new section on civil rights issues affecting Asian Americans. Updated discussions of same-sex marriage, pay equity legislation, and living wage campaigns on campus are also included. **Chapter 7** includes complete coverage of the outcome of the 2008 congressional elections and the makeup of the 111th Congress; the chapter also features a discussion of increased congressional oversight of the Bush administration during the 110th Congress. **Chapter 8** considers the impact of President George W. Bush's two terms in office and discusses the 2008 presidential election in the context of the Bush legacy. The "Politics Now" feature examines the debate over the constitutionality of presidential signing statements. The section on executive orders has also been expanded. **Chapter 9** includes an expanded and updated discussion of the use of private contractors to perform jobs formerly done by government employees. **Chapter 10** features a new opening vignette on the Roberts Court and offers updates on the Supreme Court's 2007–2008 term and models of judicial decision making. **Chapter 11**'s new opening vignette discusses the use of entrance polls in the 2008 Iowa caucuses and the impact of cell phones on polling practices. Updated public opinion data and examples related to the 2008 election cycle have been included throughout the chapter. **Chapter 12** features a new opening vignette on the 2008 national party conventions and differences in the Democratic and Republican platforms. The chapter also includes an updated and expanded discussion on the impact of recent debates over immigration on party affiliation decisions made by voters. **Chapter 13** has been heavily updated to account for the 2008 presidential and congressional elections. A new opening vignette discusses the party nomination battle in 2008. The outcomes of the 2008 congressional elections are discussed in detail. The chapter also discusses the

record levels of turnout in the 2008 presidential primaries and turnout for the election. A new section discusses the impact of group membership on voter turnout. **Chapter 14** features a narrative of the history-making 2008 presidential election and discusses the significant impact of the Internet on fundraising and political participation in 2008. A new opening vignette discusses the outcome of the presidential race. **Chapter 15** includes a new opening vignette on media coverage of vice presidential nominee Governor Sarah Palin of Alaska. Discussions of media trends, especially narrowcasting and consolidation, have been updated. The impact of the new media on the 2008 elections is also discussed in detail. **Chapter 16** includes streamlined coverage of interest group theory and discusses lobbying reform efforts in Congress, including the passage of the Honest Leadership and Open Government Act of 2007. **Chapter 17** features a new opening vignette on health care reform and the 2008 presidential election and includes new sections on energy and environmental policy. **Chapter 18** begins with a new opening vignette on the Bush administration's economic policies and efforts in 2008 to combat economic woes. The chapter also includes new sections on the economic ramifications of the wars in Iraq and Afghanistan, the subprime mortgage crisis and the ensuing financial credit crisis. **Chapter 19** includes updated information on controversies related to the war on terrorism and the wars in Iraq and Afghanistan.

AP* Features

The AP* Edition of *American Government*, Tenth Edition, includes additional features that will be helpful to AP* students. The **AP* Correlation Guide** that follows the Preface includes a detailed list of the Government and Politics: United States AP* topics correlated to *American Government*. By following the page references in the second column, students can find the discussion of each of the six major topic areas, and their more-specific details, in the pages of *American Government*. This AP* Correlation Guide will help students study and review for exams.

The AP* Edition also includes for each chapter a selection of multiple-choice and free-response questions. These practice drills replicate actual AP* exam questions, tied specifically to each chapter of *American Government*. To further guide students, answers are included for the multiple-choice questions and sample answers are provided for free-response questions, with explanations for the answers' scoring. The AP* exam questions and answers are at the back of the book.

AP* Correlation Guide

Government and Politics: United States AP* Topics Correlated to *American Government: Roots and Reform,* Tenth Edition, AP* Edition

Historical Perspective

Every chapter uses history to serve three purposes: first, to show how institutions and processes have evolved to their present states; second, to provide some of the color that makes information memorable; and third, to provide AP* students with a more thorough appreciation that our government was born amid burning issues of representation and power, issues that continue to smolder today. A richer historical texture helps to explain the present.

NEW! **Roots of** and **Toward Reform**
sections highlight the text's emphasis on the importance of the history of American government, as well as the dynamic cycle of reassessment and reform that allows the United States to continue to evolve. Every chapter begins with a "Roots of" section that gives a historical overview of the topic at hand, and ends with a "Toward Reform" section devoted to a particularly contentious aspect of the topic being discussed.

Toward Reform: Civil Liberties and Combating Terrorism

After September 11, 2001, the Bush administration, Congress, and th courts all operated in what Secretary of State Condoleezza Rice dubbe "an alternate reality," where Bill of Rights guarantees were suspended in a time war.[127] The USA Patriot Act, the Military Commissions Act, and a series of secr Department of Justice memos all altered the state of civil liberties in the Unite States. F affected

Roots of Civil Liberties: The Bill of Rights

In 1787, most state constitutions explicitly protected a va personal liberties such as speech, religion, freedom from unrea searches and seizures, and trial by jury. It was clear that the new federal system lished by the Constitution would redistribute power between the national gove and the states. Without an explicit guarantee of specific civil liberties, c national government be trusted to uphold the freedoms already granted to citi their states?

As discussed in chapter 2, recognition of the increased power that would by the new national government led Anti-Federalists to stress the need for

NEW! **Illustrated Timelines** provide AP* students with a clear and visual understanding of the development of key topics in American government. Timelines include key events leading to American Independence, the Supreme Court and the right to privacy, the development of American political parties, and the war on terrorism.

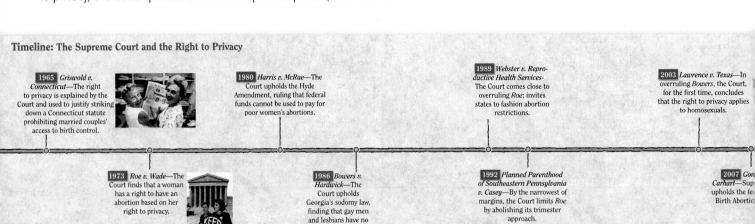

Timeline: The Supreme Court and the Right to Privacy

1965 *Griswold v. Connecticut*—The right to privacy is explained by the Court and used to justify striking down a Connecticut statute prohibiting married couples' access to birth control.

1973 *Roe v. Wade*—The Court finds that a woman has a right to have an abortion based on her right to privacy.

1980 *Harris v. McRae*—The Court upholds the Hyde Amendment, ruling that federal funds cannot be used to pay for poor women's abortions.

1986 *Bowers v. Hardwick*—The Court upholds Georgia's sodomy law, finding that gay men and lesbians have no privacy rights.

1989 *Webster v. Reproductive Health Services*-The Court comes close to overruling *Roe*; invites states to fashion abortion restrictions.

1992 *Planned Parenthood of Southeastern Pennsylvania v. Casey*—By the narrowest of margins, the Court limits *Roe* by abolishing its trimester approach.

2003 *Lawrence v. Texas*—In overruling *Bowers*, the Court, for the first time, concludes that the right to privacy applies to homosexuals.

2007 *Gor Carhart*—Sup upholds the fe Birth Abortic

The Living Constitution

The enumeration in the Constitution, of certain rights, shall not be construed to deny or disparage others retained by the people.

—NINTH AMENDMENT

The Living Constitution reflects the authors' emphasis on the origins of America's democratic system. To further support the text's emphasis on the constitutional underpinnings of government and politics, this boxed feature appears in every chapter. Each feature examines the chapter's topic in light of what the Constitution says or does not say about it.

...ment simply reiterates the belief that ...t specifically enumerated in the Bill of ...ist and are retained by the people. It ...o assuage the concerns of Federalists, ...es Madison, who feared that the enu-...so many rights and liberties in the first ...ments to the Constitution would result ...l of rights that were not enumerated. ...965, the Ninth Amendment was rarely ...by the Court. In that year, however, it ...the first time by the Court as a positive ...of a particular liberty—marital privacy. ...rivacy is not mentioned in the Constitu-...—according to the Court—o... fundamental freedoms that the drafters ...

of Rights implied as retained. Since 1965, the Court has ruled in favor of a host of fundamental liberties guaranteed by the Ninth Amendment, often in combination with other specific guarantees, including the right to have an abortion.

CRITICAL THINKING QUESTIONS

1. How can the U.S. justice system dictate the definition of a fundamental right if the Constitution does not specifically enumerate such rights?
2. How might public opinion affect judicial interpretations of the Ninth Amendment?

AMENDMENT VIII

Excessive bail shall not be required, nor excessive fines imposed, nor cruel and unusual punishments inflicted.

For an amendment of so few words, the Eighth Amendment has generated an enormous volume of commentary and litigation since its ratification. This should not be surprising, as the three major provisions of the amendment deal with some of the most sensitive and emotionally charged issues involving the rights of criminal defendants.

The Constitution of the United States of America, carefully annotated to make it accessible to students, is placed between Chapters 2 and 3, providing students with a walkthrough of this seminal document.

POLITICS NOW

Source: THE NEW YORK TIMES   August 7, 2007

Religious Accommodation on College Campuses

Universities Install Footbaths to Benefit Muslims, and Not Everyone Is Pleased

TAMAR LEWIN

DEARBORN, Mich. — When pools of water began accumulating on the floor in some restrooms at the University of Michigan-Dearborn, and the sinks pulling away from the walls, the problem was easy to pinpoint. On this campus, more ... 10 ... of ... ... Mu ...

in the new student union.

"My sister told me about it, and I didn't believe it," said Najla Malaibari, a graduate student at Eastern Michigan. "I was, 'No way,' and she said, 'Yeah, go crazy.' It really is convenient."

But after a Muslim student at Minneapolis Community and Technical College slipped and hurt herself last fall while washing her feet in a sink, word got out that the college was considering installing a footbath, and a local columnist accused the college of double standard — stopping a campus coffee cart from playing Christmas music but taking a different attitude ...

versity claims it's available for Western students as well, but, traditionally, Western students don't wash their feet five times day."

"They're building a structure for a particular religious tradition," Mr. Downs added, "and the Constitution says the government isn't supposed to endorse a particular religion."

The American Civil Liberties Union ...

Discussion Questions

1. Does the Clark County ordinance violate any First Amendment guarantees? If it does, how can the statute be altered so that it is no longer unconstitutional?

Politics Now boxes provide in-depth examinations of contemporary issues, showcasing the book's currency and serving as a counterbalance to the text's thorough treatment of America's origins and history. Excerpts from news articles are followed by Discussion Questions that allow AP* students to analyze current political issues for themselves.

Thinking Globally

Saudi Arabia and Free Exercise of Religion

In Saudi Arabia, public demonstration of religious affiliation or sentiment is forbidden except for Sunni Muslims who follow the austere Wahhabi interpretation of Islam. Public worship by non-Muslims is banned, and places of worship other than mosques are not permitted. The kingdom's Shi'a Muslim minority's religious practice is tightly controlled, and the construction of Shi'a mosques and religious community centers is restricted.

- Is it surprising that some countries officially support one religion at the expense of others? Why or why not?
- To what extent, should the United States pressure its allies, such as Saudi Arabia, to adhere more closely to American constitutional values of freedom of religion?
- What criteria would you use to evaluate the level of religious freedom in a country?

NEW! **Thinking Globally** features underscore the commonalities and differences between the United States and other nations to provide AP* students with a comparative perspective on a range of issues, including global environmentalism, indigenous legal systems in nations like Australia, and parliamentary systems and their impact on parties and the executive branch. Thinking Globally features occur three or more times in each chapter and consist of a brief overview of a key comparative topic followed by critical thinking questions.

Putting It into Action

The new and revised pedagogical features help AP* students actively engage the material, focus on key concepts, and become stronger political participants.

★ **WHAT SHOULD I KNOW ABOUT . . .**
- the roots of civil liberties and the Bill of Rights?
- First Amendment guarantees of freedom of religion?
- First Amendment gua[rantees of freedom of] speech, press, assembl[y]
- the Second Amendmen[t] bear arms?
- the rights of criminal d[efendants]
- the right to privacy?
- civil liberties and comb[at]

★ Third, we will consider the meanings of other *First Amend[ment]* *freedoms of speech, press, assembly, and petition.*

★ Fourth, we will Review *the Second Amendment* and *the ri[ght to]* *arms.*

★ Fifth, we will analyze *the rights of criminal defendants* four[nd] and how those rights have Court.

★ Sixth, we will explore *the right[s]*

★ Finally, we will examine ho[w] *liberties.*

First Amendment Guarantees: Freedom of Religion

Many of the Framers were religious men, but they knew wha[t] new nation was not founded with religious freedom as one of i[ts] many colonists had fled Europe to escape religious persecution[.] persecuted those who d[iffered] theless, in 1774, the col[onies] passed a law establishing the colonies. The First announcing its "astonish[ing]" lish . . . a religion [Cath[olic]] bigotry, persecution, mu[rder]

★ **WHAT SHOULD I HAVE LEARNED?**
- **What are the roots of civil liberties and the Bill of Rights i[n]**
  Most of the Framers originally opposed the Bill of Rights. A[...] however, continued to stress the need for a bill of rights dur[ing] ratification of the Constitution, and some states tried to ma[ke] contingent on the addition of a bill of rights. Thus, during i[...] Congress sent the first ten amendments to the Constitution[...] the states for their ratification. Later, the addition of the Fo[...] allowed the Supreme Court to apply some of the amendmen[ts] through a process called selective incorporation.
- **What are the First Amendment guarantees of freedom of [...]**
  The First Amendment guarantees freedom of religion. The [...] which prohibits the national government from establishing [...] according to Supreme Court interpretation, create an absolu[te] church and state. While the national and state governments [...] give direct aid to religious groups, many forms of aid, especi[...] children, have been held to be constitutionally permissible. [...] has generally barred organized prayer in public schools. The [...] adopted an accommodationist approach when interpreting t[...]

NEW! ## What Should I Know?
and
What Should I Have Learned?

sections allow students to preview and review the key topics and concepts explored in each chapter. Every chapter begins with a set of "What Should I Know?" questions tied to the sections within the chapter. These questions, as well as a bulleted list of section descriptions that follows the opening vignette, preview the key content of the chapter and help to focus student attention on the overall chapter structure. A "What Should I Have Learned?" section at the end of every chapter revisits each "What Should I Know?" question and answers it with a succinct summary paragraph.

TO LEARN MORE—
—TO DO MORE
To learn more about the Supreme Court's decision in *District of Columbia* v. *Heller* (2008), go to www.oyez.org and search on the name of the case.

NEW! ## To Learn More—
To Do More features serve as a capstone to every chapter's opening vignette and provide AP* students with an online reference for participation in or further information about the vignette's topic.

The Death Penalty

Overview: Challenges to the use of the death penalty are rising. In 2007, the U.S. Supreme Court agreed to take the case of *Baze v. Rees*, which questioned whether the method of lethal injection used by thirty-six states was potentially so painful as to violate the Eighth Amendment ban on cruel and unusual punishment. When the Court took the case, it in effect put a moratorium on executions until it ruled in the spring of 2008 that the method did not violate the Constitution. In 2007, forty-one people were put to death, the fewest since 1999, and New Jersey became the first state since 1965 to abolish the use of the death penalty. Although individuals and some government entities are having second thoughts about the death penalty, not everyone agrees that there is a problem. The federal government and thirty-eight states use the death penalty.

The debate over the use of capital punishment raises issues about the fundamental fairness of our system of justice. A major concern is that innocent people might be put to death, despite all the procedural safeguards in our court system to prevent mistakes. It is, of course, regrettable when someone is convicted of a crime he or she did not commit, even when they are only fined or imprisoned. Obviously there is no way of making amends when someone is executed.

Some of the current controversy related to the death penalty comes from advances in the use of DNA evidence. The Innocence Project, a nonprofit organization, has been working since 1992 to use DNA evidence to exonerate those wrongly convicted of crimes.[a] As of March 2008, the group's efforts have led to the release of 214 people, 16 of them on death row. In addition, between 1977 and 2007, another 108 people have been released from death rows because mistakes were made in eyewitness accounts, line-ups, police questioning,

and court proceedings. The obvious question is whether there were others who should have been released.

The major justification for the death penalty is captured in the slogan: "A life for a life." The consequence for taking someone else's life is the loss of the criminal's life. In turn, supporters of the death penalty believe that such a grave consequence will deter people from committing murder. There does not, however, appear to be a correlation between the death penalty and low homicide rates. Texas, for example, executes more people than all the rest of the states combined. Yet, Texas consistently has one of the highest murder rates in the country. And, as a whole, southern states use the death penalty more than any other region. The homicide rate in 2007 for the South was 42 per 100,000 people, in contrast to the rate of 17 per 100,000 people in the Northeast and Midwest.

Another concern with the death penalty is the racial and gender disparities in those who are executed. It is extremely

rare for a woman to be sent to the death chamber. And, a person is less likely to be executed if he or she is white. In 2007, for example, 53 percent of the 41 people executed were white, 37 percent were African American, and 10 percent were Hispanic—figures that do not match the racial composition of the general population. A crucial aspect of the debate regarding the death penalty is disagreement about whether the court system is biased and if convictions and executions reflect more general patterns of discrimination in society.

Arguments IN FAVOR of the Death Penalty

- The death penalty is just because it is used primarily to execute those who take the lives of others. Killing someone is the most egregious crime and act of violence, and societies must respond with the most severe punishment possible for murderers.
- The death penalty will deter at least some people from committing

capital offenses. Although some murders will occur in a fit of rage and passion, we need to make those who plot to kill another human being think about the possible consequences if they go ahead with their plan.

- It is costly to keep convicted murderers in prison for the rest of their lives. The cost to taxpayers to keep someone in prison is about $30,000 per year. It makes little economic sense for society to clothe, feed, and care for a murderer for the rest of his or her life.

Arguments AGAINST the Death Penalty

- Mistakes are inevitably going to be made, and innocent people are going to be put to death for crimes they did not commit. The consequence of executing an innocent person is beyond remedy. We simply cannot risk mistakes when life is at stake.
- The United States is alone among Western countries in continuing to have the death penalty. Canada, Australia, and all European nations are among the 91 countries that have completely abolished the death penalty. The United States is in the company of repressive nations such as China, Saudi Arabia, and Malaysia in its use of the death penalty.
- It actually costs more to execute someone than it does to imprison the person for life. The Urban Institute released a study on March 6, 2008, that showed the state of Maryland spent an average of $37.2

million for each of the five executions it conducted since it reinstated the death penalty in 1978. Although this figure is higher than those cited in other studies, the general finding is consistent with analyses that cite the high costs of appeals in capital cases and the high costs of running death rows.

Continuing the Debate

1. Should the states and the federal government abolish the death penalty? If not, for what crimes should the death penalty be allowed?
2. How, if at all, can mistakes in our criminal justice system be avoided? Do gender and racial disparities in executions suggest that the system is unfair?

To Follow the Debate Online, Go To:

www. prodeathpenalty.com, which advocates keeping and expanding the use of the death penalty and includes a list of print and media resources plus links to other supportive sites.

www. deathpenaltyinfo.org for a wide array of studies and statistics on the death penalty as well as coverage of current events related to the death penalty and arguments

pewforum.org/death-penalty/, which provides information, statistics, and arguments related to the death penalty.

[a]www.innocenceproject.org

How do states vary in their application of the death penalty? This cartoon offers a social commentary on the administration of the death penalty in Texas, which leads the nation in the number of executions.

Join the Debate boxes explore provocative, student-oriented topics and provide extensive, well-balanced coverage of both sides of a debate. Each box begins with a topic overview, provides accessible and detailed summaries of opposing arguments related to the issue, and ends with critical thinking questions that allow AP* students to examine their own stance on the topic and suggested readings for further research. New topics in this edition include the death penalty, the living wage movement, budget allocations for the Iraq War, and voting rights for felons.

Ideas Into Action

Celebrating the Constitution

In late 2004, Senator Robert C. Byrd (D–WV) introduced legislation that called on all educational institutions receiving federal funds—from kindergarten through grade 12 to colleges, universities, and even law schools—to set aside September 17 of each year to conduct educational programs concerning the U.S. Constitution. When Public Law 108-447 passed, educational institutions around the United States began to question just what types of programs were required. The selection of September 17 was not random; the U.S. Constitution was sent to the states for ratification on that date.

Since 2005, educational institutions around the United States have chosen to celebrate what is now called Constitution Day in a variety of ways. The National Constitution Center has taken the lead in publicizing unique

and thoughtful ways for schools to observe Constitution Day. Among those highlighted are "celebrate your state" events, discussions on how the U.S. Supreme Court can change the law and make policy, grade school celebrations where students wear red, white, and blue and learn about the Preamble; and interactive Web-based activities for all ages.

- Visit the C-SPAN classroom Web site at www.c-spanclassroom.org. What activities might you and your classmates use to teach about the Constitution at a local elementary school?
- What kinds of activities celebrate Constitutio
- What programs or pro government class engage Constitution Day to your
- For more Constitution Da www.constitutionday.us.

NEW! **Ideas into Action** boxes emphasize political participation by highlighting current issues of interest to AP* students and providing discussion questions, online resources for further research, and concrete suggestions for active involvement. Topics include celebrating Constitution Day, becoming a Congressional intern, and filing an *amicus curiae* brief.

Analyzing Visuals

Visual literacy—the ability to analyze, interpret, synthesize, and apply visual information—is essential in today's world. We receive much information from the written and spoken word, but much also comes in visual forms. We are used to thinking about reading written texts critically, but we do not always think about "reading" visuals in this way. We should, for images and informational graphics can tell us a lot if we read and consider them carefully. In order to emphasize these skills, the *Analyzing Visuals* feature in each chapter prompts students to think about the images and informational graphics they will encounter throughout this text, as well as those they see every day in the newspaper, in magazines, on the Web, on television, and in books. Critical thinking questions assist students in learning how to analyze visuals.

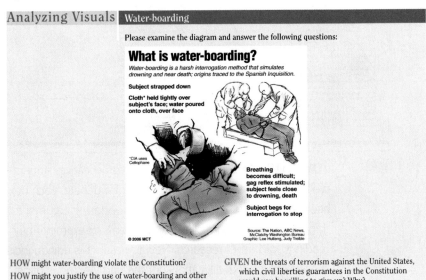

Analyzing Visuals — Water-boarding

Please examine the diagram and answer the following questions:

What is water-boarding?
Water-boarding is a harsh interrogation method that simulates drowning and near death; origins traced to the Spanish Inquisition.

Subject strapped down

Cloth* held tightly over subject's face; water poured onto cloth, over face

*CIA uses Cellophane

Breathing becomes difficult; gag reflex stimulated; subject feels close to drowning, death

Subject begs for interrogation to stop

Source: The Nation, ABC News, McClatchy Washington Bureau
Graphic: Lee Hulteng, Judy Treible
© 2006 MCT

HOW might water-boarding violate the Constitution?

HOW might you justify the use of water-boarding and other interrogation techniques that many nations classify as torture?

GIVEN the threats of terrorism against the United States, which civil liberties guarantees in the Constitution would you be willing to give up? Why?

Tables

Tables are the least "visual" of the visuals, and consist of textual information and/or numerical data arranged in tabular form, in columns and rows. Tables are frequently used when exact information is required and when orderly arrangement is necessary to locate and, in many cases, to compare the information.

Here are a few questions to guide students' analysis of the tables in this book:

- What is the purpose of the table? What information does it show? There is usually a title that offers a sense of the table's purpose.
- What information is provided in the column headings (provided in the top row)? How are the rows labeled?
- Is there a time period indicated, such as January to June 2007? Or, are the data as of a specific date, such as June 30, 2007?
- If the table shows numerical data, what do these data represent? In what units? Does a table show, for example, dollars a special interest lobby provides to a political party? Estimated life expectancy in years?
- What is the source of the information presented in the table?

TABLE 4.3 Major Forms of Municipal Government

Form of Government	1984	2002
Council–Manager	3,387 (48.5%)	2,290 (34.7%)
Mayor–Council	3,011 (43.1%)	3,686 (55.8%)
Commission	143 (2.0%)	176 (2.7%)
Town Meeting	337 (4.8%)	370 (5.6%)
Representative Town Meeting	63 (.9%)	81 (1.2%)
Total[a]	6,981 (100%)	6,603 (100%)

[a] Totals for U.S. local governments represent only those municipalities with populations of 2,500 and greater. There are close to 30,000 local governments with populations under 2,500.
Source: Statistics from "Inside the Year Book: Cumulative Distributions of U.S. Municipalities," *The Municipal Year Books* 1984–2002, International City/County Management Association (ICMA), Washington, DC.

Charts and Graphs

Charts and graphs depict numerical data in visual forms. Examples that students will encounter throughout this text are line graphs, pie charts, and bar graphs. Line graphs show a progression, usually over time (as in Social Security Costs and Revenues, 1970–2008). Pie charts (such as the distribution of federal civilian employment) demonstrate how a whole (total federal civilian employment) is divided into its parts (employees in each branch). Bar graphs compare values across categories, showing how proportions are related to each other (as in the numbers of women and minorities in Congress). Bar graphs can present data either horizontally or vertically.

Here are a few questions to guide student analysis:

- What is the purpose of the chart or graph? What information does it provide? Or, what is being measured? There is usually a title that indicates the subject and purpose of the figure.
- Is there a time period shown, such as January to June 2008? Or, are the data as of a specific date, such as June 30, 2008? Are the data shown at multiple intervals over a fixed period, or at one particular point in time?
- What do the units represent? Do they show dollars a candidate spends on a campaign? Number of voters versus number of nonvoters in Texas? If there are two or more sets of figures, what are the relationships among them?
- What is the source? Is it government information? Private polling information? Is the source a newspaper? A private organization? A corporation? An individual?
- Is the type of chart or graph appropriate for the information that is provided? For example, a line graph assumes a smooth progression from one data point to the next. Is that assumption valid for the data shown?
- Is there distortion in the visual representation of the information? Are the intervals equal? Does the area shown distort the actual amount or the proportion?

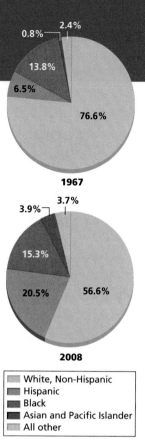

1967

2008

White, Non-Hispanic
Hispanic
Black
Asian and Pacific Islander
All other

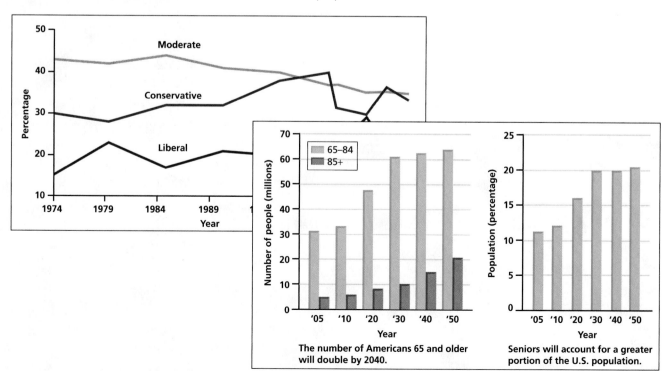

The number of Americans 65 and older will double by 2040.

Seniors will account for a greater portion of the U.S. population.

Maps

Maps—of the United States, of particular regions, or of the world—are frequently used in political analysis to illustrate demographic, social, economic, and political issues and trends.

Here are a few questions to guide student analysis:

- Is there a title that identifies the purpose or subject of the map?
- What does the map key/legend show? What are the factors that the map is analyzing?
- What is the region being shown?
- What source is given for the map?
- Maps usually depict a specific point in time. What is the point in time being shown on the map?

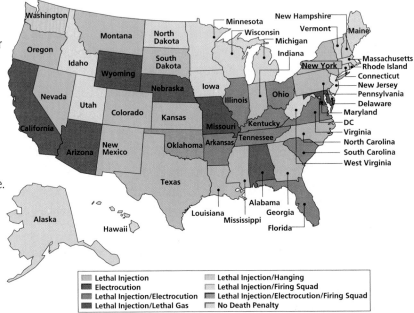

▨ Lethal Injection	▨ Lethal Injection/Hanging
▨ Electrocution	▨ Lethal Injection/Firing Squad
▨ Lethal Injection/Electrocution	▨ Lethal Injection/Electrocution/Firing Squad
▨ Lethal Injection/Lethal Gas	▨ No Death Penalty

News Photographs

Photos can have a dramatic—and often immediate—impact on politics and government. Visual images usually evoke a stronger emotional response from people than do written descriptions. For this reason, individuals and organizations have learned to use photographs as a means to document events, make arguments, offer evidence, and even in some cases to manipulate the viewer into having a particular response.

Here are a few questions to guide student analysis:

- When was the photograph taken?
- What is the subject of the photograph?

- Why was the photo taken? What appears to be the purpose of the photograph?
- Is it spontaneous or posed? Did the subject know he or she was being photographed?
- Who was responsible for the photo? (An individual, agency, an organization?) Can you discern the photographer's attitude toward the subject?
- Is there a caption? If so, what kind of information does it provide? Does it identify the subject of the photo? Does it provide an interpretation of the subject?

Political Cartoons

Some of the most interesting commentary on American politics takes place in the form of political cartoons. The cartoonist's goal is to comment on or criticize political figures, policies, or events. The cartoonist uses several techniques to accomplish this goal, including exaggeration, irony, and juxtaposition. For example, the cartoonist may point out how the results of governmental policies are the opposite of their intended effects (irony). In other cartoons, two people, ideas, or events that don't belong together may be joined to make a point (juxtaposition). Knowledge of current events is helpful in interpreting political cartoons.

Here are a few questions to guide student analysis:

- What labels appear on objects or people in the cartoon? Cartoonists will often label some of the elements. For example, a building with columns might be labeled "U.S. Supreme Court."
- What does the caption or title contribute to the meaning or impact of the cartoon?
- Can you identify any of the people shown? Presidents, well-known members of Congress, and world leaders are often shown with specific characteristics that help to identify them.
- Can you identify the event being depicted? Historical events, such as the American Revolution, or contemporary events, such as the 2008 presidential election, are often the subject matter for cartoons.
- What are the elements of the cartoon? Objects often represent ideas or events. For example, a donkey is often used to depict the Democratic Party.
- How are the characters interacting? What do the speech bubbles contribute to the cartoon?
- What is the overall message of the cartoon? Can you determine what the cartoonist's position is on the subject?

Resources in Print and Online

Most of the teacher supplements and resources for this book are available electronically on the Instructor Resource Center. Upon adoption or to preview, please go to PearsonSchool.com/Advanced and click "Online Teacher Supplements". You will be required to complete a one-time registration subject to verification before being emailed access information to download materials.

The following supplements are available to qualified adopters:

Name of Supplement	Available in Print	Available Online	Instructor or Student Supplement	Description
American Government Study Site		✔	Both	Online set of practice tests, Web links, and flashcards organized by major topics and arranged according to this book's table of contents. www.pearsonamericangovernment.com.
AP* Test Prep: US Government and Politics 0131363379	✔		Student	This student study tool, created for use specifically with *American Government, AP* Edition*, contains a wealth of resources for students, including practice tests questions with answers and applications for each chapter, and sample AP* practice exams with answers. Available for purchase.
Study Guide 0205684173	✔		Student	Contains learning objectives, chapter summaries, and practice tests. Available for purchase.
Study Card for American Government 0321291859	✔		Student	Course information is distilled down to the basics, helping AP* students quickly master the fundamentals, review a subject for understanding, or prepare for an exam. Laminated for durability. Available for purchase.
Instructor's Manual 0205684157	✔	✔	Teacher	Offers chapter overviews and outlines, teaching ideas, and discussion topics and Web activities incorporating recent political news.
AP* Test Bank 0205684165	✔	✔	Teacher	Contains over 200 questions per chapter in multiple-choice, true-false, short-answer, and essay format. Questions address all levels of Bloom's taxonomy and all multiple-choice test questions have five answer choices, conforming to the format of the AP* exam.
PowerPoint® Presentation 0205684181		✔	Teacher	Slides include a lecture outline of the text along with graphics from the book. Available on the Instructor Resource Center.
Digital Transparency Masters 0205684092		✔	Teacher	These PDF slides contain all maps, figures, and tables found in the text. Available on the Instructor Resource Center.
Instructor's Resource CD 0137153236		✔	Teacher	Contains the Instructor's Manual, PowerPoint Presentations, Digital Transparency Masters, Test Bank. The CD also contains the TestGen Computerized Testing System, which allows teachers to edit existing questions and add their own items. Tests can be printed in several different formats and can include features such as graphs and tables.
You Decide! Current Debates in American Politics, 2009 Edition	✔		Student	This debate-style reader by John Rourke of the University of Connecticut examines provocative issues in American politics today by presenting various sides of key important issues. Available for purchase.
Voices of Dissent: Critical Readings in American Politics, Eighth Edition 0205697976	✔		Student	This collection of critical essays assembled by William Grover of St. Michael's College and Joseph Peschek of Hamline University goes beyond the debate between mainstream liberalism and conservatism to fundamentally challenge the status quo. Available for purchase.
Writing in Political Science, Third Edition 0321217357	✔		Student	This guide by Diane Schmidt of California StateUniversity–Chico takes students through all aspects of writing in political science step-by-step. Available for purchase.
Choices: An American Government Database Reader		✔	Both	This customizable reader allows instructors to choose from a database of over 300 readings to create a reader that exactly matches their course needs. Available for purchase. Go to www.pearsoncustom.com/highschool for more information.
American Government: Readings and Cases, Eighteenth Edition 0205697984	✔		Student	Edited by Peter Woll of Brandeis University, this longtimebest-selling reader provides a strong, balanced blend of classic readings and cases that illustrate and amplify important concepts in American government, alongside extremely current selections drawn from today's issues and literature. Available for purchase.

Improve Results With

Designed to amplify a traditional course in numerous ways or to administer a course online, **MyPoliSciLab** combines pedagogy and assessment with an array of multimedia activities—videos, simulations, exercises, and online newsfeeds—to make learning more effective for all types of students. Now featuring the combined resources, assets, and activities of both Prentice Hall and Longman Publishers, this new release of **MyPoliSciLab** is visually richer and even more interactive than previous iterations—a quantum leap forward in design with more points of assessment and interconnectivity between concepts.

TEACHING AND LEARNING TOOLS

✓ **Assessment**: Comprehensive online diagnostic tools—learning objectives, study guides, flashcards, and pre- and post-tests—help students gauge and improve their understanding.

✓ **E-book:** Identical in content and design to the printed text, an e-book provides students access to their text wherever and whenever they need it.

✓ *UPDATED!* **PoliSci News Review:** A series of weekly articles and video clips—from traditional and non-traditional news sources—recaps the most important political news stories, followed by quizzes that test students' understanding.

✓ *NEW!* **ABC News RSS feed:** MyPoliSciLab provides an online feed from ABC News, updated hourly, to keep students current.

✓ **ABC News Video Clips**: Over 60 high-interest 2- to 4-minute clips provide historical snapshots in each chapter of key political issues and offer opportunities to launch discussions.

✓ *UPDATED!* **Roundtable and Debate Video Clips**: These video clips feature professors discussing key concepts from ideologically diverse perspectives and debating politically charged issues.

✓ **Student Polling:** Updated weekly with timely, provocative questions, the polling feature lets students voice their opinions in nationwide polls and view how their peers across the country see the same issue.

✓ **Political Podcasts:** Featuring some of Pearson's most respected authors, these video podcasts present short, instructive—and even entertaining—lectures on key topics that students can download and play at their convenience.

✓ *NEW!* **Student Podcasts:** The new MyPoliSciLab allows students to record and download their own videos for peer-to-peer learning.

INTERACTIVE ACTIVITIES

✓ **New and Updated Simulations:** Featuring an appealing new graphic interface, these role-playing simulations help students experience political decision-making in a way they never have before—including new "mini activities" that prepare students to make the right decisions.

✓ *NEW!* **Debate Exercises:** These provocative new exercises present classic and contemporary views on core controversies, ask students to take a position, and then show them the potential consequences of taking that stand.

✓ **More Focused Comparative Exercises:** These exercises have been revised in scope to concentrate on a more specific issue when comparing the US to other political systems, giving students a more concrete foundation on which to analyze key similarities and differences.

✓ **More Interactive Timelines:** With redesigned media and graphics, these timelines let students step through the evolution of some aspect of politics and now include more interactive questions throughout.

✓ **More Dynamic Visual Literacy Exercises:** These revised exercises offer attractive new graphs, charts, and tables and more opportunities to manipulate and interpret political data.

✓ **Expanded Participation Activities:** Reflecting our county's growing political interest, these expanded activities give students ideas and instructions for getting involved in all aspects of politics.

Icons in the margin of this book direct students to the activities on MyPoliSciLab related to the topics they are studying.

ONLINE ADMINISTRATION

No matter what course management system you use—or if you do not use one at all, but still wish to easily capture your students grades and track their performance—Pearson has a **MyPoliSciLab** option to suit your needs. Contact your local Pearson sales representative for more information or assistance.

High school teachers can obtain teacher and student preview or adoption access in one of two ways:

✓ By registering online at **www.pearsonschool.com/access_request.**

✓ Through the use of a physical pincode card. High school adopters will receive an adopter access pincode card (ISBN 0130343919) with their textbook order.

Preview access pincode cards may be requested using ISBN 0131115989. Both adopter and preview pincode cards include follow-on directions and provide teacher and student access.

For questions concerning access, please contact your local Pearson sales representative or email **PHwebaccess@pearsoned.com.**

Acknowledgments

Karen O'Connor thanks the thousands of students in her American Government courses at Emory and American University who, over the years, have pushed her to learn more about American government and to have fun in the process. She also thanks her American University colleagues who offered books and suggestions for this most recent revision—especially David Lublin. Her former professor and longtime friend and co-author, Nancy E. McGlen, has offered support for more than three decades. Her former students, too, have contributed in various ways to this project, especially John R. Hermann, Sue Davis, and Laura van Assendelft.

For the last four editions of the book, Alixandra B. Yanus of the University of North Carolina, Chapel Hill, has offered invaluable assistance and unflagging support. Her fresh perspectives on politics and ideas about things of interest to students, as well as her keen eye for the typo, her research abilities, and her unbelievably hard work, have made this a much better book. For this edition of the book, Jon L. Weakley, an American politics student who had the foresight (or the stupidity) to offer help during the 2006 election updates process, provided necessary reinforcement and enthusiasm. Jon's copyediting skills, love of the electoral process, and unlimited patience have significantly improved this text.

Larry J. Sabato would like to acknowledge all of the students from his University of Virginia Introduction to American Politics classes and the many student interns at the UVA Center for Politics who have offered valuable suggestions and an abundance of thoughtful feedback. A massive textbook project like this one needs the very best assistance an author can find, and this author was lucky enough to find some marvelously talented people. Jeff Gulati, assistant professor of political science at Bentley University, worked endless hours researching the new edition and weaving together beautifully constructed sections on recent American politics. His original contributions to sections on new campaign technologies, technological innovations transforming the traditional news media, and the rise of the Internet and other forms of "new media" are particularly noteworthy. As always, the staff of the University of Virginia Center for Politics and a team of extraordinary interns contributed in many important ways toward the successful completion of this volume, especially my chief of staff Ken Stroupe, Mary Brown, Cordel Faulk, Rhodes Cook, Dan Keyserling, Paul Wiley, Isaac Wood and Brandon Gould. Their commitment to excellence is also obvious in their work for the Center's Crystal Ball website (www.centerforpolitics.org/crystalball)—a very useful resource in completing this volume. Finally, Larry extends his thanks to the faculty and staff of the Department of Politics at UVA, especially Debbie Best and Department Chairman Jeffrey Legro.

Particular thanks go to Dennis L. Dresang at the University of Wisconsin–Madison, who has once again brought a keen eye and insightful analysis to chapter 4 (State and Local Government) and has written new Join the Debate features in the book; Christopher Borick at Muhlenberg College, who thoroughly revised chapters 17 and 18 (Domestic Policy and Economic Policy); and Kiki Caruson of the University of South Florida, who tackled the rapidly shifting landscape of chapter 19 (Foreign and Defense Policy) for this edition and also drafted the Thinking Globally features. Our continued thanks go to Steven Koven at the University of Louisville and Daniel S. Papp of the University System of Georgia, whose earlier work on the policy chapters continues to serve as such a strong foundation. We also thank Brian Bearry of the University of Texas at Dallas for his past help with many of the Join the Debate features.

In the now many years we have been writing and rewriting this book, we have been blessed to have been helped by many people at Longman. Eric Stano has been a fantastic editor as well as fun to work with. Our development editor, Melissa Mashburn, has been a stern taskmaster with a political junkie's eye for extensive updating. Our marketing manager, Lindsey Prudhomme, has done a terrific job. We would also like to acknowledge the tireless efforts of the Pearson Education sales force. In the end, we hope that all of these talented people see how much their work and support have helped us to write a better book.

Many of our peers reviewed past editions of the book and earned our gratitude in the process. We list a number who reviewed recent editions here:

Danny Adkison, *Oklahoma State University*
Weston H. Agor, *University of Texas at El Paso*
Victor Aikhionbare, *Salt Lake Community College*
James Anderson, *Texas A&M University*
William Arp, *Southern University, Baton Rouge*
Judith Baer, *Texas A&M University*
Vanessa Baird, *University of Colorado, Boulder*
Ruth Bamberger, *Drury College*
Christine Barbour, *Indiana University*
Ken Baxter, *San Joaquin Delta College*
Brian Bearry, *University of Texas at Dallas*
Jon Bond, *Texas A&M University*
Stephen A. Borrelli, *University of Alabama*

Ann Bowman, *University of South Carolina*
Robert C. Bradley, *Illinois State University*
Holly Brasher, *University of Alabama, Birmingham*
Michelle Brophy-Baermann, *University of Wisconsin*
Gary Brown, *Montgomery College*
John Francis Burke, *University of Houston–Downtown*
Kevin Buterbaugh, *Northwest Missouri State University*
Mark Byrnes, *Middle Tennessee State University*
Greg Caldeira, *Ohio State University*
John H. Calhoun, *Palm Beach Atlantic University*
David E. Camacho, *Northern Arizona University*
Alan R. Carter, *Schenectady County Community College*
Carl D. Cavalli, *North Georgia College and State University*

Steve Chan, *University of Colorado*
Richard Christofferson Sr. *University of Wisconsin–Stevens Point*
David Cingranelli, *SUNY Binghamton*
Clarke E. Cochran, *Texas Tech University*
Paul W. Cook, *Cy-Fair College*
Tracy Cook, *Central Texas College*
Kevin Corder, *Western Michigan University*
Anne N. Costain, *University of Colorado*
Cary Covington, *University of Iowa*
Lorrie Clemo, *SUNY Oswego*
Stephen C. Craig, *University of Florida*
Lane Crothers, *Illinois State University*
Abraham L. Davis, *Morehouse College*
Robert DiClerico, *West Virginia University*
John Dinan, *Wake Forest University*
John Domino, *Sam Houston State University*
Keith L. Dougherty, *University of Georgia*
David E. Dupree, *Victor Valley College*
Craig F. Emmert, *Texas Tech University*
Walle Engedayehu, *Prairie View A&M University*
Alan S. Engel, *Miami University*
Timothy Fackler, *University of Nevada, Las Vegas*
Frank B. Feigert, *University of North Texas*
Terri S. Fine, *University of Central Florida*
Evelyn Fink, *University of Nebraska*
Scott R. Furlong, *University of Wisconsin–Green Bay*
James D. Gleason, *Victoria College*
Dana K. Glencross, *Oklahoma City Community College*
Sheldon Goldman, *University of Massachusetts, Amherst*
Doris Graber, *University of Illinois at Chicago*
Jeffrey D. Green, *University of Montana*
Roger W. Green, *University of North Dakota*
James Michael Greig, *University of North Texas*
Charles Hadley, *University of New Orleans*
Mel Hailey, *Abilene Christian University*
William K. Hall, *Bradley University*
Robert L. Hardgrave Jr. *University of Texas at Austin*
Chip Hauss, *George Mason University/University of Reading*
Stacia L. Haynie, *Louisiana State University*
John R. Hermann, *Trinity University*
Marjorie Hershey, *Indiana University*
Justin Holmes, *University of Minnesota*
Steven Alan Holmes, *Bakersfield College*
Jerry Hopkins, *East Texas Baptist University*
Tim Howard, *North Harris College*
John C. Hughes, *Oklahoma City Community College*
Jon Hurwitz, *SUNY Buffalo*
Thomas Hyde, *Pfeiffer University*
Joseph Ignagni, *University of Texas at Arlington*
Willoughby Jarrell, *Kennesaw State College*
Susan M. Johnson, *University of Wisconsin–Whitewater*
Dennis Judd, *University of Missouri–St. Louis*
Ngozi Kamalu, *Fayetteville State University*
Carol J. Kamper, *Rochester Community College*

David Kennedy, *Montgomery College*
Kenneth Kennedy, *College of San Mateo*
Donald F. Kettl, *University of Wisconsin*
Quentin Kidd, *Christopher Newport University*
John Kincaid, *Lafayette College*
Karen M. King, *Bowling Green State University*
Alec Kirby, *University of Wisconsin–Stout*
Aaron Knight, *Houston Community College*
John F. Kozlowicz, *University of Wisconsin–Whitewater*
Jonathan E. Kranz, *John Jay College of Criminal Justice*
John C. Kuzenski, *The Citadel*
Mark Landis, *Hofstra University*
Sue Lee, *North Lake College*
Ted Lewis, *Collin County Community College*
Matt Lindstrom, *St. John's University*
Brad Lockerbie, *University of Georgia*
Susan MacFarland, *Gainesville College*
Cecilia Manrique, *University of Wisconsin–La Crosse*
Larry Martinez, *California State University–Long Beach*
Lynn Mather, *SUNY Buffalo*
Laurel A. Mayer, *Sinclair Community College*
Steve Mazurana, *University of Northern Colorado*
Clifton McCleskey, *University of Virginia*
Percival Robert McDonagh, *Catholic University*
James L. McDowell, *Indiana State University*
Carl E. Meacham, *SUNY Oneonta*
Stephen S. Meinhold, *University of North Carolina–Wilmington*
John Mercurio, *San Diego State University*
Mark C. Miller, *Clark University*
Kenneth F. Mott, *Gettysburg College*
Joseph Nogee, *University of Houston*
John O'Callaghan, *Suffolk University*
Bruce Oppenheimer, *Vanderbilt University*
Richard Pacelle, *Georgia Southern University*
Marian Lief Palley, *University of Delaware*
David R. Penna, *Gallaudet University*
Ron Pettus, *St. Charles Community College*
Richard M. Pious, *Columbia University*
David H. Provost, *California State University–Fresno*
Lawrence J. Redlinger, *University of Texas at Dallas*
James A. Rhodes, *Luther College*
Leroy N. Rieselbach, *Indiana University*
David Robertson, *Public Policy Research Centers, University of Missouri–St. Louis*
David Robinson, *University of Houston–Downtown*
Norman Rodriguez, *John Wood Community College*
David W. Rohde, *Duke University*
Frank Rourke, *Johns Hopkins University*
Thomas Rowan, *Chicago State University*
Donald Roy, *Ferris State University*
Ronald Rubin, *City University of New York, Borough of Manhattan Community College*
Bruce L. Sanders, *MacComb Community College*
Denise Scheberle, *University of Wisconsin–Green Bay*

Gaye Lynn Scott, *Austin Community College*
Martin P. Sellers, *Campbell University*
Daniel M. Shea, *University of Akron*
John N. Short, *University of Arkansas–Monticello*
Michael Eric Siegel, *American University*
Mark Silverstein, *Boston University*
James R. Simmons, *University of Wisconsin–Oshkosh*
Andrea Simpson, *University of Richmond*
Philip M. Simpson, *Cameron University*
Elliott E. Slotnick, *Ohio State University*
Michael W. Sonnleitner, *Portland Community College*
Frank J. Sorauf, *University of Minnesota*
David Sprick, *University of Missouri, Kansas City*
Gerald Stanglin, *Cedar Valley College*
C. S. Tai, *University of Arkansas–Pine Bluff*
Leena Thacker-Kumer, *University of Houston–Downtown*
Richard J. Timpone, *SUNY Stony Brook*
Albert C. Waite, *Central Texas College*
Brian Walsh, *University of Maryland*

Shirley Anne Warshaw, *Gettysburg College*
Matt Wetstein, *San Joaquin Delta College*
Richard Whaley, *Marian College*
Rich Whisonant, *York Technical College*
Harold Wingfield, *Kennesaw State University*
Martin Wiseman, *Mississippi State University*
Kevan Yenerall, *Bridgewater College*

Finally, we would also like to thank our peers who reviewed and aided in the development of the current edition:
Brian Dille, *Odessa College*
Robert Locander, *North Harris College*
Billy Monroe, *University of Texas at Dallas*
Dana Morales, *Montgomery College*
Katarina Moyon, *Winthrop University*
Kathleen Sedille, *College of DuPage*
Robert Sullivan, *Dallas Baptist University*
Ron Velten, *Grayson County College*

1 The Political Landscape

We the People of the United States, in Order to form a more perfect Union, establish Justice, insure domestic Tranquility, provide for the common defence, promote the general Welfare, and secure the Blessings of Liberty to ourselves and our Posterity, do ordain and establish this Constitution for the United States of America.

These are the words that begin the Preamble to the United States Constitution. Written in 1787 by a group of men we today refer to as the Framers, this document, which expresses sentiment which echoed in later written statements such as the Pledge of Allegiance and the American's Creed, has guided our nation, its government, its politics, its institutions, and its inhabitants for over 200 years.

When the Preamble to the U.S. Constitution was written, the phrases "We the People" and "ourselves" meant something very different from what they do today. After all, voting largely was limited to property-owning white males. Indians, slaves, and women could not vote. Today, through the expansion of the right to vote, the

■ Since the earliest days of the new Republic, the flag has stood as one of the foremost symbols of the United States.

phrase "the People" encompasses men and women of all races, ethnic origins, and social and economic statuses—a variety of peoples and interests. The Framers could not have imagined the range of people today who are eligible to vote. The Framers would be amazed, as well, at the array of services and programs the government—especially the national government—provides. They further would be surprised to see how the physical boundaries and the composition of the population have changed over the past 200 plus years. And, they might well wonder, "How did we get here?"

In the goals it outlines, the Preamble to the Constitution describes what the people of the United States can expect from their government. The Pledge of Allegiance, adopted in 1892 during a time of political turmoil and a great influx of immigrants, calls on all to profess their dedication to the American flag and for all it stands: *"I pledge allegiance to the Flag of the United States of America, and to the Republic for which it stands, one Nation, indivisible, with liberty and justice for all."* (The phrasing was changed to "one Nation under God" in 1954.)

Americans believe that each generation should hand down to the next not only a better America, but an improved economic, educational, and social status. In general, Americans long have been optimistic about their nation, its institutions, and its future. Thomas Jefferson saw the United States as the world's

WHAT SHOULD I KNOW ABOUT . . .

- the roots of American government?
- the philosophical origins of American government?
- American political culture and the characteristics of American democracy?
- political ideology, its role in the world, and its role in American politics?
- the changing characteristics of the American people?
- population changes and Americans' attitudes toward government?

3

"best hope"; Abraham Lincoln echoed these sentiments when he called it the "last, best hope on earth."[1]

But, in the wake of the September 11, 2001, terrorist attacks; the wars in Iraq and Afghanistan; and natural disasters and economic troubles at home, citizens today question how well the U.S. government can deliver on the goals set out in the Preamble and the Pledge of Allegiance. Few Americans classify the union as "perfect"; many feel excluded from "Justice" and the "Blessings of Liberty," and even our leaders do not believe that our domestic situation is particularly tranquil, as evidenced by the continuing debates about the best means to protect America. Still, in appraising how well government functions, it is imperative to look at not only the roots of the political system, but also how it has been reformed over time through amendment, legislation, common usage, and changing social mores.

Perhaps because reform is usually incremental and takes so much time, some Americans put little faith in government or do not care much at all about it. Many believe that they have no influence in its decision making, or they do not see any positive benefits from it in their lives. Yet, ironically, in times of emergency, be it a terrorist attack, a natural disaster, or in the face of rising food and gas prices, many people immediately look to their government for help. And when citizens are concerned about their lives and the state of the nation, they often call for reform. During the 2008 presidential nominating season, candidates made much of the need for "change." Yet how that change was to be accomplished remained quite vague.

TO LEARN MORE—
—TO DO MORE
Learn about the history of the Pledge of Allegiance at www.home-ofheroes.com. Search "Pledge of Allegiance" from the site's home page. Discuss if it is time, again, to refocus on American ideals as the government debates immigration and citizenship issues.

In this text, we present you with the tools that you need to understand how our political system has evolved and to prepare you to understand the changes that are yet to come. If you approach the study of American government and politics with an open mind, it should help you become a better citizen. We hope that you learn to ask questions, to understand how various issues have come to be important, and to see why a particular law was enacted, how it was implemented, and if it is in need of reform. We further hope that, with such understanding, you will learn not to accept at face value everything you see on the television news, hear on the radio, or read in the newspaper and on the Internet, especially in the blogosphere. Work to understand your government, and use your vote and other forms of participation to help ensure that your government works for you.

We recognize that the discourse of politics has changed dramatically even in the last few years: it is easier to become informed about the political process and to get involved in campaigns and elections than ever before. We also believe that a thorough understanding of the workings of government will allow you to question and think about the political system—the good parts and the bad—and decide for yourself the advantages and disadvantages of possible changes and reforms. Equipped with such an understanding, you likely will become a better informed and more active participant in the political process.

Every long journey begins with a single step. In this chapter, we will examine the following topics:

★ First, we will discuss *the roots of American government: what they are and why they are important*. Governments perform a range of well-known and not so well-known functions that affect citizens' lives on a daily basis.

★ Second, we will look at *the origins of our ideas about government*. To understand how the U.S. government and our political system work, it is critical to understand the philosophies that guided the American colonists as they created a system of government different from those then in existence.

★ Third, we will explore *American political culture and the basic tenets of American democracy*. A number of enduring values have defined American democracy since its beginning and continue to influence our nation's government and politics today.

★ Fourth, we will discuss *political ideology, its role in the world, and its role in American politics*. Political ideology has a profound impact on the public policies that Americans support or oppose.

★ Fifth, we will explore *the changing characteristics of the American people*. Because the government derives its power from the people, an understanding of who the American people are is critical.

★ Finally, we will discuss *population changes and Americans' attitudes toward government*.

Roots of American Government: What Are They and Why Are They Important?

Throughout history, all sorts of societies have organized themselves into a variety of governments, small and large, simple and complex, democratic and nondemocratic, elected and nonelected. A **government** is the formal vehicle through which policies are made and affairs of state are conducted. In fact, the term "government" is derived from the Greek for "to pilot a ship," which is appropriate, since we expect governments to guide "the ship of state." As we explore throughout this text, governments are often a result of trial and error, experiment, compromise, and sometimes bloodshed.

Unlike schools, banks, or corporations, the actions of government are binding on all citizens. A **citizen**, by law, is a member of the political community who, by nature of being born in a particular nation or having become a naturalized citizen, is entitled to all of the security and freedoms guaranteed by the government. In exchange, citizens must obey the government, its laws, and its constitution. Citzens also are expected to support their government through exercising their right to vote, paying taxes, and, if they are eligible, submitting themselves to military service.

Only governments legitimately can use force to keep order, and without governments, societies may descend into chaos, as has been evident in Kenya and Pakistan. In Kenya, the disputed 2007 presidential election resulted in deadly clashes between different ethnic groups. The assassination of former prime minister and

government
The formal vehicle through which policies are made and affairs of state are conducted.

citizen
Member of the political community to whom certain rights and obligations are attached.

Photo courtesy: Shakil Adil/AP/Wide World Photos

What happens when governments fail to enforce the rule of law? This photo of former Pakistani Prime Minister Benazir Bhutto was taken shortly before she was assassinated in December 2007. Muslim terrorists in Pakistan considered Bhutto's moderate, secular political agenda a threat to their beliefs. Many believe that Pakistan's government failed to provide adequate protection to Bhutto, and some have alleged government involvement in her assassination.

politics
The study of who gets what, when, and how—or how policy decisions are made.

opposition party leader Benazir Bhutto just weeks before the 2007 national election in Pakistan also led to violence. These examples vividly show the need for a strong government to enforce the rule of law.

As we explore American government in this text, we are referring to the web of formal administrative structures that exist on the national, state, and local levels. But, these governments do not exist in a vacuum. A variety of external forces such as the media, political parties, and interest groups influence the day-to-day workings of governments. Thus, we explore government in the context of **politics**, the study of what has been called "who gets what, when, and how," or more simply, the process of how policy decisions get made.

The study of "who gets what, when, and how" can be a fascinating process. While all governments share to greater or lesser degrees the need to provide certain key functions, to whom they provide these benefits, which benefits they provide, when they provide them, and how they are provided vary tremendously across as well as within nations. One need only look to recent debates on the war in Iraq, tax policy, and health care to realize that there are many questions involving who, what, when, and how during policy debates.

Functions of Government

COMPARATIVE

Comparing Political Landscapes

The Framers of the Constitution clearly recognized the need for a new government. As our opening vignette underscores, in attempting "to form a more perfect Union," the Framers, through the Constitution, set out several key functions of government, as well as governmental guarantees to the people, that have continuing relevance today. As discussed below, several of the Framers' ideas centered on their belief that the major function of government was creating mechanisms to allow individuals to solve conflicts in an orderly and peaceful manner. Just how much authority one must give up to governments in exchange for this kind of security, however, has vexed political philosophers as well as politicians for ages. Still, several enduring principles are evident in the Declaration of Independence, the Constitution, the Pledge of Allegiance, and the American's Creed. (To learn more about the enduring principles of the United States, see Ideas into Action: The American's Creed.) Moreover, it is important to note that each of these principles has faced challenges over time, restricting or expanding the underlying notion of a "more Perfect Union."

Thinking Globally

The European Union

The European Union (EU) was established in 1993. It is now composed of twenty-seven countries, including fifteen Western European nations, eight Eastern European nations, and the island nations of Malta and Cyprus. The European Union has achieved a great deal of cross-national integration with respect to economic, diplomatic, and technical matters. Political and military integration of the member nations has been more difficult to accomplish.

- If the United States were to enter into a union of nations similar to the European Union, which countries would be its natural partners?
- What functions of government might such a union of countries facilitate if the United States were a party to it?

ESTABLISHING JUSTICE One of the first things expected from governments is a system of laws that allows individuals to abide by a common set of principles. Societies adhering to the rule of law allow for the rational dispensing of justice by acknowledged legal authorities. Thus, today, the Bill of Rights entitles people to a trial by jury, to be informed of the charges against them, and to be tried in a courtroom presided over by an impartial judge. The Constitution created a federal judicial system to dispense

The American's Creed

Times of war often lead to patriotic displays intended to bolster support for home and country. As dissension among Americans swirled around U.S. involvement in World War I, a national contest was held to codify an "American's Creed." The winning entry, written by William Tyler Page in 1917 and adopted by the U.S. House of Representatives in 1918, states:

> I believe in the United States of America as a Government of the people, by the people, for the people, whose just powers are derived from the consent of the government; a democracy in a Republic; a sovereign Nation of many sovereign States; a perfect Union, one and inseparable; established upon those principles of freedom, equality, justice and humanity for which American patriots sacrificed their lives and fortunes.
>
> I therefore believe it is my duty to my country to love it, to support its Constitution, to obey its laws, to respect its flag and to defend it against all enemies.

The similarities between the American's Creed and the Declaration of Independence are clear, but in times of political disagreement over American policies abroad, such statements of solidarity can lead to disagreements over what American citizens owe their nation and how best they can defend it against "all enemies." Are politicians who wear flag pins on their lapels more patriotic than those who do not? To what extent may citizens actively oppose their governments' policies while still remaining loyal citizens? Does citizenship require voiced disagreement as well as support? The spirited debate on these issues will continue.

- How would you change the American's Creed to make it more relevant to twenty-first-century America? Does the creed omit or underplay aspects of citizenship that you believe are important? Does it emphasize aspects of citizenship that should be downplayed or left out?
- Examine the language of the American's Creed and research the myriad allusions it makes to other historical documents. How are these documents important to modern American society?
- Draft a new version of the American's Creed, making it both specific to the United States and also relevant to twenty-first-century America.

---

justice, but the Bill of Rights specified a host of rights guaranteed to all citizens in an effort to establish justice. (To learn more about these rights, see chapter 5.)

INSURING DOMESTIC TRANQUILITY As we will discuss throughout this text, the role of government in insuring domestic tranquility is a subject of much debate. In times of crisis such as the terrorist attacks of September 11, 2001, the U.S. government, as well as state and local governments, took extraordinary measures to contain the threat of terrorism from abroad as well as within the United States. The creation of the Department of Homeland Security and the passage of legislation giving the national government nearly unprecedented ability to ferret out potential threats show the degree to which the government takes seriously its charge to preserve domestic tranquility. On an even more practical front, local governments have police forces, the states have national guards, and the federal government can always call up troops to quell any threats.

PROVIDING FOR THE COMMON DEFENSE The Constitution calls for the president to be the commander in chief of the armed forces, and Congress is given the authority to raise an army. The Framers recognized that one of the major purposes of government is to provide for the defense of its citizens. As highlighted in Figure 1.1, the defense budget is a considerable proportion of all federal outlays.

PROMOTING THE GENERAL WELFARE When the Framers added "promoting the general Welfare" to their list of key government functions, they never envisioned how the involvement of the government at all levels would expand so tremendously. In fact, promoting the general welfare was more of an ideal than a mandate for the new national government. Over time, however, our notions of what governments should do have

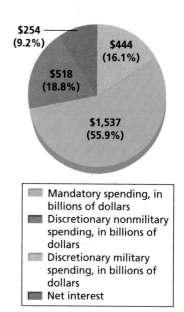

- Mandatory spending, in billions of dollars
- Discretionary nonmilitary spending, in billions of dollars
- Discretionary military spending, in billions of dollars
- Net interest

FIGURE 1.1 Allocation of the Federal Budget, 2008

Source: Fiscal Year 2008 Budget, www.whitehouse.gov/omb/budget/fy2008/pdf/spec.pdf, Table 25-1.

TABLE **1.1** Important Symbols of the United States

TABLE 1.1 Important Symbols of the United States

The U.S. flag
The seal of the United States
The Star Spangled Banner (national anthem)
The bald eagle (national bird)
The Pledge of Allegiance
The American's Creed

expanded along with the number and size of governments. As we discuss throughout this text, however, there is no universal agreement on the scope of what governments should do. There is no doubt that Social Security income programs as well as governmental programs providing health care are designed to promote the general welfare. These programs also make up a significant proportion of the federal budget, as highlighted in Figure 1.1.

SECURING THE BLESSINGS OF LIBERTY A well-functioning government that enjoys the support of its citizenry is one of the best ways to "secure the Blessings of Liberty" for its people. In a free society, citizens enjoy a wide range of liberties and freedoms and feel free to prosper. They are free to criticize the government and to petition it when they disagree with its policies or have a grievance.

The Pledge of Allegiance and the American's Creed reflect another hallmark of our democracy: protecting the American flag, which has come to be one of the most revered symbols in our nation. (To learn more about national symbols, see Table 1.1.) Such symbols can hold us together as a nation in times of crisis, as witnessed by the widespread flying of American flags throughout the nation in the wake of the September 11, 2001, terrorist attacks. Calls to display and honor the flag become especially prominent in times of war, when patriotism can become an issue. Flag burning in protest of governmental action remains controversial, but the U.S. Supreme Court has upheld its constitutionality several times, based on the right of free speech.

Taken together, these principal functions of government and the guarantees they provide to citizens permeate our lives. Whether it is your ability to obtain a low-interest student loan, buy a formerly prescription-only drug such as Claritin or Plan B over the counter, or be licensed to drive a car at a particular age, government plays a major role. And, without government-sponsored research, we would not have cellular telephones, the Internet, four-wheel-drive vehicles, or even Velcro.

Types of Government

Early theorists such as Plato and Aristotle tried to categorize governments by who participates, who governs, and how much authority those who govern enjoy. As revealed in Table 1.2, a **monarchy**, the form of government explicitly rejected by the Framers, is defined by the rule of one in the interest of all of his or her subjects. The Framers also rejected adopting an aristocracy, which is defined as government by the few in the service of the many.

The least appealing of Aristotle's classifications of government is **totalitarianism**, a form of government that he considered rule by "tyranny." Tyrants rule their countries to benefit themselves. This was the case in Iraq under Saddam Hussein. In tyrannical or totalitarian systems, the leader exercises unlimited power, and individuals have no personal rights or liberties. Generally, these systems tend to be ruled in the name of a particular religion or orthodoxy, an ideology, or a personality cult organized around a supreme leader.

Another unappealing form of government, an **oligarchy**, occurs when a few people rule in their own interest. In an oligarchy, participation in government is conditioned on the possession of wealth, social status, military position, or achievement. Oligarchies are rare today.

monarchy
A form of government in which power is vested in hereditary kings and queens who govern in the interests of all.

totalitarianism
A form of government in which power resides in a leader who rules according to self-interest and without regard for individual rights and liberties.

oligarchy
A form of government in which the right to participate is conditioned on the possession of wealth, social status, military position, or achievement.

TABLE 1.2 Aristotle's Classifications of Government

Rule by	In Whose Interest?	
	Public	Self
One	Monarchy	Tyranny
The Few	Aristocracy	Oligarchy
The Many	Polity	Democracy

Source: Aristotle, *Politics* 3, 7.

Aristotle called rule of the many for the benefit of all citizens a "polity" and referred to rule of the many to benefit themselves as a "democracy." The term **democracy** is derived from the Greek words *demos* (the people) and *kratia* (power or authority) and may be used to refer to any system of government that gives power to the people, either directly, or indirectly through elected representatives. Ironically, Aristotle was quite troubled by the idea of democracy, although he believed it better than tyranny or oligarchy. He strongly believed that the collective judgment of the many was preferable to that of a few.

The majority of governments worldwide are democracies to one extent or another. In most democracies, contrary to Aristotle's fears, the "many"—or in the case of the United States and as noted in our chapter opening vignette, "the People"—are the ruling power, albeit through their elected leaders.

democracy
A system of government that gives power to the people, whether directly or through elected representatives.

The Philosophical Origins of American Government

The current American political system did not spring into being overnight. It is the result of philosophy, trial and error, and even luck. To begin our examination of why we have the type of government we have today, we will look at the theories of government that influenced the Framers who drafted the Constitution and created the United States of America.

The Reformation and the Enlightenment: Questioning the Divine Right of Kings

In the third century, as the Roman Empire began to fall, kings throughout Europe began to rule their countries absolutely, claiming their right to govern came directly from God. Thus, since it was thought to be God's will that a particular monarch ruled a country, the people in that country had no right to question their monarch's authority or agitate for a voice in their government's operation.

During the Enlightenment period, the ideas of philosophers and scientists such as Isaac Newton (1642–1727) radically changed people's views of government. Newton and others argued that the world could be improved through the use of human reason, science, and religious toleration. He and other theorists directly challenged earlier notions that fate alone controlled an individual's destiny and that kings ruled by divine right.

The intellectual and religious developments of the Reformation and Enlightenment periods of the sixteenth and seventeenth centuries encouraged people to seek alternatives to absolute monarchies and to ponder new methods of governance. In the late sixteenth century, radical Protestants split from the Church of England, which was created by King Henry VIII when the Roman Catholic Church forbade him to divorce and remarry. Known as Puritans, these new Protestants believed in their ability to speak directly to God, and they established self-governing congregations. But, they were persecuted for their religious beliefs by the English monarchy. The Pilgrims were the first group of these Protestants to flee religious persecution and settle in America. There they established self-governing congregations and were responsible for the first widespread appearance of self-government in

Where did American ideas about government come from? Isaac Newton and other Enlightenment thinkers challenged people's ideas about the nature of government.

Photo courtesy: E.R.L./Sipa

Mayflower Compact
Document written by the Pilgrims while at sea enumerating the scope of their government and its expectations of citizens.

social contract
An agreement between the people and their government signifying their consent to be governed.

social contract theory
The belief that people are free and equal by natural right, and that this in turn requires that all people give their consent to be governed; espoused by John Locke and influential in the writing of the Declaration of Independence.

the American colonies. The **Mayflower Compact**, the document setting up their new government, was deemed sufficiently important to be written while the Pilgrims were still at sea. It took the form of a **social contract**, or agreement between the people and their government signifying their consent to be governed.

Hobbes, Locke, and the Social Contract Theory of Government

Two English theorists of the seventeenth century, Thomas Hobbes (1588–1679) and John Locke (1632–1704), built on conventional notions about the role of government and the relationship of the government to the people in proposing a **social contract theory** of government. They argued that all individuals were free and equal by natural right. This freedom, in turn, required that all men and women give their consent to be governed.

Hobbes was influenced greatly by the chaos of the English Civil War during the mid-seventeenth century. Its impact is evident in his most famous work, *Leviathan* (1651), a treatise on government that states his views on humanity and citizenship. *Leviathan* is commonly described as a book about politics, but it also deals with religion and moral philosophy. In *Leviathan*, Hobbes argued pessimistically that humanity's natural state was one of war. Government, Hobbes theorized, particularly a monarchy, was necessary to restrain humanity's bestial tendencies because life without government was but a "state of nature." Without written, enforceable rules, people would live like animals—foraging for food, stealing, and killing when necessary. To escape the horrors of the natural state and to protect their lives, Hobbes argued, people must give up certain rights to government. Without government, Hobbes warned, life would be "solitary, poor, nasty, brutish, and short"—a constant struggle to survive against the evil of others. For these reasons, governments had to intrude on people's rights and liberties to better control society and to provide the necessary safeguards for property.

Hobbes argued strongly for a single ruler, no matter how evil, to guarantee the rights of the weak against the strong. Leviathan, a biblical sea monster, was his characterization of an all-powerful government. Strict adherence to Leviathan's laws, however all-encompassing or intrusive on liberty, was a small price to pay for living in a civilized society.

In contrast to Hobbes, John Locke, like many other political philosophers of the era, took the basic survival of humanity for granted. Locke argued that a government's major responsibility was the preservation of private property, an idea that ultimately found its way into the U.S. Constitution. In two of his works—*Second Treatise on Civil Government* (1689) and *Essay Concerning Human Understanding* (1690)—Locke not only denied the divine right of kings to govern but argued that individuals were born equal and with natural rights that no king had the power to void. Under Locke's conception of social contract theory, the consent of the people is the only true basis of any sovereign's right to rule. According to Locke, people form governments largely to preserve life, liberty, and property, and to ensure justice. If governments act improperly, they break their contract with the people and therefore no longer enjoy the consent of the governed. Because he believed that true justice comes from the law, Locke argued that the branch of government that makes laws—as opposed to the one that enforces or interprets laws—should be the most powerful.

Locke believed that having a chief executive to administer laws was important, but that he should necessarily be limited by law or by the social contract with the governed. Locke's writings influenced many American colonists, especially Thomas Jeffer-

Why did Hobbes support rule by a monarch? The title page from Thomas Hobbes's *Leviathan* (1651) depicts a giant ruler whose body consists of the bodies of his subjects. This is symbolic of the people coming together under one ruler.

Photo courtesy: Bettmann/CORBIS

son, whose original draft of the Declaration of Independence noted the rights to "life, liberty, and property" as key reasons to separate from England.[2] This document was "pure Locke" because it based the justification for the split with England on the English government's violation of the social contract with the American colonists.

Devising a National Government in the American Colonies

Although social contract theorists agreed on the need for government, they did not necessarily agree on the form that a government should take. Thomas Hobbes argued for a single leader; John Locke and Jean-Jacques Rousseau (1712–1778), a French philosopher, saw the need for less centralized power.

The American colonists rejected a system with a strong ruler, like the British monarchy, when they declared their independence. Many of the colonists had fled Great Britain to avoid religious persecution and other harsh manifestations of power wielded by King George II. They viewed King George as a malevolent despot who failed to govern in their interests and were reluctant to put themselves in the same position in their new nation. The colonists also were fearful of replicating the landed and titled system of the British aristocracy. They viewed the formation of a representative form of government as far more in keeping with the ideas of social contract theorists.

The colonists were quick to create participatory forms of government in which most men were allowed to take part. The New England town meeting, where all citizens gather to discuss and decide issues facing the town, today stands as a surviving example of a **direct democracy**, in which the people rather than their elected representatives make political decisions. This system was used in ancient Greece when all free, male citizens came together periodically to pass laws and elect leaders by lot.

Direct democracies soon proved unworkable in the colonies. As more and more settlers came to the New World, many town meetings were replaced by a system of **indirect democracy**, or representative democracy, in which representatives of the people are chosen by ballot. The Virginia House of Burgesses, created in 1619, was the first representative assembly in North America. Representative government was considered undemocratic by ancient Greeks, who believed that all citizens must have a direct say in their governance.[3] And, in the 1760s, Jean-Jacques Rousseau argued that true democracy is impossible unless all citizens participate in governmental decision making. Nevertheless, indirect democracy was the form of government used throughout most of the colonies.

Many citizens were uncomfortable with the term democracy because it conjured up Hobbesian fears of the people and mob rule. Instead, they preferred the term **republic**, which implied a system of government in which the interests of the people were represented by more educated or wealthier citizens who were responsible to those who elected them. Today, representative democracies are more commonly called republics, and the words democracy and republic often are used interchangeably.

direct democracy
A system of government in which members of the polity meet to discuss all policy decisions and then agree to abide by majority rule.

indirect (representative) democracy
A system of government that gives citizens the opportunity to vote for representatives who will work on their behalf.

republic
A government rooted in the consent of the governed; a representative or indirect democracy.

American Political Culture and the Basic Tenets of American Democracy

As described previously, the Framers devised a representative democratic system to govern the United States. This system is based on a number of underlying concepts and distinguishing characteristics that sometimes conflict with one another. Taken together, these ideas lie at the core of American political culture. More specifically, **political culture** can be defined as commonly shared attitudes, beliefs, and core values about how government should operate. American political culture emphasizes the

political culture
Commonly shared attitudes, beliefs, and core values about how government should operate.

values of personal liberty, equality, popular consent and majority rule, popular sovereignty, civil society, individualism, and religious faith.

Personal Liberty

personal liberty
A key characteristic of U.S. democracy. Initially meaning freedom *from* governmental interference, today it includes demands for freedom *to* engage in a variety of practices without governmental interference or discrimination.

Personal liberty is perhaps the single most important characteristic of American democracy. The Constitution itself was written to ensure life and liberty. Over the years, however, our concepts of liberty have changed and evolved from freedom *from* to freedom *to*. The Framers intended Americans to be free from governmental infringements on freedom of religion and speech, from unreasonable searches and seizure, and so on (see chapter 5). The addition of the Fourteenth Amendment to the Constitution and its emphasis on due process and on equal protection of the laws as well as the subsequent passage of laws guaranteeing civil rights, however, expanded Americans' concept of liberty to include demands for freedom to work or go to school without discrimination. Debates over how much the government should do to guarantee these rights and liberties illustrate the conflicts that continue to occur in our democratic system.

Equality

political equality
The principle that all citizens are equal in the political process, as implied by the phrase "one person, one vote."

Another key characteristic of our democracy is **political equality**. A belief in political equality reflects Americans' emphasis on the importance of the individual. Although some individuals clearly wield more political clout than others, the adage "one person, one vote" implies a sense of political equality for all. The American emphasis on individuality is often at odds with notions of political equality. Is it for the person or the group? Historically, after being excluded from full political participation, African American men and later all women were given the right to vote, but it hardly brought with it political equality in representation. Today, the United States ranks behind China, an authoritarian government, in the number of women in its national legislature!

Moreover, notions of political equality have changed dramatically over time. The U.S. Constitution once treated slaves as equal to but three-fifths of a white man for purposes of assessing state population. No one could have imagined that in 2008, Barack Obama, the only African American in the U.S. Senate, would be elected president by large margins. President Obama even won Virginia, which is home to Richmond, the former capital of the Confederate States of America.

Although in theory most Americans today are eligible to seek elective office, few can afford the cost of a campaign. Thus, while political equality is a key component of American political theory, it still remains a dream far short of reality.

Popular Consent, Majority Rule, and Popular Sovereignty

popular consent
The principle that governments must draw their powers from the consent of the governed.

Popular consent, the idea that governments must draw their powers from the consent of the governed, is another distinguishing characteristic of American democracy. Derived from John Locke's social contract theory, the notion of popular consent was central to the Declaration of Independence. Today, a citizen's willingness to vote represents his or her consent to be governed and is thus an essential premise of democracy. Large numbers of nonvoters can threaten the operation and legitimacy of a truly democratic system.

majority rule
The central premise of direct democracy in which only policies that collectively garner the support of a majority of voters will be made into law.

Majority rule, another core political value, means that the majority (normally 50 percent of the total votes cast plus one) of citizens in any political unit should elect officials and determine policies. This principle holds for both voters and their elected representatives. Yet, the American system also stresses the need to preserve minority rights, as evidenced by the myriad protections of individual rights and liberties found in the Bill of Rights.

The concept of the preservation of minority rights has changed dramatically in the United States. It wasn't until after the Civil War that slaves were freed and African Americans began to enjoy minimal citizenship rights. By the 1960s, however, anger at America's failure to guarantee minority rights in all sections of the nation fueled the civil rights movement. This ultimately led to congressional passage of the Civil Rights Act of 1964 and the Voting Rights Act of 1965, both designed to further minority rights.

Popular sovereignty, or the notion that the ultimate authority in society rests with the people, has its basis in **natural law**. Ultimately, political authority rests with the people, who can create, abolish, or alter their governments. The idea that all governments derive their power from the people is found in the Declaration of Independence and the U.S. Constitution, but the term popular sovereignty did not come into wide use until pre–Civil War debates over slavery. At that time, supporters of popular sovereignty argued that the citizens of new states seeking admission to the union should be able to decide whether or not their states would allow slavery within their borders.

popular sovereignty
The notion that the ultimate authority in society rests with the people.

natural law
A doctrine that society should be governed by certain ethical principles that are part of nature and, as such, can be understood by reason.

Civil Society

Several of these hallmarks of our political culture also are fundamental to what many commentators now term **civil society**. This term is used to describe the society created when citizens are allowed to organize and express their views publicly as they engage in an open debate about public policy.[4] The fall of the Soviet Union "accelerated the global trend toward democracy . . . which pushed democracy to the top of the political agenda."[5] In Russia, for example, the U.S. government has used a variety of initiatives to train people how to act in a new democratic system.

Independent and politically active citizens are key to the success of any democracy, yet people who have not lived in democratic systems often are unschooled, reluctant, or afraid to participate after years in communist or totalitarian systems. The U.S. government routinely makes grants to nongovernmental organizations, professional associations, civic education groups, and women's groups to encourage the kind of participation in the political system that Americans often take for granted. U.S. efforts to assist Afghanistan and Iraq, for example, include not only public works projects but also development of their new democratic governments.

civil society
Society created when citizens are allowed to organize and express their views publicly as they engage in an open debate about public policy.

Individualism

Although many core political tenets concern protecting the rights of others, tremendous value is placed on the individual in American democracy. This emphasis on individualism makes Americans quite different from citizens of other democracies such as Canada, which practices a group approach to governance. Group-focused societies reject the American emphasis on individuals and try to improve the lives of their citizens by making services and rights available on a group or universal basis, as is the case with universal health care. In contrast, in the U.S. system, all individuals are deemed rational and fair and endowed, as Thomas Jefferson proclaimed in the Declaration of Independence, "with certain unalienable rights." Even today, many view individualism, which holds that the primary function of government is to enable the individual to achieve his or her highest level of development, as a mixed blessing. It is also a concept whose meaning has changed over time. The rugged individualism of the western frontier, for example, was altered as more citizens moved westward, cities developed, and demands for government services increased as many individuals no longer could exist independently of others.

What Are American Civic Values?

Religious Faith and Religious Freedom

Religion and religious faith are often at the forefront of how many Americans perceive political and policy issues. As the nation waged war in Iraq and attempted to export democracy to the Middle East, an increasing number of Americans, for example, considered Islam "a religion that encourages violence" and did not view Islam as having

Why is religious freedom a tenet of American democracy? Many of the first settlers came to the U.S. to escape religious persecution. Here, American Catholics greet Pope Benedict XVI during his visit to the United States.

Photo courtesy: Chang W. Lee, Pool/AP/Wide World Photos

much in common with their own religion.[6] In the 2008 presidential nominating process, some clerics and voters questioned whether Mitt Romney, a Mormon, was a Christian or a member of a religious cult. Controversial statements condemning U.S. policy in sermons given by Barack Obama's minister, the Reverend Jeremiah Wright, were also given significant coverage, prompting Obama to publicly repudiate Wright's statements. Controversial statements at his church by another pastor later led Obama to resign as a member.

Still, many Americans are quite comfortable with religion playing an important role in public policy. President George W. Bush's frequent references to his faith as guiding his decisions received the support of 60 percent of the American public in one 2005 poll.[7] In fact, although the First Amendment to the Constitution creates a wall of separation between church and state (see chapter 5), 69 percent of respondents in 2007 agreed with the statement "The president should have strong religious beliefs."[8]

Most Americans profess to have strong religious beliefs, and the United States is the most churchgoing nation in the world. It is overwhelmingly Christian, with a growing number of Christian evangelicals who, since 1980, have played an exceptionally important role in American politics, defining the political positions of the Republican Party, in particular. People of religious faith often have very firm beliefs on social issues such as contraception and abortion, same-sex marriage, the right of homosexual people to adopt children, and the use of stem cells for medical research. The concerns of people of strong religious faith continue to play a major role in shaping the political agenda of the nation.

Political Ideology: Its Role in the World and in American Politics

On September 11, 2001, nineteen terrorists, all of Middle Eastern origin and professing to be devout Muslims engaged in a "holy war" against the United States, hijacked four airplanes and eventually killed nearly 3,000 people. The terrorists' self-described holy war, or *jihad*, was targeted at Americans, whom they considered infidels. Earlier, in 1995, a powerful bomb exploded outside the Murrah Federal Building in Oklahoma City, killing nearly 170 people, including many children. This terrorist attack was launched not by those associated with radical Islam, but with an American anti-government brand of neo-Nazism. Its proponents hold the U.S. government in contempt and profess a hatred of Jews and others they believe are "inferior" ethnic groups and races.

political ideology
The coherent set of values and beliefs about the purpose and scope of government held by groups and individuals.

These are but two extreme examples of the powerful role of **political ideology**—the coherent set of values and beliefs people hold about the purpose and scope of government—in the actions of individuals.[9] Ideologies are sets or systems of beliefs that shape the thinking of individuals and how they view the world, especially in regard to issues of "race, nationality, the role and function of government, the relations between men and women, human responsibility for the natural environment, and many other matters."[10] They have been recognized increasingly as a potent political force. Isaiah Berlin, a noted historian and philosopher, noted that two factors above all others shaped human history in the twentieth century: "one is science and technology; the other is ideological battles—totalitarian tyrannies of both right and left and the explosions of nationalism, racism, and religious bigotry that the most perceptive social thinkers of the nineteenth century failed to predict."[11]

It is easier to understand how ideas get turned into action when one looks at the four functions political scientists attribute to ideologies. In a rapidly changing world, they help many better organize their thoughts about government and its role. These include:

1. *Explanation*. Ideologies can provide us with reasons for why social and political conditions are the way they are, especially in time of crisis. Knowing that Saddam Hussein ruled Iraq as a totalitarian society helps explain, at least in part, why he chose to use chemical weapons on his own people.

2. *Evaluation*. Ideologies can provide the standards for evaluating social conditions and political institutions and events. As medical costs skyrocket and more and more individuals lack health insurance, Americans' belief in the importance of the individual's abilities and personal responsibilities helps explain the reluctance of some to offer health insurance to all.

3. *Orientation*. Ideologies can provide a sense of identity, whether you are male, female, native born, or foreign born, for example. Much like a compass, ideologies provide individuals with an orientation toward issues and a position within the world. When many African American women, Oprah Winfrey among them, decided to campaign for Barack Obama and not Hillary Clinton in the 2008 Democratic presidential primary, their sense of identity as African Americans may have trumped their identity as women.

4. *Political Program*. Ideologies help people to make political choices and guide their political actions. Thus, since the Republican Party is identified with a steadfast opposition to abortion, anyone with strong pro-life views would find the party's stance on this issue a helpful guide in voting.

Thinking Globally
Christianity and Islam

Christianity is the largest and most widely spread religion in the world. Christianity is most prevalent in Europe, Latin America, and North America. Muslims represent the second largest group and the most rapidly growing religion. The Muslim religion is concentrated in the Middle East, Asia, and Africa.

- In what ways has religious faith united countries and in what ways has it divided them?
- Identify some of the different ways religion plays a role in public policy making—either in the United States or in other countries.

Prevailing American Political Ideologies

In America today, one most often hears about conservative, moderate, or liberal political ideologies. (To learn more about the distribution of ideologies in the United States, see Figure 1.2.) These ideologies often translate into political party support, which in turn affects how one votes at the polls. A small proportion of Americans

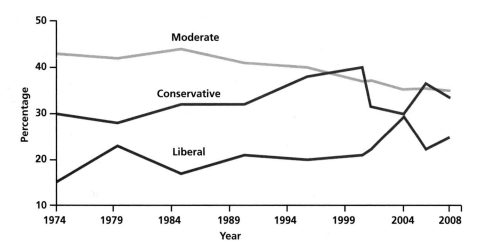

FIGURE 1.2
Adult Ideological Self-Identification 1974–2008

Source: Roper Center at the University of Connecticut, *Public Opinion Online*, Roper iPoll.

libertarian
One who favors a free market economy and no governmental interference in personal liberties.

conservative
One who believes that a government is best that governs least and that big government can only infringe on individual, personal, and economic rights.

social conservative
One who believes that traditional moral teachings should be supported and furthered by the government.

liberal
One who favors governmental involvement in the economy and in the provision of social services and who takes an activist role in protecting the rights of women, the elderly, minorities, and the environment.

also refer to themselves as **libertarian**, which means they oppose government interference in personal liberties, but pollsters rarely offer respondents the opportunity to label themselves as such. However, Representative Ron Paul (R–TX), a Republican Party candidate for the presidential nomination in 2008, was the Libertarian Party's presidential candidate in 1988 and still identifies himself as a libertarian. Much more common are the ideologies discussed below, but it is important to remember that conservatives may be liberal on some issues and vice versa.

CONSERVATISM According to William Safire's *New Political Dictionary*, a **conservative** "is a defender of the status quo who, when change becomes necessary in tested institutions or practices, prefers that it come slowly, and in moderation."[12] Conservatives tend to believe that a government is best when it governs least. They want less government, especially in terms of regulation of the economy. Conservatives favor local and state action over federal intervention, and they emphasize fiscal responsibility, most notably in the form of balanced budgets. Ironically, however, it was Republican Presidents Ronald Reagan and George W. Bush who ran record deficits, while Bill Clinton, a moderate Democrat, balanced the budget during his two terms as president.

Conservatives are likely to support smaller, less activist governments and believe that domestic problems such as homelessness, poverty, and discrimination are better dealt with by the private sector than by the government. Since the 1970s, a growing number of **social conservative** voters (sometimes referred to as the Religious Right) increasingly have affected politics and policies in the United States. Social conservatives believe that moral decay must be stemmed and that traditional moral teachings should be supported and furthered by the government. Social conservatives support government intervention to regulate sexual and social behavior and have mounted effective efforts to restrict abortion and ban same-sex marriage. While a majority of social conservatives are evangelical Protestants and Roman Catholics, some Jews and many Muslims are also social conservatives.

LIBERALISM A **liberal** is one who seeks to change the political, economic, and social status quo to foster the development of equality and the well-being of individuals.[13] The meanings of the words liberal and liberalism have changed over time, but in the modern United States, liberals generally value equality over other aspects of shared political culture. They are supportive of well-funded government social welfare programs that seek to protect individuals from economic disadvantages or to correct past injustices, and they generally oppose government efforts to regulate private behavior or infringe on civil rights and liberties.

Problems with Political Labels

In a perfect world, liberals would be liberal and conservatives would be conservative. Studies reveal, however, that many people who call themselves conservative actually take fairly liberal positions on many policy issues. In fact, anywhere from 20 percent to 60 percent of people will take a traditionally conservative position on one issue and a traditionally liberal position on another.[14] People who take conservative stances against "big government," for example, often support increases in spending for the elderly, education, or health care. It is also not unusual to encounter a person who could be considered a liberal on social issues such as abortion and civil rights but a conservative on economic or pocketbook issues. And, as Figure 1.3 makes clear, states are not uniformly "red" or "blue," even though they are often portrayed that way in the media. Today, most Americans' positions on specific issues cut across liberal/conservative ideological boundaries, and most people prefer to be categorized as moderates.

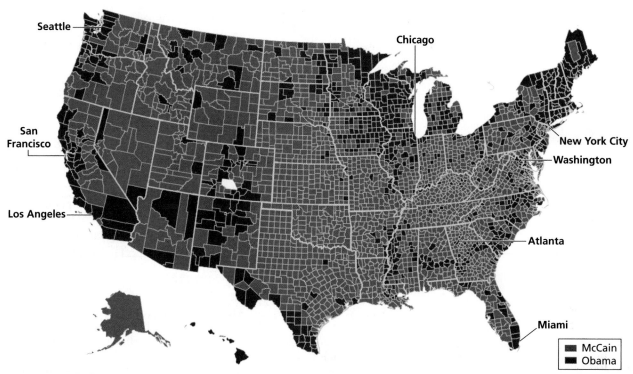

FIGURE 1.3 A Divided Nation? 2008 Presidential Election Results by County

Since the 2000 presidential election, analysts have spoken of a growing split in ideology occuring throughout the United States. After the 2008 presidential election, a quick look at the U.S. map in which each state's Electoral College result was colored red (for Republican John McCain) or blue (for Democrat Barack Obama) made clear the split between more liberal voters on the West Coast and in the Northeast and more conservative voters in the Southeast and Midwest. However, as this map showing the popular vote by county highlights, numerous blocks of counties within states such as Texas and South Carolina where McCain won the Electoral College votes actually went to Democratic candidate Obama. A similar pattern can be identified in blue states such as New York that went to Obama. McCain won a significant number of counties there.

Source: Washington Post.

Changing Characteristics of the American People

Americans have many things in common beyond their political culture, including their high regard for the symbols of government highlighted earlier in Table 1.1. Most Americans share a common language—English—and have similar aspirations for themselves and their families. Most agree that they would rather live in the United States than anywhere else, and that an indirect democracy, with all of its warts, is still the best system of government. Most Americans highly value education and want to send their children to the best schools possible, viewing a good education as the key to success. Despite these similarities, politicians, media commentators, and citizens themselves tend to focus on differences among Americans, in large part because these differences contribute to political conflicts among the electorate. Even journalists covering the U.S. Supreme Court are more likely to report on split decisions than unanimous ones.

Although it is true that the United States and its population are undergoing rapid change, this is not necessarily a new phenomenon. It is simply new to most of us. In the pages that follow, we take a look at some of the characteristics of the American populace. Because the people of the United States are the basis of political power and authority, their characteristics, which often affect their political, social, and cultural attitudes, have important implications for how America is governed and what policies are made.

Changing Size and Population

One year after the U.S. Constitution was ratified, fewer than 4 million Americans lived in the thirteen states. Most were united by a single language and a shared Protestant-Christian heritage, and those who voted were white male property owners. The Constitution mandated that each of the sixty-five members of the original House of Representatives should represent 30,000 people. However, because of rapid population growth, that number often was much higher.

As the nation grew larger with the addition of new states, as revealed in Figure 1.4, the population also grew. Although the geographic size of the United States has remained stable since the addition of Alaska and Hawaii in 1959, in 2008 there were more than 304 million Americans, and a single member of the House of Representatives from Montana represented more than 944,000 people. As a result of this population growth, most citizens today feel far removed from the national government and their elected representatives. Members of Congress, too, feel this change. Often they represent diverse constituencies with a variety of needs, concerns, and expectations, and they can meet only a relative few of these people face to face.

Changing Demographics of the U.S. Population

As the physical size and population of the United States have changed, so have many of the assumptions on which it was founded. Much of this dynamism actually stems from changes in demographics, or the characteristics of the American population, which have occurred throughout our history. Below, we look at some of these demo-

Using the Census to Understand Who Americans Are

FIGURE 1.4 U.S. Population, 1880–2040

Since around 1890, when large numbers of immigrants began arriving in America, the United States has seen a sharp increase in population. The major reasons for this increase are new births and increased longevity, although immigration has also been a contributing factor.

Source: U.S. Census Bureau Population Projections, www.census.gov.

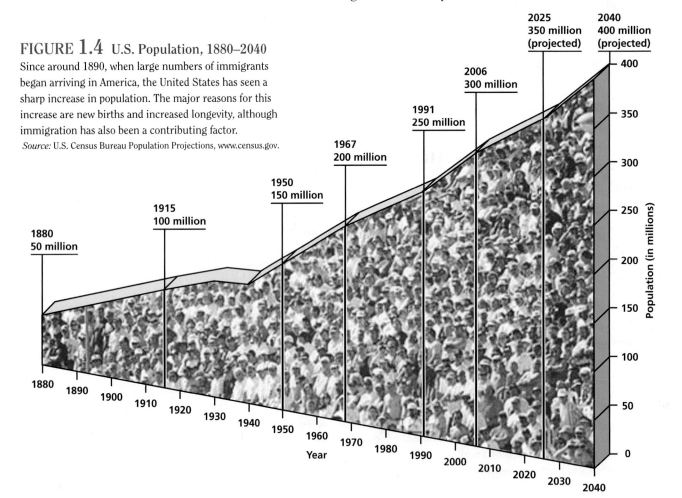

1880 / 50 million
1915 / 100 million
1950 / 150 million
1967 / 200 million
1991 / 250 million
2006 / 300 million
2025 / 350 million (projected)
2040 / 400 million (projected)

graphic characteristics and then discuss some of the implications of these changes for how our nation is governed.

CHANGES IN RACIAL AND ETHNIC COMPOSITION From the start, the American population has been altered constantly by the arrival of immigrants from various regions—Western Europeans fleeing religious persecution in the 1600s to early 1700s, Chinese laborers arriving to work on the railroads following the Gold Rush in 1848, Irish Catholics escaping the potato famine in the 1850s, Northern and Eastern Europeans from the 1880s to 1910s, and most recently, South and Southeast Asians, Cubans, and Mexicans, among others.

Immigration to the United States peaked in the first decade of the 1900s, when nearly 9 million people, many of them from Eastern Europe, entered the country. The United States did not see another major wave of immigration until the late 1980s, when nearly 2 million immigrants were admitted in one year. Today, nearly 40 million people in the United States are considered immigrants. And, contrary to the assumptions of many, they are assimilating into American culture more quickly than ever before.[15]

While immigration has been a continual source of changing demographics in America, race and ethnicity have also played major roles in the development and course of politics in the United States. As revealed in Figure 1.5, the racial and ethnic balance in America has changed dramatically, with the proportion of Hispanics growing at the quickest rate and taking over as the second most common racial or ethnic group in the United States. More importantly, what the figure does not show is that 40 percent of Americans under age twenty-five are members of a minority group, a fact that will have a significant impact not only on the demographics of the American polity but also on how America "looks." In 2008, for example, nonwhites made up one-third of the population yet came nowhere close to that kind of representation in the halls of Congress or on the U.S. Supreme Court. (To learn more about immigration debates today, see Join the Debate: The Huntington Theory of Hispanization.)

CHANGES IN AGE COHORT COMPOSITION Just as the racial and ethnic composition of the American population is changing, so too is the average age. "For decades, the U.S. was described as a nation of the young because the number of persons under the age of twenty greatly outnumber[ed] those sixty-five and older," but this is no longer the case.[16] (To learn more about the aging population, see Figure 1.6.) Because of changes in patterns of fertility, life expectancy, and immigration, the nation's age profile has changed drastically. When the United States was founded, the average life expectancy

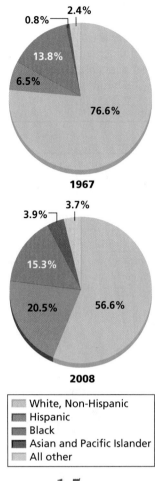

FIGURE 1.5 Race and Ethnicity in America, 1967 and 2008

Source: U.S. Census Bureau, 2008 Statistical Abstract of the United States.

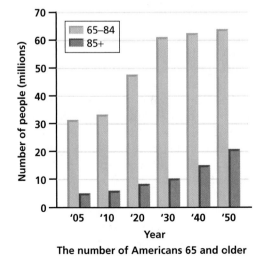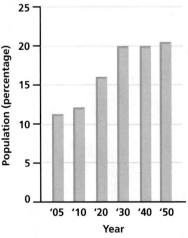

FIGURE 1.6 America Is Getting Older America is aging—and doing so rapidly. By 2050, as shown here, more than 20 percent of the U.S. population will be senior citizens, with about 65 million people age 65–84 and about 20 million people 85 and older.

Source: USA Today (October 25, 2005): 2B.

TABLE 1.3 Government, Health Care, and Costs

Examine the costs associated with the medical interventions listed in the table. Does the government have a role in providing the latest health care options to its citizens, regardless of cost? Should access to expensive new technologies and treatments like these be limited to those who can afford them or those who have health insurance policies willing to pay for such interventions?

Costs per New Medical Intervention

Treatment	What It Does or Would Do	Cost to Medicare per Additional Year of Life
Anti-aging compound for healthy people	$1-a-day compound adds 10 years to life	$11,245
Treatment for acute stroke	New drug reduces cell death after stroke	$28,024
Anti-aging compound for unhealthy people	$1-a-day compound adds 10 years to life	$38,105
Alzheimer's prevention	New drug delays onset of disease	$102,774
Implantable cardioverter defibrillator	Controls heart rhythm	$131,892
Diabetes prevention	Insulin-sensitizing drug reduces disease	$188,316
Pacemakers for atrial fibrillation	New generation of pacemakers	$1,795,850

Source: Rand and *USA Today* (October 25, 2005): 2B.

was thirty-five years; by 2008, it was eighty years for women and seventy-five years for men.

An aging population increases a host of costly demands on the government. In 2008, the first of the Baby Boomers (the 76.8 million people who were born between 1946 and 1964) reached age sixty-two and qualified for Social Security; in 2011, they will reach sixty-five and qualify for Medicare.[17] As Table 1.3 reveals, an aging America poses a great financial burden on working Americans, whose proportion of the population is rapidly declining.

These dramatic changes could potentially pit younger people against older people and result in dramatic cuts in benefits to the elderly and increased taxes for younger workers. Moreover, the elderly often vote against programs favored by younger voters, such as money for new schools and other items that they no longer view as important. At the same time, younger voters are less likely to support some things important to seniors, such as Medicare and prescription drug reform, and they favored the Bush administration's plans for Social Security reform in higher numbers than did seniors.

You Are the Mayor and Need to Get a Town Budget Passed

CHANGES IN FAMILY AND FAMILY SIZE Family size and household arrangements can be affected by several factors, including age at first marriage, divorce rates, economic conditions, longevity rates, and improvements in health care. In the past, familial gender roles were clearly defined. Women did housework and men worked in the fields. Large families were imperative; children were a source of cheap farm labor.

Industrialization and knowledge of birth control methods began to put a dent in the size of American families by the early 1900s. No longer needing children to work for the survival of the household unit on the farm, couples began to limit the sizes of their families.

By 1949, 49 percent of those polled thought that four or more children was the "ideal" family size; in 2007, only 9 percent favored large families, and 56 percent responded that no children to two children was "best."[18] As chronicled in the popular press as well as by the U.S. Department of Commerce,

How big is too big? The members of the Gosselin family, stars of *Jon and Kate Plus Eight*, show that a large family can still be a typical American suburban household.

Photo courtesy: Laura Pedrick/Discovery Health

the American family no longer looks like a television sitcom. In 1940, nine out of ten households were traditional family households. By 2006, just 67.4 percent of children under eighteen lived with both parents. In fact, almost 25 percent of children under eighteen lived with just one of their parents; the majority of those children lived with their mother. Moreover, by 2006, almost 27 percent of all households consisted of a single person, a trend that is in part illustrative of the aging American population and declining marriage rate.

These changes in composition of households, lower birthrates, and prevalence of single-parent families affect the kinds of demands people place on government as well as their perceptions of the role that government should play in their lives. Single-parent families, for example, may be more likely to support government-subsidized day care or after-school programs.

Toward Reform: Population Changes and Americans' Attitudes Toward Government

Today, 86 percent of Americans believe that illegal immigration is a serious problem, and several states have attempted to deny drivers' licenses or access to other public services to undocumented immigrants.[19] Many believe that the numbers of immigrants, legal and illegal, arriving at our shores will lead to disastrous consequences.

Such anti-immigration sentiments are hardly new. In fact, American history is replete with examples of Americans set against any new immigration. In the 1840s, for example, the Know Nothing Party arose in part to oppose immigration from Roman Catholic nations, charging that the pope was going to organize the slaughter of all Protestants in the United States. In the 1920s, the Ku Klux Klan, which had over 5 million members, called for barring immigration to stem the tide of Roman Catholic and Jewish immigrants into the nation.

Changing racial, ethnic, and even age and family demographics seem to intensify—at least for some—an us versus them mentality. For example, government affirmative action programs, which were created in the 1960s to redress decades of overt racial discrimination, continue to be under attack and were on the ballot in two states in 2008. As discussed in chapter 6, vocal critics of affirmative action believe that these programs give minorities and women unfair advantages in the job market, as well as in access to higher education.

Demographics also affect politics and government because an individual's perspective influences how he or she hears debates on various issues. Thus, African Americans, for example, viewed the government's initial slow response to the plight of the poor and displaced after Hurricane Katrina more unfavorably than did whites.[20] These feelings were exacerbated when the Bush administration took such quick action to save the homes of millionaires living in California that were jeopardized by fire.[21]

These cleavages and the emphasis many politicians put on our demographic differences play out in many ways in American politics. Baby Boomers and the elderly object to changes in Social Security or Medicare that adversely affect them, while young Americans are more likely to vote for politicians who support change. Many policies are targeted at one group or the other, further exacerbating differences—real or imagined—and lawmakers often find themselves the target of many different factions. This diversity can make it difficult to devise coherent policies to "promote the general Welfare," as promised in the Constitution.

Join the Debate

The Huntington Theory of Hispanization

OVERVIEW: Many observers of American culture and politics argue that one of the United States' greatest strengths is its ability to absorb and assimilate into the social body the diverse customs and values of different peoples. These commentators highlight the contributions to politics, the arts and sciences, national defense, and the common good made by American Indians and by various waves of immigrants—including those brought against their will during the years of slavery. Traditionalists such as Harvard professor Samuel Huntington contend that the American melting pot has been successful in part because, historically, the new Americans have absorbed the fundamental political principles of the United States as their own. Though there are numerous cultures within the country, Huntington insists that there is one shared American culture based on the values espoused in the Declaration of Independence—that is, American political culture is based on the fundamental principles of equality, individual rights, and government by consent. In order for the love of freedom and self-government to be nurtured and maintained, he would argue, American core principles must be accepted and protected by all citizens.

Huntington argues that during the latter part of the twentieth and into the twenty-first century, there has been a new wave of immigration into the United States unlike any other; he considers immigration from Mexico and Latin America to be potentially destructive of original American political principles. According to Huntington's highly controversial thesis, this immigration wave is unique in that there is a political agenda within part of the Hispanic community to "reclaim" the lands ceded to the United States after both the Texas war for independence and the Mexican-American War.

Furthermore, Huntington argues, no other nation has had to contend with a long, contiguous border that immigrants can cross rather freely to maintain familial, economic, and cultural ties, thereby fostering a type of dual national or cultural allegiance (or, at worst, immigrant loyalty to the home country) that can weaken ties to American core values. Finally, he

contends, Hispanic immigrants have created linguistic and cultural enclaves within the United States (areas of Los Angeles and Miami, for example) in which there is no need to learn the language, history, and political values of their adopted nation, thus further eroding social and political bonds between citizens.

Huntington's thesis raises serious questions. Are American core ideals so exceptional that only people who share those values should be allowed citizenship? Do new immigrants from Latin America have political and social beliefs different from or opposed to America's core values? Has American history shown that, ultimately, most immigrants and their descendents embrace the principles that underlie the U.S. Constitution and American political culture? If Huntington is right, how might we reconcile the apparent demand by U.S. employers for workers from Latin America with the threat that Huntington describes?

Arguments IN FAVOR of Huntington's Thesis

- The core political values found in the Declaration of Independence and the Constitution are essential to maintain freedom and protect rights. It may be that original American principles run the risk of being replaced by ideals that advocate forms of government or politics opposed to liberty, self-government, and individual rights, thus changing the character of the American regime.

- American institutions and political culture pursue "justice as the end of government . . . as the end of civil society." American ideals can be a guide for all to live together effectively in peace and harmony, rather than an end in themselves. These principles allow most individuals to pursue their unique conception of the American dream, relatively free from interference by the government and others.

- A shared language and civic education bind citizens together. Teaching multiple languages and cultural viewpoints denies common civic education and creates competing sources of identity that will weaken citizens' attachments to one another and to their government.

Arguments AGAINST Huntington's Thesis

- Historically, certain waves of immigrants were incorrectly thought to be opposed to American values. Benjamin Franklin expressed concerns that German immigrants could not be assimilated into colonial American life because of their culture and history, and Irish Catholic immigrants were accused of both giving allegiance to the pope and being anti-republican in political outlook—fears that proved to be unfounded.

- Bilingualism in the Hispanic community does not indicate the creation of competing sources of social and political identity. Bilingual people who use English and Spanish—or any other language—are not differing from or opposing American core political values. These values, in fact, have roots in French, Greek, and German philosophies, not just British ones.

- American political culture is more than its Anglo-Protestant core. A strength of the American experience is its ability to absorb different cultures and values and transform them into one unique political society. It took both the successive waves of immigration

THE HIGH TIDE OF IMMIGRATION—A NATIONAL MENACE.

Immigration statistics for the past year show that the influx of foreigners was the greatest in our history and that the hard-working peasants are now being supplanted by the criminals and outlaws of all Europe.

Photo courtesy: The New York Public Library/Art Resource, NY

Have Americans only recently worried about immigration? Concern over immigration is not a new phenomenon, as this cartoon from the early 1900s depicts.

and the freeing of the slaves to move the United States toward the realization of the ideals espoused in the Declaration of Independence.

Continuing the Debate

1. Does the issue of Hispanic immigration threaten American sovereignty and values? Do demonstrations by pro- and anti-immigrant groups signal a significant shift in U.S. history? Explain your thinking.

2. Is American political culture more than its core principles and institutions? What other values and institutions add to the United States' claim that it is a true "melting pot" or multicultural society?

To Follow the Debate Online, Go To:

www.whitehouse.gov to research the current administration's immigration policies.

www.aila.net, the Web site of the American Immigration Lawyer's Association, which provides information on the status of the immigration issue in court.

www.fairus.org for the views of the Federation for American Immigration Reform, which generally has advocated against allowing undocumented immigrants living in the United States to stay.

www.immigrationadvocates.org, the Web site of the Immigration Advocates Network, a partnership of religious, legal, and policy groups that works to strengthen the rights of immigrants by providing an online resource and communication site.

Attitudinal Change and Reform

Americans' views about, and expectations of, government and democracy affect the political system at all levels. It has now become part of our political culture to expect negative campaigns, dishonest politicians, and political pundits who make their living bashing politicians and the political process. In fact, the calls for change made by presidential candidates in 2008 reflect the general desire of the American populace for no more politics as usual. How Americans view politics, the economy, and their ability to achieve the **American dream**—an American ideal of a happy and successful life, which often includes wealth, a house, a better life for one's children, and for some, the ability to grow up to be president—is influenced by their political ideology as well as by their social, economic, educational, and personal circumstances and was reflected in voter turnout and voting patterns in 2008.

Since the early 1990s, the major sources of most individuals' news—the four major networks (ABC, CBS, FOX, and NBC) along with CNN and C-SPAN—have been supplemented dramatically as the number of news and quasi-news outlets has grown exponentially. First there were weekly programs such as *Dateline* on the regular networks. Next came FOX News, MSNBC, and CNBC—all competing for similar audiences. During the 2008 election, more people turned to a cable news program than to the regular networks for their political coverage.

The Internet, has also developed as an instantaneous source of news, as well as rumor, about politics. The growth of blogs has allowed consumers to report the news themselves, commenting on events as they occur, sometimes in an unflattering manner. Between bloggers and pundits, who discuss political news on a regular basis, politics has become more personal than ever.

As more and more news programs develop, each network or news program is under pressure to be the first with breaking news. The competition for news stories, as well as the instantaneous nature of these communications, often highlights the negative, the sensational, the sound bite, and the extreme. It's hard to remain upbeat about America or politics amid the media's focus on personality and scandal. It's hard to remain positive about the fate of Americans and their families if you watch news shows that feature guests trying to outshout each other or campaign ads that highlight only the negative.

We also cannot ignore how Americans are now viewed abroad. For centuries, immigrants have come to our shores to be part of the American dream—but now, to some people in Europe, the Middle East, and elsewhere, America is no longer the beacon it once was. The spread of American culture as embodied by fast-food chains and American television programs such as *Sex and the City* and *Will and Grace* to other nations, along with the United States' unpopular involvement in Iraq, has intensified the stereotype of the "ugly American." Negative perceptions of the United States increasingly affect America's relations around the world, with important effects on Americans' expectations.

High Expectations

Reform becomes difficult when expectations are unrealistically high. Economist Charles Lindbloom argues that most political change is incremental. Thus, quick change is unlikely to happen regardless of the public's views

American dream
An American ideal of a happy, successful life, which often includes wealth, a house, a better life for one's children, and for some, the ability to grow up to be president.

TIMELINE

Major Technological Innovations That Have Changed the Political Landscape

How has the face of the United States changed?
Barack Obama was the first African American to be elected to the U.S. presidency.

Photo courtesy: Chris Hondros/Getty Images

and desires. In March 2008, for example, 61 percent of Americans supported removing most U.S. troops from Iraq.[22] Yet, the Bush administration continued high troop levels, and Congress could not muster enough votes to invoke change.

In roughly the first 150 years of our nation's history, the federal government had few responsibilities, and citizens had few expectations of it beyond national defense, printing money, and collecting tariffs and taxes. The state governments were generally far more powerful than the federal government in matters affecting the everyday lives of Americans (see chapters 3 and 4).

As the nation and its economy grew in size and complexity, the federal government took on more responsibilities, such as regulating some businesses, providing poverty relief, and inspecting food. Then, in response to the Great Depression of the 1930s, President Franklin D. Roosevelt's New Deal government programs proliferated in almost every area of American life, including job creation, income security, and aid to the poor. Since then, many Americans have looked to the government for solutions to all kinds of problems.

Politicians, too, have often contributed to rising public expectations by promising far more than they or government could deliver. Although President George W. Bush vowed to "leave no child behind," the high costs of waging war, a failing economy, and increases in the cost of homeland security left little money to fund that ambitious program to implement nationwide educational standards.

In 2008, approval rates for Congress and President George W. Bush were at all time lows, and voters were faced with continued wars in Iraq and Afghanistan and a severe economic crisis. Instead of leading to apathy, however, these problems resulted in a record number of voters turning out to vote, as they looked to government to take the country in a new direction. Approximately 62 percent of eligible voters went to the polls to cast a vote in the presidental election. Experts estimated that this level of turnout was the highest percentage of voters casting ballots since at least 1964.

Thinking Globally
America's Image

In 2001, America was viewed favorably by people in many nations. Since the U.S. invasion of Iraq, however, America's image has declined around the globe, even among key allies such as Great Britain, Germany, and Japan. When surveyed, the citizens of these and many other countries have a less favorable opinion of the United States than in the past.

- What factors have contributed to the decline in America's image among traditional allies?
- What specific steps might the United States take to improve how citizens of other nations view America?

Redefining Our Expectations Concerning Reform

Today, many Americans lack faith in the country's institutions. (To learn more about Americans' confidence in institutions, see Analyzing Visuals: Faith in Institutions.) And, a 2008 poll revealed that eight in ten Americans think the country is headed in the wrong direction.[23] These concerns make it even easier for citizens to blame the government for all kinds of woes—personal as well as societal—or to fail to credit governments for the things they do well. Many Americans, for example, enjoy a remarkably high standard of living, and much of it is due to governmental programs and protections.

Even in the short time between when you get up in the morning and when you leave for classes or work, the government—or its rulings or regulations—pervades your life. National or state governments, for example, set the standards for whether you wake up on Eastern, Central, Mountain, or Pacific Standard Time. The national government regulates the airwaves and licenses the radio and television broadcasts you might listen to or glance at as you eat and get dressed. States, too, regulate and tax telecommunications. Whether the water you use as you brush your teeth contains fluoride is a state or local governmental issue. The federal Food and Drug Administration inspects your breakfast meat and sets standards for the advertising on your cereal

Analyzing Visuals   Faith in Institutions

This line graph shows the percentages of Americans declaring they had a "great deal" of confidence in American institutions. Examine the graph and answer the following questions:

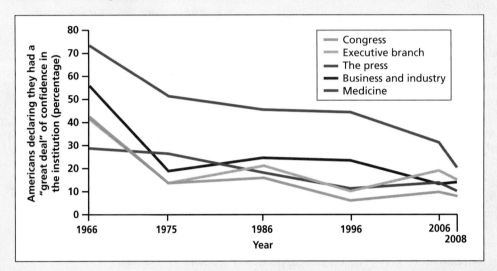

WHAT institution receives the highest rating? The lowest rating?

WHAT institution has shown the steepest decline in ratings since 1966?

WHAT institution has shown the least decline in ratings since 1966?

WHAT factors might explain the overall decline in faith in American institutions?

Sources: Newsweek (January 8, 1996): 32; *Public Perspective* 8 (February/March 1994): 4; Lexis-Nexis RPOLL; *Washington Post* (June 13, 2006): A2; Roper Center iPoll, 2008.

box, orange juice carton, and other food packaging. And, when thousands of pets were poisoned by tainted food from China and toys manufactured in China were found to have toxic levels of lead paint, calls went out from all quarters to have government do more.

Although all governments have problems, it is important to stress the good they can do. In the aftermath of the Great Depression in the United States, for example, the federal government created the Social Security program, which dramatically decreased poverty among the elderly. Our contract laws and judicial system provide an efficient framework for business, while assuring consumers some recourse in the courts should someone fail to deliver as promised. Government-guaranteed student loan programs make it possible for many students to attend college. Government-sponsored research has contributed to the development of new medicines to improve life expectancy. Thus, Americans live longer today than ever before, far more are high school graduates, and the Internet and the development of cable television have dramatically changed how Americans live and work. And, as more women have equal opportunities with men in the labor force, more families also own their own homes, although the economic downturn has made this more difficult.

Just as it is important to recognize that governments serve many important purposes, it is also important to recognize that government and politics are not static. Politics, moreover, involves conflicts over different and sometimes opposing ideologies, and these ideologies are very much influenced by one's racial, economic, and historical experiences. These divisions are real and affect the political process at all levels. It is clear to most Americans today that politics and government no longer can be counted on to cure all of America's ills. Government, however, will always play a major role. True political leaders will need to help Americans come to terms with America as it is today—not as it was in the past—real or imaginary. Perhaps a discussion on how "community" is necessary for everyone to get along—and necessary for democracy—is in order. Some democratic theorists suggest that the citizen-activist must bear ultimate responsibility for the resolution of these divisions.

The current frustration and dissatisfaction with politics and government may be just another phase, as the changing American body politic seeks to redefine its ideas about and expectations of government and how it can be reformed. This process is likely to define politics well into the future, but the individualistic nature of the American system will have long-lasting consequences on how that redefinition can be accomplished. Many Americans say they want less government, but as they get older, they don't want less Social Security. They want lower taxes and better roads, but they don't want to pay road tolls. They want better education for their children but lower expenditures on schools. They want greater security at airports but low fares and quick boarding. Some clearly want less for others but not themselves, a demand that puts politicians in the position of nearly always disappointing voters.

Politicians, as well as their constituents, are looking for ways to redefine the role of government, in much the same way that the Framers did when they met in Philadelphia to forge a solution between Americans' quest for liberty and freedom tempered by order and governmental authority. While citizens charge that it is still government as usual, a change is taking place in Washington, D.C. Sacrosanct programs such as Social Security and welfare are being reexamined, and some powers and responsibilities are being slowly returned to the states. Thus, the times may be different, but the questions about government and its role in our lives remain the same.

Although national crises such as the Civil War, the Great Depression, Watergate, and the 9/11 terrorist attacks create major turmoil, they demonstrate that our system can survive and even change in the face of enormous political, societal, and institutional pressures. Often, these crises produce considerable reforms. The Civil War led to the dismantling of the slavery system and to the passage of the Thirteenth, Fourteenth, and Fifteenth Amendments (see chapter 6), which planted the seeds of recognition of African Americans as full American citizens. The Great Depression led to the New Deal and the creation of a government more actively involved in economic and social regulation. In the 1970s, the Watergate scandal and resignation of President Richard M. Nixon resulted in stricter ethics laws that have led to the resignation or removal of many unethical elected officials. Following 9/11, Americans seem more willing to accept limits on civil liberties to battle terrorism. At the same time, they are more aware of the nation's interdependence with the rest of the world. Yet, they still seek reform of many institutions of government as well as their practices as they look to make America a "more perfect union."

★ WHAT SHOULD I HAVE LEARNED?

In this chapter, we have answered the followed questions:

■ **What are the roots of American government?**

Governments, which are made up of individuals and institutions, are the vehicles through which policies are made and affairs of state are conducted. We need governments to maintain order because governments alone can use force legitimately. Governments have many functions. In the U.S. context, most of these are included in the Preamble to the Constitution. Governments take many forms depending on the number who rule as well as whose interests are represented.

■ **What are the philosophical origins of American government?**

The American political system is based on several principles that have their roots in classical Greek ideas about democracy. The ideas of social contract theorists

John Locke and Thomas Hobbes, who held the belief that people are free and equal by natural right, have continuing implications for our ideas of the proper role of government in our indirect democracy.

■ **What defines American political culture and what are the tenets of American democracy?**

Key tenets of Americans' shared political culture are personal liberty, equality, popular consent and majority rule, popular sovereignty, civil society, individualism, and religious faith.

■ **What is the role of political ideology in the United States and the world?**

Ideologies, the belief systems that shape the thinking of individuals and how they view the world, play a powerful role in politics here and abroad. Most Americans identify themselves as conservatives, liberals, or moderates.

■ **What are the changing characteristics of the American people?**

Several characteristics of the American electorate can help us understand how the system continues to evolve and change. Chief among these are changes in size, population, and demographics.

■ **How do population changes and Americans' attitudes toward government affect policies and efforts toward reform?**

Shifts in population have created controversy in the American electorate throughout America's history. Membership in a demographic group is likely to affect one's outlook on government policies. Moreover, Americans have high and often unrealistic expectations of government yet often fail to appreciate how much their government actually does for them. Americans' failing trust in institutions also explains some of the apathy evidenced in the electorate.

Key Terms

American dream, p. 24
citizen, p. 5
civil society, p. 13
conservative, p. 16
democracy, p. 9
direct democracy, p. 11
government, p. 5
indirect (representative)
    democracy, p. 11
liberal, p. 16

libertarian, p. 16
majority rule, p. 12
Mayflower Compact, p. 10
monarchy, p. 8
natural law, p. 13
oligarchy, p. 8
personal liberty, p. 12
political culture, p. 11
political equality, p. 12
political ideology, p. 14

politics, p. 6
popular consent, p. 12
popular sovereignty, p. 13
republic, p. 11
social conservative, p. 16
social contract, p. 10
social contract theory, p. 10
totalitarianism, p. 8

Researching the Political Landscape

In the Library

Almond, Gabriel A., and Sidney Verba. *Civic Culture: Political Attitudes and Democracy in Five Nations*, new ed. New York: Sage, 1989.

Ball, Terence, and Richard Dagger. *Political Ideologies and the Democratic Ideal*, 7th ed. New York: Longman, 2008.

Dahl, Robert A. *Polyarchy: Participation and Opposition*. New Haven, CT: Yale University Press, 1972.

Elshtain, Jean Bethke. *Democracy on Trial*. New York: Basic Books, 1995.

Fiorina, Morris P., Samuel J. Abrams, and Jeremy C. Pope. *Culture War? The Myth of a Polarized America*, 2nd ed. New York: Longman, 2006.

Fournier, Ron, Douglas B. Sosnick, and Matthew J. Dowd. *Applebee's America: How Successful Political, Business, and Religious Leaders Connect with the New American Community*. New York: Simon and Schuster, 2006.

Jamieson, Kathleen Hall. *Everything You Think You Know About Politics...and Why You're Wrong*. New York: Basic Books, 2000.

Hobbes, Thomas. *Leviathan*. Ed. Richard Tuck. New York: Cambridge University Press, 1996.

Hochschild, Jennifer L. *Facing Up to the American Dream: Race, Class, and the Soul of the Nation*. Princeton, NJ: Princeton University Press, 1996.

Locke, John. *Two Treatises of Government*. Ed. Peter Lasleti. New York: Cambridge University Press, 1988.

Nye, Joseph S., Jr. *The Paradox of American Power: Why the World's Superpower Can't Go It Alone*. New York: Oxford University Press, 2002.

Putnam, Robert D. *Bowling Alone: Collapse and Revival of the American Community*. New York: Simon and Schuster, 2001.

Skocpol, Theda, and Morris P. Fiorina, eds. *Civic Engagement in American Democracy*. Washington, DC: Brookings Institution Press, 1999.

Verba, Sidney, Kay Schlozman, and Henry Brady. *Voice and Equality: Civic Volunteerism in American Politics*, 2nd ed. Cambridge, MA: Harvard University Press, 2002.

Zakaria, Fareed. *The Future of Freedom: Illiberal Democracy at Home and Abroad*. New York: Norton, 2004.

On the Web

To learn more about Thomas Hobbes and John Locke, do key word searches on their names or see **www.iep.utm.edu/h/hobmoral.htm** and **www.utm.edu/research/iep/l/locke.htm.**

To learn more about your political ideology, go to the Political Compass at **www.politicalcompass.org.**

To learn about the policy positions and attitudes of American conservatives, go to the American Conservative Union home page at **www.conservative.org.** To learn more about the policy positions and attitudes of American liberals, go to the Liberal Oasis home page at **www.liberaloasis.com.**

To learn more about the policy positions and attitudes of American libertarians, go to the *Rational Review* home page at **www.rationalreview.com/.**

To learn more about shifts in the American population, go to the U.S. Census Bureau's home page at **www.census.gov.** Notice the population clocks in the upper-right corner of the home page that show the current population of the United States as well as the world population. Detailed information about population projections and on families and household composition may be accessed here.

The Constitution

2

A t age eighteen, all American citizens are eligible to vote in state and national elections. This has not always been the case. It took an amendment to the U.S. Constitution—one of only seventeen that have been added since the Bill of Rights was ratified in 1791—to guarantee the vote to those under twenty-one years of age.

In 1942, during World War II, Representative Jennings Randolph (D–WV) proposed that the voting age be lowered to eighteen, believing that since young men were old enough to be drafted to fight and die for their country, they also should be allowed to vote. He continued to reintroduce his proposal during every session of Congress, and in 1954, President Dwight D. Eisenhower endorsed the idea in his State of the Union message. Presidents Lyndon B. Johnson and Richard M. Nixon—men who had also called upon the nation's young men to fight on foreign shores—echoed his appeal.[1]

During the 1960s, the campaign to lower the voting age took on a new sense of urgency as hundreds of thousands of young men were drafted to fight in Vietnam, and thousands of men and women were killed in action. "Old Enough to Fight, Old Enough to Vote," was one popular slogan of the day. By 1970, four states–the U.S. Constitution allows states to set the eligibility requirements for their voters–had

■ The U. S. Constitution, written in 1787, has proved to be an enduring and flexible document.

lowered their voting ages to eighteen. Later that year, Congress passed legislation lowering the voting age in national, state, and local elections to eighteen.

The state of Oregon, however, challenged the constitutionality of the law in court, arguing that Congress had not been given the authority to establish a uniform voting age in state and local government elections by the Constitution. The U.S. Supreme Court agreed.[2] The decision from the sharply divided Court meant that those under age twenty-one could vote in national elections but that the states were free to prohibit them from voting in state and local elections. The decision presented the states with a logistical nightmare. States setting the voting age at twenty-one would be forced to keep two sets of registration books: one for voters twenty-one and over, and one for voters under twenty-one.

Jennings Randolph, by then a senator from West Virginia, reintroduced his proposed amendment to lower the national voting age to eighteen.[3] Within three months of the Supreme Court's decision, Congress sent the proposed Twenty-Sixth Amendment to the states for their ratification. The required three-fourths of the states approved the amendment within three months—making its adoption on June 30, 1971, the quickest in the history of the constitutional amending process.

However, until the 2008 election cycle, issues of concern to those under the age of twenty-one, including a possible draft,

WHAT SHOULD I KNOW ABOUT . . .

- the roots of the new American nation?
- the Articles of Confederation?
- the writing of the U.S. Constitution?
- the basic principles of the U.S. Constitution?
- the drive for ratification of the U.S. Constitution?
- methods of amending the U.S. Constitution?

TO LEARN MORE—
—TO DO MORE
Find out more about voter registration in your state by going to Rock the Vote at www.RocktheVote.com or to the League of Women Voters voter information site at www.vote411.org/.

Internet privacy, reproductive rights, credit card and cell phone rules and regulations, rising college tuition, and the continuance of student loan programs, seemed to do little to energize young voters. While voter registration drives and voter awareness campaigns by groups such as Rock the Vote helped some, it was the Democratic primary race where young voters for the first time began to make a difference in electoral outcomes. Barack Obama's campaign for the Democratic presidential nod energized young people in a way never before seen. In Iowa, for example, young people accounted for 22 percent of caucus goers—the same percentage as those over age sixty-five!

At its roots, the U.S. Constitution was never indended to be easy to change. The process by which it could be changed or amended was made time consuming and difficult. Over the years, thousands of amendments—including those to prohibit child labor, provide equal rights for women, grant statehood to the District of Columbia, balance the federal budget, and ban flag burning—have been debated or sent to the states for their approval, only to die slow deaths. Only twenty-seven amendments have successfully made their way into the Constitution. What the Framers wrote in Philadelphia has continued to work, in spite of increasing demands on and dissatisfaction with our national government. Although Americans often clamor for reform, perhaps they are happier with the system of government created by the Framers than they realize.

The ideas that went into the making of the Constitution and the ways that it has evolved to address the problems of a growing and changing nation are at the core of our discussion in this chapter.

★ First, we will examine *the roots of the new American nation* and the circumstances surrounding the Declaration of Independence and the break with Great Britain.
★ Second, we will discuss *the first attempt at American government* created by the *Articles of Confederation*.
★ Third, we will examine the circumstances surrounding *writing the U.S. Constitution* in Philadelphia.
★ Fourth, we will review the results of the Framers' efforts—*the U.S. Constitution*.
★ Fifth, we will present *the drive for ratification of the U.S. Constitution*.
★ Finally, we will address *methods of amending the U.S. Constitution*.

Roots of the New American Nation

Starting in the early seventeenth century, colonists came to the New World for a variety of reasons. Often, as detailed in chapter 1, it was to escape religious persecution. Others came seeking a new start on a continent where land was plentiful. The independence and diversity of the settlers in the New World made the question of how best to rule the new colonies a tricky one. More than merely an ocean separated England from the colonies; the colonists were independent people, and it soon became clear that the crown could not govern its subjects in the colonies with the same close rein used at home. King James I thus allowed some local participation in decision making through arrangements such as the first elected colonial assembly, the Virginia House of Burgesses formed in 1619, and the

Photo courtesy: Kelly Fogel/Rock the Vote

What will it take to rock the youth vote? The genius of the U.S. Constitution is evident in how few times it has been amended as the courts have interpreted it to meet changing times. The Twenty-Sixth Amendment enfranchised young people eighteen to twenty-one. During the 2008 presidential election, the Democratic Party made strides with young voters. Many commentators noted that they "Barack-ed" the vote.

elected General Court that governed the Massachusetts Bay colony after 1629. Almost all of the colonists agreed that the king ruled by divine right, but English monarchs allowed the colonists significant liberties in terms of self-government, religious practices, and economic organization. For 140 years, this system worked fairly well.[4]

By the early 1760s, however, a century and a half of physical separation, development of colonial industry, and the relative self-governance of the colonies led to weakening ties with—and loyalties to—the crown. By this time, each of the thirteen colonies had drafted its own written constitution, which provided the fundamental rules or laws for each colony. Moreover, many of the most oppressive British traditions—feudalism, a rigid class system, and the absolute authority of the king—were absent in the New World. Land was abundant. The guild and craft systems that severely limited entry into many skilled professions in England did not exist in the colonies. Although religion was central to the lives of most colonists, there was no single state church, and the British practice of compulsory tithing (giving a fixed percentage of one's earnings to the state-sanctioned and -supported church) was nonexistent.

Trade and Taxation

Mercantilism, an economic theory designed to increase a nation's wealth through the development of commercial industry and a favorable balance of trade, justified Britain's maintenance of strict import/export controls on the colonies. After 1650, for example, Parliament passed a series of navigation acts to prevent its chief rival, Holland, from trading with the English colonies. From 1650 until well into the 1700s, England tried to regulate colonial imports and exports, believing that it was critical to export more goods than it imported as a way of increasing the gold and silver in its treasury. These policies, however, were difficult to enforce and were widely ignored by the colonists, who saw little self-benefit in them. Thus, for years, an unwritten agreement existed. The colonists relinquished to the crown and the British Parliament the authority to regulate trade and conduct international affairs, but they retained the right to levy their own taxes.

This fragile agreement was soon put to the test. The French and Indian War, fought from 1756 to 1763 on the western frontier of the colonies and in Canada, was part of a global war initiated by the British. This American phase of what was called the Seven Years' War was fought between England and France with its Indian allies. In North America, its immediate cause was the rival claims of those two European nations for the lands between the Allegheny Mountains and the Mississippi River. The first Treaty of Paris, signed in 1763, not only signaled the end of this war but also greatly increased the size of land claimed by Great Britain in North America, as shown in Figure 2.1. The colonists expected that with the Indian problem on the western frontier now under control, westward migration and settlement could begin in earnest. In 1763, they were shocked when the crown decreed that there was to be no further

mercantilism
An economic theory designed to increase a nation's wealth through the development of commercial industry and a favorable balance of trade.

FIGURE 2.1 British North America, 1763 This map shows the boundaries of the British colonies in North America after the Treaty of Paris was signed in 1763, as well as the extent of colonial settlements at that time.

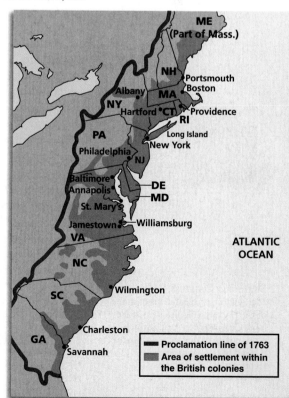

Timeline: Key Events Leading to American Independence

1763 The Treaty of Paris—ends the French and Indian War. France cedes its claims to any lands east of the Mississippi River, greatly expanding the size of the land claimed by Great Britain in North America.

1767 The Townshend Acts are passed by British Parliament—These acts impose duties on a host of colonial imports, including the colonists' favorite drink, tea.

1765 At the urging of Samuel Adams, the Stamp Act Congress convenes in New York—Adams later begins the Committees of Correspondence.

1770 The Boston Massacre—British troops open fire on a mob, killing five colonists.

---

westward movement by British subjects. Parliament believed that expansion into Indian territory would lead to new expenditures for the defense of the settlers, draining the British treasury, which had yet to recover from the high cost of waging the French and Indian War.

To raise money to pay for the war as well as the expenses of administering the colonies, Parliament enacted the Sugar Act in 1764. This act placed taxes on sugar, wine, coffee, and other products commonly exported to the colonies. A postwar colonial depression heightened resentment of the tax. Major protest, however, failed to materialize until imposition of the Stamp Act by the British Parliament in 1765. This law required that all paper items bought and sold in the colonies carry a stamp mandated by the crown. The tax itself was not offensive to the colonists. However, they feared this act would establish a precedent for the British Parliament not only to regulate commerce in the colonies, but also to raise revenues from the colonists without the approval of the colonial governments. Around the colonies, the political cry "no taxation without representation" became prominent. To add insult to injury, in 1765, Parliament passed the Quartering Act, which required the colonists to furnish barracks or provide living quarters within their own homes for British troops.

Most colonists, especially those in New England, where these acts hit merchants hardest, were outraged. Men throughout the colonies organized the Sons of Liberty, under the leadership of Samuel Adams and Patrick Henry. Women formed the Daughters of Liberty. Protests against the Stamp Act were violent and loud. Riots, often led by the Sons of Liberty, broke out. They were especially violent in Boston, where the colonial governor's home was burned by an angry mob, and British stamp agents charged with collecting the tax were threatened. A boycott of goods needing the stamps as well as British imports also was organized.

First Steps Toward Independence

In 1765, at the urging of Samuel Adams, nine of the thirteen colonies sent representatives to a meeting in New York City, where a detailed list of crown violations of the colonists' fundamental rights was drafted. Known as the **Stamp Act Congress**, this gath-

Stamp Act Congress
Meeting of representatives of nine of the thirteen colonies held in New York City in 1765, during which representatives drafted a document to send to the king listing how their rights had been violated.

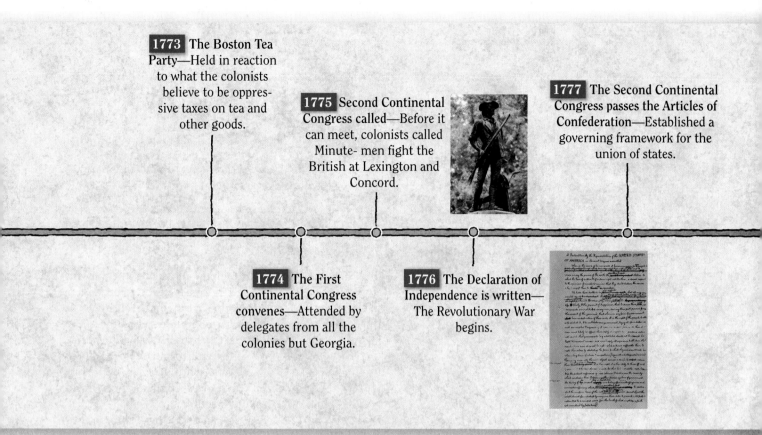

1773 The Boston Tea Party—Held in reaction to what the colonists believe to be oppressive taxes on tea and other goods.

1775 Second Continental Congress called—Before it can meet, colonists called Minute- men fight the British at Lexington and Concord.

1777 The Second Continental Congress passes the Articles of Confederation—Established a governing framework for the union of states.

1774 The First Continental Congress convenes—Attended by delegates from all the colonies but Georgia.

1776 The Declaration of Independence is written— The Revolutionary War begins.

ering was the first official meeting of the colonies and the first step toward creating a unified nation. Attendees defined what they thought to be the proper relationship between colonial governments and the British Parliament; they ardently believed Parliament had no authority to tax them without colonial representation in that body. In contrast, the British believed that direct representation of the colonists was impractical and that members of Parliament represented the best interests of all the English, including the colonists.

The Stamp Act Congress and its petitions to the crown did little to stop the onslaught of taxing measures. Parliament did, however, repeal the Stamp Act and revise the Sugar Act in 1766, largely because of the uproar made by British merchants who were losing large sums of money as a result of the boycotts. Rather than appeasing the colonists, however, these actions emboldened them to increase their resistance. In 1767, Parliament enacted the Townshend Acts, which imposed duties on all kinds of colonial imports, including tea. Responses from the Sons and Daughters of Liberty were immediate. Another boycott was announced, and almost all colonists gave up their favorite drink in a united show of resistance to the tax and British authority.[5] Tensions continued to run high, especially after the British sent 4,000 troops to Boston. On March 5, 1770, English troops opened fire on a mob that included disgruntled dock workers, whose jobs had been taken by British soldiers, and members of the Sons of Liberty, who were taunting the soldiers in front of the Boston Customs House. Five colonists were killed in what became known as the Boston Massacre. Following this confrontation, all duties except those on tea were lifted. The tea tax, however, continued to be a symbolic irritant. In 1772, at the suggestion of Samuel Adams, colonists created **Committees of Correspondence** to keep each other abreast of developments with the British. These committees also served as powerful molders of public opinion against the British.

Meanwhile, despite dissent in England over the treatment of the colonies, Parliament passed another tea tax designed to shore up the sagging sales of the East India Company, a British exporter of tea. The colonists' boycott had left that British trading house with more than 18 million pounds of tea in its warehouses. To rescue British merchants from disaster, in 1773 Parliament passed the Tea Act, granting a monopoly to the financially strapped East India Company to sell the tea imported from Britain. The company was allowed to funnel business to American

Committees of Correspondence Organizations in each of the American colonies created to keep colonists abreast of developments with the British; served as powerful molders of public opinion against the British.

THE BLOODY MASSACRE perpetrated in King—s—Street BOSTON on March 5th 1770 by a party of the 29th REGT

Unhappy Boston! see thy Sons deplore,
Thy hallow'd Walks besmear'd with guiltless Gore
While faithless P——n and his savage Bands,
With murd'rous Rancour stretch their bloody Hands;
Like fierce Barbarians grinning o'er their Prey,
Approve the Carnage and enjoy the Day.

If scalding drops from Rage from Anguish Wrung
If speechless Sorrows lab'ring for a Tongue,
Or if a weeping World can ought appease
The plaintive Ghosts of Victims such as these;
The Patriot's copious Tears for each are shed,
A glorious Tribute which embalms the Dead.

But know Fate summons to that awful Goal,
Where Justice strips the Murd'rer of his Soul
Should venal C——ts the scandal of the Land,
Snatch the relentless Villain from her Hand,
Keen Execrations on this Plate inscrib'd,
Shall reach a Judge who never can be brib'd.

The unhappy Sufferers were Mess. SAM¹ GRAY SAM¹ MAVERICK JAM⁵ CALDWELL CRISPUS ATTUCKS & PAT⁵ CARR

Killed. Six wounded; two of them (CHRIST⁵ MONK & JOHN CLARK) *Mortally*

Engrav'd Printed & Sold by PAUL REVERE BOSTON

Photo courtesy: Collection of the New York Historical Society

What really happened at the Boston Massacre? Paul Revere's famous engraving of the Boston Massacre played fast and loose with the facts. While the event occurred on a cold winter's night, the engraving features a clear sky and no ice or snow. Crispus Attucks, the Revolution's first martyr, was African American, though the engraving depicts him as a white man. Popular propaganda such as this engraving did much to stoke anti-British sentiment in the years leading up to the Revolutionary War.

merchants loyal to the crown, thereby undercutting colonial merchants, who could sell only tea imported from other nations. The effect was to drive down the price of tea and to hurt colonial merchants, who were forced to buy tea at the higher prices from other sources.

When the next shipment of tea arrived in Boston from Great Britain, the colonists responded by throwing the Boston Tea Party. Similar tea parties were held in other colonies. When the news of these actions reached King George III, he flew into a rage against the actions of his disloyal subjects. "The die is now cast," the king told his prime minister. "The colonies must either submit or triumph."

King George's first act of retaliation was to persuade Parliament to pass the Coercive Acts of 1774. Known in the colonies as the Intolerable Acts, they contained a key provision calling for a total blockade of Boston Harbor until restitution was made for the tea. Another provision reinforced the Quartering Act. It gave royal governors the authority to house British soldiers in the homes of private citizens, allowing Britain to send an additional 4,000 soldiers to patrol Boston.

The First Continental Congress

The British could never have guessed how the cumulative impact of these actions would unite the colonists. Samuel Adams's Committees of Correspondence spread the word, and food and money were sent to the people of Boston from all over the thirteen colonies. The tax itself was no longer the key issue; now the extent of British authority over the colonies was the far more important question. At the request of the colonial assemblies of Massachusetts and Virginia, all but Georgia's colonial assembly agreed to select a group of delegates to attend a continental congress authorized to communicate with the king on behalf of the now-united colonies.

The **First Continental Congress** met in Philadelphia from September 5 to October 26, 1774. It was made up of fifty-six delegates. The colonists had yet to think of breaking with Great Britain; at this point, they simply wanted to iron out their differences with the king. By October, they had agreed on a series

Who was Samuel Adams?
Today, Samuel Adams (1722–1803) is well known for the beer that bears his name. His original claim to fame was as a leader against the British and loyalist oppressors (although he did bankrupt his family's brewery business).

Painting by John Singleton Copley. Courtesy, Museum of Fine Arts, Boston. Reproduced with permission. © 2001, Museum of Fine Arts, Boston. All rights reserved.

of resolutions to oppose the Coercive Acts and to establish a formal organization to boycott British goods. The Congress also drafted a Declaration of Rights and Resolves, which called for colonial rights of petition and assembly, trial by peers, freedom from a standing army, and the selection of representative councils to levy taxes. The Congress further agreed that if the king did not capitulate to their demands, they would meet again in Philadelphia in May 1775.

The Second Continental Congress

King George refused to yield, tensions continued to rise, and a **Second Continental Congress** was deemed necessary. Before it could meet, fighting broke out early in the morning of April 19, 1775, at Lexington and Concord, Massachusetts, with what Ralph Waldo Emerson called "the shot heard round the world." Eight colonial soldiers, called Minutemen, were killed, and 16,000 British troops besieged Boston.

When the Second Continental Congress convened in Philadelphia on May 10, 1775, delegates were united by their increased hostility to Great Britain. In a final attempt to avert conflict, the Second Continental Congress adopted the Olive Branch Petition on July 5, 1775, asking the king to end hostilities. King George rejected the petition and sent an additional 20,000 troops to quell the rebellion. As a precautionary measure, the Congress already had appointed George Washington of Virginia as commander in chief of the Continental Army. The selection of a southern leader was a strategic decision, because up to that time British oppression largely was felt in the Northeast. In fact, the war essentially had begun with the shots fired at Lexington and Concord in April 1775.

In January 1776, Thomas Paine, with the support and encouragement of Benjamin Franklin, issued (at first anonymously) *Common Sense*, a pamphlet forcefully arguing for independence from Great Britain. In frank, easy-to-understand language, Paine denounced the corrupt British monarchy and offered reasons to break with Great Britain. "The blood of the slain, the weeping voice of nature cries 'Tis Time to Part,'" wrote Paine. *Common Sense*, widely read throughout the colonies, was instrumental in changing minds in a very short time. In its first three months of publication, the forty-seven-page *Common Sense* sold 120,000 copies, the equivalent of almost 22 million books, given the current U.S. population. One copy of *Common Sense* was in distribution for every thirteen people in the colonies—a truly astonishing number, given the low literacy rate.

Common Sense galvanized the American public against reconciliation with England. On May 15, 1776, Virginia became the first colony to call for independence, instructing one of its delegates to the Second Continental Congress to introduce a resolution to that effect. On June 7, 1776, Richard Henry Lee of Virginia rose to move "that these United Colonies are, and of right ought to be, free and independent States, and that all connection between them and the State of Great Britain is, and ought to be, dissolved." His three-part resolution—which called for independence, the formation of foreign alliances, and preparation of a plan of confederation—triggered hot debate among the delegates. A proclamation of independence from Great Britain was treason, a crime punishable by death. Although six of the thirteen colonies had already instructed their delegates to vote for independence, the Second Continental Congress was suspended to allow its delegates to return home to their respective colonial legislatures for final instructions. Independence was not a move to be taken lightly.

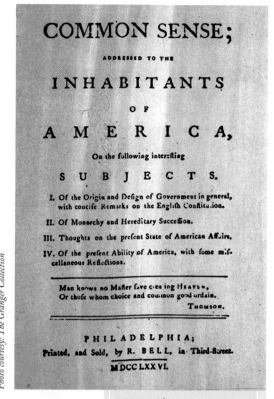

Photo courtesy: The Granger Collection

How much can one essay accomplish? *Common Sense*, by Thomas Paine, forcefully argued for independence from Great Britain. The pamphlet became a colonial best seller and was instrumental in rallying people to oppose British rule.

First Continental Congress
Meeting held in Philadelphia from September 5 to October 26, 1774, in which fifty-six delegates (from every colony except Georgia) adopted a resolution in opposition to the Coercive Acts.

Second Continental Congress
Meeting that convened in Philadelphia on May 10, 1775, at which it was decided that an army should be raised and George Washington of Virginia was named commander in chief.

Where did the ideas of the Declaration of Independence come from? The draft of Thomas Jefferson's document drew heavily from the ideas of social contract theorist John Locke.

Photo courtesy: The Granger Collection

Declaration of Independence
Document drafted by Thomas Jefferson in 1776 that proclaimed the right of the American colonies to separate from Great Britain.

The Declaration of Independence

Committees were set up to consider each point of Richard Henry Lee's proposal. A committee of five was selected to begin work on the **Declaration of Independence**. The Congress selected Benjamin Franklin of Pennsylvania, John Adams of Massachusetts, Robert Livingston of New York, and Roger Sherman of Connecticut as members of the committee. Adams lobbied hard for a Southerner to add balance. Thus, owing to his southern origin as well as his "peculiar felicity of expression," Thomas Jefferson of Virginia was selected as chair.

On July 2, 1776, twelve of the thirteen colonies (with New York abstaining) voted for independence. Two days later, the Second Continental Congress voted to adopt the Declaration of Independence largely penned by Thomas Jefferson. On July 9, 1776, the Declaration, now with the approval of New York, was read aloud in Philadelphia.[6]

In simple but eloquent language, Jefferson set out the reasons for the colonies' separation from Great Britain. Most of his stirring rhetoric drew heavily on the works of seventeenth- and eighteenth-century political philosophers, particularly the English philosopher John Locke (see chapter 1). Locke had written South Carolina's first constitution, a colonial charter drawn up in 1663 when that colony was formed by King Charles II and mercantile houses in England. In fact, many of the words in the opening of the Declaration of Independence closely resemble passages from Locke's *Second Treatise on Civil Government*.

Locke was a proponent of social contract theory, which holds that governments exist based on the consent of the governed. According to Locke, people agree to set up a government largely for the protection of property rights, to preserve life and liberty, and to establish justice. Furthermore, argued Locke, individuals who give their consent to be governed have the right to resist or remove rulers who deviate from those purposes. Such a government exists for the good of its subjects and not for the benefit of those who govern. Thus, rebellion is the ultimate sanction against a government that violates the rights of its citizens.

It is easy to see the colonists' debt to John Locke. In ringing language, the Declaration of Independence proclaims:

> We hold these truths to be self-evident, that all men are created equal, that they are endowed by their Creator with certain unalienable Rights, that among these are Life, Liberty and the pursuit of Happiness.

Jefferson and others in attendance at the Second Continental Congress wanted to have a document that would stand for all time, justifying their break with Great Britain and clarifying their notions of the proper form of government. So, Jefferson continued:

That to secure these rights, Governments are instituted among Men, deriving their just powers from the consent of the governed. That whenever any Form of Government becomes destructive of these ends, it is the Right of the People to alter or abolish it, and to institute new Government, laying its foundation on such Principles and organizing its Powers in such form, as to them shall seem most likely to effect their Safety and Happiness.

After this stirring preamble, the Declaration enumerates the wrongs that the colonists suffered under British rule. All pertain to the denial of personal rights and liberties, many of which would later be guaranteed by the U.S. Constitution through the Bill of Rights.

After the Declaration was signed and transmitted to the king, the Revolutionary War was fought with a greater vengeance. At a September 1776 peace conference on Staten Island (New York), British General William Howe demanded revocation of the Declaration of Independence. Washington's Continental Army refused, and the war raged on while the Continental Congress attempted to fashion a new united government.

The First Attempt at Government: The Articles of Confederation

As noted earlier, the British had no written constitution. The delegates to the Second Continental Congress were attempting to codify arrangements that had never before been put into legal terminology. To make things more complicated, the delegates had to arrive at these decisions in a wartime atmosphere. Nevertheless, in late 1777, the **Articles of Confederation**, creating a loose "league of friendship" between the thirteen sovereign or independent colonies, were passed by the Congress and presented to the states for their ratification.

The Articles created a type of government called a **confederation** or confederacy. Unlike Great Britain's unitary system of government, wherein all of the powers of the government reside in the national government, the national government in a confederation derives all of its powers directly from the states. Thus, the national government in a confederacy is weaker than the sum of its parts, and the states often consider themselves independent nation-states linked together only for limited purposes such as national defense. So, the Articles of Confederation proposed the following:

- A national government with a Congress empowered to make peace, coin money, appoint officers for an army, control the post office, and negotiate with Indian tribes.

- Each state's retention of its independence and sovereignty, or ultimate authority, to govern within its territories.

- One vote in the Continental Congress for each state, regardless of size.

- The vote of nine states to pass any measure (a unanimous vote for any amendment).

- The selection and payment of delegates to the Congress by their respective state legislatures.

The Articles, finally ratified by all thirteen states in March 1781, fashioned a government that reflected the political phi-

Articles of Confederation
The compact among the thirteen original colonies that created a loose league of friendship, with the national government drawing its powers from the states.

confederation
Type of government where the national government derives its powers from the states; a league of independent states.

Thinking Globally

India's Independence

In 1947, following 150 years of British colonial rule, India became an independent nation. Unlike the United States, India achieved independence without a military revolution. Instead, India's people won their independence through mass nonviolent resistance to British rule, which led to political compromise and British withdrawal.

- The colonists' desire for independence led to war; India's did not. What factors facilitate a country's path to independence and what factors complicate it?
- Was the Revolutionary War inevitable? Was a political solution between the American colonies and Great Britain possible? Why or why not?

losophy of the times.[7] Although it had its flaws, the government under the Articles of Confederation saw the nation through the Revolutionary War. However, once the British surrendered in 1781, and the new nation found itself no longer united by the war effort, the government quickly fell into chaos.

Problems Under the Articles of Confederation

In today's America, we ship goods, travel by car and airplane across state lines, make interstate phone calls, and more. Over 250 years ago, Americans had great loyalties to their states and often did not even think of themselves as Americans. This lack of national sentiment or loyalty in the absence of a war to unite the citizenry fostered a reluctance to give any power to the national government. By 1784, just one year after the Revolutionary Army was disbanded, governing the new nation under the Articles of Confederation proved unworkable.[8] In fact, historians refer to the chaotic period from 1781 to 1789 when the former colonies were governed under the Articles of Confederation as the critical period. Congress rarely could assemble the required quorum of nine states to conduct business. Even when it did meet, there was little agreement among the states on any policies. To raise revenue to pay off war debts and run the government, various land, poll, and liquor taxes were proposed. But, since Congress had no specific power to tax, all these proposals were rejected. At one point, Congress was even driven out of Philadelphia (then the capital of the new national government) by its own unpaid army.

Although the national government could coin money, it had no resources to back up the value of its currency. Continental dollars were worth little, and trade between states became chaotic as some states began to coin their own money. Another weakness was that the Articles of Confederation did not allow Congress to regulate commerce among the states or with foreign nations. As a result, individual states attempted to enter into agreements with other countries, and foreign nations were suspicious of trade agreements made with the Congress of the Confederation. In 1785, for example, Massachusetts banned the export of goods in British ships, and Pennsylvania levied heavy duties on ships of nations that had no treaties with the U.S. government.

Fearful of a chief executive who would rule tyrannically, the draftees of the Articles made no provision for an executive branch of government that would be responsible for executing, or implementing, laws passed by the legislative branch. Instead, the president was merely the presiding officer at meetings. John Hanson, a former member of the Maryland House of Delegates and of the First Continental Congress, was the first person to preside over the Congress of the Confederation. Therefore, he is often referred to as the first president of the United States.

The Articles of Confederation, moreover, had no provision for a judicial system to handle the growing number of economic conflicts and boundary disputes among the individual states. Several states claimed the same lands to the west, and Pennsylvania and Virginia went to war with each other.

The Articles' greatest weakness, however, was the lack of a strong central government. Although states had operated independently before the war, during the war they acceded to the national government's authority to wage armed conflict. Once the war was over, however, each state resumed its sovereign status and was unwilling to give up rights, such as the power to tax, to an untested national government. Consequently, the government was unable to force the states to abide by the provisions of the Treaty of Paris, signed in 1783, which officially ended the Revolutionary war. For example, states passed laws to allow debtors who owed money to Great Britain to postpone payment. States also opted not to restore property to citizens who had remained loyal to Britain during the war. Both actions violated the treaty.

The crumbling economy was made worse by a series of bad harvests that failed to produce cash crops, thus making it difficult for farmers to get out of debt quickly.

George Washington and Alexander Hamilton, both interested in the questions of trade and frontier expansion, soon saw the need for a stronger national government with the authority to act to solve some of these problems. They were not alone. In 1785 and 1786, some state governments began to discuss ways to strengthen the national government.

Shays's Rebellion

Before action to strengthen the government could take place, new unrest broke out in America. In 1780, Massachusetts adopted a constitution that appeared to favor the interests of the wealthy. Property-owning requirements barred the lower and middle classes from voting and office holding. And, as the economy of Massachusetts worsened, banks foreclosed on the farms of many Massachusetts Continental Army veterans who were waiting for promised bonuses that the national government had no funds to pay. The last straw came in 1786, when the Massachusetts legislature enacted a new law requiring the payment of all debts in cash. Frustration and outrage at the new law caused Daniel Shays, a former Continental Army captain, and 1,500 armed, disgruntled farmers to march to Springfield, Massachusetts. This group forcibly restrained the state court located there from foreclosing on the mortgages on their farms.

The Congress immediately authorized the secretary of war to call for a new national militia. A $530,000 appropriation was made for this purpose, but every state except Virginia refused Congress's request for money. The governor of Massachusetts then tried to raise a state militia, but because of the poor economy, the state treasury lacked the necessary funds to support his action. Frantic attempts to collect private financial support were made, and a militia finally was assembled. By February 4, 1787, this privately paid force put a stop to what was called **Shays's Rebellion**. The failure of the Congress to muster an army to put down the rebellion provided a dramatic example of the weaknesses inherent in the Articles of Confederation and shocked the nation's leaders into recognizing the new national government's inadequacies. And, it finally prompted several states to join together to call for a convention in Philadelphia in 1787.

Photo courtesy: Bettmann/CORBIS

What happened during Shays's Rebellion? With Daniel Shays in the lead, a group of farmers who had served in the Continental Army marched on the courthouse in Springfield, Massachusetts, to stop the state court from foreclosing on their farms.

Shays's Rebellion
A 1786 rebellion in which an army of 1,500 disgruntled and angry farmers led by Daniel Shays marched to Springfield, Massachusetts, and forcibly restrained the state court from foreclosing mortgages on their farms.

The Miracle at Philadelphia: Writing the U.S. Constitution

On February 21, 1787, in the throes of economic turmoil and with domestic tranquility gone haywire, the Congress passed an official resolution. It called for a Constitutional Convention in Philadelphia for "the sole and express purpose of revising the Articles of Confederation." However, many delegates that gathered in sweltering Philadelphia on May 25, 1787, were prepared to take potentially treasonous steps to preserve the union. For example, on the first day the convention was in session, Edmund Randolph and James Madison of Virginia proposed fifteen resolutions creating an entirely new government (later known as the Virginia Plan). Their enthusiasm, however, was not universal. Many delegates, including William Paterson of New Jersey, considered these resolutions to be in violation of the convention's charter, and proposed the New Jersey Plan, which took greater steps to preserve the Articles.

These proposals met heated debate on the convention's floor. Eventually the Virginia Plan triumphed following a declaration from Randolph that, "When the

Analyzing Visuals | Framers or Troublemakers?

This political cartoon was published during the controversy surrounding revelations that President George W. Bush had authorized domestic surveillance activities as part of his proclaimed "War on Terror." Look at the cartoon and consider the following questions:

Photo courtesy: Nick Anderson/Cartoonist Group

WHAT meeting is the cartoonist depicting in this illustration?

WHAT activity are the "troublemakers" engaged in?

WHAT point is the cartoonist trying to communicate in this cartoon?

salvation of the Republic is at stake, it would be treason not to propose what we found necessary."

Though the basic structure of the new government was established, the work of the Constitutional Convention was not complete. These differences were resolved through a series of compromises, and less than one hundred days after the meeting convened, the Framers had created a new government to submit to the electorate for its approval.

The Characteristics and Motives of the Framers

The fifty-five delegates who attended the Constitutional Convention labored long and hard that hot summer. Owing to the high stakes of their action, all of the convention's work was conducted behind closed doors. George Washington of Virginia, who was unanimously elected the convention's presiding officer, cautioned delegates not to reveal details of the convention even to their family members. The delegates agreed to accompany Benjamin Franklin of Pennsylvania to all of his meals. They feared that the normally gregarious gentleman might get carried away with the mood or by liquor and inadvertently let news of the proceedings slip from his tongue. (To learn about a humorous modern take on the convention, see Analyzing Visuals: Framers or Troublemakers?)

All of the delegates to the Constitutional Convention were men; hence, they often are referred to as the "Founding Fathers." In this text, we generally refer to them as the Framers, because their work provided the framework for the new United States government. Most of them were quite young; many were in their twenties and thirties, and only one—Franklin at eighty-one—was quite old. Seventeen owned slaves, with George Washington, George Mason, and John Rutledge owning the most. Thirty-one went to college, and seven signed both the Declaration of Independence and the Constitution.

The Framers brought with them a vast amount of political, educational, legal, and business experience. It is clear that they were an exceptional lot who ultimately produced a brilliant **constitution**, or document establishing the structure, functions, and limitations of a government.

constitution
A document establishing the structure, functions, and limitations of a government.

However, debate about the Framers' motives filled the air during the ratification struggle and has provided grist for the mill of historians and political scientists over the years. In his *Economic Interpretation of the Constitution of the United States* (1913), Charles A. Beard argued that the 1780s were a critical period not for the nation as a whole, but rather for business owners who feared that a weak, decentralized government could harm their economic interests.[9] Beard argued that the merchants wanted a strong national government to promote industry and trade, to protect private property, and to ensure payment of the public debt—much of which was owed to them. Therefore, according to Beard, the Constitution represents "an economic document drawn with superb skill by men whose property interests were immediately at stake."[10]

By the 1950s, this view had fallen into disfavor when other historians were unable to find direct links between wealth and the Framers' motives for establishing the Constitution. Others faulted Beard's failure to consider the impact of religion and individual views about government.[11] In the 1960s, however, another group of historians began to argue that social and economic factors were, in fact, important motives for supporting the Constitution. In *The Anti-Federalists* (1961), Jackson Turner Main posited that while the Constitution's supporters might not have been the united group of creditors suggested by Beard, they were wealthier, came from higher social strata, and had greater concern for maintaining the prevailing social order than the general public.[12] In 1969, Gordon S. Wood's *The Creation of the American Republic* resurrected this debate. Wood deemphasized economics to argue that major social divisions explained different groups' support for (or opposition to) the new Constitution. He concluded that the Framers were representative of a class that favored order and stability over some of the more radical ideas that had inspired the American Revolutionary War and the break with Britain.[13]

The Virginia and New Jersey Plans

The less populous states were concerned with being lost in any new system of government where states were not treated as equals regardless of population. It is not surprising that a large state and then a small one, Virginia and New Jersey, respectively weighed in with ideas about how the new government should operate.

The **Virginia Plan**, proposed by James Madison and Edmund Randolph, called for a national system based heavily on the European nation-state model, wherein the national government derives its powers from the people and not from the member states.

Its key features included:

Virginia Plan
The first general plan for the Constitution offered in Philadelphia. Its key points were a bicameral legislature, and an executive and a judiciary chosen by the national legislature.

- Creation of a powerful central government with three branches—the legislative, executive, and judicial.

- A two-house legislature with one house elected directly by the people, the other chosen from among persons nominated by the state legislatures.
- A legislature with the power to select the executive and the judiciary.

In general, smaller states such as New Jersey and Connecticut felt comfortable with the arrangements under the Articles of Confederation. These states offered another model of government, the **New Jersey Plan**. Its key features included:

New Jersey Plan
A framework for the Constitution proposed by a group of small states. Its key points were a one-house legislature with one vote for each state, a Congress with the ability to raise revenue, and a Supreme Court with members appointed for life.

- Strengthening the Articles, not replacing them.
- Creating a one-house legislature with one vote for each state and with representatives chosen by state legislatures.
- Giving Congress the power to raise revenue from duties on imports and from postal service fees.
- Creating a Supreme Court with members appointed for life by the executive officers.

Constitutional Compromises

The most serious disagreement between the Virginia and New Jersey plans concerned state representation in Congress. When a deadlock loomed, Connecticut offered its own compromise. Representation in the House of Representatives would be determined by population and each state would have an equal vote in the Senate. Again, there was a stalemate.

Great Compromise
The final decision of the Constitutional Convention to create a two-house legislature with the lower house elected by the people and with powers divided between the two houses. It also made national law supreme.

A committee to work out an agreement soon reported back what became known as the **Great Compromise**. Taking ideas from both the Virginia and New Jersey plans, it recommended:

- A two-house, or bicameral, legislature.
- In one house of the legislature (later called the House of Representatives), there would be fifty-six representatives—one representative for every 30,000 inhabitants. Representatives would be elected directly by the people.
- That house should have the power to originate all bills for raising and spending money.
- In the second house of the legislature (later called the Senate), each state should have an equal vote, and representatives would be selected by the state legislatures.
- In dividing power between the national and state governments, national power would be supreme.[14]

As Benjamin Franklin summarized it:

The diversity of opinions turns on two points. If a proportional representation takes place, the small states contend that their liberties will be in danger. If an equality of votes is to be put in its place, large states say that their money will be in danger. . . . When a broad table is to be made and the edges of a plank do not fit, the artist takes a little from both sides and makes a good joint. In like manner, both sides must part with some of their demands, in order that they both join in some accommodating position.[15]

The Great Compromise ultimately met with the approval of all states in attendance. The smaller states were pleased because they got equal representation in the Senate; the larger states were satisfied with the proportional representation in the House of Representatives. The small states then would dominate the Senate while the large states, such as Virginia and Pennsylvania, would control the House. But, because both houses had to pass any legislation, neither body could dominate the other.

The Great Compromise dealt with one major concern of the Framers—how best to treat the differences in large and small states—but other problems stemming largely from regional differences remained. Slavery, which formed the basis of much of the southern states' cotton economy, was one of the thorniest issues to address. To reach an agreement on the Constitution, the Framers had to craft a compromise that balanced southern commercial interests with comparable northern concerns. Eventually the Framers agreed that Northerners would support continuing the slave trade for twenty more years, as well as a twenty-year ban on taxing exports to protect the cotton trade, while Southerners consented to a provision requiring only a majority vote on navigation laws, and the national government was given the authority to regulate foreign commerce. It was also agreed that the Senate would have the power to ratify treaties by a two-thirds majority, which assuaged the fears of southern states, who made up more than one-third of the nation.

Another sticking point concerning slavery remained: how to determine state population for purposes of representation in the House of Representatives. Slaves could not vote, but the southern states wanted them included for purposes of determining population. After considerable dissension, it was decided that population for purposes of representation and the apportionment of direct taxes would be calculated by adding the "whole Number of Free Persons" to "three-fifths of all other Persons." "All other Persons" was the delegates' euphemistic way of referring to slaves. Known as the **Three-Fifths Compromise**, this highly political deal assured that the South would hold 47 percent of the House—enough to prevent attacks on slavery but not so much as to foster the spread of slavery northward.

Three-Fifths Compromise Agreement reached at the Constitutional Convention stipulating that each slave was to be counted as three-fifths of a person for purposes of determining population for representation in the U.S. House of Representatives.

Unfinished Business Affecting the Executive Branch

The Framers next turned to fashioning an executive branch. While they agreed on the idea of a one-person executive, they could not settle on the length of the term of office, nor on how the chief executive should be selected. With Shays's Rebellion still fresh in their minds, the delegates feared putting too much power, including selection of a president, into the hands of the lower classes. At the same time, representatives from the smaller states feared that the selection of the chief executive by the legislature would put additional power into the hands of the large states.

Amid these fears, the Committee on Unfinished Portions, whose sole responsibility was to iron out problems and disagreements concerning the office of chief executive, conducted its work. The committee recommended that the presidential term of office be fixed at four years instead of seven, as had earlier been proposed. By choosing not to mention a period of time within which the chief executive would be eligible for reelection, they made it possible for a president to serve more than one term.

The Framers also created the Electoral College as a mechanism for selecting the chief executive of the new nation. The Electoral College system gave individual states a key role, because each state would select electors equal to the number of representatives it had in the House and Senate. It was a vague compromise that removed election of the president and vice president from both the Congress and the people and put it in the hands of electors whose method of selection would be left to the states. As Alexander Hamilton noted in *Federalist No. 68*, the Electoral College was fashioned to avoid the "tumult and disorder" that the Framers feared could result if the masses were allowed to vote directly for president. Instead, the selection of the president was left to a small number of men (the Electoral College) who "possess[ed] the information and discernment requisite" to decide, in Hamilton's words, the "complicated" business of selecting the president. (To learn more about the Electoral College, see chapter 13.)

In drafting the new Constitution, the Framers also were careful to include a provision for removal of the chief executive. The House of Representatives was given the sole responsibility of investigating and charging a president or vice president with "Treason, Bribery, or other high Crimes and Misdemeanors." A majority vote then would result in issuing articles of impeachment against the president or vice president. In turn, the Senate was given sole responsibility to try the president or vice president on the charges issued by the House. A two-thirds vote of the Senate was required to convict and remove the president or the vice president from office. The chief justice of the United States was to preside over the Senate proceedings in place of the vice president (that body's constitutional leader) to prevent any conflict of interest on the vice president's part (see chapter 7).

The U.S. Constitution

Comparing Constitutions

After the compromise on the presidency, work proceeded quickly on the remaining resolutions of the Constitution. The Preamble to the Constitution, the last section to be drafted, contains exceptionally powerful language that forms the bedrock of American political deals. The Preamble originally read:

> We the People of the States of New Hampshire, Massachusetts, Rhode Island and the Providence Plantations, Connecticut, New Jersey, New York, Pennsylvania, Delaware, Maryland, Virginia, North Carolina, South Carolina and Georgia, do ordain, declare and establish the following Constitution for the government of ourselves and our Posterity.

Its opening line, "We the People," ended, at least for the time being, the question of from where the government derived its power: it came directly from the people. This phrase was later followed by "the United States" instead of a list of the individual states. This substitution boldly proclaimed that a loose confederation of states no longer existed. Instead, there was but one American people and one nation.

The Constitution's final draft next explained the need for the new outline of government: "in Order to form a more perfect Union" indirectly acknowledged the weaknesses of the Articles of Confederation in governing a growing nation. Next, the optimistic goals of the Framers for the new nation were set out: to "establish Justice, insure domestic Tranquility, provide for the common defence, promote the general Welfare, and secure the Blessings of Liberty to ourselves and our Posterity;" followed by the formal creation of a new government: "do ordain and establish this Constitution for the United States of America."

On September 17, 1787, the Constitution was approved by the delegates from all twelve states in attendance. While the completed document did not satisfy all the delegates, of the fifty-five delegates who attended some portion of the meetings, thirty-nine ultimately signed it. The sentiments uttered by Benjamin Franklin probably well reflected those of many others: "Thus, I consent, Sir, to this Constitution because I expect no better, and because I am not sure that it is not the best."[16]

The Basic Principles of the Constitution

separation of powers
A way of dividing the power of government among the legislative, executive, and judicial branches, each staffed separately, with equality and independence of each branch ensured by the Constitution.

The proposed structure of the new national government owed much to the writings of the French philosopher Montesquieu (1689–1755), who advocated distinct functions for each branch of government, called **separation of powers**, with a system of **checks and balances** between each branch. The Constitution's concern with the distribution of power between states and the national government also reveals the heavy influence of political philosophers, as well as the colonists' experience under the Articles of Confederation.[17]

checks and balances
A constitutionally mandated structure that gives each of the three branches of government some degree of oversight and control over the actions of the others.

FEDERALISM The question before and during the convention was how much power states would give up to the national government. Given the nation's experiences under the Articles of Confederation, the Framers believed that a strong national government was necessary for the new nation's survival. However, they were reluctant to create a powerful government after the model of Britain, the country from which they had just won their independence. Its unitary system was not even considered by the colonists. Instead, they employed a system (now known as the **federal system**) that divides the power of government between a strong national government and the individual states, with national power being supreme. This system was based on the principle that the

federal system
Plan of government in which power is divided between the national government and the state governments and in which independent states are bound together under one national government, whose power is supreme.

federal, or national, government derived its power from the citizens, not the states, as the national government had done under the Articles of Confederation.[18]

Opponents of this system feared that a strong national government would infringe on their liberty. But, supporters of a federal system, such as James Madison, argued that a strong national government with distinct state governments could, if properly directed by constitutional arrangements, actually be a source of expanded liberties and national unity. The Framers viewed the division of governmental authority between the national government and the states as a means of checking power with power, and providing the people with double security against governmental tyranny. Later, the passage of the Tenth Amendment, which stated that powers not given to the national government were reserved by the states or the people, further clarified the federal structure (see chapter 3).

SEPARATION OF POWERS James Madison and many of the Framers clearly feared putting too much power into the hands of any one individual or branch of government. Madison's famous words, "Ambition must be made to counteract ambition," were widely believed at the Constitutional Convention.

Separation of powers is simply a way of parceling out power among the three branches of government. Its three key features are:

1. Three distinct branches of government: the legislative, the executive, and the judicial.
2. Three separately staffed branches of government to exercise these functions.
3. Constitutional equality and independence of each branch.

As illustrated in Figure 2.2, the Framers were careful to create a system in which law-making, law-enforcing, and law-interpreting functions were assigned to indepen-

FIGURE 2.2 Separation of Powers and Checks and Balances under the U.S. Constitution

Legislative Checks on the Executive
Impeach the president
Reject legislation or funding the president wants
Refuse to confirm nominees or approve treaties
Override the president's veto by a two-thirds vote

LEGISLATIVE BRANCH POWERS
Pass all federal laws
Pass the federal budget
Declare war
Approve treaties and
 presidential appointments
Establish lower federal courts
 and the number of judges

Executive Checks on the Legislative
Veto legislation
Call Congress into special session
Implement (or fail to implement) laws
passed by Congress

EXECUTIVE BRANCH POWERS
Enforce federal laws and court orders
Propose legislation to Congress
Make foreign treaties
Nominate officers of the United
 States government and federal
 judges
Serve as commander in chief of the
 armed forces
Pardon people convicted in federal
 courts or grant reprieves

Judicial Checks on the Legislative
Rule federal and state laws unconstitutional

Judicial Checks on the Executive
Declare executive branch actions unconstitutional
Chief justice presides over impeachment trial

Legislative Checks on the Judicial
Change the number and jurisdiction of federal courts
Impeach federal judges
Propose constitutional amendments to override judicial decisions

JUDICIAL BRANCH POWERS
Interpret federal laws and U.S. Constitution
Review the decisions of lower state and federal courts

Executive Checks on the Judicial
Appoint federal judges
Refuse to implement decisions

dent branches of government. On the national level (and in most states), only the legislature has the authority to make laws; the chief executive enforces laws; and the judiciary interprets them. Moreover, initially, members of the House of Representatives, members of the Senate, the president, and members of the federal courts were selected by and were therefore responsible to different constituencies. Madison believed that the scheme devised by the Framers would divide the offices of the new government and their methods of selection among many individuals, providing each office holder with the "necessary means and personal motives to resist encroachment" on his or her power. The Constitution originally placed the selection of senators directly with state legislators, making them more accountable to the states. The Seventeenth Amendment, ratified in 1913, however, called for direct election of senators by the voters, making them directly accountable to the people, thereby making the system more democratic.

The Framers could not have foreseen the intermingling of governmental functions that has since evolved. Locke, in fact, cautioned against giving a legislature the ability to delegate its powers. In Article I of the Constitution, the legislative power is vested in the Congress. But, the president is also given legislative power via his ability to veto legislation, although his veto can be overridden by a two-thirds vote in Congress. Judicial interpretation, including judicial review, a process cemented by the 1803 decision in *Marbury* v. *Madison*, then helps to clarify the implementation of legislation enacted through this process.

So, instead of a pure system of separation of powers, a symbiotic, or interdependent, relationship among the three branches of government has existed from the beginning. Or, as one scholar has explained, there are "separated institutions sharing powers."[19] While Congress still is entrusted with making the laws, the president, as a single person who can easily capture the attention of the media and the electorate, retains tremendous power in setting the agenda and proposing legislation. And, although the Supreme Court's major function is to interpret the Constitution, its involvement in the 2000 presidential election, which effectively decided the election in favor of George W. Bush, and its decisions affecting criminal procedure, abortion, and other issues has led many to charge that it has surpassed its constitutional authority and become, in effect, a law-making body.

CHECKS AND BALANCES The separation of powers among the three branches of the national government is not complete. According to Montesquieu and the Framers, the powers of each branch (as well as the two houses of the national legislature and between the states and the national government) could be used to check the powers of the other two branches of government. The power of each branch of government is checked, or limited, and balanced because the legislative, executive, and judicial branches share some authority and no branch has exclusive domain over any single activity. The creation of this system allowed the Framers to minimize the threat of tyranny from any one branch. Thus, for almost every power granted to one branch, an equal control was established in the other two branches. For example, although President George W. Bush, as the commander in chief, had the power to deploy American troops to Iraq in 2003, he needed authorization from Congress, under the War Powers Act passed in 1973, to keep the troops in the Middle East for longer than ninety days. Similarly, to pay for this mission, the president had to ask Congress to appropriate funds, which it did in the form of an initial $87 billion supplemental appropriations bill and additional funds.

The American System of Checks and Balances

The Articles of the Constitution

The document finally signed by the Framers condensed numerous resolutions into a Preamble and seven separate articles remedying many of the deficiencies within the Articles of Confederation. (To learn more about the differences between the Articles of Confederation and the Constitution, see Table 2.1.) The first three articles established the three branches of government, defined their internal operations, and clarified their relationships with one another. All branches of government were technically considered equal, yet some

TABLE 2.1 Comparing the Articles of Confederation and the U.S. Constitution

The United States has operated under two constitutions. The first, the Articles of Confederation, was in effect from March 1, 1781, when it was ratified by Maryland. The second, the Constitution, replaced the Articles when it was ratified by New Hampshire on June 21, 1788. The two documents have much in common—they were established by the same people (sometimes literally the same exact people, though mostly just in terms of contemporaries). But, they differ more than they resemble each other, when one looks at the details.

	Articles of Confederation	Constitution
Formal name of the nation	The United States of America	Not specified, but referred to in the Preamble as "the United States of America"
Legislature	Unicameral, called Congress	Bicameral, called Congress, divided into the House of Representatives and the Senate
Members of Congress	Between two and seven members per state	Two senators per state, representatives apportioned according to population of each state
Voting in Congress	One vote per state	One vote per representative or senator
Appointment of members	All appointed by state legislatures, in the manner each legislature directed	Representatives elected by popular vote; senators appointed by state legislatures
Term of legislative office	One year	Two years for representatives, six for senators
Term limit for legislative office	No more than three out of every six years	None
Congressional pay	Paid by states	Paid by the federal government
When Congress is not in session	A Committee of States had the full powers of Congress	The President of the United States can call for Congress to assemble
Chair of legislature	President of Congress	Speaker of the House of Representatives; U.S. vice president is president of the Senate
Executive	None	President
National judiciary	Maritime judiciary established—other courts left to states	Supreme Court established, as well as other courts Congress deems necessary
Adjudicator of disputes between states	Congress	U.S. Supreme Court
New states	Admitted upon agreement of nine states (special exemption provided for Canada)	Admitted upon agreement of majority of Congress
Amendment	When agreed upon by all states	When agreed upon by three-fourths of the states
Navy	Congress authorized to build a navy; states authorized to equip warships to counter piracy	Congress authorized to build a navy; states not allowed to keep ships of war
Army	Congress to decide on size of force and to requisition troops from each state according to population	Congress authorized to raise and support armies
Power to coin money	United States and the states	United States only
Ex post facto laws	Not forbidden	Forbidden of both the states and the Congress
Bills of attainder	Not forbidden	Forbidden of both the states and the Congress
Taxes	Apportioned by Congress, collected by the states	Laid and collected by Congress
Ratification	Unanimous consent required	Consent of nine states required

initially appeared more equal than others. The order of the articles, and the detail contained in the first three, reflects the Framers' concern that these branches of government might abuse their powers. The four remaining articles define the relationships among the states, declare national law to be supreme, and set out methods of amending the Constitution.

ARTICLE I: THE LEGISLATIVE BRANCH Article I vests all legislative powers in the Congress and establishes a bicameral legislature, consisting of the Senate and the House of Representatives. It also sets out the qualifications for holding office in each house, the terms of office, the methods of selection of representatives and senators, and the system of apportionment among the states to determine membership in the House of Representatives. Article I, section 2, specifies that an "enumeration" of the citizenry must take place every ten years in a manner to be directed by the U.S. Congress.

One of the most important sections of Article I is section 8. It carefully lists the powers the Framers wished the new Congress to possess. These specified or **enumerated powers** contain many key provisions that had been denied to the Continental Congress under the Articles of Confederation. For example, one of the

enumerated powers
Seventeen specific powers granted to Congress under Article I, section 8, of the Constitution.

Join the Debate

The Equal Opportunity to Govern Amendment

OVERVIEW: Article II, section 1, clause 5, of the U.S. Constitution declares: "No person except a natural-born citizen, or a citizen of the United States at the time of the Adoption of this Constitution, shall be eligible to the Office of President." Why would the Framers put such a restriction on the qualifications for president of the United States? In a letter to George Washington, John Jay, who later became Chief Justice of the Supreme Court, argued that the duty of commander in chief was too important to be given to a foreign-born person—the potential for conflict of interest, danger, and appearance of impropriety in matters of war and foreign policy should not be left to chance. Charles Pinckney, a South Carolina delegate to the Constitutional Convention, expressed concern that foreign governments would use whatever means necessary to influence international events, and he cited the example of Russia, Prussia, and Austria manipulating the election of Stanislaus II to the Polish throne—only to divide Polish lands among themselves. Furthermore, Pinckney contended that the clause would ensure the "experience" of American politics and principles and guarantee "attachment to the country" so as to further eliminate the potential for mischief and foreign intrigue.

As soon as it became clear that Senator John McCain (R-AZ) was going to be the 2008 presidential candidate of the Republican Party, legal scholars and political figures began to debate whether he was eligible under Article II, section 1, of the U.S. Constitution. John McCain was born in the Panama Canal Zone, where his parents—U.S. citizens—were stationed. McCain's father was a U.S. Navy officer. There is no clear legislative or judicial definition of "natural-born." Other presidential candidates, such as Barry Goldwater, George Romney, and Lowell Weicker Jr. were also born outside the United States to parents who were citizens, but they were not elected president. The common assumption, however, is that "natural-born" includes the circumstances of McCain's birth.

More controversial is whether naturalized citizens (those who were citizens of a foreign country but became U.S. citizens and pledged allegiance to this country) should be allowed to serve as president. The election of Austrian-born Arnold Schwarzenegger and of Canadian-born Jennifer Granholm to the governorships of California and Michigan, respectively, reopened this debate. Why shouldn't naturalized citizens be eligible for president? Many naturalized citizens have performed great service to their adopted country; both Henry Kissinger (born in Germany) and Madeleine Albright (born in Czechoslovakia) performed admirably as secretary of state, and over 700 foreign-born Congressional Medal of Honor recipients have demonstrated patriotism and the willingness to die for the country they embraced. With these

viewpoints in mind, in July 2003, Senator Orrin Hatch (R–UT) introduced the Equal Opportunity to Govern Amendment to strike the natural-born citizen clause from the Constitution. The proposed amendment takes into account the Framers' fear of foreign intervention and of divided loyalty by placing a lengthy citizenship requirement—twenty years—before naturalized citizens become eligible to run for presidential office.

Arguments IN FAVOR of the Equal Opportunity to Govern Amendment

- The United States is in part composed of its immigrant population, and they should have the opportunity to run for all political offices. America is a nation of immigrants and many of the

necessary and proper clause
The final paragraph of Article I, section 8, of the Constitution, which gives Congress the authority to pass all laws "necessary and proper" to carry out the enumerated powers specified in the Constitution; also called the elastic clause.

major weaknesses of the Articles was Congress's lack of authority to deal with trade wars. The Constitution remedied this problem by authorizing Congress to "regulate Commerce with foreign Nations, and among the several States." Congress was also given the authority to coin money.

After careful enumeration of seventeen powers of Congress in Article I, section 8, a final, general clause authorizing Congress to "make all Laws which shall be necessary and proper for carrying into Execution the foregoing Powers" was added to Article I. Often referred to as the elastic clause, the **necessary and proper clause** has been a

Framers were foreign born, notably Alexander Hamilton, who helped shape Washington's administration and the executive branch. The Constitution allows for naturalized citizens to attain other high political office, such as Speaker of the House, senator, or Supreme Court justice; why should naturalized citizens be denied the presidency?

- **The natural-born citizen clause has outlived its usefulness.** The problems that existed in 1787 either have changed or do not exist in the twenty-first century. The amendment process was created to allow for historical and political change, and ratification of the Equal Opportunity to Govern Amendment will increase the talent pool of presidential nominees, thus increasing the quality and choice of presidential aspirants for the American people.

- **The natural-born citizen clause is discriminatory.** The clause is un-American in that it denies equality of opportunity for all American citizens. Naturalized citizens serve in the military, pay taxes, run for local, state, and federal office, endure the same national hardships and crises, and add to the overall quality of American life; thus, naturalized citizens should have the same rights and privileges as the native born.

Arguments AGAINST the Equal Opportunity to Govern Amendment

- **Foreign governments still attempt to have undue influence in American politics.** The Framers were correct in assuming foreign governments attempt to manipulate American politics. For example, in 1999, the Democratic National Committee returned over $600,000 in campaign contributions to Chinese nationals attempting to gain influence with the Clinton administration. The clause was meant to be another institutional safeguard against presidential corruption.

- **Running for president is not a right.** The office of the president is an institution designed for republican purposes. The Framers strongly believed that foreign influence within the U.S. government must be restricted (the language was unanimously adopted by the Constitutional Convention) and thus they restricted the right to run for presidential office.

- **There is no public movement or outcry to remove this clause from the Constitution.** Many constitutional scholars argue the Constitution should be amended only for pressing reasons, and amendments should be construed with a view to the well-being of future generations. Foreign policy and events are too fluid and too volatile to risk undermining the president's foreign policy and commander-in-chief authority. Until the American people determine otherwise, the clause should remain.

Continuing the Debate

1. Is the natural-born citizen clause of the U.S. Constitution discriminatory? Should the Constitution be amended to realize the principle of political equality? Explain your answer.
2. Did the Framers create a true institutional barrier to help prevent corruption by foreign governments? Explain your answer.

To Follow the Debate Online, Go To:

writ.news.findlaw.com/dean/20041008.html and read John W. Dean's essay "The Pernicious 'Natural Born' Clause of the Constitution: Why Immigrants like Governors Schwarzenegger and Granholm Ought to Be Able to Become Presidents," which provides legal analyses of this issue, discusses the history of the natural-born citizen clause, and argues for change.

lawreview.kentlaw.edu/ articles/81-1/ Herlihy.pdf and read a law review article by Sarah P. Herlihy, "Amending the Natural Born Citizen Requirement: Globalization as the Impetus and the Obstacle," which reviews the history and weighs the arguments for and against changing this clause in the Constitution.

www.nytimes.com/2008/02/ 28/us/ politics/28mccain.html for a *New York Times* article that discusses the application of the natural-born citizens clause to John McCain.

source of tremendous congressional activity never anticipated by the Framers, including the passage of laws that regulate the environment, welfare programs, education, and communication.

The necessary and proper clause, also called the elastic clause, is the basis for the **implied powers** that Congress uses to execute its other powers. Congress's enumerated power to regulate commerce has been linked with the necessary and proper clause in a variety of U.S. Supreme Court cases. As a result, laws banning prostitution where travel across state lines is involved, regulating trains and planes, establishing federal

implied powers
Powers derived from the enumerated powers and the necessary and proper clause. These powers are not stated specifically but are considered to be reasonably implied through the exercise of delegated powers.

minimum-wage and maximum-hour laws, and mandating drug testing for certain workers have passed constitutional muster.

ARTICLE II: THE EXECUTIVE BRANCH   Article II vests the executive power, that is, the authority to execute the laws of the nation, in a president of the United States. Section 1 sets the president's term of office at four years and explains the Electoral College. It also states the qualifications for office and describes a mechanism to replace the president in case of death, disability, or removal.

The powers and duties of the president are set out in section 3. Among the most important of these are the president's role as commander in chief of the armed forces, the authority to make treaties with the consent of the Senate, and the authority to "appoint Ambassadors, other public Ministers and Consuls, the Judges of the supreme Court, and all other Officers of the United States." Other sections of Article II instruct the president to report directly to Congress "from time to time," in what has come to be known as the State of the Union Address, and to "take Care that the Laws be faithfully executed." Section 4 provides the mechanism for removal of the president, vice president, and other officers of the United States for "Treason, Bribery, or other high Crimes and Misdemeanors" (see chapter 8).

Article II also limits the presidency to natural-born citizens. A more new amendment would be needed to change that qualification. (To learn about the natural-born citizen clause, see Join the Debate: The Equal Opportunity to Govern Amendment.)

ARTICLE III: THE JUDICIAL BRANCH   Article III establishes a Supreme Court and defines its jurisdiction. During the Philadelphia meeting, the small and large states differed significantly as to the desirability of an independent judiciary and on the role of state courts in the national court system. The smaller states feared that a strong unelected judiciary would trample on their liberties. In compromise, Congress was permitted, but not required, to establish lower national courts. Thus, state courts and the national court system would exist side by side with distinct areas of authority. Federal courts were given authority to decide cases arising under federal law. The U.S. Supreme Court was also given the power to settle disputes between states, or between a state and the national government. Ultimately, it was up to the Supreme Court to determine what provisions of the Constitution actually meant.

Although some delegates to the convention urged that the president be allowed to remove federal judges, ultimately judges were given appointments for life, presuming "good behavior." And, like the president's, their salaries cannot be lowered while they hold office. This provision was adopted to ensure that the legislature did not attempt to punish the Supreme Court or any other judges for unpopular decisions.

ARTICLES IV THROUGH VII   The remainder of the articles in the Constitution attempted to anticipate problems that might occur in the operation of the new national government as well as its relations to the states. Article IV begins with what is called the **full faith and credit clause**, which mandates that states honor the laws and judicial proceedings of the other states. Article IV also includes the mechanisms for admitting new states to the union.

Article V (discussed in greater detail on p. 65) specifies how amendments can be added to the Constitution. The Bill of Rights, which added ten amendments to the Constitution in 1791, was one of the first items of business when the First Congress met in 1789. Since then, only seventeen additional amendments have been ratified.

Article VI contains the supremacy clause, which asserts the basic primacy of the Constitution and national law over state laws and constitutions. The **supremacy clause** provides that the "Constitution, and the laws of the United States" as well as all treaties are to be the supreme law of the land. All national and state officers and

full faith and credit clause
Provision of the Constitution that mandates states to honor the laws and judicial proceedings of other states.

supremacy clause
Portion of Article VI of the U.S. Constitution mandating that national law is supreme to (that is, supersedes) all other laws passed by the states or by any other subdivision of government.

judges are bound by national law and take oaths to support the federal Constitution above any state law or constitution. Because of the supremacy clause, any legitimate exercise of national power supersedes any state laws or action, in a process that is called preemption, further discussed in chapter 3. Without the supremacy clause and the federal courts' ability to invoke it, the national government would have little actual enforceable power; thus, many commentators call the supremacy clause the linchpin of the entire federal system.

Mindful of the potential problems that could occur if church and state were too enmeshed, Article VI also specifies that no religious test shall be required for holding any office. This mandate is strengthed by the separation of church and state guarantee that was quickly added to the Constitution when the First Amendment was ratified.

The seventh and final article of the Constitution concerns the procedures for ratification of the new Constitution: nine of the thirteen states would have to agree to, or ratify, its new provisions before it would become the supreme law of the land.

Photo courtesy: Rex May/Cartoonist Group

"What do you want to watch — the State of the Union address or a reality show?"

How does the president's State of the Union Address affect the average American? When the Framers, in Article II of the Constitution, required the president to report directly to Congress "from time to time" they never imagined that a televised audience of millions would tune in each year to watch and listen to the president's report. Of course, as this cartoon makes clear, not everyone considers the State of the Union ideal prime time viewing.

The Drive for Ratification of the U.S. Constitution

While delegates to the Constitutional Convention labored in Philadelphia, the Congress of the Confederation continued to govern the former colonies under the Articles of Confederation. The day after the Constitution was signed, William Jackson, the secretary of the Constitutional Convention, left for New York City, then the nation's capital, to deliver the official copy of the document to the Congress. He also took with him a resolution of the delegates calling upon each of the states to vote on the new Constitution. Anticipating resistance from the representatives in the state legislatures, however, the Framers required the states to call special ratifying conventions to consider the proposed Constitution.

Jackson carried a letter from General George Washington with the proposed Constitution. In a few eloquent words, Washington summed up the sentiments of the Framers and the spirit of compromise that had permeated the long weeks in Philadelphia:

> That it will meet the full and entire approbation of every state is not perhaps to be expected, but each [state] will doubtless consider, that had her interest alone been consulted, the consequences might have been particularly disagreeable or injurious to others; that it is liable to as few exceptions as could reasonably have been expected, we hope and believe; that it may promote lasting welfare of that country so dear to us all, and secure her freedom and happiness is our ardent wish.[20]

The Second Continental Congress immediately accepted the work of the convention and forwarded the proposed Constitution to the states for their vote. It was by no means certain, however, that the new Constitution would be adopted. From the fall of 1787 to the summer of 1788, the proposed Constitution was debated hotly around the nation. State politicians understandably feared a strong central government. Farmers and other working-class people were fearful of a distant national government. Those who had accrued substantial debts during the economic chaos following the Revolutionary War feared that a new government with a new financial policy would plunge them into even greater debt. The public in general was very leery of taxes—these were the same people who had revolted against the king's taxes. At the heart of many of their concerns was an underlying fear of the massive changes that would be brought about by a new system. Favoring the Constitution were wealthy merchants, lawyers, bankers, and those who believed that the new nation could not continue to exist under the Articles of Confederation. For them, it all boiled down to one simple question offered by James Madison: "Whether or not the Union shall or shall not be continued."

Federalists versus Anti-Federalists

Federalists
Those who favored a stronger national government and supported the proposed U.S. Constitution; later became the first U.S. political party.

Almost as soon as the ink was dry on the last signature to the Constitution, those who favored the new strong national government chose to call themselves **Federalists**. They were well aware that many people still generally opposed the notion of a strong national government. They did not want to risk being labeled nationalists, so they tried to get the upper hand in the debate by nicknaming their opponents **Anti-Federalists**. Those put in the latter category insisted that they were instead Federal Republicans, who believed in a federal system. As noted in Table 2.2, Anti-Federalists argued that they simply wanted to protect state governments from the tyranny of a too powerful national government.[21]

Anti-Federalists
Those who favored strong state governments and a weak national government; opposed the ratification of the U.S. Constitution.

Federalists and Anti-Federalists participated in the mass meetings that were held in state legislatures to discuss the pros and cons of the new plan. Tempers ran high at these meetings, and fervent debates were published in newspapers, which played a powerful role in the adoption process. The entire Constitution, in fact, was printed in the *Pennsylvania Packet* just two days after the convention's end. Other major papers quickly followed suit. Soon, opinion pieces on both sides of the adoption issue began to appear around the nation, often written under pseudonyms such as "Caesar" or "Constant Reader," as was the custom of the day.

The Federalist Papers

The Federalist Papers
A series of eighty-five political papers written by Alexander Hamilton, James Madison, and John Jay in support of ratification of the U.S. Constitution.

One name stood out from all the rest: "Publius" (Latin for "the people"). Between October 1787 and May 1788, eighty-five articles written under that pen name routinely appeared in newspapers in New York, a state where ratification was in doubt. Most were written by Alexander Hamilton and James Madison. Hamilton, a young, fiery New Yorker born in the British West Indies, wrote fifty-one; Madison, a Virginian who later served as the fourth president, wrote twenty-six; jointly they penned another three. John Jay, also of New York, and later the first chief justice of the United States, wrote five of the pieces. These eighty-five essays became known as ***The Federalist Papers***.

Today, *The Federalist Papers* are considered masterful explanations of the Framers' intentions as they drafted the new Constitution. At the time, although

TABLE 2.2 Federalists and Anti-Federalists Compared

	Federalists	Anti-Federalists
Who were they?	Property owners, landed rich, merchants of Northeast and Middle Atlantic states	Small farmers, shopkeepers, laborers
Political philosophy	Elitist: saw themselves and those of their class as most fit to govern (others were to be governed)	Believed in the decency of "the common man" and in participatory democracy; viewed elites as corrupt; sought greater protection of individual rights
Type of government favored	Powerful central government; two-house legislature; upper house (six-year term) further removed from the people, whom they distrusted	Wanted stronger state governments (closer to the people) at the expense of the powers of the national government; sought smaller electoral districts, frequent elections, referendum and recall, and a large unicameral legislature to provide for greater class and occupational representation
Alliances	Pro-British, anti-French	Anti-British, pro-French

they were reprinted widely, they were far too theoretical to have much impact on those who would ultimately vote on the proposed Constitution. Dry and scholarly, they lacked the fervor of much of the political rhetoric that was then in use. *The Federalist Papers* did, however, highlight the reasons for the structure of the new government and its benefits. According to *Federalist No. 10*, for example, the new Constitution was called "a republican remedy for the disease incident to republican government." These musings of Madison, Hamilton, and Jay continue to be the clearest articulation of the political theories and philosophies that lie at the heart of our Constitution.

Why were *The Federalist Papers* written? *The Federalist Papers* highlighted the reasons for the structure of the new government and its benefits.

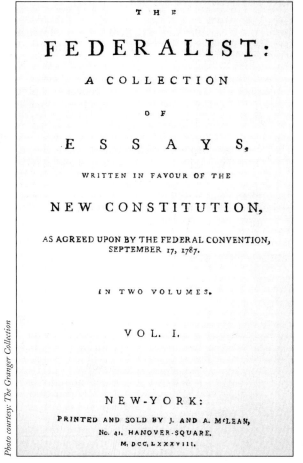

Photo courtesy: The Granger Collection

THE

FEDERALIST:

A COLLECTION

OF

ESSAYS,

WRITTEN IN FAVOUR OF THE

NEW CONSTITUTION,

AS AGREED UPON BY THE FEDERAL CONVENTION,
SEPTEMBER 17, 1787.

IN TWO VOLUMES.

VOL. I.

NEW-YORK:

PRINTED AND SOLD BY J. AND A. McLEAN,
No. 41, HANOVER-SQUARE.
M, DCC, LXXXVIII.

Forced on the defensive, the Anti-Federalists responded to *The Federalist Papers* with their own series of letters written under the pen names "Brutus" and "Cato," two ancient Romans famous for their intolerance of tyranny. These letters (actually essays) undertook a line-by-line critique of the Constitution.

Anti-Federalists argued that a strong central government would render the states powerless.[22] They stressed the strengths the government had been granted under the Articles of Confederation, and argued that the Articles, not the proposed Constitution, created a true federal system. Moreover, they argued that the strong national government would tax heavily, that the Supreme Court would overwhelm the states by invalidating state laws, and that the president eventually would have too much power, as commander in chief of a large and powerful army.[23]

In particular, the Anti-Federalists feared the power of the national government to run roughshod over the liberties of the people. They proposed that the taxing power of Congress be limited, that the executive be curbed by a council, that the military consist of state militias rather than a national force, and that the jurisdiction of the Supreme Court be limited to prevent it from reviewing and potentially overturning the decisions of state courts. But, their most effective argument concerned the absence of a bill of rights in the Constitution. James Madison answered these criticisms in *Federalist Nos. 10 and 51*. (The texts of these two essays are printed in Appendices III and IV.) In *Federalist No. 10*, Madison pointed out that the voters would not always succeed in electing "enlightened statesmen" as their representatives. The greatest threat to individual liberties would therefore come from factions within the government, who might place narrow interests above broader national interests and the rights of citizens. While recognizing that no form of government could protect the country from unscrupulous politicians, Madison argued that the organization of the new government would minimize the effects of political factions. The great advantage of a federal system, Madison maintained, was that it created the "happy combination" of a national government too large to be controlled by any single faction, and several state governments that would be smaller and more responsive to local needs. Moreover, he argued in *Federalist No. 51* that the proposed federal government's separation of powers would prohibit any one branch from either dominating the national government or violating the rights of citizens.

Ratifying the Constitution

Debate continued in the thirteen states as votes were taken from December 1787 to June 1788, in accordance with the ratifying process laid out in Article VII of the proposed Constitution. Three states acted quickly to ratify the new Constitution. Two small states, Delaware and New Jersey, voted to ratify before the large states could

SIMULATION

You Are James Madison

Celebrating the Constitution

In late 2004, Senator Robert C. Byrd (D–WV) introduced legislation that called on all educational institutions receiving federal funds—from kindergarten through grade 12 to colleges, universities, and even law schools—to set aside September 17 of each year to conduct educational programs concerning the U.S. Constitution. When Public Law 108-447 passed, educational institutions around the United States began to question just what types of programs were required. The selection of September 17 was not random; the U.S. Constitution was sent to the states for ratification on that date.

Since 2005, educational institutions around the United States have chosen to celebrate what is now called Constitution Day in a variety of ways. The National Constitution Center has taken the lead in publicizing unique and thoughtful ways for schools to observe Constitution Day. Among those highlighted are "celebrate your state" events, discussions on how the U.S. Supreme Court can change the law and make policy, grade school celebrations where students wear red, white, and blue and learn about the Preamble; and interactive Web-based activities for all ages.

- Visit the C-SPAN classroom Web site at **www.c-spanclassroom.org**. What activities might you and your classmates use to teach about the Constitution at a local elementary school?
- What kinds of activities are planned on your campus to celebrate Constitution Day?
- What programs or projects could your American government class engage in to bring recognition of Constitution Day to your campus?
- For more Constitution Day suggestions, go to **www.constitutionday.us**.

rethink the notion of equal representation of the states in the Senate. Pennsylvania, where Federalists were well organized, was also one of the first three states to ratify. Massachusetts assented to the new government but tempered its support by calling for an immediate addition of amendments, including one protecting personal rights. New Hampshire became the crucial ninth state to ratify on June 21, 1788. This action completed the ratification process outlined in Article VII of the Constitution and marked the beginning of a new nation. But, New York and Virginia, which at that time accounted for more than 40 percent of the new nation's population, had not yet ratified the Constitution. Thus, the practical future of the new nation remained in doubt.

Hamilton in New York and Madison in Virginia worked feverishly to convince delegates to their state conventions to vote for the new government. In New York, sentiment against the Constitution ran high. In Albany, fighting resulting in injuries and death broke out over ratification. When news of Virginia's acceptance of the Constitution reached the New York convention, Hamilton finally was able to convince a majority of those present to follow suit by a narrow margin of three votes. Both states also recommended the addition of a series of structural amendments and a bill of rights.

North Carolina and Rhode Island continued to hold out against ratification. Both had recently printed new currencies and feared that values would plummet in a federal system where the Congress was authorized to coin money. On August 2, 1788, North Carolina became the first state to reject the Constitution on the grounds that no Anti-Federalist amendments were included. Soon after, in September 1789, owing much to the Anti-Federalist pressure for additional protections from the national government, Congress submitted the Bill of Rights to the states for their ratification. North Carolina then ratified the Constitution by a vote of 194–77. Rhode Island, the only state that had not sent representa-

Thinking Globally
The British System

Unlike the United States, Great Britain does not have a written constitution, nor is there a document comparable to the Bill of Rights that guarantees certain individual liberties to the British people. In the United States, the ultimate arbiter of what is constitutional is the U.S. Supreme Court. In Britain, the ultimate authority is Parliament, and the country's unwritten constitution can easily be changed by a majority vote of that legislative body.

- If the U.S. Constitution could be altered by a majority vote in Congress, what kinds of changes might you predict?
- Does the United States Supreme Court have too much power to decide what the government may or may not do? Explain your answers.

What does a grassroots activist look like? In 1982, Gregory Watson, an undergraduate at the University of Texas, Austin, discovered an unratified amendment originally proposed by James Madison in 1789. Madison's amendment would ensure that any salary increase for members of Congress could not take effect until the next session of Congress. Watson began a ten-year, $6,000 self-financed crusade to renew interest in the compensation amendment, which had languished after the approval of only six states. Watson's perseverance paid off: in May 1992 the amendment was ratified by the requisite thirty-eight states and became part of the Constitution.

Photo courtesy: Ziggy Kaluzny/People Magazine Syndication

tives to Philadelphia, remained out of the new nation until 1790. Finally, under threats from its largest cities to secede from the state, the legislature called a convention that ratified the Constitution by only two votes (34–32)—one year after George Washington became the first president of the United States. (To learn more about the Constitution, see Ideas into Action: Studying the Constitution.)

Amending the Constitution: The Bill of Rights

Once the Constitution was ratified, elections were held. When Congress convened, it immediately sent a set of amendments to the states for their ratification. An amendment authorizing the enlargement of the House of Representatives and another to prevent members of the House from raising their own salaries failed to garner favorable votes in the necessary three-fourths of the states. The remaining ten amendments, known as the **Bill of Rights**, were ratified by 1791 in accordance with the procedures set out in the Constitution. Sought by Anti-Federalists as a protection for individual liberties, they offered numerous specific limitations on the national government's ability to interfere with a wide variety of personal liberties, some of which were already guaranteed by many state constitutions (see chapters 5 and 6).

Bill of Rights
The first ten amendments to the U.S. Constitution, which largely guarantee specific rights and liberties.

The Bill of Rights includes numerous specific protections of personal rights. Freedom of expression, speech, press, religion, and assembly are guaranteed by the First Amendment. The Bill of Rights also contains numerous safeguards for those accused of crimes.

Two of the amendments of the Bill of Rights were reactions to British rule—the right to bear arms (Second Amendment) and the right not to have soldiers quartered in private homes (Third Amendment). More general rights are also included in the Bill of Rights. The Ninth Amendment notes that these enumerated rights are not inclusive, meaning they are not the only rights to be enjoyed by the people, and the Tenth Amendment states that powers not given to the national government are reserved by the states or the people.

Toward Reform: Methods of Amending the U.S. Constitution

The Framers did not want to fashion a government that could be too influenced by the whims of the people. Therefore, they made the formal amendment process a slow one to ensure that the Constitution was not impulsively amended. In keeping with this intent, only seventeen amendments have been added since the addition of the Bill of Rights. However, informal amendments, prompted by judicial interpretation and cultural and social change, have had a tremendous impact on the Constitution.

You Are Proposing a Constitutional Amendment

Formal Methods of Amending the Constitution

Article V of the Constitution creates a two-stage amendment process: proposal and ratification.[24] The Constitution specifies two ways to accomplish each stage. As illustrated in Figure 2.3, amendments to the Constitution can be proposed by: (1) a vote of two-thirds of the members in both houses of Congress; or, (2) a vote of two-thirds of the state legislatures specifically requesting Congress to call a national convention to propose amendments. (To learn more about the amendment process, see The Living Constitution.)

The second method has never been used. Historically, it has served as a fairly effective threat, forcing Congress to consider amendments that might otherwise never have been debated. In the 1980s, for example, several states called on Congress to enact a balanced budget amendment. To forestall the need for a special constitutional convention, in 1985 Congress enacted the Gramm-Rudman-Hollings Act, which called for a balanced budget by the 1991 fiscal year. But, Congress could not meet that target. The act was amended repeatedly until 1993, when Congress postponed the call for a balanced budget, the need for which faded in light of surpluses that occurred late in Clinton administration. The act was later ruled unconstitutional by a three-judge district court that declared that the law violated separation of powers principles.

The ratification process is fairly straightforward. When Congress votes to propose an amendment, the Constitution specifies that the ratification process must occur in one of two ways: (1) a favorable vote in three-fourths of the state legislatures; or, (2) a favorable vote in specially called ratifying conventions in three-fourths of the states.

Thinking Globally

Changing Constitutions

The U.S. Constitution, ratified in 1788, has been amended only twenty-seven times, and the idea of making wholesale changes to the Constitution is offensive to most Americans. In contrast, the oldest German citizens have lived under at least four constitutions—two democratic and two authoritarian. Venezuela is currently operating under the country's twenty-sixth constitution.

- How can a constitution as old as that of the United States remain relevant over time?
- Why would it make sense to draft a new constitution after major political change in a country?
- What are the advantages and disadvantages to a system where wholesale change to the national constitution is considered normal?

The Constitution itself was ratified by the favorable vote of nine states in specially called ratifying conventions. The Framers feared that the power of special interests in state legislatures would prevent a positive vote on the new Constitution. Since ratification of the Constitution, however, only one ratifying convention has been called. The Eighteenth Amendment, which outlawed the sale of alcoholic beverages nationwide, was ratified by the first method—a vote in state legislatures. Millions of people broke the law, others died from drinking homemade liquor, and still others made their fortunes selling bootleg or illegal liquor. After a decade of these problems, Congress decided to act. An additional amendment—the Twenty-First—was proposed to repeal the Eighteenth Amendment. It was sent to the states for ratification, but with a call for ratifying conventions, not a vote in the state legislatures.[25] Members of Congress correctly predicted that the move to repeal the Eighteenth Amendment would encounter opposition in the statehouses,

FIGURE **2.3** Methods of Amending the Constitution

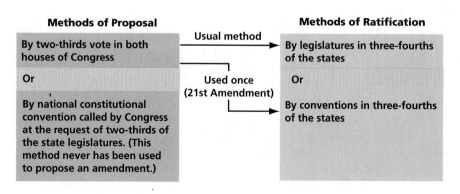

The Living Constitution

The Congress, whenever two thirds of both houses shall deem it necessary, shall propose amendments to this Constitution, or, on the application of the legislatures of two thirds of the several states, shall call a convention for proposing amendments, which, in either case, shall be valid to all intents and purposes, as part of this Constitution, when ratified by the legislatures of three fourths of the several states, or by conventions in three fourths thereof, as the one or the other mode of ratification may be proposed by the Congress.

—ARTICLE V

With this article, the Framers acknowledged the potential need to change or amend the Constitution. This article provides for two methods to propose amendments: by a two-thirds vote of both houses of Congress or by a two-thirds vote of the state legislatures. It also specifies two alternative methods of ratification of proposed amendments: by a three-quarters vote of the state legislatures, or by a similar vote in specially called state ratifying conventions.

During the Constitutional Convention in Philadelphia, the Framers were divided as to how frequently or how easily the Constitution was to be amended. The original suggestion was to allow the document to be amended "when soever it shall seem necessary." Some delegates wanted to entrust this authority to the state legislatures; however, others feared that it would give states too much power. James Madison alleviated these fears by suggesting that both Congress and the states have a role in the process.

In the late 1960s and early 1970s, leaders of the new women's rights movement sought passage of the Equal Rights Amendment (ERA). Their efforts were rewarded when the ERA was approved in the House and Senate by overwhelming majorities in 1972 and then sent out to the states for their approval. In spite of tremendous lobbying, a strong anti-ERA movement emerged and the amendment failed to gain approval in three-quarters of the state legislatures.

The failed battles for the ERA as well as other amendments, including one to prohibit child labor and another to grant statehood to the District of Columbia, underscore how difficult it is to amend the Constitution. Thus, unlike the constitutions of individual states or many other nations, the U.S. Constitution rarely has been amended.

Still, the ERA has been proposed in every session of Congress since 1923. In 2007, it was renamed the Women's Equality Amendment by its sponsors.

CRITICAL THINKING QUESTIONS

1. Should women's rights advocates press for a women's equality amendment? Why or why not?
2. Does your state already have an equal rights amendment? What does it guarantee?

which were largely controlled by elected conservative rural legislators. Thus, Congress's decision to use the convention method led to quick approval of the Twenty-First Amendment.

The intensity of efforts to amend the Constitution has varied considerably, depending on the nature of the change proposed. Whereas the Twenty-First Amendment took only ten months to ratify, an equal rights amendment (ERA) was introduced in every session of Congress from 1923 until 1972, when Congress finally voted favorably for it. Even then, years of lobbying by women's groups were insufficient to garner necessary state support. By 1982, the congressionally mandated date for ratification, only thirty-five states—three short of the number required—had voted favorably on the amendment.[26]

TIMELINE

The History of Constitutional Amendments

Why are constitutional amendments repealed? For all its moral support from groups such as the Women's Christian Temperance Union (WCTU), whose members invaded bars to protest the sale of alcoholic beverages, the Eighteenth (Prohibition) Amendment was a disaster. Among its side effects was the rise of powerful crime organizations responsible for illegal sales of alcoholic beverages. Once proposed, it took only ten months to ratify the Twenty-First Amendment, which repealed the Prohibition Amendment.

Photo courtesy: U.S. Department of Interior. National Park Service. Edison National Historical Site.

One of the most recent, concerted efforts would amend the Constitution to prohibit flag burning. In 1989, the U.S. Supreme Court ruled in *Texas* v. *Johnson* that burning the American flag was a form of speech protected under the First Amendment. Since the Court's initial ruling, passing a constitutional amendment to prohibit flag burning has become one of the social issues Republicans have used to mobilize their base. So far, anti-flag-burning amendments have been unsuccessful. Although the House of Representatives passed such an amendment, it has yet to garner the required two-thirds vote necessary for passage in the Senate. (To learn more about the flag-burning amendment, see Politics Now: Politics and the Flag.)

Informal Methods of Amending the Constitution

The formal amendment process is not the only way that the Constitution has been changed over time. Judicial interpretation and cultural and social change also have had a major impact on the way the Constitution has evolved.

JUDICIAL INTERPRETATION As early as 1803, the Supreme Court declared in *Marbury* v. *Madison* that the federal courts had the power to nullify acts of the nation's government when they were found to be in conflict with the Constitution.[27] Over the years, this check on the other branches of government and on the states has increased the authority of the Court and significantly altered the meaning of various provisions of the Constitution, a fact that prompted President Woodrow Wilson to call the Supreme Court "a constitutional convention in continuous session." (More detail on the Supreme Court's role in interpreting the Constitution is found in chapters 5, 6, and 10 especially, as well as in other chapters in this book.)

Today, some analysts argue that the original intent of the Framers, as evidenced in *The Federalist Papers*, as well as in private notes taken by James Madison at the Constitutional Convention, should govern judicial interpretation of the Constitution.[28] Others argue that the Framers knew that a changing society needed an elastic, flexible document that could adapt to the ages.[29] In all likelihood, the vagueness of the document was purposeful. Those in attendance in Philadelphia recognized that they could not agree on everything and that it was wiser to leave interpretation to future generations.

Recently, law professor Mark V. Tushnet has offered a particularly stinging criticism of judicial review and our reliance on the courts to interpret the law. He believes that under our present system, Americans are unwilling to enforce the provisions of the Constitution because they believe this is the sole province of the court system. If we were to eliminate the deference given to court decisions, Tushnet argues, citizens would be compelled to become involved in enforcing their Constitution, thereby creating a system of populist constitutional law, and a more representative government.[30]

SOCIAL AND CULTURAL CHANGE Even the most far-sighted of those in attendance at the Constitutional Convention could not have anticipated the vast changes that have occurred in the United States. For example, although many people were uncomfortable with the Three-Fifths Compromise and others hoped for the abolition of slavery, none could have imagined that an African American would one day

Source: WASHINGTON POST   June 28, 2006   Page A1

Politics and the Flag

Senate Rejects Flag Desecration Amendment

CHARLES BABINGTON

The Senate rejected by a single vote yesterday an effort to amend the Constitution to allow Congress to ban desecration of the American flag, after a two-day debate freighted with political calculations and sharp disputes over the limits of free speech.

The 66 to 34 vote fell just short of the two-thirds majority required to approve a constitutional amendment and submit it to the states for ratification. It marked the latest setback for congressional attempts to supersede Supreme Court decisions in 1989 and 1990. Justices narrowly ruled that burning and other desecrations of the flag are protected as free speech under the First Amendment. . . .

GOP [Republican] congressional leaders have offered up several measures in recent weeks that are important to their conservative political base—including an amendment banning same-sex marriage and further cuts in the estate tax—culminating with yesterday's vote on flag burning.

Polls show that most Americans want flag desecration outlawed, and the amendment's proponents said they were trying to stop justices from thwarting the public's will. They said that burning a U.S. flag in public—while rare these days—is a reprehensible insult to the nation's founders and a dishonor to the Americans who died fighting tyranny.

The amendment's opponents agreed that flag burning is repugnant, but argued that U.S. troops died to preserve freedoms that include controversial political statements.

Discussion Questions

1. *If the only approved way to dispose of an American flag is through burning, how can the government differentiate between appropriate and illegal flag burning?*
2. *Since a majority of the American public is opposed to flag desecration, how might lawmakers prohibit the practice in light of the Supreme Court's ruling that burning the flag is constitutionally protected speech?*

---

become president of the United States. Likewise, few of the Framers could have anticipated the diverse roles that women would play in American society. The Constitution has evolved to accommodate such social and cultural changes. Thus, although there is no specific amendment guaranteeing women equal protection of the law, the federal courts have interpreted the Constitution to prohibit many forms of gender discrimination, thereby recognizing cultural and societal change.

Social change has also caused changes in the way institutions of government act. As problems such as the Great Depression appeared national in scope, Congress took on more and more power at the expense of the states. In fact, Yale law professor Bruce Ackerman argues that extraordinary times call for extraordinary measures such as the New Deal that, in effect, amend the Constitution. Thus, congressional passage (and the Supreme Court's eventual acceptance) of sweeping New Deal legislation that altered the balance of power between the national government and the states truly changed the Constitution without benefit of amendment.[31] Still, in spite of massive changes such as these, the Constitution survives, changed and ever changing after more than 200 years.

WHAT SHOULD I HAVE LEARNED?

The U.S. Constitution has proven to be a remarkably enduring document. In explaining how and why the Constitution came into being, this chapter has answered the following questions:

■ **What were the roots of the new American nation?**

While settlers came to the New World for a variety of reasons, most remained loyal to Great Britain and considered themselves subjects of the king. Over the years, as new generations of Americans were born on colonial soil, those ties weakened. A series of taxes levied by the crown ultimately led the colonists to convene a Continental Congress and to declare their independence.

■ **What is the significance of the Articles of Confederation?**

The Articles of Confederation (1781) created a loose league of friendship between the new national government and the states. Numerous weaknesses in the new government quickly became apparent. Among the major flaws were Congress's inability to tax or regulate commerce, the absence of an executive to administer the government, the lack of a strong central government, and no judiciary.

■ **How did the writing of the U. S. Constitution come about?**

When the weaknesses under the Articles of Confederation became apparent, the states called for a meeting to reform them. The Constitutional Convention (1787) quickly threw out the Articles of Confederation and fashioned a new, more workable form of government. The Constitution was the result of a series of compromises, including those over representation, over issues involving large and small states, and over how to determine population. Compromises were also made about how members of each branch of government were to be selected. The Electoral College was created to give states a key role in the selection of the president.

■ **What ideas and principles are embodied in the U.S. Constitution?**

The proposed U.S. Constitution created a federal system that drew heavily on Montesquieu's ideas about separation of powers. These ideas concerned a way of parceling out power among the three branches of government, and checks and balances to prevent any one branch from having too much power.

■ **How was the U.S. Constitution ratified?**

The drive for ratification became a fierce fight between Federalists and Anti-Federalists. Federalists lobbied for the strong national government created by the Constitution; Anti-Federalists favored greater state power.

■ **How can the U. S. Constitution be amended?**

The Framers did not want to fashion a government that could respond to the whims of the people. Therefore, they designed a deliberate two-stage formal amendment process that required approval on the federal and state levels; this process has rarely been used. However, informal amendments, prompted by judicial interpretation and by cultural and social change, have had a tremendous impact on the Constitution.

Key Terms

Anti-Federalists, p. 54
Articles of Confederation, p. 39
Bill of Rights, p. 57
checks and balances, p. 46
Committees of Correspondence, p. 35
confederation, p. 39
constitution, p. 43
Declaration of Independence, p. 38
enumerated powers, p. 49

federal system, p. 46
The Federalist Papers, p. 54
Federalists, p. 54
First Continental Congress, p. 37
full faith and credit clause, p. 52
Great Compromise, p. 44
implied powers, p. 51
mercantilism, p. 33
necessary and proper clause, p. 50

New Jersey Plan, p. 44
Second Continental Congress, p. 37
separation of powers, p. 46
Shays's Rebellion, p. 41
Stamp Act Congress, p. 34
supremacy clause, p. 52
Three-Fifths Compromise, p. 45
Virginia Plan, p. 43

Researching the Constitution

In the Library

Ackerman, Bruce. *The Failure of the Founding Fathers: Jefferson, Marshall, and the Rise of Presidential Democracy*, new ed. Cambridge, MA: Belknap Press, 2007.

———. *We the People: Transformations*, new ed. Cambridge, MA: Belknap Press, 2000.

Beard, Charles A. *An Economic Interpretation of the Constitution of the United States*, reissue ed. Mineola, NY: Dover, 2004.

Bowen, Catherine Drinker. *Miracle at Philadelphia*. Boston: Little, Brown, 1986.

Breyer, Stephen. *Active Liberty: Interpreting Our Democratic Constitution*. New York: Vintage, 2007.

Brinkley, Alan, Nelson W. Polsby, and Kathleen M. Sullivan. *New Federalist Papers: Essays in Defense of the Constitution*. New York: Norton, 1997.

Dahl, Robert A. *How Democratic is the American Constitution?* 2nd ed. New Haven, CT: Yale University Press, 2004.

Hamilton, Alexander, James Madison, and John Jay. *The Federalist Papers*. New York: Bantam Books, 1989 (first published in 1788).

Lynch, Joseph M. *Negotiating the Constitution: The Earliest Debates over Original Intent*. Ithaca, NY: Cornell University Press, 2005.

Main, Jackson Turner. *The Anti-Federalists: Critics of the Constitution, 1781–1788*. Chapel Hill: University of North Carolina Press, 2004.

———. *The Social Structure of Revolutionary America*. Princeton, NJ: Princeton University Press, 1965.

Rossiter, Clinton. *1787: Grand Convention*, reissue ed. New York: Norton, 1987.

Sabato, Larry J. *A More Perfect Constitution*. New York: Walker 2008.

Simon, James F. *What Kind of Nation: Thomas Jefferson, John Marshall, and the Epic Struggle to Create a United States*. New York: Simon and Schuster, 2003.

Stewart, David O. *The Summer of 1787: The Men Who Invented the Constitution*. New York: Simon and Schuster, 2007.

Storing, Herbert J. *What the Anti-Federalists Were For*. Chicago: University of Chicago Press, 1981.

Sunstein, Cass R. *The Second Bill of Rights: FDR's Unfinished Revolution—And Why We Need It More Than Ever*. New York: Basic Books, 2006.

Tushnet, Mark. *Taking the Constitution Away from the Courts*. Princeton, NJ: Princeton University Press, 2002.

———. *The Constitution in Wartime: Beyond Alarmism and Complacency*. Durham, NC: Duke University Press, 2005.

Wood, Gordon S. *The Creation of the American Republic, 1776–1787*, reissue ed. New York: Norton, 1993.

On the Web

Learn more about the founding of the United States, the Articles of Confederation, and the writing and ratification of the Constitution at the educational resources page of the House of Representatives Web site, at **www.house.gov/house/Educate.shtml**.

Learn more about the Declaration of Independence, the Constitution, the Bill of Rights, and the Framers at the National Archives site, which includes biographical sketches and demographic information, at **www.archives.gov/exhibits/charters/charters.html**.

The Avalon Project at Yale Law School includes the text of eighteenth-century documents related to the national founding and the Revolutionary War, many of which are discussed in this chapter. Go to **www.yale.edu/lawweb/avalon/18th.htm**

The Constitution of the United States of America

We the People of the United States, in Order to form a more perfect Union, establish Justice, insure domestic Tranquility, provide for the common defence, promote the general Welfare, and secure the Blessings of Liberty to ourselves and our Posterity, do ordain and establish this Constitution for the United States of America.

ARTICLE I

1.

All legislative Powers herein granted shall be vested in a Congress of the United States, which shall consist of a Senate and House of Representatives.

Article I is the longest and most detailed of any of the articles, sections, or amendments that make up the United States Constitution. By *enumerating* the powers of Congress, the Framers attached limits to the enormous authority they had vested in the legislative branch. At the same time, the allocation of certain powers to Congress ensured that the legislative branch would maintain control over certain vital areas of public policy and that it would be protected from incursions by the executive and judicial branches. Moreover, by clearly vesting Congress with certain powers (for example, the power to regulate interstate commerce), Article I established a water's edge for the exercise of state power in what were now national affairs.

Originally, Article I also contained restrictions limiting the amendment of several of its provisions, a feature found nowhere else in the Constitution. Section 4 prohibited Congress from making any law banning the importation of slaves until 1808, and section 9 prohibited Congress from levying an income tax on the general population. Neither section is operative any longer. Section 4 expired on its own, and section 9 was modified by passage of the Sixteenth Amendment, which established the income tax (see page 88).

Despite the great care the Framers took to limit the exercise of congressional authority to those powers enumerated in Article I, the power of Congress has grown tremendously since the nation's founding. Under Chief Justice John Marshall (1801–1835), the U.S. Supreme Court interpreted the Constitution to favor the power of the national government over the states and to permit Congress to exercise both its *enumerated* (the power to regulate interstate commerce) and *implied* (the necessary and proper clause) powers in broad fashion. With only the occasional exception, the Court has never really challenged the legislative power vested in Congress to engage in numerous areas of public policy that some constitutional scholars (and politicians and voters) believe are the province of the states. Perhaps the only area in which legislative power has diminished over the years has been the war-making power granted to Congress, something that lawmakers, for all their occasional criticism of presidential conduct of foreign policy, have ceded to the executive branch rather willingly.

Section 2.

The House of Representatives shall be composed of Members chosen every second Year by the People of the several States, and the Electors in each State shall have the Qualifications requisite for Electors of the most numerous Branch of the State Legislature.

No person shall be a Representative who shall not have attained to the Age of twenty five Years, and been seven Years a Citizen of the United States, and who shall not, when elected, be an Inhabitant of that State in which he shall be chosen.

The qualifications clause, which sets out the age and residency requirements for individuals who wish to run for the House of Representatives, became the centerpiece of a national debate that emerged during the late 1980s and early 1990s over term limits for members of Congress. In *U.S. Term Limits* v. *Thornton* (1995), the Supreme Court ruled that section 2, clause 2, did not specify any other qualification to serve in the House other than age and residency (as did section 3, clause 3, to run for the Senate). Thus, no state could restrict an individual's right to run for Congress. The Court ruled that any modification to

the qualifications clause would have to come through a constitutional amendment.

Representatives and direct Taxes shall be apportioned among the several States which may be included within this Union, according to their respective Numbers which shall be determined by adding to the whole Number of free Persons, including those bound to Service for a Term of Years, and excluding Indians not taxed, three fifths of all other Persons. The actual Enumeration shall be made within three Years after the first Meeting of the Congress of the United States, and within every subsequent Term ten Years, in such Manner as they shall by Law direct. The Number of Representatives shall not exceed one for every thirty Thousand, but each State shall have at Least one Representative; and until such enumerations shall be made, the State of New Hampshire shall be entitled to chuse three, Massachusetts eight, Rhode-Island and Providence Plantations one, Connecticut five, New-York six, New Jersey four, Pennsylvania eight, Delaware one, Maryland six, Virginia ten, North Carolina five, South Carolina five, and Georgia three.

Under the Articles of Confederation, "direct" taxes (such as taxes on property) were apportioned based on land value, not population. This encouraged states to diminish the value of their land in order to reduce their tax burden. Prior to the Constitutional Convention of 1787, several prominent delegates met to discuss—and ultimately propose—changing the method for direct taxation from land value to the population of each state. A major sticking point among the delegates on this issue was how to count slaves for taxation purposes. Southern states wanted to diminish the value of slaves for tax purposes, while northern states wanted to count slaves as closer to a full person. On the other hand, southern states wanted to count slaves as "whole persons" for purposes of representation to increase their power in the House of Representatives, but northern states rejected this proposal. Ultimately, the delegates settled on the "Three-Fifths Compromise," which treated each slave as three-fifths of a person for tax and representation purposes.

At the beginning, the Three-Fifths Compromise enhanced southern power in the House. In 1790, when the 1st Congress convened, the South held 45 percent of the seats, despite a significantly smaller free population than the North. Over time, however, the South saw its power in the House diminish. By the 1830s, the South held just over 30 percent of House seats, which gave it just enough power to thwart northern initiatives on slavery questions and territorial issues, but not enough power to defeat the growing power of the North to control commercial and economic policy. This standoff between the North and South led to such events as South Carolina Senator John C. Calhoun's doctrine of nullification and secession, which argued that a state could nullify any federal law not consistent with regional or state interests. By the 1850s, the Three-Fifths Compromise had made the South dependent on expanding the number of slaveholding territories eligible for admission to the union and a judicial system sympathetic to slaveholding interests. The Three-Fifths Compromise was repealed by section 2 of the Fourteenth Amendment (see pages 86–87).

When vacancies happen in the Representation from any State, the Executive Authority thereof shall issue Writs of Election to fill such Vacancies.

This clause permits the governor of a state to call an election to replace any member of the House of Representatives who is unable to complete a term of office due to death, resignation, or removal from the House. In some cases, a governor will appoint a successor to fill out a term; in other cases, the governor will call a special election. A governor's decision is shaped less by constitutional guidelines and more by partisan interests. For example, a Democratic governor might choose to appoint a Democratic successor if he or she believes that a Republican candidate might have an advantage in a special election.

The House of Representatives shall chuse their speaker and other Officers; and shall have the sole Power of Impeachment.

Clause 5 establishes the only officer of the House of Representatives—the Speaker. The remaining offices (party leaders, whips, and so on) are created by the House.

The House also has the sole power of impeachment against members of the executive and judicial branches. The House, like the Senate, is responsible for disciplining its own members. In *Nixon* v. *U.S.* (1993), the Supreme Court ruled that government officials who are the subject of impeachment proceedings may not challenge them in court. The Court ruled that the sole power given to the House over impeachment precludes judicial intervention.

Section 3.

The Senate of the United States shall be composed of two Senators from each State chosen by the Legislature thereof, for six Years; and each Senator shall have one Vote.

The provision of this clause establishing the election of senators by state legislatures was repealed by the Seventeenth Amendment (see page 88).

Immediately after they shall be assembled in Consequence of the first Election, they shall be divided as equally as may be into three Classes. The Seats of the Senators of the first Class shall be vacated at the Expiration of the second year, of the second Class at the Expiration of the fourth Year, and of the third Class at the Expiration of the sixth Year, so that one third may be chosen every second Year and if Vacancies happen by Resignation, or otherwise, during the Recess of the Legislature of any State, the Executive thereof may make temporary Appointments until the next Meeting of the Legislature, which shall then fill such Vacancies.

Vacancies for senators are handled the same way as vacancies for representatives—through appointment or special election. The Seventeenth Amendment modified the language authorizing the state legislature to choose a replacement for a vacant Senate position.

No Person shall be a Senator who shall not have attained to the Age of thirty Years, and been nine Years a Citizen of the United States, and who shall not, when elected, be an Inhabitant of that State for which he shall be chosen.

The Vice President of the United States shall be President of the Senate, but shall have no Vote, unless they be equally divided.

Clause 4 gives the vice president the authority to vote to break a tie in the Senate. This is the only constitutional duty the Constitution specifies for the vice president. As president of the Senate, the vice president also presides over procedural matters of that body, although this is not a responsibility that vice presidents really have ever shouldered.

The Senate shall chuse their other Officers, and also a President pro tempore, in the Absence of the Vice President, or when he shall exercise the Office of President of the United States.

Clause 5 creates the position of *president pro tempore* (the president of the time), the only Senate office established by the Constitution to handle the duties of the vice president set out in section 3, clause 4.

The Senate shall have the sole Power to try all Impeachments. When sitting for that Purpose, they shall be on Oath or Affirmation. When the President of the United States is tried, the Chief Justice shall preside: And no Person shall be convicted without the Concurrence of two thirds of the Members present.

Judgment in Cases of Impeachment shall not extend further than to removal from Office, and disqualification to hold and enjoy any Office of honor, Trust or Profit under the United States; but the Party convicted shall nevertheless be liable and subject to Indictment, Trial, Judgment and Punishment, according to law.

Just as the House of Representatives has the sole power to bring impeachment against executive and judicial branch officials, the Senate has the sole power to try all impeachments. Unless the president is facing trial in the Senate, the vice president serves as the presiding officer. In 1998, President Bill Clinton was tried on two articles of impeachment (four were brought against him in the House) and found not guilty on each count. The presiding officer in President Clinton's impeachment trial was Chief Justice William H. Rehnquist.

A conviction results in the removal of an official from office. It does not prohibit subsequent civil or criminal action against that individual. Nor does it prohibit an impeached and convicted official from returning to federal office. In 1989, Alcee Hastings, a trial judge with ten years experience on the U.S. District Court for the Southern District of Florida, was convicted on impeachment charges and removed from office. In 1992, he ran successfully for the 23rd District seat of the U.S. House of Representatives, where he continues to serve as of this writing.

Section 4.

The Times, Places and Manner of holding Elections for Senators and Representatives, shall be prescribed in each State by the Legislature thereof; but the Congress may at any time by Law make or alter such Regulations, except as to the Places of chusing Senators.

The Congress shall assemble at least once in every Year, and such Meeting shall be on the first Monday in December, unless they shall by Law appoint a different Day.

Section 4 authorizes the states to establish the rules governing elections for members of Congress, but Congress has never hesitated to exercise its law-making power in this area when it has believed that improvements were necessary to improve the electoral process. The first such action did not come until 1842, when Congress passed legislation making elections to the House based on single-member districts, not from the general population. By the turn of the twentieth century, Congress had passed legislation establishing additional criteria such as the rough equality of population among districts and territorial compactness and contiguity. Article I, section 4, is one of the three main areas from which Congress derives the power to regulate the electoral process. The other two are the necessary and proper clause of Article I, section 8, clause 3, and section 2 of the Fifteenth Amendment.

Section 5.

Each House shall be the Judge of the Elections, Returns and Qualifications of its own Members, and a Majority of each shall constitute a Quorum to do business; but a smaller Number may adjourn from day to day, and may be authorized to compel the Attendance of absent Members, in such Manner, and under such Penalties as each House may provide.

Each House may determine the Rules of its Proceedings, punish its Members for disorderly Behaviour, and with the Concurrence of two thirds, expel a Member.

Clause 2 gives power to the House and Senate to establish the rules and decorum for each chamber. Expulsion from either the House or the Senate does not preclude a member from running for congressional office again or serving in any other official capacity. In *Powell* v. *McCormack* (1969), the Supreme Court ruled that the House's decision to exclude an individual from the chamber despite having been elected was different from the expulsion of a sitting representative.

Each House shall keep a Journal of its Proceedings, and from time to time publish the same, excepting such Parts as may in their judgment require Secrecy; and the Yeas and Nays of the Members of either House on any question shall, at the Desire of one fifth of those present, be entered on the Journal.

The *Congressional Record* is the official journal of Congress. Justice Joseph Story, in his much praised scholarly treatment of the U.S. Constitution, *Commentaries on the Constitution* (1833), said the purpose of this clause was "to insure publicity to the proceedings of the legislature, and a correspondent responsibility of the members to their respective constituents." Recorded votes (and yea-or-nay voice votes, if agreed to by one-fifth of the House or Senate), speeches, and other public business are contained in the *Congressional Record*.

Neither House, during the Session of Congress, shall, without the Consent of the other, adjourn for more than three days, nor to any other Place than that in which the two Houses shall be sitting.

Section 6.

The Senators and Representatives shall receive a Compensation for their Services, to be ascertained by Law, and paid out of the Treasury of the United States. They shall in all Cases, except Treason, Felony and Breach of the Peace, be privileged from Arrest during their Attendance at the Session of their respective Houses, and in going to and returning from the same; and for any Speech or Debate in either House, they shall not be questioned in any other Place.

The Twenty-Seventh Amendment, ratified in 1992, now governs the procedures for compensation of members of Congress. From the nation's founding until 1967, Congress had determined the salaries of its members. Then, Congress passed legislation giving the president the responsibility to recommend salary levels for members of Congress, since the president already had the responsibility to recommend pay levels for other federal officials. In 1989, as part of the Ethics Reform Act, Congress established a new system of pay raises and cost-of-living adjustments based on a particular vote.

Clause 1 also protects the right of senators and representatives from criminal prosecution for any "Speech or Debate" made in Congress. This protection stemmed from lessons drawn from the persistent conflicts between the House of Commons and the Tudor and Stuart monarchies in Great Britain, who used their power to bring civil and criminal actions against legislators whose opinions were deemed seditious or dangerous. The 1689 English Bill of Rights contained protection for legislators to conduct their business in Parliament free from such fears, and the Framers believed that such protection was essential for Congress under the Constitution. The Supreme Court has held, however, in *Gravel* v. *U.S.* (1972), that the speech or debate clause does not immunize senators or representatives from criminal inquiry if their activities in the Senate or House are the result of alleged or proven illegal action.

The privilege from arrest clause has little application in contemporary America. The clause applies only to arrests in civil suits, which were fairly common when the Constitution was ratified. The Court has interpreted the phrase "except Treason, Felony or Breach of the Peace" to make members eligible for arrest for crimes that would fall into that category. For example, a member of Congress is eligible if he or she commits a serious traffic offense, such as drunk or reckless driving, on the way to or from legislative business.

No Senator or Representative shall, during the Time for which he was elected, be appointed to any civil Office under the Authority of the United States, which shall have been created, or the Emoluments whereof shall have been encreased during such time; and no Person holding any Office under the United States, shall be a Member of either House during his Continuance in Office.

Clause 2 prohibits any senator or representative from holding a simultaneous office in the legislative or executive branches. This is one of the least controversial provisions of the Constitution. Indeed, there is no judicial interpretation of its meaning.

The general purpose of this clause is to prevent one branch of government from having an undue influence on another by creating dual incentives. It is also another safeguard in the separation of powers.

Section 7.

All Bills for raising Revenue shall originate in the House of Representatives; but the Senate may propose or concur with Amendments as on other Bills.

The power to raise revenue found in clause 1 is unique to the House of Representatives. In *Federalist No. 58*, James Madison argued that vesting such authority in the House was a key feature of the separation of powers. No bill either raising or lowering taxes may originate in the Senate. Legislation that creates incidental revenue may begin in the Senate, as long as the legislation does not involve taxation.

Every Bill which shall have passed the House of Representatives and the Senate, shall, before it become a Law, be presented to the President of the United States; If he approve he shall sign it, but if not he shall return it, with his Objections to that House in which it shall have originated, who shall enter the Objections at large on their Journal, and proceed to reconsider it. If after such Reconsideration two thirds of that House shall agree to pass the Bill, it shall be sent, together with the Objections, to the other House, by which it shall likewise be reconsidered, and if approved by two thirds of that House, it shall become a Law. But in all such Cases the Votes of both Houses shall be determined by Yeas and Nays, and the Names of the Persons voting for and against the Bill shall be entered on the Journal of each House respectively. If any Bill shall not be returned by the President within ten Days (Sundays excepted) after it shall have been presented to him, the Same shall be a Law, in like Manner as if he had signed it, unless the Congress by their

Adjournment prevent its Return, in which Case it shall not be a Law.

This clause establishes several key features of presidential-congressional relations in the flow of the legislative process. For a bill to become law, it must be passed by the House and Senate, and it must be signed by the president. The Supreme Court has ruled that the veto regulations outlined in this clause serve two purposes. First, by giving the president ten days to consider a bill for approval, clause 2 provides the president with ample time to consider legislation and protects him from having to approve legislation in the wake of congressional adjournment. But clause 2 also provides Congress with a countervailing power to override a presidential veto, a procedure that requires a two-thirds vote in each chamber.

Every Order, Resolution, or Vote to which the Concurrence of the Senate and House of Representatives may be necessary (except on a question of Adjournment) shall be presented to the President of the United States; and before the Same shall take Effect, shall be approved by him, or being disapproved by him, shall be repassed by two thirds of the Senate and House of Representatives, according to the Rules and Limitations prescribed in the Case of a Bill.

Clause 3 covers the presentation of resolutions, not actual legislation. For any resolution to have the force of law, it must be presented to the president for approval. Should the president veto the resolution, Congress may override this veto in the same manner expressed in section 7, clause 2. Resolutions that do not have the force of law do not require presidential approval. Preliminary votes taken on constitutional amendments and other legislative matters covered by clause 3 do not require presentation to the president.

This clause has been the subject of two major Supreme Court decisions dealing with the separation of powers. In *I.N.S.* v. *Chadha* (1983), the Court ruled that the House-only legislative veto, a practice begun during the 1930s to give Congress power to control power delegated to a rapidly expanding executive branch, violated both the bicameralism principles of Article I, section 1, and the presentment clause of section 7, clause 3. At the time, the ruling struck down about 200 legislative vetoes that had been included in various pieces of congressional legislation. In *Clinton* v. *New York* (1998), the Court ruled that the line-item veto passed by Congress to give the president the power to veto specific provisions of legislation rather than an entire bill violated the presentment clause of Article I, section 7, clause 3. The Court claimed that the line-item

veto permitted the president to "repeal certain laws," a power that belonged to Congress and not the president.

Section 8.

The Congress shall have Power To lay and collect Taxes, Duties, Imposts and Excises, to pay the Debts and provide for the common Defence and general Welfare of the United States; but all Duties, Imposts and Excises shall be uniform throughout the United States;

To borrow Money on the credit of the United States;

To regulate Commerce with foreign Nations, and among the several States, and with the Indian Tribes;

To establish a uniform Rule of Naturalization, and uniform Laws on the subject of Bankruptcies throughout the United States;

To coin Money, regulate the Value thereof, and of foreign Coin, and fix the Standard of Weights and Measures;

To provide for the Punishment of counterfeiting the Securities and current Coin of the United States;

To establish Post Offices and post Roads;

To promote the Progress of Science and useful Arts, by securing for limited Times to Authors and Inventors exclusive Right to their respective Writings and Discoveries;

To constitute Tribunals inferior to the supreme Court;

To define and punish Piracies and Felonies committed on the high Seas, and Offences against the Law of Nations;

To declare War, grant Letters of Marque and Reprisal, and make rules concerning Captures on Land and Water;

To raise and support Armies, but no Appropriation of Money to that Use shall be for a longer Term than two Years;

To provide and maintain a Navy;

To make Rules for the Government and Regulation of the land and naval Forces;

To provide for calling forth the Militia to execute the Laws of the Union, suppress Insurrections and repel Invasions;

To provide for organizing, arming, and disciplining, the Militia, and for governing such Part of them as may be employed in the Service of the United States, reserving to the States respectively, the Appointment of the Officers, and the Authority of training the Militia according to the discipline prescribed by Congress;

To exercise exclusive Legislation in all Cases whatsoever, over such District (not exceeding ten Miles square) as may, by Cession of particular States, and the Acceptance of Congress, become the Seat of the Government of the United States, and to exercise like Authority over all Places purchased by the Consent of the Legislature of the State in which the Same shall be for the Erection of Forts, Magazines, Arsenals, dock-Yards, and other needful Buildings;— And

Article I, section 8, clause 1, is, in many ways, the engine of congressional power. First, clause 1 gives Congress the power to tax and spend, a power the Supreme Court has interpreted as "exhaustive" and "reaching every subject." Second, in giving Congress the power to provide for the common defense and general welfare, it offers no specific constraint on what Congress may spend public funds for and how much it may spend. Third, section 8 gives Congress complete authority in numerous areas of policy that affect Americans at home and abroad on a massive scale. These powers include the power to regulate interstate commerce (which Congress has relied on to establish federal civil rights law), to make war (a power that Congress, since the end of World War II in 1945, has increasingly deferred to the president), and to establish the federal judicial system.

Clause 1 is often cited by constitutional scholars as an example of how the Constitution constrains legislative power by limiting the powers that Congress may exercise. To a certain extent, this is true. But, it is also true that the Court has granted Congress extensive power to legislate in certain areas that bear only a tangential relationship to the specific language of some of the provisions of clause 1. For example, in *Katzenbach* v. *McClung* (1964), the Court turned back a challenge to the constitutionality of the Civil Rights Act of 1964, which Congress had passed under its authority to regulate interstate commerce. The Court ruled that racial discrimination had an adverse effect on the free flow of commerce.

Clause 2 establishes the seat of the federal government—first New York City, now Washington, D.C. The clause also makes Congress the legislative body of the nation's capital, a power that extends to other federal bodies, such as forts, military bases, and other places where federal buildings are located.

To make all Laws which shall be necessary and proper for carrying into Execution the foregoing Powers, and all other Powers vested by this

Constitution in the Government of the United States, or in any Department or Officer thereof.

Better known as the necessary and proper clause, this provision of Article I was one of the most contested points between Federalists and Anti-Federalists during the ratification debates over the Constitution. Anti-Federalists feared that the language was too broad and all-encompassing, and, if interpreted by a Supreme Court sympathetic to the nationalist ambitions of the Federalist Party, would give Congress limitless power to exercise legislative authority over state and local matters. In *McCulloch* **v.** *Maryland* **(1819), Chief Justice John Marshall offered what constitutional scholars believe remains the definitive interpretation of the necessary and proper clause. While** *McCulloch* **certainly did cement the power of Congress in the federal system, the expansive definition given the necessary and proper clause by the Court is also testament to the flexible nature of the Constitution, and why so few amendments have been added to the original document.**

Section 9.

The Migration or Importation of such Persons as any of the States now existing shall think proper to admit, shall not be prohibited by the Congress prior to the Year one thousand eight hundred and eight, but a Tax or duty may be imposed on such Importation, not exceeding ten dollars for each Person.

Like the other provisions of the Constitution that refer to slavery, such as the Three-Fifths Compromise, section 9 creates policy governing the institution without ever mentioning the word. The importation clause was a compromise between slave traders, who wanted to continue the practice, and opponents of slavery, who needed southern support to ratify the Constitution. In 1808, Congress passed legislation banning the importation of slaves; until then, Congress used its power to tax slaves brought to the United States.

The Privilege of the Writ of Habeas Corpus shall not be suspended, unless when in Cases of Rebellion or Invasion the public Safety may require it.

Clause 2 is the only place where the writ of habeas corpus—the "Great Writ," as it was known to the Framers—is mentioned in the Constitution. Only the federal government is bound by clause 2. The writ may only be suspended in times of crisis and rebellion, and then it is Congress that has the power, not the president. In *Boumediene v. Bush* **(2008), the Supreme Court ruled that the provision of the Military Commissions Act of 2006 stripping the federal courts of their jurisdiction to hear habeas corpus petitions from detainees, regardless of their status as American**

citizens or foreign nationals, being held at a military prison at Guantanamo Bay, Cuba, was unconstitutional.

No Bill of Attainder or ex post facto Law shall be passed.

A bill of attainder is a legislative act punishing a person with "pains and penalties" without the benefit of a hearing or trial. The fundamental purpose of the ban on bills of attainder is to prevent trial by legislature and other arbitrary punishments for persons vulnerable to extra-judicial proceedings. An *ex post facto law* **is one passed making a previously committed civil or criminal action subject to penalty. In** *Calder* **v.** *Bull* **(1798), the Court ruled that the ban on** *ex post facto* **laws applied only to penal and criminal actions. A similar restriction on the states is found in Article I, section 10, clause 1.**

No Capitation, or other direct, Tax shall be laid, unless in Proportion to the Census or Enumeration herein before directed to be taken.

This clause, which originally prohibited Congress from levying an income tax, was modified by the Sixteenth Amendment, passed in 1913 (see page 88).

No Tax or Duty shall be laid on Articles exported from any State.

Clause 5 prohibits Congress from levying a tax on any good or article exported from a state to a foreign country or to another state. Many southern states feared that northern members of Congress would attempt to weaken the South's slave-based economy by taxing exports. This clause prohibited such action. Congress may prohibit the shipment of certain items from one state to another and to other countries.

No Preference shall be given by any Regulation of Commerce or Revenue to the Ports of one State over those of another: nor shall Vessels bound to, or from, one State, be obliged to enter, clear, or pay Duties in another.

Congress is prohibited from making laws regulating trade that favor one state over another. Clause 6 also prohibits Congress from establishing preferences for certain ports or trade centers over others, although it may, under its power to regulate interstate commerce, pass laws that incidentally benefit certain states or maritime outlets. The Supreme Court has ruled that states are not bound by the limitations on Congress expressed in this clause.

No money shall be drawn from the Treasury, but in Consequence of Appropriations made by Law; and a regular Statement and Account of the Receipts and Expenditures of all public Money shall be published from time to time.

Clause 7 serves two fundamental purposes. First, the clause prohibits any governmental body receiving federal funds from spending those funds without the approval of Congress. Once Congress has determined that federal funds are to be spent in a certain way, the executive branch may not exercise any discretion over that decision. Second, by restricting executive control of spending power, the clause firmly reinforces congressional authority over revenue and spending, a key feature of the separation of powers.

No Title of Nobility shall be granted by the United States: And no Person holding any Office of Profit or Trust under them, shall, without the Consent of the Congress, accept of any present, Emolument, Office, or Title, of any kind whatever, from any King, Prince, or foreign State.

This provision is among the first school-taught lessons about the Constitution. To reinforce the commitment to representative democracy, the Framers prohibited a title of nobility from being conferred on any public official. This clause also prohibits any government official from accepting compensation, gifts, or similar benefits from any foreign government for services rendered without the consent of Congress.

Section 10.

No state shall enter into any Treaty, Alliance, or Confederation; grant Letters of Marque and Reprisal; coin Money; emit Bills of Credit; make any Thing but gold and silver Coin a Tender in Payment of Debts; pass any Bill of Attainder, ex post facto Law, or Law impairing the Obligation of Contracts, or grant any Title of Nobility.

This clause denies several powers to the states that were once permissible under the Articles of Confederation, and it emphasizes the Framers' commitment under the Constitution to a strong national government with Congress as the centrifugal force. During the Civil War, the Union relied on this clause in support of its view that the Confederate states had no legal existence but instead were merely "states in rebellion" against the United States.

The restrictions on states passing either bills of attainder or ex post facto laws have come into play at various points in American history. During Reconstruction, several states enacted legislation prohibiting any individual who aided the Confederacy from entering certain professions or enjoying other benefits available to citizens who remained loyal to the Union. The Supreme Court struck down these laws on the grounds that they violated this clause.

The provision prohibiting states from passing any law "impairing the Obligation of Contracts," better known as the contract clause, has been the subject of considerable litigation before the Supreme Court. The contract clause was intended to bar the states from interfering in private contracts between consensual parties and was considered an important limit on the power of states to restrict the fledgling national economic order of the early republic. Early on, the Court considered many laws that restricted the terms set out in private contracts as unconstitutional. But as the United States became a more industrial society, and as citizen demands grew for government regulation of the economy, the environment, and social welfare benefits, the Court softened its position on the contract clause to permit states to make laws that served a reasonable public interest. A key case involving the contract clause is *Home Building and Loan Association* v. *Blaisdell* (1934). In *Blaisdell*, the Court ruled that a Depression-era law passed by the Minnesota legislature forgiving mortgage payments by homeowners to banks did not violate the contract clause.

No State shall, without the Consent of the Congress, lay any Imposts or Duties on Imports or Exports, except what may be absolutely necessary for executing its inspection Laws: and the net Produce of all Duties and Imposts, laid by any State on Imports or Exports, shall be for the Use of the Treasury of the United States, and all such Laws shall be subject to the Revision and Controul of the Congress.

No state may tax goods leaving or entering a state, although it may charge reasonable fees for inspections considered necessary to the public interest. The restriction on import and export taxes applies only to those goods entering from or leaving for a foreign country.

No State shall, without the Consent of Congress, lay any Duty of Tonnage, keep Troops, or Ships of War in time of Peace, enter into any Agreement or Compact with another State, or with a foreign Power, or engage in War, unless actually invaded, or in such imminent Danger as will not admit of delay.

Clause 3 cements the power of Congress to control acts of war and make treaties with foreign countries. The Framers wanted to correct any perception to the contrary gained from the Articles of Confederation that states were free to act independently of the national government on negotiated matters with foreign countries. They also wanted to ensure that any state that entered into a compact with another state—something this clause does not prohibit—must receive permission from Congress.

ARTICLE II

Section 1.

The executive Power shall be vested in a President of the United States of America. He shall hold his Office during the Term of four Years, and, together with the Vice President, chosen for the same Term, be elected as follows.

In *Federalist No. 70*, Alexander Hamilton argued for an "energetic executive" branch headed by a single, elected president not necessarily beholden to the majority party in Congress. Hamilton believed that a nationally elected president would not be bound by the narrow, parochial interests that drove legislative law-making. The president would possess both the veto power over Congress and a platform from which to articulate a national vision in both domestic and foreign affairs.

Hamilton believed that the constitutional boundaries placed on executive power through the separation of powers and the fact that the president was accountable to a national electorate constrained any possibility that the office would come to resemble the monarchies of Europe. However, most presidential scholars agree that the modern presidency has grown in power precisely because of the general nature of the enabling powers of Article II.

Each State shall appoint, in such Manner as the Legislature thereof may direct, a Number of Electors, equal to the whole Number of Senators and Representatives to which the State may be entitled in the Congress; but no Senator or Representative, or Person holding an Office of Trust of Profit under the United States, shall be appointed an Elector.

Clause 2 established the Electoral College and set the number of electors from each state at the total of senators and representatives serving in Congress.

The Electors shall meet in their respective States, and vote by Ballot for two Persons, of whom one at least shall not be an Inhabitant of the same State with themselves. And they shall make a List of all the Persons voted for, and, of the Number of Votes for each; which List they shall sign and certify, and transmit sealed to the Seat of the Government of the United States, directed to the President of the Senate. The President of the Senate shall, in the Presence of the Senate and House of Representatives, open all the Certificates, and the Votes shall then be counted. The Person having the greatest Number of Votes shall be the President, if such Number be a Majority of the whole Number of Electors appointed; and if there be more than one who have such

Majority, and have an equal Number of Votes, then the House of Representatives shall immediately chuse by Ballot one of them for President; and if no Person have a Majority, then from the five highest on the List the said House shall in like Manner chuse the President. But in chusing the President, the Votes shall be taken by States, the Representation from each State having one Vote; A quorum for this Purpose shall consist of a Member or Members from two thirds of the States, and a Majority of all the States shall be necessary to a Choice. In every Case, after the Choice of the President, the Person having the greatest Number of Votes of the Electors shall be the Vice President. But if there should remain two or more who have equal Votes, the Senate shall chuse from them by Ballot the Vice President.

This provision of section 1 described the rules for calling the Electoral College to vote for president and vice president. Originally, the electors did not vote separately for president and vice president. After the 1800 election, which saw Thomas Jefferson and Aaron Burr receive the identical number of electoral votes even though it was clear that Jefferson was the presidential candidate and Burr the vice presidential candidate, the nation ratified the Twelfth Amendment (see page 85).

The Twelfth Amendment did not resolve what many constitutional scholars today believe are the inadequacies of the Electoral College system. In 1824, the presidential election ended in a four-way tie, and the House of Representatives elected second-place finisher John Quincy Adams president. In 1876, Benjamin Harrison lost the popular vote but won the presidency after recounts awarded him an Electoral College majority. But perhaps the most controversial election of all came in 2000, when George W. Bush, who lost the popular contest to Al Gore by approximately 500,000 votes, was named the presidential victor after a six-week court battle over the vote count in Florida. After the Supreme Court ruled against the position of Al Gore that a recount of the Florida popular vote should continue until all votes had been counted, an outcome that would have left the nation without a president-elect for several more weeks, Bush was awarded Florida's electoral votes, which gave him 271, just one more than he needed to win the office. Outraged Democrats pledged to mount a case for Electoral College reform, but, as was so often the case before, nothing happened.

The Congress may determine the Time of chusing the Electors, and the Day on which they shall give their Votes; which Day shall be the same throughout the United States.

No Person except a natural born Citizen, or a Citizen of the United States, at the time of the Adoption of this Constitution, shall be eligible to the Office of President; neither shall any Person be eligible to that Office who shall not have attained to the Age of thirty five Years, and been fourteen Years a Resident within the United States.

This provision of Article II is referred to as the presidential eligibility clause. In addition to setting out the age and resident requirements of presidential aspirants, this clause defines who may *not* run for president—any foreign-born individual who has nonetheless obtained United States citizenship. For example, Michigan Governor Jennifer Granholm, who has lived in the United States since she was four years old, may not run for president because she was born in Canada. The same is true for California Governor Arnold Schwarzenegger, who was born in Austria but has lived in the United States his entire adult life. Judicial interpretation of the presidential eligibility clause has not resolved the question of whether children born to U.S. citizens are eligible to run for president if they meet the residency requirements.

In Case of the Removal of the President from Office, or of his Death, Resignation, or Inability to discharge the Powers and Duties of the said Office, the Same shall devolve on the Vice President, and the Congress may by Law provide for the Case of Removal, Death, Resignation or Inability, both of the President and Vice President, declaring what Officer shall then act as President, and such Officer shall act accordingly, until the Disability be removed, or a President shall be elected.

This presidential succession clause has been modified by the Twenty-Fifth Amendment (see page 92).

The President shall, at stated Times, receive for his Services, a Compensation, which shall neither be encreased nor diminished during the Period for which he shall have been elected, and he shall not receive within that Period any other Emolument from the United States, or any of them.

Presidential compensation, like compensation for members of Congress, may not be increased for the current occupant of the office. The president is not eligible for any other public compensation during time in office. However, the president may continue to receive income such as interest on investments or book royalties.

Before he enter on the Execution of his Office, he shall take the following Oath or Affirmation:—"I do solemnly swear (or affirm) that I will faithfully execute the Office of President of the United States, and will to the best of my Ability, preserve, protect and defend the Constitution of the United States."

Since George Washington's inaugural in 1789, each president has added the phrase "so help me God" to the end of the presidential oath. Although Abraham Lincoln cited the oath to justify his suspension of the writ of *habeas corpus* during the Civil War, no other president has relied on the oath to justify action that stretched the boundaries of executive power. Presidents taking extraordinary action either at home or abroad have relied on either the commander in chief clause of section 2, clause 1, or the provision of section 3 authorizing the president to "faithfully execut[e]" the laws of the United States.

Section 2.

The President shall be Commander in Chief of the Army and Navy of the United States, and of the Militia of the several States, when called into the actual Service of the United States; he may require the Opinion, in writing, of the principal Officer in each of the executive Departments, upon any Subject relating to the Duties of their respective Offices, and he shall have Power to grant Reprieves and Pardons for Offences against the United States, except in Cases of Impeachment.

Section 2, clause 1, establishes the president as commander in chief of the Army and Navy of the United States. In modern times, that authority has extended to the Air Force, the Marines, and all other branches of the armed forces operating under the command of the United States, including state militias, reserve units, and national guards. Article I provides that Congress, and not the president, has the power to declare war. But, since World War II, no American president has received or requested a declaration of war to commit the armed forces to military conflicts, including those clearly acknowledged as large-scale war (Korea, Vietnam, the 1991 Persian Gulf War, Afghanistan, and the Iraq War). For these conflicts, the president received congressional *authorization* to use force, but not an Article I declaration.

Although the Supreme Court has ruled that the president has *inherent* power—that is, power to carry out the essential functions of his office in times of crisis, war or emergencies that are not *expressly* spelled out under Article II—it has not concluded that such power is unlimited. In *Youngstown Sheet & Tube* v. *Sawyer* (1952), the Court ruled that President Harry S Truman did not have the power to seize control of the nation's steel mills to continue the production of munitions and

other war supplies without congressional authorization. More recently, the Court ruled in *Hamdan* v. *Rumsfeld* (2006) that President George W. Bush exceeded his authority when he established military commissions that had not been approved by Congress to try detainees and other "enemy combatants" captured in the War on Terror. The Court ruled that since Congress had not approved of President Bush's system of military tribunals, prisoners were entitled to the protections of the Geneva Convention and the procedural rights of the Uniform Code of Military Justice. Congress passed the Military Commissions Act to address the Court's concerns.

Clause 1 also implicitly creates the Cabinet by authorizing the president to request the opinion "in writing" of the principal officers of the executive branch. The power to create Cabinet-level offices resides with Congress, not the president.

Presidential power to pardon is broad and limited only in cases of impeachment. Perhaps the most controversial pardon in American political history was President Gerald R. Ford's decision to pardon former President Richard M. Nixon, who resigned his office on August 8, 1974, after news reports and congressional inquiries strongly implicated him in the Watergate scandal. A real possibility existed that President Nixon could be tried on criminal charges as the result of his alleged activities during the Watergate scandal.

He shall have Power, by and with the Advice and Consent of the Senate, to make Treaties, provided two thirds of the Senators present concur; and he shall nominate, and by and with the Advice and Consent of the Senate, shall appoint Ambassadors, other public Ministers and Consuls, Judges of the supreme Court, and all other Officers of the United States, whose Appointments are not herein otherwise provided for, and which shall be established by Law: but the Congress may by Law vest the Appointment of such inferior Officers, as they think proper, in the President alone, in the Courts of Law, or in the Heads of Departments.

The President shall have Power to fill up all Vacancies that may happen during the Recess of the Senate, by granting Commissions which shall expire at the End of their next Session.

Clause 2 describes several powers the president may exercise in conjunction with the advice and consent of the Senate. These powers include the power, upon the approval of two-thirds of the Senate, to make treaties with foreign countries. But, the Constitution is silent on the question of whether a president (or Congress) may terminate a treaty by refusing to honor it or simply repealing it outright. When President Jimmy Carter terminated a treaty with China over the objection of Congress, several members sought a judicial resolution of the action; the Court, however, did not decide the case on the merits and offered no resolution on the matter. The president does not require a two-thirds majority for approval of appointments to the federal judiciary, foreign ambassadorships, Cabinet-level positions, high-ranking positions in non-Cabinet agencies, and high-level military offices. But, the fact that the Senate must approve presidential appointments in these areas provides Congress (senators often listen to the constituents of House members on controversial choices) with an important check on presidential power to shape the contours of the executive branch.

Section 3.

He shall from time to time give to the Congress Information of the State of the Union, and recommend to their Consideration such Measures as he shall judge necessary and expedient; he may, on extraordinary Occasions, convene both Houses, or either of them, and in Case of Disagreement between them, with Respect to the Time of Adjournment, he may adjourn them to such Time as he shall think proper; he shall receive Ambassadors and other public Ministers; he shall take Care that the Laws be faithfully executed, and shall Commission all the Officers of the United States.

The president is required to deliver a State of the Union message to Congress each year. The nation's first two presidents, George Washington and John Adams, delivered their addresses in person. But the nation's third president, Thomas Jefferson, believed that the practice too closely resembled the Speech from the Throne delivered by British royalty. Instead, Jefferson prepared remarks for recitation before Congress by an assistant or clerk of Congress. Every American president after Jefferson followed suit until Woodrow Wilson renewed the original practice after his first year in office. Now, the State of the Union Address is a major media event, although it is less an assessment of the nation's health and happiness and more a presidential wish-list for policy initiatives and the touting of partisan accomplishments.

The final provision of section 3 authorizing the president to faithfully execute the laws of the United States has proven controversial over the years. Presidents have cited this broad language to justify such far-reaching action as the suspension of the writ of *habeas corpus*, as President Abraham Lincoln did during the Civil War before being rebuffed by the Supreme Court in *Ex parte McCardle* (1867), and the doctrine of executive privilege, which, as asserted by various presidents, permits the executive branch to withhold sensitive information from the public or the other branches of government for national security reasons. The Court has been of two minds about the doctrine of executive privilege. On the one hand, the Court has said in such cases as *New York Times* v. *U.S.* (1971) and *U.S.* v. *Nixon* (1974) that the president has the power to withhold information to protect vital secrets and the nation's security. On the other hand, the Court has said, in ruling against the assertion of executive privilege in these two cases, that only an exceptional and demonstrated case can justify allowing the president to withhold information.

Section 4.

The President, Vice President and all civil Officers of the United States, shall be removed from Office on Impeachment for, and Conviction of, Treason, Bribery, or other High Crimes and Misdemeanors.

Presidential impeachment, like impeachment of the other described offices in section 4, is the responsibility of the House of Representatives. There is no judicial definition to what constitutes a high crime or misdemeanor. Complicating the matter further is that only the House and Senate are given responsibility over the impeachment process. No federal official subject to impeachment may challenge the action in federal court, as the Supreme Court has ruled that the rules governing impeachment are not actionable in court. Only two presidents, Andrew Johnson in 1868 and Bill Clinton in 1998, have ever been impeached. Neither president was convicted by the Senate of the charges brought against them.

ARTICLE III

Section 1.

The judicial Power of the United States, shall be vested in one supreme Court, and in such inferior Courts as the Congress may from time to time ordain and establish. The Judges, both of the supreme and inferior Courts, shall hold their Offices during good Behaviour, and shall, at stated Times, receive for their Services, a Compensation, which shall not be diminished during their Continuance in Office.

Like the power of Congress and the executive branch under Articles I and II, respectively, of the Constitution, the power of the federal judiciary has developed as the result of constitutional silences and ambiguities. Article III establishes only one federal court, the Supreme Court, and leaves to Congress the power to establish "inferior" courts as it deems necessary. Many students are surprised to learn that the power of judicial review was established by Congress, not the Supreme Court. Although the Court did articulate the power of judicial review in *Marbury* v. *Madison* (1803), that decision only applied to the power of the federal courts to review federal laws. The power of the federal courts to review state laws that allegedly trespassed upon the Constitution was established by the Judiciary Act of 1789. But, on the fundamental question of what constitutes the foundation and scope of judicial power, there is little doubt that the Court, not Congress, has been the foremost exponent of its own authority. Often, the Court has justified its authority to limit the power of the other branches to regulate its affairs by pointing to other provisions of the Constitution, most notably the supremacy clause of Article VI and section 5 of the Fourteenth Amendment, as well as Article III.

Section 2.

The judicial Power shall extend to all Cases, in Law and Equity, arising under this Constitution, the Laws of the United States, and Treaties made, or which shall be made, under their Authority;—to all Cases affecting Ambassadors, other public Ministers and Consuls;—to all Cases of admiralty and maritime Jurisdiction;—to Controversies to which the United States shall be a Party;—to Controversies between two or more States;—between a State and Citizens of another State;—between Citizens of different States;—between Citizens of the same State claiming Lands under Grants of different States,—and between a State, or the Citizens thereof, and foreign States, Citizens or Subjects.

In all Cases affecting Ambassadors, other public Ministers and Consuls, and those in which a State shall be Party, the supreme Court shall have original Jurisdiction. In all the other Cases before mentioned, the supreme Court shall have appellate Jurisdiction, both as to Law and Fact, with such Exceptions, and under such Regulations as the Congress shall make.

The Trial of all Crimes, except in Cases of Impeachment, shall be by Jury; and such Trial shall be held in the State where the said Crimes shall have been committed; but when not committed within any State, the Trial shall be at such Place or Places as the Congress may by Law have directed.

Section 1 invests the judicial power in "one Supreme Court," but it is in section 2 that we find the source of much of the controversy of the exercise of this power since *Marbury* was decided. By extending the judicial power to all "Cases, in Law and Equity, arising under the Constitution, [and] the laws of the United States," section 2 authorizes the Court to both decide matters of law and, if necessary, mandate a remedy commensurate with the degree of a constitutional violation. For example, in *Swann* v. *Charlotte-Mecklenburg Board of Education* (1971), the Court ruled that a lower court, having found that a school system had failed to meet desegregation requirements, had the power to order busing and other remedies to the constitutional violations it found in *Brown* v. *Board of Education* (1954).

Federal judicial power no longer extends to cases involving lawsuits between a state and citizens of another state. This provision was superceded by the Eleventh Amendment.

Section 2 also includes the exceptions and regulations clause. This clause has been used by congressional opponents of some of the Court's more controversial and generally liberal decisions. Although most scholars believe the clause limits the power of Congress to create broad jurisdiction for the courts it creates, others have argued that it permits Congress to strip the federal courts of jurisdiction to hear particular cases. Some opponents of the Court's decisions legalizing abortion, authorizing school busing, and upholding affirmative action have attempted to curb the power of federal courts to rule in such areas by stripping them of jurisdiction in such cases. To date, no president has ever signed such legislation.

Section 3.

Treason against the United States, shall consist only in levying War against them, or in adhering to their Enemies, giving them Aid and Comfort. No Person shall be convicted of Treason unless on the Testimony of two Witnesses to the same overt Act, or on Confession in open Court.

The Congress shall have Power to declare the Punishment of Treason, but no Attainder of Treason shall work Corruption of Blood, or Forfeiture except during the Life of the Person attainted.

Article III defines the only crime mentioned by the Constitution: treason.

ARTICLE IV

Section 1.

Full Faith and Credit shall be given in each State to the public Acts, Records, and judicial Proceedings of every other State. And the Congress may by

general Laws prescribe the Manner in which such Acts, Records and Proceedings shall be proved, and the Effect thereof.

The full faith and credit clause rests on principles borrowed from international law that require one country to recognize contracts made in another country absent a compelling public policy reason to the contrary. Here, this principle, referred to in the law as comity, applied to the relationship between the states. For example, a driver's license issued in Ohio is good in Montana. The full and faith credit clause also requires a state to recognize public acts and court proceedings of another state. For the most part, interpretation of the full faith and credit clause has not been controversial. That may well change, as advocates of same-sex marriage have suggested that such a marriage performed in one state must be recognized in another state, as is the case with heterosexual marriage. A constitutional challenge to the clause may well center on the public policy exception recognized in other areas of law.

Section 2.

The Citizens of each State shall be entitled to all Privileges and Immunities of Citizens in the several States.

A Person charged in any State with Treason, Felony, or other Crime, who shall flee from Justice, and be found in another State, shall on Demand of the executive Authority of the State from which he fled, be delivered up, to be removed to the State having Jurisdiction of the Crime.

The extradition clause requires that the governor of one state deliver a fugitive from justice to the state from which that fugitive fled. Congress passed the Fugitive Act of 1793 to give definition to this provision, but the federal government has no authority to compel state authorities to extradite a fugitive from one state to another. A state may, however, sue another state in federal court to force the return of a fugitive.

No Person held to Service or Labour in one State under the Laws thereof, escaping into another, shall, in Consequence of any Law or Regulation therein, be discharged from such Service or Labour, but shall be delivered up on Claim of the Party to whom such Service or Labour may be due.

The fugitive slave clause, which required any state, including those outside the slave-holding states of the South, to return escaped slaves to their owners, was repealed in 1865 by the Thirteenth Amendment. Prior to 1865, Congress passed laws in 1793 and 1850 to enforce the clause, leaving states without power to make concurrent laws on the subject, ensuring that the southern states would always have the Constitution on their side to protect slavery.

Section 3.

New States may be admitted by the Congress into this Union; but no new State shall be formed or erected within the Jurisdiction of any other State; nor any State be formed by the Junction of two or more States, or Parts of States, without the Consent of the Legislatures of the States concerned as well as of the Congress.

The Congress shall have Power to dispose of and make all needful Rules and Regulations respecting the Territory or other Property belonging to the United States; and nothing in this Constitution shall be so construed as to Prejudice any Claims of the United States, or of any particular State.

Section 4.

The United States shall guarantee to every State in this Union a Republican Form of Government, and shall protect each of them against Invasion; and on Application of the Legislature, or of the Executive (when the Legislature cannot be convened) against domestic Violence.

ARTICLE V

The Congress, whenever two thirds of both Houses shall deem it necessary, shall propose Amendments to this Constitution, or, on the Application of the Legislatures of two thirds of the several States, shall call a Convention for proposing Amendments, which, in either Case, shall be valid to all Intents and Purposes, as Part of this Constitution, when ratified by the Legislatures of three fourths of the several States, or by Conventions in three fourths thereof, as the one or the other Mode of Ratification may be proposed by the Congress; Provided that no Amendment which may be made prior to the Year One thousand eight hundred and eight shall in any Manner affect the first and fourth Clauses in the Ninth Section of the first Article; and that no State, without its Consent, shall be deprived of its equal Suffrage in the Senate.

Changes to the Articles of Confederation had required the unanimous approval of the states. But, Article V of the U.S. Constitution offers multiple options—none of which require unanimity—for constitutional change. Article V was quite crucial to the ratification of the Constitution. Federalists who supported the Constitu-

tion wanted to ensure that any additions or modifications to the nation's charter would require the approval of more than a simple majority of citizens. This is why any amendment coming out of Congress requires two-thirds of the House and Senate for approval. The same is true for the rule requiring three-fourths of the states to ratify an amendment (either through conventions or state legislative action). Anti-Federalists who either opposed the Constitution or had reservations about key sections of it were soothed by the prospect of an amending process that did not require the unanimous approval of the states.

Only twenty-seven amendments since 1789 have been added to the Constitution, the first fifteen of which were added by 1870. Since 1933, when the nation repealed Prohibition by passing the Twenty-First Amendment, the Constitution has been amended only six times. In the modern constitutional era, efforts to amend the Constitution generally have centered on unhappiness with Supreme Court decisions (on school prayer, flag burning, school busing, abortion rights) or state court rulings with national implications (such as same-sex marriage) rather than any structural defect in the original Constitution (unlike woman suffrage or presidential succession) or a seismic political event (the Civil War). To date, none of these efforts have been successful.

ARTICLE VI

All Debts contracted and Engagements entered into, before the Adoption of this Constitution, shall be as valid against the United States under this Constitution, as under the Confederation.

This Constitution, and the Laws of the United States which shall be made in Pursuance thereof; and all Treaties made, or which shall be made, under the Authority of the United States, shall be the supreme Law of the Land; and the Judges in every State shall be bound thereby, any Thing in the Constitution or Laws of any State to the Contrary notwithstanding.

The Senators and Representatives before mentioned, and the Members of the several State Legislatures, and all executive and judicial Officers, both of the United States and of the several States, shall be bound by Oath or Affirmation, to support this Constitution; but no religious Test shall ever be required as a Qualification to any Office or public Trust under the United States.

Article VI made the national government responsible for all debts incurred by the Revolutionary War. This ensured that manufacturing and banking interests

would be repaid for the losses they sustained during the conflict. But the most important provisions of Article VI by far are contained in its second and third clauses.

Clause 2 took another major step forward for national power and away from the confederate approach to government structure of the Articles of Confederation. By making "this Constitution" and all laws made under its authority the "supreme Law of the Land," Article VI created what constitutional scholars call the supremacy clause. The Supreme Court has invoked the supremacy clause on several occasions to rebut challenges mounted by states to its decisions or acts of Congress. Among the more notable decisions by the Supreme Court that have cited the supremacy clause to mandate compliance with a previous ruling is *Cooper* v. *Aaron* (1958). In *Cooper*, the Court cited the supremacy clause in rejecting the argument of Governor Orval Faubus of Arkansas claiming that local schools were not obligated to follow the *Brown* v. *Board of Education* (1954) ruling. The Court said that *Brown* was the law of the land and, as such, all school boards were required to comply with its requirement to desegregate their schools.

Although most Americans rightly point to the First Amendment as the baseline for the guarantee for religious freedom, clause 3 of Article VI contains an important contribution to this principle—the ban on religious tests or qualifications to hold public office. Holders of public office, no matter how great or small, were required to affirm their allegiance to the Constitution and the laws of the United States, but they could not be required to profess a belief in God or meet any other religious qualification. Numerous states nonetheless ignored this requirement until 1961, when the Supreme Court ruled in *Torcaso* v. *Watkins* that states could not administer religious oaths to holders of public office.

ARTICLE VII

The Ratification of the Conventions of nine States, shall be sufficient for the Establishment of this Constitution between the States so ratifying the Same.

Done in Convention by the Unanimous Consent of the States present the Seventeenth Day of September in the Year of our Lord one thousand seven hundred and Eighty seven and of the Independence of the United States of America the Twelfth. IN WITNESS whereof We have hereunto subscribed our Names,

G. WASHINGTON,
Presid't. and deputy from Virginia

Attest
WILLIAM JACKSON,
Secretary

DELAWARE
George Read
Gunning Bedford, Jr.
John Dickinson
Richard Basset
Jacob Broom

MASSACHUSETTS
BAY
Nathaniel Gorham
Rufus King

CONNECTICUT
William Samuel
  Johnson
Roger Sherman

NEW YORK
Alexander Hamilton

NEW JERSEY
William Livingston
David Brearley
William Paterson
Jonathan Dayton

PENNSYLVANIA
Benjamin Franklin
Thomas Mifflin
Robert Morris
George Clymer
Thomas FitzSimons
Jared Ingersoll
James Wilson
Gouverneur Morris

NEW HAMPSHIRE
John Langdon
Nicholas Gilman

MARYLAND
James McHenry
Daniel of St. Thomas
  Jenifer
Daniel Carroll

VIRGINIA
John Blair
James Madison, Jr.

NORTH CAROLINA
William Blount
Richard Dobbs
  Spaight
Hugh Williamson

SOUTH CAROLINA
John Rutledge
Charles Cotesworth
  Pinckney
Charles Pinckney
Pierce Butler

GEORGIA
William Few
Abraham Baldwin

Articles in addition to, and amendment of the Constitution of the United States of America, proposed by Congress and ratified by the Legislatures of the several states, pursuant to the Fifth Article of the original Constitution.

(The first ten amendments were passed by Congress on September 25, 1789, and were ratified on December 15, 1791.)

AMENDMENT I

Congress shall make no law respecting an establishment of religion, or prohibiting the free exercise thereof; or abridging the freedom of speech, or of the press; or the right of the people peaceably to assemble, and to petition the Government for a redress of grievances.

For many Americans, the First Amendment represents the core of what the Bill of Rights stands for: limits on government power to limit or compel religious beliefs, the right to hold political opinions and express them, protection for a free press, the right to assemble peaceably, and the right to petition, through protest or the ballot, the government for a redress of political grievances. But it is also important to remember that the First Amendment, like most of the Bill of Rights, did not apply to state governments until the Supreme Court began to apply their substantive guarantees through the Fourteenth Amendment, a process that did not begin until 1925 in *Gitlow* v. *New York*.

Until then, state and local governments often failed to honor the rights and liberties that Congress, and by extension the national government, was expressly forbidden by the Constitution from withholding. For example, southern states, prior to the Civil War, outlawed pro-abolition literature; numerous states continued to collect taxes on behalf of state-sponsored churches and religious education; newspapers often were forbidden from publishing exposes on industry or political leaders because such speech was considered seditious and thus subject to prior restraint; and public protests on behalf of unpopular causes were often banned by state breach of peace laws.

The Supreme Court has recognized other important rights implied by the enumerated guarantees of the First Amendment. These include the right to association, even when such association might come in the form of clubs or organizations that discriminate on the basis of race, sex, or religion, and the right to personal privacy, which the Supreme Court held in *Griswold* v. *Connecticut* (1965) was based in part on the right of married couples to make decisions about contraception, a decision protected by one's personal religious and political beliefs.

AMENDMENT II

A well regulated Militia, being necessary to the security of a free State, the right of the people to keep and bear Arms, shall not be infringed.

Few issues in American politics generate as much emotional heat as the extent to which Americans have a right to keep and bear arms. Supporters of broad gun ownership rights, such as the National Rifle Association, argue that the Second Amendment protects an almost absolute individual right to own just about any small arm that can be manufactured, whether for reasons of sport or self-defense. Proponents of gun control, such as the Brady Campaign to Prevent Gun Violence, argue that the amendment creates no such individual right, but refers instead to the Framers' belief—now outdated—that citizen militias had the right to form to protect themselves against other states and, if need be, the national government. Under this view, Congress and the states are free to regulate gun ownership and use as they see fit, provided that the national and state governments are within their constitutional orbit of power to do so.

In 1939, the Supreme Court, for the first time, offered an interpretation of the Second Amendment. There, a unanimous Court upheld a federal law requiring the registration of sawed-off shotguns purchased for personal use. The justices also rejected the argument the Second Amendment established an individual right to keep and bear arms; the Court did, however, leave open the question by holding that not all weapons were intended for militia use only. Almost seventy years later, the Court revisited the question in *D.C.* v. *Heller* (2008), holding this time that a local law banning the possession of handguns in the home was unconstitutional. The justices also ruled that another provision of the same law requiring that all "long guns" be kept unloaded and non-functional was unconstitutional.

AMENDMENT III

No Soldier shall, in time of peace be quartered in any house, without the consent of the Owner, nor in time of war, but in a manner to be prescribed by law.

Among the complaints directed at King George III in the Declaration of Independence was the colonial-era practice of quartering large numbers of troops in private homes. The practice of quartering soldiers, along with the forced maintenance of British standing armies in times of peace without the consent of the colonial legislatures, formed a major component of the political grievances directed at the British crown. The Third Amendment was intended to protect individuals

and their property from the abuse common to the practice of quartering soldiers.

AMENDMENT IV

The right of the people to be secure in their persons, houses, papers, and effects, against unreasonable searches and seizures, shall not be violated, and no warrants shall issue, but upon probable cause, supported by Oath or affirmation, and particularly describing the place to be searched, and the persons or things to be seized.

Although the Fourth Amendment is often discussed in tandem with the Fifth, Sixth, and Eighth Amendments—the other major provisions of the Bill of Rights outlining the criminal due process guarantees of citizens—it shares a similar undercurrent that motivated the adoption of the Third Amendment: to eliminate the practice of British officers from using the general writ of assistance to enter private homes, conduct searches, and seize personal property. British officers had not been required to offer a specific reason for a search or justify the taking of particular items. In most cases, the writ of assistance was used to confiscate items considered to have violated the strict British customs laws of the colonial era.

The twin pillars of the Fourth Amendment, the probable cause and warrant requirements, are a direct reflection of the disdain the Framers had for the Revolutionary-era practices of the British. But, like the First Amendment, the guarantees of the Fourth Amendment did not apply to state and local law enforcement practices until well after the ratification of the Fourteenth Amendment. Until *Wolf* v. *Colorado* (1949), when the Court ruled that the Fourteenth Amendment made the Fourth Amendment binding on the states, evidence seized in violation of the probable cause or warrant requirements could be used against a criminal suspect. The Court's best-known decision on the Fourth Amendment, *Mapp* v. *Ohio* (1961), which established the exclusionary rule, also marked the high-water point in the rights afforded to criminal suspects challenging an unlawful search. Since the late 1970s, the Court has steadily added exceptions to the Fourth Amendment to permit law enforcement officers to engage in warrantless searches and seizures, provided that such practices meet a threshold of reasonableness in the context of the circumstances under which they are undertaken.

AMENDMENT V

No person shall be held to answer for a capital, or otherwise infamous crime, unless on a presentment or indictment of a Grand Jury, except in cases arising in the land or naval forces, or in the Militia, when in actual service in time of War or public danger; nor shall any person be subject for the same offence to be twice put in jeopardy of life or limb; nor shall be compelled in any criminal case to be a witness against himself, nor be deprived of life, liberty, or property, without due process of law; nor shall private property be taken for public use, without just compensation.

The Fifth Amendment, along with the Sixth Amendment, is the legacy of the ruthless and secretive tactics that figured prominently in the colonial-era system of British justice. By requiring that no person could be held for a "capital, or otherwise infamous" crime except upon indictment by a grand jury, the Fifth Amendment took an important step toward making the criminal indictment process a public function. Along with the public trial and trial by jury guarantees of the Sixth Amendment, the grand jury provision of the Fifth Amendment established that the government would have to make its case against the accused in public. Also, by guaranteeing that no person could be compelled to testify against himself or herself in a criminal proceeding, the Fifth Amendment highlighted the adversarial nature of the American criminal justice system, a feature that is distinct from its British counterpart. "Pleading the Fifth" is permissible in any criminal, civil, administrative, judicial, or investigatory context. *Miranda* v. *Arizona* (1966), one of the most famous rulings of the Supreme Court, established a right to silence that combined the ban against self-incrimination of the Fifth Amendment with the Sixth Amendment's guarantee of the assistance of counsel. The right to silence, unlike the ban against self-incrimination, extends to any aspect of an interrogation.

The Fifth Amendment also forbids double jeopardy, which prohibits the prosecution of a crime against the same person in the same jurisdiction twice, and prevents the government from taking life, liberty, or property without due process of law. This phrase was reproduced in the Fourteenth Amendment, placing an identical set of constraints on the states. The Court has applied all the guarantees of the Fifth Amendment, with the exception of the grand jury provision, to the states through the due process clause of the Fourteenth Amendment. Some constitutional scholars also consider the due process clause of the Fifth Amendment to embrace an equal protection provision when applied to federal cases.

The final provision of the Fifth Amendment prohibits the government from taking private property for public use without just compensation. Litigation on the takings clause, as some scholars refer to this provision, has generally centered on two major questions. The first is what constitutes a taking, either by the government's decision to seize private property or by regulating it to the point where its value is greatly diminished. The second question centers on what the appropriate level of compensation is for owners who have successfully established a taking.

The Supreme Court has taken an expansive definition of what it means to "take" private land for "public use." In *Kelo* v. *New London* (2004), the Court ruled that government could take private property and then sell it to private developers so long as that property was slated for economic development that would benefit the surrounding community. This marked the first time the Court had authorized a taking for something other than public use by governmental authorities.

AMENDMENT VI

In all criminal prosecutions, the accused shall enjoy the right to a speedy and public trial, by an impartial jury of the State and district wherein the crime shall have been committed, which district shall have been previously ascertained by law, and to be informed of the nature and cause of the accusation; to be confronted with the witnesses against him; to have compulsory process for obtaining witnesses in his favor, and to have the assistance of counsel for his defence.

The centerpiece of the constitutional guarantees afforded to individuals facing criminal prosecution, the Sixth Amendment sets out eight specific rights, more than any other provision of the Bill of Rights. As with the Fifth Amendment, the core features of the Sixth Amendment build upon the unfortunate legacy of the repressive practices of colonial-era Britain. The very first provision of the Sixth Amendment mandates that individuals subject to criminal prosecution receive "a speedy and public trial"; it then requires that all such trials take place in public, with the defendant informed of the cause and nature of the accusation against him or her. The common theme underlying these sections of the Sixth Amendment, as well as those requiring witnesses for the prosecution to testify in public, allowing the defendant to produce witnesses on his or her own behalf, and securing the assistance of counsel, is that any citizen threatened with the deprivation of liberty is entitled to have the case made against him or her in public. The Fifth Amendment also required the government to produce evidence that did not rely on confessions and self-incrimination. And, it required that any such evidence must be acquired lawfully and

with the knowledge of a public magistrate. The Sixth Amendment establishes, in principle, the American criminal justice system as one that is open and public.

Since the vast majority of criminal prosecutions in the United States are undertaken by state and local authorities, the parchment promises of the Sixth Amendment did not extend to most Americans until the Supreme Court began incorporating the guarantees of the Bill of Rights to the states through the Fourteenth Amendment. Perhaps the best-known case involving the Sixth Amendment is *Gideon* v. *Wainwright* (1963), which held that all persons accused of a serious crime are entitled to an attorney, even if they cannot afford one, a rule that was soon extended to cover misdemeanors as well. Three years later, the Supreme Court fused the right to counsel rule established in *Gideon* with the Fifth Amendment ban against self-incrimination to create the principles animating *Miranda* v. *Arizona*. For a long time, the Court had never interpreted the Fifth and Sixth Amendments to mean that individuals had rights to criminal due process guarantees if they did not know about them or could not afford them. Decisions such as *Gideon* and *Miranda* offered a clear departure from this position.

The speedy and public trial clauses only require that criminal trials take place in public within a reasonable amount of time after the period of indictment, and that juries in such cases are unbiased. Americans also often cite the Sixth Amendment as entitling them to a trial by a "jury of one's peers." This is true to the extent individuals are entitled to a trial in the jurisdiction where the crime is alleged to have been committed. It does not mean, however, that they are entitled to a trial by persons of a similar age or background, for example.

AMENDMENT VII

In Suits at common law, where the value in controversy shall exceed twenty dollars, the right of trial by jury shall be preserved, and no fact tried by a jury, shall be otherwise re-examined in any Court of the United States, than according to the rules of the common law.

One feature of the British courts that the Framers sought to preserve in the American civil law system was the distinction between courts of common law and courts of equity. Common law courts heard cases involving strict legal rules, while equity courts based their decisions on principles of fairness and totality of circumstances. Common law courts featured juries that were authorized to return verdicts entitling plaintiffs to financial compensation for losses incurred, whereas equity courts relied upon judges to make determinations about appropriate relief for successful parties. Relief in equity courts did not consist of monetary awards, but injunctions, cease-and-desist orders, and so on. The Seventh Amendment carried over this British feature into the Constitution.

In 1938, Congress amended the Federal Rules of Civil Procedure to combine the function of civil common law and equity courts. In cases involving both legal and equitable claims, a federal judge must first decide the issue of law before moving to the equitable relief, or remedy, component of the trial. Judges are permitted to instruct juries on matters of law and fact, and may emphasize certain facts or legal issues to the jury in their instructions to the jury. But, the jury alone decides guilt or innocence. In some extraordinary cases, a judge may overturn the verdict of a jury. This happens only when a judge believes the jury has disregarded completely the facts and evidence before it in reaching a verdict.

Congress has also changed the $20 threshold for the right to a trial by jury. The amount is now $75,000. Finally, the Seventh Amendment has never been incorporated to the states through the Fourteenth Amendment.

AMENDMENT VIII

Excessive bail shall not be required, nor excessive fines imposed, nor cruel and unusual punishments inflicted.

For an amendment of so few words, the Eighth Amendment has generated an enormous volume of commentary and litigation since its ratification. This should not be surprising, as the three major provisions of the amendment deal with some of the most sensitive and emotionally charged issues involving the rights of criminal defendants.

The origin of the excessive bail clause stems from the reforms to the British system instituted by the 1689 English Bill of Rights. Having had limited success in preventing law enforcement officials from detaining suspects by imposing outrageous bail requirements, Britain amended previous laws to say that "excessive bail ought not to be required." Much like the British model, the Eighth Amendment does not state what an "excessive bail" is or the particular criminal offense that warrants a high bail amount. The Supreme Court has offered two fundamental rules on the excessive bail clause. First, a judge has the discretion to decide if a criminal offense is sufficiently serious to justify high bail. Second, a judge has the power, under U.S. v. Salerno (1987), to deny a criminal defendant bail as a "preventative measure." In both such cases, a judge's action must be considered proportionate to the nature of the criminal offense for which an individual stands accused.

Like the excessive bail clause, the excessive fines clause is rooted in the English Bill of Rights. The clause applies only to criminal proceedings, not civil litigation. For example, a tobacco company cannot appeal what it believes is an excessive jury award under this clause. An indigent criminal defendant, however, can challenge a fine levied in connection with a criminal conviction.

The most controversial section of the Eighth Amendment is the clause forbidding cruel and unusual punishments. The absence of such a guarantee from the Constitution was a major impetus for the adoption of the Bill of Rights. While most historians agree that the Framers wanted to prohibit barbaric forms of punishment, including torture, as well as arbitrary and disproportionate penalties, there is little consensus on what specific punishments met this definition. By the late 1800s, the Supreme Court had ruled that such punishments as public burning, disembowelment, and drawing and quartering crossed the Eighth Amendment barrier. In Weems v. U.S. (1910), the Court went the additional of step of concluding that any punishment considered "excessive" would violate the cruel and unusual punishment clause. And, in Solem v. Helm (1983), the Court developed a "proportionality" standard that required punishments, even simple incarceration, to bear a rational relationship to the offense.

The Court has never ruled, however, that the death penalty per se violates the Eighth Amendment. It has developed certain rules and exceptions governing the application of the death penalty, such as requiring a criminal defendant actually to have killed, or attempted to have killed, a victim. It has also ruled that the mentally retarded, as a class, are exempt from the death penalty. But it has also issued highly controversial decisions concluding, for example, that neither racial disparities in the application of capital punishment nor juvenile status at the time the offense was committed violate the Eighth Amendment. Except for a four-year ban on the practice between 1972 and 1976, the death penalty has always been an available punishment in the American criminal justice system.

AMENDMENT IX

The enumeration in the Constitution, of certain rights, shall not be construed to deny or disparage others retained by the people.

A major point of contention between the Federalists and Anti-Federalists was the need for a bill of rights. In Federalist No. 84, Alexander Hamilton argued that a bill of rights was unnecessary, as there was no need to place limits on the power of government to do things that it was not authorized by the Constitution to do. Hamilton also argued that it would be impossible to list all the rights "retained by the people." Protecting some rights but not others would suggest that Americans had surrendered certain rights to their government when, in Hamilton's view, the Constitution did nothing of the sort.

Given his well-deserved reputation for unbridled national power, Hamilton's views have often been dismissed as a cynical ploy to sidestep any meaningful discussion of the Bill of Rights and speed along the ratification process. But, James Madison, along with Thomas Jefferson, held a much deeper belief in the need for a bill of rights. Madison also believed that the enumeration of certain rights and liberties in the Constitution should not be understood to deny others that exist as a condition of citizenship in a free society. Madison, the primary author of the Bill of Rights, included the Ninth Amendment to underscore this belief.

The Supreme Court has never offered a clear and definitive interpretation of the Ninth Amendment, primarily because it has been wary of giving such general language any substantive definition. The amendment has been cited in such decisions as *Griswold* v. *Connecticut* (1965) and *Richmond Newspapers* v. *Virginia* (1980) along with other constitutional amendments to bolster the case on behalf of an asserted constitutional right. The difficulty in constructing a specific meaning for the Ninth Amendment can be illustrated by the fact that both supporters and opponents of legal abortion have cited it to defend the feasibility of their respective positions.

AMENDMENT X

The powers not delegated to the United States by the Constitution, nor prohibited by it to the States, are reserved to the States respectively, or to the people.

The Tenth Amendment generated little controversy during the ratification process over the Bill of Rights. As the Supreme Court later ruled in *U.S.* v. *Darby Lumber Co.* (1941), the Tenth Amendment states a truism about the relationship between the boundaries of national and state power—that the states retain those powers not specifically set out in the Constitution as belonging to the national government. There is little in the history in the debate over the Tenth Amendment to suggest that its language is anything other than declaratory. Indeed, the refusal of the 1st Congress to insert the word "expressly" before "delegated" strongly suggests that James Madison, who offered the most thorough explanation of the amendment during the floor debates, intended to leave room for this relationship to evolve as future events made necessary.

The earliest political and constitutional developments involving the Tenth Amendment tilted the balance of power firmly in favor of national power. Alexander Hamilton's vision for a national bank to consolidate the nation's currency and trading position was realized in *McCullough* v. *Maryland* (1819), in which the Court held that Article I granted Congress broad power to make all laws "necessary and proper" to the exercise of its legislative power. By no means, however, did *McCullough* settle the argument over the power reserved to the states. Led by Chief Justice Roger B. Taney, the Court handed down several decisions in the three decades leading up to the Civil War that offered substantial protection to the southern states on the matters closest to their hearts: slavery and economic sovereignty. From the period after the Civil War until the New Deal, the Court continued to shield states from congressional legislation designed to regulate the economy and promote social and political reform. After the constitutional revolution of 1937, when the Court threw its support behind the New Deal, Congress received a blank constitutional check to engage in the regulatory action that featured an unprecedented level of federal intervention in economic and social matters once the purview of the states, one that would last almost sixty years.

Beginning in *New York* v. *U.S.* (1992), however, the Court, in striking down a key provision of a federal environmental law, began to revisit the New Deal assumptions that underlay its modern interpretation of the Tenth Amendment. A few years later, in *U.S.* v. *Lopez* (1995), it invalidated a federal gun control law on the ground that Congress lacked authority under the commerce clause to regulate gun possession. And, in *U.S.* v. *Printz* (1997), the Tenth Amendment explicitly was cited to strike down an important section of the Brady Bill, a congressional law that required states to conduct background checks on prospective gun buyers. Although the Court has not returned to the dual federalism posture on the Tenth Amendment that it built from the years between the Taney Court and the triumph of the New Deal, these decisions make clear that the constitutional status of the states as actors in the federal system has been dramatically strengthened.

AMENDMENT XI
(Ratified on February 7, 1795)

The Judicial power of the United States shall not be construed to extend to any suit in law or equity, commenced or prosecuted against one of the United States by Citizens of another State, or by Citizens or Subjects of any Foreign State.

The Eleventh Amendment was prompted by one of the earliest notable decisions of the Supreme Court, *Chisolm* v. *Georgia* (1793). In *Chisolm*, the Court held that Article III and the enforcement provision of the Judiciary Act of 1789 permitted a citizen of one state to bring suit against another state in federal court. Almost immediately after *Chisolm*, the Eleventh Amendment was introduced and promptly ratified, as the states saw this decision as a threat to their sovereignty under the new Constitution. The amendment was passed in less than a year, which, by the standards of the era, was remarkably fast.

The Eleventh Amendment nullified the result in *Chisolm* but did not completely bar a citizen from bringing suit against a state in federal court. Citizens may bring lawsuits against state officials in federal court if they can satisfy the requirement that their rights under federal constitutional or statutory law have been violated. The Eleventh Amendment has not been extensively litigated in modern times, but the extent to which states are immune under federal law from citizen lawsuits has reemerged as an important constitutional question in recent years. For example, the Court has said in several cases that the doctrine of sovereign immunity prevents citizens from suing state agencies under the Americans with Disabilities Act of 1990. But, as recently as 2003, the Court, in *Nevada* v. *Hibbs*, ruled that the Family and Medical Leave Act of 1993 did not immunize state government agencies against lawsuits brought by former state employees. States are also free to waive their immunity and consent to a lawsuit.

AMENDMENT XII
(Ratified on June 15, 1804)

The Electors shall meet in their respective states, and vote by ballot for President and Vice-President, one of whom, at least, shall not be an inhabitant of the same state with themselves; they shall name in their ballots the person voted for as President, and in distinct ballots the person voted for as Vice-President, and they shall make distinct lists of all persons voted for as President, and of all persons voted for as Vice-President, and of the number of votes for each, which lists they shall sign and certify, and transmit sealed to the seat of the government of the United States, directed to the President of the Senate;—The President of the Senate shall, in the presence of the Senate and House of Representatives, open all the certificates and the votes shall then be counted;—The person having the greatest number of votes for President, shall be the President, if such number be a majority of the whole number of Electors appointed; and if no person have such majority; then from the persons having the highest numbers not exceeding three on the list of those voted for as President, the House of Representatives shall choose immediately, by ballot, the President. But in choosing the President, the votes shall be taken by states, the representation from each state having one vote; a quorum for this purpose shall consist of a member or members from two-thirds of the states, and a majority of all the states shall be necessary to a choice. And if the House of Representatives shall not choose a President whenever the right of choice shall devolve upon them, before the fourth day of March next following, then the Vice-President shall act as President, as in the case of the death or other constitutional disability of the President.—The person having the greatest number of votes as Vice-President, shall be the Vice-President, if such number be a majority of the whole number of Electors appointed, and if no person have a majority, then from the two highest numbers on the list, the Senate shall choose the Vice-President; a quorum for the purpose shall consist of two-thirds of the whole number of Senators, and a majority of the whole number shall be necessary to a choice. But no person constitutionally ineligible to the office of President shall be eligible to that of Vice-President of the United States.

The Twelfth Amendment was added to the Constitution after the 1800 presidential election was thrown into the House of Representatives. Thomas Jefferson and Aaron Burr, running on the Democratic-Republican Party ticket, each received seventy-three electoral votes for president, even though everyone knew that Jefferson was the presidential candidate and Burr the vice presidential candidate. This was possible because Article II, section 1, did not require electors to vote for president and vice president separately. The Twelfth Amendment remedied this deficiency by requiring electors to cast their votes for president and vice president separately.

Whether it intended to or not, the Twelfth Amendment took a major step toward institutionalizing the party system in the United States. The 1796 election yielded a president and vice president from different parties, a clear indication that partisan differences were emerging in a distinct form. The 1800 election simply highlighted the problem further. By requiring electors to make their presidential and vice presidential choices separately, the Twelfth Amendment conceded that a party system in American politics had indeed evolved, an inevitable but nonetheless disappointing development to the architects of the original constitutional vision.

AMENDMENT XIII
(Ratified on December 6, 1865)

Section 1.

Neither slavery nor involuntary servitude, except as a punishment for crime whereof the party shall have been duly convicted, shall exist within the United States, or any place subject to their jurisdiction.

Section 2.

Congress shall have power to enforce this article by appropriate legislation.

The Thirteenth, Fourteenth, and Fifteenth Amendments are known collectively as the Civil War Amendments.

In anticipation of a Union victory, the Thirteenth Amendment was passed by Congress and sent to the states for ratification before the end of the Civil War. The amendment not only formally abolished slavery and involuntary servitude; it also served as the constitutional foundation for the nation's first major civil rights legislation, the Civil Rights Act of 1866. This law extended numerous rights to African Americans previously held in servitude as well as those having "free" status during the Civil War, including the right to purchase, rent, and sell personal property, to bring suit in federal court, to enter into contracts, and to receive the full and equal benefit of all laws "enjoyed by white citizens." The Thirteenth Amendment overturned the pre–Civil War decision of the Supreme Court, *Dred Scott* v. *Sandford* (1857), which held that slaves were not people entitled to constitutional rights, but property subject to the civil law binding them to their masters.

In modern times, the Court has ruled that the Thirteenth Amendment prohibits any action that recognizes a "badge" or "condition" of slavery, such as housing discrimination and certain forms of employment discrimination. The Department of Justice also has used the Thirteenth Amendment to file lawsuits against manufacturing sweatshops and other criminal enterprises in which persons are forced to work without compensation.

AMENDMENT XIV
(Ratified on July 9, 1868)

Section 1.

All persons born or naturalized in the United States, and subject to the jurisdiction thereof, are citizens of the United States and of the State wherein they reside. No State shall make or enforce any law which shall abridge the privileges or immunities of citizens of the United States; nor shall any State deprive any person of life, liberty, or property, without due process of law; nor deny to any person within its jurisdiction the equal protection of the laws.

Many constitutional scholars believe the Fourteenth Amendment is the most important addition to the Constitution since the Bill of Rights was ratified in 1791. In addition to serving as a cornerstone of Reconstruction policy, section 1 eliminated the distinction between the rights and liberties of Americans as citizens of their respective states and those to which they were entitled under the Bill of Rights as citizens of the United States. The Republican leadership that drafted and steered the Fourteenth Amendment to passage left no doubt that the three major provisions of section 1, which placed express limits on state power to abridge rights and liberties protected as a condition of national citizenship, were intended to make the Bill of Rights binding upon the states, thus overruling *Barron* v. *Baltimore* (1833). Although the Supreme Court has never endorsed this view, the selective incorporation of the Bill of Rights to the states during the twentieth century through the Fourteenth Amendment ultimately made the Reconstruction-era vision of the Republicans a reality. The former Confederate states were required to ratify the Fourteenth Amendment to qualify for readmission into the Union.

Section 2.

Representatives shall be apportioned among the several States according to their respective numbers, counting the whole number of persons in each State, excluding Indians not taxed. But when the right to vote at any election for the choice of electors for President and Vice President of the United States, Representatives in Congress, the Executive and Judicial officers of a State, or the members of the Legislature thereof, is denied to any of the male inhabitants of such State, being twenty-one years of age, and citizens of the United States, or in any way abridged, except for participation in rebellion, or other crime, the basis of representation therein shall be reduced in the proportion which the number of such male citizens shall bear to the whole number of male citizens twenty-one years of age in such State.

Section 2 established two major changes to the Constitution. First, by stating that representatives from each state would be apportioned based on the number of "whole" persons in each state, section 2 modified the Three-Fifths Compromise of Article 1, section 2, clause 3, of the original Constitution. Note, however, that section 2 still called for the exclusion of Indians "not taxed" from the apportionment criteria. Second, section 2, for

the first time anywhere in the Constitution, mentions that only "male" inhabitants of the states age twenty-one or older would be counted toward representation in the House of Representatives and eligible to vote.

The Military Reconstruction Act of 1867 had strengthened Republican power in the southern states by stripping former Confederates of the right to vote, a law that, in conjunction with the gradual addition of blacks to the voting rolls, made enactment of the Fourteenth Amendment possible. Section 2 temporarily solidified the Republican presence in the South by eliminating from apportionment counts any person that participated in the rebellion against the Union.

Section 3.

No person shall be a Senator or Representative in Congress, or elector of President and Vice President, or hold any office, civil or military, under the United States, or under any State, who, having previously taken an oath, as a member of Congress, or as an officer of the United States, or as a member of any State legislature, or as an executive or judicial officer of any State, to support the Constitution of the United States, shall have engaged in insurrection or rebellion against the same, or given aid or comfort to the enemies thereof. But Congress may by a vote of two-thirds of each House, remove such disability.

Section 3 also reflected the power of the Reconstruction-era Republicans over the South. By eliminating the eligibility of former Confederates for public office or to serve as an elector for president or vice president, the Republicans strengthened their presence in Congress and throughout national politics. This measure also allowed African Americans to run for and hold office in the South, which they were doing by 1870, the same year the Fifteenth Amendment was ratified.

In December 1868, five months after the ratification of the Fourteenth Amendment, President Andrew Johnson declared universal amnesty for all former Confederates. This measure had the effect of returning white politicians and by extension the Democratic Party to power in the South. Republican concern over this development was a major force behind the adoption of the Fifteenth Amendment, which was viewed as an instrument to protect Republican political power by securing black enfranchisement. However, Republican president Ulysses S. Grant, who defeated Johnson in 1868, pardoned all but a few hundred remaining Confederate sympathizers by signing the Amnesty Act of 1872. Decisions such as these began the gradual undoing of Republican commitment to black civil rights in the South.

Section 4.

The validity of the public debt of the United States, authorized by law, including debts incurred for payment of pensions and bounties for services in suppressing insurrection or rebellion, shall not be questioned. But neither the United States nor any State shall assume or pay any debt or obligation incurred in aid of insurrection or rebellion against the United States, or any claim for the loss or emancipation of any slave, but all such debts, obligations and claims shall be held illegal and void.

Section 4 repudiated the South's desire to have Congress forgive the Confederacy's war debts. It also rejected any claim that former slaveholders had to be compensated for the loss of their slaves.

Section 5.

The Congress shall have power to enforce, by appropriate legislation, the provisions of this article.

By giving Congress the power to enforce the provisions of the Fourteenth Amendment, section 5 reiterated the post–Civil War emphasis on national citizenship and the limit on state power to deny individuals their constitutional rights. Section 5 also extended congressional law-making power beyond those areas outlined in Article I. But, the Court has taken a mixed view of the scope of congressional power to enforce the Fourteenth Amendment. In *Katzenbach* v. *Morgan* (1966), for example, the Supreme Court offered a broad ruling on the section 5 power of Congress. It held that Congress could enact laws establishing rights beyond what the Court said the Constitution required, as long as such laws were designed to establish a remedial constitutional right or protect citizens from a potential constitutional violation. In other cases, such as *City of Boerne* v. *Flores* (1997) and *U.S.* v. *Morrison* (2000), the Court ruled that Congress may not intrude upon the authority of the judicial branch to define the meaning of the Constitution or intrude on the power of the states to make laws within their own domain.

AMENDMENT XV
(Ratified on February 3, 1870)

Section 1.

The right of citizens of the United States to vote shall not be denied or abridged by the United States or by any State on account of race, color, or previous condition of servitude.

Section 2.

The Congress shall have power to enforce this article by appropriate legislation.

The Fifteenth Amendment was the most controversial of the Civil War Amendments, both for what it did and did not do. Although the adoption of the Thirteenth and Fourteenth Amendments made clear that blacks could not be returned to their pre–Civil War slavery, enthusiasm for a constitutional right of black suffrage, even among the northern states, was another matter. On the one hand, the extension of voting rights to blacks was the most dramatic outcome of the Civil War. The former Confederate states had to ratify the Fifteenth Amendment as a condition for readmission into the Union. On the other hand, the rejection of proposed language forbidding discrimination on the basis of property ownership, education, or religious belief gave states the power to regulate the vote as they wished. And, with the collapse of Reconstruction after the 1876 election, southern states implemented laws created by this opening with full force, successfully crippling black voter registration for generations to come in the region where most African Americans lived. Full enfranchisement for African Americans would not arrive until the passage of the Voting Rights Act of 1965, almost one hundred years after the ratification of the Fifteenth Amendment.

The Fifteenth Amendment also divided woman's rights organizations that had campaigned on behalf of abolition and black enfranchisement. Feminists such as Elizabeth Cady Stanton and Susan B. Anthony were furious over the exclusion of women from the Fifteenth Amendment and opposed its ratification, while others, such as Lucy Stone, were willing to support black voting rights at the expense of woman suffrage, leaving that battle for another day. The Supreme Court sided with those who opposed female enfranchisement, ruling in *Minor* v. *Happersett* (1875) that the Fourteenth Amendment did not recognize among the privileges and immunities of American citizenship a constitutional right to vote.

AMENDMENT XVI
(Ratified on February 3, 1913)

The Congress shall have power to lay and collect taxes on incomes, from whatever source derived, without apportionment among the several States, and without regard to any census or enumeration.

The Sixteenth Amendment was a response to the Supreme Court's sharply divided ruling in *Pollock* v. *Farmers' Loan & Trust Co.* (1895), which struck down the Income Tax Act of 1894 as unconstitutional. The Court, by a 5–4 margin, held that the law violated Article I, section 9, which prevented Congress from enacting a direct tax (on individuals) unless in proportion to the U.S. Census. In some ways, this was a curious holding, since the Court had permitted Congress to enact a direct tax on individuals during the Civil War. Between the *Pollock* decision and the enactment of the Sixteenth Amendment, the Court approved of taxes levied on corporations, as such taxes were not really taxes but "excises" levied on "incidents of ownership."

Anti-tax groups have claimed the Sixteenth Amendment was never properly ratified and is thus unconstitutional. The federal courts have rejected that view and have sanctioned and fined individuals who have brought such frivolous challenges to court.

AMENDMENT XVII
(Ratified on April 8, 1913)

The Senate of the United States shall be composed of two Senators from each State, elected by the people thereof, for six years; and each Senator shall have one vote. The electors in each State shall have the qualifications requisite for electors of the most numerous branch of the State legislatures.

When vacancies happen in the representation of any State in the Senate, the executive authority of such State shall issue writs of election to fill such vacancies: Provided, That the legislature of any State may empower the executive thereof to make temporary appointments until the people fill the vacancies by election as the legislature may direct.

This amendment shall not be so construed as to affect the election or term of any Senator chosen before it becomes valid as part of the Constitution.

The Seventeenth Amendment repealed the language in Article I, section 3, of the original Constitution, which called for the election of U.S. senators by state legislatures. This method had its roots in the selection of delegates to the Constitutional Convention, who were chosen by the state legislatures. It was also the preferred method of the Framers, who believed that having state legislatures elect senators would strengthen the relationship between the states and the national government, and also contribute to the stability of Congress by removing popular electoral pressure from the upper chamber.

Dissatisfaction set in with this method during the period leading up to the Civil War, especially by the 1850s. Indiana, for example, deeply divided between Union supporters in the northern part of the state and

Confederate sympathizers in the southern part, could not agree on the selection of senators and was without representation for two years. After the Civil War, numerous Senate elections were tainted by corruption, and many more resulted in ties that prevented seating senators in a timely fashion. In 1899, Delaware's election was so mired in controversy that it did not have representation in the Senate for four years.

The ratification of the Seventeenth Amendment was the result of almost two decades of persistent efforts at reform. By 1912, twenty-nine states had changed their election laws to require the popular election of senators. In the years before that, constitutional amendments were introduced on a regular basis calling for the popular election of senators. Although many powerful legislators entrenched in the Senate resisted such change, the tide of reform, now aided by journalists and scholars sympathetic to the cause, proved too powerful to withstand. One year after the Seventeenth Amendment was sent to the states for ratification, all members of the Senate were elected by the popular vote.

AMENDMENT XVIII
(Ratified on January 16, 1919)

Section 1.

After one year from the ratification of this article the manufacture, sale, or transportation of intoxicating liquors within, the importation thereof into, or the exportation thereof from the United States and all territory subject to the jurisdiction thereof for beverage purposes is hereby prohibited.

Section 2.

The Congress and the several States shall have concurrent power to enforce this article by appropriate legislation.

Section 3.

This article shall be inoperative unless it shall have been ratified as an amendment to the Constitution by the legislatures of the several States, as provided in the Constitution, within seven years from the date of the submission hereof to the States by the Congress.

The Eighteenth Amendment was the end result of a crusade against the consumption of alcoholic beverages than began during the early nineteenth century. A combination of Christian organizations emboldened by the second Great Awakening and women's groups, who believed alcohol contributed greatly to domestic violence and poverty, campaigned to abolish the manufacture, sale, and use of alcoholic beverages in the United States. Their campaign was moderately successful in the pre–Civil War era. By 1855, thirteen states had banned the sale of "intoxicating" beverages. By the end of the Civil War, however, ten states had repealed their prohibition laws.

Another wave of anti-alcohol campaigning soon emerged, however, as the Women's Christian Temperance Union, founded in 1874 and 250,000 strong by 1911, and the Anti-Saloon League, founded in 1913, pressed the case for Prohibition. Among the arguments offered by supporters of Prohibition were that the cereal grains used in the manufacture of beer and liquor diverted valuable resources from food supplies and that the malaise of drunkenness sapped the strength of manufacturing production at home and the conduct of America's soldiers in World War I. Underneath the formal case for Prohibition was a considerable anti-immigrant sentiment, as many Prohibitionists considered the waves of Italian, Irish, Poles, and German immigrants unduly dependent on alcohol.

In 1919, Congress passed the Eighteenth Amendment over President Woodrow Wilson's veto. That same year, Congress passed the Volstead Act, which implemented Prohibition and authorized law enforcement to target illegal shipments of alcohol into the United States (mostly from Canada, which, ironically, also mandated Prohibition in most of its provinces during this time) as well as alcoholic beverages illegally manufactured in the United States. Evidence remains inconclusive over just how successful the Eighteenth Amendment was in reducing alcohol consumption in the United States. More certain was the billion-dollar windfall that Prohibition created for organized crime, as well as small-time smugglers and bootleggers.

AMENDMENT XIX
(Ratified on August 18, 1920)

The right of citizens of the United States to vote shall not be denied or abridged by the United States or by any State on account of sex.

Congress shall have power to enforce this article by appropriate legislation.

The two major woman's rights organizations of the nineteenth century most active in the battle for female enfranchisement were the National Woman Suffrage Association (NWSA) and the American Woman Suffrage Association (AWSA). NWSA campaigned for a constitutional amendment modeled on the Fifteenth Amendment, which had secured African American voting rights, while AWSA preferred to pursue women's voting rights through state-level legislative initiatives. In 1890, the two organizations combined to form the National American Woman Suffrage Association. By 1919, the NAWSA, the newer, more radical National Woman's Party, and other activists had secured congressional passage of the Nineteenth Amendment by a broad margin. It was ratified by the states just over a year later.

The Nineteenth Amendment, however, did not free black women from the voting restrictions that southern states placed in the way of African Americans. They and other minorities were not protected from such restrictions until the passage of the Voting Rights Act of 1965.

AMENDMENT XX
(Ratified on February 6, 1933)

Section 1.

The terms of the President and Vice President shall end at noon on the 20th day of January, and the terms of Senators and Representatives at noon on the 3d day of January, of the years in which such terms would have ended if this article had not been ratified; and the terms of their successors shall then begin.

Section 2.

The Congress shall assemble at least once in every year, and such meeting shall begin at noon on the 3d day of January, unless they shall by law appoint a different day.

Section 3.

If, at the time fixed for the beginning of the term of the President, the President elect shall have died, the Vice President elect shall become President. If a President shall not have been chosen before the time fixed for the beginning of his term, or if the President elect shall have failed to qualify, then the Vice President elect shall act as President until a President shall have qualified; and the Congress may by law provide for the case wherein neither a President elect nor a Vice President elect shall have qualified, declaring who shall then act as President, or the manner in which one who is to act shall be selected, and such person shall act accordingly until a President or Vice President shall have qualified.

Section 4.

The Congress may by law provide for the case of the death of any of the persons from whom the House of Representatives may choose a President whenever the rights of choice shall have devolved upon them, and for the case of the death of any of the persons from whom the Senate may choose a Vice President whenever the right of choice shall have devolved upon them.

Section 5.

Sections 1 and 2 shall take effect on the 15th day of October following the ratification of this article.

Section 6.

This article shall be inoperative unless it shall have been ratified as an amendment to the Constitution by the legislatures of three-fourths of the several States within seven years from the date of its submission.

The Twentieth Amendment is often called the lame duck amendment because its fundamental purpose was to shorten the time between the November elections, particularly in a presidential election year, and the starting date of the new presidential term and the commencement of the new congressional session. The amendment modified section 1 of the Twelfth Amendment by moving the beginning of the annual legislative session from March 4 to January 3. This change meant that the newly elected Congress would decide any presidential election thrown into the House of Representatives. It also eliminated the possibility that the nation would have to endure two additional months without a chief executive.

The Twentieth Amendment also modified Article I of the Constitution by placing a fixed time—noon—to begin the congressional session.

AMENDMENT XXI
(Ratified on December 5, 1933)

Section 1.

The eighteenth article of amendment to the Constitution of the United States is hereby repealed.

Section 2.

The transportation or importation into any State, Territory, or possession of the United States for delivery or use therein of intoxicating liquors, in violation of the laws thereof, is hereby prohibited.

Section 3.

This article shall be inoperative unless it shall have been ratified as an amendment to the Constitution by conventions in the several States, as provided in the Constitution, within seven years from the date of the submission hereof to the States by the Congress.

The Twenty-First Amendment repealed the Eighteenth Amendment, which was the first and last time that a constitutional amendment has been repealed. The Twenty-First Amendment is also the only amendment to the Constitution approved by state ratifying conventions rather than a popular vote.

By the late 1920s, Americans had tired of Prohibition, and the arrival of the Great Depression in 1929 did nothing to lift their spirits. Few public officials, well aware of the extensive criminal enterprises that had grown up around Prohibition and had made a mockery of the practice, attempted to defend Prohibition as a success. Indeed, Franklin D. Roosevelt, in his initial bid for the presidency in 1932, made the repeal of Prohibition a campaign promise. In January 1933, Congress amended the Volstead Act to permit the sale of alcoholic beverages with an alcohol content of 3.2 percent. The ratification of the Twenty-First Amendment in December returned absolute control of the regulation of alcohol to the states. States are now free to regulate alcohol as they see fit. They may, for example, limit the quantity and type of alcohol sold to consumers, or ban alcohol sales completely. The Supreme Court, in *South Carolina* v. *Dole* (1984), ruled that Congress may require the states to set a certain age for the consumption of alcohol in return for participation in a federal program without violating the Twenty-First Amendment.

AMENDMENT XXII
(Ratified on February 27, 1951)

Section 1.

No person shall be elected to the office of the President more than twice, and no person who has held the office of President, or acted as President, for more than two years of a term to which some other person was elected President shall be elected to the office of the President more than once. But this Article shall not apply to any person holding the office of President when this Article was proposed by the Congress, and shall not prevent any person who may be holding the office of President, or acting as President, during the term within which this Article becomes operative from holding the office of President or acting as President during the remainder of such term.

Section 2.

This article shall be inoperative unless it shall have been ratified as an amendment to the Constitution by the legislatures of three-fourths of the several States within seven years from the date of its submission to the States by the Congress.

Thomas Jefferson, who served as the third president of the United States, was the first person of public stature to suggest a constitutional provision limiting presidential terms. "If some termination to the services of the chief Magistrate be not fixed by the Constitution," said Jefferson, "or supplied by practice, his office, nominally four years, will in fact become for life." Until Ulysses S. Grant's unsuccessful attempt to secure his party's nomination to a third term, no other president attempted to extend the two-term limit that had operated in principle. Theodore Roosevelt, having ascended to the presidency after the assassination of William McKinley in 1901, was elected to his second term in 1904. He then sat out a term, and then ran against Woodrow Wilson in the 1912 election and lost.

The first president to serve more than two terms was Franklin D. Roosevelt, and it was his success that inspired the enactment of the Twenty-Second Amendment. In 1946, Republicans took control of Congress for the first time in sixteen years and were determined to guard against such future Democratic dynasties. A year later, Congress, in one of the most party-line votes in the history of the amending process, approved the Twenty-Second Amendment. Every Republican member of the House and Senate who voted on the amendment voted for it. The remaining votes came almost exclusively from southern Democrats, whose relationship with Roosevelt was never more than a marriage of convenience. Ironically, some Republicans began to call for the repeal of the Twenty-Second Amendment toward the end of popular Republican Dwight D. Eisenhower's second term in 1956. A similar movement emerged in the late 1980s toward the end of Republican Ronald Reagan's second term. The American public at large, however, has shown little enthusiasm for repealing the Twenty-Second Amendment.

AMENDMENT XXIII
(Ratified on March 29, 1961)

Section 1.

The District constituting the seat of Government of the United States shall appoint in such manner as the Congress may direct:

A number of electors of President and Vice President equal to the whole number of Senators and Representatives in Congress to which the District would be entitled if it were a State, but in no event more than the least populous State; they shall be in addition to those appointed by the States, but they shall be considered, for the purposes of the election of President and Vice President, to be electors appointed by a State; and they shall meet in the District and perform such duties as provided by the twelfth article of amendment.

Section 2.

The Congress shall have power to enforce this article by appropriate legislation.

Article II, section 2, of the Constitution limits participation in presidential elections to citizens who reside in the states. The Twenty-Third Amendment amended this provision to include residents of the District of Columbia. Since the District was envisioned as the seat of the national government with a transient population, the Constitution afforded no right of representation to its residents in Congress. By the time the Twenty-Third Amendment was ratified, the District had a greater population than twelve states.

In 1978, Congress introduced a constitutional amendment to give the District of Columbia representation in the House and the Senate. By 1985, the ratification period for the amendment expired without the necessary three-fourths approval from the states.

AMENDMENT XXIV
(Ratified on January 23, 1964)

Section 1.

The right of citizens of the United States to vote in any primary or other election for President or Vice President, for electors for President or Vice President, or for Senator or Representative in Congress, shall not be denied or abridged by the United States or any State by reason of failure to pay any poll tax or other tax.

Section 2.

The Congress shall have power to enforce this article by appropriate legislation.

The Twenty-Fourth Amendment continued the work of the Fifteenth Amendment. By abolishing the poll tax, the amendment eliminated one of the most popular tools used by voting registrars to prevent most African Americans and other minorities from taking part in the electoral process. Property ownership and literacy tests as conditions of the franchise extended back to the colonial era and were not particular to any region of the United States. But, the poll tax was a southern invention, coming after the enactment of the Fifteenth Amendment. By the fall of Reconstruction in 1877, eleven southern states had enacted poll tax laws. The poll tax was disproportionately enforced against poor African American voters and, in some cases, poor whites.

Congress had begun to debate a constitutional amendment to abolish the poll tax as far back as 1939, but it took the momentum of the civil rights movement to move this process forward. Shortly after the ratification of the Twenty-Fourth Amendment, Congress enacted the Civil Rights Act of 1964, the most sweeping and effective federal civil rights law to date. By the time of ratification of the Twenty-Fourth Amendment, only five states had poll taxes on their books. Spurred on by the spirit of the times, Congress enacted the Voting Rights Act of 1965, which enforced the poll tax ban of the Twenty-Fourth Amendment and also abolished literacy tests, property qualifications, and other obstacles to voter registration. In 1966, in *Harper* v. *Board of Elections*, the Supreme Court rejected a constitutional challenge to the historic voting rights law.

AMENDMENT XXV
(Ratified on February 10, 1967)

Section 1.

In case of the removal of the President from office or of his death or resignation, the Vice President shall become President.

Section 2.

Whenever there is a vacancy in the office of the Vice President, the President shall nominate a Vice President who shall take office upon confirmation by a majority vote of both Houses of Congress.

Section 3.

Whenever the President transmits to the President pro tempore of the Senate and the Speaker of the House of Representatives his written declaration that he is unable to discharge the powers and duties of his office, and until he transmits to them a written declaration to the contrary, such powers and duties shall be discharged by the Vice President as Acting President.

Section 4.

Whenever the Vice President and a majority of either the principal officers of the executive departments or of such other body as Congress may by law provide, transmit to the President pro tempore of the Senate and the Speaker of the House of Representatives their written declaration that the President is unable to discharge the powers and duties of his office, the Vice President shall immediately assume the powers and duties of the office as Acting President.

Thereafter, when the President transmits to the President pro tempore of the Senate and the Speaker of the House of Representatives his written declaration that no inability exists, he shall resume the powers and duties of his office unless the Vice President and a majority of either the principal officers of the executive department or of such other body as Congress may by law provide, transmit within four days to the President pro tempore of the Senate and the Speaker of the House of Representatives their written declaration that the President is unable to discharge the powers and duties of his office. Thereupon Congress shall decide the issue, assembling within forty-eight hours for that purpose if not in session. If the Congress, within twenty-one days after receipt of the latter written declaration, or, if Congress is not in session, within twenty-one days after Congress is required to assemble, determines by two-thirds vote of both Houses that the President is unable to discharge the powers and duties of his office, the Vice President shall continue to discharge the same as Acting President; otherwise, the President shall resume the powers and duties of his office.

Several tragedies to the men who occupied the offices of president and vice president and the lack of constitutional clarity about the path of succession in event of presidential and vice presidential disability spurred the enactment of the Twenty-Fifth Amendment.

Whether the vice president was merely an acting president or assumed the permanent powers of the office for the remainder of the term upon the death of a president was answered in 1841 when John Tyler became president upon the death of William Henry Harrison, who died only a month after his inauguration. Seven more presidents died in office before the enactment of the Twenty-Fifth Amendment,

and in each case the vice president assumed the presidency without controversy. What this amendment answered that the original Constitution did not was the method of vice presidential succession. The vice presidency often went unfilled for months at a time as the result of constitutional ambiguity. Since the enactment of the amendment, there have been two occasions when the president appointed a vice president. Both took place during the second term of President Richard M. Nixon. For the first time in United States history, the nation witnessed a presidential term served out by two men, President Gerald R. Ford and Vice President Nelson A. Rockefeller, neither of whom had been elected to the position.

The Twenty-Fifth Amendment also settled the path of succession in the event of presidential disability. This provision of the amendment was prompted by the memories of James Garfield lying in a coma for eighty days after being struck by an assassin's bullet and Woodrow Wilson's bedridden state for the last eighteen months of his term after a stroke. The first president to invoke the disability provision of the Twenty-Fifth Amendment was Ronald Reagan, who made Vice President George Bush acting president for eight hours while he underwent surgery. The only other time a president invoked this provision came in 2002, when George W. Bush underwent minor surgery and transferred the powers of his office to Vice President Dick Cheney.

The provision authorizing the vice president, in consultation with Congress and members of the Cabinet, to declare the president disabled has never been invoked.

AMENDMENT XXVI
(Ratified on July 1, 1971)

Section 1.

The right of citizens of the United States, who are eighteen years of age or older, to vote shall not be denied or abridged by the United States or by any State on account of age.

Section 2.

The Congress shall have power to enforce this article by appropriate legislation.

The Twenty-Sixth Amendment was a direct response to the unpopularity of the Vietnam War and was spurred by calls to lower the voting age to eighteen so that draft-eligible men could voice their opinion on the war through the ballot box. In 1970, Congress had amended

the Voting Rights Act of 1965 to lower the voting age to eighteen in all national, state, and local elections. Many states resisted compliance, claiming that Congress, while having the power to establish the voting age in national elections, had no such authority in state and local elections. In *Oregon* v. *Mitchell* (1970), the Supreme Court agreed with that view. Congress responded by drafting the Twenty-Sixth Amendment, and the states ratified it quickly and without controversy.

AMENDMENT XXVII
(Ratified on May 7, 1992)

No law, varying the compensation for the services of the Senators and Representatives shall take effect until an election of Representatives shall have intervened.

The Twenty-Seventh Amendment originally was introduced in 1789 during the 1st Congress as one of the original twelve amendments to the Constitution. Only six of the necessary eleven (of thirteen) states had ratified the amendment by 1791. As more states came into the union, the prospect of the amendment's passage only dwindled. No additional state ratified the amendment until 1873, when Ohio approved its addition to the Constitution.

Sometime in the early 1980s, a University of Texas student discovered the amendment and launched an intensive effort to bring it to the public's attention for ratification. The amendment's core purpose, preventing members of Congress from raising their salaries during the terms in which they served, meshed well with another grassroots movement that began during this time, the campaign to impose term limits on members of the House and Senate. Nothing in the nation's constitutional or statutory law prohibited the resurrection of the Twenty-Seventh Amendment for voter approval. In 1939, the Supreme Court had ruled in *Coleman* v. *Miller* that amendments could remain indefinitely before the public unless Congress had set a specific time limit on the ratification process. By 1992, the amendment had received the necessary three-fourths approval of the states, making it the last successful effort to amend the Constitution. The Twenty-Seventh Amendment has not, however, barred Congress from increasing its compensation through annual cost-of-living-adjustments.

3

Federalism

On August 26, 2005, New Orleans, Louisiana, and other low-lying Gulf Coast areas in Mississippi and Alabama braced for a Category 5 hurricane named Katrina. In preparation for the coming storm, Louisiana Governor Kathleen Blanco and Mississippi Governor Haley Barbour declared states of emergency in their jurisdictions and asked President George W. Bush to follow suit at the federal level. The White House responded by authorizing the Federal Emergency Management Agency (FEMA) "to identify, mobilize, and provide at its discretion, equipment and resources necessary to alleviate the impacts of the emergency."[1]

On Sunday, August 28, Mayor Ray Nagin issued the first-ever mandatory evacuation of New Orleans amid warnings that the levees, built by the U.S. Army Corps of Engineers, might not hold, thereby flooding the city. As massive evacuations of the coast occurred, Marty Bahamonde, a Boston-based FEMA official, was sent to New Orleans to be the eyes and ears of FEMA Director Michael Brown. The Louisiana National Guard asked FEMA for 700 buses to help evacuate the poor who had no other method of transportation; FEMA sent 100.

■ **Residents of the Gulf Coast are no strangers to natural disaster.** At left, a scene in Louisiana after the Great Mississippi Flood of 1927. At right, Governor Kathleen Blanco, President George W. Bush, and Mayor Ray Nagin survey damage in New Orleans in the wake of Hurricane Katrina.

When the storm hit land on August 29 as a Category 3 storm, it looked as if damages might not be as bad as predicted. Still, thousands of largely poor and elderly New Orleans citizens were forced to take refuge in the Superdome and the Convention Center. As feared, the levees gave way, flooding entire sections of New Orleans and basically destroying one of the poorest areas of the city. Many residents were stranded in their homes, some on their rooftops.

The situation quickly deteriorated when a large proportion of New Orleans police failed to show up for work and Mayor Nagin and Governor Blanco seemed unable to agree on strategies to deal with the colossal disaster. Both, however, pleaded for more federal assistance, but their pleas fell on deaf ears. Various levels of government appeared either paralyzed or unaware of the disaster in Louisiana and other coastal areas. One government official who was not able to ignore the situation was FEMA agent Bahamonde, who sent increasingly desperate e-mails back to the FEMA director. Using his Blackberry, Bahamonde, who was in the Superdome with thousands of evacuees, told Brown: "Sir, I know that you know the situation is past critical .... Hotels are kicking people out, thousands gathering in the streets with no food or water .... Estimates are that many will die within hours. We are out of food and running out of water." Still, assistance did not come quickly.

★ **WHAT SHOULD I KNOW ABOUT . . .**

■ the roots of the federal system and the constitutional allocation of governmental powers?

■ federalism and the Marshall Court?

■ dual federalism before and after the Civil War?

■ cooperative federalism during the New Deal and the growth of national government?

■ New Federalism and returning power to the states?

■ Supreme Court rulings related to a new judicial federalism?

By Thursday, September 1, New Orleans Homeland Security Director Terry Ebbert said, "This is a national disgrace. FEMA has been here three days yet there is not command and control." Mayor Nagin sent out an SOS to FEMA and was told that Brown had heard "no reports of unrest."

With many local and state employees without homes or ways to get to work, and with nearly all forms of communication failing, hundreds died in New Orleans. The official response made clear that there was no effective coordination between the local, state, and national governments, nor any real agreement as to which level of government was responsible for what in this tragedy. [2]

TO LEARN MORE—
—TO DO MORE
Find out how you can get involved with hurricane rebuilding efforts by visiting the Hands on Network at www.handsonnetwork.org/hurricane-relief.

This breakdown in intergovernmental communications, as well as other difficulties in coordinating post-Katrina recovery efforts, led local, state, and national governments to reevaluate their emergency response and disaster relief plans. Citizens, too, voiced their dissatisfaction with the way the various governments responded to Hurricane Katrina. Governor Blanco, for example, chose not to run for a second term out of fear that she would not win.

Almost exactly three years after Katrina hit the Gulf Coast, the reformed emergency response plans throughout the Gulf region, as well as the new levees around the city of New Orleans constructed by the Army Corps of Engineers were tested by a Category 2 hurricane named Gustav. Much to the pleasant surprise of citizens and observers alike, the lessons offered by Katrina appeared to have been learned.

Local, state, and national governments had prepared for a worst-case scenario, establishing a clear chain of command and cooperating with one another to assure the safety of the citizens. Evacuations throughout Texas, Louisiana, Alabama, and Mississippi went smoothly.

President Bush, who had faced heavy criticism for his administration's handling of Hurricane Katrina, summarized the various governments' response to Hurricane Gustav by saying, "The coordination on this storm [was] a lot better than during Katrina. It was clearly a spirit of sharing assets, of listening to somebody's problems and saying, "How can we best address them?" [3]

From its very beginning, the challenge for the United States of America was to preserve the traditional independence and rights of the states while establishing an effective national government. In *Federalist No. 51*, James Madison highlighted the unique structure of governmental powers created by the Framers: "The power surrendered by the people is first divided between two distinct governments, and then . . . subdivided among distinct and separate departments. Hence, a double security arises to the rights of the people."

The Framers, fearing tyranny, divided powers between the state and the national governments. At each level, moreover, powers were divided among executive, legislative, and judicial branches. The people are the ultimate source of power for the national and state governments.

Although most of the delegates to the Constitutional Convention favored a strong federal government, they knew that some compromise about the distribution of powers would be necessary. Some of the Framers wanted to continue with the confederate form of government defined in the Articles of Confederation; others wanted a more centralized system, similar to that of Great Britain. Their solution was to create the world's first federal system (although the word "federal" never appears in the U.S. Constitution). The thirteen sovereign or independent states were bound together under one national government.

Today, the Constitution ultimately binds more than 89,000 different governments at the national, state, and local levels (To learn more about governments in the United States, see Figure 3.1). The Constitution lays out the duties, obligations, and powers of each of these units. Throughout history, however, this relationship has been reshaped continually by crises, historical evolution, public expectations, and judicial interpretation. All these forces have had tremendous influence on who makes policy decisions and how these decisions get made, as is underscored in our opening vignette.

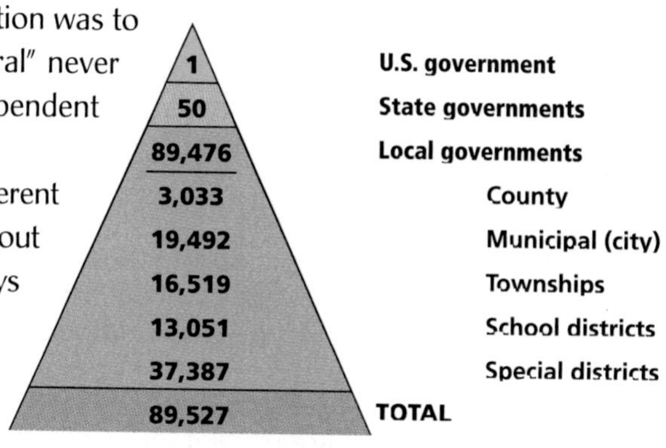

1	U.S. government
50	State governments
89,476	Local governments
3,033	County
19,492	Municipal (city)
16,519	Townships
13,051	School districts
37,387	Special districts
89,527	TOTAL

FIGURE 3.1 Number of Governments in the United States

Source: U.S. Census Bureau, www.census.gov/govs/cog/GovOrgTab033ss.html

Issues involving the distribution of power between the national government and the states affect you on a daily basis. You do not, for example, need a passport to go from Texas to Oklahoma. There is but one national currency and a national minimum wage. But, many differences exist among the laws of the various states. The age at which you may marry is a state issue, as are laws governing divorce, child custody, and most criminal laws, including how—or if—the death penalty is implemented. Other policies or programs, such as air traffic regulation, are solely within the province of the national government.[3] In areas such as education, however, the national and state governments work together in a system of shared powers.

To understand the current relationship between the states and the federal government and to better grasp some of the issues that arise from this constantly changing relationship, in this chapter, we will examine the following topics:

★ First, we will look at *the roots of the federal system and the constitutional allocation of governmental powers* created by the Framers.

★ Second, we will explore the relationship between *federalism and the Marshall Court.*

★ Third, we will examine the development of *dual federalism before and after the Civil War.*

★ Fourth, we will analyze *cooperative federalism and the growth of national government.*

★ Fifth, we will discuss *New Federalism,* the movement to *return power to the states.*

★ Finally, we will examine the Supreme Court's efforts toward *reform and a new judicial federalism.*

Roots of the Federal System and the Constitutional Allocation of Governmental Powers

As discussed in chapter 2, the United States was the first country to adopt a **federal system** of government. This system of government, where the national government

federal system
System of government where the national government and state governments share power, derive all authority from the people, and the powers of the government are specified in a Constitution.

and state governments derive all authority from the people, was designed to remedy many of the problems experienced under the Articles of Confederation. Under the Articles, the United States was governed as a **confederation** where the national government derived all of its powers from the states. This led to a weak national government that was often unable to respond to even small crises, such as Shays's Rebellion.

Thinking Globally

Federal and Unitary Systems

The United States, Germany, Russia, Nigeria, and Brazil are just some of the countries that have a federal system of government. Most of the world's nations, including Great Britain, France, China, Japan, and Iran, have unitary systems of power with authority concentrated in the central government. Although federal states are relatively few in number, they tend to be large and politically important.

- What factors encourage the adoption of a federal system rather than a unitary one?
- What features do the federal countries listed have in common? How are they different?

The new system of government also had to be different from the **unitary system** found in Great Britain, where the local and regional governments derived all their power from a strong national government. (To learn more about these forms of government, see Figure 3.2.) Having been under the rule of English kings, whom they considered tyrants, the Framers feared centralizing power in one government or institution. Therefore, they made both the state and the federal government accountable to the people at large. While the governments shared some powers, such as the ability to tax, each government was supreme in some spheres, as described in the following section.

The federal system as conceived by the Framers has proven tremendously effective. Since the creation of the U.S. system, many other nations, including Canada (1867), Mexico (1917), and Russia (1993), have adopted federal systems in their constitutions.

confederation
Type of government where the national government derives its powers from the states; a league of independent states.

unitary system
System of government where the local and regional governments derive all authority from a strong national government.

enumerated powers
Specific powers granted to Congress under Article I, section 8, of the Constitution; these powers include taxation, coinage of money, regulation of commerce, and the authority to provide for a national defense.

necessary and proper clause
The final paragraph of Article I, section 8, of the Constitution, which gives Congress the authority to pass all laws "necessary and proper" to carry out the enumerated powers specified in the Constitution; also called the elastic clause.

implied powers
Powers derived from enumerated powers and the necessary and proper clause. These powers are not stated specifically but are considered to be reasonably implied through the exercise of delegated powers.

supremacy clause
Portion of Article VI of the Constitution mandating that national law is supreme to (that is, supersedes) all other laws passed by the states or by any other subdivision of government.

National Powers Under the Constitution

Chief among the exclusive powers of the national government are the authorities to coin money, conduct foreign relations, provide for an army and navy, declare war, and establish a national court system. All of these powers set out in Article I, section 8, of the Constitution are called **enumerated powers**. Article I, section 8, also contains the **necessary and proper clause** (also called the elastic clause), which gives Congress the authority to enact any laws "necessary and proper" for carrying out any of its enumerated powers. These powers derived from enumerated powers and the necessary and proper clause are known as **implied powers.**

The federal government's right to tax was also clearly set out in the Constitution. The Framers wanted to avoid the financial problems that the national government experienced under the Articles of Confederation. If the new national government was to be strong, its power to raise revenue had to be unquestionable. Although the new national government had no power under the Constitution to levy a national income tax, that was changed by the passage of the Sixteenth Amendment in 1913. Eventually, as discussed later in this chapter, this new taxing power became a powerful catalyst for further expansion of the national government.

Article VI of the federal Constitution underscores the notion that the national government is to be supreme in situations of conflict between state and national law. It declares that the U.S. Constitution, the laws of the United States, and its treaties, are to be "the supreme Law of the Land; and the Judges in every State shall be bound thereby."

In spite of this explicit language, the meaning of what is called the **supremacy clause** has been subject to continuous judicial interpretation. In 1920, for example, Missouri sought to prevent a U.S. game warden from enforcing the Migratory Bird Treaty Act of 1918, which prohibited the killing or capturing of many species of birds as they made their annual migration across the international border from Canada to parts of the United States.[4] Missouri argued that the Tenth Amendment, which reserved a state's powers to legislate for the general welfare of its citizens, allowed Missouri to regulate hunting. But, the Court ruled that since the treaty was legal, it must be considered the supreme law of the land. (To learn more about national

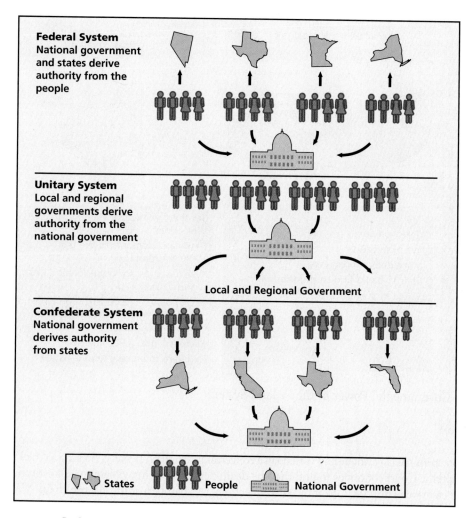

FIGURE 3.2 The Federal, Unitary, and Confederate Systems of Government
The source of governmental authority and power differs dramatically in various systems of government.

supremacy, see the discussion of *McCulloch* v. *Maryland* [1819] that follows later in the chapter.)

State Powers Under the Constitution

Because states had all the power at the time the Constitution was written, the Framers felt no need, as they did for the new national government, to list and restate the powers of the states. Article I, however, allows states to set the "Times, Places, and Manner, for holding elections for senators and representatives." Article II requires that each state appoint electors to vote for president. And, Article IV provides each state a "Republican Form of Government," meaning one that represents the citizens of the state.

It was not until the **Tenth Amendment,** the final part of the Bill of Rights, that the states' powers were described in greater detail: "The powers not delegated to the United States by the Constitution, nor prohibited by it to the States, are reserved to the States respectively, or to the people." These powers, often called the states' **reserve** or **police powers,** include the ability to legislate for the public health, safety, and morals of their citizens. Today, the states' rights to legislate under their police powers are used as the rationale for many states' restrictions on abortion. Similarly, some states now fund stem-cell research, in sharp contrast to the federal government. Police powers are also the basis for

Comparing Federal and Unitary Systems

Tenth Amendment
The final part of the Bill of Rights that defines the basic principle of American federalism in stating: "The powers not delegated to the United States by the Constitution, nor prohibited by it to the States, are reserved to the States respectively, or to the people."

reserve (or police) powers
Powers reserved to the states by the Tenth Amendment that lie at the foundation of a state's right to legislate for the public health and welfare of its citizens.

NATIONAL POWERS (ENUMERATED POWERS)	CONCURRENT POWERS	STATE POWERS (RESERVE POWERS)
Coin money	Tax	Set time, place, and manner of elections
Conduct foreign relations	Borrow money	Ratify amendments to the U.S. Constitution
Regulate commerce with foreign nations and among the states	Establish courts	Take measures for public health, safety, and morals
Provide for an army and a navy	Make and enforce laws	Exert powers the Constitution does not delegate to the national government or prohibit the states from using
Declare and conduct war	Charter banks and corporations	Establish local governments
Establish a national court system	Spend money for the general welfare	Regulate commerce within a state
Make laws necessary and proper to carry out the foregoing powers		

FIGURE 3.3 The Distribution of Governmental Power in the Federal System

state criminal laws, including varied laws concerning the death penalty. As long as the U.S. Supreme Court continues to find that the death penalty does not violate the Constitution, the states may impose it, be it by lethal injection, gas chamber, or the electric chair.

Concurrent Powers Under the Constitution

concurrent powers
Authority possessed by both the state and national governments that may be exercised concurrently as long as that power is not exclusively within the scope of national power or in conflict with national law.

As revealed in Figure 3.3, national and state powers overlap. The area where the systems overlap represents **concurrent powers**—powers shared by the national and state governments. States already had the power to tax; the Constitution extended this power to the national government as well. Other important concurrent powers include the right to borrow money, establish courts, and make and enforce laws necessary to carry out these powers.

Powers Denied Under the Constitution

bill of attainder
A law declaring an act illegal without a judicial trial.

Some powers are explicitly denied to the national government or the states under Article I of the Constitution. In keeping with the Framers' desire to forge a national economy, for example, states are prohibited from entering treaties, coining money, or impairing obligation of contracts. States also are prohibited from entering into compacts with other states without express congressional approval. In a similar vein, Congress is barred from favoring one state over another in regulating commerce, and it cannot lay duties on items exported from any state.

State governments (as well as the national government) are denied the authority to take arbitrary actions affecting constitutional rights and liberties. Neither national nor state governments may pass a **bill of attainder,** a law declaring an act illegal

Photo courtesy: Judy Gelles/Stock Boston

How does federalism affect our everyday lives? Here, endangered species are protected by state and federal law.

without a judicial trial. The Constitution also bars the national and state governments from passing *ex post facto* **laws,** laws that make an act punishable as a crime even if the action was legal at the time it was committed. (To learn more about civil rights and liberties, see chapters 5 and 6.)

Relations Among the States

In addition to delineating the relationship of the states with the national government, the Constitution provides a mechanism for resolving interstate disputes and facilitating relations among states. To avoid any sense of favoritism, it provides that disputes between states be settled directly by the U.S. Supreme Court under its original jurisdiction as mandated by Article III of the Constitution (see chapter 10). Moreover, Article IV requires that each state give "Full Faith and Credit . . . to the public Acts, Records and judicial Proceedings of every other State." The **full faith and credit clause** ensures that judicial decrees and contracts made in one state will be binding and enforceable in another, thereby facilitating trade and other commercial relationships. Full faith and credit cases continue to make their way through the judicial system.

For example, a state's refusal to honor same-sex marriage contracts poses interesting constitutional questions. States can vary considerably on social issues. (To learn more about the full faith and credit clause, see The Living Constitution: Article IV, Section 1.)

Article IV also contains the **privileges and immunities clause**, guaranteeing that the citizens of each state are afforded the same rights as citizens of all other states. In addition, Article IV contains the **extradition clause**, which requires states to extradite, or return, criminals to states where they have been convicted or are to stand trial.

To facilitate relations among states, Article 1, section 10, clause 3, of the U.S. Constitution sets the legal foundation for interstate cooperation in the form of **interstate compacts**, contracts between states that carry the force of law. It reads, "No State shall, without the consent of Congress . . . enter into any Agreement or Compact with another state." Before 1920, interstate compacts were largely bistate compacts that addressed boundary disputes or acted to help two states accomplish some objective.

More than 200 interstate compacts exist today. While some deal with rudimentary items such as state boundaries, others help states carry out their policy objectives, and administrative functions. Although several bistate compacts still exist, other compacts have as many as fifty signatories.[5] The Drivers License Compact, for example, was signed by all fifty states to facilitate nationwide recognition of licenses issued in the respective states.

States today find that interstate compacts help them maintain control because compacts with other states allow for sharing resources, expertise, and responses that often are available more quickly than those from the federal government. The Emergency Management Assistance Compact, for example, allows states to cooperate and to share resources in the event of natural and man-made disasters. After the terrorist attacks on September 11, 2001, assistance to New York and Virginia came from a host of states surrounding the areas of the attacks. (To learn more about interstate compacts, see Table 3.1.)

Thinking Globally

Mexico's Federal System

Mexico has a federal structure of government, but in practice, the central government is much more powerful than its thirty-one state and numerous municipal governments, in part because it controls a significant proportion of the nation's total revenue. Over the past twenty years, Mexico has taken some steps to decentralize power. Movement toward a U.S.-style system of government, however, has been met with opposition from federal officials and state governors who remain resistant to the idea of sharing power with local governments.

- What steps could Mexico's central government take to empower local governments and foster local control?
- How might Mexico's central government encourage those in state government to view local governments and municipalities as partners and not as competitors?

ex post facto law
Law that makes an act punishable as a crime even if the action was legal at the time it was committed.

full faith and credit clause
Section of Article IV of the Constitution that ensures judicial decrees and contracts made in one state will be binding and enforceable in any other state.

privileges and immunities clause
Part of Article IV of the Constitution guaranteeing that the citizens of each state are afforded the same rights as citizens of all other states.

extradition clause
Part of Article IV of the Constitution that requires states to extradite, or return, criminals to states where they have been convicted or are to stand trial.

interstate compacts
Contracts between states that carry the force of law; generally now used as a tool to address multistate policy concerns.

TABLE 3.1 Compacts by the Numbers

Interstate compacts with 25 or more members	13
Least compact memberships by a state (HI & WI)	14
Most compact memberships by a state (NH & VA)	42
Average compact memberships by a state	27
Compacts developed prior to 1920	36
Compacts developed since 1920	150+
Interstate compacts currently in operation	200+

Source: Council of State Governments, http://www.csg.org.

The Living Constitution

Full Faith and Credit shall be given in each State to the public Acts, Records, and judicial Proceedings of every other State. And the Congress may by general Laws prescribe the Manner in which such Acts, Records, and Proceedings shall be proved, and the Effect thereof.

—ARTICLE IV, SECTION 1

The full faith and credit clause in Article IV of the Constitution rests on principles borrowed from international law that require one country to recognize contracts made in another country absent a compelling public policy reason to the contrary. In the United States, this principle applies to the relationship between the states.

The full faith and credit clause requires a state to recognize public acts and court proceedings of another state. In 1997, the Supreme Court ruled that the full faith and credit clause mandates that state courts always honor the judgments of other state courts, even if to do so is against state public policy or existing state laws. Failure to do so would allow a single state to "rule the world," said Supreme Court Justice Ruth Bader Ginsburg during oral argument.[a]

For the most part, interpretation of the full faith and credit clause has not been controversial. That is likely to change, however, as advocates of same-sex marriage have suggested that marriages of same-sex couples performed and legally sanctioned in one state must be recognized in another state, as is the case with heterosexual marriages.

In the mid 1990s, the possible legalization of marriage between same-sex couples threw numerous state legislatures and the U.S. Congress into a virtual frenzy. Twenty-five states passed laws in 1996 or 1997 to bar legal recognition of same-sex marriages. The U.S. Congress also got into the act by passing what is called the Defense of Marriage Act (DOMA), which President Bill Clinton signed into law in 1996. It was designed to undercut possible state recognition of same-sex marriages. This federal law permits states to disregard same-sex marriages even if they are legal in other states. The U.S. Constitution, however, doesn't give Congress the authority to create exceptions to the full faith and credit clause of the Constitution. With the legalization of same-sex marriages in Massachusetts in 2004 and in Connecticut in 2008, years of litigation are likely to ensue in states that refuse to recognize same-sex unions.

CRITICAL THINKING QUESTIONS

1. How should the Suprene Court rule on a challenge to a state's refusal to recognize a legally valid marriage from Connecticut or Massachusetts? Explain your reasoning.
2. Is a federal law such as DOMA consistent with the wishes of the Framers, who left regulation of marriage largely to the states?

[a]Oral argument by Thomas in *Baker* v. *General Motors Corporation*, 522 U.S. 222 (1998), noted in Linda Greenhouse, "Court Weighs Whether One State Must Obey Another's Courts," *New York Times* (October 16, 1997): A25.

Relations within the States: Local Government

The Constitution gives local governments, including counties, municipalities, townships, and school districts, no independent standing. Thus, their authority is not granted directly by the people but through state governments, which establish, or charter, administrative subdivisions to execute the duties of the state government on a smaller scale. To learn more about the relationship between state and local governments, see chapter 4.

Federalism and the Marshall Court

The nature of federalism, including its allocation of power between the national government and the states, has changed dramatically over the past two hundred years. Much of this change is due to the rulings of the U.S. Supreme Court, which has played a major role in defining the nature of the federal system because the distribution of power between the national and state governments is not clearly delineated in the Constitution. Few Supreme Courts have had a greater impact on the federal–state relationship than the one headed by Chief Justice John Marshall (1801–1835). In a series of decisions, he and his associates carved out an important role for the Court in defining the balance of power between the national government and the states. Two rulings in the early 1800s, *McCulloch* v. *Maryland* (1819) and *Gibbons* v. *Ogden* (1824), were particularly important.

Federalism and the Supreme Court

McCulloch v. *Maryland* (1819)

McCulloch* v. *Maryland (1819) was the first major Supreme Court decision to define the relationship between the national and state governments. In 1816, Congress chartered the Second Bank of the United States. (The charter of the First Bank had been allowed to expire.) In 1818, the Maryland state legislature levied a tax requiring all banks not chartered by Maryland (that is, the Second Bank of the United States) to: (1) buy stamped paper from the state on which the Second Bank's notes were to be issued; (2) pay the state $15,000 a year, or, (3) go out of business. James McCulloch, the head cashier of the Baltimore branch of the Bank of the United States, refused to pay the tax, and Maryland brought suit against him. After losing in a Maryland state court, McCulloch appealed the decision to the U.S. Supreme Court by order of the U.S. secretary of the treasury. In a unanimous opinion, the Court answered the two central questions that had been presented to it: Did Congress have the authority to charter a bank? If it did, could a state tax it?

Chief Justice John Marshall's answer to the first question—whether Congress had the right to establish a bank or another type of corporation—continues to stand as the classic exposition of the doctrine of implied powers and as a reaffirmation of the authority of a strong national government. Although the word "bank" cannot be found in the Constitution, the Constitution enumerates powers that give Congress the authority to levy and collect taxes, issue a currency, and borrow funds. From these enumerated powers, Marshall found, it was reasonable to imply that Congress had the power to charter a bank, which could be considered "necessary and proper" to the exercise of its aforementioned enumerated powers.

Marshall next addressed the question of whether a federal bank could be taxed by any state government. To Marshall, this was not a difficult question. The national government was dependent on the people, not the states, for its powers. In addition, Marshall noted, the Constitution specifically calls for the national law to be supreme. "The power to tax involves the power to destroy," wrote Marshall.[6] Thus, the state tax violated the supremacy clause, because individual states cannot interfere with the operations of the national government, whose laws are supreme.

The Court's decision in *McCulloch* has far-reaching consequences even today. The necessary and proper clause is used to justify federal action in many areas, including social welfare problems. Furthermore, had Marshall allowed the state of Maryland to tax the federal bank, it is possible that states could have attempted to tax all federal agencies located within their boundaries, a costly proposition that could have driven the federal government into insurmountable debt.

McCulloch v. *Maryland* (1819)
The Supreme Court upheld the power of the national government and denied the right of a state to tax the federal bank using the Constitution's supremacy clause. The Court's broad interpretation of the necessary and proper clause paved the way for later rulings upholding expansive federal powers.

Gibbons v. *Ogden* (1824)

Gibbons v. *Ogden* (1824)
The Supreme Court upheld broad congressional power to regulate interstate commerce. The Court's broad interpretation of the Constitution's commerce clause paved the way for later rulings upholding expansive federal powers.

Shortly after *McCulloch*, the Marshall Court had another opportunity to rule in favor of a broad interpretation of the scope of national power. *Gibbons* v. *Ogden* (1824) involved a dispute that arose after the New York State legislature granted to Robert Fulton the exclusive right to operate steamboats on the Hudson River. Simultaneously, Congress licensed a ship to sail on the same waters. By the time the case reached the Supreme Court, it was complicated both factually and procedurally. Suffice it to say that both New York and New Jersey wanted to control shipping on the lower Hudson River. But, *Gibbons* actually addressed one simple, very important question: what was the scope of Congress's authority under the commerce clause? The states argued that "commerce," as mentioned in Article I, should be interpreted narrowly to include only direct dealings in products. In *Gibbons*, however, the Supreme Court ruled that Congress's power to regulate interstate commerce included the power to regulate commercial activity as well, and that the commerce power had no limits except those specifically found in the Constitution. Thus, New York had no constitutional authority to grant a monopoly to a single steamboat operator, an act that interfered with interstate commerce.[7] Like the necessary and proper clause, today the commerce clause has been used by Congress—with varying degrees of success—to justify federal legislation concerning regulation of highways, the stock market, and violence against women.

Dual Federalism: The Taney Court, Slavery, and the Civil War

dual federalism
The belief that having separate and equally powerful levels of government is the best arrangement.

In spite of nationalist Marshall Court decisions such as *McCulloch* and *Gibbons*, strong debate continued in the United States over national versus state power. It was under the leadership of Chief Justice Marshall's successor, Roger B. Taney (1835–1863), that the Supreme Court articulated the notions of concurrent power and **dual federalism.** Dual federalism posits that having separate and equally powerful state and national governments is the best arrangement. Adherents of this theory typically believe that the national government should not exceed its constitutionally enumerated powers, and as stated in the Tenth Amendment, all other powers are, and should be, reserved to the states or to the people.

Dred Scott and the Advent of the Civil War

During the Taney Court era, the role of the Supreme Court as the arbiter of competing national and state interests became troublesome when the justices were called upon to deal with the controversial issue of slavery. In cases such as *Dred Scott* v. *Sandford* (1857), the Court tried to manage the slavery issue by resolving questions of ownership,

Photo courtesy: The Granger Collection

Who was Dred Scott? Born into slavery around 1795, Dred Scott became the named plaintiff in a case with major ramifications for the federal system. In 1833, Scott was sold by his original owners, the Blow family, to Dr. Emerson in St. Louis, Missouri. When Emerson died in 1843, Scott tried to buy his freedom. Before he could, however, he was transferred to Emerson's widow, who moved to New York, leaving Scott in the custody of his first owners, the Blows. Some of the Blows (Henry Blow later founded the anti-slavery Free Soil Party) and other abolitionists gave money to support a test case seeking Scott's freedom. They believed that Scott's residence with the Emerson family in Illinois and later in the Wisconsin Territory, which both prohibited slavery, made Scott a free man. After many delays, the U.S. Supreme Court ruled 7–2 in 1857 that Scott was not a citizen of the United States. "Slaves," said the Court, "were never thought of or spoken of except as property." Despite this ruling, Dred Scott was given his freedom when the Emerson family permanently returned him to the anti-slavery Blows. He died of tuberculosis less than one year later.

the status of fugitive slaves, and slavery in the new territories.[8] These cases generally were settled in favor of slavery and states' rights within the framework of dual federalism. In *Dred Scott*, for example, the Taney Court, in declaring the Missouri Compromise unconstitutional, ruled that Congress lacked the authority to ban slavery in the territories. This decision seemed to rule out any nationally legislated solution to the slavery question, leaving the problem in the hands of the state legislatures and the people, who did not have the power to impose their will on other states.

The Civil War, Its Aftermath, and the Continuation of Dual Federalism

The Civil War (1861–1865) forever changed the nature of federalism. In the aftermath of the war, the national government grew in size and power. It also attempted to impose its will on the state governments through the Thirteenth, Fourteenth, and Fifteenth Amendments. These three amendments, known collectively as the Civil War Amendments, prohibited slavery and granted civil and political rights, including voting rights, to African Americans.

The U.S. Supreme Court, however, continued to adhere to its belief in the concept of dual federalism. Therefore, in spite of the growth of the national government's powers, the importance of the state governments' powers was not diminished until 1933, when the next major change in the federal system occurred. Generally, the Court upheld any laws passed under the states' police powers, which allow states to pass laws to protect the general welfare of their citizens. These laws affected commerce, labor relations, and manufacturing. After the Court's decision in *Plessy* v. *Ferguson* (1896), in which the Court ruled that state maintenance of "separate but equal" facilities for blacks and whites was constitutional, most civil rights and voting cases also became state matters, in spite of the Civil War Amendments.[9]

The Court also developed legal doctrine in a series of cases that reinforced the national government's ability to regulate commerce. By the 1930s, these two somewhat contradictory approaches led to confusion: states, for example, could not tax gasoline used by federal vehicles,[10] and the national government could not tax the sale of motorcycles to city police departments.[11] In this period, the Court, however, did recognize the need for national control over new technological developments, such as the telegraph.[12] And, beginning in the 1880s, the Court allowed Congress to regulate many aspects of economic relationships, such as monopolies, an area of regulation formerly thought to be in the exclusive realm of the states. Passage of laws such as the Interstate Commerce Act in 1887 and the Sherman Anti-Trust Act in 1890 allowed Congress to establish itself as an important player in the growing national economy.

Despite finding that most of these federal laws were constitutional, the Supreme Court did not enlarge the scope of national power consistently. In 1895, for example, the United States filed suit against four sugar refiners, alleging that their sale would give their buyer control of 98 percent of the U.S. sugar-refining business. The Supreme Court ruled that congressional efforts to control monopolies (through passage of the Sherman Anti-Trust Act) did not give Congress the authority to prevent the sale of these sugar-refining businesses, because manufacturing was not commerce. Therefore, the companies and their actions were beyond the scope of Congress's authority to regulate.[13]

Setting the Stage for a Stronger National Government

In 1895, the U.S. Supreme Court found a congressional effort to tax personal incomes unconstitutional, although an earlier Court had found a similar tax levied during the Civil War constitutional.[14] Thus, Congress and the state legislatures were moved to ratify the **Sixteenth Amendment.** The Sixteenth Amendment gave Congress the power to levy and collect taxes on incomes without apportioning them among the

Sixteenth Amendment
Authorized Congress to enact a national income tax.

states. The revenues taken in by the federal government through taxation of personal income "removed a major constraint on the federal government by giving it access to almost unlimited revenues."[15] If money is power, the income tax and the revenues it generated greatly enhanced the power of the federal government and its ability to enter policy areas where it formerly had few funds to spend.

Seventeenth Amendment
Made senators directly elected by the people; removed their selection from state legislatures.

The **Seventeenth Amendment,** ratified in 1913, similarly enhanced the power of the national government at the expense of the states. This amendment terminated the state legislatures' election of senators and put their election in the hands of the people. With senators no longer directly accountable to the state legislators who elected them, states lost their principal protectors in Congress. Coupled with the Sixteenth Amendment, this amendment paved the way for more drastic changes in the relationship between national and state governments in the United States.

Cooperative Federalism: The New Deal and the Growth of National Government

The era of dual federalism came to an abrupt end in the 1930s. While the ratification of the Sixteenth and Seventeenth Amendments set the stage for expanded national government, the catalyst for dual federalism's demise was a series of economic events that ended in the cataclysm of the Great Depression:

- Throughout the 1920s, bank failures were common.
- In 1921, the nation experienced a severe slump in agricultural prices.
- In 1926, the construction industry went into decline.
- In the summer of 1929, inventories of consumer goods and automobiles were at an all-time high.
- On October 29, 1929, stock prices, which had risen steadily since 1926, crashed, taking with them the entire national economy.

Despite the severity of these indicators, Presidents Calvin Coolidge and Herbert Hoover took little action, believing that the national depression was an amalgamation of state economic crises that should be dealt with by state and local governments. However, by 1933, the situation could no longer be ignored.

The New Deal

Rampant unemployment (historians estimate it was as high as 40 to 50 percent) was the hallmark of the Great Depression. In 1933, to combat severe problems facing the nation, newly elected President Franklin D. Roosevelt (FDR) proposed a variety of innovative programs, collectively called the "New Deal," and ushered in a new era in American politics. FDR used the full power of the office of the president as well as his highly effective communication skills to sell the American public and Congress on a new level of government intervention intended to stabilize the economy and reduce suffering. Most politicians during the New Deal period (1933–1939) agreed that to find national solutions to the Depression, which was affecting the citizens of every state in the union, the national government would have to exercise tremendous authority.

In the first few weeks of the legislative session after FDR's inauguration, Congress passed a series of acts creating new federal agencies and programs proposed by the president. These new agencies, often known by their initials, created what many termed an alphabetocracy. Among the more significant programs were the Federal

Photo courtesy: Bettmann/Corbis

How did the New Deal change federalism? The New Deal included a variety of public works programs such as the Works Progress Administration, shown here. These new programs were symbolic of increasing federal-state interactions and the end of dual federalism.

Housing Administration (FHA), which provided federal financing for new home construction; the Civilian Conservation Corps (CCC), a work relief program for farmers and homeowners; the Agricultural Adjustment Administration (AAA) and the National Recovery Administration (NRA), which imposed restrictions on production in agriculture and many industries while also providing subsidies to farmers.

New Deal programs forced all levels of government to work cooperatively with one another. Indeed, local governments—mainly in big cities—became a third partner in the federal system as FDR relied on big-city Democratic political machines to turn out voters to support his programs. Cities were embraced as equal partners in an intergovernmental system for the first time and became players in the national political arena because many members of Congress wanted to bypass state legislatures, where urban interests usually were underrepresented.

New Deal programs also enlarged the scope of the national government. Those who feared this unprecedented use of national power quickly challenged the constitutionality of the programs in court. And, at least initially, the U.S. Supreme Court often agreed with them.

Through the mid-1930s, the Supreme Court continued to rule that certain aspects of New Deal programs went beyond the authority of Congress to regulate commerce. The Court's *laissez-faire*, or hands-off, attitude toward the economy was reflected in a series of decisions ruling various aspects of New Deal programs unconstitutional.

FDR and the Congress were livid. FDR's frustration with the Court prompted him to suggest what ultimately was nicknamed his "Court-packing plan." Knowing that he could do little to change the minds of those already on the Court, FDR suggested enlarging its size from nine to thirteen justices. This would have given him the opportunity to pack the Court with a majority of justices predisposed toward the constitutional validity of the New Deal.

Even though Roosevelt was popular, the Court-packing plan was not. Congress and the public were outraged that he even suggested tampering with an institution of

Photo courtesy: Hulton Archive/Getty Images

How many justices does the Supreme Court need? This cartoon pokes fun at FDR (with his aide, Harold Ickes) and his unpopular "Court-packing plan" to expand the size of the Supreme Court. This plan would have allowed FDR to add justices to undo the Court's anti–New Deal decisions.

government. Nevertheless, the Court appeared to respond to this threat. In 1937, it reversed its series of anti–New Deal decisions, concluding that Congress (and therefore the national government) had the authority to legislate in any area so long as what was regulated affected commerce in any way. The Court also upheld the constitutionality of the bulk of the massive New Deal relief programs, including the National Labor Relations Act of 1935, which authorized collective bargaining between unions and employees;[16] the Fair Labor Standards Act of 1938, which prohibited the interstate shipment of goods made by employees earning less than the federally mandated minimum wage;[17] and the Agricultural Adjustment Act of 1938, which provided crop subsidies to farmers.[18] Congress then used this newly recognized power to legislate in a wide array of areas, including maximum hour and minimum wage laws and regulation of child labor.

The Changing Nature of Federalism: From Layer Cake to Marble Cake

Before the Depression and the New Deal, most political scientists likened the federal system to a layer cake: each level or layer of government—national, state, and local—had clearly defined powers and responsibilities. After the New Deal, however, the nature of the federal system changed. Government now looked something like a marble cake:

> Wherever you slice through it you reveal an inseparable mixture of differently colored ingredients. . . . Vertical and diagonal lines almost obliterate the horizontal ones, and

in some places there are unexpected whirls and an imperceptible merging of colors, so that it is difficult to tell where one ends and the other begins.[19]

The metaphor of marble cake federalism refers to what political scientists call **cooperative federalism,** a term that describes the intertwined relationship among the national, state, and local governments that began with the New Deal. (To learn more about cooperative federalism in practice, see Join the Debate: Protecting the Environment.) States began to take a secondary, albeit important, cooperative role in the scheme of governance, as did many cities. Nowhere is this shift in power from the states to the national government clearer than in the growth of federal grant programs that began in earnest during the New Deal. Between the New Deal and the 1990s, the tremendous growth in these programs, and in federal government spending in general, changed the nature and discussion of federalism from "How much power should the national government have?" to "How much say in the policies of the states can the national government buy?" During the 1970s energy crisis, for example the national government initially imposed a national 55 mph speed limit on the states. Subsequent national efforts forced states to adopt minimum-age drinking restrictions in order to obtain federal transportation funds.

cooperative federalism
The interwined relationship between the national, state and local governments that began with the New Deal.

Thinking Globally
Sweden's Social Welfare System

Sweden has an extensive social welfare system that provides a wide range of benefits and services to its citizens, from child care to retirement funds. Sweden has long maintained one of the world's lowest poverty levels and one of the highest rates of egalitarianism in terms of income distribution. Many claim that Sweden is a successful example of what is referred to as "social democracy."

■ To what degree should government policy emphasize egalitarianism over individualism?
■ Is a more comprehensive government-sponsored system of social benefits a possibility in the United States? If so, what would such a system look like? If not, why not?

Federal Grants and National Efforts to Influence the States

As early as 1790, Congress appropriated funds for the states to pay debts incurred during the Revolutionary War. But, it wasn't until the Civil War that Congress enacted its first true federal grant program, which allocated federal funds to the states for a specific purpose. Most commentators believe the start of this redistribution of funds began with the Morrill Land Grant Act of 1862, which gave each state 30,000 acres of public land for each representative in Congress. Income from the sale of these lands was to be earmarked for the establishment and support of agricultural and mechanical arts colleges. Sixty-nine land-grant colleges—including Texas A&M University, the University of Georgia, and Michigan State University—were founded or significantly assisted, making this grant program the single most important piece of education legislation passed in the United States up to that time.

As we have seen, Franklin D. Roosevelt's New Deal program increased the flow of federal dollars to the states with the infusion of massive federal dollars for a variety of public works programs, including building and road construction. In the boom times of World War II, even more new federal programs were introduced. By the 1950s and 1960s, federal grant-in-aid programs were well entrenched. They often defined federal/state relationships and made the national government a major player in domestic policy. Until the 1960s, however, most federal grant programs were constructed in cooperation with the states and were designed to assist the states in the furtherance of their traditional responsibilities to protect the health, welfare, and safety of their citizens.

Most of these programs were **categorical grants,** ones for which Congress appropriates funds for specific purposes. Categorical grants allocate federal dollars by a precise formula and are subject to detailed conditions imposed by the national government, often on a matching basis; that is, states must contribute money to match federal funds, although the national government may pay as much as 90 percent of the total.

categorical grant
Grants that allocated federal funds to states for a specific purpose.

Photo courtesy: Ronald Reagan Presidential Library

What was the Reagan Revolution? This movement, led by President Ronald Reagan, advocated the return of power to state governments. Here, President Reagan delivers his 1988 State of the Union Address.

By the early 1960s, as concern about the poor and minorities rose, and as states (especially in the South) were blamed for perpetuating discrimination, those in power in the national government saw grants as a way to force states to behave in ways desired by the national government.[20] If the states would not cooperate with the national government to further its goals, it would withhold funds.

In 1964, the Democratic administration of President Lyndon B. Johnson (LBJ) launched its "Great Society" program, which included what LBJ called a "War on Poverty." The Great Society program was a broad attempt to combat poverty and discrimination. In a frenzy of activity in Washington not seen since the New Deal, federal funds were channeled to states, to local governments, and even directly to citizen action groups in an effort to alleviate social ills that the states had been unable or unwilling to remedy. Money was allocated for urban renewal, education, and poverty programs, including Head Start and job training. The move to fund local groups directly was made by the most liberal members of Congress to bypass not only conservative state legislatures, but also conservative mayors and councils in cities such as Chicago, who were perceived as disinclined to help their poor, often African American, constituencies. Thus, these programs often pitted governors and mayors against community activists, who became key players in the distribution of federal dollars.

These new grants altered the fragile federal/state balance of power that had been at the core of many older federal grant programs. During the Johnson administration, the national government began to use federal grants as a way to further what federal (and not state) officials perceived to be national needs. Grants based on what states wanted or believed they needed began to decline, while grants based on what the national government wanted states to do to foster national goals increased dramatically. From pollution to economic development and law enforcement, creating a federal grant seemed like the perfect solution to every problem.[21]

Not all federal programs mandating state or local action came with federal money, however. And, while presidents during the 1970s voiced their opposition to big government, their efforts to rein it in were largely unsuccessful.

New Federalism: Returning Power to the States

In 1980, former California Governor Ronald Reagan was elected president, pledging to advance what he called **New Federalism** and a return of power to the states. This policy set the tone for the federal–state relationship that was maintained from the 1980s until 2001. Presidents and Congresses took steps to shrink the size of the federal government in favor of programs administered by state governments. President Bill Clinton, a Democrat, lauded the demise of big government. And, on the campaign trail in 2000, Republican candidate George W. Bush also seemed committed to this devolution. The September 11, 2001, terrorist attacks, however, led to substantial growth in the power and scope of the federal government.

New Federalism
Federal–state relationship proposed by Reagan administration during the 1980s; hallmark is returning administrative powers to the state governments.

The Reagan Revolution

The Reagan Revolution had at its heart strong views about the role of states in the federal system. While many Democrats and liberal interest groups argued that federal grants were an effective way to raise the level of services provided to the poor; many Republicans, including Reagan, attacked them as imposing national priorities on the states. In part to curtail federal spending, Reagan almost immediately proposed massive cuts in federal domestic programs and drastic income tax cuts. Declining federal revenues dramatically altered the relationships among federal, state, and local governments. For the first time in thirty years, federal aid to state and local governments declined.[22] Reagan persuaded Congress to consolidate many categorical grants into far fewer, less restrictive **block grants**—broad grants to states for specific activities such as secondary education or health services, with few strings attached. He also ended general revenue sharing, which had provided significant restricted funds to the states.

block grant
Broad grant with few strings attached; given to states by the federal government for general categories of activity, such as secondary education or health services.

By the end of the presidencies of Ronald Reagan and George Bush in 1993, most block grants fell into one of four categories: health, income security, education, or transportation. Yet, many politicians, including most state governors, urged the consolidation of even more programs into block grants. Calls to reform the welfare system, particularly to allow the states more latitude in an effort to get back to the Hamiltonian notion of states as laboratories of democracy, seemed popular with citizens and governments alike. New Federalism had taken hold.

The Devolution Revolution

In 1992, Bill Clinton was elected president—the first Democrat in twelve years. Although Clinton was a former governor, he was more predisposed to federal programs than his Republican predecessors. His ability to make changes in the federal system, however, was limited.

In 1994, Republican candidates for the House of Representatives joined together in their support for the Contract with America, a campaign document proposed by then House Minority Whip Newt Gingrich (R–GA). In it, Republican candidates pledged to force a national debate on the role of the national government in regard to the states. A top priority

What was the devolution revolution? Here, then House Minority Whip Newt Gingrich (R–GA) promotes the tenets of the Contract with America in 1994. A top priority of the program was to scale back the scope and size of the federal government. Though some of the Contract's proposals became law, most of its goals remained unfulfilled.

Photo courtesy: John Duricka/AP/Wide World Photos

Join the Debate

Protecting the Environment

Overview: The Environmental Protection Act, passed during Richard M. Nixon's presidency, provided the federal government with responsibility for protecting the environment. Because pollution is inherently interstate, there is good reason to defer to the federal government for environmental protection. The Interstate Commerce Clause of the Constitution provides the legal foundation for the federal government to play the dominant role in this arena. But, should this prevent states from regarding federal standards as minimum requirements and going further if they are so inclined? And, what if state officials are convinced that the federal government is not fulfilling its responsibilities? Should federal standards act as a floor or a ceiling for state laws?

States, particularly on the West Coast and in the Northeast, have repeatedly sued the federal government over powers and responsibilities to protect the In 2006, when the George W. Bush administration relaxed restrictions on the amount of pollution allowed after industries repaired or modernized their plants, twelve states in the Northeast filed suit. Some of these same states plus California, Arizona, Minnesota, and Illinois filed a suit in 2007 when the federal Environmental Protection Agency (EPA) weakened regulations requiring businesses and industries to report the toxic chemicals they use, store, and release. In late 2007 and early 2008, states and the federal government went head-to-head on two other environmental issues. First, California led nine states in requiring cars and trucks to get more miles per gallon than the federal government mandated. President Bush objected and the EPA asserted that the federal rules prevailed. Second, fifteen states established higher standards than the federal government in curbing greenhouse-gas emissions from the tailpipes of cars, thereby defying a

federal edict that only Washington can impose such rules.

The concerns raised by environmental issues apply more broadly to public policy and the governance of our society. The federal government funds Medicare, the major health care program for the elderly. States and the federal government jointly provide health care for the poor, with the federal government establishing minimum standards and guidelines for how much states can provide above the minimum. Education is the primary responsibility of states, but—as pointed out in the Politics Now feature in this chapter—the federal government is seeking to set standards through the No Child Left Behind Act.

The question of the power of the federal government in contrast to the power of state governments is central to the concept and the realities of federalism. Should the federal government set limits on how much a state wants to do for its citizens? Can policy makers in Washington, D.C., be responsive to the different opportunities and needs throughout the country?

Arguments IN FAVOR of Federal Dominance in Environmental Protection

- The intergovernmental nature of pollution requires a national approach to environmental issues. A state can have lax pollution standards in order to minimize costs to the industries within its boundaries and suffer minimal consequences while causing more serious hazards for its neighbors. Federal regulations protect everyone.

- Industries cannot be expected to produce vehicles, appliances, and other goods that meet a wide variety of standards set by different states. Car manufacturers, as an example, might have to design and build several different vehicles to comply with a mosaic of requirements. This would necessarily result in inefficiencies likely to hurt the competitiveness of U.S. companies and increase costs to consumers.

- Environmental issues require a level of scientific expertise that is

was scaling back the federal government, an effort that some commentators called the devolution revolution.

Running under a clear set of priorities contained in the Contract, Republican candidates took back the House of Representatives for the first time in more than forty years. A majority of the legislative proposals based on the Contract passed the House of Representatives during the first one hundred days of the

most likely to reside in the federal government. The identification of toxic substances and the design of strategies to reduce or eliminate these substances is a matter of scientific inquiry and discovery. Federal, not state, resources should support the expansion and application of scientific knowledge.

Arguments AGAINST Federal Dominance in Environmental Protection

- Political dynamics make the federal government an unreliable advocate for environmental protection. Not all presidents put a premium on environmental protection. Congress is susceptible to pressures from lobbyists that are more concerned with short-term profits for corporations than with the long-term consequences of pollution.

- States should be able to exceed federal standards. State governments should have discretion to respond to the needs of different regions of the country by going above minimal requirements. It is appropriate for the federal government to establish basic national standards, but it should not place limits on states who, for whatever reason, wish to do better.

- The federal government should allow states to exert leadership in public policy. California led the way in establishing higher automobile standards for pollution control in the 1960s. California has a large share of the nation's automobile market and thus was able to exert this kind of influence. Smaller states, by themselves, are not likely to exert pressure to establish new national standards, so fears of change being driven by any one state are unwarranted. States are more likely to act in coalition with others, and the largest states, like California, are likely to exert the most influence.

Continuing the Debate

1. What policy roles should states play on the one hand and the federal government play on the other?
2. Have technological developments and the development of a national and even global economy relegated states in our federal system to relatively meaningless positions?

To Follow the Debate Online Go To:

www.epa.gov, the Web site of the Environmental Protection Agency, the major federal body responsible for developing and enforcing environmental policies.

www.sierraclub.org, the Web site of the Sierra Club, a national, grassroots organization that is one of the major advocates for environmental protection and has joined lawsuits against the federal government and state governments, depending on the specific issues.

www.uschamber.com, the Web site of the U.S. Chamber of Commerce, one of the major advocates for businesses. It posts policy positions on its site and lobbies the federal government on behalf of its member businesses.

Photo courtesy: Laura Lombardi/Greenpeace/Zuma Press

What role should government play in protecting the environment? Environmental groups favor stronger actions by all levels of government to protect air and water quality and promote clean energy. Here, members of Greenpeace hang a banner at a coal burning power plant to protest the Bush Administration's energy policies.

104th Congress. However, very few of the Contract's proposals, including acts requiring a balanced budget, tax reforms, and term limits, passed the Senate and became law.

On some issues, however, the Republicans were able to achieve their goals. For example, before 1995, **unfunded mandates,** national laws that direct state or local governments to comply with federal rules or regulations (such as clean air or water stan-

unfunded mandates
National laws that direct state or local governments to comply with federal rules or regulations (such as clean air or water standards) but contain little or no federal funding to defray the cost of meeting these requirements.

No Child Left Behind

Test Scores Are Stagnant Despite No Child Left Behind

JULIA SELLERS

Aiken County pupils' scores have remained the same over the years—even with No Child Left Behind. Schools are being labeled as "failing" because administrators are having a hard time meeting requirements under the federal act, school officials said.

"When people see, 'Oh, it's a failing school,' they don't look to see that everybody's giving their best effort," said Sarah Emerling, a Busbee Elementary School special-education teacher.

David Mathis, the associate superintendent for administration, said the district's curriculum is correctly aligned and the test scores remain above state averages. The biggest frustration for the county is in the fine details of the federal act. "I don't see where No Child Left Behind has helped the system because the playing field from state to state is not level," Dr. Mathis said. "When we can play on a level playing field, I think it will have more substance to it. The concept of No Child Left Behind is a good one—no one has a desire to leave a child behind—but good policy should be supported by good practice."

The lack of federal funding hinders districts in improving low-scoring areas. "There are four-year-old programs that are organized out of federal funds, but it is never enough," Dr. Mathis said. "If the federal government fully funded programs they mandate, then we could close that gap."

Ms. Emerling, however, said the government will never change the policy if more people aren't vocal about the inconsistencies. "A parent has so much more power to make their concerns known; you always see teachers rallying against this, but not enough parents are," Ms. Emerling said. "Get in touch with legislators and local politicians."

Discussion Questions

1. *What oversight role should the federal government play with regard to powers left to the states, such as education?*
2. *What should be the source of funding for schools? Less affluent school districts and states contend that more funds should come from the federal level, while more affluent districts and states tend to believe that funding decisions should be left to state and local governments. What compromise might ensure that every child in the United States has an equal opportunity to a quality education?*

Federalism and Regulations

dards) but contain no federal funding to defray the cost of meeting these requirements, absorbed nearly 30 percent of some local budgets. Republicans in Congress, loyal to the concerns of these governments, secured passage of the Unfunded Mandates Reform Act of 1995. This act prevented Congress from passing costly federal programs without debate on how to fund them and addressed a primary concern for state governments.

Another important act passed by the Republican-controlled Congress and signed into law by President Bill Clinton was the Personal Responsibility and Work Opportunity Reconciliation Act of 1996. This legislation replaced the existing welfare program, known as Aid to Families with Dependent Children (AFDC), with a program known as Temporary Assistance for Needy Families (TANF). TANF returned much of the administrative power for welfare programs to the states and became a hallmark of the devolution revolution.

In the short run, these and other programs, coupled with a growing economy, produced record federal and state budget surpluses. States were in the best fiscal shape they had been in since the 1970s. According to the National Conference of State Legislatures, total state budget surpluses in 1998 exceeded $30 billion. These tax surpluses allowed many states to increase spending, while other states offered their residents steep tax cuts. Mississippi, for example, increased its per capita spending by 42.4 percent, while Alaska opted to reduce taxes by 44.2 percent.[23]

Despite these strong economic conditions, Vice President Al Gore failed to turn the success of the Clinton administration into a Gore presidency in 2000. His opponent, Texas Governor George W. Bush, campaigned on a platform of even more limited federal government, arguing that state and local governments should have extensive administrative powers over programs such as education and welfare.

Federalism Under the Bush Administration

On the campaign trail in 2000, then Governor George W. Bush (R–TX) made it clear that he would follow in the tradition of former President Ronald Reagan in moving to return power to the states.[24] Yet, no one could have foreseen the circumstances that would surround much of Bush's presidency. A struggling economy, terrorist attacks on the World Trade Center and the Pentagon, the invasion of Afghanistan, and the continuing costly war in Iraq, as well as the rising costs of education and welfare, produced state and federal budget deficits that would have been unimaginable only a few years before.

By 2003, many state governments faced budget shortfalls of more than $30 billion. Because state governments, unlike the federal government, are required to balance their budgets, governors and legislators struggled to make ends meet. Some states raised taxes, and others cut services, including school construction and infrastructure repairs. These dramatic changes helped nearly all of the states to project surpluses—albeit small—for fiscal year 2006.

The federal government was not so lucky; by November 2007, it struggled with a record $9.1 trillion debt, with the wars in Iraq and Afghanistan estimated to cost each American as much as $8,000.[25] This deficit had a number of sources, including President Bush's 2001 tax cuts, spending on the wars in Iraq and Afghanistan, costs associated with the dramatic expansion of the federal government after the September 11, 2001, terrorist attacks, and Hurricanes Katrina and Rita. In addition, the No Child Left Behind Act, which imposed a host of federal requirements on everything from class size to accountability testing, increased burdens on the federal coffers at rates not seen since President Lyndon B. Johnson's Great Society program.[26]

The No Child Left Behind Act was viewed by many as an unprecedented usurpation of state and local powers. However, this trend of **preemption**, or allowing the national government to override state or local actions in certain areas, is not new. The growth of preemption statutes, laws that allow the federal government to assume partial or full responsibility for state and local governmental functions, began in 1965 during the Johnson administration. Since then, Congress has used its authority under the Commerce Clause to preempt state laws. However, until recently, preemption statutes generally were supported by Democrats in Congress and the White House, not Republicans. The Bush administration's support of this law reflects a new era in preemption. (To learn more about preemption, see Politics Now: No Child Left Behind.)

preemption
A concept derived from the Constitution's supremacy clause that allows the national government to override or preempt state or local actions in certain areas.

How does the Supreme Court affect the federal–state relationship?
Since 1989, the Supreme Court has often deferred to state courts as well as judgments of the state legislatures.

Toward Reform: A New Judicial Federalism?

The role of the Supreme Court of the United States in determining the parameters of federalism cannot be underestimated. Neither can the role of the executive branch in advocating certain positions before the Court. Although in the 1930s Congress passed sweeping New Deal legislation, it was not until the Supreme Court finally reversed itself and found those programs constitutional that any real change occurred in the federal–state relationship. From the New Deal until the 1980s, the Supreme Court's impact on the federal system generally was to expand the national government's authority at the expense of the states.

Photo courtesy: Herblock/The Herb Block Foundation

Ideas Into Action

Violence on Campus

Violence is not a new trend on college campuses, but only recently has it been under the public eye. In 1990, Congress passed the Jeanne Clery Disclosure of Campus Security Policy and Campus Crime Statistics Act, which requires campuses to report all incidences of violence to students, to the community, and the U.S. Department of Education. According to the data, nearly 200,000 instances of crime were reported on campuses in 2005.[a] The prevalence of certain crimes on U.S. college and university campuses is surprising. For example, the American Association of University Women (AAUW) reports that nearly one-third of college women have been sexually harassed in a physical manner.[b]

One issue that hinders crime prevention is the coordination of federal, state, local, and campus officials. Following a mass shooting in 2007 at Virginia Tech, for example, it was revealed that the student gunman had been deemed mentally ill by state courts and that multiple complaints from fellow students had led to psychological counseling. Because much of this information was confidential and not shared among the various levels of administration, many students concluded that they were not warned about a potential danger and, furthermore, not enough was done to prevent the tragedy.[c]

In response to the wake-up call caused by the shooting, many universities reevaluated their crime prevention and emergency preparedness programs. Many universities across the country are turning to a technology that over 95 percentage of college students carry with them on a daily basis: cell phones.[d]

Hundreds of colleges and universities have begun to use text message alerts, sent to warn students of emergency situations. While proponents say the messages will help minimize disaster, others warn that not all students will receive the notifications because many professors prohibit cell phone use in class.

- Find out what program your college or university has put into place to prepare for emergency situations.
- Acquaint yourself with crisis protocol so that you and other students can be informed about what to do in emergency situations. Encourage your school to test its systems, and make suggestions on how to improve the process it has implemented.

---

[a]*Crime in the United States 2005*, Department of Justice, Federal Bureau of Investigation, September 2006.
[b]Catherine Hill and Elena Silva, *Drawing the Line: Sexual Harassment on Campus*, Washington, DC, AAUW Educational Foundation, 2006.
[c]"Killer's Manifesto: 'You Forced Me Into A Corner,'" *Massacre at Virginia Tech*, CNN.com, April 18, 2007, www.cnn.com/2007/US/04/18/vtech.shooting/index.html.
[d]Thomas Frank, "Schools Weigh Text Alerts for Crises," USAtoday.com, April 23, 2007, www.usatoday.com/tech/news/techpolicy/2007-04-23-text-alerts-vt_n.htm.

Beginning in the late 1980s, however, the Court's willingness to allow Congress to regulate in a variety of areas waned. Once Ronald Reagan was elected president, he attempted to appoint new justices committed to the notion of states' rights and to rolling back federal intervention in matters that many Republicans believed were state responsibilities.

Mario M. Cuomo, a former Democratic New York governor, has referred to the decisions of what he called the Reagan-Bush Court as creating "a kind of new judicial federalism." According to Cuomo, this new federalism could be characterized by the Court's withdrawal of "rights and emphases previously thought to be national."[27] Illustrative of this trend are many of the Supreme Court's decisions in abortion cases. In *Webster* v. *Reproductive Health Services* (1989), for example, the Court first gave new latitude—and even encouragement—to the states to fashion more restrictive abortion laws.[28] Since *Webster*, most states have enacted new restrictions on abortion, with parental consent, informed consent or waiting periods, or bans on late-term or "partial birth" abortions being the most common. (To learn more, see Analyzing Visuals: State-by-State Report Card on Access to Abortion.) The Court consistently has upheld the authority of the individual states to limit a minor's access to abortion through imposition of parental consent or notification laws. Still, as discussed in chapter 5, in *Stenberg* v. *Carhart* (2000) the Supreme Court under Chief Justice William H. Rehnquist ruled that a state law limiting "partial birth" abortions without any provision to save a woman's health was unconstitutional.[29] And, in 2006, a unani-

Examine the map created by NARAL Pro-Choice America, a liberal interest group, and answer the following questions:

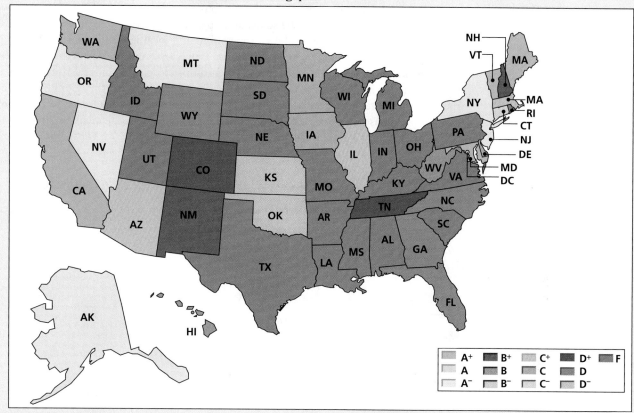

A+	B+	C+	D+	F
A	B	C	D	
A−	B−	C−	D−	

WHAT, if anything, do the states that receive A's have in common? What, if anything, do the states that receive D's and F's have in common?

HOW might factors such as political culture, geography, and characteristics of the population influence a state's laws concerning abortion?

WHAT criteria would a group opposing abortion, such as the National Right to Life Committee, use to grade the states? How would its criteria differ from those of NARAL Pro-Choice America?

Source: NARAL Pro-Choice America/NARAL Foundation, "Who Decides? A State-by-State Review of Abortion and Reproductive Rights, 2007," http://www.prochoiceamerica.org. Reprinted by permission.

mous Roberts Court ruled that states seeking to restrict minors' access to abortion must allow for some exceptions for medical emergencies.[30] But, in 2007, the Roberts Court upheld the constitutionality of the federal Partial Birth Abortion Act, the provisions of which were nearly identical to those struck down in *Stenberg*.[31]

Since 1989, the Supreme Court has also decided numerous cases in other issue areas related to federalism. From 1995–2005, especially, the Rehnquist Court made a number of closely divided decisions related to the balance of power between the federal and state governments. For example, in *U.S. v. Lopez* (1995), which involved the conviction of a student charged with carrying a concealed handgun onto school property, a five-person majority of the Court ruled that Congress lacked constitutional authority under the commerce clause to regulate guns within 1,000 feet of a school.[32] The majority concluded that local gun control laws, even those involving schools, were a state, not a federal, matter.

One year later, again a badly divided Rehnquist Court ruled that Congress lacked the authority to require states to negotiate with Indian tribes about gaming and casinos.[33] The U.S. Constitution specifically gives Congress the right to deal with Indian tribes, but the

You Are a Federal Judge

sovereign immunity
The right of a state to be free from a lawsuit unless it gives permission to the suit. Under the Eleventh Amendment, all states are considered sovereign.

Court found that Florida's **sovereign immunity** protected the state from this kind of congressional directive about how to conduct its business. In 1997, the Court decided two more major cases dealing with the scope of Congress's authority to regulate in areas historically left to the province of the states: zoning and local law enforcement. In one, a majority of the Court ruled that sections of the Religious Freedom Restoration Act were unconstitutional because Congress lacked the authority to meddle in local zoning regulations, even if a church was involved.[34] Another 5–4 majority ruled that Congress lacked the authority to require local law enforcement officials to conduct background checks on handgun purchasers until the federal government was able to implement a national system.[35] In 1999, in another case involving sovereign immunity, a slim majority of the

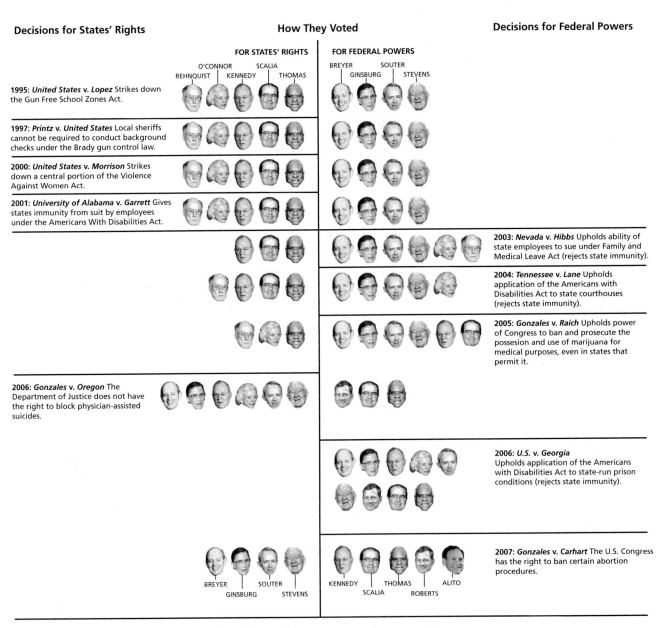

Decisions for States' Rights   **How They Voted**   **Decisions for Federal Powers**

1995: *United States* v. *Lopez* Strikes down the Gun Free School Zones Act.

1997: *Printz* v. *United States* Local sheriffs cannot be required to conduct background checks under the Brady gun control law.

2000: *United States* v. *Morrison* Strikes down a central portion of the Violence Against Women Act.

2001: *University of Alabama* v. *Garrett* Gives states immunity from suit by employees under the Americans With Disabilities Act.

2003: *Nevada* v. *Hibbs* Upholds ability of state employees to sue under Family and Medical Leave Act (rejects state immunity).

2004: *Tennessee* v. *Lane* Upholds application of the Americans with Disabilities Act to state courthouses (rejects state immunity).

2005: *Gonzales* v. *Raich* Upholds power of Congress to ban and prosecute the possession and use of marijuana for medical purposes, even in states that permit it.

2006: *Gonzales* v. *Oregon* The Department of Justice does not have the right to block physician-assisted suicides.

2006: *U.S.* v. *Georgia* Upholds application of the Americans with Disabilities Act to state-run prison conditions (rejects state immunity).

2007: *Gonzales* v. *Carhart* The U.S. Congress has the right to ban certain abortion procedures.

FIGURE **3.4** The Rehnquist and Roberts Courts and Federalism

Source: New York Times (June 12, 2005): 3; *New York Times* (July 2, 2006): A18; Legal Information Institute at Cornell University Law School.

Supreme Court ruled that Congress lacked the authority to change patent laws in a manner that would negatively affect a state's right to assert its immunity from lawsuits.[36] And, in 2000, the Court ruled that Congress had exceeded its powers in enacting some provisions of the Violence Against Women Act.[37] (To learn more, see Ideas into Action: Violence on Campus.)

When Republican George W. Bush entered the White House in 2001, it looked as if the Rehnquist Court was well on its way to supporting the Republican Congress's devolution revolution. But, many commentators now question what was really happening. At times, the Bush administration took positions clearly on the side of expanded federal powers. The administration argued, for example, that Congress had the right to prosecute individuals who used or purchased medical marijuana legalized by a state law. In 2005, the Court agreed, upholding the power of Congress to prohibit states from allowing the use of medical marijuana.[38]

As *New York Times* Supreme Court reporter Linda Greenhouse noted, "a hallmark of the Rehnquist Court has been a re-examination of the country's most basic constitutional arrangements, resulting in decisions that demanded a new respect for the sovereignty of the states and placed corresponding restrictions on the powers of Congress."[39] A careful analysis of Figure 3.4 demonstrates this point. During the 2002–2003 term, however, the Court took an unexpected turn in its federalism devolution revolution.[40] In a case opening states to lawsuits for alleged violations of the federal Family and Medical Leave Act (FMLA), writing for a six-person majority, Chief Justice William H. Rehnquist rejected Nevada's claim that it was immune from suit under FMLA. Rehnquist noted that the law was an appropriate exercise of Congress's power to combat sex-role stereotypes about the domestic responsibilities of female workers and "thereby dismantle persisting gender-based barriers that women faced in the workplace."[41] But, as also is reflected in Figure 3.4, the Roberts Court's first decision involving federalism supported state power by limiting the federal government's right to block Oregon's physician assisted suicide law.[42]

Also in 2006, however, was the Court's unanimous decision in *U.S. v. Georgia.*[43] In that case, the Court supported federal authority by ruling that Congress had the power to interfere with state powers in situations where violations of the Eighth Amendment were alleged. In *U.S. v. Georgia*, the Court rejected Georgia's claim that the Eleventh Amendment prevented it from being liable for violations of the Americans with Disabilities Act in the context of prison conditions. The extent to which the Roberts Court will ultimately throw its support to national or to state authority in our federal system remains to be seen, but the Court is clearly in a strong position to arbitrate the contentious balance of power in the American Republic.

 ## WHAT SHOULD I HAVE LEARNED?

The inadequacies of the confederate form of government created by the Articles of Confederation led the Framers to create a federal system of government that divided power between the national and state governments, with each ultimately responsible to the people. In describing the evolution of this system throughout American history, we have answered the following questions:

- **What are the roots of the federal system and how does the U.S. Constitution allocate governmental powers?**

The national government has both enumerated and implied powers under the Constitution. An additional group of concurrent powers are shared by national and state governments. Other powers are reserved to the states or the people or expressly denied to both governments, although the national government is ultimately declared supreme. The Constitution also lays the groundwork for the Supreme Court to be the arbiter in disagreements between states.

■ **What effect did the Marshall Court have on federalism?**

Early on, the Supreme Court played a key role in defining the relationship and powers of the national government through its broad interpretations of the supremacy and commerce clauses.

■ **What was the role of dual federalism before and after the Civil War?**

For many years, dual federalism, as articulated by the Taney Court, tended to limit the national government's authority in areas such as slavery and civil rights, and was the norm in relations between the national and state governments. However, the beginnings of a departure from this view became evident with the ratification of the Sixteenth and Seventeenth Amendments in 1913.

■ **What was the role of cooperative federalism during the New Deal and the growth of the national government?**

The notion of a limited federal government ultimately fell by the wayside in the wake of the Great Depression and Franklin D. Roosevelt's New Deal. This growth in the size and role of the federal government escalated during the Lyndon B. Johnson administration and into the mid to late 1970s. Federal grants became popular solutions for a host of state and local problems.

■ **How did a New Federalism return power to the states?**

After his election in 1980, Ronald Reagan tried to shrink the size and powers of the federal government through what he termed New Federalism. This trend continued through the 1990s, most notably through the Contract with America. Initially, George W. Bush's administration seemed committed to this devolution, but the September 11, 2001 terrorist attacks led to substantial growth in the size of the federal government.

■ **How have Supreme Court rulings created reform through a new judicial federalism?**

The Rehnquist and Roberts Courts have redefined the parameters of federalism. While many of the decisions rendered in the 1990s supported states' rights, several recent decisions have expanded the powers of Congress. Thus, the Court has set an ambiguous course in determining the definition and role of federalism.

Key Terms

bill of attainder, p. 100

block grant, p. 111

categorical grant, p. 109

concurrent powers, p. 100

confederation, p. 98

cooperative federalism, p. 109

dual federalism, p. 104

enumerated powers, p. 98

ex post facto law, p. 101

extradition clause, p. 101

federal system, p. 97

full faith and credit clause, p. 101

Gibbons v. *Ogden* (1824), p. 104

implied powers, p. 98

interstate compacts, p. 101

McCulloch v. *Maryland* (1819), p. 103

necessary and proper clause, p. 98

New Federalism, p. 111

preemption, p. 115

privileges and immunities clause, p. 101

reserve (or police) powers, p. 99

Seventeenth Amendment, p. 106

Sixteenth Amendment, p. 105

sovereign immunity, p. 118

supremacy clause, p. 98

Tenth Amendment, p. 99

unfunded mandates, p. 113

unitary system, p. 98

Researching Federalism

In the Library

Campbell, Tom. *Separation of Powers in Practice.* Stanford, CA: Stanford University Press, 2004.

Chemerinsky, Erwin. *Enhancing Government: Federalism for the 21st Century.* Stanford, CA: Stanford Law Books, 2008.

Derthick, Martha. *The Influence of Federal Grants.* Cambridge, MA: Harvard University Press, 1970.

Elazar, Daniel J., and John Kincaid, eds. *The Covenant Connection: From Federal Theology to Modern Federalism.* Lexington, MA: Lexington Books, 2000.

Finegold, Kenneth, and Theda Skocpol. *State and Party in America's New Deal.* Madison: University of Wisconsin Press, 1995.

Gerston, Larry N. *American Federalism: A Concise Introduction.* Armonk, NY: M.E. Sharpe, 2007.

Grodzins, Morton. *The American System: A View of Government in the United States.* Chicago: Rand McNally, 1966.

Kincaid, John, ed. *The Encyclopedia of American Federalism.* Washington, DC: CQ Press, 2005.

Manna, Paul. *School's In: Federalism and the National Education Agenda.* Washington, DC: Georgetown University Press, 2006.

McCabe, Neil Colman, ed. *Comparative Federalism in the Devolution Era.* Lanham, MD: Rowman and Littlefield, 2003.

Nagel, Robert F. *The Implosion of American Federalism.* New York: Oxford University Press, 2002.

O'Toole, Laurence, ed. *American Intergovernmental Relations: Foundations, Perspectives, and Issues.* Washington, DC: CQ Press, 2007.

Purcell, Edward, A. *Originalism, Federalism, and the American Constitutional Enterprises: A Historical Inquiry.* New Haven: Yale University Press, 2007.

Stephens, G. Ross, and Nelson Wikstrom. *American Intergovernmental Relations: A Fragmented Federal Polity.* New York: Oxford University Press, 2006.

Zimmerman, Joseph F. *Interstate Cooperation: Compacts and Administrative Agreements.* New York: Praeger, 2002.

On the Web

For a directory of federalism links, go to the American Council on Intergovernmental Relations at **govinfo.library.unt.edu/ amcouncil/index.html**

To learn more about your state and local governments, go to State and Local Government on the Net, **www.statelocalgov.net/**, which has links for thousands of state agencies and state and local governments.

The Landmark Supreme Courts cases site at **www. landmarkcases.org** provides the full text of *McCulloch v. Maryland* (1819) and *Gibbons v. Ogden* (1824).

The Oyez Project site at **www.oyez.org** provides a wealth of information on recent Supreme Court cases highlighted in the Toward Reform section of this chapter.

4

State and Local Government

One of the notable features of the 2008 elections was that neither the Republican nor the Democratic Party nominated a governor as its presidential candidate. Although Governor Sarah Palin of Alaska was the GOP vice-presidential nominee, 2008 was the first time since Georgia Governor Jimmy Carter won the presidency in 1976 that the top of the Republican and the Democratic tickets didn't include a governor. Even when governors are not candidates, they play critical roles in national as well as state politics. Governors are leaders of state parties as well as state governments. Their support can make the difference in close races for Congress or in presidential nomination battles and general elections.

Gubernatorial support was of obvious importance in the contest between Senators Barack Obama and Hillary Clinton for the Democratic presidential nomination in 2008. Governor Kathleen Sebelius of Kansas campaigned heavily for Barack Obama, while Governor Edward G. Rendell of Pennsylvania did the same for Hillary Clinton. Former Arkansas Governor Mike Huckabee drew on the support of other Republican governors in his unsuccessful attempt to secure his party's presidential nomination. After Senator

John McCain won the Republican nomination for president, Huckabee as well as Mitt Romney, the former governor of Massachusetts who was also a Republican presidential nomination contender, threw their support behind their party's choice for president.

Only eleven states elect governors on the same four-year cycle that the country elects a president. In each of those states in 2008, the key issues were, as for the country generally, related to the economy. The four Republican and four Democratic governors running for reelection had to respond to families that struggled to cope with sharp rises in food and energy costs, with incomes that were declining, jobs that were disappearing, and home loans that could not be paid.

Governor Christine Gregoire of Washington, a Democrat and former Washington State Attorney General, won her 2004 race against Dino Rossi by a razor thin 129 votes. Gregoire was Washington's second woman governor and the twenty-eighth female governor in United States history—Governor Sarah Palin of Alaska, John McCain's running mate for vice president, was the 29th. Gregoire faced Rossi again in 2008 and beat him much more decisively than in their first contest. While both the 2004 and 2008 campaigns were unusually bitter and heated, the 2008 contest included a lawsuit initiated by two former state supreme court justices that Rossi and the Building Industry Association of

■ **What do woman governors have in common?** Lurleen Wallace, shown at left, was elected as Governor of Alabama in 1966, after her husband, Governor George Wallace, was prevented from running for re-election. The Wallaces made it clear that George would continue to make policy and administrative decisions if Lurleen was elected. In 2004, Christine Gregoire, shown at right, became the second woman to be elected governor of the state of Washington. Elected by a margin of only 129 votes, Gregoire was re-elected in 2008 by a more comfortable margin of almost 200,000 votes (54 to 46 percent).

WHAT SHOULD I KNOW ABOUT . . .

- the roots of state and local governments?
- the structure and roles of state governments?
- the different types of local governments?
- the opportunities to participate in grassroots governance?
- the relations that federal, state, and local governments have with Indian nations?
- reforms in state and local finances?

TO LEARN MORE—
—TO DO MORE
Volunteer or intern with a campaign or political party in your state or local community. Get information and contacts at www.votesmart.org

Washington had illegally collaborated to defeat Governor Gregoire. Divisions in the state of Washington were, in part, regional, with the east supporting the Republican Rossi and the more urbanized west supporting the governor. Exit polls in 2008 indicated that the Washington electorate was generally pleased with Governor Gregoire's leadership and that she, like other Democrats running for state offices, benefited from the voter turnout efforts of the Barack Obama campaign. Among the new Democratic governors was Beverly Perdue, the first woman elected to that office in North Carolina. Perdue had been serving as the state's Lieutenant Governor. The four Republican governors running for reelection in 2008 won their contests, while the seven remaining contests resulted in Democratic victories.

Voters in 22 states cast ballots for 153 policy proposals as well as for candidates running for office in 2008. California, Florida, and Arizona approved bans on same-sex marriage, while the electorate in these same states, plus North Dakota and Colorado, rejected measures that would have restricted the reproductive rights of women. Michigan voters approved the medical use of marijuana and Massachusetts legalized the possession of small amounts of marijuana. Washington voters decided to join Oregon in allowing terminally ill people to end their lives with the assistance of physicians. In the context of a widespread economic downturn and rising unemployment, the electorates in Massachusetts, North Dakota and Oregon decided the need for government intervention was important and rejected major tax cuts. Tax hikes, on the other hand, did not garner support in Colorado or Florida, but they did win approval in Minnesota and Montana.

When there is an emergency in the community, who responds? The local police quickly established order and security in response to the tragic shooting on the campus of Northern Illinois University on February 14, 2008. They applied lessons from the experience at Virginia Tech in 2007.

State and local politics plays a critical role in the governance of our country. State and local governments are crucial to the health, safety, and security of the American people. State and local officials—on their own and at times in partnership with the federal government—educate our children, maintain law and order, care for those in need, clean and maintain the streets, license healthcare, legal, and other professionals, and generally provide for many of the basic services and structures we rely on.

This chapter will present the basic patterns and principles of state and local governance so that you may readily understand how public policies in your community are made and applied.

★ First, we will review *the roots of state and local governments*.

★ Second, we will describe the major institutions and roles of *state governments*, including trends in state elections.

★ Third, we will examine the different types of *local governments*, the bases for their authority, and the special traits of their institutions.

Photo courtesy: Jim Killam/Northern Star/AP/Wide World Photos

⭑ Fourth, we will identify the nature of *grassroots power and politics*.

⭑ Fifth, we will discuss *state and local government relations with Indian nations*.

⭑ Finally, we will examine the *varying challenges and proposals for reforming how state and local governments pay the bills*.

Roots of State and Local Governments

As pointed out in chapter 3, the basic, original unit of government in this country was the state. The thirteen colonial governments became thirteen state governments, and their constitutions preceded the U.S. Constitution. The states initially were loosely tied together in the Articles of Confederation but then formed a closer union and more powerful national government.

State governments also determined the existence of local governments. As we will later discuss in more detail, in some cases—such as counties and, for most states, school districts—state laws *create* local governments. In others, such as towns and cities, states *recognize* and *authorize* local governments in response to petitions from citizens.

In other words, although the power of governments at all levels is derived from the people, governmental institutions in the United States are not built from the bottom. Local towns, villages, school districts, and similar smaller units do not form states that then form the United States. Instead, states are the basic units that on the one hand establish local governments and on the other hand are the building blocks of the federal government.

In the past, state and local governments were primarily part-time governments. Except for governors and a handful of big-city mayors, people in office were farmers, teachers, lawyers, and shop owners who did public service during their spare time. This was true as well for many judges and local government bureaucrats.

As the responsibilities and challenges of government grew, more state and local jobs became full-time. Increases in the need for urban services led to more full-time local governments. Despite this trend, states with high levels of urbanization did not always have governments that responded to the specific needs of urban populations. The boundaries of districts from which state legislators got elected did not change in response to population shifts in the post–Civil War period. As a result, state legislatures did not represent the character of their respective states. One legislator from a rural area might represent 50,000 people, whereas a legislator from an urban setting might represent as many as 500,000 constituents. Such a pattern led to low priority for urban needs.

This kind of misrepresentation remained in place until the 1960s. The ruling by the U.S. Supreme Court in *Baker* v. *Carr* (1962) became a watershed in the evolution of state and local governments. The Court applied the Fourteenth Amendment of the U.S. Constitution and decreed that equal protection and the **one-person, one-vote** principles required that there be the same number of people in each of the legislative districts within a single state. As a result, state legislatures became more representative, and the agendas of state governments became much more relevant to the needs of all constituents.

The 1960s and 1970s were a period in which the federal government added to the responsibilities of state and local governments. Federal programs to combat poverty, revitalize urban areas, and protect the environment were designed to be administered by state and local officials rather than federal agencies. With these programs came federal assistance and sometimes mandates to improve the capacities and the efficiency of subnational governments.

one-person, one-vote
The principle that each legislative district within a state should have the same number of eligible voters so that representation is equitably based on population.

Since the 1970s, some trends in federalism have enhanced the importance of state and local governments while others have expanded the scope of the federal government. Conscious efforts since the Nixon administration were made to reverse the aggregation of power and authority in Washington, D.C. In part, this was philosophical, but it was also necessary. During the Reagan administration, the debt of the federal government more than tripled, and the flow of federal money and mandates that fueled much of the growth of state and local governments was reduced.

But, as noted in chapter 3, not all recent developments have enhanced the powers of state and local governments. The legacy of the administration of President George W. Bush includes a federal government that plays a major role in areas once the domain of grassroots governance, such as education, public health, and law enforcement. Federal and state partnerships in environmental and health policy have been replaced with unequal relationships in which states have less discretion and flexibility. The U.S. Supreme Court under the new leadership of Chief Justice John G. Roberts Jr. has rejected presidential intervention in a Texas death penalty conviction but ruled that federal agency approval of drugs and medical devices preempts state laws on liability for distributing harmful products.

Despite the conflicting messages, it is still clear that state and local governments have roles and responsibilities of fundamental importance. Most of the public services and regulations that affect us on a daily basis continue to be the responsibility of state and local governments. Even when there is heavy federal involvement, the actual face-to-face applications of public policy are conducted by officials at the grassroots level.

State Governments

State governments have primary responsibility for education, public health, transportation, economic development, and criminal justice. The state is also the unit of government that licenses and regulates various professions, such as doctors, lawyers, barbers, and architects. More recently, state governments have been active in welfare and the environment, in part as agents administering federal policies and programs and in part on their own. (To learn more about some of the tensions that exist between the federal and state governments, see The Living Constitution: Eleventh Amendment.)

state constitution
The document that describes the basic policies, procedures, and institutions of the government of a specific state, much as the U.S. Constitution does for the federal government.

State Constitutions

Whereas a major goal of the writers of the U.S. Constitution in 1787 was to *empower* the national government, the authors of the original **state constitutions** wanted to *limit* government. The Constitutional Convention in Philadelphia was convened, as you recall from chapter 2, because of the perception that the national government under the Articles of Confederation was not strong enough. The debates were primarily over how strong the national, or federal, government should be.

In contrast, the assumption of the authors of the first thirteen state constitutions, based on their backgrounds in the philosophy and experiences of monarchical rule, was that government should not be all powerful, so the question was how to limit it. The state constitutions were written and adopted before the Constitutional Convention and included provisions that government may not interfere with basic individual liberties. Although these

Thinking Globally

The Canadian Provinces

Canada has a federal democracy much like that of the United States. While Canada's ten provincial governments are politically strong, not one has a written constitution similar to that of an American state. In addition, each province has only one legislative house.

- Since the political power of Canadian provinces does not come from a constitution, what might be the bases for this power?
- Do states in the United States need constitutions to distinguish themselves from other states and from the federal government? Explain your answer.

The Living Constitution

The Judicial Power of the United States shall not be construed to extend to any suit in law or equity, commenced or prosecuted against one of the United States by Citizens of another State, or by Citizens or Subjects of any foreign State.

—ELEVENTH AMENDMENT

The Eleventh Amendment to the U.S. Constitution has been interpreted to grant the several states *sovereign immunity*; that is, a state cannot be sued in federal or state court without its consent. This amendment further defines the distribution of authority between federal and state governments, and it has been construed to give the states protection from the encroachment of federal power.

The Eleventh Amendment was a response to the angry public outcry regarding the Supreme Court's decision in *Chisholm v. Georgia* (1793)—a decision in which the Court held that the Judiciary Act of 1789 gave it original jurisdiction in cases regarding suits between states and citizens of other states. The *Chisholm* decision was not only widely regarded as being an untenable intrusion on state authority, but it was also considered a confirmation of Anti-Federalist fears that such a reading of Article III would "prove most pernicious and destructive" to states' rights.

The amendment was proposed at the very first meeting of Congress following the *Chisholm* decision in March 1794, and it was consequently ratified with "vehement speed" by February 1795. Interpretation of the Eleventh Amendment has subsequently been subject to inconsistent and obscure construction, and it has been a source of considerable dispute for constitutional scholars. Beginning with the New Deal, however, the federal government began to use the commerce clause to considerably expand its authority; the result was the increasing centralization and importance of the national government at the expense of substantial state power.

Under Chief Justice Rehnquist, the Supreme Court used the Eleventh Amendment to protect states from lawsuits and to return numerous powers from the federal government to the states. It is not clear whether the Court under Chief Justice Roberts will continue the trend of reestablishing a strong state sovereignty within the federal system.

CRITICAL THINKING QUESTIONS

1. Given our highly mobile, globalized society, does it make sense that states should be immune from lawsuits by citizens of another state or a foreign country? Why or why not?
2. Would you limit the use of the Eleventh Amendment to certain policy areas that you would designate as the primary responsibility of the states? If yes, which policy areas? If no, would that weaken the federal government?

provisions were integral parts of each of the state constitutions, they were added to the federal constitution as the first ten amendments: the Bill of Rights.

The first state constitutions provided for the major institutions of government, such as executives (the governors), legislatures, and courts, with an emphasis on limiting the authority of each institution.[1] The office of governor was designed to be particularly weak. The most powerful institution was each state's legislature. These constitutions did not, moreover, fully embrace the principle of checks and balances that is found in the U.S. Constitution. For example, initially only South Carolina, New York, and Massachusetts gave their governors the authority to veto legislation.

The first state constitutions set the pattern for what was to come. In one of its last actions, the national congress under the Articles of Confederation passed the

Northwest Ordinance of 1787, which addressed how new states might join the union. Lawmakers were responding primarily to settlers in what is now Ohio, but they extended coverage to the territory that includes Wisconsin, Illinois, Michigan, and Indiana—which the people in the original thirteen states considered the "northwest." The basic blueprint included in the ordinance was that a territory might successfully petition for statehood if it had at least 60,000 free inhabitants (slaves and American Indians did not count) and a constitution that was both similar to the documents of existing states and compatible with the national constitution. The first white settlers in the territory covered by the Northwest Ordinance were primarily from New York and Massachusetts. Not surprisingly, the initial constitutions of these states were almost identical to those of New York and Massachusetts.[2]

What is the legacy of the Progressive movement? Wisconsin's Robert M. La Follette, a Republican, championed Progressive reforms both as governor from 1901 to 1906 and as a U.S. senator for nearly twenty years.

Photo courtesy: Wisconsin Historical Society

The Civil War had a profound impact on the constitutions of southern states. Southern states adopted new constitutions when they seceded and formed the Confederacy. After the Civil War, they had to adopt new constitutions acceptable to the Republican-controlled Congress in Washington, D.C. These Reconstruction-era constitutions typically provided former male slaves with considerable power and disenfranchised those males who had been active in the Confederacy. (Women, as discussed in chapter 6, would not win the right to vote under the U.S. Constitution until 1920.) Because they divorced political power from economic wealth and social status and formal authority from informal influence, these were not workable constitutions. White communities simply ignored government and ruled themselves informally as much as possible. After less than ten years, whites reasserted political control and rewrote state constitutions.

The new documents reflected white distrust of government control and provided for a narrow scope of authority for state governments. Governors could serve for only two-year terms. Legislatures could meet for only short periods of time and in some cases only once every other year. Law enforcement authority, both police and justices of the peace, rested squarely in local community power structures.

Western states entered the union with constitutions that also envisioned weak governments. Here the central concern was to avoid the development of **political machines,** organizations that solicit votes from certain neighborhoods or communities for a particular political party in return for services and jobs if that party wins. (Political machines are discussed more fully later in the chapter.) In large cities in the Northeast and Midwest, machines based on bloc voting by new immigrants wrested political control from traditional elites. New states in the West sought to keep machine politics from ever getting started in the first place.

The most effective national anti-machine effort was the **Progressive movement,** led by such figures as Woodrow Wilson, Theodore Roosevelt, and Robert M. La Follette, who advocated changes that involved direct voter participation and bypassed traditional institutions.[3] These reforms included the use of primaries for nominating candidates instead of closed party processes, the initiative for allowing voters to enact laws directly rather than go through legislatures and governors, and the recall for constituents to remove officials from office in the middle of a term. Progressives suc-

---

VISUAL LITERACY

Explaining Differences in State Laws

political machine
An organization designed to solicit votes from certain neighborhoods or communities for a particular political party in return for services and jobs if that party wins.

Progressive movement
Advocated measures to destroy political machines and instead have direct participation by voters in the nomination of candidates and the establishment of public policy.

ceeded in getting their proposals adopted as statutes in existing states and in the constitutions of new states emerging from western territories. In California, progressive reforms allowed state residents to recall their governor, Gray Davis, in 2003 and replace him with movie star Arnold Schwarzenegger.

Though weak state government institutions may have been a reasonable response to earlier concerns, the trend since the 1960s, throughout the United States, has been to amend state constitutions in order to enhance the ability of governors, legislatures, and courts to address problems. In the 1970s alone, over 300 amendments to state constitutions were adopted. Most were to lengthen the terms of governors and provide chief executives with more authority over spending and administration, to streamline courts, and to make legislatures professional and full-time.[4]

Constitutional changes have also reflected some ambivalence. While there has been widespread recognition that state governments must be more capable, there is also concern about what that might mean in taxes and in the entrenchment of power. Thus, reforms have included severe restrictions on the ability of state and local governments to raise taxes and limits on how long legislators in some states may serve. Historic distrust of a powerful government continues.

Compared with the U.S. Constitution, state constitutions are relatively easy to amend. Every state allows for the convening of a constitutional convention, and over 200 have been held. Also, every state has a process whereby the legislature can pass an amendment to the state constitution, usually by a two-thirds or three-fourths vote, and then submit the change to the voters for their approval in a referendum. Seventeen states, mostly in the West, allow for amendments simply by getting the proposal on a statewide ballot, without involvement of the legislature or governor.

An implication of the relatively simple amendment processes is frequent changes. All but nineteen states have adopted wholly new constitutions since they were first admitted to the union, and almost 6,000 specific amendments have been adopted. Another effect of the process is that state constitutions tend to be longer than the U.S. Constitution and include provisions that more appropriately should be statutes or administrative rules. The California constitution, for example, not only establishes state government institutions and protects individual rights but also defines how long a wrestling match may be. Florida's constitution stipulates that it is a misdemeanor to confine a pregnant pig.

You Are Attempting to Revise the California Constitution

You Are Attempting to Revise the Texas Constitution

Governors

Governors have always been the most visible elected officials in state governments. Initially, that visibility supported the ceremonial role of governors as their primary function. Now that visibility serves governors as they set the agenda and provide leadership for others in state governments. (To learn about the party affiliations of governors in 2009, see Figure 4.1.)

The most important role that governors currently play is in identifying the most pressing problems facing their respective states and proposing solutions to those problems. Governors first establish agendas when they campaign for office. After inauguration, the most effective way for the chief executive to initiate policy changes is when submitting the budget for legislative approval.

Budgets are critical to the business of state governments. How money is raised and spent says a lot about the priorities of decision makers. Until the 1920s, state legislatures commonly compiled and passed budgets and then submitted them for gubernatorial approval or veto. As part of the efforts since the 1960s to strengthen the effectiveness of state governments, governors were, like presidents, given the major responsibility for starting the budget process. Now nearly all states have their governors propose budgets.

The role of governor as budget initiator is especially important when coupled with the governor's veto authority and executive responsibilities. Like presidents, gov-

governor
Chief elected executive in state government.

FIGURE 4.1 Political Party of State Governors, 2009 Democrats picked up one governorships in the 2008 elections and now control the corner offices in twenty-nine states.
Source: National Council of State Legislatures, http://www. ncsl. org, updated by the authors.

package or general veto
The authority of a chief executive to void an entire bill that has been passed by the legislature. This veto applies to all bills, whether or not they have taxing or spending components, and the legislature may override this veto, usually with a two-thirds majority of each chamber.

line-item veto
The authority of a chief executive to delete part of a bill passed by the legislature that involves taxing or spending. The legislature may override a veto, usually with a two-thirds majority of each chamber.

ernors have **package** or **general veto** authority, which is the power to reject a bill in its entirety. In addition, governors in all but seven states may exercise a **line-item veto** on bills that involve spending or taxing. A line-item veto strikes only part of a bill that has been passed by the legislature. It allows a chief executive to delete a particular pro-gram or expenditure from a budget bill and let the remaining provisions become law. The intent of this authority is to enable governors to revise the work of legislators in order to produce a balanced budget.

When Tommy Thompson, U.S. secretary of health and human services from 2001 to 2004, was governor of Wisconsin, he was the most extensive and creative user of the line-item veto. He reversed the intent of legislation by vetoing the word "not" in a sentence and created entirely new laws by eliminating specific letters and numerals to make new words and numbers. Voters in Wisconsin were so upset with this free use of the veto pen that in 1993 they passed the "Vanna White amendment" to the state constitution, prohibiting the governor from striking letters within words and numerals within numbers. Governor Thompson and his successors nonetheless strategically vetoed words from adjoining sen-tences to create new sentences or even law that the legislature never debated. In 2008, Wisconsin voters again amended the constitution to prohibit this practice.

While the Wisconsin case is extreme, it illustrates the significant power that veto authority can provide. Legislators can override vetoes, usually with a two-thirds vote in each of the chambers, but this rarely happens.

The executive responsibilities of governors provide an opportunity to affect public policies after laws have been passed. Agencies are responsible for implementing the laws. That may mean improving a road, enforcing a regulation, or providing a service. The speed and care with which implementation occurs are often under the influence of the governor.[5] Likewise, governors can affect the many details and interpretations that must be decided. State statutes require drivers of vehicles to have a license, but they typ-ically let an agency decide exactly what one must do to get a license, where one can take the tests, and what happens if someone fails a test. Governors can influence these kinds of decisions primarily through appointing the heads of state administrative agencies.

One of the methods of limiting gubernatorial power is to curtail appointment authority.[6] Unlike the federal government, for example, states have some major agencies headed by individuals who are elected rather than appointed by the chief executive. Forty-three states, for example, elect their attorney general, secretary of state, treasurer, and auditor. Some states elect their head of education, agriculture, or labor. The movement throughout states to strengthen the institutions of their governments has included increasing the number of senior positions that are filled by gubernatorial appointments so that governors, like heads of major corporations, can assemble their own policy and management teams.

Another position that is filled by presidential appointment in the federal government but elected in most state governments is judge. This is one more example of approaches that have been taken to restrict the authority of governors. Nonetheless, governors are major actors in the judicial system. With the legislature, they define what a crime within a state is and attach penalties that should be meted out to those convicted of committing crimes. After being convicted, a person will be institutionalized or supervised by an agency that is, in every state, headed by a gubernatorial appointment. Moreover, governors have authority to grant a **pardon** to someone who has been convicted, thereby eliminating all penalties and voiding the court action on an individual's record. Governors may also **commute** all or part of a sentence, which leaves the conviction on record even though the penalty is reduced. In addition, governors grant **parole** to prisoners who have served part of their terms. Typically, governors are advised by a parole board on whether or not to grant a parole.

Finally, under the U.S. Constitution, governors have the discretion to **extradite** individuals. This means that a governor may decide to send someone, against his or her will, to another state to face criminal charges. In December 2007, Governor Matt Blunt of Missouri asked Governor Rod Blagojevich of Illinois to extradite Timothy Krajcir so that he might stand trial and perhaps be executed for raping and murdering five women in Cape Girardeau, Missouri. Krajcir was imprisoned in Illinois for unrelated sex crimes and the murder of a student at Southern Illinois University. Governor Blagojevich had extended the moratorium on executions in Illinois begun by his predecessor and did not want to send Krajcir to a death chamber in a neighboring state. The issue was resolved when Krajcir, who was sixty-three in 2007, pled guilty to the murders in Missouri and yet another in Illinois and was sentenced to serve two consecutive forty-year terms.

Gubernatorial participation in the judicial process has led to some of the most colorful controversies in state politics. James E. Ferguson, as governor of Texas, granted 2,253 pardons between 1915 and 1917. His successor, William P. Hobby, granted 1,518 during the next two years, and then Governor Miriam "Ma" Ferguson outdid her husband by issuing almost 3,800 during her term. Texans were used to shady wheeling and dealing in politics, but this volume of pardons seemed a bit excessive. The Texas constitution was amended to remove authority to grant pardons and paroles from the governor; this power was placed in the hands of a board. Governors of the Lone Star State now have the lowest amount of authority among the fifty state chief executives to check actions of the judiciary.[7]

The general trend since the 1960s has been an increase rather than decrease in the power and authority of governors.[8] This enhancement of gubernatorial powers has come at the cost of the prerogatives of other institutions, especially state legislatures.

State Legislatures

The principles of representative democracy are embodied primarily in the legislature. Legislatures, as mentioned above, were initially established to be the most powerful of the institutions of state government. In over half of the original states, legislatures began without the check of a gubernatorial veto. Until the twentieth century, most state legislatures were responsible for executive chores such as formulating a budget and making administrative appointments.

pardon
The authority of a governor to cancel someone's conviction of a crime by a court and to eliminate all sanctions and punishments resulting from the conviction.

commute
The action of a governor to cancel all or part of the sentence of someone convicted of a crime, while keeping the conviction on the record.

parole
The authority of a governor to release a prisoner before his or her full sentence has been completed and to specify conditions that must be met as part of the release.

extradite
To send someone against his or her will to another state to face criminal charges.

You Are a Governor

POLITICS NOW

Source: VIRGINIAN-PILOT March 28, 2008

Driver Fees

Kaine Signs Bill to Repeal Abusive Driver Fees, Give Refunds

BY JULIAN WALKER

The highly unpopular abusive driver fees approved by the state legislature last year are officially roadkill. Gov. Timothy M. Kaine signed two bills Thursday that rescind the fines. The repeal is effective immediately. The bills provide a mechanism to refund individuals who have already paid the fines. The legislation also gives motorists an opportunity to restore their drivers licenses if they were revoked for failure to pay the fees.

Lawmakers last year passed the higher-than-normal fines for certain driving convictions as part of a plan to finance road projects throughout Virginia. In some instances, the abusive driver fines—which sparked online petitions that collected thousands of signatures—were as much as $3,000.

The fees also faced several challenges in courts across the state. In separate rulings last year, judges in Portsmouth and Virginia Beach upheld the legality of the fines.

"After six months of implementation, it was clear that the fees did not improve the safety of Virginia highways," Kaine said in a written statement announcing action on the two bills. "The citizens of Virginia expressed concerns regarding these fees, and based on these concerns, I have signed the bills that repeal the fees."

One of the repeal bills was sponsored by Sen. Edward Houck, D-Spotsylvania. "Back in the summer when I announced I would be filing the bill for the repeal, I talked about driving a stake in this beast's heart," Houck said Thursday. "To me, today the stake is finally in the beast's heart," he said. Kaine's repeal of the bills is the end of a serious mistake by the legislature, Houck said.

Similar legislation sponsored by Del. Tim Hugo, R-Fairfax, was also signed by the governor Thursday.

Individuals who have already paid the fees will receive refunds from the state. Outstanding balances still owed will be forgiven. However, court fines owed in connection to driving convictions that carried an abuser fee still must be paid. Drivers who lost licenses for nonpayment of bad driver fees can have their privileges restored by the state Department of Motor Vehicles.

Abusive driver fees were supposed to raise about $65 million annually towards state road costs. Since July 1, when they were enacted, only about $13 million were assessed, of which $4 million was collected.

More than 37,000 convictions carried abusive driver fees from July through December, according to the Virginia Supreme Court.

Discussion Questions

1. *When the legislature and governor enacted the stiff penalties for abusive drivers, they were responding to Virginia drivers. Is the repeal of this legislation a response to abusive drivers? Explain your answer.*
2. *Was it appropriate to repeal the law after it had been in effect for only six months? Why or why not?*
3. *If you were a governor or state legislator, what lessons would you take from Virginia's experience clamping down on abusive drivers?*

These tasks were, even more than was envisioned for the U.S. Congress, to be done by "citizen legislators" as a part-time responsibility. The assumption was that individuals would convene in the state capitol for short periods of time to conduct the state's business. State constitutions and statutes specified the part-time operation of the legislature and provided only limited compensation for those who served.

As mentioned earlier, the one-person, one-vote ruling of the U.S. Supreme Court in *Baker* v. *Carr* (1962) marked a turning point in the history of state government. Once legislatures more accurately represented their states, agendas became more relevant and policies that were adopted reflected the needs and wishes of the people.[9] (To learn about one state's response to its citizens, see Politics Now: Driver Fees.) State legislatures not only became more representative; they became more professional. Legislators worked more days—some of them full-time. In 1960, only eighteen state legislatures met annually. As of 2009, forty-three met every year and only seven every other year. Moreover, floor sessions were longer, and between sessions legislators and their staff increasingly did committee work and conducted special studies.[10] In 2004, California's newly elected governor, Arnold Schwarzenegger, criticized the full-time role of state legislators, arguing that this made legislators think they had to enact more laws: "Spending so much time in Sacramento, without anything to do, then out of that comes strange bills."[11] His attempts to enact reforms, however, were decisively rejected by the people of California in 2006.

All states except Nebraska have two legislative houses. One, the senate, typically has fewer members than the other, usually called the "house" or the "assembly." The most common ratio between the two chambers is 1:3. In fourteen states, the ratio is 1:2; in New Hampshire, it is 1:16. Another difference between the two bodies in thirty-four of the states is that senators serve four-year terms, whereas representatives in the larger house serve two-year terms. In eleven states, everyone in both houses serves two-year terms, and in the remaining five, including Nebraska, everyone serves for four years.

Although it has been common to have limits on how many terms someone may serve as governor, **term limits** for legislators did not gain widespread support until the 1980s and 1990s. By 1999, twenty states had laws limiting the number of years one might be a state legislator. Although there has been a slow but steady increase in the number of local governments with term limits, a number of states have abolished their term limits for state legislators. By 2008, the number of states was down to fifteen. Depending on the state, limits vary between six and twelve years. (To learn more about states with term limits, see Table 4.1.)

State legislatures are still primarily part-time, citizen bodies.[12] Every election puts new members in about one-fourth of the seats. Only a handful of legislators in each state envision careers as state lawmakers. Those with long-term political aspirations tend to view service in a state chamber as a step on a journey to some other office, in the state capital or in Washington, D.C. For some, their goal is to don a black robe and preside in a courtroom.

Photo courtesy: Oliphant © Universal Press Syndicate. Reprinted with permission. All Rights Reserved.

STILL THE BEST CONGRESSIONAL TERM-LIMITING DEVICE.

Should voters force politicians out of office by refusing to reelect them, or should elected officials serve only for a period of time that is established by law? Is it realistic to think that incumbents can be beaten in their bids for reelection?

State Courts

Almost everyone is in a courtroom at some point. It may be as a judge, a juror, an attorney, a court officer, or a litigant. It may also be for some administrative function such as an adoption, a name change, or the implementation of a will. Few of us will ever be in a federal court; almost all of us will be in a state court (except people who live in Washington, D.C., where *all* courts are federal courts).

The primary function of courts is to settle disputes, and most disputes are matters of state, not federal, laws. For the most part, criminal behavior is defined by state

term limits
Restrictions that exist in some states about how long an individual may serve in state or local elected offices.

TABLE **4.1** States with Term Limits for State Legislators

	House		Senate	
	Effective Date	Limit (years)	Effective Date	Limit (years)
Maine	1996	8	1996	8
California	1996	6	1998	8
Colorado	1998	8	1998	8
Arkansas	1998	6	2000	8
Michigan	1998	6	2002	8
Florida	2000	8	2000	8
Ohio	2000	8	2000	8
South Dakota	2000	8	2000	8
Montana	2000	8	2000	8
Arizona	2000	8	2000	8
Missouri[a]	2002	8	2002	8
Oklahoma	2004	12	2004	12
Louisiana	2007	12	2007	12
Nebraska	n/a	n/a	2008	8
Nevada	2010	12	2010	12

[a] Because of special elections, term limits were effective in 1998 for one senator and in 2001 for five House members.
Source: National Council of State Legislatures, http://www.ncsl.org.

legislatures. Family law, dealing with marriage, divorce, adoption, child custody, and the like, is found in state statutes. Contracts, liability, land use, and much that is fundamental to everyday business activity and economic development also are part of state governance.

A common misunderstanding is that the courts in the United States are all part of a single system, with the U.S. Supreme Court at the head. In fact, state and federal courts are separate, with their own rules, procedures, and routes for appeal. The only time state and federal courts converge is when a case involves a claim that a state law or practice violates a federal law or the Constitution or a state court judge has interpreted the Constitution. (See chapter 10 for more on the judiciary.)

Sometimes federal and state laws are directly related. If there is a contradiction between the two, then federal law usually prevails. A state statute that allowed or encouraged racial discrimination, for example, would directly conflict with the 1964 federal Civil Rights Act and the Fourteenth Amendment to the U.S. Constitution. Through a rule known as **inclusion,** state courts are obliged to enforce the federal law.

Since the 1970s, the U.S. Supreme Court has generally taken the position that state courts should be encouraged to regard the federal government as setting only minimal standards for protecting the constitutional rights of individuals.[13] If state constitutions and laws provide additional protections or benefits, then state courts should enforce those standards.

Like other state government institutions, courts have modernized in the past few decades. Many states reorganized their court systems in the 1970s to follow a model that relied on full-time, qualified judges and simplified appeal routes, which enabled state supreme courts to have a manageable workload. (To learn about the typical structure of state courts, see Figure 4.2.)

Most court cases in urban areas begin in a court that specializes in issues such as family disputes, traffic, small claims (less than $500 or $1,000), or probate (wills) or in a general jurisdiction municipal court. Small towns and rural areas usually do not have specialized courts. If they do, the position of judge is part-time. Cases here start in county-level courts that deal with the full array of disputes.

Specialized courts do not use juries. A single judge hears the case and decides the case. General courts at this level do have juries if requested by the litigants (parties in a case). A major responsibility of the judges and juries that deliberate on cases when they are originated is to evaluate the credibility of the witnesses and evidence. When cases are heard on appeal, the only individuals making presentations are attorneys.

Appellate courts have panels of judges. There are no juries in these courtrooms. An important feature of the court reorganizations of the 1970s is that a court of appeals exists between the circuit or county courts and the state supreme court. This court is to cover a region in the state and is supposed to accept all appeals. In part, this appellate level is to

inclusion
The principle that state courts will apply federal laws when those laws directly conflict with the laws of a state.

FIGURE 4.2 State Court Structure Most state courts have the basic organization shown here.

	Jury or Bench Trials	Jurisdiction	Judges
STATE SUPREME COURT	Bench only	Appeal (limited)	Panel of judges, elected/appointed for fixed term
APPEALS COURTS	Bench only	Appeal (readily granted)	Panel of judges, elected/appointed for fixed term
CIRCUIT OR COUNTY COURTS	Jury and bench	Original and appeal	One judge per court, elected/appointed for fixed term
MUNICIPAL AND SPECIAL COURTS	Jury and bench	Original	One judge per court, elected/appointed for fixed term

allow supreme courts to decide whether or not they will hear a case. The basic principle is that all litigants should have at least one opportunity to appeal a decision. If the state supreme court is the only place where an appeal can be lodged, that court is almost inevitably going to have too heavy a caseload and unreasonable backlogs will develop.

Most state judges are elected to the bench for a specific term. This differs from the federal government, where the president appoints judges for indefinite terms. Only three states use gubernatorial appointments. The first states had their legislatures elect judges, and that is still the case in Connecticut, Rhode Island, South Carolina, and Virginia. In thirteen states, voters elect judges and use party identification. In their efforts to limit and even destroy political machines, Progressives at the turn of the twentieth century advocated electing judges without party labels. Today, nineteen states use nonpartisan elections for selecting their judges. The remaining states went a step further and allowed for the election of judges but only after screening for qualifications. This process is referred to as the **Missouri** (or Merit) **Plan**. (To learn more about how states select judges, see Table 4.2.) The governor selects someone from a list prepared by an independent panel and appoints him or her as a judge for a specific term of years. If a judge wishes to serve for an additional term, he or she must receive approval from the voters, who express themselves on a "yes/no" ballot. If a majority of voters cast a "no" ballot, the process starts all over. Six states (Kansas, Missouri, New York, Rhode Island, South Dakota, and Tennessee) use the Missouri Plan for some judicial positions and elections or appointments for the others.

Missouri (Merit) Plan
A method of selecting judges in which a governor must appoint someone from a list provided by an independent panel. Judges are then kept in office if they get a majority of "yes" votes in general elections.

Elections and Political Parties

Elections are the vehicle for determining who will fill major state government positions and who will direct the institutions of state government. Almost all contests for state government posts are partisan. The major exceptions are judicial elections in many states, as noted above, and the senate in Nebraska's unicameral legislature. Although party labels are not used and political parties are not formally participants in nonpartisan races, the party identity of some candidates may be known and may have some influence.

TABLE 4.2 Judicial Selection Patterns

Partisan Election	Nonpartisan Election		Election by Legislature	Appointment by Governor
Alabama	Arkansas	North Dakota	Connecticut	California
Arkansas	California	Oregon	Rhode Island	Maine
Illinois	Florida	South Dakota	South Carolina	New Jersey
Indiana	Georgia	Utah	Virginia	
Kansas	Idaho	Washington		
Louisiana	Indiana	Wisconsin		
Missouri	Kentucky			
New York	Michigan			
Ohio	Minnesota			
Pennsylvania	Mississippi			
Tennessee	Montana			
Texas	Nevada			
West Virginia	North Carolina			

Merit Plan		
Alaska	Iowa	New York
Arizona	Kansas	Oklahoma
Colorado	Maryland	Rhode Island
Connecticut	Massachusetts	South Dakota
Delaware	Missouri	Tennessee
Florida	Nebraska	Vermont
Hawaii	New Hampshire	Wyoming
Indiana	New Mexico	

Note: Some states use different selection systems for different courts.
Source: Adapted from *The Book of the States, 2008* (Lexington, KY: Council of State Governments, 2008), 253–56.

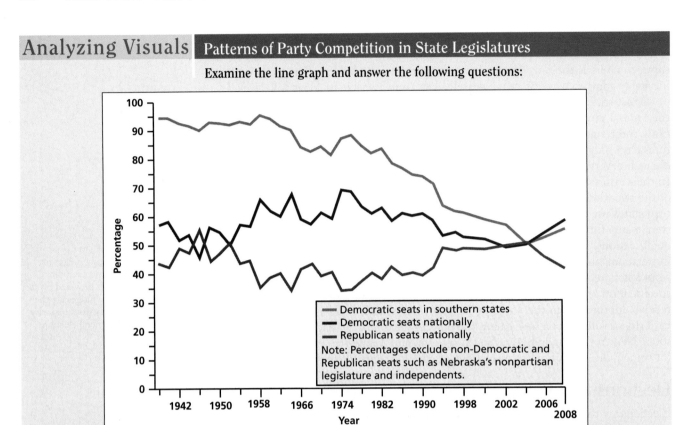

Analyzing Visuals   Patterns of Party Competition in State Legislatures

Examine the line graph and answer the following questions:

WHAT trends do you see in the regional patterns of party competition?

WHAT major movement nationally led to the decline of Democratic Party dominance in southern states?

WHAT major national event contributed to a surge in Democratic strength in the mid-1970s?

HOW would you explain the even competitiveness of the Republicans and Democrats since the mid-1990s?

Source: National Conference of State Legislatures, http://www. ncsl. org. Updated by the authors.

TIMELINE
Initiatives and Referendums

Political parties have different histories and roles in the various states. The line graph in Analyzing Visuals: Patterns of Party Competition in State Legislatures shows the trends in the number of state legislative seats won by Republicans and Democrats. Most states have experienced significant competition between Republicans and Democrats since the Civil War. These states often have party control split between the two houses of the legislature and the governor's office or have frequent changes in party control of state government.

From 1994 to 2002, Republicans made gains in state elections. One of the reasons for Republican success is that voters in the South who had been voting for conservative Democrats began voting for conservative Republicans. Southerners have supported Republican presidential candidates since the Democratic Party began asserting leadership for civil rights following World War II. Alignment with Republicans in contests for state and congressional positions was a more gradual process, however. Today, Southerners no longer represent a significant minority within the national Democratic Party but instead are part of the majority within the Republican Party—nationally and regionally.

It is easy to exaggerate the importance of partisanship in state elections. While party labels and organizations matter, state campaigns are primarily centered on individual candidates. A common strategy of candidates is to downplay their party identification, both to emphasize their strengths as individuals and to appeal to independent voters. After the election, party labels are important in determining who is in the majority in the legislature and therefore who will control committees and who will preside. That affects the agenda and the dynamics of policy making.

Elections since the 1960s have led increasingly to ethnic and racial and gender diversity among state and local officials. It is now common for African Americans, Hispanic Americans, Asian and Pacific Americans, and women to be mayors, including in some of the largest cities. In 2002, Mee Moua was elected to the state senate in Minnesota, becoming the first Hmong elected to any state legislature in the country. Two years later, another Hmong, Cy Thao, was elected to the Minnesota Assembly, and Asian Americans and Pacific Islanders, who had won offices in states such as Arizona, California, and Hawaii, won for the first time in states such as Connecticut and South Carolina.

In 2006, Massachusetts elected its first African American governor, Deval Patrick, and, in 2008, David Patterson became the first African American governor of New York. Patterson is also the first legally blind governor of a state. Nine states had women governors in 2009. While women have made some gains in gubernatorial contests, there has been virtually no change in state legislatures, where women have held 22–24 percent of the seats since 1980.

Photo courtesy: Richard Masoner

Direct Democracy

As mentioned earlier, a Progressive reform meant to weaken parties and protect against the development of political machines was to provide opportunities for voters to legislate directly and not have to go through state legislatures and governors.[14] That process, known as the **direct initiative,** is available in eighteen states, most of them in the West. Citizens in these states have been able to enact laws as wide ranging as legalizing physician assisted suicide, limiting property taxes, building mass transit systems, and outlawing cock fighting. (See Join the Debate: Direct Democracy and State Government.)

A disadvantage of the direct initiative is the possibility that a law may be passed solely because of public opinion shaped largely by thirty-second television commercials and simplistic slogans. Unlike the process when a legislative body debates a measure, there is no opportunity for making amendments to direct initiatives.

Sometimes initiatives are passed and then set aside by courts because they violate the state or federal constitution or because the federal government preempts the state. When California, for example, passed Proposition 187 in 1994, denying most public services to unregistered immigrants, federal courts kept the state from implementing the law because it trespassed on federal immigration policy and violated the U.S. Constitution.

Debate, deliberation, and amendment are included in the **indirect initiative.** In this process, legislatures first consider the issue and then pass a bill that will become law if approved by the voters. The governor plays no role. Of the eleven states that have the indirect initiative, five also have the direct initiative.

Voters in twenty-three states have the opportunity to veto some bills. This is known as a **direct** or **popular referendum.** In May 2006, the South Dakota legislature and governor enacted a law that would have made it almost impossible for a woman in that state to get an abortion. In large part, this law was passed to give the U.S. Supreme Court, with two new justices, an opportunity to overturn *Roe* v. *Wade* (1973). However, the voters of South Dakota used a direct referendum in November 2006 to repeal the law, providing South Dakota women with reproductive choice and eliminating a test case.

All state and local legislative bodies may place an **advisory referendum** on a ballot. As the name implies, this is a device to take the pulse of the voters on a particular issue and has no binding effect. In addition, voter approval is required in a referendum to amend constitutions and, in some cases, to allow a governmental unit to borrow money through issuing bonds.

What is the significance of having members of minority groups in public office? Yoriko Kishimoto was born and raised in Japan and has lived in Palo Alto, CA, since 1988. She was elected to the city council in 2001 and her colleagues on the council voted to name her Mayor of Palo Alto in 2007. Here, Mayor Kishimoto discusses the positive environmental impact of her city's participation in the 2008 Amgen Tour of California—a bicycling race.

direct initiative
A process in which voters can place a proposal on a ballot and enact it into law without involving the legislature or the governor.

indirect initiative
A process in which the legislature places a proposal on a ballot and allows voters to enact it into law, without involving the governor or further action by the legislature.

direct (popular) referendum
A process in which voters can veto a bill recently passed in the legislature by placing the issue on a ballot and expressing disapproval.

advisory referendum
A process in which voters cast nonbinding ballots on an issue or proposal.

recall
A process in which voters can petition for a vote to remove office holders between elections.

Finally, eighteen states provide for some form of **recall** election. Voters in these states have the power to petition for an election to remove an office holder before the next scheduled election. Judges, state legislators, and other office holders are occasionally the subject of a recall campaign. Most states require that the official serve in office for at least one year before being subject to a recall.[15]

Local Governments

The institutions and politics of local governance are even more individualized than those of state governments. In part this is because officials are friends, neighbors, and acquaintances living in the communities they serve. Except in large cities, most elected officials fulfill their responsibilities on a part-time basis. The personal nature of local governance is also due to the immediacy of the issues. The responsibilities of local governments include public health and safety in their communities, education of children in the area, jobs and economic vitality, zoning land for particular uses, and assistance to those in need. Local government policies and activities are the stuff of everyday living.

Thinking Globally

Direct Democracy in Venezuela

In December of 2007, Venezuelan President Hugo Chavez narrowly lost his bid to change the country's constitution in ways that would have given him expansive new powers, including the chance to stay in office indefinitely. Chavez's proposed constitutional changes were put to the test in a national referendum. Three years earlier, Chavez prevailed over an attempt to recall his presidency, winning 59 percent of the vote in an election that was certified by international monitors as free and fair.

- Should the United States have national initiatives and referendums, or should we keep these methods at the state level? Explain your reasoning.
- Recall elections are uncommon in the United States. Should all U.S. states provide for some form of recall election? Recall elections are not an option at the federal level, but should they be?

Charters

Romantic notions of democracy in America regard local governments as the building blocks of governance by the people. Alexis de Tocqueville, the critic credited with capturing the essence of early America, described government in the new country as a series of social contracts starting at the grass roots. He said, "the township was organized before the county, the county before the state, the state before the union."[16] It sounds good, but it's wrong. A more accurate description comes from Judge John F. Dillon, who in an 1868 ruling known as **Dillon's Rule** proclaimed: "The true view is this: Municipal corporations owe their origins to and derive their power and rights wholly from the [state] legislature. It breathes into them the breath without which they cannot exist. As it creates, so it may destroy. If it may destroy, it may abridge and control."[17] Dillon's Rule applies to all types of local governments.

Dillon's Rule
A court ruling that local governments do not have any inherent sovereignty but instead must be authorized by state government.

There are many categories of local governments. Some of these are created in a somewhat arbitrary way by state governments. Counties and school districts are good examples. State statutes establish the authority for these jurisdictions, set the boundaries, and determine what these governments may and may not do and how they can generate funds.

Cities, towns, and villages are not established arbitrarily by state governments but emerge as people locate in a particular place. These local governments, however, need a **charter** that is acceptable to the state legislature, much as states must have a constitution acceptable to Congress in order to pass laws and levy taxes and fees. Charters describe the institutions of government, the processes used to make legally binding decisions, and the scope of issues and services that fall within the jurisdiction of the governmental body being chartered. There are five basic types of charters:

charter
A document that, like a constitution, specifies the basic policies, procedures, and institutions of a municipality.

1. *Special charters.* Historically, as urban areas emerged, each one developed and sought approval for its own charter. To avoid inconsistencies, most state constitutions now prohibit the granting of special charters.

Campaign Against Hunger and Homelessness

On April 5, 2008, university students around the country worked at local food pantries and homeless shelters to do chores and help raise money for programs helping the growing number of hungry and homeless people. This one-day event was part of the National Student Campaign Against Hunger and Homelessness, sponsored in part by over 100 student chapters of U.S. PIRG, a federation of state Public Interest Research Groups (PIRGs).

In addition to the day of assisting local government agencies and nonprofit organizations, students in the campaign completed research papers (sometimes for course credit) and lobbied by presenting the findings of their research to relevant committees of city, county, and state governments. Students also spoke before campus and community groups to raise awareness of the problems of hunger and homelessness, to get signatures on petitions for government assistance, and to solicit funds.

While one usually associates issues of hunger and homelessness with large cities, poverty and its effects exist in small towns and rural areas, as well. Local concerns and the need for action are similar across the nation, regardless of the state or region.

- What problems of hunger and homelessness exist in your college community? How might charitable organizations provide assistance? Are there efforts underway?
- What kinds of responses might governments provide?
- How can students help encourage community and government action?
- Conduct research on hunger and on the circumstances that cause homelessness or substandard housing in your college community and share your findings with government, community, and campus organizations.
- Roll up your sleeves and volunteer to help community and government agencies that are addressing hunger and homelessness.
- Organize a food drive, perhaps with food donations as a requirement for admission to a campus sport or music event.

---

2. *General charters.* Some states use a standard charter for all jurisdictions, regardless of size or circumstance.

3. *Classified charters.* This approach classifies cities according to population and then has a standard charter for each classification.

4. *Optional charters.* A more recent development is for the state to provide several acceptable charters and then let voters in a community choose from these.

5. *Home-rule charters.* Increasingly, states specify the major requirements that a charter must meet and then allow communities to draft and amend their own charters. State government must still approve the final product.

An important feature of home rule is that the local government is authorized to legislate on any issue that does not conflict with existing state or federal laws. Other charter approaches list the subjects that a town or city may address. (For a discussion of student involvement in local government efforts to meet the needs of the hungry and homeless, see Ideas into Action: Campaign Against Hunger and Homelessness.)

Types of Local Governments

There are about 87,000 local governments in the United States. The four major categories are as follows.

1. *Counties.* Every state has **counties,** although in Louisiana they are called parishes, and in Alaska, boroughs. With few exceptions, counties have very broad responsibilities and are used by state governments as basic administrative units for welfare and environmental programs, courts, and the registration of land, births, and deaths. County and city boundaries may overlap. State actions have merged city and county in New York, San Francisco, Denver, St. Louis, Nashville, and Honolulu.

county
A geographic district created within a state with a government that has general responsibilities for land, welfare, environment, and, where appropriate, rural service policies.

Direct Democracy and State Government:
Initiative and Referendum Movements

Overview: Citizens in twenty-four states have initiated and passed or repealed laws without involving their governors or legislatures. These laws have ranged from limiting how much property owners can be taxed to allowing physicians to help the terminally ill commit suicide. Proponents of the opportunity for voters to make and repeal laws directly cite the virtues of democracy and problems with wheeling and dealing by politicians. Detractors note that when voters decide to vote yes or no on a proposal, citizens miss the deliberative process of elected representatives debating and amending policy proposals.

Initiative and referendum mechanisms originated in the Progressive movement. Through the initiative process, citizens are able to place a proposal on a ballot and enact it into law; through the referendum process, voters can veto recently passed legislation. The first state to inaugurate an initiative and referendum system was South Dakota in 1898. Currently, twenty-four states have some form of initiative and referendum system in place. Scholars offer different explanations for the use of these electoral processes. Some argue that the use of the initiative and referendum is a result of citizen grassroots mobilization to force action by unresponsive governments; others believe wealthy individuals and interest groups use these mechanisms to gain from voters what legislators are unwilling to grant.

Detractors of the initiative and referendum argue that these processes do not truly facilitate quality democratic politics. They argue that most people have neither the time nor inclination to study and deliberate on proposed initiatives, and they point to the generally dismal turnout for state and local elections as proof of an apathetic citizenry. Supporters maintain that these mechanisms are truly democractic. Voters unhappy with their government only have to show up at the ballot box to effect change.

Arguments That Initiatives and Referendums ENHANCE Democratic Practices

■ **Initiative and referendum elections help circumvent an unresponsive state government.** Citizens can use the initiative process to implement new laws, policies, and constitutional amendments that legislators are unable or unwilling to implement, and they can use the referendum to reject legislation they don't like. Voters in California, Colorado, and Oklahoma used the initiative process to impose term limits on state legislators, and voters in Washington State approved a measure that requires performance audits of government agencies. Initiatives are thus a check on legislators and hold them accountable to their constituents.

■ **Initiative and referendum elections allow for the expansion of democratic processes.** The initiative and referendum allow average citizens to participate in law-making and policy-making processes. Voters have used these processes to control state tax and spending policy and to direct their governments on social policy. Voters in Washington State approved an initiative to ban smoking inside public facilities, and voters in Maine rejected a call to repeal their law prohibiting discrimination based on sexual orientation.

■ **Initiative and referendum elections help voters counter the influence of powerful interest groups.** The influence of interest group activities and expenditures on state and local government is undeniable. Initiative and referendum mechanisms give citizens a tool to circumvent the vote trading and logrolling that go on in the legislative process due to interest group pressure. Laws passed through the initiative process do not have all the pork and amendments that typically come attached to legislation.

---

municipality
A government with general responsibilities, such as a city, town, or village government, that is created in response to the emergence of relatively densely populated areas.

2. *Towns.* In the first states and in the Midwest, "town" officially refers to a form of government in which everyone in a community is invited to an annual meeting to elect officers, adopt ordinances, and pass a budget.

3. *Municipalities.* Villages, towns, and cities are established as **municipalities** and authorized by state governments as people congregate and form communities. Some of the most intense struggles among governments within the United States

Arguments That Initiative and Referendums HINDER Democratic Practices

- **Initiative and referendum elections impede effective government.** Initiatives and referendums prevent legislators from developing consistent and coherent policy. Initiatives that restrict legislatures from raising certain types of revenue may prevent legislators from adequately budgeting to meet changing needs and priorities. Many policy makers believe that because California voters used an initiative to place severe limits on property taxes, California state legislators have been unable to sufficiently fund the state's social service programs and educational system.

- **Initiatives and referendums may lead to unforeseen and undesirable consequences.** Many drafters of initiatives do not have the requisite legal or political expertise to skillfully craft legislation. Legislators tend to make better laws, since they are usually expert in their office and have professional staffs for the research and drafting of legislation. Citizens do not have the necessary experience to understand the relationship between a given initiative and existing statutes and policy.

- **Initiatives and referendums may be anti-democratic.** In states with historically low voter turnout, those who do vote may represent only small, well-organized groups or wealthy individuals who are able to unduly influence voters, and this can result in minority tyranny.

Many of the ballot initiatives of the past twenty-five years are not the result of grassroots efforts. Those with money hire someone to collect the necessary number of signatures and then sponsor television advertisements to get voters to pass an initiative. In 2008, African Americans, Hispanics, and women in Colorado complained in court that they were misled into supporting a measure to prohibit affirmative action programs by wording on the initiative that appeared to be prohibiting discrimination.

Continuing the Debate

1. Does the initiative and referendum system create bad law? Should citizens have such a direct input in drafting or rejecting legislation? Why or why not?

2. Do initiative and referendum mechanisms give citizens a way to restrain their government and counter the influence of interest groups, or are these instruments simply tools for organized interests? Explain your answer.

To Follow the Debate Online Go To:

www.ncsl.org/programs/ legismgt/elect/initiat.htm, where the National Council of State Legislatures, a nonpartisan organization serving legislators, tracks the intro-

Photo courtesy: Pool/Getty Images

Are referendums a good use of taxpayer funds? Governor Arnold Schwarzenegger and his wife Maria Schriver prepare to vote in a California special election supported by the governor. Schwarzenegger failed to convince voters to support his slate of referendum measures and the election cost state municipalities millions of dollars.

duction and fate of initiatives and referendums.

www.iandrinstitute.org, the site of the Initiative and Referendum Institute, which promotes the expansion of these forms of direct democracy and provides relevant research and information.

www.cpr.org, the Center for Responsive Politics site, which provides information on who is funding campaigns for and against initiatives.

---

are over the boundaries, scope of authority, and sources of revenue for municipal governments.

4. ***Special Districts.*** **Special districts** are the most numerous form of government. A special district is restricted to a particular policy or service area. School districts are the most common form of special district. Others exist for library service, sewerage, water, and parks. Special districts are governed through a variety of struc-

special district
A local government that is responsible for a particular function, such as K–12 education, water, sewerage, or parks.

Photo courtesy: Kevin Jacobus/Image Works

Are public hearings and open meetings an effective way for citizens to influence public policy? One type of informal local government body is the neighborhood association.

COMPARATIVE

Comparing State and Local Governments

town meeting
Form of local government in which all eligible voters are invited to attend a meeting at which budgets and ordinances are proposed and voted on.

tures. Some have elected heads, and others, appointed. Some of these jurisdictions levy a fee to generate their revenues, whereas others depend on appropriations from a state, city, or county. A reason for the recent proliferation of special districts is to avoid restrictions on funds faced by municipalities, schools, or other jurisdictions. The creation of a special park district, for example, may enable the park to have its own budget and sources of funding and relieve a city or county treasury.

A particular municipality or special district may have been established for good reasons, but having multiple governments serving the same community and controlling the same area can create confusion. The challenge is to bridge the separation between municipalities, school districts, counties, and state agencies to effectively address an issue. A specific response to youth violence, for example, may be to provide a youth center or skateboard rink for young people in a community so they can hang out in a safe and healthy setting. Such a project poses questions about which jurisdictions will provide funding and ensure staffing. Land may have to be rezoned and building permits acquired. Will a park district be involved? Will schools count on this facility for after-school programming? What will be the role and approach of the police department? Who will be in charge?

Formal and informal arrangements among local governments exist that allow them to cooperate and coordinate their work in a single area. Miami and Dade County in Florida have been an early and visible example. The two jurisdictions have merged their public health services, jointly administer parks, operate a unified mass transit system, and together plan for development and land use. The establishment of the 911 emergency service can be a catalyst for cooperation by various police, fire, and paramedical agencies in a metropolitan area. Still, there continues to be conflict between governments on occasion and often a failure to even communicate. The past actions that created a local government can present a serious challenge for local officials and citizens alike.

Executives and Legislatures

Except for the traditional New England **town meeting,** where anyone who attends may vote on policy and management issues, local governments have some or all of the following decision-making offices:

- Elected executive, such as a mayor, village president, or county executive.
- Elected council or commission, such as a city council, school board, or county board.
- Appointed manager, such as a city manager or school superintendent.

Local government institutions are not necessarily bound to the principles of separation of powers or checks and balances that the U.S. Constitution requires of the federal government and most state constitutions require of their governments. School boards, for example, commonly have legislative, executive, and judicial authority. School board members are, with few exceptions, part-time officials, so they hire superintendents and rely heavily on them for day-to-day management and for new policy ideas. It is the school board, however, that makes the policies regarding instruction and facilities. The board also does the hiring and contracting to implement those policies. Similarly, the school board sets student conduct rules, determines if a student should be expelled, and then hears appeals from those who are disciplined.

The patterns of executive and legislative institutions in local government have their roots in the same profound events in our history that influenced state government. As mentioned earlier, the influx of immigrants into urban areas in the North after the Civil War prompted the growth of political machines.[18] New immigrants needed help getting settled. They naturally got much of that help from ethnic neighborhoods, where, for example, a family from Poland would find people who spoke Polish, restaurants with Polish food, and stores and churches with links to the old country. Politicians dealt with these ethnic neighborhoods. If the neighborhood voted to help provide victory for particular candidates for **mayor** (the chief elected official of a city) and **city council** (the legislature in a city government), then city jobs and services would be provided. Political machines were built on these quid pro quo arrangements. The bosses of those machines were either the elected officials or people who controlled the elected officials.

As part of their efforts to destroy the political machines, Progressives sought reforms that minimized the politics in local government institutions.[19] Progressives favored local governments headed by professional **managers** instead of elected executives. Managers would be appointed by councils, the members of which were elected on a nonpartisan ballot, thus removing the role of parties.

As another way of sapping the strength of ethnic bloc voting, Progressive reformers advocated that council members be elected from the city at large rather than from neighborhood districts. The choice between **district-based elections** and **at-large elections** now, however, raises concerns about discrimination against racial and ethnic minorities. At-large elections may keep minority representatives from being elected. Elections by districts is not necessarily the answer, however, because boundaries can be drawn to split ethnic neighborhoods and make an ethnic group a minority in several districts, rather than drawing a district where they are in the majority.

Progressives argued that the **commission** form of government was an acceptable alternative to mayors and boss politics. The commission evolved as a response to a hurricane in 1900 that killed almost 10,000 people in southern Texas. After the disaster, a group of prominent business leaders in Galveston formed a task force, with each member assuming responsibility for a specific area, such as housing, public safety, and finance. Task-force members essentially assumed the roles of both legislators making policy and managers implementing policy. The citizens of Galveston were so impressed with how well this worked that they amended their charter to replace the mayor and city council with a commission, elected at large and on a nonpartisan basis. The model spread quickly, and by 1917 almost 500 cities had adopted the commission form of government.

Between 1984 and 2002, there was a trend away from the council–manager form of city government toward the mayor–council form. (To learn more about changes in the forms of municipal governments, see Table 4.3.) Now half of all U.S. cities have an elected mayor and a council. Mayors differ in how much authority they have. Some are strong and have the power to veto city council action, appoint agency heads, and initiate as well as execute budgets. The charters of other cities do not provide mayors with these formal powers. Except for the largest cities, mayors serve on a part-time basis.

Slightly more than one-third of the municipalities have the Progressive model of government, with an appointed, professional manager and an elected city council. This is the most common pattern among medium-sized cities, whereas the very large

Photo courtesy: Bettmann/CORBIS

What are the most effective forms of local government? In the aftermath of the devastating 1900 hurricane in Galveston, Texas, the commission form of city government came into being. Although later abandoned by Galveston, the model spread quickly; by 1917, almost 500 cities had adopted the commission form of government.

mayor
Chief elected executive of a city.

city council
The legislature in a city government

manager
A professional executive hired by a city council or county board to manage daily operations and to recommend policy changes.

district-based election
Election in which candidates run for an office that represents only the voters of a specific district within the jurisdiction.

at-large election
Election in which candidates for office must compete throughout the jurisdiction as a whole.

commission
Form of local government in which several officials are elected to top positions that have both legislative and executive responsibilities.

TABLE 4.3 Major Forms of Municipal Government

Form of Government	1984	2002
Council–Manager	3,387 (48.5%)	2,290 (34.7%)
Mayor–Council	3,011 (43.1%)	3,686 (55.8%)
Commission	143 (2.0%)	176 (2.7%)
Town Meeting	337 (4.8%)	370 (5.6%)
Representative Town Meeting	63 (.9%)	81 (1.2%)
Total[a]	6,981 (100%)	6,603 (100%)

[a] Totals for U.S. local governments represent only those municipalities with populations of 2,500 and greater. There are close to 30,000 local governments with populations under 2,500.
Source: Statistics from "Inside the Year Book: Cumulative Distributions of U.S. Municipalities," *The Municipal Year Books* 1984–2002, International City/County Management Association (ICMA), Washington, DC.

public corporation (authority)
Government organization established to provide a particular service or run a particular facility that is independent of other city or state agencies and is to be operated like a business. Examples include a port authority or a mass transit system.

and the very small have mayors and councils. Some jurisdictions have both mayors and managers. Only 2 percent of U.S. cities use the commission form of government. Portland, Oregon, is the largest city run by a commission. Galveston, however, has abandoned this structure.

Over 1,800 of the almost 3,000 county governments are run by boards or councils that are elected from geographic districts and without any executive. Committees of the county board manage personnel, finance, roads, parks, social services, and the like. Almost 400 counties elect an executive as well as a board, and thus follow the mayor–council model. Almost 800 hire a professional manager.

School districts, with very few exceptions, follow the council–manager model. Other special districts have boards, sometimes called **public corporations** or **authorities,** that are elected or appointed by elected officials. If the district is responsible for services such as water, sewerage, or mass transit, the board is likely to hire and then supervise a manager.

Officials at the various levels of government also draw on a number of intergovernmental groups for information, expertise, and networking. (To learn more about the major intergovernmental associations, see Table 4.4.) These groups include the National Governors Association, the National Conference of State Legislatures, and the International City/County Management Association.

Grassroots Power and Politics

Political participation in state and, especially, local politics is more personal and more issue-oriented than at the national level. Much of what happens is outside the framework of political parties. Elections for some state and local government offices, in fact, are **nonpartisan elections,** which means parties do not nominate candidates and ballots do not include any party identification of those running for office. Access and approaches are usually direct. School board members receive phone calls at their homes. Members of

nonpartisan election
A contest in which candidates run without formal identification or association with a political party.

TABLE 4.4 The "Big Seven" Intergovernmental Associations

Association	Date Founded	Membership
National Governors Association (NGA)	1908	Incumbent governors
Council of State Governments	1933	Direct membership by states and territories; serves all branches of government; has dozens of affiliate organizations of specialists
National Conference of State Legislatures (NCSL)	1948	State legislators and staff
National League of Cities (NLC)	1924	Direct membership by cities and state leagues of cities
National Association of Counties (NAC)	1935	Direct membership by counties; loosely linked state associations; affiliate membership for county professional specialists
United States Conference of Mayors (USCM)	1933	Direct membership by cities with population over 30,000
International City/County Management Association (ICMA)	1914	Direct membership by appointed city and county managers and other professionals

Source: Allan J. Cigler and Burdett A. Loomis, *Interest Group Politics*, 4th ed. (Washington, DC: CQ Press, 1995), 135. Reprinted by permission of Congressional Quarterly Inc.

the city council and county board bump into constituents while shopping for groceries or cheering their children in youth sports. The concerns that are communicated tend to be specific and neither partisan nor ideological: a particular schoolteacher is unfair and ineffective; playground equipment is unsafe; it seems to be taking forever for the city to issue a building permit so that you can get started on a remodeling project.

In this setting, local news media invariably play a key role. The major newspaper in the state and what might be the only newspaper in a community can shape the agendas of government bodies and the images of government officials. The mere fact that a problem is covered by the media makes it an issue. If gang or cult activity is just a group of kids acting weird and dressing the same way, public officials might ignore it. News coverage of this or certainly of a violent incident involving members of such a group, on the other hand, assures attention. Then the question is how the media define the issue—is it an isolated and unusual event or a signal that certain needs are not being met?

The most powerful and influential people in a state or community are not necessarily those who hold offices in government. While there is always a distinction between formal and informal power, the face-to-face character of governance at the grassroots level almost invites informal ties and influence. The part-time officials in particular have a more ambiguous identity than do full-time government officials.

In small to medium-sized communities, it is common for a single family or a traditional elite to be the major decision maker, whether or not one of their members has a formal governmental position.[20] In another frequent pattern, the owners or managers of the major business in town dominate public decision making. If you want to advocate for some improvements in a local park, a curriculum change in the schools, or a different set of priorities for the police department, it may be more important to get the support of a few key community leaders than the sympathy of the village president or the head of the school board. A newcomer interested in starting a business in a town likewise would be well advised to identify and court the informal elite and not just focus on those who hold a formal office.

Ad hoc, issue-specific organizations are prevalent in state and local governments.[21] Individuals opposed to the plans of a state department of transportation to expand a stretch of highway from two to four lanes will organize, raise funds, and lobby hard to stop the project. Once the project is stopped or completed, that organization will go out of existence. Likewise, neighbors will organize to support or oppose specific development projects or to press for revitalization assistance, and then they will disband once the decision is made. The sporadic but intense activity focused on specific local or regional concerns is an important supplement to the ongoing work of parties and interest groups in state and local governments. A full understanding of what happens at the grass roots requires an appreciation of ad hoc, issue-specific politics as well as the institutions and processes through which state and local governments make and implement public policies.

SIMULATION

You Are a Restaurant Owner

Relations with Indian Nations

Treaties between the federal government and American Indian nations directly affect thirty-four states. Most of these states are west of the Mississippi River, but New York, Michigan, Florida, Connecticut, and Wisconsin are also included. Although the treaties were signed by both the United States and an American Indian tribal nation, invariably the tribal leaders signed because of actual or threatened military defeat. The legal status of the various

Thinking Globally
Australia's Indigenous People

Australia's indigenous people, Aborigines, represent about 2 percent of Australia's total population. A policy of forced assimilation begun in the 1800s marginalized the aboriginal population and brought about the extinction of some tribes. Until 1969, tens of thousands of Aborigine children were forcibly taken to be raised in white foster families or institutions under the guise of cultural assimilation. More recently, Australia has pursued measures designed to return autonomy to the Aborigine people.

- How important is it to preserve the way of life of indigenous peoples? Why?
- To what extent should governments, such as the United States and Australia, compensate indigenous peoples for past injustices?

Timeline: Relations with American Indian Nations

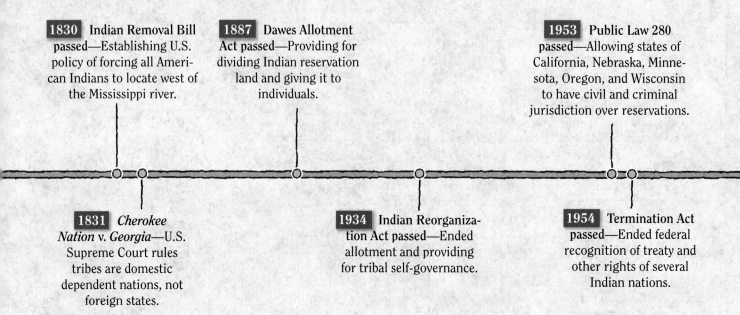

1830 Indian Removal Bill passed—Establishing U.S. policy of forcing all American Indians to locate west of the Mississippi river.

1887 Dawes Allotment Act passed—Providing for dividing Indian reservation land and giving it to individuals.

1953 Public Law 280 passed—Allowing states of California, Nebraska, Minnesota, Oregon, and Wisconsin to have civil and criminal jurisdiction over reservations.

1831 *Cherokee Nation* v. *Georgia*—U.S. Supreme Court rules tribes are domestic dependent nations, not foreign states.

1934 Indian Reorganization Act passed—Ended allotment and providing for tribal self-governance.

1954 Termination Act passed—Ended federal recognition of treaty and other rights of several Indian nations.

domestic dependent nation
A type of sovereignty that makes an Indian tribe in the United States outside the authority of state governments but reliant on the federal government for the definition of tribal authority.

trust relationship
The legal obligation of the United States federal government to protect the interests of Indian tribes.

compact
A formal, legal agreement, as that between a state and a tribe.

reservation land
Land designated in a treaty that is under the authority of an Indian nation and is exempt from most state laws and taxes.

trust land
Land owned by an Indian nation and designated by the federal Bureau of Indian Affairs as exempt from most state laws and taxes.

tribes in the United States is that of a **domestic dependent nation,** by which they retain their individual identity and sovereignty but must rely on the U.S. federal government for the interpretation and application of treaty provisions. Under the formal **trust relationship** between the United States and the Indian nations, the federal government is legally and morally obligated to protect Indian interests. State and local governments are clearly affected by federal–tribal relations but have little influence and virtually no legal authority over these relations.

The policy approach of the federal government toward Indians has varied widely. (To learn more about relationships between the federal government and Indian nations, see Timeline: Relations with American Indian Nations.) From 1830 to 1871, a major goal was to move all Indians to land west of the Mississippi. Between 1871 and today, the policy of the federal government has vacillated between assimilating American Indians and encouraging tribal self-sufficiency. Indian nations increasingly express concern about the unilateral nature of policy making concerning tribes and charge that the federal government is not being responsible about the trust relationship established by the treaties. In 2007, the federal Department of the Interior was in court in *Cobell* v. *Kempthorne* and more than 100 other suits by Indian nations citing mismanagement of Indian lands and funds. The department offered a $7 billion settlement, but the Indian nations vowed to continue legal proceedings. In 2005, the U.S. attorney general, Alberto Gonzales, estimated the federal government might be liable for $200 billion in damages.[22]

States are not parties to the treaties between the United States and American Indian nations and have no direct legal authority over tribes. The federal government has in several specific areas granted some powers to states. The Indian Gaming Regulatory Act of 1988, for example, gives state governments limited authority to negotiate agreements, called **compacts,** with tribes who wish to have casino gambling. Also, in 1953, Congress passed Public Law 280, which allows some states to pursue Indians suspected of criminal behavior even if they are on reservation land.

For the most part, however, federal–tribal relations provide given constraints and opportunities as states and communities engage in planning and problem solving. The two most important features of federal–tribal relations for state and local governments are land rights and treaty provisions for hunting, fishing, and gathering. Tribes have **reservation land** and **trust land,** neither of which is subject to taxation or regulation by state or local governments. The reservation land was designated in a treaty. Tribes can acquire trust land by securing ownership of a parcel and then petitioning to have

1968 American Indian Movement (AIM) formed—Protested U.S. government treatment of Indian people and nations.

1988 Indian Gaming Regulatory Act passed—Provided American Indians the right to have bingo and casino operations in states that allow those types of games.

1996 Federal government cedes some control—Federal government delegates authority for administering welfare and some environmental programs to Indian nations.

1973 Repeal of Termination Act— This marks the establishment of policy to encourage self-governance by Indian nations.

1995 *Seminole Tribe of Florida* v. *Florida*—U.S. Supreme Court rules that under the Eleventh Amendment, states have immunity from being sued by tribes for not negotiating gaming agreements in good faith.

2007 Federal government attempts to settle a multibillion-dollar suit—Cites the Department of the Interior with mismanagement of Indian lands and funds.

it placed in trust status by the secretary of the Department of the Interior. The acquisition of trust land has the potential for disruption of a community's development plans or tax base and an obvious challenge to cordial, working relationships between tribes, the federal government, and state or local government.

Hunting, fishing, and gathering activities have important cultural and religious significance for many American Indian nations. Treaty provisions giving rights to tribes to hunt, fish, and gather wild rice or berries on their own land and on public lands and waterways in land they once owned are key to tribal identity and dignity. These treaty rights supersede state regulations enacted for environmental and recreational purposes. Non-Indian anglers and hunters sometimes protest that Indians have special privileges. Environmental planners worry about the potential implications of unregulated Indian activity. In 1999, for example, the Makah tribe in the Northwest celebrated the successful capture and killing of a whale. While the tribe applauded the preservation of an important cultural tradition, wildlife advocates bemoaned the treaty rights that allowed this destruction of a valued animal. Incidents like this notwithstanding, generally American Indian nations have a deeper commitment to environmental protection than the state and federal governments.

Since Congress passed the Indian Self-Determination and Education Assistance Act in 1975, the federal government has been trying to strengthen tribal governments by encouraging the adoption of constitutions. The Bureau of Indian Affairs offers assistance in writing the constitutions, and other federal agencies, such as the Environmental Protection Agency, are willing to devolve some of their authority for regulating water and air pollution to tribes that have constitutions.

While tribes may include some traditional patterns of governance in their constitutions, the basic concept of a constitution is alien to Indian tribes. The documents read very much like state constitutions, with preambles that espouse principles of

How did the federal government secure land from Indian nations and make it available for settlement and private ownership? Here, an advertisement from the Department of the Interior (c. 1911) encourages individuals to purchase land designated as surplus after tribal allotments were made to Indians.

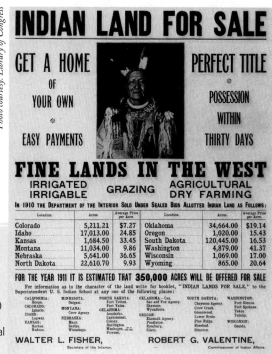

Photo courtesy: Library of Congress

INDIAN LAND FOR SALE

GET A HOME OF YOUR OWN * EASY PAYMENTS

PERFECT TITLE * POSSESSION WITHIN THIRTY DAYS

FINE LANDS IN THE WEST

IRRIGATED IRRIGABLE — GRAZING — AGRICULTURAL DRY FARMING

IN 1910 THE DEPARTMENT OF THE INTERIOR SOLD UNDER SEALED BIDS ALLOTTED INDIAN LAND AS FOLLOWS:

Location.	Acres.	Average Price per Acre.	Location.	Acres.	Average Price per Acre.
Colorado	5,211.21	$7.27	Oklahoma	34,664.00	$19.14
Idaho	17,013.00	24.85	Oregon	1,020.00	15.43
Kansas	1,684.50	33.45	South Dakota	120,445.00	16.53
Montana	11,034.00	9.86	Washington	4,879.00	41.37
Nebraska	5,641.00	36.65	Wisconsin	1,069.00	17.00
North Dakota	22,610.70	9.93	Wyoming	865.00	20.64

FOR THE YEAR 1911 IT IS ESTIMATED THAT **350,000 ACRES** WILL BE OFFERED FOR SALE

For information as to the character of the land write for booklet, "INDIAN LANDS FOR SALE," to the Superintendent U. S. Indian School at any one of the following places:

WALTER L. FISHER, Secretary of the Interior.

ROBERT G. VALENTINE, Commissioner of Indian Affairs.

You Are the Director of Economic Development for the City of Los Angeles, California

democracy and clauses that provide for a familiar separation of powers among executive, legislative, and judicial branches. Not surprisingly, some nations struggle with the mandates of their constitutions and the informal but real power of traditional rule by elders.

Toward Reform: State and Local Finances

State, tribal, and local governments must, of course, have money. Getting that money is one of the most challenging and thankless tasks of public officials. Unlike the federal government, state and local governments must balance their budgets. Unlike private businesses, state and local governments may not spend less money than they have. Whereas the goal of a private business is to have significantly more income than expenses, a governor, mayor, or other local public executive would be criticized for taxing too heavily if something akin to profits appeared on the books.

State and local governments depend on different types of taxes and fees. (To learn more about the sources of state and local government revenues, see Figure 4.3.) Unlike the federal government, which relies primarily on the income tax, state governments rely almost equally on income taxes and sales taxes. States differ among themselves, of course. Alaska, Delaware, Montana, New Hampshire, and Oregon have no sales tax, whereas some of the southern states have a double-digit sales tax. Alaska, Florida, Nevada, New Hampshire, South Dakota, Tennessee, Texas, Washington, and Wyoming do not tax personal incomes. Tax rates differ among those states that do have an income tax, but the levels are generally less than 10 percent.

Local governments rely primarily on property taxes, have little from levies on sales, and receive virtually nothing from income. Schools, in particular, depend on property taxes for funding.

In general, taxes can be evaluated according to how much money they can raise, whether the revenue is certain, and who bears the burden. Income taxes generate large sums of money, although the amount of money generated will fluctuate according to economic conditions and levels of employment. Of all the taxes, those based on income are the most **progressive taxes,** which means that they are based on the ability to pay.

Sales taxes also generate lots of money, but the amounts raised vary with how well the economy is doing. Sales taxes are not based on earnings but on purchases. Since those with a low income must spend virtually all that they earn in order to live, sales taxes are **regressive taxes.** To counter the regressive nature of sales taxes, some states exempt food, medicine, clothing, and other necessities.

Property taxes vary with the value of one's property, not one's current income or spending. Thus, farmers and those with a fixed income, such as retired persons, may bear more of a burden than their current wealth suggests they should carry. The property tax can be a good revenue earner and is stable, since a jurisdiction can set a tax rate that virtually guarantees a certain level of revenue, regardless of economic trends. The local officials who set these rates invariably hear complaints about the regressive nature of property taxes.

Both local and state governments levy user fees, such as admission to parks, licenses for hunting and fishing, tuition for public universities, and charges based on water use. User fees are typically placed in **segregated funds,** which means the funds are restricted to a specific use. A fishing license, for example, provides money to be used in stocking streams and conserving natural resources. The license revenue cannot be allocated for the general running of state government. Most people

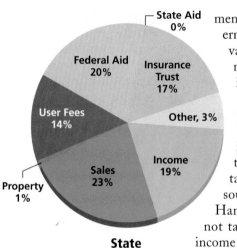

State

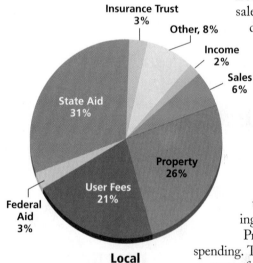

Local

FIGURE 4.3 State and Local Government Revenues (Percentage of Total Revenues) State governments depend primarily on sales and income taxes and funds from the federal government, while local governments are dependent on property taxes, user fees, and funds from state governments.

Source: Statistical Abstract of the United States, 2006 (Washington, DC: Census Bureau, 2006), 291–300.

Photo courtesy: Paul J. Richards/AFP/Getty Images

accept user fees as the fairest type of taxation. The problem is that user fees do not generate very much revenue (usually less than 5 percent of a state's budget).

Included in Figure 4.3 is income from retirement funds administered by states for their employees and former employees. This, too, is a segregated fund, and money in this category is not available for any use other than paying retirement benefits.

When governments, like businesses, establish budgets, officials make projections of expenses and revenues. State and local officials face some special uncertainties and have special risks when they make these guesses. One important factor is the health of the economy. If one is taxing sales or income, revenue will vary with levels of employment and economic activity. State and local governments face a double challenge when the economy declines, especially unexpectedly. Not only do tax revenues go down, but expenses go up as more families and individuals qualify for assistance during harsh times. State and local governments faced these challenges with the housing mortgage crisis and the signs of an economic recession that became evident in early 2008. As the interest rates on some mortgages ballooned and the value of housing declined in many areas, home owners fell behind on payments and banks began foreclosing on homes. Municipalities were faced with vacant, boarded-up houses that made neighborhoods less attractive to potential buyers, and local governments lost crucial property tax income. Moreover, with more people either out of work or in lower-paying jobs, states had less income to tax, and lower levels of spending by consumers resulted in a decline in state sales tax revenues.

Another important factor affecting state and local government budgets is the level of funding that governments give to one another. States have been getting about one-fourth of their funds from Washington, D.C. That level has declined with the deficit spending and increasing debt of the federal government since 2000. President Bush in 2008 asked states to pick up $25 billion of the $196 billion that the federal government pays for Medicaid, a program for providing low-income people with health care. The states already contribute over $150 billion to Medicaid. The general decline in the economy in 2008 is projected to make a record 28 million people eligible for food stamps, a federal program, and 8.5 million poor women and children eligible for food from the Special Supplemental Nutrition Program for Women, Infants, and Children (WIC), administered by states.[23]

Local governments rely on their respective state legislators and governors for generally one-third to two-thirds of their budgets. The federal government funds 10–20 percent. Not surprisingly, local governments are vulnerable when states face financial difficulties. Federal funds to local governments have declined steadily since 1984.

Not only is federal funding for state and local governments generally declining, but Congress and the president frequently require communities to spend their money for national programs and concerns. The National Governors Association, for example, estimated that states spend up to $4 billion each year to enhance security at airports, power plants, water sources, and vital infrastructure in the aftermath of the September 11 terrorist attacks.[24] The federal government has reimbursed state and local jurisdictions for less than one-third of their costs.

Reform proposals to meet the increased costs and decrease in revenues during harsh economic times pose political risks for officials. During the recession from 2001 to 2003, most states made tough adjustments to balance their budgets, typically opting for program cuts and user fee increases rather than tax increases.[25] But the fear of severe

How does a downturn in the economy affect state and local governments? The mortgage foreclosure crisis of 2008 squeezed state and local governments: they lost revenue because of lower incomes and lower house values, yet they had to help communities and individuals in distress.

progressive tax
The tax level increases with the wealth or ability of an individual or business to pay.

regressive tax
The tax level increases as the wealth or ability of an individual or business to pay decreases.

segregated funds
Money that comes in from a certain tax or fee and then is restricted to a specific use, such as a gasoline tax that is used for road maintenance.

damage to education, health care, and public safety led Republican Governor Bob Riley of Alabama to propose $2.3 billion in increased taxes, only to suffer a resounding defeat in a 2003 referendum. The Republican-dominated Virginia legislature decided in the spring of 2004 to support a series of unpopular tax increases proposed by the Democratic governor, Mark Warner. Both Democrats and Republicans faced voter unhappiness in Virginia in 2006, but maintained the close balance of power in that state.[26]

In 2008, state and local officials faced fiscal challenges with fewer options. Spending cuts five years earlier made further reductions considerably more difficult. Governors Deval Patrick and Steve Beshear, of Massachusetts and Kentucky, respectively, had campaigned on platforms that included casinos as a new source of revenue. Legislators, however, blocked this reform in both states. Like officials in forty-six other states, they focused on finding ways of reducing or deferring costs and raising fees—like those for driver's licenses, fishing, and hunting—rather than taxes. Simultaneously, state and local governments simply had to help communities distressed by mortgage foreclosures and individuals out of work.

WHAT SHOULD I HAVE LEARNED?

In this chapter, we have examined the changing character of governance at the state and local levels in order to appreciate both the variation and the common patterns in subnational governments. The questions you should be able to answer are:

■ **What are the roots of state and local governments?**

The initial intent of the Founders was to limit the scope of state and local governments. That changed with the increased complexity of our society and economy and with the ruling of the U.S. Supreme Court that legislative districts within a state must each have the same number of people. The trend since the 1960s has been for more representative and more professional state and local governments. These jurisdictions and the federal government are forming partnerships with each other and with the private sector to address issues and provide services.

■ **What is the structure and what are the roles of state governments?**

State governments have traditionally had primary responsibility for criminal justice, education, public health, and economic development. Recently, state officials have assumed a larger role in welfare and environmental policy. State constitutions, which reflect major historical developments in American society, provide the basic framework of institutions and values in which state governments fulfill their roles. Since the 1960s, these governments have dramatically become more competent, professional, and accessible to the general public.

■ **What are the different types of local governments?**

Local governance in the United States is conducted by a varied collection of over 87,000 units, most of which are run by part-time officials. These governments range from general jurisdictions covering densely urbanized areas to special districts functioning for a specific, narrow purpose. The forms of local governments also differ. There are town meetings in which all eligible voters in a community gather to conduct business, elected and appointed boards that have both executive and legislative powers, and governments with distinct legislative councils, elected executives, and professional managers. Local politics is frequently nonpartisan, thanks in part to conscious efforts to prevent control by political party machines.

■ **What opportunities exist to participate in grassroots governance?**

There are formal and informal ways of participating in state and community governance. Some states allow voters to place proposals on the ballot and make law directly, without a governor or legislature. In local communities, those who wield the most influence over the making and implementation of public policy are not always the ones elected to formal offices. Sometimes power is in the hands of a family, a major business, a small number of individuals, or the local media. Whether or not those who are most powerful are the ones in government offices, governance at the grass roots is face to face, between neighbors, friends, and former high school classmates.

■ **What are the relations between federal, state, and local governments and Indian nations?**

Due to treaty rights and the domestic dependent sovereignty of the tribes, the Indian nations have a special relationship with the federal government. Tribes have important protections from the potential vagaries of state and local governments. Conversely, the special status of the tribes poses challenges to coherent and consistent policies in a community. Currently, the federal government is encouraging tribal governments to move to self-determination economically and politically and to enter into agreements with state and local governments on financial and policy matters.

■ **What financial reforms are currently being considered at state and local levels?**

Funding government is complex. Revenues are hard to project because governments tax personal and business incomes, sales, and property value—making governments highly dependent on the health of the economy. State, local, and tribal governments also rely heavily on money given to them by other jurisdictions, including the federal government. During recessions and other economic hard times, budget reformers must balance the need for less spending and for more revenue against the political unpopularity of taxes and the pressure for helping communities and individuals in distress.

Key Terms

advisory referendum, p. 137
at-large election, p. 143
charter, p. 138
city council, p. 143
commission, p. 143
commute, p. 131
compact, p. 146
county, p. 139
Dillon's Rule, p. 138
direct initiative, p. 137
direct (popular) referendum, p. 137
district-based election, p. 143
domestic dependent nation, p. 146
extradite, p. 131

governor, p. 129
inclusion, p. 134
indirect initiative, p. 137
line-item veto, p. 130
manager, p. 143
mayor, p. 143
Missouri (Merit) Plan, p. 135
municipality, p. 140
nonpartisan election, p. 144
one-person, one-vote, p. 125
package or general veto, p. 130
pardon, p. 131
parole, p. 131
political machine, p. 128

Progressive movement, p. 128
progressive tax, p. 149
public corporation (authority) p. 144
recall, p. 138
regressive tax, p. 149
reservation land, p. 146
segregated funds, p. 149
special district, p. 141
state constitution, p. 126
term limits, p. 133
town meeting p. 142
trust land, p. 146
trust relationship, p. 146

Researching State and Local Government

In the Library

Burns, Nancy E. *The Formation of American Local Governments: Private Values in Public Institutions*. New York: Oxford University Press, 1994.

Council of State Governments. *The Book of the States*. Lexington, KY: Council of State Governments, annual.

Clucas, Richard A. *Readings and Cases in State and Local Politics*. Boston: Houghton Mifflin, 2006.

Erikson, Robert S., Gerald C. Wright, and John P. McIver. *Statehouse Democracy: Public Opinion and Policy in the American States*. Cambridge: Cambridge University Press, 1993.

Gerston, Larry N., and Terry Christensen. *Recall: California's Political Earthquake*. Armonk, NY: M. E. Sharpe, 2004.

International City/County Management Association. *The Municipal Year Book*. Washington, DC: ICMA, annual.

Jewell, Malcolm E., and Marcia Lynn Whicker. *Legislative Leadership in the American States*. Ann Arbor: University of Michigan Press, 1994.

Renzulli, Diane. *Capitol Offenders: How Private Interests Govern Our States*. Washington, DC: Public Integrity, 2000.

Rosenthal, Alan. *Heavy Lifting: The Job of the American Legislature*. Washington, DC: CQ Press, 2004.

Smith, Kevin. *State and Local Government, 2007–2008*. Washington, D.C.: CQ Press, 2008.

Woliver, Laura R. *From Outrage to Action: The Politics of Grass-Roots Dissent*. Urbana: University of Illinois Press, 1993.

Wright, Ralph G. *Inside the Statehouse: Lessons from the Speaker*. Washington, DC: CQ Press, 2005.

On the Web

To find statistics on any branch of government in the fifty states, go to the Council of State Governments at **www.csg.org**.

To learn about issues that governors nationwide deem most important, go to the National Governor's Association at **www/nga.org**.

To learn about the policy issues being addressed in state legislatures, go to the National Conference of State Legislatures at **www.ncsl.org**.

To learn more about American Indian nations and specific tribes go to **www.nativeweb.org**.

To follow state issues, go to **www.stateline.org**

LIVE SAFELY...LIVE HAPPILY!

How to Clean a Gun and Keep Your Head...

5 Civil Liberties

The Supreme Court is frequently called upon to adjudicate disputes related to the scope of civil liberties protections in the United States. Issues such as free speech, trial by jury, and cruel and unusual punishment come before the Court at regular intervals. And, as a result, the judiciary has played a major role in defining the boundaries of these rights.

The right to bear arms has, however, received relatively little attention from the Supreme Court. In fact, before 2008, the Court had not directly considered the Second Amendment in nearly 70 years.

Despite the lack of Supreme Court intervention, gun control has remained a hot button issue in the federal and state legislatures. The federal government has placed waiting periods on the purchase of weapons, and prohibited the ownership of certain types of automatic and semi-automatic weapons. And, many states have enacted similar restrictions. Washington, D.C., for example, passed a total ban on handgun ownership in 1976.

For much of its 32-year history, this law went relatively unchallenged. But, in 2003, Robert A. Levy, a lawyer who worked as a constitutional fellow for the

libertarian Cato Institute, decided it was time to test the legality of the statute. Levy, who had never personally owned a gun, financed the litigation, recruited co-counsel, and hand-picked six plaintiffs who were willing to bring suit against D.C. To illustrate the scope of the effects of the law, Levy assured that the plaintiffs were diverse in many ways. They included three men and three women, whose ages varied from 20 to 60. Four of the plaintiffs were white, while the other two were black. They lived in a variety of neighborhoods, and had a wide range of jobs, from lawyer to security guard.[1]

The case took five years to weave its way through the federal judicial system, eventually reaching the Supreme Court in time for its 2007–08 term. The justices chose to hear oral arguments in the case, and in June of 2008, they handed down a 5-4 decision in the case of *D.C. v. Heller*. Writing for the majority, Justice Antonin Scalia acknowledged the problems that gun violence poses in American cities, but declared that the District of Columbia's ban on handgun ownership was unconstitutional.

The Court's majority opinion also included language declaring that the Second Amendment guaranteed "the right of law abiding, responsible citizens to use arms in defense of hearth and home." This statement clarified a longstanding dispute about whether the Amendment had been written to assure for the preservation of a

■ **The right to bear arms is an enduring civil liberty established by the Second Amendment.** At left, a gun safety pamphlet from the 1950s references the recreational aspects of hunting that were once taken for granted in the United States. At right, Dick Heller, the lead plaintiff in *D.C. v. Heller*, awaits the Supreme Court's ruling, with pro- and anti-gun protesters surrounding him.

WHAT SHOULD I KNOW ABOUT . . .

- the roots of civil liberties and the Bill of Rights?
- First Amendment guarantees of freedom of religion?
- First Amendment guarantees of freedom of speech, press, assembly, and petition?
- the Second Amendment right to keep and bear arms?
- the rights of criminal defendants?
- the right to privacy?
- civil liberties and combating terrorism?

well-trained militia, or whether the right to own a weapon also extended to ownership for private use. The majority's view was not well-received by the four dissenting justices, who charged that the opinion of the Court created a "dramatic upheaval in the law."[2]

Legal scholars expect that the D.C. case will lead to additional challenges out of other states and communities with restrictive legislation. The Supreme Court may also be asked to review these cases in the very near future. The question of whether the justices will decide to hear these cases, and if so, what decisions they will make, rests heavily on the composition and interests of the Court. In this way, Second Amendment rights are quite similar to many of the other rights and liberties we will consider in this chapter.

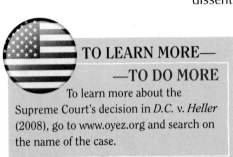

TO LEARN MORE—
—TO DO MORE
To learn more about the Supreme Court's decision in *D.C. v. Heller* (2008), go to www.oyez.org and search on the name of the case.

civil liberties
The personal guarantees and freedoms that the federal government cannot abridge by law, constitution, or judicial interpretation.

civil rights
The goverment-protected rights of individuals against arbitrary or discriminatory treatment.

When the Bill of Rights, which contains many of the most important protections of individual liberty, was written, its drafters were not thinking about issues such as abortion, gay rights, physician-assisted suicide, or many of the other personal liberties discussed in this chapter.

The Constitution is nonabsolute in the nature of most **civil liberties.** Civil liberties are the personal guarantees and freedoms that the federal government cannot abridge, either by law or judicial interpretation. As guarantees of "freedom to" action, they place limitations on the power of the government to restrain or dictate individual's actions. **Civil rights**, in contrast, provide "freedom from" a host of discriminatory actions and place the burden of protecting individuals on the government. (Civil rights are discussed in chapter 6.)

Questions of civil liberties often present complex problems. We must decide how to determine the boundaries of speech and assembly. We must also consider how much infringement on our personal liberties we want to give the police or other government actors. Moreover, in an era of a war on terrorism, it is important to consider what liberties should be accorded to those suspected of terrorist activity.

Civil liberties issues often fall to the judiciary, who must balance the competing interests of the government and the people. Thus, in many of the cases discussed in this chapter, there is a conflict between an individual or group of individuals seeking to exercise what they believe to be a liberty, and the government, be it local, state, or national, seeking to control the exercise of that liberty in an attempt to keep order and preserve the rights (and safety) of others. In other cases, two liberties are in conflict, such as a physician's and her patients' rights to easy access to a medical clinic versus a pro-life advocate's liberty to picket that clinic. Many of the Supreme Court's recent decisions, as well as the actions of George W. Bush's administration in the aftermath of the September 11, 2001, terrorist attacks, are discussed in this chapter as we explore the various dimensions of civil liberties guarantees contained in the U.S. Constitution and the Bill of Rights.

★ First, we will discuss *the roots of civil liberties and the Bill of Rights.*

★ Second, we will survey the meaning of one of *the First Amendment guarantees: freedom of religion.*

★ Third, we will consider the meanings of other *First Amendment guarantees: the freedoms of speech, press, assembly, and petition.*

★ Fourth, we will review *the Second Amendment* and *the right to keep and bear arms.*

★ Fifth, we will analyze *the rights of criminal defendants* found in the Bill of Rights and how those rights have been expanded and contracted by the U.S. Supreme Court.

★ Sixth, we will explore *the right to privacy.*

★ Finally, we will examine how reforms to *combat terrorism* have affected *civil liberties.*

Roots of Civil Liberties: The Bill of Rights

Balancing Liberty and Security in a Time of War

In 1787, most state constitutions explicitly protected a variety of personal liberties such as speech, religion, freedom from unreasonable searches and seizures, and trial by jury. It was clear that the new federal system established by the Constitution would redistribute power between the national government and the states. Without an explicit guarantee of specific civil liberties, could the national government be trusted to uphold the freedoms already granted to citizens by their states?

As discussed in chapter 2, recognition of the increased power that would be held by the new national government led Anti-Federalists to stress the need for a bill of rights. Anti-Federalists and many others were confident that they could control the actions of their own state legislators, but they didn't trust the national government to be so protective of their civil liberties.

The notion of adding a bill of rights to the Constitution was not a popular one at the Constitutional Convention. When George Mason of Virginia proposed that such a bill be added to the preface of the proposed Constitution, his resolution was defeated unanimously.[3] In the subsequent ratification debates, Federalists argued that a bill of rights was unnecessary. Not only did most state constitutions already contain those protections, but Federalists believed it was foolhardy to list things that the national government had no power to do.

Some Federalists, however, supported the idea. After the Philadelphia convention, for example, James Madison conducted a lively correspondence about the need for a national bill of rights with Thomas Jefferson. Jefferson was far quicker to support such guarantees than was Madison, who continued to doubt their utility. Madison believed that a list of protected rights might suggest that those not enumerated were not protected. Politics soon intervened, however, when Madison found himself in a close race against James Monroe for a seat in the House of Representatives in the First Congress. The district was largely Anti-Federalist. So, in an act of political expediency, Madison issued a new series of public letters similar to *The Federalist Papers* in which he vowed to support a bill of rights.

Once elected to the House, Madison made good on his promise and became the prime author of the Bill of Rights. Still, he considered Congress to have far more important matters to handle and viewed his work on the Bill of Rights as "a nauseous project."[4]

The insistence of Anti-Federalists on a bill of rights, the fact that some states conditioned their ratification of the Constitution on the addition of these guarantees,

Bill of Rights
The first ten amendments to the U.S. Constitution, which largely guarantee specific rights and liberties.

Ninth Amendment
Part of the Bill of Rights that reads "The enumeration in the Constitution, of certain rights, shall not be construed to deny or disparage others retained by the people."

Tenth Amendment
Part of the Bill of Rights that reiterates that powers not delegated to the national government are reserved to the states or to the people.

due process clause
Clause contained in the Fifth and Fourteenth Amendments. Over the years, it has been construed to guarantee to individuals a variety of rights ranging from economic liberty to criminal procedural rights to protection from arbitrary governmental action.

and the disagreement among Federalists about writing specific liberty guarantees into the Constitution led to prompt congressional action to put an end to further controversy. This was a time when national stability and support for the new government particularly were needed. Thus, in 1789, Congress sent the proposed Bill of Rights to the states for ratification, which occurred in 1791.

The **Bill of Rights,** the first ten amendments to the Constitution, contains numerous specific guarantees, including those of free speech, press, and religion (for the full text, see the annotated Constitution that begins on page 64). The Ninth and Tenth Amendments, favored by the Federalists, note that the Bill of Rights is not exclusive. The **Ninth Amendment,** strongly favored by James Madison, makes it clear that this special listing of rights does not mean that others don't exist. The **Tenth Amendment** reiterates that powers not delegated to the national government are reserved to the states or to the people.

The Incorporation Doctrine: The Bill of Rights Made Applicable to the States

The Bill of Rights was intended to limit the powers of the national government to infringe on the rights and liberties of the citizenry. In *Barron* v. *Baltimore* (1833), the Supreme Court ruled that the national Bill of Rights limited only the actions of the U.S. government and not those of the states.[5] In 1868, however, the Fourteenth Amendment was added to the U.S. Constitution. Its language suggested the possibility that some or even all of the protections guaranteed in the Bill of Rights might be interpreted to prevent state infringement of those rights. Section 1 of the Fourteenth Amendment reads: "No State shall . . . deprive any person of life, liberty, or property, without due process of law." Questions about the scope of "liberty" as well as the meaning of "due process of law" continue even today to engage legal scholars and jurists.

Until nearly the turn of the century, the Supreme Court steadfastly rejected numerous arguments urging it to interpret the **due process clause** found in the Fourteenth Amendment as making various provisions contained in the Bill of Rights applicable to the states. In 1897, however, the Court began to increase its jurisdiction over the states.[6] It began to hold states to a **substantive due process** standard whereby states had the legal burden to prove that their laws were a valid exercise of their power to regulate the health, welfare, or public morals of their citizens. Interferences with state power, however, were rare. As a consequence, states continued to pass sedition laws (laws that made it illegal to speak or write any political criticism that threatened to diminish respect for the government, its laws, or public officials), anticipating that the Supreme Court would uphold their constitutionality. When Benjamin Gitlow, a member of the Socialist Party, printed 16,000 copies of a manifesto in which he urged workers to overthrow the U.S. government, he was convicted of violating a New York law that prohibited such advocacy. Although his conviction was upheld, in *Gitlow* v. *New York* (1925), the Supreme Court noted that the states were not completely free to limit forms of political expression:

Photo courtesy: AP Wide World Photos

When were the states compelled to honor the protections of the Bill of Rights?
Until *Gitlow* v. *New York* (1925), involving Benjamin Gitlow, the executive secretary of the Socialist Party, it generally was thought that, despite the Fourteenth Amendment, the protections of the Bill of Rights did not apply to the states. Here Gitlow, right, is shown testifying before a congressional committee, investigating un-American activities.

For present purposes we may and do assume that freedom of speech and of the press—which are protected by the First Amendment from abridgement by Congress—are among the *fundamental personal rights and "liberties"* protected by the due process clause of the Fourteenth Amendment from impairment by the states [emphasis added].[7]

Gitlow, with its finding that states could not abridge free speech protections, was the first step in the slow development of what is called the **incorporation doctrine.** After *Gitlow*, it took the Court six more years to incorporate another First Amendment freedom—that of the press. *Near* v. *Minnesota* (1931) was the first case in which the Supreme Court found that a state law violated freedom of the press as protected by the First Amendment. The Supreme Court ruled that "The fact that the liberty of the press may be abused by miscreant purveyors of scandal does not make any the less necessary the immunity of the press from previous restraint."[8]

Selective Incorporation and Fundamental Freedoms

Not all the specific guarantees in the Bill of Rights have been made applicable to the states through the due process clause of the Fourteenth Amendment, as revealed in Table 5.1. Instead, the Court has used the process of **selective incorporation** to limit the rights of states by protecting against abridgement of **fundamental freedoms**. Fundamental freedoms are those liberties defined by the Court as essential to order, liberty, and justice. These freedoms are subject to the Court's most rigorous standard of review.

substantive due process
Judicial interpretation of the Fifth and Fourteenth Amendments' due process clauses that protects citizens from arbitrary or unjust laws.

incorporation doctrine
An interpretation of the Constitution that holds that the due process clause of the Fourteenth Amendment requires that state and local governments also guarantee those rights.

selective incorporation
A judicial doctrine whereby most but not all of the protections found in the Bill of Rights are made applicable to the states via the Fourteenth Amendment.

fundamental freedoms
Those rights defined by the Court to be essential to order, liberty, and justice and therefore entitled to the highest standard of review, strict scrutiny.

TABLE 5.1 The Selective Incorporation of the Bill of Rights

Amendment	Right	Date	Case Incorporated
I	Speech	1925	*Gitlow* v. *New York*
	Press	1931	*Near* v. *Minnesota*
	Assembly	1937	*DeJonge* v. *Oregon*
	Religion	1940	*Cantwell* v. *Connecticut*
II	Bear arms	2008	*D.C.* v. *Heller*
III	No quartering of soldiers		Not incorporated (The quartering problem has not recurred since colonial times.)
IV	No unreasonable searches or seizures	1949	*Wolf* v. *Colorado*
	Exclusionary rule	1961	*Mapp* v. *Ohio*
V	Just compensation	1897	*Chicago, B&Q RR Co.* v. *Chicago*
	Self-incrimination	1964	*Malloy* v. *Hogan*
	Double jeopardy	1969	*Benton* v. *Maryland* (overruled *Palko* v. *Connecticut*)
	Grand jury indictment		Not incorporated (The trend in state criminal cases is away from grand juries.)
VI	Public trial	1963	*Gideon* v. *Wainwright*
	Right to counsel	1968	*Duncan* v. *Louisiana*
	Confrontation of witnesses	1967	*Klopfer* v. *North Carolina*
	Impartial trial	1965	*Pointer* v. *Texas*
	Speedy trial	1948	*In re Oliver*
	Compulsory trial	1967	*Washington* v. *Texas*
	Criminal jury trial	1966	*Parker* v. *Gladden*
VII	Civil jury trial		Not incorporated (Chief Justice Warren Burger wanted to abolish these trials.)
VIII	No cruel and unusual punishment	1962	*Robinson* v. *California*
	No excessive fines or bail		Not incorporated

Selective incorporation requires the states to respect freedoms of press, speech, and assembly, among other rights. Other guarantees contained in the Third and Seventh Amendments, have not been incorporated because the Court has yet to consider them sufficiently fundamental to national notions of liberty and justice.

The rationale for selective incorporation was set out by the Court in *Palko* v. *Connecticut* (1937).[9] Frank Palko was charged with first-degree murder for killing two Connecticut police officers, found guilty of a lesser charge of second-degree murder, and sentenced to life imprisonment. Connecticut appealed. Palko was retried, found guilty of first-degree murder, and sentenced to death. Palko then appealed his second conviction, arguing that it violated the Fifth Amendment's prohibition against double jeopardy because the Fifth Amendment had been made applicable to the states by the due process clause of the Fourteenth Amendment.

The Supreme Court upheld Palko's second conviction and the death sentence. They also chose not to bind states to the Fifth Amendment's double jeopardy clause and concluded that protection from being tried twice (double jeopardy) was not a fundamental freedom. Palko died in Connecticut's gas chamber one year later. The Court's decision was overruled in 1969.

First Amendment Guarantees: Freedom of Religion

Many of the Framers were religious men, but they knew what evils could arise if the new nation was not founded with religious freedom as one of its core ideals. Although many colonists had fled Europe to escape religious persecution, most colonies actively persecuted those who did not belong to their predominant religious groups. Nevertheless, in 1774, the colonists uniformly were outraged when the British Parliament passed a law establishing Anglicanism and Roman Catholicism as official religions in the colonies. The First Continental Congress immediately sent a letter of protest announcing its "astonishment that a British Parliament should ever consent to establish . . . a religion [Catholicism] that has deluged [England] in blood and dispersed bigotry, persecution, murder and rebellion through every part of the world."[10]

In President Thomas Jefferson's view, there was to be a near impenetrable wall of separation between church and state. Moreover, the Framers' distaste for a national church or religion was reflected in the Constitution. Article VI, for example, provides that "no religious Test shall ever be required as a Qualification to any Office or Public Trust under the United States." This simple statement, however, did not completely reassure those who feared the new Constitution would curtail individual liberty. Thus, the First Amendment to the Constitution soon was ratified to allay those fears.

The **First Amendment** to the Constitution begins, "Congress shall make no law respecting an establishment of religion, or prohibiting the free exercise thereof." This statement sets the boundaries of governmental action. The **establishment clause** ("Congress shall make no law respecting an establishment of religion") directs the national government not to involve itself in religion. The **free exercise clause** ("or prohibiting the free exercise thereof") guarantees citizens that the national government will not interfere with their practice of religion. These guarantees, however, are not absolute. In the mid-1800s, Mormons traditionally practiced and preached polygamy, the taking of multiple wives. In 1879, when the Supreme Court was first called on to interpret the free exercise clause, it upheld the conviction of a Mormon under a federal law barring polygamy. The Court reasoned that to do otherwise would provide constitutional protections to a full range of religious beliefs, including those as extreme as human sacrifice. "Laws are made for the government of actions," noted the Court, "and while they cannot interfere with mere religious belief and opinions,

First Amendment
Part of the Bill of Rights that imposes a number of restrictions on the federal government with respect to the civil liberties of the people, including freedom of religion, speech, press, assembly, and petition.

establishment clause
The first clause in the First Amendment; it prohibits the national government from establishing a national religion.

free exercise clause
The second clause of the First Amendment; it prohibits the U.S. government from interfering with a citizen's right to practice his or her religion.

they may with practices."[11] Later, in 1940, the Supreme Court observed that the First Amendment "embraces two concepts—freedom to believe and freedom to act. The first is absolute, but in the nature of things, the second cannot be. Conduct remains subject to regulation of society."[12]

The Establishment Clause

The separation of church and state has always been a thorny issue in American politics. A majority of Americans clearly value the moral teachings of their own religions, especially Christianity. U.S. coins are embossed with "In God We Trust." The U.S. Supreme Court asks God's blessing on the Court. Every session of the U.S. House and Senate begins with a prayer, and both the House and Senate have their own chaplains. Over the years, the Court has been divided over how to interpret the establishment clause. Does this clause erect a total wall between church and state, as favored by Thomas Jefferson, or is some governmental accommodation of religion allowed? While the Supreme Court has upheld the constitutionality of many kinds of church/state entanglements such as public funding to provide sign language interpreters for deaf students in religious schools,[13] the Court has held fast to the rule of strict separation between church and state when issues of prayer in school are involved. In *Engel* v. *Vitale* (1962), for example, the Court ruled that the recitation in public school classrooms of a brief nondenominational prayer drafted by the local school board was unconstitutional.[14]

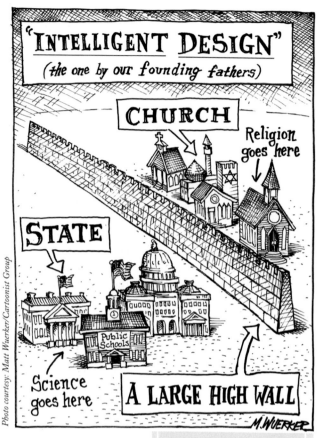

Photo courtesy: Matt Wuerker/Cartoonist Group

Why is separation of church and state important? The above cartoon speaks to the First Amendment issue of separation of church and state. What point is the cartoonist trying to communicate? Do you agree with the cartoonist's depiction? Where did the Democratic and Republican 2008 presidential candidates stand on this issue?

The Court has gone back and forth in its effort to come up with a workable way to deal with church/state questions. In 1971, in *Lemon* v. *Kurtzman*, the Court tried to carve out a three-part test for laws dealing with religious establishment issues. According to the *Lemon* test, a practice or policy was constitutional if it: (1) had a secular purpose; (2) neither advanced nor inhibited religion; and, (3) did not foster an excessive government entanglement with religion.[15] But, since the early 1980s, the Supreme Court often has sidestepped the *Lemon* test altogether and has appeared more willing to lower the wall between church and state so long as school prayer is not involved. In 1981, for example, the Court ruled unconstitutional a Missouri law prohibiting the use of state university buildings and grounds for "purposes of religious worship." The law had been used to ban religious groups from using school facilities.[16]

This decision was taken by many members of Congress as a sign that this principle could be extended to secondary and even primary schools. In 1984, Congress passed the Equal Access Act, which bars public schools from discriminating against groups of students on the basis of "religious, political, philosophical or other content of the speech at such meetings." The constitutionality of this law was upheld in 1990.[17] In 1993, the Court also ruled that religious groups must be allowed to use public schools after hours if that access is also given to other community groups.[18]

In 1995, the Court signaled that it was willing to lower the wall even further. In a case involving the University of Virginia, a 5–4 majority held that the university violated the free speech rights of a fundamentalist Christian group when it refused to fund the group's student magazine. The importance of this decision was highlighted by Justice David Souter, who noted in dissent: "The Court today, for the first time, approves direct funding of core religious activities by an arm of the state."[19]

For more than a quarter century, the Supreme Court basically allowed "books only" as an aid to religious schools, noting that the books go to children, not to the schools. But, in 2000, the Court voted 6–3 to uphold the constitutionality of a federal aid provision that allowed the government to lend books and computers to religious schools.[20] And, in 2002, by a bitterly divided 5–4 vote, the Supreme Court concluded that governments can give money to parents to allow them to send their children to private or religious schools.[21] Basically, the Court now appears willing to support programs so long as they provide aid to religious and nonreligious schools alike, and the money goes to persons who exercise free choice over how it is used.

Prayer in school also continues to be an issue. In 1992, the Court continued its unwillingness to allow organized prayer in public schools by finding unconstitutional the saying of prayer at a middle school graduation.[22] And, in 2000, the Court ruled that student-led, student-initiated prayer at high school football games violated the establishment clause.

Establishment issues, however, do not always focus on education. In 2005, for example, the Supreme Court in a 5–4 decision narrowly upheld the continued vitality of the *Lemon* test in holding that a privately donated courthouse display, which included the Ten Commandments and 300 other historical documents illustrating the evolution of American law, was a violation of the First Amendment's establishment clause. Court watchers now are waiting to see how the addition of two new justices to the Court will affect these closely divided opinions.[23]

The Free Exercise Clause

The free exercise clause of the First Amendment proclaims that "Congress shall make no law . . . prohibiting the free exercise [of religion]." Although the free exercise clause of the First Amendment guarantees individuals the right to be free from governmental interference in the exercise of their religion, this guarantee, like other First Amendment freedoms, is not absolute. When secular law comes into conflict with religious law, the right to exercise one's religious beliefs is often denied—especially if the religious beliefs in question are held by a minority or by an unpopular or "suspicious" group. (To learn about academic efforts to support free exercise, see Politics Now: Religious Accomodation on College Campuses.)

The U.S. Supreme Court has interpreted the Constitution to mean that governmental interests can outweigh free exercise rights. State statutes barring the use of certain illegal drugs, snake handling, and polygamy—all practices once part of some religions—have been upheld as constitutional when states have shown compelling reasons to regulate or ban them. Nonetheless, the Court has made it clear that the free exercise clause requires that a state or the national government remain neutral toward religion. In 1993, for example, the Court ruled that members of the Santería Church, an Afro-Cuban religion, had the right to sacrifice animals during religious services. In upholding that practice, the Court ruled that a city ordinance banning such practices was unconstitutionally aimed at the group, thereby denying its members the right to free exercise of their religion.[24] Earlier, however, in 1990, the Court ruled that the free exercise clause allowed Oregon to ban the use of sacramental peyote (an illegal hallucinogenic drug) in some Native American tribes' traditional religious services.[25]

This decision prompted a dramatic outcry. Congressional response was passage of the Religious Freedom Restoration Act, which specifically made the use of peyote in religious services legal.[26] As recently as 2006, the U.S. Supreme Court by a vote of 8–0, found that the use of hoasca tea, well-known for its hallucinogenic properties, was permissible free exercise of religion for members of a

Thinking Globally

Saudi Arabia and Free Exercise of Religion

In Saudi Arabia, public demonstration of religious affiliation or sentiment is forbidden except for Sunni Muslims who follow the austere Wahhabi interpretation of Islam. Public worship by non-Muslims is banned, and places of worship other than mosques are not permitted. The kingdom's Shi'a Muslim minority's religious practice is tightly controlled, and the construction of Shi'a mosques and religious community centers is restricted.

- Is it surprising that some countries officially support one religion at the expense of others? Why or why not?
- To what extent, should the United States pressure its allies, such as Saudi Arabia, to adhere more closely to American constitutional values of freedom of religion?
- What criteria would you use to evaluate the level of religious freedom in a country?

POLITICS NOW

Source: THE NEW YORK TIMES   August 7, 2007

Religious Accommodation on College Campuses

Universities Install Footbaths to Benefit Muslims, and Not Everyone Is Pleased

TAMAR LEWIN

DEARBORN, Mich. — When pools of water began accumulating on the floor in some restrooms at the University of Michigan-Dearborn, and the sinks pulling away from the walls, the problem was easy to pinpoint. On this campus, more than 10 percent of the students are Muslims, and as part of ritual ablutions required before their five-times-a-day prayers, some were washing their feet in the sinks.

The solution seemed straightforward. After discussions with the Muslim Students' Association, the university announced that it would install $25,000 foot-washing stations in several restrooms.

But as a legal and political matter, that solution has not been quite so simple. When word of the plan got out this spring, it created instant controversy, with bloggers going on about the Islamification of the university, students divided on the use of their building-maintenance fees, and tricky legal questions about whether the plan is a legitimate accommodation of students' right to practice their religion — or unconstitutional government support for that religion.

Nationwide, more than a dozen universities have footbaths, many installed in new buildings. On some campuses, like George Mason University in Virginia, and Eastern Michigan University in Ypsilanti, Mich., there was no outcry. At Eastern Michigan, even some Muslim students were surprised by the appearance of the footbath — a single spigot delivering 45 seconds of water — in a partitioned corner of the restroom in the new student union.

"My sister told me about it, and I didn't believe it," said Najla Malaibari, a graduate student at Eastern Michigan. "I was, 'No way,' and she said, 'Yeah, go crazy.' It really is convenient."

But after a Muslim student at Minneapolis Community and Technical College slipped and hurt herself last fall while washing her feet in a sink, word got out there that the college was considering installing a footbath, and a local columnist accused the college of a double standard — stopping a campus coffee cart from playing Christmas music but taking a different attitude toward Islam.

"After the column, a Christian conservative group issued an action alert to its members, which prompted 3,000 e-mail and 600 voice messages to me and/or legislators," said Phil Davis, president of the college.

Mr. Davis said that after a legal briefing, the board concluded that installing footbaths was constitutional, and that the college hoped to have a plan in place by the next school year.

Here in Dearborn, the university called the footbaths a health and safety measure, not a religious decision. And it argued that while the footbaths may benefit Muslim students, they will be available to others, like lacrosse players who want to wash their feet.

Still, the plans are controversial.

On her Web site, Debbie Schlussel, a conservative lawyer and blogger in Southfield, Mich., posted, "Forget about the Constitutionally mandated separation of church and state ... at least when it comes to mosque and state."

And in an editorial, the student newspaper, The Michigan Journal, worried that opponents would turn their hostility "on Muslim students at the university and Islam as a whole."

Hal Downs, president of the Michigan chapter of Americans United for Separation of Church and State, said, "The university claims it's available for Western students as well, but, traditionally, Western students don't wash their feet five times day."

"They're building a structure for a particular religious tradition," Mr. Downs added, "and the Constitution says the government isn't supposed to endorse a particular religion."

The American Civil Liberties Union says the footbath issue is complex.

"Our policy is to object whenever public funds are spent on any brick and mortar component of religion," said Kary Moss, director of the Michigan Civil Liberties Union. "What makes this different, though, is that the footbaths themselves can be used by anyone, don't have any symbolic value and are not stylized in a religious way. They're in a regular restroom, and could be just as useful to a janitor filling up buckets, or someone coming off the basketball court, as to Muslim students."

Then, too, Ms. Moss said, the health and safety component is not normally part of religious accommodation cases.

"This came from the maintenance staff, which was worried about the wet floors," she said. "We were also aware that if the university said students could not wash their feet in the sink anymore, that could present a different civil liberties problem, interfering with Muslim students' ability to practice their religion."

Discussion Questions

1. *Do you agree with administrators at the University of Michigan that installation of footbaths are a health and safety issue and do not run afoul of First Amendment guarantees? Why or why not?*

2 *Do you believe that the same groups would object to the installation of footbaths if they were an accommodation for students practicing a religion other than Islam?*

Brazilian-based church. The Court noted that Congress had overruled its earlier decision and specifically legalized the use of other sacramental substances including peyote. Queried Justice Ruth Bader Ginsburg regarding the religious uses of hoasca tea and peyote, "if the government must accommodate one, why not the other?"[27]

Although conflicts between religious beliefs and the government are often difficult to settle, the Court has attempted to walk the fine line between the free exercise and establishment clauses. In the area of free exercise, the Court often has had to confront questions of "What is a god?" and "What is a religious faith?"—questions that theologians have grappled with for centuries. In 1965, for example, in a case involving three men who were denied conscientious objector deferments during the Vietnam War because they did not subscribe to "traditional" organized religions, the Court ruled unanimously that belief in a supreme being was not essential for recognition as a conscientious objector.[28] Thus, the men were entitled to the deferments because their views paralleled those who objected to war and who belonged to traditional religions. In contrast, despite the Court's having ruled that Catholic, Protestant, Jewish, and Buddhist prison inmates must be allowed to hold religious services,[29] the Court ruled that Islamic prisoners can be denied the same right for security reasons.[30]

Comparing Civil Liberties

First Amendment Guarantees: Freedoms of Speech, Press, Assembly, and Petition

Today, some members of Congress criticize the movie industry and reality television shows for pandering to the least common denominator of society. Other groups criticize popular musicians for lyrics that denigrate women. Such criticism often comes with calls for increased restrictions and greater regulation of media outlets. This leads many civil libertarians to believe that the rights to speak, print, and assemble freely are being seriously threatened.[31]

Freedom of Speech and the Press

A democracy depends on a free exchange of ideas, and the First Amendment shows that the Framers were well aware of this fact. Historically, one of the most volatile areas of constitutional interpretation has been in the interpretation of the First Amendment's mandate that "Congress shall make no law . . . abridging the freedom of speech or of the press." Like the establishment and free exercise clauses of the First Amendment, the speech and press clauses have not been interpreted as absolute bans against government regulation. A lack of absolute meaning has led to thousands of cases seeking both broader and narrower judicial interpretations of the scope of the amendment. Over the years, the Court has employed a hierarchical approach in determining what the government can and cannot regulate, with some items getting greater protection than others. Generally, thoughts have received the greatest protection, and actions or deeds the least. Words have come somewhere in the middle, depending on their content and purpose.

prior restraint
Constitutional doctrine that prevents the government from prohibiting speech or publication before the fact; generally held to be in violation of the First Amendment.

THE ALIEN AND SEDITION ACTS   When the First Amendment was ratified in 1791, it was considered to protect against **prior restraint** of speech or expression, or to guard against the prohibition of speech or publication before the fact. However, in 1798, the Federalist Congress with President John Adams's blessing enacted the Alien and Sedition Acts, which were designed to ban any criticism of the Federalist government by the growing numbers of Democratic-Republicans. These acts made the publication of "any false, scandalous writing against the government of the United States" a criminal offense. Although the law clearly ran in the face of the First Amendment's ban on prior restraint, the Adams administration and partisan Federalist judges successfully prosecuted and imposed fines and jail terms on at least ten Democratic-Republican newspaper editors. The acts became a major issue in the 1800 presidential election campaign, which led to the election of Thomas Jefferson, a vocal opponent of the acts. He quickly pardoned all who had been convicted under their provisions and the Democratic-Republican Congress allowed the acts to expire before the Federalist-controlled Supreme Court had an opportunity to rule on the constitutionality of these First Amendment infringements.

SLAVERY, THE CIVIL WAR, AND RIGHTS CURTAILMENTS After the public outcry over the Alien and Sedition Acts, the national government largely refrained from regulating speech. But, in its place, the states, which were not yet bound by the Bill of Rights (through selective incorporation), began to prosecute those who published articles critical of governmental policies. In the 1830s, at the urgings of abolitionists (those who sought an end to slavery), the publication or dissemination of any positive information about slavery became a punishable offense in the North. In the opposite vein, in the South, supporters of slavery enacted laws to prohibit publication of any anti-slavery sentiments. Southern postmasters, for example, refused to deliver northern abolitionist papers, a step that amounted to censorship of the federal mail.

During the Civil War, President Abraham Lincoln took several steps that actually were unconstitutional. He made it unlawful to print any criticisms of the national government or of the Civil War, effectively suspending the free press protections of the First Amendment. Lincoln went so far as to order the arrest of several newspaper editors critical of his conduct of the war and ignored a Supreme Court decision saying that these practices were unconstitutional.

After the Civil War, states also began to prosecute individuals for seditious speech if they uttered or printed statements critical of the government. Between 1890 and 1900, for example, there were more than one hundred state prosecutions for sedition.[32] Moreover, by the dawn of the twentieth century, public opinion in the United States had grown increasingly hostile toward the commentary of Socialists and Communists who attempted to appeal to growing immigrant populations. Groups espousing socialism and communism became the targets of state laws curtailing speech and the written word. By the end of World War I, over thirty states had passed laws to punish seditious speech, and more than 1,900 individuals and over one hundred newspapers were prosecuted for violations.[33] In 1925, however, states' authority to regulate speech was severely restricted by the Court's decision in *Gitlow* v. *New York*.

WORLD WAR I AND ANTI-GOVERNMENTAL SPEECH The next major national efforts to restrict freedom of speech and the press did not occur until Congress, at the urging of President Woodrow Wilson during World War I, passed the Espionage Act in 1917. Nearly 2,000 Americans were convicted of violating its various provisions, especially those that made it illegal to urge resistance to the draft or to prohibit the distribution of anti-war leaflets. In *Schenck* v. *U.S.* (1919), the Supreme Court upheld this act, ruling that Congress had a right to restrict speech "of such a nature as to create a clear and present danger that will bring about the substantive evils that Congress has a right to prevent."[34] Under this **clear and present danger test,** the circumstances surrounding an incident are important. Under *Schenck*, anti-war leaflets, for example, may be permissible during peacetime, but during World War I they were considered to pose too much of a danger to be permissible.

For decades, the Supreme Court wrestled with what constituted a danger. Finally, in *Brandenburg* v. *Ohio* (1969), the Court fashioned a new test for deciding whether certain kinds of speech could be regulated by the government: the **direct incitement test.** Now, the government could punish the advocacy of illegal action only if "such advocacy is directed to inciting or producing imminent lawless action and is likely to incite or pro-

TIMELINE

Civil Liberties and National Security

clear and present danger test
Test articulated by the Supreme Court in *Schenck* v. *U.S.* (1919) to draw the line between protected and unprotected speech; the Court looks to see "whether the words used" could "create a clear and present danger that they will bring about substantive evils" that Congress seeks "to prevent."

direct incitement test
Test articulated by the Supreme Court in *Brandenburg* v. *Ohio* (1969) that holds that advocacy of illegal action is protected by the First Amendment unless imminent lawless action is intended and likely to occur.

The New York Times

"All the News That's Fit to Print"

The New York Times

LATE CITY EDITION
Weather: Partly cloudy today; cool tonight. Partly sunny tomorrow.
Temp. range: Today 57–69; Friday 55–73. Full U.S. report on Page 86.

VOL. CXXII...No. 42,112   © 1973 The New York Times Company   NEW YORK, SATURDAY, MAY 12, 1973   15 CENTS

PENTAGON PAPERS CHARGES ARE DISMISSED; JUDGE BYRNE FREES ELLSBERG AND RUSSO, ASSAILS 'IMPROPER GOVERNMENT CONDUCT'

White House Says Attacks Will Continue in Cambodia

GRAY CALL TO NIXON

Said to Inform Inquiry It Came 3 Weeks After Watergate

NEW TRIAL BARRED

But Decision Does Not Solve Constitutional Issues in Case

Photo Courtesy: The Granger Collection

Why was the *Pentagon Papers* case important? A headline from the *New York Times* details legal proceedings in the *Pentagon Papers* case, formally called *New York Times Co.* v. *U.S. (1971)*, which was an important decision in establishing the boundaries of prior restraint.

duce such action."[35] The requirement of "imminent lawless action" makes it more difficult for the government to punish speech and publication and is consistent with the Framers' notion of the special role played by these elements in a democratic society.

Protected Speech and Publications

As discussed, the Supreme Court has refused to uphold the constitutionality of legislation that amounts to prior restraint of the press. Other types of speech and publication are also protected by the Court, including symbolic speech and hate speech.

VISUAL LITERACY

What Speech is Protected by the Constitution?

PRIOR RESTRAINT With only a few exceptions, the Court has made it clear that it will not tolerate prior restraint of speech. For example, in *New York Times Co.* v. *U.S.* (1971) (also called the *Pentagon Papers* case), the Supreme Court ruled that the U.S. government could not block the publication of secret Department of Defense documents illegally furnished to the *Times* by anti-war activists.[36] In 1976, the Supreme Court went even further, noting in *Nebraska Press Association* v. *Stuart* (1976) that any attempt by the government to prevent expression carried "'a heavy presumption' against its constitutionality."[37] In this case, a trial court issued a gag order barring the press from reporting the lurid details of a crime. In balancing the defendant's constitutional right to a fair trial against the press's right to cover a story, the Nebraska trial judge concluded that the defendant's right carried greater weight. The Supreme Court disagreed, holding the press's right to cover the trial paramount. Still, judges are often allowed to issue gag orders affecting parties to a lawsuit or to limit press coverage of a case.

In 2005, for example, the Court ruled that a judge's injection banning all futures comments made by client against his attorney, in this case the high-profile attorney Johnnie Cochran, did not extend beyond Cochran death.[38] The Court found that, in light of his death, Cochran's had a diminished need for protection. Thus the prohibition was an overly broad exercise of prior restraint.

symbolic speech
Symbols, signs, and other methods of expression generally also considered to be protected by the First Amendment.

SYMBOLIC SPEECH In addition to the general protection accorded to pure speech, the Supreme Court has extended the reach of the First Amendment to **symbolic speech**, a means of expression that includes symbols or signs. In the words of Justice John Marshall Harlan, these kinds of speech are part of the "free trade in ideas."[39] (To learn more about symbolic speech, see Ideas into Action: Political Speech and Mandatory Student Fees.)

The Supreme Court first acknowledged that symbolic speech was entitled to First Amendment protection in *Stromberg* v. *California* (1931).[40] There, the Court overturned a communist youth camp director's conviction under a state statute prohibiting the display

Ideas Into Action

Political Speech and Mandatory Student Fees

Universities across the United States often charge mandatory student fees that are used to pay for various activities and services across campus. These may include a range of health services (including sex education), student unions, technology, student publications, transportation, community service groups, and political organizations. Mandatory fees have increased in recent years at most universities, sometimes more sharply than tuition increases, especially at public universities. At the University of Wisconsin, Madison, for example, mandatory student fees increased nearly 20 percent in 2007, while tuition increased about 5 percent.[a]

The practice of charging mandatory fees can be controversial.[b] In March 2000, the U.S. Supreme Court ruled unanimously in *Board of Regents* v. *Southworth* that public universities could charge students a mandatory activity fee that could be used to facilitate extracurricular student political speech as long as the programs are neutral in their application.[c]

Scott Southworth, a law student at the University of Wisconsin, believed that the university's mandatory fee was a violation of his First Amendment right to free speech. He, along with several other law students, objected that their fees went to fund liberal groups. They particularly objected to the support of eighteen of the 125 various groups on campus that benefited from the mandatory activity fee, including the Lesbian, Gay, Bisexual, and Transgender Center, the International Socialist Organization, and the campus women's law center.[d] The Court ruled against Southworth and for the university, underscoring the importance of universities being a forum for the free exchange of political and ideological ideas and objectives.

- Should universities be allowed to charge mandatory fees to all students, even those who do not use some of the services?
- Visit the Web site of your university or a university near you. What kind of mandatory fees are currently in place, and where do such fees go? How difficult is it to find information on the subject?
- Are you aware of any student organizations whose request for school funding has been rejected? If so, what reasons were given?.
- How is paying for student organizations a way universities can reinforce rights guaranteed by the First Amendment?

---

[a]Heather LaRoi, "Mandatory Student Fees Have Been Rising Faster than Tuition at UW Campuses," *Wisconsin State Journal* (November 4, 2007).
[b]Jordan Lorence, *FIRE's Guide to Student Fees and Legal Equality on Campus*. (Philadelphia: Foundation for Individual Rights in Education, 2003), 3–4.
[c]*Board of Regents* v. *Southworth*, 529 U.S. 217 (2000).
[d]"U.S. Court Upholds Student Fees Going to Controversial Groups," *Toronto Star* (March 23, 2000): NEXIS.

---

of a red flag, a symbol of opposition to the U.S. government. In a similar vein, the right of high school students to wear black armbands to protest the Vietnam War was upheld in *Tinker* v. *Des Moines Independent Community School District* (1969).[41] Burning the American flag also has been held a form of protected symbolic speech, as discussed in chapter 2.

HATE SPEECH, UNPOPULAR SPEECH, AND SPEECH ZONES "As a thumbnail summary of the last two or three decades of speech issues in the Supreme Court," wrote eminent First Amendment scholar Harry Kalven Jr. in 1966, "we may come to see the Negro as winning back for us the freedoms the Communists seemed to have lost for us."[42] Still, says noted African American scholar Henry Louis Gates Jr., Kalven would be shocked to see the stance that some blacks now take toward the First Amendment, which once protected protests, rallies, and agitation in the 1960s: "The byword among many black activists and black intellectuals is no longer the political imperative to protect free speech; it is the moral imperative to suppress 'hate speech.' "[43]

In the 1990s, a particularly thorny First Amendment issue emerged as cities and universities attempted to prohibit what they viewed as offensive hate speech. In *R.A.V.* v. *City of St. Paul* (1992), a St. Paul, Minnesota, ordinance that made it a crime to engage in speech or action likely to arouse "anger," "alarm," or "resentment" on the basis of race, color, creed, religion, or gender was at issue. The Court ruled 5–4 that a

Photo courtesy: Dana Summers/© Tribune Media Services, Inc. All rights reserved. Reprinted with permission.

Whose actions does the Bill of Rights protect? As this cartoon suggests, the Bill of Rights protects a wide range of citizens and activities, many of which may be considered objectionable.

Thinking Globally

Free Speech or Hate Speech?

In 2007, as part of efforts to combat racism and hate crimes, the twenty-seven nations that comprise the European Union (EU) agreed to criminalize statements that deny or trivialize the Holocaust, the mass killing of Jews during World War II. The proposed rules call for the EU to impose up to three-year prison sentences for those convicted. A German court recently sentenced Ernst Zundel to five years in prison for inciting racial hatred and for his denial of the Holocaust.

■ Is the European Union's ban on statements that deny the Holocaust too restrictive of free speech? Why or why not?
■ Would such a ban be possible in the United States? Should such a ban be possible in the United States? Explain your answers.

white teenager who burned a cross on a black family's front lawn, thereby committing a hate crime under the ordinance, could not be charged under that law because the First Amendment prevents governments from "silencing speech on the basis of its content."[44] In 2003, the Court narrowed this definition, ruling that state governments could constitutionally restrict cross burning when it occurred with the intent of racial intimidation.[45]

Two-thirds of colleges and universities have banned a variety of forms of speech or conduct that creates or fosters an intimidating, hostile, or offensive environment on campus. To prevent disruption of university activities, some universities have also created free speech zones that restrict the time, place, or manner of speech. Critics, including the ACLU, charge that free speech zones imply that speech can be limited on other parts of the campus, which they see as a violation of the First Amendment. They have filed a number of suits in district court, but to date none of these cases has been neared by the Supreme Court.

Unprotected Speech and Publications

Although the Supreme Court has allowed few governmental bans on most types of speech, some forms of expression are not protected. In 1942, the Supreme Court set out the rationale by which it would distinguish between protected and unprotected speech. According to the Court, libel, fighting words, obscenity, and lewdness are not protected by the First Amendment because "such expressions are no essential part of any exposition of ideals, and are of such slight social value as a step to truth that any benefit that may be derived from them is clearly outweighed by the social interest in order and morality."[46]

libel
False written statement or a written statement tending to call someone's reputation into disrepute.

slander
Untrue spoken statements that defame the character of a person.

LIBEL AND SLANDER Libel is a written statement that defames the character of a person. If the statement is spoken, it is **slander.** In many nations—such as Great Britain, for example—it is relatively easy to sue someone for libel. In the United States, however, the standards of proof are much higher. A person who believes that he or she has been a victim of libel must show that the statements made were untrue. Truth is an absolute defense against the charge of libel, no matter how painful or embarrassing the revelations.

It is often more difficult for individuals the Supreme Court considers "public persons or public officials" to sue for libel or slander. ***New York Times Co. v. Sullivan* (1964)** was the first major libel case considered by the Supreme Court.[47] An Alabama state court found the *Times* guilty of libel for printing a full-page advertisement accusing Alabama officials of physically abusing African Americans during various civil rights protests. (The ad was paid for by civil rights activists, including former First Lady Eleanor Roosevelt.) The Supreme Court overturned the conviction and established that a finding of libel against a public official could stand only if there was a showing of "actual malice," or a knowing disregard for the truth. Proof that the statements were false or negligent was not sufficient to prove actual malice.

New York Times Co. v. *Sullivan* (1964)
The Supreme Court concluded that "actual malice" must be proved to support a finding of libel against a public figure.

FIGHTING WORDS In the 1942 case of *Chaplinsky* v. *New Hampshire*, the Court stated that **fighting words**, or words that, "by their very utterance inflict injury or tend or incite an immediate breach of peace" are not subject to the restrictions of the First Amendment.[48] Fighting words, which include "profanity, obscenity, and threats," are therefore able to be regulated by the federal and state governments.

These words do not necessarily have to be spoken; fighting words can also come in the form of symbolic expression. For example, in 1968, a California man named Paul Cohen wore a jacket that said "Fuck the Draft. Stop the War" into a Los Angeles county courthouse. He was arrested and charged with disturbing the peace and engaging in offensive conduct, which the police feared would incite others to act violently toward Cohen. The trial court convicted Cohen, and this conviction was upheld by a state appellate court. However, when the case reached the Supreme Court in 1971, the Court reversed the lower courts' decisions and ruled that forbidding the use of certain words amounted to little more than censorship of ideas.[49]

fighting words
Words that, "by their very utterance inflict injury or tend to incite an immediate breach of peace." Fighting words are not subject to the restrictions of the First Amendment.

OBSCENITY Through 1957, U.S. courts often based their opinions of what was obscene on an English common-law test that had been set out in 1868: "Whether the tendency of the matter charged as obscenity is to deprive and corrupt those whose minds are open to such immoral influences and into whose hands a publication of this sort might fall."[50] In *Roth* v. *U.S.* (1957), however, the Court abandoned this approach and held that, to be considered obscene, the material in question had to be "utterly without redeeming social importance," and articulated a new test for obscenity: "whether to the average person, applying contemporary community standards, the dominant theme of the material taken as a whole appeals to the prurient interests."[51]

In many ways, the *Roth* test brought with it as many problems as it attempted to solve. Throughout the 1950s and 1960s, "prurient" remained hard to define, as the Supreme Court struggled to find a standard for judging actions or words. Moreover, it was very difficult to prove that a book or movie was "*utterly* without redeeming social value." In general, even some hardcore pornography passed muster under the *Roth* test, prompting some to argue that the Court fostered the increase in the number of sexually oriented publications designed to appeal to those living during the sexual revolution.

Richard M. Nixon made the growth in pornography a major issue when he ran for president in 1968. Nixon pledged to appoint to federal judgeships only those who would uphold law and order and stop coddling criminals and purveyors of porn. Once elected president, Nixon made four appointments to the Supreme Court, including Chief Justice Warren Burger, who wrote the opinion in *Miller* v. *California* (1973). There, the Court set out a test that redefined obscenity. To make it easier for states to regulate obscene materials, the justices concluded that lower courts must ask "whether the work depicts or describes, in a patently offensive way, sexual conduct specifically defined by state law." The courts also were to determine "whether the work, taken as a whole, lacks serious literary, artistic, political, or scientific value." And, in place of the contemporary community standards gauge used in *Roth*, the Court defined community

What are the boundaries of free assembly? Members of an activist group calling itself the Granny Peace Brigade exercise their constitutional right to assemble in New York City to protest the Iraq War. In April of 2006, eighteen members of the group ranging in age from 59 to 91 were acquitted of two counts of disorderly conduct stemming from a protest against the war at a military recruitment center in Times Square. The judged ruled that the "grannies" had been wrongly arrested because there was credible evidence that they had left room for people to enter and leave the recruitment center.

Photo courtesy: Mel Evans/AP Wide World Photos

standards to refer to the locality in question, under the rationale that what is acceptable in New York City might not be acceptable in Maine or Mississippi.[52]

Time and contexts clearly have altered the Court's and, indeed, much of America's perceptions of what works are obscene. But, the Supreme Court has allowed communities great leeway in drafting statutes to deal with obscenity and, even more importantly, other forms of questionable expression. In 1991, for example, the Court voted 5–4 to allow Indiana to ban totally nude erotic dancing, concluding that the statute furthered a substantial governmental interest, and therefore was not in violation of the First Amendment.[53]

While lawmakers have been fairly effective in restricting the sale and distribution of obscene materials, monitoring the Internet has proven difficult for Congress. Since 1996, Congress has passed several laws designed to prohibit the transmission of obscene or "harmful" materials over the Internet to anyone under age eighteen.

The U.S. Supreme Court has repeatedly found these laws unconstitutional.[54] Yet, in 2008, a seven-justice majority decided in *U.S.* v. *Williams* that the Protect Act, which outlawed the printing of material believed to be child pornography, was not overly broad and did not abridge the freedom of speech guaranteed by the First Amendment.[55]

Freedoms of Assembly and Petition

"Peaceful assembly for lawful discussion cannot be made a crime," Chief Justice Charles Evans Hughes wrote in the 1937 case of *DeJonge* v. *Oregon*, which incorporated the First Amendment's freedom of assembly clause to apply to the states.[56] Despite this clear declaration, and an even more ringing declaration in the First Amendment, the fundamental freedoms of assembly and petition have been among the most controversial, especially in times of war. As with other First Amendment freedoms, the Supreme Court often has become the arbiter between the freedom of the people to express dissent and government's authority to limit controversy in the name of national security.

Because the freedom to assemble is hinged on peaceful conduct, the freedoms of assembly and petition are related directly to the freedoms of speech and of the press.

If the words or actions taken at any event cross the line of constitutionality, the event itself may no longer be protected by the Constitution. Absent that protection, leaders and attendees may be subject to governmental regulation and even criminal arrest, incarceration, or civil fines.

The Second Amendment: The Right to Keep and Bear Arms

Gun Rights and Gun Control

During colonial times, the colonists' distrust of standing armies was evident. Most colonies required all white men to keep and bear arms, and all white men in whole sections of the colonies were deputized to defend their settlements against Indians and European powers. These local militias were viewed as the best way to keep order and protect liberty.

The Second Amendment was added to the Constitution to ensure that Congress could not pass laws to disarm state militias. This amendment appeased Anti-Federalists, who feared that the new Constitution would cause them to lose the right to "keep and bear arms" as well as an unstated right—the right to revolt against governmental tyranny.

Through the early 1920s, few state statutes were passed to regulate firearms (and generally these laws dealt with the possession of firearms by slaves). The Supreme Court's decision in *Barron* v. *Baltimore* (1833), which refused to incorporate the Bill of Rights to the state governments, prevented federal review of those state laws.[57] Moreover, in *Dred Scott* v. *Sandford* (1857) (see chapter 3), Chief Justice Roger B. Taney listed the right to own and carry arms as a basic right of citizenship.[58]

In 1934, Congress passed the National Firearms Act in response to the increase in organized crime that occurred in the 1920s and 1930s as a result of Prohibition. The act imposed taxes on automatic weapons and sawed-off shotguns. In *U.S.* v. *Miller* (1939), a unanimous Court upheld the constitutionality of the act, stating that the Second Amendment was intended to protect a citizen's right to own ordinary militia weapons and not sawed-off shotguns.[59] "For nearly seventy years following *Miller*, the Court did not directly address the Second Amendment. Then, in the 2008 case of *D.C.* v. *Heller*, the Court ruled that the Second Amendment protects an individual's right to own a firearm for personal use.[60]

Congress and the executive branch, however, have been consistent players in the gun control debate. In the aftermath of the assassination attempt on President Ronald Reagan in 1981, many lawmakers called for passage of gun control legislation. At the forefront of that effort was Sarah Brady, the wife of James Brady, the presidential press secretary who was badly wounded and left partially disabled by John Hinckley Jr., President Reagan's assailant. In 1993, her efforts helped to win passage of the Brady Bill, which imposed a federal mandatory five-day waiting period on the purchase of handguns.

Perhaps more important than the Brady Bill was the ban on assault weapons signed by President Bill Clinton in 1994. This provision, which prohibited Americans from owning many of the most powerful types of guns, carried a ten-year time limit. It expired just before the 2004 presidential and congressional elections. Neither President George W. Bush nor the Republican-controlled Congress made any serious efforts to renew it.

Thinking Globally
Gun Control in Europe

Many European countries have very strict laws governing gun ownership. In Great Britain, it is illegal to own a handgun. In France, citizens may apply for a three-year permit only after demonstrating a clear need and completing an exhaustive background check. Laws in Switzerland and Germany are equally restrictive.

■ Why is the issue of gun control so polarizing in the United States but not in Europe?
■ Do you support any restrictions on the right to keep and bear arms? If so, what? If not, why?

The Rights of Criminal Defendants

writs of *habeas corpus*
Court orders in which a judge requires authorities to prove that a prisoner is being held lawfully and that allows the prisoner to be freed if the judge is not persuaded by the government's case. *Habeas corpus* rights imply that prisoners have a right to know what charges are being made against them.

***ex post facto* law**
From the Latin for "after the fact," a law that applies to actions committed before the law was passed. Prohibited by the Constitution.

bill of attainder
A legislative act that inflicts punishment on individuals without any kind of judicial action. Prohibited by the Constitution.

Article I of the Constitution guarantees a number of rights for those accused of crimes. The Constitution guarantees **writs of *habeas corpus*,** court orders in which a judge requires authorities to prove that a prisoner is being held lawfully and that allows the prisoner to be freed if the judge is not persuaded by the government's case. Habeas corpus rights also imply that prisoners have a right to know what charges are being made against them.

Article I of the Constitution also prohibits ***ex post facto* laws,** or laws that apply to actions committed before the laws were passed. And, Article I prohibits **bills of attainder,** legislative acts that inflict punishment on individuals without judicial action.

The Fourth, Fifth, Sixth, and Eighth Amendments supplement these rights with a variety of procedural guarantees, often called due process rights. In this section, we examine how the courts have interpreted and applied these guarantees in an attempt to balance personal liberty and national safety and security.

Over the years, many individuals criticized liberal Warren Court decisions of the 1950s and 1960s, arguing that its rulings gave criminals more liberties than their victims. The Warren Court made several provisions of the Bill of Rights dealing with the liberties of criminal defendants applicable to the states through the Fourteenth Amendment. It is important to remember that most procedural guarantees apply to individuals charged with crimes—that is, they apply before the individuals have been tried. These liberties were designed to protect those wrongfully accused, although, of course, they often have helped the guilty. But, as Justice William O. Douglas once noted, "Respecting the dignity even of the least worthy citizen . . . raises the stature of all of us."[61]

Many commentators continue to argue, however, that only the guilty are helped by the American system and that criminals should not go unpunished because of simple police error. The dilemma of balancing the liberties of the individual against those of society permeates the entire debate. This debate has been further fueled by the passage of the USA Patriot Act and the Military Commissions Act. The impact of these laws on Americans' civil liberties is discussed in the Toward Reform section at the end of this chapter.

The Fourth Amendment and Searches and Seizures

Fourth Amendment
Part of the Bill of Rights that reads: "The right of the people to be secure in their persons, houses, papers, and effects, against unreasonable searches and seizures, shall not be violated, and no Warrants shall issue, but upon probable cause, supported by Oath or affirmation, and particularly describing the place to be searched, and the persons or things to be seized."

The **Fourth Amendment** to the Constitution protects people from unreasonable searches by the federal government. Moreover, in some detail, it sets out what may not be searched unless a warrant is issued, underscoring the Framers' concern with preventing government abuses.

The purpose of this amendment was to deny the national government the authority to make general searches. But, still, the language that the Framers chose left numerous questions to be answered, including the definition of an unreasonable search.

Over the years, in a number of decisions, the Supreme Court has interpreted the Fourth Amendment to allow the police to search: (1) the person arrested; (2) things in plain view of the accused person; and, (3) places or things that the arrested person could touch or reach or are otherwise in the arrestee's immediate control. In 1995, the Court resolved a decades-old constitutional dispute by ruling unanimously that, barring reasonable exceptions, police must knock and announce their presence before entering a house or apartment to execute a search.[62] But, in 2006, the Court ruled in a 5–4 decision that even if police refused to knock, evidence improperly seized could be used in cases where police had a valid warrant.[63]

You Are a Police Officer

Warrantless searches often occur if police suspect that someone is committing or is about to commit a crime. In these situations, police may stop and frisk the individual under suspicion. In 1989, the Court ruled that there need be only a "reasonable suspicion" for stopping a suspect—a much lower standard than probable cause.[64] Thus, a suspected drug courier may be stopped for brief questioning but only a frisk search (for weapons) is permitted. A person's answers to the questions may shift reasonable suspicion to probable cause, thus permitting the officer to search further. But, except at borders between the United States and Mexico and Canada (or international airports within U.S. borders), searches require probable cause.

Searches can also be made without a warrant if consent is obtained, and the Court has ruled that consent can be given by a variety of persons. It has ruled, for example, that police can search a bedroom occupied by two persons as long as they have the consent of one of them.[65] The same standard, however, does not apply to houses. In 2006, the Court ruled that the police could not conduct a warrantless search of a home if one of the occupants objected.[66]

In situations where no arrest occurs, police must obtain search warrants from a "neutral and detached magistrate" prior to conducting more extensive searches of houses, cars, offices, or any other place where an individual would reasonably have some expectation of privacy.[67] Police cannot get search warrants, for example, to require you to undergo surgery to remove a bullet that might be used to incriminate you, since your expectation of bodily privacy outweighs the need for evidence.[68] But, courts do not require search warrants in possible drunk driving situations. Thus, the police in some states can require you to take a Breathalyzer test to determine whether you have been drinking in excess of legal limits.[69] In some states, refusing a test may result in the automatic loss of your license.

Until passage of the USA Patriot Act, homes, too, were presumed to be private. Firefighters can enter your home to fight a fire without a warrant. But, if they decide to investigate the cause of the fire, they must obtain a warrant before their reentry.[70] In contrast, under the open fields doctrine first articulated by the Supreme Court in 1924, if you own a field, and even if you post "No Trespassing" signs, the police can search your field without a warrant to see if you are illegally growing marijuana, because you cannot reasonably expect privacy in an open field.[71]

In 2001, in a decision that surprised many commentators, by a vote of 5–4, the Supreme Court ruled that drug evidence obtained by using a thermal imager (without a warrant) on a public street to locate the defendant's marijuana hothouse was obtained in violation of the Fourth Amendment.[72] In contrast, the use of low-flying aircraft and helicopters to detect marijuana fields or binoculars to look in a yard have been upheld because officers simply were using their eyesight, not a technological tool.[73]

Cars have proven problematic for police and the courts because of their mobile nature. As noted by Chief Justice William H. Taft as early as 1925, "the vehicle can quickly be moved out of the locality or jurisdiction in which the warrant must be sought."[74] Over the years, the Court has become increasingly lenient about the scope of automobile searches.

In 2002, an unusually unanimous Court ruled that when evaluating if a border patrol officer acted lawfully in stopping a suspicious minivan, the totality of the circumstances had to be considered. Wrote Chief Justice William H. Rehnquist, the "balance between the public interest and the individual's right to personal security," tilts in favor of a "standard less than probable cause in brief investigatory stops." This ruling gave law enforcement officers more leeway to pull over suspicious motorists.[75]

Testing for drugs is an especially thorny search and seizure issue. If the government can require you to take a Breathalyzer test, can it require you to be tested for

Photo courtesy: X17online.com

Should parents be required to undergo drug tests in order to see their children? The issue of drug testing in family law gained increased national salience as Britney Spears and Kevin Federline fought over custody of their two sons. A California judge ordered Spears to undergo mandatory drug tests; after reports that she failed or missed most of these tests, Spears's visitation rights were revoked temporarily.

Fifth Amendment
Part of the Bill of Rights that imposes a number of restrictions on the federal government with respect to the rights of persons suspected of committing a crime. It provides for indictment by a grand jury and protection against self-incrimination, and prevents the national government from denying a person life, liberty, or property without the due process of law. It also prevents the national government from taking property without just compensation.

Miranda v. *Arizona* (1966)
A landmark Supreme Court ruling that held the Fifth Amendment requires that individuals arrested for a crime must be advised of their right to remain silent and to have counsel present.

drugs? In the wake of growing public concern over drug use, in 1986, President Ronald Reagan signed an executive order requiring many executive branch employees to undergo drug tests. In 1997, Congress passed a similar law authorizing random drug searches of all congressional employees.

While many private employers and professional athletic organizations routinely require drug tests upon application or as a condition of employment, governmental requirements present constitutional questions about the scope of permissible searches and seizures. In 1989, the Supreme Court ruled that mandatory drug and alcohol testing of employees involved in accidents was constitutional.[76] In 1995, the Court upheld the constitutionally of random drug testing of public high school athletes.[77] And, in 2002, the Court upheld the constitutionality of a Tecumseh, Oklahoma, policy that required mandatory drug testing of high school students participating in any extracurricular activities. Thus, prospective band, choir, debate, or drama club members were subject to the same kind of random drug testing undergone by athletes.[78]

In general, all employers can require pre-employment drug screening. However, because governments are unconditionally bound by the constitutional search provisions of the Fourth Amendment, public employees enjoy more protection in the area of drug testing than do employees of private enterprises.[79]

Another issue is the constitutionality of drug testing in regard to family law. In 2001, in a 6–3 decision, the Court ruled that compulsory testing of women for cocaine use and reporting positive results to law enforcement officials to generate evidence for law enforcement officials and not to give medical treatment to the women was unconstitutional.[80]

The Fifth Amendment: Self-Incrimination and Double Jeopardy

The **Fifth Amendment** provides that "No person shall be . . . compelled in any criminal case to be a witness against himself." "Taking the Fifth" is shorthand for exercising one's constitutional right not to self-incriminate. The Supreme Court has interpreted this guarantee to be "as broad as the mischief against which it seeks to guard," finding that criminal defendants do not have to take the stand at trial to answer questions, nor can a judge make mention of their failure to do so as evidence of guilt.[81] Moreover, lawyers cannot imply that a defendant who refuses to take the stand must be guilty or have something to hide.

This right not to incriminate oneself also means that prosecutors cannot use as evidence in a trial any of a defendant's statements or confessions that were not made voluntarily. As is the case in many areas of the law, however, judicial interpretation of the term voluntary has changed over time.

In earlier times, it was not unusual for police to beat defendants to obtain their confessions. In 1936, however, the Supreme Court ruled that convictions for murder based solely on confessions given after physical beatings were unconstitutional.[82] Police then began to resort to other measures to force confessions. Defendants, for example, were given the third degree—questioned for hours on end with no sleep or food, or threatened with physical violence until they were mentally beaten into giving confessions. In other situations, family members were threatened. In one case, a young mother accused of marijuana possession was told that her welfare benefits would be terminated and her children taken away from her if she failed to talk.[83]

***Miranda* v. *Arizona* (1966)** was the Supreme Court's response to these coercive efforts to obtain confessions that were not truly voluntary. On March 3, 1963, an eighteen-year-old girl was kidnapped and raped on the outskirts of Phoenix, Arizona.

Ten days later, police arrested Ernesto Miranda, a poor, mentally disturbed man with a ninth-grade education. In a police-station lineup, the victim identified Miranda as her attacker. Police then took Miranda to a separate room and questioned him for two hours. At first he denied guilt. Eventually, however, he confessed to the crime and wrote and signed a brief statement describing the crime and admitting his guilt. At no time was he told that he did not have to answer any questions or that he could be represented by an attorney.

After Miranda's conviction, his case was appealed on the grounds that his Fifth Amendment right not to incriminate himself had been violated because his confession had been coerced. Writing for the Court, Chief Justice Earl Warren, himself a former district attorney and a former California state attorney general, noted that because police have a tremendous advantage in any interrogation situation, criminal suspects must be given greater protection. A confession obtained in the manner of Miranda's was not truly voluntary; thus, it was inadmissible at trial.

To provide guidelines for police to implement *Miranda*, the Court mandated that: "Prior to any questioning, the person must be warned that he has a right to remain silent, that any statements he does make may be used as evidence against him, and that he has a right to the presence of an attorney, either retained or appointed." In response to this mandate from the Court, police routinely began to read suspects what are now called their **Miranda rights**, a practice you undoubtedly have seen repeated over and over in movies and TV police dramas.

Although the Burger Court did not enforce the reading of *Miranda* rights as vehemently as had the Warren Court, Chief Justice Warren Burger, Warren's successor, acknowledged that they had become an integral part of established police procedures.[84] The Rehnquist Court, however, was more tolerant of the use of coerced confessions and employed a much more flexible standard to allow their admissibility.

In 2003, the Court was faced with a new twist on *Miranda* rights. Samuel Patane was arrested in his home for violating a restraining order taken out by his girlfriend. As he was being arrested and was about to be read his rights, Patane interrupted the officers, saying that he knew them. The officers subsequently found guns in Patane's home, which as an ex-felon he was not allowed to possess. Patane later argued that the search was illegal because he was not Mirandized. A majority of the Court concluded that the guns could be used as evidence against Patane.[85]

The Fifth Amendment also mandates: "nor shall any person be subject for the same offense to be twice put in jeopardy of life or limb." This is called the **double jeopardy clause** and it protects individuals from being tried twice for the same crime in the same jurisdiction. Thus, if a defendant is acquitted by a jury of a charge of murder, he or she cannot be retried for the offense even if new information is unearthed that could further point to guilt.

The Fourth and Fifth Amendments and the Exclusionary Rule

In *Weeks* v. *U.S.* (1914), the U.S. Supreme Court adopted the **exclusionary rule,** which bars the use of illegally seized evidence at trial. Thus, although the Fourth and Fifth Amendments do not prohibit the use of evidence obtained in violation of their provisions, the exclusionary rule is a judicially created remedy to deter constitutional violations. In *Weeks*, for example, the Court reasoned that allowing police and prosecutors to use the "fruits of a poisonous tree" (a tainted search) would only encourage that activity.[86]

In balancing the need to deter police misconduct against the possibility that guilty individuals could go free, the Warren Court decided that deterring police misconduct

Photo courtesy: AP/Wide World Photos

Who was Ernesto Miranda?
Even though Ernesto Miranda's confession was not admitted as evidence at his retrial, the testimony of his ex-girlfriend and the victim were enough to convince the jury of his guilt. He served nine years in prison before he was paroled. After his release, he routinely sold autographed cards inscribed with what are called the *Miranda* rights now read to all suspects. In 1976, four years after his release, Miranda was stabbed to death in a Phoenix bar fight during a card game. Two *Miranda* cards were found on his body, and the person who killed him was read his *Miranda* rights upon his arrest.

Miranda rights
Statements that must be made by the police informing a suspect of his or her constitutional rights protected by the Fifth Amendment, including the right to an attorney provided by the court if the suspect cannot afford one.

double jeopardy clause
Part of the Fifth Amendment that protects individuals from being tried twice for the same offense.

exclusionary rule
Judicially created rule that prohibits police from using illegally seized evidence at trial.

was most important. In *Mapp* v. *Ohio* (1961), the Warren Court ruled that "all evidence obtained by searches and seizures in violation of the Constitution, is inadmissible in a state court."[87] This historic and controversial case put law enforcement officers on notice that if they found evidence in violation of any constitutional rights, those efforts would be for naught because the tainted evidence could not be used in federal or state trials.

In 1976, the Court noted that the exclusionary rule "deflects the truth-finding process and often frees the guilty."[88] Since then, the Court has carved out a variety of limited "good faith exceptions" to the exclusionary rule, allowing the use of tainted evidence in a variety of situations, especially when police have a search warrant and, in good faith, conduct the search on the assumption that the warrant is valid even though it is subsequently found invalid. Since the purpose of the exclusionary rule is to deter police misconduct, and in this situation there is no police misconduct, the courts have permitted the introduction at trial of the seized evidence. Another exception to the exclusionary rule is "inevitable discovery." Evidence illegally seized may be introduced if it would have been discovered anyway in the course of continuing investigation.

The Court has continued to uphold the exclusionary rule. In a 2006 victory for advocates of defendants' rights, the Court ruled unanimously that the Fourth Amendment requires that any evidence collected under an anticipatory warrant—one presented by the police yet not authorized by a judge—would be inadmissible at trial as a violation of the exclusionary rule.[89]

The Sixth Amendment and the Right to Counsel

Sixth Amendment
Part of the Bill of Rights that sets out the basic requirements of procedural due process for federal courts to follow in criminal trials. These include speedy and public trials, impartial juries, trials in the state where crime was committed, notice of the charges, the right to confront and obtain favorable witnesses, and the right to counsel.

The **Sixth Amendment** guarantees to an accused person "the Assistance of Counsel in his defense." In the past, this provision meant only that an individual could hire an attorney to represent him or her in court. Since most criminal defendants are too poor to hire private lawyers, this provision was of little assistance to many who found themselves on trial. Recognizing this, Congress required federal courts to provide an attorney for defendants who could not to afford one. This was first required in capital cases (where the death penalty is a possibility); eventually, attorneys were provided to the poor in all federal criminal cases.[90] Similarly, in 1932, the Supreme Court directed states to furnish lawyers to defendants in capital cases.[91] The Court also began to expand the right to counsel to other state offenses but did so in a piecemeal fashion that gave the states little direction. Given the high cost of providing legal counsel, this ambiguity often made it cost-effective for the states not to provide counsel at all.

These ambiguities came to an end with the Court's decision in *Gideon* v. *Wainwright* (1963).[92] Clarence Earl Gideon, a fifty-one-year-old drifter, was charged with breaking into a Panama City, Florida, pool hall and stealing beer, wine, and some change from a vending machine. At his trial, he asked the judge to appoint a lawyer for him because he was too poor to hire one himself. The judge refused, and Gideon was convicted and given a five-year prison term for petty larceny. The case against Gideon had not been strong, but as a layperson unfamiliar with the law and with trial practice and procedure, he was unable to point out its weaknesses.

The apparent inequities in the system that had resulted in Gideon's conviction continued to bother him. Eventually, he requested some paper from a prison guard, consulted books in the prison library, and then drafted and mailed a *habeas corpus* petition to the U.S. Supreme Court asking it to overrule his conviction.

In a unanimous decision, the Supreme Court agreed with Gideon and his court-appointed lawyer, Abe Fortas, a future associate justice of the Supreme Court. Writing for the Court, Justice Hugo Black explained that "lawyers in criminal courts are necessities, not luxuries." Therefore, the Court concluded, the state must provide an attorney to indigent defendants in felony cases. Underscoring the Court's point, Gideon was acquitted when he was retried with a lawyer to argue his case.

The Burger and Rehnquist Courts gradually expanded the *Gideon* rule. The justices first applied this standard to cases that were not felonies[93] and, later, to many cases where probation and future penalties were possibilities. In 2008, the Court also ruled that the right to counsel began at the accused's first appearance before a judge.[94]

The issue of legal representation also extends to questions of competence. Various courts have held that lawyers who fell asleep during trial, failed to put on a defense, or were drunk during the proceedings were "adequate." In 2005, however, the Supreme Court ruled that the Sixth Amendment's guarantees required lawyers to take reasonable steps to prepare for their clients' trial and sentencing, including examining their prior criminal history.

The Sixth Amendment and Jury Trials

The Sixth Amendment (and, to a lesser extent, Article III of the Constitution) provides that a person accused of a crime shall enjoy the right to a speedy and public trial by an impartial jury—that is, a trial in which a group of the accused's peers act as a fact-finding, deliberative body to determine guilt or innocence. It also provides defendants the right to confront witnesses against them. The Supreme Court has held that jury trials must be available if a prison sentence of six or more months is possible.

Impartiality is a requirement of jury trials that has undergone significant change, with the method of selecting jurors being the most frequently challenged part of the process. Although potential individual jurors who have prejudged a case are not eligible to serve, no groups can be systematically excluded from serving. In 1880, for example, the Supreme Court ruled that African Americans could not be excluded from state jury pools (lists of those eligible to serve).[95] And, it was not until 1975 that the Court ruled that barring women from jury service violated the mandate that juries be made up of a "fair cross section" of the community.[96]

In 1986, the Court expanded the requirement that juries reflect a fair cross section of the community. Historically, lawyers had used peremptory challenges (those for which no cause needs to be given) to exclude African Americans from juries, especially when African Americans were criminal defendants. In *Batson* v. *Kentucky* (1986), the Court ruled that the use of peremptory challenges specifically to exclude African American jurors violated the equal protection clause of the Fourteenth Amendment.[97]

Photo courtesy: Supreme Court Historical Society

What was the impact of *Gideon* v. *Wainwright* (1963)? When Clarence Earl Gideon wrote his petition for a writ of *certiorari* to the Supreme Court, (asking the Court, in its discretion, to hear his case), he had no way of knowing that his case would lead to the landmark ruling on the right to counsel, *Gideon* v. *Wainwright* (1963). Nor did he know that Chief Justice Earl Warren actually had instructed his law clerks to be on the lookout for a *habeas corpus* petition (literally, "you have the body," which argues that the person in jail is there in violation of some statutory or constitutional right) that could be used to guarantee the assistance of counsel for defendants in criminal cases.

In 1994, the Supreme Court answered the major remaining unanswered question about jury selection: can lawyers exclude women from juries through their use of peremptory challenges? This question came up frequently because in rape trials and sex discrimination cases, one side or another often considers it advantageous to select jurors on the basis of their sex. The Supreme Court ruled that the equal protection clause prohibits discrimination in jury selection on the basis of gender. Thus, lawyers cannot strike all potential male jurors based on the belief that males might be more sympathetic to the arguments of a man charged in a paternity suit, a rape trial, or a domestic violence suit, for example.[98]

The right to confront witnesses at trial also is protected by the Sixth Amendment. In 1990, however, the Supreme Court ruled that this right was not absolute. In *Maryland* v. *Craig* (1990), the Court ruled that, constitutionally, the testimony of a six-year-old alleged child abuse victim via one-way closed circuit television was permissible. The clause's central purpose, said the Court, was to ensure the reliability of testimony by subjecting it to rigorous examination in an adversarial proceeding.[99] In this case, the child was questioned out of the presence of the defendant, who was in communication with his defense and prosecuting attorneys. The defendant, along with the judge and jury, watched the testimony.

The Eighth Amendment and Cruel and Unusual Punishment

Eighth Amendment
Part of the Bill of Rights that states: "Excessive bail shall not be required, nor excessive fines imposed, nor cruel and unusual punishments inflicted."

The **Eighth Amendment** prohibits "cruel and unusual punishments," a concept rooted in the English common-law tradition. Interestingly, today the United States is the only Western nation to put people to death for committing crimes. Not surprisingly, there are tremendous regional differences in the imposition of the death penalty, with the South leading in the number of men and women executed each year.

In the 1500s, religious heretics and those critical of the English Crown were subjected to torture to extract confessions and then condemned to an equally hideous death by the rack, disembowelment, or other barbarous means. The English Bill of Rights, written in 1687, safeguarded against "cruel and unusual punishments" as a result of public outrage against those practices. The same language found its way into the U.S. Bill of Rights. Prior to the 1960s, however, little judicial attention was paid to the meaning of that phrase, especially in the context of the death penalty.

The death penalty was in use in all of the colonies at the time the U.S. Constitution was adopted, and its constitutionality went unquestioned. In fact, in two separate cases in the late 1800s, the Supreme Court ruled that deaths by public shooting[100] and electrocution were not "cruel and unusual" forms of punishment in the same category as "punishments which inflict torture, such as the rack, the thumbscrew, the iron boot, the stretching of limbs and the like."[101]

In the 1960s, the NAACP Legal Defense Fund (LDF), believing that the death penalty was applied more frequently to African Americans than to members of other groups, orchestrated a carefully designed legal attack on its constitutionality.[102] Public opinion polls revealed that in 1971, on the eve of the LDF's first major death sentence case to reach the Supreme Court, public support for the death penalty had fallen to below 50 percent. With the timing just right, in *Furman* v. *Georgia* (1972), the Supreme Court effectively put an end to capital punishment, at least in the short run.[103] The Court ruled that because the death penalty often was imposed in an arbitrary manner, it constituted cruel and unusual punishment in violation of the Eighth and Fourteenth Amendments. Following

Furman, several state legislatures enacted new laws designed to meet the Court's objections to the arbitrary nature of the sentence. In 1976, in *Gregg* v. *Georgia*, Georgia's rewritten death penalty statute was ruled constitutional by the Supreme Court in a 7–2 decision.[104] (To learn more about the controversy over the death penalty, see Join the Debate: The Death Penalty.)

This ruling did not deter the LDF from continuing to bring death penalty cases before the Court. In 1987, a 5–4 Court ruled that imposition of the death penalty—even when it appeared to discriminate against African Americans—did not violate the equal protection clause.[105] It noted that even if statistics show clear discrimination, there must be a showing of racial discrimination in the case at hand.

Four years later, a case involving the same defendant produced an equally important ruling on the death penalty and criminal procedure from the U.S. Supreme Court. In the second case, the Court found that new issues could not be raised on appeal, even if there was some state error. The case, *McCleskey* v. *Zant*, produced new standards designed to make it much more difficult for death-row inmates to file repeated appeals.[106] Justice Lewis Powell, one of those in the five-person majority, later said (after his retirement) that he regretted his vote and should have voted the other way.

The Supreme Court has exempted two key classes of people from the death penalty: those who are mentally retarded and those under the age of eighteen. In 2002, the Court ruled that mentally retarded convicts could not be executed.[107] This 6–3 decision reversed what had been the Court's position on executing the retarded since 1989, a thirteen-year period when several retarded men were executed. In 2005, the Court ruled in a 5–4 decision that standards of decency had evolved sufficiently in the United States, as well as internationally, so that executing those who committed murders as minors was against the Eighth Amendment's ban on cruel and unusual punishment.[108]

At the state level, a move to at least stay executions took on momentum in March 2000 when Governor George Ryan (R–IL) ordered a moratorium on all executions. Ryan, a death penalty proponent, became disturbed by new evidence collected as a class project by Northwestern University students. The students unearthed information that led to the release of thirteen men on the state's death row. The specter of allowing death sentences to continue in light of evidence showing so many men were wrongly convicted prompted Ryan's much publicized action. Soon thereafter, the Democratic governor of Maryland followed suit after receiving evidence that blacks were much more likely to be sentenced to death than whites; however, the Republican governor who succeeded him lifted the stay. Before leaving office in January 2003, Illinois Governor Ryan continued his anti-death-penalty crusade by commuting the sentences of 167 death-row inmates, giving them life in prison instead. This action constituted the single largest anti-death-penalty action since the Court's decision in *Gregg*, and it spurred national conversation on the death penalty, which, in recent polls, has seen its lowest levels of support since 1978.

In another effort to verify that those on death row are not there wrongly, several states offer free DNA testing to death-row inmates. The U.S. Supreme Court recognized the potential exculpatory power of DNA evidence in *House* v. *Bell* (2006), in which the Court ruled a Tennessee death-row inmate who had exhausted other federal appeals was entitled to an exception to

VISUAL LITERACY

Race and the Death Penalty

Thinking Globally

The Death Penalty and Extradition

Mexico, which has no death penalty, will not extradite anyone facing possible execution to the United States. To guarantee extradition of criminals, U.S. prosecutors must agree to seek no more than life in prison. Other countries, including France and Canada, also demand such assurances from the U.S. government.

- Were you surprised to learn that international agreements between nations can limit the types of sentences handed down to fugitives from the law? Why would justice officials agree to forgo the death penalty in such cases?
- Canada, Australia, the European Union, and most of Central and South America have abolished the death penalty. What makes the United States so different in this regard?

Join the Debate

The Death Penalty

Overview: Challenges to the use of the death penalty are rising. In 2007, the U.S. Supreme Court agreed to take the case of *Baze* v. *Rees*, which questioned whether the method of lethal injection used by thirty-six states was potentially so painful as to violate the Eighth Amendment ban on cruel and unusual punishment. When the Court took the case, it in effect put a moratorium on executions until it ruled in the spring of 2008 that the method did not violate the Constitution. In 2007, forty-one people were put to death, the fewest since 1999, and New Jersey became the first state since 1965 to abolish the use of the death penalty. Although individuals and some government entities are having second thoughts about the death penalty, not everyone agrees that there is a problem. The federal government and thirty-eight states use the death penalty.

The debate over the use of capital punishment raises issues about the fundamental fairness of our system of justice. A major concern is that innocent people might be put to death, despite all the procedural safeguards in our court system to prevent mistakes. It is, of course, regrettable when someone is convicted of a crime he or she did not commit, even when they are only fined or imprisoned. Obviously there is no way of making amends when someone is executed.

Some of the current controversy related to the death penalty comes from advances in the use of DNA evidence. The Innocence Project, a nonprofit organization, has been working since 1992 to use DNA evidence to exonerate those wrongly convicted of crimes.[a] As of March 2008, the group's efforts have led to the release of 214 people, 16 of them on death row. In addition, between 1977 and 2007, another 108 people have been released from death rows because mistakes were made in eyewitness accounts, line-ups, police questioning, and court proceedings. The obvious question is whether there were others who should have been released.

The major justification for the death penalty is captured in the slogan: "A life for a life." The consequence for taking someone else's life is the loss of the criminal's life. In turn, supporters of the death penalty believe that such a grave consequence will deter people from committing murder. There does not, however, appear to be a correlation between the death penalty and low homicide rates. Texas, for example, executes more people than all the rest of the states combined. Yet, Texas consistently has one of the highest murder rates in the country. And, as a whole, southern states use the death penalty more than any other region. The homicide rate in 2007 for the South was 42 per 100,000 people, in contrast to the rate of 17 per 100,000 people in the Northeast and Midwest.

Another concern with the death penalty is the racial and gender disparities in those who are executed. It is extremely rare for a woman to be sent to the death chamber. And, a person is less likely to be executed if he or she is white. In 2007, for example, 53 percent of the 41 people executed were white, 37 percent were African American, and 10 percent were Hispanic—figures that do not match the racial composition of the general population. A crucial aspect of the debate regarding the death penalty is disagreement about whether the court system is biased and if convictions and executions reflect more general patterns of discrimination in society.

Arguments IN FAVOR of the Death Penalty

- The death penalty is just because it is used primarily to execute those who take the lives of others. Killing someone is the most egregious crime and act of violence, and societies must respond with the most severe punishment possible for murderers.

- The death penalty will deter at least some people from committing

more stringent federal appeals rules due to DNA and related evidence suggesting his innocence.[109] The Court also revisited what can be considered cruel and unusual punishment in 2006 when it unanimously ruled that death-row inmates could challenge the drugs and procedures involved in lethal injections.[110] This "invitation" was followed by the Court's acceptance of a case challenging the cocktail of drugs used in capital offenses. Although some murders will occur in a fit of rage and passion, we need to make those who plot to kill another human being think about the possible consequences if they go ahead with their plan.

■ It is costly to keep convicted murderers in prison for the rest of their lives. The cost to taxpayers to keep someone in prison is about $30,000 per year. It makes little economic sense for society to clothe, feed, and care for a murderer for the rest of his or her life.

Arguments AGAINST the Death Penalty

■ Mistakes are inevitably going to be made, and innocent people are going to be put to death for crimes they did not commit. The consequence of executing an innocent person is beyond remedy. We simply cannot risk mistakes when life is at stake.

■ The United States is alone among Western countries in continuing to have the death penalty. Canada, Australia, and all European nations are among the 91 countries that have completely abolished the death penalty. The United States is in the company of repressive nations such as China, Saudi Arabia, and Malaysia in its use of the death penalty.

■ It actually costs more to execute someone than it does to imprison the person for life. The Urban Institute released a study on March 6, 2008, that showed the state of Maryland spent an average of $37.2

Photo courtesy Nick Anderson/Cartoonist Group

How do states vary in their application of the death penalty? This cartoon offers a social commentary on the administration of the death penalty in Texas, which leads the nation in the number of executions.

million for each of the five executions it conducted since it reinstated the death penalty in 1978. Although this figure is higher than those cited in other studies, the general finding is consistent with analyses that cite the high costs of appeals in capital cases and the high costs of running death rows.

Continuing the Debate

1. Should the states and the federal government abolish the death penalty? If not, for what crimes should the death penalty be allowed?
2. How, if at all, can mistakes in our criminal justice system be avoided? Do gender and racial disparities in executions suggest that the system is unfair?

To Follow the Debate Online, Go To:

www. prodeathpenalty.com, which advocates keeping and expanding the use of the death penalty and includes a list of print and media resources plus links to other supportive sites.

www. deathpenaltyinfo.org for a wide array of studies and statistics on the death penalty as well as coverage of current events related to the death penalty and arguments

pewforum.org/death-penalty/, which provides information, statistics, and arguments related to the death penalty.

ᵃwww.innocenceproject.org.

lethal injections. Kentucky (and a number of other states). Many states issued a moratorium on the death penalty until the Court decided the case. In April 2008, the Court ruled that the combination of drugs used in these lethal injections did not constitute cruel and unusual punishment.[111] (To learn more about the methods used by each state to execute death row inmates, see Figure 5.1).

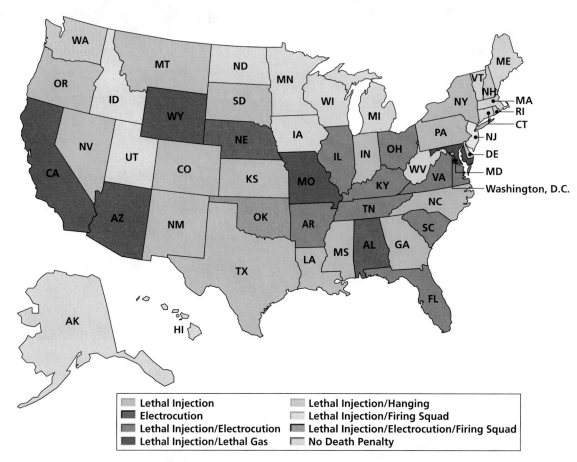

Lethal Injection	Lethal Injection/Hanging
Electrocution	Lethal Injection/Firing Squad
Lethal Injection/Electrocution	Lethal Injection/Electrocution/Firing Squad
Lethal Injection/Lethal Gas	No Death Penalty

FIGURE 5.1   **Methods of Execution In the United States**
Look at this map detailing methods of execution in the United States. What trends do you observe? What methods of execution are most common and least common? What do you notice about states that do not employ the death penalty?

Source: *USA Today*, http://usatoday.com/news/science/stuffworks/2001-05-10-lethal-injection.html

Privacy and Government Surveillance Powers

right to privacy
The right to be left alone; a judicially created principle encompassing a variety of individual actions protected by the penumbras or shadows cast by several constitutional amendments, including the First, Third, Fourth, Ninth, and Fourteenth Amendments.

The Right to Privacy

To this point, we have discussed rights and freedoms that have been derived fairly directly from specific guarantees contained in the Bill of Rights. However, the Supreme Court also has given protection to rights not enumerated specifically in the Constitution or Bill of Rights.

Although the Constitution is silent about the **right to privacy,** the Bill of Rights contains many indications that the Framers expected that some areas of life were off limits to governmental regulation. The liberty to practice one's religion guaranteed in the First Amendment implies the right to exercise private, personal beliefs. The guarantee against unreasonable searches and seizures contained in the Fourth Amendment similarly implies that persons are to be secure in their homes and should not fear that police will show up at their doorsteps without cause. As early as 1928, Justice Louis Brandeis hailed privacy as "the right to be left alone—the most comprehensive of rights and the right most valued by civilized men."[112] It was not until 1965, however, that the Court attempted to explain the origins of this right. (To learn more about the Ninth Amendment, see The Living Constitution.)

Birth Control

Today, most Americans take access to birth control as a matter of course. Condoms are sold in the grocery store, and some television stations air ads for them. Easy access to birth control, however, wasn't always the case. Many states often barred the sale of contraceptives to minors, prohibited the display of contraceptives, or even banned their sale altogether. One of the last states to do away with these kinds of laws was Connecticut. It outlawed the sale of all forms of birth control and even prohibited physicians from discussing it with their married patients until the Supreme Court ruled its restrictive laws unconstitutional.

Photo courtesy: Bettmann/Corbis

What was the outcome of *Griswold* v. *Connecticut* (1965)? In this photo, Estelle Griswold (left), executive director of the Planned Parenthood League of Connecticut, and Cornelia Jahncke, its president, celebrate the Supreme Court's ruling *Griswold* v. *Connecticut* (1965). *Griswold* invalidated a Connecticut law that made selling contraceptives or disseminating information about contraception illegal.

Griswold v. *Connecticut* (1965) involved a challenge to the constitutionality of an 1879 Connecticut law prohibiting the dissemination of information about and/or the sale of contraceptives.[113] In *Griswold*, seven justices decided that various portions of the Bill of Rights, including the First, Third, Fourth, Ninth, and Fourteenth Amendments, cast what the Court called "penumbras" (unstated liberties on the fringes or in the shadow of more explicitly stated rights), thereby creating zones of privacy, including a married couple's right to plan a family. Thus, the Connecticut statute was ruled unconstitutional because it violated marital privacy, a right the Court concluded could be read into the U.S. Constitution through interpreting several amendments.

Later, the Court expanded the right of privacy to include the right of unmarried individuals to have access to contraceptives. "If the right of privacy means anything," wrote Justice William J. Brennan Jr., "it is the right of the individual, married or single, to be free from unwarranted governmental intrusion into matters so fundamentally affecting a person as the decision to bear or beget a child."[114] This right to privacy was to be the basis for later decisions from the Court, including the right to secure an abortion.

Abortion

In the early 1960s, two birth-related tragedies occurred. Severely deformed babies were born to European women who had been given the drug thalidomide while pregnant, and, in the United States, a nationwide measles epidemic resulted in the birth of more babies with severe problems. The increasing medical safety of abortions and the growing women's rights movement combined with these tragedies to put pressure on the legal and medical establishments to support laws that would guarantee a woman's access to a safe and legal abortion.

By the late 1960s, fourteen states had voted to liberalize their abortion policies, and four states decriminalized abortion in the early stages of pregnancy. But, many women's rights activists wanted more. They argued that the decision to carry a pregnancy to term was a woman's fundamental right. In 1973, in one of the most controversial decisions ever handed down, seven members of the Court agreed with this position.

The woman whose case became the catalyst for pro-choice and pro-life groups was Norma McCorvey, an itinerant circus worker. The mother of a toddler she was unable to care for, McCorvey could not leave another child in her mother's care. So,

Timeline: The Supreme Court and the Right to Privacy

1965 *Griswold v. Connecticut*—The right to privacy is explained by the Court and used to justify striking down a Connecticut statute prohibiting married couples' access to birth control.

1980 *Harris v. McRae*—The Court upholds the Hyde Amendment, ruling that federal funds cannot be used to pay for poor women's abortions.

1973 *Roe v. Wade*—The Court finds that a woman has a right to have an abortion based on her right to privacy.

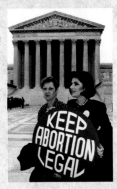

1986 *Bowers v. Hardwick*—The Court upholds Georgia's sodomy law, finding that gay men and lesbians have no privacy rights.

Roe v. *Wade* (1973)
The Supreme Court found that a woman's right to an abortion was protected by the right to privacy that could be implied from specific guarantees found in the Bill of Rights applied to the states through the Fourteenth Amendment.

she decided to terminate her second pregnancy. She was unable to secure a legal abortion and was frightened by the conditions she found when she sought an illegal abortion. McCorvey turned to two young Texas lawyers who were looking for a plaintiff to bring a lawsuit to challenge Texas's restrictive statute. The Texas law allowed abortions only when they were necessary to save the life of the mother. McCorvey, who was unable to obtain a legal abortion, later gave birth and put the baby up for adoption. Nevertheless, she allowed her lawyers to proceed with the case using her as their plaintiff. Here lawyers used the pseudonym Jane Roe for McCorvey as they challenged the Texas law as enforced by Henry Wade, the district attorney for Dallas County, Texas.

When the case finally came before the Supreme Court, Justice Harry A. Blackmun, a former lawyer at the Mayo Clinic, relied heavily on medical evidence to rule that the Texas law violated a woman's constitutionally guaranteed right to privacy, which he argued included her decision to terminate a pregnancy. Writing for the majority in ***Roe v. Wade* (1973),** Blackmun divided pregnancy into three stages. In the first trimester, a woman's right to privacy gave her an absolute right (in consultation with her physician), free from state interference, to terminate her pregnancy. In the second trimester, the state's interest in the health of the mother gave it the right to regulate abortions—but only to protect the woman's health. Only in the third trimester—when the fetus becomes potentially viable—did the Court find that the state's interest in potential life outweighed a woman's privacy interests. Even in the third trimester, however, abortions to save the life or health of the mother were to be legal.[115]

Roe v. *Wade* unleashed a torrent of political controversy. Anti-abortion groups, caught off guard, scrambled to recoup their losses in Congress. Representative

1989 *Webster v. Reproductive Health Services*- The Court comes close to overruling *Roe*; invites states to fashion abortion restrictions.

2003 *Lawrence v. Texas*—In overruling *Bowers*, the Court, for the first time, concludes that the right to privacy applies to homosexuals.

1992 *Planned Parenthood of Southeastern Pennsylvania v. Casey*—By the narrowest of margins, the Court limits *Roe* by abolishing its trimester approach.

2007 *Gonzales v. Carhart*—Supreme Court upholds the federal Partial Birth Abortion Ban Act.

Post abortive women say, **ABORTION HURTS WOMEN**

Who was Jane Roe? Norma McCorvey first stepped into the national spotlight as the "Jane Roe" of *Roe* v. *Wade* (1973). But, in 1995, McCorvey made a surprising announcement—she had become pro-life. The left photo shows McCorvey before the Court's ruling on *Roe*. The right photo shows her at a pro-life rally.

Photos courtesy: (*left*) Greg Gibson/AFP/Getty Images; (*right*) Tony Gutierrez/AFP/Wide World Photos

Henry Hyde (R–IL) persuaded Congress to ban the use of Medicaid funds for abortions for poor women, and the constitutionality of the Hyde Amendment was upheld by the Supreme Court in 1977 and again in 1980.[116] The issue also polarized both major political parties.

The Living Constitution

The enumeration in the Constitution, of certain rights, shall not be construed to deny or disparage others retained by the people.

—NINTH AMENDMENT

This amendment simply reiterates the belief that rights not specifically enumerated in the Bill of Rights exist and are retained by the people. It was added to assuage the concerns of Federalists, such as James Madison, who feared that the enumeration of so many rights and liberties in the first eight amendments to the Constitution would result in the denial of rights that were not enumerated.

Until 1965, the Ninth Amendment was rarely mentioned by the Court. In that year, however, it was used for the first time by the Court as a positive affirmation of a particular liberty—marital privacy. Although privacy is not mentioned in the Constitution, it was—according to the Court—one of those fundamental freedoms that the drafters of the Bill of Rights implied as retained. Since 1965, the Court has ruled in favor of a host of fundamental liberties guaranteed by the Ninth Amendment, often in combination with other specific guarantees, including the right to have an abortion.

CRITICAL THINKING QUESTIONS

1. How can the U.S. justice system dictate the definition of a fundamental right if the Constitution does not specifically enumerate such rights?
2. How might public opinion affect judicial interpretations of the Ninth Amendment?
3. What others implied rights should be protected by the Ninth Amendment?

From the 1970s through the present, the right to an abortion and its constitutional underpinnings in the right to privacy have been under attack by well-organized pro-life groups. The administrations of Ronald Reagan and George Bush were strong abortion opponents, and their Justice Departments regularly urged the Court to overrule *Roe*. They came close to victory in *Webster* v. *Reproductive Health Services* (1989).[117] In *Webster*, the Court upheld state-required fetal viability tests in the second trimester, even though these tests increased the cost of an abortion considerably. The Court also upheld Missouri's refusal to allow abortions to be performed in state-supported hospitals or by state-funded doctors or nurses. Perhaps most noteworthy, however, was that four justices seemed willing to overrule *Roe* v. *Wade* and that Justice Antonin Scalia publicly rebuked his colleague, Justice Sandra Day O'Connor, then the only woman on the Court, for failing to provide the critical fifth vote to overrule *Roe*.

After *Webster*, states began to enact more restrictive legislation. In *Planned Parenthood of Southeastern Pennsylvania* v. *Casey* (1992), Justices O'Connor, Anthony Kennedy, and David Souter, in a jointly authored opinion, wrote that Pennsylvania could limit abortions so long as its regulations did not pose "an undue burden" on pregnant women.[118] The narrowly supported standard, by which the Court upheld a twenty-four-hour waiting period and parental consent requirements, did not overrule *Roe*, but clearly limited its scope by abolishing its trimester approach and substituting the undue burden standard for the judicial standard used by the Court in *Roe*.

In 1993, newly elected pro-choice President Bill Clinton, a Democrat, ended bans on fetal tissue research, abortions at military hospitals, and federal financing for overseas population control programs. He also lifted the federal gag rule, a regulation enacted in 1987 that barred public health clinics receiving federal dollars from discussing abortion. (These policies were later reversed by George W. Bush).[119] Clinton also ended the ban on testing RU-486, or mifepristone, a pill for medically induced, nonsurgical abortions, which ultimately was made available in the United States to wo0men with a doctor's prescription late in 2000. President Clinton also appointed two supporters of abortion rights, Ruth Bader Ginsburg and Stephen Breyer, to the Supreme Court.

While President Clinton was attempting to shore up abortion rights through judicial appointments, Republican Congresses made repeated attempts to restrict abortion rights. In March 1996 and again in 1998, Congress passed and sent to President Clinton a bill to ban—for the first time—a specific procedure used in late-term abortions.[120] The president vetoed the federal Partial Birth Abortion Act over the objections of many of its supporters, including the National Right to Life Committee. Many state legislatures, nonetheless, passed their own versions of the act. In 2000, the Supreme Court, however, ruled 5–4 in *Stenberg* v. *Carhart* that a Nebraska partial birth abortion statute was unconstitutionally vague because it failed to contain an exemption for a woman's health. The law, therefore, was unenforceable and called into question the partial birth abortion laws of twenty-nine other states.[121]

By October 2003, however, Republican control of the White House and both houses of Congress facilitated passage of the federal Partial Birth Abortion Ban Act. Pro-choice groups such as Planned Parenthood, the Center for Reproductive Rights, and the American Civil Liberties Union immediately filed lawsuits challenging the constitutionality of this law. The Supreme Court heard oral arguments on the challenge to the federal ban the day after the 2006 midterm elections. In a 5–4 decision, *Gonzales* v. *Carhart* (2007), the Roberts Court revealed the direction it was heading in abortion cases. Over the strong objections of Justice Ruth Bader Ginsburg, Justice Anthony Kennedy's opinion for the majority upheld the federal act although, like the law at issue in *Stenberg*, it contained no exceptions for the health of the mother. This ruling was viewed as a significant step toward reversing *Roe* v. *Wade* altogether.

Homosexuality

It was not until 2003 that the U.S. Supreme Court ruled that an individual's constitutional right to privacy, which provided the basis for the *Griswold* (contraceptives) and *Roe* (abortion) decisions, prevented the state of Texas from criminalizing private sexual behavior. This monumental decision invalidated the laws of fourteen states.

In *Lawrence* v. *Texas* (2003), six members of the Court overruled its decision in *Bowers* v. *Hardwick* (1986) which had upheld anti-sodomy laws—and found that the Texas law was unconstitutional; five justices found it violated fundamental privacy rights.[122] Justice Sandra Day O'Connor agreed that the law was unconstitutional, but concluded that it was an equal protection violation. (To learn more about the equal protection clause of the Fourteenth Amendment, see chapter 6). Although Justice Antonin Scalia issued a stinging dissent, charging that "the Court has largely signed on to the so-called homosexual agenda," the majority of the Court was unswayed.[123]

Photo Courtesy: David J. Phillips/AP/World Wide Photos

Do all Americans deserve the same freedoms and liberties? Tyron Garner (left) and John Geddes Lawrence (center), the plaintiffs in *Lawrence* v. *Texas* (2003), are shown here with their attorney.

The Right to Die

In 1990, the Supreme Court ruled 5–4 that parents could not withdraw a feeding tube from their comatose daughter after her doctors testified that she could live for many more years if the tube remained in place. Writing for the majority, Chief Justice William H. Rehnquist rejected any attempts to expand the right of privacy into this thorny area of social policy. The Court did note, however, that individuals could terminate medical treatment if they were able to express, or had done so in writing via a living will, their desire to have medical treatment terminated in the event they became incompetent.[124]

In 1997, the U.S. Supreme Court ruled unanimously that terminally ill persons do not have a constitutional right to physician assisted suicide. The Court's action upheld the laws of New York and Washington State that make it a crime for doctors to give life-ending drugs to mentally competent but terminally ill patients who wish to die.[125] But, Oregon enacted a right-to-die or assisted suicide law approved by Oregon voters that allows physicians to prescribe drugs to terminally ill patients.

In November 2001, however, U.S. Attorney General John Ashcroft issued a legal opinion determining that assisted suicide is not "a legitimate medical purpose," thereby putting physicians following the Oregon law in jeopardy of federal prosecution.[126] His memo also called for the revocation of physicians' prescription drug licenses, putting the state and the national government in conflict in an area that Republicans historically have argued is the province of state authority. Oregon officials immediately (and successfully) sought a court order blocking Ashcroft's attempt to interfere with implementation of Oregon law. Later, a federal judge ruled that Ashcroft had overstepped his authority on every point.[127]

The U.S. Supreme Court agreed with the lower court on many points.[128] In *Gonzales* v. *Oregon* (2006), the Court upheld the Oregon act. In so doing, the justices affirmed the lower court's decision by a 6-3 margin.[129] Other states viewed this decision as an invitation to enact similar legislation. In 2008, for example, voters in Washington State overwhelmingly approved an initiative allowing physician assisted suicide in that state.

Toward Reform: Civil Liberties and Combating Terrorism

After September 11, 2001, the Bush administration, Congress, and the courts all operated in what Secretary of State Condoleezza Rice dubbed "an alternate reality," where Bill of Rights guarantees were suspended in a time of war.[130] The USA Patriot Act, the Military Commissions Act, and a series of secret Department of Justice memos all altered the state of civil liberties in the United States. Here, we detail the provisions of these actions and explain how they have affected the civil liberties discussed in this chapter.

The First Amendment

Both the 2001 USA Patriot Act and the 2006 Military Commissions Act contain a variety of major and minor interferences with the civil liberties that Americans, as well as those visiting our shores, have come to expect. The USA Patriot Act, for example, violates the First Amendment's free speech guarantees by barring those who have been subject to search orders from telling anyone about those orders, even in situations where no need for secrecy can be proven. It also authorizes the FBI to investigate citizens who choose to exercise their freedom of speech with no need to prove that any parts of their speech might be labeled illegal.

Another potential infringement of the First Amendment occurred right after the September 11, 2001, terrorist attacks, when it was made clear that members of the media were under strong constraints to report only positive aspects of U.S. efforts to combat terrorism. And, while the Bush administration decried any leaks of information about its deliberations or actions, the administration selectively leaked information that led to conservative columnist Robert Novak revealing the identity of Valerie Plame, a CIA operative.

In addition, respect for religious practices fell by the wayside in the wake of the war on terrorism. For example, many Muslim detainees captured in Iraq and Afghanistan were fed pork, a violation of basic Muslim religious rules. Some were stripped naked in front of members of the opposite sex, another religious violation.

The Fourth Amendment

The USA Patriot Act enhances the ability of the government to curtail specific search and seizure restrictions in four areas. First, it allows the government to examine an individual's private records held by third parties. This includes allowing the FBI to force anyone, including physicians, libraries, bookshops, colleges and universities, and Internet service providers, to turn over all records they have on a particular individual. Second, it expands the government's right to search private property without notice to the owner. Third, according to the American Civil Liberties Union, the Act "expands a narrow exception to the Fourth Amendment that had been created for the collection of foreign intelligence information."[131] Finally, the Act expands an exception for spying that collects "addressing information" about where and to whom communications are going, as opposed to what is contained in the documents.

Judicial oversight of these new governmental powers is virtually nonexistent. Proper governmental authorities need only certify to a judge, without any evidence, that the requested search meets the statute's broad criteria. Moreover, the legislation deprives judges of the authority to reject such applications.

Other Fourth Amendment violations include the ability to conduct searches without a warrant. The government also does not have to demonstrate probable cause that a person has, or might, commit a crime. Thus, the USA Patriot Act goes against key elements of the due process rights guaranteed by the Fifth Amendment.

Who is most responsible for protecting civil liberties? In 2007, questions about Central Intelligence Agency interrogation techniques led to the resignation of Attorney General Alberto Gonzales. His successor, Michael Mukasey, is shown here testifying before the Senate Judiciary Committee.

Photo Courtesy: Susan Etheridge/The New York Times/Redux Pictures

Analyzing Visuals   Water-boarding

Please examine the diagram and answer the following questions:

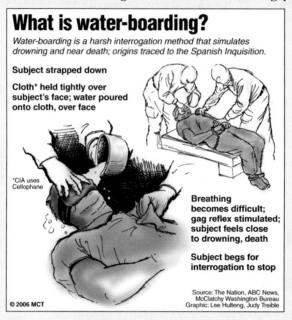

What is water-boarding?

Water-boarding is a harsh interrogation method that simulates drowning and near death; origins traced to the Spanish Inquisition.

Subject strapped down

Cloth* held tightly over subject's face; water poured onto cloth, over face

*CIA uses Cellophane

Breathing becomes difficult; gag reflex stimulated; subject feels close to drowning, death

Subject begs for interrogation to stop

Source: The Nation, ABC News, McClatchy Washington Bureau
Graphic: Lee Hulteng, Judy Treible

© 2006 MCT

HOW might water-boarding violate the Constitution?

HOW might you justify the use of water-boarding and other interrogation techniques that many nations classify as torture?

GIVEN the threats of terrorism against the United States, which civil liberties guarantees in the Constitution would you be willing to give up? Why?

Due Process Rights

Illegal incarceration and torture are federal crimes, and the Supreme Court ruled in 2004 that detainees have a right to *habeas corpus*.[132] However, the Bush administration argued that under the Military Commissions Act of 2006, alien victims of torture had significantly reduced rights of *habeas corpus*. The Military Commission Act also eliminated the right to bring any challenge to "detention, transfer, treatment, trial, or conditions of confinement" of detainees. It allowed the government to declare permanent resident aliens to be enemy combatants and enabled the government to jail these people indefinitely without any opportunity to file a writ of *habeas corpus*. In 2008, in a surprising setback for the Bush Administration the Roberts Court ruled parts of the act unconstitutional, finding that any detainees could challenge their extended incarceration in federal court.[133]

Many suspected terrorists have also been held against their will in secret offshore prisons, known as black sites. In September 2006, President Bush acknowledged the existence of these facilities, moving fourteen such detainees to the detention facility at Guantanamo Bay, Cuba.

The Sixth Amendment right to trial by jury has also been curtailed by recent federal activity. Although those declared enemy combatants can no longer be held indefinitely for trial by military tribunals, they still do not have access to the evidence against them, and the evidence can be obtained through coercion or torture. These trials are closed, and people tried in these courts do not have a right to an attorney of their choosing. The federal government's activity in these tribunals was limited by the Supreme Court,[134] but the Military Commissions Act returned these powers to the executive branch.

Finally, the Eighth Amendment's prohibition on cruel and unusual punishment has been the subject of great controversy. Since shortly after the terrorist attacks of September 11, 2001, there were rumors that many of the prisoners detained by the U.S. government were treated in ways that violated the Geneva Convention. In 2004, for example, photos of cruel treatment of prisoners held by the U.S. military in Abu Ghraib prison in Iraq surfaced. These photos led to calls for investigations at all levels of government. On the heels of this incident, the Justice Department declared torture "abhorrent" in a December 2004 legal memo. That position lasted but a short time. After Alberto Gonzales was sworn in as attorney general in February 2005, the department issued a secret memo. Provisions of this memo leaked to the press constituted "an expansive endorsement of the harshest interrogation techniques ever used by the Central Intelligence Agency."[135] According to one Justice Department memo, interrogation practices were not to be considered illegal unless they produced pain equivalent to organ failure or death. Among the techniques authorized by the government were combinations of "painful physical and psychological tactics, including head-slapping, simulated drowning, and frigid temperatures."[136] The most controversial of these techniques is water-boarding, which simulates drowning. (To learn more about this technique, see Analyzing Visuals: Water-boarding.)

The controversy over these interrogation techniques was one of the reasons for the resignation of Attorney General Gonzales, in 2007. Questions about the appropriateness of such interrogation techniques were the main focus of the confirmation hearings of his successor, Michael Mukasey.

WHAT SHOULD I HAVE LEARNED?

■ **What are the roots of civil liberties and the Bill of Rights in the United States?**

Most of the Framers originally opposed the Bill of Rights. Anti-Federalists, however, continued to stress the need for a bill of rights during the drive for ratification of the Constitution, and some states tried to make their ratification contingent on the addition of a bill of rights. Thus, during its first session, Congress sent the first ten amendments to the Constitution, the Bill of Rights, to the states for their ratification. Later, the addition of the Fourteenth Amendment allowed the Supreme Court to apply some of the amendments to the states through a process called selective incorporation.

■ **What are the First Amendment guarantees of freedom of religion?**

The First Amendment guarantees freedom of religion. The establishment clause, which prohibits the national government from establishing a religion, does not, according to Supreme Court interpretation, create an absolute wall between church and state. While the national and state governments may generally not give direct aid to religious groups, many forms of aid, especially many that benefit children, have been held to be constitutionally permissible. In contrast, the Court has generally barred organized prayer in public schools. The Court largely has adopted an accommodationist approach when interpreting the free exercise clause by allowing some governmental regulation of religious practices.

■ **What are the First Amendment guarantees of freedom of speech, press, assembly, and petition?**

Historically, one of the most volatile areas of constitutional interpretation has been in the interpretation of the First Amendment's mandate that "Congress shall make no law . . . abridging the freedom of speech or of the press." Like the establishment and free exercise clauses of the First Amendment, the speech and press clauses have not been interpreted as absolute bans against government regulation.

Some areas of speech and publication are unconditionally protected by the First Amendment. Among these are prior restraint, symbolic speech, and hate speech. Other areas of speech and publication, however, are unprotected by the First Amendment. These include libel, fighting words, and obscenity and pornography. The freedoms of peaceable assembly and petition are directly related to the freedoms of speech and of the press. As with other First Amendment rights, the Supreme Court has often become the arbiter between the right of the people to express dissent and government's right to limit controversy in the name of security.

■ **What is the Second Amendment right to keep and bear arms?**

Initially, the right to bear arms was envisioned as one dealing with state militias. Over the years, states and Congress have enacted various gun ownership restrictions with little Supreme Court interpretation. In 2008, the Court ruled that gun ownership is a constitutionally protected individual right.

■ **What rights are guaranteed to criminal defendants in the United States?**

The Fourth, Fifth, Sixth, and Eighth Amendments provide a variety of procedural guarantees to individuals accused of crimes. In particular, the Fourth Amendment prohibits unreasonable searches and seizures, and the Court has generally refused to allow evidence seized in violation of this safeguard to be used at trial.

Among other rights, the Fifth Amendment guarantees that "no person shall be compelled to be a witness against himself." The Supreme Court has interpreted this provision to require that the government inform the accused of his or her right to remain silent. This provision has also been interpreted to require that illegally obtained confessions must be excluded at trial.

The Sixth Amendment's guarantee of "assistance of counsel" has been interpreted by the Supreme Court to require that the government provide counsel to defendants unable to pay for it in cases where prison sentences may be imposed. The Sixth Amendment also requires an impartial jury, although the meaning of impartial continues to evolve through judicial interpretation.

The Eighth Amendment's ban against "cruel and unusual punishments" has been held not to bar imposition of the death penalty or the use of lethal injection.

■ **What does the right to privacy encompass and what is the U.S. Supreme Court's rationale for this right?**

The right to privacy is a judicially created right carved from the penumbras (unstated liberties implied by more explicitly stated rights) of several amendments, including the First, Third, Fourth, Ninth, and Fourteenth Amendments. Statutes limiting access to birth control or abortion or banning homosexual acts have been ruled unconstitutional violations of the right to privacy. The Court, however, appears poised to allow some states to opt to allow their citizens the right to die under a physician's supervision.

■ **How have reforms to combat terrorism affected civil liberties?**

After the terrorist attacks of September 11, 2001, reform enacted by the Bush administration and Congress have dramatically altered civil liberties in the United States. Critics charge that a host of constitutional guarantees have been significantly compromised, while supporters say that these reforms are necessary to protect national security in a time of war.

Key Terms

bill of attainder, p. 170
Bill of Rights, p. 156
civil liberties, p. 154
civil rights, p. 154
clear and present danger test, p. 163
direct incitement test, p. 163
double jeopardy clause, p. 173
due process clause, p. 156
Eighth Amendment, p. 176
establishment clause, p. 158
exclusionary rule, p. 173
ex post facto law, p. 170

Fifth Amendment, p. 172
fighting words, p. 167
First Amendment, p. 158
Fourth Amendment, p. 170
free exercise clause, p. 158
fundamental freedoms, p. 158
incorporation doctrine, p. 157
libel, p. 166
Miranda rights, p. 173
Miranda v. *Arizona* (1966), p. 172
New York Times Co. v. *Sullivan*
  (1964), p. 166

Ninth Amendment, p. 156
prior restraint, p. 162
right to privacy, p. 180
Roe v. *Wade* (1973), p. 182
selective incorporation, p. 157
Sixth Amendment, p. 174
slander, p. 166
substantive due process, p. 157
symbolic speech, p. 164
Tenth Amendment, p. 156
writ of *habeas corpus*, p. 170

Researching Civil Liberties

In the Library

Abrams, Floyd. *Trials of the First Amendment*. New York: Viking, 2006.

Ackerman, Bruce. *Before the Next Attack: Preserving Civil Liberties in an Age of Terrorism*. New Haven, CT: Yale University Press, 2007.

Cole, David, and James X. Dempsey. *Terrorism and the Constitution: Sacrificing Civil Liberties in the Name of National Security*, 3rd ed. Washington, DC: First Amendment Foundation, 2006.

Darmer, M. Katherine B., Robert M. Baird, Stuart E. Rosenbaum, eds. *Civil Liberties vs. National Security in a Post 9/11 World*. New York: Prometheus, 2004.

Etzoni, Amitai, and Jason H. Marsh, eds. *Rights vs. Public Safety after 9/11: America in the Age of Terrorism*. Lanham, MD: Rowman and Littlefield, 2003.

Fiss, Owen M. *The Irony of Free Speech*, reprint ed. Cambridge, MA: Harvard University Press, 1998.

Gates, Henry Louis, Jr., ed. *Speaking of Race, Speaking of Sex: Hate Speech, Civil Rights, and Civil Liberties*. New York: New York University Press, 1995.

Ivers, Gregg, and Kevin T. McGuire, eds. *Creating Constitutional Change*. Charlottesville: University Press of Virginia, 2004.

Leone, Richard C., and Greg Anrig Jr., eds. *The War on Our Freedoms: Civil Liberties in an Age of Terrorism*. Public Affairs, 2003.

Lewis, Anthony. *Gideon's Trumpet*, reissue ed. New York: Vintage Books, 1989.

———. *Make No Law: The Sullivan Case and the First Amendment*, reprint ed. New York: Random House, 1992.

Lichtblau, Eric. *Bush's Law: The Remaking of American Justice*. New York:/Pantheon, 2008.

O'Brien, David M. *Animal Sacrifice and Religions Freedom: Church of the Lukumi Babalu Aye* v. *City of Hialeah*. Lawrence: University Press of Kansas, 2004.

———. *Constitutional Law and Politics, vol. 2: Civil Rights and Civil Liberties*, 6th ed. New York: Norton, 2005.

O'Connor, Karen. *No Neutral Ground: Abortion Politics in an Age of Absolutes*. Boulder, CO: Westview, 1996.

Romero, Anthony D., and Dina Temple-Raston. *In Defense of Our America: The Fight for Civil Liberties in the Age of Terror*. New York: William Morrow, 2007.

Sando, Philippe. *Torture Teams: Rumsfeld's Memo and the Betrayal of American Values*. New York: Palgrave Macmillan, 2008.

Weddington, Sarah. *A Question of Choice*, reprint ed. New York: Grosset/Putnam, 1993.

On the Web

To compare differing views on civil liberties, including debates related to the war on terrorism, go to the home pages for the following groups:
  The American Civil Liberties Union, **www.aclu.org**
  People for the American Way, **www.pfaw.org**
  The American Center for Law and Justice, **www.aclj.org**
  The Federalist Society, **www.fed-soc.org**
To learn more about the Supreme Court cases discussed in this chapter, go to Oyez: U.S. Supreme Court Media, **www.oyez.org**, and search on the case name. Or, go to the Legal Information Institute of Cornell University's Law School, **www.law.cornell.edu/supet/cases/topic. htm,** where you can search cases by topic.
To compare the different sides of the abortion debate, go to FLITE (Federal Legal Information Through Electronics) at **www.fedworld.gov/supcourt/.**
For more on civil liberties protections for homosexuals, go to Human Rights Campaign at **www.hrc.org**, and Lambda Legal at **www.lambdalegal.org.**

Civil Rights

For many years, the U.S. government has played an important role in enforcing civil rights in the nation. The passage of the Thirteenth, Fourteenth, and Fifteenth Amendments, for example, abolished slavery, guaranteed citizens equal protection of the laws, and granted the right to vote to newly freed male slaves. Much later, after a prolonged civil rights movement sparked by years of discrimination against African Americans, particularly in the South, the U.S. Congress passed sweeping anti-discrimination legislation in the Civil Rights Act of 1964 and the Voting Rights Act of 1965. The Civil Rights Act, in particular, banned discrimination in employment, public accommodations, and education based on race, creed, color, religion, national origin, or sex. Over the years, Congress has added prohibitions based on pregnancy and disability to the act.

The Civil Rights Act and all federal statutes prohibiting discrimination are enforced by the Civil Rights Division of the Department of Justice. The division is headed by an assistant attorney general, a political appointee, who reports to the chief law enforcement official of the United States, the attorney general.

In 2006, the Civil Rights Division was in turmoil. Almost 20 percent of its lawyers, a record number, left in 2005 when many took advantage of a buyout program that allowed them to retire early; other career lawyers took positions elsewhere because they were upset by what they perceived as the politicization of the division. Many of the lawyers, all career civil servants, believed they were being pressured to leave because they "did not share the administration's conservative view on civil rights laws."[1] Veteran lawyers charged that the political appointees in the division made hiring and policy decisions without consulting staff members with more expertise. Their allegations were supported when it was revealed in 2007 that Attorney General Alberto Gonzales, along with the White House, had interfered in the work of regional U.S. attorneys. Eight of these attorneys appeared to have been fired without just cause spurring congressional hearings and the indictment of a Gonzales aide.[2]

In addition to these personnel changes, since President George W. Bush took office and appointed those who shared his beliefs to key division spots, prosecutions of race and sex discrimination have decreased by 40 percent. Many division lawyers found their workloads shifted to immigration and deportation cases.[3]

Voting Rights Act enforcement, too, was politicized, according to many nonpolitical career lawyers in the division's voting rights section. According to them, those "who remain are barred from offering

■ **Who protects the civil rights of American citizens?** At left, non-violent protestors demanding voting rights for African Americans march across the Edmund Pettus Bridge on their way from Selma to Montgomery, Alabama, in March of 1965. At right, some of the U. S. attorneys who were fired by the Justice Department in 2006. the firings raised questions about the extent to which partisan politics rather than the rule of law was the guiding force during Alberto Gonzales's tenure as attorney general.

WHAT SHOULD I KNOW ABOUT . . .

- the roots of suffrage: 1800–1890?
- the push for equality: 1890–1954?
- the civil rights movement?
- the women's rights movement?
- how other groups have mobilized for civil rights?
- reforms affecting civil rights, affirmative action, and pay equity?

recommendations in major voting rights cases."[4] And, when the section involved itself in cases in Georgia, Mississippi, and Texas, it supported actions favoring the election of Republicans. With regard to the controversial Texas redistricting plan discussed in chapter 13, for example, the attorney general acknowledged in December 2005 that Department of Justice officials had overruled a unanimous finding that aspects of the Texas plan would violate the Voting Rights Act of 1965.[5] In 2006, the U.S. Supreme Court ruled that states did not have to wait for a new U.S. Census to redraw district lines. The Court also found that one of the districts diluted the voting power of Hispanics and thus violated the Voting Rights Act.[6] The Obama administration is likely to refocus the agency's energies on civil rights enforcement.

TO LEARN MORE—

—TO DO MORE

Go to the Civil Rights Division section of the Department of Justice's Web site, www.usdoj.gov/crt, to examine the types of discrimination prioritized by the Obama administration.

The Declaration of Independence, written in 1776, boldly proclaims: "We hold these truths to be self-evident, that all men are created equal, that they are endowed by their Creator with certain unalienable rights." And, although the Framers considered some equality issues, one entire class of citizens—slaves—were treated in the new Constitution more as property than as people. Delegates to the Constitutional Convention put political expediency before the immorality of slavery. Moreover, the Constitution considered white women full citizens for purposes of determining state population, but voting qualifications were left to the states, and none allowed women to vote at the time the Constitution was ratified.

civil rights
The government-protected rights of individuals against arbitrary or discriminatory treatment by governments or individuals.

Since the Constitution was written, concepts of **civil rights,** the government-protected rights of individuals against arbitrary or discriminatory treatment by governments or individuals based on categories such as race, sex, national origin, age, religion, or sexual orientation, have changed dramatically. The addition of the Fourteenth Amendment, one of three Civil War Amendments ratified from 1865 to 1870, introduced the notion of equality into the Constitution by specifying that a state could not deny "any person within its jurisdiction equal protection of the laws." Throughout history, the Fourteenth Amendment's equal protection guarantees have been the linchpin of efforts to expand upon the original intent of the amendment to allow its provisions to protect a variety of other groups from discrimination.

The Fourteenth Amendment has generated more litigation to determine and specify its meaning than any other provision of the Constitution. Within a few years of its ratification, women—and later, African Americans and other minorities and disadvantaged groups—took to the courts to seek expanded civil rights in all walks of life. But, the struggle to augment rights was not limited to the courts. Public protest, civil disobedience, legislative lobbying, and appeals to public opinion have been part of the arsenal of those seeking equality.

Since passage of the Civil War Amendments, there has been a fairly consistent pattern of expansion of civil rights to more and more groups. In this chapter, we will explore how notions of equality and civil rights have changed in this country.

★ First, we will discuss *the roots of suffrage* from *1800 to 1890*.

★ Second, we will examine African Americans' and women's *push for equality* from *1890 to 1954*, using two of the Supreme Court's most famous decisions,

Plessy v. Ferguson (1896) and Brown v. Board of Education (1954), as bookends for our discussion.

★ Third, we will analyze *the civil rights movement* as well as the Civil Rights Act of 1964 and its effects.

★ Fourth, we will discuss the development of a new *women's rights movement* and its push for an equal rights amendment to the U.S. Constitution.

★ Fifth, we will present the efforts of *other groups*, including Hispanic and Latino/a Americans, American Indians, Asian and Pacific Americans, gays and lesbians, and Americans with disabilities, to *mobilize for rights* using methods often modeled after the actions of African Americans and women.

★ Finally, we will explore reform efforts related to *civil rights, affirmative action, and pay equity*.

Roots of Suffrage: 1800–1890

Today, we take for granted the voting rights of women and African Americans. Since 1980, women have outvoted men at the polls in presidential elections; in the 1990s, African Americans and women became the core of the Democratic Party. But, it wasn't always this way. The period from 1800 to 1890 was one of tremendous change and upheaval in America. Despite the Civil War and the freeing of the slaves, the promise of equality guaranteed to African Americans by the Civil War Amendments failed to become a reality. Women's rights activists also began to make claims for equality, often using the arguments enunciated for the abolition of slavery, but they too fell far short of their goals.

The Struggle for Equal Protection

Slavery and Congress

Congress banned the slave trade in 1808, after the expiration of the twenty-year period specified by the Constitution. In 1820, blacks made up twenty-five percent of the U.S. population and were in the majority in some southern states. By 1840, that figure had fallen to twenty percent. After the introduction of the cotton gin (a machine invented in 1793 that separated seeds from cotton very quickly), the South became even more dependent on agriculture and cheap slave labor as its economic base. At the same time, technological advances were turning the northern states into an increasingly industrialized region, which deepened the cultural and political differences and animosity between the North and the South.

As the nation grew westward in the early 1800s, conflicts between northern and southern states intensified over the admission of new states to the union with free or slave status. The first major crisis occurred in 1820, when Missouri applied for admission to the union as a slave state—that is, one in which slavery would be legal. Missouri's admission would have weighted the Senate in favor of slavery and therefore was opposed by northern senators. To resolve this conflict, Congress passed the Missouri Compromise of 1820. The Compromise prohibited slavery north of the geographical boundary at 36 degrees latitude. This act allowed Missouri to be admitted to the union as a slave state, and to maintain the balance of slave and free states, Maine was carved out of a portion of Massachusetts.

Photo courtesy: Library of Congress

Who was Frederick Douglass?
Frederick Douglass (1817–1895) was born into slavery but learned how to read and write. Once he escaped to the North (where 250,000 free blacks lived), he became a well-known orator and journalist. In 1847, he started a newspaper, the *North Star*, in Rochester, New York. The paper quickly became a powerful voice against slavery, and he urged President Abraham Lincoln to emancipate the slaves. Douglass was also a firm believer in woman suffrage.

The First Civil Rights Movements: Abolition and Women's Rights

The Missouri Compromise solidified the South in its determination to keep slavery legal, but it also fueled the fervor of those who opposed slavery. William Lloyd Garrison, a white New Englander, galvanized the abolitionist movement in the early 1830s. Garrison, a newspaper editor, founded the American Anti-Slavery Society in 1833; by 1838, it had more than 250,000 members. Given the U.S. population today, the National Association for the Advancement of Colored People (NAACP) would need 3.8 million members to have the same kind of overall proportional membership. (In 2008, NAACP membership slightly exceeded 500,000.)

Slavery was not the only practice that people began to question in the decades following the Missouri Compromise. In 1840, for example, Garrison and Frederick Douglass, a well-known black abolitionist writer, left the Anti-Slavery Society when it refused to accept their demand that women be allowed to participate equally in all its activities. Custom dictated that women not speak out in public, and most laws made women second-class citizens. In most states, for example, women could not divorce their husbands or keep their own wages and inheritances. And, of course, they could not vote.

Elizabeth Cady Stanton and Lucretia Mott, who were to found the first women's rights movement, attended the 1840 meeting of the World Anti-Slavery Society in London with their husbands. After their long journey, they were not allowed to participate in the convention because they were women. As they sat in the balcony, apart from the male delegates, they paused to compare their status to that of the slaves they sought to free. They concluded that women were not much better off than slaves, and they resolved to meet to address these issues. In 1848, they finally sent out a call for the first woman's rights convention. Three hundred women and men, including Frederick Douglass, attended the first meeting for women's rights, which was held in Seneca Falls, New York.

The Seneca Falls convention in 1848 attracted people from all over New York State and other states as well who believed that men and women should be able to enjoy all rights of citizenship equally. Attendees passed resolutions calling for the abolition of legal, economic, and social discrimination against women. All of the resolutions reflected the attendees' dissatisfaction with contemporary moral codes, divorce and criminal laws, and the limited opportunities for women in education, the church, medicine, law, and politics. Ironically, only the call for "woman suffrage" (a call to give women the right to vote) failed to win unanimous approval. Most who attended the Seneca Falls meeting continued to press for women's rights along with the abolition of slavery. Moreover, similar conventions were held across the Northeast and Mid-

What was the Seneca Falls Convention? This is the announcement that was placed in a local newspaper about the upcoming Seneca Falls Convention for the civil and political rights of women.

THE FIRST CONVENTION

EVER CALLED TO DISCUSS THE

Civil and Political Rights of Women,

SENECA FALLS, N. Y., JULY 19, 20, 1848.

———

WOMAN'S RIGHTS CONVENTION.

———

A Convention to discuss the social, civil, and religious condition and rights of woman will be held in the Wesleyan Chapel, at Seneca Falls, N. Y., on Wednesday and Thursday, the 19th and 20th of July current; commencing at 10 o'clock A. M. During the first day the meeting will be exclusively for women, who are earnestly invited to attend. The public generally are invited to be present on the second day, when Lucretia Mott, of Philadelphia, and other ladies and gentlemen, will address the Convention.*

———
* This call was published in the *Seneca County Courier*, July 14, 1848, without any signatures. The movers of this Convention, who drafted the call, the declaration and resolutions were Elizabeth Cady Stanton, Lucretia Mott, Martha C. Wright, Mary Ann McClintock, and Jane C. Hunt.

Photo courtesy: Library of Congress

west. At an 1851 meeting in Akron, Ohio, for example, former slave Sojourner Truth delivered her famous "Ain't I a Woman?" speech calling on women to recognize the plight of their black sisters.

The 1850s: The Calm Before The Storm

By 1850, much had changed in America: the Gold Rush had spurred westward migration, cities grew as people were lured from their farms, railroads and the telegraph increased mobility and communication, and immigrants flooded into the United States. The woman's movement gained momentum, and slavery continued to tear the nation apart. Harriet Beecher Stowe's *Uncle Tom's Cabin*, a novel that depicted the evils of slavery, further inflamed the country. *Uncle Tom's Cabin* sold more than 300,000 copies in 1852. Equivalent sales today would top 4 million copies.

The tremendous national reaction to Stowe's work, which later prompted President Abraham Lincoln to call Stowe "the little woman who started the big war," had not yet faded when a new controversy over the Missouri Compromise of 1820 became the lightning rod for the first major civil rights case to be addressed by the U.S. Supreme Court. As discussed in chapter 3, in *Dred Scott* v. *Sandford* (1857), the Court ruled that the Missouri Compromise, which prohibited slavery north of a set geographical boundary, was unconstitutional. Furthermore, the Court went on to add that slaves were not U.S. citizens, and as a consequence, slaves could not bring suits in federal court.

The Civil War and Its Aftermath: Civil Rights Laws and Constitutional Amendments

The Civil War had many causes, but slavery was clearly a key issue. During the war (1861–1865), abolitionists continued to press for an end to slavery. They were partially rewarded when President Abraham Lincoln issued the Emancipation Proclamation, which provided that all slaves in states still in active rebellion against the United States would be freed automatically on January 1, 1863. Designed as a measure to gain favor for the war in the North, the Emancipation Proclamation did not free all slaves—it freed only those who lived in the Confederacy. Complete abolition of slavery did not occur until congressional passage and ultimate ratification of the Thirteenth Amendment in 1865.

The **Thirteenth Amendment** was the first of the three Civil War Amendments. It banned all forms of "slavery [and] involuntary servitude." (To learn more about the Thirteenth Amendment, see The Living Constitution: Thirteenth Amendment, Section 1.) Although southern states were required to ratify the Thirteenth Amendment as a condition of their readmission to the Union after the war, most of the former Confederate states quickly passed laws that were designed to restrict opportunities for newly freed slaves. These **Black Codes** prohibited African Americans from voting, sitting on juries, or even appearing in public places. Although Black Codes differed from state to state, all empowered local law-enforcement officials to arrest unemployed blacks, fine them for vagrancy, and hire them out to employers to satisfy their fines. Some state codes went so far as to require African Americans to work on plantations or to be domestics. The Black Codes laid the groundwork for Jim Crow laws, which later would institute segregation in all walks of life in the South.

An outraged Congress enacted the Civil Rights Act of 1866 to invalidate some state Black Codes. President Andrew Johnson vetoed the legislation, but—for the first time in history—Congress overrode a presidential veto. The Civil Rights Act formally made African Americans citizens of the United States and gave the Congress and the federal courts the power to intervene when states attempted to restrict

Photo courtesy: The Granger Collection

What was Uncle Tom's Cabin? This advertisement attests to the popularity of *Uncle Tom's Cabin, or Life Among the Lowly,* by Harriet Beecher Stowe. By the 1960s, "Uncle Tom" had become a derogatory term for blacks who were perceived as subservient to whites.

Thirteenth Amendment
One of the three Civil War Amendments; specifically bans slavery in the United States.

Black Codes
Laws denying most legal rights to newly freed slaves; passed by southern states following the Civil War.

The Living Constitution

Neither slavery nor involuntary servitude, except as a punishment for crime whereof the party shall have been duly convicted, shall exist within the United States, or any place subject to their jurisdiction.

—THIRTEENTH AMENDMENT, SECTION 1

This amendment, the first of three Civil War Amendments, abolished slavery throughout the United States and its territories. It also prohibited involuntary servitude.

Based on his wartime authority, in 1863 President Abraham Lincoln issued the Emancipation Proclamation abolishing slavery in the states that were in rebellion against the United States. Because Congress was considered to lack the constitutional authority to abolish slavery, after one unsuccessful attempt to garner the two-thirds vote necessary, the proposed Thirteenth Amendment was forwarded to the states on February 1, 1865. With its adoption, said one of its sponsors, it relieved Congress "of sectional strifes." Initially, some doubted if any groups other than newly freed African slaves were protected by the provisions of the amendment. Soon, however, the Supreme Court went on to clarify this question by noting: "If Mexican peonage or the Chinese coolie labor system shall develop slavery of the Mexican or Chinese race within our territory, this amendment may safely be trusted to make it void."

In the early 1990s, the Supreme Court was called on several times to construe section 1 of the amendment, especially in regard to involuntary servitude. Thus, provisions of an Alabama law that called for criminal sanctions and jail time for defaulting sharecroppers were considered unconstitutional, and Congress enacted a law banning this kind of involuntary servitude. More recently, the Court has found that compulsory high school community service programs do not violate the ban on involuntary servitude.

The Supreme Court and a host of lower federal and state courts have upheld criminal convictions of those who psychologically coerced mentally retarded farm laborers into service or who lured foreign workers to the United States with promises of jobs and then forced them to work long hours at little or no pay. Human trafficking, in fact, was targeted by the Bush administration as an especially onerous form of involuntary servitude. The U.S. Department of Justice began hundreds of investigations in an attempt to end this system.

CRITICAL THINKING QUESTIONS

1. Why would the Supreme Court rule that compulsory high school community service programs do not violate the Thirteenth Amendment?
2. Is forcing prison inmates to work as part of a "chain gang" a form of involuntary servitude? Why or why not?

the citizenship rights of male African Americans in matters such as voting. Congress reasoned that African Americans were unlikely to fare well if they had to file discrimination complaints in state courts, where most judges were elected. Passage of a federal law allowed African Americans to challenge discriminatory state practices in the federal courts, where judges were appointed for life by the president.

Because controversy remained over the constitutionality of the act (since the Constitution gives states the right to determine qualifications of voters), the **Fourteenth Amendment** was proposed simultaneously with the Civil Rights Act to guarantee, among other things, citizenship to all freed slaves. Other key provisions of the Fourteenth Amendment barred states from abridging "the privileges or immunities of citizenship" or depriving "any person of life, liberty, or property without due process of law," or denying "any person within its jurisdiction the equal protection of the laws."

Fourteenth Amendment
One of the three Civil War Amendments; guarantees equal protection and due process of the law to all U.S. citizens.

Unlike the Thirteenth Amendment, which had near-unanimous support in the North, the Fourteenth Amendment was opposed by many women because it failed to guarantee suffrage for women. During the Civil War, woman's rights activists put aside their claims for expanded rights for women, most notably the right to vote, and threw their energies into the war effort. They were convinced that once slaves were freed and given the right to vote, women similarly would be rewarded with the franchise. They were wrong.

In early 1869, after ratification of the Fourteenth Amendment (which specifically added the word "male" to the Constitution for the first time), woman's rights activists met in Washington, D.C., to argue against passage of any new amendment that would extend suffrage to black males and not to women. The convention resolved that "a man's government is worse than a white man's government, because, in proportion as you increase the tyrants, you make the condition of the disenfranchised class more hopeless and degraded."

In spite of these arguments, the **Fifteenth Amendment** was passed by Congress in early 1869. It guaranteed the "right of citizens" to vote regardless of their "race, color or previous condition of servitude." Sex was not mentioned.

Woman's rights activists were shocked. Abolitionists' continued support of the Fifteenth Amendment, which was ratified by the states in 1870, prompted many woman's rights supporters to leave the abolition movement and to work solely for the cause of women's rights. Twice burned, Susan B. Anthony and Elizabeth Cady Stanton decided to form their own group, the National Woman Suffrage Association (NWSA), to achieve that goal. (Another, more conservative group, the American Woman Suffrage Association, also was formed.) In spite of the NWSA's opposition, however, the Fifteenth Amendment was ratified by the states in 1870.

Thinking Globally
European Policies on Slavery

Slavery was outlawed in many nations long before ratification of the Thirteenth Amendment to the U.S. Constitution. In 1794, during the French Revolution, the French National Convention emancipated all slaves in French colonies. Napoleon reintroduced the practice of slavery in 1802, but by 1818 slavery was once again illegal. In Great Britain, the Great Emancipation Act of 1833 freed all slaves on British soil.

- In the United States, the issue of slavery helped to ignite a civil war. What factors contributed to this outcome?
- Why were Great Britain, France, and other European nations able to abolish slavery without igniting a civil war?

Fifteenth Amendment
One of the three Civil War Amendments; specifically enfranchised newly freed male slaves.

Civil Rights, Congress, and the Supreme Court

Continued southern resistance to African American equality led Congress to pass the Civil Rights Act of 1875, designed to grant equal access to public accommodations such as theaters, restaurants, and transportation. The act also prohibited the exclusion of African Americans from jury service. By 1877, however, national interest in the legal condition of African Americans waned. Most white Southerners and even some Northerners never had believed in true equality for "freedmen," as former slaves were called. Any rights that freedmen received had been contingent on federal enforcement. Federal occupation of the South ended in 1877. National troops were no longer available to guard polling places and to prevent whites from excluding black voters, and southern states quickly moved to limit African Americans' access to the ballot. Other forms of discrimination also were allowed by judicial decisions upholding **Jim Crow laws**, which required segregation in public schools and facilities, including railroads, restaurants, and theaters. Some Jim Crow laws, specifically known as miscegenation laws, barred interracial marriage.

All these laws, at first glance, appeared to conflict with the Civil Rights Act of 1875. In 1883, however, a series of cases decided by the Supreme Court severely damaged the vitality of the 1875 act. The ***Civil Rights Cases* (1883)** were five separate cases involving the convictions of private individuals found to have violated the Civil Rights Act by refusing to extend accommodations to African Americans in theaters, a hotel, and a railroad.[7] In deciding these cases, the Supreme Court ruled that Congress could prohibit only state or governmental action and not private acts of discrimination. The Court thus seriously limited the scope of the Civil Rights Act by concluding that Congress had no authority to prohibit private discrimination in public accommodations. The Court's

Jim Crow laws
Laws enacted by southern states that discriminated against blacks by creating "whites only" schools, theaters, hotels, and other public accommodations.

***Civil Rights Cases* (1883)**
Name attached to five cases brought under the Civil Rights Act of 1875. In 1883, the Supreme Court decided that discrimination in a variety of public accommodations, including theaters, hotels, and railroads, could not be prohibited by the act because such discrimination was private discrimination and not state discrimination.

Photo courtesy: Bettmann/Corbis

What did Jim Crow laws do?
Throughout the South, examples of Jim Crow laws abounded. One such law required separate public drinking fountains, shown here. Notice the obvious difference in quality.

poll tax
A tax levied in many southern states and localities that had to be paid before an eligible voter could cast a ballot.

grandfather clause
Voting qualification provision in many southern states that allowed only those whose grandfathers had voted before Reconstruction to vote unless they passed a wealth or literacy test.

Plessy v. *Ferguson* (1896)
Supreme Court case that challenged a Louisiana statute requiring that railroads provide separate accommodations for blacks and whites. The Court found that separate but equal accommodations did not violate the equal protection clause of the Fourteenth Amendment.

opinion in the *Civil Rights Cases* provided a moral reinforcement for the Jim Crow system. Southern states viewed the Court's ruling as an invitation to gut the reach and intent of the Thirteenth, Fourteenth, and Fifteenth Amendments.

In devising ways to make certain that African Americans did not vote, southern states had to avoid the intent of the Fifteenth Amendment. This amendment did not guarantee suffrage; it simply said that states could not deny anyone the right to vote on account of race or color. To exclude African Americans in a seemingly racially neutral way, southern states used three devices before the 1890s: (1) **poll taxes** (small taxes on the right to vote that often came due when poor African American sharecroppers had the least amount of money on hand); (2) some form of property-owning qualifications; and, (3) "literacy" or "understanding" tests, which allowed local voter registration officials to administer difficult reading-comprehension tests to potential voters whom they did not know.

These voting restrictions had an immediate impact. By the late 1890s, black voting fell by 62 percent from the Reconstruction period, while white voting fell by only 26 percent. To make certain that these laws did not further reduce the numbers of poor or uneducated white voters, many southern states added a **grandfather clause** to their voting qualification provisions, granting voting privileges to those who failed to pass a wealth or literacy test only if their grandfathers had voted before Reconstruction. Grandfather clauses effectively denied the descendents of slaves the right to vote.

While African Americans continued to face wide-ranging racism on all fronts, women also confronted discrimination. During this period, married women, by law, could not be recognized as legal entities. Women often were treated in the same category as juveniles and imbeciles, and in many states they were not entitled to wages, inheritances, or custody of their children.

The Push for Equality, 1890–1954

The Progressive era (1890–1920) was characterized by a concerted effort to reform political, economic, and social affairs. Evils such as child labor, the concentration of economic power in the hands of a few industrialists, limited suffrage, political corruption, business monopolies, and prejudice against African Americans all were targets of progressive reform efforts. Distress over the inferior legal status of African Americans was aggravated by the U.S. Supreme Court's decision in *Plessy* v. *Ferguson* (1896), a case that some commentators point to as the Court's darkest hour.[8]

In 1892, a group of African Americans in Louisiana decided to test the constitutionality of a Louisiana law mandating racial segregation on all public trains. They convinced Homer Plessy, a man Louisiana designated as black because he was one-eighth African, to board a train in New Orleans and proceed to the "whites only" car.[9] He was arrested when he refused to take a seat in the car reserved for African Americans as required by state law. Plessy challenged the law, arguing that the Fourteenth Amendment prohibited racial segregation.

The Supreme Court disagreed. After analyzing the history of African Americans in the United States, the majority concluded that the Louisiana law was constitutional. The justices based their decision on their belief that separate facilities for blacks and whites provided equal protection of the laws. After all, they reasoned, African Americans were not prevented from riding the train; the Louisiana statute required only that the races travel separately. Justice John Marshall Harlan was the lone dissenter. He argued that "the Constitution is colorblind" and that it was senseless to hold constitutional a law "which, practically, puts the badge of servitude and degradation upon a large class of our fellow citizens."

Not surprisingly, the separate-but-equal doctrine enunciated in *Plessy* v. *Ferguson* soon came to mean only separate, as new legal avenues to discriminate against African Americans were enacted into law throughout the South. The Jim Crow system soon expanded and became a way of life and a rigid social code in the American South. Journalist Juan Williams notes in *Eyes on the Prize:*

> There were Jim Crow schools, Jim Crow restaurants, Jim Crow water fountains, and Jim Crow customs—blacks were expected to tip their hats when they walked past whites, but whites did not have to remove their hats even when they entered a black family's home. Whites were to be called "sir" and "ma'am" by blacks, who in turn were called by their first names by whites. People with white skin were to be given a wide berth on the sidewalk; blacks were expected to step aside meekly.[10]

By 1900, equality for African Americans was far from the promise first offered by the Civil War Amendments. Again and again, the Supreme Court nullified the intent of the amendments and sanctioned racial segregation while the states avidly followed its lead.[11] Yet, the Supreme Court did take a step toward progress when it ruled that peonage laws, which often affected poor blacks, amounted to debt bondage or indentured servitude and were unconstitutional.[12]

The Founding of the National Association for the Advancement of Colored People

In 1909, a handful of individuals active in a variety of progressive causes, including woman suffrage and the fight for better working conditions for women and children, met to discuss the idea of a group devoted to the problems of the Negro. Major race riots had occurred in several American cities, and progressive reformers were concerned about these outbreaks of violence and the possibility of others. Oswald Garrison Villard, the influential publisher of the *New York Evening Post*—and the grandson of William Lloyd Garrison—called a conference to discuss the problem. This group soon evolved into the National Association for the Advancement of Colored People (NAACP). Along with Villard, its first leaders included W. E. B. Du Bois, a founder of the Niagara Movement, a group of African American intellectuals who took their name from their first meeting place in Niagara Falls, Ontario, Canada.

Key Women's Groups

The struggle for women's rights was revitalized in 1890 when the National and American Woman Suffrage Associations merged. The new organization, the National American Woman Suffrage Association (NAWSA), was headed by Susan B. Anthony. Unlike NWSA, which had

Why was the Niagara Movement founded? W. E. B. Du Bois (second from left in the second row, facing right) is pictured with the other original leaders of the Niagara Movement. This 1905 photo was taken on the Canadian side of Niagara Falls because no hotel on the U.S. side would accommodate the group's African American members. At the meeting, a list of injustices suffered by African Americans was detailed.

Photo courtesy: The New York Public Library/Art Resource, NY

Photo courtesy: Picture History

Who were the leaders of the suffrage movement? Alice Paul and other members of the National Woman's Party picketed outside the White House to support woman suffrage. Although they were arrested, jailed, and force-fed, their efforts ultimately were successful; they are shown here celebrating.

suffrage movement
The drive for voting rights for women that took place in the United States from 1890 to 1920.

Nineteenth Amendment
Amendment to the Constitution that guaranteed women the right to vote.

sought a wide variety of expanded rights for women, this new association was devoted largely to securing woman suffrage. Its task was greatly facilitated by the proliferation of women's groups that emerged during the Progressive era. In addition to the rapidly growing temperance movement—the move to ban the sale of alcohol, which many women blamed for a variety of social ills—women's groups were created to seek protective legislation in the form of maximum hour or minimum wage laws for women and to work for improved sanitation, public morals, education, and the like. Other organizations that were part of what was called the club movement were created to provide increased cultural and literary experiences for middle-class women. With increased industrialization, for the first time some women found that they had the opportunity to pursue activities other than those centered on the home.

One of the most active groups lobbying on behalf of women during this period was the National Consumers' League (NCL), which successfully lobbied the state of Oregon for legislation limiting women to ten hours of work a day. Soon after the law was enacted, Curt Muller was charged and convicted of employing women more than ten hours a day in his small laundry. When he appealed his conviction to the U.S. Supreme Court, the NCL sought permission from the state to conduct the defense of the statute.

At the urging of NCL attorney and future U.S. Supreme Court Justice Louis Brandeis, NCL members amassed an impressive array of sociological and medical data that were incorporated into what became known as the Brandeis brief. This contained only three pages of legal argument. More than a hundred pages were devoted to nonlegal, sociological data that were used to convince the Court that Oregon's statute was constitutional. In agreeing with the NCL in *Muller* v. *Oregon* (1908), the Court relied heavily on these data to document women's unique status as mothers to justify their differential legal treatment.[13]

Women seeking the vote used reasoning reflecting the Court's opinion in *Muller*. Discarding earlier notions of full equality, NAWSA based its claim to the right to vote largely on the fact that women, as mothers, should be enfranchised. Furthermore, although many members of the suffrage movement were NAACP members, the new women's movement—called the **suffrage movement** because of its focus on the vote alone and not on broader issues of women's rights—took on racist overtones. Suffragists argued that if undereducated African American men could vote, why couldn't women? Some NAWSA members even argued that "the enfranchisement of women would ensure immediate and durable white supremacy."

Diverse attitudes clearly were present in the growing suffrage movement, which often tried to be all things to all people. Its roots in the Progressive movement gave it an exceptionally broad base that transformed NAWSA from a small organization of just over 10,000 members in the early 1890s to a true social movement of more than 2 million members in 1917. By 1920, a coalition of women's groups, led by NAWSA and the newer, more radical National Woman's Party, was able to secure ratification of the **Nineteenth Amendment** to the Constitution. It guaranteed all women the right to vote—fifty years after African American males were enfranchised by the Fifteenth Amendment.

After passage of the suffrage amendment in 1920, the fragile alliance of diverse women's groups that had come together to fight for the vote quickly disintegrated. Women returned to their home groups, such as the NCL or the Women's Christian Temperance Union, to pursue their individualized goals. In fact, after the tumult of the suffrage movement, widespread organized activity on behalf of women's rights did not reemerge until the 1960s. In the meantime, the NAACP continued to fight racism and racial segregation. Its activities and those of others in the civil rights movement would later give impetus to a new women's movement.

Litigating for Equality

During the 1930s, leaders of the NAACP began to sense that the time was right to launch a full-scale challenge in the federal courts to the constitutionality of *Plessy*'s separate-but-equal doctrine. Clearly, the separate-but-equal doctrine and the proliferation of Jim Crow laws were a bar to any hope of full equality for African Americans. Traditional legislative channels were unlikely to work, given African Americans' limited or nonexistent political power. Thus, the federal courts and a litigation strategy were the NAACP's only hopes. The NAACP mapped out a long-range plan that would first target segregation in professional and graduate education.

TEST CASES The NAACP opted first to challenge the constitutionality of Jim Crow law schools. In 1935, all southern states maintained fully segregated elementary and secondary schools. Colleges and universities also were segregated, and most states did not provide for postgraduate education for African Americans. NAACP lawyers chose to target law schools because they were institutions that judges could well understand, and integration there would prove less threatening to most whites.

Lloyd Gaines, a graduate of Missouri's all-black Lincoln University, sought admission to the all-white University of Missouri Law School in 1936. He was immediately rejected. In the separate-but-equal spirit, the state offered to build a law school at Lincoln (although no funds were allocated for the project) or, if he didn't want to wait, to pay his tuition at an out-of-state law school. Gaines rejected the offer, sued, lost in the lower courts, and appealed to the U.S. Supreme Court.

Gaines's case was filed at an auspicious time. As discussed in chapter 3, a constitutional revolution of sorts occurred in Supreme Court decision making in 1937. Before this time, the Court was most receptive to and interested in the protection of economic liberties. In 1937, however, the Court reversed itself in a series of cases and began to place individual freedoms and personal liberties on a more protected footing. Thus, in 1938, Gaines's lawyers pleaded his appeal to a far more sympathetic Supreme Court. NAACP attorneys argued that the creation of a separate law school of a lesser caliber than that of the University of Missouri would not and could not afford Gaines an equal education. The justices agreed and ruled that Missouri had failed to meet the separate-but-equal requirements of *Plessy*. The Court ordered Missouri either to admit Gaines to the school or to set up a law school for him.[14]

Recognizing the importance of the Court's ruling, in 1939 the NAACP created a separate, tax-exempt legal defense fund to devise a strategy that would build on the Missouri case and bring about equal educational opportunities for all African American children. The first head of the NAACP Legal Defense and Educational Fund, commonly referred to as the LDF, was Thurgood Marshall, who later became the first African American to serve on the U.S. Supreme Court. Sensing that the Court would be more amenable to the NAACP's broader goals if it were first forced to address a variety of less threatening claims to educational opportunity, Marshall and the LDF brought a series of carefully crafted test cases to the Court.

The first case involved H. M. Sweatt, a forty-six-year-old African American mail carrier, who applied for admission to the all-white University of Texas Law School in 1946. Rejected on racial grounds, Sweatt sued. The judge gave the state six months to establish a law school or to admit Sweatt to the university. The state legislature saw the handwriting on the wall and authorized $3 million for the creation of the Texas State University for Negroes. One hundred thousand dollars of that money was to be for a new law school in Austin across the street from the state capitol building. It consisted

Photo courtesy: Bettmann/Corbis

What did "separate but equal" look like? Here, George McLaurin, the plaintiff in one of the LDF's challenges to the "separate but equal doctrine," is shown outside his classroom. This was the university's shameful accommodation when a federal district court ordered his admission into the University of Oklahoma's doctoral program.

of three small basement rooms, a library of 10,000 books, access to the state law library, and three part-time first-year instructors as the faculty. Sweatt declined the opportunity to obtain an education there and instead chose to continue his legal challenge.

While working on the Texas case, the LDF also decided to pursue a case involving George McLaurin, a retired university professor who had been denied admission to the doctoral education program at the University of Oklahoma. Marshall reasoned that McLaurin, at age sixty-eight, would be immune from the charges that African Americans wanted integration in order to intermarry with whites. After a lower court ordered McLaurin's admission, the university reserved a dingy alcove in the cafeteria for him to eat in during off-hours, and he was given his own table in the library behind a shelf of newspapers. In what surely "was Oklahoma's most inventive contribution to legalized bigotry since the adoption of the 'grandfather clause,' " McLaurin was forced to sit outside classrooms while lectures and seminars were conducted inside.[15]

The Supreme Court handled these two cases together.[16] The eleven southern states filed an *amicus curiae* (friend of the court) brief, in which they argued that *Plessy* should govern both cases. The LDF received assistance, however, from an unexpected source— the U.S. government. In a dramatic departure from the past, the administration of President Harry S Truman filed a friend of the court brief, urging the Court to overrule *Plessy*. Earlier, Truman had issued an executive order desegregating the military.

Since the late 1870s, the U.S. government never had sided against the southern states in a civil rights matter and never had submitted an *amicus* brief supporting the rights of African American citizens. President Truman believed that because many African Americans had fought and died for their country in World War II, this kind of executive action was proper.

Although the Court did not overrule *Plessy*, the justices found that the measures taken by the states in each case failed to live up to the strictures of the separate-but-equal doctrine. The Court unanimously ruled that the remedies to each situation were inadequate to afford a sound education. In the *Sweatt* case, for example, the Court declared that the "qualities which are incapable of objective measurement but which make for greatness in a law school . . . includ[ing] the reputation of the faculty, experience of the administration, position and influence of the alumni, standing in the community, traditions and prestige" made it impossible for the state to provide an equal education in a segregated setting.[17]

In 1950, after these decisions were handed down, the LDF concluded that the time had come to launch a full-scale attack on the separate-but-equal doctrine. The decisions of the Court were encouraging, and the position of the U.S. government and the population in general appeared to be more receptive to an outright overruling of *Plessy*.

Brown v. *Board*
of Education (1954)
U.S. Supreme Court decision holding that school segregation is inherently unconstitutional because it violates the Fourteenth Amendment's guarantee of equal protection.

equal protection clause
Section of the Fourteenth Amendment that guarantees that all citizens receive "equal protection of the laws."

BROWN v. BOARD OF EDUCATION *Brown* v. *Board of Education* (1954) actually was four cases brought from different areas of the South and border states involving public elementary or high school systems that mandated separate schools for blacks and whites.[18] In *Brown*, LDF lawyers, again led by Thurgood Marshall, argued that *Plessy*'s separate-but-equal doctrine was unconstitutional under the **equal protection clause** of the Fourteenth Amendment, and that if the Court was still reluctant to overrule *Plessy*, the only way to equalize the schools was to integrate them. A major component of the LDF's strategy was to prove that the intellectual, psychological, and financial damage that befell African Americans as a result of segregation precluded any court from finding that equality was served by the separate-but-equal policy.

In *Brown*, the LDF presented the Supreme Court with evidence of the harmful consequences of state-imposed racial discrimination. To buttress its claims, the LDF introduced the now-famous doll study, conducted by Kenneth Clark, a prominent African American sociologist who had long studied the negative effects of segregation on African American children. His research revealed that black children not only preferred white dolls when shown black dolls and white dolls, but that many added that the black doll looked "bad." This information was used to illustrate the negative impact of racial segregation and bias on an African American child's self-image.

The LDF's legal briefs were supported by important *amicus curiae* briefs submitted by the U.S. government, major civil rights groups, labor unions, and religious groups decrying racial segregation. On May 17, 1954, Chief Justice Earl Warren delivered the fourth opinion of the day, *Brown* v. *Board of Education*. Writing for the Court, Warren stated:

> To separate [some school children] from others . . . solely because of their race generates a feeling of inferiority as to their status in the community that may affect their hearts and minds in a way very unlikely ever to be undone. We conclude, unanimously, that in the field of public education the doctrine of "separate but equal" has no place.

There can be no doubt that *Brown* was the most important civil rights case decided in the twentieth century.[19] It immediately evoked an uproar that shook the nation. Some segregationists called the day the decision was handed down Black Monday. The governor of South Carolina denounced the decision, saying, "Ending segregation would mark the beginning of the end of civilization in the South as we know it."[20] The LDF lawyers who had argued these cases as well as the cases leading to *Brown*, however, were jubilant.

Remarkable changes had occurred in the civil rights of Americans since 1890. Women won the right to vote, and after a long and arduous trail of litigation in the federal courts, the Supreme Court finally overturned its most racist decision of the era, *Plessy* v. *Ferguson*. The Court boldly proclaimed that separate but equal (at least in education) would no longer pass constitutional muster. The question then became how *Brown* would be interpreted and implemented. Could it be used to invalidate other Jim Crow laws and practices? Would African Americans ever be truly equal under the law?

The Civil Rights Movement

Our notion of civil rights has changed profoundly since the *Brown* decision in 1954. *Brown* served as a catalyst for change, sparking the development of the modern civil rights movement. Women's work in that movement and the student protest movement that arose in reaction to the U.S. government's involvement in Vietnam gave women the experience needed to form their own organizations to press for full equality. As African Americans and women became more and more successful, they served as models for other groups who sought equality—Hispanic Americans, American Indians, Asian and Pacific Americans, homosexuals, the disabled, and others.

The Civil Rights Movement

School Desegregation After *Brown*

One year after *Brown*, in a case referred to as *Brown* v. *Board of Education II* (1955), the Court ruled that racially segregated systems must be dismantled "with all deliberate speed."[21] To facilitate implementation, the Court placed enforcement of *Brown* in the hands of appointed federal district court judges, who were considered more immune to local political pressures than were elected state court judges.

The NAACP and its LDF continued to resort to the courts to see that *Brown* was implemented, while the South entered into a near conspiracy to avoid the mandates of *Brown II*. In Arkansas, for example, Governor Orval Faubus, who was facing a reelection bid, announced that he would not "be a party to any attempt to force acceptance of change to which people are overwhelmingly opposed."[22] The day before school was to begin, he announced that National Guardsmen would surround Little Rock's Central High School to prevent African American students from entering. While the federal courts in Arkansas continued to order the admission of African American children, the governor remained adamant. Finally, President Dwight D. Eisenhower sent federal troops to Little Rock to protect the rights of the nine students attending Central High.

In reaction to the governor's outrageous conduct, the Court broke with tradition and issued a unanimous decision in *Cooper* v. *Aaron* (1958), which was filed by the Little Rock School Board asking the federal district court for a two-and-one-half-year delay in implementation of its desegregation plans. Each justice signed the opinion individually, underscoring his individual support for the notion that "no state legislator or executive or judicial officer can war against the Constitution without violating his undertaking to support it."[23] The state's actions thus were ruled unconstitutional and its "evasive schemes" illegal.

A New Move for African American Rights

In 1955, soon after *Brown II*, the civil rights movement took another step forward—this time in Montgomery, Alabama. Rosa Parks, the local NAACP's Youth Council adviser, decided to challenge the constitutionality of the segregated bus system. First, Parks and other NAACP officials began to raise money for litigation and made speeches around town to garner public support. Then, on December 1, 1955, Rosa Parks made history when she refused to leave her seat on a bus to move to the back to make room for a white male passenger. She was arrested for violating an Alabama law banning integration of public facilities, including buses. After she was freed on bond, Parks and the NAACP decided to enlist city clergy to help her cause. At the same time, they distributed 35,000 handbills calling for African Americans to boycott the Montgomery bus system on the day of Parks's trial. Black ministers used Sunday services to urge their members to support the boycott. On Monday morning, African Americans walked, carpooled, or used black-owned taxicabs. That night, local ministers decided that the boycott should be continued. A new, twenty-six-year-old minister, the Reverend Martin Luther King Jr., was selected to lead the newly formed Montgomery Improvement Association.

As the boycott dragged on, Montgomery officials and local business owners began to harass the city's African American citizens. The residents held out, despite suffering personal hardship for their actions, ranging from harassment to job loss to bankruptcy. In 1956, a federal court ruled that the segregated bus system violated the equal protection clause of the Fourteenth Amendment. After a year of walking, black Montgomery residents ended their protest when city buses were ordered to integrate. The first effort at nonviolent protest had been successful. Organized boycotts and other forms of nonviolent protest, including sit-ins at segregated restaurants and bus stations, were to follow.

Formation of New Groups

The recognition and respect that the Reverend Martin Luther King Jr. earned within the African American community helped him to launch the Southern Christian Leadership Conference (SCLC) in 1957, soon after the end of the Montgomery bus boycott. Unlike the NAACP, which had northern origins and had come to rely largely on litigation as a means of achieving expanded equality, the SCLC had a southern base and was rooted more closely in black religious culture. The SCLC's philosophy reflected King's growing belief in the importance of nonviolent protest and civil disobedience.

On February 1, 1960, students at the all-black North Carolina Agricultural and Technical College participated in the first sit-in. The students marched to a local lunch counter, sat down, and ordered cups of coffee. They were refused service and sat at the counter until police arrived. When the students refused to leave, they were arrested and jailed. Soon thereafter, African American college students around the South did the same. Their actions were the subject of extensive national media attention.

Over spring break 1960, with the assistance of an $800 grant from the SCLC, 200 student delegates—black and white—met at Shaw University in North Carolina to consider recent sit-in actions and to plan for the future. Later that year, the Student Nonviolent Coordinating Committee (SNCC) was formed.

Whereas the SCLC generally worked with church leaders in a community, SNCC was much more of a grassroots organization. Always perceived as more radical than the SCLC, SNCC tended to focus its organizing activities on the young, both black and white.

In addition to joining the sit-in bandwagon, SNCC also came to lead what were called freedom rides, designed to focus attention on segregated public accommodations. Bands of college students and other civil rights activists traveled by bus throughout the South in an effort to force bus stations to desegregate. Often these protesters were met by angry mobs of segregationists and brutal violence, as local police chose not to defend protesters' basic constitutional rights to free speech and peaceful assembly. African Americans were not the only ones to participate in freedom rides; increasingly, white college students from the North began to play an important role in SNCC.

Photo courtesy: Chicago Defender

While SNCC continued to sponsor sit-ins and freedom rides, in 1963 the Reverend Martin Luther King Jr. launched a series of massive nonviolent demonstrations in Birmingham, Alabama, long considered a major stronghold of segregation. Thousands of blacks and whites marched to Birmingham in a show of solidarity. Peaceful marchers were met there by the Birmingham police commissioner, who ordered his officers to use dogs, clubs, and fire hoses on the marchers. Americans across the nation were horrified as they witnessed the brutality and abuse heaped on the protesters on television. As the marchers hoped, the shocking scenes helped convince President John F. Kennedy to propose important civil rights legislation. (To learn more about the Civil Rights Movement, see Analyzing Visuals: Police Confront Civil Rights Demonstrators in Birmingham.)

The Civil Rights Act of 1964

Both the SCLC and SNCC sought full implementation of Supreme Court decisions dealing with race and an end to racial segregation and discrimination. The cumulative effect of collective actions including sit-ins, boycotts, marches, and freedom rides—as well as the tragic bombings and deaths inflicted in retaliation—led Congress to pass the first major piece of civil rights legislation since the post–Civil War era, the Civil Rights Act of 1964, followed the next year by the Voting Rights Act of 1965. Several events led to the consideration of the two pieces of legislation.

How did Emmett Till's murder awaken a nation to racial injustice? The brutal 1955 murder of Emmett Till, a fourteen-year-old boy from Chicago, Illinois, heightened awareness of the injustices of the Jim Crow system in the South and helped to coalesce the nascent Civil Rights Movement. Till, who was visiting relatives in Mississippi, was accused of whistling at a white woman. He was kidnapped, beaten, mutilated, shot, and thrown in a river. His mother insisted on an open casket funeral, so that news media and mourners would understand the violence visited upon her child. Two suspects were acquitted of the killings, but later confessed their crime to a reporter.

Analyzing Visuals   Police Confront Civil Rights Demonstrators in Birmingham

Examine the May 1963 photograph by Charles Moore reprinted here. It was taken during a civil rights demonstration in Birmingham, Alabama, and was frequently reprinted and also discussed on the floor Congress during debate over the Civil Rights Act of 1964. After examining the photograph, answer the following questions:

Photo courtesy: Charles Moore/Black Star/Stock Photo

WHAT do you observe about the scene and the various people shown in the photograph?

WHAT do you notice about the man who is being attacked by the dogs? The other demonstrators? The police?

WHAT emotions does the picture evoke? Why do you think this image was an effective tool in the struggle for African Americans' civil rights?

In 1963, President John F. Kennedy requested that Congress pass a law banning discrimination in public accommodations. Seizing the moment, the Reverend Martin Luther King Jr. called for a monumental march on Washington, D.C., to demonstrate widespread support for far-ranging anti-discrimination legislation. It was clear that national legislation outlawing discrimination were the only answer: southern legislators would never vote to repeal Jim Crow laws. The March on Washington for Jobs and Freedom was held in August 1963, only a few months after the Birmingham demonstrations. More than 250,000 people heard King deliver his famous "I Have a Dream" speech from the Lincoln Memorial. Before Congress had the opportunity to vote on any legislation, however, John F. Kennedy was assassinated on November 22, 1963, in Dallas, Texas.

When Vice President Lyndon B. Johnson, a southern-born, former Senate majority leader, succeeded Kennedy as president, he put civil rights reform at the top of his legislative priority list, and civil rights activists gained a critical ally. Thus, through the 1960s, the movement subtly changed in focus from peaceful protest and litigation to legislative lobbying. Its focus broadened from integration of school and public facilities and voting rights to preventing housing and job discrimination and alleviating poverty.

The push for civil rights legislation in the halls of Congress was helped by changes in public opinion. Between 1959 and 1965, southern attitudes toward integrated schools changed enormously. The proportion of Southerners who responded that they would not mind their child's attendance at a racially balanced school doubled.

In spite of strong presidential support and the sway of public opinion, the Civil Rights Act of 1964 did not sail through Congress. Southern senators, led by South Carolina's Strom Thurmond, a Democrat who later switched to the Republican Party, conducted the longest filibuster in the history of the Senate. For eight weeks, Thurmond led the effort to hold up voting on the civil rights bill until cloture was invoked and the filibuster ended. Once passed, the **Civil Rights Act of 1964**:

- Outlawed arbitrary discrimination in voter registration and expedited voting rights lawsuits.
- Barred discrimination in public accommodations engaged in interstate commerce.
- Authorized the Department of Justice to initiate lawsuits to desegregate public facilities and schools.
- Provided for the withholding of federal funds from discriminatory state and local programs.
- Prohibited discrimination in employment on grounds of race, creed, color, religion, national origin, or sex.
- Created the Equal Employment Opportunity Commission (EEOC) to monitor and enforce the bans on employment discrimination.

Civil Rights Act of 1964
Wide-ranging legislation passed by Congress to outlaw segregation in public facilities and discrimination in employment, education, and voting; created the Equal Employment Opportunity Commission.

As challenges were made to the Civil Rights Act of 1964, other changes continued to sweep the United States. African Americans in the North, who believed that their brothers and sisters in the South were making progress against discrimination, found themselves frustrated. Northern blacks were experiencing high unemployment, poverty, discrimination, and little political clout. Some, including Black Muslim leader Malcolm X, even argued that, to survive, African Americans must separate themselves from white culture in every way. These increased tensions resulted in riots in many major cities from 1964 to 1968, when many African Americans in the North took to the streets, burning and looting to vent their rage. The assassination of the Reverend Martin Luther King Jr. in 1968 triggered a new epidemic of race riots.

Who was the Reverend Martin Luther King Jr.? The Reverend Martin Luther King Jr. is perhaps the most recognizable leader of the civil rights movement. Here, he delivers his famous "I Have a Dream" speech in Washington, D.C., on August 28, 1963. King was assassinated in 1968 at age thirty-nine in Memphis, Tennessee.

The Impact of the Civil Rights Act of 1964

Many Southerners were adamant in their belief that the Civil Rights Act of 1964 was unconstitutional because it went beyond the scope of Congress's authority to legislate under the Constitution, and lawsuits were quickly brought to challenge the act. In 1965, the Supreme Court upheld its constitutionality when it found that Congress was within the legitimate scope of its commerce power as outlined in Article I.[24]

EDUCATION One of the key provisions of the Civil Rights Act of 1964 authorized the Department of Justice to bring actions against school districts that failed to comply with *Brown v. Board of Education*. By 1964, a full decade after *Brown*, fewer than 1 percent of African American children in the South attended integrated schools.

Photo courtesy: AP Wide World Photos

de jure discrimination
Racial segregation that is a direct result of law or official policy.

de facto discrimination
Racial discrimination that results from practice (such as housing patterns or other social or institutional, non-governmental factors) rather than the law.

In *Swann* v. *Charlotte-Mecklenburg School District* (1971), the Supreme Court ruled that all vestiges of state-imposed segregation, called ***de jure* discrimination**, or discrimination by law, must be eliminated at once. The Court also ruled that lower federal courts had the authority to fashion a wide variety of remedies including busing, racial quotas, and the pairing of schools to end dual, segregated school systems.[25]

In *Swann*, the Court was careful to distinguish *de jure* from ***de facto* discrimination**, which is discrimination that results from practice, such as housing patterns or private acts, rather than the law. The Court noted that its approval of busing was a remedy for intentional, government imposed or sanctioned discrimination only.

Over the years, forced, judicially imposed busing found less and less favor with the Supreme Court, even in situations where *de jure* discrimination had existed. In 1992, the Supreme Court ruled that an all-black school could continue to exist so long as the segregation was not a result of the school board's actions. In 1995, the Court ruled 5–4 that city school boards can use plans to attract white suburban students to mostly minority urban schools only if both city and suburban schools still show the effects of segregation, thus reversing a lower court desegregation order.[26] And, in 2007, in a badly divided opinion, the Supreme Court abolished the use of voluntary school desegregation plans based on race.[27]

What has busing achieved? In the late 1960s, court-ordered busing to achieve racial integration frequently required police escorts.

Photo courtesy: Bettmann/Corbis

EMPLOYMENT Title VII of the Civil Rights Act of 1964 prohibits employers from discriminating against employees for a variety of reasons, including race, sex, age, and national origin. (In 1978, the act was amended to prohibit discrimination based on pregnancy.) In 1971, in one of the first major cases decided under the act, the Supreme Court ruled that employers could be found liable for discrimination if the effect of their employment practices was to exclude African Americans from certain positions.[28] African American employees were allowed to use statistical evidence to show that they had been excluded from all but one department of the Duke Power Company, because it required employees to have a high school education or pass a special test to be eligible for promotion.

The Supreme Court ruled that although the tests did not appear to discriminate against African Americans, their effects—that there were no African American employees in any other departments—were sufficient to shift to the employer the burden of proving that no discrimination occurred. Thus, the Duke Power Company would have to prove that the tests were a business necessity that had a "demonstrable relationship to successful performance" of a particular job.

The notion of "business necessity," as set out in the Civil Rights Act of 1964 and interpreted by the federal courts, was especially important for women. Women long had been kept out of many occupations on the strength of the belief that customers preferred to deal with male personnel. Conversely, males were barred from flight-attendant positions because the airlines believed that passengers preferred to be served by young, attractive women. Similarly, many large factories, manufacturing establishments, and police and fire departments avoided hiring women by subjecting them to arbitrary height and weight requirements. Like the tests declared illegal by the Court, these requirements often could not be shown to be related to job performance and were eventually ruled illegal by the federal courts.

The Women's Rights Movement

Just as in the abolition movement in the 1800s, women from all walks of life participated in the civil rights movement. Women were important members of new groups such as SNCC and the SCLC as well as more traditional groups such as the NAACP, yet they often found themselves treated as second-class citizens. At one point during a SNCC national meeting, its chair proclaimed: "The only position for women in SNCC is prone."[29] Statements and attitudes such as these led some women to found early women's liberation groups that generally were quite radical but small in membership. Others founded more traditional groups such as the National Organization for Women (NOW). Some groups sought improved rights for women through lobbying for specific laws or a constitutional amendment to guarantee women equal rights; other groups, following the model of the NAACP LDF, turned to the courts.

TIMELINE

Women's Struggle for Equality

Litigation for Equal Rights

As discussed earlier, initial efforts to convince the Supreme Court to enfranchise women under the equal protection clause of the Fourteenth Amendment were uniformly unsuccessful. The paternalistic attitudes of the Supreme Court, and perhaps society as well, continued well into the 1970s. As late as 1961, Florida required women who wished to serve on juries to travel to the county courthouse and register for that duty. In contrast, all men who were registered voters automatically were eligible to serve. When Gwendolyn Hoyt was convicted of bludgeoning her adulterous husband to death with a baseball bat, she appealed her conviction, claiming that the exclusion of women from her jury prejudiced her case. She believed that female jurors—her peers—would have been more sympathetic to her and the emotional turmoil that led to her attack on her husband and her claim of temporary insanity. She therefore argued that her trial by an all-male jury violated her rights as guaranteed by the Fourteenth Amendment.

In rejecting her contention, Justice John Harlan wrote in *Hoyt* v. *Florida* (1961): "Despite the enlightened emancipation of women from the restrictions and protections of bygone years, and their entry into many parts of community life formerly considered to be reserved to men, a woman is still regarded as the center of home and family life."[30]

These kinds of attitudes and decisions (*Hoyt* was unanimously reversed in 1975) were insufficient to forge a new movement for women's rights. Shortly after *Hoyt*, however, three events occurred to move women to action. In 1961, soon after his election, President John F. Kennedy created the President's Commission on the Status of Women, which was headed by former first lady Eleanor Roosevelt. The commission's report, *American Women*, released in 1963, documented pervasive discrimination against women in all walks of life. In addition, the civil rights movement and the publication of Betty Friedan's *The Feminine Mystique* (1963), which led some women to question their lives and status in society, added to their dawning recognition that something was wrong.[31] Soon after, the Civil Rights Act of 1964 prohibited discrimination based not only on race but also on sex. Ironically, that provision had been added to Title VII of the Civil Rights Act by southern Democrats. These senators saw a prohibition against sex discrimination in employment as a joke, and viewed

---

Thinking Globally

Saudi Arabia and Women's Rights

In Saudi Arabia, women are prohibited from voting and driving and may only travel abroad or work with the permission of a male relative. In schools and universities, women are segregated from their male colleagues.

■ Saudi Arabia is considered a strong U.S. ally. Should Saudi Arabia's lack of support for women's civil rights affect U.S. foreign policy toward Saudi Arabia? Explain your answer.

■ What should be considered "women's rights"? Are they the same rights afforded to men or not?

its addition as a means to discredit the entire act and ensure its defeat. Thus, it was added at the last minute and female members of Congress seized the opportunity to garner support for the measure.

In 1966, after the **Equal Employment Opportunity Commission** failed to enforce the law as it applied to sex discrimination, female activists formed the National Organization for Women. NOW was modeled closely on the NAACP. Its founders sought to work within the system to prevent discrimination. Initially, most of this activity was geared toward two goals: achievement of equality either by passage of an equal rights amendment to the Constitution, or by judicial decision.

Not all women agreed with the notion of full equality for women. Members of the National Consumers' League, for example, feared that an equal rights amendment would invalidate protective legislation of the kind specifically ruled constitutional in *Muller* v. *Oregon* (1908). Nevertheless, from 1923 to 1972, a proposal for an equal rights amendment was made in every session of every Congress. Every president between Harry S Truman and Richard M. Nixon backed it, and by 1972 public opinion favored its ratification.

Finally, in 1972, in response to pressure from NOW, the National Women's Political Caucus, and a wide variety of other feminist groups, Congress voted in favor of the Equal Rights Amendment (ERA) by overwhelming majorities (84–8 in the Senate; 354–24 in the House). The amendment provided that:

> Equality of rights under the law shall not be denied or abridged by the United States or by any state on account of sex.
>
> The Congress shall have the power to enforce, by appropriate legislation, the provisions of this article.

Within a year, twenty-two states ratified the amendment, most by overwhelming margins, but the tide soon turned. In *Roe* v. *Wade* (1973), the Supreme Court decided that women had a constitutionally protected right to privacy that included the right to terminate a pregnancy. Almost overnight, *Roe* gave the ERA's opponents political fuel. Although privacy rights and the ERA have nothing to do with each other, opponents effectively persuaded many people in states that had yet to ratify the amendment that the two were linked. They also claimed that the ERA and feminists were anti-family and that the ERA would force women out of their homes and into the workforce because husbands would no longer be responsible for their wives' support.

These arguments and the amendment's potential to make women eligible for the military draft brought the ratification effort to a near standstill. In 1974 and 1975, the amendment only squeaked through the Montana and North Dakota legislatures, and two states—Nebraska and Tennessee—voted to rescind their earlier ratifications. By 1978, one year before the deadline for ratification was to expire, thirty-five states had voted for the amendment—three short of the three-fourths necessary for ratification. Efforts in key states such as Illinois and Florida failed as opposition to the ERA intensified. Faced with the prospect of defeat, ERA supporters heavily lobbied Congress to extend the deadline for ratification. Congress extended the ratification period by three years, but to no avail. No additional states ratified the amendment, and three more rescinded their votes.

Equal Employment Opportunity Commission
Federal agency created to enforce the Civil Rights Act of 1964, which forbids discrimination on the basis of race, creed, national origin, religion, or sex in hiring, promotion, or firing.

Who continues to fight for the ERA? Members of Congress led by Representative Carolyn B. Maloney (D–NY) have reintroduced the Equal Rights Amendment in all recent sessions of Congress. Here, Representative Maloney (at podium), her co-sponsors, and women's group leaders hold a press conference in March of 2005 announcing the reintroduction of the ERA in the 109th Congress. In 2007, the ERA was renamed the Women's Equality Amendment.

Photo courtesy: Office of Congresswoman Carolyn Maloney

What began as a simple correction to the Constitution turned into a highly controversial proposed change. Even though large percentages of the public favored the ERA, opponents needed to stall ratification in only thirteen states while supporters had to convince legislators in thirty-eight. The success that women's rights activists were having in the courts was hurting the effort. When women first sought the ERA in the late 1960s, the Supreme Court had yet to rule that women were protected by the Fourteenth Amendment's equal protection clause from any kind of discrimination, thus highlighting the need for an amendment. But, as the Court widened its interpretation of the Constitution to protect women from some sorts of discrimination, many felt the need for a new amendment was less urgent. The proposed amendment died without being ratified on June 30, 1982.

While several women's groups worked toward passage of the ERA, which was renamed the **Women's Equality Amendment** in 2007, NOW and other groups, including the American Civil Liberties Union (ACLU), formed litigating arms to pressure the courts. But, women faced an immediate roadblock in the Supreme Court's interpretation of the equal protection clause of the Fourteenth Amendment.

Women's Equality Amendment
Proposed amendment to the Constitution that states "Equality of rights under the law shall not be denied or abridged by the United States or any state on account of sex."

The Equal Protection Clause and Constitutional Standards of Review

The Fourteenth Amendment protects all U.S. citizens from state action that violates equal protection of the laws. Most laws, however, are subject to what is called the rational basis or minimum rationality test. This lowest level of scrutiny means that governments must allege a rational foundation for any distinctions they make. Early on, however, the Supreme Court decided that certain freedoms were entitled to a heightened standard of review. As early as 1937, the Supreme Court recognized that certain freedoms were so fundamental that a very heavy burden would be placed on any government that sought to restrict those rights. As discussed in chapter 5, when fundamental freedoms such as those guaranteed by the First Amendment or **suspect classifications** such as race are involved, the Court uses a heightened standard of review called **strict scrutiny** to determine the constitutional validity of the challenged practices, as detailed in Table 6.1.

suspect classification
Category or class, such as race, that triggers the highest standard of scrutiny from the Supreme Court.

strict scrutiny
A heightened standard of review used by the Supreme Court to determine the constitutional validity of a challenged practice.

TABLE **6.1** The Equal Protection Clause and Standards of Review

Type of Classification: What kind of statutory classification is at issue?	Standard of Review: What standard of review will be used?	Test: What does the Court ask?	Example: How does the Court apply the test?
Fundamental freedoms (including religion, speech, assembly, press, privacy); Suspect classifications (including race, alienage, and national origin)	Strict scrutiny or heightened standard	Is classification necessary to the accomplishment of a permissible state goal? Is it the least restrictive way to reach that goal?	*Brown* v. *Board of Education* (1954): Racial segregation not necessary to accomplish the state's goal of educating its students.
Gender	Intermediate standard	Does the classification serve an important governmental objective, and is it substantially related to those ends?	*Craig* v. *Boren* (1976): Keeping drunk drivers off the roads may be an important governmental objective, but allowing eighteen- to twenty-one-year-old women to drink alcoholic beverages while prohibiting men of the same age from drinking is not substantially related to that goal.
Others (including age, wealth, mental retardation, and sexual orientation)	Minimum rationality standard	Is there any rational foundation for the discrimination?	*Romer* v. *Evans* (1996): Colorado state constitutional amendment denying equal rights to homosexuals is unconstitutional.

Beginning with *Korematsu* v. *U.S.* (1944), which involved a constitutional challenge to the internment of Japanese Americans as security risks during World War II, Justice Hugo Black noted that "all legal restrictions which curtail the civic rights of a single racial group are immediately suspect," and should be given "the most rigid scrutiny."[32] In *Brown* v. *Board of Education* (1954), the Supreme Court again used the strict scrutiny standard to evaluate the constitutionality of race-based distinctions. In legal terms, this means that if a statute or governmental practice makes a classification based on race, the statute is presumed to be unconstitutional unless the state can provide "compelling affirmative justifications": that is, unless the state can prove the law in question is necessary to accomplish a permissible goal and that it is the least restrictive means through which that goal can be accomplished. (In *Korematsu*, however, the Court concluded that the national risks posed by Japanese Americans were sufficient to justify their internment.)

During the 1960s and into the 1970s, the Court routinely struck down as unconstitutional practices and statutes that discriminated on the basis of race. "Whites-only" public parks and recreational facilities, tax-exempt status for private schools that discriminated, and statutes prohibiting interracial marriage were declared unconstitutional. In contrast, the Court refused to consider whether the equal protection clause might apply to discrimination against women. Finally, in a case argued in 1971 by Ruth Bader Ginsburg (now an associate justice of the Supreme Court) as director of the Women's Rights Project of the ACLU, the Supreme Court ruled that an Idaho law granting a male parent automatic preference over a female parent as the administrator of their deceased child's estate violated the equal protection clause of the Fourteenth Amendment. *Reed* v. *Reed* (1971), the Idaho case, turned the tide in terms of constitutional litigation. Although the Court did not rule that sex was a suspect classification, it concluded that the equal protection clause of the Fourteenth Amendment prohibited unreasonable classifications based on sex.[33]

In 1976, the Court ruled that sex-discrimination complaints would be judged by a new, judicially created intermediate standard of review a step below strict scrutiny.[34] In *Craig* v. *Boren* (1976), the Court carved out a new test to be used in examining claims of sex discrimination: "to withstand constitutional challenge, ... classifications by gender must serve important governmental objectives and must be substantially related to achievement of those objectives." According to the Court, an intermediate standard of review was created within what previously was a two-tier distinction—strict scrutiny and rational basis.

Men, too, can use the Fourteenth Amendment to fight gender-based discrimination. Since 1976, the Court has applied the intermediate standard of constitutional review to most claims that it has heard involving gender. Thus, the following kinds of practices have been found to violate the Fourteenth Amendment:

- Single-sex public nursing schools.[35]
- Laws that consider males adults at twenty-one years but females at eighteen years.[36]
- Laws that allow women but not men to receive alimony.[37]
- State prosecutors' use of peremptory challenges to reject men or women to create more sympathetic juries.[38]
- Virginia's maintenance of an all-male military college, the Virginia Military Institute.[39]
- Different requirements for a child's acquisition of citizenship based on whether the citizen parent is a mother or a father.[40]

In contrast, the Court has upheld the following governmental practices and laws:

- Draft registration provisions for males only.[41]
- State statutory rape laws that apply only to female victims.[42]

The level of review used by the Court is crucial. Clearly, a statute excluding African Americans from draft registration would be unconstitutional. But, because gender is not subject to the same higher standard of review that is used in racial discrimination cases, the exclusion of women from the requirements of the Military Selective Service Act was ruled permissible because the government policy was considered to serve "important governmental objectives."[43]

This history has perhaps clarified why women's rights activists continue to argue that until the passage of the Women's Equality Amendment, women will never enjoy the same rights as men. An amendment would raise the level of scrutiny that the Court applies to gender-based claims, although there are clear indications that the Supreme Court favors requiring states to show "exceedingly persuasive justifications" for their actions.[44]

'Three-fourths of a penny for your thoughts...'

What are the practical consequences of pay equity? This cartoon pokes fun at a serious issue in gender equality: pay equity. In 2007, women earned an average of 77 cents for every $1.00 earned by their male counterparts.

Statutory Remedies for Sex Discrimination

In part because of the limits of the intermediate standard of review and the fact that the equal protection clause applies only to governmental discrimination, women's rights activists began to bombard the courts with sex-discrimination cases. The Equal Pay Act of 1963 requires employers to pay women and men equal pay for equal work. Women have won important victories under the act, but a large wage gap between women and men continues to exist. Women's earnings in 2007 equaled only 77 percent of their male counterparts' earnings.

Other cases have been filed under Title VII of the Civil Rights Act, which prohibits discrimination by private (and, after 1972, public) employers. Key victories under Title VII include:

- Consideration of sexual harassment as sex discrimination.[45]
- Inclusion of law firms, which many argued were private partnerships, in the coverage of the act.[46]
- A broad definition of what can be considered sexual harassment, which includes same-sex harassment.[47]
- Allowance of voluntary affirmative action programs to redress historical discrimination against women.[48]

Other victories have come under **Title IX** of the Education Amendments of 1972, which bars educational institutions receiving federal funds from discriminating against female students. Holding school boards or districts responsible for sexual harassment of students by teachers, for example, was ruled actionable under Title IX by the U.S. Supreme Court.[49]

Title IX, which parallels Title VII, greatly expanded the opportunities for women in elementary, secondary, and postsecondary institutions. It bars educational institutions receiving federal funds from discriminating against female students. Since women's groups saw eradication of educational discrimination as key to improving other facets of women's lives, they lobbied for it heavily. Most of today's college students do not go through school being excluded from home economics or industrial arts or technology education classes because of their sex. Nor, probably, do many attend schools that have no team sports for females. Yet, this was commonly the case in the United States prior to passage of Title IX.[50] Nevertheless, sport facilities, access to premium playing times, and quality equipment remain unequal in many high schools and colleges. Moreover,

Title IX
Provision of the Educational Amendments of 1972 that bars educational institutions receiving federal funds from discriminating against female students.

THE GRAPES of WRATH
John Steinbeck

Photo courtesy: The Granger Collection

Can literature affect social movements? John Steinbeck's *The Grapes of Wrath*, published in 1939, focused national attention on the plight of migrant workers in California's grape-growing industry.

the Bush administration actively opposed many of Title IX's provisions and repeatedly allowed colleges and universities to reduce the number of women's sports teams, as well as scholarships and general spending on these teams. But, in 2005, the Supreme Court ruled that Title IX allows retaliatory lawsuits based on a complaint made by a basketball coach on behalf of his players who had been denied equal treatment by the school board.[51]

Other Groups Mobilize for Rights

African Americans and women are not the only groups that have suffered unequal treatment under the law. Denial of civil rights has led many other disadvantaged groups to mobilize. Their efforts have many parallels to the efforts made by African Americans and women. Many groups also recognized that litigation and the use of test-case strategies would be key to further civil rights gains. Others have opted for more direct, traditional forms of activism.

Hispanic Americans

Hispanic Americans—Latino/as—are the largest and fastest growing minority group in the United States. But, Latino/a immigration to the United States is not a new phenomenon. In 1910, the Mexican Revolution forced Mexicans seeking safety and employment into the United States. And, in 1916, New Mexico entered the union as an officially bilingual state—the only one in the United States.

These early immigrants, many of whom were from families who had owned land when parts of the Southwest were still in Mexico's control, formed the League of United Latin American Citizens (LULAC) in 1929. LULAC continues to be the largest Latino/a group in the United States, with local councils in every state and Puerto Rico. Latinos returning home from fighting in World War II also formed the American G.I. Forum in Texas to fight discrimination and improve the legal status of Latinos.

As large numbers of immigrants from Mexico and Puerto Rico came to the United States, they quickly became a source of cheap labor, with Mexicans initially tending to settle in the Southwest, where they most frequently were employed as migratory farm workers, and Puerto Ricans mainly moving to New York City. Both groups tended to live in their own neighborhoods, where life was centered around the Roman Catholic Church and the customs of their homeland, and both groups largely lived in poverty. Still, in 1954, the same year as *Brown*,

TIMELINE

The Mexican-American Civil Rights Movement

Photo courtesy: Library of Congress

What was the significance of the Supreme Court's decision in *Hernandez v. Texas*? *Hernandez v. Texas* (1954) was a landmark decision for Latino/a rights groups. Here, a San Antonio newspaper celebrates the Court's decision.

How many protesters are needed to affect public policy? More than 1 million immigrants and their supporters took to the streets across the nation to rally for immigrants' civil rights on May 1, 2006. The march was held in the wake of proposed immigration legislation in Congress that would have cracked down on illegal immigrants and toughened border security with Mexico. Here, an estimated 400,000 people march in Chicago, Illinois.

Photo courtesy: John Zich/zimages.com

Latinos won a major victory when in *Hernandez* v. *Texas*, the Supreme Court struck down discrimination based on ethnicity and class.[52] In *Hernandez*, the Court ruled unanimously that Mexican Americans were entitled to a jury that included other Mexican Americans.

A push for greater Hispanic rights began in the mid-1960s, just as a wave of Cuban immigrants began to establish homes in Florida, dramatically altering the political and social climate of Miami and other neighboring towns and cities. This new movement, marked by the establishment of the National Council of La Raza in 1968, included many tactics drawn from the African American civil rights movement, including sit-ins, boycotts, marches, and other activities designed to attract publicity to their cause. In one earlier example, in 1965, Cesar Chavez and Dolores Huerta organized migrant workers into the United Farm Workers Union, which would become the largest farm worker's union in the nation, and led them in a strike against growers in California. This strike was eventually coupled with a national boycott of several farm products.

Latinos/as also have relied heavily on litigation to secure legal change. Key groups are the Mexican American Legal Defense and Educational Fund (MALDEF) and the Puerto Rican Legal Defense and Educational Fund. MALDEF was founded in 1968 after members of LULAC met with NAACP LDF leaders and, with their assistance, secured a $2.2-million start-up grant from the Ford Foundation. MALDEF was originally created to bring test cases before the Supreme Court to force school districts to allocate more funds to schools with predominantly low-income minority populations, to implement bilingual education programs, to force employers to hire Latino/as, and to challenge election rules and apportionment plans that undercount or dilute Latino/a voting power.

MALDEF has been successful in its efforts to expand voting rights and opportunities to Hispanic Americans under the Voting Rights Act of 1965 (renewed in 2006 for ten years) and the U.S. Constitution's equal protection clause. In 1973, for

Timeline: Important Moments in Hispanic American Rights

1910 Mexican Revolution—Political turmoil during the Mexican Revolution forces Mexicans to seek safety and employment in the United States.

1929 League of United Latin American Citizens Formed—Several service organizations unite, creating LULAC, the largest Latino/a service organization in the country.

1954 *Hernandez v. Texas*—Supreme Court rules that the Fourteenth Amendment's equal protection rights apply to other racial groups, including Latino/as.

1916 New Mexico Becomes a State—New Mexico is granted statehood as an officially bilingual member of the union.

1939 *Grapes of Wrath* Published—John Steinbeck's novel draws attention to the plight of migrant farm workers.

1965 United Farm Workers Union Founded—The United Farm Workers Union, the largest farm workers union in the United States, has been important in coordinating strikes in California.

example, it won a major victory when the Supreme Court ruled that multimember electoral districts (in which more than one person represents a single district) in Texas discriminated against African Americans and Latino/as.[53] In multimember systems, legislatures generally add members to larger districts instead of drawing smaller districts in which a minority candidate could get a majority of the votes necessary to win.

MALDEF's success in educational equity cases came more slowly. In 1973, for example, in *San Antonio Independent School District* v. *Rodriguez*, the Supreme Court refused to find that a Texas law under which the state appropriated a set dollar amount to each school district per pupil, while allowing wealthier districts to enrich educational programs from other funds, violated the equal protection clause of the Fourteenth Amendment.[54] In 1989, however, MALDEF won a case in which a state district judge elected by the voters of only a single county declared the state's entire method of financing public schools to be unconstitutional under the state constitution.[55] And, in 2004, it entered into a settlement with the state of California in a case brought four years earlier to address, in MALDEF's words, "the shocking inequities facing public school children across the state."[56]

MALDEF continues to litigate in a wide range of areas of concern to Latinos/as. High on its agenda today are affirmative action, the admission of Latino/a students to state colleges and universities, health care for undocumented immigrants, and challenging redistricting practices that make it more difficult to elect Latino/a legislators. It also litigates to challenge many state redistricting plans to ensure that Hispanics are adequately represented. In 2006, for example, MALDEF and other Hispanic rights

1965 Voting Rights Act of 1965—The Voting Rights Act of 1965, among other innovations, requires bilingual ballots in Spanish speaking communities.

1973 *San Antonio Independent School District* v. *Rodriguez*—MALDEF fails to convince the Supreme Court that educational funds should be distributed equally among school districts.

2006 *LULAC* v. *Perry*—The Supreme Court decides in Texas that a redistricting plan does not intentionally limit Latino/a representation.

1968 Legal Lobbying Groups Created—MALDEF and the Puerto Rican Legal Defense and Education Fund are founded in the image of the NAACP LDF.

2006 Day Without Immigrants—More than 1 million immigrants leave their jobs to march in cities across the United States to illustrate the importance of Latino/as and other immigrants to the American economy.

groups played a major role in challenging a redistricting plan created by the Texas legislature, charging that the legislature's plan was designed intentionally to limit Latino/a representation in South Texas.

MALDEF is also at the fore of legislative lobbying for expanded rights. Since 2002, it has worked to oppose restrictions concerning driver's license requirements for undocumented immigrants, to gain greater rights for Latino/a workers, and to ensure that redistricting plans do not silence Latino/a voters. MALDEF also focuses on the rights of Latino/a workers.

In 2006, MALDEF, LULAC, and hundreds of ad hoc groups of Latinos, many encouraged from the pulpits of Roman Catholic Churches around the nation, rallied to show their concern about various governmental proposals being offered concerning immigrants. Not only had President George W. Bush proposed legislation that would affect immigration and strengthen the border with Mexico, but forty-three states were considering various laws to deal with illegal immigrants. Thus, on May 1, 2006, legal and illegal immigrants, supported by many American citizens, took the day off in what originally was to be an economic boycott called "Day Without Immigrants." Ultimately, more than 1 million marchers took to the streets in at least forty states to draw attention to the plight of immigrants, the vast majority of them of Hispanic origin.

Immigration issues continue to divide Americans. In 2006, President Bush signed a bill authorizing an additional 700 miles of fencing along the U.S. border with Mexico; 1.2 billion dollars was designated for enhanced border security. There is no mandate that these funds be used specifically to build a border barrier.

American Indians

Americans Indians are the first true Americans, and their status under U.S. law is unique. Under the U.S. Constitution, Indian tribes are considered distinct governments, a situation that has affected American Indians' treatment by the Supreme Court in contrast to other groups of ethnic minorities.

It is estimated that there were as many as 10 million Indians in the New World at the time Europeans arrived in the 1400s. The actual number of Indians is hotly contested, with estimates varying from a high of 150–200 million to a low of 20–50 million throughout North and South America. By 1900, the number of Indians in the continental United States had plummeted to less than 2 million. Today, there are approximately 2.8 million.

For years, Congress and the courts manipulated Indian law to promote the westward expansion of the United States. The Northwest Ordinance of 1787, passed by the Continental Congress, specified that "good faith should always be observed toward the Indians; their lands and property shall never be taken from them without their consent, and their property rights, and liberty, they shall never be invaded or disturbed, unless in just and lawful wars authorized by Congress." These strictures were not followed. Instead, over the years, "American Indian policy has been described as 'genocide-at-law' promoting both land acquisition and cultural extermination."[57] During the eighteenth and nineteenth centuries, the U.S. government isolated Indians on reservations as it confiscated their lands and denied them basic political rights. Indian reservations were administered by the federal government, and American Indians often lived in squalid conditions.

With passage of the Dawes Act in 1887, however, the government switched policies to promote assimilation over separation. Each Indian family was given land within the reservation; the rest was sold to whites, thus reducing Indian lands from about 140 million acres to about 47 million. Moreover, to encourage American Indians to assimilate, their children were sent to boarding schools off the reservation, and native languages and rituals were banned. American Indians did not become U.S. citizens nor were they given the right to vote until 1924.

At least in part because tribes were small and scattered (and the number of Indians declining), American Indians formed no protest movement in reaction to these drastic policy changes. It was not until the 1960s that Indians began to mobilize. During this time, Indian activists, many trained by the American Indian Law Center at the University of New Mexico, began to file hundreds of test cases in the federal courts involving tribal fishing rights, tribal land claims, and the taxation of tribal profits. The Native American Rights Fund (NARF), founded in 1970, became the NAACP LDF of the Indian rights movement.

American Indians have won some very important victories concerning hunting, fishing, and land rights. American Indian tribes all over America have sued to reclaim lands they say were stolen from them by the United States, often more than 200 years ago. Today, these land rights allow American Indians to play host to a number of casinos across the country, a phenomenon that has resulted in billions of dollars for Indian tribes. These improvements in Indians' economic affairs have helped to increase their political clout. Tribes are donating to political campaigns of candidates who seem predisposed to policies favorable to tribes. The Agua Caliente Band of Cahuilla Indians, for example, donated $7.5 million to political campaigns in just one year alone. These large expenditures, Indians claim, are legal, because as sovereign nations they are immune from federal and state campaign finance disclosure laws.[58] It is likely that the political involvement of Indian tribes will continue to grow as their casinos—and the profits of those ventures—continue to proliferate.

American Indians have not fared particularly well in areas such as religious freedom, especially where tribal practices come into conflict with state law. As noted in chapter 5, the Supreme Court used the rational basis test to rule that a state could infringe on reli-

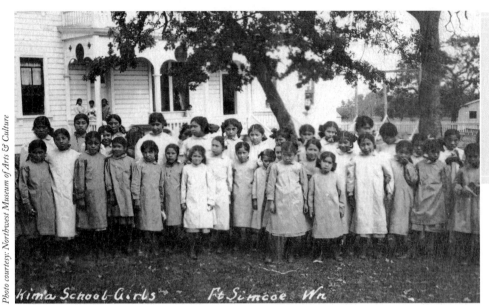

Photo courtesy: Northwest Museum of Arts & Culture

Kima School Girls   Ft Simcoe Wa

How were American Indians treated by the U.S. government? Indian children were forcibly removed from their homes beginning in the late 1800s and sent to boarding schools where they were pressured to give up their cultural traditions and tribal languages. Here, girls from the Yakima Reservation in Washington State are pictured in front of such a school in 1913.

gious exercise (use of peyote as a sacrament in religious ceremonies) by a neutral law, and limited Indian access to religious sites during timber harvesting.[59] Congress attempted to restore some of those rights through passage of the Religious Freedom Restoration Act. Parts of the law, however, were later ruled unconstitutional by the Supreme Court.[60]

Like the civil rights and women's rights movements, the movement for American Indian rights has had a radical as well as a more traditional branch. In 1973, for example, national attention was drawn to the plight of Indians when members of the radical American Indian Movement took over Wounded Knee, South Dakota, the site of the massacre of 150 Indians by the U.S. Army in 1890. Just two years before the protest, the treatment of Indians had been highlighted in the best-selling *Bury My Heart at Wounded Knee*, which in many ways served to mobilize public opinion against the oppression of American Indians in the same way *Uncle Tom's Cabin* had against slavery.[61]

More recently, Indian tribes have found themselves locked in a controversy with the Department of the Interior over its handling of Indian trust funds, which are to be paid out to Indians for the use of their lands. In 1996, several Indian tribes filed suit to force the federal government to account for the billions of dollars it has collected over the years for its leasing of Indian lands, which it took from the Indians and has held in trust since the late nineteenth century, and to force reform of the system.[62] As the result of years of mismanagement, the trust, administered by the Department of the Interior, has no records of monies taken in or how they were disbursed. The ongoing class action lawsuit includes 500,000 Indians, who claim that they are owed more than $10 billion. The trial judge found massive mismanagement of the funds, which generate up to $500 million a year, and at one time threatened to hold the secretary of the interior in contempt. Although this case has been largely deadlocked, in early 2004 a mediator was appointed to help bring greater resolution to the conflict.[63]

Indians also are attempting to have their voices heard by electing more Native Americans to office. In 2005, the Indigenous Democratic Network (INDN) was founded. Its

Thinking Globally

Equality for Indigenous People in Mexico

Chiapas is one of the poorest states in Mexico; it also boasts one of the largest concentrations of indigenous peoples. In 1994, a rebel movement known as the Zapatistas took control of several Chiapas cities. Its leaders demanded better treatment by the federal government for the Chiapas people. The rebels' actions focused the world's attention on the plight of many indigenous groups in Central and South America.

■ What is the level of a country's responsibility to its indigenous people?
■ Should indigenous peoples enjoy distinct or special rights because of their position as descendants of the original settlers of a particular region? Explain your reasoning.

campaign finance arm, INDN's List, is modeled after other political action committees and its purpose is to elect Indians and Democrats at the state and national level. INDN also trains candidates in "Campaign Camp" and encourages Indians to run for office.[64] To learn more about political action committees, see chapter 16.

Asian and Pacific Americans

Like African Americans and Latino/as, Asian and Pacific Americans have confronted significant discrimination in the United States. For example, as Representative David Wu (D–OR) was attempting to enter the U.S. Department of Energy where he was to give a speech, guards refused to believe he was an American citizen, even though he produced his congressional identification.[65]

One of the most significant difficulties for Asian and Pacific Americans has been finding a Pan-Asian identity. Originally, Asian and Pacific Americans were far more likely to identify as Japanese, Chinese, Korean, or Filipino.[66] It was not until 1977 that the U.S. government decided to use the nomenclature "Asian and Pacific Islanders." Even this identity has been challenged by some subgroups; in the 1990s, native Hawaiians unsuccessfully requested to be categorized with American Indians, with whom they felt greater affinity.

Discrimination against Asian and Pacific immigrants developed over time in the United States. In 1868, Congress passed a law allowing free migration from China, but in 1882, Congress passed the Chinese Exclusion Act, which was the first to restrict the immigration of any identifiable nationality. This legislation implicitly invited more discriminatory laws against the Chinese, which closely paralleled the Jim Crow laws affecting African Americans.

Several Supreme Court cases also slowed the progress of Asian and Pacific Americans. But, in 1886, the Court decided the landmark case of *Yick Wo* v. *Hopkins* using the rational basis test highlighted in Table 6.1. A number of events precipitated this decision. Discriminatory provisions in the California Constitution prevented Chinese people from practicing many professions. However, the Chinese in California were allowed to open laundries. And, many immigrants did. In response to this growing trend, the city of San Francisco passed a ban on cleaners operating in wooden buildings, two-thirds of which were owned by persons of Chinese ancestry. The Court in *Yick Wo* found that the law violated the Fourteenth Amendment in its application.[67]

In 1922, the Court took a step backwards, ruling that Asian and Pacific Americans were not white and therefore not entitled to full citizenship rights.[68] Conditions became even worse, especially for those of Japanese descent, after the Japanese invasion of Pearl Harbor in 1941. In response to this action, President Franklin D. Roosevelt issued Executive Order 9066, which led to the internment of 120,000 Japanese Americans. Over two-thirds of those confined to internment camps were U.S. citizens.[69] The Supreme Court upheld the constitutionality of these camps in *Korematsu* v. *U.S.* (1944). The justices applied the strict scrutiny standard of review and ruled that these internments served an important governmental objective and were not discriminatory on their face. According to Justice Hugo Black:

Korematsu was not excluded from the Military Area because of hostility to him or his race. He was excluded because we are at war with the Japanese Empire, because the properly constituted military authorities feared an invasion of our West Coast and felt constrained to take proper security measures, because they decided that the military

How were Japanese Americans treated during World War II? The internment of Japanese Americans during World War II was a low point in American history. In *Korematsu* v. *U.S.* (1944), the U.S. Supreme Court upheld the constitutionality of this action.

Photo courtesy: Russell Lee/Corbis

urgency of the situation demanded that all citizens of Japanese ancestry be segregated from the West Coast temporarily, and, finally, because Congress, reposing its confidence in this time of war in our military leaders—as inevitably it must—determined that they should have the power to do just this.[70]

In sharp contrast, as a goodwill gesture to an ally, the U.S. government offered Chinese immigrants the opportunity to apply for U.S. citizenship. At the end of the war, President Harry S Truman extended the same privilege to Filipino immigrants, many of whom had aided in the war effort.

During the 1960s and 1970s, Asian and Pacific Americans, like many other groups discussed in this chapter, began to organize for equal rights. Filipino farm workers, for example, joined with Mexicans to form the United Farm Workers Union. In 1973, the Movement for a Free Philippines emerged to oppose the government of Ferdinand Marcos, the president of the Philippines. Soon, it joined forces with the Friends of Filipino People, which ultimately established the Congress Education Project, a Washington, D.C.-based lobbying group. The Congress Education Project, and other Asian and Pacific Americans constituent groups largely were opposed to the Vietnam War.

In the 1970s and 1980s, Japanese Americans mobilized, lobbying the courts and Congress for reparations for their treatment during World War II. In 1988, Congress passed the Civil Liberties Act, which apologized to the interned and their descendants and offered reparations to them and their families.

Today, myriad Asian and Pacific American groups target diverse political venues. In California, in particular, they have been successful in seeing more men and women elected at the local and state level. (To learn more about states with large Asian and Pacific Americans populations, see Table 6.2.)

TABLE 6.2	States with Largest Asian and Pacific American Populations, 2007
California	5,036,849
New York	1,437,979
Hawaii	918,606
Texas	901,439
New Jersey	692,542
Illinois	600,127
Washington	548,690
Florida	496,005
Virginia	426,196
Massachusetts	344,768

Source: Data based on U.S. Census Bureau data, http://www.census.gov/popest/states/asth/SC-EST200704.html.

Gays and Lesbians

Until very recently, gays and lesbians have had an even harder time than other groups in achieving anything approximating equal rights.[71] However, gays and lesbians have, on average, far higher household incomes and educational levels than other minority groups, and they are beginning to convert these advantages into political clout at the ballot box and recently have benefited from changes in public opinion. As discussed in chapter 5, like African Americans and women, gays and lesbians initially did not fare well in the Supreme Court. In the late 1970s, the Lambda Legal Defense and Education Fund, the Lesbian Rights Project, and Gay and Lesbian Advocates and Defenders were founded by gay and lesbian activists dedicated to ending legal restrictions on the civil rights of homosexuals.[72] Although these groups have won important legal victories concerning HIV/AIDS discrimination, insurance policy survivor benefits, and even some employment issues, they generally were not as successful as other historically disadvantaged groups.[73]

In 1993, for example, President Bill Clinton tried to ban discrimination against homosexuals in the armed services. Congressional and military leaders led the effort against Clinton's proposal. Eventually, Clinton and Senate leaders compromised on what was called the "Don't Ask, Don't Tell" policy. It stipulated that gays and lesbians would no longer be asked if they were homosexual, but they were barred from revealing their sexual orientation (under threat of discharge from the service).[74] Although this policy was initially viewed as a successful compromise, it has been called into question in recent years, as the wars in Iraq and Afghanistan have increased America's need for active-duty military personnel. Since the policy was adopted in 1994, at least 11,000 soldiers have been discharged for their sexual orientation.[75]

POLITICS NOW

Source: OMAHA WORLD-HERALD   May 23, 2007   Page 1A

Gay and Lesbian Rights

Gay Discrimination Ban Again Fails to Become Nebraska Law

MARTHA STODDARD

State lawmakers Tuesday decided that Nebraska should not join Iowa and other states in prohibiting job discrimination against gays and lesbians. A 24–15 vote killed Legislative Bill 475, which had been introduced by State Sen. Ernie Chambers of Omaha. He sponsored the measure because of what he said is a need for its proposed protections. LB 475 would give homosexuals "what all of us take for granted: the right to earn an honest living," Chambers said. "We're not talking about anything other than the right to get a job."

Sen. Bill Avery of Lincoln said the bill had limited scope. It would have applied only to hiring, firing and promotions in the workplace, and it only covered people based on sexual orientation. Opposing the measure were Sen. Tony Fulton of Lincoln and others, who argued against giving special protections to gay and lesbian people in state law.

Fulton questioned whether the bill's protections would extend to pedophiles or transvestites wanting to be teachers. He said studies that show gay households have higher average incomes demonstrate that job discrimination is not a problem.

Sen. Tom Carlson of Holdrege said the bill is not needed as long as people keep private what goes on in their bedrooms. "I don't think we should unleash such things on the unsuspecting public," he said. "We're talking here about values. We're talking here about behavior. We're talking here about ethics."

LB 475 would have exempted small businesses and religious organizations from its provisions.

Nebraska law offers specific legal protection to gays and lesbians in two instances. The state's hate crimes law enhances penalties for crimes committed against people based on their sexual orientation. Language added to the state budget in 2005 bars recipients of biomedical research money from discriminating against gays and lesbians.

A state constitutional amendment bars same-sex couples from marrying.

Chambers said his bill would pass easily if senators were not afraid of political repercussions. When asked directly by Chambers, even some opponents of the bill said they did not believe an employer should be able to discriminate against a gay or lesbian person.

Discussion Questions

1. *Is a person's sexual orientation relevant to employment? Why or why not?*
2. *Are anti-discrimination laws "special protection," and if so, do they violate the Fourteenth Amendment?*
3. *To what extent should policy makers be able to impose their personal values in formulating civil rights laws and regulations?*

Civil Rights and Gay Adoption

The public's views toward homosexuality have also changed, as signaled by the Court's 1996 decision in *Romer* v. *Evans*.[76] In this case, the Court ruled that an amendment to the Colorado constitution that denied homosexuals the right to seek protection from discrimination was unconstitutional under the equal protection clause of the Fourteenth Amendment.

In 2000, Vermont became the first state to recognize civil unions, marking another landmark in the struggle for equal rights for homosexuals. However, it was the Supreme Court's decision in *Lawrence* v. *Texas* (2003) that really put homosexual rights on the public agenda (see chapter 5). In this case, the Court reversed an earlier ruling by finding a Texas statute that banned sodomy to be unconstitutional. Writing for the majority, Justice Anthony Kennedy stated, "[homosexuals'] right to liberty under the due process clause gives them the full right to engage in their conduct without intervention of the government."[77]

Following the Court's ruling in *Lawrence*, many Americans were quick to call for additional rights for homosexuals. Many corporations also responded to this amplified call for equal rights. For example, Wal-Mart announced it would ban job discrimination based on sexual orientation. In addition, editorial pages across the country praised the Court's ruling, arguing that the national view toward homosexuality had changed.[78] In November 2003, the Massachusetts Supreme Court further agreed when it ruled that denying homosexuals the right to civil marriage was unconstitutional under the state's constitution. The U.S. Supreme Court later refused to hear an appeal of this case, paving the way for the legality of marriage.

In 2004, many conservative groups and Republican politicians made same-sex marriage a key issue. Referenda or amendments prohibiting same-sex marriage were placed on eleven state ballots, and all were passed overwhelmingly by voters.

President George W. Bush again renewed his call for a constitutional amendment to ban same-sex marriage in the summer of 2006. This effort failed in the U.S. Senate, where supporters did not gain a simple majority of votes in support of a ban, let alone the two-thirds vote necessary to send a proposed amendment to the states. Same-sex marriage bans were on several state ballots in the 2006 midterm elections, but the issue seemed to lack the emotional punch of the 2004 effort in the context of plummeting presidential approval and the ongoing war in Iraq.

In 2008, California and Connecticut joined Massachusetts in legalizing same-sex marriages. Same-sex couples traveled to California, especially, to legally marry. But, in November 2008, California voters passed a ballot proposition amending the state constitution in a manner that makes same-sex marriages illegal again; several organized interests have announced their intention to litigate on the legality of this proposition.

Photo courtesy: Marcio Jose Sanchez/AFP/Getty Images

Americans with Disabilities

Americans with disabilities also have lobbied hard for anti-discrimination legislation as well as equal protection under the Constitution. In the aftermath of World War II, many veterans returned to a nation unequipped to handle their disabilities. The Korean and Vietnam Wars made the problems of disabled veterans all the more clear. These veterans saw the successes of African Americans, women, and other minorities, and they too began to lobby for greater protection against discrimination.[79] In 1990, in coalition with other disabled people, veterans finally were able to convince Congress to pass the Americans with Disabilities Act (ADA). The statute defines a disabled person as someone with a physical or mental impairment that limits one or more "life activities," or who has a record of such impairment. It thus extends the protections of the Civil Rights Act of 1964 to all of those with physical or mental disabilities. It guarantees access to public facilities, employment, and communication services. It also requires employers to acquire or modify work equipment, adjust work schedules, and make existing facilities accessible to those with disabilities. Thus, for example, buildings must be accessible to people in wheelchairs, and telecommunications devices must be provided for deaf employees.

In 1999, the U.S. Supreme Court issued a series of four decisions redefining and limiting the scope of the ADA. The cumulative impact of these decisions was to limit dramatically the number of people who can claim coverage under the act. Moreover, these cases "could profoundly affect individuals with a range of impairments—from diabetes and hypertension to severe nearsightedness and hearing loss—who are able to function in society with the help of medicines or aids but whose impairments may still make employers consider them ineligible for certain jobs."[80] Thus, pilots who need glasses to correct their vision cannot claim discrimination when employers fail to hire them even though their vision is correctable.[81] In the 2004 case of *Tennessee* v. *Lane*, however, the Court ruled 5–4 that disabled persons could sue states that failed to make reasonable accommodations to assure that courthouses are handicapped

Why is same-sex marriage controversial? The legalization of same-sex marriage in California in 2008 allowed gay couples committed to one another for decades to finally tie the knot. Here, lesbian activists Del Martin (87) and Phyllis Lyon (83)—partners for more than 50 years--are married by San Francisco Mayor Gavin Newsom. Unions such as this are opposed by many religious conservatives, who believe homosexuality is a sin and support only the rights of heterosexual couples to marry. Del Martin died in August of 2008, only a few months after her wedding, and the legal status of same-sex marriage in California is now in question.

SIMULATION

You are the Mayor and Need to Make Civil Rights Decisions

Accommodating College Students with Disabilities

Since the Americans with Disabilities Act (ADA) of 1990, universities across the United States have been trying to make facilities and services on campus more accessible to students with disabilities. According to the ADA, a disabled student is one who "has a physical or mental impairment that substantially limits major life activities." Not only are there testing and instructional modifications for students with learning disabilities, but wheelchair ramps, lifts, handlebars, and other accommodations have been put into place to assist those with physical disabilities.

The number of disabled students at colleges or universities has increased rapidly in recent years. Nearly 10 percent of the students in the State University of New York's system are considered disabled.[a] However, few universities have been fully effective in adapting facilities and services to meet the individual needs of these students. Many educational institutions lack formal structures and methods to help accommodate students with disabilities.[b] Failure to provide adequately maintained sidewalks, lack of benches and elevators, and the absence of listening systems in classrooms and auditoriums are among the many lapses. Fixing these problems has proven to be an expensive venture for educational systems, and some students have to pay for the services themselves.[c]

- How should schools pay for the staffing and equipment required to accommodate students with disabilities?
- Look for physical accommodations across your campus. Also, what programs or service are available for students with disabilities? Are the accommodations meeting the needs of the individuals who require them?

---

[a]National Council on Disability, *People with Disabilities and Postsecondary Education*.
[b]Robert A. Stodden, L. M. Galloway, and Norma Jean Stodden, "Secondary School Curricula Issues: Impact on Postsecondary Students with Disabilities," *Exceptional Children* 70 (2003): 9–25.
[c]Sara D. Knapp, "Disability Access at SUNY Campuses: 10 Years After the ADA," United University Professions' Disability Rights and Concerns Committee, April 2004, 19.

---

accessible.[82] (To learn more about the ADA's impact on college campuses, see Ideas into Action: Accommodating College Students with Disabilities.)

The largest national nonprofit organization lobbying for expanded civil rights for the disabled is the American Association of People with Disabilities (AAPD). Acting on behalf of the over 56 million Americans who suffer from some form of disability, it works in coalition with other disability organizations to assure that the ADA is implemented fully. AAPD was founded by activists who lobbied for the ADA and who recognized that "beyond national unity for ADA and our civil rights, people with disabilities did not have a venue or vehicle for working together for common goals."[83]

Civil rights groups such as the AAPD often find themselves working in concert with more radical disability rights groups such as Not Dead Yet. Not Dead Yet is one of many other disability groups actively opposing assisted suicide and euthanasia laws, believing that they infringe on the civil rights of people with disabilities, especially those who cannot advocate for themselves. Other groups, such as the National Right to Life Committee, best known for its anti-abortion work, also work to protect the rights of the disabled and elderly, believing that any attempts to withhold nourishment or treatment or to otherwise end life are basic violations of civil rights.

Who does the Americans with Disabilities Act protect? George Lane was the appellant *Tennessee v. Lane* (2004), which involved the scope of the Americans with Disabilities Act. Lane was forced to crawl up two flights of stairs to attend a state court hearing on a misdemeanor charge. Had he not, he could have been jailed.

Photo courtesy: Jason R. Davis/AP Wide World Photos

Toward Reform: Civil Rights, Affirmative Action, and Pay Equity

Since passage of major civil rights legislation in the 1960s and the Supreme Court's continued interest in upholding the civil rights of many groups, African Americans, women, Latino/as, American Indians, Asian and Pacific Americans, gays and lesbians, and the disabled have come much closer to the attainment of equal rights. Yet, all of these groups remain far from enjoying full equality under the Constitution and continue to seek reform by pushing for rights from all three branches of government. Enforcement of anti-discrimination laws varies, based on administration priorities as well as the resources of private individuals to fund challenges to perceived discriminatory practices. Private discrimination, which cannot be legislated against, is perhaps the major continuing source of discrimination.

Affirmative Action

The civil rights debate centers on the question of equality of opportunity versus equality of results. Most civil rights and women's rights organizations argue that the lingering and pervasive burdens of racism and sexism can be overcome only by taking race or gender into account in fashioning remedies for discrimination. They argue that the Constitution is not and should not be blind to color or sex.

Other groups believe that if it was once wrong to use labels to discriminate against a group, it should be wrong to use those same labels to help a group. They argue that laws should be neutral, or color-blind. According to this view, quotas and other forms of **affirmative action**, policies designed to give special attention or compensatory treatment to members of a previously disadvantaged group, should be illegal. (To learn more about affirmative action, see Figure 6.1.)

The debate over affirmative action and equality of opportunity became particularly intense during the presidential administration of Ronald Reagan. Shortly before his election, two court cases were generally decided in favor of affirmative action. In 1978, the Supreme Court for the first time fully addressed the issue of affirmative

affirmative action
Policies designed to give special attention or compensatory treatment to members of a previously disadvantaged group.

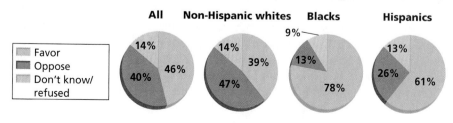

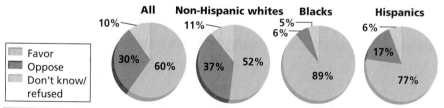

"Do you generally favor or oppose affirmative action programs for racial minorities?"

All — 10%, 30%, 60%
Non-Hispanic whites — 11%, 37%, 52%
Blacks — 5%, 6%, 89%
Hispanics — 6%, 17%, 77%

Favor / Oppose / Don't know/refused

"In order to overcome past discrimination, do you favor or oppose affirmative action programs, which give special preferences to qualified blacks in hiring and education?"

All — 14%, 40%, 46%
Non-Hispanic whites — 14%, 47%, 39%
Blacks — 9%, 13%, 78%
Hispanics — 13%, 26%, 61%

Favor / Oppose / Don't know/refused

FIGURE 6.1 Public Opinion on Affirmative Action

These pie charts present the results of two versions of a question about affirmative action in a survey conducted by the Pew Research Center. Which group of those who were polled is most supportive of affirmative action? Which group is least supportive? Describe how the "special preferences" wording in the second question affects support for affirmative action in each group surveyed.

Source: Pew Research Center, "Optimism About Black Progress Declines: Blacks See Growing Values Gap Between Poor and Middle Class," November 13, 2007.

Join the Debate

Determining a Living Wage

OVERVIEW: When the Reverend Martin Luther King Jr. was assassinated, he was visiting Memphis, Tennessee, to support African Americans in their struggle to raise poverty-level wages and to secure collective bargaining rights. As this chapter points out, there are various dimensions to civil rights. Economic justice is one of them. An example of such an economic justice issue is how best to determine the level of pay that workers should receive.

Most people are familiar with the concept of a minimum wage, which is the lowest hourly rate that employers can legally pay their workers. The federal government and all state governments except for Tennessee, Alabama, Mississippi, Louisiana, and South Carolina have passed laws setting a minimum wage. The federal minimum wage as of July 24, 2008, is $6.55 an hour. Thirty-four states mandate a higher rate than the federal minimum. A limitation of the minimum wage is that it is arbitrary and, because of political stalemates in Congress, may not change from year to year. The federal minimum wage was $5.15 per hour from 1997 to 2007—and because of inflation, the 2007 rate was worth only $4.04 when compared to a decade earlier.

In contrast to the minimum wage, a living wage refers to how much a person needs to earn in order to pay for a satisfactory level of housing, food, utilities, transportation, and health care. Since costs vary over time and vary depending on where you live, the living wage differs from place to place and changes over time.

College students around the country have been visible in the campaign for the adoption of living wage policies. United Students Against Sweatshops (USAS) has organized chapters on over sixty campuses and helped organize protests and other activities to get universities to commit to paying their employees at least a living wage. USAS has won victories at Georgetown, Stanford, Harvard, Washington University, and the University of Wisconsin–Madison.

The Association of Community Organizations for Reform Now (ACORN) is the nation's oldest and largest grassroots organization of low- and moderate-income people. ACORN'S over 200,000 members have pressed in almost ninety cities to get living wage ordinances adopted. These efforts have been successful in places like San Francisco, California; Madison, Wisconson, and Baltimore, Maryland. In 2007, Maryland enacted a living wage law covering the entire state.

Chambers of Commerce and other representatives of businesses warn that the victories achieved by living wage advocates are temporary and costly. The general philosophical argument is that market forces, not politics and government, should set wages.

Living wage opponents also argue that there are alternatives to living wage mandates if one is concerned about low-income people. There are public programs providing food stamps, energy and housing assistance, and other welfare programs for needy families and individuals. Those concerned about the adoption of living wage laws object in part because they do not see why a change is necessary.

Another concern with the concept of a living wage is the complexity of incorporating geographic variation. In response to this concern, Amy Glasmeier, director of the Pennsylvania State University Center for Policy Research on Energy, Environment, and Community Well-Being, has developed an online calculator that determines a living wage for specific communities throughout the United States. She uses federal government data from the Census Bureau, the Department of Agriculture, and the Department of Housing and Urban Development and includes a sample list of jobs and wages for each community.

action. Alan Bakke, a thirty-one-year-old paramedic, sought admission to several medical schools and was rejected because of his age. The next year, he applied to the University of California at Davis and was placed on its waiting list. The Davis Medical School maintained two separate admission committees—one for white students and another for minority students. Bakke was not admitted to the school, although his grades and standardized test scores were higher than those of all of the African American students admitted to the school. In *Regents of the University of California* v. *Bakke* (1978), a sharply divided Court concluded that Bakke's rejection had been illegal because the use of strict quotas was inappropriate.[84] The medical school, however, was free to "take race into account," said the Court.

Arguments IN FAVOR of a Living Wage

- If people are working full-time, they should at least be able to afford basic housing, food, and other necessities for life. This is an issue of fairness and common sense, as has long been recognized. In 1891, for example, Pope Leo XIII issued an encyclical on economic justice. A fundamental right of individuals is to be able to survive if they work full-time for someone else.

- The living wage is sensitive to geographic variations in costs and changes in costs over time. The living wage concept is superior to the minimum wage because it is not static or arbitrary. Public policy supporting a living wage is essentially reminding employers to be realistic in setting wages, and to be responsive to local conditions rather than a national or statewide standard.

- Living wages will eliminate the need for many government welfare programs. The current system is unfair not only toward workers but also toward taxpayers. In the absence of a living wage requirement, employers are able to pay extremely low wages while their workers turn to the government for food stamps, housing assistance, and the like. This system essentially provides government subsidies so that companies may have low labor costs and higher profits.

Arguments AGAINST a Living Wage

- Governments should not be setting wages; that is the role of the market. The lowest wages go to the most unskilled and plentiful labor. Individuals who want to increase their earnings should select a job or career path where their labor is more valued in the economy, instead of putting political pressure on the government. The government sets artificial wages and is bound to disrupt natural market forces.

- Adoption of a living wage policy will result in loss of business and unemployment. By increasing labor costs through a living wage policy, government will force businesses to reduce the number of workers or to move to a community that doesn't have such a requirement. A business has to make a profit in order to survive and grow. Governments and communities benefit much more by encouraging business growth and development than by forcing businesses to reduce their workforce or close altogether.

- A living wage policy is going to hurt consumers. If government arbitrarily and artificially increases labor costs for businesses, some of those businesses are going to close, and consumers will no longer have access to those services or products. When businesses close, that affects general competition, which is important in keeping prices down and quality up. Again, consumers lose. And, as businesses pass their increased labor costs along to consumers by raising prices, consumers will not get more, but they will pay more.

Continuing the Debate

1. Is it the role of government to ensure a living wage for all workers? Why are why not?
2. Is it likely that employers will close or move their businesses rather than comply with a living wage law? Explain your reasoning.

To Follow the Debate Online, Go To:

www.livingwagecampaign.org, Association of Community Organizations for Reform Now (ACORN), which includes information about their campaign for a living wage and instructions for organizing at a local level.

www.ncpa.org, National Center for Policy Analysis, a nonprofit, nonpartisan organization that advocates for policy alternatives to government regulation and involvement in American business. They oppose living wage policies.

www.livingwage.geog.psu.edu, An online calculator identifies the living wage for a specific community. The information for each community includes housing, food, and other costs that determine the living wage and a sample list of jobs and wages in the community.

Bakke was followed by a 1979 case in which the Court ruled that a factory and a union could voluntarily adopt a quota system in selecting black workers over more senior white workers for a training program. These kinds of programs outraged blue-collar Americans who traditionally had voted for the Democratic Party. In 1980, they abandoned the party in droves to support Ronald Reagan, an ardent foe of affirmative action.

For a while, despite the addition of Reagan-appointed Justice Sandra Day O'Connor to the Court, the Court continued to uphold affirmative action plans, especially when there was clear-cut evidence of prior discrimination. In 1987, for example, the Court ruled for the first time that a public employer could use a voluntary plan to promote women even if there was no judicial finding of prior discrimination.[85]

In all these affirmative action cases, the Reagan administration strongly urged the Court to invalidate the plans in question, but to no avail. With changes on the Court, however, including the 1986 elevation of William H. Rehnquist, a strong opponent of affirmative action, to chief justice, the continued efforts of the Reagan administration finally began to pay off as the Court heard a new series of cases signaling an end to the advances in civil rights law. In a three-month period in 1989, the Supreme Court handed down five civil rights decisions limiting affirmative action programs and making it harder to prove employment discrimination.

In February 1990, congressional and civil rights leaders unveiled legislation designed to overrule the Court's rulings, which, according to the bill's sponsor, "were an abrupt and unfortunate departure from its historic vigilance in protecting the rights of minorities."[86] The bill passed both houses of Congress but was vetoed by President Reagan's successor, George Bush, and Congress failed to override the veto. In late 1991, however, Congress and the White House reached a compromise on a weaker version of the civil rights bill, which was passed by overwhelming majorities in both houses of Congress. The Civil Rights Act of 1991 overruled the five Supreme Court rulings noted above.

The Supreme Court, however, has not stayed silent on the issue. In 1995, the Court ruled that Congress, like the states, must show that affirmative action programs meet the strict scrutiny test outlined in Table 6.1.[87] In 1996, the 5th U.S. Circuit Court of Appeals also ruled that the University of Texas Law School's affirmative action admissions program was unconstitutional, throwing the college and university admissions programs in Texas, Oklahoma, and Mississippi into turmoil. Later that year, the U.S. Supreme Court refused to hear the case, thereby allowing the Court of Appeals decision to stand.[88]

By 2002, the U.S. Supreme Court once again found the affirmative action issue ripe for review. In *Grutter* v. *Bollinger* (2003), the Court voted to uphold the constitutionality of the University of Michigan's law school admissions policy, which gave preference to minority applicants.[89] However, in a companion case, the Court struck down Michigan's undergraduate point system, which gave minority applicants twenty automatic points simply because they were minorities.[90]

Taken together, these cases set the stage for a new era in affirmative action in the United States. Although the use of strict quotas and automatic points is not constitutional, the Court clearly believes that there is a place for some preferential treatment, at least until greater racial and ethnic parity is achieved. However, as Justice Sandra Day O'Connor noted in *Grutter*, "a program must remain flexible enough to ensure that each applicant is evaluated as an individual and not in a way that makes an applicant's race or ethnicity the defining feature of his or her application."[91]

Pay Equity and Other Issues of Workplace Discrimination

Comparing Civil Rights

Race is not the only issue that continues to breed civil rights controversies. In fact, one of the largest barriers faced by minority groups living in the United States is the issue of pay equity, which, as already discussed, has an especially significant impact on female workers. The issue of pay equity for women received national attention through a lawsuit filed against the nation's largest employer, Wal-Mart. Six California women filed a claim against the chain, charging that they were the victims of gender discrimination.[92] These women asserted that they were paid lower wages and offered fewer opportunities for advancement than their male colleagues. In June 2004, a federal judge broadened their class action suit to include 1.6 million women. The lawsuit is still pending before the 9th Circuit Court of Appeals. Meanwhile, similar suits have been filed by employees at other big box stores, including Costco. (To learn more about a controversy related to pay equity, see Join the Debate: Determining a Living Wage.)

In 2007, the Supreme Court took up the issue of pay equity. The justices heard the case of Lilly Ledbetter, the lone female supervisor at a Goodyear tire factory in Alabama. Ledbetter charged that sex discrimination throughout her career had led her to earn substantially less than her male counterparts. In a 5–4 decision, the Court ruled that Ledbetter and other women could not seek redress of grievances for discrimination that had occurred over a period of years. Justice Ruth Bader Ginsburg, who litigated many landmark women's rights cases as an attorney for the ACLU Women's Rights Project, took the uncommon action of reading her dissent from the bench. Speaking for herself and Justices David Souter, John Paul Stevens, and Stephen Breyer, she noted, "In our view, the court does not comprehend, or is indifferent to, the insidious way in which women can be victims of pay discrimination."[93]

Pay equity has also been a concern for Lationo/as and other immigrants. Nine illegal immigrants who worked as janitors at Wal-Marts in New Jersey are suing the company for discriminating against them by paying them lower wages and giving them fewer benefits based solely on their ethnic origin. Another group of Wal-Mart employees from twenty-one states is also suing the corporation, claiming that executives knowingly conspired to hire illegal immigrants and, in doing so, violated the workers' civil rights by refusing to pay Social Security and other wage compensation benefits.[94] These suits are representative of a growing trend in discrimination suits filed by immigrants who believe they have been persecuted or disadvantaged following changes in security and immigration law since the September 11, 2001, terrorist attacks.

In fact, many of the Latino/a and other groups discussed in this chapter have been forced to devote significant portions of their time to immigration cases rather than workplace discrimination issues because the Civil Rights Division, as noted in our opening vignette, continues to allocate lawyers' resources toward immigration issues.

 ## WHAT SHOULD I HAVE LEARNED?

While the Framers and other Americans basked in the glory of the newly adopted Constitution and Bill of Rights, their protections did not extend to all Americans. In this chapter, we have shown how rights have been expanded to ever-increasing segments of the population. To that end, we have addressed the following questions:

■ **What should I know about the roots of suffrage from 1800 through 1890?**
When the Framers tried to compromise on the issue of slavery, they only postponed dealing with a volatile question that eventually would rip the nation apart. Ultimately, the Civil War was fought to end slavery. Among its results were the triumph of the abolitionist position and the adoption of the Thirteenth, Fourteenth, and Fifteenth Amendments. During this period, women also sought expanded rights, especially the right to vote, but to no avail.

■ **How did African Americans and women push for equality from 1890 through 1954?**
Although the Civil War Amendments were added to the Constitution, the Supreme Court limited their application. As Jim Crow laws were passed throughout the South, the NAACP was founded in the early 1900s to press for equal rights for African Americans. Women's groups also were active during this period, successfully lobbying for passage of the Nineteenth Amendment, which assured them the right to vote. Groups such as the National Consumers' League (NCL) began to view litigation as a means to an end, and went court to to argue for the constitutionality of legislation protecting women workers.

■ **What should I know about the civil rights movement?**
In 1954, the U.S. Supreme Court ruled in *Brown v. Board of Education* that racially-segregated state school systems were unconstitutional. This victory empowered African Americans as they sought an end to other forms of pervasive

discrimination. Bus boycotts, sit-ins, freedom rides, pressure for voting rights, and massive nonviolent demonstrations became common tactics. This activity culminated in the passage of the Civil Rights Act of 1964, which gave African Americans another weapon in their legal arsenal.

■ **What should I know about the women's rights movement?**
After passage of the Civil Rights Act, a new women's rights movement arose. Several women's rights groups were created, and while some sought a constitutional amendment, others attempted to litigate under the equal protection clause. Over the years, the Supreme Court developed different tests to determine the constitutionality of various forms of discrimination. In general, strict scrutiny, the most stringent standard, was applied to race-based claims. An intermediate standard of review was developed to assess the constitutionality of sex discrimination claims.

■ **How did other groups mobilize for their civil rights?**
Building on the successes of African Americans and women, other groups, including Latino/as, American Indians, Asian and Pacific Americans, gays and lesbians, and the disabled, organized to litigate for expanded civil rights as well as to lobby for anti-discrimination laws.

■ **What should I know about reforms related to affirmative action and pay equity?**
The groups discussed in this chapter have yet to reach full equality. One policy, affirmative action, which was designed to remedy education and employment discrimination, continues to be very controversial. Gays, women, and immigrants continue to use the courts to seek remedies for costly employment discrimination.

Key Terms

affirmative action, p. 227
Black Codes, p. 197
Brown v. *Board of Education* (1954), p. 204
civil rights, p. 194
Civil Rights Act of 1964, p. 209
Civil Rights Cases (1883), p. 199
de facto discrimination, p. 210
de jure discrimination, p. 210

Equal Employment Opportunity Commission, p. 212
equal protection clause, p. 204
Fifteenth Amendment, p. 199
Fourteenth Amendment, p. 198
grandfather clause, p. 200
Jim Crow laws, p. 199
Nineteenth Amendment, p. 202
Plessy v. *Ferguson* (1896), p. 200

poll tax, p. 200
strict scrutiny, p. 213
suffrage movement, p. 202
suspect classification, p. 213
Thirteenth Amendment, p. 197
Title IX, p. 215
Women's Equality Amendment, p. 213

Researching Civil Rights

In the Library

Anderson, Terry H. *The Pursuit of Fairness: A History of Affirmative Action*. New York: Oxford University Press, 2005.

Delgado, Richard. *Justice at War: Civil Liberties and Civil Rights During Times of Crisis*. New York: New York University Press, 2005.

Freeman, Jo. *The Politics of Women's Liberation*. New York: Backinprint.com, 2000.

Guinier, Lani, and Susan Sturm. *Who's Qualified?* Boston: Beacon, 2001.

Kluger, Richard. *Simple Justice*, reprint ed. New York: Vintage, 2004.

Longmore, Paul, and Lauri Umansky. *The New Disability History: American Perspectives*. New York: New York University Press, 2001.

Mansbridge, Jane J. *Why We Lost the ERA*. Chicago: University of Chicago Press, 1986.

McClain, Paula D., and Joseph Stewart Jr. *"Can We All Get Along?": Racial and Ethnic Minorities in American Politics*, 4th ed. Boulder, CO: Westview, 2005.

McGlen, Nancy E., et al. *Women, Politics, and American Society*, 4th ed. New York: Longman, 2004.

Ramakrishnan, S. Karthick. *Democracy in Immigrant America: Changing Demographics and Political Participation*. Stanford, CA: Stanford University Press, 2005.

Reed, Adolph, Jr., ed. *Without Justice for All: The New Liberalism and Our Retreat from Racial Equity*. Boulder, CO: Westview, 2001.

Rodriguez, Clara E. *Changing Race: Latinos, the Census, and the History of Ethnicity in the United States*. New York: New York University Press, 2000.

Rosales, F. Arturo. *Chicano! The History of the Mexican American Civil Rights Movement*. Houston, TX: Arte Publico, 1996.

Wilkins, David E. *American Indian Politics and the American Political System*. New York: Rowman and Littlefield, 2006.

Williams, Juan. *Eyes on the Prize: America's Civil Rights Years, 1954–1965*. New York: Penguin, 1987.

Wilson, William Julius. *The Bridge over the Racial Divide: Rising Inequality and Coalition Politics*, 2nd ed. Berkeley: University of California Press, 2001.

Zia, Hellen. *Asian American Dreams: The Emergence of an American People*. New York: Farrar, Straus and Giroux, 2000.

On the Web

To learn more about the Civil Rights Division of the Department of Justice and its priorities, go to **www.usdoj.gov/crt/**.

To learn more about civil rights issues in the United States, go to **www.civilrights.org,** where a coalition of 150 civil rights organizations provides coverage of a host of civil rights issues as well as links to breaking news related to civil rights.

To read the full text of *Brown v. Board of Education* (1954) and other civil rights Supreme Court opinions, go to **www.oyez.org** and search the case name.

To learn more about the civil rights era, go to the African American Odyssey section of the Library of Congress, **memory.loc.gov/ammem/aaohtml/exhibit/aointro.html,** and click on the last section, Civil Rights.

To learn more about the ACLU Women's Rights Project, go to **www.aclu.org/womensrights/index.html.**

To learn more about MALDEF, go to **www.maldef.org.**

To learn more about Asian and Pacific American civil rights, go to the Web site for the Asian American Justice Center, **www.napalc.org.**

To learn more about the Native American Rights Fund, go to **www.narf.org.**

To learn more about the controversy surrounding same-sex marriage go to the Pew Forum on Religion and Public Life site, **pewforum.org/gay-marriage/.**

To learn more about disability advocacy groups, go to the Web site for the American Association of People with Disabilities, **www.aapd.com.**

7

Congress

On February 6, 2002, Representative Nancy Pelosi (D–CA) broke through a glass ceiling when she was sworn in as the Democratic House whip, becoming the first woman in history to win an elected position in the formal leadership of the U.S. House of Representatives.[1] The whip position has long been viewed as a stepping stone to becoming the Speaker of the House. House Speakers Tip O'Neill (D–MA) and Newt Gingrich (R–GA) were both former whips. As whip, it was Pelosi's responsibility to convince Democratic members of the House to vote together on the full range of bills before the 107th Congress.

First elected to Congress from California in 1986, Pelosi quickly made her mark as an advocate for human rights in China and as an effective fundraiser. Her fund-raising skills and years of experience in the House, in fact, helped her win the hotly contested race for the whip position. As part of the House leadership, she became the first woman to attend critical White House meetings, where, said Pelosi, "Susan B. Anthony and others are with me."[2]

Although the president's party traditionally loses seats in midterm elections, in 2002 House Republicans actually increased their majority. Critics charged that the Democrats lacked a consistent message. Therefore, soon after the election results were in, House Minority Leader Richard Gephardt (D–MO) resigned from his position, leaving Pelosi in line to succeed him. Representative Harold Ford (D–TN), one of the youngest members of the House, threw his hat into the ring to oppose Pelosi's campaign for the leader's position. Ford, a moderate, charged that Pelosi, who already was being referred to by conservatives as a "San Francisco liberal," was simply too liberal to lead the Democrats back to political viability in the 2004 elections. A majority of the members of the House Democratic Caucus, however, did not appear fazed by these charges; Pelosi was elected minority leader by an overwhelming majority of the caucus members.

In 2006, when Democrats regained control of Congress, Pelosi was catapulted into the role of Speaker. In shattering what she termed "the marble ceiling" as Speaker of the House, Pelosi became the first woman to hold that position and is second in line of succession to the presidency. Thus, more than 150 years after women first sought the right to vote, a female member of Congress now leads the House of Representatives.

■ The position of Speaker of the House has changed dramatically in the last 200 years. At left is House Speaker Henry Clay of Kentucky, the first powerful Speaker of the House. At right is current House Speaker Nancy Pelosi, shown celebrating Democratic gains in the 2006 congressional elections.

WHAT SHOULD I KNOW ABOUT . . .

■ the roots of the legislative branch of government?
■ how Congress is organized?
■ the members of Congress?
■ how members of Congress make decisions?
■ the law-making function of Congress?
■ congressional checks on the executive and judicial branches of government?

235

TO LEARN MORE—

—TO DO MORE

Go to www.opensecrets.org to learn if candidates receiving financial support from House Speaker Nancy Pelosi were successful.

The Framers' original conception of the representational function of Congress was much narrower than it is today. Instead of regarding members of Congress as representatives of the people, those in attendance at the Constitutional Convention were extremely concerned with creating a legislative body that would be able to make laws to govern the new nation. Over time, Congress has attempted to maintain the role of a law- and policy-making institution, but changes in the demands made on the national government have allowed the executive and judicial branches to gain powers at the expense of the legislative. Moreover, the power and the importance of individual members have grown. Thus, the public doesn't think much about Congress itself, but somewhat ironically, citizens hold their own elected representatives in high esteem.

The dual roles that Congress plays contribute to this divide in public opinion. Members of Congress must combine and balance the roles of lawmaker and policy maker with being a representative of their district, their state, their party, and sometimes their race, ethnicity, or gender. Not surprisingly, this balancing act often results in role conflict.

In this chapter, we will analyze the powers of Congress and the competing roles members of Congress play as they represent the interests of their constituents, make laws, and oversee the actions of the other two branches of government. We will also see that as these functions have changed throughout U.S. history, so has Congress itself.

★ First, we will examine *the roots of* Congress—*the legislative branch of government*.

★ Second, we will describe *how Congress is organized*. We will compare the two chambers and how their differences affect the course of legislation.

★ Third, we will look at *the members of Congress*, including how members get elected, and how they spend their days.

★ Fourth, we will examine the various factors that influence *how members* of Congress *make decisions*.

★ Fifth, we will outline *the law-making function of Congress*.

★ Finally, we will examine *reform efforts* and *congressional checks on the executive and judicial branches of government*.

Roots of the Legislative Branch of Government

Article I of the Constitution describes the structure of the legislative branch of government we know today. As discussed in chapter 2, the Great Compromise at the Constitutional Convention resulted in the creation of an upper house, the Senate, and a lower house, the House of Representatives. Any two-house legislature, such as the one created by the Framers, is called a **bicameral legislature.** Each state is represented in the Senate by two senators, regardless of the state's population. The number of representatives each state sends to the House of Representatives, in contrast, is determined by that state's population.

The U.S. Constitution sets out the formal, or legal, requirements for membership in the House and Senate. As agreed to at the Constitutional Convention, House mem-

bicameral legislature
A legislature divided into two houses; the U.S. Congress and the state legislatures are bicameral except Nebraska, which is unicameral.

bers are to be at least twenty-five years of age; senators, thirty. Members of the House are required to be citizens of the United States for at least seven years; those elected to the Senatemust have been citizens for at least nine years. Both representatives and senators must be legal residents of the states from which they are elected. Historically, many members of Congress have moved to their states specifically to run for office. In 1964, U.S. Attorney General Robert Kennedy moved to New York to launch a successful campaign for the Senate, as did Hillary Clinton in 2000. Less successful was former Republican presidential hopeful Alan Keyes, who moved from Maryland to run unsuccessfully for the U.S. Senate in Illinois against Barack Obama in 2006.

Senators are elected for six-year terms, and originally they were elected by state legislatures because the Framers intended for senators to represent their states' interests in the Senate. State legislators lost this influence over the Senate with the ratification of the Seventeenth Amendment in 1913, which provides for the direct election of senators by voters. Then, as now, one-third of all senators are up for reelection every two years.

Members of the House of Representatives are elected to two-year terms by a vote of the eligible electorate in each congressional district. The Framers expected that House members would be more responsible to the people, both because they were elected directly by them and because they were up for reelection every two years.

The U.S. Constitution requires that a census, which entails the counting of all Americans, be conducted every ten years. Until the first census could be taken, the Constitution fixed the number of representatives in the House of Representatives at sixty-five. In 1790, one member represented about 30,000 people. But, as the population of the new nation grew and states were added to the union, the House became larger and larger. In 1910, it expanded to 435 members, and in 1929, its size was fixed at that number by statute. When Alaska and Hawaii became states in the 1950s, the number of seats was increased to 437. The number reverted back to 435 in 1963. In 2008, the average number of people in a district was 693,000.

Thinking Globally

Bicameral and Unicameral Legislatures Worldwide

Among the nations of the world, the most common legislative model is the bicameral parliament, congress, or assembly, with a lower chamber and an upper chamber—as in the United Kingdom, Canada, Australia, and the United States. However, a unicameral system—a single legislative body—is used in several established democracies, including Denmark, Sweden, Israel, New Zealand, South Korea, and Singapore.

- How would replacing the U.S. House and Senate with a single body affect the legislative process?
- Are unicameral systems likely to be more or less powerful than their bicameral counterparts? What are the potential weaknesses of a unicameral system? What are the potential weaknesses of a bicameral system?

Photo courtesy: Brendan Smialowski/The New York Times

Who runs for the U.S. Senate?
Cousins Tom Udall (D–NM) and Mark Udall (D–CO) ran for and won seats in the U.S. Senate in 2008. Here, they are shown on Capitol Hill posing in front of a photo of former presidential candidate Morris Udall, Mark's father.

Congressional Redistricting

apportionment
The process of allotting congressional seats to each state following the decennial census according to their proportion of the population.

redistricting
The redrawing of congressional districts to reflect increases or decreases in seats allotted to the states, as well as population shifts within a state.

bill
A proposed law.

Each state is allotted its share of these 435 representatives based on its population. After each U.S. Census, the number of seats allotted to each state is adjusted by a constitutionally mandated process called **apportionment.** After seats are apportioned, congressional districts must be redrawn by state legislatures to reflect population shifts to ensure that each member in Congress represents approximately the same number of residents. This process of redrawing congressional districts to reflect increases or decreases in the number of seats allotted to a state, as well as population shifts within a state, is called **redistricting.** The Supreme Court has ruled that states may redraw districts more frequently than after each U.S. Census. The legal controversies and effects of redistricting are discussed in chapter 13.

The Constitution specifically gives Congress its most important power: the authority to make laws. (To learn more about the powers of Congress, see Table 7.1.) No **bill** (proposed law) can become law without the consent of both houses. Examples of other powers shared by both houses include the power to declare war, raise an army and navy, coin money, regulate commerce, establish the federal courts and their jurisdiction, establish rules of immigration and naturalization, and "make all Laws which shall be necessary and proper for carrying into Execution the foregoing Powers." As interpreted by the U.S. Supreme Court, the necessary and proper clause, found at the end of Article I, section 8, when coupled with one or more of the specific powers enumerated in Article I, section 8, has allowed Congress to increase the scope of its authority, often at the expense of the states and into areas not necessarily envisioned by the Framers.

Congress alone is given formal law-making powers in the Constitution. But, it is important to remember that presidents issue proclamations and executive orders with the force of law (see chapter 8), bureaucrats issue quasi-legislative rules and are charged with enforcing laws, rules, and regulations (see chapter 9), and the Supreme Court and lower federal courts render opinions that generate principles that also have the force of law (see chapter 10).

Reflecting the different constituencies and size of each house of Congress (as well as the Framers' intentions), Article I gives special, exclusive powers to each house in addition to their shared role in law-making. For example, as noted in Table 7.2, the Constitution specifies that all revenue bills must originate in the House of Representatives. Over the years, however, this mandate has been blurred, and it is not unusual to

TABLE **7.1**   The Powers of Congress

The powers of Congress, found in Article I, section 8, of the Constitution, include the power to:

- Lay and collect taxes and duties
- Borrow money
- Regulate commerce with foreign nations and among the states
- Establish rules for naturalization (that is, the process of becoming a citizen) and bankruptcy
- Coin money, set its value, and fix the standard of weights and measures
- Punish counterfeiting
- Establish a post office and post roads
- Issue patents and copyrights
- Define and punish piracies, felonies on the high seas, and crimes against the law of nations
- Create courts inferior to (that is, below) the U.S. Supreme Court
- Declare war
- Raise and support an army and navy and make rules for their governance
- Provide for a militia (reserving to the states the right to appoint militia officers and to train militias under congressional rules)
- Exercise legislative powers over the seat of government (the District of Columbia) and over places purchased to be federal facilities (forts, arsenals, dockyards, and "other needful buildings")
- "Make all Laws which shall be necessary and proper for carrying into Execution the foregoing Powers, and all other Powers vested by this Constitution in the government of the United States" (Note: This "necessary and proper," or "elastic," clause has been interpreted expansively by the Supreme Court, as explained in chapter 2 and in the Annotated Constitution.)

see budget bills being considered simultaneously in both houses, especially since, ultimately, each must approve all bills, whether or not they involve revenues. The House also has the power to charge the president, vice president, or other "civil officers," including federal judges, with "Treason, Bribery, or other high Crimes and Misdemeanors." Only the Senate is authorized to conduct trials of **impeachment,** with a two-thirds yea vote being necessary before a federal official can be removed from office.

While the House and Senate share in the impeachment process, the Senate has the sole authority to approve major presidential appointments, including federal judges, ambassadors, and Cabinet- and sub-Cabinet-level positions. The Senate, too, must approve all presidential treaties by a two-thirds vote. Failure by the president to court the Senate can be costly. At the end of World War I, for example, President Woodrow Wilson worked hard to get other nations to accept the Treaty of Versailles, which contained the charter of the proposed League of Nations. He overestimated his support in the Senate, however. That body refused to ratify the treaty, dealing Wilson and his international stature a severe setback.

impeachment
The power delegated to the House of Representatives in the Constitution to charge the president, vice president, or other "civil officers," including federal judges, with "Treason, Bribery, or other high Crimes and Misdemeanors." This is the first step in the constitutional process of removing such government officials from office.

How Congress Is Organized

Every two years, a new Congress is seated. After ascertaining the formal qualifications of new members, the Congress organizes itself as it prepares for the business of the coming session. Among the first items on its agenda are the election of new leaders and the adoption of rules for conducting its business. Each house has a hierarchical leadership structure that is closely tied to the key role of political parties in organizing Congress.

TABLE 7.2 Key Differences Between the House of Representatives and the Senate

Constitutional Differences	
House	**Senate**
435 voting members (apportioned by population)	100 voting members (two from each state)
Two-year terms	Six-year terms (one-third up for reelection every two years)
Initiates all revenue bills	Offers "advice and consent" on many major presidential appointments
Initiates impeachment procedures and passes articles of impeachment	Tries impeached officials
	Approves treaties

Differences in Operation	
House	**Senate**
More centralized, more formal; stronger leadership	Less centralized, less formal; weaker leadership
Committee on Rules fairly powerful in controlling time and rules of debate (in conjunction with the Speaker of the House)	No rules committee; limits on debate come through unanimous consent or cloture of filibuster
More impersonal	More personal
Power distributed less evenly	Power distributed more evenly
Members are highly specialized	Members are generalists
Emphasizes tax and revenue policy	Emphasizes foreign policy

Changes in the Institution	
House	**Senate**
Power centralized in the Speaker's inner circle of advisers	Senate workload increasing and institution becoming more formal; threat of filibusters more frequent than in the past
House procedures becoming more efficient	Becoming more difficult to pass legislation
Turnover is relatively high, although those seeking reelection almost always win	Turnover is moderate

majority party
The political party in each house of
Congress with the most members.

minority party
The political party in each house of
Congress with the second most
members.

The Role of Political Parties in Organizing Congress

As demonstrated in Figure 7.1, the organization of both houses of Congress is closely tied to political parties and their strength in each house. The basic division in Congress is between majority and minority parties. The **majority party** is the party in each house with the most members. The **minority party** is the party in each house with the second most members. (To learn more about the 111th Congress, see Figure 7.2.)

Parties play a key role in the committee system, an organizational feature of Congress that facilitates its law-making and oversight functions. The committees, controlled by the majority party in each house of Congress, often set the agendas, although in recent years chairs' power eroded substantially in the House of Representatives as the Speaker's power was enhanced.[3]

At the beginning of each new Congress—the 111th Congress, for example, will sit in two sessions, one in 2009 and one in 2010—the members of each party gather in their party caucus or conference. Historically, these caucuses have enjoyed varied powers, but today the party caucuses—now called caucus by House Democrats and conference by House and Senate Republicans and Senate Democrats—have several roles, including nominating or electing party officers, reviewing committee assignments, discussing party policy, imposing party discipline, setting party themes, and coordinating

The Power of
the Speaker of the House

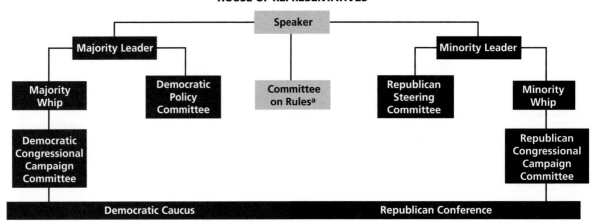

FIGURE 7.1 Organizational Structure of the House of Representatives and the Senate in the 111th Congress

Source: Adapted from Roger H. Davidson and Walter J. Oleszek, *Congress and its Members,* 10th ed. (Washington, DC: CQ Press, 2006.) Updated by the authors.

media, including talk radio. Conference and caucus chairs are recognized party leaders who work with other leaders in the House or Senate.[4]

Each caucus or conference has specialized committees that fulfill certain tasks. House Republicans, for example, have a Committee on Committees that makes committee assignments. The Democrats' Steering Committee performs this function. Each party also has congressional campaign committees to assist members in their reelection bids.

The House of Representatives

Even in the first Congress in 1789, the House of Representatives was almost three times larger than the Senate. It is not surprising, then, that from the beginning the House has been organized more tightly, structured more elaborately, and governed by stricter rules. Traditionally, loyalty to the party leadership and voting along party lines has been more common in the House than in the Senate. House leaders also play a key role in moving the business of the House along. Historically, the Speaker of the

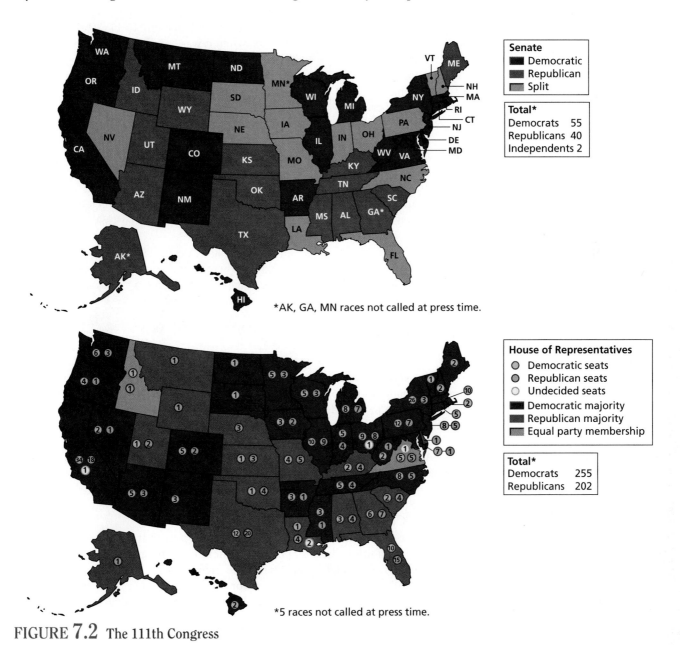

FIGURE 7.2 The 111th Congress

The Living Constitution

The Congress shall have power . . . to establish a uniform Rule of Naturalization.

—ARTICLE 1, SECTION 8, CLAUSE 4

This article reiterates the sovereign power of the nation and places authority to draft laws concerning naturalization in the hands of Congress. Congress's power over naturalization is exclusive—meaning that no state can bestow U.S. citizenship on anyone. Citizenship is a privilege and Congress may make laws limiting or expanding the criteria.

The word *citizen* was not defined constitutionally until ratification in 1868 of the Fourteenth Amendment, which sets forth two kinds of citizenship: by birth and through naturalization. Throughout American history, Congress has imposed a variety of limits on naturalization, originally restricting it to "free, white persons." "Orientals" were excluded from eligibility in 1882. At one time those affiliated with the Communist Party and those who lacked "good moral character" (a phrase that was construed to bar homosexuals, drunkards, gamblers, and adulterers) were deemed unfit for citizenship. These restrictions no longer carry the force of law, but they do underscore the power of Congress in this matter.

Congress continues to retain the right to naturalize large classes of individuals, as it did in 2000 when it granted automatic citizenship rights to all

minor children adopted abroad as long as both adoptive parents were American citizens. Naturalized citizens, however, do not necessarily enjoy the full rights of citizenship enjoyed by other Americans. Congress at any time, subject only to Supreme Court review, can limit the rights and liberties of naturalized citizens, especially in times of national crisis. In the wake of the September 11, 2001, terrorist attacks, when it was revealed that one-third of the forty-eight al-Qaeda-linked operatives who took part in some sort of terrorist activities against the United States were lawful permanent residents or naturalized citizens, Congress called for greater screening by the U.S. Citizenship and Immigration Service for potential terrorists.

CRITICAL THINKING QUESTIONS

1. Is Congress the appropriate institution to have the power over immigration and naturalization? Why or why not?
2. Is racial profiling by the U.S. Citizenship and Immigration Service and other government entities an appropriate action in the name of national security? Why or why not?

House, the majority and minority leaders, and the Republican and Democratic House whips have made up the party leadership that runs Congress. This group now has been expanded to include deputy whips of both parties, as well as those who head the Democratic Caucus and the Republican Conference.

Speaker of the House
The only officer of the House of Representatives specifically mentioned in the Constitution; elected at the beginning of each new Congress by the entire House; traditionally a member of the majority party.

THE SPEAKER OF THE HOUSE The **Speaker of the House** is the only officer of the House of Representatives specifically mentioned in the Constitution. The office, the chamber's most powerful position, is modeled after a similar one in the British Parliament—the Speaker was the one who spoke to the king and conveyed the wishes of the House of Commons to the monarch.[5]

The entire House of Representatives elects the Speaker at the beginning of each new Congress. Traditionally, the Speaker is a member of the majority party, as are all committee chairs. Although typically not the member with the longest service, the Speaker generally has served in the House for a long time and in other House leadership positions as an apprenticeship. The current Speaker, Nancy Pelosi (D–CA), spent almost twenty years in the House; her predecessor, Dennis Hastert (R–IL), was in office twelve years before being elected to the position.

The Speaker presides over the House of Representatives, oversees House business, and is the official spokesperson for the House, as well as being second in the line of presidential succession. Moreover, the Speaker is the House liaison with the president and generally has great political influence within the chamber. The Speaker is also expected to smooth the passage of party-backed legislation through the House.

The first powerful Speaker was Henry Clay (R–KY). Serving in Congress at a time when turnover was high, he was elected to the position in 1810, his first term in office. He was the Speaker of the House for a total of six terms—longer than anyone else in the nineteenth century.

By the late 1800s, the House ceased to have a revolving door and the length of members' average stays in the House increased. With this new professionalization of the House came professionalization in the position of Speaker. Between 1896 and 1910, a series of Speakers initiated changes that brought more power to the office as the Speaker largely took control of committee assignments and the appointing of committee chairs. Institutional and personal rule reached its height during the 1903–1910 tenure of Speaker Joe Cannon (R–IL).

Negative reaction to those strong Speakers eventually led to a revolt in 1910 and 1911 in the House and to a reduction of the formal powers of the Speaker. As a consequence, many Speakers between Cannon and Newt Gingrich, who became Speaker in 1995, often relied on more informal powers that came from their personal ability to persuade members of their party. Gingrich, the first Republican Speaker in forty years, convinced fellow Republicans to return important formal powers to the position. These formal changes, along with his personal leadership skills, allowed Gingrich to exercise greater control over the House and its agenda than any other Speaker since the days of Cannon.

In time, Gingrich's highly visible role as a revolutionary transformed him into a negative symbol outside of Washington, D.C., and his public popularity plunged, causing him to resign as Speaker in 1998. Gingrich was replaced by J. Dennis Hastert (R–IL), a "pragmatic and cautious politician" known for his low-profile leadership style.[6] Hastert's passive style, however, was called into

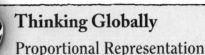

Thinking Globally
Proportional Representation

America's winner-take-all system for determining election outcomes effectively marginalizes minor parties. Independents serving in Congress generally caucus (assemble) with either the Democrats or the Republicans. In contrast, many countries with a parliamentary system of government rely on proportional representation. For example, Israel's unicameral parliament, the Knesset, awards seats to political parties in exact proportion to their share of the popular vote. The Knesset has operated successfully with numerous different parties represented and with no single party holding a majority.

- How would a proportional representation system affect the U.S. Congress?
- What are the advantages of a legislative system based on two or three major parties compared to one that incorporates many parties? What are the disadvantages?

Photo courtesy: Library of Congress

What was Congress like in the early years of the nation?
Throughout Congress's first several decades, partisan, sectional, and state tensions often found their way onto the floors of the U.S. House and Senate. This eighteenth-century cartoon depicts a showdown that took place in the House on February 15, 1798, between Federalist Roger Griswold of Connecticut and Republican Matthew Lyon of Vermont. Griswold, at right, is attempting to club Lyon with a hickory walking stick. Lyon, at left, is shown defending himself with a pair of fire tongs grabbed from the chamber's fireplace. The skirmish came as a surprise to few House members. Tensions between the two parties were high and attacks on the character of individual members often led to escalating violence.

question just before the 2006 midterm elections when it appeared that he had failed to act on information that a Republican member of the House had made improper advances toward young male pages.

In 2007, Democrat Nancy Pelosi became the first female Speaker when Democrats won control of the House. Despite fears that she was "too liberal" for the job, her leadership style has been inclusive and accommodating, as highlighted in Politics Now: Leadership Styles of the Speaker of the House.

OTHER HOUSE LEADERS After the Speaker, the next most powerful people in the House are the majority and minority leaders, who are elected in their individual **party caucuses** or **conferences.** The **majority leader** is the second most important person in the House; his or her counterpart on the other side of the aisle (the House is organized so that if you are facing the front of the chamber, Democrats sit on the left side and Republicans on the right side of the center aisle) is the **minority leader.** The majority leader helps the Speaker schedule proposed legislation for debate on the House floor. In the past, both leaders worked closely with the Speaker. When Republicans took control of the House in 1995, however, they steadily decreased any efforts to consult Democratic leaders.[7] With the Democrats in control since 2007, Republicans now argue that they are shut out of the process.

The Republican and Democratic **whips,** who are elected by party members in caucuses, assist the Speaker and majority and minority leaders in their leadership efforts. The position of whip originated in the British House of Commons, where it was named after the "whipper in," the rider who keeps the hounds together in a fox hunt. Party whips—who were first designated in the U.S. House of Representatives in 1899 and in the Senate in 1913—do, as their name suggests, try to whip fellow Democrats or Republicans into line on partisan issues. They try to maintain close contact with all members on important votes, prepare summaries of content and implications of bills, get "nose counts" during debates and votes, and in general get members to toe the party line. Whips and their deputy whips also serve as communications links, distributing word of the party line from leaders to rank-and-file members and alerting leaders to concerns in the ranks. Whips can be extraordinarily effective. In 1998, for example, President Bill Clinton was stunned to learn that moderate Republicans on whom he had counted to vote against his impeachment were "dropping like flies." The reason? Then House Republican Whip Tom DeLay (R–TX) had threatened Republicans that they would be denied coveted committee assignments and would even face Republican challengers in the next primary season unless they voted the party line.

The Senate

The Constitution specifies that the presiding officer of the Senate is the vice president of the United States. Because he is not a member of the Senate, he votes only in the case of a tie. The official chair of the Senate is the **president pro tempore,** or pro tem, who is selected by the majority party and presides over the Senate in the absence of the vice president. The position of pro tem today is primarily an honorific office that generally goes to the most senior senator of the majority party. Once elected, the pro tem stays in that office until there is a change in the majority party in the Senate. Since presiding over the Senate can be a rather perfunctory duty, neither the vice president nor the president pro tempore actually perform the task very often. Instead, the duty of presiding over the Senate rotates among junior members of the chamber, allowing more senior members to attend more important meetings.

The true leader of the Senate is the majority leader, elected to the position by the majority party. Because the Senate is a smaller and more collegial body, the majority leader is not nearly as powerful as the Speaker of the House. The minority leader and the Republican and Democratic whips round out the leadership positions in the Senate and perform functions similar to those of their House counterparts. But, leading and

party caucus or conference
A formal gathering of all party members.

majority leader
The elected leader of the party controlling the most seats in the House of Representatives or the Senate; is second in authority to the Speaker of the House and in the Senate is regarded as its most powerful member.

minority leader
The elected leader of the party with the second highest number of elected representatives in the House of Representatives or the Senate.

whip
Key member who keeps close contact with all members of his or her party and takes nose counts on key votes, prepares summaries of bills, and in general acts as communications link within a party.

president pro tempore
The official chair of the Senate; usually the most senior member of the majority party.

Source: POLITICO.COM   June 27, 2007

Leadership Styles of the Speaker of the House

Pelosi Forging Quieter Path than Gingrich

JOSEPHINE HEARN

Nancy Pelosi would never have made the mistake Newt Gingrich did in late 1995, when he complained to reporters over breakfast that President Clinton had not invited him to sit in the front of Air Force One. The *New York Daily News* had a field day, emblazoning on the next day's front page, "Cry Baby: Newt's Tantrum; He closed down the government because Clinton made him sit at the back of the plane." The remark kicked off the worst public relations episode of the Gingrich speakership.

Pelosi, six months into a speakership similar to Gingrich's in timing and national significance, is no fan of freewheeling breakfasts with three dozen reporters. The California Democrat is more press-shy than the former Republican Speaker from Georgia, who reveled in his often unscripted role. Pelosi, though not immune to blunders, manages her image more carefully, limiting her media availabilities.

Though she and Gingrich came to power under similar circumstances—after widespread discontent with the ruling party swept the underdogs into power— Pelosi is developing a leadership style all her own. Either by natural temperament or political calculation, she has averted Gingrich's early missteps.

She polls ahead of Democratic leaders and Congress as a whole—and until recently enjoyed a roughly 15-point lead in approval ratings over Gingrich. Lately, she has about the same approval ratings as Gingrich did at this time, but her disapproval ratings are lower.

To be sure, Pelosi has made her own mistakes. Her drop in the polls coincided with Democrats' failed showdown with the White House over withdrawing U.S. troops from Iraq. Her trip to Syria was widely panned. She famously miscalculated in backing Rep. John P. Murtha (D–PA) in the race for majority leader last fall. She has picked a nasty fight with House Energy and Commerce Chairman John Dingell (D–MI) over global warming legislation. And congressional approval ratings are lower than ever.

But the Pelosi model has shown that a new majority need not hinge on a larger-than-life charismatic figure, as Gingrich was until his fall. Facing a hostile president of another party, much like Gingrich did, Pelosi is a quieter speaker. Among the public, twice as many people are unaware of Pelosi than were unaware of Gingrich.

Gingrich held 33 news conferences in his first three months, according to *Congressional Quarterly*. Many of them were solo events, televised nationally and loaded with colorful commentary. Pelosi conducted fewer than half that number during the same period, a rough count showed. And she has most often invited other lawmakers to join her.

To her critics, Pelosi's cloistered style is a weakness. "She's handled and protected like a prize fighter," said Rep. Jack Kingston (R–GA). "She has a good agent who only puts her in comfortable situations. Newt would go behind enemy lines and not think twice about it."

But even Gingrich later regretted his penchant for the limelight. "I should have had much more media discipline," he said in 2003. "There's a side of me that's permanently analytical, that likes coming and giving the speech, and that side of me should not have been allowed out of the box for the entire time I was speaker."

Discussion Questions

1. *What are the effects of a Speaker's leadership style on the day-to-day operations of the House of Representatives?*
2. *What effect does a Speaker's leadership have on his or her party caucus?*
3. *Why is the Speaker's relationship with the press important?*

---

whipping in the Senate can be quite a challenge. Senate rules always have given tremendous power to individual senators; in most cases senators can offer any kind of amendments to legislation on the floor, and an individual senator can bring all work on the floor to a halt indefinitely through a filibuster unless three-fifths of the senators vote to cut him or her off.[8]

Because of the Senate's smaller size, organization and formal rules never have played the same role that they do in the House. Through the 1960s, it was a gentlemen's club whose folkways—unwritten rules of behavior—governed its operation. One such folkway, for example, stipulated that political disagreements not become personal criticisms. A senator who disliked another referred to that senator as "the

How do congressional leaders handle a crisis? Senate Majority Leader Harry Reid (D-NV) and Senate Minority Leader Mitch McConnell (R-KY) hold a press conference announcing the Senate's successful passage of controversial financial bailout legislation on October 1, 2008. The House leadership passed the bill on Friday, October 3, after a failed initial attempt.

Photo courtesy: Mark Wilson/Getty Images

able, learned, and distinguished senator." A member who really couldn't stand another called that senator "my very able, learned, and distinguished colleague."

In the 1960s and 1970s, senators became more and more active on a variety of issues on and off the Senate floor, and extended debates often occurred on the floor without the rigid rules of courtesy that had once been the hallmark of the body. These changes have made the majority leader's role as coalition-builder extraordinarily challenging.[9]

The Committee System

The saying "Congress in session is Congress on exhibition, whilst Congress in its committee rooms is Congress at work" may not be as true today as it was when Woodrow Wilson wrote it in 1885.[10] Still, "the work that takes place in the committee and subcommittee rooms of Capitol Hill is critical to the productivity and effectiveness of Congress."[11] Standing committees are the first and last places to which most bills go. Usually committee members play key roles in floor debate in the full House or Senate about the merits of bills that have been introduced. When different versions of a bill are passed in the House and Senate, a conference committee with members of both houses meets to iron out the differences. The organization and specialization of committees are especially important in the House of Representatives because of its size. The establishment of subcommittees allows for even greater specialization.

Congress created an institutionalized committee system in 1816, and more and more committees were added over time. The large number of committees resulted in duplication of duties and jurisdictional battles.[12] When Republicans took control of the House in 1995, they cut several committees and subcommittees. And, when House Democrats regained control in 2007, they renamed some committees and subcommittees to stress their importance.

TYPES OF COMMITTEES There are four types of congressional committees: (1) standing; (2) joint; (3) conference; and, (4) select, or special.[13]

1. **Standing committees,** so called because they continue from one Congress to the next, are the committees to which bills are referred for consideration.
2. **Joint committees** are set up to expedite business between the houses and to help focus public attention on major matters, such as the economy, taxation, or scandals. They include members from both houses of Congress who conduct investigations or special studies.
3. **Conference committees** are special joint committees that reconcile differences in bills passed by the House and Senate. A conference committee is made up of those members from the House and Senate committees that originally considered the bill.
4. **Select (or special) committees** are temporary committees appointed for specific purposes. Generally such committees are established to conduct special investigations or studies and to report back to the chamber that established them.

In the 111th Congress, the House had nineteen standing committees, as shown in Table 7.3, each with an average of thirty-one members. Together, these standing committees had roughly ninety subcommittees that collectively act as the eyes, ears, and hands of the House. They consider issues roughly parallel to those of the departments represented in the president's Cabinet. For example, there are committees on agriculture, education, the judiciary, veterans affairs, transportation, and commerce.

Although most committees in one house parallel those in the other, the House Committee on Rules, for which there is no counterpart in the Senate, plays a key role in the House's law-making process. Indicative of the importance of the Committee on Rules, majority party members are appointed directly by the Speaker. This committee reviews most bills after they come from a committee and before they go to the full chamber for consideration. Performing a traffic cop function, the Committee on Rules gives each bill what is called a rule, which contains the date the bill will come up for

standing committee
Committee to which proposed bills are referred; continues from one Congress to the next.

joint committee
Committee that includes members from both houses of Congress to conduct investigations or special studies.

conference committee
Special joint committee created to iron out differences between Senate and House versions of a specific piece of legislation.

select (or special) committee
Temporary committee appointed for specific purpose, such as conducting a special investigation or study.

debate and the time that will be allotted for discussion, and often specifies what kinds of amendments can be offered. Bills considered under a closed rule cannot be amended.

Standing committees have considerable power. They can kill bills, amend them radically, or hurry them through the process. In the words of former President Woodrow Wilson, once a bill is referred to a committee, it "crosses a parliamentary bridge of sighs to dim dungeons of silence from whence it never will return."[14] Committees report out to the full House or Senate only a small fraction of the bills assigned to them. Bills can be forced out of a House committee by a **discharge petition** signed by a majority (218) of the House membership.

In the 111th Congress, the Senate had seventeen standing committees ranging in size from fifteen to twenty-nine members. It also had roughly seventy subcommittees, which allowed all majority party senators to chair at least one.

In contrast to the House, whose members hold few committee assignments (an average of 1.8 standing and three subcommittees), senators each serve on an average of three to four committees and seven subcommittees. Whereas the committee system allows House members to become policy or issue specialists, Senate members often are generalists. In the 111th Congress, Senator Kay Bailey Hutchison (R–TX), for example, served on several committees, including Appropriations; Commerce, Science, and Transportation; Veterans Affairs; and Rules and Administration. She also served on ten subcommittees, and was the chair of the Republican Policy Committee.

Senate committees enjoy the same power over framing legislation that House committees do, but the Senate, being an institution more open to individual input

discharge petition
Petition that gives a majority of the House of Representatives the authority to bring an issue to the floor in the face of committee inaction.

TABLE **7.3**   Committees of the 111th Congress (with Subcommittee Examples in Italics)

Standing Committees	
House	Senate
Agriculture	Agriculture, Nutrition, & Forestry
Appropriations	Appropriations
Armed Services	Armed Services
Budget	Banking, Housing, & Urban Affairs
Education & Labor	Budget
Energy & Commerce	Commerce, Science, & Transportation
Financial Services	Energy & Natural Resources
Foreign Affairs	Environment & Public Works
Homeland Security	Finance
House Administration	Foreign Relations
Judiciary	Health, Education, Labor, & Pensions
Commercial & Administrative Law	Homeland Security & Governmental Affairs
The Constitution, Civil Rights, & Civil Liberties	Indian Affairs
Courts, the Internet, & Intellectual Property	Judiciary
Crime, Terrorism, & Homeland Security	*Administrative Oversight & the Courts*
Immigration, Citizenship, Refugees, Border	*Antitrust, Competition Policy, & Consumer Rights*
Security, & International Law	*The Constitution*
Natural Resources	*Crime & Drugs*
Oversight & Government Reform	*Human Rights & the Law*
Rules	*Immigration, Refugees, & Border Security*
Science & Technology	*Terrorism, Technology, & Homeland Security*
Small Business	Rules & Administration
Standards of Official Conduct	Small Business & Entrepreneurship
Transportation & Infrastructure	Veterans Affairs
Veterans Affairs	
Ways & Means	

Select, Special, and Other Committees		
House	Senate	Joint Committees
Permanent Select Intelligence	Select Ethics	Economics
Select Committee on Energy	Select Intelligence	Taxation
Independence & Global Warming	Special Aging	

than the House, gives less deference to the work done in committees. In the Senate, legislation is more likely to be rewritten on the floor, where all senators can participate and add amendments at any time.

COMMITTEE MEMBERSHIP   Many newly elected members of Congress come into the body with their sights on certain committee assignments. Others are more flexible. Many legislators seeking committee assignments inform their party's selection committee of their preferences. They often request assignments based on their own interests or expertise or on a particular committee's ability to help their prospects for reelection. One political scientist has noted that committee assignments are to members what stocks are to investors—they seek to acquire those that will add to the value of their portfolios.[15]

Representatives often seek committee assignments that have access to what is known as **pork,** legislation that allows representatives to bring money and jobs to their districts in the form of public works programs, military bases, or other programs. In the past, a seat on the Armed Services Committee, for example, would allow a member to bring lucrative defense contracts back to his or her district, or to discourage base closings within his or her district or state. Many of these programs are called **earmarks** because they are monies that an appropriations bill designates—"earmarks"—for specific projects within a member's district or state.

Legislators who bring jobs and new public works programs back to their districts are hard to defeat when up for reelection. But, ironically, these are the programs that attract much of the public criticism directed at the federal government in general and Congress in particular. Thus, it is somewhat paradoxical that pork improves a member's chances for reelection.

Pork isn't the only motivator for those seeking strategic committee assignments.[16] Some committees, such as Energy and Commerce, facilitate reelection by giving House members influence over decisions that affect large campaign contributors. Other committees, such as Education and the Workforce or Judiciary, attract members eager to work on the policy responsibilities assigned to the committee even if the appointment does them little good at the ballot box. Another motivator for certain committee assignments is the desire to have power and influence within the chamber. The Appropriations and Budget Committees provide that kind of reward for some members, given the monetary impact of the committees. Congress can approve programs, but unless money for them is appropriated in the budget, they are largely symbolic.

In both the House and the Senate, committee membership generally reflects the party distribution within that chamber. For example, at the outset of the 111th Congress, Democrats held a majority of House seats and thus claimed about a 58 percent share of the seats on several committees. On committees more critical to the operation of the House or to the setting of national policy, the majority often takes a disproportionate share of the

pork
Legislation that allows representatives to bring home the bacon to their districts in the form of public works programs, military bases, or other programs designed to benefit their districts directly.

earmark
Funds in appropriations bill that provide dollars for particular purposes within a state or congressional district.

How many committees do members of Congress serve on? Senator Kay Bailey Hutchison (R–TX) served on five committees and ten subcommittees in the 110th Congress. She also chaired the Republican Policy Committee.

Photo courtesy: Office of U.S. Senator Kay Bailey Hutchinson

slots. Since the Committee on Rules regulates access to the floor for legislation approved by other standing committees, control by the majority party is essential for it to manage the flow of legislation. For this reason, no matter how narrow the majority party's margin in the chamber, it makes up more than two-thirds of the Committee on Rules' membership.

COMMITTEE CHAIRS   Committee chairs enjoy tremendous power and prestige. They are authorized to select all subcommittee chairs, call meetings, and recommend majority members to sit on conference committees. Committee chairs may even opt to kill a bill by refusing to schedule hearings on it. They also have a large committee staff at their disposal and are often recipients of favors from lobbyists, who recognize the chair's unique position of power. Personal skill, influence, and expertise are a chair's best allies.

Historically, committee chairs were the majority party members with the longest continuous service on the committee. Committee chairs in the House, unlike the Senate, are no longer selected by **seniority,** or time of continuous service on the committee. Instead, potential chairs are interviewed by party leaders to ensure that candidates demonstrate loyalty to the party.

The seniority system is also affected by term limits enacted by the House and Senate in 1995 and 1997, respectively. This term limit of six years for all committee chairs has forced many longtime committee chairs to step down or take over other committees.

seniority
Time of continuous service on a committee.

The Members of Congress

Today, many members of Congress find the job exciting in spite of public criticism of the institution. But, it wasn't always so. Until Washington, D.C., got air-conditioning and drained its swamps, it was a miserable town. Most representatives spent as little time as possible there, viewing the Congress, especially the House, as a stepping stone to other political positions back home. It was only after World War I that most House members became congressional careerists who viewed their work in Washington as long term.[17]

Members must attempt to appease two constituencies—party leaders, colleagues, and lobbyists in Washington, D.C., and constituents at home.[18] In attempting to do so, members spend full days at home as well as in D.C. According to one study of House members, average representatives made about forty trips back home to their districts each year.[19] One journalist has aptly described a member's days as a "kaleidoscopic jumble: breakfast with reporters, morning staff meetings, simultaneous committee hearings to juggle, back-to-back sessions with lobbyists and constituents, phone calls, briefings, constant buzzers interrupting office work to make quorum calls and votes on the run, afternoon speeches, evening meetings, receptions, fundraisers, all crammed into four days so they can race home for a weekend gauntlet of campaigning. It's a rat race."[20] (To learn more about a day in the life of a member of Congress, see Table 7.4.)

Running for and Staying in Office

Despite the long hours and hard work required of senators and representatives, thousands aspire to these jobs every year. Yet, only 535 men and women (plus five nonvoting delegates) actually serve in the U.S. Congress. Membership in one of the two major political parties is almost always a prerequisite for election, because election

Mr. Chairman

Who chairs congressional committees? Representative Charles B. Rangel (D–NY) became chair of the powerful House Ways and Means Committee after Democrats won control of the House in the 2006 elections.

Photo courtesy: Fred R. Conrad/The New York Times

incumbency
The fact that being in office helps a person stay in office because of a variety of benefits that go with the position.

VISUAL LITERACY

Why is it So Hard to Defeat an Incumbent?

laws in various states often discriminate against independents (those without party affiliation) and minor-party candidates. As discussed in chapter 14, the ability to raise money often is key to any member's victory, and many members spend nearly all of their free time on the phone dialing for dollars or attending fundraisers.

Incumbency helps members stay in office once they are elected.[21] It's often very difficult for outsiders to win because they don't have the advantages (enumerated in Table 7.5) enjoyed by incumbents, including name recognition, access to free media, an inside track on fund-raising, and a district drawn to favor the incumbent. As illustrated in Analyzing Visuals: Approval Ratings of Congress and Individual Representatives, most Americans have higher regard for their own members of Congress than for Congress collectively.

It is not surprising, then, that an average of 96 percent of the incumbents who seek reelection win their primary and general election races.[22] One study concluded that unless a member of Congress was involved in a serious scandal, his or her chances of defeat were minimal.[23]

Congressional Demographics

Congress is better educated, richer, more male, and more white than the general population. All but three senators are college graduates; 399 representatives share that honor. Over two-thirds of the members of each body also hold advanced degrees.[24] Many members of both houses have significant inherited wealth, but given their educational attainment, which is far higher than the average American's, it is not surprising to find so many wealthy members of Congress.

Almost 250 members of Congress are millionaires. The Senate, in fact, is often called the Millionaires Club, and its members sport names including Rockefeller, Kennedy, and Clinton. The median net worth of a senator in 2008 was $1.7 million, while the median net worth of a House member was $75,000.[25]

TABLE **7.4** A Day in the Life of a Member of Congress

8:30 a.m.	Breakfast with a former member.
9:30 a.m.	Science Committee: Hearing.
10:00 a.m.	Private briefing by NASA officials for afternoon subcommittee hearing.
10:00 a.m.	Commerce Committee: Markup session of pending legistation
12:00 p.m.	Photo opportunity with Miss Universe.
12:00 p.m.	Lunch with visiting friend at Watergate Hotel.
1:30 p.m.	Science Committee: Subcommittee hearing.
1:30 p.m.	Commerce Committee: Subcommittee markup session of pending legislation.
2:00 p.m.	House convenes.
3:00 p.m.	Meeting with National Alliance for Animal Legislation official.
4:30 p.m.	Meeting with American Jewish Congress delegates.
5:00 p.m.	State University reception.
5:00 p.m.	Briefing by the commissioner of the Bureau of Labor Statistics on the uninsured.
5:30 p.m.	Reception/fundraiser for party whip.
6:00 p.m.	Reception/fundraiser for fellow member from the same state.
6:00 p.m.	Cajun foods reception sponsored by Louisiana member.
6:00 p.m.	Winetasting reception on behalf of New York wine industry sponsored by New York member.
10:45 p.m.	House adjourns.

TABLE 7.5 The Advantages of Incumbency

- Name recognition gained through previous campaigns and repeated visits (many of them government paid) to the district to make appearances at various public events.
- Credit claimed for bringing federal money to the district in the form of grants and contracts.
- Positive evaluations from constituents earned by doing favors (casework) such as helping cut red tape and tracking down federal aid, and tasks handled by government-salaried professional staff members.
- Distribution of newsletters and other noncampaign materials free through the mail by using the "frank" (an envelope that contains the legislator's signature in place of a stamp).
- Access to media—incumbents are newsmakers who provide reporters with tips and quotes.
- Greater ease in fundraising—members' high reelection rates make them a good bet for people or groups willing to give campaign contributions in hopes of having access to powerful decision makers.
- Experience in running a campaign, putting together a campaign staff, making speeches, understanding constituent concerns, and connecting with people.
- Superior knowledge about a wide range of issues gained through work on committees, review of legislation, and previous campaigns.
- A record for supporting locally popular policy positions.
- In the House, a district drawn to enhance electability.

Comparing Legislatures

The average age of senators in the 111th Congress was sixty-two. Mark Pryor (D–AR) is the youngest senator. The average age of House members is fifty-six; Representative Aaron Schock (R–IL) was first elected to the House in 2008 and is the youngest member of Congress.

As revealed in Figure 7.3, the 1992 elections saw a record number of women, African Americans, and other minorities elected to Congress. By the 111th Congress, the total number of women members increased to at least seventy-four in the House and seventeen in the Senate. In 2009, the number of African Americans serving in the House held steady at thirty-nine. Until his election to the presidency, Barack Obama (D–IL) was the only African American in the Senate. In the 111th Congress, only twenty-four Hispanics serve in the House. Three Hispanics serve in the Senate. Also serving in the 111th Congress are two members of Asian or Pacific Islander heritage in the Senate and five in the House of Representatives. Only one American Indian, Tom Cole (R–OK), serves in the 111th Congress.

Interestingly, the 111th Congress includes a historic number of Jewish members. Forty-five Jews served in the Senate and thirty-two served in the House of Representatives.

Theories of Representation

Over the years, political theorists have offered various ideas about how constituents' interests are best represented in any legislative body. Does it make a difference if the members of Congress come from or are members of a particular group? Are they bound to vote the way their constituents expect them to vote even if they personally favor another policy? Your answer to these questions may depend on your view of the representative function of legislators.

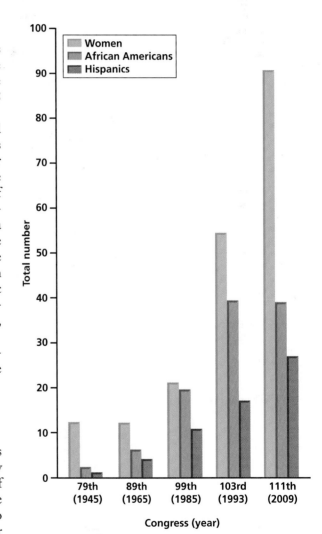

FIGURE 7.3 Female and Minority Members of Congress, Selected Years

Photo courtesy: The Office of U.S. Senator Daniel Akaka

How diverse is Congress?
Senator Daniel Akaka (D–HI) is one of seven members of Congress whose ethnic background is Asian or Pacific American.

trustee
Role played by elected representatives who listen to constituents' opinions and then use their best judgment to make final decisions.

delegate
Role played by elected representatives who vote the way their constituents would want them to, regardless of their own opinions.

politico
Role played by elected representatives who act as trustees or as delegates, depending on the issue.

British political philosopher Edmund Burke (1729–1797), who also served in the British Parliament, believed that although he was elected from Bristol, it was his duty to represent the interests of the entire nation. He reasoned that elected officials were obliged to vote as they personally thought best. According to Burke, a representative should be a **trustee** who listens to the opinions of constituents and then can be trusted to use his or her own best judgment to make final decisions.

A second theory of representation holds that a representative should be a **delegate.** True delegates are representatives who vote the way their constituents would want them to, whether or not those opinions are the representative's. Delegates, therefore, must be ready and willing to vote against their conscience or personal policy preferences if they know how their constituents feel about a particular issue.

Not surprisingly, members of Congress and other legislative bodies generally don't fall neatly into either category. It is often unclear how constituents feel about a particular issue, or there may be conflicting opinions within a single constituency. With these difficulties in mind, a third theory of representation holds that a **politico** alternately dons the hat of a trustee or delegate, depending on the issue. On an issue of great concern to their constituents, representatives most likely will vote as delegates; on other issues, perhaps those that are less visible, representatives will act as trustees and use their own best judgment. Research by political scientists supports this view.[27]

How a representative views his or her role—as a trustee, delegate, or politico—may still not answer the question of whether it makes a difference if a representative or senator is male or female, African American, Latino/a, or Caucasian, young or old, gay or straight. Burke's ideas about representation don't even begin to address more practical issues of representation. Can a man, for example, represent the interests of women as well as a woman? Can a rich woman represent the interests of the poor? Are veterans more sensitive to veterans' issues?

Interestingly, one NBC/*Wall Street Journal* poll found that a majority of people agreed that it would be "better for society" if "most of the members of Congress were women."[28] Many voters believe that women are not only more interested in, but better suited to deal with, a wide range of domestic issues, such as education and health care.[29] Moreover, women representatives often have played prominent roles in advancing issues of concern to women.[30] One study by the Center for American Women and Politics, for example, found that most women in the 103rd Congress "felt a special responsibility to represent women, particularly to represent their life experiences. . . . They undertook this additional responsibility while first, and foremost, like all members of Congress, representing their own districts." However, more recent research finds that Republican women "may be willing to downplay their commitment to women's issues in order to make gains on other district and policy priorities that conform more easily to the Republican agenda."[31]

The actions of the lone American Indian who served in the Senate until 2005 underscore the representative function that members can play in Congress. Senator Ben Nighthorse Campbell (R–CO) not surprisingly served on the Committee on Indian Affairs. Earlier, as a member of the House, he fought successfully for legislation to establish the National Museum of the American Indian on the Mall in Washington, D.C.

Analyzing Visuals | Approval Ratings of Congress and Individual Representatives

Examine the line graph tracking approval ratings of Congress in general as well as of the respondents' individual representatives. Consider the following questions:

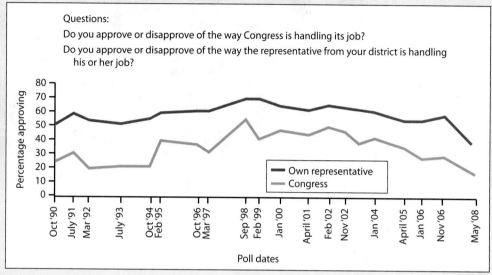

Questions:
Do you approve or disapprove of the way Congress is handling its job?
Do you approve or disapprove of the way the representative from your district is handling his or her job?

Source: Data derived from Lexis-Nexis RPOLL.

DO the data for approval of Congress and approval of one's own representative show similar trends over the period covered in the figure?

WHAT factors might account for the differences in the ratings of Congress as a whole and one's own representative?

IN general, why would the approval ratings for Congress be significantly lower than those for individual members?

How Members Make Decisions

As a bill makes its way through the labyrinth of the law-making process, members are confronted with the question: "How should I vote?" Members adhere to their own personal beliefs on some matters, but their views often are moderated by other considerations. To avoid making any voting mistakes, members look to a variety of sources for cues.

Party

Members often look to party leaders for indicators of how to vote. Indeed, the whips in each chamber reinforce the need for party cohesion, particularly on issues of concern to the party. In fact, from 1970 to the mid-1990s, the incidence of party votes in which majorities of the two parties took opposing sides roughly doubled to more than 60 percent of all roll-call votes.[32] Describing this phenomenon, former political scientist turned representative David E. Price (D-NC) notes, "in rereading *Congressional Government* [written by then political scientist and later U.S. President Woodrow Wilson] certain Wilsonian themes struck me with much more force than they did [in 1994]: the balances of power between Congress and the executive in the federal government and between the committees and the parties within the Congress. Those balances were in better repair, I believe—not perfect repair, but better repair—in the 1990s than they are today."[33]

Under unified Republican control in the 107th Congress, for example, there was perfect party unity on all major votes taken in the House.[34] In the 108th Congress,

Can a man represent the interests of a woman as well as a woman? The sixteen women senators of the 110th Congress, pictured here, don't think so. The 2008 elections saw their numbers increase by one—Jeanne Shaheen (D-NH), while Elizabeth Dole (R-NC) was defeated by Kay Hagan (D-NC).

Photo courtesy: The Office of U.S. Senator Barbara Mikulski

Democratic senators demonstrated unanimity in filibustering several presidential judicial nominations to the U.S. Courts of Appeals. While some charged that this was not evidence of party unity, but instead elected officials taking their direction from liberal special-interest groups, there can be no doubt that in both closely divided houses, party reigns supreme.[35]

With the election of George W. Bush, a Republican president determined to govern from the "right in" rather than the "center out," congressional Republicans, especially those in the House, took on a harder edge. New tactics were devised to eliminate dependence on or participation by Democrats. At the same time, members of the narrow Republican majority were kept in line largely by threats of poor committee assignments or loss of committee or subcommittee chairs. According to Price, "Most obvious is the practice of going to the floor with a narrow whip count and holding the vote open as long as necessary to cajole the last few Republican members to vote yes. The most notorious example was the vote on the Republicans' privatized Medicare drug benefit, held open for almost three hours on November 22, 2003, but the tactic was [also] utilized . . . on the post-Katrina bill dealing with refinery construction and price-gouging."[36]

After years of Congress and the presidency being controlled by the Republican Party, in 2006 voters voiced their discontent over what many viewed as the excessive partisanship of the 109th Congress. A poll taken on Election Day 2006 found that 52 percent of voters preferred **divided government,** the political condition in which different parties control the White House and Congress. Historically, divided government has led to a situation called gridlock, which often results in very little important legislation being enacted into law. In an attempt to avert a gridlock scenario, Democratic Leader Nancy Pelosi (D–CA), soon to become the new Speaker of the House, met with President George W. Bush two days after the 2006 election. Nevertheless, Democrats found it difficult to pass legislation during the 110th Congress as Bush began to veto bills for the first time in his presidency.

divided government
The political condition in which different political parties control the White House and Congress.

Constituents

Constituents—the people who live and vote in a representative's home district or state—are always in a member's mind when casting votes.[37] Studies by political scientists show that members vote in conformity with prevailing opinion in their districts about two-thirds of the time.[38] On average, Congress passes laws that reflect national public opinion at about the same rate.[39] It is rare for a legislator to vote against the wishes of his or her constituents regularly, particularly on issues of welfare rights, domestic policy, or other highly salient issues. For example, during the 1960s, representatives from southern states could not hope to keep their seats for long if they voted in favor of proposed civil rights legislation.

Gauging how voters feel about any particular issue often is not easy. Because it is virtually impossible to know how the folks back home feel on all issues, a representative's perception of their constituents' preferences is important. Even when voters have opinions, legislators may get little guidance if their district is narrowly divided. Abortion is an issue about which many voters feel passionately, but a legislator whose district has roughly equal numbers of pro-choice and pro-life advocates can satisfy only a portion of his or her constituents.

In short, legislators tend to act on their own preferences as trustees when dealing with topics that have come through the committees on which they serve or with issues that they know about as a result of experience in other contexts, such as their vocation. On items of little concern to people back in the district or for which the legislator has little first-hand knowledge, the tendency is to turn to other sources for voting cues. But with regard to particularly charged topics like same-sex marriage, abortion restrictions, and flag burning—often called "wedge issues," given their ability to divide or drive a wedge between voters—members are always keenly aware of the consequences of voting against their constituents' views.

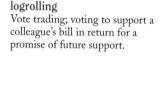

SIMULATION

The Prepared Voter Kit

Colleagues and Caucuses

The range and complexity of issues confronting Congress mean that no one can be up to speed on more than a few topics. When members must vote on bills about which they know very little, they often turn for advice to colleagues who have served on the committee that handled the legislation. On issues that are of little interest to a legislator, **logrolling,** or vote trading, often occurs. Logrolling often takes place on specialized bills targeting money or projects to selected congressional districts. An unaffected member often will exchange a yea vote now for the promise of a future yea vote on a similar piece of specialized legislation.

logrolling
Vote trading; voting to support a colleague's bill in return for a promise of future support.

Members may also look to other representatives who share common interests. Special-interest caucuses created around issues, home states, regions, congressional class, or other commonalities facilitate this communication. Prior to 1995, the power of these groups was even more evident, as several caucuses enjoyed formal status within the legislative body and were provided staff, office space, and budgets. Today, however, all caucuses are informal in nature, although some, such as the Black and Hispanic Caucuses, are far more organized than others. The Congressional Caucus for Women's Issues, for example, has formal elections of its Republican and Democratic co-chairs and vice chairs, its members provide staff to work on issues of common concern to caucus members, and staffers meet regularly to facilitate support for legislation of interest to women.

Interest Groups, Lobbyists, and Political Action Committees

A primary function of most lobbyists, whether they work for interest groups, trade associations, or large corporations,

Photo courtesy: George Bridges/KRT/Newscom

Who says sisters think alike? U.S. Representatives Loretta and Linda Sanchez (D–CA), the first sisters to hold seats in the House of Representatives, split when it came to their choices for the Democratic presidential nominees in 2008. Linda, at right, was a staunch supporter of Barack Obama, while Loretta put her support behind Hillary Clinton.

is to provide information to supportive or potentially supportive legislators, committees, and their staffs.[40] It is likely, for example, that a representative knows the National Rifle Association's (NRA) position on gun control legislation. What the legislator needs to get from the NRA is information and substantial research on the feasibility and impact of such legislation. How could the states implement such legislation? Is it constitutional? Will it really have an impact on violent crime or crime in schools? Organized interests can win over undecided legislators or confirm the support of their friends by providing information that legislators use to justify the position they have embraced. They also can supply direct campaign contributions, volunteers, and publicity to members seeking reelection. And, they may urge supporters to deluge their representatives with e-mails or even to visit members' D.C. or district offices.

Interest groups also use grassroots appeals to pressure legislators by urging their members in a particular state or district to call, write, fax, or e-mail their senators or representatives. Lobbyists can't vote, but constituents back home can and do.

While a link to a legislator's constituents may be the most effective way to influence behavior, it is not the only path of interest-group influence on members' decision making.[41] The high cost of campaigning has made members of Congress, especially those without huge personal fortunes, attentive to those who help pay the tab for the high cost of many campaigns. The almost 5,000 political action committees (PACs) organized by interest groups are a major source of most members' campaign funding. When an issue comes up that is of little consequence to a member's constituents, there is, not surprisingly, a tendency to support the positions of those interests who helped pay for the last campaign. After all, who wants to bite the hand that feeds him or her? (To learn more about PACs and interest groups, see chapters 14 and 16.)

You Are an Informed Voter Helping Your Classmates Decide How to Vote

Staff and Support Agencies

Members of Congress rely heavily on members of their staffs for information on pending legislation.[42] House members have an average of seventeen staffers; senators have an average of forty. Staff are divided between D.C. and district offices. When a bill is nonideological or one on which the member has no real position, staff members can be very influential. In many offices, they are the greatest influence on their boss's votes. In many cases, lobbyists are just as likely to contact key staffers as they are members. And, in many of the recent major House lobbying scandals, it was staffers who ultimately faced criminal investigations or prosecutions for influence buying. (To learn about work opportunities in Congress, see Ideas into Action: Be a Congressional Intern.)

Congressional committees and subcommittees also have their own dedicated staff to assist committee members. Additional support for members comes from support personnel at the Congressional Research Service (CRS) at the Library of Congress, the Government Accountability Office (GAO), and the Congressional Budget Office (CBO). (To learn more about congressional support agencies, see Table 7.6.)

How do staffers affect congressional decision making? Members of the Congressional Muslim Staffers Association like Sarah Bassal (left) and Amina Rubin (right) work to educate policy makers about Islam and Islamic beliefs.

Photo courtesy: Jamie Rose/The New York Times

The Law-Making Function of Congress

The organization of Congress allows it to fulfill its constitutional responsibilities, chief among which is

Be a Congressional Intern

Senators and representatives cannot do their jobs by themselves. With so many demands on their time, both in Washington and their districts, these elected members rely on their staffs on a daily basis.

But, even professional staffers cannot do everything members of Congress require. Thus, advanced high school and college students are hired as interns to help with basic tasks. Interns answer phones, help with casework, respond to constituent letters and e-mails, and attend events on behalf of members. They work in both Washington, D.C., and district offices, and they are invaluable resources.

Internships provide students with an invaluable opportunity to learn about the day-to-day operations of Congress. In fact, a significant number of current members of Congress began their political careers as interns.

Explore the Web site of your senator or representative and learn what internship opportunities might be available to you. Then, consider the following questions:

- Do you know anyone who has worked for a member of Congress or a state legislator? What tasks did they perform?
- What skills might you learn as a congressional intern?
- How do your political views align with those of your representative or senator? How might this affect your experience as an intern in that person's office?

its law-making function. It is through this power that Congress affects the day-to-day lives of all Americans and sets policy for the future. Proposals for legislation—be they about terrorism, Medicare, or tax policy—can come from the president, executive agencies, committee staffs, interest groups, or even private individuals. Only members of the House or Senate, however, can formally submit a bill for congressional consideration (although many are initially drafted by lobbyists). Once a bill is introduced by a member of Congress, it usually reaches a dead end. Of the approximately 10,000 bills introduced during the 110th session of Congress, fewer than 5 percent were made into law.

It is probably useful to think of Congress as a system of multiple vetoes, which was what the Framers desired. They wanted to disperse power, and as Congress has evolved it has come closer and closer to the Framers' intentions. As a bill goes through Congress, numerous roadblocks to passage must be surmounted. In addition to realistic roadblocks, caution signs and other opportunities for delay abound. A member who sponsors a bill must get through every obstacle. In contrast, successful opposition means winning at only one of many stages, including: (1) the House subcommittee; (2) the full House committee; (3) the House Committee on Rules; (4) the House; (5) the Senate subcommittee; (6) the full Senate committee; (7) the Senate; (8) floor leaders in both Houses; (9) the House-Senate conference committee; and, (10) the president.

TABLE 7.6 Congressional Support Agencies

Congressional Research Service (CRS)	Government Accountability Office (GAO)	Congressional Budget Office (CBO)
Created in 1914 as the Legislative Research Service (LRS), CRS is administered by the Library of Congress. It responds to more than a quarter of a million congressional requests for information each year. Its staff conducts nonpartisan studies of public issues and conducts major research projects for committees at the request of members. CRS also prepares summaries and tracks the progress of all bills introduced.	The Government Accountability Office (GAO) was established in 1921 as an independent regulatory agency for the purpose of auditing the financial expenditures of the executive branch and federal agencies. The GAO performs four additional functions: it sets government standards for accounting, it provides a variety of legal opinions, it settles claims against the government, and it conducts studies upon congressional request.	The CBO was created in 1974 to evaluate the economic effect of different spending programs and to provide information on the cost of proposed policies. It is responsible for analyzing the president's budget and economic projections. The CBO provides Congress and individual members with a valuable second opinion to use in budget debates.

The story of how a bill becomes a law in the United States can be told in two different ways. The first is the textbook method, which provides a greatly simplified road map of the process to make it easier to understand. We'll review this method first. The real-life process, the second method, is obviously much more complicated and is discussed after the textbook version of the process.

How A Bill Becomes A Law: The Textbook Version

A bill must survive several stages or roadblocks before it becomes a law. It must be approved by one or more standing committees and both chambers, and, if House and Senate versions differ, each house must accept a conference report resolving those differences. These multiple points of approval provide many opportunities for members to revise the content of legislation and may lead representatives to alter their views on a particular piece of legislation several times over. Thus, it is much easier to defeat a bill than it is to get one passed. As revealed in Figure 7.4, roadblocks (indicated by stop signs in the figure) exist at nearly every stage of the process.

The House and Senate have parallel processes, and often the same bill is introduced in each chamber at the same time. A bill must be introduced by a member of Congress, but, in an attempt to show support for the aims of the bill, it is often sponsored by several other members (called co-sponsors).[43] Once introduced, the bill is sent to the clerk of the chamber, who gives it a number (for example, HR 1 or S 1—indicating House or Senate bill number one). The bill is then printed, distributed, and sent to the appropriate committee or committees for consideration.

The first action takes place within the committee, after a bill is referred there by the Speaker of the House or by the Senate majority leader. The committee usually refers the bill to one of its subcommittees, which researches the bill and decides whether to hold hearings on it. The subcommittee hearings provide the opportunity for those on both sides of the issue to voice their opinions. Since the passage of sunshine laws in the 1970s, most of these hearings are now open to the public. After the hearings, the bill is revised in subcommittee, and then the subcommittee votes to approve or defeat the bill. If the subcommittee votes in favor of the bill, it is returned to the full committee. There, during **markup,** committee members can add items to the bill and send it to the House or Senate floor with a favorable recommendation. It can also reject the bill.

The second stage of action takes place on the House or Senate floor. As previously discussed, in the House, before a bill may be debated on the floor, it must be approved by the Committee on Rules and given a rule and a place on the calendar, or schedule. (House budget bills, however, don't go to the Committee on Rules.) In the House, the rule given to a bill determines the limits on the floor debate and specifies what types of amendments, if any, may be attached to the bill. Once the Committee on Rules considers the bill, it is put on the calendar.

When the day arrives for floor debate, the House may choose to form a Committee of the Whole. This procedure allows the House to deliberate with only one hundred members present, to expedite consideration of the bill. On the House floor, the bill is debated, amendments are offered, and a vote ultimately is taken by the full House. If the bill survives, it is sent to the Senate for consideration if it was not considered there simultaneously.

Unlike the House, where debate is necessarily limited given the size of the body, bills may be held up by a hold or a filibuster in the Senate. A **hold** is a tactic by which a senator asks to be informed before a particular bill is brought to the floor. This request signals the Senate leadership and the sponsors of the bill that a colleague may have objections to the bill and should be consulted before further action is taken.

Holds are powerful tools. In 2002, for example, then Senator Joe Biden (D–DE) became so upset with congressional failure to fund Amtrak security (Biden took Amtrak back and forth to his home in Delaware when the Senate was in session) that he put holds on two Department of Transportation nominees, whom he called "fine, decent, and competent people." This meant that their nominations could not be considered until he removed his hold. In return, the Bush administration retaliated by withholding a third of

How a Bill Becomes a Law

You Are a Member of Congress

markup
A process in which committee members offer changes to a bill before it goes to the floor in either house for a vote.

hold
A tactic by which a senator asks to be informed before a particular bill is brought to the floor. This allows the senator to stop the bill from coming to the floor until the hold is removed.

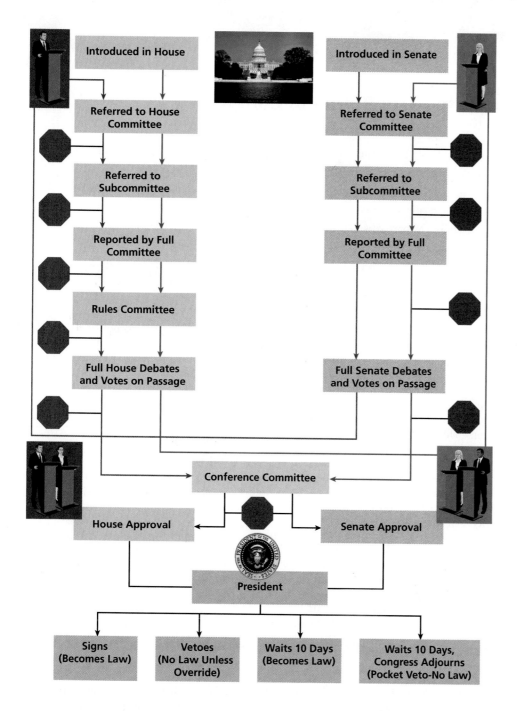

FIGURE **7.4** How A Bill Becomes A Law

the funding for a University of Delaware research project on high-speed trains. As the *Washington Post* noted in reporting this story, "Welcome to the wild wacky world of Washington politics, where people sometimes destroy a village to save it."[44] Holds are still important weapons, but Senator Biden, now the vice president, looks instead for ways to cooperate with the Senate on behalf of the Obama administration.

Filibusters, which allow for unlimited debate on a bill (or on presidential appointments), grew out of the absence of rules to limit speech in the Senate. In contrast to a hold, a filibuster is a more formal and public way of halting action on a bill. There are no rules on the content of a filibuster as long as a senator keeps talking. A senator may read from a phone book, recite poetry, or read cookbooks to delay a vote. Often, a team of senators takes turns speaking to keep the filibuster going in the hope that a bill will be tabled or killed. In 1964, for example, a group of northern liberal

filibuster
A formal way of halting action on a bill by means of long speeches or unlimited debate in the Senate.

Minority Party Rights in Congress

OVERVIEW: Some political commentators have concluded that the United States may be viewed as divided into two significant minorities representing the Republican and Democratic Party faithful. It follows, so the logic goes, that in the event of close elections, the governing process should strive to reflect the policy and political desires of the relatively nonpartisan "moderate middle" of the American electorate. Representatives typically are chosen by partisans in primary elections, however, and elected officials are compelled to at least try to enact party preferences. Should law-making rules be written to prevent legislative majorities from enforcing their agendas over the objections of the minority party? What rights should the minority party in a two-party system have to pursue its interests?

Article I, section 5, of the Constitution gives both chambers of Congress the authority to "determine the Rules of its Proceedings" and declares that a "Majority of each [chamber] shall constitute a Quorum to do business" (a quorum is the number of members required to transact affairs). Other than giving a legislative minority the right to "compel the Attendance of absent Members" (to ensure that a majority of representatives are available to conduct legislative business), the Constitution does not speak to minority party rights. And, the language of the Constitution plainly gives each chamber the power to determine its own manners of procedure, and hence the power to make rules governing the legislative process.

Nevertheless, the Framers did not foresee the rise of ideological political parties and their resulting political maneuvering. In fact, James Madison, in *Federalist No. 10*, argued that the Constitution would tend "to break and control the violence of faction." However, since parties have grown and developed, many observers believe that minority safeguards like the Senate's filibuster rule may be necessary to ensure that congressional governance reflects the policy desires of the broad majority of American voters. Other commentators see the filibuster as an opportunity for the minority party to obstruct the will of a majority. When in the minority in a closely divided Senate, both Republicans and Democrats have blocked legislation on a wide variety

of issues. In effect, as political scientists have observed, a supermajority of sixty votes is often needed to pass a bill, since it takes sixty votes to break a filibuster.

Arguments IN FAVOR of Minority Party Rights in Congress

- **Legislative majorities can be unjust.** Many people consider actions by legislative majorities to be harmful to the rights or lives of citizens. For example, some observers believe the Defense of Marriage Act, which gives states the authority to deny the legitimacy of same-sex marriages made in other states, is an infringement on the rights of individual citizens to marry.

senators continued a filibuster for eighty-two days in an effort to prevent amendments that would weaken a civil rights bill. Still, filibusters often are more of a threat than an actual event on the Senate floor, although members may use them in extreme circumstances. (To learn more about minority-majority relationships in Congress, see Join the Debate: Minority Party Rights in Congress.)

There is only one way to end a filibuster. Sixty senators must sign a motion for **cloture.** After a cloture motion passes the Senate floor, members may spend no more than thirty additional hours debating the legislation at issue.

The third stage of action takes place when the two chambers of Congress approve different versions of the same bill. When this happens, they establish a conference committee to iron out the differences between the two versions. The conference committee, whose members are from the original House and Senate committees, hammers out a compromise, which is returned to each chamber for a final vote. Sometimes the conference committee fails to agree and the bill dies

cloture
Mechanism requiring sixty senators to vote to cut off debate.

Allowing a minority party the right to impede legislation could provide a means for preventing unjust or unfair legislation.

- **Giving the minority party legislative rights helps the deliberative process.** Allowing a minority party the right to slow down the legislative process will result in a better law. Giving the minority party assured rights would make certain there will be compromise and negotiation in the legislative process, and as a result, law and policy would be further filtered through deliberation and conciliation.

- **Legislation should reflect the preferences of the electorate as a whole.** Representative democracy means representation for all, not just for a political majority. Giving the minority party the right to block legislation will ensure legislation and policy are crafted to reflect the diverse and broad policy preferences of the American electorate. Otherwise, legislation will reflect the ideological desires of only a portion of the American people.

Arguments AGAINST Minority Party Rights in Congress

- **The Constitution is explicit where it requires supermajorities for political action.** The Constitution plainly states when a supermajority is necessary for an act of government, and there are seven instances in the Constitution where this is necessary. For example, Article I requires that a two-thirds vote of each chamber is necessary to override a presidential veto, and Article II requires that a two-thirds vote of the Senate is necessary to ratify treaties. If the Framers wanted more than a simple majority vote to make law and policy, it would be embodied in the Constitution's text.

- **Voters have the ability to unseat members of Congress.** If voters don't care for the legislative and political agenda of the majority party in Congress, they are competent enough to vote the party out of power. Voter disaffection with forty years of Democratic Party dominance of Congress, for example, led to the party being voted out of majority status in the 1994 midterm elections.

- **Giving a legislative minority authority to stop legislation frustrates the will of the electorate.** Even in a closely divided electorate, the majority principle remains. Echoing the sentiment expressed in the Constitutional Convention, Thomas Jefferson argued that majority rule must necessarily be the rule for democratic government. The Framers believed that giving legislative minorities rights was essentially giving democratic government over to the rule of small elites.

Continuing the Debate

1. Should minority parties have the right to slow down or derail the passage of legislation sponsored by the majority party? Is this a violation of the Framers' majority principle? Why or why not?

2. Given that minority party representatives are duly elected by a majority of their constituents, what minority party protections seem appropriate?

To Follow the Debate Online, Go To:

www.fairvote.org

Advocates for majority rule and for limiting the rights of minority parties.

www.votesmart.org

Project Vote Smart, a nonprofit, nonpartisan organization, encourages participation in elections and provides information on topics like the role and strategies of minority and majority parties in Congress.

---

there. No changes or amendments to the compromise version are allowed. If the bill is passed, it is sent to the president, who either signs it or **vetoes** it. If the bill is not passed in both houses, it dies.

The president has ten days to consider a bill. He has four options:

1. The president can sign the bill, at which point it becomes law.

2. The president can veto the bill, which is more likely to occur when the president is of a different party from the majority in Congress; Congress may override the president's veto with a two-thirds vote in each chamber, a very difficult task.

3. The president can wait the full ten days, at the end of which time the bill becomes law without his signature if Congress is still in session.

4. If the Congress adjourns before the ten days are up, the president can choose not to sign the bill, and it is considered pocket vetoed.

veto
Formal constitutional authority of the president to reject bills passed by both houses of the legislative body, thus preventing the bill from becoming law without further congressional activity.

pocket veto
If Congress adjourns during the ten days the president has to consider a bill passed by both houses of Congress, the bill is considered vetoed without the president's signature.

A **pocket veto** figuratively allows bills stashed in the president's pocket to die. The only way for a bill then to become law is for it to be reintroduced in the next session and be put through the process all over again. Because Congress sets its own date of adjournment, technically the session could be continued the few extra days necessary to prevent a pocket veto. Extensions are unlikely, however, as sessions are scheduled to adjourn close to the November elections or the December holidays.

How A Bill Really Becomes A Law: The China Trade Act of 2000

For each bill introduced in Congress, enactment is a longshot. A bill's supporters struggle to get from filing in both houses of Congress to the president's signature, and each bill follows a unique course. The progress of the trade legislation described below is probably even quirkier than most bills that actually become law.

Under the Trade Act of 1974, part of a two-decades-old American Cold War policy, the president of the United States was empowered to grant any nation "most favored" trade status, a designation that brings favorable U.S. tariff treatment. By law, however, the president was limited to extending that status to communist countries on a year by year (instead of permanent) basis subject to congressional review. Thus, since passage of that act, China, as a communist nation, could receive this status only a year at a time, even though it provided a huge potential market for U.S. goods. President Bill Clinton and many members of the business community wanted this year by year reauthorization dropped once China was scheduled to join the World Trade Organization. To do that required a new act of Congress. Ironically, the Clinton administration's push for this bill also allied President Clinton with many Republicans who favored opening trade to a nation with billions of new consumers. Many of the Republicans' biggest financial and political supporters would benefit from opening Chinese markets and removing barriers to service providers such as banks and telecommunications companies, although not all Republicans were in agreement. Unions, however, traditionally a Democratic constituency, feared further loss of jobs to foreign shores.

Legislation to extend what is called permanent normal trade relations (PNTR) was viewed by Clinton as a means of putting "his imprint on foreign policy [as] the president who cemented in place the post-Cold-War experiment of using economic engagement to foster political change among America's neighbors and its potential adversaries."[45] He had begun this effort in 1993 after he pushed through Congress passage of the North American Free Trade Agreement (NAFTA) with Mexico and Canada. Now, as his time in office was coming to an end, he wanted Congress to act to allow him to cement PNTR with China.

As soon as the United States completed a bilateral agreement to make China a member of the World Trade Organization in November 1999 and early 2000, Clinton met with more than one hundred lawmakers individually or in groups, called scores more on the phone, and traveled to the Midwest and California to build support for the proposed legislation, which was necessary to implement this agreement. While Clinton was setting the stage for congressional action, the U.S. Chamber of Commerce and the Business Roundtable launched a $10 million ad campaign—the largest ever for a single legislative issue.[46]

On March 8, 2000, Clinton transmitted the text of legislation he was requesting to Congress. This proposed legislation, called S 2277, was formally introduced in the Senate on March 23 by Senator William Roth Jr. (R–DE). It was then read twice and referred to the Finance Committee. In the House, hearings on the China trade policy were held throughout the spring, even before the Clinton legislation formally was introduced. Anticipating concern from colleagues about China's human rights abuses, labor market issues, and the rule of law, some members proposed that Congress create (under separate legislation) a U.S. Congressional-Executive Commission on China to monitor those issues. HR 4444, the bill that Clinton sought, was introduced formally in the House on May 15, 2000, by Representative Bill Archer (R–TX). It was referred to the House Ways and Means Committee shortly thereafter and a mark-up session was held

Photo courtesy: Richard A. Bloom/Bloom/Corbis

How does a bill become a law? To enact a piece of legislation, Congress and the president must work together to build consensus. Here, union workers protest efforts to pass the China Trade Act of 2000.

on May 17. It was reported out of committee on the same day by a vote of 34–4. On May 23, 2000, HR 4444 received a rule from the Committee on Rules allowing for three hours of debate. The bill was closed to amendments except motions to recommit, and the House Republican leadership "closed ranks behind the bill," claiming that economic change would foster political change.[47] But, they still had to sell this idea to their colleagues, many of whom balked at extending trade advantages to a communist government with a history of rights violations, including religious persecution and the denial of political rights. The rights legislation was designed to assuage those fears.

While the House Committee on International Relations was holding hearings (and even before), the Clinton administration sprang into action. Secretary of Commerce William Daley and several other Cabinet members were sent out to say the same thing over and over again: the bill will mean jobs for Americans and stability in Asia. Republican leaders got Chinese dissidents to say that the bill would improve human rights in China, and televangelist Billy Graham was recruited by the leadership to endorse the measure. At the same time, interest groups on both sides of the debate rushed to convince legislators to support their respective positions. Organized labor, still stinging from its NAFTA loss, was the biggest opponent of the bill. Teamsters and members of the United Auto Workers roamed the halls of Congress, trying to lobby members of the House.[48] Vice President Al Gore, knowing that he would need union support in the upcoming presidential election, broke ranks with the president and said that the bill would only serve to move American jobs to China.

On the other side, lobbyists from large corporations, including Procter and Gamble, and interest groups such as the Business Roundtable, used their cell phones and personal contacts to cajole legislators. "It's like a big wave hitting the shore," said one uncommitted Republican legislator from Staten Island, New York.[49] For the first time, he was lobbied by rank-and-file office workers at the request of their corporate offices, as well as union members. Another member of Congress was contacted by former President George Bush and Secretary of Defense William Cohen, and he received a special defense briefing from the Central Intelligence Agency. The president of the AFL-CIO also personally visited him. All stops were out, and this was the kind of treatment most undecided members received.

House debate on the bill began on May 24, 2000. That morning, House Republican Whip Tom DeLay (R–TX) didn't know if he had enough votes to support the measure to ensure its passage. The bare minimum he needed was 150 Republicans if he was to push the bill over the top.[50] DeLay lined up lots of assistance. Texas Governor George W. Bush and retired General Colin Powell were enlisted to help convince wavering Republicans to support the Democratic president's goals. Powell, in particular, was called on to assuage national security concerns of several conservative representatives. Scores of pro-trade lobbyists spread out over Capitol Hill like locusts looking to light on any wavering legislators. A last-minute amendment to create a twenty-three-member commission to monitor human rights and a second to monitor surges in Chinese imports helped garner the votes of at least twenty more legislators.

Debate then came on a motion from House Democratic Whip David Bonior (D–MI) to recommit the bill to the Ways and Means and International Relations Committees to give them the opportunity to add an amendment to the bill to provide conditions under which withdrawals of normal trade relations with China could occur should China attack or invade Taiwan. This motion failed on a vote of 176–258. As lobbyists stepped up their efforts, their actions and those of the Republican leadership and the Clinton administration bore fruit. Every single uncommitted Republican voted for the bill, joining seventy-three Democrats to grant China permanent normal trade status as the bill passed by a surprisingly large margin of 237–197. "Frankly, they surprised me a bit. Members in the last few hours really turned around and understood how important this was," said DeLay. Stunned labor leaders admitted that they were outgunned. "The business community unleashed an unprecedented campaign that was hard for anyone to match," said the president of the United Auto Workers.[51]

As the bill was transmitted to the Senate, critics sprang into action. Senator Jesse Helms (R–NC), chair of the Foreign Relations Committee and a major critic of the Beijing government, immediately put fellow Republicans on notice that he would not rubber stamp the actions of the House. Although amendments were not allowed in the House, Senate rules that permit amendment were seen as a way of changing the nature of the bill and causing the amended version to go back to the House for a vote. Secretary Daley immediately went to see the Senate majority leader and members of the Senate Finance Committee, which had jurisdiction over the bill, to ask their assistance in fending off amendments.

While hearings on China were being held in the House, the Senate Finance Committee had been considering the bill. Once it passed the House, however, it was reported out of the Senate Finance Committee immediately on May 25. On that day, Senators Fred Thompson (R–TN) and Robert Torricelli (D–NJ) held a press conference to announce that they would offer parallel legislation based on their concerns about Chinese proliferation of weapons of mass destruction to continue a yearly review of China as a condition of open trade with that nation. They viewed the opening of PNTR to China as a national security as well as a trade issue.

The Senate began debating S 2277 on July 26, 2000. The next day, after a filibuster was begun by several opponents of the bill, including Senators Robert Byrd (D–WV), Jesse Helms (R–NC), Barbara Mikulski (D–MD), and Ben Nighthorse Campbell (R–CO), a move to invoke cloture was brought by the majority leader and several others. Cloture then was invoked by a vote of 86–12, well over the sixty votes required. The Senate recessed shortly thereafter. Debate on S 2277 began anew on September 5, after the Labor Day recess. At that time, until the final vote on September 19, 2000, scores of amendments were offered by senators; all failed by various margins. On September 19, 2000, the bill passed without amendment on an 83–15 vote with most senators voting as they had done on the cloture motion. Throughout that period, however, lobbyists kept up their pressure on the committed to make sure that no amendments were added to the bill that would require House reconsideration.

The bill was signed by President Clinton on October 10, 2000, amid considerable fanfare. Throughout the course of this bill becoming law, Clinton used his office in a way reminiscent of Lyndon B. Johnson's cajoling of recalcitrant legislators. One member got a new zip code for a small town and another got a natural gas pipeline for his district.[52] In the end, these kinds of efforts were crucial to House passage of the bill.

China became a member of the World Trade Organization on December 11, 2001. On December 28, 2001, President George W. Bush signed a formal proclamation granting normal trading status to China, ending annual reviews. In 2004, however, the United States and the European Union lodged WTO complaints against China, charging that it had failed to fulfill promises to open its markets to other nations.[53] Complaints from Washington and around the world have continued since that time. In early 2006, for example, President Bush filed a complaint with the WTO charging that Chinese officials were not fully opening their markets to American auto parts and manufacturers.[54]

The issue of trade relations with China resurfaced during the 2008 presidential election. Campaigning for the Democratic presidential nomination, New York Senator Hillary Clinton was at the forefront of criticizing the Bush administration's policies. "Over the course of the last seven years, Bush policies have allowed the Chinese government to become our banker," Clinton said. "Today, China's steel comes here and our jobs go there. We play by the rules and they manipulate their currency. We get tainted fish and lead-laced toys and poison pet food in return."

Photo courtesy: Paul Sakama/AP World Wide Photos

Is the China trade agreement working? In 2007 and 2008, the American public was shocked to learn that dog food, toys, and fish imported from China contained exceedingly high levels of lead and other chemicals. The Curious George dolls shown here were among the many toys recalled by their manufacturer.

Toward Reform: Congressional Checks on the Executive and Judicial Branches

The Constitution envisioned that the Congress, the president, and the judiciary would have discrete powers, and that one branch would be able to hold the other in check. Over the years, and especially since the 1930s, the president often has held the upper hand. In times of crisis or simply when it was unable to meet public demands for solutions, Congress willingly has handed over its authority to the chief executive. Even though the chief executive has been granted greater latitude, Congress does, of course, retain ultimate legislative authority to question executive actions and to halt administration activities by cutting off funds for programs a president wants. Congress also wields ultimate power over the president, since it can impeach and even remove him from office. Similar checks and balances affect relations between Congress and the courts.

The Shifting Balance of Power

The balance of power between Congress and the president has seesawed over time. The post–Civil War Congress attempted to regain control of the vast executive powers that President Abraham Lincoln, recently slain, had assumed. Angered at the refusal of Lincoln's successor, Andrew Johnson, to go along with its radical "reforms" of the South, Congress passed the Tenure of Office Act, which prevented the president, under the threat of civil penalty, from removing any Cabinet-level appointees of the previous administration. Johnson accepted the challenge and fired Lincoln's secretary of war, who many believed was guilty of heinous war crimes. The House voted to impeach Johnson, but the desertion of a handful of Republican senators prevented him from being removed from office. (The effort fell short by one vote.) Nonetheless, the president's power had

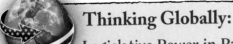

Thinking Globally:

Legislative Power in Parliamentary Systems

The executive branch in most parliamentary systems is dependent upon the direct support of the legislative branch—the parliament. In the bulk of parliamentary systems, the head of government (typically called the prime minister) is chosen by the governing party or coalition of parties in the parliament.

- Do the principles of separation of powers and checks and balances that characterize American government help or hinder effective governance? In what ways?
- Under which system is the legislative branch more powerful? Why?

been greatly weakened, and the Congress again became the center of power and authority in the federal government.

Beginning in the early 1900s, however, a series of strong presidents acted at the expense of congressional power. Theodore Roosevelt, Franklin D. Roosevelt, and Lyndon B. Johnson viewed the presidency as carrying with it enormous powers. Especially since the presidency of Franklin D. Roosevelt, Congress has ceded to the president a major role in the legislative process. Today, Congress often finds itself responding to executive-branch proposals. Critics of Congress point to its slow and unwieldy nature as well as the complexity of national problems as reasons that it often does not seem to act on its own. Many commentators have concluded that this power void allowed President George W. Bush to claim unprecedented presidential powers, as is discussed further below and in chapter 8.

The Bush administration made it clear, more than any administration before it, that it believed that Congress had limited oversight function, especially in times of war. In a further display of dominance, the Bush administration, which refused to honor subpoenas for information from Congress, was the first administration to enter a member of Congress's office to execute a search warrant. In 2006, FBI agents searched the office of Representative William J. Jefferson (D–LA) and removed files as part of an investigation of bribe-taking. This unprecedented action was criticized by House Speaker Dennis Hastert (R–IL), who "pushed Bush strongly on the issue."[55]

Congressional Oversight of the Executive Branch

oversight
Congressional review of the activities of an agency, department, or office.

From the the 1960s through the election of President George W. Bush, Congress increased its **oversight** of the executive branch. Oversight subcommittees became particularly prominent in the 1970s and 1980s as a means of promoting investigation and program review, to determine if an agency, department, or office is carrying out its responsibilities as intended by Congress.[56] Congressional oversight also includes checking on possible abuses of power by members of the military and governmental officials, including the president. The Republican-controlled Congress was especially mindful of its oversight duties during the Clinton administration. Not only did it regularly hold oversight hearings involving Cabinet secretaries, but it also launched several investigations of the Clintons themselves, such as Travelgate, the Clintons' investments in the failed Whitewater development in Arkansas, and, of course, President Bill Clinton's involvement with intern Monica Lewinsky, which led to his impeachment in the House and trial in the Senate.

Historically, the key to Congress's performance of its oversight function is its ability to question members of the administration to see if they are enforcing and interpreting the laws as intended by Congress. These committee hearings, now routinely televised, are among Congress's most visible and dramatic actions. The hearings are not used simply to gather information. Hearings may focus on particular executive-branch actions and often signal that Congress believes changes in policy need to be made before an agency next comes before the committee to justify its budget. Hearings also are used to improve program administration. Since most members of House and Senate committees and subcommittees are interested in the issues under their jurisdiction, they often want to help and not hinder policy makers.

Although most top government officials appear before various House and Senate committees regularly to update them on their activities, this is not necessarily the case for those who do not require Senate confirmation. Moreover, sometimes members of the administration are reluctant to appear before Congress.

With the election of President George W. Bush, a highly partisan, Republican-controlled Congress worked to lessen the oversight role of Congress as "centralized power was deployed uncritically in the service of the White House agenda."[57] A bipartisan team of congressional scholars concluded that the Bush administration preferred to keep Democratic lawmakers out of the loop, and had "aggressively fought to expand executive power vis-à-vis Congress. . . . Strong majority leadership in Congress had not led to vigorous exercise of congressional authority and responsibility but to a general obeisance to presidential initiative and passivity in the face of presidential power."[58]

Thus, the Bush years saw an unprecedented decline in congressional oversight. Democrats grew increasingly frustrated by what they perceived first as the Republican majority's failure to investigate thoroughly a host of issues, including the September 11, 2001 terrorist attacks, Medicare prescription drug costs, abuse of detainees in Iraq and Afghanistan, and the government's responses to Hurricanes Katrina and Rita. Winning both the House and Senate in 2007 resulted in Democrats trying to reassert their responsibility to exercise this important constitutional check on the executive branch. Still, the Bush White House claimed that Congress lacked the authority to compel testimony or review documents, especially those involving conduct of the Iraq War.

As Congress has moved to reclaim its traditional oversight function, members have additional means of oversight at their disposal. Legislators may augment their formal oversight of the executive branch by allowing citizens to appeal adverse bureaucratic decisions to agencies, Congress, and even the courts. The Congressional Review Act of 1996 allows Congress to nullify agency regulations by joint resolutions of legislative disapproval. This process, called **congressional review,** is another method of exercising congressional oversight.[59] The act provides Congress with sixty days to disapprove newly announced agency regulations, often passed to implement some congressional action. A regulation is disapproved if the resolution is passed by both chambers and signed by the president, or when Congress overrides a presidential veto of a disapproving resolution. Since its passage, only thirty-seven joint resolutions of disapproval relating to twenty-eight rules have been introduced.[60] To date, this act has been used only once—in 2001—when Congress and the president reversed Clinton administration ergonomics regulations, which were intended to prevent job-related repetitive stress injuries.

Photo courtesy: Chip Somodevilla/Getty Images

How does congressional oversight function? Then Senate Armed Services Committee Chair John Warner (R–VA), ranking Democrat Carl Levin (D–MI), and committee members Robert Byrd (D–WV) and John McCain (R–AZ) caucus before holding a markup hearing about the Military Commissions Act of 2006. The act provides the president with unprecedented powers to detain and interrogate citizens and noncitizens accused of terrorism. While some observers believe that the compromise eventually worked out between the White House and members of Congress indicated appropriate congressional oversight, others believe that a number of the act's provisions are unconstitutional and compromise Congress's ability to review executive branch actions.

congressional review
A process whereby Congress can nullify agency regulations by a joint resolution of legislative disapproval.

FOREIGN POLICY AND NATIONAL SECURITY The Constitution divides foreign policy powers between the executive and the legislative branches. The president has the power to wage war and negotiate treaties, whereas the Congress has the power to declare war and the Senate has the power to ratify treaties. The executive branch, however, has become preeminent in foreign affairs despite the constitutional division of powers. This supremacy is partly due to a series of crises and the development of nuclear weapons in the twentieth century; both have necessitated quick decision making and secrecy, which are much easier to manage in the executive branch. Congress, with its 535 voting members, has a more difficult time reaching a consensus and keeping secrets.

After years of playing second fiddle to a series of presidents from Theodore Roosevelt to Richard M. Nixon, a "snoozing Congress" was "aroused" and seized for itself the authority and expertise necessary to go head to head with the chief executive.[61] In a delayed response to Lyndon B. Johnson's conduct of the Vietnam War, in 1973 Congress passed the **War Powers Act** over President Nixon's veto. This act requires presi-

War Powers Act
Passed by Congress in 1973; the president is limited in the deployment of troops overseas to a sixty-day period in peacetime (which can be extended for an extra thirty days to permit withdrawal) unless Congress explicitly gives its approval for a longer period.

July 17, 2003

Dear Mr. Vice President,

I am writing to reiterate my concern regarding the sensitive intelligence issues we discussed today with the DCI, DIRNSA, Chairman Roberts and our House Intelligence Committee counterparts.

Most respectfully,

Jay Rockefeller

Photo courtesy: bottom, Alex Wong/Getty Images; top, Office of Jay Rockefeller

How do members of Congress assert their authority? Senator Jay Rockefeller (D–WV) went public with his criticisms of the Bush administration's domestic surveillance program in December of 2005. Rockefeller sent a handwritten letter voicing his concerns to Vice President Dick Cheney in 2003 (see excerpt above), noting that he was placing a handwritten copy of the letter in a safe to insure that his concerns and recollection of events were recorded for posterity. When the administration subsequently argued that Congress had been adequately briefed on the program and implied members had raised no concerns about it, Rockefeller released his letter to the press.

dents to obtain congressional approval before committing U.S. forces to a combat zone. It also requires them to notify Congress within forty-eight hours of committing troops to foreign soil. In addition, the president must withdraw troops within sixty days unless Congress votes to declare war. The president also is required to consult with Congress, if at all possible, prior to committing troops.

The War Powers Act has been of limited effectiveness in claiming a larger congressional role in international crisis situations. Presidents Gerald R. Ford, Jimmy Carter, and Ronald Reagan never consulted Congress in advance of committing troops, citing the need for secrecy and swift movement, although each president did notify Congress shortly after the incidents. They contended that the War Powers Act was probably unconstitutional because it limits presidential prerogatives as commander in chief, as discussed in greater detail in chapter 8.

The issue of oversight is particularly thorny for a nation at war. As early as July 17, 2003, for example, Senator Jay Rockefeller (D–WV), the ranking member on the Senate Intelligence Committee, wrote to Vice President Dick Cheney that he was very troubled by what he had heard at a secret intelligence briefing. These secret briefings, which usually involved the White House revealing information to House and Senate members on the respective Intelligence Committees, are part of the oversight process, yet committee members are prohibited from telling anyone—even other members of Congress or key staffers—of the contents of the meetings. At this particular briefing, Rockefeller had been apprised that the National Security Agency was monitoring Americans' phone and e-mail communications without the judicial oversight called for by law. "Clearly," wrote Rockefeller, "the activities we discussed raise profound oversight issues."[62]

CONFIRMATION OF PRESIDENTIAL APPOINTMENTS   The Senate plays a special oversight function through its ability to confirm key members of the executive branch, as well as presidential appointments to the federal courts. As discussed in chapters 9 and 10, although the Senate generally confirms most presidential nominees, it does not always do so. A wise president considers senatorial reaction before nominating potentially controversial individuals to his administration or to the federal courts.

THE IMPEACHMENT PROCESS   As discussed earlier, the impeachment process is Congress's ultimate oversight of the U.S. president (as well as of federal court judges). The U.S. Constitution is quite vague about the impeachment process, and much of the debate about it concerns what is an impeachable offense. The Constitution specifies that a president can be impeached for treason, bribery, or other "high crimes and misdemeanors." Most commentators agree that this phrase was meant to mean significant abuses of power.

House and Senate rules control how the impeachment process operates. (To learn move about the impeachment process, see Table 7.7.) Yet, because the process is used so rarely, and under such disparate circumstances, there are few hard and fast rules. The U.S. House of Representatives has voted to impeach only seventeen federal officials. Of those, seven were convicted and removed from office and three resigned before the process described below was completed.

Only four resolutions against presidents have resulted in further action: (1) John Tyler, charged with corruption and misconduct in 1843; (2) Andrew Johnson, charged with serious misconduct in 1868; (3) Richard M. Nixon, charged with obstruction and the abuse of power in 1974; and, (4) Bill Clinton, charged with perjury and obstruction of justice in 1998. The House rejected the charges against Tyler; Johnson was acquitted by the Senate by a one-vote margin; Nixon resigned before the full House voted on the articles of impeachment; and Clinton was acquitted by the Senate by a vote of 55–45 against impeachment.

Congress and the Judiciary

As part of our system of checks and balances, the power of judicial review (discussed in chapters 2 and 10) gives the Supreme Court the power to review the constitutionality of acts of Congress. This is a potent power because Congress must ever be mindful to make sure that the laws that it passes are in accord with the U.S. Constitution. That is not to say, however, that Congress always does this. In spite of a 2000 Supreme Court case that indicated that a Nebraska state law banning partial birth abortion was unconstitutional, the U.S. Congress passed its own version outlawing the procedure. And, ultimately, the Roberts Court upheld the constitutionality of the federal law.

Congress exercises its control over the judiciary in a variety of ways. Not only does it have the constitutional authority to establish the size of the Supreme Court, its appellate jurisdiction, the structure of the federal court system, and to allocate its budget, but the Senate also has the authority to accept or reject presidential nominees to the federal courts (as well as top executive branch appointments).

In the case of federal district court appointments, senators often have considerable say in the nomination of judges from their states through **senatorial courtesy,** a

senatorial courtesy
A process by which presidents, when selecting district court judges, defer to the senator in whose state the vacancy occurs.

TABLE 7.7 The Eight Stages of the Impeachment Process

1. **The Resolution.** A resolution, called an inquiry of impeachment, is sent to the House Judiciary Committee. Members also may introduce bills of impeachment, which are referred to the Judiciary Committee.
2. **The Committee Vote.** After the consideration of voluminous evidence, the Judiciary Committee votes on the resolution or bill of impeachment. A positive vote from the committee indicates its belief that there is sufficiently strong evidence for impeachment in the House.
3. **The House Vote.** If articles of impeachment are recommended by the House Judiciary Committee, the full House votes to approve (or disapprove) a Judiciary Committee decision to conduct full-blown impeachment hearings.
4. **The Hearings.** Extensive evidentiary hearings are held by the House Judiciary Committee concerning the allegations of wrongdoing. Witnesses may be called and the scope of the inquiry may be widened at this time.
5. **The Report.** The committee votes on one or more articles of impeachment. Reports supporting this finding (as well as dissenting views) are forwarded to the House and become the basis for its consideration of specific articles of impeachment.
6. **The House Vote.** The full House votes on each article of impeachment. A simple majority vote on any article is sufficient to send that article to the Senate for its consideration.
7. **The Trial in the Senate.** A trial is conducted on the floor of the Senate with the House Judiciary Committee bringing the case against the president, who is represented by his own private attorneys. The Senate, in essence, acts as the jury, with the chief justice of the United States presiding over the trial.
8. **The Senate Vote.** The full Senate votes on each article of impeachment. If there is a two-thirds vote on any article, the president automatically is removed from office and the vice president assumes the duty of the president.

process by which presidents generally defer to the senators who represent the state where the vacancy occurs. The judicial nominees of both Presidents Bill Clinton and George W. Bush encountered a particularly hostile Senate. "Appointments have always been the battleground for policy disputes," says one political scientist. But now, "what's new is the rawness of it—all of the veneer is off."[63] (Nominations to the Supreme Court and lower federal courts are discussed in chapter 10.)

An equally potent form of congressional oversight of the judicial branch that involves both the House and the Senate is the setting of the jurisdiction of the federal courts. Originally, the jurisdiction, or ability of the federal courts to hear cases, was quite limited. Over time, however, as Congress legislated to regulate the economy and even crime, the caseload of the courts skyrocketed. But, no matter how busy federal judges are, it is ultimately up to the Congress to determine the number of judges on each court.

During the 109th Congress, several members, unhappy with Supreme Court decisions and the Senate's failure to pass a proposed constitutional amendment to ban same-sex marriage, began to push for a bill to prevent federal courts from hearing challenges to the federal Defense of Marriage Act. In the House, the Republican majority leader pledged to promote similar legislation to bar court challenges to the Pledge of Allegiance and other social issues, including abortion. When Congress rears the ugly head of jurisdiction, it is signaling to the federal courts that Congress believes federal judges have gone too far.

WHAT SHOULD I HAVE LEARNED?

The size and scope of Congress, and the demands put on it, have increased tremendously over the years. In presenting the important role that Congress plays in American politics, we have answered the following questions:

■ **What are the roots of the legislative branch of government?**
The Constitution created a bicameral legislature with members of each body to be elected differently, and thus to represent different constituencies. Article I of the Constitution sets forth qualifications for office, states age minimums, and specifies how legislators are to be distributed among the states. The Constitution also requires seats in the House of Representatives to be apportioned by population. Thus, after every U.S. Census, district lines must be redrawn to reflect population shifts. The Constitution also provides a vast array of enumerated and implied powers to Congress. Some, such as law-making and oversight, are shared by both houses of Congress; others are not.

■ **How is Congress organized?**
Political parties play a major role in the way Congress is organized. The Speaker of the House is traditionally a member of the majority party, and members of the majority party chair all committees. Because the House of Representatives is large, the Speaker enforces more rigid rules on the House than exist in the Senate. In addition to the party leaders, Congress has a labyrinth of committees and subcommittees that cover the entire range of government policies, often with a confusing tangle of shared responsibilities. Each legislator serves on one or more committees and multiple subcommittees. It is in these environments that many policies are shaped and that members make their primary contributions to solving public problems.

■ **Who are the members of Congress?**
Members of Congress live in two worlds—in their home districts and in the District of Columbia. They must attempt to appease two constituencies—party leaders, colleagues, and lobbyists in Washington, D.C., and constituents in their home districts.

■ **How do the members of Congress make decisions?**
A multitude of factors affect legislators as they decide policy issues. These include political party, constituents, colleagues and caucuses, staff and support agencies and interest groups, lobbyists, and political action committees.

■ **How does Congress make laws?**
The road to enacting a bill into law is long and strewn with obstacles, and only a small share of the proposals introduced become law. Legislation must be approved by committees in each house and on the floor of each chamber. In addition, most House legislation initially is considered by a subcommittee and must be approved by the House Committee on Rules before getting to the floor. Legislation that is passed in different forms by the two chambers must be resolved in a conference before going back to each chamber for a vote and then to the president, who can sign the proposal into law, veto it, or allow it to become law without his signature. If Congress adjourns within ten days of passing legislation, that bill will die if the president does not sign it.

What are the major congressional checks on the executive and judicial branches? Congress has attempted to oversee the actions of the president and the executive branch through committee hearings, the War Powers Act, and the power to confirm or reject presidential appointments. Its ultimate weapon is the power of impeachment and conviction. Congress also exercises its control over the judiciary in a variety of ways. It has the constitutional authority to establish the size of the Supreme Court, its appellate jurisdiction, and the structure of the federal court system.

Key Terms

apportionment, p. 238
bicameral legislature, p. 236
bill, p. 238
cloture, p. 260
conference committee, p. 246
congressional review, p. 267
delegate, p. 252
discharge petition, p. 247
divided government, p. 254
earmark, p. 248
filibuster, p. 259
hold, p. 258
impeachment, p. 239

incumbency, p. 250
joint committee, p. 246
logrolling, p. 255
majority leader, p. 244
majority party, p. 240
markup, p. 258
minority leader, p. 244
minority party, p. 240
oversight, p. 266
party caucus or conference, p. 244
pocket veto, p. 262
politico, p. 252
pork, p. 248

president pro tempore, p. 244
redistricting, p. 238
select (or special) committee, p. 246
senatorial courtesy, p. 269
seniority, p. 249
Speaker of the House, p. 242
standing committee, p. 246
trustee, p. 252
veto, p. 261
War Powers Act, p. 267
whip, p. 244

Researching Congress
In the Library

Adler, E. Scott, and John S. Lapinski. *The Macropolitics of Congress.* Princeton, NJ: Princeton University Press, 2006.

Bianco, William T., ed. *Congress on Display, Congress at Work.* Ann Arbor: University of Michigan Press, 2000.

Binder, Sarah A. *Stalemate: Causes and Consequences of Legislative Gridlock.* Washington, DC: Brookings Institute, 2003.

Cox, Gary W., and Mathew D. McCubbins. *Setting the Agenda: Responsible Party Government in the U.S. House of Representatives.* New York: Cambridge University Press, 2005.

Davidson, Roger H., Walter Oleszek, and Frances E. Lee. *Congress and Its Members*, 11th ed. Washington, DC: CQ Press, 2007.

Dodd, Lawrence C., and Bruce I. Oppenheimer, eds. *Congress Reconsidered*, 8th ed. Washington, DC: CQ Press, 2007.

Evans, Diana. *Greasing the Wheels: Using Pork Barrel Projects to Build Majority Coalitions in Congress.* New York: Cambridge University Press, 2004.

Fenno, Richard F., Jr. *Home Style: House Members in Their Districts*, reprint ed. New York: Longman, 2002.

Gertzog, Irwin N. *Women and Power on Capitol Hill: Reconstructing the Congressional Women's Caucus.* Boulder, CO: Lynne Rienner, 2004.

Mayhew, David R. *Congress: The Electoral Connection*, 2nd ed. New Haven, CT: Yale University Press, 2004.

O'Connor, Karen, ed. *Women in Congress: Running, Winning, and Ruling.* New York: Haworth, 2004.

Oleszek, Walter J. *Congressional Procedures and the Policy Process*, 7th ed. Washington, DC: CQ Press, 2007.

Price, David E. *The Congressional Experience: A View from the Hill*, 3rd ed. Boulder, CO: Westview, 2005.

Quirk, Paul J., and Sarah A. Binder, eds. *Institutions of American Democracy: The Legislative Branch.* New York: Oxford University Press, 2006.

Rosenthal, Cindy Simon, ed. *Women Transforming Congress.* Norman: University of Oklahoma Press, 2003.

Smith, Steven S. *Party Influence in Congress.* New York: Cambridge University Press, 2007.

Theriault, Sean M. *Party Polarization in Congress.* New York: Cambridge University Press, 2008.

On the Web

To learn more about the legislative branch, go to the official Web site of the Senate, **www.senate.gov,** and of the House of Representatives, **www.house.gov.**

The Library of Congress's home page for information related to the legislative branch is named Thomas, in honor of President Thomas Jefferson. From the home page at **thomas.loc.gov,** you can research roll call votes, committee reports, and the Congressional Record.

Project Vote Smart is a nonpartisan group dedicated to providing U.S. citizens with the factual information they need to be informed voters. The Web site **www.votesmart.org** provides biographical information about members of Congress and lists the grades given to elected representatives by a range of interest groups.

THE NATION MOURNS.

8

The Presidency

When Ronald Reagan died on June 5, 2004, many Americans, first in California and then in Washington, D.C., lined up for hours to pay their respects to the man who had been the fortieth president of the United States. Many people were able to see, for the first time in recent memory, the grandeur of a presidential state funeral. Reagan was the first president to lie in state in the Rotunda of the Capitol since Lyndon B. Johnson did in January 1973, and one of only nine American presidents to receive that honor.

Presidential funerals underscore the esteem with which most Americans accord the office of the president, regardless of its occupant. Just before the first president, George Washington, died, he made it known that he wanted his burial to be a quiet one, "without parade or funeral oration." He also asked that he not be buried for three days; at that time, it was not without precedent to make this kind of request out of fear of being buried alive. Despite these requests, Washington's funeral was a state occasion as hundreds of soldiers, with their rifles held backward, marched to Mount Vernon, Virginia, where he was interred. Across the nation, imitation funerals were held, and the military wore black armbands for six months.[1] It was during

Washington's memorial service that Henry Lee declared that the former president was "first in war, first in peace, and first in the hearts of his countrymen."[2]

When Abraham Lincoln died in 1865 after being wounded by an assassin's bullet, more than a dozen funerals were held for him. Hundreds of thousands of mourners lined the way as the train carrying his open casket traveled the 1,700 miles to Illinois, where he was buried next to the body of his young son, who had died three years earlier. Most presidents' bodies were transported to their final resting place by train, allowing ordinary Americans the opportunity to pay their respects as the train traveled long distances. When Franklin D. Roosevelt died in Warm Springs, Georgia, his body was transported to Washington, D.C., and then to Hyde Park, New York, where he, like Washington, was buried on his family's estate.

Today, one of the first things a president is asked to do upon taking office is to consider funeral plans. The military has a book 138 pages long devoted to the kind of ceremony and traditions that were so evident in the Reagan funeral: a horse-drawn caisson; a riderless horse with boots hung backward in the stirrups to indicate that the deceased will ride no more; a twenty-one-gun salute; a flyover by military aircraft. Each president's family, however, has personalized their private, yet also public opportunity to mourn. The Reagan family, for example, filed a 300-page plan for the

■ **Presidential funerals have been occasions for national mourning since the death of the United States' first president, George Washington.** At left, the nation mourns President Abraham Lincoln, the first American president to be assassinated. At right, current and former presidents and their wives attend a funeral service for President Ronald Reagan in the National Cathedral prior to his interment in California.

WHAT SHOULD I KNOW ABOUT ...
- the roots of the office of the president of the United States?
- the constitutional powers of the president?
- the development and expansion of presidential power?
- the presidential establishment?
- presidential leadership and the importance of public opinion?
- the president as policy maker?

TO LEARN MORE—

—TO DO MORE

Find out more about President Gerald R. Ford's funeral at the Ford Presidential Library, www.fordlibrarymuseum.gov.

funeral in 1989 and updated it regularly. Former president Gerald R. Ford filed a plan that was enacted after his death 2006. Presidents Jimmy Carter and George Bush have also filed formal plans; Bill Clinton and George W. Bush have yet to do so.

The Reagan funeral also created a national time-out from the news of war, and even presidential campaigns were halted in respect for the deceased president. One historian commented that the event gave Americans the opportunity to "rediscover . . . what holds us together instead of what pulls us apart."[3] This is often the role of presidents—in life or in death.

Comparing Executive Branches

The authority granted to the president by the U.S. Constitution and through subsequent congressional legislation makes it a position with awesome power and responsibility. Not only did the Framers not envision such a powerful role for the president, but they could not have foreseen the skepticism with which many presidential actions are now greeted in the press, on talk radio, and on the Internet. Presidents have gone into policy arenas never dreamed of by the Framers. Imagine, for example, what the Framers might have thought about President George W. Bush's 2004 State of the Union message, in which he advocated colonizing Mars and addressed steroid use; or his 2006 address, in which he asked legislators to prohibit "the most egregious abuse of medical research—human cloning."

The modern media, used by successful presidents to help advance their agendas, have brought us closer to our presidents and made them seem more human, a mixed blessing for those trying to lead. Only two photographs exist of President Franklin D. Roosevelt in a wheelchair—his paralysis was a closely guarded secret. Five decades later, Bill Clinton was asked on national TV what kind of underwear he preferred (briefs). Later, revelations about his conduct with intern Monica Lewinsky made this disclosure seem tame. This demystification of the office of the president and increasing mistrust of government make governing a difficult job.

A president relies on more than the formal powers of office to lead the nation: public opinion and confidence are key components of his ability to get his programs adopted and his vision of the nation implemented. As political scientist Richard E. Neustadt has noted, the president's power often rests on his power to persuade.[4] To persuade, he not only must be able to forge links with members of Congress, but he also must have the support of the American people and the respect of foreign leaders.

The abilities to persuade and to marshal the informal powers of the presidency have become more important over time. In fact, the presidency of George W. Bush and the circumstances that surround it were dramatically different from the presidency of his father, George Bush (1989–1993). America is changing dramatically and so are the responsibilities of the president as well as people's expectations of the person who holds that office. Presidents in the last century battled the Great Depression, fascism, communism, and several wars involving American soldiers.

The nation's forty-fourth president, Barack Obama, took office in 2009 with a number of pressing issues to tackle, including the wars in Iraq and Afganistan, and the global economic crisis.

The tension between public expectations about the presidency and the formal powers of the president permeate our discussion of how the office has evolved from its humble origins in Article II of the Constitution to its current stature. In this chapter:

★ First, we will examine *the roots of the office of president of the United States* and discuss how the Framers created a chief executive officer for the new nation.

★ Second, we will discuss *the constitutional powers of the president.*

★ Third, we will examine *the development and expansion of presidential power* and a more personalized presidency.

★ Fourth, we will discuss the development of *the presidential establishment*, the myriad departments, special assistants, and advisers who help the president but also make it easier for a president to lose touch with the common citizen.

★ Fifth, we will examine *presidential leadership and the importance of public opinion,* including the effect that public opinion has on the American presidency and the role the president plays in molding public opinion.

★ Finally, we will focus on *the president's role as policy maker.*

Roots of the Office of President of the United States

The earliest example of executive power in the colonies was the position of royal governor. These appointees of the king of England governed each colony and normally were entrusted with the "powers of appointment, military command, expenditure, and—within limitations—pardon, as well as with large powers in connection with the powers of law making."[5] Royal governors often found themselves at odds with the colonists and especially with elected colonial legislatures. As representatives of the crown, the governors were distrusted and disdained by the people, many of whom had fled from Great Britain to escape royal domination. Others, generations removed from England, no longer felt strong ties to the king and his power over them.

When the colonists declared their independence from Great Britain in 1776, their distrust of a strong chief executive remained. Most state constitutions reduced the once-powerful office of governor to a symbolic post elected annually by the legislature. However, some states did entrust wider powers to their chief executives. The governor of New York, for example, was elected directly by the people. Perhaps because he then was accountable to the people, he was given the power to pardon, the duty to execute the laws faithfully to the best of his ability, and the power to act as commander in chief of the state militia.

Under the Articles of Confederation, there was no executive branch of government; the eighteen different men who served as the president of the Continental Congress of the United States of America were president in name only—they held no actual authority or power in the new nation. When the delegates to the Constitutional Convention met in Philadelphia to fashion a new government, there was little dissention about the need for an executive branch to implement the laws made by Congress. Although some delegates suggested there should be multiple executives, eventually the Framers agreed that executive authority should be vested in one person. This agreement was relatively seamless because the Framers were sure that George Washington—whom they had trusted with their lives during the Revolutionary War—would become the first president of the new nation.

The Framers also had no problem in agreeing on a title for the new office. Borrowing from the constitutions of several states, the Framers called the new chief executive the president. How the president was to be chosen and by whom was a major stumbling block. James Wilson of Philadelphia suggested a single, more powerful president, who would be elected by the people and "independent of the legislature." Wilson also suggested giving the executive an absolute veto over the acts of Congress. "Without such a defense," he wrote, "the legislature can at any moment sink it [the executive] into non-existence."[6]

The manner of the president's election haunted the Framers for some time, and their solution to the dilemma—the creation of the Electoral College—is described in detail in chapter 13. We leave the resolution of that issue aside for now and turn instead to details of the issues the Framers resolved quickly.

Presidential Qualifications and Terms of Office

Comparing Chief Executives

The Constitution requires that the president (and the vice president, whose major function is to succeed the president in the event of his death or disability) be a natural-born citizen of the United States, at least thirty-five years old, and a resident of the United States for at least fourteen years. In the 1700s, those engaged in international diplomacy were often out of the country for substantial periods of time, and the Framers wanted to make sure that prospective presidents spent significant time on this country's shores before running for its highest elective office. Most presidents have prior elective experience, too, as revealed in Table 8.1. While there is no constitutional bar to a woman or member of a minority group seeking the presidency, Barack Obama is the only non-white male to be elected to this office.

Although only two of the last six presidents failed to win election to a second term, at one time the length of a president's term was controversial. Four-, seven-, and eleven-year terms with no eligibility for reelection were suggested by various delegates to the Constitutional Convention. The Framers ultimately reached agreement on a four-year term with eligibility for reelection.

The first president, George Washington (1789–1797), sought reelection only once, and a two-term limit for presidents became traditional. Although Ulysses S. Grant unsuccessfully sought a third term, the two terms established by Washington remained the standard for 150 years, avoiding the Framers' much-feared "constitutional monarch," a perpetually reelected tyrant. In the 1930s and 1940s, however, Franklin D. Roosevelt ran successfully in four elections as Americans fought first the Great Depression and then World War II. Despite Roosevelt's popularity, negative reaction to his long tenure in office ultimately led to passage (and ratification in 1951) of the **Twenty-Second Amendment.** It limits presidents to two four-year terms. A vice president who succeeds a president due to death, resignation, or impeachment is eligible for a total of ten years in office: two years of a

Who serves as president of the United States? Before Barack Obama, all of the people who served as president were white men. Here, five former presidents—Richard M. Nixon, Gerald R. Ford, Jimmy Carter, Ronald Reagan and George Bush—gather to celebrate the opening of the Reagan Presidential Library in 1991.

Photo courtesy: Marcy Nighswander/AP/Wide World Photos

TABLE **8.1** Personal Characteristics of the U.S. Presidents

President	Place of Birth	Higher Education	Occupation	Years in Congress	Years as Governor	Years as Vice President	Age at Becoming President
George Washington	VA	William & Mary	Farmer/surveyor	2	0	0	57
John Adams	MA	Harvard	Farmer/lawyer	5	0	4	61
Thomas Jefferson	VA	William & Mary	Farmer/lawyer	5	3	4	58
James Madison	VA	Princeton	Farmer	15	0	0	58
James Monroe	VA	William & Mary	Farmer/lawyer	7	4	0	59
John Quincy Adams	MA	Harvard	Lawyer	0[a]	0	0	58
Andrew Jackson	SC	None	Lawyer	4	0	0	62
Martin Van Buren	NY	None	Lawyer	8	0	4	55
William H. Harrison	VA	Hampden	Military	0	0	0	68
John Tyler	VA	William & Mary	Lawyer	12	2	0	51
James K. Polk	NC	North Carolina	Lawyer	14	3	0	50
Zachary Taylor	VA	None	Military	0	0	0	65
Millard Fillmore	NY	None	Lawyer	8	0	1	50
Franklin Pierce	NH	Bowdoin	Lawyer	9	0	0	48
James Buchanan	PA	Dickinson	Lawyer	20	0	0	65
Abraham Lincoln	KY	None	Lawyer	2	0	0	52
Andrew Johnson	NC	None	Tailor	14	4	0	57
Ulysses S. Grant	OH	West Point	Military	0	0	0	47
Rutherford B. Hayes	OH	Kenyon	Lawyer	3	6	0	55
James A. Garfield	OH	Williams	Educator/lawyer	18	0	0	50
Chester A. Arthur	VT	Union	Lawyer	0	0	1	51
Grover Cleveland	NJ	None	Lawyer	0	2	0	48
Benjamin Harrison	OH	Miami (Ohio)	Lawyer	6	0	0	56
Grover Cleveland	NJ	None	Lawyer	0	2	0	53
William McKinley	OH	Allegheny	Lawyer	14	4	0	54
Theodore Roosevelt	NY	Harvard	Lawyer/author	0	2	1	43
William H. Taft	OH	Yale	Lawyer	0	0	0	52
Woodrow Wilson	VA	Princeton	Educator	0	2	0	56
Warren G. Harding	OH	Ohio Central	Newspaper editor	6	0	0	56
Calvin Coolidge	VT	Amherst	Lawyer	0	2	3	51
Herbert Hoover	IA	Stanford	Engineer	0	0	0	55
Franklin D. Roosevelt	NY	Harvard/Columbia	Lawyer	0	4	0	49
Harry S Truman	MO	None	Clerk/store owner	10	0	0	61
Dwight D. Eisenhower	TX	West Point	Military	0	0	0	63
John F. Kennedy	MA	Harvard	Journalist	14	0	0	43
Lyndon B. Johnson	TX	Southwest Texas State Teachers' College	Educator	24	0	3	55
Richard M. Nixon	CA	Whittier/Duke	Lawyer	6	0	8	56
Gerald R. Ford	NE	Michigan/Yale	Lawyer	25	0	2	61
Jimmy Carter	GA	Naval Academy	Farmer/business owner	0	4	0	52
Ronald Reagan	IL	Eureka	Actor	0	8	0	69
George Bush	MA	Yale	Business owner	4	0	8	64
Bill Clinton	AR	Georgetown/Yale	Lawyer	0	12	0	46
George W. Bush	CT	Yale/Harvard	Business owner	0	6	0	54
Barack Obama	HI	Columbia/Harvard	Community organizer	3	0	0	48

[a] Adams served in the U.S. House for six years after leaving the presidency.

Source: Adapted from *Presidential Elections Since 1789*, 4th ed. (Washington, DC: CQ Press, 1987), 4; Norman Thomas, Joseph Pika, and Richard Watson, *The Politics of the Presidency*, 3rd ed. (Washington, DC: CQ Press, 1993), 490; Harold W. Stanley and Richard G. Niemi, eds., *Vital Statistics on American Politics 2001–2002* (Washington, DC: CQ Press, 2001). Updated by the authors.

president's remaining term and two elected terms, or more than two years of a president's term followed by one elected term.

The Framers paid little attention to the office of vice president beyond the need to have an immediate official stand-in for the president. Initially, for example, the vice president's one and only function was to assume the office of president in the case of the death of the president or some other emergency. After further debate, the delegates made the vice president the presiding officer of the Senate (except in cases of presidential impeachment). They feared that if the Senate's presiding officer were

Twenty-Second Amendment
Adopted in 1951, prevents a president from serving more than two terms, or more than ten years if he came to office via the death or impeachment of his predecessor.

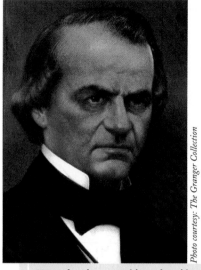

Photo courtesy: The Granger Collection

Photo courtesy: AP/Wide World Photos

Photo courtesy: Tim Sloan/AFP/Getty Images

How often have presidents faced impeachment proceedings? Only two presidents, Andrew Johnson (left) and Bill Clinton (right) have been formally impeached by the House. Richard M. Nixon (center) chose to resign from office rather than face certain impeachment and conviction.

impeachment
The power delegated to the House of Representatives in the Constitution to charge the president, vice president, or other "civil officers," including federal judges, with "Treason, Bribery, or other high Crimes and Misdemeanors." This is the first step in the constitutional process of removing such government officials from office.

executive privilege
An implied presidental power that allows the president to refuse to disclose information regarding confidential conversations or national security to Congress or the judiciary.

chosen from the Senate itself, one state would be short a representative. The vice president was given the authority to vote in that body in the event of a tie.

During the Constitutional Convention, Benjamin Franklin was a staunch supporter of including a provision allowing for **impeachment,** the first step in a formal process to remove a specified official from office. He noted that "historically, the lack of power to impeach had necessitated recourse to assassination."[7] Not surprisingly, then, Franklin urged the rest of the delegates to formulate a legal mechanism to remove the president and vice president.

The impeachment provision ultimately included in Article II was adopted as a check on the power of the president. As we discussed in detail in chapter 7, each house of Congress was given a role to play in the impeachment process to assure that the chief executive could be removed only for "Treason, Bribery, or other high Crimes and Misdemeanors." The House is empowered to vote to impeach the president by a simple majority vote. The Senate then acts as a court of law and tries the president for the charged offenses. A two-thirds majority vote in the Senate on any count contained in the articles of impeachment is necessary to remove the president from office. Only two presidents, Andrew Johnson and Bill Clinton, have been impeached by the House of Representatives. Neither man, however, was removed from office by the Senate. (To learn more about how the impeachment process works, see Table 7.7).

In 1974, President Richard M. Nixon resigned from office rather than face the certainty of impeachment, trial, and removal from office for his role in covering up details about a break-in at the Democratic Party's national headquarters in the Watergate office complex. What came to be known simply as Watergate also produced a major decision from the Supreme Court on the scope of what is termed **executive privilege.** In *U.S. v. Nixon* **(1974),** the Supreme Court ruled unanimously that there was no overriding executive privilege that sanctioned the president's refusal to comply with a court order to produce information for use in the trial of the Watergate defendants. Since then, presidents have varied widely in their use of the claim of executive privilege. President Bill Clinton asserted it several times, especially during the impeachment proceedings against him. President George W. Bush made such claims less frequently, instead often arguing that he and the vice president had what he called "constitutional perogatives."[8]

Rules of Succession

Through 2009, eight presidents have died in office from illness or assassination. William H. Harrison was the first

Thinking Globally

Impeachment in the Philippines

In the United States, use of the impeachment process by the Congress to remove the president is rare. In contrast, in the Philippines, opponents of President Gloria Macapagal Arroyo have filed an impeachment complaint alleging corruption against her every year since she won a disputed election in 2004.

■ Is the impeachment process an effective tool for regulating presidential conduct? Why or why not?
■ Should others in the executive branch be subject to impeachment? Should members of Congress be subject to impeachment? Explain your reasoning.

The Living Constitution

Whenever there is a vacancy in the office of the Vice President, the President shall nominate a Vice President who shall take office upon confirmation by a majority vote of both Houses of Congress.

—TWENTY-FIFTH AMENDMENT, SECTION 2

This clause of the Twenty-Fifth Amendment allows a president to fill a vacancy in the office of vice president with the consent of a simple majority of both Houses of Congress. The purpose of this amendment, which also deals with vacancies in the office of the president, was to remedy some structural flaws in Article II. When this amendment to the Constitution was proposed in 1965, (it was ratified in 1967), seven vice presidents had died in office and one had resigned. For over 20 percent of the nation's history there had been no vice president to assume the office of the president in case of his death or infirmity. When John F. Kennedy was assassinated, Vice President Lyndon B. Johnson became president and the office of vice president was vacant. Since Johnson had suffered a heart attack as vice president, members of Congress were anxious to remedy the problems that might occur should there be no vice president.

Richard M. Nixon followed Johnson as president, and during Nixon's presidency, the office of the vice president became empty twice! First, Nixon's vice president, Spiro T. Agnew, was forced to resign in the wake of charges of bribe taking,

corruption, and income-tax evasion while an elected official in Maryland; he was replaced by popular House Minority Leader Gerald R. Ford (R–MI), who had no trouble getting a majority vote in both houses of Congress to confirm his nomination. When Nixon resigned rather than face sure impeachment, Ford became president and selected the former governor of New York, Nelson A. Rockefeller, to be his vice president. This chain of events set up for the first time in U.S. history a situation in which neither the president nor the vice president had been elected to those positions.

CRITICAL THINKING QUESTIONS

1. Why wasn't the Twenty-Fifth Amendment proposed until 1965? Why might a vice president be more necessary today than in the past?

2. Is it appropriate in a representative democracy to ever have a situation where both the president and the vice president have not been popularly elected?

president to die in office—he caught a cold at his inauguration in 1841 and died one month later. (John Tyler thus became the first vice president to succeed to the presidency.) In 1865, Abraham Lincoln became the first president to be assassinated.

The Framers were aware that a system of orderly transfer of power was necessary; this was the primary reason they created the office of the vice president. To further clarify the order of presidential succession, in 1947, Congress passed the Presidential

U.S. v. Nixon (1974)
Key Supreme Court ruling on power of the president, finding that there is no absolute constitutional executive privilege to allow a president to refuse to comply with a court order to produce information needed in a criminal trial.

TABLE 8.2 Presidential Line of Succession

1. Vice President	10. Secretary of Commerce
2. Speaker of the House	11. Secretary of Labor
3. President Pro Tempore of the Senate	12. Secretary of Health and Human Services
4. Secretary of State	13. Secretary of Housing and Urban Development
5. Secretary of the Treasury	14. Secretary of Transportation
6. Secretary of Defense	15. Secretary of Energy
7. Attorney General	16. Secretary of Education
8. Secretary of the Interior	17. Secretary of Veterans Affairs
9. Secretary of Agriculture	18. Secretary of Homeland Security

Succession Act, which lists—in order—those in line (after the vice president) to succeed the president. (To learn more about the order of succession see Table 8.2.)

The Succession Act has never been used because there has always been a vice president to take over when a president died in office. The **Twenty-Fifth Amendment,** in fact, was added to the Constitution in 1967 to assure that this will continue to be the case. Should a vacancy occur in the office of the vice president, the Twenty-Fifth Amendment directs the president to appoint a new vice president, subject to the approval (by a simple majority) of both houses of Congress. (To learn more, see The Living Constitution: Twenty-Fifth Amendment, Section 2.)

The Twenty-Fifth Amendment also contains a section that allows the vice president and a majority of the Cabinet (or some other body determined by Congress) to deem a president unable to fulfill his duties. It sets up a procedure to allow the vice president to become acting president if the president is incapacitated. The president also voluntarily can relinquish his power. In 2002, for example, President George W. Bush briefly made Vice President Dick Cheney acting president while he underwent a colonoscopy.

Twenty-Fifth Amendment
Adopted in 1967 to establish procedures for filling vacancies in the office of president and vice president as well as providing for procedures to deal with the disability of a president.

Cabinet
The formal body of presidential advisers who head the fifteen executive departments. Presidents often add others to this body of formal advisers.

The Constitutional Powers of the President

Though the Framers largely agreed about the need for a strong central government and a greatly empowered Congress, they did not agree about the proper role of the president or the sweep of his authority. In contrast to Article I's laundry list of enumerated powers for the Congress, Article II details few presidential powers. Perhaps the most important section of Article II is its first sentence: "The executive Power shall be vested in a President of the United States of America." Nonetheless, the sum total of the president's powers, enumerated below, allows him to become a major player in the policy process.

The Appointment Power

To help the president enforce laws passed by Congress, the Constitution authorizes him to appoint, with the advice and consent of the Senate, "Ambassadors, other public Ministers and Consuls, judges of the supreme Court, and all other Officers of the United States, whose Appointments are not herein otherwise provided for, and which shall be established by Law." Although this section of the Constitution deals only with appointments, behind that language is a powerful policy-making tool. The president has the authority to make nearly 3,000 appointments to his administration (of which just over 1,000 require Senate confirmation). He also has the power to remove many of his appointees at will. In addition, he technically appoints more than 75,000 military personnel. Many of these appointees are in positions to wield substantial authority over the course and direction of public policy. Although Congress has the authority "to make all laws," through the president's enforcement power—and his chosen assistants—he often can set the policy agenda for the nation. And, especially in the context of his ability to make appointments to the federal courts, his influence can be felt far past his term of office.

It is not surprising, then, that selecting the right people is often one of a president's most important tasks. Presidents look for a blend of loyalty, competence, and integrity. Identifying these qualities in people is a major challenge that every new president faces. Recent presidents, especially Bill Clinton and George W. Bush, have made an effort to create a Cabinet and staff that, in President Clinton's terms, looks "more like America." (To learn more about the proportion of women appointees, see Table 8.3.)

In the past, when a president forwarded a nomination to the Senate for its approval, his selections traditionally were given great respect—especially

Who takes responsibility for a president's failures? In the wake of Democratic wins that some attributed to President George W. Bush's low approval ratings, Secretary of Defense Donald Rumsfeld surprised observers when he resigned a day after the 2006 midterm elections. Here, President Bush escorts Rumsfeld to the door of the Oval Office after the president introduced his nominee for Rumsfeld's replacement, Robert Gates.

Photo courtesy: Tim Sloan/Getty Images

those for the **Cabinet,** an advisory group selected by the president to help him make decisions and execute the laws. In fact, until the Clinton administration, the vast majority (97 percent) of all presidential nominations were confirmed.[9]

Rejections of presidential nominees as well as onerous delays in their approval can have a major impact on the course of an administration. Rejections leave a president without first choices, affect a president's relationship with the Senate, and affect how the president is perceived by the public. Rejections and delays also have a chilling effect on other potential nominees. Still, President George W. Bush had little problem getting two nominees for the U.S. Supreme Court approved by the Republican-controlled Senate.

Photo courtesy: Morteza Nikoubazl/Reuters/Landov

The Power to Convene Congress

The Constitution requires the president to inform the Congress periodically of "the State of the Union," and authorizes the president to convene either or both houses of Congress on "extraordinary Occasions." In *Federalist No. 77*, Hamilton justified the latter by noting that because the Senate and the chief executive enjoy concurrent powers to make treaties, "It might often be necessary to call it together with a view to this object, when it would be unnecessary and improper to convene the House of Representatives." The power to convene Congress was important when Congress did not sit in nearly year-round sessions.

The Power to Make Treaties

The president's power to make treaties with foreign nations is checked by the Constitution's stipulation that all treaties must be approved by at least two-thirds of the members of the Senate. The chief executive can also "receive ambassadors," wording that has been interpreted to allow the president to recognize the existence of other nations.

Historically, the Senate ratifies about 70 percent of the treaties submitted to it by the president.[10] Only sixteen treaties that have been put to a vote have been rejected, often under highly partisan circumstances. Perhaps the most notable example of the Senate's refusal to ratify a treaty was its defeat of the Treaty of Versailles submitted by President Woodrow Wilson in 1919. The treaty was an agreement among the major nations to end World War I. At Wilson's insistence, it also called for the creation of the League of Nations—a precursor of the United Nations—to foster continued peace and international disarmament. In struggling to gain international acceptance for the

How does a president use his appointment power? The president's power to nominate justices to the Supreme Court serves as a key check on the judiciary. In 2005, President George W. Bush nominated White House counsel and long-time political aide Harriet E. Miers to replace Justice Sandra Day O'Connor. Miers later withdrew her name from consideration following questions from social conservatives about her policy positions and concern about her legal qualifications.

SIMULATION

You Are the President and Need to Appoint a Supreme Court Justice

TABLE **8.3** Women on Presidential Teams: Carter to G. W. Bush

	Total Appointments	Total Women	Percentage Women
Jimmy Carter	1,087	191	17.6%
Ronald Reagan	2,349	277	11.8%
George Bush	1,079	215	19.9%
Bill Clinton	2,479	1,125	45.0%
George W. Bush[a]	2,786	1,017	36.0%

[a] Bush data include all political appointees through 2005 when his administration stopped making numbers public.

Sources: "Insiders Say White House Has Its Own Glass Ceiling," *Atlanta Journal and Constitution* (April 10, 1995): A1F; Judi Hasson, "Senate GOP Leader Lott Says He'll Work with Clinton," *USA Today* (December 4, 1996): 8A; and "The Growth of Political Appointees in the Bush Administration," U.S. House of Representatives, Committee on Government Reform—Minority Staff, May 2006.

TABLE **8.4**   Treaties and Executive Agreements Concluded by the United States, 1789–2006

Years	Number of Treaties	Number of Executive Agreements
1789–1839	60	27
1839–1889	215	238
1889–1929	382	763
1930–1932	49	41
1933–1944 (F. Roosevelt)	131	369
1945–1952 (Truman)	132	1,324
1953–1960 (Eisenhower)	89	1,834
1961–1963 (Kennedy)	36	813
1964–1968 (L. Johnson)	67	1,083
1969–1974 (Nixon)	93	1,317
1975–1976 (Ford)	26	666
1977–1980 (Carter)	79	1,476
1981–1988 (Reagan)	125	2,840
1989–1992 (G. Bush)	67	1,350
1993–2000 (Clinton)	209	2,047
2001–2008 (G.W. Bush)	45	612

Note: Number of treaties includes those concluded during the indicated span of years. Some of these treaties did not receive the consent of the U.S. Senate. Varying definitions of what an executive agreement comprises and their entry-into-force date make the above numbers approximate.
Sources: 1789–1980: *Congressional Quarterly's Guide to Congress*, 291; 1981–2002: Office of the Assistant Legal Adviser for Treaty Affairs. U.S. Department of State; 2002–2006: www.saramitchell.org/MarshallPrins.pdf/

executive agreement
Formal government agreement entered into by the president that does not require the advice and consent of the U.S. Senate.

veto power
The formal, constitutional authority of the president to reject bills passed by both houses of Congress, thus preventing them from becoming law without further congressional action.

League, Wilson had taken American support for granted. This was a dramatic miscalculation. Isolationists, led by Senator Henry Cabot Lodge (R–MA), opposed U.S. participation in the League on the grounds that the League would place the United States in the center of every major international conflict. Proponents countered that, League or no League, the United States had emerged from World War I as a world power and that membership in the League of Nations would enhance its new role. The vote in the Senate for ratification was very close, but the isolationists prevailed—the United States stayed out of the League, and Wilson was devastated.

The Senate also may require substantial amendment of a treaty prior to its consent. When President Jimmy Carter proposed the controversial Panama Canal Treaty in 1977 to turn the canal over to Panama, for example, the Senate required several conditions to be ironed out before approving the canal's return. Presidents may also "unsign" treaties, a practice often met with dismay from other signatories. For example, the Bush administration formally withdrew its support for the International Criminal Court (ICC). In a short, three-sentence letter to United Nations Secretary General Kofi Annan, the United States withdrew from efforts to create the first permanent court to prosecute war crimes, genocide, and other crimes against humanity. This treaty was formerly signed by President Bill Clinton and was scheduled to take effect July 1, 2002. Critics of the treaty argued that it could lead to politically motivated charges against U.S. troops in Afghanistan and Iraq.[11]

When trade agreements are at issue, presidents often are forced to be mindful of the wishes of Congress. What is called congressional "fast track" authority protects a president's ability to negotiate trade agreements with confidence that the accords will not be altered by Congress. Trade agreements submitted to Congress under fast track procedures bar amendments and require an up or down vote in Congress within ninety days of introduction.

Presidents also often try to get around the constitutional "advice and consent" of the Senate requirement for ratification of treaties and the congressional approval requirement for trade agreements by entering into an **executive agreement,** which allows the president to form secret and highly sensitive arrangements with foreign nations without Senate approval. Presidents have used these agreements since the days of George Washington, and their use has been upheld by the courts. Although executive agreements are not binding on subsequent administrations, since 1900 they have been used far more frequently than treaties, further cementing the role of the president in foreign affairs, as revealed in Table 8.4.

Veto Power

Presidents can affect the policy process through the **veto power,** the authority to reject any congressional legislation. The threat of a presidential veto often prompts members of Congress to fashion legislation that they know will receive presidential acquiescence, if not support. Thus, simply threatening to veto legislation often gives a president another way to influence law-making.

During the Constitutional Convention, proponents of a strong executive argued that the president should have an absolute and final veto over acts of Congress. Opponents of this idea, including Benjamin Franklin, countered that in their home states the executive veto "was constantly made use of to extort money" from legislators. James Madison made the most compelling argument for a compromise on the issue:

> Experience has proven a tendency in our governments to throw all power into the legislative vortex. The Executives of the States are in general little more than Ciphers, the legislatures omnipotent. If no effectual check be devised for restraining the instability and encroachments of the latter, a revolution of some kind or other would be inevitable.[12]

In keeping with the system of checks and balances, then, the president was given the veto power, but only as a "qualified negative." Although the president was given the authority to veto any act of Congress (with the exception of joint resolutions that propose constitutional amendments), Congress was given the authority to override an executive veto by a two-thirds vote in each house. The veto is a powerful policy tool because Congress cannot usually muster enough votes to override a veto. Thus, in over 200 years, there have been approximately 2,500 presidential vetoes and only about a hundred have been overridden, as revealed in Table 8.5.

As early as 1873, in his State of the Union message, President Ulysses S. Grant proposed a constitutional amendment to give to presidents a **line-item veto,** a power to disapprove of individual items within a spending bill and not just the bill in its entirety. Many governors have this authority. Over the years, 150 resolutions calling for a line-item veto were introduced in Congress. Finally, in 1996, Congress enacted legislation that gave the president the authority to veto specific spending provisions within a bill without vetoing the bill in its entirety. The city of New York soon challenged the line-item veto law when President Bill Clinton used it to stop payment of some congressionally authorized funds to the city. In *Clinton* v. *City of New York* (1998), the U.S. Supreme Court ruled that the line-item veto was unconstitutional because it gave powers to the president denied him by the U.S. Constitution. Significant alterations of executive/congressional powers, said the Court, require constitutional amendment.[13]

TABLE 8.5 Presidential Vetoes

President	Regular Vetoes	Pocket Vetoes	Total Vetoes	Vetoes Overridden
Washington	2	.....	2	.....
J. Adams	.....	.....	.....	.....
Jefferson	.....	.....	.....	.....
Madison	5	2	7	.....
Monroe	1	.....	1	.....
J. Q. Adams	.....	.....	.....	.....
Jackson	5	7	12	.....
Van Buren	.....	1	1	.....
W. H. Harrison	.....	.....	.....	.....
Tyler	6	4	10	1
Polk	2	1	3	.....
Taylor	.....	.....	.....	.....
Fillmore	.....	.....	.....	.....
Pierce	9	.....	9	5
Buchanan	4	3	7	.....
Lincoln	2	5	7	.....
A. Johnson	21	8	29	15
Grant	45	48	93	4
Hayes	12	1	13	1
Garfield	.....	.....	.....	.....
Arthur	4	8	12	1
Cleveland	304	110	414	2
B. Harrison	19	25	44	1
Cleveland	42	128	170	5
McKinley	6	36	42	.....
T. Roosevelt	42	40	82	1
Taft	30	9	39	1
Wilson	33	11	44	6
Harding	5	1	6	.....
Coolidge	20	30	50	4
Hoover	21	16	37	3
F. Roosevelt	372	263	635	9
Truman	180	70	250	12
Eisenhower	73	108	181	2
Kennedy	12	9	21	.....
L. Johnson	16	14	30	.....
Nixon	26	17	43	7
Ford	48	18	66	12
Carter	13	18	31	2
Reagan	39	39	78	9
G. Bush[a]	29	15	44	1
Clinton	36	1	38	2
G. W. Bush[b]	11	1	12	4
Total	**1495**	**1067**	**2562**	**110**

[a] President George Bush attempted to pocket veto two bills during intrasession recess periods. Congress considered the two bills enacted into law because of the president's failure to return the legislation. The bills are not counted as pocket vetoes in this table.
[b] George W. Bush information as of January 1, 2008.
Source: Clerk of the House, http://clerk.house.gov.

line-item veto
The authority of a chief executive to delete part of a bill passed by the legislature that involves taxing or spending. Ruled unconstitutional by the U.S. Supreme Court.

The Power to Preside Over the Military as Commander in Chief

One of the most important constitutional executive powers is the president's authority over the military. Article II states that the president is "Commander in Chief of

THE PRESIDENT'S MANY HATS

Photo courtesy: Bettmann/Corbis

Chief law enforcer: Troops sent by President Dwight D. Eisenhower enforce a federal court decision ordering the integration of public schools in Little Rock, Arkansas.

Photo courtesy: Matt Reinstein/The Image Works

Leader of the party: Ronald Reagan mobilized conservatives and changed the nature of the Republican Party.

Commander in Chief: President George. W. Bush speaks about the War in Iraq.

Shaper of public policy: President Richard M. Nixon cheers on the efforts of Apollo 11 astronauts.

Photo courtesy: Hulton Archive/Getty Images

Key player in the legislative process: President Bill Clinton at a bill signing ceremony.

Photo courtesy: Ruth Frenson/AP/Wide World Photos

Chief of state: President John F. Kennedy and his wife, Jacqueline, with the president of France and his wife during the Kennedys' widely publicized 1961 trip to that nation.

the Army and Navy of the United States." While the Constitution specifically grants Congress the authority to declare war, presidents since Abraham Lincoln have used the commander in chief clause in conjunction with the chief executive's duty to "take Care that the Laws be faithfully executed" to wage war (and to broaden various powers).

Modern presidents' continually clash with Congress over the ability to commence hostilities. The Vietnam War, in which 58,000 American soldiers were killed and 300,000 were wounded, was conducted (at a cost of $150 billion) without a congressional declaration of war. In fact, acknowledging President Lyndon B. Johnson's claim to war-making authority, in 1964 Congress passed—with only two dissenting votes—the Gulf of Tonkin Resolution, which authorized a massive commitment of U.S. forces in South Vietnam.

During that highly controversial war, Presidents Johnson and then Nixon routinely assured members of Congress that victory was near. In 1971, however, publication of what were called *The Pentagon Papers* revealed what many people had suspected all along: Lyndon B. Johnson systematically had altered casualty figures and distorted key facts to place the progress of the war in a more positive light. Angered by this misinformation that had led Congress largely to defer to the executive in the conduct of the Vietnam War, in 1973 Congress passed the **War Powers Act** to limit the president's authority to introduce American troops into hostile foreign lands without congressional approval. President Nixon vetoed the act, but it was overridden by a two-thirds majority in both houses of Congress.

Presidents since Nixon have continued to insist that the War Powers Act is an unconstitutional infringement of their executive power. Still, in 2001, President George W. Bush complied with the act when he sought, and both houses of Congress approved, a joint resolution authorizing the use of force against "those responsible for the recent [September 11] attacks launched against the United States." This resolution actually gave the president more open-ended authority to wage war than his father had received in 1991 to conduct the Persian Gulf War or President Johnson had received after the Gulf of Tonkin Resolution in 1964.[14] Later, in October 2002, after President Bush declared Iraq to be a "grave threat to peace," the House (296–133) and Senate (77–23) voted overwhelmingly to allow the president to use force in Iraq "as he determines to be necessary and appropriate," thereby conferring tremendous authority on the president to wage war. (To learn more about the controversies related to this law, see Join the Debate: The War Powers Act.)

The Pardoning Power

Presidents can exercise a check on judicial power through their constitutional authority to grant reprieves or pardons. A **pardon** is an executive grant releasing an individual from the punishment or legal consequences of a crime before or after conviction, and restores all rights and privileges of citizenship. Presidents exercise complete pardoning power for federal offenses except in cases of impeachment, which cannot be pardoned. President Gerald R. Ford granted the most famous presidential pardon when he pardoned former President Richard M. Nixon—who had not been formally charged with any crime—"for any offenses against the United States, which he, Richard Nixon, has committed or may have committed while in office." This unilateral, absolute pardon prevented the former president from ever being tried for any crimes he may have committed. It also unleashed a torrent of public criticism against Ford and questions about whether Nixon had discussed the

Thinking Globally

The Executive Branch and Military Leadership

In the United States, the president serves as the commander in chief of the armed forces but is not a member of any branch of the military. Other countries, such as Pakistan, have a long history of presidents who simultaneously served as military leaders while in office. Former president of Pakistan Pervez Musharraf, for example, achieved power through a military coup in 1999 and relinquished his role as chief of the Pakistani Army with great reluctance after extensive pressure from Pakistani and foreign leaders.

- Is it necessary to draw a distinction between civilian leadership and military leadership as we do in the United States? Why or why not?
- Can you imagine a situation where a military overthrow of the government might occur in the United States? Explain your answer.

War Powers Act
Passed by Congress in 1973; the president is limited in the deployment of troops overseas to a sixty-day period in peacetime (which can be extended for an extra thirty days to permit withdrawal) unless Congress explicitly gives its approval for a longer period.

Presidential Leadership: Which Hat Do You Wear?

pardon
An executive grant providing restoration of all rights and privileges of citizenship to a specific individual charged or convicted of a crime.

Join the Debate

The War Powers Act

OVERVIEW: While the Constitution divides the power to wage war between Congress and the president, scholars and politicians disagree on the specifics of the division. They also disagree on how this division should play out in specific circumstances. The Constitution gives Congress the authority to declare war, to make the rules that govern military forces, and to provide appropriations to the armed services. Yet, the president's constitutional jurisdiction over war powers has steadily increased since the nation's founding. Although President James Madison would not go to war with Great Britain in 1812 without a war declaration from Congress, the last six major American conflicts were conducted without formal declarations of war.

The War Powers Act of 1973, passed in the aftermath of the Vietnam War, was an attempt to rein in the war-making authority of the president by demanding, among other things, that the executive notify Congress when committing the U.S. military to hostile action. The War Powers Act requires the president to report to Congress "in every possible instance" within forty-eight hours after deploying the armed forces in combat. Implied in the law is the understanding that the information Congress receives will be timely and accurate. President Richard M. Nixon's veto of the act was overridden by both houses of Congress, but presidential administrations since Nixon's, Democratic and Republican alike, have agreed that the act infringes on the president's constitutional duty as commander in chief.

The intelligence the president and Congress receive is critically important when determining whether or not to engage in and support armed conflict but sometimes intelligence sources are flawed. For instance, in 1998, President Bill Clinton ordered the destruction of a pharmaceutical plant in Sudan based on faulty intelligence that the site produced nerve gas. In 2002–2003, President George W. Bush made the case for invading Iraq by asserting that the country harbored terrorists and possessed weapons of mass destruction (WMDs) that posed an imminent threat to the United States and the countries neighboring Iraq. These assertions, although not supported by evidence, loomed large in the national debate regarding whether to intervene in Iraq.

Complying with the War Powers Act, President Bush asked for and received authorization from Congress to use military force against Iraq if diplomatic efforts failed. Critics have charged that congressional authorization would not have been as forthcoming had the president and his administration not ignored or downplayed intelligence reports that contradicted their beliefs in the existence of WMDs and links between the Iraq government and terrorist organizations. The fact that WMDs were not found undermined the administration's credibility with many Americans, including members of Congress, as well as foreign nations. Some constitutional scholars have noted that intelligence failures, the rising death toll, and costs related to military action in Iraq suggest it is time for Congress to increase its oversight of the executive in foreign policy matters. Other scholars disagree, siding with executive-branch officials who consider the War Powers Act an infringement on the president's constitutional authority.

Arguments IN FAVOR of the War Powers Act

- The War Powers Act reflects the will of the American people. The doctrine of civilian supremacy places ultimate war-making authority with the American people, and the War Powers Act reflects the will of the people as expressed through the representative institution of Congress.

- The War Powers Act is an attempt by Congress to restore the balance of shared control of the military with the executive. The act's stated purpose is to "fulfill the intent of the framers . . . and insure that the collective judgment of both the Congress and the president will apply to the introduction of United States Armed Forces into hostilities . . . and to the continued use of such forces." This is an attempt to return to the constitutional principle that waging war is to be shared by both branches of government.

pardon with Ford before Nixon's resignation. Many analysts attribute Ford's defeat in his 1976 bid for the presidency to that pardon.

Even though pardons are generally directed toward a specific individual, presidents have also used them to offer general amnesties. Presidents George Washington, John Adams, James Madison, Abraham Lincoln, Andrew Johnson, Theodore Roo-

- The War Powers Act is an additional check on the president's authority as commander in chief. The act is an attempt to prevent future presidents from engaging in hostilities of questionable importance to U.S. national security and to force deliberation within the government with regard to armed conflict. For example, had Congress known of President Lyndon B. Johnson's use of faulty or intentionally misleading information to increase U.S. military involvement in Vietnam, U.S. involvement in Southeast Asia may have taken a different, less costly, path in both lives and expenditures.

What authority do presidents have during wartime? President Lyndon B. Johnson's action during the Vietnam War led to the passage of the War Powers Act, which, at least in theory, restricts presidential power to deploy troops.

Source: Yoichi R. Okamoto/Picture History

Arguments AGAINST the War Powers Act

- International relations can be so volatile that the president must be able to act quickly and without hindrance to protect the nation and its people. The American executive was created in part to act quickly without relative interference during exceptional times of crisis. During extraordinary times, the president must take extraordinary means to defend the nation without undue interference from Congress. *Federalist No. 8* argues: "It is the nature of war to increase the executive at the expense of the legislative authority" as this is considered a natural shift in power.

- The Supreme Court has upheld an expanded interpretation of the president's authority. In *U.S.* v. *Curtiss-Wright* (1936), the Court argued that the president and "not

Congress has the better opportunity of knowing the conditions which prevail in foreign countries, and especially this is true during times of war. He has his confidential sources of information. . . . Secrecy in respect of information gathered by them may be highly necessary and the premature disclosure of it productive of harmful results." Thus, the Court concluded that the president is uniquely responsible in the area of foreign policy and war making.

- The Constitution has clearly defined the roles Congress should play in military action and there is no need to extend these powers. Congress has the authority to declare war, to establish military policies, and to fund military action. These are the appropriate checks on executive powers. Congress, for example, used the power of the purse to bring U.S. military activity to an end in Vietnam and in Somalia. The system of checks and balances is not broken, and thus does not need to be fixed.

Continuing the Debate

1. Is the War Powers Act constitutional? If Congress has the power to limit the war-making power of the executive, what implications does this have for U.S. national security?

2. Should Congress have access to the same information and intelligence regarding national security that is available to the president? Are there any circumstances where such information should be restricted to just the president and his or her closest advisers? Explain your answers.

To Follow the Debate Online, Go To:

www.fas.org/search.html

National security reports of the Congressional Research Service, an official agency of the U.S. Congress. The reports are listed when one enters "War Powers Act" into the search engine.

www.americansecurityproject.org/ iraq_and_the_war_powers_act

Studies, resources, and position papers on foreign policy issues, including arguments about checks on the president, especially with regard to Iraq.

sevelt, Harry S Truman, and Jimmy Carter used general pardons to grant amnesty to large classes of individuals for illegal acts. Carter, for example, incurred the wrath of many veterans' groups when he made an offer of unconditional amnesty to approximately 10,000 men who had fled the United States or gone into hiding to avoid being drafted for military service in the Vietnam War.

The Development and Expansion of Presidential Power

Every president brings to the position not only a vision of America, but also expectations about how to use presidential authority. But, most presidents find accomplishing their goals much more difficult than they envisioned. After President John F. Kennedy was in office two years, for example, he noted publicly that there were "greater limitations upon our ability to bring about a favorable result than I had imagined."[15] Similarly, as he was leaving office, President Harry S Truman mused about what surprises awaited his successor, Dwight D. Eisenhower, a former general: "He'll sit here and he'll say, 'Do this! Do that!' And nothing will happen. Poor Ike—it won't be a bit like the army. He'll find it very frustrating."[16]

A president's authority is limited by the formal powers enumerated in Article II of the Constitution and by the Supreme Court's interpretation of those constitutional provisions. How a president wields these powers is affected by the times in which the president serves, his confidantes and advisers, and the president's personality and leadership abilities. The 1950s postwar era of good feelings and economic prosperity presided over by the grandfatherly Eisenhower, for instance, called for a very different leader from the one needed by the Civil War–torn nation governed by Abraham Lincoln. Furthermore, not only do different times call for different kinds of leaders; they also often provide limits, or conversely, wide opportunities, for whoever serves as president at the time. Crises, in particular, trigger expansions of presidential power. The danger to the Union posed by the Civil War in the 1860s required a strong leader to take up the reins of government. Because of his leadership during this crisis, Lincoln is generally ranked by historians as the best president (To learn more about presidential rankings, see Table 8.6).

TABLE 8.6 Ranking U.S. Presidents

Who was the best president and who was the worst? Many surveys of scholars have been taken over the years to answer this question, and virtually all have ranked Abraham Lincoln among the best. A C-SPAN survey of fifty-eight historians from across the political spectrum came up with these results:

Five Best Presidents	Five Worst Presidents
1. Lincoln (best)	1. Buchanan (worst)
2. F. Roosevelt	2. A. Johnson
3. Washington	3. Pierce
4. T. Roosevelt	4. Harding
5. Truman	5. W. Harrison

Source: C-SPAN Survey of Presidential Leadership. www.cspan.com.

Establishing Presidential Authority: The First Presidents

The first three presidents—George Washington, John Adams and Thomas Jefferson—and their conceptions of the presidency continue to have a profound impact on American government. When President George Washington was sworn in on a cold, blustery day in New York City on April 30, 1789, he took over an office and a government that were yet to be created. Eventually, a few hundred postal workers were hired and Washington appointed a small group of Cabinet advisers and clerks. During Washington's two terms, the entire federal budget was only about $40 million, or approximately $10 for every citizen in America. In contrast, in 2007, the federal budget was $2.8 trillion, or $9,300, for every man, woman, and child.

George Washington set several important precedents for future presidents:

- He took every opportunity to establish the primacy of the national government. In 1794, for example, Washington used the militia of four states to put down the Whiskey Rebellion, an uprising of 3,000 western Pennsylvania farmers opposed to the payment of a federal excise tax on liquor. Leading those 1,500 troops was Secretary of the Treasury Alexander Hamilton, whose duty it was to collect federal taxes. Washington's action helped establish the idea of federal supremacy and the authority of the executive branch to collect the taxes levied by Congress.

- He began the practice of regular meetings with his advisers, thus establishing the Cabinet system.

- He asserted the prominence of the role of the chief executive in the conduct of foreign affairs. He sent envoys to negotiate the Jay Treaty to end continued hostilities with Great Britain. Then, over senatorial objection, he continued to assert his authority first to negotiate treaties and then simply to submit them to the Senate for its approval. Washington made it clear that the Senate's function was limited to approval of treaties and did not include negotiation with foreign powers.

- He claimed the powers of the presidency as the basis for proclaiming a policy of strict neutrality when the British and French were at war. Although the Constitution is silent about a president's authority to declare neutrality, Washington's supporters argued that the Constitution granted the president **inherent powers**—that is, powers that belong to the national government simply because it is a sovereign body. Thus, they argued, the president's power to conduct diplomatic relations could be inferred from the Constitution. Since neither Congress nor the Supreme Court later disagreed, this power was implicitly added to the list of specific, enumerated presidential powers found in Article II.

inherent powers
Powers that belong to the national government simply because it is a sovereign body.

Like Washington, the next two presidents, John Adams and Thomas Jefferson, acted in ways that were critical to the development of the presidency as well as to the president's role in the political system. Adams's poor leadership skills, for example, heightened the divisions between Federalists and Anti-Federalists and probably quickened the development of political parties (see chapter 12). Jefferson took critical steps to expand the role of the president in the legislative process. Like Washington, he claimed that certain presidential powers were inherent and used those inherent powers to justify his expansion of the size of the nation through the Louisiana Purchase in 1803.

Incremental Expansion of Presidential Powers: 1809–1933

Although the first three presidents made enormous contributions to the office of the chief executive, the way government had to function in its formative years caused the balance of power to be heavily weighted in favor of a strong Congress. Americans routinely had close contacts with their representatives in Congress, while to most citizens the president seemed a remote figure. Members of Congress frequently were at home, where they were seen by voters; few citizens ever even gazed on a president. By the end of Jefferson's first term, it was clear that the Framers' initial fear of an all-powerful, monarchical president was unfounded. The strength of Congress and the relatively weak presidents who came after Jefferson allowed Congress quickly to assert itself as the most powerful branch of government.

Andrew Jackson was the first president to act as a strong national leader who represented more than just a landed, propertied elite. By the time Jackson ran for president in 1828, eleven new states had been added to the union, and the number of white males eligible to vote had increased dramatically as property requirements for voting were removed by nearly all states. The election of Jackson, a Tennessean, as the seventh president signaled the end of an era: he was the first president not to be either a Virginian or an Adams. His election launched the beginning of Jacksonian democracy, a concept that embodied the western, frontier, egalitarian spirit personified by Jackson, the first common man to be elected president. The masses loved him, and legends were built around his down-to-earth image. Jackson, for example, once was asked to give a position to a soldier who had lost his leg on the battlefield

and needed the job to support his family. When told that the man hadn't voted for him, Jackson responded: "If he lost his leg fighting for his country, that is vote enough for me."[17]

Jackson used his image and personal power to buttress the developing party system by rewarding loyal followers of his Democratic Party with presidential appointments. Frequently at odds with Congress, he made use of the veto power against twelve bills, surpassing the combined total of nine vetoes used by his six predecessors. Jackson also reasserted the supremacy of the national government (and the presidency) by facing down South Carolina's nullification of a federal tariff law.

Abraham Lincoln's approach to the presidency was similar to Jackson's. To combat the unprecedented emergency of the Civil War, Lincoln assumed powers that no president before him had claimed. Because Lincoln believed he needed to act quickly for the very survival of the union, he frequently took action without first obtaining the approval of Congress. Among many of Lincoln's legally questionable acts:

What makes a great president? President Abraham Lincoln is regarded as one of the best presidents, largely because of his leadership during the Civil War. Here, Lincoln visits Union leaders at Antietam, Maryland, in 1862 just weeks after the bloodiest single day in U.S. history.

Photo courtesy: Alexander Gardner/Granger Collection

- He suspended the writ of *habeas corpus*, which allows those in prison to petition to be released, citing the need to jail persons even suspected of disloyal practices.
- He expanded the size of the U.S. army above congressionally mandated ceilings.
- He ordered a blockade of southern ports, in effect initiating a war without the approval of Congress.
- He closed the U.S. mail to treasonable correspondence.

Lincoln argued that the inherent powers of his office allowed him to circumvent the Constitution in a time of war or national crisis. Since the Constitution conferred on the president the duty to make sure that the laws of the United States are faithfully executed, reasoned Lincoln, the acts enumerated above were constitutional. He simply refused to allow the nation to crumble because of what he viewed as technical requirements of the Constitution.

The Growth of the Modern Presidency

Before the days of instantaneous communication, the nation could afford to allow Congress, with its relatively slow deliberative processes, to make most decisions. Furthermore, decision making might have been left to Congress because its members, and not the president, were closest to the people. As times and technology have changed, however, so have the public's expectations of anyone who becomes president. The breakneck speed with which so many cable news networks and Internet sites report national and international events has intensified the public's expectation that, in a crisis, the president will be the individual to act quickly and decisively on behalf of the entire nation. Congress often is unable to respond to fast-changing events—especially in foreign affairs.

In the twentieth and twenty-first centuries, the general trend has been for presidential—as opposed to congressional—decision making to be more and more important. The start of this trend can be traced to the four-term presidency of Franklin D. Roosevelt (FDR), who led the nation through several crises. This growth of presiden-

SIMULATION

You Are a President During a Nuclear Meltdown

tial power and the growth of the federal government and its programs in general are now criticized by many people. To understand the basis for many of the calls for reform of the political system being made today, it is critical to understand how the growth of government and the role of the president occurred.[18]

FDR took office in 1933 in the midst of a major crisis—the Great Depression—during which a substantial portion of the U.S. workforce was unemployed. Noting the sorry state of the national economy in his Inaugural Address, FDR concluded: "This nation asks for action and action now." To jump-start the American economy, FDR asked Congress for and was given "broad executive powers to wage a war against the emergency, as great as the power that would be given to me if we were in fact invaded by a foreign foe."[19]

Just as Abraham Lincoln had taken bold steps upon his inauguration, Roosevelt also acted quickly. He immediately fashioned a plan for national recovery called the **New Deal**, a package of bold and controversial programs designed to invigorate the failing American economy (these are discussed in detail in chapter 3).

Roosevelt served an unprecedented twelve years in office; he was elected to four terms but died shortly after the beginning of this fourth term. During his years in office, the nation went from the economic war of the Great Depression to the real international conflict of World War II. The institution of the presidency changed profoundly and permanently as new federal agencies were created to implement New Deal.

Not only did FDR create a new bureaucracy to implement his pet programs, but he also personalized the presidency by establishing a new relationship between the president and the people. In his radio addresses, or fireside chats, as he liked to call them, he spoke directly to the public in a relaxed and informal manner about serious issues.

To his successors, FDR left the modern presidency, including a burgeoning federal bureaucracy (see chapter 9), an active and usually leading role in both domestic and foreign policy and legislation, and a nationalized executive office that used technology—first radio, then television, and now the Internet—to bring the president closer to the public than ever before.

Thinking Globally

Executive Power in North Korea

The differences between the American and the North Korean executives could not be more extreme. The government of North Korea is a highly secretive communist dictatorship controlled by Kim Jong Il. Kim Jong Il serves as both head of state and head of the one viable political party. He also exercises control over the judiciary, the military, and the economy.

- Should absolute power be entrusted to a single political institution or individual? Why or why not?
- Under what circumstances might it be beneficial to invest it must a single institution or individual with a broad spectrum of powers?

New Deal
The name given to the program of "Relief, Recovery, Reform" begun by President Franklin D. Roosevelt in 1933 to bring the United States out of the Great Depression.

The Presidential Establishment

As the responsibilities and scope of presidential authority grew over the years, so did the executive branch, including the number of people working directly for the president in the White House. The vice president and his staff, the Cabinet, the first lady and her staff, the Executive Office of the President, and the White House staff all help the president fulfill his duties as chief executive.

The Vice President

For many years the vice presidency was considered a sure place for a public official to disappear into obscurity. When John Adams wrote to his wife, Abigail, about his position as America's first vice president, he said it was "the most insignificant office that was the invention of man . . . or his imagination conceived."[20]

Historically, presidents chose their vice presidents largely to balance—politically, geographically, or otherwise—the presidential ticket, with little thought given to the

THE TIMES·PICAYUNE © 2008

cartoonistgroup.com

DO YOU PREFER THE ATTRACTIVE NOVICE AND THE SEASONED OLD GUY, OR THE SEASONED OLD GUY AND THE ATTRACTIVE NOVICE?

OBAMA BIDEN / McCAIN PALIN

Photo courtesy: Steve Kelley/Cartoonist Group

Why are vice presidents selected? Governor Sarah Palin (R–AK) and Senator Joe Biden (D–DE) were chosen as vice presidential nominees for very different reasons. Both, however, helped to balance two historic presidential tickets.

possibility that the vice president would become president. Franklin D. Roosevelt, for example, a liberal New Yorker, selected John Nance Garner, a conservative Texan, to be his running mate in 1932. After serving two terms, Garner—who openly disagreed with Roosevelt over many policies, including Roosevelt's decision to seek a third term—unsuccessfully sought the 1940 presidential nomination himself.

In 2000, most commentators agreed that Dick Cheney was added to the ticket to provide "gravitas"—a sense of national governmental experience, especially in foreign affairs, that Governor George W. Bush neither had nor claimed.

In 2008, Senator John McCain surprised most commentators when he selected Alaska Governor Sarah Palin to be his running mate. Palin, a virtual unknown outside her home state, energized social conservatives who had not been firmly behind McCain. Barack Obama, who was accused of lacking foreign policy experience, chose Senator Joe Biden (D–DE) to provide balance to the democratic ticket. In the end, several commentators believed that Palin cost McCain the presidency when she appeared to be unfamiliar with many significant policy issues.

How much power a vice president has depends on how much the president is willing to give him. Jimmy Carter was the first president to give his vice president, Walter Mondale, more than ceremonial duties. In fact, Walter Mondale was the first vice president to have an office in the White House. No vice presidents, however, have ever enjoyed the access to, and ear of, the president to the extent of Vice President Cheney. Some commentators argued that Cheney had a clearer agenda of where the United States should be moving, especially in terms of foreign affairs, than President Bush.

The Cabinet

The Cabinet, which has no basis in the Constitution, is an informal institution based on practice and precedent whose membership is determined by tradition and presidential discretion. By custom, this advisory group selected by the president includes the heads of major executive departments. Presidents today also include their vice presidents in Cabinet meetings, as well as any other agency heads or officials to whom they would like to accord Cabinet-level status.

As a body, the Cabinet's major function is to help the president execute the laws and assist him in making decisions. Although the Framers discussed the idea of some form of national executive council, they did not include a provision for one in the Constitution. They did recognize, however, the need for departments of government and departmental heads.

As revealed in Table 8.7, over the years the Cabinet has grown alongside the responsibilities of the national government. As interest groups, in particular, pressured Congress and the president to recognize their demands for services and governmental action, they often were rewarded by the creation of an executive department. Since each was headed by a secretary who automatically became a member of the president's Cabinet, powerful clientele groups including farmers (Agriculture), business people (Commerce), workers (Labor), and teachers (Education) saw the creation of a department as increasing their access to the president.

While the size of the president's Cabinet has increased over the years, most presidents' reliance on their Cabinet secretaries has decreased. Some individual members of

TABLE 8.7 The U.S. Cabinet and Responsibilities of Each Executive Department

Department Head	Department	Date of Creation	Responsibilities
Secretary of State	Department of State	1789	Responsible for the making of foreign policy, including treaty negotiation
Secretary of the Treasury	Department of the Treasury	1789	Responsible for government funds and regulation of alcohol, firearms, and tobacco
Secretary of Defense	Department of Defense	1789	Responsible for national defense; current department created by consolidating the former Departments of War, the Army, the Navy, and the Air Force in 1947
Attorney General	Department of Justice	1870	Represents U.S. government in all federal courts, investigates and prosecutes violations of federal law
Secretary of the Interior	Department of the Interior	1849	Manages the nation's natural resources, including wildlife and public lands
Secretary of Agriculture	Department of Agriculture	1889	Assists farmers, oversees food-quality programs, administers food stamp and school lunch programs
Secretary of Commerce	Department of Commerce	1903	Aids businesses and conducts the U.S. Census (originally the Department of Commerce and Labor)
Secretary of Labor	Department of Labor	1913	Runs labor programs, keeps labor statistics, aids labor through enforcement of laws
Secretary of Health and Human Services	Department of Health and Human Services	1953	Runs health, welfare, and Social Security programs (originally the Department of Health, Education, and Welfare, lost its education function in 1979)
Secretary of Housing and Urban Development	Department of Housing and Urban Development	1965	Responsible for urban and housing programs
Secretary of Transportation	Department of Transportation	1966	Responsible for mass transportation and highway programs
Secretary of Energy	Department of Energy	1977	Responsible for energy policy and research, including atomic energy
Secretary of Education	Department of Education	1979	Responsible for the federal government's education programs
Secretary of Veterans Affairs	Department of Veterans Affairs	1989	Responsible for programs aiding veterans
Secretary of Homeland Security	Department of Homeland Security	2002	Responsible for all issues pertaining to homeland security

a president's Cabinet, however, may be very influential. To learn more about the Cabinet's role in executing U.S. policy, see chapter 9.

The First Lady

From the time of Martha Washington, first ladies (a term coined during the Civil War) have assisted presidents as informal advisers while making other, more public, and significant contributions to American society. Abigail Adams, for example, was a constant sounding board for her husband, John. An early feminist, in 1776 she cautioned him "to Remember the Ladies" in any new code of laws.

Edith Bolling Galt Wilson was probably the most powerful first lady. When President Woodrow Wilson

Photo courtesy: Stock Montage, Inc.

How important is the First Lady? In 1919, President Woodrow Wilson had what many believed to be a nervous collapse in the summer and a debilitating stroke in the fall that incapacitated him for several months. His wife, Edith Bolling Galt Wilson, refused to admit his advisers to his sickroom, and rumors flew about the "First Lady President," as many suspected it was his wife and not Wilson who was issuing the orders.

collapsed and was left partly paralyzed in 1919, she became his surrogate and decided whom and what the stricken president saw. Her detractors dubbed her "Acting First Man."

Eleanor Roosevelt also played a powerful and much criticized role in national affairs. Not only did she write a nationally syndicated daily newspaper column, but she traveled and lectured widely, worked tirelessly on countless Democratic Party matters, and raised six children. After FDR's death, she shone in her own right as U.S. delegate to the United Nations, where she headed the commission that drafted the covenant on human rights. Later, she headed President John F. Kennedy's Commission on the Status of Women.

More recently, Laura Bush, a former librarian, seemed to be following the path of her mother-in-law, former First Lady Barbara Bush. She adopted a behind-the-scenes role and made literacy the focus of her activities. In the aftermath of the tragedy of September 11, 2001, the first lady took on a more public role, speaking out in support of improvements in the legal status of women in Afghanistan and Iraq. She also took to the campaign trail in 2002, 2004, and 2006, very effectively fund-raising on behalf of her husband as well as other Republican candidates, but returned to a behind-the-scenes role in 2008 as her husband's popularity plummeted.

The Executive Office of the President (EOP)

Executive Office of the President (EOP)
Created in 1939 to help the president oversee the executive branch bureaucracy.

The **Executive Office of the President (EOP)** was established by FDR in 1939 to oversee his New Deal programs. It was created to provide the president with a general staff to help him direct the diverse activities of the executive branch. In fact, it is a mini-bureaucracy of several advisers and offices located in the ornate Executive Office Building next to the White House on Pennsylvania Avenue, as well as in the White House itself, where the president's closest advisers often are located.

The EOP has expanded over time to include several advisory and policy-making agencies and task forces. Over time, the units of the EOP have become the prime policy makers in their fields of expertise as they play key roles in advancing the president's policy preferences. Among the EOP's most important members are the National Security Council, the Council of Economic Advisers, the Office of Management and Budget, the Office of the Vice President, and the Office of the U.S. Trade Representative.

The National Security Council (NSC) was established in 1947 to advise the president on American military affairs and foreign policy. The NSC is composed of the president, the vice president, and the secretaries of state and defense. The chair

What does the National Security Council do? President George W. Bush meets with his National Security Council in 2006. The Council's handling of the war in Iraq received increasing criticism as the war continued.

Photo courtesy: The White House/Handout/Getty Images

of the Joint Chiefs of Staff and the director of the Central Intelligence Agency also participate. Others such as the White House chief of staff and the general counsel may attend. The national security adviser runs the staff of the NSC, coordinates information and options, and advises the president.

Although the president appoints the members of each of these bodies, they must perform their tasks in accordance with congressional legislation. As with the Cabinet, depending on who serves in key positions, these mini-agencies may not be truly responsible to the president.

Presidents can give clear indications of their policy preferences by the kinds of offices they include in the EOP. President George W. Bush, for example, not only moved or consolidated several offices when he became president in 2001, but he created a new Office of Faith-Based and Community Initiatives to help him achieve his goal of greater religious involvement in matters of domestic policy.

The White House Staff

Often more directly responsible to the president are the members of the White House staff: the personal assistants to the president, including senior aides, their deputies, assistants with professional duties, and clerical and administrative aides. As personal assistants, these advisers are not subject to Senate confirmation, nor do they have divided loyalties. Their power is derived from their personal relationship to the president, and they have no independent legal authority.

Although presidents organize the White House staff in different ways, they typically have a chief of staff whose job is to facilitate the smooth running of the staff and the executive branch of government. Successful chiefs of staff also have protected the president from mistakes and helped implement policies to obtain the maximum political advantage for the president. Other key White House aides include the counselor to the president; domestic, foreign, and economic policy strategists; communications staff; White House counsel; and a lobbyist who acts as a liaison between the president and Congress.

As presidents have tried to consolidate power in the White House, and as public demands on the president have grown, the size of the White House staff has increased—from fifty-one in 1943, to 247 in 1953, to a high of 583 in 1972. Since that time, staffs have been trimmed, generally running around 500. During his 1992 presidential campaign, Bill Clinton promised to cut the size of the White House staff and that of the Executive Office of the President, and eventually he reduced the size of his staff by approximately 15 percent. The Bush White House had approximately 450 staffers.

Although White House staffers prefer to be located in the White House in spite of its small offices, many staffers are relegated to the Dwight David Eisenhower Executive Office Building, formerly called the old Executive Office Building, next door because White House office space is limited. In Washington, the size of the office is not the measure of power that it often is in corporations. Instead, power in the White House goes to those who have the president's ear and the offices closest to the Oval Office.

Presidential Leadership and the Importance of Public Opinion

A president's ability to get his programs adopted or implemented depends on many factors, including his leadership abilities, his personality and powers of persuasion, his ability to mobilize public opinion to support his actions, the public's perception of his performance, and Congress's perception of his public support.

TABLE 8.8 Barber's Presidential Personalities

Political scientist James David Barber defines presidential character as the "way the president orients himself toward life." Barber believes that there are four presidential character types, based on energy level (whether the president is active or passive) and the degree of enjoyment a president finds in the job (whether the president has a positive or negative attitude). Barber believes that active and positive presidents are more successful than passive and negative presidents. Active-positive presidents, he argues, approach the presidency with a characteristic zest for life and have a drive to lead and succeed. In contrast, passive-negative presidents find themselves reacting to circumstances, are likely to take directions from others, and fail to make full use of the enormous resources of the executive office.

	Active	Passive
Positive	F. Roosevelt	Taft
	Truman	Harding
	Kennedy	Reagan
	Ford	
	Carter[a]	
	G. Bush	
Negative	Wilson	Coolidge
	Hoover	Eisenhower
	L. Johnson	
	Nixon	

[a] Some scholars think that Carter better fits the active-negative typology.
Source: James David Barber, *The Presidential Character: Predicting Performance in the White House*, 5th ed. (New York: Longman, 2008).

Presidential Leadership

Leadership is not an easy thing to exercise, and it remains an elusive concept for scholars to identify and measure, but it is important to all presidents seeking support for their programs and policies. Moreover, ideas about the importance of effective leaders have deep roots in our political culture. The leadership abilities of the great presidents—Washington, Jefferson, Lincoln, and FDR—have been extolled over and over again, leading us to fault modern presidents who fail to cloak themselves in the armor of leadership. Americans thus have come to believe that "if presidential leadership works some of the time, why not all of the time?"[21] This attitude, in turn, directly influences what we expect presidents to do and how we evaluate them. (To learn more about presidential personalities, see Table 8.8.)

Research by political scientists shows that presidents can exercise leadership by increasing public attention to particular issues. Analyses of presidential State of the Union Addresses, for example, reveal that mentions of particular policies translate into more Americans mentioning those policies as the most important problems facing the nation.[22] Political scientist Richard E. Neustadt calls the president's ability to influence members of Congress and the public "the power to persuade." Neustadt believes this power is crucial to presidential leadership.[23]

Frequently, the difference between great and mediocre presidents centers on their ability to grasp the importance of leadership style. Truly great presidents, such as Lincoln and FDR, understood that the White House was a seat of power from which decisions could flow to shape the national destiny. They recognized that their day-to-day activities and how they went about them should be designed to bolster support for their policies and to secure congressional and popular backing that could translate their intuitive judgment into meaningful action. Mediocre presidents, on the other hand, have tended to regard the White House as "a stage for the presentation of performances to the public" or a fitting honor to cap a career.[24]

Going Public: Mobilizing Public Opinion

Even before radio, television, and the Internet, presidents tried to reach out to the public to gain support for their programs through what President Theodore Roosevelt called the bully pulpit. The development of commercial air travel and radio, newsreels, television, and computers have made direct communication to larger numbers of voters easier. Presidents, first ladies, and other presidential advisers travel all over the world to publicize their views and to build personal support as well as support for administration programs.

Direct, presidential appeals to the electorate like those often made by recent presidents are referred to as "going public."[25] Going public means that a president goes over the heads of members of Congress to gain support from the people, who can then place pressure on their elected officials in Washington. (To learn more about this tactic, see Ideas into Action: Exploring Presidential Visits.)

Bill Clinton was keenly aware of the importance of maintaining his connection with the public. Beginning with his 1992 campaign, Clinton often appeared on *Larry King Live* on CNN. Even after becoming president, Clinton continued

Photo courtesy: Cecil Stoughton/The John F. Kennedy Presidential Library, Boston

What role do presidential speeches serve? President John F. Kennedy gave one of the most famous presidential commencement addresses when he spoke at American University on June 10, 1963. In this speech, he called on the Soviet Union to work with the United States to craft a nuclear test ban treaty.

to take his case directly to the people. He launched his health care reform proposals, for example, on a prime-time edition of *Nightline* hosted by Ted Koppel. Moreover, at a black-tie dinner honoring radio and television correspondents, Clinton responded to criticisms leveled against him for not holding traditional press conferences by pointing out how clever he was to ignore the traditional press. "You know why I can stiff you on the press conferences? Because Larry King liberated me from you by giving me to the American people directly," quipped Clinton.[26] George W. Bush continued in the Clinton tradition of rarely holding press conferences yet trying to go directly to the people. He chose, for example, to give important speeches on the ongoing war in Iraq before receptive audiences at the National War College and the U.S. Air Force Academy.

The Public's Perception of Presidential Performance

For presidents and other public figures, approval ratings are often used as tacit measures of their political capital: their ability to enact public policy simply because of their name and their office. Presidents who have high approval ratings, as President George W. Bush did in the immediate aftermath of the September 11, 2001 terrorist attacks, are assumed to be more powerful leaders with a mandate for action that comes largely by virtue of the high levels of public support they enjoy. They are often able to use their clout to push controversial legislation, such as the USA Patriot Act, through Congress. A public appearance from a popular president can even deliver a hotly contested congressional seat or gubernatorial contest to the president's party.

In sharp contrast, presidents with low approval ratings are often crippled in the policy arena. Their low ratings can actually prevent favored policies from being enacted on Capitol Hill, even when their party controls the legislature, as many of their partisans locked in close elections shy away from being seen or affiliated with an unpopular president. This was the case in 2008 when House Republicans did not want to be affiliated with the president's emergency financial bailout plan.

Presidential popularity, however, generally follows a cyclical pattern. These cycles have been recorded since 1938, when pollsters first began to track presidential popularity. Typically, presidents enjoy their highest level of public approval at the beginning of their terms and try to take advantage of this honeymoon period to get their programs passed by Congress as soon as possible. Each action a president takes,

Presidential Success in Polls and Congress

Exploring Presidential Visits

President Richard M. Nixon was the first president to visit all fifty states. Since Nixon's administration, chief executives have made a significant effort to visit each state during their term in office. President Bill Clinton, for example, took a one-day trip to Nebraska in November of 2000 in order to be able to say that he had visited each of the states. And, as of August 2008, President George W. Bush had visited every state but Vermont.

These visits may occur for any number of reasons—campaign events, policy speeches, or ceremonial visits. Presidents, for example, are often asked to give college commencement addresses. They may visit places of historical significance, commemorate historical events, or visit with foreign ambassadors.

State and local officials do not take presidential visits lightly. These visits often require significant preparation of security, although some events may not be accessible to the public.

Explore the history of your state or locality to learn more about presidential visits, both past and present.

■ What presidents have visited your area? Did you attend any of these events? If so, what were they like?
■ What local attractions or commemorations might be appropriate events for attracting the president? How might you go about bringing these events to the president's attention?

How do presidents prepare to use their honeymoon period?
Even before his election as the forty-fourth president of the United States, Barack Obama worked to fill key staff and cabinet positions. Obama named Congressman Rahm Emanuel (D–IL) as his chief of staff a mere two days after his election.

however, is divisive—some people will approve, and others will disapprove. Disapproval tends to have a negative cumulative effect on a president's approval rating.

Since Lyndon B. Johnson's presidency, only four presidents have left office with approval ratings of more than 50 percent. (To learn more, see Analyzing Visuals: Presidential Approval Ratings Since 1981.) Many people attribute this trend to events such as Vietnam, Watergate, and the Iraq War, which have made the public increasingly skeptical of presidential performance.

However, recent presidents, including George Bush, Bill Clinton, and George W. Bush, have experienced a surge in their approval ratings during the course of their presidencies. Popularity surges allow presidents to achieve some policy goals that they believe are for the good of the nation, even though the policies are unpopular with the public. Usually coming on the heels of a domestic or international crisis such as the 1991 Persian Gulf War or the 9/11 terrorist attacks, these increased approval ratings generally don't last long, as the cumulative effects of governing once again catch up with the president.

President George Bush's rapid rise in popularity occurred after the major and, perhaps more important, quick victory in the 1991 Persian Gulf War. His popularity, however, plummeted as the good feelings faded and Americans began to feel the pinch of recession. In contrast, President Bill Clinton's approval scores skyrocketed after the 1996 Democratic National Convention. More interestingly, Clinton's high approval ratings continued in the wake of allegations of wrongdoing in the Oval Office, his eventual admission of inappropriate conduct, and through his impeachment proceedings. In fact, when Clinton went to the American public and admitted that he misled them about his relationship with Monica Lewinsky, an ABC poll conducted immediately after his speech showed a 10-point jump in his job approval rating.[27]

Photo courtesy: Ben Baker/Redux Pictures

Analyzing Visuals   Presidential Approval Ratings Since 1981

Examine the line graph, which shows the percentage of the American public approving of presidents' performances from 1981 through 2008, and consider the following questions:

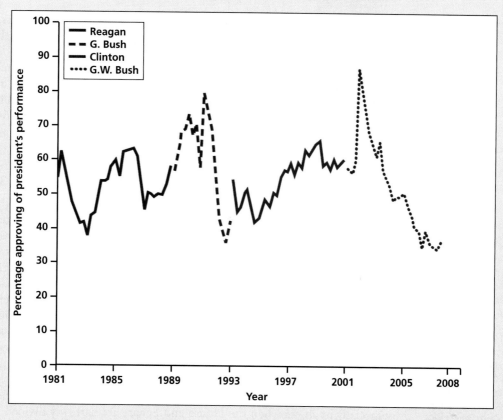

DO you notice a pattern in the approval ratings for two-term presidents Ronald Reagan, Bill Clinton, and George W. Bush?

WHICH president left office with the highest approval rating? The lowest approval rating?

BASED on your knowledge of President George W. Bush's terms in office, how would you explain the rise and fall of his approval ratings from 2001 to 2008?

Source: Roper Center, University of Connecticut.

George W. Bush enjoyed one of the longest rallies in history. But, by 2005, his approval ratings hovered around 50 percent in the wake of political scandals, escalating violence in Iraq, and rising gas prices. The president's approval ratings dropped even lower in 2006; by the midterm elections they were a scant 35 percent. As one Republican pollster commented, "[Bush] has no political capital. Slowly but surely it's been unraveling. There's been a direct correlation between the trajectory of his approval numbers and the—I don't want to call it disloyalty—the independence on the part of the Republicans in Congress."[28] In many states, voters viewed the elections as a referendum on Bush, leading to widespread Democratic victories that resulted in Democrats gaining control of both the House and the Senate. By the 2008 elections, President Bush's approval rating had dropped to a staggeringly low 26 percent.

Toward Reform: The President as Policy Maker

When FDR sent his first legislative package to Congress, he broke the traditional model of law-making.[29] As envisioned by the Framers, it was to be Congress that made the laws. Now FDR was claiming a leadership role for the president in the legislative process. Said the president of this new relationship: "It is the duty of the President to propose and it is the privilege of the Congress to dispose."[30] With those words and the actions that followed, FDR shifted the presidency into a law- and policy-maker role. Now the president and the executive branch not only executed the laws but generally suggested them, too.

The President's Role in Proposing and Facilitating Legislation

From FDR's presidency to the Republican-controlled 104th Congress, the public looked routinely to the president to formulate concrete legislative plans to propose to Congress, which subsequently adopted, modified, or rejected his plans for the nation. Then, in 1994, it appeared for a while that the electorate wanted Congress to reassert itself in the legislative process. In fact, the Contract with America was a Republican call for Congress to take the reins of the law-making process. But several Republican Congresses failed to pass many of the items of the Contract, and President Bill Clinton's continued forceful presence in the budgetary process made a resurgent role for Congress largely illusory. The same scenario held true for President George W. Bush, although by 2006, even some Republicans were concerned with Bush's continued deficit spending requests.

Modern presidents continue to play a major role in setting the legislative agenda, especially in an era when the House and Senate are narrowly divided along partisan lines. Without working majorities, "merely placing a program before Congress is not enough," as President Lyndon B. Johnson (LBJ) once explained. "Without constant attention from the administration, most legislation moves through the congressional process at the speed of a glacier."[31] Thus, the president's most important power (and often the source of his greatest frustration), in addition to support of the public, is his ability to construct coalitions within Congress that will work for passage of his legislation. FDR and LBJ were among the best presidents at working Congress, but they were helped by Democratic majorities.[32]

On the whole, presidents have a hard time getting Congress to pass their programs.[33] Passage is especially difficult if the president presides over a divided government, which occurs when the presidency and Congress are controlled by different political parties (see chapter 7). Recent research by

How does the president affect policy? President Lyndon B. Johnson signs the long-awaited Civil Rights Act of 1964. To his immediate right is Senator Edward Brooke (R–MA), the first African American to be popularly elected as a U.S. senator. To his left is Senator Walter Mondale (D–MN), who later served as vice president. To Mondale's left is Thurgood Marshall, whom Johnson later appointed to the U.S. Supreme Court, where he became its first African American member.

Photo courtesy: Bettmann/Corbis

political scientists, however, shows that presidents are much more likely to win on bills central to their announced agendas, such as President George W. Bush's victory on the Iraq war resolution, than to secure passage of legislation proposed by others.[34]

Because presidents generally experience declining support for policies they advocate throughout their terms, it is important that a president propose key plans early in his administration, during the honeymoon period, a time when the good-will toward the president often allows a president to secure passage of legislation that he would not be able to gain at a later period. Even President Lyndon B. Johnson, who was able to get nearly 60 percent of his programs through Congress, noted: "You've got to give it all you can, that first year . . . before they start worrying about themselves. . . . You can't put anything through when half the Congress is thinking how to beat you."[35]

Another way a president can bolster support for his legislative package is to call on his political party. As the informal leader of his party, he should be able to use that position to his advantage in Congress, where party loyalty is very important. This strategy works best when the president has carried members of his party into office on his coattails, as was the case in the Johnson and Reagan landslides of 1964 and 1984, respectively. In fact, many scholars regard President Lyndon B. Johnson as the most effective legislative leader.[36] Not only had he served in the House and as Senate majority leader, but he also enjoyed a comfortable Democratic Party majority in Congress, and many Democrats owed their victories to his landslide win over his Republican challenger, Senator Barry Goldwater (R–AZ).[37]

The Budgetary Process and Legislative Implementation

Closely associated with a president's ability to pass legislation is his ability to secure funding for new and existing programs. A president sets national policy and priorities through his budget proposals and his continued insistence on their congressional passage. The budget proposal not only outlines the programs he wants but indicates the importance of each program by the amount of funding requested for each and for its associated agency or department.

How important is a balanced budget? President Bill Clinton and Vice President Al Gore celebrate the first balanced budget in years, a feat not likely to be repeated soon in light of the federal tax cuts and huge spending increases under President George W. Bush. In October 2008, the White House announced that the federal budget deficit was up from 2006's $161 billion to a record $458.8 billion, due in large part to the crippling economic downturn in 2008.

Photo courtesy: J. Scott Applewhite/AP Wide World Photos

Because the Framers gave Congress the power of the purse, Congress had primary responsibility for the budget process until 1930. The economic disaster set off by the stock market crash of 1929, however, gave FDR, once elected in 1932, the opportunity to assert himself in the congressional budgetary process, just as he inserted himself in the legislative process. In 1939, the Bureau of the Budget, which had been created in 1921 to help the president tell Congress how much money it would take to run the executive branch of government, was made part of the newly created Executive Office of the President. In 1970, President Nixon changed its name to the **Office of Management and Budget (OMB)** to clarify its function in the executive branch.

The OMB works exclusively for the president and employs hundreds of budget and policy experts. Key OMB responsibilities include preparing the president's annual budget proposal, designing the president's program, and reviewing the progress, budget, and program proposals of the executive department agencies. It also supplies economic forecasts to the president and conducts detailed analyses of proposed bills and agency rules. OMB reports allow the president to attach price tags to his legislative proposals and defend the presidential budget. The OMB budget is a huge document, and even those who prepare it have a hard time deciphering all of its provisions. Even so, the expertise of the OMB directors often gives them an advantage over members of Congress.

Office of Management and Budget (OMB)
The office that prepares the president's annual budget proposal, reviews the budget and programs of the executive departments, supplies economic forecasts, and conducts detailed analyses of proposed bills and agency rules.

Policy Making Through Executive Order

Proposing legislation and using the budget to advance policy priorities are not the only ways that presidents can affect the policy process, especially in times of highly divided government. Major policy changes may be instituted when a president has issued an **executive order,** a rule or regulation issued by the president that has the effect of law. Presidents Franklin D. Roosevelt and Harry S Truman used executive orders to seize mills, mines, and factories whose production was crucial to World War II and the Korean War efforts. Roosevelt and Truman argued that these actions were necessary to preserve national security. The Supreme Court, however, eventually disagreed with the Truman administration in *Youngstown Sheet and Tube* v. *Sawyer* (1952). In that case, the Court unequivocally stated that Truman had overstepped the boundaries of his office as provided by the Constitution.[38] While many executive orders are issued to help clarify or implement legislation enacted by Congress, other executive orders have the effect of making new policy. President Truman also used an executive order to end segregation in the military, and affirmative action was institutionalized as national policy through Executive Order 11246, issued by Lyndon B. Johnson in 1966.

executive order
A rule or regulation issued by the president that has the effect of law. All executive orders must be published in the *Federal Register*.

The Executive Order Over Time

Executive orders have been used since the 1980s to set national policies toward abortion. President Ronald Reagan, for example, used an executive order to stop federal funding of fetal tissue research and to end federal funding of any groups providing abortion counseling. President Bill Clinton immediately rescinded those orders when he became president. One of President George W. Bush's first acts upon taking office was to issue an executive order reversing those Clinton orders.

George W. Bush also used executive orders to put his policy stamp on a wide array of important issues. After much soul searching, for example, he signed an executive order limiting federal funding of stem cell research to the sixty or so cell lines currently in the possession of scientific researchers.[39] An executive order also was used to allow military tribunals to try any foreigners captured by U.S. forces in Afghanistan or linked to the 9/11 terrorist acts. One of President Bush's more controversial executive orders eviscerated the 1978 Presidential Records Act, which "established that the records of presidents belong to the American people."[40] Now, scholars, journalists, and other interested persons must demonstrate a specific "need to know" when requesting presidential or vice presidential documents.[41] For whatever reason the order was issued, it demonstrates how easily presidents may thwart the wishes of

POLITICS NOW

Source: THE BOSTON GLOBE   April 30, 2006

Are Signing Statements Constitutional?

George W. Bush Challenges Hundreds of Laws

CHARLIE SAVAGE

President Bush has quietly claimed the authority to disobey more than 750 laws enacted since he took office, asserting that he has the power to set aside any statute passed by Congress when it conflicts with his interpretation of the Constitution. Among the laws Bush said he can ignore are military rules and regulations, affirmative action provisions, requirements that Congress be told about immigration services problems, "whistle-blower" protections for nuclear regulatory officials, and safeguards against political interference in federally funded research.

Legal scholars say the scope and aggression of Bush's assertions that he can bypass laws represent a concerted effort to expand his power at the expense of Congress, upsetting the balance between the branches of government. The Constitution is clear in assigning to Congress the power to write the laws and to the president a duty "to take care that the laws be faithfully executed." Bush, however, has repeatedly declared that he does not need to "execute" a law he believes is unconstitutional. . . .

Far more than any predecessor, Bush has been aggressive about declaring his right to ignore vast swaths of laws—many of which he says infringe on power he believes the Constitution assigns to him

alone as the head of the executive branch or the commander in chief of the military. . . .

For the first five years of Bush's presidency, his legal claims attracted little attention in Congress or the media. Then, twice in recent months, Bush drew scrutiny after challenging new laws: a torture ban and a requirement that he give detailed reports to Congress about how he is using the Patriot Act. Bush administration spokesmen declined to make White House or Justice Department attorneys available to discuss any of Bush's challenges to the laws he has signed. Instead, they referred a *Globe* reporter to their response to questions about Bush's position that he could ignore provisions of the Patriot Act. They said at the time that Bush was following a practice that has "been used for several administrations" and that "the president will faithfully execute the law in a manner that is consistent with the Constitution.". . .

Bush . . .has signed every bill that reached his desk, often inviting the legislation's sponsors to signing ceremonies at which he lavishes praise upon their work.

Then, after the media and the lawmakers have left the White House, Bush quietly files "signing statements"—official documents in which a president lays out his legal interpretation of a bill for the federal bureaucracy to follow when implementing the new law. The statements are recorded in the *Federal Register.*

In his signing statements, Bush has repeatedly asserted that the Constitution gives him the right to ignore numerous sections of the bills—sometimes including provisions that were the subject of negotiations with Congress in order to get

lawmakers to pass the bill. He has appended such statements to more than one of every 10 bills he has signed....

Though Bush has gone further than any previous president, his actions are not unprecedented. Since the early 19th century, American presidents have occasionally signed a large bill while declaring that they would not enforce a specific provision they believed was unconstitutional. On rare occasions, historians say, presidents also issued signing statements interpreting a law and explaining any concerns about it. But it was not until the mid-1980s, midway through the tenure of President Reagan, that it became common for the president to issue signing statements. . . .

Reagan's successors continued this practice. George H.W. Bush challenged 232 statutes over four years in office, and Bill Clinton objected to 140 laws over his eight years. . . .

Many of the challenges involved longstanding legal ambiguities and points of conflict between the president and Congress.

Discussion Questions

1. *Are signing statements a constitutional exercise of presidential power, or do they upset the system of checks and balances between the branches? Why or why not?*
2. *Why might presidents favor signing statements over the exercise of the veto power?*
3. *What other ways might presidents go about achieving the policy reforms they desire?*

Congress and substitute their own policy preferences through executive orders, which require congressional legislation to make them unenforceable.

Presidents may also issue "signing statements" when signing legislation. Often these written statements merely comment on the bill signed, but they sometimes include controversial claims by the president that some part of the legislation is unconstitutional and that he intends to disregard it or to implement it in other ways. (To learn more about signing statements, see Politics Now: Are Signing Statements Constitutional?)

WHAT SHOULD I HAVE LEARNED?

Because the Framers feared a tyrannical monarch, they gave considerable thought to the office of the chief executive. Since ratification of the Constitution, the office has changed considerably—more through practice and need than from changes in the Constitution. In chronicling these changes, we have answered the following questions:

■ **What are the roots of the office of the president of the United States?**

Distrust of a too powerful leader led the Framers to create an executive office with limited powers. They mandated that a president be at least thirty-five years old, a natural-born citizen, and a resident of the United States for at least fourteen years, and they opted not to limit the president's term of office. To further guard against tyranny, they made provisions for the removal of the president.

■ **What are the constitutional powers of the president?**

The Framers gave the president a variety of specific constitutional powers in Article II, including the appointment power, the power to convene Congress, and the power to make treaties. The Constitution also gives the president the power to grant pardons and to veto acts of Congress. In addition, the president derives considerable power from being commander in chief of the military.

■ **How did presidential power develop and expand?**

The development of presidential power has depended on the personal force of those who have held the office. George Washington, in particular, took several actions to establish the primacy of the president in national affairs and as true chief executive of a strong national government. But, with only a few exceptions, subsequent presidents often let Congress dominate in national affairs. With the election of FDR, however, the power of the president increased, and presidential decision making became more important in national and foreign affairs.

■ **What offices make up the presidential establishment?**

As the responsibilities of the president have grown, so has the executive branch of government. Franklin D. Roosevelt established the Executive Office of the President to help him govern. Perhaps the most key policy advisers are those closest to the president: the vice president, the White House staff, some members of the Executive Office of the President, and sometimes, the first lady.

■ **How do public opinion and public perceptions of presidential leadership affect presidential success?**

To gain support for his programs or proposed budget, the president uses a variety of skills, including personal leadership and direct appeals to the public. How the president goes about winning support is determined by his leadership and personal style, affected by his character and his ability to persuade. Since the 1970s, however, the American public has been increasingly skeptical of presidential actions, and few presidents have enjoyed extended periods of the kind of popularity needed to help win support for programmatic change.

■ **How do presidents use their legislative proposals to affect and reform policy?**

Since FDR, the public has looked to the president to propose legislation to Congress. Through proposing legislation, advancing budgets, and involvement in the regulatory process, presidents make policy.

Key Terms

Cabinet, p. 280

executive agreement, p. 282

Executive Office of the President
(EOP), p. 294

executive order, p. 302

executive privilege, p. 278

impeachment, p. 278

inherent powers, p. 289

line-item veto, p. 283

New Deal, p. 291

Office of Management and Budget
(OMB), p. 302

pardon, p. 285

Twenty-Fifth Amendment, p. 280

Twenty-Second Amendment, p. 277

U.S. v. *Nixon* (1974), p. 279

veto power, p. 282

War Powers Act, p. 285

Researching the Presidency

In the Library

Barber, James David. *The Presidential Character: Predicting Presidential Performance in the White House*, 5th ed. New York: Longman, 2008.

Cooper, Philip J. *By Order of the President: The Use and Abuse of Executive Direct Action*. Lawrence: University Press of Kansas, 2002.

Cronin, Thomas E., and Michael A. Genovese. *The Paradoxes of the American Presidency*, 2nd ed. New York: Oxford University Press, 2006.

Edwards, George C., III, and Desmond King. *The Polarized Presidency of George W. Bush*. New York: Oxford University Press, 2007.

Greenstein, Fred I. *The Presidential Difference: Leadership Style from FDR to George W. Bush*, 2nd ed. Princeton, NJ: Princeton University Press, 2004.

Martin, Janet M. *The American Presidency and Women: Promise, Performance, and Illusion*. College Station: Texas A&M University Press, 2003.

Milkis, Sidney M., and Michael T. Nelson. *The American Presidency: Origins and Development, 1776–2007*, 5th ed. Washington, DC: CQ Press, 2007.

Neustadt, Richard E. *Presidential Power and the Modern Presidents*. New York: Free Press, 1991.

Pfiffner, James P. *The Character Factor: How We Judge America's Presidents*. College Station: Texas A&M University Press, 2004.

———. *The Modern Presidency*, 5th ed. Belmont, CA: Wadsworth, 2007.

Pika, Joseph A., and John Anthony Maltese. *The Politics of the Presidency*, 7th ed. Washington, DC: CQ Press, 2008.

Rossiter, Clinton. *The American Presidency*, reprint ed. Baltimore, MD: Johns Hopkins University Press, 1987.

Skowronek, Stephen. *The Politics Presidents Make: Leadership from John Adams to Bill Clinton*. Cambridge, MA: Harvard University Press, 1997.

Warshaw, Shirley Anne. *The Keys to Power: Managing the Presidency*, 2nd ed. New York: Longman, 2005.

Wood, B. Dan. *The Politics of Economic Leadership: The Causes and Consequences of Presidential Rhetoric*. Princeton, NJ: Princeton University Press, 2007.

On the Web

To learn more about the office of the president, go to the official White House Web site, **www.whitehouse.gov.** There you can track current presidential initiatives and legislative priorities, read press briefings, and learn more about presidential nominations and executive orders.

To learn more about past presidents, go to the National Archives at **www.archives.gov/index.html,** where you can learn about the presidential libraries, view presidential documents, and hear audio of presidents speaking.

To learn more about the office of the vice president, go to **www.whitehouse.gov/vicepresident.**

To learn more about the initiatives favored by the first lady, go to **www.whitehouse.gov/firstlady.**

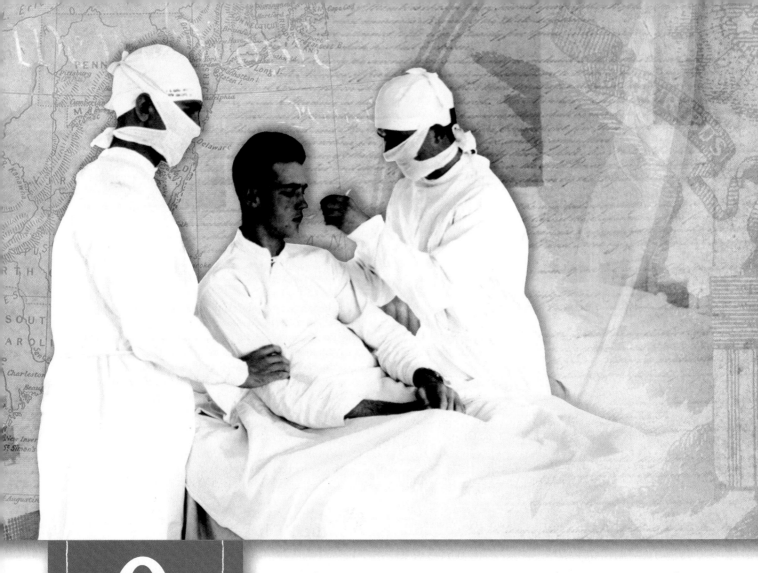

9 The Executive Branch and the Federal Bureaucracy

To maintain a secure homeland, planning is critical. And, at a time when federal resources are stretched to their limit given the high cost of military interventions in Iraq and Afghanistan, the U.S. government—especially its bureaucracy—is trying to prepare for what some are calling the next pandemic: avian flu.

Avian influenza, or H5N1—the designation scientists have given this particular strain of the influenza virus—has infected domesticated and migratory birds in more than fifty nations across Asia, Africa, and Europe. It has infected more than 250 people worldwide, with an astonishingly high death rate of more than 50 percent. Flu viruses mutate rapidly, and experts believe it is highly likely that this particular strain of avian flu could become a global threat to humanity. The last major influenza pandemic occurred in 1918 and killed tens of millions of people worldwide.

Since it takes time to culture a reliable vaccine to protect people from getting easily transmitted viruses, a pandemic caused by a virus like H5N1, could outpace the abilities of governments to vaccinate their citizens or contain the outbreak. Even if the first widespread infections occurred in China, given the global travel patterns of U.S. citizens, a deadly virus likely would be on the ground in the United States within weeks. "If such an outbreak occurred, hospitals would become overwhelmed, riots would engulf vaccination clinics, and even power and food would be in short supply," concludes a draft of a plan the Bush administration developed as part of its initial planning to handle avian flu.[1]

On May 3, 2006, Frances Townsend, President George W. Bush's homeland security advisor, issued the administration's Pandemic Influenza Strategic Plan to get the nation ready for a 1918-style flu disaster, which left more than one-half million Americans dead. The new government plan outlined the responsibilities of every federal department and agency should the flu begin to spread quickly among humans. The secretary of health and human services was given major responsibility for health issues, and nonmedical emergency efforts and coordination were given to the secretary of homeland security. The secretary of state was given responsibility for international response issues.[2]

Critics were quick to point out that none of the secretaries were given emergency powers to spend additional monies, such

■ **Governments have been called upon to deal with public health crises for many years.** At left, doctors tend to a patient during the 1918 Spanish flu epidemic. At right, Homeland Security Advisor Frances Townsend announces the Bush Administration's plan for a strategic response to the threat of avian flu.

★ **WHAT SHOULD I KNOW ABOUT . . .**
■ the roots of the federal bureaucracy?
■ the modern bureaucracy?
■ how the bureaucracy works?
■ making agencies accountable?

as granting emergency medical coverage to the uninsured. Priorities as to how to allot any vaccines or interventional medicines were also left unanswered, as was any potential role for the military. "The real shortcoming of the plan is that it doesn't say who's in charge," said a top health official who fears the consequences of a disorganized response from the federal government.[3] Possibly further complicating a "national plan of action," the administration's plan places tremendous responsibility on state and local governments, who often are first responders in any emergency, and it has been criticized by the National Association of County and City Health Officials, who view the administration's plan as "the mother of all unfunded mandates."[4]

The plan, which suggests steps that state and local governments can take to prepare for a pandemic, calls for quarantine and travel restrictions, but the administration admits that such steps are largely stopgap measures. Its worst-case scenario foresees the deaths of nearly 2 million Americans and the need to hospitalize an additional 8.5 million people.

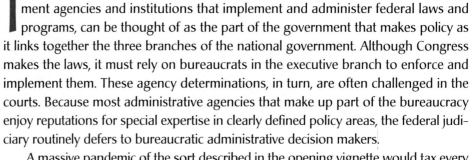

TO LEARN MORE—
—TO DO MORE
To learn more about U.S. preparedness in the event of a possible avian flu outbreak, go to the U.S. government avian and pandemic flu information site at www.pandemicflu.gov.

bureaucracy
A set of complex hierarchical departments, agencies, commissions, and their staffs that exist to help a chief executive officer carry out his or her duties. Bureaucracies may be private organizations or governmental units.

SIMULATION

You Are Deputy Director of the Census Bureau

In the American system, the **bureaucracy**, or the thousands of federal government agencies and institutions that implement and administer federal laws and programs, can be thought of as the part of the government that makes policy as it links together the three branches of the national government. Although Congress makes the laws, it must rely on bureaucrats in the executive branch to enforce and implement them. These agency determinations, in turn, are often challenged in the courts. Because most administrative agencies that make up part of the bureaucracy enjoy reputations for special expertise in clearly defined policy areas, the federal judiciary routinely defers to bureaucratic administrative decision makers.

A massive pandemic of the sort described in the opening vignette would tax every agency of the federal bureaucracy, whether it was directly involved in health issues or not. If quarantines were put into effect, for example, the U.S. Postal Service would close down, Social Security checks would not be printed or mailed, banks might close, and commerce could come to a stop. Such is the tremendous scope of what the federal government and the bureaucrats and political appointees who run it do.

The federal bureaucracy often is called the "fourth branch of government." Critics often charge that the bureaucracy is too large, too powerful, and too unaccountable to the people or even to elected officials. Many politicians, elected officials, and voters complain that the federal bureaucracy is too wasteful. However, few critics discuss the fact that laws and policies also are implemented by state and local bureaucracies and bureaucrats whose numbers are proportionately far larger, and often far less accountable, than those working for the federal government.

Many Americans are uncomfortable with the large role of the federal government in policy making. Nevertheless, recent studies show that most users of federal agencies rate quite favorably the agencies and the services they receive. Many of those polled by the Pew Research Center were frustrated by complicated rules and the slowness of a particular agency. Still, a majority gave most agencies overall high marks. Most of those polled drew sharp distinctions between particular agencies and the government as a whole. For example, 84 percent of physicians and pharmacists rated the Food and Drug Administration favorably, whereas only one-half of all those sampled were positive about the government in general.[5]

Harold D. Lasswell once defined political science as the "study of who gets what, when, and how."[6] It is by studying the bureaucracy that those questions can perhaps best be answered. To allow you to understand the role of the bureaucracy, this chapter explores the following issues:

★ First, we will examine *the roots of the federal bureaucracy.*

★ Second, we will examine *the modern bureaucracy* by discussing bureaucrats and the formal organization of the bureaucracy.

★ Third, we will discuss *how the bureaucracy works.*

★ Finally, we will discuss *efforts intended to make agencies accountable.*

Roots of the Federal Bureaucracy

In 1789, only three departments existed under the Articles of Confederation: Foreign Affairs, War, and Treasury. President George Washington inherited those departments, and soon, the head of each department was called its secretary and Foreign Affairs was renamed the Department of State. To provide the president with legal advice, Congress also created the office of attorney general. From the beginning, individuals appointed as Cabinet secretaries (as well as the attorney general) were subject to approval by the U.S. Senate, but they could be removed from office by the president alone. Even the First Congress realized how important it was that a president be surrounded by those in whom he had complete confidence and trust.

From 1816 to 1861, the size of the federal executive branch and the bureaucracy grew as increased demands were made on existing departments and new departments were created. The Post Office, for example, which Article I constitutionally authorized Congress to create, was forced to expand to meet the needs of a growing and westward-expanding population. President Andrew Jackson removed the Post Office from the jurisdiction of the Department of the Treasury in 1829 and promoted the postmaster general to Cabinet rank.

The Post Office quickly became a major source of jobs President Jackson could fill by presidential appointment, as every small town and village in the United States had its own postmaster. In commenting on Jackson's wide use of political positions to reward friends and loyalists, one fellow Jacksonian Democrat commented: "to the victors belong the spoils." From that statement came the term **spoils system**, which describes an executive's ability to fire public office holders of the defeated political party and replace them with party loyalists. The spoils system was a form of **patronage**: jobs, grants, or other special favors given as rewards to friends and political allies for their support. Political patronage often is defended as an essential element of the party system because it provides rewards and inducements for party workers.

TIMELINE

The Evolution of the Federal Bureaucracy

spoils system
The firing of public-office holders of a defeated political party in order to replace them with loyalists of the newly elected party.

patronage
Jobs, grants, or other special favors that are given as rewards to friends and political allies for their support.

What was the Pony Express? In 1860, advertisements were placed in newspapers that read: "Wanted: Young, skinny, wiry fellows not over 18. Must be expert riders willing to risk death daily. Orphans preferred." Thus was born the Pony Express, a private, for-profit attempt to deliver mail faster and more efficiently across the United States that remains a popular chapter in American history. The United States Postal Service, the federal government's solution to the need for fast and efficient mail delivery, trademarked "Pony Express" in 2006.

Photo courtesy: Hulton Archive/Getty Images

Which U.S. president popularized the spoils system? Here, a political cartoonist depicts how President Andrew Jackson might have been immortalized for his use of the spoils system.

Photo courtesy: Bettman/Corbis

The Civil War and the Growth of Government

As discussed in chapter 3, the Civil War (1861–1865) permanently changed the nature of the federal bureaucracy. As the nation geared up for war, thousands of additional employees were added to existing departments. The Civil War also spawned the need for new government agencies. A series of poor harvests and distribution problems led President Abraham Lincoln (who understood that you need well-fed troops to conduct a war) to create the Department of Agriculture in 1862, although it was not given full Cabinet-level status until more than twenty years later.

The Pension Office was established in 1866 to pay benefits to the thousands of Union veterans who had fought in the war (more than 127,000 veterans initially were eligible for benefits). Justice, headed by the attorney general, was made a cabinet department in 1870, and other departments were added through 1900. Agriculture became a full-fledged department in 1889 and began to play an important role in informing farmers about the latest developments in soil conservation, livestock breeding, and planting.

From the Spoils System to the Merit System

The spoils system reached a high-water mark during Abraham Lincoln's presidency. By the time James A. Garfield, a former distinguished Civil War officer, was elected president in 1880, many reformers were calling for changes in the patronage system. Garfield's immediate predecessor, Rutherford B. Hayes, had favored the idea of the replacement of the spoils system with a merit system based on test scores and ability. Congress, however, failed to pass the legislation he proposed. Possibly because potential job seekers wanted to secure positions before Congress had the opportunity to act on an overhauled civil service system, thousands pressed Garfield for positions. This siege prompted Garfield to record in his diary: "My day is frittered away with the personal seeking of people when it ought to be given to the great problems which concern the whole country."[7] Garfield resolved to reform the civil service, but his life was cut short by the bullets of an assassin who, ironically, was a frustrated job seeker.

Public reaction to Garfield's death and increasing criticism of the spoils system prompted Congress to pass the Civil Service Reform Act in 1883, more commonly known as the **Pendleton Act**, named in honor of its sponsor, Senator George H. Pendleton (D–OH). It established the principle of federal employment on the basis of open, competitive exams and created a bipartisan three-member Civil Service Commission, which operated until 1978. Initially, only about 10 percent of the positions in the federal **civil service system** were covered by the law, but later laws and executive orders extended coverage of the act to over 90 percent of all federal employees. This new system was called the **merit system**.

Regulating the Economy

As the nation grew, so did the bureaucracy (To learn more, see Analyzing Visuals: Federal Employees in the Executive Branch, 1789–2005). In the wake of the tremendous growth of big business (especially railroads), widespread price fixing, and other unfair business practices that occurred after the Civil War, Congress created the Interstate Commerce Commission (ICC) in 1887. In creating the ICC, Congress was reacting

Pendleton Act
Reform measure that created the Civil Service Commission to administer a partial merit system. The act classified the federal service by grades, to which appointments were made based on the results of a competitive examination. It made it illegal for federal political appointees to be required to contribute to a particular political party.

civil service system
The legal system by which many federal bureaucrats are selected.

merit system
The system by which federal civil service jobs are classified into grades or levels, and appointments are made on the basis of performance on competitive examinations.

to public outcries over the exorbitant rates charged by railroad companies for hauling freight. It became the first **independent regulatory commission**, an agency outside a major executive department. Independent regulatory commissions such as the ICC, generally concerned with particular aspects of the economy, are created by Congress to be independent of direct presidential authority. Commission members are appointed by the president and hold their jobs for fixed terms, but they are not removable by the president unless they fail to uphold their oaths of office. The creation of the ICC also marked a shift in the focus of the bureaucracy from service to regulation. Its creation gave the government—in the shape of the bureaucracy—vast powers over individual and property rights.

Photo courtesy: Bettman/Corbis

What led to the assassination of President James A. Garfield? This artist's interpretation shows President Garfield's assassination at the hands of an unhappy job seeker.

independent regulatory commission
An agency created by Congress that is generally concerned with a specific aspect of the economy.

When Theodore Roosevelt, a progressive Republican, became president in 1901, the movement toward governmental regulation of the economic sphere was strengthened. The size of the bureaucracy was further increased when, in 1903, Roosevelt asked Congress to establish a Department of Commerce and Labor to oversee employer-employee relations. At the turn of the twentieth century, many workers toiled long hours for low wages in substandard conditions. Many employers refused to recognize the rights of workers to join unions, and many businesses had grown so large and powerful that they could force workers to accept substandard conditions. The progressives wanted new government regulations to cure some of the ills suffered by workers and to control the power of the increasingly monopolistic corporations.

In 1913, when it became clear that one agency could not well represent the interests of both employers and employees, President Woodrow Wilson divided the Department of Commerce and Labor, creating two separate departments. One year later, Congress created the Federal Trade Commission (FTC) to protect small businesses and the public from unfair competition, especially from big business.

As discussed in chapter 3, the ratification of the Sixteenth Amendment to the Constitution in 1913 affected the size and growth potential of government. It gave Congress the authority to implement a federal income tax to supplement the national treasury and provided a huge infusion of funds to support new federal agencies, services, and programs.

The Growth of Government in the Twentieth Century

The economy appeared to boom as U.S. involvement in World War I caused an increase in manufacturing, but ominous events were just over the horizon. Farmers were in trouble after a series of bad harvests, the nation experienced a severe slump in agricultural prices, the construction industry went into decline, and, throughout the 1920s, bank failures became common. After stock prices crashed in 1929, the nation plunged into the Great Depression. To combat the resultant high unemployment and weak financial markets, President Franklin D. Roosevelt created hundreds of new government agencies to regulate business practices and various aspects of the national economy. Roosevelt believed that a national economic depression called for national intervention. Thus, the president proposed, and the Congress enacted, far-ranging economic legislation. The desperate mood of the nation supported these moves, as most Americans began to reconsider their ideas about the proper role of government and the provision of governmental services. Formerly, most Americans had believed

Analyzing Visuals | Federal Employees in the Executive Branch, 1789–2005

Examine the line graph tracking the number of federal employees in the executive branch of the U.S. government from the eighteenth to the twenty-first century. After reviewing the data and balloons in the line graph and reading the material in this chapter on the origins and development of the executive branch and federal bureaucracy, answer the following questions:

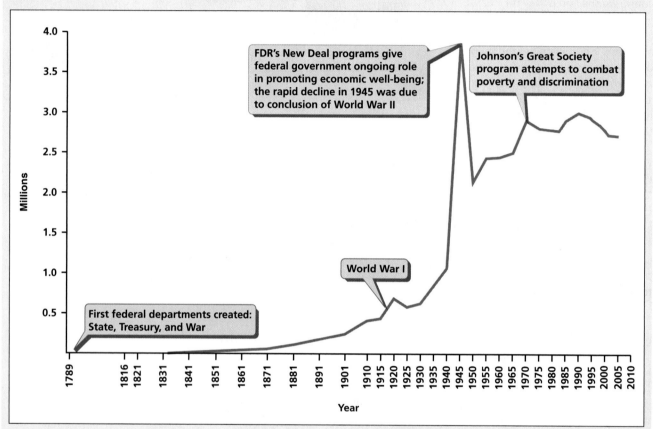

BEFORE the United States' involvement in World War II, what was the principal reason for the growth in the number of federal employees?

THE rapid decline in federal employees between 1945 and 1950 was a result of the end of World War II, but why

do you think the number of federal employees declined after 1970? Why might it have increased between 1975 and 1990?

WOULD you expect the Obama administration to hire more or fewer federal employees? Why?

Source: Office of Personnel Management, *The Fact Book*, http://www. opm.gov/feddata/factbook/2005/factbook2005.pdf.

in a hands-off approach; now they considered it the federal government's job to get the economy going and get Americans back to work.

As the nation struggled to recover from the Great Depression, the United States was forced into World War II on December 7, 1941, when Japan attacked U.S. ships at Pearl Harbor, in Hawaii. The war immediately affected the economy: healthy, eligible men went to war and women went to work at factories or in other jobs to replace the men. Factories operated around the clock to produce the armaments, material, and clothes necessary to equip, shelter, and dress an army.

During World War II, the federal government also continued to grow tremendously to meet the needs of a nation at war. Tax rates were increased to support the war, and they never again fell to prewar levels. After the war, this infusion of new monies and veterans' demands for services led to a variety of new programs and a much bigger government. The G.I. (Government Issue) Bill, for example, provided college loans for returning veterans and reduced mortgage rates to allow them to buy homes. The national government's involvement in these programs not only affected more people but also led to its greater involvement in more regulation. Homes bought with Veterans Housing Authority loans, for example, had to meet certain specifications. With these programs, Americans became increasingly accustomed to the national government's role in entirely new areas such as affordable middle-class housing and scholarships that allowed lower- and middle-class men their first opportunities for higher education.

Photo courtesy: AP Wide World Photos

Within two decades after World War II, the civil rights movement and President Lyndon B. Johnson's Great Society programs produced additional growth in the bureaucracy. The Equal Employment Opportunity Commission (EEOC) was created in 1965 by the Civil Rights Act of 1964. The Departments of Housing and Urban Development (HUD) and Transportation were created in 1965 and 1966, respectively. These expansions of the bureaucracy corresponded to increases in the president's power and his ability to persuade Congress that new agencies would be an effective way to solve pressing social problems.

What led to the growth of government in the 1930s?
During the New Deal, President Franklin D. Roosevelt suggested and Congress enacted the Emergency Relief Appropriation Act, which authorized the Works Progress Administration (WPA) to hire thousands of unemployed workers to complete numerous public works projects. These WPA workers are widening a road.

The Modern Bureaucracy

The national government differs from private business in numerous ways. Governments exist for the public good, not to make money. Businesses are driven by a profit motive; government leaders, but not bureaucrats, are driven by reelection. Businesses get their money from customers; the national government gets its money from taxpayers. Another difference between a bureaucracy and a business is that it is difficult to determine to whom bureaucracies are responsible. Is it the president? Congress? The citizenry? Still, governments can learn much from business, and recent reform efforts have tried to apply business solutions to create a government that works better and costs less.

The different natures of government and business have a tremendous impact on the way the bureaucracy operates. Because all of the incentive in government "is in the direction of not making mistakes," public employees view risks and rewards very differently from their private-sector counterparts.[8] There is little reason for government employees to take risks or go beyond their assigned job tasks. In contrast, private employers are far more likely to reward ambition. The key to the modern bureaucracy is to understand who bureaucrats are, how the bureaucracy is organized, how organization

Thinking Globally

Bureaucratic Independence in India and China

In India, the bureaucracy is considered the backbone of the country's government. It enjoys a high degree of autonomy and plays an important role in the public policy process. In contrast, China's civil servants have limited decision-making authority as the Communist Party functions as the principal policy-making organization.

- What level of independence should be extended to a government's bureaucracy? How might an independent bureaucracy facilitate the public policy process? How might it complicate it?
- Should civil service employees act as autonomous agents of government policy or as agents of the political party in power?

and personnel affect each other, and how bureaucrats act within the political process. It also is key to understand that government cannot be run entirely like a business. An understanding of these facts and factors can help in the search for ways to motivate positive change in the bureaucracy.

Who Are Bureaucrats?

Federal bureaucrats are career government employees who work in the executive branch in the Cabinet-level departments and independent agencies that comprise more than 2,000 bureaus, divisions, branches, offices, services, and other subunits of the federal government. There are more than 2.7 million federal workers in the executive branch. Nearly one-third of all civilian employees work in the U.S. Postal Service, as illustrated in Figure 9.1. The remaining federal civilian workers are spread out among the various executive departments and agencies throughout the United States. Most of these federal employees are paid according to what is called the "General Schedule" (GS). They advance within fifteen GS grades (as well as steps within those grades), moving into higher GS levels and salaries as their careers progress.

As a result of reforms during the Truman administration that built on the Pendleton Act, most civilian federal governmental employees today are selected by merit standards, which include tests (such as civil service or foreign service exams) and educational criteria. Merit systems also protect federal employees from being fired for political reasons.

At the lower levels of the U.S. Civil Service, most positions are filled by competitive examinations. These usually involve a written test. Mid-level to upper ranges of federal positions do not normally require tests; instead, applicants submit resumes online. Personnel departments then evaluate potential candidates and rank candidates according to how well they fit a particular job opening. Only the names of those deemed "qualified" are then forwarded to the official filling the vacancy. This can be a time-consuming process; it often takes six to nine months before a position can be filled in this manner.

The remaining 10 percent of the federal workforce is made up of persons not covered by the civil service system. These positions generally fall into three categories:

1. *Appointive policy-making positions.* Nearly 3,000 people are presidential appointees. Some of these, including Cabinet secretaries and under- and assistant secretaries, are subject to Senate confirmation. These appointees, in turn, are responsible for appointing high-level policy-making assistants who form the top of the bureaucratic hierarchy. These are called "Schedule C" political appointees, and their numbers were increased by over 300 by the Bush administration.

2. *Independent regulatory commissioners.* Although each president gets to appoint as many as one hundred commissioners, they become independent of his direct political influence once they take office.

3. *Low-level, nonpolicy patronage positions.* These types of positions generally concern secretarial assistants to policy makers.

More than 15,000 job skills are represented in the federal government. Government employees, whose average age is forty-seven, have an average length of service of seventeen years. They include forest rangers, FBI agents, foreign service officers, computer programmers, security guards, librarians, administrators, engineers, plumbers, lawyers, doctors, postal carriers, and zoologists, among others. The diversity of government jobs

Total Employed: 2,713,200

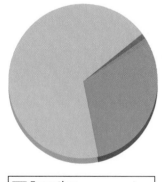

- Executive: 1,881,700 (69.3%)
- U.S. Postal Service: 767,600 (28.3%)
- Judicial: 33,800 (1.2%)
- Legislative: 30,000 (1.1%)

FIGURE 9.1

Distribution of Federal Civilian Employment, 2004

Source: Office of Personnel Management, *2005 Fact Book.*

mirrors the diversity of jobs in the private sector. The federal workforce, itself, is also diverse but under-represents African Americans and Hispanics, in particular, and the overall employment of women lags behind that of men. (To learn more about the distribution of the federal workforce, see Figure 9.2.) Women make up more than 60 percent of the lowest GS levels but raised their proportion of positions in the GS 13–15 ranks from 18 percent in 1990 to over 30 percent in 2004.[9]

There are about 332,500 federal workers in the nation's capital; the rest are located in regional, state, and local offices scattered throughout the country. To enhance efficiency, the United States is broken up into several regions, with most agencies having regional offices in one city in that region. (To learn more about agency regions, see Figure 9.3.) The decentralization of the bureaucracy facilitates accessibility to the pub-

Comparing Bureaucracies

The Changing Face of the Federal Bureaucracy

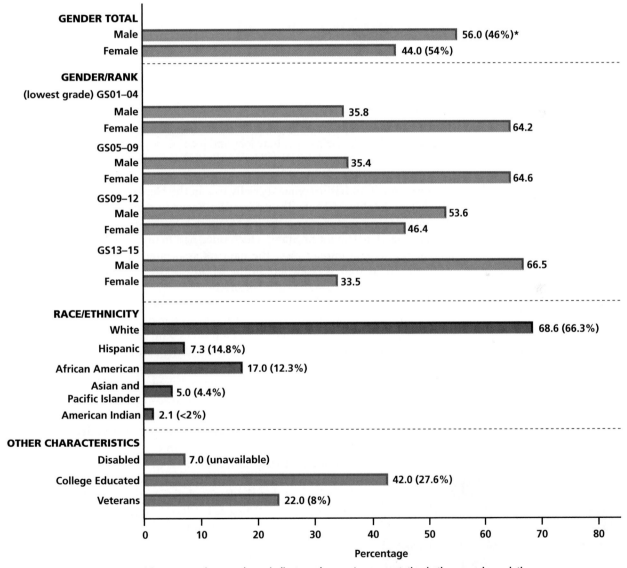

* Percentages in parentheses indicate each group's representation in the general population.

FIGURE 9.2 Characteristics and Rank Distribution of Federal Civilian Employees, 2004.

This figure depicts the percentage of the federal civilian workforce in several categories. As you review the data displayed in the graph, consider the trends you observe across GS levels and overall.

Source: Office of Personnel Management, *2005 Fact Book*.

FIGURE **9.3** Federal Agency Regions and City Headquarters

Source: Department of Health and Human Services, http://www.hhs.gov/images/regions.gif.

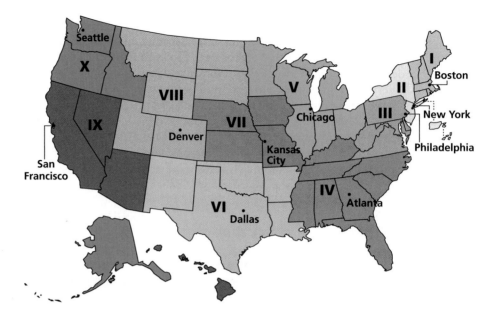

lic. The Social Security Administration, for example, has numerous offices so that its clients can have a place nearby to take their paperwork, questions, and problems. Decentralization also helps distribute jobs and incomes across the country.

Many people complain that jobs in the federal government, especially highly skilled ones, are difficult to fill because they pay less than comparable positions in the private sector. This has become especially true in the Department of Homeland Security. Many employees of its Transportation Security Administration, for example, leave after only a short time on the job for more lucrative careers outside government. And, at the Department of State, which once had many of the most highly coveted jobs in the federal bureaucracy, the dangers associated with postings in Iraq and Afghanistan, as well as elsewhere in the Middle East, are making it harder to find well-qualified people to staff critical positions.[10]

Consequently, the military has enlisted private contractors at unprecedented rates to fill many bureaucratic positions in Iraq and other dangerous sites. Many of these private contractors are former government employees who can make much more money working for private companies. With a portion of the cost of the war in Iraq going to private contractors, one commentator likened the practice to "a school district hiring taxi drivers to pick kids up and drive them home when a school bus route runs right past their door."[11] The Blackwater scandal, which involved private contractors killing Iraqi civilians with seeming impunity in the Middle East, cast a new eye on the prevalence of the hiring of outsiders to perform military duties. From 2005 to 2007, Blackwater employees were implicated in nearly 200 shootings of Iraqi civilians.[12]

While the exact number of private contractors is unknown, it is estimated that the Bush administration added 2.4 million contractors to the existing 5.3 million contractors performing government work. This more than tripled the number of total military personnel and civil servants combined.[13]

The graying of the federal workforce is another concern. More than two-thirds of those in the highest nonpolitical positions as well as a large number of mid-level managers are eligible to retire.[14] Many in government hope that the Presidential Management Fellows Program, which was begun in 1977 to hire and train future managers and executives, will be enhanced to make up for the shortfall in experienced managers that the federal government is

What are the proper roles of government contractors? Private contractors perform duties once performed by federal employees. This security guard, an employee of the Blackwater contracting firm, is seen protecting L. Paul Bremer III in Iraq. At the time, Bremer was the administrator of Iraq's transitional government after the overthrow of Saddam Hussein.

Photo courtesy: Watniq Khuzaie/Pool/epa/Corbis

now facing. Agencies even are contemplating ways to pay the college loans of prospective recruits while at the same time trying to enhance benefits to attract older workers.[15]

Formal Organization

While even experts can't agree on the exact number of separate governmental agencies, commissions, and departments that make up the federal bureaucracy, there are at least 1,150 civilian agencies.[16] A distinctive feature of the executive bureaucracy is its traditional division into areas of specialization. For example, the Occupational Safety and Health Administration (OSHA) handles occupational safety, and the Department of State specializes in foreign affairs. It is not unusual, however, for more than one agency to be involved in a particular issue or for one agency to be involved in myriad issues. The vast authority and range of activities of the Department of Homeland Security are probably the best example of this phenomenon. In fact, numerous agencies often have authority in the same issue areas, making administration even more difficult.

Agencies fall into four general types: (1) Cabinet departments; (2) government corporations; (3) independent executive agencies; and, (4) independent regulatory commissions.

CABINET DEPARTMENTS   The fifteen Cabinet **departments** are major administrative units that have responsibility for conducting a broad area of government operations. (To learn more about the Cabinet, see The Living Constitution: Article II, Section 2, Clause 1.) Cabinet departments account for about 60 percent of the federal workforce. The vice president, the heads of all of the departments, as well as the heads of the Environmental Protection Agency (EPA), Office of Management and Budget (OMB), Office of National Drug Control Policy, the U.S. Trade Representative, and the president's chief of staff make up his formal Cabinet.

The executive branch departments depicted in Figure 9.4 are headed by Cabinet members called secretaries (except the Department of Justice, which is headed by the attorney general). The secretaries are responsible for establishing their department's

departments
Major administrative unit with responsibility for a broad area of government operations. Departmental status usually indicates a permanent national interest in a particular governmental function, such as defense, commerce, or agriculture.

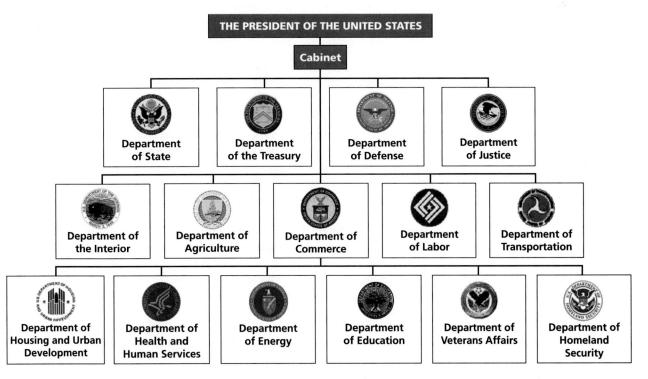

FIGURE **9.4** The Cabinet Departments

The Living Constitution

The President . . . may require the Opinion, in writing, of the principal Officer in each of the executive Departments, upon any subject relating to the Duties of their respective Office.

—ARTICLE II, SECTION 2, CLAUSE 1

This clause, along with additional language designating that the president shall be the commander in chief, notes that the heads of departments are to serve as advisers to the president. There is no direct mention of the Cabinet in the Constitution.

This meager language is all that remains of the Framers' initial efforts to create a council to guide the president. Those in attendance at the Constitutional Convention largely favored the idea of a council but could not agree on who should be a part of that body. Some actually wanted to follow the British parliamentary model and create the Cabinet from members of the House and Senate, who would rotate into the bureaucracy; most, however, appeared to support the idea of the heads of departments along with the chief justice, who would preside when the president was unavailable. The resulting language above depicts a one-sided arrangement whereby the heads of executive departments must simply answer in writing questions put to them by the president.

The Cabinet of today differs totally from the structure envisioned by the Framers. George Washington was the first to convene a meeting of what he called his Cabinet. Some presidents have used their Cabinets as trusted advisers; others have used them to demonstrate that they are committed to political, racial, ethnic, or gender diversity, and have relied more on White House aides than particular Cabinet members. Who is included in the Cabinet, as well as how it is used, is solely up to the discretion of the sitting president with the approval of the U.S. Senate, although executive departments cannot be created or abolished without approval of both houses of Congress.

CRITICAL THINKING QUESTIONS

1. What are the advantages and disadvantages of having a Cabinet composed of heads of the departments?
2. What issues arise from requiring senatorial approval for Cabinet positions, and how does the Constitution remedy these issues?

general policy and overseeing its operations. As discussed in chapter 8, Cabinet secretaries are responsible directly to the president but are often viewed as having two masters—the president and those affected by their department. Cabinet secretaries also are tied to Congress, due to the appropriations process and given their discretion in implementing legislation and making rules and policy.

Although departments vary considerably in size, prestige, and power, they share certain features. Department status generally signifies a strong permanent national interest to promote a particular function. Each department covers a broad area of responsibility generally reflected by its name. Each secretary is assisted by one or more deputies or undersecretaries who take part of the administrative burden off the secretary's shoulders, as well as by several assistant secretaries who direct major programs within the department. In addition, each secretary has numerous assistants who help with planning, budgeting, personnel, legal services, public relations, and their key staff functions. Most departments are subdivided into bureaus, divisions, sections, or other smaller units, and it is at this level that the real work of each agency is done. Most departments are subdivided along functional lines, but the basis for division may be geography, work processes (for example, the Transportation Security Administration is housed in the Department of Homeland Security), or clientele (such as the Bureau of Indian Affairs in the Department of the Interior). Clientele agencies are particularly subject to outside lobbying from organized interests in Washington. The clientele agencies and groups also are active at the regional level, where the agencies devote a substantial part of their resources to program implementation.

GOVERNMENT CORPORATIONS **Government corporations** are the most recent addition to the bureaucracy. Dating from the early 1930s, they are businesses established by Congress to perform functions that could be provided by private businesses. The corporations are formed when the government chooses to engage in commercial activities that produce revenue and require greater flexibility than Congress generally allows regular departments. Some of the better-known government corporations include Amtrak and the Federal Deposit Insurance Corporation (FDIC). Unlike other governmental agencies, government corporations charge for their services. The Tennessee Valley Authority (TVA) provides electricity at reduced rates to millions of Americans in Appalachia, generally a low-income area that had failed to attract private utility companies to provide service there.

    In cases such as the TVA, where the financial incentives for private industry to provide services are minimal, Congress often believes that it must act. In other cases, it steps in to salvage valuable public assets. For example, when passenger rail service in the United States became unprofitable, Congress stepped in to create Amtrak, nationalizing the passenger-train industry to keep passenger trains running, especially in the Northeast corridor.

INDEPENDENT EXECUTIVE AGENCIES **Independent executive agencies** closely resemble Cabinet departments but have narrower areas of responsibility. Generally speaking, independent agencies perform services rather than regulatory functions. The heads of these agencies are appointed by the president and serve, like Cabinet secretaries, at his pleasure.

government corporations
Businesses established by Congress to perform functions that can be provided by private businesses.

independent executive agencies
Governmental units that closely resemble a Cabinet department but have narrower areas of responsibility (such as the Central Intelligence Agency) and are not part of any Cabinet department.

What do government corporations do? Workers install housing for turbines during the 1941 construction of the Tennessee Valley Authority's Cherokee Dam in Tennessee. Today, the TVA continues to provide electricity at reduced rates to millions of Americans living in Appalachia.

Photo courtesy: AP Wide World Photos

Thinking Globally

Nationalizing Venezuela's Oil Reserves

During the 1990s, Venezuela opened its economy to privatization, including the state-owned oil industry. Under President Hugo Chávez's leadership in 2007, Venezuela renationalized the nation's oil reserves, taking control of at least 60 percent of the shares in all oil operations in the country. Chávez maintains that this move ensures that the people of Venezuela profit from their nation's natural resources.

- Are there sectors of the U.S. economy that should be controlled or managed by the government, especially in light of the recent finanacial crisis? Why or why not?
- What is the proper balance between private ownership and government management of key sectors of the economy such as oil and gas production?

Independent agencies exist apart from executive departments for practical or symbolic reasons. The National Aeronautics and Space Administration (NASA), for example, could have been placed within the Department of Defense. Such positioning, however, could have conjured up thoughts of a space program dedicated solely to military purposes, rather than to civilian satellite communication or scientific exploration. Similarly, the Environmental Protection Agency (EPA) could have been created within the Department of the Interior but instead was created as an independent agency in 1970 to administer federal programs aimed at controlling pollution and protecting the nation's environment. As an independent agency, the EPA is less indebted to the president on a day-to-day basis than it would be if it were within a Cabinet department, although the president still has the ability to appoint its director and often intervenes on high-profile decisions.

INDEPENDENT REGULATORY COMMISSIONS As noted earlier, independent regulatory commissions are agencies created by Congress to exist outside the major departments to regulate a specific economic activity or interest. Because of the complexity of modern economic issues, Congress sought to create commissions that could develop expertise and provide continuity of policy with respect to economic issues because neither Congress nor the courts have the time or specific talents to do so. Examples include the National Labor Relations Board (NLRB), the Federal Reserve Board , the Federal Communications Commission (FCC), and the Securities and Exchange Commission (SEC).[17]

Older boards and commissions, such as the SEC and the Federal Reserve Board, generally are charged with overseeing a certain industry. Most were created specifically to be free from partisan political pressure. Each is headed by a board composed of five to seven members (always an odd number, to avoid tie votes) who are selected by the president and confirmed by the Senate for fixed, staggered terms to increase the chances of a bipartisan board. Unlike executive department heads, they cannot easily be removed by the president. In 1935, the U.S. Supreme Court ruled that in creating independent commissions, Congress had intended that they be independent panels of experts as far removed as possible from immediate political pressures.[18]

Photo courtesy: Karen Bleier/AFP/Getty Images

What government entity protects miners? The Mine Safety and Health Administration, part of the Department of Labor, has been responsible for protecting the safety and health of miners since 1978. A rash of mining disasters in West Virginia led to increased pressure for greater government oversight of mining companies. Here, Senator Robert Byrd (D–WV) meets with the family of Marty Bennet, one of twelve miners killed in a 2006 mine explosion.

Newer regulatory boards are more concerned with how the business sector relates to public health and safety. The Occupational Safety and Health Administration (OSHA), for example, promotes job safety. These boards and commissions often lack autonomy and freedom from political pressures; they are generally headed by a single administrator who can be removed by the president. Thus, they are far more susceptible to the political wishes of the president who appoints them.

Government Workers and Political Involvement

As the number of federal employees and agencies grew during the 1930s, many Americans began to fear that the members of the civil service would play major roles not only in implementing public policy but also in electing members of Congress and even the president. Consequently, Congress enacted the Political Activities Act of 1939, commonly known as the **Hatch Act**, named in honor of its main sponsor, Senator Carl Hatch (D–NM). It was designed to prohibit federal employees from becoming directly involved in working for political candidates. Although this act allayed many critics' fears, other people argued that the Hatch Act was too extreme.

Today, government employees' political activity is regulated by the **Federal Employees Political Activities Act** of 1993. This liberalization of the Hatch Act allows employees to run for public office in nonpartisan elections, contribute money to political organizations, and campaign for or against candidates in partisan elections. Federal employees still, however, are prohibited from engaging in political activity while on duty, soliciting contributions from the general public, or running for office in partisan elections. (To learn more about the Federal Employees Political Activities Act, see Table 9.1.)

You Are the President of MEDICORP

Hatch Act
The 1939 act to prohibit civil servants from taking activist roles in partisan campaigns. This act prohibited federal employees from making political contributions, working for a particular party, or campaigning for a particular candidate.

Federal Employees Political Activities Act
The 1993 liberalization of the Hatch Act. Federal employees are now allowed to run for office in nonpartisan elections and to contribute money to campaigns in partisan elections.

TABLE **9.1** The Federal Employees Political Activities Act

Here are some examples of permissible and prohibited activities for federal employees under the Federal Employees Political Activities Act of 1993. Federal employees:

- **May** be candidates for public office in nonpartisan elections
- **May** assist in voter registration drives
- **May** express opinions about candidates and issues
- **May** contribute money to political organizations
- **May** attend political fund-raising functions
- **May** attend and be active at political rallies and meetings
- **May** join and be active members of a political party or club
- **May** sign nominating petitions
- **May** campaign for or against referendum questions, constitutional amendments, and municipal ordinances
- **May** campaign for or against candidates in partisan elections
- **May** make campaign speeches for candidates in partisan elections
- **May** distribute campaign literature in partisan elections
- **May** hold office in political clubs or parties
- **May not** use their official authority or influence to interfere with an election
- **May not** collect political contributions unless both individuals are members of the same federal labor organization or employee organization and the one solicited is not a subordinate employee
- **May not** knowingly solicit or discourage the political activity of any person who has business before the agency
- **May not** engage in political activity while on duty
- **May not** engage in political activity in any government office
- **May not** engage in political activity while wearing an official uniform
- **May not** engage in political activity while using a government vehicle
- **May not** solicit political contributions from the general public
- **May not** be candidates for public office in partisan elections

Source: U.S. Special Counsel's Office.

How the Bureaucracy Works

German sociologist Max Weber believed bureaucracies were a rational way for complex societies to organize themselves. Model bureaucracies, said Weber, are characterized by certain features, including:

1. A chain of command in which authority flows from top to bottom.
2. A division of labor whereby work is apportioned among specialized workers to increase productivity.
3. Clear lines of authority among workers and their superiors.
4. A goal orientation that determines structure, authority, and rules.
5. Impersonality, whereby all employees are treated fairly based on merit and all clients are served equally, without discrimination, according to established rules.
6. Productivity, whereby all work and actions are evaluated according to established rules.[19]

Clearly, this Weberian idea is somewhat idealistic, and even the best-run government agencies don't always work this way, but most are trying.

When Congress creates any kind of department, agency, or commission, it is actually delegating some of its powers listed in Article I, section 8, of the U.S. Constitution. Therefore, the laws creating departments, agencies, corporations, or commissions carefully describe their purpose and give them the authority to make numerous policy decisions, which have the effect of law. Congress recognizes that it does not have the time, expertise, or ability to involve itself in every detail of every program; therefore, it sets general guidelines for agency action and leaves it to the agency to work out the details. How agencies execute congressional wishes is called **implementation**, the process by which a law or policy is put into operation.

Historically, political scientists attempting to study how the bureaucracy made policy investigated what they termed **iron triangles,** a term refering to the relatively stable relationships and patterns of interaction that occurred among federal workers in agencies or departments, interest groups, and relevant congressional committees and subcommittees. (To learn more about iron triangles, see Figure 9.5.) Today, iron triangles no longer dominate most policy processes. Some do persist, however, such as the relationship between the Department of Veterans' Affairs, the House Committee on Veterans' Affairs, and the American Legion and the Veterans of Foreign Wars, the two largest veterans groups.

Many political scientists examining external influences on the modern bureaucracy prefer to examine **issue networks.** In general, issue networks, like iron triangles, include agency officials, members of Congress (and committee staffers), and interest group lobbyists. But, they also include lawyers, consultants, academics, public relations specialists, and sometimes even the courts. Unlike iron triangles, issue networks constantly are changing as members with technical expertise or newly interested parties become involved in issue areas.

As a result of the increasing complexity of many policy domains, many alliances have also been created within the bureaucracy. One such example is **interagency councils,** working groups that bring together representatives of several departments and agencies to facilitate the coordination of policy making and implementation. Depending on how well these councils are funded, they can be the prime movers of administration policy in any area where an interagency council exists. The U.S. Interagency Council on the Homeless,

implementation
The process by which a law or policy is put into operation by the bureaucracy.

iron triangles
The relatively stable relationships and patterns of interaction that occur among agencies, interest groups, and congressional committees or subcommittees.

issue network
The loose and informal relationships that exist among a large number of actors who work in broad policy areas.

interagency councils
Working groups created to facilitate coordination of policy making and implementation across a host of governmental agencies.

SIMULATION

You Are a Government Affairs Consultant in Texas

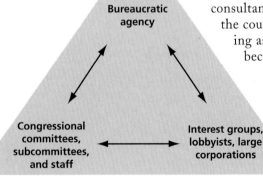

FIGURE **9.5** An Iron Triangle

for example, was created in 1987 to coordinate the activities of the more than fifty governmental agencies and programs that work to alleviate homelessness.

In areas where there are extraordinarily complex policy problems, recent presidential administrations have created policy coordinating committees (PCCs) to facilitate interaction among agencies and departments at the subcabinet level. These PCCs gained increasing favor after the September 11, 2001 terrorist attacks. For example, the PCC on Terrorist Financing, which includes representatives from the Departments of Treasury, State, Defense, and Justice, along with the CIA and FBI, conducted a study that recommended to the president that he ask the Saudi government to take action against alleged terrorist financiers.[20] In 2002, the Strategic Communications Policy Coordinating Committee was created to formulate U.S. public diplomacy communication efforts. And, in 2004, a Muslim World Outreach PCC was established "to target more specifically efforts to smooth diplomatic relations with Muslim nations."[21]

Making Policy

The end product of all of these decision-making bodies is policy making. Policy making and implementation take place on both informal and formal levels. Practically, many decisions are left to individual government employees on a day-to-day basis. Department of Justice lawyers, for example, make daily decisions about whether or not to prosecute someone. Similarly, street-level Internal Revenue Service agents make many decisions during personal audits. These street-level bureaucrats make policy on two levels. First, they exercise wide discretion in decisions concerning citizens with whom they interact. Second, taken together, their individual actions add up to agency behavior.[22] Thus, how bureaucrats interpret and how they apply (or choose not to apply) various policies are equally important parts of the policy-making process.

Administrative discretion, the ability to make choices concerning the best way to implement congressional or executive intentions, also allows decision makers (whether they are in a Cabinet-level position or at the lowest GS levels) a tremendous amount of leeway. It is exercised through two formal administrative procedures: rule making and administrative adjudication.

administrative discretion
The ability of bureaucrats to make choices concerning the best way to implement congressional intentions.

RULE MAKING **Rule making** is a quasi-legislative administrative process that results in regulations and has the characteristics of a legislative act. **Regulations** are the rules that govern the operation of all government programs and have the force of law. In essence, then, bureaucratic rule makers often act as lawmakers as well as law enforcers when they make rules or draft regulations to implement various congressional statutes. (To learn more about rule-making, see Figure 9.6.) Some political scientists say that rule making "is the single most important function performed by agencies of government."[23]

Because regulations often involve political conflict, the 1946 Administrative Procedures Act established rule-making procedures to give everyone the chance to participate in the process. The act requires that: (1) public notice of the time, place, and nature of the rule-making proceedings be provided in the *Federal Register*; (2) interested parties be given the opportunity to submit written arguments and facts relevant to the rule; and, (3) the statutory purpose and basis of the rule be stated. Once rules are written, thirty days generally must elapse before they take effect.

rule making
A quasi-legislative administrative process that has the characteristics of a legislative act.

regulations
Rules that govern the operation of a particular government program that have the force of law.

You Are a Federal Administrator

Sometimes an agency is required by law to conduct a formal hearing before issuing rules. Evidence is gathered, and witnesses testify and are cross-examined by opposing interests. The process can take weeks, months, or even years, at the end of which agency administrators must review the entire record and then justify the new rules. Although cumbersome, the process has reduced criticism of some rules and bolstered the deference given by the courts to agency decisions. Many Americans are unaware of the opportunities available to them to influence government at this stage. As illustrated in Ideas into Action: Enforcing Gender Equity in College Athletics,

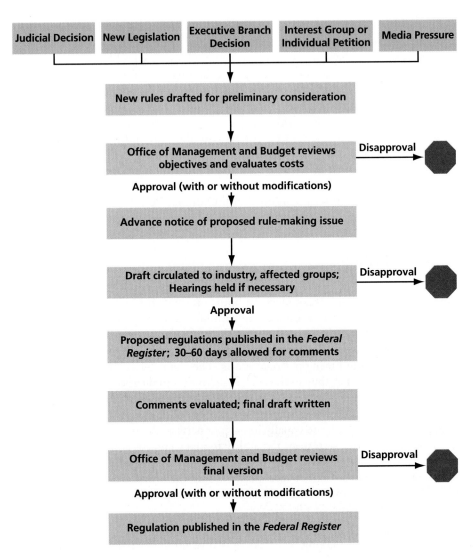

FIGURE 9.6 How a Regulation is Made

women's groups and female athletes testified at hearings held around the country urging then Secretary of Education Roderick Paige not to revise existing Title IX regulations, although the Bush administration ultimately did.

administrative adjudication
A quasi-judicial process in which a bureaucratic agency settles disputes between two parties in a manner similar to the way courts resolve disputes.

ADMINISTRATIVE ADJUDICATION   **Administrative adjudication** is a quasi-judicial process in which a bureaucratic agency settles disputes between two parties in a manner similar to the way courts resolve disputes. Administrative adjudication is referred to as quasi judicial, because law-making by any body other than Congress or adjudication by any body other than the judiciary would be a violation of the constitutional principle of separation of powers.

Agencies regularly find that persons or businesses are not in compliance with the federal laws the agencies are charged with enforcing, or that they are in violation of an agency rule or regulation. To force compliance, some agencies resort to administrative adjudication, which generally is less formal than a trial. Several agencies and boards employ administrative law judges to conduct the hearings. Although these judges are employed by the agencies, they are strictly independent and cannot be removed except for gross misconduct. Congress, for example, empowers the Federal Trade Commission to determine what constitutes an unfair trade practice.[24] Its actions, however, are

Ideas Into Action

Enforcing Gender Equity in College Athletics

During the late 1960s and early 1970s, women students at colleges and universities had few opportunities to participate in sports. To address the lack of athletic programs for women, the federal government passed Title IX of the Education Amendments Act of 1972. Title IX prohibits discrimination on the basis of sex in any education program receiving federal financial assistance. In order for a university to demonstrate compliance with the act, it must show that:

1. The university provides opportunities to women similar to the proportion of their enrollment in the student body; or
2. The university has developed programs for the underrepresented; or
3. The university has attempted to accommodate the interests of women who may want to become involved in affected programs.

By most measures, the law has achieved its goal and increased opportunities for women at educational institutions, especially in athletics. In the thirty years since the federal bureaucracy implemented Title IX, women have made significant gains in sports. By 2005, for example, there were 2.8 million girls playing high school sports, up from 294,000 in 1971. Similarly, there has been a five-fold increase in the number of women playing sports at the college level.[a]

Title IX has not gone without criticism. Some male alumni, for example, have protested when men's sports programs are cut to free up funds for athletic opportunities for women students. And, a number of federal regulations have loosened or reinterpreted Title IX. The Bush administration established a panel that held hearings on the implementation of Title IX. This panel clarified the standards for compliance with Title IX and decided that universities could demonstrate that they were meeting the needs of female students through e-mail surveys inquiring about their

Photo courtesy: Doug Mills/The New York Times

Who lobbies for Title IX enforcement? Soccer Olympian Julie Foudy joins members of the Congressional Women's Caucus to save Title IX.

interest in playing sports. Notably, the committee stated that if a student did not respond to the survey, the students would be counted as uninterested. Supporters of Title IX, however, argue that women who wish to play college sports don't simply decide to do so once they are enrolled in a university. The NCAA, too, has voiced its opposition to the survey, and through 2008, few universities have used surveys to demonstrate compliance.

- Is your college or university bound by the regulations of Title IX? Why or why not?
- How does your university demonstrate compliance with Title IX? Is this compliance consistent with what you observe on campus? In what ways?
- How might you increase awareness of women's sports programs on your campus? What assistance might you expect from the Obama administration?

[a]Katrina Vanden Heuvel, "Bush Targets Women's Sports," http://www.thenation.com/blogs/edcut/2310.

reviewable in the federal courts, as are the findings of the Equal Employment Opportunity Commission and Social Security Administration judges.

Toward Reform: Making Agencies Accountable

The question of to whom bureaucrats should be responsible is one that continually comes up in any debate about governmental accountability. Should the bureaucracy be answerable to itself? To organized interest groups? To its clientele? To the president? To Congress? Or to some combination of all of these? At times an agency becomes so removed from the public it serves that Congress must step in. This is what happened with the Internal Revenue Service (IRS). Throughout 1997 and 1998, Congress held extensive hearings about abuses at the IRS, one of the most hated and feared federal agencies in America. Senate hearings in particular exposed abuses of ordinary citizens who found themselves in a nightmare of bureaucratic red tape and agency employee abuse of power. As a result of these hearings, Congress ordered the new IRS commissioner to overhaul the way the IRS deals with the public.[25] The IRS's attempt to ease online tax filing in 2002 was another example of the use of technology to improve relations with the public. The IRS also redesigned its Web site, www.irs.gov. The public responded positively to these changes, and by 2003, 52 percent of the American public reported that they had confidence in the IRS.[26]

Although many critics of the bureaucracy argue that federal employees should be responsive to the public interest, the public interest is difficult to define. As it turns out, several factors work to control the power of the bureaucracy, and to some degree, the same kinds of checks and balances that operate among the three branches of government serve to check the bureaucracy. (To learn more about agency accountability, see Table 9.2.)

Many political scientists argue that the president should be in charge of the bureaucracy because it is up to him to see that popular ideas and expectations are translated into administrative action. But, under our constitutional system, the president is not the only actor in the policy process. Congress creates the agencies, funds them, and establishes the broad rules of their operation. Moreover, Congress continually reviews the various agencies through oversight committee investigations, hearings, and its power of the purse. And, the federal judiciary, as in most other matters, has the ultimate authority to review administrative actions.

Executive Control

As the size and scope of the American national government, in general, and of the executive branch and the bureaucracy, in particular, have grown, presidents have delegated more and more power to bureaucrats. But, most presidents have continued to try

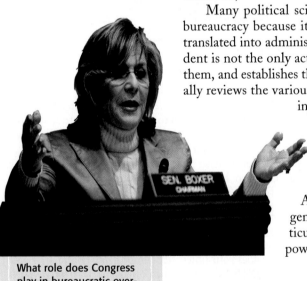

Photo courtesy: Chip Somodevilla/Getty Images

What role does Congress play in bureaucratic oversight? Senator Barbara Boxer (D–CA), chair of the Senate Environmental and Public Works Committee, makes a statement at a committee hearing.

TABLE **9.2** Making Agencies Accountable

The president has the authority to:
- Appoint and remove agency heads and other top bureaucrats.
- Reorganize the bureaucracy (with congressional approval).
- Make changes in an agency's annual budget proposals.
- Ignore legislative initiatives originating within the bureaucracy.
- Initiate or adjust policies that would, if enacted by Congress, alter the bureaucracy's activities.
- Issue executive orders.
- Reduce an agency's annual budget.

Congress has the authority to:
- Pass legislation that alters the bureaucracy's activities.
- Abolish existing programs.
- Refuse to appropriate funds for certain programs.
- Investigate bureaucratic activities and compel bureaucrats to testify about them.
- Influence presidential appointments of agency heads and other top bureaucratic officials.
- Write legislation to limit the bureaucracy's discretion.

The judiciary has the authority to:
- Rule on whether bureaucrats have acted within the law and require policy changes to comply with the law.
- Force the bureaucracy to respect the rights of individuals through hearings and other proceedings.
- Rule on the constitutionality of all challenged rules and regulations.

POLITICS NOW

Source: THE WASHINGTON POST   August 20, 2007   Page A01

The Bush Administration and Bureaucratic Control

As Democracy Push Falters, Bush Feels Like a 'Dissident'

PETER BAKER

By the time he arrived in Prague in June for a democracy conference, President Bush was frustrated. He had committed his presidency to working toward the goal of "ending tyranny in our world," yet the march of freedom seemed stalled. Just as aggravating was the sense that his own government was not committed to his vision.

As he sat down with opposition leaders from authoritarian societies around the world, he gave voice to his exasperation. "You're not the only dissident," Bush told Saad Eddin Ibrahim, a leader in the resistance to Egyptian President Hosni Mubarak. "I too am a dissident in Washington. Bureaucracy in the United States does not help change. It seems that Mubarak succeeded in brainwashing them."

If he needed more evidence, he would soon get it. In his speech that day, Bush vowed to order U.S. ambassadors in unfree nations to meet with dissidents and boasted that he had created a fund to help embattled human rights defenders. But the State Department did not send out the cable directing ambassadors to sit down with dissidents until two months later. And to this day, not a nickel has been transferred to the fund he touted.

Two and a half years after Bush pledged in his second inaugural address to spread democracy around the world, the grand project has bogged down in a bureaucratic and geopolitical morass, in the view of many activists, officials and even White House aides. Many in his administration never bought into the idea, and some undermined it, including his own vice president. The Iraq war has distracted Bush and, in some quarters, discredited his aspirations. And while he focuses his ire on bureaucracy, Bush at times has compromised the idealism of that speech in the muddy reality of guarding other U.S. interests.

Discussion Questions

1. *How does this excerpt underscore presidents' difficulties in controlling the bureaucracy?*
2. *How does the structure of the bureaucracy help or hinder policy making?*
3. *What remedies might be useful in solving the problems inherent in the U.S. bureaucracy? Consider whether particular remedies might create additional problems.*

---

to exercise some control over the bureaucracy, although they have often found that task more difficult than they first envisioned. President John F. Kennedy, for example, once lamented that to give anyone at the Department of State an instruction was comparable to putting your request in a dead-letter box.[27] No response would ever be forthcoming. (To learn more, see Politics Now: The Bush Administration and Bureaucratic Control.)

Recognizing these potential problems, presidents try to appoint the best possible people to carry out their wishes and policy preferences. Presidents make hundreds of appointments to the executive branch; in doing so, they have the opportunity to appoint individuals who share their views on a range of policies. Although presidential appointments make up a very small proportion of all federal jobs, presidents or the Cabinet secretaries usually fill most top policy-making positions.

Presidents, with the approval of Congress, can reorganize the bureaucracy. They also can make changes in an agency's annual budget requests and ignore legislative initiatives originating within the bureaucracy. Several presidents have made it a priority to try to tame the bureaucracy to make it more accountable. Thomas Jefferson was the first president to address the issue of accountability. He attempted to cut waste and bring about a "wise and frugal government." But, it wasn't until the Progressive era (1890–1920) that calls for reform began to be taken seriously. Later, President Calvin Coolidge urged spending cuts and other reforms. His Correspondence Club was designed to reduce bureaucratic letter writing by 30 percent.[28]

As discussed in chapter 8, presidents also can shape policy and provide direction to bureaucrats by issuing executive orders.[29] **Executive orders** are rules or regulations issued by the president that have the effect of law. For example, even before Congress acted to protect women from discrimination by the federal government, the National Organization for Women convinced President Lyndon B. Johnson to sign a 1967 executive order that amended an earlier one prohibiting the federal government from discriminating on the basis of race, color, religion, or national origin in the awarding

executive order
Rules or regulations issued by the president that have the effect of law. All executive orders must be published in the *Federal Register*.

of federal contracts, by adding to it the category of "gender." Although the president signed the order, the Office of Federal Contract Compliance, part of the Department of Labor's Employment Standards Administration, failed to draft appropriate guidelines for implementation of the order until several years later.[30] A president can direct an agency to act, but it may take some time for the order to be carried out. Given the many jobs of any president, few can ensure that all their orders will be carried out or that they will like all the rules that are made.

Congressional Control

You Are the Head of FEMA

Congress, too, historically has played an important role in checking the power of the bureaucracy. Constitutionally, it possesses the authority to create or abolish departments and agencies as well as to transfer agency functions, as was the case in the protracted debate over the creation of the Department of Homeland Security. In addition, it can expand or contract bureaucratic discretion. The Senate's authority to confirm (or reject) presidential appointments also gives Congress a check on the bureaucracy. Legally, Congress has considerable oversight over the bureaucracy in several ways.

Congress uses many of its constitutional powers to exercise control over the bureaucracy. These include its investigatory powers. It is not at all unusual for a congressional committee or subcommittee to hold hearings on a particular problem and then direct the relevant agency to study the problem or find ways to remedy it. Representatives of the agencies also appear before these committees on a regular basis to inform members about agency activities and ongoing investigations. In the aftermath of Hurricane Katrina, for example, several congressional committees held hearings ordering then Federal Emergency Management Agency (FEMA) chief Michael Brown, as well as Secretary Michael Chertoff of the Department of Homeland Security, to appear before them to explain the series of bad decisions that contributed to the disaster, not only for purposes of accountability, but also so that Congress and the administration could learn from the mistakes made. Indeed, the Senate Committee on Homeland Security found FEMA to be so inadequate that it was "beyond repair" and should be replaced with a new agency.[31]

Political scientists distinguish between two different forms of congressional oversight: police patrol and fire alarm oversight.[32] As the names imply, police patrol oversight is proactive and allows Congress to set its own agenda for programs or agencies to review. In contrast, fire alarm oversight is reactive and generally involves a congressional response to a complaint filed by a constituent or politically significant actor.

Given the prevalence of iron triangles, issue networks, and policy coordinating committees, it is not surprising that the most frequently used form of oversight is fire alarm oversight and the most effective communication is between House staffers and agency personnel. Various forms of program evaluations make up the next most commonly used forms of congressional control. Members of Congress and their staff routinely conduct evaluations of programs and conduct oversight hearings.

Congress also has the power of the purse. To control the bureaucracy, Congress uses its ability to fund or not to fund an agency's activities much like the proverbial carrot and stick. The House Appropriations Committee routinely holds hearings to allow agency heads to justify their budget requests. Authorization legislation originates in the various legislative committees that oversee particular agencies (such as Agriculture, Veterans Affairs, Education, and Labor) and sets the maximum amounts that agencies can spend on particular programs. While some authorizations, such as those for Social Security, are permanent, others, including the Departments of State and Defense procurements, are watched closely and are subject to annual authorizations. For example, spending on the war in Iraq must be approved by Congress on an annual basis. For fiscal year 2008, in response to President Bush's request for $200 billion to fund the war, Congress allocated $196 billion. (To learn more about controversies related to funding the Iraq War, see Join the Debate: Funding the War in Iraq.)

Photo courtesy: Justin Sullivan/Getty Images

Once programs are authorized, funds for them must be appropriated before they can be spent. Appropriations originate with the House Appropriations Committee, not the specialized legislative committees. Often the Appropriations Committee allocates sums smaller than those authorized by legislative committees. Thus, the Appropriations Committee, a budget cutter, has an additional oversight function.

To help Congress's oversight of the bureaucracy's financial affairs, in 1921 Congress created the General Accounting Office, now called the Government Accountability Office (GAO), at the same time that the Office of the Budget, now the Office of Management and Budget (OMB), was created in the executive branch. With the establishment of the GAO, the Congressional Research Service (CRS), and later, the Congressional Budget Office (CBO), Congress essentially created its own bureaucracy to keep an eye on what the executive branch and bureaucracy were doing. Today, the GAO not only tracks how money is spent in the bureaucracy, but it also monitors how policies are implemented. The CBO also conducts oversight studies. If it or the GAO uncovers problems with an agency's work, Congress is notified immediately.

Legislators also augment their formal oversight of the executive branch by allowing citizens to appeal adverse bureaucratic decisions to agencies, Congress, and even the courts. Congressional review, a procedure adopted by the 104th Congress, by which agency regulations can be nullified by joint resolutions of legislative disapproval, is another method of exercising congressional oversight. This form of oversight is discussed in greater detail in chapter 7.

Judicial Control

Whereas the president's and Congress's ongoing control over the actions of the bureaucracy is very direct, the judiciary's oversight function is less apparent. Still, federal judges, for example, can issue injunctions or orders to an executive agency even before a rule is promulgated formally, giving the federal judiciary a potent check on the bureaucracy.

The courts also have ruled that agencies must give all affected individuals their due process rights guaranteed by the U.S. Constitution. A Social Security recipient's checks cannot be stopped, for example, unless that individual is provided with reasonable notice and an opportunity for a hearing. On a more informal, indirect level, litigation,

What sorts of executive-branch programs does Congress review? Roy Dillon mows the lawn in front of his FEMA trailer in the Lower Ninth Ward of New Orleans. By 2008, the Federal Emergency Management Agency had purchased 102,000 trailers at a cost of $60,000 each for a total of more than $6 billion to house people who lost their homes to Hurricane Katrina. Reports that tens of thousands of empty trailers were warehoused in Arkansas and other states led to calls for increased congressional oversight of how funds were being spent and why the trailers were not being distributed.

Join the Debate

Funding the War in Iraq

OVERVIEW: Funding and accountability are two of the issues raised by the military action and ensuing presence of the United States in Iraq. The operations of any government bureaucracy, civilian or military, depend on how much money there is to spend, the source of the money, and how the money is spent. In the federal government, the president typically proposes the amount and the source of funding, while Congress approves—perhaps with amendments and conditions—the request for funding. Then the relevant agency makes detailed spending decisions and proceeds with its operations, and Congress provides oversight to be sure the funds have been spent appropriately. The funding of the Iraq war has followed this general pattern with some important exceptions. President George W. Bush separated his requests for funding from the regular annual budgets, and the war in Iraq has been funded by borrowing money, rather than using current revenues. The Departments of Defense and State have relied very heavily on contracting with private companies for U.S. operations in Iraq, which has complicated oversight and accountability. Clearly, fundamental differences exist between the war in Iraq and the activities common to most other federal agencies. Do these differences necessitate the need for unusual funding arrangements?

When the United States began combat operations in Afghanistan in fiscal year 2002 and in Iraq in 2003, President George W. Bush made emergency requests for appropriating $18 billion and $78 billion respectively. Congress approved those requests. Although there had been planning prior to the commencement of military action, there were no requests for funding made in the regular budget process. To do so would have been highly unusual and might have compromised strategic and safety considerations about exactly when and how to begin the attacks.

As operations have continued, funding requests from the president have continued to be outside the regular budget process. Except for a slight decrease in 2004 to $74 billion, appropriations for continuing operations in Iraq and Afghanistan (funding requests since 2003 have combined the two operations) have increased steadily each year. As of March 2008, the total costs were $752 billion, with a pending request for another $101 billion. This is almost twelve times the total cost

predicted at the beginning of military action. Spending in Iraq in 2008 was at the rate of $2 billion per week. Despite these sums and the administration's intention of a long-term commitment, all funding requests were still for "emergency appropriations." Some senators and representatives in Congress sought, unsuccessfully, to amend the legislation funding operations in Iraq by requiring the administration to submit plans for withdrawing troops or by setting deadlines for cutting back on U.S. involvement.

An issue with both administrative and political implications is the source of funding. According to analyses by the Congressional Budget Office, only $16 billion (2 percent) of the money allocated for Iraq and Afghanistan comes from the regular budget of the Department of Defense. The rest is borrowed. On the one hand, this means that taxpayers currently are not sacrificing either by paying higher taxes or suffering cuts in other federal programs in order to pay for operations in Iraq and Afghanistan. However, this also means that taxpayers in the future

will have to pay the amounts borrowed, plus interest.

Congress relies on reports and evaluations prepared by members of the federal bureaucracy to oversee these expenditures. However, the extensive use of private contractors in Iraq makes oversight and accountability more challenging. Contractors have been used to provide logistical support for troops, to construct military bases and a new U.S. embassy in Iraq, to provide services to civilians, and to protect American diplomats and other officials. Using private vendors for many of the duties traditionally performed by military personnel frees soldiers for combat missions and avoids the creation of more government agencies and jobs. By 2008, the Government Accountability Office had completed over 130 studies of contracts used in operations in Iraq, frequently finding it difficult to trace where the money flowed and for what purpose it was spent. When instances of corruption or misbehavior were identified, contractors usually were not liable because they were not subject to either

U.S. domestic law or to Iraqi law. Congressional hearings and investigations began focusing on concerns about contracting in 2007, after Democrats gained control of both houses of Congress. Republicans questioned whether this was oversight or partisan posturing.

Arguments IN FAVOR of Special Arrangements for Funding the War in Iraq

- **National security is essential.** The need to protect the United States from acts of terrorism and aggression is so fundamental that it trumps business-as-usual procedures. The government should spend what it takes to provide for national security, and if that means borrowing money and making emergency appropriations, then that is what it must do.

- **It is not possible to predict what must be spent to achieve peace and stability in various regions of the world.** The planning and budgeting that federal agencies do to protect the environment, maintain transportation networks, and perform other activities are irrelevant for national security and military activities. The government must respond to threats as they emerge and to developments in countries like Iraq as they occur.

- **Private companies can provide services more efficiently and less expensively than public bureaucracies, and in military situations they help soldiers focus on combat and security missions.** A strength of the United States is the quality and competitiveness of its businesses. Contracts with private companies build on this strength and avoid some of the problems associated with public bureaucracies. It is especially important to use private vendors to support military operations. The armed forces no longer rely on a draft, which means the military is leaner and must be more focused on its core mission.

Arguments AGAINST Special Arrangements for Funding the War in Iraq

- **The security of the United States is not so dependent on what happens to Iraq that a blank check is justified.** The justifications for attacking Iraq were based on faulty intelligence and flawed reasoning. The government must now proceed based on a plan that considers Iraq along with other national security and domestic needs. This means including funding for future operations in Iraq in the regular budget process and ending the policy of open-ended borrowing and spending.

- **The future of Iraq should be determined by the people of Iraq, not the government of the United States.** It is not appropriate to ask American taxpayers to fund operations that are constantly being undermined by violence among Iraqi groups and corruption among Iraqi officials. Funding should be limited and focused, and the U.S. government should let the Iraqis solve their own problems.

- **Contractors operating in Iraq make huge profits and are not held accountable for their actions and expenditures.** The argument that the government benefits from contracts with private companies fails to recognize that many of the most lucrative contracts were issued without a competitive bidding process. Reports by the inspectors general of the Department of Defense and Department of State revealed performance problems and missing funds related to contracting in Iraq. Likewise, congressional investigations and reports by the Government Accountability Office cite waste and abuse.

Continuing the Debate

1. Should funding the war in Iraq be separate from the regular budget process? Should we continue to borrow money for operations in Iraq, or should we make cuts in other federal programs or raise taxes? Explain your reasoning.
2. Is it appropriate for Congress to tie funding for operations in Iraq to a requirement for preparing a withdrawal of some or all U.S. troops? Why or why not?
3. What changes do you expect the Obama administration will place on the use of private contractors in Iraq?

To Follow the Debate Online, Go To:

www.cbo.gov/ to find Congressional Budget Office analyses of funding the war in Iraq.

www.gao.gov/docsearch/featured/oif.html, where the Governmental Accountability Office provides more than 130 reports on contracts for services and construction projects related to the war in Iraq.

www.iraqwarveterans.org for information about support to military veterans of the Iraq War and their families and continuing U.S. efforts in Iraq.

www.mfso.org, the Web site of Military Families Speak Out, which advocates ending funding in order to halt U.S. involvement and casualties in Iraq.

or even the threat of litigation, often exerts a strong influence on bureaucrats. Injured parties can bring suit against agencies for their failure to enforce a law, and can challenge agency interpretations of any law. In general, however, the courts give great weight to the opinions of bureaucrats and usually defer to their expertise.[33]

The development of specialized courts, however, has altered the relationship of some agencies with the federal courts, apparently resulting in less judicial deference to agency rulings. Research by political scientists reveals that specialized courts such as the Court of International Trade, because of its jurists' expertise, defer less to agency decisions than do more generalized federal courts. Conversely, decisions from executive agencies are more likely to be reversed than those from more specialized independent regulatory commissions.[34]

WHAT SHOULD I HAVE LEARNED?

The bureaucracy plays a major role in America as a shaper of public policy, earning it the nickname the "fourth branch" of government. To explain the evolution and scope of bureaucratic power, in this chapter we have answered the following questions:

■ **What are the roots of the federal bureaucracy?**

The federal bureaucracy has changed dramatically since George Washington's time, when the executive branch had only three departments—State, War, and Treasury—through the Civil War. Significant gains occurred in the size of the federal bureaucracy as the government geared up to conduct a war. As employment opportunities within the federal government increased, concurrent reforms in the civil service system assured that more and more jobs were filled according to merit and not by patronage. By the late 1800s, reform efforts led to further increases in the size of the bureaucracy, as independent regulatory commissions were created. In the wake of the Depression, many new agencies were created to get the national economy back on course as part of President Franklin D. Roosevelt's New Deal.

■ **What are the key characteristics of the modern bureaucracy?**

The modern bureaucracy is composed of more than 2.7 million civilian workers from all walks of life. In general, bureaucratic agencies fall into four categories: departments, government corporations, independent agencies, and independent regulatory commissions. The political activity of employees in the federal government is regulated by the Federal Employees Political Activities Act.

■ **How does the bureaucracy work?**

The bureaucracy gets much of its power from the Congress delegating its powers. A variety of formal and informal mechanisms have been created to help the bureaucracy work more efficiently. These mechanisms help the bureaucracy and bureaucrats make policy.

■ **What controls are in place to make bureaucratic agencies accountable?**

Agencies enjoy considerable discretion, but they are also subjected to many formal controls. The president, Congress, and the judiciary all exercise various degrees of control over the bureaucracy.

Key Terms

administrative adjudication, p. 324
administrative discretion, p. 323
bureaucracy, p. 308
civil service system, p. 310
departments, p. 317
executive order, p. 327
Federal Employees Political
    Activities Act, p. 321

government corporations, p. 319
Hatch Act, p. 321
implementation, p. 322
independent executive
    agencies, p. 319
independent regulatory commission,
    p. 311
interagency council, p. 322

iron triangle, p. 322
issue network, p. 322
merit system, p. 310
patronage, p. 309
Pendleton Act, p. 310
regulations, p. 323
rule making, p. 323
spoils system, p. 309

Researching the Executive Branch and the Federal Bureaucracy

In the Library

Aberbach, Joel D., and Bert A. Rockman. *In the Web of Politics: Three Decades of the U.S. Federal Executive.* Washington, DC: Brookings Institution, 2000.

Borrelli, MaryAnne. *The President's Cabinet: Gender, Power, and Representation.* Boulder, CO: Lynne Rienner, 2002.

Brehm, John, and Scott Gates. *Working, Shirking, and Sabotage: Bureaucratic Response to a Democratic Public.* Ann Arbor: University of Michigan Press, 1997.

Dolan, Julie A., and David H. Rosenbloom. *Representative Bureaucracy: Classic Readings and Continuing Controversies.* Armonk, NY: M. E. Sharpe, 2003.

Felbinger, Claire L., and Wendy A. Haynes, eds. *Outstanding Women in Public Administration: Leaders, Mentors, and Pioneers.* Armonk, NY: M. E. Sharpe, 2004.

Goodsell, Charles T. *The Case for Bureaucracy: A Public Administration Polemic,* 4th ed. Washington, DC: CQ Press, 2003.

Gormley, William T., and Steven J. Balla. *Bureaucracy and Democracy: Accountability and Perform,* 2nd ed. Washington, DC: CQ Press, 2007.

Ingraham, Patricia Wallace. *The Foundation of Merit: Public Service in American Democracy.* Baltimore, MD: Johns Hopkins University Press, 1995.

Ingraham, Patricia Wallace, and Laurence E. Lynn Jr. *The Art of Governance: Analyzing Management and Administration.* Washington, DC: Georgetown University Press, 2004.

Kerwin, Cornelius M. *Rulemaking: How Government Agencies Write Law and Make Policy,* 3rd ed. Washington, DC: CQ Press, 2003.

Meier, Kenneth J., and John Bohte. *Politics and the Bureaucracy,* 5th ed. Belmont, CA: Wadsworth, 2006.

Nigro, Lloyd G. et al. *The New Public Personnel Administration,* 6th ed. Belmont, CA: Wadsworth, 2006.

Peters, B. Guy. *The Politics of Bureaucracy,* 5th ed. New York: Routledge, 2001.

Richardson, William D. *Democracy, Bureaucracy and Character.* Lawrence: University Press of Kansas, 1997.

Stivers, Camilla. *Gender Images in Public Administration: Legitimacy and the Administrative State,* 2nd ed. Thousand Oaks, CA: Sage, 2002.

Twight, Charlotte. *Dependent on DC: The Rise of Federal Control over the Lives of Ordinary Americans.* New York: Palgrave Macmillan, 2002.

Wilson, James Q. *Bureaucracy: What Government Agencies Do and Why They Do It,* reprint ed. New York: Basic Books, 2000.

On the Web

To learn more about federal employees go to the Office of Personnel Management Web site at **www. opm.gov** or to the page listing demographic information, **www.opm.gov/feddata/factbook/.** What percentage of federal employees share your gender? Your racial and ethnic background?

To learn more about rules, proposed rules, and notices of federal agencies and organizations, go to the home page for the *Federal Register* at **www.gpoaccess.gov/fr/index. html.**

To learn more about the Government Accountability Office, go to **www.gao.gov.** What resources are available to Congress? To the media? To the general public?

To learn more about the Congressional Budget Office, **www.cbo.gov.** How does the information on the CBO site differ from the information on the GAO site? After comparing information about the missions of both organizations, do you consider one or the other more important to the efficient, transparent functioning of the bureaucracy?

10

The Judiciary

The nine justices of the U.S. Supreme Court must work together to reach consensus on which cases to hear, how opinions are written, and ultimately, what precedents are established. Therefore, changing one or two justices on a nine-person court can have an important impact on the direction of the Court's decisions. In a body as closely divided as recent Courts, these changes can be particularly significant.

Thus, when Chief Justice John G. Roberts Jr. and Justice Samuel A. Alito Jr. were confirmed by the Senate to join the Court during its 2005–2006 term, many Court watchers began to speculate about how the Court's decisions would change. Most observers expected that with the addition of Roberts and Alito, the Court would become more conservative than the earlier Court led by Chief Justice William H. Rehnquist.

Roberts and Alito's first full term on the Court appeared to validate the speculation of Court watchers. The nation's highest court seemed increasingly

■ The Supreme Court's power has increased markedly since the founding of the United States. At left, the Warren Court (1953–1969) greatly expanded civil rights and liberties as well as judicial and federal government powers. At right, Court justices attend the funeral of Chief Justice William H. Rehnquist.

conservative. Among other decisions, the Roberts Court upheld the first federal restriction on abortion procedures, limited employees' ability to sue for employment discrimination, and allowed school officials to limit speech that appeared to advocate drug use. All of these decisions—and a full one-third of those handed down by the Court during its 2006–2007 term—were decided by a 5–4 margin.[1] Conservative Justices Antonin Scalia, Clarence Thomas, and Anthony Kennedy joined Roberts and Alito in opposing the liberal bloc of Justices John Paul Stevens, David Souter, Stephen Breyer, and Ruth Bader Ginsburg.

During the Roberts Court's second full term, however, the Court seemed to step back from the conservative rulings of the previous term. Although the Court handed down a significant victory for conservative gun rights advocates, the liberal bloc won major victories in a wide range of issue areas, including criminal rights, presidential power, and employment discrimination. More surprisingly, the deep divisions that marked the Roberts Court's first term were often absent. Many of the Court's major decisions were decided by 6–3 or even 7–2 margins.[2]

WHAT SHOULD I KNOW ABOUT . . .

- the roots of the federal judiciary?
- the American legal system?
- the federal court system?
- the selection of federal court judges?
- the Supreme Court today?
- judicial philosophy and decision making?
- the judiciary's power to affect policy?

335

Thus, two full terms into the Roberts Court, observers were still struggling to define the difference that Chief Justice Roberts and Justice Alito have made on the decisions of the Supreme Court. Chief Justice Roberts's effect on the number and kinds of cases heard by the Court, on the other hand, is much clearer.

During the 2006–2007 term, the Roberts Court decided only seventy-five cases. In 2007–2008, the Court decided seventy-four cases. These numbers are the lowest since 1953, when the Court was asked to hear about half as many cases as today.[3] They represent a significant reduction in the activity of the Court and suggest that the justices may be struggling to agree on which cases are most important. (As discussed later in this chapter, for the Court to hear a case, four justices must agree that it presents an important legal question.)

The issues addressed by these cases are also drastically different from those that were the focus of much of the work of the Rehnquist Court. While the Rehnquist Court favored cases on issues such as federalism and the Fourth Amendment, the Roberts Court seems to be focusing on topics such as discrimination, sentencing, and *habeas corpus,* going head to head with the Bush administration to come out against its use of war powers to justify the curtailment of the rights of prisoners at Guantanamo Bay.

It is clearly too early to completely understand the direction of the Court under Chief Justice Roberts. But, leaders from John Marshall to Earl Warren to Rehnquist have demonstrated the inherent power that comes with the office of chief justice of the United States. These officials and their associate justices have led the country through significant periods of political and legal change. In so doing, they have carved a significant role for the Supreme Court in the American policy-making process.

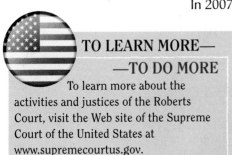

TO LEARN MORE—
—TO DO MORE
To learn more about the activities and justices of the Roberts Court, visit the Web site of the Supreme Court of the United States at www.supremecourtus.gov.

In 1787, when Alexander Hamilton wrote articles urging support for the U.S. Constitution, he firmly believed that the judiciary would prove to be the weakest of the three departments of government. In its formative years, the judiciary was, in Hamilton's words, "the least dangerous" branch. The judicial branch seemed so inconsequential that when the young national government made its move to the District of Columbia in 1800, Congress actually forgot to include any space to house the justices of the Supreme Court! Last-minute conferences with Capitol architects led to the allocation of a small area in the basement of the Senate wing of the Capitol building for a courtroom. Noted one commentator, "A stranger might traverse the dark avenues of the Capitol for a week, without finding the remote corner in which justice is administered to the American Republic."[4]

Today, the role of the courts, particularly the Supreme Court of the United States, is significantly different from that envisioned when the national government came into being. The "least dangerous branch" now is perceived by many as having too much power.

Historically, Americans have been unaware of the political power held by the courts. They have been raised to think of the federal courts as above the fray of politics. That, however, has never been the case. Elected presidents nominate judges to the federal courts and justices to the Supreme Court, and elected senators ultimately confirm (or decline to confirm) presidential nominees to the federal bench. The process by which cases ultimately get heard—if they are heard at all—by the Supreme Court often is political as well. Interest groups routinely seek out good test cases to advance their policy positions. Even the U.S. government, generally through the Department of Justice and the U.S. solicitor general (a political appointee in that department), seeks to advance its position in court. Interest groups then often line up on opposing sides to advance their positions, much in the same way lobbyists do in Congress.

In this chapter, we will explore these issues and the scope and development of judicial power:

★ First, we will look at *the roots of the federal judiciary*. Article III of the Constitution created a Supreme Court but left it to Congress to create any other federal courts, a task it took up quickly.

★ Second, we will discuss *the American legal system* and the concepts of civil and criminal law.

★ Third, we will discuss *the federal court system*. The federal court system is composed of specialized courts, district courts, courts of appeals, and the Supreme Court, which is the ultimate authority on all federal law.

★ Fourth, we will examine *how federal court judges are selected*. All appointments to the federal district courts, courts of appeals, and the Supreme Court are made by the president and are subject to Senate confirmation.

★ Fifth, we will look at *the Supreme Court today*. Only a few of the millions of cases filed in courts around the United States every year eventually make their way to the Supreme Court through the lengthy appellate process.

★ Sixth, we will examine *judicial philosophy and decision making* and discuss how judicial decision making is based on a variety of legal and extra-legal factors.

★ Finally, we will discuss reform efforts and *the judiciary's power to affect policy*.

A note on terminology: When we refer to the "Supreme Court," the "Court," or the "high Court" here, we always mean the U.S. Supreme Court, which sits at the pinnacle of the federal and state court systems. The Supreme Court is referred to by the name of the chief justice who presided over it during a particular period. For example, the Marshall Court is the Court presided over by John Marshall from 1801 to 1835, and the Roberts Court is the current Court that began in late 2005. When we use the term "courts," we refer to all federal or state courts unless otherwise noted.

Roots of the Federal Judiciary

The detailed notes James Madison took at the Constitutional Convention in Philadelphia make it clear that the Framers devoted little time to writing Article III, which created the judicial branch of government. The Framers believed that a federal judiciary posed little threat of tyranny. One scholar has even suggested that, for at least some delegates to the Constitutional Convention, "provision for a national judiciary was a matter of theoretical necessity . . . more in deference to the maxim of separation [of powers] than in

Comparing Judicial Systems

response to clearly formulated ideas about the role of a national judicial system and its indispensability."[5]

Alexander Hamilton argued in *Federalist No. 78* that the judiciary would be the least dangerous branch of government. Anti-Federalists, however, did not agree with Hamilton. They particularly objected to a judiciary whose members had life tenure and the ability to define "the supreme law of the land," a phrase that Anti-Federalists feared would give the Supreme Court too much power.

As discussed in chapter 2, the Framers also debated the need for any federal courts below the Supreme Court. Some argued in favor of deciding all cases in state courts, with only appeals going before the Supreme Court. Others argued for a system of federal courts. A compromise left the final choice to Congress, and Article III, section 1, begins simply by vesting "The judicial Power of the United States . . . in one supreme Court, and in such inferior Courts as the Congress may from time to time ordain and establish."

Article III, section 2 specifies the judicial power of the Supreme Court (To learn more about the Court's jurisdiction, see Table 10.1) and discusses the Court's original and appellate jurisdiction. This section also specifies that all federal crimes, except those involving impeachment, shall be tried by jury in the state in which the crime was committed. The third section of the article defines treason, and mandates that at least two witnesses appear in such cases.

Had the Supreme Court been viewed as the potential policy maker it is today, it is highly unlikely that the Framers would have provided for life tenure with "good behavior" for all federal judges in Article III. This feature was agreed on because the Framers did not want the justices (or any federal judges) subject to the whims of politics, the public, or politicians. Moreover, Alexander Hamilton argued in *Federalist No. 78* that the "independence of judges" was needed "to guard the Constitution and the rights of individuals." (To learn more about Article III and judicial compensation, see The Living Constitution: Article III, Section 1.)

Some checks on the power of the judiciary were nonetheless included in the Constitution. The Constitution gives Congress the authority to alter the Court's jurisdiction (its ability to hear certain kinds of cases). Congress can also propose constitutional amendments that, if ratified, can effectively reverse judicial decisions, and it can impeach and remove federal judges. In one further check, it is the president who, with the "advice and consent" of the Senate, appoints all federal judges. (To learn more, see Join the Debate: Senate Advice and Consent on Judicial Nominations.)

The Court can, in turn, check the presidency by presiding over presidential impeachment. Article I, section 3, notes in discussing impeachment, "When the President of the United States is tried, the Chief Justice shall preside."

The Constitution, however, is silent on the Court's power of **judicial review**, which allows the judiciary to review acts of the other branches of government and the state. This question was not resolved until *Marbury* v. *Madison* (1803),[6] regarding acts of the national government, and *Martin* v. *Hunter's Lessee* (1816), regarding state law.[7]

judicial review
Power of the courts to review acts of other branches of government and the states.

TABLE **10.1** **The Judicial Power of the United States Supreme Court**

The following are the types of cases the Supreme Court was given the jurisdiction to hear as initially specified in Article III, section 2, of the Constitution:

- All cases arising under the Constitution and laws or treaties of the United States
- All cases of admiralty or maritime jurisdiction
- Cases in which the United States is a party
- Controversies between a state and citizens of another state (later modified by the Eleventh Amendment)
- Controversies between two or more states
- Controversies between citizens of different states
- Controversies between citizens of the same states claiming lands under grants in different states
- Controversies between a state, or the citizens thereof, and foreign states or citizens thereof
- All cases affecting ambassadors or other public ministers

The Living Constitution

The Judges both of the supreme and inferior Courts, shall . . . receive for their services, a compensation, which shall not be diminished during their continuance in office.

—ARTICLE III, SECTION 1

This section of Article III guarantees that the salaries of all federal judges will not be reduced during their service on the bench. During the Constitutional Convention, there was considerable debate over how to treat the payment of federal judges. Some believed that Congress should have an extra check on the judiciary by being able to reduce their salaries. This provision was a compromise after James Madison suggested that Congress have the authority to bar increases as well as decreases in the salaries of these unelected jurists. The delegates recognized that decreases, as well as no opportunity for raises, could negatively affect the perks associated with life tenure.

There has not been much controversy over this clause of the Constitution. When the federal income tax was first enacted, some judges unsuccessfully challenged it as a diminution of their salaries. Much more recently, Chief Justices William H. Rehnquist and John G. Roberts Jr. have repeatedly urged Congress to increase salaries for federal judges. As early as 1989, Rehnquist noted that "judicial salaries are the single greatest problem facing the federal judiciary today." Roberts, in his first state of the judiciary message, pointed out that the comparatively low salaries earned by federal judges drive away many well-qualified and diverse lawyers, compromising the independence of the American judiciary.

More and more federal judges are leaving the bench for more lucrative private practice. While a salary of $217,400 (for the chief justice) or $208,100 (for the other justices) may sound like a lot to most people, lawyers in large urban practices routinely earn more than double and triple that amount annually. Supreme Court clerks, moreover, now regularly receive $200,000 signing bonuses (in addition to large salaries) from law firms anxious to pay for their expertise.

CRITICAL THINKING QUESTIONS

1. What other checks on judicial power does Congress have?
2. Do you agree with Chief Justice Roberts's contention that judges are underpaid? Why or why not?

The Judiciary Act of 1789 and the Creation of the Federal Judicial System

In spite of the Framers' intentions, the pervasive role of politics in the judicial branch quickly became evident with the passage of the Judiciary Act of 1789. Congress spent nearly the entire second half of its first session deliberating the various provisions of the act to give form and substance to the federal judiciary. As one early observer noted, "The convention has only crayoned in the outlines. It left it to Congress to fill up and colour the canvas."[8]

The **Judiciary Act of 1789** established the basic three-tiered structure of the federal court system. At the bottom are the federal district courts—at least one in each state. If the people participating in a lawsuit (called litigants) are unhappy with the district court's verdict, they can appeal their case to one of three circuit courts. Each circuit court, initially created to function as a trial court for important cases, was composed of one district court judge and two itinerant Supreme Court justices who met as a circuit court twice a year. It wasn't until 1891 that circuit courts (or, as we know them today, courts of appeals) took on their exclusively appellate function. The third tier of

Judiciary Act of 1789
Established the basic three-tiered structure of the federal court system.

Join the Debate

Senate Advice and Consent On Judicial Nominations

OVERVIEW: Article II of the Constitution gives the president sole authority to make judicial and executive appointments, and it gives the Senate the power to confirm the chief executive's choices. Article I of the Constitution gives the Senate authority to determine its own rules including procedural devices such as the filibuster to slow or stop legislative and political action. Any senator can use the filibuster to delay a vote on a political nominee. A two-thirds majority vote is needed to invoke cloture, thereby ending the filibuster, while only a simple majority (50 percent plus one) is needed to confirm a nominee. Historically, the Senate generally has confirmed the president's nominees, and it was only in 1955 that the tradition of judicial appointees regularly appearing before the Senate Judiciary Committee began (the first potential justice to appear before the Senate did so in 1916). The Senate generally has played a narrow role in the confirmation process and usually has deferred to the president's wishes. Precedent for filibustering Supreme Court nominees, however, was set in 1968 when President Lyndon B. Johnson's choice for chief justice, Abe Fortas, was blocked by the Republican minority. But it was with the controversial Supreme Court nomination of Judge Robert H. Bork in 1987 that confirmation politics took a contentious turn. The Senate voted against Bork's nomination after unprecedented pressure from civil and women's rights groups who believed his conservative judicial views would roll back civil liberties protections.

Senate Democrats, while in the minority in 2005 and 2006, argued that the use of the filibuster is necessary to help moderate the ideological make-up of the federal bench, noting that Republicans made similar arguments when they were in the minority and opposed some of former President Bill Clinton's judicial nominees. During this time, the Senate's Republican majority threatened to use the somewhat arcane rules of the chamber to bar filibusters on judicial nominations. Those opposed to judicial filibusters argue that the minority party has no right to thwart the majority's constitutional advice and consent role. They argue that the Constitution requires a simple majority to confirm nominees—the Constitution is explicit when it requires a two-thirds or three-quarters supermajority vote—and judicial filibusters have the effect of denying the Senate majority its right to exercise consent.

Arguments AGAINST Allowing Filibusters in the Senate's Confirmation Process

- Article II of the Constitution gives the president sole authority to make judicial nominations. Some scholars argue that the president has full power over the nomination process. The Senate's role is merely to provide advice and consent on already chosen nominees with a vote approving or blocking a nominee

- There is nothing in the Constitution creating or giving protection to judicial filibusters. Article I, section 5, gives each chamber the authority to determine its own rules of procedure by a simple majority vote. If the Senate, in order to change with the times, wishes to abolish the filibuster, it has the full authority of the Constitution behind it.

- The Constitution's Framers intended only a simple majority vote for the advice and consent clause. Alexander Hamilton explains in *Federalist Nos. 76* and *77* that the advice and

the federal judicial system created by the Judiciary Act of 1789 was the Supreme Court of the United States. Although the Constitution mentions "the supreme Court," it was silent on its size. In the Judiciary Act, Congress set the size of the Supreme Court at six—the chief justice plus five associate justices. After being reduced to five members in 1801, it later expanded and contracted, and finally the Court's size was fixed at nine in 1869.

consent function would be exercised "by the whole body, by [the] entire branch of the legislature." That is, the advice and consent would reflect the majority's will. A faction should not be allowed to thwart a legitimate majority's will.

Arguments IN FAVOR of Filibusters in the Senate's Confirmation Process

■ **Filibusters are necessary to maintain the ideological balance of the federal courts.** Filibusters on judicial nominees allow the minority party to check a president's attempt to stack the judiciary with members espousing one political philosophy. Maintaining ideological diversity will allow different constitutional interpretations and understandings, thus adding depth to our knowledge of constitutional jurisprudence.

■ **The Framers intended for the Senate to be a deliberative body.** The Constitution's writers intended for Senate debate to be slow, deliberate, and reasoned. The idea was to create a small legislative body in which all views would be aired in the marketplace of ideas. The filibuster keeps the debate open. Besides, if two-thirds of the Senate support cloture, the filibuster ends.

How far should the Senate go in blocking a president's judicial nominees? President George W. Bush meets with conservative judge Priscilla Owen at the White House. It took more than four years to confirm Owen to a position on the Fifth Circuit Court of Appeals.

■ **Senate rules benefit both political parties and their partisans.** No party remains in the majority forever. History shows that both parties spend significant time in both majority and minority status. Altering the rules to suit partisan politics practically ensures that minority party members will engage in the same tactics and politics once they regain majority standing and the cycle of bitter partisan politics will continue.

Continuing the Debate

1. Should a dedicated minority be able to delay the will of the majority? Why or why not?
2. Should a president strive to place nonpartisan judges on the federal bench? Why or why not?

To Follow the Debate Online, Go To:

www.senate.gov/reference/reference_index_subjects/Filibuster_vrd.htm, where the Senate provides a link to several reports on the use and implications of the filibuster.

www.civilrights.org/issues/nominations, a Web site developed by coalition of over 180 civil rights groups to advocate for a number of issues, including the preservation of the filibuster rule in the Senate as a way of preventing a president from appointing judges opposed to civil rights.

www.committeeforjustice.org, which favors the appointment of conservative judges and argues for changing Senate rules so that the filibuster rule no longer would apply to the confirmation of judicial nominees.

Photo courtesy: J. Scott Applewhite/AP Wide World Photos

When the justices met in their first public session in New York City in 1790, they were garbed magnificently in black and scarlet robes in the English fashion. The elegance of their attire, however, could not make up for the relative ineffectiveness of the Court. Its first session—presided over by John Jay, who was appointed chief justice of the United States by George Washington—initially had to be adjourned when less than half the justices attended. Later, once a sufficient number of justices assembled, the

Timeline: The Development of the Supreme Court

1787 Writing a Constitution— U.S. Constitution makes provisions for a federal judiciary in Article III.

1790 First Session— Court meets for the first time in New York City.

1803 *Marbury* v. *Madison*— The Court asserts that the power of judicial review can be implied from Constitution's supremacy clause.

1869 Nine Member Court— The Court's size is set at nine: eight associate justices and one chief justice.

1789 Judiciary Act— Act gives form and substance to the federal judiciary, establishing the three-tiered system that exists today.

1801 John Marshall becomes Chief Justice— The Marshall Court increases the power of the Court, discontinues the practice of *seriatim*, and expands the power of the Court over the states.

Court decided only one major case—*Chisholm* v. *Georgia* (1793). Moreover, as an indication of its lowly status, one associate justice left the Court to become chief justice of the South Carolina Supreme Court. (Although such a move would be considered a step down today, keep in mind that in the early years of the United States, many people viewed the states as more important than the national government.)

Hampered by frequent changes in personnel, limited space for its operations, no clerical support, and no system of reporting its decisions, the early Court did not impress many people. From the beginning, the circuit court duties of the Supreme Court justices presented problems for the prestige of the Court. Few good lawyers were willing to accept nominations to the high Court because circuit court duties entailed a substantial amount of travel— most of it on horseback over poorly maintained roads. Southern justices often rode as many as 10,000 miles a year on horseback. President George Washington tried to prevail on several friends and supporters to fill vacancies on the Court, but most refused the "honor." John Adams, the second president of the United States, ran into similar problems. When Adams asked John Jay to resume the position of chief justice after Jay resigned to become governor of New York, Jay declined the offer.

In spite of these problems, in its first decade, the Court took several actions to mold the new nation. First, by declining to give George Washington advice on the legality of some of his actions, the justices attempted to establish the Supreme Court as an independent, nonpolitical branch of government. Although John Jay frequently gave the president private advice, the Court refused to answer questions Washington posed to it concerning the construction of international laws and treaties.

Thinking Globally

Judicial Review in Great Britain

The process of judicial review in Great Britain is less than fifty years old. It consists of a review by courts of the legality (not constitutionality) of a decision by an administrative authority. For example, an action by the Prime Minister may be negated if it is illegal, irrational, or involves a procedural impropriety.

- How important is judicial review to the governing process? Is it surprising that a country such as Great Britain only recently adopted the power of judicial review?
- Does the power of judicial review give the courts too much power? Why or why not?

342

1935 Supreme Court Building Opens—The Court moves into its own building.

1986 William H. Rehnquist becomes Chief Justice—The Rehnquist Court makes a series of important decisions on federalism and significantly reduced the Court's caseload.

1882 Justice Horace Gray Hires a Clerk—Clerks greatly facilitate the work of the justices; today each justice has four clerks.

1953 Earl Warren becomes Chief Justice—The Warren Court is noted for its broad expansions of civil rights and liberties.

2005 John G. Roberts Jr. becomes Chief Justice—The current Court is viewed as moderate to conservative.

Where did the Supreme Court hear cases in the eighteenth and nineteenth centuries? From 1819 to 1860, the Supreme Court met in this small room in the basement of the U.S. Capitol building. It is now known as the "Old Supreme Court Chamber." This was far from its only meeting place, however. The Supreme Court first met on February 1, 1790, in the Merchants Exchange Building in New York City. When the nation's capital moved to Philadelphia in 1790, the Court moved with it, establishing chambers first in the state house (Independence Hall) and later in City Hall. After the federal government established Washington, D.C., as the permanent capital in 1800, the Court changed its meeting place a half-dozen times before it moved into its own building in 1935.

Photo courtesy: Architect of the U.S. Capitol

The early Court also tried to advance principles of nationalism and to maintain the national government's supremacy over the states. As circuit court jurists, the justices rendered numerous decisions on such matters as national suppression of the Whiskey Rebellion, which occurred in 1794 after a national excise tax was imposed on whiskey, and the constitutionality of the Alien and Sedition Acts, which made it a crime to criticize national governmental officials or their actions (see chapter 5).

During the ratification debates, Anti-Federalists had warned that Article III extended federal judicial power to controversies "between a State and Citizens of another State"—meaning that a citizen of one state could sue any other state in federal court, a prospect unthinkable to defenders of state sovereignty. Although Federalists, including Alexander Hamilton and James Madison, had scoffed at the idea, the nationalist Supreme Court quickly proved them wrong in *Chisholm* v. *Georgia* (1793). In *Chisholm*, the justices interpreted the Court's jurisdiction under Article III, section 2, to include the right to hear suits brought by a citizen against a state in which he did not reside. Writing in *Chisholm*, Justice James Wilson denounced the "haughty notions of state independence, state sovereignty, and state supremacy."[9] The states' reaction to this perceived attack on their authority led to passage and ratification in 1798 of the Eleventh Amendment to the Constitution, which specifically limited judicial power by stipulating that the authority of the federal courts could not "extend to any suit . . . commenced or prosecuted against one of the United States by citizens of another State."

The Marshall Court: *Marbury* v. *Madison* (1803) and Judicial Review

John Marshall, who headed the Court from 1801 to 1835, brought much-needed respect and prestige to the Court. Marshall was appointed chief justice by President John Adams in 1801, three years after he declined to accept a nomination as associate justice. An ardent Federalist, Marshall is considered the most important justice to serve on the high Court. Part of his reputation is the result of the duration of his service and the historical significance of this period in our nation's history.

Photo courtesy: Boston Athenaeum

As chief justice, Marshall helped to establish the Court as a co-equal branch of government. The Marshall Court, for example, discontinued the practice of *seriatim* (Latin for "in a series") opinions, which was the custom of the King's Bench in Great Britain. Prior to the Marshall Court, the justices delivered their individual opinions in order. For the Court to take its place as an equal branch of government, Marshall believed, the justices needed to speak as a Court and not as six individuals. In fact, during Marshall's first four years in office, the Court routinely spoke as one, and the chief justice wrote twenty-four of its twenty-six opinions.

The Marshall Court also established the authority of the Supreme Court over the judiciaries of the various states.[10] In addition, the Court established the supremacy of the federal government and Congress over state governments through a broad interpretation of the necessary and proper clause in *McCulloch* v. *Maryland* (1819), discussed in detail in chapter 3.[11]

Finally, the Marshall Court claimed the right of judicial review, from which the Supreme Court derives much of its day-to-day power and impact on the policy process. This established the Court as the final arbiter of constitutional questions, with the right to declare congressional acts void.[12]

Who was John Marshall? A single person can make a major difference in the development of an institution. Such was the case with John Marshall (1755–1835), who dominated the Supreme Court during his thirty-four years as chief justice. More of a politician than a lawyer, Marshall served as a delegate to the Virginia legislature and played an instrumental role in Virginia's ratification of the U.S. Constitution in 1787. He became secretary of state in 1800 under John Adams. When Oliver Ellsworth resigned as chief justice of the United States in 1800, Adams nominated Marshall. Marshall served on the Court until the day he died, participating in more than 1,000 decisions and authoring more than 500 opinions.

The American Legal System

Alexander Hamilton first publicly endorsed the idea of judicial review in *Federalist No. 78*, noting, "Whenever a particular statute contravenes the Constitution, it will be the duty of the judicial tribunals to adhere to the latter and disregard the former." Nonetheless, because judicial review is not mentioned in the U.S. Constitution, the actual authority of the Supreme Court to review the constitutionality of acts of Congress was an unsettled question. But, in **Marbury v. Madison (1803)**, Chief Justice John Marshall claimed this sweeping authority for the Court by asserting that the right of judicial review could be implied from the Constitution's supremacy clause.[13]

Marbury v. Madison arose amid a sea of political controversy. In the final hours of the Adams administration, William Marbury was appointed a justice of the peace for the District of Columbia. But, in the confusion of winding up matters, Adams's secretary of state failed to deliver Marbury's commission. Marbury then asked James Madison, Thomas Jefferson's secretary of state, for the commission. Under direct orders from Jefferson, who was irate over the Adams administration's last-minute appointment of several Federalist judges (quickly confirmed by the Federalist Senate), Madison refused to turn over the commission. Marbury and three other Adams appointees who were in the same situation then filed a writ of *mandamus* (a legal motion) asking the Supreme Court to order Madison to deliver their commissions.

Political tensions ran high as the Court met to hear the case. Jefferson threatened to ignore any order of the Court. Marshall realized that he and the prestige of the Court could be devastated by any refusal of the executive branch to comply with the decision. Responding to this challenge, in a brilliant opinion that in many sections reads more like a lecture to Jefferson than a discussion of the merits of Marbury's claim, Marshall concluded that although Marbury and the others were entitled to their commissions, the Court lacked the power to issue the writ sought by Marbury. In *Marbury* v. *Madison*, Marshall further ruled that the parts of the Judiciary Act of 1789 that extended the original jurisdiction of the Court to allow it to issue writs were inconsistent with the Constitution and therefore unconstitutional.

Although the immediate effect of the decision was to deny power to the Court, its long-term effect was to establish the implied power of judicial review. Said Marshall, writing for the Court, "it is emphatically the province and duty of the judicial department to say what the law is." Since *Marbury*, the Court has routinely exercised the power of judicial review to determine the constitutionality of acts of Congress, the executive branch, and the states.

Marbury v. Madison (1803)
Case in which the Supreme Court first asserted the power of judicial review by finding that the congressional statute extending the Court's original jurisdiction was unconstitutional.

Chief Justices of the Supreme Court

The American Legal System

The judicial system in the United States can best be described as a dual system consisting of the federal court system and the judicial systems of the fifty states, as illustrated in Figure 10.1 and described in chapter 4. Cases may arise in either system. Both systems are basically three-tiered. At the bottom of the system are **trial courts**, where litigation begins. In the middle are appellate courts in the state systems and the courts of appeals in the federal system. At the top of each pyramid sits a court of last resort. The federal courts of appeals and Supreme Court as well as state courts of appeals and supreme courts are **appellate courts** that, with few exceptions, review on appeal only cases that already have been decided in lower courts. These courts generally hear matters of both civil and criminal law.

Comparing Judiciaries

trial court
Court of original jurisdiction where cases begin.

appellate court
Court that generally reviews only findings of law made by lower courts.

Jurisdiction

Before a state or federal court can hear a case, it must have **jurisdiction**, or the authority to hear and decide the issues in that case. The jurisdiction of the federal courts is controlled by the U.S. Constitution and by statute. Jurisdiction is conferred

jurisdiction
Authority vested in a particular court to hear and decide the issues in any particular case.

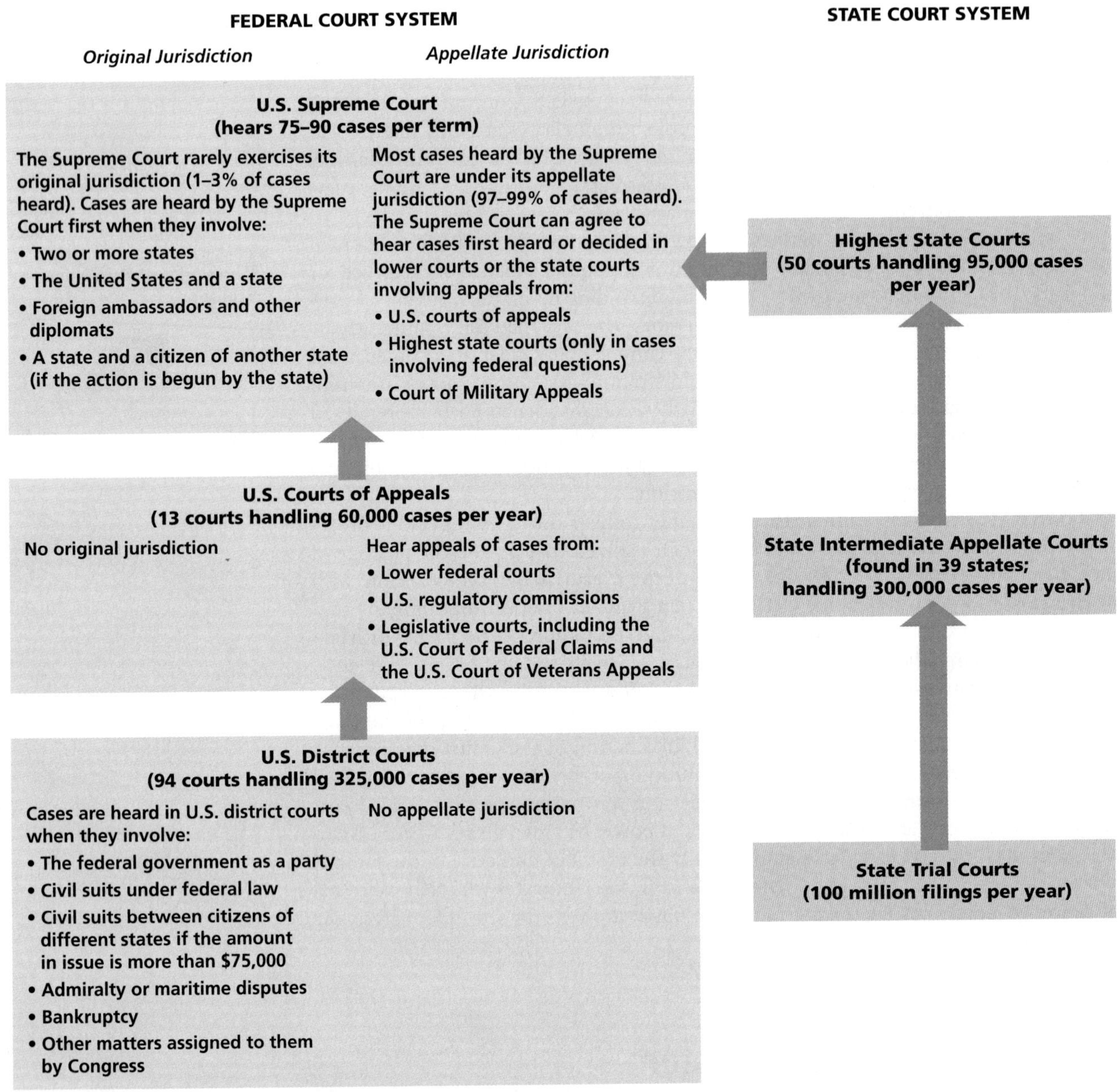

FEDERAL COURT SYSTEM

Original Jurisdiction   *Appellate Jurisdiction*

STATE COURT SYSTEM

U.S. Supreme Court
(hears 75–90 cases per term)

The Supreme Court rarely exercises its original jurisdiction (1–3% of cases heard). Cases are heard by the Supreme Court first when they involve:

• Two or more states

• The United States and a state

• Foreign ambassadors and other diplomats

• A state and a citizen of another state (if the action is begun by the state)

Most cases heard by the Supreme Court are under its appellate jurisdiction (97–99% of cases heard). The Supreme Court can agree to hear cases first heard or decided in lower courts or the state courts involving appeals from:

• U.S. courts of appeals

• Highest state courts (only in cases involving federal questions)

• Court of Military Appeals

Highest State Courts
(50 courts handling 95,000 cases per year)

U.S. Courts of Appeals
(13 courts handling 60,000 cases per year)

No original jurisdiction

Hear appeals of cases from:

• Lower federal courts

• U.S. regulatory commissions

• Legislative courts, including the U.S. Court of Federal Claims and the U.S. Court of Veterans Appeals

State Intermediate Appellate Courts
(found in 39 states; handling 300,000 cases per year)

U.S. District Courts
(94 courts handling 325,000 cases per year)

Cases are heard in U.S. district courts when they involve:

• The federal government as a party

• Civil suits under federal law

• Civil suits between citizens of different states if the amount in issue is more than $75,000

• Admiralty or maritime disputes

• Bankruptcy

• Other matters assigned to them by Congress

No appellate jurisdiction

State Trial Courts
(100 million filings per year)

FIGURE **10.1** The Dual Structure of the American Court System

original jurisdiction
The jurisdiction of courts that hear a case first, usually in a trial. These courts determine the facts of a case.

appellate jurisdiction
The power vested in particular courts to review and/or revise the decision of a lower court.

based on issues, the amount of money involved in a dispute, or the type of offense. Procedurally, we speak of two types of jurisdiction: original and appellate. **Original jurisdiction** refers to a court's authority to hear disputes as a trial court and may occur on the federal or state level. For example, the child custody case between Britney Spears and Kevin Federline began in a California state trial court of original jurisdiction. In contrast, the legal battle over the constitutionality of the federal Partial Birth Abortion Ban Act began in several federal district courts. More than 90 percent of all cases, whether state or federal, end in a court of original jurisdiction. **Appellate jurisdiction** refers to a court's ability to review cases already decided by a trial court. Appellate courts ordinarily do not review the factual record. Instead, they review legal procedures to make certain that the law was applied properly to the issues presented in the case.

Criminal and Civil Law

Criminal law is the body of law that regulates individual conduct and is enforced by the state and national governments.[14] Crimes are graded as felonies, misdemeanors, or offenses, according to their severity. Some acts—for example, murder, rape, and robbery—are considered crimes in all states. Although all states outlaw murder, their penal, or criminal, codes treat the crime quite differently; some states, for example, allow the death penalty for murder, while others prohibit the use of capital punishment. Other practices—such as gambling—are illegal only in some states.

Criminal law assumes that society itself is the victim of the illegal act; therefore, the government prosecutes, or brings an action, on behalf of an injured party (acting as a plaintiff) in criminal but not civil cases. Criminal cases are traditionally in the purview of the states. But, a burgeoning set of federal criminal laws is contributing significantly to delays in the federal courts.

Civil law is the body of law that regulates the conduct and relationships between private individuals or companies. Because the actions at issue in civil law do not constitute a threat to society at large, people who believe they have been injured by another party must take action on their own to seek judicial relief. Civil cases, then, involve lawsuits filed to recover something of value, whether it is the right to vote, fair treatment, or monetary compensation for an item or service that cannot be recovered.

Most legal disputes that arise in the United States never get to court. Individuals and companies involved in civil disputes routinely settle their disagreements out of court. Often these settlements are not reached until minutes before the case is to be tried. Many civil cases that go to trial are settled during the course of the trial—before the case can be handed over to the jury or submitted to a judge for a decision or determination of responsibility or guilt.

Each civil or criminal case has a plaintiff, or petitioner, who brings charges against a defendant, or respondent. Sometimes the government is the plaintiff. The government may bring civil charges on behalf of the citizens of the state or the national government against a person or corporation for violating the law, but it is always the government that brings a criminal case. When cases are initiated, they are known first by the name of the petitioner. In *Marbury* v. *Madison*, William Marbury was the plaintiff, suing the defendants, the U.S. government and James Madison as its secretary of state, for not delivering Marbury's judicial commission.

During trials, judges often must interpret the intent of laws enacted by Congress and state legislatures. To do so, they read reports, testimony, and debates on the relevant legislation and study the results of other similar legal cases. They also rely on the presentations made by lawyers in their briefs and at trial.

Another important component of most civil and criminal cases is the jury. This body acts as the ultimate finder of fact and plays an important role in determining the culpability of the individual on trial. The composition of juries has been the subject of much controversy in the United States. In the past, women and blacks often were excluded from jury service because many states selected jurors from those registered to vote. Although the Supreme Court ruled in 1888 that African American citizens could not be barred from serving as jurors,[15] it was not until 1979 that the Court extended this ruling to women.[16]

Until recently, however, it was not all that unusual for lawyers to use their peremptory challenges (those made without a reason) to systematically dismiss women or African Americans if lawyers believed that they would be hostile to their case. In two opinions, however, the Supreme

criminal law
Codes of behavior related to the protection of property and individual safety.

civil law
Codes of behavior related to business and contractual relationships between groups and individuals.

You Are a Young Lawyer

Thinking Globally
Customary Courts

Tribal, or customary, courts continue to serve an important role in many nations, including Ghana and Australia. Customary courts encourage participation by the public in the decision-making process. Tribal chiefs or bodies of elders who are believed to be unfair typically lose popular support. Customary courts often exist side by side with a nation's formal, statutory judicial system.

- Historically, jurisdiction has been a contentious issue between customary and statutory systems. What kinds of cases might be decided in each type of court?
- Are the decisions of customary courts likely to differ significantly from those of more formal, statutory courts? Why or why not?

Court concluded that race or gender could not be used as a reason to exclude potential jurors.[17] Thus, today, juries are more likely to be representative of local populations than in the past, providing litigants in civil or criminal trial with a true jury of their peers.

The Federal Court System

constitutional courts
Federal courts specifically created by the U.S. Constitution or by Congress pursuant to its authority in Article III.

legislative courts
Courts established by Congress for specialized purposes, such as the Court of Military Appeals.

The federal district courts, courts of appeals, and the Supreme Court are called **constitutional** (or Article III) **courts** because Article III of the Constitution either established them or authorized Congress to establish them. Judges who preside over these courts are nominated by the president (with the advice and consent of the Senate), and they serve lifetime terms, as long as they engage in "good behavior."

In addition to constitutional courts, **legislative courts** are set up by Congress, under its implied powers, generally for special purposes. The U.S. territorial courts (which hear federal cases in the territories) and the U.S. Court of Veterans Appeals are examples of legislative courts, or what some call Article I courts. The judges who preside over these federal courts are appointed by the president (subject to Senate confirmation) and serve fixed, limited terms.

District Courts

As we have seen, Congress created U.S. district courts when it enacted the Judiciary Act of 1789. District courts are federal trial courts of original jurisdiction. There are currently ninety-four federal district courts. No district court cuts across state lines. Every state has at least one federal district court, and the most populous states—

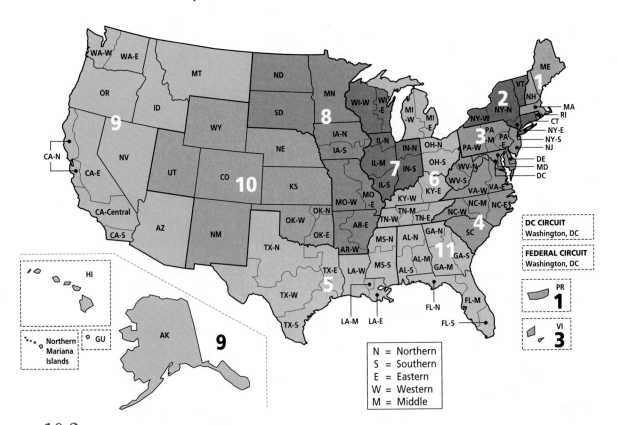

FIGURE **10.2** The Federal Court System
This map shows the location of the U.S. courts of appeals and the boundaries of the federal district courts in states with more than one district.

California, Texas, and New York—each have four.[18] (To learn more about federal district courts, see Figure 10.2.)

Federal district courts, where the bulk of the judicial work takes place in the federal system, have original jurisdiction over only specific types of cases. Although the rules governing district court jurisdiction can be complex, cases heard in federal district courts by a single judge (with or without a jury) generally fall into one of three categories:

1. They involve the federal government as a party.
2. They present a federal question based on a claim under the U.S. Constitution, a treaty with another nation, or a federal statute. This is called federal question jurisdiction and it can involve criminal or civil law.
3. They involve civil suits in which citizens are from different states, and the amount of money at issue is more than $75,000.[19]

Each federal judicial district has a U.S. attorney, who is nominated by the president and confirmed by the Senate. The U.S. attorney in each district is that district's chief law enforcement officer. The number of assistant U.S. attorneys in each district depends on the amount of litigation. U.S. attorneys, like district attorneys within the states, have a considerable amount of discretion as to whether they pursue criminal or civil investigations or file charges against individuals or corporations. These highly visible positions often serve as springboards for elective office. Former New York City mayor and 2008 presidential candidate Rudy Giuliani once served as the U.S. attorney for the Southern District of New York.

The Courts of Appeals

The losing party in a case heard and decided in a federal district court can appeal the decision to the appropriate court of appeals. The United States courts of appeals (known as the circuit courts of appeals prior to 1948) are the intermediate appellate courts in the federal system and were established in 1789 to hear appeals from federal district courts. There are currently eleven numbered courts of appeals. A twelfth, U.S. Court of Appeals for the D.C. Circuit, handles most appeals involving federal regulatory commissions and agencies, including, for example, the National Labor Relations Board and the Securities and Exchange Commission. The thirteenth federal appeals court is the U.S. Court of Appeals for the Federal Circuit, which deals with patents and contract and financial claims against the federal government.

The number of judges within each Court of Appeals varies—depending on the workload and the complexity of the cases—and ranges from six to nearly thirty. Each court is supervised by a chief judge, the most senior judge in terms of service below the age of sixty-five, who can serve no more than seven years. In deciding cases, judges are divided into rotating three-judge panels, made up of the active judges within the Court of Appeals, visiting judges (primarily district judges from the same court), and retired judges. In rare cases, all the judges in a Court of Appeals may choose to sit together (*en banc*) to decide a case by majority vote.

The courts of appeals have no original jurisdiction. Rather, Congress has granted these courts appellate jurisdiction over two general categories of cases: appeals from criminal and civil cases from the district courts, and appeals from administrative agencies. Criminal and civil case appeals constitute about 90 percent of the workload of the courts of appeals, with appeals from administrative agencies about 10 percent. Because so many agencies are located in Washington, D.C., the U.S. Court of Appeals for the D.C. Circuit hears an inordinate number of such cases. The D.C. Circuit, then, is considered the second most important court in the nation because its decisions govern the regulatory agencies. Supreme Court Chief Justice John G. Roberts Jr. and Justices Antonin Scalia, Clarence Thomas, and Ruth Bader Ginsburg sat on the U.S. Court of Appeals for the D.C. Circuit before their nomination to the Supreme Court.

Once a decision is made by a federal court of appeals, a litigant no longer has an automatic right to an appeal. The losing party may submit a petition to the U.S. Supreme Court to hear the case, but the Court grants few of these requests. The courts of appeals, then, are the courts of last resort for almost all federal litigation. Keep in mind, however, that most cases, if they actually go to trial, go no further than the district court level.

In general, courts of appeals try to correct errors of law and procedure that have occurred in lower courts or administrative agencies. Courts of appeals hear no new testimony; instead, lawyers submit written arguments in what is called a **brief** (also submitted in trial courts), and they then appear to present and argue the case orally to the court.

Decisions of any court of appeals are binding on only the courts within its geographic confines, but decisions of the U.S. Supreme Court are binding throughout the nation and establish national **precedents**. This reliance on past decisions or precedents to formulate decisions in new cases is called ***stare decisis*** (a Latin phrase meaning "let the decision stand"). The principle of *stare decisis* allows for continuity and predictability in our judicial system. Although *stare decisis* can be helpful in predicting decisions, at times judges carve out new ground and ignore, decline to follow, or even overrule precedents to reach a different conclusion in a case involving similar circumstances. This is a major reason why so much litigation exsists in America today. Parties to a suit know that the outcome of a case is not always predictable; if such prediction were possible, there would be little reason to go to court.

The Supreme Court

The U.S. Supreme Court, as we saw in the opening vignette, is often at the center of the storm of highly controversial issues that have yet to be resolved successfully in the political process. It reviews cases from the U.S. courts of appeals and state supreme courts (as well as other courts of last resort) and acts as the final interpreter of the U.S. Constitution. The Court not only decides major cases with tremendous policy significance each year, but it also ensures uniformity in the interpretation of national laws and the Constitution, resolves conflicts among the states, and maintains the supremacy of national law in the federal system.

Since 1869, the U.S. Supreme Court has consisted of eight associate justices and one chief justice, who is nominated by the president specifically for that position. There is no special significance about the number nine, and the Constitution is silent about the size of the Court. Between 1789 and 1869, Congress periodically altered the size of the Court. The lowest number of justices on the Court was six; the most, ten. Through December 2008, only 110 justices had served on the Court, and there had been seventeen chief justices. (To learn more about chief justices of the Supreme Court, see Appendix IV.)

Compared with the president or Congress, the Supreme Court operates with few support staff. Along with the four clerks each justice employs, there are about 400 staff members at the Supreme Court.

How Federal Court Judges Are Selected

The selection of federal judges is often a very political process with important political ramifications because judges are nominated by the president and must be confirmed by the U.S. Senate. Presidents, in general, try to select well-qualified men and women for the bench. But, these appointments also provide a president with the opportunity to put his philosophical stamp on the federal courts. (To

brief
A document containing the legal written arguments in a case filed with a court by a party prior to a hearing or trial.

precedent
A prior judicial decision that serves as a rule for settling subsequent cases of a similar nature.

stare decisis
In court rulings, a reliance on past decisions or precedents to formulate decisions in new cases.

TABLE 10.2 How A President Affects the Federal Judiciary

The table depicts the number of judges appointed by each president and shows how quickly a president can make an impact on the make-up of the courts.

President	Appointed to Supreme Court	Appointed to Courts of Appeals[a]	Appointed to District Courts[b]	Total Appointed	Total Number of Judgeships[c]	Percentage of Judgeships Filled by President
Johnson (1963–1969)	2	40	122	164	449	37
Nixon (1969–1974)	4	45	179	228	504	45
Ford (1974–1977)	1	12	52	65	504	13
Carter (1977–1981)	0	56	202	258	657	39
Reagan (1981–1989)	3	78	290	368	740	50
Bush (1989–1993)	2	37	148	185	825	22
Clinton (1993–2001)	2	66	305	373	841	44
G. W. Bush (2001–2009)[d]	2	57	287	344	866	40

[a]Does not include the U. S. Court of Appeals for the Federal Circuit
[b]Includes district courts in the territories
[c]Total judgeships authorized in president's last year in office
[d]George W. Bush data through September 1, 2008

Source: "Imprints on the Bench," *CQ Weekly Report* (January 19, 2001): 173. Reprinted by permission of Copyright Clearance Center on behalf of Congressional Quarterly, Inc. Updated by authors.

learn more about how presidents affect the judiciary, see Table 10.2.) Nominees, however, while generally members of the nominating president's party, usually are vetted through the senator's offices of the states where the district court or court of appeals vacancy occurs. In the Clinton White House, candidates for district court generally came from recommendations by Democratic senators, "or in the absence of a Democratic senator, from the Democratic members of the House of Representatives or other high ranking Democratic Party politicians."[20] This process by which presidents generally defer selection of district court judges to the choice of senators of their own party who represent the state where the vacancy occurs is known as **senatorial courtesy**.

Despite the Clinton administration's attempts to appoint moderate justices, so that they might win approval in a Republican-controlled Senate, the Senate leadership took steps to prevent many of these nominees from winning approval. Thus, when George W. Bush took office in 2001, Democrats responded to his nominees with a similar level of scrutiny. Almost immediately, Senate Democrats charged that many of Bush's appointees were too conservative, and even filibustered several nominations.

In 2003, the Republican leadership held a forty-hour talkathon to bring attention to the Senate's failure to confirm these nominees. This event received a good deal of press, but it achieved little success. President Bush further irritated Senate Democrats when he made several recess appointments of contested appointees, which allowed them to serve for the remainder of the 108th Congress. In 2004, President Bush and Senate Democrats reached an agreement that no further recess appointments would occur if the Senate confirmed twenty-five of the president's nominees.[21] These accords fell apart in 2005 as the Bush administration continued to nominate judges perceived by Democrats as too ideological. Bitter confrontations over the Democrats' threats as well as use of the filibuster to block votes on several more Bush nominees led a bipartisan "Gang of Fourteen" senators to band together. Their aim was to make sure that well-qualified nominees would be brought to a vote except in extraordinary circumstances, such as when a nominee had ideological views far outside the mainstream. This group of moderates from both parties worked across the aisle to prevent the Republican leadership from exercising what had been nicknamed the "nuclear option" by changing Senate rules so that votes on all judicial nominees would be immune from filibuster.[22]

senatorial courtesy
Process by which presidents generally defer selection of district court judges to the choice of senators of their own party who represent the state where the vacancy occurs.

Who are Federal Judges?

Typically, federal district court judges have held other political offices, such as those of state court judge or prosecutor, as illustrated in Table 10.3. Most have been involved in politics, which is what usually brings them into consideration for a position on the federal bench. Griffin Bell, a former federal court of appeals judge (who later became U.S. attorney general in the Carter administration), once remarked, "For me, becoming a federal judge wasn't very difficult. I managed John F. Kennedy's presidential campaign in Georgia."[23]

Increasingly, most judicial nominees have had prior judicial experience. White males continue to dominate the federal courts, but since the 1970s, most presidents have pledged (with varying degrees of success) to do their best to appoint more African Americans, Hispanics, women, and other underrepresented groups to the federal bench. (To learn more, see Analyzing Visuals: Race, Ethnicity, and Gender of District Court Appointees.)

Appointments to the U.S. Supreme Court

The Constitution is silent on the qualifications for appointment to the Supreme Court (as well as to other constitutional courts), although Justice Oliver Wendell Holmes once remarked that a justice should be a "combination of Justinian, Jesus Christ and John Marshall."[24] However, like other federal court judges, the justices of the Supreme Court are nominated by the president and must be confirmed by the Senate.

Presidents always have realized how important their judicial appointments, especially their Supreme Court appointments, are to their ability to achieve all or many of their policy objectives. But, even though most presidents have tried to appoint jurists with particular political or ideological philosophies, they often have been wrong in

TABLE 10.3 Characteristics of District Court Appointees from Carter to Bush

	Carter	Reagan	Bush	Clinton	G. W. Bush[a]
Occupation					
Politics/government	5.0%	13.4%	10.8%	11.5%	12.3%
Judiciary	44.6	36.9	41.9	48.2	46.8
Lawyer	49.9	49.0	45.9	38.7	40.7
Other	0.5	0.7	1.4	2.6	2.0
Experience					
Judicial	54.0%	46.2%	46.6%	52.1%	51.7%
Prosecutorial	38.1	44.1	39.2	41.3	43.8
Neither	30.7	28.6	31.8	28.9	26.1
Political Affiliation					
Democrat	91.1%	4.8%	6.1%	87.5%	6.9%
Republican	4.5	91.7	88.5	6.2	84.7
Other/None	4.5	3.4	5.4	6.2	8.4
ABA Rating					
Extremely/Well Qualified	51.0%	53.5%	57.4%	59.0%	60.9%
Qualified	47.5	46.6	42.6	40.0	29.1
Not Qualified	1.5	—	—	1.0	2.0
Net Worth					
Under $200,000	35.8%	17.6%	10.1%	13.4%	5.9%
$200,000–499,999	41.2	37.6	31.1	21.6	18.2
$500,000–999,999	18.9	21.7	26.4	26.9	22.7
$1,000,000+	4.0	23.1	32.4	32.4	53.2
Average age at nomination (years)	49.6	48.6	48.2	49.5	50.0
Total number of appointees	202	290	148	305	203

Note that percentages do not always add to 100 because some nominees fit in more than one category (i.e., they have been judges and prosecutors).

[a]George W. Bush appointee data are through January 20, 2007.

Source: Sheldon Goldman et al. "Picking Judges in a Time of Turmoil: W. Bush's Judiciary during the 109th Congress." *Judicature* (2007): 252.

Analyzing Visuals   Race, Ethnicity, and Gender of Federal Court Appointees

Examine the bar graphs, which show some of the characteristics of federal court appointees from President Jimmy Carter to President George W. Bush, and consider the following questions:

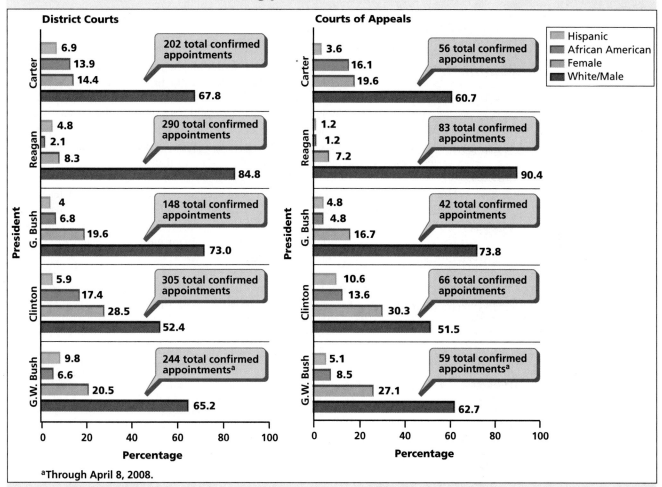

District Courts

Carter
- Hispanic: 6.9
- African American: 13.9
- Female: 14.4
- White/Male: 67.8

202 total confirmed appointments

Reagan
- Hispanic: 4.8
- African American: 2.1
- Female: 8.3
- White/Male: 84.8

290 total confirmed appointments

G. Bush
- Hispanic: 4
- African American: 6.8
- Female: 19.6
- White/Male: 73.0

148 total confirmed appointments

Clinton
- Hispanic: 5.9
- African American: 17.4
- Female: 28.5
- White/Male: 52.4

305 total confirmed appointments

G.W. Bush
- Hispanic: 9.8
- African American: 6.6
- Female: 20.5
- White/Male: 65.2

244 total confirmed appointments[a]

Courts of Appeals

Carter
- Hispanic: 3.6
- African American: 16.1
- Female: 19.6
- White/Male: 60.7

56 total confirmed appointments

Reagan
- Hispanic: 1.2
- African American: 1.2
- Female: 7.2
- White/Male: 90.4

83 total confirmed appointments

G. Bush
- Hispanic: 4.8
- African American: 4.8
- Female: 16.7
- White/Male: 73.8

42 total confirmed appointments

Clinton
- Hispanic: 10.6
- African American: 13.6
- Female: 30.3
- White/Male: 51.5

66 total confirmed appointments

G.W. Bush
- Hispanic: 5.1
- African American: 8.5
- Female: 27.1
- White/Male: 62.7

59 total confirmed appointments[a]

Legend: Hispanic, African American, Female, White/Male

President / Percentage

[a]Through April 8, 2008.

ARE there differences between appointments made by Democratic presidents (Carter and Clinton) and Republican presidents? Can you identify any trends in appointees over time?

WHICH groups are most underrepresented?

SHOULD race, ethnicity, and gender matter in presidential appointments? Why or why not?

Source: Federal Judges Biographical database, www.fjc.gov/public/home.nsf/hisj.

their assumptions about their appointees. President Dwight D. Eisenhower, a moderate conservative, was appalled by the liberal opinions written by his appointee to chief justice, Earl Warren, concerning criminal defendants' rights. Similarly, Justices John Paul Stevens and David Souter, appointed by Presidents Gerald R. Ford and George Bush, respectively, are not as conservative as some commentators predicted. Souter, in particular, has surprised many commentators with his moderate to liberal decisions in a variety of areas, including free speech, criminal rights, race and gender discrimination, and abortion.

Historically, because of the special place the Supreme Court enjoys in our constitutional system, its nominees have encountered more opposition than have district court or court of appeals nominees. As the role of the Court has increased over time, so too has the amount of attention given to nominees. With this increased attention has come greater opposition, especially to nominees with controversial views.

Nomination Criteria

Justice Sandra Day O'Connor once remarked that "You have to be lucky" to be appointed to the Court.[25] Although luck is certainly important, over the years nominations to the bench have been made for a variety of reasons. Depending on the timing of a vacancy, a president may or may not have a list of possible candidates or even a specific individual in mind. Until recently, presidents often looked within their circle of friends or their administration to fill a vacancy. Nevertheless, whether the nominee is a friend or someone known to the president only by reputation, at least six criteria are especially important: competence, ideology or policy preferences, rewards, pursuit of political support, religion, and race and gender.

COMPETENCE Most prospective nominees are expected to have had at least some judicial or governmental experience. For example, John Jay, the first chief justice, was one of the authors of *The Federalist Papers* and was active in New York politics. In 2008, all nine sitting Supreme Court justices had prior judicial experience. (To learn more about the current Court, see Table 10.4.)

IDEOLOGY OR POLICY PREFERENCES Most presidents seek to appoint individuals who share their policy preferences, and almost all have political goals in mind when they

TABLE 10.4 The Supreme Court, 2008

	Year of Birth	Year of Appointment	Political Party	Law School	Appointing President	Religion	Prior Judicial Experience	Prior Government Experience
John G. Roberts Jr.	1955	2005	R	Harvard	G. W. Bush	Roman Catholic	U.S. Court of Appeals	Dept. of Justice, White House counsel
John Paul Stevens	1920	1975	R	Chicago	Ford	Nondenominational Protestant	U.S. Court of Appeals	Associate Counsel, House Judiciary Committee
Antonin Scalia	1936	1986	R	Harvard	Reagan	Roman Catholic	U.S. Court of Appeals	Assistant attorney general, Office of Legal Counsel
Anthony Kennedy	1936	1988	R	Harvard	Reagan	Roman Catholic	U.S. Court of Appeals	
David Souter	1939	1990	R	Harvard	Bush	Episcopalian	U.S. Court of Appeals	New Hampshire assistant attorney general
Clarence Thomas	1948	1991	R	Yale	Bush	Roman Catholic	U.S. Court of Appeals	Chair, Equal Employment Opportunity Commission
Ruth Bader Ginsburg	1933	1993	D	Columbia/ Harvard	Clinton	Jewish	U.S. Court of Appeals	
Stephen Breyer	1938	1994	D	Harvard	Clinton	Jewish	U.S. Court of Appeals	Chief counsel, Senate Judiciary Committee
Samuel A. Alito Jr.	1950	2006	R	Yale	G. W. Bush	Roman Catholic	U.S. Court of Appeals	Dept. of Justice, U.S. Attorney.

appoint a justice. Presidents Franklin D. Roosevelt, Richard M. Nixon, and Ronald Reagan were very successful in molding the Court to their own political beliefs.

REWARDS Historically, many of those appointed to the Supreme Court have been personal friends of presidents. Abraham Lincoln, for example, appointed one of his key political advisers to the Court. Lyndon B. Johnson appointed his longtime friend Abe Fortas to the bench. Most presidents also select justices of their own party affiliation. Chief Justice John G. Roberts Jr. and Justice Samuel A. Alito Jr., for example, both Republicans, worked in the Department of Justice during the Reagan and George Bush administrations. Roberts also served as associate White House counsel under Reagan.

PURSUIT OF POLITICAL SUPPORT During Ronald Reagan's successful campaign for the presidency in 1980, some of his advisers feared that the gender gap would hurt him. Polls repeatedly showed that he was far less popular with female voters than with men. To gain support from women, Reagan announced during his campaign that should he win, he would appoint a woman to fill the first vacancy on the Court. When Justice Potter Stewart, a moderate, announced his retirement from the bench, under pressure from women's rights groups, President Reagan nominated Sandra Day O'Connor of the Arizona Court of Appeals to fill the vacancy. Similarly, it probably did not hurt President Bill Clinton's popularity with woman voters that his first appointment (Ruth Bader Ginsburg) was female.

RELIGION Ironically, religion, which historically has been an important issue, was hardly mentioned during the most recent Supreme Court vacancies. For years, traditionally, there was a Catholic and a Jewish seat on the Court.

Through early 2009, of the 110 justices who served on the Court, almost all have been members of traditional Protestant faiths.[26] Only eleven have been Catholic and only seven have been Jewish.[27] Today, more Catholics—Roberts, Scalia, Kennedy, Thomas, and Alito—serve on the court than at any other point in history. Ironically, there was a time in history when no one could have imagined that Roman Catholics would someday make up a majority of the Court, given historical discrimination against Catholics through the 1950s.

RACE, ETHNICITY, AND GENDER Through 2008, only two African Americans and two women have served on the Court. Race was undoubtedly a critical issue in the appointment of Clarence Thomas to replace Thurgood Marshall, the first African American justice. But, President George Bush refused to acknowledge his wish to retain a black seat on the Court. Instead, he announced that he was "picking the best man for the job on the merits," a claim that was met with considerable skepticism by many observers. Many commentators assumed that George W. Bush would appoint a Hispanic to fill the next vacancy on the bench in recognition of their growing proportion in the general population and their underrepresentation in national politics. This plan, however, was derailed by questions from the right as well as the left about the ideology and activities of the front-runners for the nomination, Attorney General Alberto Gonzales and lawyer Miguel Estrada.

Although the role of gender was crucial to the nomination of Sandra Day O'Connor, when O'Connor resigned, George W. Bush nominated Judge John G. Roberts Jr. to replace her. When Chief Justice William H. Rehnquist died soon after, Bush nominated Roberts to fill the vacant chief justice position. Though his next choice to fill O'Connor's seat was a woman, White House counsel Harriet Miers, her nomination was short-lived after it met with significant criticism from conservatives. O'Connor's vacancy eventually was filled by Judge Samuel A. Alito Jr., much to O'Connor's public chagrin. The departing justice noted that one woman on the Supreme Court was hardly proportional to women's representation within the legal profession.

The Supreme Court Confirmation Process

The Constitution gives the Senate the authority to approve all nominees to the federal bench. Before 1900, about one-fourth of all presidential nominees to the Supreme Court were rejected by the Senate. In 1844, for example, President John Tyler sent six nominations to the Senate, and all but one were defeated. In 1866, Andrew Johnson nominated his brilliant attorney general, Henry Stanberry, but the Senate's hostility to Johnson led it to reduce the size of the Court from nine to six seats to prevent Johnson from filling any vacancies.

Ordinarily, nominations are referred to the Senate Judiciary Committee. This committee investigates the nominees, holds hearings, and votes on its recommendation for Senate action. At this stage, the committee may reject a nominee or send the nomination to the full Senate for a vote. The full Senate then deliberates on the nominee before voting. A simple majority vote is required for confirmation.

INVESTIGATION   As a president begins to narrow the list of possible nominees to the Supreme Court, those names are sent to the Federal Bureau of Investigation for a background check. The names of prospective nominees are also forwarded to the American Bar Association (ABA), the politically powerful organization that represents the interests of the legal profession. Republican President Dwight D. Eisenhower started this practice, believing it helped "insulate the process from political pressure."[28] After its own investigation, the ABA rates each nominee, based on his or her qualifications, as Well Qualified (previously "Highly Qualified"), Qualified, or Not Qualified. (The same system is used for lower federal court nominees.)

David Souter, George Bush's first nominee to the Court, received a unanimous rating of Highly Qualified from the ABA, as did both of Bill Clinton's nominees, Ruth Bader Ginsburg and Stephen Breyer. In contrast, another Bush nominee, Clarence Thomas, was given only a Qualified rating (well before sexual harassment charges against him became public). Two ABA members even voted him Not Qualified. Thomas was the first nominee to receive less than a unanimous Qualified rating by the ABA.

After a formal nomination is made and sent to the Senate, the Senate Judiciary Committee begins its own investigation. (The same process is used for nominees to the lower federal courts, although such investigations rarely are as extensive as for Supreme Court nominees.) To begin its task, the Senate Judiciary Committee asks each nominee to complete a lengthy questionnaire detailing previous work (dating as far back as high school summer jobs), judicial opinions written, judicial philosophy, speeches, and even all interviews ever given to members of the press. Committee staffers also contact potential witnesses who might offer testimony concerning the nominee's fitness for office.

LOBBYING BY INTEREST GROUPS Many groups are keenly interested in the nomination process. In 1987, for example, the nomination of Judge Robert H. Bork to the Supreme Court led liberal groups to launch an exten-

What does the confirmation process entail? When Samuel A. Alito Jr. was nominated for a seat on the Supreme Court, the result was a high-stakes confirmation battle that involved a number of interest groups. Here, Alito signs autographs for supporters on the way to his confirmation hearing.

Photo courtesy: Joshua Roberts/Reuters/Landov

sive radio, television, and print media campaign against the nominee. These interest groups decried Bork's actions as solicitor general, especially his firing of the Watergate special prosecutor at the request of President Richard M. Nixon, as well as his political beliefs.

More and more, interest groups are also getting involved in district court and court of appeals nominations. They recognize that these appointments often pave the way for future nominees to the Supreme Court. For example, a coalition of conservative evangelical Christian organizations, including Focus on the Family and the Family Research Council, have held a series of "Justice Sunday" events featuring televangelists and politicians promoting the confirmation of judges with conservative and religious records.

THE SENATE COMMITTEE HEARINGS AND SENATE VOTE Not all nominees inspire the kind of intense reaction that kept Bork from the Court and almost blocked the confirmation of Clarence Thomas. Until 1929, all but one Senate Judiciary Committee hearing on a Supreme Court nominee was conducted in executive session— that is, closed to the public. The 1916 hearings on Louis Brandeis, the first Jewish justice, were conducted in public and lasted nineteen days, although Brandeis himself never was called to testify. In 1939, Felix Frankfurter became the first nominee to testify in any detail before the committee.[29]

Since the 1980s, it has become standard for senators to ask the nominees probing questions. Most nominees have declined to answer most of these questions on the grounds that the issues raised ultimately might come before the Court.

After hearings are concluded, the Senate Judiciary Committee usually makes a recommendation to the full Senate. Any rejections of presidential nominees to the Supreme Court generally occur only after the Senate Judiciary Committee has recommended against a nominee's appointment. Few recent confirmations have been close; Clarence Thomas's 52–48 vote in 1991 and Samuel A. Alito Jr.'s 58–42 vote in 2006 were the closest in recent history. (To learn more about interest group participation in Supreme Court nominations, see Table 10.5.)

What role does the Senate play in judicial nominations? The Senate has the power to offer advice and consent on judicial nominees. They often hold hearings to assure that they have full information about prospective nominees. Here, Justice Felix Frankfurter testifies before the Judiciary Committee.

Photo courtesy: Thomas D. McAvoy/Time & Life Pictures/Getty Images

TABLE 10.5 Interest Groups Appearing in Selected Senate Judiciary Committee Hearings

Nominee	Year	Liberal	Conservative	ABA Rating	Senate Vote
Stevens	1976	2	3	Well-Q	98–0
Scalia	1986	5	7	Well-Q	98–0
Bork	1987	18	68	Well-Q[a]	42–58
Kennedy	1987	12	14	Well-Q	97–0
Souter	1990	13	8	Well-Q	90–9
Thomas	1991	30	46	Q[b]	52–48
Ginsburg	1993	6	5	Well-Q	96–3
Breyer	1994	8	3	Well-Q	87–9
Roberts	2005	5	4	Well-Q	78–22
Alito	2005	2	1	Well-Q	58–42

[a]Four ABA committee members evaluated him as Not Qualified.
[b]Two ABA committee members evaluated him as Not Qualified.
Source: Karen O'Connor, Alixandra B. Yanus, and Linda Mancillas Patterson, "Where Have All the Interest Groups Gone? An Analysis of Interest Group Participation in Presidential Nominations to the Supreme Court of the United States," in Allan J. Cigler and Burdett A. Loomis, eds., *Interest Group Politics*, 7th ed. (Washington, DC: CQ Press, 2007).

The Supreme Court Today

Given the judicial system's vast size and substantial, although often indirect, power over so many aspects of our lives, it is surprising that so many Americans know next to nothing about the judicial system, in general, and the U.S. Supreme Court, in particular.

Even after the attention the Court received during the nominations of John G. Roberts Jr. and Samuel A. Alito Jr., more than half of those Americans surveyed in early 2006 could not name one member of the Court; virtually no one could name all nine members of the Court. As revealed in Table 10.6, Sandra Day O'Connor, the first woman appointed to the Court, was the most well-known justice. Still, only about a quarter of those polled could name her.

While much of this ignorance can be blamed on the American public's lack of interest, the Court has also taken great pains to ensure its privacy and sense of decorum. Its rites and rituals contribute to the Court's mystique and encourage a "cult of the robe."[30] Consider, for example, the way Supreme Court proceedings are conducted. Oral arguments are not televised, and deliberations concerning the outcome of cases are conducted in utmost secrecy. In contrast, C-SPAN brings us daily coverage of various congressional hearings and floor debate on bills and important national issues, and CNN (and sometimes other networks) provides extensive coverage of many important state court trials. The Supreme Court, however, remains adamant in its refusal to televise its proceedings—including public oral arguments, although it now allows the release of same-day audio tapes of oral arguments. (To learn about efforts to open Supreme Court proceedings to the media, see Politics Now: Should Supreme Court Proceedings Be Televised?)

TABLE **10.6** Don't Know Much About the Supreme Court

Supreme Court Justice	Percentage Who Could Name
Sandra Day O'Connor	27
Clarence Thomas	21
John G. Roberts Jr.	16
Antonin Scalia	13
Ruth Bader Ginsburg	12
Anthony Kennedy	7
David Souter	5
Stephen Breyer	3
John Paul Stevens	3

Source: Findlaw.com poll, January 10, 2006, http://company.findlaw.com/pr/2006/011006.supremes.html.

Case Overload

You Are a Supreme Court Justice Deciding a Free Speech Case

Deciding to hear a case

Just over 9,600 cases were filed at the Supreme Court in its 2007–2008 term; 75 were heard, and 74 decisions were issued. In contrast, from 1790 to 1801, the Court heard only 87 cases under its appellate jurisdiction.[31] In the Court's early years, most of the justices' workload involved their circuit-riding duties. From 1862 to 1866, only 240 cases were decided. Creation of the courts of appeals in 1891 resulted in an immediate reduction in Supreme Court filings—from 600 in 1890 to 275 in 1892.[32] As recently as the 1940s, fewer than 1,000 cases were filed annually. Filings increased at a dramatic rate until the mid 1990s, shot up again in the late 1990s, and generally have now leveled off. (To learn more about the Court's caseload, see Figure 10.3.)

The content of the Court's docket is every bit as significant as its size. During the 1930s, cases requiring the interpretation of constitutional law began to take a growing portion of the Court's workload, leading the Court to take a more important role in the policy-making process. At that time, only 5 percent of the Court's cases involved questions concerning the Bill of Rights. By the late 1950s, one-third of filed cases involved such questions; by the 1960s, half did.[33]

Justices can also exercise a significant role in policy making and politics by opting not to hear a case. For example, in late 2004, after the Court refused to hear an appeal of a Massachusetts Supreme Court decision requiring the state to sanction same-sex marriages, President George W. Bush and others renewed their calls for a constitutional amendment to ban same-sex marriage.

As discussed earlier in the chapter, the Court has two types of jurisdiction. The Court has original jurisdiction in "all Cases affecting Ambassadors, other public Ministers and Consuls, and those in which a State shall be a party." It is rare for more than two or three of these cases to come to the Court in a year. The second kind of

POLITICS NOW

Source: CQ WEEKLY – WEEKLY REPORT, LEGAL AFFAIRS   December 10, 2007   Page 3665

Should Supreme Court Proceedings Be Televised?

Supreme Court TV Bill Snags on Procedure

CAITLIN WEBBER AND KEITH PERINE

The Senate Judiciary Committee endorsed legislation last week that would compel the Supreme Court to televise its public proceedings, but the panel will have to revisit the issue this week because of a procedural snag.

Members voted, 11–7, in favor of the bill (S 344), which would require TV coverage of the Court's open sessions unless a majority of justices vote to block cameras for a particular case. Currently, the Court releases only transcripts and audio recordings.

Technically, however, the panel did not approve the measure. Under committee rules, which allow for proxy voting, a majority of senators must vote in person for a bill in order for it to be approved. The tally of those senators who were present was 5–5. The committee has scheduled another vote for Dec. 13 to ratify last week's vote.

A majority of justices on the bench have spoken out against allowing cameras. Justice Anthony M. Kennedy told the Judiciary Committee in February that televised Court proceedings would "change our collegial dynamic. And we hope that this respect that separation of powers and checks and balances implies would persuade you to accept our judgment in this regard."

Dianne Feinstein of California was the only Democrat to vote against the measure, saying it would "have a negative impact on the way justices relate to each other."

"Congress should not tell the Court how to run its operations, just as the Court should not tell us how to run Congress," she said.

Judiciary's ranking Republican, Arlen Specter of Pennsylvania, who introduced the bipartisan bill in January, disagreed. "We have substantial authority . . . .Congress has also established time limits that the Supreme Court and the other federal courts have to observe," he said.

Chief Justice John G. Roberts Jr. has moved to better publicize the court's proceedings. The Court now publishes same-day transcripts and some audio recordings of oral arguments.

Discussion Questions

1. *Should Congress have the authority to compel the Supreme Court to televise its proceedings? Why or why not?*
2. *How might television cameras change the dynamics of legal proceedings before the Supreme Court?*
3. *What are other possible reasons that would explain why the justices are resistant to having cameras in the courtroom?*

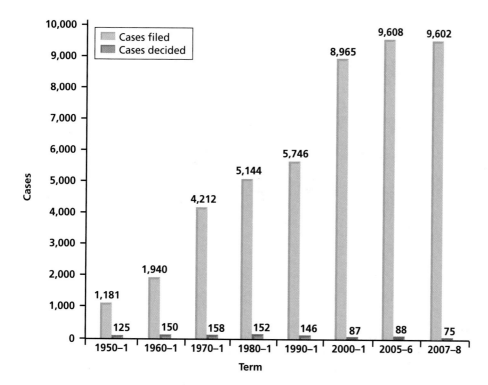

FIGURE 10.3 Supreme Court Caseload, 1950–2008 Terms Cases the Supreme Court chooses to hear (represented by brown bars) represent a tiny fraction of the total number of cases filed with the Court (represented by green bars).

Source: Administrative Office of the Courts; Supreme Court Public Information Office.

jurisdiction enjoyed by the Court is its appellate jurisdiction. The Court is not expected to exercise its appellate jurisdiction simply to correct errors of other courts. Instead, appeal to the Supreme Court should be taken only if the case presents important issues of law, or what is termed "a substantial federal question." Since 1988, nearly all appellate cases that have gone to the Supreme Court arrived there on a petition for a **writ of *certiorari*** (from the Latin "to be informed"), which is a request for the Supreme Court—at its discretion—to order up the records of the lower courts for purposes of review. (To learn more about this process, see Figure 10.4.)

writ of *certiorari*
A request for the Court to order up the records from a lower court to review the case.

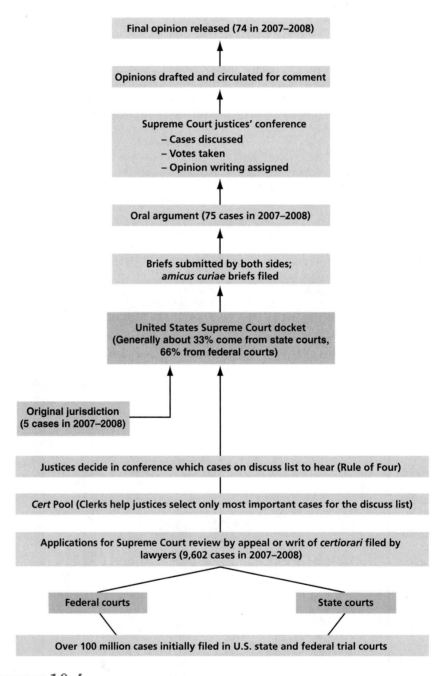

FIGURE 10.4 How a Case Gets to the Supreme Court
This figure illustrates both how cases get on the Court's docket and what happens after a case is accepted for review.

WRITS OF *CERTIORARI* AND THE RULE OF FOUR   The Supreme Court controls its own caseload through the *certiorari* process, deciding which cases it wants to hear, and rejecting most cases that come to it. All petitions, or writs of *certiorari*, must meet two criteria:

1. The case must come from either a U.S. court of appeals, a special three-judge district court, or a state court of last resort.
2. The case must involve a federal question. Thus, the case must present questions of federal constitutional law or involve a federal statute, action, or treaty. The reasons that the Court should accept the case for review and legal argument supporting that position are set out in the petition for a writ of *certiorari*.

The clerk of the Court transmits petitions for writs of *certiorari* first to the chief justice's office, where clerks review the petitions, and then to the individual justices' offices. On the Roberts Court, all of the justices except Justice John Paul Stevens (who allows his clerks great individual authority in selecting the cases for him to review) participate in what is called the *cert* pool.[34] Pool participants review their assigned fraction of petitions and share their notes with each other. Those cases that the justices deem noteworthy are then placed on what is called the discuss list prepared by the chief justice's clerks and circulated to the chambers of the other justices. All others are dead listed and go no further. Only about 30 percent of submitted petitions make it to the discuss list. During one of the justices' weekly conference meetings, the cases on the discuss list are reviewed. The chief justice speaks first, then the rest of the justices, according to seniority. The decision process ends when the justices vote, and by custom, *certiorari* is granted according to the **Rule of Four**—when at least four justices vote to hear a case.

Rule of Four
At least four justices of the Supreme Court must vote to consider a case before it can be heard.

THE ROLE OF CLERKS   As early as 1850, the justices of the Supreme Court beseeched Congress to approve the hiring of a clerk to assist each justice. Congress denied the request, so when Justice Horace Gray hired the first law clerk in 1882, he paid the clerk himself. Justice Gray's clerk was a top graduate of Harvard Law School whose duties included cutting Justice Gray's hair and running personal errands. Finally, in 1886, Congress authorized each justice to hire a stenographer clerk for $1,600 a year.

Who sits on the Roberts Court? Back row, from left to right: Justices Stephen Breyer, Clarence Thomas, Ruth Bader Ginsburg, and Samuel A. Alito Jr. Front row, from left to right: Justices Anthony Kennedy and John Paul Stevens, Chief Justice John G. Roberts Jr., Justices Antonin Scalia and David Souter.

Photo courtesy: Supreme Court Historical Society

You Are a Clerk to Supreme Court Justice Judith Gray

Clerks typically are selected from candidates at the top of the graduating classes of prestigious law schools. They perform a variety of tasks, ranging from searching for arcane facts to playing tennis or taking walks with the justices. Clerks spend most of their time researching material, reading and summarizing cases, and helping justices write opinions. Clerks also make the first pass through the petitions that come to the Court, undoubtedly influencing which cases get a second look. Just how much help they provide in the writing of opinions is unknown.[35] (To learn more about what clerks do, see Table 10.7.)

TABLE 10.7 What do Supreme Court Clerks Do?

Supreme Court clerks are among the best and brightest recent law school graduates. Almost all first clerk for a judge on one of the courts of appeals. After their Supreme Court clerkship, former clerks are in high demand. Firms often pay signing bonuses of up to $200,000 to attract clerks, who earn over $180,000 their first year in private practice.

Tasks of a Supreme Court clerk include the following:

- Perform initial screening of the 9,000 or so petitions that come to the Court each term
- Draft memos to summarize the facts and issues in each case, recommending whether the case should be accepted by the Court for full review
- Write "bench memos" summarizing an accepted case and suggesting questions for oral argument
- Write the first draft of an opinion
- Serve as informal conduit for communicating and negotiating with other justices' chambers as to the final wording of an opinion

Over time, the number of clerks employed by the justices has increased. Through the 1946 to 1969 terms, most justices employed two clerks. By 1970, most had three clerks, and by 1980, all but three justices had four clerks. In 2009, the nine active justices and retired Justice Sandra Day O'Connor employed a total of thirty-eight clerks. This growth in the number of clerks has had many interesting ramifications for the Court. As the number of clerks has grown, so have the number and length of the Court's opinions.[36] And, until recently, the number of cases decided annually increased as more help was available to the justices.

The relationship between clerks and the justices for whom they work is close and confidential, and many aspects of the relationship are kept secret.[37] Clerks may sometimes talk among themselves about the views and personalities of their justices, but rarely has a clerk leaked such information to the press. In 1998, a former clerk to Justice Harry A. Blackmun broke the silence. Edward Lazarus published an insider's account of how the Court really works.[38] He argued that the justices give their young, often ideological, clerks far too much power.

How Does a Case Survive the Process?

It can be difficult to determine why the Court decides to hear a particular case. Sometimes it involves a perceived national emergency, as was the case with appeals concerning the outcome of the 2000 presidential election. The Court does not offer reasons, and "the standards by which the justices decide to grant or deny review are highly personalized and necessarily discretionary," noted former Chief Justice Earl Warren.[39] Political scientists nonetheless have attempted to determine the characteristics of the cases the Court accepts; not surprisingly, they are similar to those that help a case get on the discuss list. Among the cues are the following:

- The federal government is the party asking for review.
- The case involves conflict among the courts of appeals.
- The case presents a civil rights or civil liberties question.
- The case involves the ideological or policy preferences of the justices.
- The case has significant social or political interest, as evidenced by the presence of interest group *amicus curiae* briefs.

solicitor general
The fourth-ranking member of the Department of Justice; responsible for handling all appeals on behalf of the U.S. government to the Supreme Court.

THE FEDERAL GOVERNMENT One of the most important cues for predicting whether the Court will hear a case is the solicitor general's position. The **solicitor general**, appointed by the president, is the fourth-ranking member of the Department of Justice and is responsible for handling most appeals on behalf of the U.S. government to the Supreme Court. The solicitor's staff resembles a small, specialized law firm within the Department of Justice. But, because this office has such a special relationship with the Supreme Court, even having a suite of offices within the Supreme Court building, the solicitor general often is referred to as the Court's "ninth and a half member."[40] Moreover, the solicitor general, on behalf of the U.S. government, appears as a party or as an *amicus curiae* in more than 50 percent of the cases heard by the Court each term. **Amicus curiae** means friend of the court. *Amici* may file briefs or even appear to argue their interests orally before the Court.

amicus curiae
"Friend of the court"; *amici* may file briefs or even appear to argue their interests orally before the court.

This special relationship helps to explain the overwhelming success the solicitor general's office enjoys before the Supreme Court. The Court generally accepts 70 to 80 percent of the cases where the U.S. government is the petitioning party, compared with about 5 percent of all others.[41] But, because of this special relationship, the solicitor general often ends up playing two conflicting roles: representing in Court both the president's policy interests and the broader interests of the United States. At times, solicitors find these two roles difficult to reconcile. Former Solicitor General Rex E. Lee (1981–1985), for example, noted that on more than one occasion he refused to make arguments in Court that had been advanced by the Reagan administration (a stand that ultimately forced him to resign his position).[42]

CONFLICT AMONG THE COURTS OF APPEALS Conflict among the lower courts is another reason that the justices take cases. When interpretations of constitutional or federal law are involved, the justices seem to want consistency throughout the federal court system. Often these conflicts occur when important civil rights or civil liberties questions arise. Political scientists have noted that the justices' ideological leanings play a role.[43] It is not uncommon to see conservative justices voting to hear cases to overrule liberal lower court decisions, or vice versa. Justices also take cases when several circuit courts are in disagreement over a main issue.

INTEREST GROUP PARTICIPATION A quick way for the justices to gauge the ideological ramifications of a particular civil rights or liberties case is by the nature and amount of interest group participation. Richard C. Cortner has noted that "Cases do not arrive on the doorstep of the Supreme Court like orphans in the night."[44] Instead, most cases heard by the Supreme Court involve either the government or an interest group—either as the sponsoring party or as an *amicus curiae*. Liberal groups, such as the American Civil Liberties Union, People for the American Way, or the NAACP Legal Defense Fund, and conservative groups, including the Washington Legal Foundation, Concerned Women for America, and the American Center for Law and Justice, routinely sponsor cases or file *amicus* briefs either urging the Court to hear a case or asking it to deny *certiorari*.

The positions of both parties in a case are often echoed or expanded in *amicus curiae* briefs filed by interested parties, especially interest groups. Interest groups also provide the Court with information not necessarily contained in the party briefs, help write briefs, and assist in practice oral arguments during moot court sessions. In these moot court sessions, the lawyer who will argue the case before the nine justices goes through several complete rehearsals, with prominent lawyers and law professors role playing the various justices.

Since the 1970s, interest groups increasingly have used the *amicus* brief as a way to lobby the Court. Because litigation is so expensive, few individuals have the money (or time or interest) to pursue a perceived wrong all the way to the U.S. Supreme Court. All sorts of interest groups, then, find that joining ongoing cases through *amicus* briefs is a useful way of advancing their policy preferences. Major cases such as *Brown* v. *Board of Education* (1954) (see chapter 6), *Planned Parenthood of Southeastern Pennsylvania* v. *Casey* (1992) (see chapter 5), and *Grutter* v. *Bollinger* (2003) (see chapter 6) all attracted large numbers of *amicus* briefs as part of interest groups' efforts to lobby the judiciary and bring about desired political objectives.[45] (To learn more about the types of groups that participate before the Court, see Table 10.8.)

Research by political scientists has found that "not only does [an *amicus*] brief in favor of *certiorari* significantly improve the chances of a case being accepted, but two,

TABLE **10.8**   Amicus Curiae Briefs in Companion Affirmative Action Cases: *Grutter* v. *Bollinger* and *Gratz* v. *Bollinger* (2003)

For the Petitioners

Asian American Legal Foundation	Claremont Institute Center for	Pacific Legal Foundation
Cato Institute	Constitutional Jurisprudence	Reason Foundation
Center for Equal Opportunity et al.	Law Professors	State of Florida and Governor Jeb Bush
Center for Individual Freedom	Massachusetts School of Law	United States
Center for the Advancement of Capitalism	Michigan Association of Scholars	Ward Connerly
Center for New Black Leadership	National Association of Scholars	

For the Respondents

65 Leading American Businesses	Deans of Law Schools	National Coalition of Blacks for Reparations in
AFL-CIO	General Motors Corporation	America et al.
American Bar Association	Graduate Management Admission Council et al.	National Education Association
American Council on Education et al.	Harvard Black Law Students Association et al.	National School Boards Association
American Educational Research Association et al.	Harvard University et al.	National Urban League et al.
American Jewish Committee et al.	Hayden Family	New America Alliance
American Law Deans Association	Hispanic National Bar Association	New Mexico Hispanic Bar Association et al.
American Media Companies	Howard University	New York City Council Members
American Psychological Association	Human Rights Advocates et al.	New York State Black and Puerto Rican Legislative
American Sociological Association	Indiana University	Caucus
Amherst College et al.	King County Bar Association	Northeastern University
Arizona State University College of Law	Latino Organizations	NOW Legal Defense and Education Fund et al.
Association of American Law Schools	Lawyers Committee for Civil Rights Under	School of Law of the University of North Carolina
Association of American Medical Colleges	Law et al.	Social Scientists
Authors of the Texas Ten Percent Plan	Leadership Conference on Civil Rights et al.	Society of American Law Teachers
Bay Mills Indian Community et al.	Massachusetts Institute of Technology et al.	State of New Jersey
Black Women Lawyers Association of Greater	Members of Congress (3 briefs)	State of Maryland et al.
Chicago	Members of the Pennsylvania General	Students of Howard University Law School
Boston Bar Association et al.	Assembly et al.	UCLA School of Law Students of Color
Carnegie Mellon University et al.	Michigan Black Law Alumni Association	United Negro College Fund et al.
City of Philadelphia et al.	Michigan Governor Jennifer Granholm	University of Michigan Asian Pacific American Law
Clinical Legal Educational Association	Military Leaders	Students Association
Coalition for Economic Equity et al.	MTV Networks	University of Pittsburgh et al.
Columbia University et al.	NAACP Legal Defense and Education Fund et al.	Veterans of the Southern Civil Rights Movement
Committee of Concerned Black Graduates of	National Asian Pacific American Legal	et al.
ABA Accredited Law Schools	Consortium et al.	
Current Law Students at Accredited Law Schools	National Center for Fair and Open Testing	

For Neither Party

Anti-Defamation League	Equal Employment Opportunity Council
BP America	Exxon Mobil Corporation
Criminal Justice Legal Foundation	

three and four briefs improve the chances even more."[46] Clearly, it's the more the merrier, whether the briefs are filed for or against granting review.[47] (To learn how you can participate in court cases, see Ideas into Action: Be a Friend of the Court.)

Hearing and Deciding the Case

Once a case is accepted for review, a flurry of activity begins. Lawyers on both sides of the case begin to prepare their written arguments for submission to the Court. In these briefs, lawyers cite prior case law and make arguments as to why the Court should find in favor of their client.

ORAL ARGUMENTS   Once a case is accepted by the Court for full review, and after briefs and *amicus* briefs are submitted on each side, oral argument takes place. The Supreme Court's annual term begins the first Monday in October, as it has since the

Be a Friend of the Court

Amicus curiae briefs have become an increasingly popular way for interest groups and individuals to express their points of view to state supreme courts as well as the U.S. Supreme Court. This form of judicial lobbying allows citizens to become active participants in what is often viewed as the most insulated branch of government.

State supreme courts and the U.S. Supreme Court adjudicate a number of issues of concern to students. A number of state high courts, for example, have dealt with an ongoing stream of cases dealing with how to finance public education. And, the U.S. Supreme Court has dealt with cases involving mandatory student fees and school vouchers (see chapter 5).

Recently, a number of student groups, including Students for Sensible Drug Policy, participated in the U.S. Supreme Court case of *Morse* v. *Frederick* (2007). This case, also known

as the "bong hits for Jesus" case, asked whether the First Amendment allows public schools to restrict the display of signs promoting drug use at school-sponsored events. As a free speech issue, *Morse* was a matter of concern for students and student rights groups across the country. The Court eventually ruled that schools could prohibit such signage.

Explore the docket of the U.S. Supreme Court or your state's high court and identify the cases that may be relevant to students like you. Then, consider:

- What rules govern *amicus* briefs in your state's high court? In the U.S. Supreme Court?
- Are you active in any groups that might file a relevant *amicus* brief? How would you go about preparing this sort of brief? What resources would you need?
- What other ways might you get involved in litigation in your state's high court? The U.S. Supreme Court?

late 1800s, and generally runs through late June. Justices hear oral arguments from the beginning of the term until early April. Special cases, such as *U.S.* v. *Nixon* (1974), which involved President Richard M. Nixon's refusal to turn over tapes of Oval Office conversations to a special prosecutor investigating a break-in at the Democratic Party headquarters in the Watergate building, have been heard even later in the year.[48] During the term, "sittings," periods of about two weeks in which cases are heard, alternate with "recesses," also about two weeks long. Oral arguments usually are heard Monday through Wednesday.

Oral argument generally is limited to the immediate parties in the case, although it is not uncommon for the U.S. solicitor general to appear to argue orally as an *amicus curiae*. Oral argument at the Court is fraught with time-honored tradition and ceremony. At precisely ten o'clock every morning when the Court is in session, the Court marshal, dressed in a formal morning coat, emerges to intone "Oyez! Oyez! Oyez!" as the nine justices emerge from behind a reddish-purple velvet curtain to take their places on the raised and slightly angled bench. The chief justice sits in the middle. The remaining justices sit to the left and right alternating in seniority.

Almost all attorneys are allotted one half hour to present their cases, and this time includes that required to answer questions from the bench. As a lawyer approaches the mahogany lectern, a green light goes on, indicating that the attorney's time has begun. A white light flashes when five minutes remain. When a red light goes on, Court practice mandates that counsel stop immediately. One famous piece of Court lore told to all attorneys concerns a counsel who continued talking and reading from his prepared argument after the red light went on. When he looked up, he found an empty bench—the justices had risen quietly and departed while he continued to talk. On another occasion, Chief Justice Charles Evans Hughes stopped a leader of the New York bar in the middle of the word "if."

Although many Court watchers have tried to figure out how a particular justice will vote based on the questioning at oral argument, most researchers find that the nature and number of questions asked do not help much in predicting the outcome of a case. Nevertheless, many scholars believe that oral argument has several important functions. First, it is the only opportunity for even a small portion of the public (who may attend the hearings) and the press to observe the workings of the Court. Second, it assures lawyers that the justices have heard the parties' arguments, and it forces lawyers to focus on arguments believed important by the justices. Last, it provides the Court with additional information, especially concerning the Court's broader political role, an issue not usually addressed in written briefs. For example, the justices can ask how many people might be affected by its decision or where the Court (and country) would be heading if a case were decided in a particular way. Justice Stephen Breyer also notes that oral arguments are a good way for the justices to try to highlight certain issues for other justices.

THE CONFERENCE AND THE VOTE   The justices meet in closed conference once a week when the Court is hearing oral arguments. Since the ascendancy of Chief Justice Roger B. Taney to the Court in 1836, the justices have begun each conference session with a round of handshaking. Once the door to the conference room closes, no others are allowed to enter. The justice with the least seniority acts as the doorkeeper for the other eight, communicating with those waiting outside to fill requests for documents, water, and any other necessities.

Conferences highlight the importance and power of the chief justice, who presides over them and makes the initial presentation of each case. Each individual justice then discusses the case in order of his or her seniority on the Court, with the most senior justice speaking next. Most accounts of the decision-making process reveal that at this point some justices try to change the minds of others, but that most enter the conference room with a clear idea of how they will vote on each case.

During the Rehnquist Court, the justices generally voted at the same time they discussed each case, with each justice speaking only once. Initial conference votes were not final, and justices were allowed to change their minds before final votes were taken later. The Roberts Court is much more informal than the Rehnquist Court. The justices' regular Friday conferences now last longer and, unlike the conferences headed by Rehnquist, the new chief justice encourages discussion.[49]

WRITING OPINIONS   After the Court has reached a decision in conference, the justices must formulate a formal opinion of the Court. If the chief justice is in the majority, he selects the justice who will write the opinion. This privilege enables him to wield tremendous power and is a very important strategic decision. If the chief justice is in the minority, the assignment falls to the most senior justice in the majority.

The opinion of the Court can take several different forms. Most decisions are reached by a majority opinion written by one member of the Court to reflect the views of at least five of the justices. This opinion usually sets out the legal reasoning justifying the decision, and this legal reasoning becomes a precedent for deciding future cases. The reasoning behind any decision is often as important as the outcome. Under the system of *stare decisis*, both are likely to be relied on as precedent later by lower courts confronted with cases involving similar issues.

In the process of creating the final opinion of the Court, informal caucusing and negotiation often take place, as justices may hold out for word changes or other modifications as a condition of their continued support of the majority opinion. This negotiation process can lead to divisions in the Court's majority. When this occurs, the Court may be forced to decide cases by plurality opinions, which attract the support of three or four justices. While these decisions do not have the precedential value of majority opinions, they nonetheless have been used by the Court to decide many major cases.

Justices who agree with the outcome of the case but not with the legal rationale for the decision may file concurring opinions to express their differing approach. For example, Justice Stephen Breyer filed a concurring opinion in *Clinton* v. *Jones* (1997). Although a unanimous Court ruled that a sitting president was not immune to civil lawsuits, Breyer wanted to express his belief that a federal judge could not schedule judicial proceedings that might interfere with a president's public duties.[50]

Justices who do not agree with the outcome of a case file dissenting opinions. Although these opinions have little direct legal value, they can be an important indicator of legal thought on the Court and are an excellent platform for justices to note their personal and legal disagreements with other members of the Court. Justice Antonin Scalia is often noted for writing particularly stinging dissents. In his dissent in *Atkins* v. *Virginia*, a 2002 death penalty case, for example, Justice Scalia attacked Justice John Paul Stevens's reference to international norms in the majority opinion, writing, "But the Prize for the Court's Most Feeble Effort to fabricate 'national consensus' must go to its appeal (deservedly relegated to a footnote) to the views of . . . the so-called 'world community.' . . . We must never forget that it is a Constitution for the United States of America that we are expounding . . . . [W]here there is not first a settled consensus among our own people, the views of other nations, however enlightened the Justices of this Court may think them to be, cannot be imposed upon Americans through the Constitution."[51]

Judicial Philosophy and Decision Making

Justices do not make decisions in a vacuum. Principles of *stare decisis* dictate that the justices follow the law of previous cases in deciding cases at hand. But, a variety of legal and extra-legal factors have also been found to affect Supreme Court decision making.

Judicial Philosophy, Original Intent, and Ideology

Legal scholars long have argued that judges decide cases based on the Constitution and their reading of various statutes. Determining what the Framers meant—if that is even possible today—often appears to be based on an individual jurist's philosophy.

One of the primary issues concerning judicial decision making focuses on what is called the activism/restraint debate. Advocates of **judicial restraint** argue that courts should allow the decisions of other branches to stand, even when they offend a judge's own principles. Restraintists defend their position by asserting that the federal courts are composed of unelected judges, which makes the judicial branch the least democratic branch of government. Consequently, the courts should defer policy making to other branches of government as much as possible.

Restraintists refer to *Roe* v. *Wade* (1973), the case that liberalized abortion laws, as a classic example of **judicial activism** run amok. They maintain that the Court should have deferred policy making on this sensitive issue to the states or to the elected branches of the federal government.

Advocates of judicial restraint generally agree that judges should be **strict constructionists**; that is, they should interpret the Constitution as it was written and intended by the Framers. They argue that in determining the constitutionality of a statute or policy, the Court should rely on the explicit meanings of the clauses in the document, which can be clarified by looking at the intent of the Framers.

Advocates of judicial activism contend that judges should use their power broadly to further justice, especially in the areas of equality and personal liberty. Activists argue that it is appropriate for the courts to correct injustices committed by the other branches of government. Implicit in this argument is the notion that courts need to protect oppressed minorities.[52]

Activists point to *Brown* v. *Board of Education* (1954) as an excellent example of the importance of judicial activism.[53] In *Brown*, the Supreme Court ruled that racial

judicial restraint
A philosophy of judicial decision making that argues courts should allow the decisions of other branches of government to stand, even when they offend a judge's own sense of principles.

judicial activism
A philosophy of judicial decision making that argues judges should use their power broadly to further justice, especially in the areas of equality and personal liberty.

strict constructionist
An approach to constitutional interpretation that emphasizes the Framers' original intentions.

segregation in public schools violated the equal protection clause of the Fourteenth Amendment. Segregation nonetheless was practiced after passage of the Fourteenth Amendment. An activist would point out that if the Court had not reinterpreted provisions of the amendment, many states probably would still have laws or policies mandating segregation in public schools.

Although judicial activists are often considered politically liberal and restraintists politically conservative, in recent years a new brand of conservative judicial activism has become prevalent. Liberal activist decisions often expanded the rights of political and legal minorities. But, conservative activist judges view their positions as an opportunity to issue broad rulings that impose their own political beliefs and policies on the country at large.

Some scholars argue that this increased conservative judicial activism has had an effect on the Court's reliance on *stare decisis* and adherence to precedent. Chief Justice William H. Rehnquist noted that while "*stare decisis* is a cornerstone of our legal system . . . it has less power in constitutional cases."[54]

Models of Judicial Decision Making

Most political scientists who study judicial behavior conclude that a variety of forces shape judicial decision making. Many have attempted to explain how judges vote by integrating a variety of models to offer a more complete picture of how judges make decisions.[55] Many of those models attempt to take into account justices' individual behavioral characteristics and attitudes as well as the fact patterns of the case. The explanatory power of these models is often difficult to discern, and even those who have built their careers on constructing models note their inadequacies. Passage of time, the internal dynamics of the Court, and assumptions of presumed political values often can wreak havoc with these models.[56] Still, it is important to recognize the ways in which political scientists have attempted to evaluate and predict how justices will vote.

BEHAVIORAL CHARACTERISTICS Originally, some political scientists argued that social background differences, including childhood experiences, religious values, education, earlier political and legal careers, and political party loyalties, are likely to influence how a judge evaluates the facts and legal issues presented in any given case. Justice Harry A. Blackmun's service at the Mayo Clinic often is pointed to as a reason that his opinion for the Court in *Roe* v. *Wade* (1973) was grounded so thoroughly in medical evidence. Similarly, Justice Potter Stewart, who was generally considered a moderate on most civil liberties issues, usually took a more liberal position on cases dealing with freedom of the press. Why? It may be that Stewart's early job as a newspaper reporter made him more sensitive to these claims.

THE ATTITUDINAL MODEL The attitudinal approach links judicial attitudes with decision making.[57] The attitudinal model holds that Supreme Court justices decide cases according to their personal preferences toward issues of public policy. Among some of the factors used to derive attitudes are a justice's party identification,[58] the party of the appointing president, and the liberal/conservative leanings of a justice.[59] For example, under the attitudinal model, a liberal justice appointed by a Democratic president would be more likely to decide an abortion case in favor of the pro-choice point of view. Similarly, a conservative justice appointed by a Republican president would favor measures to support a free-market economy. Both justices would adapt their interpretations of the law to support these ideological beliefs.

THE STRATEGIC MODEL   The strategic model argues that justices temper legal doctrine and their own policy beliefs with concerns about how other internal and external variables will affect and be affected by their decision. In sharp contrast to the attitudinal model, the strategic model suggests that justices are prospective thinkers who act to achieve and preserve their policy and personal goals over the long term. Scholars have accumulated a body of evidence in support of the strategic model. They have found, for example, that justices are strategic in their votes for *certiorari*.[60] Justices may not vote to hear a case, no matter how interesting, if they suspect they will lose in the final decision.

Other internal and external factors may influence strategic decisions. Evidence shows that the chief justice often assigns final opinions to justices based on the organizational needs of the Court.[61] And, at least under some conditions, justices pay attention to their colleagues' preferences in crafting majority opinions.[62] Finally, the Supreme Court appears to be responsive to public opinion,[63] other courts,[64] and other institutions.[65]

Public Opinion

Many political scientists have examined the role of public opinion in Supreme Court decision making. Not only do the justices read legal briefs and hear oral arguments, but they also read newspapers, watch television, and have some knowledge of public opinion—especially on controversial issues.

Whether or not public opinion actually influences justices, it can act as a check on the power of the courts and as an energizing factor. Activist periods on the Supreme Court generally have corresponded to periods of social or economic crisis. For example, the Marshall Court supported a strong national government, much to the chagrin of a series of pro-states' rights Democratic-Republican presidents in the early crisis-ridden years of the republic. Similarly, the Court capitulated to political pressures and public opinion when, after 1936, it reversed many of its earlier decisions that had blocked President Franklin D. Roosevelt's New Deal legislation.

The courts, especially the Supreme Court, also can be the direct target of public opinion. When *Webster* v. *Reproductive Health Services* (1989) was about to come before the Supreme Court, the Court was subjected to unprecedented lobbying as groups and individuals on both sides of the abortion issue marched and sent appeals to the Court. Mail at the Court, which usually averaged about 1,000 pieces a day, rose to an astronomical 46,000 pieces per day, virtually paralyzing normal lines of communication.

The Supreme Court also appears to affect public opinion. Political scientists have found that the Court's initial rulings on controversial issues such as abortion or capital punishment positively influence public opinion in the direction of the Court's opinion. However, this research also finds that subsequent decisions have little effect.[66] The extent to which the public and the Court are in agreement on a variety of controversial issues is shown in Table 10.9.

TABLE **10.9** The Supreme Court and the American Public

In recent years, the Court's rulings have agreed with or diverged from public opinion on various questions, such as:

Issue	Case	Court Decision	Public Opinion
Should homosexual relations between consenting adults be legal?	*Lawrence* v. *Texas* (2003)	Yes	Maybe (50%)
Should local school boards be restricted in using race to assign children to schools?	*Parents Involved in Community Schools* v. *Seattle School District 1* (2007)	Yes	No (56%)
Should the procedure known as partial-birth abortion be banned except when a woman's life is at risk?	*Gonzales* v. *Carhart* (2007)	Yes	Yes (55%)
Is the death penalty constitutional?	*Gregg* v. *Georgia* (1976)	Yes	Yes (72% favor)

Source: Table compiled from Lexis-Nexis RPOLL.

The Court also is dependent on the public for its prestige as well as for compliance with its decisions. In times of war and other emergencies, for example, the Court frequently has decided cases in ways that commentators have attributed to the sway of public opinion and political exigencies. In *Korematsu* v. *U.S.* (1944), for example, the high Court upheld the obviously unconstitutional internment of Japanese American citizens during World War II.[67] Moreover, Chief Justice William H. Rehnquist himself once suggested that the Court's restriction on presidential authority in *Youngstown Sheet & Tube Co.* v. *Sawyer* (1952), which invalidated President Harry S Truman's seizure of the nation's steel mills, was largely attributable to Truman's unpopularity in light of the Korean War.[68]

Public confidence in the Court, as with other institutions of government, has ebbed and flowed. Public support for the Court was highest after the Court issued *U.S.* v. *Nixon* (1974).[69] At a time when Americans lost faith in the presidency due to the Watergate scandal, they could at least look to the Supreme Court to do the right thing. Although the numbers of Americans with confidence in the courts has fluctuated over time, in 2006, 40 percent of those sampled by Gallup International had a "great deal" or "quite a lot" of confidence in the Supreme Court.[70]

Toward Reform: Power, Policy Making, and the Court

All judges, whether they recognize it or not, make policy. The decisions of the Supreme Court, in particular, have a tremendous impact on American politics and policy. Over the last 250 years, the justices have helped to codify many of the major rights and liberties guaranteed to the citizens of the United States. Although justices need the cooperation of the executive and legislative branches to implement and enforce many of their decisions, it is safe to say that many policies we take for granted in the United States would not have come to fruition without the support of the Supreme Court. These include the right to privacy (see chapter 5) and equal rights for African Americans, women, Latino/as, gays and lesbians, and other minority groups (see chapter 6).

Several Courts have played particularly notable roles in the development of the judiciary's policy making role. As discussed earlier in the chapter, the Marshall Court played an important role in establishing the Supreme Court as a co-equal branch, including establishing the power of judicial review in *Marbury* v. *Madison* (1803). The Warren Court decided a number of civil rights cases that broadly expanded civil and political rights. These decisions drew a great deal of criticism but played a major role in broadening public understanding of the Court as a policy maker. The Rehnquist Court made numerous decisions related to federalism (see chapter 3), which caused observers to take note of the Court's ability to adjudicate conflicts between the federal government and the states. And, the Roberts Court reversed the general trend of the Court agreeing with executive actions during times of war by finding in 2008 that the Bush administration's denial of *habeas corpus* rights to prisoners being held at Guantanamo Bay was an unconstitutional exercise of presidential power.[71]

Policy Making

One measure of the power of the courts and their ability to make policy is that more than one hundred federal laws have been declared unconstitutional. Although many of these laws have not been particularly significant, others have. For example, in

Ashcroft v. *Free Speech Coalition* (2002), the Court ruled that the Child Online Protection Act, designed to prevent minors from viewing pornography over the Internet, was unconstitutional.[72] But, as noted in chapter 5, the Supreme Court upheld the Protect Act, a federal statute that criminalizes the pandering or soliciting of child pornography.[73]

Another measure of the policy-making power of the Supreme Court is its ability to overrule itself. Although the Court generally abides by the informal rule of *stare decisis*, by one count, it has overruled itself in more than 200 cases.[74] *Brown* v. *Board of Education* (1954), for example, overruled *Plessy* v. *Ferguson* (1896), thereby reversing years of constitutional interpretation concluding that racial segregation was not a violation of the Constitution. Moreover, in the past few years, the Court repeatedly has reversed earlier decisions in the areas of criminal defendants' rights, women's rights, and the establishment of religion, revealing its powerful role in determining national policy.

A measure of the growing power of the federal courts is the degree to which they now handle issues that had been considered political questions more appropriately left to the other branches of government to decide. Prior to 1962, for example, the Court refused to hear cases questioning the size (and population) of congressional districts, no matter how unequal they were.[75] The boundary of a legislative district was considered a political question. Then, in 1962, writing for the Court, Justice William Brennan Jr. concluded that simply because a case involved a political issue, it did not necessarily involve a political question. This opened up the floodgates to cases involving a variety of issues that the Court formerly had declined to address.[76]

Photo courtesy: Bettmann/Corbis

Do unpopular Supreme Court rulings threaten the nation? The Warren Court's broad expansions of civil and political rights led to a great deal of criticism, including a movement to impeach the chief justice. Here, two California billboards present contrasting views of Warren's performance.

Implementing Court Decisions

President Andrew Jackson, annoyed about a particular decision handed down by the Marshall Court, is alleged to have said, "John Marshall has made his decision; now let him enforce it." Jackson's statement raises a question: how do Supreme Court rulings translate into public policy? In fact, although judicial decisions carry legal and even moral authority, all courts must rely on other units of government to carry out their directives. If the president or members of Congress, for example, don't like a particular Supreme Court ruling, they can underfund programs needed to implement a decision or seek only lax enforcement. **Judicial implementation** refers to how and whether judicial decisions are translated into actual public policies affecting more than the immediate parties to the lawsuit.

How well a decision is implemented often depends on how well crafted or popular it is. Hostile reaction in the South to *Brown* v. *Board of Education* (1954) and the absence of precise guidelines to implement the decision meant that the ruling went largely unenforced for years. The *Brown* experience also highlights how much the Supreme Court needs the support of both federal and state courts as well as other governmental agencies to carry out its judgments. For example, you probably graduated from high school after 1992, when the Supreme Court ruled that public middle

judicial implementation
How and whether judicial decisions are translated into actual public policies affecting more than the immediate parties to a lawsuit.

Photo courtesy: Joe Raedle/Newsmakers/Getty Images

Can the Supreme Court ensure compliance with its decisions? This photo, taken in September 2000, illustrates the difficulty in implementing judicial decisions. Although the Supreme Court ruled in June 2000 that school-sponsored pre-game prayers at public schools were unconstitutional, prayers continued at many public school sporting events across the country.

school and high school graduations could not include a prayer, yet your own commencement ceremony may have included one.

The implementation of judicial decisions involves what political scientists call an implementing population and a consumer population.[77] The implementing population consists of those people responsible for carrying out a decision. It varies, depending on the policy and issues in question, but can include lawyers, judges, public officials, police officers and police departments, hospital administrators, government agencies, and corporations. In the case of school prayer, the implementing population could include teachers, school administrators, or school boards. The consumer population consists of those people who might be directly affected by a decision, that is, in this case, students and parents.

For effective implementation of a judicial decision, the first requirement is that the members of the implementing population must act to show that they understand the original decision. For example, the Supreme Court ruled in *Reynolds* v. *Sims* (1964) that every person should have an equally weighted vote in electing governmental representatives.[78] This "one person, one vote" rule might seem simple enough at first glance, but in practice it can be very difficult to understand. The implementing population in this case consists chiefly of state legislatures and local governments, which determine voting districts for federal, state, and local offices. If a state legislature draws districts in such a way that African American or Hispanic voters are spread thinly across a number of separate constituencies, the chances are slim that any particular district will elect a representative who is especially sensitive to minority concerns. Does that violate "equal representation"? (In practice, through the early 1990s, courts and the Department of Justice intervened in many cases to ensure that elected officials would include minority representation, only ultimately to be overruled by the Supreme Court.)[79]

The second requirement is that the implementing population actually must follow Court policy. Thus, when the Court ruled that men could not be denied admission to a state-sponsored nursing school, the implementing population—in this case, university administrators and the state board of regents governing the nursing school—had to enroll qualified male students.[80]

Judicial decisions are most likely to be implemented smoothly if responsibility for implementation is concentrated in the hands of a few highly visible public officials, such as the president or a governor. By the same token, these officials also can thwart or impede judicial intentions. Recall from chapter 6, for example, the effect of Governor Orval Faubus's initial refusal to allow black children to attend all-white public schools in Little Rock, Arkansas.

The third requirement for implementation is that the consumer population must be aware of the rights that a decision grants or denies them. Teenagers seeking an abortion, for example, are consumers of the Supreme Court's decisions on abortion. They need to know that most states require them to inform their parents of their intention to have an abortion or to get parental permission to do so. Similarly, criminal defendants and their lawyers are consumers of Court decisions and need to know, for instance, the implications of recent Court decisions for evidence presented at trial.

Thinking Globally
Judicial Independence in Pakistan

In November 2007, President Pervez Musharraf of Pakistan removed several Supreme Court justices and four judges from the provincial high courts immediately following his imposition of emergency rule in the country. A newly reconstituted Supreme Court legalized the dismissal of the judges, but opposition groups in the parliament vowed to reinstate the fired judges, who might be asked to rule on the constitutionality of the president's most recent election. Musharraf was later removed from office.

- How would the role of the Supreme Court change in the United States if the president was able to remove justices who did not support his or her policy agenda?
- How independent should the Supreme Court be? Does today's Court exercise too much influence over the policy-making process, or too little? Explain your reasoning.

WHAT SHOULD I HAVE LEARNED?

The judiciary and the legal process—on both the national and state levels—are complex and play a far more important role in the setting of policy than the Framers ever envisioned. To explain the judicial process and its evolution, we have asked the following questions:

- **What are the roots of the federal judiciary?**

  Many of the Framers viewed the judicial branch of government as little more than a minor check on the other two branches, ignoring Anti-Federalist concerns about an unelected judiciary and its potential for tyranny. The Judiciary Act of 1789 established the basic federal court system we have today. It was the Marshall Court (1801–1835), however, that interpreted the Constitution to include the Court's major power, that of judicial review.

- **What is the structure of the American legal system?**

  Ours is a dual judicial system consisting of the federal court system and the separate judicial systems of the fifty states. In each system there are two basic types of courts: trial courts and appellate courts. Each type deals with cases involving criminal and civil law. Original jurisdiction refers to a court's ability to hear a case as a trial court; appellate jurisdiction refers to a court's ability to review cases already decided by a trial court.

- **How is the federal court system organized?**

  The federal court system is made up of constitutional and legislative courts. Federal district courts, courts of appeals, and the Supreme Court are constitutional courts.

- **How are federal court judges selected?**

  District court and court of appeals judges are nominated by the president and subject to Senate confirmation. Supreme Court justices are nominated by the president and must also win Senate confirmation. Important criteria for selection include competence, standards, ideology, rewards, pursuit of political support, religion, race, ethnicity, and gender.

■ **How does the Supreme Court function today?**

Several factors influence the Court's decision to hear a case. Not only must the Court have jurisdiction, but at least four justices must vote to hear the case. Cases with certain characteristics are most likely to be heard. Once a case is set for review, briefs and *amicus curiae* briefs are filed and oral argument scheduled. The justices meet after oral argument to discuss the case, votes are taken, and opinions are written, circulated, and then announced.

■ **What are the key aspects of judicial philosophy and decision making?**

Judges' philosophy and ideology have an extraordinary impact on how they decide cases. Political scientists consider these factors in identifying models of how judges make decisions, including the behavioral, attitudinal, and strategic models.

■ **How does the judiciary affect policy and what efforts have been made to reform its policy-making powers?**

The Supreme Court is an important participant in the policy-making process. The power to interpret the laws gives the Court tremendous policy-making power never envisioned by the Framers.

Key Terms

amicus curiae, p. 363
appellate court, p. 345
appellate jurisdiction, p. 346
brief, p. 350
civil law, p. 347
constitutional court, p. 348
criminal law, p. 347
judicial activism, p. 367

judicial implementation, p. 371
judicial restraint, p. 367
judicial review, p. 338
Judiciary Act of 1789, p. 339
jurisdiction, p. 345
legislative court, p. 348
Marbury v. *Madison* (1803), p. 345
original jurisdiction, p. 346

precedent, p. 350
Rule of Four, p. 361
senatorial courtesy, p. 351
solicitor general, p. 362
stare decisis, p. 350
strict constructionist, p. 367
trial court, p. 345
writ of *certiorari*, p. 360

Researching the Judiciary

In the Library

Baum, Lawrence. *Judges and Their Audiences: A Perspective on Judicial Behavior*. Princeton, NJ: Princeton University Press, 2005.

———. *The Puzzle of Judicial Behavior*. Ann Arbor: University of Michigan Press, 1997.

Epstein, Lee, and Jeffrey A. Segal. *Advice and Consent: The Politics of Judicial Appointments*. New York: Oxford University Press, 2005.

Epstein, Lee, et al. *The Supreme Court Compendium*, 4th ed. Washington, DC: CQ Press, 2007.

Hall, Kermit L., ed. *The Oxford Companion to the Supreme Court of the United States*, 2nd ed. New York: Oxford University Press, 2005.

Hall, Kermit L., and Kevin T. McGuire, eds. *Institutions of American Democracy: The Judicial Branch*. New York: Oxford University Press, 2005.

Lazarus, Edward. *Closed Chambers: The First Eyewitness Account of the Epic Struggles Inside the Supreme Court*. New York: Times Books, 1998.

O'Brien, David M. *Storm Center: The Supreme Court in American Politics*, 8th ed. New York: Norton, 2008.

Perry, H. W. *Deciding to Decide: Agenda Setting in the United States Supreme Court*, reprint ed. Cambridge, MA: Harvard University Press, 2005.

Segal, Jeffrey A., and Harold J. Spaeth. *The Supreme Court and the Attitudinal Model Revisited*. New York: Cambridge University Press, 2002.

Slotnick, Elliot E., and Jennifer A. Segal. *Television News and the Supreme Court: All the News That's Fit to Air*. Boston: Cambridge University Press, 1998.

Sunstein, Cass R., et al. *Are Judges Political? An Empirical Analysis of the Federal Judiciary*. Washington, DC: Brookings Institution, 2006.

Ward, Artemus, and David L. Weiden. *Sorcerer's Apprentices: 100 Years of Law Clerks at the United States Supreme Court*. New York: New York University Press, 2006.

Whittington, Keith E. *Political Foundations of Judicial Supremacy: The Presidency, the Supreme Court, and Constitutional Leadership in U.S. History*. Princeton, NJ: Princeton University Press, 2007.

Woodward, Bob, and Scott Armstrong. *The Brethren: Inside the Supreme Court*, 2nd reprint ed. New York: Avon, 2005.

On the Web

To take a virtual tour of the U.S. Supreme Court and examine current cases on the Court's docket, go to **www.supremecourtus.gov**.

To learn more about the workings of the U.S. justice system, go to the Department of Justice Website at **www.usdoj.gov**.

To learn about the U.S. Senate Judiciary Committee and judicial nominations currently under review, go to the Senate's home page at **www.senate.gov**. You may also find information about pending nominations at the president's Web site at **www.whitehouse.gov**.

To learn about the American Bar Association's legislative and government advocacy, go to **www.abanet.org**.

To examine major Supreme Court decisions from the past to the present, go to Cornell Law School's Supreme Court Collection at **www.law.cornell.edu/supct/**.

Streaming audio of oral arguments before the Court may be accessed at Oyez: U.S. Supreme Court Media at **www.oyez.org**.

Political Socialization and Public Opinion

11

E xit polls have long received attention for their ability to help media outlets predict the outcome of elections before state agencies completely tabulate the results. But, during the 2008 Iowa caucuses, a different, related way to gauge public opinion—the entrance poll—gained prevalence. In an entrance poll, voters are asked about which candidate they are going to vote for and why before they walk into the actual caucus. These polls are favored in caucuses because their results can be released immediately after they are collected. This allows networks to predict what might happen in a caucus while the events is actually occurring.

During the 2008 Iowa caucuses, five major television and cable networks (ABC, CBS, NBC, CNN, and FOX News) and the Associated Press banded together to collect information through an agency known as the National Election Pool. This agency sent pollsters to 40 caucuses for each political party, a total of 80 different meetings.

Entrance polls in Iowa immediately set the tone for the 2008 contest, showing record numbers of first-time caucus goers and young voters. They emphasized the importance of independent voters and correctly predicted strong support for Democratic candidate Barack Obama and Republican candidate Mike Huckabee, both of whom won their party's caucuses. Caucus voters, in addition, seemed to have a widespread interest in political change.

The 2008 entrance polls were notable for a number of other reasons, as well. First, they were the first entrance polls to include a correction to take into account caucus-goers who refused to participate in the survey; evidence shows that younger people are more likely to complete a whole entrance poll than their older counterparts. This correction, which had previously been implemented in exit polls, requires pollsters to collect the demographic information of all of the people who elect not to participate in the poll. This information is used to weight the collected data to accurately represent the population that comes to the polling place or party caucus.

Second, the polling firms charged with conducting the entrance poll made a concerted effort to recruit and train a broader cross-section of interviewers. This, too, was directed at improving the representativeness of the sample; pollsters believe that people

■ Polling has been used to gauge public opinion on presidential elections since the early 20th Century. At left, George Gallup, the godfather of scientific polling, appears on a television program in 1948. At right, Iowa Caucus-goers register inside Waukee High School in Waukee, Iowa, in 2008.

WHAT SHOULD I KNOW ABOUT...
- political socialization?
- public opinion and polling?
- the reasons we form and express political opinions?
- the effects of public opinion on government and politics?

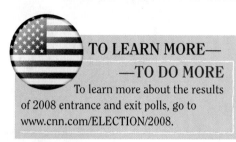

TO LEARN MORE—
—TO DO MORE
To learn more about the results of 2008 entrance and exit polls, go to www.cnn.com/ELECTION/2008.

Comparing Governments and Public Opinion

political socialization
The process through which individuals acquire their political beliefs and values.

are more likely to participate in a poll conducted by someone like them. For example, women may be more likely to respond to a poll conducted by a woman, and young people may be more likely to respond to a poll conducted by a young person.

In 1787, John Jay wrote glowingly of the sameness of the American people. He and the other authors of *The Federalist Papers* believed that Americans had more in common than not. Wrote Jay in *Federalist No. 2*, we are "one united people—a people descended from the same ancestors, speaking the same language, professing the same religion, attached to the same principles of government, very similar in manners and customs." Many of those who could vote in Jay's time were of English heritage; almost all were Christian. Moreover, most believed that certain rights—such as freedom of speech, association, and religion—were rights that could not be revoked. Jay also spoke of shared public opinion and of the need for a national government that reflected American ideals.

Today, however, Americans are a far more varied lot. Election after election and poll after poll reveal this diversity, but, nonetheless, Americans appear to agree on many things. Most want less government, particularly at the national level. So did many citizens in 1787. Most want a better nation for their children. So did the Framers.

People develop their political views through **political socialization**, "the process through which an individual acquires his particular political orientations—his knowledge, feeling, and evaluations regarding his political world."[1] The political beliefs developed through the political socialization process affect public opinion, which is based on the sum total of a selection of individuals' views on issues, candidates, and various public policies.

The process and role of political socialization and public opinion and their role in the making of public policy are explored in this chapter:

★ First, we will discuss *political socialization and the roots of political values*, including the broad array of factors that influence this process.

★ Second, we will examine *public opinion and polling*, explaining the role of public opinion polls in determining public perception of political issues.

★ Third, we will examine *why we form and express political opinions*.

★ Finally, we will describe *the effects of public opinion on government and politics*. Since the writing of *The Federalist Papers*, parties, candidates, and public officials have tried to gauge, sway and reform public opinion for political purposes.

Roots of Political Values: Political Socialization

Political scientists believe that many of our attitudes about issues are grounded in our political values. We learn these values through political socialization. Family, school, peers, and the mass media are often important influences or agents of political socialization. For example, try to remember your earliest memory of the president of the United States. It was most likely Bill

Clinton (older students probably remember earlier presidents). What did you think of the president? Of the Republican or Democratic Party? It is likely that your earliest feelings or attitudes were shaped by what your parents thought about that particular president and his party. Your experiences at school and your friends also probably influence your political beliefs today. Similar processes also apply to your early attitudes about the American flag, or the police. Other factors, too, often influence how political opinions are formed or reinforced. These include religious beliefs, race and ethnicity, gender, age, the region of the country in which you live, and even political events. Your own political knowledge may also shape your ideals.

The Family

The influence of the family on political socialization can be traced to two factors: communication and receptivity. Children, especially during their preschool years, spend tremendous amounts of time with their parents; early on, they learn their parents' political values, even though these concepts may be vague. (To learn more about political socialization, see Ideas into Action: Be a Socialization Agent.) One study found that the most important visible public figures for children under the age of ten were police officers and, to a much lesser extent, the president.[2] Young children almost uniformly view both as "helpful." But, by the age of ten or eleven, children become more selective in their perceptions of the president. By this age, children raised in Democratic households are much more likely to be critical of a Republican president than are those raised in Republican households. In 1988, for example, 58 percent of children in Republican households identified themselves as Republicans, and many had developed strong positive feelings toward Ronald Reagan, the Republican president.

Photo courtesy: Laura van Assendelft

When are political values shaped? Political values begin to form during childhood.

School and Peers

Researchers report mixed findings concerning the role of schools in the political socialization process. (To learn more about schools and the socialization process, see Join the Debate: Teaching Civics in American High Schools.) There is no question that, in elementary school, children are taught respect for their nation and its symbols. Most school days begin with the Pledge of Allegiance, and patriotism and respect for country are important components of most school curricula. Support for flag and country create a foundation for national allegiance that prevails despite the negative views about politicians and government institutions that many Americans develop later in life. For example, though many Americans debated U.S. action in Iraq in 2003, large numbers of schoolchildren were encouraged to send letters and packages to troops there and elsewhere. In some states, teachers were encouraged to limit anti-war discussion.[3] Measures such as these, however controversial, help to build a sense of patriotism at a young age.

The *Weekly Reader*, read by elementary students nationwide, not only attempts to present young students with newsworthy stories but also tries to foster political awareness and a sense of civic duty. In presidential election years, students get the opportunity to vote for actual presidential candidates in the nationwide *Weekly Reader* election. These elections, which have been held since 1956, have been remarkably accurate. *Weekly Reader* has been wrong only

Thinking Globally

Civic Education

In the United States, citizenship education is valued in primary and secondary grades. In Malaysia and Hong Kong, civic education is a compulsory subject throughout a student's academic career. In contrast, civics classes are not mandatory in the education curricula of Great Britain and Australia.

■ How important are civics classes in kindling political awareness and interest among young people? Should citizenship education be an institutionalized component of a country's education system?

■ Why might citizenship education be compulsory in some countries but not in others?

Ideas Into Action

Be a Socialization Agent

Children begin to learn about politics and political values as early as preschool. Thus, political scientists and advocates for civic education argue that it is important for even the youngest Americans to be aware—even if superficially—of the importance of elections in American democracy.

A number of efforts are geared to engaging children in the electoral process, especially during presidential election years. These include *Weekly Reader* elections and the Girl Scouts' Ms. President badge, both discussed in the text. Another group, Kids Voting USA, works to educate children and their parents about issues and ideas through mock elections, classroom activities, and community outreach. The group has a number of local chapters and affiliates

nationwide and has had significant success in increasing rates turnout.

Explore the programs that exist in your community to help preschool and elementary students learn about candidates and elections on the local, state, and national levels. Then, consider:

- What existing programs can you join? If there are no programs in your community, how might you go about building your own civic outreach program to get children involved in politics?
- What concerns might you need to be sensitive to as you teach children about political issues?
- How might you make politics interesting and relevant to young children? How did you learn about elections and politics as a child?

once, in the 1992 election of Bill Clinton. These returns were skewed by prominent independent candidate Ross Perot.

A child's peers—that is, children about the same age—also seem to have an important effect on the socialization process. While parental influences are greatest from birth to age five, a child's peer group becomes increasingly important as the child gets older, especially as he or she gets into middle school or high school.[4] Groups such as the Girl Scouts of the USA recognize the effect of peer pressure and are trying to influence more young women to participate in, and have a positive view of, politics. The Girl Scouts' Ms. President merit badge encourages girls as young as five to learn "herstory" and to emulate women leaders.

High schools also can be important agents of political socialization. They continue the elementary school tradition of building good citizens and often reinforce textbook learning with trips to the state or national capital. They also offer courses on current U.S. affairs. Many high schools impose a compulsory service learning requirement, which some studies report positively affects later political participation.[5]

Although the formal education of some Americans ends with high school, research shows that better-informed citizens vote more often as adults. Therefore, presentation of civic information is especially critical at the high school level, where it reinforces views about participation.

At the college level, teaching style often changes. Many college courses and texts like this one are designed in part to provide you with the information necessary to think critically about issues of major political consequence. It is common in college for students to be called on to question the appropriateness of certain

How do you get young women to think about careers in politics? The Girl Scouts of the USA is reaching out to all girls and offers a Ms. President badge for social action. Farheen Hakeem, shown right, leads a Girl Scout troop in Minneapolis.

Photo courtesy: Allen Brisson-Smith/The New York Times/Redux Pictures

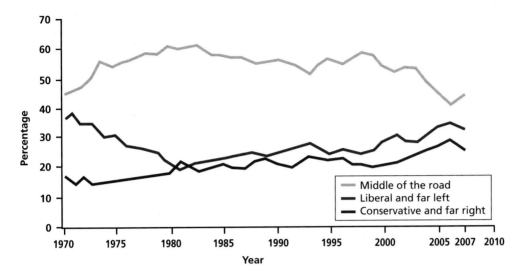

FIGURE 11.1 The Ideological Self-Identification of First-Year College Students

A majority of first-year college students describe themselves as middle of the road; this number has been fairly consistent since the early 1990s although it decreased beginning in the early 2000s. The number of students identifying themselves as liberal and far left declined dramatically during the 1970s and early 1980s but is currently on the rise. The number of students identifying themselves as conservative and far right has also increased, but at a slower rate.

Sources: Reprinted from Harold W. Stanley and Richard G. Niemi, *Vital Statistics on American Politics, 2007–2008* (Washington, DC: CQ Press, 2008), 124. 2005 data from Cooperative Institutional Research Program, "The American Freshman: National Norms for Fall 2005," December 2005.

political actions or to discuss underlying reasons for certain political or policy decisions. Therefore, most researchers believe that college has a liberalizing effect on students. Since the 1920s, studies have shown that students become more liberal each year they are in college.

Figure 11.1, however, reveals that students entering college in the 1980s were more conservative than in past years. The 1992 and 1996 victories of Bill Clinton and his equally youthful running mate Al Gore, who went out of their way to woo the youth vote, probably contributed to the small bump in the liberal ideological identification of first-year college students in those years. But, in 2007, 25 percent of freshmen identified themselves as conservative or far right; this was the highest percentage of conservative identifiers in more than thirty years. The number of students identifying themselves as liberal or far left increased from 24.2 percent in 2003 to 32 percent in 2007, however. More students continue to identify themselves as liberal than conservative, as they have done in nearly every year since studies of incoming freshmen began in 1965.[6] And, a big jump in students identifying themselves as liberal was expected in 2008 as young people registered and voted for Barack Obama in large numbers. In fact, a significant majority of those aged eighteen to twenty-nine— 66 percent—voted for Obama.

The Mass Media

The media today are taking on a growing role as socialization agents. Adult Americans spend nearly thirty hours a week in front of their television sets; children spend even more.[7] Television has a tremendous impact on how people view politics, government, and politicians. Television can serve to enlighten voters and encourage

Join the Debate

Teaching Civics in American High Schools

OVERVIEW: Civic education is considered an essential component of political socialization. In many classrooms, for example, children elect the students who will erase chalkboards or serve as class leaders; by participating in classroom elections, students are thus socialized to accept electoral politics as part of legitimate political behavior. Most democratic societies have some form of civic education, if only to teach citizens social norms, virtues, and the "rules of the game" of the democratic process. Historically low voter turnout and close election outcomes have been cited by supporters of civic education as a sign that more needs to be done to teach young people the importance of political participation. Recently, civic education requirements have taken on additional urgency in light of debates about immigration policy and questions regarding the extent to which civic education efforts should focus exclusively on U.S. norms or emphasize commonalities and differences among democratic nations worldwide.

Civic education in secondary education has declined over the last thirty years. The National Assessment of Educational Progress (NAEP) has determined that only 26 percent of all high school seniors may be considered "proficient" in American political knowledge, and a Roper survey discovered that the majority of graduates from America's elite universities were incapable of identifying James Madison (a principal architect of the Constitution and the fourth president) or words from President Abraham Lincoln's Gettysburg Address. As a corrective, the federal government has instituted increased spending and guidelines for secondary American history and government education under the National Endowment for the Humanities' We the People Initiative, a program created to reaffirm and reinstitute civic education in America's classrooms.

French political commentator Alexis de Tocqueville argued that without common values and virtues, there can be no common action and social stability. What is the best way to teach American history, government, and political principles so that all who have contributed to the American experiment are recognized? Is a common civic education necessary, or should political socialization be left to the family? What can be done to increase interest in democratic politics and participation, and how can civic knowledge be restored to the American electorate?

Arguments IN FAVOR of Civic Education in High Schools

- **There may be a relationship between political participation and civic education.** A Carnegie Corporation study contends that student participation in the management of schools and classrooms, as well as in simulations of democratic institutions and processes, may increase involvement in the American political process.

voter turnout. For example, MTV began coverage of presidential campaigns in 1992 and had reporters traveling with both major candidates to heighten young people's awareness of the stakes in the campaign. Its "Choose or Lose" and "Rock the Vote" campaigns are designed to change the abysmal turnout rates of young voters.

Over the years, more and more Americans have turned away from traditional sources of news such as nightly news broadcasts on the major networks and daily newspapers in favor of different outlets. In 2008, one study estimated that the same percentage of viewers watched alternative sources such as *The Tonight Show, The Late Show,* or *The Daily Show* as watched more traditional cable news such as CNN or FOX News.[8] TV talk shows, talk radio, online magazines, listservs, and blogs are important sources of information about politics for many, yet the information that people get from these sources often is skewed.

- Civic education teaches citizens how to participate in a democratic society. Students become politically socialized by taking part in school elections, activities, and extracurricular activities (such as participating in debate teams and publishing school newspapers). Civic education teaches not only cooperation, but also tolerance of dissent and opposing views, as well as political compromise. This prepares students for the realities of pluralistic democratic life.

- Civic education is a complement to political socialization. The primary influence on a person's political development comes from family and friends, and mass media and culture also help to shape political values and attitudes. The role of a formal civic education is to teach American history and governmental and political structures and principles, as well as to provide a forum for students to hone their political skills, practice public debate, and learn civic engagement.

Arguments AGAINST Increased Civic Education in High Schools

- Civic education is innately biased by promoting certain values over others. In a free, multicultural society, it is inherently wrong to press upon individuals a certain political and social view. Modern democratic governments gather their strength from the many diverse cultures and political views that make up their respective societies. Teaching one sociopolitical view stifles the contributions of different cultures. To this end, the American Historical Society advocates teaching comparative and world history.

- Parents should be responsible for civic education. A government-sanctioned education will likely be partial to the government's interests and views. It is proper that parents introduce their children to the nation's political culture. This will help ensure a diversity of views in regard to the nature of government, thereby fostering debate and compromise in the marketplace of political ideas.

- It is difficult to determine what should constitute a civic education curriculum in a pluralistic society. Which understanding of American history, politics, and government is to be taught? Different groups have different interpretations and understanding of the historical unfolding of American society. To promote the views of one group over another would be unfair, and to teach all views would overwhelm students with information; the effect may be actually to *discourage* political engagement by subjecting students to information overload.

Continuing the Debate

1. Is there a correlation between civic participation and civic education? Why or why not?
2. Is it the proper place of public schools to engage in civic education, or is this the duty of family and friends?

To Follow the Debate Online, Go To:

www. civiced. org, the Web site of the Center for Civic Education, a group partially funded by the Pew Charitable Trusts to provide resources and programs to promote civic education.

www.carnegie.org/reporter/07/civic/demo_low. html, a page from the Carnegie Foundation web site discussing a number of studies that link civic education and patterns of participation in governance.

Some of the movement toward alternative news sources may be attributed to the increasing use of the sound bite. In the 2004 election, for example, the average sound bite was just six seconds, which gives the electorate little opportunity to evaluate a candidate. In sharp contrast, talk shows allow candidates ample time to discuss issues and present themselves as people. Thus, in 2008, presidential candidates Barack Obama and John McCain, as well as their spouses Michelle Obama and Cindy McCain, made individual appearances on a variety of popular programs.

Since the 2004 presidential election, major party candidates have used another form of media to sway and inform voters: the Internet. Candidates running for office in 2008 launched their own Internet sites, and the major networks and newspapers had their own Internet sites reporting on the election. Blogs and social networking sites also played an important role. The Obama campaign relied heavily on Facebook.

Religious Beliefs

Throughout our history, religion has played an extraordinary role in political life. Many colonists came to American shores seeking religious liberty, yet many quickly moved to impose their religious beliefs on others, and some made participation in local politics contingent on religiosity. Since political scientists began to look at the role of religion, numerous scholars have found that organized religion influences the political beliefs and behaviors of its adherents. The effects of organized religion are magnified in American culture, as 82 percent of respondents in a 2007 Gallup poll considered religion an important part of their lives.[9]

Through much of the twentieth century, social scientists found that faith-based political activity occurred largely on the left. From the civil rights movement, to efforts to improve the living standards of farmers and migrant workers, to abolition of the death penalty, religious leaders were evident. The civil rights movement, in particular, was led by numerous religious men, including the Reverend Martin Luther King Jr. and the Reverend Andrew Young (who later became mayor of Atlanta, Georgia, and the U.S. ambassador to the United Nations), as well as more recently the Reverend Jesse Jackson and the Reverend Al Sharpton.

In 1972, for the first time, a religious gap appeared in voting and public opinion. President Richard M. Nixon's re-election campaign was designed to appeal to what he termed "the Silent Majority," who wanted a return to more traditional values after the tumult of the 1960s. After Nixon's campaign, conservative religious leaders established organizations whose effective fund-raising and get out the vote efforts allowed them to gain significant national political influence within the Republican Party. In 1979, televangelist Jerry Falwell became the widely recognized face of the Moral Majority, a group of conservative religious political action committees. Falwell, along with conservative Catholic and Jewish leaders, helped to ensure Republican candidate Ronald Reagan's election to the presidency in 1980. The Reverend Pat Robertson, host of television's widely watched *700 Club*, established the Christian Coalition as a political advocacy and voter mobilization effort after his failed 1988 bid for the U.S. presidency. Each election cycle, the Christian Coalition distributes voter guides evaluating candidates on a range of issues to conservative evangelical churches throughout the United States. Today, religion is the second largest predictor of vote choice, after party identification. Regular church-goers have conservative views and vote Republican by a 2 to 1 margin.

In 2006, 55 percent of Americans identified themselves as Protestant, 26 percent as Catholic, and 4 percent as Jewish, while 14 percent claimed to have no religious affiliation. As shown in Figure 11.2, Protestants, especially evangelicals, are the most conservative and Jews the most liberal. And, as liberals, Jews tend to vote Democratic. In 2008, for example, Barack Obama and his running mate, Joe Biden, captured 78 percent of the Jewish vote.[10]

Shared religious attitudes tend to affect voting and stances on particular issues. Catholics as a group, for example, favor aid to parochial schools, while many fundamentalist Protestants support organized prayer in public schools as well as abstinence-only education.

www.mikehuckabee.com

Photo courtesy: Huckabee Campaign/AP/Wide World Photos

What role does religion play in politics? Southern Baptist minister Mike Huckabee ran for the Republican nomination for president in 2008. A former governor of Arkansas, Huckabee says his political opinions are deeply rooted in and reflect his Christian faith. This Christmas campaign advertisement was controversial because critics believed the arrangement of the bookcase in the background resembled a cross.

Race and Ethnicity

Another reliable predictor of people's political attitudes is their race or ethnicity. Differences in political socialization appear at a very early age. Young African American children, for example, generally show very positive feelings about American society and political processes, but this attachment lessens considerably over time. Historically, black children have had less positive views of the president than white

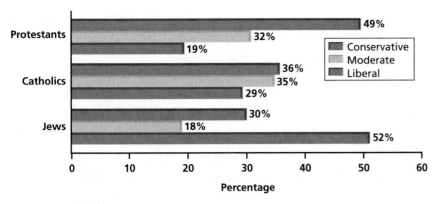

FIGURE 11.2 The Ideological Self-Identification of Protestants, Catholics, and Jews

Source: Data compiled and analyzed by Alixandra B. Yanus from the 2004 American National Election Study.

children.[11] The election of Barack Obama to the presidency should produce dramatic changes in these views.

Differences in racial attitudes were starkly evident in the wake of Hurricane Katrina. As revealed in Figure 11.3, while both blacks and whites said they believed that the federal government's response to the disaster was slow because most of the affected were poor or black, far more blacks (77 percent) than whites (44 percent) viewed the looters as "mostly desperate people." And, while 67 percent of the whites polled by *USA Today*/Gallup reported they believed that "President Bush cares about black people," only 21 percent of blacks agreed with this statement.[12]

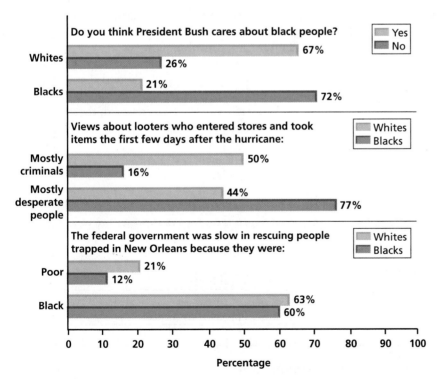

FIGURE 11.3 Views of Whites and Blacks in Wake of Hurricane Katrina

Note: Margins of sampling error: overall results ± 3 percentage points: whites ± 4 percentage points; blacks ± 7 percentage points.

Source: *USA Today*/CNN/Gallup poll of 1,110 people taken September 8–11, 2005.

Race and ethnicity are exceptionally important factors in elections and in the study of public opinion. The direction and intensity of African American opinion on a variety of hot-button issues often are quite different from those of whites. As revealed in Analyzing Visuals: Racial and Ethnic Attitudes on Selected Issues, whites are much more likely to support the war in Iraq than are blacks or Latino/as.

Likewise, differences can be seen in other issue areas, including support for preferential treatment to improve the position of minorities.[13] Government-sponsored health insurance for the working poor, for example, is a hot-button issue with Latino/a voters, with 94 percent favoring it. Unlike many non-Latino/a Americans, Hispanics also favor bilingual education and liberalized immigration policies.[14] Asian and Pacific Americans, and American Indians also often respond differently to issues than do whites.

Gender

Poll after poll reveals that women hold very different opinions from men on a variety of issues. Women, and particularly unmarried women, are more likely to be Democrats, while white men are increasingly becoming the core of the Republican Party.[15]

From the time that the earliest public opinion polls were taken, women have held more liberal attitudes about social welfare issues such as education, juvenile justice, capital punishment, and the environment. Some analysts suggest that women's more nurturing nature and their prominent role as mothers lead women to have more liberal attitudes on issues affecting the family or children. Research by political scientists, however, finds no support for a maternal explanation.[16]

Historically, public opinion polls have also found that women hold more negative views about war and military intervention. However, the gender gap on military issues began to disappear in the late 1990s, when the United States intervened in Kosovo. Many speculated that this occurred because of the increased participation of women in the workforce and the military, the "sanitized nature of much of the war footage" shown on TV, and the humanitarian reasons for involvement.[17]

The gender gap in military affairs also was less visible following the terrorist attacks of September 11, 2001. Right after the attacks, polls showed that 47 percent of women and 53 percent of men voiced their support for the U.S. military intervention in Afghanistan.[18] However, as the memory of 9/11 has receded, the war in Iraq has resulted in a renewed gender gap on foreign affairs. (To learn more about the gender gap, see Table 11.1.)

Age

Age seems to have a decided effect on political socialization. Our view of the proper role of government, for example, often depends on the era in which we were born and

TABLE 11.1 Gender Differences on Political Issues

Public opinion polls reveal that men and women tend to hold different views on a number of political issues. Yet, as this table also reveals, on some political issues, little difference is evident.

	Men (%)	Women (%)
Think Iraq War worth the cost	42	35
Favor increased federal spending on war on terrorism	50	36
Favor increased federal spending on Social Security	57	67
Favor ban on late-term (partial birth) abortion	57	60
Think federal government should make it more difficult to buy guns	48	67
Voted for Barack Obama in 2008	49	56

Source: Data compiled and analyzed by Alixandra B. Yanus from the 2004 American National Election Study.

Analyzing Visuals   Racial and Ethnic Attitudes on Selected Issues

Political opinions held by racial and ethnic groups in the United States differ on many issues. Look at the bar graph comparing the opinions of whites, blacks, and Latino/as on a number of political issues and ask yourself the following questions:

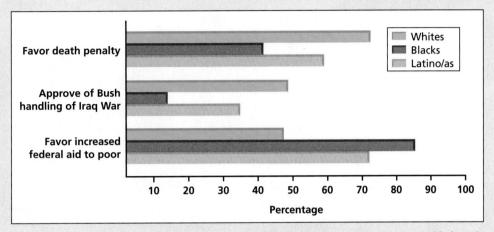

WHAT do you observe about the differences and similarities in opinions among the three different groups?

ON which issues do blacks and whites, Latino/as and blacks, and Latino/as and whites have the most divergent opinions?

ON which issues are these groups likely to have the most similar opinions?

Source: Data compiled and analyzed by Alixandra B. Yanus from the 2004 American National Election Study.

our individual experiences with a variety of social, political, and economic forces. Older people continue to be affected by having lived through the Great Depression and World War II. One political scientist predicts that as Baby Boomers age, the age gap in political beliefs about political issues, especially governmental programs, will increase.[19] Young people, for example, resist higher taxes to fund Medicare, while the elderly resist all efforts to limit Medicare or Social Security.

In states such as Florida, to which many northern retirees have flocked seeking relief from cold winters and high taxes, the elderly have voted as a bloc to defeat school tax increases and to pass tax breaks for themselves. As a group, senior citizens are much more likely to favor an increased governmental role in the area of medical insurance.

Region

Regional and sectional differences have been important factors in the development and maintenance of political beliefs since colonial times. As the United States developed into a major industrial nation, waves of immigrants with different religious traditions and customs entered the United States and often settled in areas where other immigrants from their region already lived. For example, thousands of Scandinavians settled in Minnesota, and many Irish settled in the urban centers of the Northeast, as did many Italians and Jews. All brought with them unique views about numerous issues, as well as about the role of government. These political views often have been transmitted through the generations, and many regional differences continue to affect public opinion today.

One of the most long-standing and dramatic regional differences in the United States is that between the South and the North. Recall that during the Constitutional Convention, most Southerners staunchly advocated a weak national government.

Photo courtesy: Ken Basant

Are young people disinterested in politics? Young people are participating in the political process more than ever before. Their voter turnout increased substantially in the 2004 and 2008 presidential elections. Here, students at Prairie View A&M University in Waller County, Texas, protest the lack of early voter registration centers in their precinct.

Nearly a hundred years later, the Civil War was fought in part because of basic differences in philosophy toward government (states' rights in the South versus national rights in the North). As we know from the results of modern political polling, the South has continued to lag behind the rest of the nation in support for civil rights, while continuing to favor return of power to the states at the expense of the national government.

The South also is much more religious than the rest of the nation, as well as more Protestant. About two-thirds of the South is Protestant (versus about 45 percent for the rest of the nation), and church attendance is highest in the South, where 46 percent report weekly visits. In contrast, only 34 percent of those living in the Northeast go to church or synagogue on a weekly basis.[20] Given the South's higher churchgoing rates, it is not surprising that the Christian Coalition (also discussed in chapter 16) has been very successful at mobilizing voters in that region.

The West, too, appears different from other sections of the nation. Some people have moved there to avoid city life; other residents have an anti-government bias. Many who have sought refuge there are staunchly against any governmental action, especially on the national level. One need only look at a map of the vote distribution in the 2008 presidential election to see stark differences in candidate appeal. Barack Obama carried almost every large city in America; John McCain carried 53 percent of the rural and small-town voters as well as most of America's heartland.[21] Republicans won the South, the West, and much of the Midwest; Democrats carried the Northeast and West Coast.

The Impact of Events

Key political events play a very important role in a person's political socialization. You probably have teachers or professors who remember what they were doing on the day that President John F. Kennedy was killed—November 22, 1963. This dramatic event is indelibly etched in the minds of virtually all people who were old

TIMELINE

War, Peace, and Public Opinion

enough to be aware of it. Similarly, most college students today remember where they were when they heard about the September 11, 2001 attacks on the World Trade Center and the Pentagon. These attacks on American shores evoked a profound sense of patriotism and national unity as American flags were displayed from windows, doors, balconies, and cars. For many Americans, the attacks were life-changing political events.

One problem in discussing the impact of events on political socialization is that many of the major studies on this topic were conducted in the aftermath of Watergate, which, along with the civil rights movement and the Vietnam War, produced a marked increase in Americans' distrust of government. The findings reported in Analyzing Visuals: Faith in Institutions (see page 26) reveal the dramatic drop-off of trust in government that began in the mid-1960s.

Public Opinion and Polling

At first glance, **public opinion** seems to be a very straightforward concept: it is what the public thinks about a particular issue or set of issues at a particular time. Since the 1930s, governmental decision makers have relied heavily on **public opinion polls**—interviews with samples of citizens that are used to estimate what the public is thinking. According to George Gallup (1901–1983), an Iowan who is considered the founder of modern-day polling, polls have played a key role in defining issues of concern to the public, shaping administrative decisions, and helping "speed up the process of democracy" in the United States.[22]

Gallup further contended that leaders must constantly take public opinion—no matter how short-lived—into account. This does not mean that leaders must follow the public's view slavishly; it does mean that they should have an available appraisal of public opinion and take some account of it in reaching their decisions.[23]

Even though Gallup undoubtedly had a vested interest in fostering reliance on public opinion polls, his sentiments accurately reflect the feelings of many political thinkers concerning the role of public opinion and governance. Some, like Gallup, believe that the government should do what a majority of the public wants done. Others argue that the public as a whole doesn't have consistent opinions on day-to-day issues but that subgroups within the public often hold strong views on some issues. These pluralists believe that the government must allow for the expression of these minority opinions and that democracy works best when these different voices are allowed to fight it out in the public arena.

The History of Public Opinion Research

As early as 1824, one Pennsylvania newspaper tried to predict the winner of that year's presidential contest. In 1883, the *Boston Globe* sent reporters to selected election precincts to poll voters as they exited voting booths in an effort to predict the results of key contests. But, public opinion polling as we know it today did not begin to develop until the 1930s. Much of this growth was prompted by Walter Lippmann's seminal work, *Public Opinion* (1922). In this piece, Lippmann

public opinion
What the public thinks about a particular issue or set of issues at any point in time.

public opinion polls
Interviews or surveys with samples of citizens that are used to estimate the feelings and beliefs of the entire population.

Thinking Globally
Public Opinion Regarding Terrorism

Public opinion regarding the degree to which terrorism represents an important national problem differs significantly across countries. In the United States, 44 percent of citizens surveyed in 2007 by the Pew Charitable Trust reported terrorism was a very important problem. Among Canadians, only 24 percent agreed that terrorism was a major concern. In Western Europe, 31 percent of Germans, 54 percent of French, 66 percent of Spanish, and 73 percent of Italians considered terrorism a major problem.

■ What factors might account for the different opinions about the danger posed by terrorism across countries?

■ Are you surprised that more Americans aren't worried about terrorism? Why are opinions about the importance of terrorism so different across neighboring countries in Western Europe?

observed that research on public opinion was far too limited, especially in light of its importance. Researchers in a variety of disciplines, including political science, heeded Lippmann's call to learn more about public opinion. Some tried to use scientific methods to measure political thought through the use of surveys or polls. As methods for gathering and interpreting data improved, survey data began to play an increasingly important role in all walks of life, from politics to retailing.

Literary Digest, a popular magazine that first began presidential polling in 1916, was a pioneer in the use of **straw polls**, unscientific surveys used to gauge public opinion, to predict the popular vote in those four presidential elections. Its polling methods were hailed widely as "amazingly right" and "uncannily accurate."[24] In 1936, however, its luck ran out. *Literary Digest* predicted that Republican Alfred M. Landon would beat incumbent President Franklin D. Roosevelt by a margin of 57 percent to 43 percent of the popular vote. Roosevelt, however, won in a landslide election, receiving 62.5 percent of the popular vote and carrying all but two states.

Literary Digest's 1936 straw poll had three fatal errors. First, its **sample**, a subset of the whole population selected to be questioned for the purposes of prediction or gauging opinion, was drawn from telephone directories and lists of automobile owners. This technique oversampled the upper middle class and the wealthy, groups heavily Republican in political orientation. Moreover, in 1936, voting polarized along class lines. Thus, the oversampling of wealthy Republicans was particularly problematic because it severely underestimated the Democratic vote.

Literary Digest's second problem was timing. Questionnaires were mailed in early September. It did not measure the changes in public sentiment that occurred as the election drew closer.

Its third error occurred because of a problem we now call self-selection. Only highly motivated individuals sent back the cards—a mere 22 percent of those surveyed responded. Those who respond to mail surveys (or today, online surveys) are quite different from the general electorate; they often are wealthier and better educated and care more fervently about issues. *Literary Digest*, then, failed to observe one of the now well-known cardinal rules of survey sampling: "One cannot allow the respondents to select themselves into the sample."[25]

At least one pollster, however, correctly predicted the results of the 1936 election: George Gallup. Gallup had written his dissertation in psychology at the University of Iowa on how to measure the readership of newspapers. He then expanded his research to study public opinion about politics. He was so confident about his methods that he gave all of his newspaper clients a money-back guarantee: if his poll predictions weren't closer to the actual election outcome than those of the highly acclaimed *Literary Digest*, he would refund their money. Although Gallup underpredicted Roosevelt's victory by nearly 7 percent, the fact that he got the winner right was what everyone remembered, especially given *Literary Digest's* dramatic miscalculation.

Through the late 1940s, polling techniques became more sophisticated. The number of polling groups also dramatically increased, as businesses and politicians began to rely on polling information to market products and candidates. But, in 1948, the polling industry suffered a severe, although fleeting, setback when Gallup and many other pollsters incorrectly predicted that Thomas E. Dewey would defeat President Harry S Truman.

Nevertheless, as revealed in Figure 11.4, the Gallup Organization continues to predict the winners of the presidential popular vote successfully. In 2008, for example, Gallup not only predicted the winner, it also accurately predicted Barack Obama's popular vote.

Recent efforts to measure public opinion also have been aided by social science surveys such as the National Election Study (NES), conducted by researchers at the University of Michigan since 1952. NES surveys focus on the political attitudes and the behavior of the electorate, and they include questions about how respondents voted, their party affiliation, and their opinions of major political parties and candidates. In addition, NES surveys include questions about interest in politics and political participation.

straw polls
Unscientific surveys used to gauge public opinion on a variety of issues and policies.

sample
A subset of the whole population selected to be questioned for the purposes of prediction or gauging opinion.

Is polling always accurate? Not only did advance polls in 1948 predict that Republican nominee Thomas E. Dewey would defeat Democratic incumbent President Harry S Truman, but based on early and incomplete vote tallies, some newspapers' early editions published the day after the election declared Dewey the winner. Here a triumphant Truman holds aloft the *Chicago Daily Tribune*.

Photo courtesy: Bettmann/CORBIS

These surveys are conducted before and after midterm and presidential elections and often include many of the same questions. This format enables researchers to compile long-term studies of the electorate and facilitates political scientists' understanding of how and why people vote and participate in politics. (To learn about one of the most recent obstacles to survey research, see Politics Now: Cell Phones Challenge Pollsters.)

Traditional Public Opinion Polls

The polling process most often begins when someone says, "Let's find out about X and Y." Potential candidates for local office may want to know how many people have heard of them (the device used to find out is called a name recognition survey). Better-known candidates contemplating running for higher office might want to

You Are a Polling Consultant

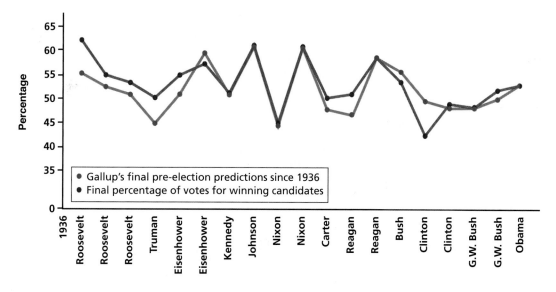

FIGURE 11.4 The Success of the Gallup Poll in Presidential Elections, 1936–2008
As seen here, Gallup's final predictions have been remarkably accurate. Furthermore, in each of the years where there is a significant discrepancy between Gallup's prediction and the election's outcome, there was a prominent third candidate. In 1948, Strom Thurmond ran on the Dixiecrat ticket; in 1980, John Anderson ran as the American Independent Party candidate; in 1992, Ross Perot ran as an independent.

Sources: Marty Baumann, "How One Polling Firm Stacks Up," *USA Today* (October 27, 1992): 13A; 1996 data from Mike Mokrzycki, "Pre-election Polls' Accuracy Varied," *Atlanta Journal and Constitution* (November 8, 1996): A12; 2000 data from Gallup Organization, "Poll Releases," November 7, 2000; 2004 and 2008 data from *USA Today* and CNN/Gallup Tracking Poll, USAToday.com.

POLITICS NOW

Source: ST. LOUIS POST DISPATCH   December 9, 2007

Cell Phones Challenge Pollsters

Pollsters Face New Hurdles: Cell Phones

BILL LAMBRECHT

Pollsters taking the pulse of voters this political season are confronting growing obstacles from cell phones—and an electorate that is increasingly walling itself off with caller ID and answering machines. The response rate in phone surveys has plunged from about 40 percent in the 1980s to 20 percent or less now, making it harder and more expensive for pollsters to secure the samples they need. These changes are causing some to wonder about the accuracy of poll results this year, especially when it comes to young adults, who are 50 percent more likely than the rest of the population to use cell phones but who are voting in ever-greater numbers. . . .

According to the most recent government figures, nearly 13 percent of American homes were categorized as cell phone only—meaning that they had no land line. A quarter of young adults are reachable by cell phone only, and that number continues to rise.

Pollsters tend to shun cell phones for several reasons. Among them:

- Cell phone users are able to automatically screen calls and are less likely to answer.

- Area codes of cell phones don't necessarily indicate where the user lives.
- Directories for cell phones are not available, and blocks of numbers available for purchase may not represent the geographical region being polled.
- Mobile phones are typically used by people on the go, perhaps in their cars or in situations where they are distracted and unable to complete long interviews.

Besides narrowing the traditional random sample pool, the switch to cell phones makes it less likely that people reached by pollsters on land lines will be between 18 and 34 years old—a group that is voting more heavily than it used to.

As recently as the 2000 presidential election, pollsters had a nearly 1-in-3 chance of encountering a young adult in a phone call. By the 2006 congressional elections, the percentage of young people in land-line homes had dropped to 20 percent, and by earlier this year, the percentage had dipped into the teens.

For pollsters, this means extrapolating from the responses of young people they do reach—meaning they are talking to fewer young people than their surveys might suggest—or trying to reach people on cell phones.

Del Ali is president of Research 2000, which conducts polls for the [St. Louis] *Post-Dispatch* and other news organizations. He uses cell phone numbers in polls but says he takes extra care to make sure that young people reached on their cell phones are registered voters in the state or locale targeted. Ali is among pollsters who say a bigger worry is Internet polling.

Pollster John Zogby, a pioneer in Internet surveys, acknowledges that cyberspace polling is still in its infancy. He has been working for years to build a database of 350,000 e-mail addresses of people that he regards as representative of the nation. When conducting a national poll, he'll e-mail 50,000-75,000 people to take part. From the thousands who respond, he'll randomly select people for the poll.

Skeptics say Internet polling is flawed because an e-mail database may not be representative of the population at large. Zogby, who also uses phone surveys, professes confidence in his Internet results and argues that survey research must change with society.

"I know that it is the next wave," he said. "The telephone is becoming ungainly. It's still a useful tool (for polling), but we're anticipating that it won't continue to be a useful tool."

Discussion Questions

1. *How can pollsters surmount the problems that come with a growing population of cell phone users?*
2. *What additional shortcomings might Internet polling have?*
3. *How might you make more people aware of the shortcomings of traditional polling techniques?*

---

know how they might fare against an incumbent. Polls also can be used to gauge how effective particular ads are or if a candidate is being well (or negatively) perceived by the public. Political scientists have found that public opinion polls are critical to successful presidents and their staffs, who use polls to "create favorable legislative environment(s) to pass the presidential agenda, to win reelection, and to be judged favorably by history."[26] These polls and others have several key phases, including: (1) determining the content and phrasing the questions; (2) selecting the sample; and, (3) contacting respondents.

DETERMINING THE CONTENT AND PHRASING THE QUESTIONS Once a candidate, politician, or news organization decides to use a poll to measure the public's attitudes, special care has to be taken in constructing the questions to be asked. For example, if

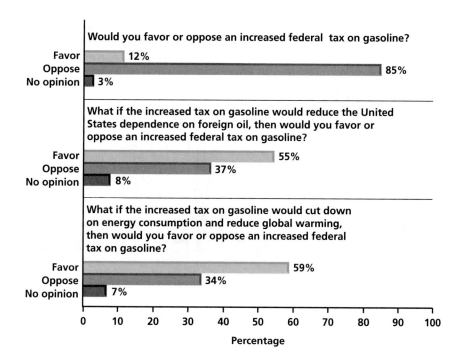

FIGURE **11.5** American Opinions on Gasoline Taxes
Source: New York Times and *CBS* News telephone interviews with 1,018 adults, February 22–26, 2008.

your professor asked you, "Do you think my grading procedures are fair?" rather than asking, "In general, how fair do you think the grading is in your American Politics course?" you might give a slightly different answer. The wording of the first question tends to put you on the spot and personalize the grading style; the second question is more neutral. Even more obvious differences appear in the real world of polling, especially when interested groups want a poll to yield particular results. Responses to highly emotional issues such as abortion, same-sex marriage, and affirmative action often are skewed depending on the wording of a particular question. Even in unbiased polls, limited responses can skew results, as reflected in Figure 11.5, a *New York Times*/CBS News Poll on gasoline taxes.

SELECTING THE SAMPLE Once the decision is made to take a poll, pollsters must determine the universe, or the entire group whose attitudes they wish to measure. This universe could be all Americans, all voters, all city residents, all Latino/as, or all Republicans. In a perfect world, each individual would be asked to give an opinion, but such comprehensive polling is not practical. Consequently, pollsters take a sample of the universe in which they are interested. One way to obtain this sample is by **random sampling**. This method of selection gives each potential voter or adult the same chance of being selected. In theory, this sounds good, but it is actually impossible to achieve because no one has lists of every person in a group. Thus, the method of representative poll taking is extremely important in determining the validity and reliability of the results.

Most national surveys and commercial polls use samples of 600 to 1,000 individuals and use a variation of the random sampling method called **stratified sampling**. Simple random, nonstratified samples are not very useful at predicting voting because they may undersample or oversample key populations that are not likely to vote. To avoid these problems, reputable polling organizations use stratified sampling (the most rigorous sampling technique) based on census data that provide the number of residences in an area and their location. Researchers divide the country into four sampling regions. They then randomly select a set of counties and standard metropolitan statistical areas in proportion to the total national population. Once certain primary

random sampling
A method of poll selection that gives each person in a group the same chance of being selected.

stratified sampling
A variation of random sampling; census data are used to divide the country into four sampling regions. Sets of counties and standard metropolitan statistical areas are then randomly selected in proportion to the total national population.

Doonesbury
BY GARRY TRUDEAU

Photo courtesy: DOONESBURY © G.B. Trudeau. Reprinted with permission of Universal Press Syndicate. All Rights Reserved.

What impact does the wording of questions have? How the questions in an opinion poll are worded can affect the results of a poll. Here, the cartoonist questions the polling source itself.

sampling units are chosen, they often are used for many years, because it is cheaper for polling companies to train interviewers to work in fixed areas.

About twenty respondents from each primary sampling unit are picked to be interviewed. Generally four or five city blocks or areas are selected, and then four or five target families from each district are used. Large, sophisticated surveys such as the National Election Study and General Social Survey, which produce the data commonly used by political scientists, attempt to sample from lists of persons living in each household. The key to the success of the stratified sampling method is not to let people volunteer to be interviewed—volunteers as a group often have different opinions from those who do not volunteer.

CONTACTING RESPONDENTS After selecting the methodology to conduct the poll, the next question is how to contact those to be surveyed. Television stations often ask people to call in, and some surveyors hit the streets. Telephone polls, however, are the most frequently used mechanism by which to gauge the temper of the electorate.

The most common form of telephone polls are random-digit dialing surveys, in which a computer randomly selects telephone numbers to be dialed. (To learn more about how random-digit surveys are conducted, see Figure 11.6.) In spite of some problems (such as the fact that many people do not want to be bothered, especially at dinner time or do not have home phones), most polls done for newspapers and news magazines are conducted in this way. Pollsters are exempt from federal and state do-not-call lists because poll-taking is a form of constitutionally protected speech.

Individual, in-person interviews are conducted by some groups, such as the National Election Study. Some analysts favor such in-person surveys, but others argue that the unintended influence of the questioner or pollster is an important source of errors. How the pollster dresses, relates to the person being interviewed, and even asks the questions can affect responses. (Some of these factors, such as tone of voice or accent, can also affect the results of telephone surveys.)

Political Polls

As polling has become increasingly sophisticated and networks, newspapers, and magazines compete with each other to report the most up-to-the-minute changes in public opinion on issues or politicians, new types of polls have been suggested and put into use. Each type of poll has contributed to our knowledge of public opinion and its role in the political process.

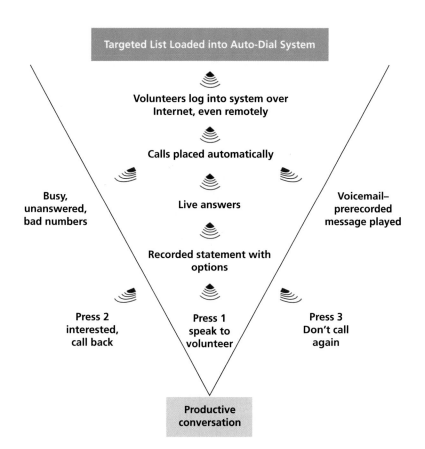

Targeted List Loaded into Auto-Dial System

Volunteers log into system over
Internet, even remotely

Calls placed automatically

Busy,
unanswered,
bad numbers

Live answers

Voicemail–
prerecorded
message played

Recorded statement with
options

Press 2
interested,
call back

Press 1
speak to
volunteer

Press 3
Don't call
again

Productive
conversation

FIGURE **11.6** How
Random-Digit Telephone
Surveys Are Conducted

PUSH POLLS All good polls for political candidates contain questions intended to produce information that helps campaigns judge their own strengths and weaknesses as well as those of their opponents.[27] They might, for example, ask if you would be more likely to vote for candidate X if you knew that candidate was a strong environmentalist. These kinds of questions are accepted as an essential part of any poll, but there are concerns as to where to draw the line. Questions that go over the line are called **push polls** and often are a result of ulterior motives. Push polls are designed to give respondents some negative or even untruthful information about a candidate's opponent to push them away from that candidate and toward the one paying for the poll. Reputable polling firms eschew these tactics. A typical push poll might ask a question such as "If you knew Candidate X beat his wife, would you vote for him?" Push poll takers don't even bother to record the responses because they are irrelevant. The questions are designed simply to push as many voters away from a candidate as possible. Although campaign organizations generally deny conducting push polls, research shows that more than three-quarters of political candidates have been a subject of push polling. Push poll calls are made to thousands; legitimate polls survey much smaller samples.

push polls
Polls taken for the purpose of providing information on an opponent that would lead respondents to vote against that candidate.

TRACKING POLLS During the 1992 presidential elections, **tracking polls**, which were taken on a daily basis by some news organizations, were first introduced to allow presidential candidates to monitor short-term campaign developments and the effects of their campaign strategies. Today, tracking polls involve small samples (usually of registered voters contacted at certain times of day) and are conducted every twenty-four hours. The results are then combined into moving three- to five-day averages, as illustrated in Figure 11.7. Even though these surveys are fraught with reliability problems and are vulnerable to bias, many major news organizations continue their use. As revealed in Figure 11.7, the 2008 tracking polls, performed very well and predicted an Obama Electoral College and popular vote victory.

tracking polls
Continuous surveys that enable a campaign to chart its daily rise or fall in support.

exit polls
Polls conducted as voters leave selected
polling places on Election Day.

EXIT POLLS In contrast to the entrance polls discussed in the opening vignette, **exit polls** are polls conducted as voters leave selected polling places on Election Day. Generally, large news organizations send pollsters to selected precincts to sample every tenth voter as he or she emerges from the polling site. The results of these polls are used to help the media predict the outcome of key races, often just a few minutes after the polls close in a particular state and generally before voters in other areas—sometimes in a later time zone—have cast their ballots. They also provide an independent assessment of why voters supported particular candidates.

In 1980, President Jimmy Carter's own polling and the results of network exit polls led him to concede defeat three hours before the polls closed on the West Coast. Many Democratic Party officials and candidates criticized Carter and network predictions for harming their chances at victories, arguing that with the presidential election already called, voters were unlikely to go to the polls. In the aftermath of that controversy, all networks agreed not to predict the results of presidential contests until all polling places were closed.

Shortcomings of Polling

The information derived from public opinion polls has become an extremely important part of governance. When the results of a poll are accurate, they express the feelings of the electorate and help guide policymakers. However, when the results of a poll are inaccurate, disastrous consequences often result. For example, during the 2000 presidential election, Voter News Service (VNS), the conglomerate organization that provided the major networks with their exit poll data, made a host of errors in estimating the results of the election in Florida, calling the state for Al Gore, which would have provided him with the votes necessary to win the presidency. Not only did VNS fail to estimate the

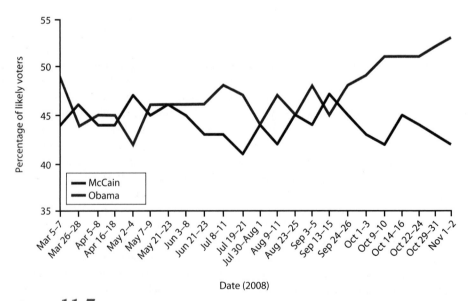

FIGURE 11.7 A Daily Tracking Poll for the 2008 Presidential Election
The day-to-day fluctuations in presidential and congressional races are often shown through tracking polls. This figure shows the ups and downs of the 2008 presidential election.
Source: USA Today and CNN/Gallup poll results, www.usatoday.com/news/politicselections/nation/polls/usatodaypolls.htm.

number of voters accurately, but it also used an inaccurate exit poll model and incorrectly estimated the number of African American and Cuban voters.

In November 2004, the major networks and the Associated Press joined in a new polling consortium, the National Election Pool. Its data, like that of VNS, also were riddled with errors. Its subscribers were quite unhappy and the fate of exit polls on Election Day remains in doubt, given their poor track record in predicting winners in the past three national elections. Reports on the 2006 midterm elections found the exit polls more reliable than in past years. In 2008, many commentators were skeptical that polling results were reliable because for the first time, an African American was running for president. Some feared that respondents would not admit to a prejudiced response against Barack Obama and would claim support when in fact they were not supporting him. That was not the case, however, and most polls were remarkably accurate.

MARGIN OF ERROR All polls contain errors. Typically, the margin of error in a sample of 1,000 will be about 4 percent. If you ask 1,000 people "Do you like ice cream?" and 52 percent say yes and 48 percent say no, the results are too close to tell whether more people like ice cream than not. Why? Because the **margin of error** implies that somewhere between 56 percent (52 + 4) and 48 percent (52 − 4) of the people like ice cream, while between 52 percent (48 + 4) and 44 percent (48 − 4) do not. The margin of error in a close election makes predictions very difficult.

SAMPLING ERROR The accuracy of any poll depends on the quality of the sample that was drawn. Small samples, if properly drawn, can be very accurate if each unit in the universe has an equal opportunity to be sampled. If a pollster, for example, fails to sample certain populations, his or her results may reflect that shortcoming. Often the opinions of the poor and homeless are underrepresented because insufficient attention is given to making certain that these groups are sampled representatively.

Perhaps the most common form of unrepresentative sampling is the kind of straw poll used today by local television news programs or online services. Many have regular features asking viewers to call in their sentiments (with one phone number for pro and another for con) or asking those logged on to indicate their preferences. The results of these unscientific polls are not very accurate because only those who feel very strongly about the issue will vote, sometimes more than once.

LIMITED RESPONDENT OPTIONS Polls can be inaccurate when they limit responses. If you are asked "How do you like this class?" and are given only like or dislike options, your full sentiments may not be tapped if you like the class very much or feel only so-so about it.

LACK OF INFORMATION Public opinion polls may also be inaccurate when they attempt to gauge attitudes about issues that some or even many individuals do not care about or about which the public has little information. Most academic public opinion research organizations, such as the National Election Study, use some kind of filter question that first asks respondents whether or not they have thought about the question. These screening procedures generally allow surveyors to exclude as many as 20 percent of their respondents, especially on complex issues like the federal budget. Questions on more personal issues such as moral values, drugs, crime, race, and women's role in society get far fewer "no opinion" or "don't know" responses.

Photo courtesy: Peter Steiner/Cartoon Bank

How can sampling affect polling results? This cartoon pokes fun at a serious shortcoming of polling—sampling error.

margin of error
A measure of the accuracy of a public opinion poll.

Can public opinion polling measure intensity?
One of the difficulties of public opinion researchers is measuring how strongly people hold their opinons.

Photo courtesy: Justin Sullivan/Getty Images

DIFFICULTY MEASURING INTENSITY Another shortcoming of polls concerns their inability to measure intensity of feeling about particular issues. Whereas a respondent might answer affirmatively to any question, it is likely that his or her feelings about issues such as abortion, the death penalty, or support for U.S. troops in Afghanistan or Iraq are much more intense than are his or her feelings about the Electoral College or types of voting machines.

Why We Form and Express Political Opinions

Often, the sentiments we express in public opinion polls can be traced to our political socialization. However, most people also are influenced by a number of other factors, including: (1) personal benefits; (2) political knowledge; (3) cues from various leaders or opinion makers; and, (4) their political ideology.

Personal Benefits

Most polls reveal that Americans are growing more and more "I" centered. This perspective often leads people to agree with policies that will benefit them personally. You've probably heard the adage "People vote with their pocketbooks." Taxpayers generally favor lower taxes, hence the popularity of candidates pledging "No new taxes." They also begin to question policies such as the war in Iraq as it costs billions and billions of dollars, causing national economic woes. (To learn more about public opinion on the war in Iraq, see Figure 11.8.)

Some government policies, however, don't really affect us individually. Legalized prostitution and the death penalty, for example, are often perceived as moral issues that directly affect few citizens. Individuals' attitudes on these issues often are based on underlying values they have acquired through the years.

When we are faced with policies that don't affect us personally and don't involve moral issues, we often have difficulty forming an opinion. Foreign policy is an area in which this phenomenon is especially true. Most Americans often know little of the world around them. Unless major issues of national importance are involved, American public opinion on foreign affairs is likely to be volatile in the wake of any new information.

Political Knowledge

Political knowledge and political participation have a reciprocal effect on one another—an increase in one will increase the other.[28] Knowledge about the political system is essential to successful political involvement, which, in turn, teaches citizens about politics and increases their interest in public affairs.[29] And, although few citizens know everything about all of the candidates and issues in a particular election, they can, and often do, know enough to impose their views and values as to the general direction the nation should take.[30]

This is true despite the fact that most Americans' level of knowledge about history and politics is quite low (To learn more about political knowledge, see Table 11.2). According to the Department of Education, today's college graduates have less civic knowledge than high school graduates did fifty years ago.[31]

Americans also don't appear to know much about foreign policy; some critics would even argue that many Americans are geographically illiterate. An astounding 49 percent of young Americans could not find New York on a map, and 10 percent of all Americans could not locate the United States.[32]

There are also significant gender differences in political knowledge. For example, one 2004 study done by the Annenberg Public Policy Center found that men were consistently more able than women to identify the candidates' issue positions.[33] This gender gap in knowledge, which has existed for the last fifty years, perplexes scholars, because women consistently vote in higher numbers than males of similar income and education levels.

Cues from Leaders or Opinion Makers

As early as 1966, noted political scientist V. O. Key Jr. argued in *The Responsible Electorate* that voters "are not fools."[34] Still, low levels of knowledge can lead to rapid opinion shifts on issues. The ebb and flow of popular opinion can be affected dramatically (some cynics might say manipulated) by political leaders. Given the visibility of political leaders and their access to the media, it is easy to see the important role they play in influencing public opinion. Political leaders, members of the news media, and a host of other experts have regular opportunities to influence public opinion because of the lack of deep conviction with which most Americans hold many of their political beliefs.[35]

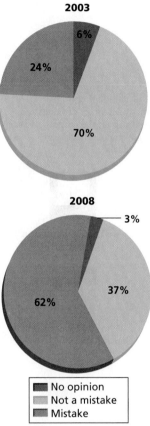

FIGURE 11.8
Public Opinion on the War in Iraq, 2003 Versus 2008
Source: Data provided by The Roper Center for Public Opinion Research, University of Connecticut

TABLE **11.2** Americans' Political Knowledge

	Percentage Unable to Identify
Number of senators (2002)	52
Representative in the House (2002)	53
Speaker of the House (2004)	89
British Prime Minister (2004)	35
Chief Justice of the Supreme Court (2004)	69

Sources: "A Nation That Is in the Dark," *San Diego Union-Tribune* (November 3, 2002): E3; John Wilkens, "America Faces a Crisis of Apathy," *San Diego Union-Tribune* (November 3, 2002): E3; and data compiled by Alixandra B. Yanus from the 2004 American National Election Study.

The president, especially, is often in a position to mold public opinion through effective use of the bully pulpit, as discussed in chapter 8.[36] One political scientist concludes that there is a group of citizens—called followers—who are inclined to rally to the support of the president no matter what he does.[37]

The president's strength, especially in the area of foreign affairs (where public information is lowest), derives from the majesty of his office and his singular position as head of state. Recognizing this phenomenon, presidents often take to television in an effort to drum up support for their programs.[38] President George W. Bush took his case for the wars in Afghanistan and Iraq as well as Social Security privatization directly to the public, urging citizens to support his efforts. These efforts, however, are not always successful, and public support may not last. The Iraq War and failing economy, for example, contributed to President Bush's declining approval ratings.

Political Ideology

political ideology
The coherent set of values and beliefs about the purpose and scope of government held by groups and individuals.

As discussed in chapter 1, an individual's coherent set of values and beliefs about the purpose and scope of government is called his or her **political ideology**. Americans' attachment to strong ideological positions has varied over time. In sharp contrast to spur-of-the-moment responses, these sets of values, which are often greatly affected by political socialization, can prompt citizens to favor a certain set of policy programs and adopt views about the proper role of government in the policy process.

Conservatives generally are likely to support smaller, less activist governments, limited social welfare programs, and reduced government regulation of business. Increasingly, they also have very strong views on social issues, including abortion and same-sex marriage. In contrast, liberals generally believe that the national government has an important role to play in a wide array of areas, including helping the poor and the disadvantaged. Unlike most conservatives, they generally favor activist governments. Most Americans today, however, identify themselves as moderates.

Political scientists and politicians often talk in terms of liberal, moderate, and conservative ideologies. Moreover, most Americans believe that their beliefs are best described by one of these three labels. In terms of elections, these values or beliefs often lead to individuals labeling themselves Democrats, independents, or Republicans.

Are You a Liberal or a Conservative?

Who Are Liberals and Conservatives? What's the Difference?

Toward Reform: The Effects of Public Opinion on Government and Politics

As early as the founding period the authors of *The Federalist Papers* noted that "all government rests on public opinion," and as a result, public opinion inevitably influences the actions of politicians and public officials. The public's perception of the need for change, for example, was the driving force behind the victories of both former Governor Mike Huckabee and Senator Barack Obama in the 2008 Iowa caucuses, and change eventually became the mantra of both the Obama and John McCain presidential campaigns.

Although politicians and government officials spend millions of dollars each year taking the pulse of the public, it is difficult to determine how much they rely on this data. Several political scientists have attempted to study whether public policy is responsive to public opinion, with mixed results.[39] As we have seen, public opinion can fluctuate, making it difficult for a politician or policy maker to assess. Some critics of polls and of their use by politicians argue that polls hurt democracy and make leaders weaker. Political scientist Benjamin Ginsberg, one of these critics, argues that widespread use of polling by politicians weakens democracy.[40] He claims that polls allow governments and politicians to say that they have considered public opinion even though polls don't always measure the intensity of feeling on an issue or might overreflect the views of the public because of responders who lack sufficient information to make educated choices. Ginsberg further argues that democracy is better served by politicians' reliance on telephone calls and letters—active signs of interest—than on the passive voice of public opinion. Some observers worry that politicians rely on poll results rather than a thoughtful debate of the issues to determine their actions, arguing that the outcome of polls determines individual policy positions. In response to this argument, George Gallup retorted, "One might as well insist that a thermometer makes the weather."[41]

By permission of Mike Luckovich and Creators Syndicate, Inc.

How susceptible are polls to short-term forces? This cartoon is a humorous take on the frequent fluctuations many political polls demonstrate as the electorate responds to changing events.

Polls can clearly distort the election process by creating what are called bandwagon and underdog effects. In a presidential campaign, an early victory in the Iowa caucuses or the New Hampshire primary, for example, can boost an underdog candidate's standings in the polls as the rest of the nation begins to think of him or her in a more positive light. New supporters jump on the bandwagon. A strong showing in the polls, in turn, can generate more and larger donations, the lifeblood of any campaign. However, the opposite can also happen, turning a front-runner into an underdog. One political scientist has noted that "bad poll results, as well as poor primary and caucus standings, may deter potential donors from supporting a failing campaign."[42]

★ WHAT SHOULD I HAVE LEARNED?

Public opinion is a subject constantly mentioned in the media, especially in presidential election years or when important policies are under consideration. What public opinion is, where it comes from, how it is measured, and how it is used are aspects of a complex subject. To that end, this chapter has explored the following questions:

■ **What is political socialization and how is it the root of political values?**

The first step in forming opinions occurs through a process called political socialization. Our family, school, peers, social groups—including religion, race, ethnicity, gender, and age—as well as where we live and the impact of events all affect how we view political events and issues. Even the views of other people affect our ultimate opinions.

■ **How does polling seek to measure and influence public opinion and how are polls conducted?**

Public opinion is what the public thinks about an issue or a particular set of issues. Public opinion polls are used to estimate public opinion. Almost since the beginning of the United States, various attempts have been made to influence public opinion about particular issues or to sway elections. Modern-day polling did not begin until the 1930s, however.

Over the years, polling to measure public opinion has become increasingly sophisticated and more accurate because pollsters are better able to sample the public in their effort to determine their attitudes and positions on issues. Polls, however, have several shortcomings, including sampling error, limited respondent options, lack of information, and difficulty measuring intensity.

■ **How do we form and express political opinions?**

Myriad factors enter our minds as we form opinions about political matters. These include a calculation about the personal benefits involved, degree of personal political knowledge, cues from leaders, and political ideology.

■ **What are the effects of public opinion on government and politics?**

Knowledge of the public's views on issues is often used by politicians to tailor campaigns or to drive policy decisions.

Key Terms

exit polls, p. 396
margin of error, p. 397
political ideology, p. 400
political socialization, p. 378

public opinion, p. 389
public opinion polls, p. 389
push polls, p. 395
random sampling, p. 393

sample, p. 390
stratified sampling, p. 393
straw polls, p. 390
tracking polls, p. 395

Researching Political Socialization and Public Opinion

In the Library

Althaus, Scott L. *Collective Preferences in Democratic Politics: Opinion Surveys and the Will of the People*. New York: Cambridge University Press, 2003.

Alvarez, R. Michael, and John Brehm. *Easy Answers, Hard Choices: Values, Information, and American Public Opinion*. Princeton, NJ: Princeton University Press, 2002.

Asher, Herbert. *Polling and the Public: What Every Citizen Should Know*, 7th ed. Washington, DC: CQ Press, 2007.

Clawson, Rosalee A., and Zoe M. Oxley. *Public Opinion: Democratic Ideals, Democratic Practice*. Washington, DC: CQ Press, 2008.

Erikson, Robert S., and Kent L. Tedin. *American Public Opinion: Its Origins, Contents, and Impact*, 7th ed. New York: Longman, 2006.

Erikson, Robert S., Gerald C. Wright, and John P. McIver. *Statehouse Democracy: Public Opinion and the American States*. New York: Cambridge University Press, 1993.

Erikson, Robert S., Michael B. MacKuen, and James A. Stimson. *The Macro Polity*. New York: Cambridge University Press, 2002.

Jamieson, Kathleen Hall. *Everything You Think You Know About Politics . . . And Why You Were Wrong*. New York: Basic Books, 2000.

Key, V. O., Jr. *Public Opinion and American Democracy*. New York: Knopf, 1961.

Manza, Jeff, ed. *Navigating Public Opinion: Polls, Policy, and the Future of American Democracy*. New York: Oxford University Press, 2002.

Mutz, Diana Carole. *Impersonal Influence: How Perceptions of Mass Collectives Affect Political Attitudes*. New York: Cambridge University Press, 1998.

Stimson, James A. *The Tides of Consent: How Public Opinion Shapes American Politics*. New York: Cambridge University Press, 2004.

Zaller, John. *The Nature and Origin of Mass Opinions*. New York: Cambridge University Press, 1992.

On the Web

To learn more about the history of the Gallup Organization and poll trends, go to **www.gallup.com**.

To compare state and national political polling results, go to Real Clear Politics at **www.realclearpolitics.com/polls/**. This site combines polling results from all the major polling organizations and also tabulates averages across polls.

To learn more about the American National Election Study (ANES), including the history of this public opinion research project, go to **www.electionstudies.org**.

For the most recent Roper Center polls, go to the Roper Center's public opinion archives page at **www.ropercenter.uconn.edu**.

12

Political Parties

I n August 2008, the Democrats used the city of Denver to formally launch the nomination of Senator Barack Obama as their candidate for president of the United States. A few weeks later, from Minneapolis, the Republicans followed by formally nominating John McCain as their candidate. The televised convention proceedings and morning papers focused on the nominations of these two people and their personal attributes. Less attention, however, was paid to the importance of the party platforms, the official statements that detail each party's positions on key public policy issues. Party platforms are often taken for granted, certainly by the news media, and even by many political activists. They are rarely noted by American voters, many of whom are more concerned about the personalities of candidates than the details of their policy positions and are also cynical about politicians and political parties, in general.

How wrong the cynics are. Party platforms reflect significant policy differences and worldviews. The 2008 Democratic platform criticized the Republican Bush administration, claiming that President George W. Bush had overextended the military by rushing into an ill-considered war in Iraq. Democrats also charged that

Republican economic policies had put the American Dream at risk by allowing incomes to fall and foreclosures and gas prices to rise. The Democratic platform pledged to renew America's promise and provide leadership on the world stage.

The Republican platform noted that the tragedy of September 11 had not been repeated on American soil and that the Republican Party remained committed to victory in Iraq. The Republican platform also pledged that the men and women on the front lines of the war on terrorism would be given the authority and resources they needed to protect the country and the platform promised to further reduce the tax burden of all Americans.

In addition to seeking to place blame for policy failures (the Democrats) or lay claim to policy successes (the Republicans), detailed policy positions were laid out in each platform. The Democrats advocated cutting taxes for middle class families and most senior citizens, closing corporate loopholes, and restoring fairness to the tax code by raising taxes on the richest Americans. The Republicans vowed to make President Bush's 2001 and 2003 tax cuts permanent; to reduce a variety of taxes on individuals, families, and small businesses; and to eliminate the practice of congressional earmarks and attack wasteful government spending. The Democrats pledged to lead the nation towards energy independence by investing in renewable energy technologies and

■ **National party conventions generate excitement and enthusiasm from dedicated delegates.** At left, members of the Democratic Party's Texas delegation celebrate the re-nomination of Franklin Delano Roosevelt for president in 1936. At right, avid supporters of Senator John McCain and Governor Sarah Palin attends the 2008 Republican National Convention in Minneapolis.

 WHAT SHOULD I KNOW ABOUT . . .

- the roots of the American party system?
- the functions of the American party system?
- the organizational structure of American political parties?
- how political parties help organize the branches and layers of American government?
- party identification?
- party dealignment and the continuing strength of parties in America?

TO LEARN MORE—
—TO DO MORE

To learn more about the Democratic and Republican party platforms, go to www.democrats.org and www.rnc.org. To learn about the platforms of two of the leading third parties, the Libertarians and the Greens, go to www.lp.org and www.gp.org.

advanced biofuels and increasing the fuel efficiencies of automobiles. They also pledged to lower gasoline prices by cracking down on speculators artificially driving up oil prices. The Republicans advocated accelerating domestic oil exploration and drilling offshore and on federal lands, constructing more oil refineries and nuclear power plants, and offering tax credits to encourage the development of alternative energy sources. The Democrats reiterated their support for *Roe* v. *Wade* and preserving a woman's right to choose a safe and legal abortion. The Republicans continued their strong pro-life stance and advocated for the passage of a Constitutional amendment to outlaw abortion. (To learn more about the party platforms, see Table 12.1.)

Long after memories of the national conventions have faded, the issues embodied by the party platforms persist. In fact, the policy differences outlined in the platforms stretch well beyond presidential politics. In elections to Congress, these same themes are echoed throughout the country. Candidates running for the Senate and the House also differ on issues related to foreign policy and national security, taxation, and social issues such as same-sex marriage and abortion.

As this chapter will discuss, party positions really matter, as they give voters important choices in the electoral process and help guide the direction of the nation. Political parties have been influencing American life for over two centuries and, in one form or another, they most likely will continue to direct American politics in the future. In this chapter we will address contemporary party politics by examining them from many vantage points. Our discussion of political parties will trace their roots in the late 1700s to the status of parties today. We will also discuss the reforms to party politics that have been sought throughout American history.

★ First, we will answer the question "What is a political party?" and trace *the roots of the American party system.*

★ Second, we will examine *the functions of the American party system.*

★ Third, we will explore *the organizational structure of American political parties.*

★ Fourth, we will uncover how political parties help *organize the branches and layers of American government.*

★ Fifth, we will analyze the concept of *party identification,* discussing how current trends and patterns affect American politics.

★ Finally, we will discuss the *continuing strength of parties* in the United States and recent attempts to reform the party system.

Roots of the American Party System

political party
An organized effort by office holders, candidates, activists, and voters to pursue their common interests by gaining and exercising power through the electoral process.

At the most basic level, a **political party** is an organized effort by office holders, candidates, activists, and voters to pursue their common interests by gaining and exercising power through the electoral process. Notice how pragmatic this concept of party is. The goal is to win office so as to exercise power, not just to compete for office. While the party label carries with it messages about ideology and issue positions, political parties are not narrowly focused interest groups—organized groups that try to influence public policy (see chapter 16). Interest groups exist to pursue issue outcomes, while political parties have traditionally existed to win elections. The difference is a matter of emphasis, with parties stressing the role of elections in gaining and exercising power. Indeed, as one observer noted, parties and interest group allies now work together so closely that "the traditional lines of demarcation between parties and interest groups are no longer clear."[1]

TABLE **12.1** Party Platforms: Moderate but Different

As most Americans have moderate political views and the aim of political parties is to attract voters, the platforms of the two dominant parties tend to be moderate in tone and occasionally similar in substance, though the differences below the rhetoric are significant.

	Democratic Platform	Republican Platform
Abortion	The Democratic Party strongly and unequivocally supports *Roe v. Wade* and a woman's right to choose a safe and legal abortion, regardless of ability to pay, and we oppose any and all efforts to weaken or undermine that right. The Democratic Party also strongly supports access to comprehensive affordable family planning services and age-appropriate sex education which empower people to make informed choices and live healthy lives.	We assert the inherent dignity and sanctity of all human life and affirm that the unborn child has a fundamental individual right to life which cannot be infringed. We support a human life amendment to the Constitution, and we endorse legislation to make clear that the Fourteenth Amendment's protections apply to unborn children. We oppose using public revenues to promote or perform abortion and will not fund organizations which advocate it. We support the appointment of judges who respect traditional family values and the sanctity and dignity of innocent human life.
Energy	Democrats are committed to fast-track investment of billions of dollars over the next ten years to establish a green energy sector that will create up to five million jobs. We'll create an energy focused youth job program to give disadvantaged youth job skills for this emerging industry. We must invest in research and development, and deployment of renewable energy technologies as well as technologies to store energy through advanced batteries and clean up our coal plants.	We must draw more American oil from American soil. We will encourage refinery construction and modernization and, with sensitivity to environmental concerns, an expedited permitting process. Republicans will pursue dramatic increases in the use of all forms of safe nuclear power. We must continue to develop alternative fuels, such as biofuels, especially cellulosic ethanol, and hasten their technological advances to next-generation production.
Taxation	We will shut down the corporate loopholes and tax havens and use the money so that we can provide an immediate middle-class tax cut. We'll eliminate federal income taxes for millions of retirees, because all seniors deserve to live out their lives with dignity and respect. For families making more than $250,000, we'll ask them to give back a portion of the Bush tax cuts to invest in health care and other key priorities. We will expand the Earned Income Tax Credit, and dramatically simplify tax filings so that millions of Americans can do their taxes in less than five minutes.	Republicans will lower the tax burden for families by doubling the exemption for dependents. We will continue our fight against the federal death tax. Republicans support tax credits for health care and medical expenses. We support a major reduction in the corporate tax rate so that American companies stay competitive with their foreign counterparts and American jobs can remain in this country. We support a plan to encourage employers to offer automatic enrollment in tax-deferred savings programs.
National Security	We must first bring the Iraq war to a responsible end. We will defeat Al Qaeda in Afghanistan and Pakistan, where those who actually attacked us on 9-11 reside and are resurgent. We will fully fund and implement the recommendations of the bipartisan 9-11 Commission. We must invest still more in human intelligence and deploy additional trained operatives with specialized knowledge of local cultures and languages. We will review the current Administration's warrantless wiretapping program.	We must regularly exercise our ability to quickly respond to acts of bioterrorism and other WMD-related attacks. We must develop and deploy both national and theater missile defenses to protect the American homeland, our people, our Armed Forces abroad, and our allies. We must increase the ranks and resources of our human intelligence capabilities, integrate technical and human sources, and get that information more quickly to the war-fighter and the policy maker.

Note: Excerpts are taken directly from the relevant sections of the 2008 party platforms.
Sources: http://www.democrats.org/a/party/platform.html and http://platform.gop.com/2008Platform.pdf.

Political scientists sometimes describe political parties as consisting of three separate but related entities: (1) the office holders who organize themselves and pursue policy objectives under a party label (the **governmental party**); (2) the workers and activists who make up the party's formal organization structure (the **organizational party**); and, (3) the voters who consider themselves allied or associated with the party (the **party in the electorate**).[2] Later in this chapter, we examine all three components of political parties—the organizational party, the governmental party, and the party in the electorate.

The broad structure and pragmatic purpose of political parties have been features of the American party system since the founding of the republic. By tracing the history and development of political parties in the United States, we will see that another prominent feature is a competitive two-party system, even as there have been dramatic shifts in party coalitions and reforms to democratize the system.

governmental party
The office holders who organize themselves and pursue policy objectives under a party label.

organizational party
The workers and activists who make up the party's formal organization structure.

party in the electorate
The voters who consider themselves allied or associated with the party.

TIMELINE

The Evolution of Political Parties in the United States

The Birth of American Political Parties

It is one of the great ironies of the early republic that George Washington's public farewell, which warned the nation against parties, marked the effective end of the

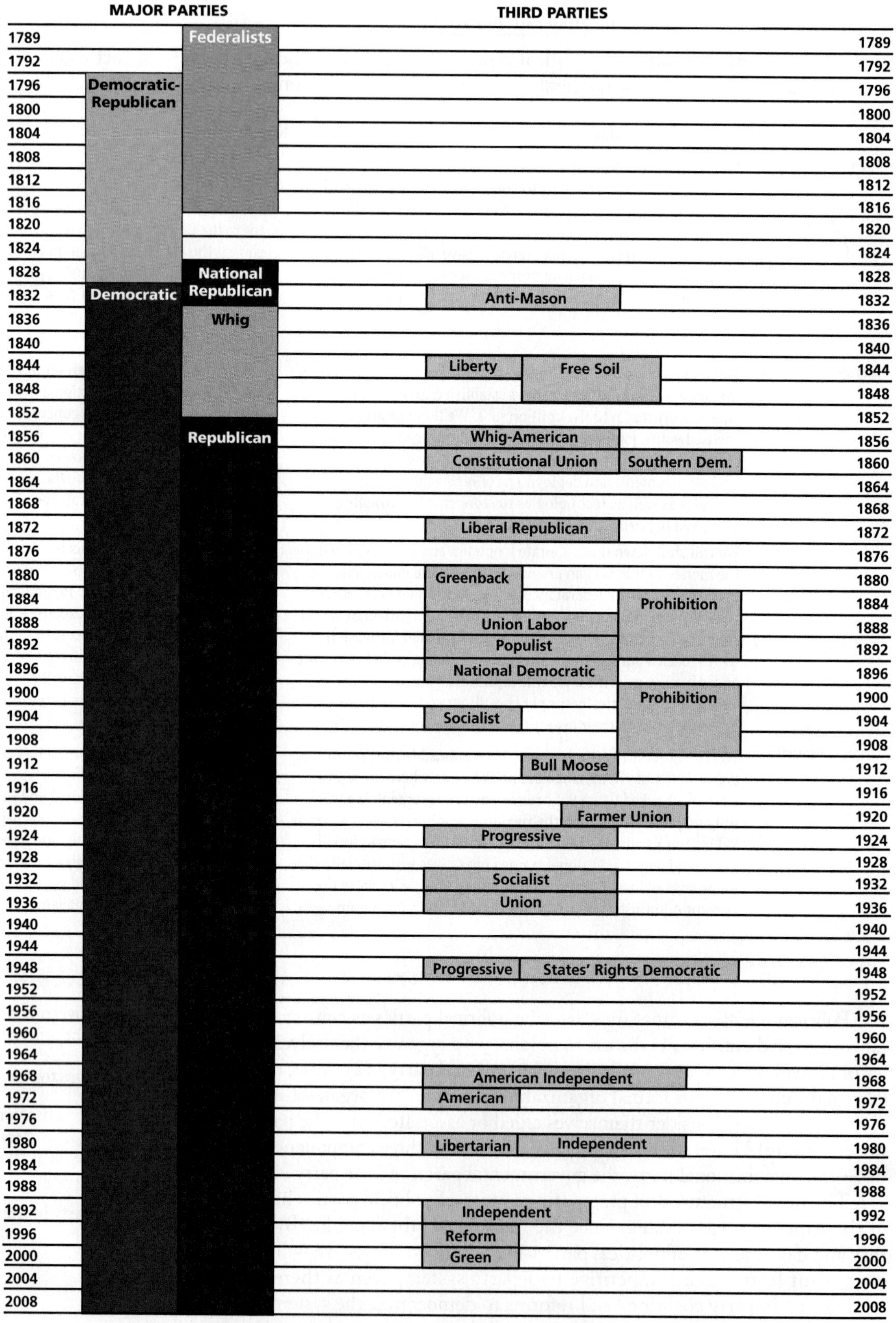

MAJOR PARTIES

THIRD PARTIES

Federalists (1789–1816)

Democratic-Republican (1796–1824)

Democratic (1828–2008)

National Republican (1828–1832)

Whig (1836–1852)

Republican (1856–2008)

Year	Third Parties
1789	
1792	
1796	
1800	
1804	
1808	
1812	
1816	
1820	
1824	
1828	
1832	Anti-Mason
1836	
1840	
1844	Liberty / Free Soil
1848	Free Soil
1852	
1856	Whig-American
1860	Constitutional Union / Southern Dem.
1864	
1868	
1872	Liberal Republican
1876	
1880	Greenback
1884	Prohibition
1888	Union Labor
1892	Populist
1896	National Democratic
1900	Prohibition
1904	Socialist
1908	
1912	Bull Moose
1916	
1920	Farmer Union
1924	Progressive
1928	
1932	Socialist
1936	Union
1940	
1944	
1948	Progressive / States' Rights Democratic
1952	
1956	
1960	
1964	
1968	American Independent
1972	American
1976	
1980	Libertarian / Independent
1984	
1988	
1992	Independent
1996	Reform
2000	Green
2004	
2008	

FIGURE 12.1 American Party History at a Glance

Note: Chart lists political parties that received at least 1 percent of the presidential vote.

Source: Harold W. Stanley and Richard G. Niemi, *Vital Statistics on American Politics, 2007–2008* (Washington, DC: CQ Press, 2007).

The Living Constitution

It is difficult to imagine modern American politics without the political parties, but where in the text of Constitution do we find the provision to establish them?

Nowhere in the Constitution do we find a provision establishing political parties. Some might point out that the First Amendment establishes the right to assemble as a constitutional right, and this right certainly helps to preserve and protect parties from governmental oppression during rallies and conventions. However, the right to assembly is not the same as permission for two organizations to mediate elections. Furthermore, James Madison, in *Federalist No. 10*, feared that one of the greatest dangers to the new American republic was a majority tyranny created by the domination of a single faction fighting for one set of interests, so he hoped that extending the sphere of representation among many members of Congress would prevent a majority of representatives from coming together to vote as a bloc.

Of course, parties are *not* like the factions Madison describes. Parties today seem to embody Madison's principle of the extended sphere of representation. Neither of the two major political parties is monolithic in its beliefs; rather, both parties constantly reconsider their platforms in light of the changes of the various constituencies they try to represent. The Republicans have Senator Olympia Snowe (ME), who is pro-choice and pro-environment, and Representative Roy Blunt (MO), who is pro-life and pro-business. Democrats have Representative Dennis Kucinich (OH), who advocates withdrawal from the North American Free Trade Agreement, and Governor Bill Richardson (NM), who balances various racial/ethnic concerns and business interests while trying to protect the border between the U.S. and Mexico. These comparisons illustrate significant differences in interests, an approach Madison supported.

Finally, Madison himself actually belonged to two early American political parties during his public service, first the Federalists and later the Democratic-Republicans. In fact, it is because of the Federalist Party that we have a Constitution today. Federalists compromised with Anti-Federalists to provide a Bill of Rights so long as the Anti-Federalists would stop opposing ratification of the Constitution. So parties are not so much *in* the Constitution as *behind* the Constitution, first behind its ratification and, today, behind its preservation of diverse interests.

CRITICAL THINKING QUESTIONS

1. How could the Constitution be amended in order to officially establish political parties as an institution of government? Would this be a good idea? Why or why not?
2. Why would candidates and office holders with very diverse views join the same political party?

brief era of partyless politics in the United States (To learn more about American party history, see Figure 12.1). Washington's unifying influence ebbed as he stepped off the national stage, and his vice president and successor, John Adams, occupied a much less exalted position. To win the presidency in 1796, Adams narrowly defeated his arch-rival Thomas Jefferson, who according to the existing rules of the Constitution became vice president. Over the course of Adams's single term, two competing congressional factions, the Federalists and Democratic-Republicans, gradually organized around these clashing men and their principles: Adams and his Federalist allies supported a strong central government; the Democratic-Republicans of Thomas Jefferson and his allies inherited the mantle of the Anti-Federalists (see chapter 2) and preferred a federal system in which the states retained the balance of power. (Jefferson actually preferred the simpler name "Republicans," a different group from today's party of the same name, but Alexander Hamilton, a leading Federalist, insisted on calling the group "Democratic-Republicans," an attempt to disparage the group by linking them to the radical democrats of the French Revolution.) In the presidential election of 1800, the Federalists supported Adams's bid for a second term, but this time the Democratic-Republicans prevailed with their nominee, Jefferson, who

Timeline: Political Parties in the United States

1788 The Federalists and Democratic-Republicans emerge— The new nation's first political parties emerge and usher in the First American Party System.

1828 Second Party System emerges— The disappearance of the Federalists and a split among Republicans pits the Whigs against the modern Democratic Party.

1856 Whig Party Dissolves—The new Republican Party, which opposes slavery, nominates John C. Frémont as their first presidential candidate.

1800 Jefferson Elected President— Voters reject the Federalists' agenda of a strong centralized government by electing Thomas Jefferson to the Presidency and a majority of Democratic-Republicans to Congress.

1832 First Presidential Nomination Convention— Democratic Party holds the first presidential nomination convention, re-nominating President Andrew Jackson for President.

1860 Lincoln Elected President— Reaction to the growing slavery crisis splits the Democratic Party and Republican Abraham Lincoln is elected president.

became the first U.S. president elected as the nominee of a political party. (To learn more about factionalism and the Framers, see The Living Constitution.)

Jefferson was deeply committed to the ideas of his party but not nearly as devoted to the idea of a party system. He regarded his party as a temporary measure necessary to defeat Adams, not a long-term political tool or an essential element of democracy. Jefferson's party never achieved widespread loyalty among the citizenry akin to that of today's Democrats and Republicans. Although Southerners were overwhelmingly partial to the Democratic-Republicans and New Englanders favored the Federalists, no broad-based party organizations existed to mobilize popular support. Rather, the congressional factions organized around Adams and Jeffer-

Was politics more collegial before the emergence of political parties? This 1793 cartoon illustrates the stark disdain that Federalist supporters of Alexander Hamilton had for Thomas Jefferson and his supporters. Federalists saw Jefferson's Democratic-Republicans as a coalition of visionaries and scoundrels who would not hesitate to sell their souls to the devil.

Photo courtesy: The Granger Collection

A Peep into the Antifederal Club

410

1912 "Bull Moose" Party wins 88 Electoral Votes— Former President Theodore Roosevelt, running as a "Bull Moose", wins the largest share of the Electoral College and highest popular vote percentage of any third-party candidate for President. Woodrow Wilson wins the presidency with 42% of the popular vote.

1992 Perot Runs for President—Texas billionaire and businessman Ross Perot wins 18.9% of the popular vote for President, the highest vote percentage for an independent candidate since T. Roosevelt in 1912.

2008 Michigan and Florida delegations sanctioned by DNC—Democratic National Committee threatens to bar MI and FL delegations from national convention for holding primaries before February 5, 2008. Delegates are ultimately seated and allowed to vote after extensive controversy and negotiation.

1944 *Smith* v. *Allwright*— The Supreme Court invalidates Texas' "white primary" and other party rules and nomination procedures that violate basic constitutional rights and liberties.

2002 Bipartisan Campaign Reform Act (BCRA)—This legislation eliminated the use of soft money by the political parties.

son primarily were designed to settle the dispute over how strong the new federal government would be.[3] Just as the nation was in its infancy, so, too, was the party system.

The Early Parties Fade

After the spirited confrontations of the republic's early years, political parties faded somewhat in importance for a quarter of a century. The Federalists ceased nominating presidential candidates by 1816, having failed to elect one of their own since Adams's victory in 1796, and by 1820 the party had dissolved. James Monroe's presidency from 1817 to 1825 produced the so-called Era of Good Feeling, when party politics was nearly suspended at the national level. Even during Monroe's tenure, however, party organizations continued to develop at the state level. Party growth was fueled in part by the enormous increase in the electorate that took place between 1820 and 1840, as the United States expanded westward and most states abolished property requirements as a condition of white male suffrage. During this twenty-year period, the number of votes cast in presidential contests rose from 300,000 to more than 2 million.

At the same time, U.S. politics was being democratized in other ways. By the 1820s, all the states except South Carolina had switched from state legislative selection of presidential electors to popular election of Electoral College members. This change helped transform presidential politics. No longer just the concern of society's upper crust, the election of the president became a matter for all qualified voters to decide.

Party membership broadened along with the electorate. After receiving criticism for being elitist and undemocratic, the small caucuses of congressional party leaders that had previously nominated candidates gave way to nominations at large party conventions. In

Photo courtesy: Museum of the City of New York/Hulton Archive/Getty Images

Who was Boss Tweed?
William M. "Boss" Tweed (1823–1878) was the leader of Tammany Hall, the Democratic Party political machine that ran New York City until his conviction on graft charges in 1873. A controversial figure, Tweed has been praised by some for using his machine to aid the sick and unemployed and fight for the rights of tenants and workers.

political machine
A party organization that recruits voter loyalty with tangible incentives and is characterized by a high degree of control over member activity.

1832, the Democratic Party, which succeeded the old Jeffersonian Democratic-Republicans, held the first national presidential nomination convention. Formed around President Andrew Jackson's popularity, the Democratic Party attracted most of the newly enfranchised voters, who were drawn to Jackson's charismatic style. His strong personality helped to polarize politics, and opposition to the president coalesced into the Whig Party. Among the Whig Party's early leaders was Henry Clay, the Speaker of the House from 1811 to 1820. The incumbent Jackson, having won a first term as president in 1828, defeated Clay in the 1832 presidential contest. Jackson was the first chief executive who won the White House as the nominee of a truly national, popularly based political party.

The Whigs and the Democrats continued to strengthen after 1832, establishing state and local organizations almost everywhere. Their competition was usually fierce and closely matched, and they brought the United States the first broadly supported two-party system in the Western world.[4] Unfortunately for the Whigs, the issue of slavery sharpened the many divisive tensions within the party, which led to its gradual dissolution and replacement by the new Republican Party. Formed in 1854 by anti-slavery activists, the Republican Party set its sights on the abolition (or at least the containment) of slavery. After a losing presidential effort for John C. Frémont in 1856, the party was able to assemble enough support primarily from former Whigs and anti-slavery northern Democrats to win the presidency for Abraham Lincoln in a fragmented 1860 vote. In that year, the South voted solidly Democratic, beginning a tradition so strong that not a single southern state voted Republican for president again until 1920.

Democrats and Republicans: The Golden Age

From the presidential election of 1860 to this day, the same two major parties, the Republicans and the Democrats, have dominated elections in the United States, and control of an electoral majority has seesawed between them. Party stability, the dominance of party organizations in local and state governments, and the impact of those organizations on the lives of millions of voters were the central traits of the era called the "Golden Age" of political parties. This era, which spanned the years 1874–1912, from the end of post–Civil War Reconstruction until the reforms of the Progressive era, featured remarkable stability in the identity of the two major political parties. Such stability has been exceptionally rare in democratic republics around the world.

Emigration from Europe (particularly from Ireland, Italy, and Germany) fueled the development in America of big-city **political machines** that gained control of local and state government during this time. A political machine is a party organization that uses tangible incentives such as jobs and favors to win loyalty among voters. Machines also are characterized by a high degree of leadership control over member activity. Party machines were a central element of life for millions of people in the United States during the Golden Age. For city-dwellers, their party and their government were virtually interchangeable during this time.

Political parties thus not only served the underlying political needs of the society, but also supplemented the population's desire for important social services. In addition to providing housing, employment, and even food to many voters, parties in most major cities provided entertainment by organizing torchlight parades, weekend picnics, socials, and other community events. Many citizens—even those who weren't particularly "political"—attended, thereby gaining some allegiance to one party or the other. The parties offered immigrants not just services but also the opportunity for upward social mobility as they rose in the organization. As a result, parties generated intense loyalty and devotion among their supporters and office holders that helped to produce startlingly high voter turnouts—75 percent or better in all presidential elections from 1876 to 1900—compared with today's 50–60 percent.[5]

The Modern Era

The modern era seems very different from the Golden Age of parties. Many social, political, technological, and governmental changes have contributed to changes in the nature of the national parties since the 1920s. Historically, the government's gradual assumption of important functions previously performed by the parties, such as printing ballots, conducting elections, and providing social welfare services, had a major impact. Beginning in the 1930s with Franklin Roosevelt's New Deal, social services began to be seen as a right of citizenship rather than as a privilege extended in exchange for a person's support of a party. Also, as the flow of immigrants slowed dramatically in the 1920s, party organizations gradually shrank in many places.

A **direct primary** system, in which party nominees were determined by the ballots of qualified voters rather than at party conventions, gained widespread adoption by the states in the first two decades of the twentieth century. Championed by the Progressive movement, direct primaries removed the power of nomination from party leaders and workers and gave it instead to a much broader and more independent electorate, thus loosening the tie between party nominees and the party organization.

direct primary
The selection of party candidates through the ballots of qualified voters rather than at party nominating conventions.

Additional Progressive movement reforms also contributed to reduced party influence in the United States. **Civil service laws,** for example, which require appointment on the basis of merit and competitive examinations, removed opportunities for much of the patronage used by the parties to reward their followers. The development of the civil service is discussed in greater detail in chapter 9.

civil service laws
These acts removed the staffing of the bureaucracy from political parties and created a professional bureaucracy filled through competition.

In the post–World War II era, extensive social changes also contributed to the move away from strong parties. A weakening of the party system gave rise to candidate and **issue-oriented politics**. Rather than a focus on party platforms, contemporary politics focuses on the individuals running for office and specific issues, such as civil rights, tax cutting, or environmentalism. Interest groups and lobbyists have stepped into the void that weaker parties have left behind. Candidates compete for endorsements and contributions from a variety of multi-issue as well as single-issue organizations. Issue politics tends to cut across party lines and encourages voters to **ticket-split**—to vote for candidates of different parties in the same election (a phenomenon we discuss in greater depth in chapter 13). Parties' diminished control over issues and campaigns also have left candidates considerable power in how they conduct themselves during election season and how they seek resources. This new **candidate-centered politics** is an outgrowth of voters focusing directly on the candidates, their particular issues, and character, rather than on their party affiliation.

issue-oriented politics
Politics that focuses on specific issues rather than on party, candidate, or other loyalties.

ticket-split
To vote for candidates of different parties for various offices in the same election.

candidate-centered politics
Politics that focuses directly on the candidates, their particular issues, and character, rather than on party affiliation.

Another post–World War II social change that has affected the parties is the population shift from urban to suburban locales. Millions of people have moved from the cities to the suburbs, where a sense of privacy and detachment can deter the most energetic party organizers. In addition, population growth in the last half-century has created districts with far more people, making it less feasible to knock on every door or shake every hand.[6]

Realignment

Periodically in election years, voters make dramatic shifts in partisan preference that drastically alter the political landscape. During these **party realignments,** existing party affiliations are subject to upheaval: many voters may change parties, and the youngest age group of voters may permanently adopt the label of the newly dominant party.[7]

party realignment
A shifting of party coalition groupings in the electorate that remains in place for several elections.

Preceding a major realignment are one or more **critical elections,** which may polarize voters around new issues and personalities in reaction to crucial developments, such as a war or an economic depression. Three tumultuous eras in particular have produced significant critical elections. First, Thomas Jefferson, in reaction against the Federalist Party's agenda of a strong, centralized federal government, formed the Democratic-Republican Party, which took the presidency and Congress in 1800. Second, in reaction to the growing crisis over slavery, the Whig Party gradually dissolved and the Republican Party gained strength and ultimately won the presidency in 1860. Third, the Great Depression of the 1930s caused large numbers

critical election
An election that signals a party realignment through voter polarization around new issues.

of voters to repudiate Republican Party policies and embrace the Democratic Party. Each of these cases resulted in fundamental and enduring alterations in the party equation. See Figure 12.2 for the electoral results of these three critical elections.

The last confirmed major realignment, then, happened in the 1928–1936 period, as Republican Herbert Hoover's presidency was held to one term because of voter anger about the Depression. In 1932, Democrat Franklin D. Roosevelt swept to power as the electorate decisively rejected Hoover and the Republicans. This dramatic vote of "no confidence" was followed by substantial changes in policy by the new president. The majority of voters responded favorably to Roosevelt's New Deal policies, accepted his vision of society, and ratified their choice of the new president's party in subsequent presidential and congressional elections.

The idea that party realignments occurred on a predictable, periodic basis beguiled many political scientists in the 1960s and 1970s, and much attention was focused on awaiting the next sea change in partisan alignment.[8] However, no uniform shift in partisan alignment has occurred in American politics since the election of Franklin D. Roosevelt in 1932. In fact, divided partisan government has been a dominant outcome of elections since World War II. Many scholars today question the value of party realignments in understanding partisanship and policy change. While critical elections share some degree of similarity, each is precipitated by distinctive political changes that are linked to the particular period and issues.[9] Nonetheless, party realignments offer a useful basis for understanding how pivotal elections may lastingly alter the direction of American politics.

A critical election is not the only occasion when changes in partisan affiliation are accommodated. In truth, every election produces realignment to some degree, since some individuals are undoubtedly pushed to change parties by events and by their reactions to the candidates. Research suggests that partisanship is much more responsive to current issues and personalities than had been believed earlier.[10]

Secular Realignment

secular realignment
The gradual rearrangement of party coalitions, based more on demographic shifts than on shocks to the political system.

Although the term *realignment* is usually applied only if momentous events such as war or economic depression produce enduring and substantial alterations in the party coalitions, political scientists have long recognized that a more gradual rearrangement of party coalitions can occur.[11] Called **secular realignment,** this piecemeal process depends not on convulsive shocks to the political system but on slow, almost barely discernible demographic shifts—the shrinking of one party's base of support and the enlargement of the other's, for example—or simple generational replacement (that is, the dying off of the older generation and the maturing of the younger generation). According to one version of this theory, in an era of weaker party attachments (such as we currently are experiencing), a dramatic, full-scale realignment may not be possible.[12] Still, a critical mass of voters may be attracted for years to one party's banner in waves or streams, if that party's leadership and performance are consistently exemplary.

The prospect of a national realignment is unlikely as long as party ties remain tenuous for so many voters.[13] However, regionally there have been slow but stable partisan realignments that have affected the power bases of the major parties. During the 1990s, the southern states, traditionally Democratic stalwarts since the Civil War, shifted dramatically toward the Republican Party. The Northeast, a longtime reliable voting bloc for Republicans, became increasingly Democratic during the same period. Many factors have contributed to these gradual regional shifts in party allegiance. Southern Democrats were the most conservative of the New Deal coalition, favoring the social status quo and opposing civil rights reform. As the Democratic Party shifted its platform toward more liberal social causes such as civil rights and social spending, many southern voters and politicians shifted their allegiance toward the Republicans. In a region where voting for a Republican was once considered taboo, the South is now one of the most reliable blocs of Republican voters.[14]

SIMULATION

You Are Redrawing the Districts in Your State

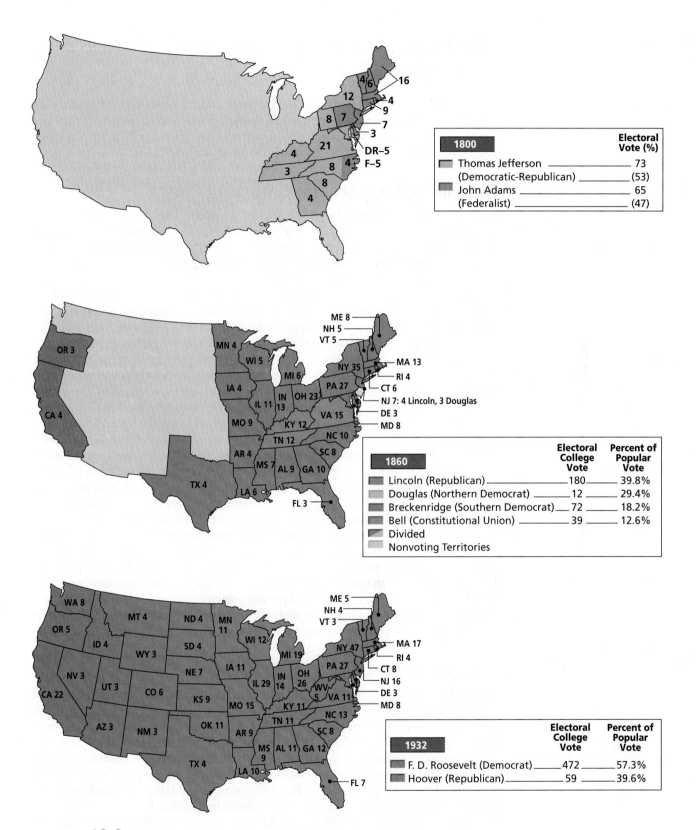

1800

	Electoral Vote (%)
Thomas Jefferson	73
(Democratic-Republican)	(53)
John Adams	65
(Federalist)	(47)

4 6
16
12
4
9
8 7
7
3
4 21
DR–5
F–5
4 8 4
3
8
4

ME 8
NH 5
VT 5
MN 4
OR 3
WI 5
MI 6
NY 35
MA 13
RI 4
IA 4
PA 27
CT 6
CA 4
IN OH 23
IL 11 13
NJ 7: 4 Lincoln, 3 Douglas
DE 3
MO 9
VA 15
MD 8
KY 12
TN 12
NC 10
AR 4
SC 8
MS 7 AL 9 GA 10
TX 4
LA 6
FL 3

1860

	Electoral College Vote	Percent of Popular Vote
Lincoln (Republican)	180	39.8%
Douglas (Northern Democrat)	12	29.4%
Breckenridge (Southern Democrat)	72	18.2%
Bell (Constitutional Union)	39	12.6%
Divided		
Nonvoting Territories		

WA 8
MT 4
ND 4
MN 11
OR 5
ID 4
WY 3
SD 4
WI 12
ME 5
NH 4
VT 3
MI 19
NY 47
MA 17
RI 4
NV 3
NE 7
IA 11
PA 27
CT 8
CA 22
UT 3
CO 6
KS 9
IL 29
IN 14
OH 26
WV 5
VA 11
NJ 16
DE 3
MD 8
AZ 3
NM 3
OK 11
MO 15
KY 11
TN 11
NC 13
AR 9
SC 8
MS 9 AL 11 GA 12
TX 4
LA 10
FL 7

1932

	Electoral College Vote	Percent of Popular Vote
F. D. Roosevelt (Democrat)	472	57.3%
Hoover (Republican)	59	39.6%

FIGURE 12.2 Electoral College Results for Three Realigning Presidential Contests

The Functions of the American Party System

For over 200 years, the two-party system has served as the mechanism American society uses to organize and resolve social and political conflict. Political parties often are the chief agents of change in our political system. They provide vital services to society, and it would be difficult to envision political life without them.

Mobilizing Support and Gathering Power

Party affiliation is enormously helpful to elected leaders. They can count on support among their fellow party members not just in times of trouble and times when they need to gather support for tight votes, but also on general political and legislative matters. Therefore the parties aid office holders by giving them room to develop their policies and by mobilizing support for them.

Because there are only two major parties in the United States, citizens who are interested in politics or public policy are mainly attracted to one or the other party, creating natural majorities or near majorities for party office holders to command. The party generates a community of interest that bonds disparate groups over time into a **coalition**. This continuing mutual interest eliminates the necessity of forming a new coalition for every campaign or every issue. Imagine the constant chaos and mad scrambles for public support that would ensue without the continuity provided by the parties.

It remains an open debate whether or not party activities that are designed to mobilize voters actually increase political participation among the general public. It is easy to see how party efforts such as voter registration drives and get out the vote (GOTV) efforts might increase voter participation. In GOTV drives, parties spend tremendous resources to identify their base voters and then motivate these people to cast a ballot through the mail or at the ballot box. GOTV drives have been an increasingly effective means of winning elections, helping to drive up the number of committed partisan voters going to the polls.[15] The Republican Party in particular has been very successful in identifying likely voters and getting them to vote. But, the overall effect of increasing the numbers of registered voters or motivating those unaffiliated with political parties to vote is not as pronounced. While the 2008 presidential election showed an upswing in voter turnout for the second consecutive presidential election, there was no clear trend toward party alignment within the electorate. Overall, however, there seem to be some signs of partisan resurgence after a historically long period of party weakness.

A Force for Stability and Moderation

As mechanisms for organizing and containing political change, the parties are a potent force for stability. They represent continuity in the wake of changing issues and personalities, anchoring the electorate in the midst of the storm of new political policies and people. Because of its overarching desire to win elections, each party in a sense acts to moderate public opinion. Traditionally, parties have tamed their own extreme elements by pulling them toward an ideological center in order to attract a majority of votes on Election Day. But, an increasingly polarized political landscape has diminished the moderating effects of partisan competition.[16]

The parties encourage stability in the type of coalitions they form. There are inherent contradictions in these coalitions that, oddly enough, strengthen the nation even as they strain party unity. Franklin D. Roosevelt's Democratic New Deal coalition, for example, included many African Americans and most southern whites, opposing groups nonetheless joined in common political purpose by economic hardship and, in the case of better-off Southerners, in longtime voting habits.[17]

coalition
A group made up of interests or organizations that join forces for the purpose of electing public officials.

While parties still serve to moderate the turbulent passions of democracy, many politicians have become increasingly strident in their partisan attacks in their struggle for power and influence in the electorate.[18] The wrangling in the Senate over President George W. Bush's judicial nominations, which inspired extended and rancorous debate over the survival of the filibuster, led many to decry a lack of decorum and moderation in party politics. However, as discussed in chapter 7, a coalition of moderate senators from both parties averted any changes to the rules governing the filibuster. Despite the tribulations of public opinion or partisan passions, the party system still manages to organize and direct effective political action.

Unity, Linkage, and Accountability

Parties are the glue that holds together the disparate elements of the U.S. governmental and political apparatus. The Framers designed a system that divides and subdivides power, making it possible to preserve individual liberty but difficult to coordinate and produce action in a timely fashion. Parties help compensate for this drawback by linking the executive and legislative branches. Although rivalry between these two branches of U.S. government is inevitable, the partisan affiliations of the leaders of each branch constitute a common basis for cooperation, as the president and his fellow party members in Congress usually demonstrate daily. When President George W. Bush proposed a major new program of tax cuts, Republican members of Congress were the first to speak up in favor of the program and to orchestrate efforts for its passage. Not surprisingly, presidential candidates and presidents are inclined to push policies similar to those advocated by their party's congressional leaders.[19]

Even within each branch, there is intended fragmentation, and the party once again helps narrow the differences between the House of Representatives and the Senate, or between the president and the department heads in the executive bureaucracy. Similarly, the division of national, state, and local governments, while always an invitation to conflict, is made more workable and more easily coordinated by the intersecting party relationships that exist among office holders at all levels. Party affiliation, in other words, is a basis for mediation and negotiation laterally among the branches of government and vertically among national, state, and local layers.

The party's linkage function does not end there. Party identification and organization foster communication between the voter and the candidate, as well as between the voter and the office holder. The party connection is one means of increasing accountability in election campaigns and in government. Candidates on the campaign trail and elected party leaders in office are required from time to time to account for their performance at party-sponsored forums, nominating primaries, and conventions.

The Electioneering Function

The election, proclaimed author H. G. Wells, is "democracy's ceremonial, its feast, its great function," and the political parties assist this ceremony in essential ways. First, the parties help to funnel eager, interested individuals into politics and government. While most candidates are self-recruited, some are also recruited each year by the two parties, as are many of the candidates' staff members—the people who manage the campaigns and go on to serve in key governmental positions once the election has been won.

Elections can have meaning in a democracy only if they are competitive, and in the United States they probably could not be competitive without the parties. (When we use the term *competitive*, we mean that both parties have sufficient organization, money, and people to run a vigorous election campaign, and to sustain their arguments through the period of governance.)

Party as a Voting and Issue Cue

A voter's party identification can act as an invaluable filter for information, a perceptual screen that affects how he or she digests political news. Parties try to cultivate a popular image and help inform the public about issues through advertising and voter contact. Therefore, party affiliation provides a useful cue for voters, particularly for the least informed and least interested, who can use the party label as a shortcut or substitute for interpreting issues and events they may not fully comprehend. Better-educated and more involved voters also find party identification helpful. After all, no one has the time to study every issue carefully or to become fully knowledgeable about every candidate seeking public office.

Policy Formulation and Promotion

national party platform
A statement of the general and specific philosophy and policy goals of a political party, usually promulgated at the national convention.

As discussed at the beginning of this chapter, the **national party platform** is the most visible instrument that parties use to formulate, convey, and promote public policy. Every four years, each party writes for the presidential nominating conventions a lengthy platform explaining its positions on key issues. In a two-party system, a platform not only explains what a party supports but also describes more clearly the important differences between the two dominant parties, giving voters meaningful policy choices through the electoral process. In other words, a party platform not only explains the party's policy preferences but also argues why its preferences are superior to those of the rival party. This is particularly true for contentious social issues on which there is little room for compromise and which divide the electorate, like abortion and same-sex marriage.

State Control and National Platforms

Scholarship suggests that about two-thirds of the promises in the victorious party's presidential platform have been completely or mostly implemented. Moreover, about one-half or more of the pledges of the losing party also tend to find their way into public policy, a trend that no doubt reflects the effort of both parties to support broad policy positions that enjoy widespread support in the general public.[20] For example, continuing the war in Iraq, which a majority of Americans supported leading into the 2004 presidential election, was endorsed in both party platforms. Both parties also supported the larger war on terrorism and the focus on homeland security, which has led some critics to point out that the two-party system, and its preference for broadly supported issues, can severely limit voter choice.

Besides mobilizing Americans on a permanent basis, then, the parties convert the cacophony of hundreds of identifiable social and economic groups into a two-part semi-harmony that is much more comprehensible, if not always on key and pleasing to the ears. The simplicity of two-party politics may be deceptive, given the enormous variety in public policy choices, but a sensible system of representation in the American context might be impossible without it.

Crashing the Party: Minor Parties in the American Two-Party System

proportional representation
A voting system that apportions legislative seats according to the percentage of the vote won by a particular political party.

winner-take-all system
An electoral system in which the party that receives at least one more vote than any other party wins the election.

Unlike many European countries that use **proportional representation** (awarding legislative seats according to the percentage of votes a political party receives), the United States has a "single-member, plurality" electoral system, often referred to as a **winner-take-all system** (a system in which the party that receives at least one more vote than any other party wins the election). To paraphrase the legendary football coach Vince Lombardi, finishing first is not everything, it is the *only* thing in U.S. politics; placing second, even by one vote, doesn't count. The winner-take-all system encourages the grouping of interests into as few parties as possible (the democratic minimum being two). Moreover, the two parties will often move to the left or right on issues in order to gain popular support. Some observers claim that parties in the United States have no permanent positions at all, only permanent interests—winning elections.[21] Regardless of one's position on this issue, it is clear that the adaptive nature of the two parties further forestalls the growth of third parties in the United States.

Smaller parties can have a role in countries that use proportional representation, which often guarantee legislative seats to any faction securing as little as 5 percent of the vote. Rather than running for individual legislative seats, candidates for each party are placed on a "party list" and voters choose among competing parties. If a party wins 50 percent of the votes nationwide, it will be awarded 50 percent of the legislative seats, with the top half of the candidates on the party's list assigned to those seats. Proportional representation encourages a multi-party system and can make it harder for one party to form a majority. While this system has been a source of instability in some parliamentary democracies, proponents of proportional representation cite its strengths, such as encouraging consensus and accommodation and allowing for a broader representation of views.[22]

Despite their disadvantages in the United States, minor parties based on causes often neglected by the major parties have significantly affected American politics. (To learn more about minor parties, see Join the Debate: Third Parties: Good or Bad for the American Political System?) Third parties find their roots in sectionalism (as did the South's states' rights Dixiecrats, who broke away from the Democrats in 1948), in economic protest (such as the agrarian revolt that fueled the Populists, an 1892 prairie-states party), in specific issues (such as the Green Party's support of the environment), in ideology (the Socialist, Communist, and Libertarian Parties are examples), and in appealing, charismatic personalities (Theodore Roosevelt's affiliation with the Bull Moose Party in 1912 is perhaps the best case). Many minor parties have drawn strength from a combination of these sources. The American Independent Party enjoyed a measure of success because of a dynamic leader (George Wallace in 1968), a firm geographic base (the South), and an emotional issue (an opposition to federal civil rights legislation). In 1992, Ross Perot, the billionaire with a folksy Texas manner, was a charismatic leader whose campaign was fueled by the deficit issue (as well as by his personal fortune).

Minor-party and independent candidates are not limited to presidential elections. Many also run in congressional elections, and the numbers appear to be growing. In the 2006 congressional elections, for example, nearly 350 minor-party and independent candidates ran for seats in the House and Senate—almost three and half times as many as in 1968 and one and a half times the number that ran in 1980. Only two members of the 111th Congress—Senator Joe Lieberman, who lost the Democratic primary but won reelection as an independent in Connecticut, and freshman Senator Bernie Sanders of Vermont—are independents, and both caucus with the Democrats. Minor-party

TIMELINE

Third Parties in American History

Why do minor parties form? In 1912, former President Theodore Roosevelt lost the Republican nomination to incumbent president William Howard Taft, a conservative. Roosevelt, who represented the progressive wing of the Republican Party and supported issues like conservation and labor protections, staged a walkout from the Republican Convention. He and other like-minded Republicans reconvened their own Progressive "Bull Moose" Party at the Chicago Coliseum in August of 1912, shown here.

Photo courtesy: Library of Congress

Join the Debate

Third Parties: Good or Bad for the American Political System?

OVERVIEW: Third parties are a recurring political phenomenon in the United States, and they originate for one of two reasons: (1) to express an alternative political platform to those held by the two major parties or (2) to launch an alternative candidate for public office.

The Socialist Party favored a dismantling of the American capitalist system and a complete overhaul of the government. The Dixiecrats, who believed in continued racial segregation, broke from the Democratic Party because it was beginning to abandon this position. These parties emerged to express ideas lacking support in the Republican and Democratic Parties.

Third parties have also, upon occasion, offered strong alternative presidential candidates. In 1911, the Bull Moose Party—known officially as the Progressive Party—was conceived to support Theodore Roosevelt's 1912 presidential campaign. In 1992, Ross Perot founded the Reform Party with the sole purpose of running for president. The Green Party, on the other hand, courted Ralph Nader, a well-known consumer advocate and political activist, to be their presidential candidate in 2000 in order to increase their exposure among voters nationwide.

These parties, and the candidates that bore their standard, gained popularity and support based on dissatisfaction with the candidates and trends in the two major parties at the time. Despite their failures at the ballot box, they all exerted pressure on the two major parties and most influenced election outcomes to some extent.

While single issues and popular candidates are successful ingredients for the creation of third parties, they lack the power to sustain a party's viability over time. In addition, the trouble with single-issue parties is that the issue is usually specific to a certain group of people or a certain area of the nation that is too small to impact a national election. If these third parties fought for more local or state representation, they would have better chances of winning, as the Vermont Socialists did when one of their own, Bernard Sanders, was elected to the U.S. House of Representatives in 1990 as an independent. Elected to the Senate in 2006, Sanders has caucused with the Democrats since coming to Congress.

The trouble with candidate-oriented third parties is that they depend utterly on their candidate. When interest in Ross Perot declined, the support for the Reform Party seemed to evaporate with it, until former professional wrestler and independent governor of Minnesota Jesse Ventura became the new candidate on which the party could focus. When arch-conservative and former Republican insider Pat Buchanan received the Reform Party nomination for president, Ventura and his independent voters backed out, leaving the Reform Party in ruins. The Green Party, on the other hand, has maintained a presence at both the national and state levels even without a notable candidate at the top of the ticket in 2004 and 2008. Like the Libertarians, the Greens have survived because of a coherent party platform and strong, enthusiastic support at the grass roots.

Arguments IN FAVOR of Third Parties

- Third parties benefit the United States because they allow for a greater diversity of opinion, beyond that of Democrats and Republicans. Often the issues promoted by third parties and the candidates that represent them gain popular support, and the major parties are then forced to address them. For example, several of the reforms proposed by the GOP's 1994 Contract with America had been part of Ross Perot's campaign platform in 1992. In cases like this, third parties are essential in guaranteeing that all voices are heard.

- The two-party system is not integral to a successful representative democracy. While American democracy quickly evolved into a

candidates for the House are most likely to emerge under three conditions: (1) when a House seat becomes open; (2) when a minor-party candidate has previously competed in the district; and, (3) when partisan competition between the two major parties in the district is close.[23]

Above all, third parties make electoral progress in direct proportion to the failure of the two major parties to incorporate new ideas or alienated groups or to nominate attractive candidates as their standard-bearers. Third parties do best when declining trust in the two major political parties plagues the electorate.[24] Usually, though, third

political system characterized by two major parties, many other successful democracies operate with multi-party systems. Spain, Germany, South Korea, and Israel, for example, have stable democratic governments that continue to provide successful leadership and progress for their citizens.

- Third parties can provide useful solutions to political problems on the local and regional level. While the major parties must incorporate a broad range of issues in order to maintain national appeal, third parties are able to focus on a single issue or on a few issues specific to a state or locality. While there has never been a third-party president, there have been several third-party state governors in recent history.

Arguments AGAINST Third Parties

- Third parties can be composed of political extremists who are uninterested in real politics. With an intense focus on a specific issue or agenda, some third parties and their candidates have been known to disregard the idea of compromise that characterizes the American political system and is the basis for progress. To energize supporters, they may use emotional appeals that many find repulsive, resulting in disenchantment with the system and less participation in the process.

- Some third parties exhibit strongly anti-democratic tendencies. In the 1940s, the Dixiecrats wanted to preserve the Jim Crow South, where African Americans were legally discriminated against and states required businesses and public buildings to separate white patrons from black patrons. Earlier in the twentieth century, the Bull Moose Party nearly became a cult of personality for Theodore Roosevelt. His supporters' hero worship prevented the party from focusing on the issue positions that he represented.

- Third parties may impact elections and produce an outcome contrary to the popular sentiment.
Frequently a third party will arise out of dissatisfaction within a major party on a specific issue, or among individuals with particular political leanings. As a result, the third party can drain support disproportionately from voters of the major party on Election Day, leading to a victory for a candidate who would not have had a majority in a two-candidate race. Ross Perot is often credited with costing then-President George Bush a second term in 1992, by appealing to a large number of conservative voters who might otherwise have voted for Bush. Some cite Ralph Nader as the primary reason for Al Gore's defeat in 2000, because he pulled much of his support from liberal voters.

Photo courtesy: Nicholas Kamm/AFP/Getty Images

What minor party candidates ran for president in 2008? Former Republican congressman Bob Barr of Georgia ran as the Libertarian Party's presidential nominee in 2008. Libertarians believe in limited government, a strong defense of civil liberties, free trade, and minimal involvement in foreign affairs.

Continuing the Debate

1. In what ways has the current political climate benefited from the presence of third parties? How have third parties harmed the system?

2. What influence did third-party candidates have on the outcome of the 2008 presidential election?

To Follow the Debate Online, Go To:

Third Party Watch:
www.thirdpartywatch.com
Open Debates:
www.opendebates.org/theissue/

parties are eventually co-opted by one of the two major parties, each of them eager to take the politically popular issue that gave rise to the third party and make it theirs in order to secure the allegiance of the third party's supporters. For example, the Republicans of the 1970s absorbed many of the states' rights planks of George Wallace's 1968 presidential bid. Both major parties have also more recently attempted to attract independent voters by sponsoring reforms of the governmental process, such as Senators John McCain and Russ Feingold's groundbreaking attempt to reform the nation's campaign finance laws.

The Party Organization

Although the distinctions might not be as clear today as they were two or three decades ago, the two major parties remain fairly loosely organized, with national, state, and local branches. (To learn more about Political Party organization, see Figure 12.3.) The different levels of each party represent diverse interests in Washington, D.C., state capitals, and local governments throughout the nation.

National Committees

The first national party committees were skeletal and formed some years after the creation of the presidential nominating conventions in the 1830s. First the Democrats in 1848 and then the Republicans in 1856 established national governing bodies—the Democratic National Committee, or DNC, and the Republican National Committee, or RNC—to make arrangements for the national conventions and to coordinate the subsequent presidential campaigns. In addition, to serve their interests, the congressional party caucuses in both houses organized their own national committees, loosely allied with the DNC and RNC. The National Republican Congressional Committee (NRCC) was started in 1866 when the Radical Republican congressional delegation was feuding with Abraham Lincoln's moderate successor, President Andrew Johnson, and wanted a counterweight to his control of the RNC. At the same time, House and Senate Democrats set up a similar committee.

After the popular election of U.S. senators was initiated in 1913 with the ratification of the Seventeenth Amendment to the Constitution, both parties organized separate Senate campaign committees. This three-part arrangement of national party

FIGURE **12.3** Political Party Organization in America: From Base to Pinnacle

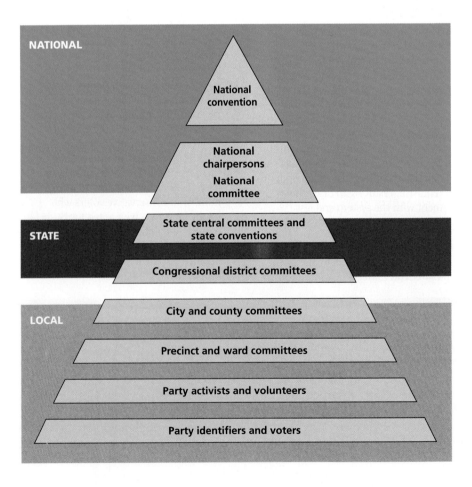

NATIONAL

National convention

National chairpersons
National committee

STATE

State central committees and state conventions

Congressional district committees

LOCAL

City and county committees

Precinct and ward committees

Party activists and volunteers

Party identifiers and voters

committee, House party committee, and Senate party committee has persisted in both parties to the present day, and each party's three committees are located in Washington, D.C. There is, however, an informal division of labor among the national committees. Whereas the DNC and RNC focus primarily on aiding presidential campaigns and conducting general party-building activities, the congressional campaign committees work primarily to maximize the number of seats held by their respective parties in Congress. In the past two decades, all six national committees have become major, service-oriented organizations in American politics.[25]

Leadership

The key national party official is the chairperson of the national committee. Although the chair is formally elected by the national committee, he or she is usually selected by the sitting president or newly nominated presidential candidate, who is accorded the right to name the individual for at least the duration of his or her campaign. Only the post-campaign, out-of-power party committee actually has the authority to appoint a chairperson independently. The committee-crowned chairpersons generally have the greatest impact on the party, because they come to their posts at times of crisis when a leadership vacuum exists. (To learn more about the importance of national party leaders, see Politics Now: The Impact of a National Committee Chair.)

The chair often becomes the prime spokesperson and arbitrator for the party during the four years between elections. He or she is called on to damp down factionalism, negotiate candidate disputes, and prepare the machinery for the next presidential election. Perhaps most critically, the chair is called upon to raise funds and keep the party financially strong. Balancing the interests of all potential White House contenders is a particularly difficult job, and strict neutrality is normally expected from the chair.

National Conventions

Every four years, each party holds a **national convention** to nominate its presidential and vice presidential candidates. Much of any party chairperson's work involves planning the presidential nominating convention, the most publicized and vital event on the party's calendar. Until 1984, gavel-to-gavel coverage was standard practice on all national television networks. Recently, however, television networks have cut back convention air time to little more than one hour a day, during which the most important speakers speak as much to viewers as they do to convention attendees. The cable networks have more extensive coverage of the evening's speeches, but little is heard over the commentary being provided by the networks' large panels of experts and pundits. Although none of the networks expanded their coverage in 2008, there was a significant increase in interest among the public. Over 39 million Americans watched Senator Barack Obama give his acceptance speech at Denver's 75,000-seat Invesco Field, which was filled to capacity. This was the largest television audience ever for a convention speech, until one week later, when over 40 million Americans watched Senator McCain accept his party's nomination at the Xcel Center in St. Paul. Large audiences of 38 million and 26 million, respectively, also tuned in to watch Governor Sarah Palin accept the Republican vice presidential nomination and Senator Hillary Clinton give a keynote address asking her Democratic supporters to support Barack Obama in the general election. Most of the recent party chairpersons, in cooperation with the incumbent president or likely nominee, have tried to orchestrate every minute of the conventions in order to project just the right image. By and large, they have succeeded, though at the price of draining spontaneity and excitement from the convention process.

In addition to nominating the presidential ticket, the convention also fulfills its role as the ultimate governing body for the party. The rules adopted and the party platform that is passed serve as durable guidelines that steer the party until the next convention.

national convention
A party meeting held in the presidential election year for the purposes of nominating a presidential and vice presidental ticket and adopting a platform.

The Impact of a National Committee Chair

The Dems, Now Dancing to His Tune

PERRY BACON JR.

When running for president in 2004, Howard Dean famously screamed at Democrats; in 2008, plenty of Democrats are screaming right back.

But Democrats have some good reasons to stop kicking Dean around. . . . If the Democrats win in 2008, they may come to thank Dr. Dean [chair of the Democratic National Committee] for providing the medicine that cured some of the party's ills.

Sen. Barack Obama's campaign has been groundbreaking on many levels, but its widely hailed use of the Internet to create a large base of small donors largely recycles the breakthrough that powered Dean's 2004 campaign. Despite having had more time to plan for her presidential run, Clinton has often found herself outmaneuvered at creative online fundraising by Obama, and Sen. John McCain may find himself at a sizable fundraising disadvantage to either Democrat. . . .

As the Democrats tried to win back Congress in 2006, Dean found himself back at the center of controversy. The new DNC chairman set out to forge what he called the "50-state strategy," spend-ing millions to start building party organizations in red states such as Alabama. That infuriated congressional Democrats who wanted to spend the money on tar-geted districts in swing states such as Ohio and Pennsylvania. The Democrats did win some congressional seats in GOP-leaning states such as Indiana, but even Dean might acknowledge that that had less to do with the small number of ground-level organizers he deployed than with weak GOP incumbents forced to defend an unpopular war. Still, Dean got some results: a study by Harvard's Elaine Kamarck found that Democratic turnout in 2006 was higher in places where Dean's new organizers were work-ing.

Dean's basic point was also some-thing Democrats may come to embrace: Far more Democrats live in some very red states than you might guess, and if the Democrats want to build a perma-nent majority in Congress, they'll need to win at least some seats in those areas.

It's no accident that Obama, not Dean, is benefiting most from some of Dean's insights. The DNC chief's check-ered track record makes it hard for some Democrats to laud him. Many Democ-rats say that he has by and large failed at building strong organizations, with the DNC finding itself with far less cash on hand than the Republican National Committee, despite the paucity of grass-roots enthusiasm for the GOP. Dean is also often described as weak in the two areas party chairs are supposed to excel at: raising money and providing "mes-sage discipline." Many Democrats still cringe when the loose-lipped former gov-ernor appears on television to push the party's message. Meanwhile, his limited relationships with many party insiders have made it harder for him to referee party disputes, such as stopping Michi-gan and Florida from moving their pri-maries up, or persuade the two Democ-ratic brawlers not to bloody each other.

But those shortcomings don't tarnish the underlying point: Howard Dean has been a man ahead of his time. When he leaves Washington for good next year, the improved fortunes he has helped bring to his party may be enough to make him want to scream.

Discussion Questions

1. In retrospect, was Howard Dean's strategy for allocating national party resources a more effective strategy for expanding the Democrats' majorities in Congress and winning the White House than targeting key districts and states?
2. Despite Barack Obama's record-breaking fund-raising totals in 2008, the DNC under Howard Dean's leadership lagged behind the RNC in raising money. What are some explanations for why there was such a disparity between Obama's and the DNC's fund-raising?

States and Localities

Although national committee activities of all kinds attract most of the media atten-tion, the party is structurally based not in Washington, D.C., but in the states and localities. Except for the campaign finance arena, virtually all government regulation of political parties is left to the states. Most importantly, the vast majority of party leadership positions are filled at subnational levels.

The arrangement of party committees provides for a broad base of support. The smallest voting unit, the precinct, usually takes in a few adjacent neighborhoods and is the fundamental building block of the party. There are more than 100,000 precincts in the United States. The precinct committee members are the foot soldiers of any party, and their efforts are supplemented by party committees above them in the wards, cities, counties, towns, villages, and congressional districts.

The state governing body supervising this collection of local party organizations is usually called the state central (or executive) committee. Its members come from all major geographic units, as determined by and selected under state law. Generally, state parties are free to act within the limits set by their state legislatures without interference from the national party, except in the selection and seating of presidential convention delegates. National Democrats have been particularly inclined to regulate this aspect of party life. With the decline of big-city political machines, few local parties are strong enough to defy national party policy positions or to select nominees against the national party's wishes.

When Democrats in Michigan and Florida scheduled their presidential primaries for January 2008, they violated their national party's rule that only Iowa, New Hampshire, Nevada, and South Carolina could hold their nomination contests prior to February 5. In response, the Democratic National Committee (DNC) voted to strip both states of their delegates to the national convention. Party leaders, however, were concerned that such severe sanctions would affect Democratic turnout in Michigan and Florida in November, jeopardizing Democrats' ability to win those crucial swing states. When the DNC Rules Committee met in May 2008, Democrats sought a way to include the renegade delegates while maintaining the integrity of the process. The Rules Committee ultimately decided that all of the Michigan and Florida delegates would be seated at the convention, but that each of their votes would count for only half a vote. Full voting rights were ultimately restored to both delegations just before the convention.

Photo courtesy: Manny Garcia/Bloomberg News/Landov

Although weaker with respect to how they affect the national party, state and local parties have become significantly more effective over the past three decades in terms of fund-raising, campaign events, registration drives, publicity of party and candidate activity, and the distribution of campaign literature.[26] Examining separately the national, state, and local parties should not lead us to overlook the increasing integration of these committees, however. The growing reliance of state parties on national party funding has fundamentally changed the balance of power in the American party system. Whereas power previously flowed up from the state and local parties to the national committees, the national committees now enjoy considerable leverage over state and local parties.[27]

The relationships among the national, state, and local party committees have been affected by the passage of the Bipartisan Campaign Reform Act (BCRA) that took effect following the 2002 midterm elections (see chapter 14 to learn more about BCRA). As a result of the new law, national party committees were able to transfer far less money to state parties to be used for shared activities. This separation has not weakened state parties, however, and only slightly reduced the influence of the national parties. State parties made up for the loss of national party transfers by raising more money from individual donors, whose contribution limits were increased by BCRA. Other national-level committees also were allowed to increase their contributions to state party organizations under the law. An increasing number of independent political committees, moreover, have been formed to circumvent the new regulations.[28]

In 2004, independent political committees spent nearly $612 million, with over two-thirds of their money directed toward federal races and the national parties. In 2008, Senator Obama's decision to decline public financing and Senator McCain's reliance on the RNC to finance a significant portion of his advertising and voter mobilization budgets helped reduce the role of independent groups. Independent groups spent approximately $400 million in 2008, with half of the expenditures directed toward state races and state parties.

How do national parties discipline unruly state parties?
On May 31, 2008, protesters gathered outside a meeting of the DNC Rules and Bylaws Committee as it debated how to treat delegates from Florida and Michigan at the upcoming Democratic National Convention. With over 591,000 votes cast in Michigan, almost 1.7 million votes cast in Florida, and both states expected to be battle ground states in the general election, the Committee's solution was to give each delegate half a vote. Before the convention, Senator Barack Obama, assured of winning the nomination, offered a motion to seat all of Michigan and Florida's delegates and grant them full voting rights.

Informal Groups

The formal structure of party organization is supplemented by numerous official and semi-official groups that attempt to affect politics through the formal party organization. Both the DNC and RNC have affiliated organizations of state and local party women (the National Federation of Democratic Women and the National Federation of Republican Women), as well as numerous college campus organizations, including the College Democrats of America and the College Republican National Committee. The youth divisions (the Young Democrats of America and the Young Republicans' National Federation) have a generous definition of "young," up to and including age thirty-five. State governors in each party have their own party associations, too: the Democratic Governors Association and the Republican Governors Association.

Just outside the party orbit are the supportive interest groups and associations that often provide money, labor, or other forms of assistance to the parties. Labor unions, progressive political action committees (PACs), teachers, African American and liberal women's groups, and Americans for Democratic Action are some of the Democratic Party's organizational groups. Business PACs, the U.S. Chamber of Commerce, fundamentalist Christian organizations, and some anti-abortion groups work closely with the Republicans.

think tank
Institutional collection of policy-oriented researchers and academics who are sources of policy ideas.

Each U.S. party has several institutionalized sources of policy ideas. Though unconnected to the parties in any official sense, these **think tanks** (institutional collections of policy-oriented researchers and academics) influence party positions and platforms. Republicans have dominated the world of think tanks, with prominent conservative groups including the Hudson Institute, American Enterprise Institute, and Heritage Foundation. And, the libertarian Cato Institute is closely aligned with the Republican Party. While generally fewer in number and enjoying far less funding than their conservative counterparts, prominent think tanks that generally align with the Democratic Party include the Center for National Policy and Open Society Institute. The Brookings Institution, founded in 1916, prides itself on a scholarly and nonpartisan approach to public policy.

The Transformation of the Party Organization

Both major political parties have supplemented labor-intensive, person-to-person operations with modern technological and communication strategies, and both parties are similar in the objectives they pursue to achieve political power. Nevertheless, each party has its strengths and weaknesses.

The contemporary national Republican Party has considerable organizational prowess, often surpassing the Democrats in fund-raising by large margins (see Figure 12.4). In recent election cycles, Democrats have worked hard to compete with the Republican Party fund-raising machine, which is fueled by a large number of wealthy donors.

soft money
The virtually unregulated money funneled through political parties for party-building purposes, such as get out the vote efforts or issue ads. Banned after 2002.

In 2004, the Republican Party outraised the Democratic Party, but the Democrats came closer to matching the Republicans than in earlier elections. This was true despite the fact that **soft money,** the virtually unregulated money funneled through political parties for party-building purposes, such as get out the vote efforts or issue ads, was banned

Photo courtesy: Mannie Garcia/Bloomberg News/Landov

What groups influence party nominations?
Republican Governor Mitt Romney of Massachusetts announced the end of his presidential campaign at the American Conservative Union's annual convention, CPAC. Before Romney's announcement, 44 percent of convention attendees indicated in a straw poll that they favored him for the nomination, while only 27 percent favored the eventual nominee, Senator John McCain.

following passage of the Bipartisan Campaign Reform Act in 2002 (campaign finance reform efforts will be discussed in more detail in chapter 14). As Republicans had long enjoyed a substantial advantage in raising **hard money,** funds that can be used for direct electioneering but that are limited and regulated by the Federal Election Commission, many Democrats feared that banning soft money would give Republicans a clear fund-raising advantage in 2004. No doubt this fear aided the Democrats in their fund-raising efforts, providing donors a strong incentive to increase their contributions and, in fact, helping to shrink the GOP fund-raising advantage in 2004.

During the 2006 midterm elections, the Democrats came still closer to matching Republican fundraising. Still, the Republican Party and its congressional campaign committees raised $438 million—$100 million more than the Democrats—in 2006. By 2008, however, the Democrats outpaced the Republicans in most key fundraising categories. The Democrats' House and Senate campaign committees raised over $250 million, which was nearly $50 million more than the amount raised by their Republican counterparts. And while the Republican National Committee maintained an edge by raising over $250 million, which was about $50 million more than the Democratic National Committee, the DNC actually spent more money than the RNC in 2008.

hard money
Funds that can be used for direct electioneering but are limited and regulated by the Federal Elections Commission.

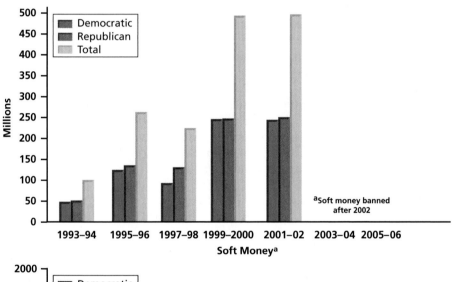

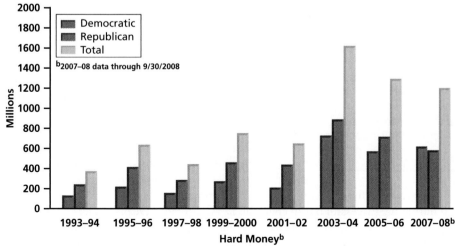

FIGURE 12.4 Political Party Finances, 1993–2008

Note how the Democratic Party had higher receipts than the Republican Party for the first time in the 2007–08 cycle. Also note how the receipts for both parties have substantially increased over time, even following the 2002 Bipartisan Campaign Reform Act (BCRA), which outlawed soft-money contributions (shown in the top graph) to the parties.

Sources: 2003–2008 from Center for Responsive Politics (http://www.opensecrets.org), and earlier years from Harold W. Stanley and Richard Niemi, *Vital Statistics on American Politics, 2003–2004* (Washington, DC: CQ Press, 2004).

The parties raise so much money because they have developed networks of donors reached by a variety of methods. Both parties have highly successful mail solicitation lists. The Republican effort to reach donors through the mail dates back to the early 1960s and accelerated in the mid-1970s, when postage and production costs were relatively low. Both the national Republican and Democratic committees have expanded their mailing lists of proven donors to several million. Republicans also pioneered the use of interactive technologies to attract voters. With these contributions, the parties have spent millions of dollars for national, state, and local public opinion surveys. Many of the surveys are provided to party nominees at a cut-rate cost. In important contests, the party frequently commissions tracking polls to chart its daily rise or fall. The information provided in such polls is invaluable in the tense concluding days of an election. Both parties operate sophisticated media divisions that specialize in the design and production of television advertisements for party nominees at all levels. And, both parties train the armies of political volunteers and paid operatives who run the candidates' campaigns. Early in each election cycle, the national parties also help prepare voluminous research reports on opponents, analyzing their public statements, votes, and attendance records.

The Republicans, moreover, have applied the principles of their sophisticated fund-raising database to help coordinate national GOTV efforts and assist Republican candidates at all levels of office. At the heart of these efforts is "micro-targeting," a practice derived from the field of consumer behavior. With data obtained from a growing volume of government census records and marketing firms, Republicans have used advanced computer models to identify potential GOP voters based on consumer preferences, personal habits, and past voting behavior. Once identified, these voters' names are stored in a database—Voter Vault—and shared with individual campaigns, whose volunteers contact voters by phone and personal visits. The detailed information that can be accessed from Voter Vault allows campaigns to carefully tailor their messages to individual voters. The voter turnout drive culminates with the seventy-two-hour project, which uses the last few days of the campaign to personally contact GOP voters and remind them to vote. Many observers credit the success of the Republicans in 2002 and 2004 to this well-organized and costly GOTV effort.

Because Democrats have been suspicious of using corporate techniques and traditionally have relied on labor unions and other interest groups to carry out voter mobilization, they have been late in creating similar programs. A number of consecutive electoral defeats made Democrats realize that their party needed not only to revitalize its organization but also rethink its approach. Thus was born the commitment to technological and fund-raising modernization that drives the Democratic Party today. As a presidential candidate in the 2004 Democratic primaries, former Vermont governor Howard Dean used an Internet Web site to coordinate "meet-ups" and to bring in an unprecedented sum of online campaign contributions. When his candidacy ended in defeat, Dean and his network of activist-contributors became a fund-raising resource for Democrats, a fact that Dean later trumpeted during his successful bid to chair the DNC.[29] Under Dean's leadership, Democrats focused on fielding competitive candidates in nearly every 2006 race, and the DNC provided organizing funds to Democrats in traditionally Republican states as part of a fifty-state grassroots organizing effort. They have also developed their own computer models to build a centralized database that will identify and mobilize new Democratic voters. These strategies, along with low approval ratings for President

Thinking Globally

Financing Parties in Europe

The governments of Austria, Belgium, Denmark, Finland, Germany, Italy, the Netherlands, and Sweden make direct payments to political parties. Payment amounts are determined by each party's share of parliamentary seats or the percentage of votes won in the last election.

- How would the American public react to a constitutional amendment authorizing the federal government to fund the operations of political parties and election campaigns?
- How would the public react if the amendment also prohibited parties and candidates from raising and spending their own money?

George W. Bush and the Republican-led Congress, resulted in significant Democratic victories in 2006. The addition of Senator Obama's extensive grassroots organization helped to further expand Democratic majorities in 2008

Until very recently, Democrats trailed Republicans by virtually every significant measure of party activity. However, Democratic candidates are now raising as much money as their Republican opponents in hard-money contributions, collectively outpacing the GOP in recent Senate and presidential contests.[30] But, the real strength of the Democratic Party is in the number of party activists. The decision in 1981 to begin a direct-mail program for the national party was a turning point for Democrats. From a list of only 25,000 donors before the program began, the DNC's support base grew to 500,000.

Photo courtesy: Ben Sklar/Getty Images

The Party in Government

In addition to their role in mobilizing voters, political parties are used to organize the branches and layers of American government.

The Congressional Party

In no segment of U.S. government is the party more visible or vital than in the Congress. In this century, political parties have dramatically increased the sophistication and impact of their internal congressional organizations. Prior to the beginning of every session, the parties in both houses of Congress gather (or "caucus") separately to select party leaders and to arrange for the appointment of members of each chamber's committees. In effect, then, the parties organize and operate the Congress. Their management systems have grown quite elaborate; the web of deputy and assistant whips for House Democrats now extends to about one-fourth of the party's entire membership. Although not invulnerable to pressure from the minority, the majority party in each house generally holds sway, even fixing the size of its majority on all committees—a proportion frequently in excess of the percentage of seats it holds in the house as a whole.

How do party activists help individual candidates in their campaigns? Staffers and volunteers call on the party faithful to vote on Election Day. Phone banks, like this one in Senator Hillary Clinton's Manchester, New Hampshire office during the Democratic primary campaign, have become a major part of party-related activity around election time.

Congressional party leaders enforce a degree of discipline in their party members in various ways. Even though seniority traditionally determined committee assignments, increasingly choice assignments have been given to the loyal or withheld from the rebellious, regardless of seniority. The Senate majority leader can decide whether a member's bill is given priority in the legislative agenda or will be dismissed with barely a hearing. Pork-barrel projects—government projects yielding rich patronage benefits that sustain many a legislator's electoral survival—may be included or deleted during the appropriations process. Small favors and perquisites (such as the allocation of desirable office space or the scheduling of floor votes for the convenience of a member) can also be useful levers. Then, too, there are the campaign aides at the command of the leadership: money from party sources, endorsements, appearances in the district or at fund-raising events, and so on.

There are, however, limits to coordinated, cohesive party action. A separate executive branch, bicameral power sharing, and the extraordinary decentralization of Congress's work all constitute institutional obstacles to effective party action. Party discipline is hurt, moreover, by the individualistic, candidate-centered nature of U.S. political campaigns and the diversity of the electoral constituencies to which members of Congress must be responsive. Another factor that undermines party cohesion is the largely private system of election financing that makes legislators indebted to wealthy individuals and nonparty interest groups. The importance to lawmakers of attracting the news media's attention—often more easily done by showmanship than by quiet, effective labor within the party system—also makes cohesive party action more unlikely.

Indeed, given the barriers to coordinated party activity, it is impressive to discover that party labels have consistently been the most powerful predictor of congressional roll-call voting. In the last few years, party-line voting has increased noticeably, as reflected in the upward trend by both Democrats and Republicans shown in Figure 12.5. Although not invariably predictive, a member's party affiliation proved to be the indicator of his or her votes about 88 percent of the time in 2007; that is, the average representative or senator sided with his or her party on about 88 percent of the votes that divided a majority of Democrats from a majority of Republicans that year. In most recent years, unanimous party-line votes have become increasingly common, with Democrats recording a record 272 unanimous roll-call votes in 2007.[31]

There are many reasons for the recent growth of congressional party unity. Both congressional parties, for instance, have gradually become more ideologically homogeneous and internally consistent. Southern Democrats today are typically moderate or liberal like their northern counterparts. Similarly, the vast majority of Republicans in Congress identify themselves as conservative. Partisan gerrymandering, redrawing congressional lines so as to create safe districts (see Figure 13.6 in chapter 13), has also increased party cohesion, as members of Congress increasingly represent congressional districts that strongly favor a single party. Party campaign committees have also played a role in this renewed cohesiveness. Each national party committee has been recruiting and training House and Senate candidates as never before, and devising themes and issues aimed at targeted districts. With numbers close in each chamber of Congress, parties are equally focused on electing a majority of legislators.

Thinking Globally

Party Loyalty in South Africa

Members of South Africa's National Assembly can change political party affiliation during two periods set aside every electoral term for what are called *floor crossings*.

- If this procedure became an annual feature of the U.S. Congress, which members would be the most likely to switch parties? Why?
- How would most voters react to a member of Congress who was running for reelection after having switched parties? How would a voter's party identification affect his or her reaction to the party switcher?

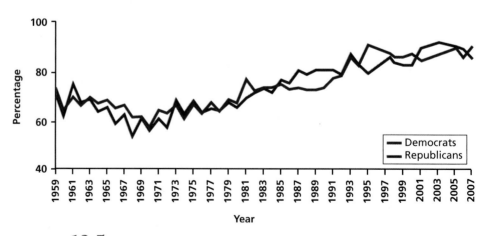

FIGURE **12.5** Congressional Party Unity Scores, 1959–2007

Note how party-based voting has increased conspicuously since the 1970s.

Source: Congressional Quarterly Almanacs (Washington, DC: CQ Press).

The Presidential Party

Political parties may be more central to the operation of the legislative branch than the executive branch, but it is the party of the president that captures the public imagination and shapes the electorate's opinion of the two parties. Voters' perceptions of the incumbent president and the presidential candidates determine to a large extent how citizens perceive the parties. The chief executive's successes are his party's successes; his failures are borne by the party as much as by the individual. The image a losing presidential candidate projects is incorporated into the party's contemporary portrait, whether wanted or not.

It is not easy for a president to juggle contradictory roles. Expected to bring the country together as ceremonial chief of state and also to forge a ruling consensus as head of government, the president must also be an effective commander of a sometimes divided party. Along with the inevitable headaches party leadership brings, though, are clear and compelling advantages. Foremost among them is a party's ability to mobilize support among voters for a president's program. Also, the executive's legislative agenda might be derailed more quickly without a shared party label uniting the chief executive and many members of Congress; all presidents appeal for some congressional support on the basis of shared party affiliation, and—depending on circumstances and their executive skill—they generally receive it. Presidents reciprocate the support they receive by appointing many activists to office, recruiting candidates, raising money for the party treasury, and campaigning extensively for party nominees during election seasons.

Some presidents have taken their party responsibilities more seriously than have others. In general, most presidents since Franklin D. Roosevelt have been less supportive of their respective political parties than were Roosevelt and his predecessors.[32] Dwight D. Eisenhower elevated nonpartisanship to a virtual art form; while this may have preserved his personal popularity, it proved a disaster for his party. Despite his two-term occupancy of the White House, the Republican Party remained mired in minority status among the electorate. Lyndon Johnson, Richard M. Nixon, and Jimmy Carter all showed similar neglect of their parties, often drawing on their party's organization for personal uses.

Nevertheless, some presidents have taken their party responsibilities extremely seriously. Democrats Woodrow Wilson and Franklin D. Roosevelt were dedicated to building their party electorally and governmentally. More recently, Republicans Ronald Reagan and George W. Bush have exemplified the "pro-party" presidency. Most of former President George W. Bush's major policy initiatives and legislative victories depended on support from his own party and near-unanimous opposition from the Democrats. This emphasis on satisfying core GOP voters was instrumental in encouraging the party's base to turn out to vote albeit wih mixed electoral success.[33]

Photo courtesy: Bettmann/CORBIS

What role do Presidents have in party building?
Despite winning two consecutive terms as president and leaving with high approval ratings, Republican Dwight D. Eisenhower, here shown in 1952 surrounded by Republican Committee women from eleven states, failed to help his party achieve majority status. Eisenhower was barred from running for a third term in 1960, and his Vice President, Richard M. Nixon, was unable to hold the White House for the Republicans.

The Parties and the Judiciary

While it is true that legislators tend to be much more partisan than judges and that legal restrictions and judicial norms often limit the partisan activities of judges, it would be wrong to assume that judges reach decisions wholly independently of partisan values. Judges are creatures of the political process, and their posts are considered patronage plums. Judges appointed by presidents or governors are chosen for their abilities but also increasingly as representatives of a certain philosophy of or approach to government. Most recent presidents have appointed judges overwhelmingly from their own party. Furthermore, Democratic executives are naturally inclined to select for the bench more liberal individuals who may be friendly to social programs or labor interests. Republican executives generally lean toward conservatives, hoping they will be tough on criminal defendants, opposed to abortion, and support business interests. President George W. Bush saw many of his judicial appointments blocked by Senate Democrats, who refused to allow a vote on the nominations. This tactic provided not only a way for Democrats to exact revenge on the Republicans, who had used similar measures during the Clinton administration, but also a means to forestall ideological changes that can last far beyond the next election cycle.

Research has long indicated that party affiliation is a moderately good predictor of judicial decisions in some areas.[34] One specific example involves judicial approval of new congressional districts created by state legislatures every ten years based on the U.S. Census. Judges tend to favor redistricting plans passed by their partisans in state legislatures rather than those of the opposition party.[35] Not surprisingly, jurists who are elected to office are often more partisan than those who are appointed. In a majority of states, at least some judicial positions are filled by election, and fourteen states hold outright partisan elections. In some rural counties across the United States, local judges are not merely partisan elected figures; they are the key party officials, controlling many patronage jobs and the party machinery.

The Parties and State Governments

Most of the conclusions just discussed about the party's relationship to the legislature, the executive, and the judiciary apply to those branches at the state level as well. The national parties, after all, are organized around state units, and the basic structural arrangement of party and government is much the same in Washington and the state capitals. Remarkably, too, the major national parties are the dominant political forces in all fifty states. This has been true consistently; unlike Great Britain or Canada, the United States has no regional or state parties that displace one or both of the national parties in local contests. Occasionally in U.S. history, a third party has proven locally potent, as did Minnesota's Farmer-Labor Party and Wisconsin's Progressives, both of which elected governors and state legislative majorities in the twentieth century. But, over time, no such party has survived.[36] Every state's two-party system mirrors national party dualism, at least as far as labels are concerned.

Governors in many states have greater influence over their parties' organizations and legislators than do presidents. Many governors have more patronage positions at their command than does a president, and these material rewards and incentives give governors added clout with party activists and office holders. In addition, tradition in some states permits the governor to play a role in selecting the legislature's committee chairs and party floor leaders, and some state executives even attend and help direct the party legislative caucuses, activities no president would ever undertake. Moreover, forty-one governors possess the power of the line-item veto, which permits the governor to veto single items (such as pork-barrel projects) in appropriations bills. The line-item veto has given governors enormous leverage with legislators, as they can now remove pork-barrel projects from members who oppose the governor's agenda.

After the 2008 election, Democrats controlled both chambers in twenty-seven state legislatures and shared control in eight states. Parties often have significant legislative influence at the state level, so the consequences of continuing Democratic control may be significant. Most state legislatures surpass the U.S. Congress in partisan unity and cohesion, with a number of state legislatures (including Massachusetts, New York, Ohio, and Pennsylvania) achieving party voting levels of 70 percent or better in some years. Not all states display party cohesion of this magnitude, of course. Nebraska has a nonpartisan legislature, elected without party labels on the ballot.

One other party distinction is notable in many state legislatures. Compared with the Congress, state legislative leaders have much more authority and power; this is one reason party unity is usually higher in the state capitols.[37] State legislative leaders, for example, often have considerable discretion in appointing committee chairs and members.

Party leaders and caucuses as well as the party organizations have more influence over legislators at the state level. State legislators depend on their state and local parties for election assistance much more than their congressional counterparts. Whereas members of Congress have large government-provided staffs and lavish perquisites to assist (directly or indirectly) their reelection efforts, state legislative candidates need party workers and, increasingly, the party's financial support and technological resources at election time.

The Party in the Electorate

Comparing Political Parties

A political party is much more than its organizational shell, however dazzling the technologies at its command, and its reach extends well beyond the small number of men and women who are the party in government. In any democracy, where power is derived directly from the people, the party's real importance and strength must come from the citizenry it attempts to mobilize. The party in the electorate—the mass of potential voters who identify with a party label—is a crucial element of the political party, providing the foundation for the organizational and governmental parties. But, in some respects, it is the weakest of the components of the U.S. political party system. Although partisan identification tends to be a reliable indicator of likely voting choices, the trend is for fewer voters to declare loyalty to a party; twenty-nine percent of voters called themselves independents on Election Day in 2008. (For a more detailed explanation of patterns in American vote choice, see chapter 13.)

Photo courtesy: Republican Party of Florida

What is the relationship between the state party and local party organizations? State parties often provide valuable financial assistance to party organizations at the local level. Here, Florida State Republican Party Chair Carole Jean Jordan of Florida presents Jefferson County Republicans with a check for $7,000 in matching funds for party development.

Party Identification

Most American voters identify with a party but do not belong to it. Universal party membership does not exist in the United States: the voter pays no prescribed dues; no formal rules govern an individual's party activities; and voters assume no enforceable obligations to the party even when they consistently vote for its candidates. A party has no real control over its adherents, and the party's voters subscribe to few or none of the commonly accepted tenets of organizational membership, such as regular participation and some measure of responsibility for the group's welfare. Rather, **party identification** or affiliation is an informal and impressionistic exercise whereby a citizen acquires a party label and accepts its standard as a summary of his or her political views and preferences. (To learn more about trends in party identification, see Analyzing Visuals: Party Identification, 1990–2008.)

party identification
A citizen's personal affinity for a political party, usually expressed by a tendency to vote for the candidates of that party.

For those Americans who do firmly adopt a party label, their party often becomes a central political reference symbol and perceptual screen. For these partisans, party identification is a significant aspect of their political personality and a way of defining and explaining themselves to others. The loyalty generated by the label can be as intense as any enjoyed by sports teams and alma maters.

Individual party identifications are reinforced by the legal institutionalization of the major parties. Because of restrictive ballot laws, campaign finance rules, the powerful inertia of political tradition, and many other factors, voters for all practical purposes are limited to a choice between a Democrat and a Republican in almost all elections—a situation that naturally encourages the pragmatic choosing up of sides. About half of the states require a voter to state a party preference (or independent status) when registering to vote, and they restrict voting in a party primary only to registrants in that particular party, making it an incentive for voters to affiliate themselves with a party.[38]

Whatever the societal and governmental forces responsible for party identification, the explanations of partisan loyalty at the individual's level are understandably more personal. Not surprisingly, parents are the single greatest influence in establishing a person's first party identification. Politically active parents with the same party loyalty raise children who will be strong party identifiers, whereas parents without party affiliations or with mixed affiliations produce offspring more likely to be independents.

Early socialization is hardly the last step in an individual's acquisition and maintenance of a party identity; marriage, economic status, and other aspects of adult life can change one's loyalty. Charismatic political personalities, particularly at the national level (such as Franklin D. Roosevelt and Ronald Reagan) can influence party identification, as can cataclysmic events (the Civil War and the Great Depression are the best examples). Hot-button social issues (for instance, abortion and same-sex marriage) can also influence party ties. Social class remains a powerful indicator of likely partisan choice in the United States, with wealthy Americans tending to prefer the Republican Party and working-class Americans tending to favor the Democratic Party, though the relationship is weaker than in other Western democracies. Not only are Americans less inclined than Europeans to perceive class distinctions, preferring instead to see themselves and most other people as members of an exceedingly broad middle class, but other factors, including sectionalism and candidate-oriented politics, tend to blur class lines in voting.

Group Affiliations

Just as individuals vary in the strength of their partisan choice, so, too, do groups vary in the degree to which they identify with the Democratic Party or the Republican Party. Variations in party identification are particularly noticeable when geographic region, gender, race and ethnicity, age, social and economic status, religion, marital

Analyzing Visuals   Party Identification, 1990–2008

Examine the table showing the percentage of Americans identifying themselves as Democrat, Republican, or independent since 1990 and answer the following questions:

	Democrat			Republican	
	Partisan	Leaner	Independent	Leaner	Partisan
1990	33	11	5	12	31
1992	33	16	6	14	28
1994	32	13	7	14	30
1996	33	16	5	13	29
1998	33	14	7	12	28
2000	33	12	6	12	28
2002	31	12	6	13	30
2004	33	14	5	12	30
2006	33	15	6	10	28
2008	35	14	6	12	28

Questions asked: In politics today, do you consider yourself a Republican, Democrat, or Independent?" If Independent: "As of today do you lean more to the Republican Party or more to the Democratic Party?" Rows do not equal 100 percent because results for respondents who did not answer the question or volunteered "no preference" or another party are not shown.
Source: Calculated by authors based on data from the Pew Research Center for the People and the Press.

HOW would you describe the general trend in the number of Americans who identify strongly or weakly as Democrats? As Republicans?

WHAT can be said about the number of "true" independents, when independents who normally support one party over the other are included as partisans?

WHAT can be said about the relative strength of the Democratic and Republican Parties when you include the percentage of independent leaners along with those who identify weakly or strongly with each party?

status, and ideology are examined. (To learn more about the party indentifications of various groups, see Table 12.2.)

GEOGRAPHIC REGION   In modern American politics, the geographic regions are relatively closely contested between the parties. The South, which was solidly Democratic as a result of party attachments that were cultivated in the nineteenth century and hardened in the fires of the Civil War, is now a competitive two-party region. While Democrats still outdo Republicans in local elections in the South, since the 1994 elections Southerners have elected Republicans to a majority of the Senate and U.S. House seats representing the states of the old Confederacy, and Republican presidential candidates have come to rely on strong support in southern states.[39]

GENDER   Some political scientists argue that the difference in the way men and women vote first emerged in 1920, when newly enfranchised women registered overwhelmingly as Republicans. It was not until the 1980 presidential election, however, that a noticeable and possibly significant gender gap emerged. When Ronald Reagan trounced incumbent Democratic President Jimmy Carter, he did so with the support of 54 percent of the men who voted but only 46 percent of the women voters. This pattern continues to predominate in presidential elections. In 2008, John McCain won the support of 48 percent of male voters but only 43 percent of women voters. (To learn more about the impact of gender on party voting patterns, see Figure 12.6.)

TABLE **12.2** Party Identification by Group Affiliation

		Democratic Identifiers	Independents	Republican Identifiers
Region	Northeast	33	45	23
	Midwest	35	44	21
	South	34	41	26
	West	33	39	29
Gender	Male	30	45	25
	Female	37	39	24
Race	Black	66	31	3
	Hispanic	37	47	17
	White	27	42	30
Age	<30	35	46	19
	30–49	30	42	28
	50+	36	40	24
Income	<30,000	41	15	44
	30,000–74,999	31	30	39
	75,000+	39	32	39
Education	High School or Less	34	24	43
	College	28	32	40
	Advanced Degree	39	22	39
Union Member	Yes	47	22	32
Military Veteran	Yes	29	27	45
Religion Type	Protestant	34	39	37
	Catholic	34	23	43
	Jewish	48	18	34
Evangelical Christian	Yes	31	33	36
Marital Status	Married	28	31	41
	Not Currently Marrried	39	19	42
Ideology	Conservative	21	33	45
	Moderate	35	48	17
	Liberal	53	42	6

Note: In this table, independent leaners are collapsed into the independent column. Partisans and strong partisans are collapsed into the party columns. Due to rounding, not all rows equal 100 percent.
Source: Pew Research Center, *Political Landscape More Favorable to Democrats: Trends in Political Values and Core Attitudes, 1987–2007,*

One of the biggest challenges facing Republicans is how to gain the support of women without alienating their male base. Besides abortion and women's rights issues, women's concerns for peace and social justice may provide much of the gap's distance. For instance, women are usually less likely than men to favor American military action and are generally more supportive of education and social welfare spending. Most researchers now explain the gender gap not by focusing on the Republican Party's difficulties in attracting female voters, but rather on the Democratic Party's inability to attract the votes of males. In other words, as one study notes, the gender gap exists because of the lack of support for the Democratic Party among men and the corresponding male preference for the Republican Party, stemming from differences in opinions about social welfare and military issues.[40]

RACE AND ETHNICITY   African Americans are the most dramatically split population subgroup in party terms. The 50-percent-plus advantage they offer the Democrats dwarfs the edge given to either party by any other signif-

Thinking Globally

Regional Parties in India

India's multi-party parliamentary system consists of several strong regional parties, which have had significant representation in the lower house of India's national parliament. These regional parties have helped national parties form winning coalitions and their members have held numerous cabinet positions.

- Under what conditions might a regional party emerge in the United States?
- Which party might be harmed the most by such a regional threat? Why?

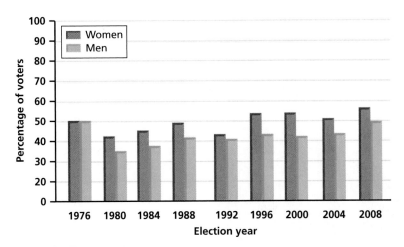

FIGURE 12.6 Support for Democratic Presidential Candidates by Gender, 1976–2008

Source: Center for American Women and Politics

icant segment of the electorate, and their proportion of strong Democrats (about 40 percent) is three times that of whites. African Americans account almost entirely for the slight lead in party affiliation that Democrats normally enjoy over Republicans, since the GOP has recently been able to attract a narrow majority of whites to its standard. Perhaps as a reflection of the massive party chasm separating blacks and whites, the two races differ greatly on many policy issues, with blacks overwhelmingly on the liberal side and whites closer to the conservative pole. The belief of most blacks that their fate is linked causes upper-income blacks generally to vote the same as lower-income blacks. Whites see no such obligation.[41] Views on abortion and gay rights provide an exception, however. Religious beliefs lead many African Americans to adopt more conservative stances on these issues than their white Democratic counterparts.

Hispanics supplement African Americans as Democratic stalwarts; by more than three to one, Hispanics prefer the Democratic Party. Voting patterns of Puerto Ricans are very similar to those of African Americans, while Mexican Americans favor the Democrats by smaller margins. An exception is the Cuban American population, whose anti–Fidel Castro tilt leads to support for the Republican Party. For example, in a 2004 pre-election survey, 81 percent of Cuban American respondents said they supported President Bush.[42] As the Hispanic population has increased rapidly in recent years and now exceeds that of African Americans, Republicans have fought to make inroads with Hispanic voters. President Bush made a number of high-ranking Hispanic appointments and selected former Texas Supreme Court Justice Alberto Gonzales to serve as attorney general. Prominent Republicans who can speak in Spanish, such as Jeb Bush, the former governor of Florida, often campaign for Republican candidates before Hispanic groups. These efforts seemed to pay off at the end of President Bush's first term: whereas only 35 percent of Hispanic voters cast a ballot for Bush in 2000, 44 percent voted to reelect him in 2004.

More recently, debates and proposals regarding immigration revealed how difficult it has been for Republicans to appeal to a potentially supportive new voting bloc while also satisfying their conservative base with immigration restrictions and increased enforcement. When President Bush supported a bipartisan Senate bill in June 2007 that would tighten enforcement and border security, introduce a temporary worker program, and allow immigrants currently in the United States illegally to continue working and potentially be eligible for citizenship, it was mainly Republicans who were opposed to the bill and killed it through procedural means.[43]

Photo courtesy: Keith Bedford/Bloomberg News/Landov

Grassroots anger at Senator John McCain, the principle Republican advocate for the bill, almost doomed the GOP front-runner's chances for the presidential nomination. At the same time, Republicans were perceived by many as anti-immigrant, while Democrats regained their large advantage in partisan identification among Hispanics. By the end of 2007, 57 percent of Hispanic voters identified themselves as Democrats, while only 23 percent identified as Republicans.

AGE Age has long been associated with party identification, as most voters develop their partisan affiliations based on formative political experiences growing up. For example, many voters who were alive during the Great Depression identify strongly with the Democratic Party, whereas many who were young during the Reagan years

How does race and ethnicity affect party identification?
A delegate to the 2008 Democratic National Convention holds a "Hispanic Voter" sign while reacting to speeches at Invesco Field in Denver, Colorado. In the wake of Republican support for strict enforcement of immigration laws, the deportation of illegal immigrants, and a border fence with Mexico, nearly two-thirds of Latinas and Latinos identified themselves as Democrats in the run-up to the 2008 election.

identify with the Republican Party. Today, generally the very youngest and very oldest voters tend to prefer the Democratic Party, while middle-aged voters disproportionately favor the Republican Party. The Democratic Party's more liberal positions on social issues tend to resonate with today's moderate but socially progressive young adults. (To learn more about the youth vote, see Ideas into Action: Party Affiliation Among College Students.) The nation's oldest voters, who tend to focus on Social Security and Medicare, tend to favor the Democratic Party's consistent support for these programs and are generally skeptical of privatization plans supported by many Republicans. Middle-aged voters, often at the height of their careers and consequently at the height of their earnings potential, tend to favor the low taxes championed by Republicans.[44]

SOCIAL AND ECONOMIC FACTORS Occupation, income, and education also influence party affiliation. The GOP remains predominant among executives, professionals, and white-collar workers, whereas the Democrats lead substantially among trial lawyers, educators, and blue-collar workers. Labor union members are also Democratic by nearly two to one. Women who do not work outside the home are less liberal and Democratic than those who do. Occupation, income, and education are closely related, of course, so many of the same partisan patterns appear in all three classifications. Democratic support drops as one climbs the income scale. Those with a college education tend to support the Republican Party, although those with advanced degrees tend to be Democratic.[45]

RELIGION Party preferences by religion are also traditional, but with modern twists. White Protestants—especially Methodists, Presbyterians, and Episcopalians—favor the Republicans, whereas Catholics and, even more so, Jewish voters tend to favor the Democratic Party. Decreased polarization is apparent all around, however.[46] Democrats have made inroads among many liberal Protestant denominations over the past three decades, and Republicans can now sometimes claim up to 25 percent of Jewish voters and a nearly equal share of the Catholic vote. Evangelical Christians are some-

Ideas Into Action

Party Affiliation Among College Students

The political turmoil over the reinstitution of the draft during the Vietnam War created a movement among young citizens for a lowering of the legal voting age to eighteen, leading to ratification of the Twenty-Sixth Amendment to the Constitution in 1971. Since that time, the vote of college-age students has been important to American politics, with each party vying for the attention of these newly eligible voters. Traditionally, these youngest voters voted the least, despite efforts by public and private organizations to register and encourage participation. Happily, in the 2004 presidential election, turnout among those age eighteen to twenty-four surged to 47 percent, or 11 percent more than in 2000. It is too soon to tell if this is an emerging trend, but it is none theless encouraging that younger voters are engaging in American politics in greater numbers.

During the 1970s, the youth vote was predominately liberal and oriented toward the Democratic Party. By the end of the 1980s, after President Ronald Reagan's two terms in office, the eighteen- to twenty-four-year-old age group was heavily Republican in affiliation.

Young people began to swing back to the Democrats in 1992. President Bill Clinton, who aggressively courted the youth vote, ran strongly among eighteen- to twenty-four-year-olds in 1992 and 1996. In 2000, young voters were almost evenly split: 48 percent voted for Al Gore and 46 percent voted for George W. Bush. In 2004, however, John Kerry won the youth vote by almost ten points, garnering 54 percent to George W. Bush's 45 percent.

It might be that young voters are more candidate-centered and less loyal to a political party than are older voters. Another line of thinking suggests that neither party currently provides a solid fit with the issues that are important to young voters. Young voters tend to hold more liberal positions on social issues, like abortion rights and same-sex marriage, but also tend to favor traditionally conservative positions like low taxes and strong national security. If parties could once again find issues that capture the imagination of young voters, then perhaps young voters might become more loyal to a party.

■ Where will you be on Election Day? If you will not be in your town to vote on the day of the election, you will need to find out from your local government what are the procedures for voting early or by absentee ballot. You also may change your voter registration to your current address and vote in the same town as your college or university.

■ Schedule an interview with representatives of the Democratic and Republican Parties. Ask them why their party is best suited to represent the views of younger voters and what mechanisms they have in place to be attentive to the policy concerns of young people. Which party seems to be the most responsive?

■ For more information on issues, turnout, and other statistics on the youth vote, see the Web site of the Center for Information and Research on Civic Learning and Engagement: www.civicyouth.org/quick/youth_voting.htm.

■ To get an idea of the issue positions and candidates that college students and other young people support, and to make your own voice heard, see Facebook's U.S. Politics Web site: www.facebook.com/politics.

---

what less Republican than commonly believed. The GOP usually has just a 10 percent edge among them, primarily because so many African Americans, who are strongly pro-Democratic, are also members of this group.[47]

MARITAL STATUS Even marital status reveals something about partisan affiliation. People who are married, a traditionally more conservative group, tend to favor the Republican Party, while single people who have never married tend to favor the Democratic Party. Taken as a group, the widowed lean toward the Democrats, probably because there are many more widows than widowers; here, the gender gap is again expressing itself. The divorced and the separated, who may be experiencing economic hardship, appear to be more liberal than the married population.[48]

dealignment
A general decline in party identification and loyalty in the electorate.

Toward Reform: Dealignment and the Strength of Political Parties

Over the past two decades, numerous political scientists as well as other observers, journalists, and party activists have become increasingly anxious about **dealignment,** a general decline in partisan identification and loyalty in the electorate.[49] Since parties traditionally provide political information and serve as an engine of political participation, it has been feared that weakening party attachments are undermining political involvement.

The Center for Political Studies/Survey Research Center (CPS/SRC) of the University of Michigan has charted the rise of self-described independents from a low of 19 percent in 1958 to a peak of 40 percent in 2000, with percentages in recent years consistently hovering just below the high-water mark of 40 percent. Before the 1950s (although the evidence for this research is more circumstantial because of the scarcity of reliable survey research data), it is believed that independents were far fewer in number and party loyalties were considerably firmer than is the case today.

Currently, the Democratic and Republican Parties can claim a roughly equal percentage of self-identified partisans, with levels fluctuating around one-third of the population each. This can seem inconsistent with voting behavior and election results, but one must pay close attention to the manner in which these data are collected. When pollsters ask for party identification information, they generally proceed in two stages. First, they inquire whether a respondent considers himself or herself to be a Democrat, Republican, or independent. Then the party identifiers are asked to categorize themselves as "strong" or "not very strong" supporters, while the independents are pushed to reveal their "leanings" with a question such as "Which party do you normally support in elections, the Democrats or the Republicans?" It may be true that some independent respondents are thereby prodded to pick a party under the pressure of the interview situation, regardless of their true feelings. But, research has demonstrated that independent "leaners" in fact vote very much like real partisans, in some elections more so than the "not very strong" party identifiers.[50] There is reason to count the independent leaners as closet partisans, though voting behavior is not the equivalent of real partisan identification.

In fact, the reluctance of leaners to admit their real party identities reveals a significant change in attitudes about political parties and their role in our society. Being a socially acceptable, integrated, and contributing member of one's community once almost demanded partisan affiliation; it was a badge of good citizenship, signifying that one was a patriot. Today, many voters consider such labels an offense to their individualism, and many Americans insist that they vote for "the person, not the party."

The reasons for these anti-party attitudes are not hard to find. The growth of issue-oriented politics that cut across party lines for voters who feel intensely about certain policy matters is partly the cause. So, too, is the emphasis on personality politics by the mass media and political consultants.

Although the underlying partisanship of the American people has not declined significantly since 1952, voter-admitted partisanship has dropped considerably. From 1952 to 1964, about three-fourths or more of the electorate volunteered a party choice without prodding, but since 1970 an average of less than two-thirds has been willing to do so. Professed independents (including leaners) have increased from around one-fifth of the electorate in the 1950s to over one-third during the last three decades. In recent years, the number of voters who identify with parties has stabilized, but the number still lags far behind historical norms.

Despite the challenges described above, the parties' decline can easily be exaggerated. When we view parties in the broad sweep of U.S. history, several strengths of parties become clear.

First, although political parties have evolved considerably and changed form from time to time, they usually have been reliable vehicles for mass participation in a representative democracy. In fact, parties orchestrated the gradual but steady expansion of suffrage in order to incorporate new supporters into the party fold.[51] Keep in mind, however, the notable exceptions in which parties or party factions attempted to contract the electorate. Southern Democrats, for example, worked to exclude African American political participation from the end of Reconstruction through the civil rights movement of the 1960s, in an effort to maintain their political power in the region.

Second, the parties' journeys through U.S. history have been characterized by the same ability to adapt to prevailing conditions that is often cited as the genius of the Constitution. Both major parties exhibit flexibility and pragmatism, which help ensure their survival and the success of the society they serve.

Third, despite massive changes in political conditions and frequent dramatic shifts in the electorate's mood, the two major parties not only have achieved remarkable longevity but also have almost always provided strong competition for each other and the voters at the national level. Of the thirty presidential elections from 1884 to 2008, for instance, the Republicans won seventeen and the Democrats fifteen. Even when calamities have beset the parties—the Great Depression of the 1930s or the Watergate scandal of the 1970s for the Republicans, and the Civil War for the Democrats—the two parties have proved tremendously resilient, sometimes bouncing back from landslide defeats to win the next election.

Fourth, while the party in the electorate might have waned in recent years, depending on whether you look at the relatively modest rise in pure independents or more robust increase in leaners evident in some surveys, the party in government and the party organizations are stronger than ever. The sharp rise in party unity scores in Congress discussed earlier in the chapter suggests that the party in government is alive and well. The unprecedented fund-raising of the party organizations suggests, moreover, that political parties are here to stay.

Perhaps most of all, history teaches us that the development of parties in the United States has been inevitable. Human nature alone guarantees conflict in any society; in a free state, the question is simply how to contain and channel conflict productively without infringing on individual liberties. The Framers' utopian hopes for the avoidance of partisan faction, Madison's chief concern, have given way to an appreciation of the parties' constructive contributions to conflict definition and resolution during the years of the American republic. Political parties have become the primary means by which society addresses its irreconcilable differences, and as such they play an essential role in democratic society.

WHAT SHOULD I HAVE LEARNED?

A political party is an organized effort by office holders, candidates, activists, and voters to pursue their common interests by gaining and exercising power through the electoral process. The goal of parties is to win office so as to exercise power and pursue policy objectives. Parties encompass three separate components: (1) the governmental party make up office holders who organize themselves and pursue policy objectives under a party label; (2) the party organization comprises the workers and activists who make up the party's formal structure; and (3) the party in the electorate refers to the voters who consider themselves allied or associated with the party. In this chapter, we have answered the following questions:

■ **What are the roots of the American party system?**

A political party is an organized effort by office holders, candidates, activists, and voters to pursue common interests by gaining and exercising power through the electoral process. The evolution of U.S. political parties has been remarkably smooth, and the stability of the Democratic and Republican groupings is a wonder, considering all the social and political tumult in U.S. history. On rare occasions, critical elections and party realignments dramatically have altered the political landscape.

■ **What are the functions of the American party system?**

For 150 years, the two-party system has served as the mechanism American society uses to organize and resolve social and political conflict. The Democratic and Republican Parties, through lengthy nominating processes, provide a screening mechanism for those who aspire to office, helping to weed out unqualified individuals, expose and test candidates' ideas on important policy questions, and ensure a measure of long-term continuity and accountability.

■ **How are political parties organized?**

The basic structure of the major parties is complex. The state and local parties are generally more important than the national ones, though campaign technologies and fund-raising concentrated in Washington, D.C., have helped to centralize power within national party committees. Political parties' use of modern technologies and communication strategies has begun to be tempered by a renewed focus on get out the vote drives, canvassing, and voter identification. Nevertheless, the capabilities of the party organizations vary widely from place to place.

■ **How do parties help organize the government?**

Political parties are not restricted to their role as grassroots organizations of voters; they also have another major role *inside* government institutions. The party in government comprises the office holders who organize themselves and pursue policy objectives under a party label.

■ **What is party identification?**

Most American voters have a personal affinity for a political party, which summarizes their political views and preferences and is expressed by a tendency to vote for the candidates of that party. This significant political party element provides the foundation for the organizational and governmental parties.

■ **What does the future hold for American political parties?**

While dealignment, a general decline in partisan identification and loyalty in the electorate, has undoubtedly occurred over the last fifty years, the future of the party system is not in doubt. Parties remain strong, adaptive, and essential players in the political process and are likely to remain so in the future.

Key Terms

candidate-centered politics, p. 413
civil service laws, p. 413
coalition, p. 416
critical election, p. 413
dealignment, p. 440
direct primary, p. 413
governmental party, p. 407
hard money, p. 427

issue-oriented politics, p. 413
national convention, p. 423
national party platform, p. 418
organizational party, p. 407
party identification, p. 434
party in the electorate, p. 407
party realignment, p. 413
political machine, p. 412

political party, p. 406
proportional representation, p. 418
secular realignment, p. 414
soft money, p. 426
think tank, p. 426
ticket-split, p. 413
winner-take-all system, p. 418

Researching Political Parties

In the Library

Aldrich, John Herbert. *Why Parties? The Origin and Transformation of Political Parties in America.* Chicago: University of Chicago Press, 1995.

Bibby, John F., and Brian Schaffner. *Politics, Parties, and Elections in America.* Boston, MA: Thomson Wadsworth, 2008.

Chhibber, Pradeep K., and Ken Kollman. *The Formation of National Party Systems: Federalism and Party Competition in Canada, Great Britain, India, and the United States.* Princeton, NJ: Princeton University Press, 2004.

Green, Donald, Bradley Palmquist, and Eric Schickler. *Partisan Hearts and Minds.* New Haven: Yale University Press, 2002.

Hershey, Marjorie. *Party Politics in America*, 12th ed. New York: Pearson Longman, 2007.

Key, V. O., Jr. *Southern Politics in State and Nation*, new edition. Knoxville: University of Tennessee Press, 1984.

Key, V. O., Jr. *Politics, Parties, and Pressure Groups*, 5th ed. New York: Crowell, 1964.

Malbin, Michael J. *The Election After Reform: Money, Politics, and the Bipartisan Campaign Reform Act.* Lanham, MD: Rowman and Littlefield, 2006.

Mayhew, David R. *Electoral Realignments.* New Haven, CT: Yale University Press, 2004.

Rosenstone, Steven J., Roy L. Behr, and Edward H. Lazarus. *Third Parties in America*, 2nd ed. Princeton, NJ: Princeton University Press, 1996.

Sabato, Larry J., and Bruce A. Larson. *The Party's Just Begun: Shaping Political Parties for America's Future*, 2nd ed. New York: Longman, 2002.

Sabato, Larry J., and Howard R. Ernst. *Encyclopedia of American Parties and Elections.* New York: Facts on File, 2005.

Schattschneider, E. E. *Party Government.* New York: Holt, Rinehart and Winston, 1942.

White, John Kenneth, and Daniel M. Shea. *New Party Politics: From Jefferson and Hamilton to the Information Age*, 2nd ed. Boston, MA: Thomson Wadsworth, 2003.

On the Web

Open Secrets tracks campaign contributions to political parties, candidates, PACs and other political committees and analyzes the effect on elections and public policy. Visit their Web site at **www.opensecrets.org/**.

C-SPAN provides a comprehensive list of public policy organizations and think tanks located in the Washington, D.C. area. Go to **www.c-span.org/resources/policy.asp.**

The Pew Research Center for the People and the Press provides a political typology of the American electorate derived from public opinion surveys, organizing voters into groups based on values, political beliefs, and party affiliation. See **people-press.org/reports/display.php3?ReportID=242**.

For a summary of the evolution, current platforms, prominent officeholders, and candidates for both major parties and nearly 50 minor and third parties, go to **www.politics1.com/parties.htm**.

The U.S. Senate maintains a large resource of historical documents, essays, and lecture transcripts pertaining to the evolution of party leadership in the Senate and the personalities holding those posts. Go to **www.senate.gov/reference/reference_index_subjects/Leadership_vrd.htm**.

13

Voting and Elections

W hile it is impossible to mark the exact beginning of the 2008 presidential contest, it is likely that the 2008 race was on the minds of several presidential hopefuls prior to the conclusion of the 2004 contest. Senator John McCain's endorsement in 2004 of George W. Bush, his arch-rival from the 2000 presidential primary, was certainly influenced by McCain's desire to gain support among the party faithful for a 2008 bid. Senator and former First Lady Hillary Rodham Clinton's decision not to run in 2004 was undoubtedly influenced by her upcoming bid for reelection to the Senate in 2006, as well as the fact that the 2008 presidential election, unlike the 2004 race, was likely be highly contested by both parties.

A year before the Democratic and Republican Parties would formally nominate their candidates for president, there seemed to be little doubt that the 2008 quest for the presidency would be the most memorable in recent history. For the first time

since 1928, none of the candidates would be either the incumbent president or vice president. Among the Democrats, former first lady and current New York Senator Hillary Clinton seemed the inevitable nominee. With her proven ability to raise money, the popularity of the Clinton brand, and a front-loaded nominating contest that seemed likely to reward an early front-runner, Senator Clinton appeared poised to make history as the first woman to lead a major party's presidential ticket. Among the Republicans, Senator John McCain was thought surely to be folding his campaign after he ran out of money in the summer of 2007 and began a free fall in the polls. When no clear front-runner emerged from the rest of the Republican pack, a protracted struggle for the GOP nomination seemed certain.

But, nomination battles often prove difficult to predict. The January 3 Iowa caucuses turned the Democratic nomination race upside down. Senator Barack Obama, who also hoped to make history by becoming the first African American nominee of a major party, was the surprise winner, while Senator Clinton finished a distant third behind John Edwards, a former senator who had been the 2004 vice presidential candidate. With fresh polls coming out of New Hampshire showing Obama surging and building an insurmountable lead, the talk in the media was about Clinton's inevitable demise. But, the voters of the Granite State gave

■ **Voting rights are a basic cornerstone of American democracy.** At left, a woman stands in a voting booth in 1920, shortly after the ratification of the Nineteenth Amendment expanded voting rights to women. At right, an Obama supporter braves a snow bank to support his candidate before the 2008 New Hampshire Primary.

WHAT SHOULD I KNOW ABOUT . . .
- the roots of voting behavior?
- elections in the United States?
- presidential elections?
- congressional elections?
- the 2008 congressional elections?
- reforming the electoral process?

445

Clinton a dramatic comeback victory, and she seemed ready to secure the nomination on Super Tuesday, February 5, when twenty-three states and territories would hold their nominating contests. The people voting on Super Tuesday, however, split their votes between Clinton and Obama, ensuring that the battle for the nomination would not end until voters in remaining states had a chance to cast their ballots.

The momentum continued to swing back and forth throughout the spring of 2008. Senator Obama won the next nine consecutive contests, while Senator Clinton won nine of the last sixteen, all the while pledging that she would fight on until all the votes had been counted in the nomination battle. It would not be until the evening of June 3, 2008, after the final contests, that Senator Obama could claim a majority of delegates and declare himself the presumptive Democratic nominee.

TO LEARN MORE—
—TO DO MORE
Track the dynamics of the nomination contests by viewing the many polls taken throughout 2007 and 2008 at Real Clear Politics: www.realclearpolitics.com/epolls/2008/president/.

Conventional wisdom also suffered at the hands of Republican primary and caucus voters. Former Massachusetts Governor Mitt Romney, who had the best-financed and most well-organized campaign among the Republican front-runners, moved to the top of the opinion polls in Iowa and New Hampshire and was in a strong position to be the beneficiary of the GOP's wide-open field. But, with a shoestring organization and little money, former Arkansas Governor and Baptist minister Mike Huckabee emerged the winner in Iowa. In New Hampshire, John McCain resurrected his campaign and won a dramatic come-from-behind victory. McCain then followed up with victories in South Carolina and Florida, where he ended the nomination hopes of former New York Mayor Rudy Giuliani. On Super Tuesday, McCain won an overwhelming share of Republican delegates, ending Romney's candidacy, and had built up a large enough lead to secure the nomination. On the day that Senator Clinton had hoped to make history, it was Senator McCain who emerged as a big winner, on his way to the Republican nomination.

Every four years, on the Tuesday following the first Monday in November, a plurality of voters, simply by casting ballots peacefully across a continent-sized nation, reelects or replaces politicians at all levels of government—from the president of the United States, to members of the U.S. Congress, to state legislators. Americans tend to take this process for granted, but in truth it is a marvel. Many other countries do not enjoy the benefit of competitive elections and the peaceful transition of political power made possible through the electoral process. American political institutions have succeeded in maintaining peaceful elections, even when they are closely contested, as was the case with the 2000 presidential election. Elections take the pulse of average people and gauge their hopes and fears, they provide direction for government action in a process that shapes and reforms all levels of government, and they hold the nation's leaders accountable.

The United States, judging from its frequent elections at all levels of government for more offices than any other nation on earth, is committed to democracy. The nation has steadily increased the size of the electorate (those citizens eligible to vote) by removing restrictions based on property ownership, religion, race, and gender. But, despite the increased access to the ballot box, and various direct democratic devices such as primaries and initiatives opened to the public in the last century, voter turnout remains historically low. After all the blood spilled and energy expended to expand voting rights, little more than half of eligible voters bother to go to the polls.

This chapter focuses on patterns of voting over time, the purposes served by elections, and the various kinds of elections held in the United States. Presidential and congressional elections are given special attention, as their rich histories tell us a great deal about the American people and their changing hopes and needs. We conclude by returning to contemporary presidential elections and addressing key aspects of electoral reform.

★ First, we will discuss *the roots of voting behavior*, focusing on distinct patterns in voter turnout and vote choice.

★ Second, we will examine *the purposes and types of elections*, pointing out that elections at all levels confer a legitimacy on regimes better than any other method of change.

★ Third, we will take a closer look at the elements of *presidential elections*, including primaries, conventions, and the Electoral College.

★ Fourth, we will explore how *congressional elections*, although they share similarities with presidential elections, are really quite different.

★ Fifth, we will discuss *the 2008 congressional elections* and their similarities and differences with other recent congressional elections.

★ Finally, we will present arguments for *reforming the electoral process* and explore the potential benefits and unintended consequences of electoral change.

Roots of Voting Behavior

By far the most accepted and common method of political participation in the United States is voting in an election at the local, state, or national level. Voting is the most widespread example of **conventional political participation**—political participation that attempts to influence the political process through well-accepted and often moderate forms of persuasion, such as writing letters to government officials, making political contributions, and, as noted above, voting.

The war in Iraq has caused a great deal of political tension and revived a venerable American tradition of protest and demonstration. **Unconventional political participation** in the United States—political participation

conventional political participation
Political participation that attempts to influence the political process through well-accepted, often moderate forms of persuasion.

unconventional political participation
Political participation that attempts to influence the political process through unusual or extreme measures, such as protests, boycotts, and picketing.

Photo courtesy: Alex Wong/Getty Images

What issues elicit unconventional political participation? To bring attention to their opposition to the Iraq War, Code Pink has staged numerous non-violent, but vocal demonstrations at political events and government meetings. Code Pink members interrupted General David Petraeus's testimony at a September 2007 congressional hearing and Senator John McCain's acceptance speech at the Republican National Convention in 2008.

Timeline: The Expansion of Voting Rights

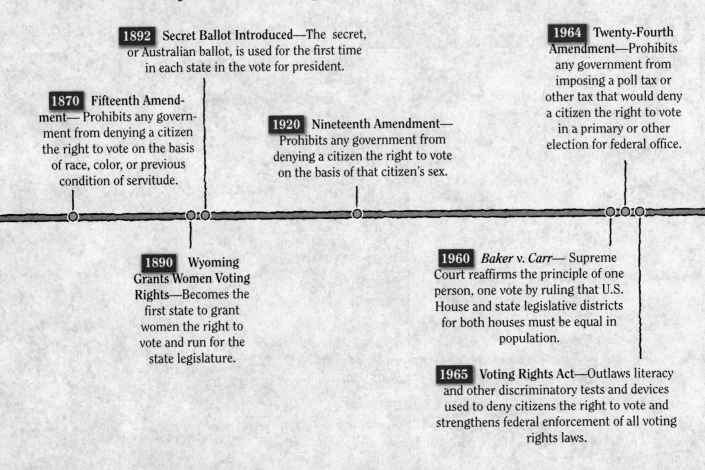

1892 Secret Ballot Introduced—The secret, or Australian ballot, is used for the first time in each state in the vote for president.

1870 Fifteenth Amendment— Prohibits any government from denying a citizen the right to vote on the basis of race, color, or previous condition of servitude.

1920 Nineteenth Amendment— Prohibits any government from denying a citizen the right to vote on the basis of that citizen's sex.

1964 Twenty-Fourth Amendment—Prohibits any government from imposing a poll tax or other tax that would deny a citizen the right to vote in a primary or other election for federal office.

1890 Wyoming Grants Women Voting Rights—Becomes the first state to grant women the right to vote and run for the state legislature.

1960 *Baker* v. *Carr*— Supreme Court reaffirms the principle of one person, one vote by ruling that U.S. House and state legislative districts for both houses must be equal in population.

1965 Voting Rights Act—Outlaws literacy and other discriminatory tests and devices used to deny citizens the right to vote and strengthens federal enforcement of all voting rights laws.

that attempts to influence the political process through unusual or extreme measures such as protests, boycotts, and picketing—is older than the nation itself and has been carried out during every period of American history. The Boston Tea Party and Shays's Rebellion are but two prominent early examples.

Elections are more common today than rebellions, however, and political scientists have devoted significant time and energy to looking at voting behavior. Research on voting behavior seeks primarily to explain two phenomena: voter turnout (that is, what factors contribute to an individual's decision to vote or not to vote) and vote choice (once the decision to vote has been made, what leads voters to choose one candidate over another). In this section, we will discuss patterns in voter turnout and analyze the relatively low level of voter participation in the United States; we will then turn our attention to patterns in vote choice.

Patterns in Voter Turnout

turnout
The proportion of the voting-age public that votes.

Turnout is the proportion of the voting-age public that votes. Those eligible to vote include all citizens of the United States who are age eighteen or older. States regulate voting eligibility in a number of ways, however. (To learn more, see Table 13.1.) About 40 percent of the eligible adult population in the United States votes regularly, whereas 25 percent are occasional voters and 35 percent rarely or never vote. According to the International Institute for Democracy and Electoral Assistance, this places

1993 The National Voter Registration Act—Requires states to offer voter registration services at drivers' license registration centers and social service, military recruiting and other public offices.

2008 Voter turnout reaches its highest level since 1964, with approximately 62% of eligible voters voting in the 2008 presidential election.

1971 Twenty-Sixth Amendment—Prohibits any government from denying a citizen who is eighteen years or older the right to vote on the basis of age.

1995 *Miller v. Johnson*—Supreme Court rules that states cannot design redistricting plans that use race as the overriding and predominant factor.

2008 *Crawford v. Marion County Election Board*—Supreme Court upholds Indiana's law requiring voters to present photo identification at polling places, finding that a state's broad interests in deterring and detecting voter fraud outweighs the burden that may be felt by poor and elderly voters.

2002 Help America Vote Act (HAVA)—Mandates that all states and localities upgrade their election procedures, including their voting machines, registration processes, and poll worker training.

the United States far below nations such as Italy, Australia, and Sweden, which regularly have voting rates that exceed 70 percent.

As discussed in chapter 12, turnout is especially important in American elections because candidates are elected in a winner-take-all system, where an election's outcome can be influenced by a single voter. Some of the factors known to influence voter

---

TABLE 13.1 State Laws Regulating Voter Eligibility in National Elections

For presidential elections and elections to the U.S. Congress, the Constitution guarantees the right to vote to all citizens 18 years of age and older. States are permitted to regulate the administration of elections and voting eligibility in some cases.

Key Ways in Which States Regulate Voting Eligibility

- Prohibiting ex-felons from voting (10 states)
- Allowing incarcerated felons to vote from prison (2 states)
- Requiring first-time voters to show some form of ID to vote (2 states)
- Requiring all voters to show some form of ID to vote (18 states)
- Requiring all voters to show a photo ID to vote (3 states)
- Requiring all voters to show a photo ID or sign an affidavit to vote (4 states)
- Allowing 17-year-olds to vote in primaries if they will be 18 on Election Day (12 states)
- Allowing Election Day registration (6 states)
- Requiring voters to register to vote at least 30 days prior to an election (12 states and DC)

Sources: http://www.felonvotingprocon.org; http://www.pewcenteronthestates.org; http://www.civicyouth.org.

POLITICS NOW

Source: CHICAGO TRIBUNE *June 25, 2008*

Can Turnout Aid One Candidate?

A *Chicago Tribune* analysis looks at battleground states as Democrats push a voter registration drive.

TURNOUT BOOST COULD FAVOR OBAMA

MIKE DORNING

Barack Obama could make major gains in at least nine states the Democratic ticket lost in 2004 if he can achieve a relatively modest increase in turnout among young and African-American voters, a *Tribune* analysis of voting data suggests. That potential helps explain why the Obama campaign chose to forgo federal funding and also why it is engaged in a massive voter registration drive. With its unprecedented resources, the campaign can fund an array of specific targeting operations, and Obama exploited early versions of those to great success during the primary campaign.

If Obama could inspire just 10 percent more Democratic voters under 30 to go to the polls than did four years ago, that alone could be enough to switch Iowa and New Mexico from red to blue, the analysis suggests. Just a 10 percent increase in turnout among blacks would make up more than 40 percent of George W. Bush's 2004 victory margin in Ohio and more than 20 percent of the Republicans' 2004 victory margin in Florida. Turnout increases of 10 percent of both young voters and African-Americans could virtually eliminate the Republicans' 2004 victory margin in Ohio and go

a long way to closing the gap in Colorado, Nevada, Missouri, Virginia and—a bit more of a stretch—possibly North Carolina.

The campaign dispatched an advance guard to the likely battlefields of the November election more than a month before Obama had even locked up the nomination. Its mission: to begin work on an ambitious national voter registration drive that advisers say is a key part of the campaign's strategy.

Campaign volunteers have been registering voters at bars and nightclubs as well as visiting hip-hop parties and even gas stations—where drivers irate over rising fuel prices are a target, said one organizer. More than 250 of the campaign's "organizing fellows" arrived last week in Virginia, a state Democrats did not seriously contest in 2004, and will spend much of the summer there on voter registration.

With the Illinois senator's enthusiastic following that regularly packs arena-sized venues for rallies, and unprecedented organizational resources from his campaign's fundraising successes, his barrier-breaking campaign sees a chance to re-shape the electorate this fall to the Democrats' advantage, possibly for several elections into the future....

There's still plenty of time between now and Election Day for the Obama hype to come crashing down. But the Obama campaign sees reason for hope after a primary season in which at least 3.5 million new voters registered and young people of voting age, typically apathetic, turned out as much as older voters in some states. . . .

The Republican Party also is hard at work mobilizing voters it believes will be especially supportive of McCain, including military veterans. The McCain campaign is opening an office even in Democratic-leaning New Jersey....And a Republican official argues that the party's well-developed expertise in "surgical" micro-targeting of narrowly sliced segments of the electorate will give the party an advantage in turnout efforts. . . .

The Obama campaign has structured its voter registration drive as a 50-state effort. But campaign officials said they will concentrate resources on states that are competitive or they hope to make competitive, as well as demographic groups supportive of their candidate that historically have turned out in low numbers. . . .

Still, Republican officials and plenty of others are skeptical. But even if the Obama campaign can force Republicans to spend limited resources to defend previously safe territory, that in itself offers an advantage, political strategists said.

Discussion Questions

1. *Was the Obama campaign's decision to target young people, African Americans, and other groups with historically low turnout rates an effective strategy, given the outcome of the 2008 presidential election? Why or why not?*
2. *What are the possible long-term implications of young voters' support for Barack Obama? Do the results suggest that 2008 was a transformative election year?*

---

turnout include education, income, age, gender, race and ethnicity, group membership, and interest in politics. (To learn about turnout considerations and the 2008 presidential election, see Politcs Now: Can Turnout Aid One Candidate?)

EDUCATION AND INCOME Highly educated people are more likely to vote than people with less education. A higher income level also increases the likelihood that a person will exercise his or her right to vote.

Other things being equal, college graduates are much more likely to vote than those with less education, and people with advanced degrees are the most likely to vote. People with more education tend to learn more about politics, are less hindered by registration requirements, and are more self-confident about their ability to affect public life.[1] Therefore, one might argue that institutions of higher education provide citizens with opportunities to learn about and become interested in politics.

A considerably higher percentage of citizens with annual incomes over $65,000 vote than do citizens with incomes under $35,000. Income level, to some degree, is connected to education level, as wealthier people tend to have more opportunities for higher education, and more education also may lead to higher income. Wealthy citizens are more likely than poor ones to think that the "system" works for them and that their votes make a difference. People with higher incomes are more likely to recognize their direct financial stake in the decisions of the government, thus spurring them into action.[2]

By contrast, lower-income citizens often feel alienated from politics, possibly believing that conditions will remain the same no matter who holds office. American political parties may contribute to this feeling of alienation. As discussed in chapter 12, unlike parties in many other countries that tend to associate themselves with specific socio-economic classes, U.S. political parties are less directly linked to socio-economic class. One consequence of "classless" parties is that the interests of the poor receive relatively little public attention, feeding feelings of alienation and apathy.

AGE   A strong correlation exists between age and voter participation rates. The Twenty-Sixth Amendment to the Constitution, ratified in 1971, lowered the voting age to eighteen. While this amendment obviously increased the number of *eligible* voters, it did so by enfranchising the group that is least likely to vote. A much higher percentage of citizens age thirty and older vote than do citizens younger than thirty, although voter turnout decreases over the age of seventy, primarily due to difficulties some older voters have getting to their polling locations. Regrettably, only 58 percent of eligible eighteen- to twenty-four-year-olds are even registered to vote.[3] The most plausible reason for this is that younger people are more mobile; they have not put down roots in a community. Because voter registration is not automatic, people who relocate have to make an effort to register. Therefore, the effect of adding this low-turnout group to the electorate has been to lower the overall turnout rate. As young people marry, have children, and settle down in a community, their likelihood of voting increases.[4] In the 2008 presidential election, one research group estimated that turnout among those eighteen to twenty-nine increased to about 53 percent, 12 percent more than in 2000 and 5 percent more than in 2004 (see http://www.civicyouth.org for the most up-to-date counts).

GENDER   With passage of the Nineteenth Amendment in 1920, women gained the right to vote in the United States (see chapter 6). While early polling numbers are not reliable enough to shed light on the voting rate among women in the years immediately following their entry into the voting process, it is generally accepted that in the period following ratification of the Nineteenth Amendment, women voted at a lower rate than men. Recent polls suggest that today women vote at the same rate as men or at a slightly higher rate. Since women comprise slightly more than 50 percent of the U.S. population, they now account for a majority of the American electorate.

RACE AND ETHNICITY   Despite substantial gains in voting rates among minority groups, especially African Americans, race remains an important factor in voter participation. Whites still tend to vote more regularly than do African Americans, Hispanics, and other minority groups.

Several factors help to explain the persistent difference in voting rates between white and black voters. One reason is the relative income and educational levels of the two racial groups. African Americans tend to be poorer and to have less formal education than whites; as mentioned earlier, both of these factors affect voter turnout. Significantly, though, highly educated and wealthier African Americans are more likely to vote than whites of similar background.[5] Another explanation focuses on the

Motivating Young Voters

In the 2008 presidential election, 53 percent of eligible voters age eighteen to twenty-nine voted—that's five percent more than in the 2004 presidential election.[a] While midterm elections typically draw fewer voters than presidential elections, exit polls suggested that the "surge" in the youth vote also was observed in 2006, when 26 percent of young people voted—2 million more than in the 2002 midterms.[b] Still, when compared to the approximately 64 percent of voters thirty and over who voted in the last presidential election, 53 percent can only be described as low.

This lower turnout should disturb young voters, since it directly impacts what issues state and federal governments address. Ongoing military action in Iraq and Afghanistan, the federal deficit, rising health costs, the long-term financial stability of Social Security, high oil prices, and climate change are all issues likely to affect young voters—if not now, then in the future. Rising tuition costs and the extent to which government supports higher education are issues that hit even closer to home, since many students must work to pay their tuition bills and are likely to have loans to repay when they graduate. The stakes are high for young voters, so why aren't they voting?

Surveys consistently have shown that young voters do not vote because they believe their votes do not make a difference, they do not have enough information to make a decision, or they are too busy. Nearly half of students polled claim not to discuss politics with their parents, and over half say that schools do not sufficiently educate them on how to vote![c] Of course, if you do not know how to vote, then you do not vote, and if you never vote, then you never discover that your vote does make a difference.

- Did the parties and candidates in the last election make a real effort to connect with younger voters? Was one party or candidate more effective than others? Explain your answers.
- As the 2010 midterm elections approach, what advice do you have for parties and candidates who want to appeal to young voters?
- Design an educational brochure that can be distributed to high school students in your community explaining how to register to vote and how to locate their polling location. Make sure that the brochure includes information on absentee and early voting. While gathering the information for the brochure, note the procedural difficulties that Americans face in order to vote, and consider possible reforms to make the process more user-friendly.
- Conduct a brief survey of students on your campus to find out how many voted in the 2008 presidential election. Ask those who did not vote why they did not vote.
- The Harvard Institute of Politics released its 14th Biannual Youth Survey on Politics and Public Service in April 2007. The survey includes responses from 2,500 U.S. citizens eighteen to twenty-four years old, half of whom were enrolled in four-year colleges and universities. You can view the full report at www.iop.harvard.edu/Research-Publications/Polling/Spring-2008-Survey/Executive-Summary.

[a]National Election Pool exit polls, www.cnn.com/ELECTION/2008/.
[b]See www.civicyouth.org for information on youth voting drawn from exit poll results in 2002 through 2008.
[c]See www.civicyouth.org/?page_id=154.

long-term consequence of the voting barriers that African Americans historically faced in the United States, especially in areas of the Deep South (see chapter 6).

Race also helps explain why the South has long had a lower turnout than the rest of the country (see Figure 13.1). As discussed in chapter 6, in the wake of Reconstruction, the southern states made it extremely difficult for African Americans to register to vote, and only a small percentage of the eligible African American population was registered throughout the South until the 1960s. The Voting Rights Act (VRA) of 1965 helped to change this situation. Often heralded as the most successful piece of civil rights legislation ever passed, the VRA was intended to guarantee voting rights to African Americans nearly a century after passage of the Fifteenth Amendment. The VRA, key provisions of which were extended for another twenty-five years in 2006, targets states that once used literacy or morality tests or poll taxes to exclude minorities from the polls. The act bans any voting device or procedure that interferes with a minority citizen's right to vote, and it requires approval for any changes in voting qualifications or procedures in certain areas where minority registration was not in proportion to the racial composition of the district. It also authorizes the federal government to monitor all elections in areas where discrimination was found to be practiced or where less than 50 percent of the voting-age public was registered to vote in the 1964 election.

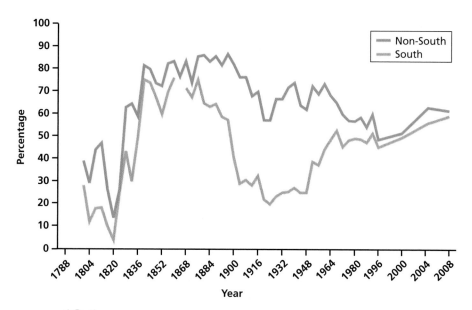

FIGURE 13.1 The South Versus the Non-South for Presidential Voter Turnout
After a century-long discrepancy caused by discrimination against African American voters in the South, regional voting turnouts have grown much closer together with the increasing enfranchisement of these voters.

Source: Compiled from data contained in the Center for the Study of the American Electorate 2004 Election Report, November 4, 2004. Data from 2008 compiled from CNN exit polls.

The 2000 Census revealed that the Hispanic community in the United States is now slightly larger in size than the African American community; thus, Latino/as have the potential to wield enormous political power. In California, Texas, Florida, Illinois, and New York, five key electoral states, Latino/a voters have emerged as powerful allies for candidates seeking office. However, just as voter turnout among African Americans is historically much lower than among whites, the turnout among Hispanic Americans is much lower than turnout among African Americans.[6] In the five largest states—California, Texas, Florida, Illinois, and New York—Hispanic voters have emerged as powerful allies for candidates seeking office. Moreover, their increasing presence in Arizona, Colorado, Nevada, and New Mexico—the latter three were key battleground states in the 2008 presidential election—have forced candidates of both parties to place more emphasis on issues that affect Hispanics. However, just as voter turnout among African Americans is historically much lower than among whites, the turnout among Hispanics is much lower than turnout among African Americans. In 2004, 67 percent of whites voted in the presidential election, while 60 percent of African Americans and only 44 percent of Hispanics turned out to vote. Turnout for Asian Americans also was quite low, with only 47 percent voting in 2004. Barack Obama's candidacy helped narrow the gap between whites and African Americans in 2008, but a similar upswing in turnout was not evident among other minority groups.[7]

Like any voting group, Hispanics are not easily categorized and voting patterns cannot be neatly generalized. However, several major factors play out as key decision-making variables: country of origin, length of time in the United States, and income levels. Although Hispanic Americans share a common history of Spanish colonialism and similar patterns of nation building, they differ in political processes and agendas. Despite having citizenship, Puerto Ricans can vote in a presidential election only if they live on the mainland and establish residency. Cuban Americans are concentrated in south Florida and tend to be conservative and vote for GOP

Does voter turnout matter?
Lines like this were common in urban areas during the 2008 elections. In 2008, 62 percent of eligible Americans, over 128 million voters, cast a ballot. Among the 14 million voting for the first time, 68 percent voted for Barack Obama.

Photo courtesy: Tom Reel/Sam Antonio News-Express/Zuma Press

candidates. Mexican Americans favor Democrats, but their voting patterns are very issue-oriented and vary according to income levels, length of time in the United States, and age.[8] As discussed in chapter 12, high-profile debates in Congress over immigration led to an upswing in Democratic support by Hispanics in 2008.

GROUP MEMBERSHIP Individuals who are members of civic organizations, trade and professional organizations, and labor unions are more likely to vote and participate in politics than those who are not members of these or similar types of groups. People who more frequently attend church or other religious services, moreover, also are more likely to vote than people who rarely attend or do not belong to religious institutions. A recent study found that 74 percent of people who say that they attend a religious service at least one a week voted in the 2006 midterm elections, while only 54 percent of those who rarely or never attend services voted.

Many of these organizations, and American churches in particular, emphasize community involvement, which often encourages voting and exposes members to requests from political parties and candidates for support. These groups also encourage participation by providing opportunities for members to develop organizational and communication skills that are relevant for political activity. Union membership is particularly likely to increase voting turnout among people who on the basis of their education or income are less likely to vote.[9]

Voting Turnout: Who Votes in the United States?

INTEREST IN POLITICS   An interest in politics must also be included as an important factor for voter turnout. Many citizens who vote have grown up in families interested and active in politics. It is believed that interest serves as a gateway that leads people to gather information about candidates and to more fully participate in the political process, including voting. People who are highly interested in politics constitute only a small minority of the U.S. population. The most politically active Americans—party and issue-group activists—make up less than 5 percent of the country's more than 300 million people. Those who contribute time or money to a party or a candidate during a campaign make up only about 10 percent of the total adult population. Although these percentages appear low, they translate into millions of Americans who contribute more than just votes to the system.

The sophisticated use of new technologies by campaigns, moreover, points to increased participation in the future. The Internet has made donating money to candidates a much simpler process, in particular for younger voters and smaller

FIGURE 13.2 Why People Don't Vote According to the U.S. Census Bureau's Current Population Survey taken after the 2004 elections, "too busy" was the single biggest reason Americans gave for not voting on Election Day.

Source: U.S. Census Bureau, Current Population Survey, November 2004.

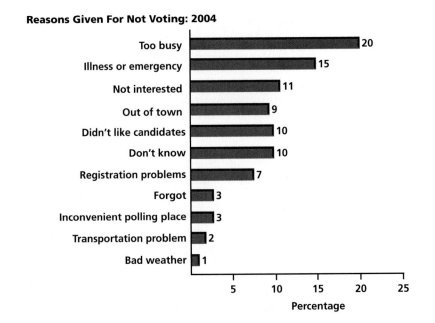

Reasons Given For Not Voting: 2004

Reason	Percentage
Too busy	20
Illness or emergency	15
Not interested	11
Out of town	9
Didn't like candidates	10
Don't know	10
Registration problems	7
Forgot	3
Inconvenient polling place	3
Transportation problem	2
Bad weather	1

Percentage

donors, with campaign Web sites offering online credit-card payment options.[10] In addition, the increased popularity of social networking sites such as Facebook and MySpace has provided campaigns with an effective tool for identifying supporters and recruiting volunteers.

Why Is Voter Turnout So Low?

The United States has one of the lowest voter participation rates of any nation in the industrialized world. In 1960, 65 percent of the eligible electorate voted in the presidential election, but by 1996, American voter participation had fallen to 51.5 percent and only 48.8 percent of the voting age population—the lowest turnout in a presidential election in modern times. Since then, however, turnout has steadily increased, to 54 percent in 2000, climbing to 60 percent in 2004, and surging to at least 62 percent in 2008. Figure 13.2 lists reasons U.S. nonvoters gave for not voting in 2004. A number of contributing factors are discussed below.

TOO BUSY   According to the U.S. Census Bureau, 20 percent of registered nonvoters reported in 2004 that they did not vote in a recent election because they were too busy or had conflicting work or school schedules (see Figure 13.2). Another 15 percent said they did not vote because they were ill, disabled, or had a family emergency. While these reasons seem to account for a large portion of the people surveyed, they may also reflect the respondents' desire not to seem uneducated about the candidates and issues or apathetic about the political process. Although some would-be voters are undoubtedly busy, infirm, or otherwise unable to make it to the polls, it is likely that many of these nonvoters are offering an easy excuse and have another reason for failing to vote.

DIFFICULTY OF REGISTRATION   Of those citizens who are registered, the overwhelming majority vote. A major reason for lack of participation in the United States remains the relatively low percentage of the adult population that is registered to vote. To learn more, see Figure 13.3. There are several reasons for the low U.S. registration rate. First, while nearly every other democratic country places the burden of registration on the government rather than on the individual, in the United States the registration process

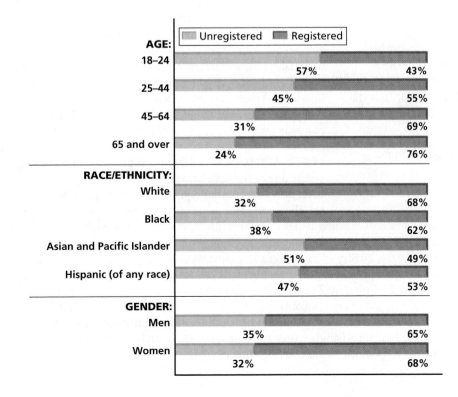

FIGURE 13.3 Percentage of Registered Voters by Age, Race/Ethnicity, and Gender, 2004 Older Americans continue to register at a much higher rate than younger voters. While increasing their representation at the ballot box, minorities still lag behind white voters in registration. Exit polls suggest that voting increased for many of these groups in 2008, especially young voters and African Americans.

Source: U.S. Census Bureau, Current Population Survey, November 2004.

still requires individual initiative—a daunting impediment in this age of political apathy. Thus, the cost (in terms of time and effort) of registering to vote is higher in the United States than it is in other industrialized democracies. Second, many nations automatically register all of their citizens to vote. In the United States, however, citizens must jump the extra hurdle of remembering on their own to register. Indeed, it is no coincidence that voter participation rates dropped markedly after reformers, desiring to combat voter fraud, pushed through strict voter registration laws in the early part of the twentieth century. Correspondingly, several recent studies of the effects of relaxed state voter registration laws show that easier registration leads to higher levels of turnout.[11] When states adopted Election Day registration of new voters, large and significant improvements in turnout occurred among younger voters and the poor.[12]

The National Voter Registration Act of 1993, commonly known as the Motor Voter Act, was a recent attempt to ease the bureaucratic hurdles associated with registering to vote. The law requires states to provide the opportunity to register through drivers' license agencies, public assistance agencies, and the mail. While a large number of Americans have yet to take advantage of the Motor Voter Act, it is likely that the law is at least partially responsible for the increases in voter participation experienced in recent elections.

DIFFICULTY OF ABSENTEE VOTING   Stringent absentee ballot laws are another factor in low voter turnout for the United States. Many states, for instance, require citizens to apply in person for absentee ballots, a burdensome requirement given that one's inability to be present in one's home state is often the reason for absentee balloting in the first place. Recent literature in political science links liberalized absentee voting rules and higher turnout. One study, for instance, concluded that generous absentee voting guidelines reduced the "costs of voting" and increased turnout when the parties mobilized their followers to take advantage of such absentee voting rules.[13]

NUMBER OF ELECTIONS   Another explanation for low voter turnout in the United States is the sheer number and frequency of elections. According to a study by the International Institute for Democracy and Electoral Assistance, the United States typically holds twice as many national elections as other Western democracies, a consequence of the relatively short two-year term of office for members of the House of Representatives.[14] American federalism (see chapter 3), with its separate elections at the local, state, and national levels, and its use of primary elections for the selection of candidates, also contributes to the number of elections in which Americans are called on to participate. With so many elections, even the most active political participants may skip part of the electoral process from time to time.

Thinking Globally

How Many Elections?

Between 1945 and 2005, the United States held thirty national elections. In contrast, Iceland held sixteen, Italy held fourteen, and Portugal held a mere nine.

- How frequently should elections be held? Does the United States hold elections too often? Explain your reasoning.
- Is the frequency of elections an important factor in the accountability of elected officials? Why or why not?

VOTER ATTITUDES   Although some low voter participation is due to the institutional factors we have just described, voter attitudes play an equally important part. Some voters are alienated, and others are just plain apathetic, possibly because of a lack of pressing issues in a particular year, satisfaction with the status quo, or uncompetitive (even uncontested) elections. Furthermore, many citizens may be turned off by the quality of campaigns in a time when petty issues and personal mudslinging are more prevalent than ever. Divided government can also affect voter turnout, with turnout declining by 2 percent in each consecutive election conducted when the presidency and Congress are controlled by different parties.[15] Some nations, such as Australia and Belgium, try to get around the effects of voter attitudes with compulsory voting laws. Not surprisingly, voter turnout rates in Australia and Belgium are often greater than 90 percent, as these nations fine citizens who fail to vote.

WEAKENED INFLUENCE OF POLITICAL PARTIES Political parties today are not as effective as they once were in mobilizing voters, ensuring that they are registered, and getting them to the polls. As we discussed in chapter 12, the parties once were grassroots organizations that forged strong party–group links with their supporters. Today, candidate-centered campaigns and the growth of expansive party bureaucracies have resulted in a somewhat more distant party with which fewer people identify very strongly. While efforts have been made in recent elections to bolster the influence of parties, in particular through sophisticated get out the vote efforts, the parties' modern grassroots activities pale in comparison to their earlier efforts.

Photo courtesy: Dennis Brack/Black Star/StockPhoto

What impact did the Motor Voter Act have on voter registration? A worker at a state motor vehicles office displays the form that makes it easy to register to vote. Motor Voter legislation increased voter registration by about four percent in the first four years of implementation.

Efforts to Improve Voter Turnout

Reformers have proposed many ideas to increase voter turnout in the United States. Always on the list is raising the political awareness of young citizens, a reform that inevitably must involve our nation's schools. The rise in formal education levels among Americans has played a significant role in preventing an even greater decline in voter turnout.[16] No less important, and perhaps simpler to achieve, are institutional reforms, though many of the reforms discussed below, if enacted, may result in only a marginal increase in turnout. (To learn more about a controversial topic related to voter turnout, see Join the Debate: Should Felons Be Allowed to Vote?)

EASIER REGISTRATION AND CONVENIENCE VOTING   Registration laws vary by state, but in most states, people must register prior to Election Day. Nine states—Idaho, Iowa, Maine, Minnesota, Montana, New Hampshire, North Carolina, Wisconsin, and Wyoming—now permit same-day Election Day registration. Turnout in these same-day registration states has averaged about 11 percentage points higher in recent elections than in other states, supporting the long-held claim by reformers that voter turnout could be increased if registering to vote were made simpler for citizens.[17] Better yet, all U.S. citizens could be registered automatically at the age of eighteen. Other proposals are that states could allow voters to vote early or make it easier to obtain absentee ballots by eliminating the in-person requirement. In thirty-one states voters can visit an election official's office and cast a vote in person without providing a reason for not being able to vote on Election Day. Some states even have established satellite locations for voting before Election Day, including, for example, in other government offices, grocery stores, and shopping malls. Oregon has become the first state in the nation to eliminate polling places, switching to all-mail balloting; after the change, turnout increased. More and more voters are choosing to vote early or vote by mail because of the convenience. Election administrators are encouraging these practices because of the savings to taxpayers and the reduction to the stress of processing ballots quickly on Election Day.

The motor-voter legislation discussed above, which requires states to permit individuals to register by mail, also allows citizens to register to vote when they visit any motor vehicles office, public assistance agency, or military recruitment office.

Join the Debate

Should Felons Be Allowed to Vote?

OVERVIEW: An estimated 5.3 million citizens could not vote in 2008 because they had been convicted of a felony. States, not the federal government, determine whether or not felons can vote, and there is considerable variation in state laws. Vermont and Maine allow convicted felons—even those in prison or on probation or parole—to vote. Convicted felons in Kentucky and Virginia, on the other hand, are barred from voting for life. In 2007, Florida, which had permanently disenfranchised almost 1 million felons, adopted rules allowing those convicted of nonviolent crimes to vote after completing their time in prison. Eighteen other states reconsidered their policies in 2007, and seven adopted changes.

In 2005, one out of every fifteen African American men of voting age and one out of every thirty-six Hispanic men were in prison. In contrast, only one out of 106 white men were incarcerated. The number of women in prisons is considerably less than the number of men, but the patterns are similar: one out every 203 African American women, one out of every 436 Hispanic women, and one out every 859 white women. The racial impact of not allowing felons to vote is even more pronounced when including those on probation and parole. Almost 17 percent of African Americans and 12 percent of Hispanics are disenfranchised because of felonies, but only 2 percent of whites.[a] While the reasons for this pattern are themselves a subject of heated debate, clearly the impact of policies taking away the voting rights of felons affects racial minorities far more heavily than whites.

When an individual commits a felony offense, he or she is demonstrating a basic disregard for the law. One way of responding to that is to focus on the illegal act or acts and another is to consider the felon as so alienated from and hostile to society that he or she should not participate in the governing process. Are we, in other words, dealing with bad behavior or a bad person? The latter perspective provides a justification for banning felons not only from the voting booth but also from serving in top government posts.

Efforts to reform state laws and allow felons the right to vote focus more on behavior than fundamental flaws in character. The assumption is that individuals who commit crimes should be punished but can be rehabilitated. Part of rehabilitation and reintegration into life outside prison walls is participation in the electoral process and in governance generally. Courts have ruled that states may pursue whatever policies they like with regard to felons. The Fourteenth Amendment to the Constitution requires states to provide "equal protection of the laws" to all citizens, which can be interpreted to mean that once someone completes a sentence, they have the same rights as others. However, the Fourteenth Amendment includes a clause that explicitly does not include this protection for persons who participate "in rebellion or other crimes."[b]

Some maintain that a partisan dimension to the debate about the voting rights of felons exists. The public debate focuses on issues of law and order, crime and punishment, but the probable implications for which party gains or loses if felons are not allowed to vote fuels suspicions of partisan strategy. As pointed out in this chapter, African Americans and those with lower levels of income and education tend to vote for Democrats. On the other hand, as also pointed out in this chapter, these same demographic groups tend to have a low rate of voter participation, thus making accusations of partisan bias in this debate somewhat suspect, at least in practice.

The widespread adoption of motor-voter by the various states has increased voter registration rates an estimated 5 to 9 percent, especially among young voters, and confirms the value of innovative election reform for state and federal lawmakers.[18]

MAKE ELECTION DAY A HOLIDAY Besides removing an obstacle to voting (the busy workday), making Election Day a national holiday might focus more voter attention on the contests in the critical final hours. The strategy might backfire, however, as people might use the day off to extend vacations or long weekends. The tradition of Tuesday elections in this country should reduce this risk.

Arguments AGAINST Voting Rights for Felons

- Part of the punishment for committing a serious crime is the revocation of the privilege of voting. The penalties for disregarding the law include a variety of restrictions and lost freedoms. Convicted felons do not enjoy the same rights as the rest of us do to privacy, employment, and movement.

- Prohibiting felons from voting is a race and class neutral policy. If racial minorities or people with lower incomes or lower education are disproportionately represented among felons, that is a social and economic issue that might demonstrate the need for certain policies, but it does not affect the justification for disenfranchising convicted criminals.

- We need to deter crime and one of the ways of doing that is to take the right to vote away from felons. There need to be consequences when someone commits a crime. One of the consequences is to revoke a criminal's right to vote.

Arguments IN FAVOR of Voting Rights for Felons

- Voting is a right of citizenship, not a reward for good behavior. One does not forfeit basic rights of citizenship when making a mistake and committing a crime. Although we incarcerate and place on probation and parole those who have been convicted of crimes, we do not revoke their basic constitutional rights to humane treatment or to freedom of expression and association. Likewise, we should not allow states to take away the right to vote.

- Felons need to be reintegrated into society, not treated like noncitizens. It is a mixed message to tell felons that they need to get a legitimate job and to act like a law-abiding citizen and then to tell them that they may not vote. Current policies treat felons, even after they have completed their sentences in prison and thus have paid their debt to society, as if they are still criminals rather than functioning members of society.

- Limiting the rights of felons to vote disproportionately affects ethnic minorities and individuals with low levels of income or education. To disenfranchise felons is to double the disadvantages already faced by members of minority groups and lower socio-economic classes. Taking away voting rights of felons works against the objective of integrating our society.

Continuing the Debate

1. When, if at all, should felons be allowed to vote again? If they are no longer incarcerated? If they are no longer on probation or parole? For a certain period after they are no longer in the correctional system? Explain your answer.
2. Is the concern about the number of felons who are poor or members of minority groups a legitimate reason for reinstating the voting rights of felons? Why or why not?

To Follow the Debate Online, Go To:

Project Vote, projectvote.org/issues/felon-voting-rights.html
The American Civil Liberties Union, www.aclu.org/votingrights/exoffenders
The Federalist Society, www.fed-soc.org/publications/PubID.185/pub_detail.asp

[a]The Pew Center on the States, *One in 100: Behind Bars in America 2008*, www.pewcenteronthestates.org/uploaded-Files/One%20in%20100.pdf; and Bureau of Justice Statistics, *Probation and Parole, 2005*, www.ojp.usdoj.gov/bjs/abstract/ppus05.htm.
[b]Christopher P. Manfredi, "Judicial Review and Criminal Disenfranchisement in the United States and Canada," *Review of Politics* 60:2 (1998): 277–305.

Photo courtesy: Robert Allred

Is voting a right or a privilege? Bill Kleiber, far right, provides voter registration information to former inmates in Texas.

STRENGTHEN PARTIES Reformers have long argued that strengthening the political parties would increase voter turnout, because parties have historically been the organizations in the United States most successful at mobilizing citizens to vote. During the late 1800s and early 1900s, the country's "Golden Age" of powerful political parties, one of their primary activities was getting out the vote on Election Day. Even today, the parties' Election Day get out the vote drives increase voter turnout by several million in national contests. The Democratic National Committee undertook an initiative proposed by its chair, Howard Dean, to canvass all fifty states prior to the 2006 election, even putting resources in states that have not been traditionally receptive to Democratic politics in an attempt to reinvigorate the party nationwide. These efforts yielded significant returns for the Democrats in the 2006 and 2008 congressional elections, when they picked up a number of seats in states and districts that had not sent a Democrat to Congress in decades by maximizing turnout among their core constituencies.

OTHER SUGGESTIONS Other ideas to increase voter turnout are less practical or feasible. For example, holding fewer elections might sound appealing, but it is difficult to see how this could be accomplished without diluting many of the central tenets of federalism and separation of powers that the Framers believed essential to the protection of liberty. One proposal to increase voter turnout is the use of a proportional representation system for congressional elections to encourage third parties and combat voter apathy toward the two major parties. Other proposals include changing Election Day to Saturday or Sunday, making voting mandatory, or providing a tax credit for those who vote. Other, perhaps more promising ideas include allowing for a longer period of time to vote (perhaps an election week), using Internet technology to ease the burden of voting, increasing the availability of mail-in voting, or simply increasing the availability of voting places.[19]

Patterns in Vote Choice

Just as there are certain predictable patterns when it comes to American voter turnout, so, too, are there predictable patterns of vote choice. Some of the most prominent correlates of vote choice include partisan identification, race and ethnicity, gender, religion, income, ideology, issues, and campaign-specific developments.

PARTY IDENTIFICATION Party identification remains the most powerful predictor of voter behavior. Stated simply, self-described Democrats tend to vote for Democratic candidates and self-described Republicans tend to vote for Republican candidates. Still, although intense partisanship has increased over the last ten years, many voters continue to be more independent of party in their vote choice. The practice of **ticket-splitting,** voting for candidates of different parties for various offices in an election, rose dramatically during the 1960s and 1970s.[20] In 1972, a year with a particularly high level of ticket-splitting, 30 percent of voters split their tickets between their presidential vote and their vote for U.S. representative. The National Elections Study estimates ticket-splitting was at 26 percent in the 2004 election, with 55 percent of respondents stating they preferred to have party control split between the president and Congress.[21]

ticket-splitting
Voting for candidates of different parties for various offices in the same election.

Scholars have posited several potential explanations for ticket-splitting. One explanation is that voters split their tickets, consciously or not, because they trust neither party to govern. Under this interpretation, ticket-splitters are aware of the differences between the two parties and split their tickets to augment the checks and balances already present in the Constitution.[22] Alternatively, voters split their tickets possibly because partisanship has become less relevant as a voting cue. Other explanations for ticket-splitting abound. The growth of issue-oriented politics and single-interest groups, the greater emphasis on candidate-centered personality politics, and broader-based education are all often cited.[23]

RACE AND ETHNICITY Just as voter turnout varies according to race and ethnicity, so does vote choice. The different racial and ethnic groups tend to vote in distinct patterns. While whites have shown an increasing tendency to vote Republican in recent elections, African American voters remain overwhelmingly Democratic in both their partisan identification and in their voting decisions. Despite the best efforts of the Republican Party to garner African American support, this pattern shows no signs of waning. In 2008, Barack Obama's candidacy accelerated this trend, and 95 percent of African Americans voted for him. John McCain received a mere 4 percent of the African American vote.[24]

Hispanics also tend to identify with and vote for Democrats, although not as monolithically as do African Americans.[25] In 2008, for example, Obama received 67 percent of the votes cast by Hispanics; McCain received only 31 percent.

The Asian and Pacific American segment of the electorate is less monolithic and more variable in its voting than either the Hispanic or African American communities. It is worth noting the considerable political diversity within this group: Chinese Americans tend to prefer Democratic candidates, but Vietnamese Americans, with a strong anti-communist leaning, tend to support Republicans. A typical voting split for the Asian and Pacific American community runs about 60 percent Democratic and 40 percent Republican, though it can reach the extreme of a 50–50 split, depending on the election.[26]

Photo courtesy: Sandy Huffaker/Getty Images

How do candidates campaign for the support of racial and ethnic minorities? Barack Obama is pictured here speaking at the 2008 National Council of La Raza conference on July 14, 2008. Candidates regularly appear at the annual meetings of civic organizations and interest groups representing ethnic minorities.

GENDER In a number of elections, gender has been touted as a factor, although precise data are not always available to prove the conventional wisdom. For example, journalists in 1920 claimed that women—voting in their first presidential election after passage of the Nineteenth Amendment—were especially likely to vote for Republican presidential candidate Warren G. Harding due to Harding's good looks and purported charm.

In most elections today, women are more likely to support the Democratic candidate and men are more likely to support the Republican candidate. Since 1980, the gender gap, the difference between the voting choices of men and women, has become a staple of American politics (see chapter 12). The size of the gender gap varies considerably from election to election, though normally the gender gap is between 5 and 7 percentage points. That is, women support the average Democrat 5 to 7 percent more than men. Some elections result in an expanded gender gap, however, such as the presidential election of 1996. Bob Dole narrowly won among men in 1996, while Bill Clinton scored a landslide among women. In 2004, George W. Bush won 55 percent of the male vote, while John Kerry received 51 percent of the female vote. In 2008, Barack Obama won 56 percent of the female vote, but only 49 percent of the male vote. (To learn more, see Figure 12.6.)[27]

A gender gap in vote choice is not confined only to contests between Democrats and Republicans but is frequently apparent in intra-party contests as well. In the 2008 Democratic primaries and caucuses, Democratic women were more likely than Democratic men to support Senator Hillary Clinton. In the California primary, for example, 59 percent of women voted for Senator Clinton while only 36 percent voted for Senator Barack Obama. Among men, 48 percent voted for Obama while 45 percent voted for Clinton. There was a similar pattern in other competitive states after Super Tuesday, such as Ohio, Texas, and Pennsylvania.[28] While there was a clear difference between Democratic women and men in this particular nomination contest, there is no evidence to suggest women and men generally vote for a candidate of their own gender in races that have both women and men running.[29] The strong, consistent support of Democratic women for Senator Clinton, in particular among blue-collar women and women over 50, may have resulted from a long-standing identification with her and her commitment to issues related to women.

461

RELIGION Religious groups also have tended to vote in distinct patterns, but some of these traditional differences have declined considerably in recent years. The most cohesive of religious groups has been Jewish voters, a majority of whom identify as Democrats and have voted for every Democratic presidential candidate since the New Deal realignment. While Republican presidents' strong support for Israel decreased Jewish voters' overwhelming preference for Democratic candidates between 1972 and 1988, recent Democratic candidates have reversed these gains. In 2004, 74 percent of Jewish voters supported John Kerry, the Democratic nominee, and in 2008, 78 percent supported Senator Obama.

While Catholics also have tended to identify with the Democratic Party, a majority are now voting for Republican candidates in most elections. Catholics first broke away from the Democratic coalition to support President Eisenhower and President Nixon's reelection bids. Since 1976, Catholics have alternated their support for the two parties, supporting the winning presidential candidate in each case and, thus, making Catholics one of the most important constituency groups in U.S. politics. In 2004, 52 percent of Catholics voted for President Bush while only 47 percent voted for Senator Kerry, who himself is Catholic. Four years later, 54 percent of Catholic voters supported Democrat Barack Obama, while only 45 percent supported Republican John McCain. Among white Catholics, however, a narrow majority voted for Senator McCain.

Since the New Deal realignment, a majority of Protestants have identified as Republicans, but there is considerable diversity among this group of voters. In 2004, for example, 59 percent of Protestants voted to reelect President Bush, while only 40 percent supported John Kerry. White Protestants, however, consistently have supported Republicans at much higher margins than African American Protestants. But, there are divisions among white Protestants as well. While George W. Bush won the support of nearly 80 percent of white Evangelical Protestants (e.g., Southern Baptists, United Methodists, Church of God), he won the support of only about 54 percent of whites from mainline Protestant denominations such as Episcopalians and Presbyterians.[30]

Photo courtesy: Laura J. Gardner/The News and Advance/AP/Wide World Photos

How do candidates campaign for the support of different religious groups? In his losing bid for the 2000 Republican presidential nomination, Senator John McCain publicly feuded with the late Reverend Jerry Falwell, a leading fundamentalist Christian political leader. In the run-up to the 2008 presidential election, however, McCain delivered the commencement address at Falwell's Liberty University.

INCOME Over the years, income has been a remarkably stable correlate of vote choice. The poor vote more Democratic; the well-to-do vote heavily Republican.[31] Indeed, in the 2004 presidential election, those voters whose household income was less than $15,000 yearly voted for Kerry over Bush by 63 percent to 36 percent, whereas those voters whose household income was more than $100,000 yearly supported Bush over Kerry by 59 to 41 percent. The split among middle-income voters was more evenly balanced between the two candidates, with President Bush winning approximately 53 percent of the vote from voters in households earning between $30,000 and $75,000.[32] Generally, the candidate who wins a majority of "middle-class" votes will win the presidency.

IDEOLOGY Ideology represents one of the most significant divisions in contemporary American politics. Liberals, generally speaking, favor government involvement in social programs (like Social Security, public education, and Medicare) and are committed to the ideals of tolerance and social justice. Liberals tend to view government as an instrument of social progress. Conservatives, on the other hand, tend to favor defense and police protection as the top priorities of government and believe that private and faith-based organizations are better suited to provide social programs than the government. Conservatives are dedicated to the ideals of individualism and market-based competition, and they tend to view government as a necessary evil rather than an agent of social improvement. Moderates, who comprise the bulk of the American electorate, lie somewhere between liberals and conservatives on the ideological spectrum, or favor conservative positions on some issues and liberal positions on others.

Not surprisingly, ideology is very closely related to vote choice. Liberals tend to vote for Democrats, and conservatives tend to vote for Republicans. In 2008, 89 percent of self-described liberals voted for Barack Obama, whereas only 10 percent voted for John McCain. Conservatives, on the other hand, voted for McCain over Obama at a rate of 79 to 20 percent.[33]

ISSUES   In addition to the underlying influences on vote choice discussed above, individual issues can have important effects in any given election year. In 1992, when Bill Clinton's chief political adviser, James Carville, established "it's the economy stupid" as Clinton's campaign mantra, he was confirming a well-established idea in American politics: perceptions of the economy drive voter decisions.[34] Voters tend to reward the party in government, usually the president's party, during good economic times and punish the party in government during periods of economic downturn. When this occurs, the electorate is exercising **retrospective judgment;** that is, voters are rendering judgment on the performance of the party in power by judging whether the economy has improved under its governance. At other times, voters might use **prospective judgment;** that is, they vote based on what they perceive to be the future direction of the economy. By looking forward, voters can evaluate if a party's positions are likely to serve their interests, while not holding the ruling party accountable for economic conditions that might be beyond the party's control (for example, the economic effects of a hurricane or terrorist attack).

retrospective judgment
A voter's evaluation of the performance of the party in power.

prospective judgment
A voter's evaluation of a candidate based on what he or she pledges to do about an issue if elected.

The 2004 and 2008 elections provide examples of how both retrospective and prospective judgment helps voters to reach their ballot decisions. Ordinarily, incumbent reelections become a referendum on the incumbent's performance, making Americans likely to think retrospectively. However, in 2004, economic conditions, which were slowly recovering following the September 11, 2001, terrorist attacks, offered no clear direction to voters. While President Bush, the incumbent, encouraged prospective evaluations by arguing his opponent would bring a tax-and-spend philosophy to the White House, economic factors seemed to be of secondary importance in this election. The ongoing war on terrorism led voters to consider how their choice of president would affect the next four years of American military policy, and Bush won with a higher percentage of the popular vote than he had received in 2000.

In 2008, voters were concerned primarily with one overarching issue: the state of the economy. On a consistent basis, Democrat Barack Obama argued that the poor economy and specific problems such as the steep drop in stock prices and crisis on Wall Street, increasing home foreclosures, and rising unemployment, resulted from the failed policies of the Bush administration. In addition, Obama argued, the cost of continuing a war that never should have been fought in Iraq not only had diverted attention from a deteriorating situation in Afghanistan, but it also had drained resources that were needed for important domestic needs. Senator Obama also sought to link Republican John McCain to the highly unpopular Republican president, citing Senator McCain's claim that he had supported President Bush 90 percent of the time. In other words, a vote for McCain was a vote for more of the same. For his part, Senator McCain emphasized Senator Obama's opposition to the troop surge in Iraq in 2007 and Obama's unwillingness to acknowledge the reduction of violence in the region. But, voters' concerns about Iraq and national security diminished (in part, some argued, as a result of the success of the troop surge that Senator McCain had vigorously supported). The financial meltdown on Wall Street that began in September left no doubt that the economy was the most important issue to Americans. McCain attempted to draw a sharper contrast between the two candidates' positions on taxes and government spending, but with limited success.

In the end, the Obama campaign's effort to link McCain to President Bush and his handling of the economy was quite successful. Exit polls showed that 63 percent of voters considered the economy the most important issue, and these voters supported Obama over McCain by a significant margin: 54 percent to 45 percent. Voters who were most concerned about terrorism, however, voted overwhelmingly for McCain, 86 percent to 13 percent, but only nine percent of the voters considered it the most important issue.

Elections in the United States

Both the ballot and the bullet are methods of governmental change around the world, and surely the ballot is preferable. Although the United States has not escaped the bullet's awful effects, as was the case when President Lincoln was shot in 1865, the election process is responsible for most leadership change in this country. Regular free elections guarantee mass political action and enable citizens to influence the actions of their government. Societies that cannot vote their leaders out of office are left with little choice other than to force them out by means of strikes, riots, or coups d'état.

The Purposes of Elections

Popular election confers on a government the legitimacy that it can achieve no other way. Elections confirm the very concept of popular sovereignty, the idea that legitimate political power is derived from the consent of the governed (see chapter 1), and they serve as the bedrock for democratic governance. Even **authoritarian systems,** such as those in North Korea, Syria, and China, which base their rule on force rather than the consent of the governed, recognize this fact and sometimes attempt to create the appearance of fair and open elections to justify their rule. From time to time, they hold "referenda" to endorse their regimes or one-party elections, even though these so-called elections offer no real choice that would ratify their rule. The symbolism of elections as mechanisms to legitimize change, then, is important, but so is their practical value.

authoritarian system
A system of government that bases its rule on force rather than consent of the governed.

electorate
The citizens eligible to vote.

mandate
A command, indicated by an electorate's votes, for the elected officials to carry out their platforms.

In a democratic society, elections are the primary means to fill public offices and staff the government. The voters' choice of candidates and parties helps to organize government as well. Regular elections ensure that government is accountable to the people it serves. At fixed intervals, the **electorate**—citizens eligible to vote—is called on to judge those in power. Even though the majority of office holders in the United States win reelection, some office holders inevitably lose power, and all candidates are exposed to the judgment of the voters. The threat of elections keeps policy makers concerned with public opinion and promotes ethical behavior, as nothing makes an incumbent more vulnerable than a scandal.

Because candidates advocate certain policies, elections also provide a choice of direction on a wide range of issues, from abortion to civil rights to national defense to the environment. If current office holders are reelected, they may continue their policies with renewed resolve. Should office holders be defeated and their challengers elected, however, a change in policies will likely result. Either way, the winners will claim a **mandate** (literally, a command) from the people to carry out their policy agenda.

Often the claim of a mandate is suspect because voters are not so much endorsing one candidate and his or her positions as rejecting his or her opponent. Moreover, elections that are won by razor-thin margins, cannot qualify as an electoral mandate. This was particularly true in 1992 when the presence of third-party candidate Ross Perot enabled Bill Clinton to win the presidency with less than 50 percent of the vote, and in 2000 when George W. Bush lost the popular vote but won the Electoral College vote as a result of a Supreme Court ruling.

On rare occasions, off-year congressional elections can produce mandates. In 1994, backlash against President Clinton's policy direction helped Representative Newt

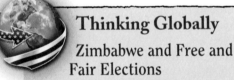

Thinking Globally

Zimbabwe and Free and Fair Elections

The international community has become increasingly active in calling for free and fair elections across the globe. The most basic requirements of free and fair elections are reasonable intervals between elections, guaranteed universal suffrage, equal access to polling places, and voting by secret ballot. Zimbabwe's 2008 presidential election caused an electoral crisis resulting in widespread rioting and violence, a vote recount, the arrest of election officials, charges from longtime President Robert Mugabe that widespread electoral fraud biased the outcome against the ruling party, and counter-claims by opposition party supporters that they had won the election.

- Identify other examples where election results have been called into question. What was the basis for the election dispute?
- Under what conditions are elections more likely to be free and fair? In what ways might the United States improve its election process?

Gingrich (R–GA) lead Republicans to gain control of the House of Representatives and claim a mandate for the "Contract with America," a series of popular policy proposals supported by Gingrich and his followers. The fact that the House Republicans were unified in support of a set policy platform and that they were able to pick up fifty-two seats in the House helped them build a strong case that the election represented a rare off-year mandate.

Types of Elections

So far, we have referred mainly to general elections at the national level, but in the U.S. system, elections happen at various levels (national, state, and local) and come in numerous types (primary elections, general elections, initiatives, referenda, and recalls). (To learn about age qualifications for the different levels of national elected office see The Living Constitution feature.)

You Are a Campaign Manager: Countdown to 270! Choose Your Candidate and Lead Him to Electoral College Victory

PRIMARY ELECTIONS In **primary elections,** voters decide which of the candidates within a party will represent the party's ticket in the general elections. There are different kinds of primaries. For example, **closed primaries** allow only a party's registered voters to cast a ballot, and **open primaries** allow independents and sometimes members of the other party to participate. Closed primaries are considered healthier for the party system because they prevent members of one party from influencing the primaries of the opposition party. Studies of open primaries indicate that **crossover voting**—participation in the primary of a party with which the voter is not affiliated—occurs frequently.[35] Nevertheless, the research shows little evidence of much **raiding**—an *organized* attempt by voters of one party to influence the primary results of the other party.[36]

In ten states, when none of the candidates in the initial primary secures a majority of the votes, there is a **runoff primary,** a contest between the two candidates with the greatest number of votes.[37] Louisiana has a novel twist on the primary system. There, all candidates for office appear on the ballot, and if one candidate receives over 50 percent of the vote, the candidate wins and no general election is necessary. If no candidate wins a majority of the vote, the top two candidates, even if they belong to the same party, face each other in a runoff election. Such a system blurs the lines between primary and general election and all but removes the political party from the selection process.

GENERAL ELECTIONS Once party members vote for their party candidates for various offices, each state holds its general election. In the **general election,** voters decide which candidates will actually fill the nation's elective public offices. These elections are held at many levels, including municipal, county, state, and national. Whereas primaries are contests between the candidates within each party, general elections are contests between the candidates of opposing parties.

INITIATIVE, REFERENDUM, AND RECALL Three other types of elections are the initiative, the referendum, and the recall. Taken together, the initiative and referendum processes are collectively known as ballot measures. **Ballot measures** provide the electorate a direct voice in the political process by allowing voters to enact public policy. An **initiative** is a process that allows citizens to propose legislation or state constitutional amendments by submitting them directly to the state electorate for popular vote, provided the initiative supporters receive a certain number of signatures on petitions supporting the placement of the proposal on the ballot. The initiative process is used in twenty-four states and the District of Columbia. A **referendum** is an election whereby the state legislature submits proposed legislation or state constitutional amendments to the state's voters for approval. Although both the referendum and the initiative provide for more direct democracy, they are not free from controversy.

primary election
Election in which voters decide which of the candidates within a party will represent the party in the general election.

closed primary
A primary election in which only a party's registered voters are eligible to vote.

open primary
A primary in which party members, independents, and sometimes members of the other party are allowed to vote.

crossover voting
Participation in the primary of a party with which the voter is not affiliated.

raiding
An organized attempt by voters of one party to influence the primary results of the other party.

runoff primary
A second primary election between the two candidates receiving the greatest number of votes in the first primary.

general election
Election in which voters decide which candidates will actually fill elective public offices.

ballot measure
An election option such as the initiative or referendum that enables voters to enact public policy.

initiative
An election that allows citizens to propose legislation and submit it to the state electorate for popular vote.

referendum
An election whereby the state legislature submits proposed legislation to the state's voters for approval.

The Living Constitution

No Person shall be a Representative who shall not have attained to the Age of twenty five Years.

ARTICLE I, SECTION 2

No Person shall be a Senator who shall not have attained to the Age of thirty Years.

ARTICLE I, SECTION 3

...neither shall any person be eligible to that Office [of the Presidency] who shall not have attained to the Age of thirty five Years.

ARTICLE II, SECTION 1

There was little debate among the Framers at the Constitutional Convention that elected officials should have enough experience in life and in politics before being qualified to take on the responsibility of representing the interests of the nation and of their district or state. It is likely that they concurred, as they so often did, with John Locke, who stated in section 118 of his *Second Treatise of Government*, "a Child is born a Subject of no Country or Government. He is under his Father's Tuition and Authority, till he come to Age of Discretion." However, a minor, who is not subject to the authority of the state in the same way as a full citizen, also could not possibly be qualified to vote. The Framers added age requirements higher than the age when one becomes a full citizen as a guarantee that individuals with the necessary experience would be elected. Notice how the age limits scale upward according to the amount of deliberation and decision making that the position involves. House members need to be only twenty-five, but the president must be at least thirty-five, giving whoever would run for that office plenty of time to acquire the political experience necessary for the central role he or she will play.

State governments usually employ similar requirements. For instance, Virginia requires that candidates for the state's House of Delegates and Senate be at least twenty-one years old, while candidates for the state's three most powerful executive positions—governor, lieutenant governor, and attorney general—must be at least thirty years old. South Dakota, however, sets the minimum age limit for its most important executive officers—governor and lieutenant governor—at twenty-one.

Amazingly, the Framers did not impose an age limit on Supreme Court justices, not even the chief justice. Perhaps the Framers thought that the president was not likely to appoint minors to the bench, or at least that they would not be approved by the Senate. Looking at the nine justices today, it is obvious that the Framers were right not to worry.

CRITICAL THINKING QUESTIONS

1. A minimum age requirement is one of the few qualifications for office that the Constitution imposes on candidates running for Congress and the presidency. What additional qualifications would you propose for candidates running for these positions? Why do you think the Framers were reluctant to include additional qualifications for office in the Constitution?

2. Some analysts have suggested imposing a maximum age limit on Supreme Court justices and other federal judges or a limit on how many years a justice or judge can serve. What are some of the advantages and disadvantages of imposing a mandatory retirement age for judges?

Ballot measures have been the subject of heated debate in the past decades. Critics charge that ballot measures—which were intended to give citizens more direct control over policy making—are now unduly influenced by interest groups and "the initiative industry—law firms that draft legislation, petition management firms that guarantee ballot access, direct-mail firms, and campaign consultants who specialize in initiative contests."[38] Critics also question the ability of voters to deal with the numerous complex issues that appear on a ballot. In the 1990 elections, for instance, California had so many referenda and initiatives on its ballot that the state printed a lengthy two-volume guide to explain them all to voters. In addition, the wording of a ballot measure can have an enormous impact on the outcome. In some cases, a "yes" vote will bring about a policy change; in other cases, a "no" vote will cause a change.[39] Moreover, ballot initiatives are not subject to the same campaign contribution limits that limit donations in candidate campaigns. Consequently, a single wealthy individual can bankroll a ballot measure and influence public policy in a manner that is not available to the individual through the normal policy process.

Supporters of ballot measures argue that critics have overstated their case, and they point out that the process has historically been used to champion popular issues that were resisted at the state level by entrenched political interests. Initiatives, for example, have been instrumental in popular progressive causes such as banning child labor, promoting environmental laws, expanding suffrage to women, and passing campaign finance reform. The process has also been used to pass popular conservative proposals such as tax relief and banning affirmative action policies.[40] Supporters point out that ballot measures can heighten public interest in elections and can increase voter participation. In general, the supporters have far more confidence in the ability of the voting public to understand and judge public policy than do the critics.

The third type of election (or "deelection") found in many states is the **recall,** in which voters can remove an incumbent from office prior to the next scheduled election. Recall elections are very rare, and sometimes they are thwarted by the official's resignation or impeachment prior to the vote. In 2003, under intense national media attention, Californians recalled Governor Grey Davis (a Democrat) and replaced him with movie star (and Republican) Arnold Schwarzenegger. Davis, who had won reelection against a weak Republican candidate, Bill Simon, faced intense criticism for his handling of the state's slumping economy and looming energy crisis. Immediately following the recall, commentators feared that voters in California had set a precedent for the people of a state to recall governors whenever things are not going well. However, no additional governors were removed from office following the Davis recall, and only one other governor besides Davis—North Dakota's Lynn J. Frazier in 1921—has been removed from office through the recall process.

recall
An election in which voters can remove an incumbent from office by popular vote.

Presidential Elections

Variety aside, no U.S. election can compare to the presidential contest. This spectacle, held every four years, brings together all the elements of politics and attracts the most ambitious and energetic politicians to the national stage. Voters in a series of state contests that run through the winter and spring of the election year select delegates who will attend each party's national convention. Following the national convention for each party, held in mid and late summer, there is a final set of fifty separate state elections all held on the Tuesday after the first Monday in November to select the president. This lengthy process exhausts candidates and voters alike, but it allows the diversity of the United States to be displayed in ways a shorter, more homogeneous presidential election process could not. (To learn more about the 2008 presidential election, see chapter 14.)

The state party organizations use several types of methods to elect national convention delegates and ultimately select the candidates who will run against each other in the general election:

1. *Winner-take-all primary*: Under this system the candidate who wins the most votes in a state secures all of that state's delegates. While Democrats no longer permit its use because it is viewed as less representative than a proportional

system, Republicans generally prefer this process as it enables a candidate to amass a majority of delegates quickly and shortens the divisive primary season.

2. *Proportional representation primary*: Under this system, candidates who secure a threshold percentage of votes are awarded delegates in proportion to the number of popular votes won. Democrats now strongly favor this system and use it in many state primaries, where they award delegates to anyone who wins more than 15 percent in any congressional district. Although proportional representation is probably the fairest way of allocating delegates to candidates, its downfall is that it renders majorities of delegates more difficult to accumulate and thus can lengthen the contest for the presidential nomination.

3. *Caucus*: Under this system, party members meet in small groups throughout a state to discuss and select the party's delegates to the national convention. While less common in recent years than in the past, this method maintains some of the characteristics of the era in which party bosses selected candidates. The first in the nation contest, the Iowa caucus, serves as the first test of candidate strength and receives a remarkable level of attention by both the candidates and the media.

Primaries Versus Caucuses

The mix of preconvention contests has changed over the years, with the most pronounced trend being the shift from caucuses to primary elections. Only seventeen states held presidential primaries in 1968; the number increased to thirty-eight in 1992, forty-two in 1996, and forty-three in 2000, but declined to forty in 2008. In recent years, the vast majority of delegates to each party's national convention have been selected through the primary system.

Iowa Caucuses

The caucus is the oldest, most party-oriented method of choosing delegates to the national conventions. Traditionally, the caucus was a closed meeting of party activists in each state who selected the party's choice for presidential candidate. In the late nineteenth and early twentieth centuries, however, many people viewed these caucuses as elitist and anti-democratic, and reformers succeeded in replacing them with direct primaries in most states. Although there are still presidential nominating caucuses today (in Iowa, for example, as noted above), they are now more open and attract a wider range of the party's membership. Indeed, new participatory caucuses more closely resemble primary elections than they do the old, exclusive party caucuses.[41]

Some people support the increase in the number of primaries because they believe that this type of election is more democratic. The primaries are open not only to party activists, but also to anyone who wants to vote. Related to this idea, advocates argue that presidential primaries are the most representative means by which to nominate presidential candidates. They are a barometer of a candidate's popular-

Photo courtesy: Reed Saxon/AP/Wide World Photos

Where are party caucuses held? While voters go to polling places located in places such as schools and community centers to vote in primary and general elections, caucuses can be held in someone's living room, a high school gym, or even in a casino. Union members supporting Senator Hillary Clinton rally for their candidate before caucuses in Nevada.

ity with the party's rank and file. While conventional wisdom holds that both primaries and caucuses attract more extreme voters in each party, recent research posits that primaries help nominate more moderate and appealing candidates—those that primary voters believe can win in the general election. For instance, scholars describe "sophisticated voting," where primary voters vote for their second or third choice because they believe the candidate will more easily win in November than will their first choice—perhaps because of less extreme policy positions.[42] Finally, the proponents of presidential primaries claim that they constitute a rigorous test for the candidates, a chance to display under pressure some of the skills needed to be a successful president.

Critics of presidential primaries argue that although primaries may attract more participants than do caucuses, this quantity does not substitute for the quality of information held by caucus participants. At a caucus, participants spend several hours learning about politics and the party. They listen to speeches by candidates or their representatives and receive advice from party leaders and elected officials, then cast a well-informed vote. Critics of the primary system argue that primary voters tend to make their decisions based on campaign advertisements or a candidate's popularity among media elites.

Critics also argue that the unfair scheduling of primaries affects their outcomes. For example, the earliest primary takes place in New Hampshire, a small, heavily white, and historically conservative state. Some argue that New Hampshire receives much more media coverage than it deserves simply because its primary is first in the nation. Such excessive coverage undoubtedly skews voter opinions in more populous states that hold their primaries later. Additionally, critics believe that the qualities tested by the primary system are by no means a complete list of those a president needs to be successful. For instance, skill at handling national and local media representatives is by itself no guarantee of an effective presidency. The exhausting primary schedule may be a better test of a candidate's stamina than of his or her brain power.

The primary schedule has been altered by a phenomenon often referred to as **front-loading,** the tendency of states to choose an early date on the primary calendar. Seventy percent of all the delegates to both party conventions are now chosen before the end of February. This trend is hardly surprising, given the added press emphasis on the first contests and the voters' desire to cast their ballots before the competition is decided. (To learn about the accelerating trend in frontloading, see Figure 13.4.)

front-loading
The tendency of states to choose an early date on the primary calendar.

Front-loading has important effects on the nomination process. First, a front-loaded primary schedule generally benefits the front-runner, since opponents have little time to turn the contest around once they fall behind. Second, front-loading gives an advantage to the candidate who wins the "invisible primary," that is, the one who can raise the bulk of the money *before* the nomination season begins. Once the primaries begin, there is less opportunity to raise money to finance campaign efforts simultaneously in many states. The consequences of front-loading seemed likely to be even more pronounced in the 2008 race for president, after the Democratic National Committee introduced a very crowded opening by adding Nevada's caucus between the contests in Iowa and New Hampshire, with South Carolina following closely behind. This move started a chain reaction in which over twenty states, including California, New York, Texas, and Ohio, moved their contests to early February. Not to be outdone, Florida and Michigan moved their primaries into January, even though their actions jeopardized seating their delegates at the national convention. Iowa and New Hampshire officials responded by moving their contests to early January. While the strong support for both Senators Hillary Rodham Clinton and Barack Obama in 2008 resulted in a nomination battle that stretched until after the last primary in June, this result is likely to be the exception rather than the rule in future elections.

However, Internet fund-raising has emerged as a means to soften the advantage of a large campaign fund going into a primary battle, since it allows candidates to raise large sums from many small donors nationwide virtually overnight. In 2008, long-shot Republican presidential candidate Ron Paul raised a record $6 million in one day, shattering his own record of $4.2 million in the previous month. All of the major 2008 presidential can-

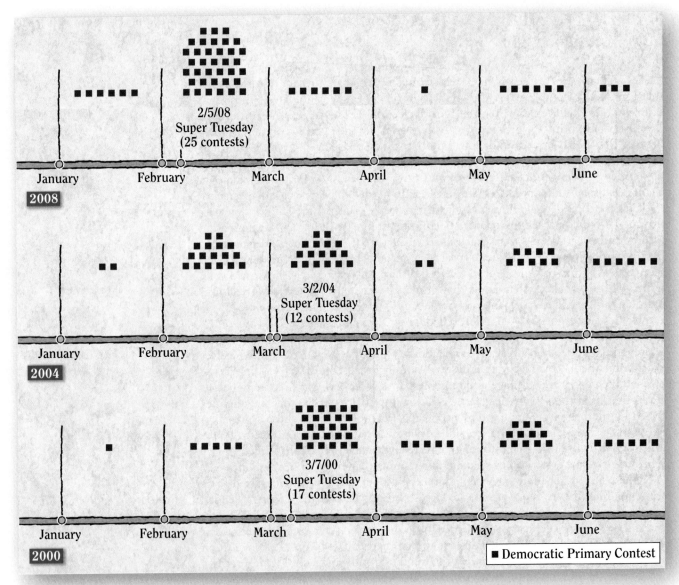

FIGURE 13.4 Frontloading in the Democratic Presidential Nominating Contests: 2000, 2004, and 2008

didates relied on online donations to finance their campaigns, but the highly compressed schedule still forced even the best-funded candidates to make difficult decisions on how to allocate their financial resources.

The Party Conventions

The seemingly endless nomination battle does have a conclusion: the national party convention held in the summer of presidential election years. The out-of-power party traditionally holds its convention first, in late July, followed in mid-August by the party holding the White House. Preempting an hour or more of prime-time network television for four nights and monopolizing the cable networks such as CNN, FOX News, and C-SPAN, these remarkable conclaves give viewers a chance to learn about the candidates.

Today, the convention is fundamentally different from what it was in the past. First, its importance as a party conclave, at which compromises on party leadership and policies can be worked out, has diminished. Second, although the convention still formally selects the presidential ticket, most nominations are settled well in advance. Third, three preconvention factors have lessened the role of the current parties and conventions: delegate selection, national candidates and issues, and the news media.

DELEGATE SELECTION As mentioned in the previous section, the selection of delegates to the conventions is no longer the function of party leaders but of primary elections and grassroots caucuses. Moreover, recent reforms, especially by the Democratic Party, have generally weakened any remaining control by local party leaders over delegates. A prime example of such reform is the Democrats' abolition of the **unit rule,** a traditional party practice under which the majority of a state delegation (say, twenty-six of fifty delegates) could force the minority to vote for its candidate. Another Democratic Party rule decrees that a state's delegates be chosen in proportion to the votes cast in its primary or caucus (so that, for example, a candidate who receives 30 percent of the vote gains about 30 percent of the convention delegates). This change has had the effect of requiring delegates to indicate their presidential preference at each stage of the selection process. Consequently, the majority of state delegates now come to the convention already committed to a candidate. Before 1972, most delegates to a Democratic National Convention were not bound by primary results to support a particular candidate for president. This freedom to maneuver meant that conventions could be exciting and somewhat unpredictable gatherings, where last-minute events and deals could sway wavering delegates.

In sum, the many complex changes in the rules of delegate selection have contributed to the loss of decision-making powers by the convention. Even though the Democratic Party initiated many of these changes, the Republicans were carried along as many Democratic-controlled state legislatures enacted the reforms as state laws.

There have been new rules to counteract some of these changes, however. For instance, since 1984, the number of unpledged delegate slots reserved for elected Democratic Party officials—**superdelegates**—has been increased. The creation of superdelegates was an attempt to maintain some level of party control over the selection process, while still allowing most delegates to be selected through the electoral process. Republicans do not bind delegates to select the candidate the party members chose during the primary; thus, delegates can vote against the will of the state party and the use of superdelegates is unnecessary.

Who the delegates are, a topic that is less important today than it was when delegates enjoyed more power in the selection process, still reveals interesting differences between the political parties. Both parties draw their delegates from an elite group whose income and educational levels are far above the average American's. Nearly 35 percent of delegates at the 2008 Democratic convention were minorities, and half were women. (To learn more about "firsts" for women at the conventions, see Table 13.2.) Only 7 percent of the delegates to the 2008 Republican convention were racial and ethnic minorities. Despite recent GOP efforts to increase minority representation at its convention, this marks a steep decline from 2004, when 17 percent of the delegates were minorities.

unit rule
A traditional party practice under which the majority of a state delegation can force the minority to vote for its candidate.

superdelegate
Delegate slot to the Democratic Party's national convention that is reserved for an elected party official.

TABLE **13.2** Historic Moments for Women at the Conventions

Since 1980, Democratic Party rules have required that women constitute 50 percent of the delegates to its national convention. The Republican Party has no similar quota. Nevertheless, both parties have tried to increase the role of women at the convention. Some "firsts" and other historic moments for women at the national conventions include:

1876	First woman to address a national convention
1890	First women delegates to conventions of both parties
1940	First woman to nominate a presidential candidate
1951	First woman asked to chair a national party
1972	First woman keynote speaker
1984	First major-party woman nominated for vice president (Democrat Geraldine Ferraro)
1996	Wives of both nominees make major addresses
2000	Daughter of a presidential candidate nominates her father
2004	Both candidates introduced by their daughters
2008	First woman nominated by the Republican Party for vice president (Governor Sarah Palin)

Source: Center for American Women in Politics. Updated by authors.

The contrast in the two parties' delegations is no accident; it reflects not only the differences in the party constituencies, but also conscious decisions made by party leaders. After the tumultuous 1968 Democratic National Convention, which was torn by dissent over the Vietnam War, Democrats formed a commission to examine the condition of the party and to propose changes in its structure. As a direct consequence of the commission's work, the 1972 Democratic convention was the most broadly representative ever of women, African Americans, and young people, because the party required these groups to be included in state delegations in rough proportion to their numbers in the population of each state. State delegations failing this test were not seated. This new mandate was very controversial, and it has since been watered down considerably. Nonetheless, women and minority groups are still more fully represented at Democratic conventions than at Republican conventions. GOP leaders have placed much less emphasis on proportional representation; instead of procedural reforms, Republicans have concentrated on strengthening their state organizations and fund-raising efforts.

NATIONAL CANDIDATES AND ISSUES The political perceptions and loyalties of voters are now influenced largely by national candidates and issues, a factor that has undoubtedly served to diminish the power of state and local party leaders at the convention. The national candidates have usurped the autonomy of state party leaders with their preconvention ability to garner delegate support. Issues, increasingly national in scope, remain central to the convention. The conventions still provide the parties with a forum for drafting their platforms and for debating their future direction (see chapter 12). But, the party professionals, who prior to the late 1960s had a monopoly on the management of party affairs, are no longer able to dominate the process.

THE NEWS MEDIA The media have helped transform the national conventions into political extravaganzas for the television audience's consumption. They have also helped to preempt the convention, by keeping count of the delegates committed to the candidates; as a result, well before the convention, the delegates and even the candidates have much more information about nomination politics than they did in the past.

How does media coverage affect public perceptions of party conventions? The 1968 Democratic Convention was beset by violent protests over the Vietnam War and clashes with Chicago police, which were extensively covered by the three major television networks' news divisions.

Photo courtesy: Bettmann/CORBIS

Television coverage has shaped the business of the convention. Desirous of presenting a unified image to kick off a strong general election campaign, the parties assign important roles to attractive speakers, and crucial party affairs are saved for primetime viewing hours. During the 1990s, the networks gradually began to reduce their convention coverage, citing low viewer ratings. The cable networks (CNN, FOX News, MSNBC, and others) have more than made up for reduced primetime coverage from the networks, and C-SPAN continues to provide gavel-to-gavel coverage.

Extensive media coverage of the convention has its pros and cons. On the one hand, such exposure helps the party launch its presidential campaign with fanfare, usually providing a boost to the party's candidate. On average, recent nominees have recorded a six-point bounce immediately following their conventions. Democratic nominee Barack Obama received a modest five-point bounce following the 2008 Democratic convention; the McCain-Palin campaign received a seven-point bounce following the Republican convention. Convention bounces typically last for about a week, but then subside as news coverage between the two nominees becomes more balanced. On the other hand, media coverage can expose rifts within a party, as happened in 1968 at the Democratic convention in Chicago. Dissension was obvious when "hawks," supporting the Vietnam War and President Lyndon B. Johnson, clashed with the anti-war "doves" both on the convention floor and in street demonstrations outside the convention hall.

Some reformers have spoken of replacing the conventions with national direct primaries, but it is unlikely that the parties would agree to this. Although its role in nominating the presidential ticket has often been reduced to formality, the convention is still valuable. After all, it is the only real arena where the national political parties can command a significant audience while they celebrate past achievements and project their hopes for the future.

The Electoral College: How Presidents Are Elected

Given the enormous amount of energy, money, and time expended to nominate two major-party presidential contenders, it is difficult to believe that the general election could be more arduous than the nominating contests, but it usually is. The actual campaign for the presidency (and other offices) is described in chapter 14, but the object of the exercise is clear: winning a majority of the **Electoral College**. This uniquely American institution consists of representatives of each state who cast the final ballots that actually elect a president. The total number of **electors**—the members of the Electoral College—for each state is equivalent to the number of senators and representatives that state has in the U.S. Congress. The District of Columbia is accorded three electoral votes making 538 the total number of votes cast in the Electoral College. Thus, the magic number for winning in the presidency is 270 votes.

The Electoral College was the result of a compromise between those Framers who argued for selection of the president by the Congress and those who favored selection by direct popular election. There are three essentials to understanding the Framers' design of the Electoral College. The system was constructed (1) to work without political parties; (2) to cover both the nominating and electing phases of presidential selection; and, (3) to produce a nonpartisan president.

The Electoral College machinery as originally designed by the Framers was somewhat complex. Each state designated electors (through appointment or popular vote) equal in number to the sum of its representation in the House and Senate. The electors met in their respective states. Each elector had two votes to cast in the Electoral College's selection for the president and vice president, although electors could not vote for more than one candidate from their state. The rules of the college stipulated that each elector was allowed to cast only one vote for any single candidate, and by extension obliged each elector to use his second vote for another candidate. There was no way to designate votes for president or vice president; instead, the candidate

Electoral College
Representatives of each state who cast the final ballots that actually elect a president.

elector
Member of the Electoral College chosen by methods determined in each state.

with the most votes (provided he also received votes from a majority of the electors) won the presidency and the runner-up won the vice presidency. If two candidates received the same number of votes and both had a majority of electors, the election was decided in the House of Representatives, with each state delegation acting as a unit and casting one vote. If no candidate secured a majority, the election would also be decided in the House, with each state delegation casting one vote for any of the top five electoral vote-getters. In both these scenarios, the candidate needed a majority of the total number of states for victory.

This system seems almost insanely unpredictable, complex, and unwieldy until one remembers that the Framers devised it specifically for the type of political system that existed when they framed the Constitution and that they (erroneously) foresaw for America in perpetuity: a nonpartisan, consensus-based, indirectly representative, multi-candidate system. In such a system, the Electoral College would function admirably. In practice, the Framers hoped that electors with a common basic political understanding would arrive at a consensus preference for president, and most, if not all, would plan to cast one of their votes for that candidate, thereby virtually guaranteeing one clear winner, who would become president (a tie was an unlikely and unhappy outcome). Each would then plan to cast his remaining vote for another candidate, the one whom the elector implicitly preferred for vice president. Consensus on the vice presidency would presumably be less clear than for the more important position of president, so there might be a closer spread among the runners-up.

THE ELECTORAL COLLEGE IN THE NINETEENTH CENTURY   The republic's fourth presidential election revealed a flaw in the Framers' Electoral College plan. In 1800, Thomas Jefferson and Aaron Burr were, respectively, the presidential and vice presidential candidates advanced by the Democratic-Republican Party, whose supporters controlled a majority of the Electoral College. Accordingly, each Democratic-Republican elector in the states cast one of his two votes for Jefferson and the other one for Burr. Since there was no way under the constitutional arrangements for electors to earmark their votes separately for president and vice president, the presidential election resulted in a tie between Jefferson and Burr. Even though most understood Jefferson to be the actual choice for president, the Constitution mandated that a tie be decided by the House of Representatives. It was, of course, and in Jefferson's favor, but only after much energy was expended to persuade lame-duck Federalists not to give Burr the presidency.

The Twelfth Amendment, ratified in 1804 and still the constitutional foundation for presidential elections today, was an attempt to remedy the confusion between the selection of vice presidents and presidents that beset the election of 1800. The amendment provided for separate elections for each office, with each elector having only one vote to cast for each. In the event of a tie or when no candidate received a majority of the total number of electors, the

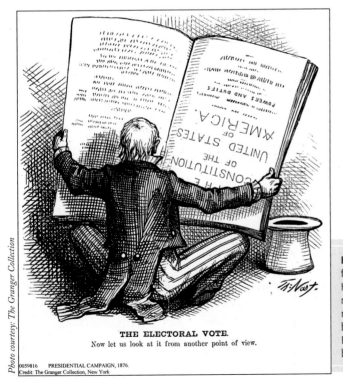

THE ELECTORAL VOTE.
Now let us look at it from another point of view.

Photo courtesy: The Granger Collection
0059816   PRESIDENTIAL CAMPAIGN, 1876.
Credit: The Granger Collection, New York

How was the 1876 presidential election resolved? This cartoon from the 1876 presidential contest between Republican Rutherford B. Hayes and Democrat Samuel J. Tilden describes the frustration of many Americans with interpreting the Constitutional procedures for resolving Electoral College disputes. An electoral commission formed by Congress to decide the matter awarded all disputed electors to Hayes, giving him the victory even though he had lost the popular vote by a 51-48 percent margin.

election still went to the House of Representatives; now, however, each state delegation would have one vote to cast for one of the three candidates who had received the greatest number of electoral votes.

The Electoral College modified by the Twelfth Amendment has fared better than the college as originally designed, but it has not been problem free. On three occasions during the nineteenth century, the electoral process resulted in the selection of a president who received fewer votes than his opponent. In 1824, neither John Quincy Adams nor Andrew Jackson secured a majority of electoral votes, throwing the election into the House. Although Jackson had more electoral and popular votes than Adams, the House voted for the latter as president. In the 1876 contest between Republican Rutherford B. Hayes and Democrat Samuel J. Tilden, no candidate received a majority of electoral votes; the House decided in Hayes's favor even though he had 250,000 fewer popular votes than Tilden. In the election of 1888, President Grover Cleveland secured about 100,000 more popular votes than did Benjamin Harrison, yet Harrison won a majority of the Electoral College vote, and with it the presidency.

THE ELECTORAL COLLEGE IN THE TWENTIETH AND TWENTY-FIRST CENTURIES

Several near crises pertaining to the Electoral College occurred in the twentieth century. For example, had third-party presidential candidate Ross Perot stayed in the 1992 presidential contest, he could have thrown the election into the House of Representatives. His support had registered from 30 percent to 36 percent in the polls in early 1992, prior to his dropping out of the race. When he reentered the race, some of that backing had evaporated, and he finished with 19 percent of the vote and carried no states. However, Perot drained a substantial number of Republican votes from George Bush, thus splitting the GOP base and enabling Bill Clinton to win many normally GOP-leaning states.[43]

Throughout the 2000 presidential campaign, many analysts foresaw that the election would likely be the closest since the 1960 race between John F. Kennedy and Richard M. Nixon. Few realized, however, that the election would be so close that the winner would not be officially declared for more than five weeks after Election Day. And, no one could have predicted that the Electoral College winner, George W. Bush, would lose the popular vote and become president after the Supreme Court's controversial decision in *Bush* v. *Gore* (2000) stopped the recount in Florida. With the margin of the Electoral College results so small (271 for Bush, 267 for Gore), a Gore victory in any number of closely contested states could have given him a majority in

TIMELINE

**Close Calls in
Presidential Elections**

Photo courtesy: Kirk Condyles

How was the 2000 presidential election resolved? Controversy over the counting of votes in Florida in the 2000 presidential election brought people to West Palm Beach, Florida, to protest on behalf of Al Gore and George W. Bush. The Supreme Court's decision in *Bush v. Gore* (2000) decided the Electoral College outcome in Bush's favor, allowed him to assume the presidency after losing the popular vote by 500,000 votes.

reapportionment
The reallocation of the number of seats in the House of Representatives after each decennial census.

the Electoral College. As it turned out, Al Gore became only the fourth person to win the popular vote and lose the presidency.

Keep in mind that through **reapportionment,** representation in the House of Representatives and consequently in the Electoral College is altered every ten years to reflect population shifts. Reapportionment is simply the reallocation of the number of seats in the House of Representatives that takes place after each national census. The number of House seats has been fixed at 435 since 1910 Since that time, the average size of congressional districts has tripled in population, from 211,000 following the 1910 Census to 647,000 in the 2000 Census.[44]

Projections for the upcoming 2010 census show a sizable population shift from the Midwest and the Democratic-dominated Northeast to the South and West, where Republicans are much stronger. If these projections hold, Texas will gain four congressional districts, and therefore four additional seats in the House of Representatives and four additional votes in the Electoral College. Arizona and Florida will gain two seats and two votes, while four other states will gain one. New York and Ohio stand to lose two seats and two votes, while eight states stand to lose a single seat and electoral vote. If Barack Obama runs for reelection and wins the same states in 2012 that he won in 2008, he will win 5 fewer votes. (To learn more about the 2008 Electoral College map, see Figure 13.5.)

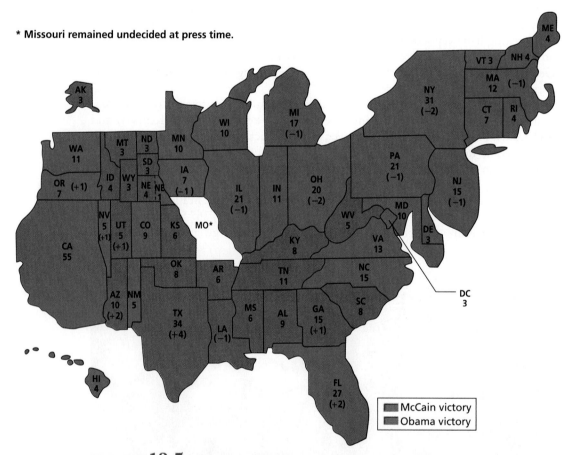

FIGURE 13.5 **The States Drawn in Proportion to Their Electoral College Votes**
This map visually represents the respective electoral weights of the fifty states in the 2008 presidential election. For each state, the projected gain or loss of Electoral College votes based on the upcoming 2010 Census is indicated in parentheses.

Note: States drawn in proportion to number of electoral votes. Total electoral votes: 538.

Source: http://synapse.princeton.edu/~sam/ev_projection_current_map.jpg and http://www.edssurvey.com/images/File/NR_Appor07wTables.pdf.

THE ELECTORAL COLLEGE RECONSIDERED Given the Electoral College's imperfections, especially those exposed by the 2000 election, reformers have seized the opportunity to suggest several proposals for improving the presidential selection process. Three major reform ideas have developed; each is described below.

POPULAR VOTE This reform would abolish the Electoral College entirely and have the president selected by popular vote, eliminating the chance of someone losing the presidency after winning the popular vote. Many critics believe that the Electoral College is archaic and that it distorts the popular vote while failing to provide the benefits that the Framers originally envisioned.

While this is the most democratic reform, it is by far the least likely to be enacted, given that the Constitution of the United States would have to be amended to abolish the Electoral College. Even assuming that the House of Representatives could muster the two-third majority necessary to pass an amendment, the proposal would almost certainly never pass the Senate. Small states have the same representation in the Senate as populous ones, and the Senate thus serves as a bastion of equal representation for all states, regardless of population—a principle generally reinforced by the existing configuration of the Electoral College, which ensures some electoral influence for even the smallest states. California, the most populous state and one that would benefit electorally from the elimination of the Electoral College, passed a bill in 2006 endorsing the popular election of the president. Certain organizations, such as National Popular Vote, continue to promote this Electoral College reform.

CONGRESSIONAL DISTRICT PLAN Under this plan, each candidate would receive one electoral vote for each congressional district that he or she wins in a state, and the winner of the overall popular vote in each state would receive two bonus votes (one for each senator) for that state. Take for example Virginia, which has eleven representatives and two senators for a total of thirteen electoral votes. If the Democratic candidate wins five congressional districts, and the Republican candidate wins the other six districts and also the statewide majority, the Democrat wins five electoral votes and the Republican wins a total of eight. This reform could be adopted without a constitutional amendment. This electoral system currently exists only in Maine and Nebraska, though neither state has ever split its electoral votes. Any state can adopt this system on its own because the Constitution gives states the right to determine the place and manner by which it selects its electors.

The congressional district plan has some unintended consequences. First, the winner of the popular vote might still lose the presidency under this plan. Under a congressional district plan, Richard M. Nixon would have won the 1960 election instead of John F. Kennedy. George W. Bush would have likely won by a wider margin if the entire nation used this system in 2000. Second, this reform would further politicize the congressional redistricting process that takes place every ten years according to U.S. Census results. If electoral votes were at stake, parties would seek to maximize the number of safe electoral districts for their presidential nominee while minimizing the number of competitive districts. A third consequence of state-by-state adoption is that the nation would quickly come to resemble a patchwork of different electoral methods, with some states being awarded by congressional districts and some states awarded solely by popular vote. Finally, candidates would not ignore entire states, but quickly learn to focus their campaigning on competitive districts while ignoring secure districts, which would contribute electoral votes only through the senatorial/statewide-majority component.

KEEP THE COLLEGE, ABOLISH THE ELECTORS This proposal calls for the preservation of the college as a statistical electoral device but would remove all voting power from actual human electors and their legislative appointers. It would eliminate the threat of so-called faithless electors—that is, electors who are appointed by state

Electoral College

legislators to vote for the candidate who won that state's vote but who then choose, for whatever reason, to vote for a different candidate. Most Americans are comfortable with making this change, although the problem of faithless electors is only a secondary and little-realized liability of the Electoral College. While in the history of presidential elections there have been 157 instances in which electors have cast their ballots in a different manner than they were directed by the state legislature, no faithless elector has ever changed the outcome of an election. A recent incident occurred in 2004, when an elector from Minnesota anonymously cast a vote for John Edwards, the Democratic vice presidential candidate, for president.[45]

Any change in the existing system would inevitably have a profound impact on the way that candidates go about the business of seeking votes for the U.S. presidency. However, if the national crisis over electoral votes in Florida in 2000 could not motivate a national outcry, the chances of Electoral College reform seem remote.

Congressional Elections

Compared with presidential elections, congressional elections receive scant national attention. Unlike major-party presidential contenders, most candidates for Congress labor in relative obscurity. There are some celebrity nominees for Congress—television stars, sports heroes, even local TV news anchors. In 2000, First Lady Hillary Rodham Clinton made history with her Senate campaign and gained the nation's attention by becoming the only first lady to win elective office. The vast majority of party nominees for Congress, however, are little-known state legislators and local office holders who receive remarkably limited coverage in many states and communities. For them, just establishing name identification in the electorate is the biggest battle.

The Incumbency Advantage

incumbency
The holding of an office.

The current system enhances the advantages of **incumbency** (that is, already being in office). Those people in office tend to remain in office. Of the 396 incumbents running for the House in 2008, only 18 lost. In a "bad" year for House incumbents, such as the Democratic wave of 2006, "only" 94 percent of incumbents will win, but the senatorial reelection rate can drop much lower on occasion (79 percent in 2006). To the political novice, these reelection rates might seem surprising, as public trust in government and satisfaction with Congress has remained remarkably low during the very period that reelection rates have been on the rise. To understand the nature of the incumbency advantage it is necessary to explore its primary causes.

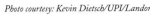
Photo courtesy: Kevin Dietsch/UPI/Landor

Did the incumbency advantage help Republican incumbents survive in a Democratic year? U.S. Senator Susan Collins (R–ME), elected to the Senate in 1996 after working as a Senate staffer for 12 years, easily won a race for reelection against Democratic Representative Tom Allen, 60 percent to 39 percent. High name recognition and a strong record of constituency service enabled Senator Collins and seven other incumbents to win in states carried by the opposing party in the presidential race.

STAFF SUPPORT   Members of the U.S. House of Representatives are permitted to hire eighteen permanent and four nonpermanent aides to work in their Washington and district offices. Senators typically enjoy far larger staffs, with the actual size determined by the number of people in the state they represent, and both House and Senate members enjoy the additional benefits provided by the scores of unpaid interns who assist with office duties. Many of the activities of staff members directly or indirectly promote the legislator by means of generating free mass mailings and *constituency services*, the term used to describe a wide array of assistance provided by a member of Congress to voters in need (for example, tracking a lost Social Security check, helping a veteran receive disputed benefits, or finding a summer internship for a college student). Having a responsive constituent service program contributes strongly to incumbency. If a House incumbent helped solve a problem for a constituent, that constituent rated the incumbent more favorably than constituents who were not assisted by the incumbent,[46] therefore providing the incumbent a great advantage over any challenger.

MEDIA AND TRAVEL   In addition to these institutional means of self-promotion, most incumbents are highly visible in their districts. They have easy access to local media, cut ribbons galore, attend important local funerals, and speak frequently at meetings and community events. Moreover, convenient schedules and generous travel allowances increase the local availability of incumbents. Nearly a fourth of the people in an average congressional district claim to have met their representative, and about half recognize their legislator's name without prompting. This visibility has an electoral payoff, as research shows district attentiveness is at least partly responsible for incumbents' electoral safety.[47]

THE "SCARE-OFF" EFFECT   Research also identifies an indirect advantage of incumbency: the ability of the office holder to fend off challenges from strong opposition candidates, something scholars refer to as the "scare-off" effect.[48] Incumbents have the ability to scare off high-quality challengers because of the institutional advantages of office, such as high name recognition, large war chests, staffs attached to legislative offices, and overall experience in running a successful campaign. Potential strong challengers facing this initial uphill battle will wait until the incumbent retires rather than challenge him or her. This tendency only strengthens the arguments for advantages to reelection related to incumbency.[49]

The "scare-off" effect also helps to explain why reelection rates tend to be lower in the Senate than in the House. Studies show that the quality of the challengers in Senate races is higher than in House races, making it more likely that an incumbent could be upset.[50] While it is impossible to say whether high-quality challengers cause the lower reelection rates, or whether the lower reelection rates attract high-quality challengers, it is clear that Senate elections attract strong challengers, and incumbents often lose reelections in the Senate.

REDISTRICTING   Because the Constitution requires that representation in the House be based on state population, and that each state have at least one representative, congressional districts must be redrawn by state legislatures to reflect population shifts, so that each member in Congress will represent approximately the same number of residents. Exceptions to this rule are states such as Wyoming and Vermont, whose statewide populations are less than average congressional districts. This process of redrawing congressional districts to reflect increases or decreases in seats allotted to the states, as well as population shifts within a state, is called **redistricting**.

Redistricting is a largely political process that the majority party in a state uses to ensure formation of voting districts that protect their majority. For example, in 2003, ten Texas Democratic state senators left the capitol in Austin for Albuquerque, New Mexico, in order to break the state Senate quorum necessary to pass a Republican-sponsored

redistricting
Redrawing congressional districts to reflect increases or decreases in seats allotted to the states as well as population shifts within a state.

redistricting bill. The Republicans, who had gained control of the state government following the 2002 election, desired to redraw the district lines that had been crafted by the judiciary when the legislature, then divided, failed to redraw the lines in time for the 2002 election. At one point in the standoff, state police were ordered to begin a search for the errant state senators. The efforts of the ten Democrats failed after one of them, John Whitmire, returned to the Texas Senate, believing that the Democrats were going to lose any future legal action against them. In the end, the Republican plan was adopted and Republicans gained seats in the 2004 election. As we discuss in greater detail below, a 2006 Supreme Court ruling upheld all but one of the redrawn districts. Hoping to avoid this sort of political high theater, some states, including Iowa and Arizona, appoint nonpartisan commissions or use some other independent means of drawing district lines. Although the processes vary in detail, most states require legislative approval of redistricting plans.

gerrymandering
The legislative process through which the majority party in each statehouse tries to assure that the maximum number of representatives from its political party can be elected to Congress through the redrawing of legislative districts.

This redistricting process often involves **gerrymandering**—the drawing of boundaries in a way to produce a particular electoral outcome without regard to the shape of the district (To learn more about gerrymandering, see Figure 13.6.) Because of enormous population growth, the partisan implications of redistricting, and the requirement under the Voting Rights Act for minorities to get an equal chance to elect candidates of their choice, legislators end up drawing oddly shaped districts to achieve their goals.[51] Redistricting plans routinely meet with court challenges across the country. Following the 2000 Census and the subsequent redistricting in 2002, the courts threw out legislative maps in a half-dozen states, primarily because of state constitutional concerns about compactness.[52]

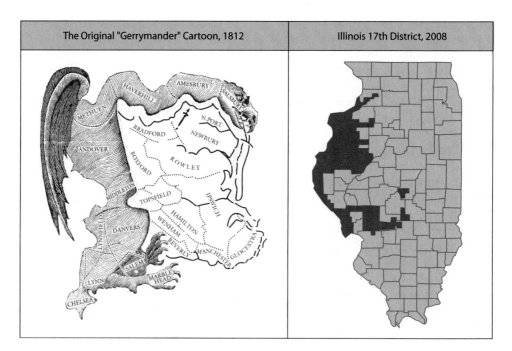

FIGURE 13.6 Gerrymandering

Two drawings—one a mocking cartoon, the other all too real—show the bizarre geographical contortions that result from gerrymandering. The term was coined by combining the last name of the Massachusetts governor first credited with politicizing the redistricting process, Elbridge Gerry, and the word salamander, which signifies the oddly shaped district that Gerry created.

Sources: David Van Biema, "Snakes or Ladders?" *Time* (July 12, 1993) © 1993, Time Inc. Reprinted by permission. Illinois General Assembly.

Over the years, the Supreme Court has ruled that:

- Congressional as well as state legislative districts must be apportioned on the basis of population.[53]
- District lines must be contiguous; you must be able to draw the boundaries of the district with one unbroken line.
- Purposeful gerrymandering of a congressional district to dilute minority strength is illegal under the Voting Rights Act of 1965.[54]
- Redrawing of districts for obvious racial purposes to enhance minority representation is constitutional if race is not the "predominate" factor over all other factors that are part of traditional redistricting, including compactness.[55]

The dominant party often uses redistricting to make their incumbents safer. This can also happen in a state with divided government, in which one party controls one part of state government and another party controls a different branch of government. In this situation, neither party has sufficient power to redistrict for partisan advantage, and consequently, both parties often work together to achieve what in the political world is the next best thing to partisan advantage, safe districts. The Supreme Court has for a long time considered political redistricting based on partisan considerations to be a political question that was not a matter of Constitutional law, but rather a question to be worked out through the regular political process.[56] However, the Court recently upheld most of the 2003 political gerrymander of Texas by state Republicans that cost Democrats five seats in Congress in the 2004 election. The same decision found that Texas's 23rd congressional district was unconstitutional because it violated federal voting rights protections for Hispanics.[57] Conservatives on the Supreme Court continue to contend that gerrymandering is primarily a political and not a judicial question, and with President Bush's two conservative appointments, it seems likely the Court will continue to affirm this position.

Thinking Globally
Gerrymandering in Other Nations

Israel and the Netherlands are not susceptible to gerrymandering in their national government elections because they use an electoral system with only one (nationwide) voting district. Other countries, such as Great Britain and Canada, attempt to prevent political manipulation of electoral districts by having constituency boundaries set by nonpartisan organizations. Gerrymandering is most common in countries such as the United States where elected officials are largely responsible for defining districts.

- Should the United States use a nonpartisan, independent commission or organization to conduct the redistricting process? Why or why not?
- It what ways would election outcomes change if the United States adopted a nonpartisan method for determining election districts?

Countervailing Forces to the Incumbency Advantage

While most incumbents win reelection, in every election cycle some members of Congress lose their positions to challengers. For the relatively few incumbent members of Congress who lose their reelection bids, there are four major reasons: redistricting efforts, scandals, presidential coattails, and midterm elections.

REDISTRICTING EFFORTS   While redistricting can be used to secure incumbent advantage (as discussed above), it can also be used to punish incumbents in the out-of-power party. Some incumbents can be put in the same districts as other incumbents, or the base of other representatives can be weakened by adding territory favorable to the opposition party. The number of incumbents who actually lose their reelections because of redistricting is lessened by the strategic behavior of redistricted members—who often choose to retire rather than wage an expensive (and likely unsuccessful) reelection battle.[58]

SCANDALS   Scandals come in many varieties in this age of investigative journalism. The old standby of financial impropriety has been supplemented by other forms of career-ending incidents, such as sexual improprieties. Incumbents implicated in scandals typically do not lose reelections—because they simply choose to retire rather than face

Photo courtesy: Matt Cilley/Bloomberg News/Landov

How do scandals affect incumbents? The full impact of scandals on incumbent politicians is hard to judge because many incumbents choose not to run for reelection. Here, Senator Larry Craig (R–ID), who was charged with disorderly conduct in an airport bathroom, announces that he will not run for reelection.

defeat.[59] Representative Mark Foley (R–FL) resigned shortly before the 2006 elections after newspaper reports that he had sent sexually explicit instant messages and emails to underage male congressional pages. The House Majority Leader, Tom DeLay (R–TX), also resigned before the election after being indicted for violating campaign finance laws, and Representative Bob Ney (R–OH) resigned after being convicted on corruption charges. Although their districts had been normally safe for Republicans, these scandals helped Democrats claim all three seats in 2006. Other incumbent Republicans under investigation or tainted with scandal, such as Senator Larry Craig (R–ID) and Representative John Doolittle (R–CA), announced their retirements early in the 2008 election cycle, helping their party retain control of their Republican-leaning districts. The man who defeated Foley in 2006, Tim Mahoney (D–FL), was himself defeated after it was revealed that he was accused of sexual harassment and it was revealed he had two extra-marital relationships with staff members.

PRESIDENTIAL COATTAILS   The defeat of a congressional incumbent can also occur as a result of the presidential coattail effect. Successful presidential candidates usually carry into office congressional candidates of the same party in the year of their election. Notice the overall decline in the strength of the coattail effect in modern times, however, as party identification has weakened and the powers and perks of incumbency have grown. Whereas Harry S Truman's party gained seventy-six House seats and nine additional Senate seats in 1948, George W. Bush's party actually lost two House seats and four Senate berths in 2000, and saw only modest gains in 2004. The gains can be minimal even in presidential landslide reelection years, such as 1972 (Nixon) and 1984 (Reagan). Occasionally, though, when the issues are emotional and the voters' desire for change is strong enough, as in Reagan's original 1980 victory, the coattail effect can still be substantial.

Midterm Elections

midterm election
An election that takes place in the middle of a presidential term.

Elections in the middle of presidential terms, called **midterm elections,** present a threat to incumbents of the president's party. Just as the presidential party usually gains seats in presidential election years, it usually loses seats in off years as shown in Table 13.3. The problems and tribulations of governing normally cost a president some popularity, alienate key groups, or cause the public to want to send the president a message of one sort or another. An economic downturn or presidential scandal can underline and expand this circumstance, as the Watergate scandal of 1974 and the recession of 1982 demonstrated. The 2002 midterm elections, however, bucked that trend, marking the first time since 1934 and Franklin D. Roosevelt that a first-term president gained seats for his party in a midterm election. The 2002 election was likely an anomaly, as it was the first election following the September 11 terrorist attacks, and voters most likely sought political stability by supporting the president's party.

TIMELINE

Critical Congressional (Mid-Term) Elections

Most apparent is the tendency of voters to punish the president's party much more severely in the sixth year of an eight-year presidency, a phenomenon associated with retrospective voting. After only two years, voters are still willing to "give the guy a chance," but after six years, voters are often restless for change. In what many saw as a referendum on President George W. Bush's policy in Iraq, for example, the Republican Party lost control of both chambers of Congress in the 2006 election. This midterm election was typical of the sixth-year itch, with voters looking for a change and punishing the incumbent president's party in Congress.

TABLE **13.3** Congressional Election Results, 1948–2008

The party of the president in power almost always loses seats in midterm elections, especially in the midterm election of the second term. In a phenomenon sometimes called the "sixth-year itch," voters are tired of the incumbent president and reward the opposition party with big gains in Congress. The recent exceptions showed the American people's unhappiness with impeachment efforts against Bill Clinton and their support for George W. Bush due to concerns related to the war on terrorism.

	Gain (+) or Loss (-) for President's Party				
	Presidential Election Years			Midterm Election Years	
President/Year	House	Senate	Year	House	Senate
Truman (D): 1948	+76[a]	+9	1950	−29	−6
Eisenhower (R): 1952	+24	+2	1954	−18	−1
Eisenhower (R): 1956	−2	0	1958	−48	−13
Kennedy (D): 1960	−20	−2	1962	−4	+3
Johnson (D): 1964	+38	+2	1966	−47	−4
Nixon (R): 1968	+7	+5	1970	−12	+2
Nixon (R): 1972	+13	−2	*Ford* (R): 1974	−48	−5
Carter (D): 1976	+2	0	1978	−15	−3
Reagan (R): 1980	+33	+12	1982	−26	+1
Reagan (R): 1984	+15	−2	1986	−5	−8
G. Bush (R): 1988	−3	−1	1990	−9	−1
Clinton (D): 1992	−10	0	1994	−52	−9[b]
Clinton (D): 1996	+10	−2	1998	+5	0
G. W. Bush (R): 2000	−2	−4	2002	+6	+2
G. W. Bush (R): 2004	+3	+4	2006	−30	−6
Obama: 2008	+19[c]	+6[c]	2010	—	—

[a] Gains and losses are the difference between the number of seats won by the president's party and the number of seats won by that party in the previous election.

[b] Includes the switch from Democrat to Republican of Alabama U.S. Senator Richard Shelby one day after the election.

[c] Does not include the results of races called after November 10, 2008.

Senate elections are less inclined to follow these off-year patterns than are House elections, although that was not the case in 2006 elections, in which Republicans lost six Senate seats. The idiosyncratic nature of Senate contests is due to their intermittent scheduling (only one-third of the seats come up for election every two years) and the existence of well-funded, well-known candidates who can sometimes swim against whatever political tide is rising. Also worth remembering is that midterm elections typically have a much lower voter turnout than presidential elections. (To learn more, see Analyzing Visuals: Turnout of Eligible Voters in Presidential Elections, 1948–2008.)

The 2008 Congressional Elections

Democrats began the 2008 congressional election cycle with momentum at their backs and a favorable electoral landscape. Just two years earlier, they had gained thirty seats in the House and six in the Senate, giving the Democratic Party control of both Houses of Congress for the first time since 1994. Moreover, Democratic candidates pulled off stunning upsets in three special elections to fill seats vacated by Republicans from conservative districts in early 2008. With twenty-nine Republicans from the House and five from the Senate not seeking re-election, but only six Democrats from the House retiring, Democrats had fewer seats to defend and could go on the offensive in more competitive races than embattled Republicans.

Democrats also benefited from a slight fundraising advantage, which reached record levels in 2008. Whereas Democratic candidates raised a combined total of approximately $500 million, Republican candidates raised a combined total of approximately $425 million. Together, the nearly $1 billion represented the most ever raised for congressional

Analyzing Visuals   Turnout of Eligible Voters in Presidential Elections, 1948–2008

Examine the line graph that shows the percentage of eligible voters (VEP) who participated in presidential contests beginning in 1948 and answer the following questions:

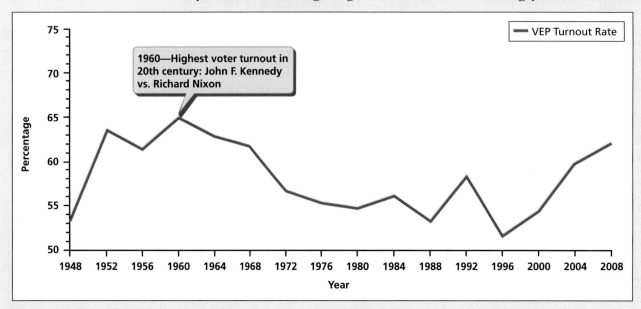

WHAT general trend do you notice about voter turnout since 1948?

WHY do you think voter turnout, generally speaking, has remained relatively low in the United States?

Source: Adapted from Harold W. Stanley and Richard G. Niemi, *Vital Statistics on American Politics, 2007–2008* (Washington, DC: CQ Press, 2008), and Michael McDonald's United States Election Project, http://elections.gmu.edu/voter_turnout.htm.

elections. The biggest fundraisers of all the congressional candidates were Senator Norm Coleman (R-MN) and his Democratic challenger, comedian Al Franken. The incumbent Coleman raised over $15 million, while Franken raised even more, over $17 million, and was the top fundraiser in 2008. The biggest fundraiser in the House was Jared Polis, running for a Democratic open seat in Colorado, who amassed almost $7.5 million to keep the seat Democratic. In addition, the Democratic Party committees in the House and Senate out-raised their Republican counterparts by over $75 million.

The national political climate also favored the Democrats, given widespread disapproval of President Bush and Republicans in Congress and an increase in Democratic partisan identification. Barack Obama also inspired great confidence among Democrats. With Obama at the top of the ticket, all Democratic candidates would benefit from increased turnout among Democratic-leaning constituencies.

Thus, it was expected that the Democrats would build on their gains from 2006, but it was not certain whether they would be able to win enough Senate races to reach sixty seats, the number of votes needed to break a filibuster. Of the 35 seats up for election in 2008, Democrats needed not only to win all the open seats, but also to defeat several vulnerable Republican incumbents in traditionally Blue States. And, to reach the magic number of sixty, they would have to pull off some upsets against incumbents in several Red States such as Alaska, Georgia, Kentucky, Mississippi, and North Carolina.

The favorable political environment helped Democrats win at least six more seats in the Senate. Pending the outcome of a recount in Minnesota, a run-off in Georgia, and late arriving absentee ballots in Alaska, Democratic gains could be as high as nine seats (for the most up-to-date status of the races not called on Election Day, go to http://elections.foxnews.com/states_map). While the Democrats were not assured of reaching their ambitious goal, they did increase their majority by at least six, unseating three incumbents and capturing three open seats that previously were held by Republicans. As expected, Democrats won open seats in Colorado, New Mexico, and Virginia. In New Hampshire, former Governor Jeanne Shaheen defeated one-term incumbent Senator John Sununu in a rematch of their 2002 contest by a decisive 52 percent to 45 percent margin. In Oregon, Democratic State House Speaker Jeff Merkley defeated two-term incumbent Gordon Smith by a margin of three percent. Sununu and Smith had two of the more moderate voting records in their party and had stressed their opposition to President Bush in their advertising. This strategy failed both incumbents in two states that have become more Democratic in recent years.

Democrats also were successful in ousting first-term incumbent Elizabeth Dole in North Carolina, a state that still tends to vote Republican. From the beginning of the campaign the Democratic nominee, State Senator Kay Hagan, questioned the effectiveness of Dole's Senate tenure. In the wake of slipping poll numbers, the Dole campaign ran an attack ad the week before the election that highlighted the Godless Americans PAC's endorsement of Hagan and suggested that Hagan, herself, was an atheist. The spot concluded with a narrator announcing: "Godless Americans and Kay Hagan; she hid from cameras; took godless money. What did Hagan promise in return?" Within days, Hagan, an elder in the Presbyterian Church and a former Sunday School teacher, fired back with her own ad, where she accused her rival of deceptive advertising and of attacking a fellow Christian. The airing of the "Godless" ad clearly backfired on Dole, and she was defeated by a convincing 54 percent to 45 percent margin. With the Hagan and Shaheen elections, there are 17 women serving in the 111th Congress, an all-time high.

TABLE 13.4 Results of Selected Congressional Elections, 2008

	Contest	Winner	Loser	Significance
Alabama	House	Bobby Bright (D)	Jay Love (R)	In an open seat held by a Republican since 1993, the Democratic Mayor of Montgomery, Bobby Bright, defeated Republican State Representative Jay Love by a mere 1,500 votes.
Colorado	House	Betsy Markey (D)	Marilyn Musgrave (R)	Businesswoman Betsy Markey defeated incumbent Marilyn Musgrave, the main sponsor of the unsuccessful Federal Marriage Amendment. Musgrave's defeat continues a trend of difficult losses for Republicans in the West.
Connecticut	House	Jim Himes (D)	Christopher Shays (R)	Shays's defeat not only ends the career of the most liberal Republican in the House, but gives the Democrats control of all 24 House seats in the five New England states.
Florida	House	Tom Rooney (R)	Tim Mahoney (D)	Democrat Tim Mahoney scored an upset in this Republican leaning district in 2006, replacing incumbent Mark Foley in the wake of a scandal. Mahoney admitted to an extramarital affair with an aide and was accused of paying her hush money to conceal the relationship. He refused to leave the race and was defeated by a 20-point margin.
New Hampshire	Senate	Jeanne Shaheen (D)	John Sununu (R)	In a rematch of their 2002 race, ex-Gov. Shaheen defeated first-term Senator Sununu by effectively linking the incumbent to President George W. Bush. New Hampshire sends its first woman and first Democrat to the Senate since 1975.
North Carolina	Senate	Kay Hagan (D)	Elizabeth Dole (R)	State Senator Kay Hagan defeated first-term Senator Elizabeth Dole by painting the incumbent as an ineffective advocate for North Carolina. In one of the most memorable ads of the 2008 contests, Dole was criticized by two elderly men in rocking chairs for being ranked as the 93rd most effective Senator even though she had over 40 years of Washington experience.
Oregon	Senate	Jeff Merkley (D)	Gordon Smith (R)	State House Speaker Jeff Merkley defeated the highly unpopular incumbent Gordon Smith, who had tried to save his seat by distancing himself from President Bush and linking himself to Barack Obama and other popular Democrats.
Pennsylvania	House	Kathy Dahlkemper (D)	Phil English (R)	Political novice Kathy Dahlkemper defeated six-term incumbent Phil English, who had pledged not to serve more than 12 years. Dahlkemper, who opposes abortion rights and additional gun control measures, is only the third Democrat to represent the 3rd District since 1893.
Texas	House	Pete Olson (R)	Nick Lampson (D)	Democrat Nick Lampson won a narrow victory in former Majority Leader Tom Delay's solidly Republican district in 2006, running against a write-in candidate. Running against Senate staffer and Navy veteran Pete Olson in 2008, Lampson was unable to retain this seat for the Democrats.
Virginia	Senate	Mark Warner (D)	James Gilmore (R)	Former Gov. Mark Warner defeated his predecessor Jim Gilmore in an open seat race in which the retiring Republican senator, John Warner, failed to endorse the Republican nominee. Virginia Democrats now control both Senate seats and the Virginia statehouse for the first time since 1968.

Photo courtesy: Ellen Ozier/Reuters/Landov

When is incumbency not an advantage? State Senator Kay Hagan celebrates after learning of her stunning upset of incumbent Senator Elizabeth Dole. Winning the open seat vacated by conservative icon Jesse Helms in 2002, Dole, the wife of former Senate Majority Leader and 1996 Republican presidential nominee Bob Dole, was poised to make a difference for North Carolinians in Washington. She had twice served as a cabinet secretary and was the former head of the American Red Cross. But, after being ranked as only the 93rd most effective Senator in the 100-member body by an independent group, Dole's considerable Washington connections and experience seemed to represent simply the status quo in an election year in which voters were demanding change.

COMPARATIVE

Comparing Voting and Elections

In the House races, Democrats captured ten open seats vacated by Republicans and defeated 13 incumbents. The Democratic gains were nationwide. Open seats were won in Alabama, Virginia, New Jersey, New York (2), Illinois, Ohio, Arizona, and New Mexico (2), while GOP incumbents were defeated in Florida (2), North Carolina, Virginia, Connecticut, New York, Pennsylvania, Michigan (2), Ohio, Colorado, Idaho, and Nevada. The GOP minimized their losses slightly by defeating four one-term Democratic incumbents who previously had scored upset wins in heavily Republican districts. Overall, the Democrats came away with a net gain of at least 19 seats and as many as 25, depending on the outcome of pending ballots and recounts in six districts (see http://clerk.house.gov/ for the most up-to-date information on partisan divisions in the 111th Congress). Over the course of two election cycles, Democrats had gained over 50 seats. As a result, the Democrats begin the 111th Congress with a commanding 75-seat advantage in the House to go with their 14-seat majority in the Senate. With Barack Obama winning the White House, Democrats now control both chambers of Congress and the presidency for the first time since the 103rd Congress. A great opportunity now exists for President Obama and the congressional leadership to move quickly on initiatives to address current problems and push forward longstanding Democratic priorities that were blocked by President Bush and Republicans in Congress. At the same time, history has shown that unified partisan control does not assure smooth process or even major policy successes. Rivalries between the executive and legislative branches are common, and a large majority in Congress usually indicates a diversity of viewpoints within the majority party. The outcome will be closely watched, as it will have a tangible impact on the president's popularity and the 2010 midterm elections.

Toward Reform: Strengthening the Electoral Process

The legitimacy of electoral outcomes and the legitimacy of the political institutions that elections serve ultimately rest in the health of the electoral process. While Americans might disagree with the policy preferences of a particular president, they take comfort in the fact that the president was chosen in a fair and open system and that they will have the chance to influence the direction of the country by participating in future elections. When the legitimacy of the electoral process itself comes into question, as was the case with the 2000 presidential contest, and to a significantly lesser extent the 2004 presidential election, the very foundation of democratic governance can be shaken to its core.

Many proposals for electoral reform in America center on the Electoral College, as discussed earlier. What the numerous ideas for reforming the electoral process have in common is the desire for elections to serve as a clearer reflection of public preference. Abolition of the Electoral College, the establishment of a congressional district plan, or the elimination of electors are the most dramatic and apparently urgent reform options, especially in light of the events of the 2000 election. They are also the least likely to succeed, given entrenched interests and the difficulty of amending the Constitution. Changes to the Electoral College, however, are not the only ways in which the election of public officials in America might be improved. Several of the numerous other plans that merit attention are described below; each is designed to cure an existing weakness in the current system.

Regional Primaries

Electoral reforms that focus on the presidential nominating process often attempt to cure the uneven playing field that currently exists among states. These reform proposals attempt to remove the disproportionate attention that some states receive by holding their contests early in the primary season. One proposal is to hold a series of **regional primaries** throughout the United States during the first week of each month, beginning in February of a presidential election year. Under this system, the country would be divided into five regions: the Southeast, Southwest, Far West, Midwest, and Northeast. In December of the year prior to the presidential election, states would hold a lottery to determine the order of the primaries, with all regional contests held on the first of every month from February through June. The goals of this reform would be twofold. First, it would end the current "permanent campaign" by preventing candidates from "camping out" in Iowa and New Hampshire for one to two years in the hopes of winning or doing better than expected in these small, unrepresentative states. Second, some rational order would be imposed on the nomination process, more equitably distributing the influence of states in the nomination process and allowing candidates to focus on each region's concerns.[60]

regional primary
A proposed system in which the country would be divided into five or six geographic areas and all states in each region would hold their presidential primary elections on the same day.

Campaign Finance Reform

Another perennial election concern focuses on the corrupting influence of money in the electoral process. The electoral reform that has attempted to address this issue and that has gained the most attention in recent years involves campaign finance reform. The Bipartisan Campaign Reform Act (BCRA), sponsored by Senators John McCain (R–AZ) and Russ Feingold (D–WI), was signed into law in March 2002. This legislation banned unregulated soft-money donations to political parties, restricted the use of political ads, and increased political contribution limits for private individuals. Supporters heralded its passage as a major victory in lessening the influence of big money on politics. Unfortunately, political consultants have found ways around the legislation, leaving many voters to wonder what improvement the BCRA brought, if any. Campaign finance will be discussed more thoroughly in chapter 14.

You Are a Campaign Manager: McCain Navigates Campaign Financing: Rules and Trends Regarding the "Mother's Milk" of Politics

Online Voting

The quest for a secure, reliable, fraud-free voting mechanism continues to elude the American voter. In the nineteenth century, political parties ran the elections, supplying not only paper ballots but also many of the poll watchers and election judges. This was a formula for fraud, of course—there was not even a truly secret ballot, as people voted on ballots of different colors, depending on their choice of party. The twentieth century saw widespread improvements in election practices and technology. The states now oversee the election process through official state boards of election, and the use of voting machines, nearly universal in America by the 1970s, permits truly secret mechanical voting. These measures helped effect enormous reductions in fraud and electoral ambiguity—though as the problems of the 2000 and 2004 elections proved, there is still a long way to go.

Democracy and the Internet

As computer technology continues to evolve, Internet voting has become a likely way to cast votes in the coming years. Rightly or wrongly, many Americans equate Internet voting with the ideals of instant democracy and greater citizen participation. Many states are formally studying the feasibility and impact of Internet voting. In 2000, Arizona pioneered online balloting by allowing citizens to vote via the Internet in the state's Democratic presidential primary. In 2004, Michigan made a similar attempt during its presidential caucus. In both cases, fears of computer hacking and voter fraud, as well as technical difficulties, limited the success of the experiments.

The Democratic Party resurrected Internet voting for the 2008 presidential nominating contests in limited form by allowing Democrats living abroad to vote absentee over the Internet. To date, persistent security concerns have hampered widespread adoption of online voting practices.

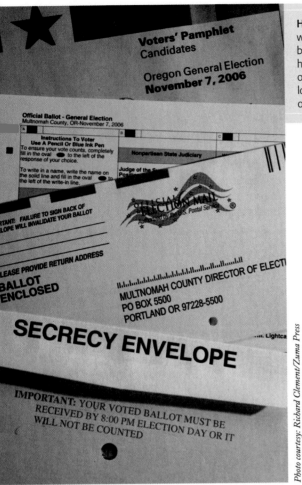

Photo courtesy: Richard Clement/Zuma Press

How does Oregon's system of voting by mail work? In 1998, Oregonians overwhelmingly approved an initiative authorizing voting by mail. Two to three weeks before an election, ballots are mailed to the registered address of the voter. The voter has two weeks to return the sealed ballot through the mail or by dropping it off at an official site. Ballots must be sealed in an envelope and then placed in another envelope that includes the voter's signature. The signature is checked against the signature on file with the elections division.

Voting by Mail

As noted earlier in the chapter, over a quarter of eligible voters who failed to vote in the 2002 election cited "too busy" as their reason. Reformers who seek to increase turnout note that the process is inconvenient and time consuming, especially having to show up at a specific polling place on a particular day. The use of mail-in ballots, whereby registered voters are mailed ballots and given several weeks to mail them back with their votes, has been found to increase participation. Currently, Oregon and Washington are the only states that vote almost entirely by mail-in ballots. However, most states have a system of absentee balloting through which voters can request that they receive their ballots at home. Voters then mail back their completed ballots. Political parties have encouraged their voters to register by absentee ballot, since it increases turnout and allows the party more time to follow up with voters. To expand voter options, more states have been allowing early voting or no longer require that a voter give a reason for voting absentee. Also referred to as "convenience voting," these practices allow voters to cast their ballots as much as several weeks prior to the election. Currently, thirty-four states and the District of Columbia allow some form of convenience voting.

While the all-mail system remains popular in Oregon and is credited with increasing voting rates in that state, voting by mail has its downside. There are concerns about decreased ballot security and increased potential for fraud with mail-in elections. Another problem with such an approach is that it delays election results. Oregon did not have its 2000 presidential results finalized until several weeks after Election Day. The state of Washington, which has extremely liberal laws regarding mail-in votes, was also much later than the rest of the country in announcing its presidential and congressional winners. Additionally, voters who voted by mail or voted early in a campaign may change their minds after obtaining new information about candidates just days prior to the election, or they may have voted for a candidate who subsequently withdrew from the race.

Modernizing the Ballot

As shown in Figure 13.7, the use of electronic voting systems such as touch-screen machines and optical scan readers has increased rapidly since 2000. Following the 2004 presidential election, many states replaced their paper ballots with electronic devices. Indeed, prior to the 2002 midterm elections, the Florida legislature under-

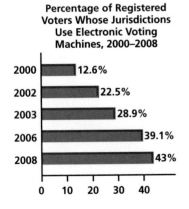

Percentage of Registered Voters Whose Jurisdictions Use Electronic Voting Machines, 2000–2008

Year	Percentage
2000	12.6%
2002	22.5%
2003	28.9%
2006	39.1%
2008	43%

FIGURE **13.7** Percentage of Voters Using Electronic Voting Machines, 2000–2008
The 2000 election disaster in Florida prevented many votes from being properly counted due to problems with voting equipment and ballot design. Beginning in 2002, many areas throughout the country adopted electronic voting machines. With concerns about reliability and fraud growing, however, some localities are abandoning the new technology in favor of old-fashioned paper ballots.

Source: Election Data Services; 2008 data based on pre-election estimates.

took massive voting reforms, including banning punch-card ballots and investing $30 million in new touch-screen voting systems, with the individual counties spending tens of millions more. Unfortunately, problems plagued the 2002 Democratic gubernatorial primary. Confusion abounded as voters and poll workers misused the expensive new machines. Election administrators had difficulty tabulating the electronic votes, leading to a week-long delay in naming an official winner. Everyone learned an important lesson: technology is not a panacea that will cure all election problems.

Supporters of electronic voting believe that emphasis must be placed on training poll workers, administrators, and voters on how to effectively use the new equipment. Critics believe that the lack of a paper trail leaves electronic machines vulnerable to fraud and worry that the machines could crash during an election. Still other critics cite the expense of the machines. Observers agree that updating election equipment and ensuring fair elections across the country should be a legislative priority. As Charles M. Vest, the president of the Massachusetts Institute of Technology, noted, "A nation that can send a man to the moon, that can put a reliable ATM machine on every corner, has no excuse not to deploy a reliable, affordable, easy-to-use voting system."[61]

WHAT SHOULD I HAVE LEARNED?

Elections continue to be the cornerstone of American government, a continual reaffirmation of the right of the people to rule. Despite lingering voter apathy, many reforms have increased citizens' access to elections. Moreover, the high turnout in the 2008 elections demonstrated a reassuring increase in the interest and intensity of American elections. In our efforts to explain the complex and multilayered U.S. electoral system, we covered these points in this chapter:

■ **What are the roots of voting behavior in the United States and what voting patterns have political scientists identified?**

Voting is the most fundamental form of electoral participation. Voter turnout in the United States is much lower than in other industrialized democracies. It is higher, however, among citizens who are white, older, more educated, have higher incomes, belong to labor unions, and attend religious services more frequently. Whether they are casting ballots in congressional or presidential elections, partisan identification is the most powerful predictor of voter choice.

■ **What types of elections occur in the United States and what purposes do they serve?**

Regular elections guarantee mass political action and governmental accountability. They also confer legitimacy on regimes better than any other method of change. When it comes to elections, the United States has an embarrassment of riches. There are various types of primary elections in the country, as well as general elections, initiatives, referenda, and recall elections.

■ **What are the key elements of presidential elections?**

Variety aside, no U.S. election can compare to the presidential contest. This spectacle, held every four years, brings together all the elements of politics and attracts the most ambitious and energetic politicians to the national stage. The parties select presidential candidates through either primary elections or caucuses, with the primary process culminating in each party's national convention, after which the general election campaign begins. The American political system uses indirect electoral representation in the form of the Electoral College.

■ **What are the key elements of congressional elections and how do they differ from presidential elections?**

Many similar elements are present in different kinds of elections. Candidates, voters, issues, and television advertisements are constants. But, there are distinctive aspects of each kind of election as well. In congressional elections incumbents have a strong advantage over their challengers. Redistricting, scandal, presidential coattails, and midterm elections serve as countervailing forces to the incumbency advantage and are the main sources of turnover in Congress.

■ **What was the outcome of the 2008 congressional elections?**

Democrats built on their 2006 successes and strengthened their control of both chambers of Congress by adding at least 19 more seats in the House and six seats in the Senate. A highly favorable political climate and electoral landscape, numerous Republican retirements, and fundraising and recruiting advantages contributed to Democrats achieving a 75-seat majority in the House and a 14-seat majority in the Senate.

■ **What efforts are being made to reform the electoral process?**

Events of the 2000 election renewed calls for change in the Electoral College. Other suggested electoral reforms are regional primaries, campaign finance limits, online voting, and voting by mail. Some states have promoted electronic voting technologies to eliminate problems with punch-card ballots, but critics point to the possibility of voter fraud.

Key Terms

authoritarian system, p. 464
ballot measure, p. 465
closed primary, p. 465
conventional political participation, p. 447
crossover voting, p. 465
elector, p. 473
Electoral College, p. 473
electorate, p. 464
front-loading, p. 469
general election, p. 465

gerrymandering, p. 480
incumbency, p. 478
initiative, p. 465
mandate, p. 464
midterm election, p. 482
open primary, p. 465
primary election, p. 465
prospective judgment, p. 463
raiding, p. 465
reapportionment, p. 476
recall, p. 467

redistricting, p. 479
referendum, p. 465
regional primary, p. 487
retrospective judgment, p. 463
runoff primary, p. 465
superdelegate, p. 471
ticket-splitting, p. 460
turnout, p. 448
unconventional political participation, p. 447
unit rule, p. 471

Researching Voting and Elections

In the Library

Abramson, Paul R., John H. Aldrich, and David W. Rohde. *Change and Continuity in the 2004 and 2006 Elections.* Washington, DC: CQ Press, 2007.

Alvarez R. Michael, and Thad E. Hall. *Electronic Elections: The Perils and Promises of Digital Democracy.* Princeton, NJ: Princeton University Press, 2008.

Campbell, Angus, Philip E. Converse, Warren E. Miller, and Donald E. Stokes. *The American Voter,* reprint ed. Chicago: University of Chicago, 1980.

Carroll, Susan J., and Richard L. Fox, eds. *Gender and Elections: Shaping the Future of American Politics.* New York: Cambridge University Press, 2006.

Crigler, Ann N., Marion Just, and Edward J. McCaffery. *Rethinking the Vote: The Politics and Prospects of American Election Reform.* New York: Oxford University Press, 2004.

Dolan, Kathleen A. *Voting for Women: How the Public Evaluates Women Candidates.* Boulder, CO: Westview, 2003.

Fiorina, Morris P. *Retrospective Voting in American National Elections.* New Haven, CT: Yale University Press, 1981.

Flanigan, William H., and Nancy H. Zingale. *Political Behavior of the American Electorate,* 11th ed. Washington, DC: CQ Press, 2006.

Herrnson, Paul S. *Congressional Elections: Campaigning at Home and in Washington,* 5th ed. Washington, DC: CQ Press, 2007.

Jacobson, Gary C. *The Politics of Congressional Elections,* 7th ed. New York: Longman, 2008.

Key, V. O., Jr., with Milton C. Cummings. *The Responsible Electorate*. Cambridge, MA: Harvard University Press, 1966.

Lawless, Jennifer L., and Richard Fox. *It Takes a Candidate: Why Women Don't Run for Office*. New York: Cambridge University Press, 2005.

Lewis-Beck, Michael S., Helmut Norpoth, William G. Jacoby, and Herbert F. Weisberg. *The American Voter Revisited*. Ann Arbor: University of Michigan Press, 2008.

Mayer, William G. *The Swing Voter in American Politics*. Washington, DC: Brookings Institution, 2007.

Niemi, Richard G., and Herbert F. Weisberg. *Classics in Voting Behavior*. Washington, DC: CQ Press, 1992.

—— *Controversies in Voting Behavior*, 4th ed. Washington, DC: CQ Press, 2001.

Nivola, Pietro, and David W Brady. *Red and Blue Nation? Consequences and Correction of America's Polarized Politics*. Washington, DC: Brookings Institution, 2008.

Sabato, Larry J. *The Sixth Year Itch: The Rise and Fall of George W. Bush's Presidency*. New York: Longman, 2007.

Sabato, Larry J., and Howard R. Ernst, eds. *The Encyclopedia of American Political Parties and Election*. New York: Facts on File, 2006.

Stanley, Harold W., and Richard G. Niemi. *Vital Statistics on American Politics, 2007–2008* Washington, DC: CQ Press, 2007.

Thomas, Sue, and Clyde Wilcox. *Women and Elective Office: Past, Present, and Future*, 2nd ed. New York: Oxford University Press, 2005.

Wattenberg, Martin P. *Is Voting for Young People? With a Postscript on Citizen Engagement*. New York: Longman, 2007.

On the Web

For comprehensive election information that includes the political biographies and issue positions of the major candidates, county-by-county election results, exit poll data, primary and caucus rules and delegate allocation, and an explanation of the Electoral College, go to **www.cnn.com/ELECTION/2008/**.

The Center for American Women and Politics site, **www.cawp.rutgers. edu**, provides lists of women currently serving in Congress and in statewide elective office, state-by-state facts about women office holders, data on the gender gap and voting patterns, a list of women's PACs and donor networks, and firsts for women in U.S. politics.

For a nonpartisan, nonadvocacy Web site that provides news and analysis on election reform and a forum for learning, discussing, and debating election administration issues, go to **www. electiononline.org**.

To learn more about the Federal Election Commission (FEC), which monitors and enforces campaign finance and election laws, go to **www.fec.gov**.

The Initiative and Referendum Institute, **www.iandrinstitute.org**, offers scholarly research reports on direct democracy, as well as resources for evaluating and debating upcoming referenda or initiatives and past election results.

Project Vote Smart, **www.vote-smart.org**, is a nonpartisan resource for researching the voting records, issue positions, public statements, and campaign finances for current office holders and candidates. The site also includes a search engine to identify your member of Congress, voter registration information, and key issues being debated in your state.

14

The Campaign Process

By the time Senator Barack Obama secured his party's nomination in June, the electoral environment was looking quite favorable for the Democrats. President George W. Bush's approval rating was around 25 percent, the Democratic base was energized, and a real hunger for change was sweeping the nation. Obama's path to the presidency was not assured, however. Democrats worried that not enough white Americans would be willing to vote for an African American for president. And, Obama's Republican opponent, Senator John McCain, was a more experienced candidate with a distinguished war record and history of breaking with his own party's policies. The decision awaiting both campaigns were how best to form an electoral majority given the advantages and disadvantages at hand.

Although the presidential election is national, candidates traditionally focus on specific states that were won by narrow margins in the most recent past elections in order to secure a majority of the Electoral College. Many of these "battleground states" are located in the Rust Belt—Michigan, Ohio, Pennsylvania, and Wisconsin—or the Southwest—Colorado, Nevada, and New Mexico. Others—such as Florida, Iowa, Minnesota, Missouri, and New Hampshire—are spread across the country. For the

Obama campaign, the road to the White House would depend on holding all of the states that John Kerry had won in 2004. By adding Iowa, which had voted Democratic in 2000, and the three Southwestern battleground states, which had been trending towards the Democrats since 2004, Obama could win with 278 electoral votes. Alternatively, the Obama campaign could concentrate on winning Florida and Ohio, the battleground states that went Republican in both 2000 and 2004 by small margins. A win in just one of those two states would allow Senator Obama to obtain an Electoral College majority. But, the Obama campaign had a third strategy in mind: pursue both of these strategies simultaneously and compete vigorously in a number of reliably Republican states, most notably Virginia, which had not voted for a Democrat for president since 1964. While this bold and ambitious plan to expand the electoral map seemed risky to many seasoned observers, the Obama campaign was confident in its decision to pursue a strategy that included organizing on the ground early in all fifty states and opting out of the public financing system, which would allow them to raise an unprecedented sum of money and to spend as much as was needed to finance their nationwide effort. For the McCain campaign, the options were much more limited and there would be little room for error. McCain would need to hold all the states George W. Bush had won in 2004 and he also would have to win in one or more states that generally do not vote Republican in order to win the presidency. McCain's challenge was made only more difficult by his

■ **Presidential campaigns leave indelible marks on the nation.** At left, Theodore Roosevelt gives a campaign speech from the back of a train in 1912. At right, President-elect Barack Obama and his family wave to over 100,000 supporters in Chicago's Grant Park after Obama was declared the winner of the 2008 presidential election.

WHAT SHOULD I KNOW ABOUT . . .
- the roots of modern political campaigns?
- political candidates and their campaign staff?
- the media's role in covering campaigns?
- campaign finance and its impact on the campaign process?
- the 2008 presidential campaign?
- campaign finance reform and the rise of 527 advocacy groups?

decisions to limit his campaign spending in return for federal financing and to focus his early attention and scarce resources only on battleground states.

TO LEARN MORE—
—TO DO MORE
To see how citizens in your region and state voted for president, go to www.cnn.com/ELECTION/2008.

On Election Day, the Obama campaign's strategy proved to be decisive. As the first returns were announced from states in the eastern and central time zones, none of the states that Kerry had won in 2004 were switching over to McCain and all of the battleground states that Bush had won remained too close to call. Even more surprising were the early returns from a number of traditionally Republican states: the outcomes in Indiana, Georgia, North Carolina, and Virginia remained in doubt for most of the evening. A similar pattern soon became apparent in the West, with the networks unwilling to make early calls on the outcomes in Montana, North Dakota and even McCain's home state of Arizona. In the end, Obama not only held on to all of the states the Democrats had won in 2004, but he also won all four of the states that he had targeted in the Southwest, Florida and Ohio, and usually reliably Republican Virginia, North Carolina and Indiana, for a total of 364 electoral votes. When looking at how the 2008 Electoral College map changed from the 2004 map, one can see that the division of the country between coastal "blue" Democratic states and interior "red" Republican states is less pronounced. Democrats are now competitive in the high-growth states of the Southwest and the New South and have increased their reach into the Midwest. Whether this is the beginning of a trend or simply a reaction to the policies of the Bush administration, however, remains to be seen.

How do party rivals unite after a long, competitive nomination contest? Senators Hillary Clinton and Barack Obama are pictured here during a heated one-on-one debate in February 2008. Clinton and Obama appeared together in 26 debates and campaigned against each other for over 15 months. While a deep resentment emerged between the two candidates and their staffs, the two set aside their differences during the Democratic National Convention in order to unify their party, and Clinton campaigned effectively for Obama during the general election.

Modern political campaigns enjoy all the trappings of a major-league sporting event, plus the added intrigue that comes from knowing that election outcomes can quite literally alter the course of history. Though campaigns have become high-stakes, high-priced extravaganzas, the basic purpose of modern electioneering remains intact: one person asking another for support.

The art of modern campaigning involves the management of a large budget and staff, the planning of sophisticated voter outreach efforts, and the creation of sophisticated Internet sites that provide continuous communication updates and organize voter and donor support. Campaigning also involves the diplomatic skill of unifying disparate individuals and groups to achieve a fragile but election-winning majority. How candidates perform these exquisitely difficult tasks is the subject of this chapter, in which we discuss the following topics:

★ First, we will explore *the roots of modern campaigns*, which are often described in terms of military strategy or sports competitions and are generally segmented into nomination and general election campaigns.

★ Second, we will look at *the key players in the modern campaign*, the people who run for office and the paid and volunteer staffs who constitute the campaign organization.

Photo courtesy: Matt Sullivan/Reuters/Landov

⋆ Third, we will examine *the media's role in covering campaigns*, exploring how the conventional news media and increasingly new media depict the political landscape and how campaigns attempt to influence media coverage.

⋆ Fourth, we will analyze *the campaign finance and its impact on the campaign process*, giving special attention to the impact of the Bipartisan Campaign Reform Act of 2002.

⋆ Fifth, we will assess *the 2008 presidential campaign* and its important lessons.

⋆ Finally, we will explore *current campaign finance reform efforts* and analyze the impact of 527 and 501(c) advocacy groups on American politics.

Comparing Political Campaigns

Roots of Modern Political Campaigns

"Campaign" is the military term for an armed struggle to achieve a specific objective. The language of modern campaigning is filled with military words. For example, political campaigns are "launched," and they include "tactics and strategy." Incumbents amass considerable "war chests," while challengers attempt to "raid" votes from the incumbent. Common sports metaphors have also infiltrated the lexicon of campaigning, with candidates "scoring touchdowns," "hitting home runs," and "landing knockout punches" when they perform well against their opponents. And, as in sports, there are the big leagues (presidential, gubernatorial, and U.S. Senate races), as well as minor leagues (state and local contests). There is a campaign "season," and ultimately every campaign has its "winners" and "losers."

No two political campaigns are the same: the players change, the political landscape evolves, and even the rules change from time to time. Each aspect of the campaign interacts with the other aspects to create a dynamic set of circumstances that make campaigns unpredictable and add to their excitement. Despite the unique qualities of each race, however, most electoral contests are similar in structure, consisting of some form of nomination campaign and a general election.

Thinking Globally

The Length of Campaigns

While many of the candidates for the 2008 U.S. presidential nominations made their first campaign visits to Iowa and New Hampshire a few days following the 2006 midterm elections, candidates in most parliamentary democracies campaign for only thirty to sixty days. Canadian law requires that the minimum length of a campaign be thirty-six days, although most national campaigns have lasted for an average of two months.

■ For the electorate, what might be the advantages and disadvantages of having a much shorter presidential campaign?
■ Are certain types of candidates given an advantage (and others left at a disadvantage) by limiting the length of a campaign? In the United States, who might benefit the most if candidates were prohibited from raising money or producing advertisements sixty days prior to an election?

The Nomination Campaign

The **nomination campaign** begins as soon as the candidate has decided to run—sometimes years prior to an official announcement—and it ends at the party convention. During the nomination campaign, the candidate targets the leaders and activists who choose nominees in primaries or conventions. Party leaders are concerned with electability, while party activists are often ideologically and issue oriented, so a candidate must appeal to both bases.

As they seek their party's nomination, candidates learn to adjust to the pressure of being in the spotlight day in and day out. This is the time for the candidates to learn that a single careless phrase could end the campaign or guarantee a defeat. This is also the time to seek the support of party leaders and interest groups and to test out themes, slogans, and strategies. The press and public take much less notice of shifts in strategy at this time than they will later in the general election campaign.

nomination campaign
That part of a political campaign aimed at winning a primary election.

Timeline: Elections and Campaign Finance Reform

1800 Election of 1800— Thomas Jefferson, the Republican Party's presidential nominee, and Aaron Burr, the Republican's Vice-Presidential nominee, win an equal number of electoral votes. After numerous votes in the House of Representatives and support from his rival, Alexander Hamilton, Jefferson secures a majority and is elected president.

1825 Election of 1825— In the only presidential election since the 12th amendment to be decided by the House of Representatives, John Quincy Adams is elected president although he failed to win a plurality in the Electoral College.

1952 Twenty-Second Amendment Ratified— Amendment prohibits a person from serving more than two terms or 10 years as president.

1971 Federal Election Campaign Act (FECA)—Law imposes limits on campaign contributions, requiring disclosure of receipts and expenditures, and establishes the Federal Election Commission to enforce election rules.

1876 Election of 1876—Rutherford B. Hayes is elected president after losing the popular vote, but winning the Electoral College by one vote after 20 disputed votes are awarded to Hayes in exchange for Republicans' promise to end Reconstruction in the South.

1975 *Buckley* v. *Valeo*— Supreme Court invalidates limits on campaign expenditures imposed by 1974 FECA amendments on the grounds that these limits place restrictions on the ability of candidates, citizens, and associations to engage in protected First Amendment free speech rights.

1804 Twelfth Amendment Ratified—Requires electors to cast one vote for President and another for Vice President. If no candidate wins a majority of the Electoral College, the House chooses among the top three vote-winners.

TIMELINE

Nominating Process

The nomination campaign is a critical time for gaining and maintaining an aura of support, both within the party and with the larger electorate. In the months leading up to the 2000 Republican convention, George W. Bush, the eventual Republican nominee for president, won support through a variety of means. Much of this support grew out of Bush's early fund-raising success and the sense of inevitability that a steady flow of cash supplies in politics—not necessarily out of support for Bush's issue positions or campaign themes.[1] In the 2008 campaign for the Democratic Party nomination, Senator Hillary Rodham Clinton was initially considered a near shoo-in for the Democratic nomination due to the large campaign war chest she had amassed. Senator Barack Obama's early success raising money and effective grassroots organizing, however, resulted in two clear frontrunners who stayed in the race through the final primaries in June.

A danger not always heeded by candidates during the nomination campaign is that, in the quest to win the party's nomination, a candidate can move too far to the right or left and appear too extreme to the electorate in November. Party activists are generally more ideologically extreme than party-identified voters in the general electorate, and activists participate in primaries and caucuses at a relatively high rate. If a candidate tries too hard to appeal to their interests, he or she jeopardizes the ultimate goal of winning the election. Conservative Barry Goldwater, the 1964 Republican nominee for president, and liberal George McGovern, the 1972 Democratic nominee

2002 The Bipartisan Campaign Reform Act (BCRA)—Legislation sponsored by McCain and Feingold increases contribution limits to candidates and political parties and eliminates the use of soft money by the political parties. Law defines issue ads run 30 days prior to primary election and 60 days prior to the general election as electioneering, making them subject to FCC regulations.

2007 *FCC* v. *Wisconsin Right to Life*—Supreme Court invalidates BCRA's ban on issue ads in the days prior to an election on the grounds that issue ads that do not explicitly urge the support or defeat of a candidate cannot be designated as electioneering

2000 2000 Election—George W. Bush is elected president without winning a plurality of the popular vote. Election does not become final, however, until the Supreme Court rules in *Bush* v. *Gore* that Florida's method for recounting ballots was unconstitutional, securing Bush the victory in Florida and a majority in the Electoral College.

2003 *McConnell* v. *FCC*—Supreme Court upholds BCRA, concluding that any restriction on free speech is minimal and justified by the government's legitimate interest in preventing both corruption and the appearance of corruption that might result from campaign contributions.

for president, both fell victim to this phenomenon in seeking their party's nomination—Goldwater going too far right, and McGovern going too far left—and they were handily defeated in the general elections by Presidents Lyndon B. Johnson and Richard M. Nixon, respectively.

The General Election Campaign

After earning the party's nomination, candidates embark on the **general election campaign**. They must seek the support of interest groups and a majority of voters and decide on the issues they will emphasize. When courting interest groups, a candidate seeks both money and endorsements, although the results are mainly predictable: liberal, labor, and minority groups usually back Democrats, while social conservatives and business organizations usually support Republicans. The most active groups often coalesce around emotional issues such as abortion and gun control, and these organizations can produce a bumper crop of money and activists for favored candidates. Virtually all candidates adopt a brief theme, or slogan, to serve as a rallying cry in their quest for office. In 2004, the Kerry-Edwards campaign adopted the slogan "A Stronger America" in order to emphasize the security issue. In 2008, John McCain adopted the slogan "Country First" in order to remind voters of his experience as a prisoner of war in Vietnam and his ability to work across party lines and defy his own party. Candidates try to

general election campaign
That part of a political campaign aimed at winning a general election.

Photo courtesy: Bettmann/CORBIS

What makes a good campaign slogan? 1964 Republican presidential candidate Barry Goldwater's famous slogan, "In your heart, you know he's right," was quickly lampooned by incumbent Democratic opponent President Lyndon B. Johnson's campaign as "In your guts, you know he's nuts."

avoid controversy in their selection of slogans, and some openly eschew ideology. The clever candidate also attempts to find a slogan that cannot be lampooned easily. In 1964, Barry Goldwater's handlers may have regretted their choice of "In your heart, you know he's right" when Lyndon B. Johnson's supporters quickly converted it into "In your guts, you know he's nuts." (Democrats were trying to portray Goldwater as a warmonger after the Republican indicated a willingness to use nuclear weapons.)

In addition to deciding which issues to focus on during the campaign, the candidate must also define his or her stance on other topics of interest to voters. A variety of factors influence candidates' positions and core issues, including personal conviction, party platform, and experience in a certain area. Candidates also use public opinion polling to gauge whether the issues that they care about are issues that the voters care about.

The Key Players: The Candidate and the Campaign Staff

Most observers agree that the most important aspect of any campaign is the quality of the candidate and the attributes of the campaign team. The ability to convey ideas in a persuasive manner, the cornerstone of all political campaigns, ultimately rests in the hands of the candidate. The ability to package and project the candidate's message in the most effective and persuasive manner, the work of the campaign staff, requires expertise in media and public relations. The ability to raise funds, which in turn provide volume to the campaign message, requires the combined effort of a strong candidate and experienced campaign staff.

The Candidate

Before there can be a campaign, there must be candidates. Candidates run for office for any number of reasons, including personal ambition, the desire to promote ideological objectives or pursue specific public policies, or simply because they think they can do a better job than their opponents.[2] In any case, to be successful, candidates must spend a considerable amount of time and energy in pursuit of their desired office, and all candidates must be prepared to expose themselves to public scrutiny and the chance of rejection by the voters.

In the effort to show voters that they are hardworking, thoughtful, and worthy of the office they seek, candidates try to meet as many citizens as possible in the course of a campaign. To some degree, such efforts are symbolic, especially for presidential candidates, since it is possible to have direct contact with only a small fraction of the nearly 125 million people who are likely to vote in a presidential contest. Moreover, at the presidential level, these "one-on-one" meetings are often staged events, meant more for the television audience than the actual participants. But, one should not discount the value of visiting numerous localities to both increase media coverage and to motivate local activists who are working for the candidate's campaign.

In a typical campaign, a candidate for high office maintains an exhausting schedule. The day may begin at 5 a.m. at the entrance gate to an auto plant with an hour or two of handshaking, followed by similar glad-handing at subway stops until 9 a.m. Strategy sessions with key advisers and preparation for upcoming presentations and forums may fill the rest of the morning. A luncheon talk, afternoon fundraisers, and a series of television and print interviews crowd the afternoon agenda. Cocktail parties are followed by a dinner speech, perhaps telephone or neighborhood canvassing of voters, and a civic-forum talk or two. More meetings with advisers and planning for the next day's events can easily take a candidate past midnight. Following only a few hours of sleep, the candidate starts all over again. The hectic pace of campaigning can strain the candidate's family life and leaves little time for reflection and long-range planning. After months of this grueling pace, candidates may be functioning on automatic pilot and often commit gaffes, from referring to the wrong city's sports team to fumbling an oft-repeated stump speech. Candidates also are much more prone to lose their tempers, responding sharply to criticism from opponents and even the media when they believe they have been characterized unfairly. These frustrations and the sheer exhaustion only get worse when a candidate believes he or she is on the verge of defeat and the end of the campaign is near.

The Campaign Staff

Paid staff, political consultants, and dedicated volunteers work behind the scenes to support the candidate. Collectively, they plan general strategy, conduct polls, write speeches, craft the campaign's message, and design the strategy for communicating that message in the form of television advertisements, radio spots, Web sites, and direct mail pieces. Others are responsible for organizing fund-raising events, campaign rallies, and direct voter contacts. The staff, professional and volunteer, keeps the candidate on message and manages the campaign's near-infinite details. The size and nature of the organizational staff varies significantly depending on the type of race. Senate and gubernatorial races, for example, are able to hire for many staff positions and employ a number of different consultants and pollsters, whereas races for state legislatures will likely have a paid campaign manager and rely more heavily on volunteer workers. Presidential campaign organizations, not surprisingly, have the most elaborate structure. (To learn more about presidential campaign organizations, see Figure 14.1.)

voter canvass
The process by which a campaign reaches individual voters, either by door-to-door solicitation or by telephone.

VOLUNTEER CAMPAIGN STAFF Volunteers are the lifeblood of every national, state, and local campaign. Volunteers answer phone calls, staff candidate booths at festivals and county fairs, copy and distribute campaign literature, and serve as the public face of the campaign. They go door to door to solicit votes, or use computerized telephone banks to call targeted voters with scripted messages, two basic methods of **voter canvass**. Most canvassing, or direct solicitation of support, takes place in the month before the election, when voters are most

Who are the senior advisors to a presidential candidate?
Charles Black, at right, served as John McCain's chief campaign advisor. Black brought considerable experience in presidential politics to the McCain campaign, having worked on Ronald Reagan's 1976 and 1980 campaigns and served as senior political advisor to George Bush in 1992. Black took a leave of absence from his role as the chief lobbyist for a major Washington, DC firm and did not draw a salary for his 2008 campaign work.

Photo courtesy: Mary Altaffer/AP/Wide World Photos

Senator Barack Obama's Campaign Organization
Obama for America

General
Campaign Manager: David Plouffe
Media Strategist: David Axelrod
Senior Strategist for Communications and
    Message: Robert Gibbs
Senior Advisor: Valerie Jarrett
Deputy Campaign Manager: Steve Hildebrand

Operations
Chief Operating Officer: Betsy Myers
Chief of Staff: Jim Messina
Chief Financial Officer: Marianne
    Markowitz
General Counsel: Bob Bauer

Finance
Finance Director: Julianna Smoot
Deputy Finance Director: Ami Copeland
Director of Grassroots Fundraising:
    Meaghan Burdick
National Finance Chair: Penny Pritzker
Direct Mail: Larry Grisolano and Erik
    Smith

Communications
Senior Communications Advisor: Anita
    Dunn
Communications Director: Dan Pfeiffer
Deputy Communications Director: Josh
    Earnest
National Press Secretary: Bill Burton
Traveling Spokeswoman: Linda Douglass
Traveling Press Secretary: Jen Psaki
Scheduling and Advance: Alyssa
    Mastromonaco
Director of Rapid Response: Christina
    Reynolds
Director of Speechwriting: Jon Favreau

Internet and Information Technology
Chief Technology Officer: Kevin Malover
New Media Director: Joe Rospars
Online Organizers: Chris Hughes, Emily
    Bokar, Gray Brooks
Blogger: Sam Graham-Felsen.
Video: Kate Albright-Hanna
E-mail: Stephen Geer, Teddy Goff, Udai
    Rohagi, Stephen Speakman
Internet Advertising: Michael Organ

Policy
Senior Policy Strategist: Heather
    Higginbottom
Economic Policy Director: Jason Furman
National Security Coordinator: Denis
    McDonough

Political
Political Director: Patrick Gaspard
Constituency Director: Brian Bond
Youth Vote Director: Hans Reimer

Field
National Field Director: Jon Carson
50-State Voter Registration Director:
    Jason Green

Research and Polling
Research Director: Devorah Adler
Pollsters: Paul Harstad and Cornell
    Belcher

Michelle Obama Staff
Senior Advisor and Chief of Staff:
    Stephanie Cutter
Communications Director: Katie
    McCormick Lelyveld

Joe Biden Staff
Chief of Staff: Patti Solis Doyle
Deputy Chief of Staff: Kathleen McGlynn
Communications Director: Ricki Seidman
Traveling Press Secretary: David Wade
Traveling Speechwriter: Jeff Nussbaum

FIGURE 14.1 Obama Campaign Organizational Chart The modern presidential campaign requires an incredible amount of organization and personnel, as is reflected in this organizational chart from President Barack Obama's 2008 campaign.

likely to be paying attention. Closer to Election Day, volunteers begin vital **get out the vote (GOTV)** efforts, calling and e-mailing supporters to remind them to vote and arranging for their transportation to the polls if necessary.

THE CANDIDATE'S PROFESSIONAL STAFF Nearly every campaign at the state and national level is run by a **campaign manager,** who coordinates and directs the campaign. The campaign manager is the person closest to the candidate, the person who delivers the good and bad news about the condition of the campaign and makes the essential day-to-day decisions, such as whom to hire and when to air which television advertisement. The campaign manager helps to determine the campaign's overall strategy, and equally important, works to keep the campaign on message throughout the race.

Most candidates also have one or more close personal advisers who may not have official titles and are not found on an organizational chart. These advisers, who could be the candidate's spouse or longtime friends and colleagues, have the candidate's ear and can influence decisions on strategy, tactics, and personnel.

Key paid positions in addition to the campaign manager, and depending on the race, include the **finance chair,** who is responsible for bringing in the large contributions that fund the campaign, the **pollster,** who takes public opinion surveys to learn what issues voters want candidates to address in speeches, and the **direct mailer,** who supervises direct mail fund-raising. The **communications director** develops the overall media strategy for the candidate, carefully blending press coverage with paid TV, radio, and mail media, not to mention advertisements on Web sites visited by those likely to favor the candidate's positions.

The **press secretary** is charged with interacting and communicating with journalists on a daily basis. It is the press secretary's job to be quoted in the newspapers or on TV explaining the candidate's positions or reacting to the actions of the opposing candidate. Good news is usually announced by the candidate. Bad news, including responding to attacks from the other side, is the preserve of the press secretary (better to have someone not on the ballot doing the dirty work of the campaign).

An indispensable part of modern political campaigns is the campaign's **Internet team,** which manages the campaign's communications, outreach, and fund-raising via the Internet, and increasingly tries to manage the candidate's online visibility. Members of the Internet team monitor and post on blogs popular with the party faithful, and they create candidate profiles intended for a more general audience on social networking sites.

Howard Dean's technology guru, Joe Trippi, took Internet campaigning to new levels in the 2004 election. Dean surged to an early lead in the polls, thanks in large part to Trippi's tremendously successful Internet-based fund-raising strategy and efforts at engaging supporters through a campaign blog and "meet-ups." Building on these successes, the candidates running for president in 2008 used the Internet in more innovative ways. Senator Hillary Rodham Clinton used her campaign Web site to post a video announcing her decision to run for president, to launch a campaign asking supporters to choose the campaign's theme song, and to conduct a series of live video Web chats with voters throughout the campaign. Senator Clinton and Governor Mitt Romney experimented extensively with Web-only ads that appeared on their Web sites and YouTube. And, Senator Barack Obama established the largest presence on numerous social networking sites, including registering support from over one million people on the campaign's own social network, MyObama.com.

Fund-raising remains the most valuable use of the Internet by political campaigns. Of the $55 million Senator Obama raised in February 2008, 90 percent of the contributions were raised over the Internet. Since making multiple appeals online for campaign contributions costs significantly less than raising funds through expensive direct-mail campaigns or pricey fund-raising events—the standard means of attaining campaign resources—the Internet is radically altering the way candidates raise funds and manage their campaigns.

get out the vote (GOTV)
A push at the end of a political campaign to encourage supporters to go to the polls.

campaign manager
The individual who travels with the candidate and coordinates the many different aspects of the campaign.

finance chair
A professional who coordinates the fund-raising efforts for the campaign.

pollster
A professional who takes public opinion surveys that guide political campaigns.

direct mailer
A professional who supervises a political campaign's direct mail fund-raising strategies.

communications director
The person who develops the overall media strategy for the candidate, blending free press coverage with paid TV, radio, and mail media.

press secretary
The individual charged with interacting and communicating with journalists on a daily basis.

Internet team
The campaign staff that makes use of Web-based resources to communicate with voters, raise funds, organize volunteers, and plan campaign events.

Does the Internet generate votes? Chris Hughes, one of the founding members of Facebook, developed the Obama campaign's social networking site, http://my.barackobama.com/. No evidence suggests that candidates who have more professional Web sites win more votes as a result. Some evidence suggests, however, that the size of a candidate's social network is associated with higher support at the polls. In most cases, the candidates' Internet presence is most important for fundraising and reinforcement of existing support.

Photo courtesy: Chicago Tribune by Phil Velasquez. All rights reserved. Used with permission.

campaign consultant
A private-sector professional who sells to a candidate the technologies, services, and strategies required to get that candidate elected.

media consultant
A professional who produces candidates' television, radio, and print advertisements.

You Are a Media Consultant to a Political Candidate

paid media
Political advertisements purchased for a candidate's campaign.

free media
Coverage of a candidate's campaign by the news media.

new media
New technologies, such as the Internet, that blur the line between paid and free media sources.

positive ad
Advertising on behalf of a candidate that stresses the candidate's qualifications, family, and issue positions, without reference to the opponent.

negative ad
Advertising on behalf of a candidate that attacks the opponent's platform or character.

THE CANDIDATE'S HIRED GUNS   Campaign consultants are the private-sector professionals and firms who sell the technologies, services, and strategies many candidates need to get elected. Consultants' numbers have grown exponentially since they first appeared in the 1930s, and their specialties and responsibilities have increased accordingly, to the point that campaign consultants are now an obligatory part of campaigns at the state and national level.[3] Candidates generally hire specialized consultants who focus on only one or two areas, such as fund-raising, polling, media relations, Internet outreach, and speech writing.

Media consultants design advertisements for distribution on TV, the Internet, radio, billboards, and flyers. More than one consultant or even an advertising company or two may be assigned to this fundamental part of the modern political campaign. The communications director, with frequent involvement from the campaign manager, pollster, and sometimes even the candidate, works with the media consultant to craft the campaign's advertising message and address key issues.

Coverage of the Game: The Media's Role in Defining the Playing Field

What voters actually see and hear of the candidate is primarily determined by the paid media, free media, and the new media. The **paid media,** are political advertisements or other pieces that the campaign creates and pays to have disseminated. The campaign staff and consultants determine the amount, form, and content of paid media. The **free media** are the stories about a campaign that news programs choose to broadcast, or newspapers and magazines choose to print, and which cost the campaign nothing. The **new media** are new technologies, such as the Internet, which blur the lines between paid and free media sources. The new media, made possible by a wide array of technological innovations, are generated in part by the campaign but are also driven by individuals from outside the campaign. These individuals may contribute to the candidate's existing online effort, maintain Web sites and groups on social networking sites, and write blogs about the candidate and his or her policies.

Paid Media

Within the media campaign, candidates and their media consultants decide on how to use the paid media, that is, which ads to air to support the campaign's strategies. **Positive ads** stress the candidate's qualifications, family and personal ties, and issue positions with no direct reference to the opponent. Positive ads are usually favored by the incumbent candidate. **Negative ads** attack the opponent's character and platform.

And, with the exception of the candidate's brief, legally required statement that he or she approved the ad, a negative ad may not even mention the candidate who is paying for the airing. **Contrast ads** compare the records and proposals of the candidates, with a bias toward the candidate sponsoring the ad.

While the lines between different types of ads are often blurry, a clear and classic example of one of the first negative advertisements aired in the 1964 presidential election. In an attempt to reinforce the view that his Republican challenger, Senator Barry Goldwater, held extreme views and would be reckless in office, President Lyndon B. Johnson's campaign produced a television ad called "Peace Little Girl" that showed a young girl counting the petals she was picking off a daisy. Once she said the number nine, a voice-over started counting down a missile launch that ended in images of a nuclear explosion and a mushroom cloud. The viewer then hears the president's voice saying, "These are the stakes," implying that the election of Goldwater would result in the destruction of the planet. The ad was considered so shocking and unfair that it was pulled after only one broadcast. Considerable discussion of the ad in the media, however, ensured that its point was made repeatedly to the electorate.

Most paid advertisements are short **spot ads** that range from ten to sixty seconds long. In a notable departure from this trend, Barack Obama purchased airtime the week before the 2008 election to broadcast a 30-minute advertisement intended to sway undecided voters.

Although negative advertisements have grown dramatically in number during the past two decades, they have been a part of American campaigns almost since the nation's founding. In 1796, Federalists portrayed presidential candidate Thomas Jefferson as an atheist and a coward. In Jefferson's bid for a second term in 1800, Federalists again attacked him, this time spreading a rumor that he was dead. The effects of negative advertising are well documented. Voters frequently vote *against* the other candidate, and negative ads can provide the critical justification for such a vote.

Before the 1980s, well-known incumbents usually ignored negative attacks from their challengers, believing that the proper stance was to be above the fray. But, after some well-publicized defeats of incumbents in the early 1980s in which negative television advertising played a prominent role,[4] incumbents began attacking their challengers in earnest. The new rule of politics became "An attack unanswered is an attack agreed to." In a further attempt to stave off brickbats from challengers, incumbents began anticipating the substance of their opponents' attacks and airing **inoculation ads** early in the campaign to protect themselves in advance from the other side's spots. Inoculation advertising attempts to counteract an anticipated attack from the opposition before such an attack is launched. For example, a senator who fears a broadside about her voting record on veterans' issues might air advertisements featuring veterans or their families praising her support.

Although paid advertising remains the most controllable aspect of a campaign's strategy, the news media are increasingly having an impact on it. Major newspapers throughout the country have taken to analyzing the accuracy of television advertisements aired during campaigns—a welcome and useful addition to journalists' scrutiny of politicians.

contrast ad
Ad that compares the records and proposals of the candidates, with a bias toward the sponsor.

spot ad
Television advertising on behalf of a candidate that is broadcast in sixty-, thirty-, or ten-second duration.

Television and Presidential Campaigns

inoculation ad
Advertising that attempts to counteract an anticipated attack from the opposition before the attack is launched.

When does a negative ad cross the line? President Lyndon B. Johnson's "Daisy Ad" broke new ground in negative campaigning by linking the election of Republican Barry Goldwater with nuclear holocaust. The ad was shown only once, but its negativity generated intense media attention that amounted to free airplay. In general, the public are more averse to negative ads that focus on personal issues rather than policy positions.

Photo courtesy: Lyndon Baines Johnson Library Collection

Thinking Globally

Campaign Advertising

In Brazil, candidates must buy advertising space in newspapers, but radio and television airtime is free and allocated equally among the registered political parties. In Guatemala, political parties and their candidates are entitled to free postal and telecommunications services beginning with the official calling of an election and ending one month after its conclusion.

- Should the United States provide free advertising access for political candidates? Why or why not?
- If free access to television and radio were extended to political candidates in the United States, how would such a change affect the campaign process? Would campaign strategy change as a result? If so, how?

**You Are a Campaign Manager:
Navigating Negativity: Help
Obama Handle Negative Attacks**

Free Media

While candidates have control over what advertisements are run (paid media), they have little control over how journalists will cover their campaign and convey it to voters. During campaign season, the news media constantly report political news. What they report is largely based on news editors' decisions of what is newsworthy or "fit to print." The press often reports what candidates are doing, such as giving speeches, holding fundraisers, or meeting with party leaders. Even better from the candidate's perspective, the news media may report on a candidate's success, perhaps giving that candidate the brand of a "winner," making him or her that much more difficult to beat. Reporters may also investigate rumors of a candidate's misdeeds or unflattering personal history, such as run-ins with the law, alleged use of drugs, or a failed marriage.

Analysts observe that not all media practices are conducive to fair and unbiased coverage of campaigns. For example, the news media often regard political candidates with suspicion—looking for possible deception even when a candidate is simply trying to share his or her message with the public. This attitude makes it difficult for candidates to explain their positions to the news media without being on the defensive. In addition, many studies have shown that the media are obsessed with the horse-race aspect of politics—who's ahead, who's behind, who's gaining—to the detriment of the substance of the candidates' issues and ideas. Public opinion polls, especially tracking polls, many of them taken by news outlets, dominate coverage, especially on network television, where only a few minutes a night are devoted to politics.[5]

The media's expectations can have an effect on how the public views the candidates. Using poll data, journalists often predict the margins by which they expect contenders to win or lose. A clear victory of 5 percentage points can be judged a setback if the candidate had been projected to win by 12 or 15 points. The tone of the media coverage—that a candidate is either gaining or losing support in polls—can affect whether people decide to give money and other types of support to a candidate.[6]

One final area in which the media tend to portray candidates in a biased way is in overemphasizing trivial parts of the campaign, such as a politician's minor gaffe, hairstyle, or wardrobe decisions. This superficial coverage displaces serious journalism on the issues. These subjects are discussed in detail in the next chapter, which deals specifically with the media.

The New Media

Since candidates began experimenting with electronic media to reach out directly to voters, the nature of campaigns has changed drastically. Labor-intensive community activities have been replaced by carefully targeted messages disseminated through the mass media, and candidates today are able to reach voters more quickly than at any time in our nation's history. The results of this technological transformation, which skyrocketed with the advent of personal computers and the Internet, are candidate-centered campaigns in which candidates build well-financed, finely tuned organizations centered around their personal aspirations, and political parties play a secondary role in the election process.

Contemporary campaigns have an impressive new array of weapons at their disposal: faster printing technologies, reliable data bases, instantaneous Internet publishing and mass e-mail, autodialed pre-recorded messages, video technology, and enhanced telecommunications and teleconferencing. As a result, candidates can gather and disseminate information more quickly and effectively than ever.

One outcome of these changes is the ability of candidates to employ "rapid-response" techniques: the formulation of prompt and informed responses to changing events on the campaign battlefield. In response to breaking news of a scandal or issue, for example, candidates can conduct background research, implement an opinion poll and tabulate the results, devise a containment strategy and appropriate "spin," and deliver a reply. This makes a strong contrast with the campaigns of the 1970s and early 1980s, dominated primarily by radio and TV advertisements, which took much longer to prepare and had little of the flexibility enjoyed by the contemporary e-campaign.[7]

In 2002, many candidates increasingly turned to recorded phone messages, or robo-calling, targeted to narrow constituencies. These messages have been used mainly to spread negative (and sometimes false) information about an opponent "under the radar" and frequently have raised the anger of the targeted candidate. But robo-calls also have been used to raise money and rally supporters. In 2008, both parties used politicians and celebrities to contact voters through prerecorded phone messages. Democrats heard from Scarlett Johansson and Jay–Z, for example, while Republicans heard from Governor Arnold Schwarzenegger. With consulting firms able to deliver 2,500 calls per minute at only six cents a call, robo-calling will continue to be common practice in campaign communication and mobilization.

The first use of the Internet in national campaigning came in 1992 when the Democratic presidential ticket of Bill Clinton and Al Gore maintained a Web site that stored electronic versions of their biographical summaries, speeches, press releases, and position papers. The Internet remained something of a virtual brochure until the 2000 elections, when candidates began using e-mail and their Web sites as vehicles for fund-raising, recruiting volunteers, and communicating with supporters. By 2006, most campaign Web sites featured downloadable and streaming video and were integrated into the candidate's overall communication and mobilization strategy. In 2008, all of the major candidates running for president and nearly 90 percent of the Democratic and Republican congressional candidates maintained a campaign Web site.

You Are a Campaign Manager: Voter Mobilization and Suppression: Political Dirty Tricks or Fair Games?

How have the new media affected campaigns? Representative Ron Paul (R–TX) was the last Republican candidate to withdraw from the 2008 Republican nomination campaign. Paul's folksy appeal and stance against the Iraq War generated a great deal of grassroots interest. His campaign set a record for most campaign funds raised over the Internet in a single day in early 2008. Up until the first week in March 2008, Paul had more supporters on Facebook than any other Republican candidate. Paul's anti-war stance drew support from across the ideological spectrum, but his opposition to the income tax, the federal reserve, and U.S. participation in the United Nations limited his electoral appeal. Online success is no substitute for a message that resonates with the majority of the public or at least a majority in your own party.

Even after a campaign has concluded, online networks can persist and keep supporters abreast of a candidate's future direction. After failing to win the 2004 presidential election, John Kerry was able to keep his base informed by maintaining his Web site and sending a steady flow of mass e-mails to supporters. After he endorsed Barack Obama for the Democratic presidential nomination, Kerry was able to use his e-mail contacts to assist the Obama campaign in expanding its e-mail list and potential pool of online donors.

With the advent of blogs, a candidate's Web site can take on a life of its own. Blogs enable supporters and the occasional stealthy opponent to post messages on the candidate's Web site and to engage in a nearly contemporaneous exchange of ideas with other supporters and with the candidate's Internet team. While it is possible that this form of dialogue can be empowering for supporters and encourage civic involvement, the way that candidates have used blogs calls this possibility into question. Most candidates who have a blog rarely offer live commentary, but rather post excerpts from recent speeches and press releases or have a moderator start a discussion. The moderator closely monitors comments in order to guide the discussion in a direction that conforms to the campaign's larger communication strategy. The lack of authenticity on most blogs and inability to control the message has made it difficult for candidates' blogs to have any real impact on a campaign.

The newest Internet tools to have emerged in campaigns are social networking sites such as Facebook and MySpace, which allow candidates to cultivate a sense of community and build a personal network of supporters. Since the 2006 midterm elections, social networking sites have created a space for candidates to develop personal profiles that allow them to list their professional qualifications and personal interests, share photographs, post campaign updates, and host free-flowing discussion forums. Members of the network can become supporters of the candidate and then receive updates, contribute content, and interact with other supporters. It is still an open question, however, whether candidate support on social networking sites can be transformed into offline activism and, ultimately, votes for the candidate.

Campaign Strategies to Control Media Coverage

Candidates, of course, want favorable media coverage but realize that they can afford to buy only a limited amount of coverage. Moreover, voters consider the news media more credible sources of information than paid advertisements or what they read on a candidate's or party's Web site. In an effort to obtain favorable coverage, candidates and their media consultants use various strategies to attempt to influence the press.

First, the campaign staff members often seek to isolate the candidate from the press, thus reducing the chances that reporters will bait a candidate into saying something that might damage his or her cause. Naturally, journalists are frustrated by such a tactic, and they demand open access to candidates.

Second, the campaign stages media events: activities designed to include brief, clever quotes called *sound bites* and staged with appealing backdrops so that they will be covered on the television news and in the newspaper. In this fashion, the candidate's staff can successfully fill the news hole reserved for campaign coverage. In this area, the incumbent president always has a tremendous advantage. The president's news events are almost always newsworthy and consequently covered by the mainstream press.

Third, campaign staff and consultants have cultivated a technique termed *spin*— they put forward the most favorable possible interpretation for their candidate (and the most negative for their opponent) on any circumstance occurring in the campaign, and they work the press to sell their point of view or at least to ensure that it is included in the reporters' stories. In the days following the nominating contests on Super Tuesday, both the Obama and Clinton campaigns tried to declare that their candidate was the "winner" and had the momentum going forward. The Obama team

Photo courtesy: Bettmann/Corbis

Photo courtesy: Frederick Bredon IV/UPI/Landov

pointed to the fact that he had won more delegates and more states than Senator Clinton, including states that he was not expected to win, such as Missouri, Connecticut, and Delaware. The Clinton campaign countered that she had won more popular votes, all the larger states except for Obama's native Illinois, and three important "Red" States—Arkansas, Oklahoma, and Tennessee—that demonstrated her appeal in the general election.

Fourth, candidates have found ways to circumvent the news media by appearing on talk shows such as *The Oprah Winfrey Show*, *The Tyra Banks Show*, and *Larry King Live*, where they have an opportunity to present their views and answer questions in a less critical forum. They also make regular appearances on comedy shows, such as *Saturday Night Live*, *The Late Show*, the *Daily Show*, and the *Colbert Report*. Former Senator Fred Thompson announced his candidacy for the 2008 Republican nomination during an interview with Jay Leno on *The Tonight Show*.

Candidate debates are a surprisingly recent aspect of presidential elections and were not a staple of electoral politics until the twentieth century. The first face-to-face presidential debate in U.S. history did not occur until 1960, and face-to-face debates did not become a regular part of presidential campaigns until the 1980s. However, they are now an established feature of presidential campaigns, as well as races for governor, U.S. senator, and many other offices, and serve as a fifth means by which campaigns seek to control (or at least to influence) media coverage. (To learn more about the impact of debates, see Ideas into Action: Presidential Debates.)

Candidates and their staffs recognize the importance of debates as a tool not only for consolidating their voter base but also for correcting misperceptions about the candidate's suitability for office. However, while candidates have complete control over what they say in debates, they do not have control over what the news media will highlight and focus on after the debates. Therefore, even though candidates prepare themselves by rehearsing their responses, they cannot avoid the perils of spontaneity. Errors or slips of the tongue in a debate can affect election outcomes. President Gerald R. Ford's erroneous insistence during an October 1976 debate with Jimmy Carter that Poland was not under Soviet domination (when in fact it was) may have cost him a close election. George Bush's bored expression and watch gazing during his 1992 debate with Bill Clinton certainly did not help Bush's electoral hopes. In an effort to put the best possible spin on debates, teams of consultants and staffers for each participant swarm the press rooms to declare victory even before their candidates finish their closing statements.

In most cases, however, debates do not alter the results of an election, but rather increase knowledge about the candidates and their respective personalities and issue positions, especially among voters who had not previously paid attention to the campaign.

How have the rules and format for presidential debates changed since the first televised debates? Presidential debates have come a long way since an ill-at-ease Richard M. Nixon was visually bested by John F. Kennedy in the first set of televised debates. John McCain and Barack Obama's second debate in 2008 was in a town meeting format, where the candidates responded to questions directly posed by audience members.

candidate debate
Forum in which political candidates face each other to discuss their platforms, records, and character.

Presidential Debates

Since the nation's first televised presidential debate in 1960, debates have offered the American electorate a unique opportunity to see and hear presidential candidates. They are a means by which millions of Americans gather information regarding each candidate's personality and platform. Recognizing the profound educational value of these debates to the voting public, the Commission on Presidential Debates was established in 1987.

The commission's formal charge is to ensure that debates are a permanent part of every general election and that they provide the best possible information to viewers and listeners. The last five presidential elections have included twenty-one debates sponsored by the commission, seventeen of which have been held on college campuses. In 2008, the University of Mississippi, Washington University in St. Louis, Belmont University in Nashville, and Hofstra University were the sites for the presidential debates sponsored by the commission.

Prospective debate hosts must conform to a rigorous set of criteria encompassing a broad range of categories, including the physical structure of the debate hall, adequate transportation and lodging networks, and the ability to raise over half a million dollars to cover production costs.

- Why would a college or university go through so much trouble to host a presidential debate, especially since only a relatively small percentage of students are able to attend, and an even smaller percentage of students are permitted to ask candidates questions?

- Would it serve the public interest if the Commission on Presidential Debates invited the leading third-party candidates to participate in one or more of the debates? Explain your reasoning.

- To access a complete video archive of the 2008 presidential and vice presidential debates, post-debate media commentary, and behind-the-scenes footage, go to C-SPAN's 2008 Vote: Presidential Debates at **www.c-span.org/resources/index.asp**.

- Go to the Museum of Broadcast Communication's History of Televised Debates, and view a few video clips from past presidential debates. Pay special attention to the candidates' rhetoric and how they attempt to persuade voters. What patterns do you see? Do candidates tend to persuade mostly by appealing to reason, to character and credibility, or to emotion?

Source: Commission on Presidential Debates, www.debates.org.

The Rules of the Game: Campaign Finance

Successful campaigns require a great deal of money. Nearly $2 billion was raised by the Democratic and Republican parties in 2008, setting a record for the national parties. In 2004, the two parties raised over $1.6 billion, a 24 percent increase in receipts over the totals of the 2000 election cycle. Presidential candidates in 2008 raised over $1.1 billion in support of their campaigns. Barack Obama, who decided to forgo public financing, raised almost $700 million (a new record in presidential fund-raising), with over 90 percent of his total coming from 3.2 million individual donors. John McCain raised almost $400 million, with around half coming from individual donors and $84 million coming from federal matching funds. The 30 incumbents in the Senate running for reelection raised an average of $6.4 million through September. Their challengers, in contrast, raised an average of $2.5 million.[8] As humorist Will Rogers once remarked early in the twentieth century, "Politics has got so expensive that it takes lots of money even to get beat with." (To learn more about Barack Obama's decision to opt out of public financing, see Politics Now: Is the Public Financing System Broken?)

While the amount expended in a single election season has recently increased, in the past the cost of elections in the United States has been less than or approximately the same as in some other nations if measured on a per-voter basis. For example, the per capita cost of Canada's 2004 elections is estimated at almost $9 per person, whereas in the United States it was around $5.50.[9]

Source: NEW YORK TIMES   June 20, 2008

Is the Public Financing System Broken?

Obama, in Shift, Says He'll Reject Public Financing

MICHAEL LUO AND JEFF ZELENY

Citing the specter of attacks from independent groups on the right, Senator Barack Obama announced Thursday that he would opt out of the public financing system for the general election. His decision to break an earlier pledge to take public money will quite likely transform the landscape of presidential campaigns, injecting hundreds of millions of additional dollars into the race and raising doubts about the future of public financing for national races.

In becoming the first major party candidate to reject public financing and its attendant spending limits, Mr. Obama contended that the public financing apparatus was broken and that his Republican opponents were masters at "gaming" the system and would spend "millions and millions of dollars in unlimited donations" smearing him. But it is not at all clear at this point in the evolving campaign season that Republicans will have the advantage when it comes to support from independent groups. In fact, the Democrats appear much better poised to benefit from such efforts. Republican activists have been fretting about the absence so far of any major independent effort, comparable to Swift Boat Veterans for Truth, which helped undermine Senator John Kerry's campaign in 2004, to boost Senator John McCain, the presumed Republican nominee, who has badly trailed Mr. Obama in raising money. . . .

Mr. Obama's decision, which had long been expected given his record-breaking money-raising prowess during the Democratic primary season, was immediately criticized by Mr. McCain, who confirmed Thursday that he would accept public financing. "This is a big, big deal," said Mr. McCain, of Arizona, who was touring flooded areas in Iowa. "He has completely reversed himself and gone back, not on his word to me, but the commitment he made to the American people.". . .

According to aides, Mr. Obama reached his decision knowing he might tarnish his desired reformist image—he pledged last year to accept public financing if his opponent did as well—but strategists for the campaign made the calculation that it was worth it, in part, because of the potential for the Republican National Committee to seriously outraise its Democratic counterpart. The Republican committee finished May with nearly $54 million in the bank, compared with just $4 million for the Democratic National Committee. . . .

Mr. Obama, who has sharply criticized the influence of money in politics and has barred contributions from federal lobbyists and political action committees to his campaign and the party, announced his decision Thursday in a videotaped message to supporters. He argued that the tens of thousands of small donors who had fueled his campaign over the Internet represented a "new kind of politics," free from the influence of special interests. The Obama campaign highlighted Thursday the fact that 93 percent of the more than 3 million contributions it had received were for $200 or less. But Mr. Obama has also benefited from a formidable high-dollar network that has collected more money in contributions of $1,000 or more than even Senator Hillary Rodham Clinton's once-vaunted team of bundlers of donations. . . .

Mr. Obama, however, cast his decision on Thursday as a necessary counter to unscrupulous supporters of Mr. McCain's. "We've already seen that he's not going to stop the smears and attacks from his allies' running so-called 527 groups, who will spend millions and millions of dollars in unlimited donations," Mr. Obama said.

Mr. McCain has been highly critical in the past of 527s and other independent groups, but he seems to have softened his rhetoric lately, saying his campaign could not be expected to "referee" such groups. Nevertheless, Republican strategists said many affluent donors who might be in a position to finance 527 groups were wary this time because of the legal headaches that bedeviled many of these groups after the 2004 election, as well as the possibility they might incur the wrath of Mr. McCain.

Discussion Questions

1. *Considering the spending not only by the candidates but also by the major parties' national committees and groups like the 527s, were the presidential campaigns more or less equally competitive?*

2. *What are the likely long-term implications for the public financing system given President Obama's campaign decision? Are future presidential candidates more or less likely to forgo public financing? Explain your reasoning.*

The Road to Reform

The United States has struggled to achieve effective campaign finance rules for well over one hundred years. One early attempt to regulate the way candidates raise campaign resources was enacted in 1883, when Congress passed civil service reform legislation that prohibited solicitation of political funds from federal workers, attempting to halt a corrupt and long-held practice. In 1907, the Tillman Act prohibited corporations from making direct contributions to candidates for federal office. The Corrupt

Thinking Globally

Campaign Finance in Japan

In contrast to multimillion-dollar U.S. political campaigns, direct expenses for the comparatively short campaigns before Japanese elections are relatively modest. The use of campaign posters and pamphlets is strictly regulated, candidates appear on Japan's noncommercial public television station to give short campaign speeches, and neither candidates nor political parties may advertise in the mass media until twelve days before an election. Unlike in the United States, most of this campaign activity is publicly funded.

- What are the advantages and disadvantages of a more regulated campaign system such as the one in place in Japan?
- Does public funding for an election make the process more fair? Why or why not?

Practices Acts (1910, 1911, and 1925), Hatch Act (1939), and Taft-Hartley Act (1947) all attempted to regulate the manner in which federal candidates finance their campaigns and to some extent limit the corrupting influence of campaign spending.

In the early 1970s, Congress enacted its most ambitious round of campaign laws to date. The Federal Election Campaign Act (FECA) and its later amendments established disclosure requirements, established the Presidential Public Funding Program, which provides partial public funding for presidential candidates who meet certain criteria, and created the Federal Election Commission (FEC), an independent federal agency tasked with enforcing the nation's election laws.

The most recent round of reforms was set in motion by Senators John McCain (R–AZ) and Russell Feingold (D–WI). McCain ran for the 2000 Republican presidential nomination on a platform to ban unregulated soft-money contributions and to take elections out of the hands of the wealthy. McCain lost to George W. Bush, who ironically used soft money in the primaries to defeat McCain. However, McCain's credibility on the issue skyrocketed. Once corporate soft-money donors at Enron, WorldCom, and Global Crossing (to name a few) became embroiled in accounting scandals and alleged criminal behavior, the issue of electoral corruption became too pervasive for Congress to ignore. McCain and Feingold co-sponsored the Bipartisan Campaign Reform Act (BCRA) of 2002 in the Senate, while Representatives Chris Shays (R–CT) and Martin Meehan (D–MA) sponsored the House version. On Valentine's Day, the bills passed, and in March 2002, President George W. Bush signed BCRA into law. Included within BCRA was a "fast track" provision that any suits challenging the constitutionality of the reforms would be immediately placed before a U.S. district court, and giving appellate powers to the U.S. Supreme Court. The reason for this provision was simple: to thwart the numerous lobbying groups and several high-profile elected officials who threatened to tie up BCRA in the courts for as long as they could. No sooner did President Bush sign BCRA than U.S. Senator Mitch McConnell (R–KY) and the National Rifle Association separately filed lawsuits claiming that the BCRA violated free speech rights.

In a 5–4 decision in *McConnell* v. *Federal Election Commission* (2003), the U.S. Supreme Court held that the government's interest in preventing corruption overrides the free speech rights to which the parties would otherwise be entitled and, thus, found that BCRA's restrictions on soft-money donations and political advertising did not violate free speech rights.[10] In *Federal Election Commission v. Wisconsin Right to Life* (2007), however, the Supreme Court invalidated BCRA's strict ban on genuine issue ads during the "blackout" period on the grounds that the timing of the ad does not automatically designate it as electioneering.[11] These two cases indicate that the Supreme Court has very narrowly upheld the BCRA measures restricting speech both in the form of political contributions (soft money) and in political advertising, but also has opened the door to challenges to how the Federal Election Commission will enforce BCRA. (To learn more about campaign finance and free speech concerns, see the Living Constitution.)

Current Rules

The Supreme Court's *McConnell* decision in 2003 means that political money is now regulated by the federal government under the terms of the BCRA, which supplanted most of the provisions of the Federal Election Campaign Act. The BCRA outlaws

The Living Constitution

Congress shall make no law . . . abridging the freedom of speech.

FIRST AMENDMENT

When the nation's Framers set about writing the Constitution and the Bill of Rights, they were not specific in their definition of free speech in the First Amendment. Therefore it has been up to subsequent Congresses, presidents, Supreme Courts, and others to interpret and expand on their very simple, elegant statement. Today, we have an elaborate campaign finance system that tries to balance free speech with the need to prevent political corruption. The Supreme Court has repeatedly addressed that difficult balance in cases such as *Buckley* v. *Valeo* (1976) and *McConnell* v. *Federal Election Commission* (2003).

Essentially, the Framers looked at campaigning as crass and beneath the dignity of office holders. At least theoretically, they believed that the office should seek the person, although in practice many of them were very ambitious and intensely sought high elected office. They did not do so in the context of a mass electorate, but rather by means of the aristocratic gentry that acted through the Electoral College to select the president and vice president.

In this era of ultra-democracy, when everyone expects to have a voice, the system must operate very differently. As a result, candidates campaign by raising hundreds of millions of dollars, visiting television studio after television studio for news coverage, holding media events, taping paid television and radio advertisements, and using the Internet for communication with their supporters. The candidates' free speech is augmented by the free speech of those interested in seeing one candidate elected and the other defeated in a particular race. Thus, political parties raise money and carry out organizational and electioneering activities as described in chapter 12.

Also being heard are political action committees (PACs)—the contributing arms of special interest groups on the left, on the right, and in the middle. And, because of loopholes in the Bipartisan Campaign Reform Act of 2002, there are 527 and 501(c) committees, which form to attack candidates through television and radio ads as well as individual voter contact. Finally, there are completely independent political committees that can raise and spend whatever they want, for whatever interests they support—so long as they have no direct or indirect contact with any campaign organizations.

It is amazing that all of these aspects have developed from the powerful words of the First Amendment regarding free speech. The Framers could hardly have imagined what massive enterprises campaigns would become, and what the few words they penned on parchment would create with the passing of two centuries.

CRITICAL THINKING QUESTIONS

1. How might increased public financing of campaigns, including support to congressional candidates and the political parties, increase citizens' engagement and participation in the political process while limiting the influence of "special interests?"
2. In general, when evaluating wealthy candidates who finance their own campaigns, would you consider them more likely or less likely to be responsive to a wider group of citizens and to serve the public interest? Explain your reasoning.

---

unlimited and unregulated contributions to parties, known as **soft money,** and limits the amounts that individuals, interest groups, and political parties can give to candidates for president, U.S. senator, and U.S. representative. (To learn more about contribution limits, see Table 14.1.) The goal of all limits is the same: to prevent any single group or individual from gaining too much influence over elected officials, who naturally feel indebted to campaign contributors.

soft money
The virtually unregulated money funneled by individuals and political committees through state and local parties.

TABLE 14.1 Individual Contribution Limits per Election Cycle Before and After Bipartisan Campaign Reform Act (2002)

	Before	After[a]
Contributions per candidate	$1,000	$2,300
Contributions per national party committee	$20,000	$38,500
Total contributions per 2-year cycle	$50,000	$108,200
Soft money	Unlimited	Banned

[a]These limits are for 2007–2008. BCRA limits are adjusted in odd-numbered years to account for inflation.
Source: Campaign Finance Institute, http://www.cfinst.org/studies/ElectionAfterReform/pdf/EAR_Appendix1.pdf.

INDIVIDUAL CONTRIBUTIONS Individual contributions are donations from individual citizens. The maximum allowable contribution under federal law for congressional and presidential elections was $2,300 per election to each candidate in 2007–2008, with primary and general elections considered separately. Individuals in 2007–2008 were also limited to a total of $108,200 in gifts to all candidates, political action committees, and parties combined per two-year election cycle. These limits will rise at the rate of inflation in subsequent cycles. Most candidates receive a majority of all funds directly from individuals, and most individual gifts are well below the maximum level. Finally, individuals who spend over $10,000 to air "electioneering communication," that is, "any broadcast, cable, or satellite communication which refers to a clearly identified candidate for Federal office" within sixty days of a general election or thirty days of a primary election, are now subject to a strict disclosure law. The rationale behind this regulation is that spending on an ad favoring a candidate is effectively the same as a contribution to the candidate's campaign and requires the same scrutiny as other large donations.[12]

political action committee (PAC) Federally mandated, officially registered fund-raising committee that represents interest groups in the political process.

POLITICAL ACTION COMMITTEE (PAC) CONTRIBUTIONS When interest groups such as labor unions, corporations, trade unions, and ideological issue groups seek to make donations to campaigns, they must do so by establishing **political action committees (PACs)**. PACs are officially recognized fund-raising organizations that are allowed by federal law to participate in federal elections. (Some states have similar requirements for state elections.) Under current rules, a PAC can give no more than $5,000 per candidate per election (primary, general, and special election), and $15,000 each year to each of the units of the national parties.

Approximately 4,000 PACs are registered with the FEC. In 2006, PACs contributed $359 million to Senate and House candidates, while individuals donated $785 million. On average, PAC contributions accounted for 37 percent of the war chests (campaign funds) of House candidates and 14 percent of the treasuries of Senate candidates. Incumbents benefit the most from PAC money; incumbents received $289 million, much more than the $70 million given to challengers during the 2006 election cycle.[13] By making these contributions, PACs hope to secure entrée to candidates after they have been elected in order to influence them on issues important to the PAC, since they might reciprocate campaign donations with loyalty to the cause. Corporate PACs give primarily to incumbents because incumbents tend to win, and lobbyists want to guarantee access for their clients. Single-issue and more ideologically based PACs are often willing to support challengers and more untried candidates who pledge to support their positions if elected.[14]

Because donations from a small number of PACs make up such a large proportion of campaign war chests, PACs have influence disproportionate to that of individuals. In an attempt to control PACs, the BCRA has a limit on the way PACs attempt to influence campaigns. The law strictly forbids PACs from using corporate or union funds for the electioneering communications discussed earlier. PACs can use corporate or labor contributions only for administrative costs. The purpose of this rule is to prevent corporations or unions from having an undue influence on the outcome of elections by heavily advertising toward specific audiences in the weeks leading up to elections.

PACs remain one of the most controversial parts of the campaign financing process. Some observers claim that PACs are the embodiment of corrupt special interests that use campaign donations to buy the votes of legislators. Studies, in fact, have shown that PACs effectively use contributions to punish legislators and affect policy, at least in the short run.[15] Legislators who vote contrary to the wishes of a PAC see their donations withheld, but those who are successful in legislating as the PAC wishes are rewarded with even greater donations.[16] However, contribution limits keep the influence of PACs to $5,000 per candidate per year, and while this amount may substantially aid an incumbent's reelection, it pales in comparison to the total budget required for victory in federal elections.

Some critics of PAC influence also argue that the less affluent and minority members of society do not enjoy equal access to these political organizations. These charges are serious and deserve consideration. Although the media relentlessly stress the role of money in determining policy outcomes, the evidence that PACs buy votes is not well supported by research.[17] Political scientists have conducted many studies to determine the impact of interest group PAC contributions on legislative voting, and the conclusions reached by these studies have varied widely.[18] Whereas some studies have found that PAC money affects legislators' voting behavior, other studies have uncovered no such correlation. It may be, of course, that interest group PAC money has an impact at earlier stages of the legislative process. One innovative study found that PAC money had a significant effect on legislators' participation in congressional committees on legislation important to the contributing group.[19] Thus, interest group PAC money may mobilize something more important than votes—the valuable time and energy of members of Congress.

Although a good number of PACs of all persuasions existed prior to the 1970s, it was during the 1970s—the decade of campaign finance reform—that the modern PAC era began. PACs grew in number from 113 in 1972 to a peak of 4,268 in 1988 and have remained near that number over the past twenty years. However, their contributions to congressional candidates have multiplied almost thirty-fold, from $8.5 million in 1971 and 1972 to $330 million in 2006. But, these numbers should not obscure a basic truth about the PAC system: that a very small group of PACs conducts the bulk of total PAC activity. A mere 5 percent of all PACs have contributed about 60 percent of the total dollars given to congressional candidates by PACs during recent election cycles.[20]

Although the widespread use of the PAC structure is relatively new, special-interest money of all types has always found its way into politics. Before the 1970s, it did so in less traceable and much more disturbing and unsavory ways, because little of the money given to candidates was regularly disclosed to public inspection. Although it is true that PACs contribute a massive sum to candidates in absolute terms as shown in Figure 14.2, it is not clear that there is proportionately more interest group money in the system than earlier. The proportion of House and Senate campaign funds provided by PACs has certainly increased since the early 1970s, but individuals, most of whom are unaffiliated with PACs, together with the political parties still supply more than 60 percent of all the money spent by or on behalf of House candidates, 75 percent of the campaign expenditures for Senate contenders, and 85 percent of the campaign expenditures for presidential candidates.[21] So, while the importance of PAC spending has grown, PACs clearly remain secondary as a source of election funding and therefore pose less of a threat to the system's legitimacy than is generally believed.

POLITICAL PARTY CONTRIBUTIONS Candidates also receive donations from the national and state committees of the Democratic and Republican Parties. As mentioned in chapter 12, political parties can give substantial contributions to their congressional

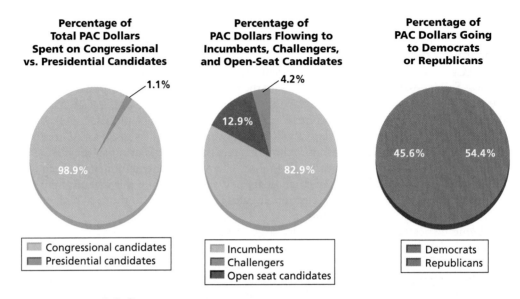

FIGURE 14.2 Expenditures by PACs in the 2008 Election Cycle

PACs contributed approximately $29 million to candidates competing in the 2008 election cycle.

Source: Federal Election Commission, http://www.fec.gov; Center for Responsive Politics, http://www.opensecrets.org/lobby.

nominees. Under the current rules, national parties can give up to $5,000 to a House candidate in the general election and $39,900 to a Senate candidate. In 2006, the Republican and Democratic parties funneled over $768 million to their standard-bearers, via direct contributions and coordinated expenditures. In competitive races, the parties may provide 15–17 percent of their candidates' total war chests.

MEMBER-TO-CANDIDATE CONTRIBUTIONS In Congress and in state legislatures, well-funded, electorally secure incumbents often contribute campaign money to their party's needy incumbent and non-incumbent legislative candidates.[22] This activity began in some state legislatures (notably California), but it is now well-established at the congressional level.[23] Generally, members contribute to other candidates by establishing their own PACs—informally dubbed "leadership" PACs—through which they distribute campaign support to candidates. In the 2006 general election cycle, 256 members of Congress established leadership PACs and contributed over $32 million to other candidates. A PAC established by Senator Barbara Boxer (D–CA), for example, contributed $71,500 to Democratic House candidates and $161,000 to Democrats running for Senate seats. Boxer's PAC spent nearly $300,000 in an attempt to help the Democrats win back the Senate and House.[24]

In general, members give their contributions to the same candidates who receive the bulk of congressional campaign committee resources. Thus, member contributions at the congressional level have emerged as a major supplement to the campaign resources contributed by the party campaign committees.[25]

CANDIDATES' PERSONAL CONTRIBUTIONS Candidates and their families may donate to the campaign. The U.S. Supreme Court ruled in *Buckley* v. *Valeo* (1976) that no limit could be placed on the amount of money candidates can spend from their own families' resources, since such spending is considered a First Amendment right of free speech.[26] (See Join the Debate: Campaign Finance: Freedom of Speech or License to Corrupt.) For wealthy politicians, this allowance may mean personal spending in the millions. For example, Mitt Romney spent a record $42 million of his own money in his failed quest for the 2008 Republican presidential nomination. In

2006, the top two self-financers were candidates for the Senate, Republican Pete Ricketts of Nebraska and Democrat Ned Lamont of Connecticut. Both lost their bids despite each spending over $10 million of their own money on their campaigns. While Lamont ran a competitive campaign, Ricketts only managed to receive 36 percent of the vote against incumbent Democrat Ben Nelson. While self-financed candidates often garner a great deal of attention, most candidates commit much less than $100,000 in family resources to their election bids.[27]

PUBLIC FUNDS **Public funds** are donations from general tax revenues to the campaigns of qualifying candidates. Only presidential candidates (and a handful of state and local contenders) receive public funds. Under the terms of the FECA (which first established public funding of presidential campaigns), a candidate for president can become eligible to receive public funds during the nominating contest by raising at least $5,000 in individual contributions of $250 or less in each of twenty states. The candidate can apply for federal **matching funds,** whereby every dollar raised from individuals in amounts less than $251 is matched by the federal treasury on a dollar-for-dollar basis. Of course, this assumes there is enough money in the Presidential Election Campaign Fund to do so. The fund is accumulated by taxpayers who designate $3 of their taxes for this purpose each year when they send in their federal tax returns. (Only about 20 percent of taxpayers check off the appropriate box, even though participation does not increase their tax burden.) During the 2008 primaries, all of the major candidates except John Edwards opted out of the federal matching funds, allowing them to raise considerably more money than the government would have provided.

For the general election, the two major-party presidential nominees can accept an $85 million lump-sum payment from the federal government after the candidate accepts his or her nomination. If the candidate accepts the money, it becomes the sole source for financing the campaign. A candidate may refuse the money and be free from the spending cap the government attaches to it, as Barack Obama did in 2008, subsequently setting a record for the most spent by a candidate for a presidential campaign.

A third-party candidate receives a smaller amount proportionate to his or her November vote total if that candidate gains a minimum of 5 percent of the vote. Note that in such a case, the money goes to third-party campaigns only *after* the election is over; no money is given in advance of the general election. Only two third-party candidates have qualified for public campaign funding: John B. Anderson in 1980 after gaining 7 percent of the vote, and Texas billionaire Ross Perot in 1992 after gaining 19 percent of the vote.

public funds
Donations from the general tax revenues to the campaigns of qualifying presidential candidates.

matching funds
Donations to presidential campaigns from the federal government that are determined by the amount of private funds a qualifying candidate raises.

The Main Event: The 2008 Presidential Campaign

The 2008 election may go down in history for being one of the nation's longest and most contentious electoral marathons. The outcome was a source of anxiety not only for millions of Americans, but also for people around the globe, many of whom viewed America's presidential choice as a referendum on George W. Bush's policies abroad. Senator Barack Obama, the 47-year-old Democratic nominee for president, initially was unable to capitalize fully on the fundamental advantages that favored the Democratic Party. Many Americans were unsure whether Obama had the experience to serve in the nation's highest office at a time of global economic instability and threats to national security. Despite his years of experience in Congress and military service, Americans also expressed doubts about 72-year-old Senator John McCain, the Republican Party's nominee. Many were unsure that McCain could understand the plight of

Join the Debate

Campaign Finance: Freedom of Speech or License to Corrupt?

OVERVIEW: Campaigns are not free. A candidate has to employ an army of staff to engage in a number of activities, from scheduling campaign stops to ordering pizza deliveries. Unless a candidate is massively wealthy, the money to pay for campaign staff and services has to come from other people, namely donors. Aside from the instrumental value of money, there is a symbolic value. Many donors believe that their contributions make a statement about their beliefs. The question is, therefore, whether campaign finance regulations are merely controlling the sources and use of money to prevent political corruption or are also prohibiting the right to free speech that belongs to all Americans.

Both the National Rifle Association and the American Civil Liberties Union agree that the regulation of campaign contributions amounts to a government violation of the very rights the government is supposed to protect. If organizations wish to air ads on behalf of an issue that interests them, then they should be able to do so under the First Amendment. Organizations such as Common Cause, however, say that the problem with the "money equals speech" argument is that money actually replaces speech. Too often, groups lacking funds are squeezed out of meetings with elected officials, who need the money for reelection more than they need to hear about the complaints of constituents.

Disallowing organizations from engaging in the political process is by definition an infringement of political freedom, but perhaps it was a freedom so thoroughly abused that it had to be taken away to protect the republic. Furthermore, there is no guarantee that increasing government regulation will make the process any more democratic. The scope of campaign finance is broad, and the implications of regulating it are far reaching. While the Supreme Court upheld the ban on soft money in the recent Bipartisan Campaign Reform Act of 2002, it continues to give limited free-speech protections to campaign contributors, including interest groups who produce express advocacy ads under the guise of issue advocacy. Still, many interest groups believe that recent legislation limits free-speech rights and are concerned that Congress may move to limit advocacy and communication on the Internet in the near future.

Arguments IN FAVOR of Campaign Finance Reform

- A government beholden to a small group of wealthy and mobilized interests is, by definition, an oligarchy and undemocratic. With millions of dollars to spare, large organizations such as unions and corporations can control candidate agendas by demanding loyalty in exchange for donations. The result is that a candidate, once elected, represents not ordinary constituents but those who got him or her elected. This is nothing more than bribery.

- Prohibiting large organizations from dominating the attention of elected officials creates greater grassroots political involvement. If candidates cannot count on big donors to finance their elections, they will have to find ways of appealing to larger numbers of people. That forces candidates back into their local communities to listen to their concerns and promise to address them. Then, communities can organize to fund-

ordinary Americans and resolve the major problems of the day; others worried about McCain's age—he would be the oldest man ever to be elected president if he won the election. Polls taken throughout the summer and fall of 2008 showed nearly 10 percent of Americans undecided between Senators Obama and McCain. Another 15 percent claimed that they could switch their support before Election Day.

The Party Nomination Battles

With no incumbent president or vice president running for reelection, the nomination contests in both parties drew a crowded field of candidates. The Democrats had former Iowa Governor Tom Vilsack; Representative Dennis Kucinich (OH); former senator and the party's 2004 vice presidential nominee, John Edwards (NC); Senator

raise for certain candidates. The winner is bound to address the local community's interests, which is what representative government is supposed to do in the first place.

- Campaign finance reform opens up the door for new challengers. Curbing the influence of wealthy interests creates a more even playing field for candidates. If incumbents must run against strong challengers, they become more accountable and, if necessary, more easily replaced.

Arguments AGAINST Campaign Finance Reform

- Campaign contributions are political speech, the most hallowed and protected speech under the First Amendment. All Americans have a right to freely state their political beliefs; just because one group has more money than another doesn't make a difference.

- Bureaucracy is never the better answer to a market-driven problem. While the intentions behind campaign finance reform are usually good, they are based on the assumption that the way to solve political problems is through regulations. More regulations create a forever expanding labyrinth of quickly out-of-date rules that only years of debate and wrangling will fix, followed by

implementing more quickly outgrown rules requiring another round of wrangling. Regulation is a dog chasing its tail.

- Campaign finance reform actually assists incumbents, not challengers. Incumbents benefit from free media, since they have name recognition and greater credibility from their experience "on the Hill." A challenger needs money to counteract this and other advantages of incumbency. Regulating campaign finance limits a challenger's competitiveness, making the government less democratic as a result.

Continuing the Debate

1. Can money, in the form of campaign contributions, be considered protected speech under the First Amendment? Why or why not?
2. Is it more democratic to centralize control of elections in order to allow more interests to be heard, or to let interests compete for attention without government interference? Explain your reasoning.

Photo courtesy: Dennis Cook/AP/Wide World Photos

How Bipartisan was the Bipartisan Campaign Reform Act of 2002? Senators Russell Feingold (D–WI) and John McCain (R–AZ) celebrate passage of the Bipartisan Campaign Reform Act in March of 2002. In the House of Representatives, only 41 of 217 Republicans voted for the bill, while 198 of 210 Democrats voted for the bill.

To Follow the Debate Online Go To:

The Campaign Finance Institute, www.cfinst.org/

The Cato Institute, www.cato.org/ researchareas.php

The Brookings Institution, www.brookings.edu/topics/campaign-finance.aspx

Joe Biden (DE); Senator Chris Dodd (CT); New Mexico Governor Bill Richardson; and former Senator Mike Gravel (AK). The most anticipated announcements came in February when first-term Senator Barack Obama (IL) and former First Lady and two-term Senator Hillary Clinton (NY) announced their candidacies.

The initial field of candidates for the Republicans was even larger. Senator Sam Brownback (KS) led the way with an announcement in January 2007. He would soon be joined by Senator John McCain (AZ); Representatives Duncan Hunter (CA), Ron Paul (TX), and Tom Tancredo (CO); former New York City Mayor Rudolph Giuliani; former Governors James Gilmore (VA); Mike Huckabee (AR), Mitt Romney (MA), and Tommy Thompson (WI); former Ambassador Alan Keyes; and businessman John Cox. Former Senator Fred Thompson (TN) became the thirteenth candidate when he announced his candidacy on the *Tonight Show* with Jay Leno.

The Democratic candidates spent the spring and summer of 2007 in the typical primary season fashion: fund-raising, debating, giving speeches and meeting personally with voters, particularly in the states with early nomination contests. Senator Clinton began the race as the clear front-runner and emerged the winner of the "invisible primary." By autumn, she had raised the most money, secured the most endorsements from major party leaders and Democratic constituencies, and was the leader in the national polls. Clinton seemed to be the focus of many of the other candidates' attacks during the 17 debates before the Iowa caucuses and any stumbles she experienced garnered intense scrutiny and attention from the media. Senator Obama, whose electrifying address to the Democratic National Convention in 2004 had catapulted him into the national spotlight, was the main beneficiary of that hostility. Obama combined a firm anti-war stance with rhetoric that tapped into Democrats' frustration with the Washington establishment and a desire for real change in terms of both policy and tone. His star power within the party and growing grassroots confidence in his electability helped Obama match Clinton's fundraising totals and climb in opinion polls.

Obama was the clear winner of the Iowa caucuses, with John Edwards finishing second, and Clinton finishing a close third. Not only did a win in Iowa generate momentum for Obama's campaign, but it also demonstrated that an African American candidate could win significant support from white voters. Also telling was the effectiveness of Obama's intricate field organization and the great enthusiasm he was generating among young voters. With the field of frontrunners narrowed to Clinton, Edwards, and Obama, the focus shifted to New Hampshire, where Senator Obama was surging ahead in the polls with the primary less than a week away. Rather than deliver the expected knockout blow to Senator Clinton's candidacy, Obama finished second to Clinton, an outcome that surprised every pollster and pundit in the field. Clinton's victory was attributed to a strong debate performance and strong turnout and support among women.

Senator Clinton next won a close popular-vote victory in Nevada but suffered a resounding defeat in South Carolina, possibly due to negative attacks on Obama by Clinton supporters, including the candidate's husband, that some perceived to be racially-tinged. Most observers assumed that the nomination would be decided on February 5, Super Tuesday, when 25 states and territories would hold primaries and caucuses. Yet, the strength of Clinton's and Obama's candidacies resulted in a close race pitting two well-funded candidates with significant numbers of avid supporters against one another. Super Tuesday resulted in a draw. After a bruising nomination battle that threatened to split the Democratic Party, the nomination contest at last came to a close on June 5, when Senator Clinton officially conceded to Senator Obama.

The Republican contest was the one that was supposed to be long and dramatic, given the absence of a front-runner among a crowded field of top-tier candidates. Through 15 debates in 2007, each candidate sought to portray himself as the conservative best able to win an election in a climate that was unfavorable to Republicans. Mitt Romney established an early lead in the polls in Iowa and New Hampshire. There did not seem to be a widespread movement towards Romney among social conservatives, however, as many had concerns about his Mormon faith and the moderate image he had presented to the public during his political career in Massachusetts. Fred Thompson seemed to be the most reliably conservative option, but his lackluster performance on the campaign trail disappointed many frustrated conservatives unable to throw their overwhelming support to any of the candidates.

Mike Huckabee, the former Arkansas governor and an ordained Baptist minister, was the big winner in Iowa, with Romney finishing second. Playing the role of underdog, McCain won a convincing victory in New Hampshire and effectively won the nomination on Super Tuesday by winning nine of 21 contests and 61 percent of Republican delegates. Romney won seven states but only 21 percent of the delegates with his best performances coming in caucuses and smaller states. Huckabee had a respectable showing, but could not seem to expand his coalition beyond his evangelical base. The Republican race officially continued for another month, until McCain had enough delegates to clinch the nomination.

The Democratic and Republican Conventions

An almost two month gap would separate the end of the primary season and the first day of the Democratic National Convention. Speculation had centered on whether Obama would ask his Democratic rival, Senator Hillary Clinton, to be his running mate. Some in the party base argued that a "dream ticket" of Obama and Clinton was needed to unify the party and win in November. In the end, Obama chose Senator Joe Biden of Delaware, whose working class upbringing and foreign policy credentials were seen as broadening the ticket's appeal.

The Democratic National Convention was held August 25-28 in Denver, Colorado. One of the most highly anticipated speeches came on the second night of the convention when Senator Clinton, who had come closer than any woman before her to winning the U.S. presidency, gave her full support to Obama in front of an enthusiastic crowd in the convention hall and 26 million viewers at home and asked her supporters to back her former opponent. Former president Bill Clinton was followed by vice presidential nominee Joe Biden on Wednesday night. On the final night of the convention, Senator Obama accepted his party's nomination in front of 86,000 supporters at Invesco Field, with another 39 million watching on television. This speech by the first African American to win the nomination of a major party for president marked the 45th Anniversary of the Reverend Martin Luther King's "I Have a Dream" speech. Observers judged it a significant achievement and an important milestone in American history.

Less than 12 hours after the Democratic convention had ended, in what most agreed was a tactic to

How do debates affect the party nomination battle? Individual campaigns negotiate with other campaigns and the major news organizations to schedule debates during the party nomination races. Here, Democratic and Republican primary presidential candidates shake hands at the request of moderator Charles Gibson of ABC News when the two parties held back-to-back debates at St. Anselm College on January 5, 2008. The debates were co-sponsored by Facebook and the local ABC affiliate. The 2008 campaign marked the first time that new media organizations such as Facebook and YouTube participated in the debate process.

Photo courtesy: Neil Hamburg/Bloomberg News/Landov

reduce Obama's post-convention bounce, Senator McCain announced the selection of Alaska Governor Sarah Palin as his running mate. Palin was only the second woman to run for the vice presidency on a major party ticket and the first Republican woman to be selected.

McCain's announcement generated great excitement among the Republican base. Governor Palin was presented to the public as a rising star in Alaskan politics with a strong record of government reform. The mother of five children, including a special needs infant, Palin's strong pro-life views connected on a very personal level with social conservatives and Evangelicals. In a brief speech after McCain introduced her as his running mate, Palin referenced Hillary Clinton's campaign for the White House, in what was seen as a clear bid to win the support of disaffected supporters of Senator Clinton. Intense media scrutiny of Palin began immediately after McCain's announcement. Over the next few days, journalists, pundits, and bloggers took part in a frenzied examination of her family, personal life, political record, and policy positions.

The 2008 Republican National Convention was held September 1-4 in the Xcel Center in St. Paul, Minnesota. Because New Orleans was again under threat of a massive hurricane, the first night of the convention was scaled back considerably. The night was to feature President Bush and Vice President Cheney as speakers, but both of their appearances were cancelled. Their absence may have benefited the McCain campaign, given that both men were widely unpopular. Moreover, the latest tracking polls showed that the Democrats were getting their post-convention bounce. By Tuesday, the Obama-Biden ticket had jumped out to a six-point advantage. Republicans hoped to turn things around on Wednesday night, when Sarah Palin addressed the convention and 38 million television viewers. In an accomplished speech, Palin introduced herself to America and delivered biting criticisms of the Democratic nominee, the mainstream media, and Washington, D.C., while touting her running mate as a fellow maverick and American hero. Palin's speech was rapturously received in the convention center and received high marks from media commentators and political analysts.

What does a historic presidential ticket look like? Senator John McCain and Governor Sarah Palin wave to the party faithful after McCain delivered his acceptance speech to the Republican National Convention in St. Paul, Minnesota. McCain, a prisoner of war during Vietnam and long-time senator, was the oldest person to run for president in the nation's history. Palin was the first woman to run for the vice presidency on the Republican ticket.

Photo courtesy: Kyodo/Landov/Landov

In a somewhat anti-climactic appearance the following night, John McCain accepted his party's nomination with a speech that revealed in very personal terms his motivation for service. McCain explained his dedication to "Country First"—the slogan for his campaign—as stemming from the lessons he had learned as a prisoner of war in Vietnam and discussed his record of doing what was right for the nation, regardless of his party's support. While McCain's speech did not have the flair or generate the enthusiasm that Obama and Palin's speeches did, it was watched by a record-breaking 40 million television viewers.

The Debates and the General Election Campaign

The first presidential debate was scheduled to take place on Friday, September 26, on the campus of the University of Mississippi. By this point, the Republicans' optimism was beginning to fade. A growing economic crisis had made the economy, not foreign policy, the primary concern for a majority of the country. Since most Americans trusted Democrats more on economic policy, this policy focus harmed McCain's standing in the polls. In addition, President Bush's proposal to address nearly frozen credit markets was met with great skepticism among the electorate and on Capitol Hill. Sensing an opportunity to demonstrate his problem-solving abilities, Senator McCain "suspended" his campaign and suggested postponing the first debate in order to work on the financial crisis until a compromise had been reached. When the initial bill failed to pass the House due to opposition mostly from conservative Republicans, McCain appeared to be an obstacle to a solution. On Friday morning, McCain announced that he would participate in the debate as planned. The format featured questions posed by the moderator, PBS host Jim Lehrer, with responses and rebuttals by the candidates. While neither candidate broke new ground on the issues, Obama consistently came across as calm, confident, and having a firm grasp of policy. McCain's performance was somewhat uneven, although he demonstrated his experience and expertise in national security matters quite convincingly. For a Friday evening, the audience for the first debate was exceptionally high, with 52.4 million Americans watching on television. Opinion polls found that a majority of viewers believed that Obama was the winner.

Another concern for the McCain campaign was the increasingly negative impression that voters were forming about Sarah Palin. After having been sheltered from major news organizations during the first weeks of the campaign, interviews were arranged with ABC World News anchor Charlie Gibson and CBS Evening News anchor Katie Couric. Neither of these interviews went well. The Couric interview was especially problematic, as Palin frequently appeared flustered by rather innocuous questions and provided confusing answers on more serious ones. Palin was able to regain her footing and reassure nervous supporters during the only Vice Presidential debate with Joe Biden, who was nevertheless considered the strongest performer of the two candidates. Over 70 million people watched the debate, the most ever for a Vice Presidential debate. Palin would continue to be a big draw in public and on television. On October 18, 14 million Americans watched her impressive appearance on Saturday Night Live, a record audience for the late night comedy show.

A town-hall format was used for the second presidential debate, which was held on October 7 at Belmont University in Nashville. Moderator Tom Brokaw of NBC News asked questions prepared by about 125 undecided registered voters selected by the Gallup polling organization. The expectations and stakes were high for Senator McCain, who was very experienced with the town-hall format and needed a strong performance in order to alter the dynamics of the race. As with the first debate, no major gaffes or new substantive information was revealed. Again, however, Senator Obama received higher marks from viewers.

A television viewing audience of 56.5 million watched the final debate on October 15 at Hofstra University on Long Island. With CBS veteran correspondent Bob Schieffer serving as moderator, this debate focused on domestic policy with the two candidates seated close together at a table. This was clearly McCain's strongest performance, as he had his opponent on the defensive for most the early part of the debate. He also introduced the country to "Joe the Plumber," an Ohio voter who was videotaped having a friendly argument with Senator Obama over Obama's tax proposals. Most of the public saw Obama as the winner, giving the Democratic ticket a clean sweep of the four debates and strong momentum into the final weeks of the campaign.

Opinion polls taken after the last debate indicated that Senator Obama had maintained a lead over Senator McCain that had begun to build during the week of the financial crisis. On the day of the first debate, the Rasmussen Reports daily presidential tracking poll showed that Obama was the choice of 50 percent of likely voters, while McCain was the choice of 45 percent. Support for both tickets fluctuated only slightly from that point forward, with Obama-Biden peaking at 52 percent several times and never dropping below 50 percent. Support for McCain-Palin, on the other hand, never reached above 47 percent. The picture for the Republicans was even more disappointing at the state level, where Obama led in all the battleground states except Missouri throughout October. But even more troubling was the numbers coming out of states that were thought to be reliably Republican. Polls showed leads averaging six percent for Obama in Virginia and only one percent leads for McCain in Indiana and North Carolina. Indiana and Virginia had not voted for a Democrat for president since 1964, while North Carolina last voted Democratic in 1976. Additional signs of trouble were apparent from the numbers coming out of Georgia, Montana, and North Dakota.

McCain's hope to change the dynamics of the race had rested on a strong showing in the debates or a major misstep by Obama. The Democrats stayed on message, however, criticizing President George W. Bush's handling of the economy and tying Senator McCain to the unpopular president and his policies. In addition to offering a general promise of "change we can believe in," Obama put forth a plan to cut taxes for 95 percent of all Americans, invest in alternative sources of energy, and make health care more accessible and affordable. He also promised to withdraw American troops from Iraq within a specified period of time and place more emphasis on capturing Osama bin Laden and funding the war against a resurgent Taliban in Afghanistan. With nearly $300 million spent on over 535,000 airings of campaign ads, including a 30-minute long advertisement aired on seven networks the week before the election, the Obama campaign not only stayed on message, but it made sure that the message was made clear to millions of swing voters across the country.

Senator McCain spent most of the campaign attempting to distance himself from President Bush and prove that he was a maverick—a more authentic agent of change than his opponent. In both cases, McCain was largely unsuccessful. In the summer, the McCain campaign had made some headway by arguing for a withdrawal from Iraq without arbitrary timetables and pushing a proposal to lift the federal ban on offshore drilling for oil. Growing stability in Iraq and falling energy prices in anticipation of a looming global recession, however, made it difficult to keep these two issues at the top of the policy agenda.

McCain also had made some progress sowing seeds of doubt in voters' minds about Obama's readiness to be president. While McCain had tax cuts and a health insurance reform plan of his own, the campaign focused on Obama's policy positions and his association with a 1960s radical in a series of highly negative attack ads throughout the fall. To the bewilderment of many observers, McCain's campaign made no mention of Obama's relationship with his former pastor, the Reverend Jeremiah Wright, whose fiery sermons had been excerpted to great effect by conservative broadcasters and pundits. Nor was there much mention of Senator McCain's numer-

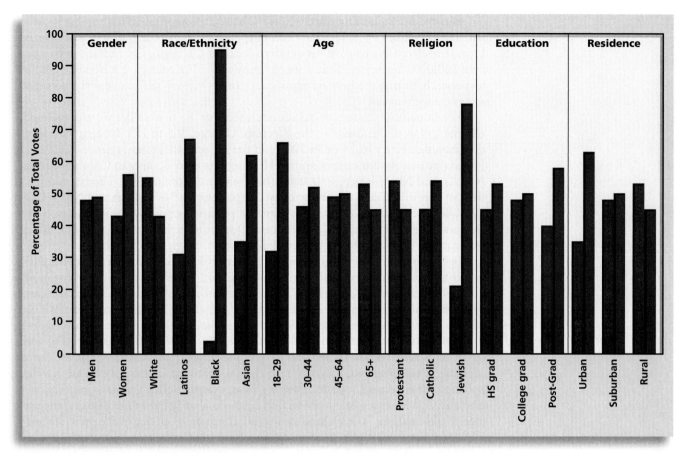

FIGURE 14.3 Group-Identified Voting Patterns in the 2008 Presidential Election

Red bars indicate the percentage of votes for John McCain; blue bars indicate the percentage of votes for Barack Obama.

Source: http://www.cnn.com/ELECTION/2008/results/polls.main/

ous bipartisan legislative achievements and initiatives. In the final two weeks of the campaign, with Samuel "Joe the Plumber" Wurzelbacher frequently by his side, McCain zeroed in on Obama's tax and spending proposals, claiming that Obama's brief conversation with Wurzelbacher provided evidence of a Democratic plan to pursue redistributive economic policies once Obama was in office.

Election Results and Analysis

As the first returns and exit polls were announced from states in the Eastern and Central time zones, it was clear that Obama's lead in the polls was accurate. The outcomes in reliably red states with early poll closings—Indiana, Georgia, North Carolina, and Virginia—were deemed by the network and cable news bureaus as "too close to call" for most of the evening. The same was true for Florida and Ohio, two battleground states that George W. Bush had won and that McCain needed to keep in order to have any chance of winning. But soon after the polls closed in New Hampshire and Pennsylvania, two states that Kerry had won in 2004 and that McCain needed to win to compensate for likely losses in Colorado and New Mexico, the news media called both states for Obama. Around 9:30 pm EST, the networks called Ohio for Obama and the only question remaining was his margin of victory. As soon as California was called for Obama at 11:00 pm EST, the networks declared Barack Obama the forty-fourth president of the United States.

Senator McCain immediately called Obama to congratulate him on his historic win and then gave a gracious concession speech in front of supporters in Phoenix. President-elect Obama gave his victory speech at Chicago's Grant Park in front of over 100,000 supporters. To chants of "Yes we did!" Obama gave a highly conciliatory speech, noting the historic significance of his victory and praising the power of American democracy.

When polls in the remaining states closed and the final tallies were completed, Obama had won a landslide in the Electoral College, 365 to 173. Obama won all of the states that Kerry had won in 2004 and the major battleground states of Ohio and Florida by narrow, but clear margins. He also won convincingly in Colorado, Iowa, Nevada, and New Mexico, four states that Bush had won in 2004. The big surprises were in Virginia, where Obama won by five percent, and in Indiana and North Carolina, both of which he won by less than one percentage point. Obama also won one electoral vote from the 2nd Congressional District in Nebraska, which is one of just two states to allocate votes by congressional district.

In the popular vote, Obama won 53 percent to McCain's 46 percent—the highest percentage of the vote won by a Democratic nominee since 1964. (Go to http://www.cnn.com/ELECTION/2008/results/president/ to see the final counts and percentages in each state). The 2008 election also had the highest voter turnout since 1964, with over 62 percent of eligible citizens casting more than 128 million votes.

Most analysts expected the 2008 election to be similar to the 2000 election, with most "red states" remaining red and most "blue states" remaining blue. The Obama campaign was convinced, however, that they had the opportunity to expand the blue portion of the electoral map by investing in an extensive field organization that covered all 50 states, much of it built on organizations already put in place during the primaries and caucuses. The Obama campaign's decision to opt out of the public financing system allowed them to raise an unprecedented sum of money to fund their ground operation and to buy extensive airtime for campaign advertisements. In contrast, the McCain campaign pursued a more traditional strategy, assuming that much of their base was secure and focused their attention on the states that had been decided by narrow margins in the past two elections. McCain's decision to agree to limits on his spending in return for federal financing also contributed to his defeat, since it resulted in an inadequate amount of resources devoted to voter mobilization. In October, for example, the McCain campaign had to abandon battleground states that Kerry had won in 2004, which allowed the Obama campaign to redirect even more resources to the states still considered in play.

Obama's impressive seven percent win was fueled by strong performances among key voting groups. Although McCain won the support of 55 percent of white voters, Obama won the support of women of all races by 13 percentage points and the support of men of all races by one percent. This was the first time that a Democrat had won a majority of men since 1976. Ninety-five percent of African Americans supported Obama. Strategically important given their status as America's fastest-growing ethnic group and concentration in key electoral states was the preference of Latino/a voters: 67 percent voted for Obama and only 31 percent for McCain. In 2004, Kerry won Latino/as by a margin of only 53 percent to 44 percent. Young voters, those between the ages of 18 and 29, also strongly supported Obama over McCain, by a margin of 66 percent to 32 percent.

Barack Obama ran a disciplined, innovative campaign in a year that strongly favored a Democratic victory. Obama was able to inspire a majority of the electorate, including numerous young people and racial and ethnic minorities, with a message of change and hope during the worse economic crisis to face the nation since the Great Depression. His election as the first African American president of the United States was seen by many as the culmination of the American dream. And, as is the tradition in American politics, Americans of all ideological stripes began uniting behind their new president in the days following the election.

Toward Reform: Campaign Finance and the 527 Loophole

Soft money, as discussed above, is campaign money raised and spent by political parties for expenses such as overhead and administrative costs and for grassroots activities such as political education and GOTV efforts. In a 1978 advisory opinion, the Federal Election Commission ruled that political parties could raise these funds without regulation. Then, in 1979, Congress passed an amendment allowing parties to *spend* unlimited sums on these same activities.[28] In the years immediately following the rule changes, the national parties began raising five-and six-figure sums from individuals and interest groups to pay for expenses such as rent, employee salaries, and building maintenance. The national parties also began transferring large sums of soft money to state parties in order to help pay for grassroots activities (such as get out the vote drives) and campaign paraphernalia (such as yard signs and bumper stickers).

However, the line separating expenditures that influence federal elections from those that do not proved to be quite blurry, and this blurriness resulted in a significant campaign finance loophole. The largest controversy came in the area of campaign advertisements. The federal courts ruled that only campaign advertisements that use explicit words or phrases—for example, "vote for," "vote against," "elect," or "support"—qualify as *express advocacy* advertisements. Political advertisements that do not use these words were considered *issue advocacy* advertisements.[29] Because express advocacy advertisements were openly intended to influence federal elections, they could be paid for only with strictly regulated **hard money**. Issue advocacy advertisements, on the other hand, were paid for with unregulated soft money. The parties' response to these rules was to create issue advocacy advertisements that very much resemble express advocacy ads, for such advertisements call attention to the voting record of the candidate supported or opposed and are replete with images of the candidate. However, the parties ensured that the magic words "vote for" or "vote against" were never uttered in the advertisements, allowing them to be paid for with unregulated soft rather than hard money.

As discussed earlier in the chapter, soft-money donations are now prohibited under the 2002 Bipartisan Campaign Finance Reform Act (BCRA), and third-party issue ads, if coordinated with a federal candidate's campaign, can now be considered campaign contributions and are thus regulated by the FEC. The last election cycle for the parties to use soft money was 2001–2002, and the amount raised, nearly $430 million for Republican and Democrats combined,[30] highlights why the reform seemed necessary. Republicans raised $219 million in soft money from pharmaceutical, insurance, and energy companies. Democrats raised just under $211 million in soft money from unions and law firms. With soft money banned, the hope was that wealthy donors and interest groups would be deprived of their privileged and potentially corrupting influence on parties and candidates. The hope was that, like every other citizen, they would have to donate within the hard-money limits placed on individuals and PACs. Unfortunately, these reforms have not worked, and the 2004 election revealed the latest campaign finance loophole.

The most significant unintended result of the BCRA in 2004 was the emergence of political entities known as **527 political committees**—the numbers come from the provisions of the Internal Revenue tax code that establish their legal status. These committees are essentially unregulated interest groups that focus on specific causes or policy positions and attempt to influence voters. (To learn more about 527 activity in 2008, see Analyzing Visuals: The Ten Most Active 527 Groups in 2008.)

According to the tax code, 527s may not directly engage in advocacy for or against a candidate, but they can advocate on behalf of political issues. This allowed them to circumvent the direct advocacy prohibition by creating what detractors called "sham issue ads" naming a particular candidate and stating how the candidate supported or

The Electoral College: Campaign Consequences and Mapping the Results

hard money
Legally specified and limited contributions that are clearly regulated by the Federal Election Campaign Act and by the Federal Election Commission.

527 political committees
Nonprofit and unregulated interest groups that focus on specific causes or policy positions and attempt to influence voters.

Analyzing Visuals   The Ten Most Active 527 Groups in 2008

Examine the table showing the most financially active 527 groups participating in the 2008 elections and answer the following questions:

Committee	Expenditures	Pro-Democratic	Pro-Republican
Service Employees International Union	$25,058,103	✔	
America Votes	$19,672,551	✔	
American Solutions Winning the Future	$17,470,711		✔
The Fund for America	$11,514,130	✔	
EMILY's List	$10,349,746	✔	
GOPAC	$8,100,840		✔
College Republican National Committee	$6,458,084		✔
Citizens United	$5,238,329		✔
Alliance for New America	$4,890,620	✔	
Working for Working Americans	$2,049,833	✔	
Gay & Lesbian Victory Fund	$5,145,721	✔	
Club for Growth	$4,246,547		✔

LOOKING at the information in the table, what conclusions can you draw about the relative success of Democratic and Republican fund-raising efforts with regard to 527 groups in 2008?

Source: http://www.opensecrets.org/527s/527cmtes.php

GIVEN what you know about some of the individual 527s listed in the table, what conclusions can you draw about the effectiveness of various 527 strategies with regard to the 2008 presidential election?

You Are a Campaign Manager: Lead Obama to Battleground State Victory

You Are a Campaign Manager: McCain and the Swingers: Help McCain Win Swing States and Swing Voters

501(c) (3) committees
Nonprofit and tax-exempt groups that can educate voters about issues and are not required to release the names of their contributors.

harmed a particular interest, but without directly stating the 527 group's opinion on how to vote in the election. Thus, money that would have entered the system as unregulated soft money in previous election cycles ended up in the hands of 527 organizations in 2004, funding several television advertisements and direct mailings.[31] To limit the influence of such ads on voters, the BCRA now forbids their airing in the thirty days before a primary and sixty days before a general election.

The 527s exist in both political camps, though the Democrats, the party out of power in 2004, were first to aggressively pursue them. Two of the largest pro-Democratic committees in the 2004 election were the Media Fund and Americans Coming Together (ACT), both raising millions of dollars from people eager to see a Democrat in the White House. These committees bought TV, radio, and print advertising to sell their message, focusing on the battleground or "swing" states that were not firmly in the Bush or Kerry camps. Even though most political observers predicted that President Bush would easily outspend Senator Kerry in the presidential contest, the Democratic 527s considerably aided the Democratic campaign. Through the end of the 2004 election, pro-Democratic 527 groups spent more than $200 million, more than double that of their Republican counterparts. Groups on both sides saw large donations from wealthy individuals, including billionaire George Soros, who gave $23.4 million to Democratic organizations, and Texas developer Bob Perry, who donated $8 million to Republican groups.[32] As fund-raising records in almost every category were shattered in 2004, the campaign reform law clearly had no effect on overall spending or in limiting the amount that wealthy individuals can contribute to influence the process. In 2006, 527 committees contributed almost $300 million to House and Senate candidates, while in 2008 527's contributed approximately $425 million, (To learn more about 527 activity in the 2008 elections, see Table 14.3.)

Another loophole that groups and individuals have used to circumvent the BCRA is to direct soft money donations to tax-exempt, non-profit **501(c)(3) committees**. These committees, also known by their designation in the federal tax code, are prohibited from conducting political campaign activities to influence elections to public office. But like 527s, 501(c)(3)s are permitted to educate voters on political issues as long as they do not overtly advocate a specific position. These committees are beginning to rival 527s in popularity as conduits for soft money, however, because they do not have to release the names of donors, who therefore can remain anonymous until their tax returns are filed in the following year. Other nonprofit committees provide greater anonymity to donors because their contributions are not tax-exempt and, thus, are not included as part of IRS records. Social welfare organizations governed by section 501(c)(4), and labor and business groups governed by 501(c)(5) also have the advantage of being permitted to lobby for a particular position on an issue, allowing for a clearer direction to voters on whom to support. The main restriction on these latter groups is that less than half of their budget can be spent on political activities.[33] This lack of disclosure makes it difficult for voters to learn who is supporting a campaign and for what purpose.

Campaign Finance Regulations

Reformers will once again attempt to reform their reforms, but the abolition of 527 committees or restrictions on 501(c)s are highly unlikely—and the money supporting them would most likely reappear in some other way. Overall, however, one lesson of the Bipartisan Campaign Reform Act is obvious: no amount of clever legislating will rid the American system of campaign money. Interested individuals and groups will always find ways to have their voices heard. The challenge is to find a way to force contributors to disclose their contributions in a timely fashion, so that the public may take this information into account when deciding how to vote. Information regarding political contributions, when revealed to the public by the press in advance of an election, provides the voters with an invaluable cue for evaluating candidates. What better way to understand who supports a candidate and who does not? As always, disclosure is the ultimate check on potential misbehavior in the realm of political money.

WHAT SHOULD I HAVE LEARNED?

While campaign rules and media coverage have a profound impact on elections, campaigns still tend to rise and fall on the strength of the individual candidate and his or her campaign team. In this chapter we have asked the following questions:

■ **What are the roots of modern political campaigns?**

While each campaign has its own unique aspects, in modern campaigns there is a predictable pathway toward elections that involves a nomination and general election strategy. At the nomination phase it is essential for candidates to secure the support of people within their party, interest groups, and political activists. In the general election, the candidates must focus on the voters and defining their candidacy in terms acceptable to a majority of voters in the district or state.

■ **Who are the key players in campaigns?**

The candidate makes appearances, meets voters, raises funds, holds press conferences, gives speeches, and is ultimately responsible for conveying the campaign message and for the success of the campaign. A professional staff organizes volunteers, produces campaign literature, organizes events, plans strategy, conducts polls, produces advertisements, raises money, and interacts with the media. Campaign staffs combine volunteers, professionals, and key political consultants, including media consultants, a pollster, a direct mailer, and an Internet team. Media consultants are particularly important, and given the cost of advertising, campaign media budgets consume the lion's share of available resources.

■ **What is the media's role in campaigns?**

Candidates for public office seek to gain favorable coverage in the media. They gain access with paid media, purchasing ad time on television and ad space in print media; and with free media, television and print media news coverage. Because candidates cannot easily control media coverage, they cannot rely on free media alone. Candidates, therefore, must spend campaign dollars on creating advertisements that deliver campaign messages without media criticism. The Internet increasingly makes this possible, since candidates can use it as a cheap medium to relate directly to voters and activists.

■ **What are the rules governing campaign finance?**

Since the 1970s, campaign financing has been governed by the terms of the Federal Election Campaign Act (FECA). Because of the rise of soft money, the FECA was amended in 2002 by the Bipartisan Campaign Reform Act (BCRA), which was promptly challenged and upheld with very few exceptions by the Supreme Court.

■ **What were the highlights and what was the outcome of the 2008 Presidential Campaign?**

A competitive and spirited Democratic nomination battle that continued through the last contest ended in victory for Barack Obama, who defeated the early frontrunner, Hillary Clinton. John McCain emerged the winner of a wide-open Republican nomination process. Both candidates had successful conventions and began the unofficial general campaign nearly even in public opinion polls. Obama built a modest lead that he would never relinquish after the two candidates' response to the collapse on Wall Street and performance in three televised debates. Turnout increased over the previous presidential election for the third consecutive time. By running a near flawless campaign, with strong support from young and first-time voters, and benefiting from an unpopular Republican president, Barack Obama managed an Electoral College landslide and impressive margin in the popular vote. Obama's victory gives Americans their first African American president.

■ **What does the future hold for campaign finance reform?**

Though the BCRA was successful in banning the unregulated soft money that flowed through the political parties, it exposed another loophole in the existing campaign finance laws, the unregulated money that now flows through 527 and 501(c) groups. While the next round of reforms will try to address these loopholes, it is clear from past attempts at reform that it is difficult to rid the American system of unregulated campaign money. Requiring candidates to disclose their contributions and expenditures in more detail and in a timely fashion is a more likely possibility.

Key Terms

campaign consultant, p. 502
campaign manager, p. 501
candidate debate, p. 507
communications director, p. 501
contrast ad, p. 503
direct mailer, p. 501
finance chair, p. 501
501(c)(3) committees, p. 526
527 political committees, p. 525
free media, p. 502

general election campaign, p. 497
get out the vote (GOTV), p. 501
hard money, p. 525
inoculation ad, p. 503
Internet team, p. 501
matching funds, p. 515
media consultant, p. 502
negative ad, p. 502
new media, p. 502
nomination campaign, p. 495

paid media, p. 502
political action committee (PAC),
   p. 512
pollster, p. 501
positive ad, p. 502
press secretary, p. 501
public funds, p. 515
soft money, p. 511
spot ad, p. 503
voter canvass, p. 499

Researching the Campaign Process

In the Library

Ansolabehere, Stephen, and Shanto Iyengar. *Going Negative: How Political Ads Shrink and Polarize the Electorate*. New York: Free Press, 1997.

Green, Donald P., and Alan S. Gerber. *Get Out the Vote: How to Increase Voter Turnout*, 2nd ed. Washington, DC: Brookings Institution, 2008.

Halperin, Mark, and John F. Harris. *The Way to Win: Taking the White House in 2008*. New York: Random House, 2006.

Holbrook, Thomas M. *Do Campaigns Matter?* Thousand Oaks, CA: Sage, 1996.

Johnson, Dennis W. *No Place for Amateurs: How Political Consultants Are Reshaping American Democracy*, 2nd ed. New York: Routledge, 2007.

Nelson, Candice J., and James A. Thurber. *Campaigns American Style*. Boulder, CO: Westview, 2004.

Sabato, Larry J. *Marathon: The 2008 Election*. New York: Longman, 2008.

———. *Divided States of America: The Slash and Burn Politics of the 2004 Presidential Election*. New York: Longman, 2005.

Sabato, Larry J., and Glenn R. Simpson. *Dirty Little Secrets: The Persistence of Corruption in American Politics*. New York: Random House, 1996.

Shaw, Daron R. *The Race to 270: The Electoral College and the Campaign Strategies of 2000 and 2004*, new edition. Chicago: University Of Chicago Press, 2006.

Shea, Daniel M., and Michael John Burton. *Campaign Craft: The Strategies, Tactics, and Art of Political Campaign Management*, 3rd ed. Westport, CT: Praeger, 2006.

Skewes, Elizabeth A. *Message Control: How News Is Made on the Presidential Campaign Trail*. Lanham, MD: Rowman and Littlefield, 2007.

Trent, Judith S., and Robert V. Friedenberg. *Political Campaign Communication: Principles and Practices*, 6th ed. Westport, CT: Praeger, 2008.

Trippi, Joe. *The Revolution Will Not Be Televised*. New York: HarperCollins, 2004.

West, M. Darrell. *Air Wars: Television Advertising in Election Campaigns 1952–2004*, 4th ed. Washington, DC: CQ Press, 2005.

On the Web

To learn more about Common Cause, a nonpartisan, nonprofit watchdog group that monitors political developments in campaign finance reform, visit their Web site at **www. commoncause.org.**

For Facebook's profiles of elected officials and candidates, debates on contemporary issues, and the latest political news and commentary, go to **www.facebook.com/politics/?us.**

For fact sheets, research reports, academic studies, and practical tools to encourage civic engagement, go to **www.civicyouth.org.**

For an archive of screen shots of the home pages of presidential campaign Web sites and a list of Web site features since 1996, go to **www.4president.us.**

15

The Media

O n the evening of August 28, 2008, Senator Barack Obama accepted the Democratic Party's nomination for President in a speech before over 84,000 people at Denver's Invesco Field and another 39 million Americans watching on television. But in less than twelve hours, the news media had turned their attention away from an event of such historical significance to Senator John McCain's announcement that he had selected Governor Sarah Palin of Alaska, a 44-year-old mother of five, to be his running mate on the Republican ticket.

The selection of a little-known politician who was only the second woman to serve as a vice presidential nominee on a major party ticket was historic in its own right, but a variety of factors made Palin a compelling source of news. The governor's oldest son was about to be deployed to Iraq and her youngest son had been born in 2008 with Down Syndrome. A skeptical media were eager to learn more about Palin's meteoric rise in Alaska politics, 21-month record as Governor, and positions on major policy issues. Their fascination with Palin seemed, however, to border on obsession: the Republican vice-presidential nominee would receive more media cov-

erage during her first week in the national spotlight than Obama received during the week of the Democratic National Convention when he became the first African American presidential candidate to be nominated by a major party.

As with all obsessions that go unchecked, the intense scrutiny of Governor Palin's past led to instances of irresponsible and erratic behavior on the part of the media. The tabloids and celebrity magazines were delving into unsubstantiated rumors about her family and personal life. Mainstream anchors and commentators were questioning whether she was a good mother and a good conservative for trying to juggle the demands of the vice presidency with a difficult family situation. Two days after Senator McCain's surprise announcement, an unsubstantiated claim that Palin had "faked" her last pregnancy and that her youngest child was actually the son of her teenage daughter was posted on the influential liberal blog Daily Kos. To put this story to rest, the McCain campaign revealed the next day that the same teenage daughter, now 17, was five months pregnant and soon would be marrying her 18-year-old boyfriend. On that same day, the campaign confirmed a story that Palin's husband had been arrested for a DUI twenty-two years ago. While most journalists were taking a closer look at Palin's public record in Alaska, including a legislative investigation into her firing of the state's head of Public Safety, one

■ The relationship between the news media and politicians may be mutually beneficial and exceedingly rocky. At left, President Franklin D. Roosevelt gives a "fireside chat" radio broadcast to the American people. At right, Governor Sarah Palin and her family wave to delegates at the Republican National Convention after Palin's acceptance of the vice-presidential nomination.

WHAT SHOULD I KNOW ABOUT . . .

- the roots of news media in the United States?
- current media trends?
- rules governing the media?
- how the media cover politics?
- media influence, media bias, and public perceptions of the media?

531

TO LEARN MORE—

—TO DO MORE

To learn more about how the media cover politics and the criticisms leveled at the media, go to mediamatters.org and www.fair.org.

study found twice as much media coverage of her personal life than of her public record.

The "Palin Phenomenon" provides insight into the media environment in which politicians now operate. Competition from new and alternative news sources and a twenty-four hour news cycle have pressured traditional news organizations to be constantly in search of newsworthy events. Increased competition and a shrinking audience also has encouraged reporters and editors to be less strict in where they draw the line between the private and public life of political figures. In an interview with a McCain aide, CNN's Campbell Brown described how blurry the line had become when she said: "You know, this a presidential election. Nothing is private. The world is watching."

Although frustration with the news media's performance has been a feature of the American political tradition since the founding, there also has been a strong appreciation for media's role in a democratic society. In a letter written in 1787, Thomas Jefferson explained that if he was forced to decide between a "government without newspapers or newspapers without a government," he "would not hesitate a moment to prefer the latter." Jefferson, like many of the nation's founders, realized the profound importance of a free press in a free society. So important was this idea that it was canonized in the First Amendment with the simple words "Congress shall make no law . . . abridging the freedom of speech, or of the press," an idea that has shaped the American republic as much as any other idea in the Constitution. With the Constitution's sanction, as interpreted by the Supreme Court over two centuries, a vigorous and highly competitive press has emerged. This freedom has been crucial in facilitating the political discourse and free flow of information necessary to maintain democracy.

A free press is a necessary component of a democratic society because it informs the public, giving them the information they need in order to choose their leaders and influence the direction of public policy. In fact, the American media have been called the "fourth branch of government" because their influence is often as great as that of the three constitutional branches: the executive, the legislative, and the judiciary. However, this term is misleading because the American media are composed of many competing private enterprises.

Throughout the world, mass media are organized around different principles from those in the United States and can serve different purposes. Under authoritarian regimes, the media serve as a carefully controlled outlet for "approved" messages from those in charge to those being governed without consent. In constitutional monarchies, the media cooperate with the monarchy in a mutually beneficial relationship. The media get interesting stories about the royal family, while the family helps support the media. In the turbulent Middle East, where there is no more influential network than al-Jazeera, news is reported from a distinct perspective, often providing militants a venue to express their ideas and casting U.S. involvement in the region in the darkest possible light.[1]

This chapter traces the historical development of the news media in the United States and then explores recent developments affecting the media. In discussing the changing role and impact of the media, we will address the following:

★ First, we will discuss *the roots of news media in the United States,* from the founding of the country to the modern period.

★ Second, we will examine *current media trends.*

★ Third, we will consider *rules governing the media,* both self-imposed rules of conduct and government regulations affecting radio, television, and the Internet.

★ Fourth, we will discuss *how the media cover politics.*

★ Finally, we will consider reforms pertaining to *media influence, media bias, and public perceptions of the media.*

Roots of News Media in the United States

The **mass media**—the entire array of organizations through which information is collected and disseminated to the general public—have become a colossal enterprise in the United States. The mass media include print sources, movies, television, radio, and Web-based material. Collectively the mass media make use of broadcast, cable, and satellite technologies to distribute information, which reaches every corner of the United States. The mass media are a powerful tool for both entertaining and informing the public. They reflect American society, but they are also the primary lens through which citizens view American culture and American politics. The **news media,** which are one component of the larger mass media, provide the public with new information about subjects of public interest and play a vital role in the political process.[2] Although often referred to as a large, impersonal whole, the media are made up of diverse personalities and institutions, and they form a spectrum of opinion. Through the various outlets that make up the news media—from newspapers to online magazines—journalists inform the public, influence public opinion, and affect the direction of public policy in our democratic society.

Throughout American history, technological advances have had a major impact on the way in which Americans receive their news. High-speed presses and more cheaply produced paper made mass-circulation daily newspapers possible. The telegraph and then the telephone made newsgathering easier and much faster. When radio became widely available in the 1920s, millions of Americans could hear national politicians instead of merely reading about them. With television—first introduced in the late 1940s, and nearly a universal fixture in U.S. homes by the mid-1950s—citizens could see and hear political candidates and presidents. And now with the rise of Web-based media, the process is once again undergoing a transformation. Never before has information been more widely distributed, and never have the lines between news producer and consumer been less clear.

mass media
The entire array of organizations through which information is collected and disseminated to the general public.

news media
Media providing the public with new information about subjects of public interest.

Three Hundred Years of American Mass Media

Print Media

The first example of news media in America came in the form of newspapers, which were published in the colonies as early as 1690. The number of newspapers grew throughout the 1700s, as colonists began to realize the value of a press free from government oversight and censorship. The battle between Federalists and Anti-Federalists over ratification of the Constitution, discussed in chapter 2, played out in various partisan newspapers in the late eighteenth century. Thus, it was not sur-

Timeline: The Development of American News Media

1893 Joseph Pulitzer launches *New York World*—Known for its sensationalism and progressive crusades, Pulitzer's approach is nicknamed "yellow journalism".

1960 Presidential debates—Debates are televised for the first time.

1833 *New York Sun* enters circulation—Single copies sell for one penny (about four dollars in today's currency). The Sun is written to appeal to a mass audience.

1848 Associated Press established—The AP becomes the nation's first wire service.

1920 KDKA in Pittsburgh—First commercial radio station launches and provides detailed campaign coverage.

1789 Rise of the Partisan Press—Alexander Hamilton's *The Gazette of the United States* and Thomas Jefferson's *The National Gazette* are established.

1912 The Columbia School of Journalism admits its first class—Students use the first journalism textbook—*The Practice of Journalism* by Williams and Martin—in their classes.

prising that one of the Anti-Federalists' demands was a constitutional amendment guaranteeing the freedom of the press (To learn more about freedom of the press, see The Living Constitution.)

The partisan press eventually gave way to the penny press. In 1833, Benjamin Day founded the *New York Sun*, which cost a penny at the newsstand. Beyond its low price, the *Sun* sought to expand its audience by freeing itself from the grip of a single political party. Inexpensive and politically independent, the *Sun* was the forerunner of modern newspapers, which rely on mass circulation and commercial advertising to produce profit. By 1861, the penny press had so supplanted partisan papers that President Abraham Lincoln announced his administration would have no favored or sponsored newspaper.

Although the print media were becoming less partisan, they were not necessarily becoming more respectable. Mass-circulation dailies sought wide readership, attracting readers with the sensational and the scandalous. The sordid side of politics became the entertainment of the times. One of the best-known examples occurred in

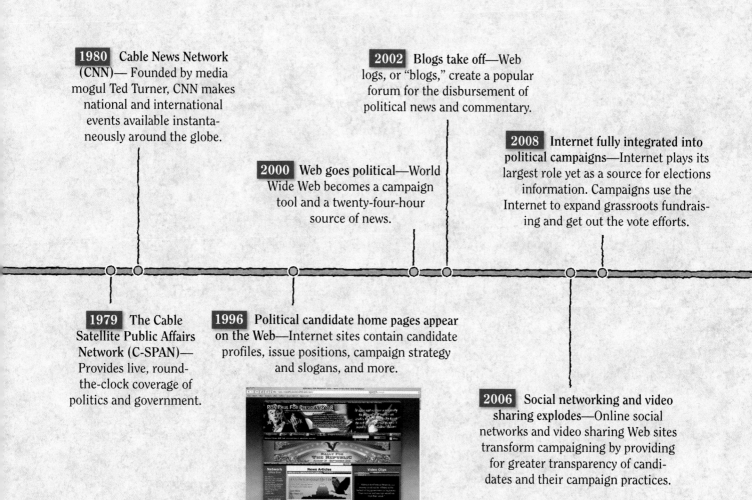

1980 Cable News Network (CNN)— Founded by media mogul Ted Turner, CNN makes national and international events available instantaneously around the globe.

2002 Blogs take off—Web logs, or "blogs," create a popular forum for the disbursement of political news and commentary.

2008 Internet fully integrated into political campaigns—Internet plays its largest role yet as a source for elections information. Campaigns use the Internet to expand grassroots fundraising and get out the vote efforts.

2000 Web goes political—World Wide Web becomes a campaign tool and a twenty-four-hour source of news.

1979 The Cable Satellite Public Affairs Network (C-SPAN)— Provides live, round-the-clock coverage of politics and government.

1996 Political candidate home pages appear on the Web—Internet sites contain candidate profiles, issue positions, campaign strategy and slogans, and more.

2006 Social networking and video sharing explodes—Online social networks and video sharing Web sites transform campaigning by providing for greater transparency of candidates and their campaign practices.

the presidential campaign of 1884, when the *Buffalo Evening Telegraph* headlined "A Terrible Tale" about Grover Cleveland, the Democratic nominee.[3] The story alleged that Cleveland, an unmarried man, had fathered a child in 1871, while sheriff of Buffalo, New York. Even though paternity was indeterminate because the child's mother had been seeing other men, Cleveland willingly accepted responsibility, since all the other men were married, and he had dutifully paid child support for years. The strict Victorian moral code that dominated American values at the time made the story even more shocking than it would be today. Fortunately for Cleveland, another newspaper, the *Democratic Sentinel*, broke a story that helped to offset this scandal: Republican presidential nominee James G. Blaine and his wife's first child had been born just three months after their wedding.

Throughout the nineteenth century, payoffs to the press were common. Andrew Jackson, for instance, gave one in ten of his early appointments to loyal reporters.[4] During the 1872 presidential campaign, the Republicans slipped cash to about 300 news-

The Living Constitution

Congress shall make no law respecting an establishment of religion, or prohibiting the free exercise thereof; or abridging the freedom of speech, or of the press; or the right of the people peaceably to assemble, and to petition the government for a redress of grievances.

FIRST AMENDMENT

The Framers knew that democracy is not easy, that a republic requires a continuous battle for rights and responsibilities. One of those rights is the freedom of the press, preserved in the First Amendment to the Constitution. To protect the press, the Framers were wise enough to keep the constitutional language simple—and a good thing, too. Their view of the press, and its required freedom, was almost certainly less broad than our conception of press freedom today.

It is difficult today to appreciate what a leap of faith it was for the Framers to grant freedom of the press when James Madison brought the Bill of Rights before Congress. Newspapers were largely run by disreputable people, since at the time editors and reporters were judged as purveyors of rumor and scandal, the reason Madison, as well as Alexander Hamilton and John Jay, published their newspaper articles advocating the ratification of the Constitution, *The Federalist Papers*, under the pseudonym "Publius."

The printed word was one of the few mediums of political communication in the young nation—it was critical for keeping Americans informed about issues. Therefore, the Framers had to hope that giving the press freedom to print all content, although certain to give rise to sensational stories, would also produce high-quality, objective reporting. Nevertheless, we should note that the Framers were not above using journalism as a way of promoting their political agendas. For example, Thomas Jefferson created a newspaper, the *National Gazette*, to report news favoring his Democratic-Republican Party. Giving the press freedom was also giving opposing politicians an open forum to attack each other.

Not much has changed since the Framers instituted the free press. We still have tabloids and partisan publications in which politicians attack each other, and we still rely on the press to give us important political information that we use to make voting decisions. The First Amendment declares the priority of free expression. The Framers recognized that all kinds of information would have to be protected to maximize opportunities for solid information to be reported. Regulations in response to what offends some people might be the first step on the slippery slope to censorship. The simple, enduring protection the Framers created in the First Amendment continues to make possible the flow of ideas that a democratic society relies upon.

CRITICAL THINKING QUESTIONS

1. While the First Amendment guarantees the rights of a free press, it is silent about their responsibilities to the public. What should the responsibilities of the media and individual journalists be? How would you suggest encouraging them to live up to their responsibilities?

2. The First Amendment was drafted in a time where the press consisted of newspapers, pamphlets, and public speakers. How relevant are the guarantees enshrined in the First Amendment to today's media environment? Are bloggers journalists? Do bloggers deserve the same constitutional protections as traditional journalists?

yellow journalism
A form of newspaper publishing in vogue in the late nineteenth century that featured pictures, comics, color, and sensationalized, oversimplified news coverage.

men.[5] Wealthy industrialists also sometimes purchased investigative cease-fires for tens of thousands of dollars.

In the late 1800s and early 1900s, prominent publishers such as William Randolph Hearst and Joseph Pulitzer expanded the reach of newspapers in their control by practicing what became known as **yellow journalism**—sensationalized reporting

Did the practice of yellow journalism contribute to the rise of objective journalism? In this 1898 cartoon titled "Uncle Sam's Next Campaign—the War Against the Yellow Press," yellow journalism is attacked for its threats, insults, filth, grime, blood, death, slander, gore, and blackmail. The cartoon was published in the wake of the Spanish-American War and the cartoonist suggests that, having won the war abroad, the government ought to attack yellow journalists at home.

Photo courtesy: Stock Montage, Inc.

that lowered journalistic standards in order to increase readership. Hearst's and Pulitzer's newspapers featured pictures and comics printed in color and sensationalized news stories designed to increase their readership and capture a share of the burgeoning immigrant population market.

The Progressive movement, discussed in chapter 4, gave rise to a new type of journalism in the early 1920s. **Muckraking** journalists—so named by President Theodore Roosevelt after a special rake designed to collect manure—were devoted to exposing misconduct by government, business, and individual politicians.[6] For Roosevelt, muckraking was a derogatory term used to describe reporters who focused on the carnal underbelly of politics rather than its more lofty pursuits. Nevertheless, much good came from these efforts. Muckrakers stimulated demands for anti-trust regulations—laws that prohibit companies, like large steel companies, from controlling an entire industry—and exposed deplorable working conditions in factories, as well as outright exploitation of workers by business owners. An unfortunate side effect of this emphasis on crusades and investigations, however, was the frequent publication of gossip and rumor without sufficient proof.

As the news business grew, so did the focus on increasing its profitability. Newspapers became more careful and less adversarial in their reporting to avoid alienating the advertisers and readers who produced their revenues. Clearer standards were applied in evaluating the behavior of people in power. Journalism also changed during this period as the industry became more professionalized. Reporters were being trained to adhere to principles of objectivity and balance and motivated by a never ending quest for the "truth."[7]

muckraking
A form of journalism, in vogue in the early twentieth century, concerned with reforming government and business conduct.

You Are the News Editor

Radio News

The advent of radio in the early part of the twentieth century was a media revolution and a revelation to the average American who rarely, if ever, had heard the voice of a president, governor, or senator. The radio became the center of most homes in the evening, when national networks broadcast the news as well as entertainment shows. Calvin Coolidge was the first president to appear on radio on a regular basis, but President Franklin D. Roosevelt made the radio appearance a must-listen by presenting "fireside chats" to promote his New Deal. The soothing voice of Roosevelt made it difficult for most Americans to believe that what the president wanted could be anything other than what was best for America.

News radio, which had begun to take a back seat to television by the mid-1950s, regained popularity with the development of AM talk radio in the mid-1980s. Controversial radio host Rush Limbaugh began the trend with his unabashed conservative views, opening the door for other conservative commentators such as Laura Ingraham, Sean Hannity, and Michael Reagan (son of the former president). Statistics show that these conservative radio hosts have resurrected the radio as a news medium by giving the information that they broadcast a strong ideological bent. In 1997, 12 percent of Americans reported getting their news from talk radio; by 2005, 22 percent did.[8] Liberal groups have attempted to break into the AM market, but to date liberal programming, like Air America, which was established in 2004 but declared bankruptcy in 2006, has had limited success. How fee-based satellite radio services will affect news radio remains to be seen. Sirius Satellite Radio, for example, offers both a conservative and a liberal political talk channel and received significant publicity when radio personality Howard Stern moved his show to Sirius's network in early 2006.

Television News

Television was first demonstrated in the United States at the 1939 Worlds Fair in New York, but it did not take off as a news source until after World War II. While most homes had televisions by the early 1960s, it would take several years more for television to replace print and radio as the nation's chief news provider. In 1963, most networks provided only fifteen minutes of news per day; only two major networks provided thirty minutes of news coverage. During this period, a substantial majority of Americans still received most of their news from newspapers. But, in 2007, 65 percent of Americans claimed to get their news from television, whereas only 27 percent read newspapers, as shown in Figure 15.1.

An important distinction exists between network and cable news stations. Network news has lost viewers since 1980, with the loss becoming even steeper after the advent of cable news. Between 2000 and 2004, viewership for all network news programming declined from 45 percent to 35 percent.[9] Cable news has seen an increase in viewership, from 34 percent in 2000 to 38 percent in 2004. This increase is due in large part to the increased availability of services providing twenty-four-hour news channels. By 2006, 58 percent of all U.S. households subscribed to a cable service, and 29 percent of households were using a direct broadcast satellite (such as DirectTV or DISH Network).[10] Thus, the vast majority of Americans receive cable news in addition to their broadcast stations.

FIGURE 15.1 Where Americans Get Most of Their National and International News: 2000, 2004, and 2007

Source: Pew Research Center for the People and the Press, "Views of Press Values and Performance: 1985–2007," http://people-press.org/reports/.

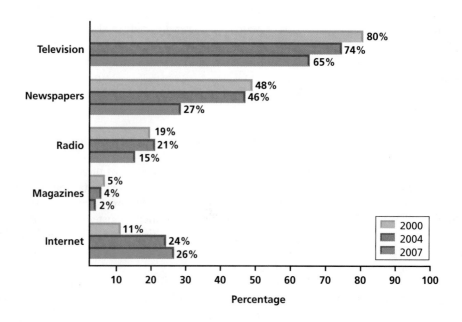

Photo courtesy: left, Marc Asnin/Corbis Saba; right, Comedy Central/Photofest

How do partisan pundits and political satirists affect political coverage? Bill O'Reilly, at left, is one of the country's most visible conservative commentators and the host of the FOX News program *The O'Reilly Factor.* Stephen Colbert, at right, hosts Comedy Central's *The Colbert Report,* which lampoons O'Reilly's conservative views and blustering approach to reporting the news. Both programs have generated loyal audiences and high ratings.

Cable and satellite providers give consumers access to a less glitzy and more unfiltered source of news with C-SPAN, a basic cable channel that offers gavel-to-gavel coverage of congressional proceedings, as well as major political events when Congress is not in session. It also produces some of its own programming, such as *Washington Journal*, which invites scholars and journalists to speak about topics pertaining to their areas of expertise. C-SPAN has expanded its brand to include C-SPAN2 and C-SPAN3, channels that air academic programming, including conferences, seminars, and book presentations. C-SPAN benefits from having no sponsors distracting from (with commercials or banners) or possibly affecting what it broadcasts. Because the content of C-SPAN can be erudite, technical, and sometimes downright tedious (such as the fixed camera shot of the Senate during a roll-call vote), audiences tend to be very small, but they are very loyal and give C-SPAN its place as a truly content-driven news source.

A recent development in television news is the growth in popularity of comedy news programs. While *Saturday Night Live* and other late-night comedy programs, like those hosted by Jay Leno and David Letterman, have mocked politicians and the news for years, more recent programs like Jon Stewart's *Daily Show* and Stephen Colbert's *Colbert Report*—a satire of FOX News's *The O'Reilly Factor*—dedicate their entire program to poking fun at world leaders and current issues. One study conducted by the Annenberg Public Policy Center of the University of Pennsylvania revealed comedy programs actually inform viewers as well as entertain them. Regular viewers of *The Daily Show* were found to know more about world events than nonviewers, even when education, party identification, watching cable news, and other factors were taken into consideration.[11]

The New Media

Increasingly, media consumers, especially those under the age of thirty-five, are abandoning traditional media outlets in favor of other sources. While cable news networks are still the most regularly viewed, the Internet is gaining ground.[10] The Internet, which began as a Department of Defense project named Advanced Research Projects Agency Network (ARPANET) in the late 1960s, has grown into an unprecedented source of public information for people throughout the world. In 2000, whereas only 9 percent of Americans claimed to receive news from the Internet, 29 percent did in 2007.[12] Of course, few people rely exclusively on the

Internet for news, although it is likely in the future that many citizens will use the video components of the World Wide Web to substitute for television news watching. All major networks and newspapers now offer their news online in text form and in video. Major cable news stations, such as CNN, MSNBC, and FOX News, have their own Web sites that also promote their television programming and provide breaking news updates. Many of the news programs on the networks and cable are available as podcasts and other portable formats. The *New York Times* and *Washington Post* are available online for free to users who register. Political magazines such as the conservative *National Review* and liberal *Nation* provide all online content free of charge; like newspaper Web sites, they earn revenue by selling online pop-up and banner advertisements.

Many people wonder if newspapers and television stations currently offering free Web sites are cutting into their own subscription revenues. However, there is very little evidence that this is happening. By and large, the people who use media Web sites are highly informed voters who devour additional information about politics and government and use the Web for updates and supplements to their traditional media services. Indeed, a 2006 study discovered that 96 percent of the daily consumers of online news sites rely on multiple sources to get their news. In short, those most interested in the news will take their news any way they can get it.[13] (To learn more about the media preferences of Americans under 30, see Ideas into Action: Where Do Young People Get Their Campaign News?)

Comparing News Media

In an attempt to assert an online presence and make government more accessible, the U.S. government provides its own news to the public over the Internet. Press releases, government forms, statistical data, and other information are available on Web sites created for all the major departments and agencies. The president and both houses of Congress also have official Web sites that offer basic information regarding the history and function of the respective bodies and current issues before them. Users can also access the complete voting record of individual members of Congress on the Senate and House sites and use the contact information found there to contact any representatives or senators. Individual members of Congress also have their own Web sites that allow them to promote their personalities, activities, and policy views. State governments and an increasing number of local governments have adopted similar online practices.[14]

The Internet also offers access to foreign news media previously unavailable to most Americans. The British Broadcasting Channel (BBC) has a Web site entirely devoted to news and available in over forty languages. International newspapers offer online content, although usually in their native languages. Al-Jazeera, a major Arabic television news source, has an English-language Web site providing news concerning the Middle East. By visiting alternative news sources like these, individuals gain a more nuanced and informed understanding of global issues.

The future relationship between the Internet and politics remains hard to predict. While there was general skepticism just a few years ago, most analysts now believe that as today's computer-literate children and young people become adult voters, the Web is likely to become the primary source of information about politics and government. (To learn more about the public's media choices by age group, see Table 15.1.) The current debate among

Thinking Globally

Internet Access in Iran

Despite the many restrictions the Iranian government places on Internet usage, several million Iranians follow political news on the Internet, and political parties have their own active Web sites. In 2006, the authorities banned high-speed Internet downloads on private computers. The government also uses sophisticated filtering equipment to block hundreds of Web sites and blogs that it considers religiously or politically inappropriate. Iran has jailed a number of bloggers and shut down dozens of Web sites.

- How effective are government restrictions on Internet access and content as a way to control the information citizens receive?
- How useful is the Internet as a source of information for people living under authoritarian governments, such as Iran?
- Under what circumstances is political information accessed from the Internet likely to be more reliable than information in more traditional print sources such as newspapers? Under what circumstances is Internet information likely to be less reliable than traditional print media sources?

Where Do Young People Get Their Campaign News?

In January 2008, the Pew Research Center for the People and the Press stated in a press release that many young voters (age eighteen to twenty-nine) rely on the Internet for campaign news: 42 percent of young voters, 26 percent of voters age thirty to forty-nine, and 15 percent of voters age fifty or older use the Internet for campaign news. Pew also found that young voters rely on comedy television shows, such as *The Daily Show* and *Saturday Night Live*, for campaign information: 21 percent of young voters use comedy television shows, much higher than the 5 percent of those thirty or older.[a] The fact that young voters might make voting decisions based on a quip from Stephen Colbert or a skit featuring Tina Fey may upset many in academia and in the media. One journalist disparagingly called the age bracket "the Young and the Newsless."[b]

But other data are quite encouraging and point toward a greater level of political awareness and engagement for today's youth. The Pew studies also have revealed that for Americans of all ages, only 4 percent rely exclusively on the Internet to get news about the campaign. Moreover, when online, voters gravitate toward the Web sites with traditional news sources, with MSNBC, CNN, and Yahoo News getting the most traffic.

Pew's most surprising finding, however, was that voters regularly watching *The Daily Show*, *The Colbert Report*, and other late-night comedy shows are more knowledgeable about current affairs than the average voter. What explains this phenomenon is that these shows tend to draw well-educated audiences and those already following politics. Well-informed young voters in particular gravitate to newer media for learning about politics.[c]

So when Jon Stewart reminds the audience, as he often does, that he anchors a fake news show, the audience will listen and, after the "Moment of Zen" segment, check the headlines on the Web site of a major newspaper. After all, when told that *The Daily Show* could be confused with an old form of satire or a new kind of journalism, Stewart said,

"Well, then, that either speaks to the sad state of comedy or the sad state of the news."[d]

- Why are traditional ways of getting the news, such as newspapers, radio, magazines, and television, less appealing to young voters than comedy shows and the Internet? How are traditional media responding to the popularity of the Internet and comedy shows as venues for the news?
- Go to the Web site of *The Daily Show* (www.thedailyshow.com) and watch an archived interview that Jon Stewart conducted with a 2008 presidential candidate. Next, visit the Web site of ABC News's *This Week* (www.abcnews.go.com/ThisWeek) and watch an interview conducted by George Stephanopoulos with the same candidate. What differences do you notice in the tone and substance of the interviews? What do you see in each format that is either beneficial or harmful to the public interest?
- Go to Comedy Central's Web site for *The Colbert Report* (www.comedycentral.com/colbertreport) and search for archived clips of the "Better Know a District" segment, where the host profiles a congressional district and interviews its member of Congress. Watch three or four of these segments, preferably those closer to where you live. Do these profiles and interviews educate the public in some way? Why or why not?
- In what ways do comedy shows and Internet news sources, including blogs and other user-generated content, enhance the media's role in a democratic society? In what ways do new media undermine the media's role in serving democracy?

[a]Pew Research Center, "Cable and Internet Loom Large in Fragmented Political News Universe" January 11, 2004, and "Social Networking and Online Videos Take Off," January 11, 2008, http://www.pewinternet.org.

[b]Melanie McFarland, "Young People Turning Comedy Shows into Serious News Source," *Seattle Post-Intelligencer*, January 22, 2004, http://seattlepi.nwsource.com.

[c]Pew Research Center, "What Americans Know: 1989–2007," April 15, 2007.

[d]Jon Stewart interview by Bill Moyers, *NOW*, PBS, July 11, 2003.

scholars is whether all the information available on the Web will be good for politics and society or not. Most believe that the availability of all this information makes for a better-informed and more active electorate.[15] Others are concerned that only the more educated and affluent will benefit from a greater reliance on technology and that this will produce new inequalities. There also is concern that the ability to view only those news sources that support one's existing views and ideological preferences and a tendency to communicate only with like-minded people will polarize Americans further, rather than allowing them to bridge differences and identify common ground.[16] A crucial question for the future is whether citizens will devote the time necessary to find valid and balanced data amidst the almost unlimited information available through the Internet.

TABLE **15.1** The News Generation Gap

	18–29 %	30–49 %	50–64 %	65+ %
Regularly watch/listen to:				
Nightly network news	9	24	38	43
Cable TV news	30	31	40	46
Local TV news	42	51	60	65
Morning news show	20	22	26	23
C-SPAN	4	4	6	9
NewsHour with Jim Lehrer	4	4	6	9
National Public Radio	15	21	18	11
Political talk radio shows	21	21	20	14
The Daily Show with Jon Stewart	11	7	4	3
The O'Reilly Factor	4	7	11	14
Did yesterday				
Read a newspaper	22	33	46	57
Watched TV news	49	53	63	69
Listened to radio news	26	43	39	27

Source: Pew Research Center for the People and the Press, "Maturing Internet New Audience—Broader Than Deep," July 30, 2006, http://people-press.org.

Current Media Trends

The editors of the first partisan newspapers could scarcely have imagined what their profession would become more than two centuries later. The number and diversity of media outlets today are stunning. The **print media** consist of many thousands of daily and weekly newspapers, magazines, newsletters, and journals. **Broadcast media** encompass traditional radio and television stations, as well as satellite and cable services. The **new media** are the latest technologies, such as the Internet, that blur the lines between media sources and create new opportunities for the dissemination of news and other information.

The Influence of Media Giants

Every newspaper, radio station, television station, and Web site is influential in its own area, but only a handful of media outlets are influential nationally, and an even smaller number of media giants have international influence. The United States has no nationwide daily newspapers to match the influence of Great Britain's *Times*, *Guardian*, and *Daily Telegraph*, all of which are avidly read in virtually every corner of the United Kingdom. The national orientation of the British print media can be traced to the smaller size of the country and also to London's role as both the national capital and that nation's largest cultural metropolis. The vastness of the United States and the existence of many large cities effectively preclude a nationally united print medium in this country.

However, the *New York Times*, the *Wall Street Journal*, *USA Today*, and the *Christian Science Monitor* are distributed nationally, and other newspapers, such as the *Washington Post* and the *Los Angeles Times*, have substantial influence from coast to coast. These six newspapers also have a pronounced effect on what the major national broadcast **networks** (ABC, CBS, NBC, and FOX) air on their evening news programs, and what the major cable news networks (CNN, FOX News, MSNBC, and CNBC) air around the clock. These news shows are carried by hundreds of local stations—called **affiliates**—that are associated with the national networks and may choose to carry their programming. **Wire services,** such as the Associated Press (AP), Reuters, and United Press International (UPI) distribute news around the globe. Most newspapers subscribe to at least one of these services, which not only produce their own news stories but also put on the wire major stories produced by other media outlets.

print media
The traditional form of mass media, comprising newspapers, magazines, newsletters, and journals.

broadcast media
Television, radio, cable, and satellite services.

new media
Technologies, such as the Internet, that blur the line between media sources and create new opportunities for the dissemination of news and other information.

network
An association of broadcast stations (radio or television) that share programming through a financial arrangement.

affiliates
Local television stations that carry the programming of a national network.

wire service
An electronic delivery of news gathered by the news service's correspondents and sent to all member news media organizations.

Several national news magazines, whose subscribers number in the millions, supplement the national newspapers, wire services, and broadcast networks. *Time*, *Newsweek*, and *U.S. News and World Report* bring the week's news into focus and headline one event or trend for special treatment. Other news magazines stress commentary from an ideological viewpoint, including the *Nation* (progressive), *New Republic* (moderate-liberal), and the *Weekly Standard* (conservative). These last three publications have much smaller circulations, but because their readerships are composed of activists and opinion leaders, they have disproportionate influence. There are now some good, exclusively Web-based magazines, such as Salon.com and Slate.com. These Web sites direct their content to a hipper, generally younger audience by emphasizing cultural forces at work within day-to-day political events.

Media Consolidation

Private ownership of the media in the United States has proven to be a mixed blessing. While private ownership assures media independence, something that cannot be said about state-controlled media in the former Soviet Union or in present-day China, it also brings market pressures to journalism that do not exist in state-run systems. The news media in the United States are multibillion-dollar, for-profit businesses that ultimately are driven by the bottom line. As with all free-market enterprises, the pressure in privately owned media is to increasingly consolidate media ownership, so as to reap the benefits that come from larger market shares and fewer large-scale competitors.

Unlike traditional industries, where the primary concern associated with consolidation is the manipulation of prices made possible by monopolies or near monopolies, the consolidation of the media poses a far greater potential risk. Should the news media become dominated by a few mega-corporations, the fear is that these groups could limit the flow of information and ideas that form the very essence of a free society and that make democracy possible. While it is unlikely that profit-driven media chains intentionally manipulate the news in favor of specific political perspectives, it is possible that market forces, aimed at expanding market shares and pleasing advertisers, lead to the focus on sensational issues, news as entertainment, and avoidance of issues that could bore or alienate their audiences.

In 1923, over 500 cities had competing daily newspapers; by 2008, that number was down to a mere eleven. Most daily newspapers are owned by large media conglomerates such as Gannett, McClatchy, and the Tribune Company. The top ten media chains account for 54 percent of daily circulation, while only 280 of the nearly 1,460 daily newspapers are independently owned; thus, chains own over 80 percent of the daily newspapers.[17] None of the three original television networks remain independent entities: General Electric owns NBC, Viacom owns CBS, and Walt Disney owns ABC. In the print media arena, Gannett, the parent company of *USA Today* and roughly 100 other newspapers in the United States, enjoys the nation's largest circulation rate. From the mid-1970s to the current period, the number of owners of full-power TV stations and daily newspapers has been cut by more than half. In radio, a single company, Clear Channel, which owns and operates nearly 1,200 radio stations, accounts for roughly 18 percent of the total market. While government officials continue to grapple with the consequences of a market-driven media industry, media outlets continue to exert considerable pressure on policy makers, demanding more, not less, media consolidation.

Increasing Use of Experts

Most journalists know a little bit about many subjects but do not specialize in any one area and certainly do not possess enough knowledge to fill the hours of airtime made possible by cable television's twenty-four-hour news cycle. Therefore, especially on cable stations, the news media employ expert consultants from a number of different disciplines ranging from medical ethics to political campaigning. These experts, also referred to as pundits, or the more derogatory term "talking heads," are hired to discuss the dominant issues of the day. For example, during the proceedings of the 9/11 Commission, which investigated the September 11, 2001, terrorist attacks on the United States, and after the release of the commission's report, with its recommendations on how to improve security and intelligence gathering, one could not turn on the television or read a newspaper without encountering a stable full of government officials, former intelligence officers, and other experts giving their thoughts. It is unclear, however, just how objective and independent many of these experts actually are. A recent investigate report in the *New York Times* revealed that a number of the military analysts who have been commenting on issues related to the Iraq War and terrorism have business ties to military contractors and were subjected to attempts by the Bush administration to influence their views during private "briefings" held for them at the White House.[18]

One 1992 study about how experts affect the views of Americans toward foreign policy says that "news from experts or research studies is estimated to have almost as great an impact" as anchorpersons, reporters in the field, or special commentators. Such findings are both good and bad for Americans. On the one hand, the "strong effects by commentators and experts are compatible with a picture of a public that engages in collective deliberation and takes expertise seriously." On the other, "one might argue that the potency of media commentators and of ostensibly nonpartisan TV 'experts' is disturbing. Who elected them to shape our views of the world? Who says they are insightful or even unbiased?"[19]

The lesson is clear. Viewers and readers must rely on the networks and newspapers to choose experts wisely. Rarely is there much discussion of the backgrounds and the credentials of the individuals who are placed on the screen. There may be biases in the commentary of these experts, but it is the hope that a diversity of expert opinion is reflected on each subject throughout the media. Nonetheless, biases do break through, and many critics claim that various media outlets consciously represent biased points of view in their reportage.

Narrowcasting

narrowcasting
Targeting media programming at specific populations within society.

In recent years, fierce competition to attract viewers and the availability of additional television channels made possible by cable and satellite television have led media outlets to move toward **narrowcasting**—targeting media programming at specific populations within society. Within the realm of cable news, the two ratings leaders, CNN and FOX News, have begun engaging in this form of niche journalism. The two stations divide audiences by ideology. FOX News emphasizes a conservative viewpoint and CNN increasingly stresses a more liberal perspective, although the FOX view is often more pronounced.[20] Table 15.2 indicates where Republicans, Democrats, and independents prefer to get their news about political campaigns.

The nation has also seen the rise of Spanish-language news programs on stations such as Univision and TeleMundo, as well as news programming geared toward African American viewers on cable's Black Entertainment Television (BET). In fact, well before cable television, African Americans benefited from a lengthy history of newspapers published specifically for the African American community (see chapter 6). And for Christian conservatives, Pat Robertson's Christian Broadcasting Network (CBN), with its flagship *700 Club*, has been narrowcasting news for over forty years.

While narrowcasting can help to promote the interests of parts of the population, especially racial and ethnic minorities who may ordinarily be left out of mainstream media coverage, it comes with a social cost. Narrowcasting increases the chance that group members will rely on news that is appealing to their preexisting views. By limiting one's exposure to a broad range of information or competing views, narrowcast-

TABLE **15.2** Main Source of Campaign News by Party Affiliation

Percentage who regularly watch/listen	Total %	Rep. %	Dem. %	Ind. %
FOX News	23	34	20	17
CNN	22	19	28	20
MSNBC	11	8	15	10
CNBC	11	9	13	8
NBC Nightly News	15	14	19	13
CBS Evening News	13	13	17	9
ABC World News	14	12	18	12
NPR	17	13	22	18
NewsHour (PBS)	5	4	7	4
O'Reilly Factor	9	16	5	7
Rush Limbaugh	5	10	3	3
Larry King	4	3	7	3
Daily Show	6	3	10	7

Note: Figures add to more than 100 percent because respondents could list more than one source.
Source: Pew Research Center for the People and the Press, "Maturing Internet New Audience—Broader Than Deep," July 30, 2006, http://people-press.org.

ing could result in the further polarization of public opinion. The polarization made possible by narrowcasting is particularly problematic when it comes to programs that are narrowcasted in a specific ideological direction.[21]

Technological Innovation

While technological innovation has been a constant throughout American history and has regularly transformed the way information travels, it is not always possible to recognize the full significance of technological changes while society is in the midst of technological upheaval, as we are today. The technological transformation that the world has experienced in the last decade, with the explosion of Web resources and electronic media outlets, continues unabated.

To date, we have seen how the new media can simultaneously work to consolidate the flow of news and to disperse news. The new media give the media giants, discussed above, the ability to project their news messages to local and regional news outlets around the world, which are often eager to reproduce or at least respond to the message of the dominant media. As technology continues to reduce the cost of producing news, making anyone with a personal computer, Internet connection, and something to say a potential news source, the value of reliable and high-quality information may continue to grow in importance, further adding to the influence of the existing media giants. Since time is limited and the available news options made possible by the new media are virtually unlimited, it is likely that information misers (information seekers who want the news but do not have time to waste) will continue to be drawn to reliable news outlets.

Ironically, the same technology that has given rise to media giants also has the ability to increase the diversity of available news. **Blogs,** which have rapidly grown in popularity in recent years, are Web-based journal entries that provide an editorial and news outlet for citizens. They have become webs of information, linking together people with common ideological or issue-specific interests.

blog
Web-based journal entries that provide an editorial and news outlet for citizens.

In some instances, information made public on blogs has been picked up by mainstream news outlets, revealing how the new media provide unprecedented opportunities for the flow of information. Following FEMA's slow response to Hurricane Katrina during the summer of 2005, bloggers on sites like Daily KOS railed against FEMA director Michael Brown for his questionable credentials and his handling of disaster relief in New Orleans. Bloggers pointed out that Brown, who prior to heading FEMA had served as the head of the International Arabian Horse Association, lacked disaster relief experience, a fact that was later echoed in the mainstream press.

Many blogs are devoted to ideological rabble-rousing and rumor mongering, while others provide reasoned discourse. The right-leaning Drudge Report (www.drudgereport.com) pioneered the spreading of newsworthy rumors during the second Clinton administration. Well-known right-leaning political Web sites include Red State (www.redstate.org) and Townhall (www.townhall.com). On the left are the Daily KOS (www.dailykos.com), the Huffington Post (www.huffingtonpost.com), and TalkingPointsMemo (www.talkingpointsmemo.com).

While blogs and their user-generated content seem to offer the public a more democratic means of engaging in public discussion, there is growing concern that the blogosphere has become dominated by a small elite. While there are over 70 million blogs on the Web, only a very small number of sites have a sizeable audience and, thus, attract most of the advertising dollars available. Moreover, most of the bloggers on the "A-list" are graduates of the nation's top colleges, and many have post-graduate degrees. But maybe more significant is that only 30 percent of Americans view blogs as an important source for news, ranking them behind not only traditional media sources, but also friends and neighbors.[22]

citizen journalism
The collecting, reporting, and analyzing of news content by ordinary individuals.

Other Web sites have taken a more inclusive and participatory approach to providing content to their users. Relying exclusively on **citizen journalists** to collect, report, and analyze news and information, these sites have become an increasingly popular means for serving local needs and filling a void left by traditional news organizations. Sites such as Backfence.com in the D.C. suburbs and iBrattleboro.com in Burlington, Vermont, keep their neighbors informed about important events in their community such as town meetings, school closings, and recycling initiatives. These sites also feature numerous posts on births, marriages and recent deaths, personal accomplishments, do-it-yourself advice, and other human-interest subjects.[23] The largest and most sophisticated site for citizen-generated content is Ohmy News International. Established in South Korea in 2000, the site is viewed by over 2.5 million unique users a month and receives content from over 60,000 citizen reporters from all over the world. In addition, Ohmy News employs a staff of sixty editors to assist contributors and monitor their posts, and it established the first journalism school for citizen reporting in 2007.[24] Today, there are over 1,500 citizen journalism sites operating worldwide, but only 20 percent of these sites earn a profit.[25]

Traditional news media outlets have begun to rely on citizen journalists for news gathering, especially in cases where the public can provide unprecedented access to events as they are unfolding. For example, people who were themselves experiencing the disasters of Hurricane Katrina in 2001, the Indian Ocean tsunami in 2004, and the terrorist bombings in London subway stations in 2005 were able to provide information to police and rescue workers about what was happening through wireless devices and digital cameras before journalists could make it to the scene. Another

Photo courtesy: Andrea Mohin/
The New York Times/Redux Pictures

Are bloggers journalists? Joshua Micah Marshall, founder of the progressive blog Talking Points Memo, began his journalistic career writing for The American Prospect. He started his blog during the 2000 Florida recount and is credited with publicizing then-Senate Majority Leader Trent Lott's praise of Strom Thurmond's 1948 presidential run as a segregationist. The ensuing controversy resulted in Lott's resignation. Marshall won The Polk Award for Legal Reporting for his coverage of the Bush administration's dismissal of several U.S. attorneys.

interesting example of citizen journalism in recent years has been the establishment of war blogs, where soldiers serving in Afghanistan and Iraq have provided firsthand accounts of their war experiences. Some newspapers such as the *Greensboro News-Record* and *Lawrence Journal-World* have made a more formal commitment to using citizen-generated content as a way to better connect with their readers and compensate for decreasing news budgets.[26]

While the future of the new media remains as unpredictable as the latest blog entry, it is likely that the new media will continue to blur the lines between print and broadcast, consumer and producer, commentary and fact, and entertainment and news. The distinctions between the Internet and broadcast and cable news are likely to shrink as the technologies merge. Wireless handheld devices that allow users to send e-mail and text messages, make phone calls, browse the Internet, and download music and video clips are increasing in popularity. The emergence of online social networks such as MySpace and Facebook, video- and photo-sharing sites like YouTube and Flickr, and the citizen-encyclopedia, Wikipedia, are also affecting the ways in which Americans share and consume the news and information. The further development of these applications offers the potential for the public to have a greater voice in public affairs and to be more engaged in civic life.

Rules Governing the Media

The First Amendment to the U.S. Constitution, which prohibits Congress from abridging the freedom of the press, does not provide the media with unlimited print and broadcast freedom. A wide array of internal and external checks governs the behavior of the modern media.

Journalistic Standards

The heaviest restrictions placed on reporters do not come from government regulations but from the industry's own professional norms and each journalist's level of integrity, as well as from the oversight provided by editors who are ultimately responsible for the accuracy of the news they produce. To help guide the ethical behavior of journalists, the Society of Professional Journalists publishes a detailed "Code of Ethics" for journalists that includes principles and standards governing issues like avoiding conflicts of interest, dealing ethically with sources, and verifying the information being reported.

As with any profession, journalism has its fair share of unscrupulous actors, people who disregard professional ethics in pursuit of self-interest. In the early 1980s, *Washington Post* reporter Janet Cook won a Pulitzer Prize for her gripping, but thoroughly fabricated story about an eight-year-old boy addicted to heroin. Stephen Glass of the *New Republic* was fired after it was discovered he embellished his articles with colorful quotes and edgy facts that were not grounded in reality. Glass even faked notes and sources to deceive his editors. Jayson Blair, another ethically challenged young reporter, was fired from the *New York Times* in 2003 when it was discovered that he, too, made up quotes and interviews to pad his reporting.

While blatant examples of journalistic fraud are rare, journalists often grapple with less obvious ethical dilemmas. Whether the issue is how to make use of a confidential source, how to deal with "off the record" comments, or simply determining what information is newsworthy, journalists are in the business of balancing competing pressures. The pressure to get the story right is often weighed against the pressure to get the story first, or at the very least to get the story finished before the next deadline. The twenty-four-hour news cycle, brought to life by cable news stations and nourished by the expansion of Web-based media, has only heightened the pressure to produce interesting copy in a timely manner.

In order to assure professional integrity, several major newspapers and magazines, including the *Washington Post* and the *New York Times*, have hired internal media critics, or ombudsmen, who assess how well their newspaper and its reporters are performing their duties. Some nonprofits, such as the Project for Excellence in Journalism and the Pew Research Center for the People and the Press in Washington, D.C., conduct scientific studies of the news and entertainment media. Other groups, including the conservative watchdog group Accuracy in Media (AIM) and its liberal counterpart Fairness and Accuracy in Reporting (FAIR), critique news stories and attempt to set the record straight on important issues that they believe have received biased coverage. All of these organizations have a role in ensuring that the media provide fair and objective coverage of topics that are of importance to citizens. (To learn about one journalist's surprising approach to insuring unbiased reporting, see Politics Now: Why I Didn't Vote Today.)

Government Regulation of the Electronic Media

The U.S. government regulates the electronic component of the media. Unlike radio or television, the print media are exempt from most forms of government regulation, although even print media must not violate community standards for obscenity, for instance. There are two reasons for this unequal treatment. First, the airwaves used by the electronic media are considered public property and are leased by the federal government to private broadcasters. Second, those airwaves are in limited supply; without some regulation, the nation's many radio and television stations would interfere with one another's frequency signals. It was not, in fact, the federal government but rather private broadcasters, frustrated by the numerous instances in which signal jamming occurred, that initiated the call for government regulation in the early days of the electronic media.

In 1996, Congress passed the sweeping Telecommunications Act, deregulating whole segments of the electronic media. The Telecommunications Act sought to provide an optimal balance of competing corporate interests, technological innovations, and consumer needs. It appeared to offer limitless opportunities for entrepreneurial companies to provide enhanced services to consumers. The result of this deregulation was the sudden merger of previously distinct kinds of media in order to create a more "multimedia" approach to communicating information and entertainment. This paved the way for the creation of multimedia corporations such as Viacom, Time Warner, and Comcast.

In June 2003, the Federal Communications Commission (FCC) attempted to build on these deregulatory changes by proposing to increase the total national audience a corporation could reach from 35 percent to 45 percent. Since total national audience is measured by how many stations a corporation owns, this increase would have allowed corporations to own more television stations.

Both Republicans and Democrats in Congress opposed the FCC changes, arguing that the country needs more and not less media diversification, given increasing media outlet consolidation. Furthermore, many ideologically opposing groups also argued against media consolidation: conservative religious groups believe that large media corporations purvey immoral content, and liberal groups believe that less diversification kills community-based media. Finally, there was a general public outcry, with legislators receiving angry letters and e-mails demanding that Congress stop the FCC.[27] At the end of the year, Congress had passed an amendment to an appropriations bill that raised the 35 percent cap on a national audience to 39 percent, a compromise that allowed the largest corporations to retain their current share—the largest corporation, Viacom, had 38.9 percent of the national audience—but prohibited any further expansion.[28]

The FCC's attempt to enact other controversial deregulatory changes related to media cross-ownership in specific markets was placed on hold. The Third Circuit

POLITICS NOW

Source: POLITICO, www.dyn.politico.com.　　　　　　　　February 13, 2008

Election Neutrality

Why I Didn't Vote Today

MIKE ALLEN

Ever since I was a journalistic sprout covering town-council races in rural Virginia, I've had an Election Day ritual of going to the polls—but not to vote. I talk to voters to get a sense of their mood and passions, then head off without going inside.

I'm part of a minority school of thought among journalists that we owe it to the people we cover, and to our readers, to remain agnostic about elections, even in private. I figure that if the news media serve as an (imperfect) umpire, neither team wants us taking a few swings.

My Mom and Grandma called voting "exercising your franchise," and it's not a privilege to forgo lightly. But I feel strongly enough about it that I've only voted in one election in my life—a Democratic primary in Virginia years ago. My roommates were working endless hours on one of the campaigns. It was their life, and I would have felt badly to let them down.

The first time I thought about the special duty journalists owe to voters and candidates was during my freshman year at Washington and Lee University, where I was covering student-body elections for the paper, which believe it or not is called The Ring-tum Phi. You voted in a big barrel in the freshman quad and I started to walk over there but then realized that if I dropped in a slip of paper, the candidates I'd been covering—and the readers who trusted me—could see me and know that I wasn't neutral in my heart.

This view was reinforced when I started covering state politics, which is much more intimate than the massive circuses that follow the presidential candidates. When you're assigned to a candidate for senator or governor, oftentimes you ride in their van. When they're tired, you're tired. When you're hungry, they're hungry. When they're sick, you're sick. I just wouldn't feel right about hanging out with—and writing about—a candidate after rendering a secret thumbs-up or thumbs-down.

The most notable proponent of this view is one of my heroes and former bosses, Leonard Downie Jr., the executive editor of The Washington Post, who is among the fairest journalists I have been lucky enough to meet. Len doesn't impose his stance on the newsroom, where it was my experience that many of the reporters and editors voted.

In an online chat on washington post.com in 2004, Downie explained: "I decided to stop voting when I became the ultimate gatekeeper for what is published in the newspaper. I wanted to keep a completely open mind about everything we covered and not make a decision, even in my own mind or the privacy of the voting booth, about who should be president or mayor, for example."

I try to convince the kids in my life that principled stands often have practical benefits. That's certainly the case with the ballot box. Putting aside the sound reasons for remaining electorally pure on behalf of our sources and readers, it's a great dodge. People make all kinds of inaccurate assumptions about the personal views of reporters. I can always say: I don't vote—and you can look it up.

Discussion Questions

1. *Does not voting seem to be an effective strategy for journalists to adopt to help them be objective in their reporting? Why or why not? What might be lost in campaign coverage if more journalists adopted this writer's point of view?*

2. *How might journalists' backgrounds and life experiences affect their reporting? What strategies could journalists use to keep their personal biases out of their reporting?*

Court of Appeals issued a stay blocking the FCC's changes and subsequently asked the FCC to revise its proposals. In December 2007, the FCC issued a revised rule lifting the cross-ownership ban for televisions and newspapers in the twenty largest markets, and it established procedures to grant waivers for combinations in smaller markets if they served the public interest.[29]

Content Regulation

The government also subjects the electronic media to substantial **content regulation** that, again, does not apply to the print media. Charged with ensuring that the airwaves "serve the public interest, convenience, and necessity," the FCC has attempted to promote equity in broadcasting. For example, the **equal time rule** requires that broadcast stations sell air time equally to all candidates in a political campaign if they choose to sell it to any, which they are under no obligation to do. An exception to this rule is a political debate: stations may exclude from this event less well-known and minor-party candidates.

Until 2000, FCC rules required broadcasters to give candidates the opportunity to respond to personal attacks and to political endorsements by the station. In October

content regulation
Government attempts to regulate the substance of the mass media.

equal time rule
The rule that requires broadcast stations to sell air time equally to all candidates in a political campaign if they choose to sell it to any.

2000, however, a federal court of appeals found these rules, long criticized by broadcasters as having a chilling effect on free speech, to be unconstitutional when the FCC was unable to justify these regulations to the court's satisfaction.[30]

The most recent controversy over regulation of media content involves the communications industry and Internet service providers. Common carriers as defined by the Communications Act of 1934, such as telephone companies, are required to be neutral in the content they carry over their networks and cannot limit or censor individuals or organizations they may disagree with. Internet service providers (ISPs), including telephone and cable companies that offer Internet service, are not subject to the common carrier definition and therefore may legally block transmission through their networks of content they find objectionable. Many free speech advocates and high-tech firms are lobbying Congress for "net neutrality" legislation, which would define ISPs as common carriers, placing on them the same obligations of content neutrality to which companies offering telephone services must adhere.

Advocates of net neutrality worry especially about the ability of some ISPs to hinder the free and open communication of political ideas by either blocking Web sites with objectionable content or forcing content providers who do not pay premium fees to run at slower speeds.[31] The ISPs counter that the inability to charge firms that use more bandwidth will make it harder to finance future enhancements to the Internet. They also reject claims that they have any intention of degrading access or restricting content, which would outrage their customers and hurt their bottom line. Congress's attempt to pass net neutrality legislation failed in 2006.[32] Verizon's initial decision to block text messages by an abortion rights group to members who had agreed to receive them in 2007, as well as Comcast's restrictions on the flow of large video and music clips on file-sharing networks in 2008, may cause Congress to revisit the issue of net neutrality if these practices become more common.[33]

Efforts to Control the News Media

In the United States, only government officials can be prosecuted for divulging classified information; no such law applies to journalists. Nor can the government, except under extremely rare and confined circumstances, impose prior restraints on the press—that is, the government cannot censor the press. This principle was clearly established in *New York Times Co. v. U.S.* (1971).[34] In this case, the Supreme Court ruled that the government could not prevent publication by the *New York Times* of the Pentagon Papers, classified government documents about the Vietnam War that had been stolen, photocopied, and sent to the *Times* and the *Washington Post* by Daniel Ellsberg, a government employee. "Only a free and unrestrained press can effectively expose deception in the government," Justice Hugo Black wrote in a concurring opinion for the Court. "To find that the President has 'inherent power' to halt the publication of news by resort to the courts would wipe out the First Amendment."

Similar concerns arose in the United States during the 1991 Persian Gulf War. Reporters were upset that the military was not forthcoming about events on and off the battlefield, while some Pentagon officials and many persons in the general public accused the press of telling the enemy too much in their dispatches. The U.S. government attempted to isolate offending reporters by keeping them away from the battlefield. This maneuver was highly controversial and very unpopular with news correspondents because it directly interfered with their job of reporting the news. Defenders of efforts to curb media coverage in war zones cite safety and intelligence con-

Thinking Globally

Censorship in North Korea

North Koreans live in the most heavily censored country in the world. The North Korean government tightly controls all domestic radio and television stations and newspapers. Radio and television receivers are locked to government-specified frequencies, and the content of all broadcasts is determined by a single government agency.

- Government censorship of the media deprives citizens of information; however, some might argue that the American press has too much freedom. Do you agree? Why or why not?
- What are the consequences of a censored media in repressive nations such as North Korea, Myanmar (Burma), and Cuba? What would you expect to happen if these countries allowed more open access to a variety of news sources?

cerns. Critics of the military's public affairs strategies during times of war resent its emphasis on controlling information and view it as an attempt to manipulate public support. Critics argue that civilian and military officials alike have a keen awareness of and desire to avoid "Vietnam syndrome," where widespread resistance to the war, some have argued, grew out of the media's unfettered access to the front lines and broadcasts of graphic footage on television.

The George W. Bush administration provided an interesting compromise to this dilemma when it gave journalists the opportunity to be embedded with various parts of the military and report about the experiences of each unit when U.S.-led forces invaded Iraq in 2003. Organizations such as the Project for Excellence in Journalism found that embedded journalists typically provided only anecdotal stories, lacked the overall context of the war, and stressed American successes without much coverage of Iraqi civilian casualties. While conceding these limitations, some scholars maintain that an embedded journalist is better than no journalist at all, especially since journalists of foreign news organizations, like al-Jazeera, are able to cover the events from different perspectives.[35]

Photo courtesy: Jill Carroll Collection/Getty Images

How well do embedded journalists report the news? This image shows Jill Carroll, at right, a freelance journalist for *The Christian Science Monitor*, embedded with U.S. troops in Iraq. Carroll was the thirty-first foreign journalist to be kidnapped in Iraq, but was safely released after three months in captivity.

Not all Western democracies provide their media the same level of freedom. In Great Britain, the state-run British Broadcasting Corporation (BBC) and the privately owned media are subject to unusually strict regulation on the publication of governmental secrets. For example, the sweeping Official Secrets Act of 1911 makes it a criminal offense for a Briton to publish any facts, material, or news collected in that person's capacity as a public minister or civil servant. The act was invoked when the British government banned the publication of *Spy Catcher*, a 1987 novel written by Peter Wright, a former British intelligence officer, who undoubtedly collected much of the book's information while on the job. On the other hand, Great Britain applies a far more liberal standard of indecency to its broadcasters, who exercise considerably more freedom than Americans with regard to explicit content. To assist the media in determining what is and is not publishable, Great Britain provides a system called D-notice, which allows journalists to submit questionable material to a review committee before its publication.

Whatever one's specific quarrel with the American news media, most Americans would probably prefer that the media tell them too much rather than not enough. Totalitarian and authoritarian societies have a tame journalism, after all. Media excesses may be considered the price of popular sovereignty.

How the Media Cover Politics

The news media focus an extraordinary amount of attention on our politicians and the day-to-day operations of our government. Since 1983, the number of print (newspaper and magazine) reporters accredited at the U.S. Capitol jumped from 2,300 to more than 4,000 today.[36] On the campaign trail, a similar phenomenon has occurred. In the 1960s, a presidential candidate in the primaries would attract a press entourage of at most a few dozen reporters, but today a hundred or more journalists can be seen tagging along with a front-runner. When a victorious candidate reaches the White

House, the media are there as well; in 2007, sixty-eight journalists were credentialed as daily White House correspondents.[37] Consequently, a politician's every public utterance is reported and intensively scrutinized and interpreted in the media.

How the Press and Public Figures Interact

Communication between elected officials or public figures and the media takes different forms. A **press release** is a written document offering an official comment or position on an issue or news event; it is usually printed on paper and faxed or handed directly to reporters, or increasingly, released by e-mail. A **press briefing** is a relatively restricted live engagement with the press, with the range of questions limited to one or two specific topics. In a press briefing, a press secretary or aide represents the elected official or public figure, who does not appear in person. In a full-blown **press conference,** an elected official appears in person to talk with the press at great length about an unrestricted range of topics. Press conferences provide a field on which reporters struggle to get the answers they need and public figures attempt to retain control of their message and spin the news and issues in ways favorable to them.

On some occasions, candidates and their aides will go on background to give trusted newspersons juicy morsels of negative information about rivals. **On background**—meaning that none of the news can be attributed to the source—is one of several journalistic devices used to elicit information that might otherwise never come to light. **Deep background** is another such device; whereas background talks can be attributed to unnamed senior officials, deep background news must be completely unsourced, with the reporter giving the reader no hint about the origin of the information. A journalist may also obtain information **off the record,** which means that nothing the official says may be printed. (If a reporter can obtain the same information elsewhere, however, he or she is free to publish it.) By contrast, if a session is **on the record,** as in a formal press conference, every word an official utters can be printed—and used against that official. Not surprisingly, office holders often prefer the other alternatives.

Clearly, these rules regarding source information are necessary for reporters to do their basic job—informing the public. Ironically, the same rules keep the press from fully informing their readers and viewers. Public officials know that journalists are pledged to protect the confidentiality of their sources, and therefore the rules can sometimes be used to an official's own benefit. Politicians and media interact in a variety of other ways as well. Politicians hire campaign consultants who use focus groups and polling in an attempt to gauge how to present the candidate to the media and to the public. Additionally, politicians can attempt to bypass the national news media through paid advertising and by appearing on talk shows and local news programs. (Some of these and other techniques for dealing with the media during a campaign are discussed in greater detail in chapter 14.) Politicians also use the media to attempt to retain a high level of name recognition and to build support for their ideological and policy ideas.

In the past, a reporter would think twice about filing a story critical of a politician's character, and the editors probably would have killed the story had the reporter been foolish enough to do so. The reason? Fear of a libel suit. (Recall from chapter 5 that libel is written defamation of character that unjustly injures a person's reputation.) The first question editors would ask about even an ambiguous or suggestive phrase about a public official was, "If we're sued, can you prove beyond a doubt what you've written?"

Such concerns were significantly reduced in 1964, when the Supreme Court ruled in ***New York Times Co. v. Sullivan*** that simply publishing a defamatory falsehood is not enough to justify a libel judgment.[38] Henceforth, a public official would have to prove "actual malice," a requirement extended three years later to all public figures, such as Hollywood stars and prominent athletes.[39] As discussed in chapter 5, the Supreme Court declared that the First Amendment requires elected officials and candidates to prove that the publisher either believed the challenged statement was

---

press release
A document offering an official comment or position.

press briefing
A relatively restricted session between a press secretary or aide and the press.

press conference
An unrestricted session between an elected official and the press.

on background
Information provided to a journalist that will not be attributed to a named source.

deep background
Information provided to a journalist that will not be attributed to any source.

off the record
Information provided to a journalist that will not be released to the public.

on the record
Information provided to a journalist that can be released and attributed by name to the source.

New York Times Co. v. Sullivan **(1964)**
The Supreme Court concluded that "actual malice" must be proved to support a finding of libel against a public figure.

false or at least entertained serious doubts about its truth and acted recklessly in publishing it in the face of those doubts. The actual malice rule has made it very difficult for public figures to win libel cases.

Covering the Presidency

The three branches of the U.S. government—the executive, the legislative, and the judicial—are roughly equal in power and authority. But, in the world of media coverage, the president is first among equals. All television cables lead to the White House, and a president can address the nation on all networks almost at will. On television, Congress and the courts appear to be divided and confused institutions—different segments contradicting others—whereas the commander in chief is in clear focus as chief of state and head of government. The situation is scarcely different in other democracies. In Great Britain, for example, all media eyes are on No. 10 Downing Street, the office and residence of the prime minister.

Since Franklin D. Roosevelt's time, chief executives have used the office and presidential press conference as a bully pulpit to shape public opinion and explain their actions, as shown in Figure 15.2. The presence of the press in the White House enables a president to appear even on very short notice and to televise live, interrupting regular programming. The White House's press briefing room is a familiar sight on the evening news, not just because presidents use it fairly often, but also because the presidential press secretary has almost daily question and answer sessions there.

The post of press secretary to the president has existed only since Herbert Hoover's administration (1929–1933), and the individual holding it is the president's main disseminator of information to the press. For this vital position, some presidents choose close aides with whom they have worked previously and who are familiar with their thinking. Press secretaries must be very adept at dealing with the news media; some worked as journalists prior to becoming a press secretary, and many go on to press jobs after their stint in the White House. For example, Lyndon B. Johnson's press secretary, Bill Moyers, has produced or hosted many PBS documentaries and series. The first female press secretary, Dee Dee Myers, served under Bill Clinton and

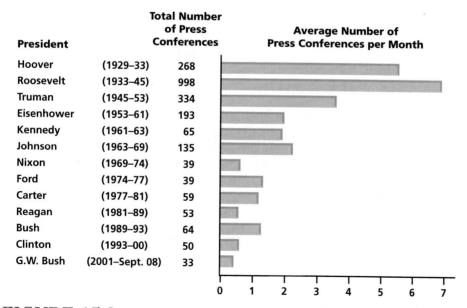

FIGURE 15.2 Presidential Press Conferences
Modern presidents have been holding increasingly fewer press conferences and rely more on their press secretaries and Cabinet officers to brief the media.
Source: White House press office.

Who conducts daily press briefings? Dana Perino served as George W. Bush's fourth press secretary. Here, Perino fields questions in the White House press briefing room, which opened in 1970 on the former site of Franklin D. Roosevelt's swimming pool.

Photo courtesy: Chip Somadevilla/Getty Images

used her experience to launch a career in political punditry. When George W. Bush's second press secretary, Scott McClellan, resigned in May 2006, the Bush administration, in an unusual move, hired political journalist and FOX News commentator Tony Snow to take his place.

While the president receives the vast majority of the press's attention, much of this focus is unfavorable. Dwight Eisenhower once opened up a press conference by inviting the press to "nail him to the cross" as they usually did, and this approach suggests the way most presidents approach their formal encounters with the press. A study in the early 1990s found coverage of George Bush's handling of important national problems was almost solely negative.[40] Analysis of the coverage of Bill Clinton's turbulent presidency found a frenzy of negative media coverage immediately following the Lewinsky scandal, followed by a longer period of more even-handed coverage.[41]

The media faced a more difficult challenge in covering the administration of George W. Bush, a president who prided himself on the tight-lipped, no leaks nature of his White House. No member of his staff appeared on television or in print without prior permission, while Bush kept his direct contact with the press to a minimum. President Bush clearly tried to control his image by controlling how much the press directly encountered him and by speaking at highly staged media events, quite often in military settings, where he delivered a scripted message and presented an interesting visual, but answered no questions from the media.[42]

Throughout his presidential campaign, Barack Obama was quite successful in controlling his image by limiting his exposure to the news media and received some of the most favorable press coverage afforded any presidential candidate in the television age. The relationship between the Obama administration and the press is unlikely to remain as harmonious if this practice is continued in the White House, as journalists become more confrontational when their access to government officials is restricted and information is not forthcoming.

Covering Congress

With 535 voting members representing distinct geographic areas, covering Congress poses a difficult challenge for the media. Nevertheless, the congressional press corps has more than 3,000 members.[43] Most news organizations solve the size and decentralization problems inherent in covering news developments in the legislative branch by concentrating coverage on three groups of individuals. First, the leaders of both parties in both houses receive the lion's share of attention because only they can speak for a majority of their party's members. Usually the majority and minority leaders in each house and the Speaker of the House are the preferred spokespersons, but the whips also receive a substantial share of air time and column inches. Second, key committee chairs command center stage when subjects in their domain are newsworthy. Heads of the most prominent committees (such as Ways and Means or Armed Services) are guaranteed frequent coverage, but even the chairs and members of minor committees or subcommittees can achieve fame when the time and issue are right. For example, a sensational scandal like steroid use in major league baseball may lead to congressional committee hearings that receive extensive media coverage. Third, local newspapers and broadcast stations normally devote some resources to covering their local senators and representatives, even when these legislators are junior and relatively lacking in influence.

As with coverage of the president, media coverage of Congress is disproportionately negative. A significant portion of the media attention given to the House and Senate focuses on conflict among members. Some political scientists believe that such reporting is at least partially responsible for the public's negative perceptions of Congress.[44]

Coverage of Congress has been greatly expanded through cable channels C-SPAN and C-SPAN2, which provide coverage of House and Senate sessions as well as many committee hearings. For the first time, Americans can watch their representatives in action without editing or interpretation.

Covering the Supreme Court

While the president and Congress interact with the media on a regular basis, the Supreme Court remains a virtual media vacuum. Despite persistent efforts by C-SPAN and other media outlets to gain access, television cameras have never been permitted to record Supreme Court proceedings. Citing the need to protect the public's perception of the Supreme Court as a nonpolitical and autonomous entity, the justices have given little evidence to suggest that they are eager to reverse their broadcast media ban. Instead, at the end of each term, they release written transcripts and audio recordings of the proceedings, which lack both the visuals and timeliness that could make them fodder for the modern press. Since 2000, however, reporters have been granted on a case-by-case basis the ability to make use of same-day audio recordings. The first instance of this occurred during *Bush* v. *Gore* (2000), which decided the presidential vote in Florida. Since this case, reporters have been granted limited audio access to the Court.

While print and broadcast reporters are granted access to the Court, even if their cameras are not, coverage of the Court remains severely limited when compared with coverage of the executive and legislative branches. There are less than a dozen full-time reporters covering the Supreme Court, and the amount of space dedicated to Court-related stories has continued to shrink. Stories involving complex legal issues are not as easy to sell as well-illustrated stories related to the Congress or president.[45]

Toward Reform: Media Influence, Media Bias, and Public Confidence

There are many important questions concerning the media's relationship with the public. For instance, how much influence do the media actually have on public opinion? Do the media have a discernable ideological bent or bias, as some people suggest? Are people able to resist information that is inconsistent with their preexisting beliefs? And, how much confidence does the public have in the news media?

**Use of the Media by
the American Public**

Media Influence

In most cases, the press has surprisingly little effect on what people believe. To put it bluntly, people tend to see what they want to see; that is, human beings will focus on parts of a report that reinforce their own attitudes and ignore parts that challenge their core beliefs. Most people also selectively tune out or ignore reports that contradict their preferences in politics and other fields. Therefore, a committed Democrat will remember certain portions of a televised news program about a current campaign—primarily the parts that reinforce his or her own choice—and an equally committed Republican will recall very different sections of the report or remember the material in a way that supports the GOP position. In other words, most voters are not empty vessels into which the media can pour their own beliefs. Indeed, many studies from the 1940s and 1950s, an era when partisan identification was very strong, suggested that the media had no influence at all on public opinion. During the last forty years, however, the decline in political identification has opened the door to greater media influence. Studies now show that the media have a definite effect on shaping public opinion, especially during elections.[46]

Some political scientists argue that the content of news coverage accounts for a large portion of the volatility and changes in public opinion and voting preferences of Americans, when measured over relatively short periods of time.[47] These changes are called **media effects.** Let's examine how these media-influenced changes might occur. First, reporting can sway people who are uncommitted and have no strong opinion in the first place. So, for example, the media have a greater influence on political independents than on strong partisans.[48] That said, the sort of politically unmotivated individual who is subject to media effects may not vote in a given election, in which case the media influence may be of little particular consequence.

Second, it is likely that the media have a greater impact on topics far removed from the lives and experiences of readers and viewers. News reports can probably shape public opinion about events in foreign countries fairly easily. Yet, what the media say about domestic issues such as rising prices, neighborhood crime, or child rearing may have relatively little effect, because most citizens have personal experience of and well-formed ideas about these subjects.

Third, in a process often referred to as **agenda setting,** news organizations can influence what we think about, even if they cannot determine what we think. Indeed, the press often sets the agenda for a campaign or for government action by focusing on certain issues or concerns.

Fourth, the media influence public opinion through **framing**—the process by which a news organization defines a political issue and consequently affects opinion about the issue. For example, an experiment conducted by one group of scholars found that if a news story about a Ku Klux Klan rally was framed as a civil rights story (i.e., a story about the right of a group to express their ideas, even if they are unpopular), viewers were generally tolerant of the rally. However, if the story was framed as a law and order issue (i.e., a story about how the actions of one group disrupted a community and threatened public safety), public tolerance for the rally decreased. In either case, the media exert subtle influence over the way people respond to the same information.[49]

Fifth, the media have the power to indirectly influence the way the public views politicians and government. For example, voters' choices in presidential elections are often related to their assessments of the economy. In general, a healthy economy motivates voters to reelect the incumbent president, whereas a weak economy motivates voters to choose the challenger. Hence, if the media paint a consistently dismal picture of the economy, that picture may well hurt the incumbent president seeking reelection. In fact, one study convincingly shows that the media's relentlessly negative coverage of the economy in 1992 shaped voters' retrospective assessments of the economy, which in turn helped lead to George Bush's defeat in the 1992 presidential election.[50]

media effects
The influence of news sources on public opinion.

agenda setting
The constant process of forming the list of issued to be addressed by government.

framing
The process by which a news organization defines a political issue and consequently affects opinion about the issue

Media Bias

Whenever the media break an unfavorable story about a politician, the politician usually counters with a cry of "biased reporting"—a claim that the press has told an untruth, has told only part of the truth, or has reported facts out of the complete context of the event. (To learn more about this topic, see Join the Debate: Are the Media Biased?) Some research suggests that candidates may charge the media with bias as a strategy for dealing with an assertive press, and that bias claims are part of the dynamic between elected officials and reporters. If a candidate can plausibly and loudly decry bias in the media as the source of his negative coverage, for example, reporters might temper future negative stories or give the candidate favorable coverage to mitigate the calls of bias.[51]

Media Bias

Are journalists biased? The answer is simple and unavoidable. Of course they are. Journalists, like all human beings, have values, preferences, and attitudes galore—some conscious, others subconscious, but all reflected at one time or another in the subjects selected for coverage or the portrayal of events or content communicated. Given that the press is biased, in what ways is it biased and when and how are the biases shown?

For much of the 1980s and 1990s, the argument was that the media had a liberal bias because of the sheer number of journalists who leaned to the left. Studies in the 1980s showed that professional journalists were drawn heavily from the ranks of highly educated social and political liberals.[52] To this day, journalists are substantially Democratic in party affiliation and voting habits, progressive and anti-establishment in political orientation, and to the left of the general public on many economic, foreign policy, and social issues. Indeed, a 2007 survey revealed that, whereas 36 percent of the general public describes themselves as being ideologically conservative, only 8 percent of those in the national media would do the same. At the same time, the majority of national journalists—53 percent—describe themselves as moderate, while only 39 percent of Americans describe themselves in the same way. Local journalists, moreover, are less liberal than their counterparts in the national media. Whereas 32 percent of the national journalists describe themselves as liberal, only 23 percent of the local journalists describe themselves as liberals, much more in line with most Americans.[53]

Some scholars argue that corporate interests play a significant role in what journalists report, and that they may counter any liberal leanings of reporters. During legislative debate over the Telecommunications Act of 1996, the passage of which would benefit media corporations with television holdings, scholars found that articles appearing in newspapers owned by media corporations with television interests typically failed to report the possible negative impact resulting from passage of the act. These scholars concluded that "very different pictures of the likely effects of this legislation were being painted by the different newspapers examined, pictures that served to further the interests of the newspapers' corporate owners rather than the interests of their readers in a fair and complete coverage of an important policy issue."[54]

Other analysts have argued that a conservative bias in the media is even more pervasive. They point to the elite background of the typical journalist, who tends to be white, male, highly educated, and relatively affluent. As a result, many of these journalists may unconsciously ignore reporting on issues that are important to racial and ethnic minorities, the poor, and others who might be critical of government and big business.[55]

Recently, many media critics have focused on the national news media's lack of skepticism about the Bush administration's arguments for waging a war in Iraq during the run-up to that conflict in 2002–2003. As we now know, those in the administration who believed the Iraqis would acquiesce to a U.S. occupation were wrong, as were those who believed that Saddam Hussein possessed weapons of mass

Join the Debate

Are the Media Biased?

OVERVIEW: The national news media often assert that journalists have the professionalism they need to be objective in their reporting. Journalistic objectivity is the reporting of the facts of an event without imposing a political or ideological slant. The objectivity of journalists is crucial, since the vast majority of Americans rely on the news media for the information they need to make political decisions. To charge bias against the news media, then, is to explode a whole learning model for American citizenship. Rather than allowing American citizens to make political decisions based on facts, the media would make the decisions for them by either reporting only certain aspects of a story or not reporting the story at all. The media would control what you know or how you know it, making all the political decisions of average Americans merely an outcome of the original bias.

Is there a systemic bias in the news media? Conservative critics charge that the media have a liberal bias because up to 90 percent of journalists vote Democratic.[a]

Moreover, they contend that many of the political reporters and analysts are hired not merely because of their political experience but also because of their Democratic experience. For example, ABC News hired former Clinton White House adviser George Stephanopoulos to host the Sunday morning political talk show *This Week*. Liberals point out that conservatives such as Pat Buchanan went from the Nixon and Reagan administrations to a career as a media pundit. And, many assert that FOX News reports news for conservatives.[b]

Other critics charge that the corporate interests of companies that own the media, regarded as fiscally conservative and strongly hesitant to criticize possible sponsors, operate as much stronger biases than do the personal beliefs of journalists.[c]

The difficulty of proving bias is that one's own biases inform one's opinion of bias. While the conservative watchdog group Accuracy in Media believes that the media reports stories of Iraqi violence too often, liberal watchdog group Fairness and Accuracy in Reporting believes that media intentionally suppress stories about Iraqi civilian casualties and prisoner abuse. However, editors have to make decisions on what to report based on newsworthiness and audience demand, not merely their own politics or interests, in order to keep viewers watching or readers reading. Therefore, to prove bias, one must disprove alternatives, such as newsworthiness, a standard as frustratingly subjective as bias itself.

Arguments IN FAVOR of Entrenched Media Bias

- Since journalists have their own personal bias, claims of professional objectivity are absurd. Journalistic professionalism is a myth sustained only by those who wish to conceal a personal agenda. Even if journalists feel bound to be objective, it is hard to believe that all of them are all of the time, especially when audiences have no other information with which to corroborate stories the media report.

- Corporate demands for the news media to make profits preclude the reporting of otherwise newsworthy

destruction. It is now clear that major newspapers, the television networks, and other news outlets did not question the administration enough about the evidence for Iraqi weapons of mass destruction and ties to terrorism. But it is also clear that the intelligence system failed in this situation and that members of the Congress, both Democrats and Republicans, failed to push the issue. Left with little conflict to report, the press echoed Washington's consensus.

It seems that much of the more recent media bias is intentional and a response to increasing fragmentation and competition among media. One-sided media, a type of narrowcasting, is gaining in popularity as networks intentionally market a one-sided message to secure a competitive edge in niche markets. Not all networks are forthright with their leanings, however. For example, the moniker for FOX News is "fair and balanced," while the reporting has a distinctly conservative bias. A comprehensive study of the news media reports that audiences are aware of news bias and seek out particular perspectives in the news they consume. While "mainstream, general interest newspapers, network television and local television news" are slowly losing

stories. Huge corporations demand that papers, television programs, and Web sites report only the stories that attract viewers rather than educating them, and that attract sponsors rather than holding them accountable. The result is that tabloid journalists report on minor scandals and not human rights abuses or the negative effects of corporate mergers, leading to further audience ignorance of important issues.

- Ideological bias aside, the American media insufficiently report news from other regions of the world. Americans lack sufficient knowledge about global events. This void is dangerous, since these events directly affect American interests. Television reports on global events are nothing more than "Around the World in 80 Seconds," while newspapers typically relegate world news not immediately pertaining to American interests to the back pages. This downplay creates an unfounded bias among audiences that places America at the center of world affairs.

Arguments AGAINST Entrenched Media Bias

- **Bias is not systemic but a problem only with particular journalists.** Even if a certain journalist is unprofessional, it does not follow

that all journalists are. The vast majority of journalists have done nothing to lead us to believe that they are somehow politically biased. Accusations of systemic bias are sometimes the product of bias, and the practice of uncovering media bias may be nothing more than a witch hunt.

- **Bias is a misunderstanding of the niche journalism trend.** Recently, all news media have begun tailoring their content to specific audiences because audiences for news have fractured into tinier and tinier pieces. Some media direct content toward specific ideologies. Calling certain newspapers or cable stations biased is wrong, not because it is not factually true, but because the stations, rather openly, have begun presenting information about matters important to liberals or to conservatives. That's how the free market works.

- **There are simply too many sources of news for an audience to suffer the influence of media bias.** Consumers have access to dozens of magazines, news Web sites, and smaller circulation newspapers that provide audiences with different views of subjects. Bias, in this context, is understood. Individuals have the

option of looking at multiple competing sources and then critically evaluating the information they have gathered in order to make informed opinions.

Continuing the Debate

1. What other kinds of bias might exist in the news media, aside from ideology? How do these biases impact American audiences? How could these biases be corrected without violating the First Amendment?
2. What does it mean for a journalist to be "objective"?

To Follow the Debate Online Go To:

The Media Research Center, a conservative watchdog group at www.mediaresearch.org

The Huffington Post, a liberal site commenting on the media at www.huffingtonpost.com

The *Columbia Journalism Review*'s "Who Owns What?" at www.cjr.org/resources/

[a]Accuracy in Media, http://www.aim.org.

[b]Pew Research Center for the People and the Press, "Maturing Internet News Audience—Broader Than Deep," July 30, 2006, http://people-press.org.

[c]Fairness and Accuracy in Reporting, http://www.fair.org.

audiences, "online, ethnic and alternative media are growing markedly" and "share the same strength—the opportunity for audiences to select tailored content and, in the case of the Internet, to do it on demand."[56] In order for various media to compete, they have to differentiate themselves from the rest, and their current method of choice is to provide content that plays to the preexisting biases of their target market.

The deepest bias among political journalists is the desire to get to the bottom of a good campaign story—which is usually negative news about a candidate. The fear of missing a good story, more than bias, leads media outlets to develop similar headlines and to frame their stories in a similar fashion. In the absence of a good story, news people may attempt to create a horse race where none exists. News people, whose lives revolve around the current political scene, naturally want to add spice and drama, minimize their boredom, and increase their audience. While the horse-race components of elections are intrinsically interesting, the limited time that television devotes to politics is disproportionately given to the competitive aspects of politics, leaving less time for adequate discussion of public policy.[57] Looking at media

Thinking Globally
Al-Jazeera and Media Bias

Al-Jazeera is an independent television station that broadcasts from the tiny, oil-rich Islamic country of Qatar—an important U.S. ally. Unlike its regional competitors, when al-Jazeera was founded in 1996, it offered more than state propaganda and limited news content. Over the years, al-Jazeera's broadcasts have caused international controversy. Saudi Arabia, Libya, Algeria, and Kuwait have all expressed outrage over the station's coverage of domestic events, while the United States has criticized al-Jazeera for broadcasting interviews with Osama bin Laden and for referring to Palestinians killed by Israeli forces as martyrs.

- Go to al-Jazeera's English-language Web site, www.aljazeera.net. How does its coverage of world news compare with that of American media outlets?
- Why would media coverage in some parts of the world tend to be very critical of the United States? Where would media coverage be most critical of the United States and where would it be most favorable?
- Think about the media outlets you rely on for news. How objective or balanced are they in their coverage? In what ways are they biased?

coverage of the 2008 presidential primaries, one study found that only 9 percent of the stories examined issue positions and candidate qualifications.[58] (To learn more about negative media coverage of the 2008 presidential candidates, see Analyzing Visuals: Partisan Bias in Media Reporting?)

Other human biases are also at work in reporting on politics. Whether the press likes or dislikes a candidate is often vital. Former Governor Howard Dean became a media darling during the 2004 Democratic primaries because his fiery speeches made for good stories, putting him on the cover of *Time* and other news magazines. His rapid fall from grace after his poor showing in Iowa and his subsequent and much criticized "scream" at a rally gave rise to the speculation that the press can make then break their favorite candidates. Senator John McCain initially received mostly positive news coverage, partly as a result of his positive relationships with and openness with the press. This made him a more viable candidate in the presidential primary and helped him to survive a potentially damaging story by the *New York Times* soon after he clinched the 2008 Republican nomination. The most favorable coverage in 2008 went to Senator Barack Obama, however, whose historic candidacy and personal appeal likely had the same effect on most journalists as it had on much of the electorate.

One other source of bias, or at least of nonobjectivity, is the increasing celebrity status of many people who report the news. In an age of media stardom and blurring boundaries between forms of entertainment, journalists in prominent media positions have unprecedented opportunities to attain fame and fortune, of which they often take full advantage. Already commanding multimillion-dollar salaries, these celebrity journalists can often secure lucrative speaker's fees. Especially in the case of journalists with highly ideological perspectives, close involvement with wealthy or powerful special-interest groups can blur the line between reporting on policy issues and influencing them. Some journalists find work as political consultants or members of government—which seems reasonable, given their prominence, abilities, and expertise, but which can become problematic when they move between spheres not once, but repeatedly. A good example of this revolving-door phenomenon is Pat Buchanan, who has repeatedly and alternately enjoyed prominent positions in media (as a host of CNN's *Crossfire* and later as a commentator on MSNBC) and politics (as an adviser in Republican administrations and as a presidential candidate). If American journalism is to retain its integrity, it is essential that key distinctions between private enterprise and conscientious public service continue to command our respect.

The Public's Perception of the Media

Americans' general assessment of the news media is considerably unfavorable and has been in a downward trend since the 1980s. According to a 2007 survey by the Pew Research Center for the People and the Press, a majority of the public gives the media low ratings on a number of indicators. Pew found that 55 percent of the respondents perceive the news media to be politically biased and 53 percent believe that the press often is inaccurate in their reporting. Moreover, there has been a steady decline in the

Analyzing Visuals   Partisan Bias in Media Reporting?

After examining the table comparing the percentage of negative stories aired about each presidential candidate over a five-week period, answer the following critical thinking questions:

Broadcast and Cable News (9/9–10/16/2008)*	Percent Negative Evaluations	
	John McCain (R)	Barack Obama (D)
Network Evening News (ABC, CBS, NBC)	48.6	21.4
PBS *NewsHour*	46.7	16.7
CNN	61.3	38.7
FOX News	39.8	40.0
MSNBC	72.8	13.5

*Based on evaluations of 785 news stories reported on ABC, CBS, NBC evening news, PBS Newshour, 12 cable evening news programs, and a sample of afternoon cable news programs where the candidate was a significant presence in the story.

WHAT do you notice about the results for each network?

GIVEN that data were collected from each network during the same time period, what explanations might exist for the differences you see in the table?

SHOULD it always be the goal of a network to have an equal number of positive and negative stories about each candidate? Explain your reasoning.

Source: Project for the Excellence in Journalism, "The Color of News: How Different Media Have Covered the Election," October 29, 2008, http://www.journalism.org/node/13436.

perceived believability of the major news organizations. In 2004, only 54 percent of the public reported that they can believe most of what they read in their daily newspaper. The ratings for the television networks and local news stations are somewhat better, around 60 percent.

There also is an increasing partisan divide between Democrats and Republicans in their assessments of the media's performance. Whereas large majorities of Republicans see the press as liberal and politically biased, only a little more than one-third of Democrats feel the same way. In addition, Republicans are much more likely to see the press as too critical of America (63 percent vs. 23 percent) and hurting democracy (70 percent vs. 39 percent).[59]

Democrats and Republicans also get their news from different sources. Recent survey data show that Democrats are more likely to watch CNN than Republicans, and Republicans are nearly twice as likely to watch FOX News as Democrats. With cable news becoming a crowded field of competitors fighting over audience share, stations have tried to differentiate themselves in order to attract audiences. The trend, however, goes beyond cable news. Research shows that nearly 40 percent of Democrats watch network news, while less than 25 percent of Republicans do. Republicans are more likely to watch cable news and listen to AM talk radio. Democrats, on the other hand, are more likely to listen to National Public Radio (NPR), which typically caters to a more liberal palate. There is only a small disparity in newspaper reading between Republicans and Democrats (43 to 41 percent, respectively). However, like radio,

Do late night comedy shows affect politics? Saturday Night Live cast members portray Senator Barack Obama and Senator Hillary Clinton, the two Democratic contenders for the presidential nomination, in a campaign debate spoof in early 2008. The skit portrayed the moderators of the debate fawning over Obama, while asking particularly harsh questions of Clinton, and mirrored charges of media bias by supporters of Clinton who believed that coverage of Obama was far less critical than coverage of their candidate. Journalists subsequently increased their examinations of Obama's record and statements.

Photo courtesy: Dana Edelson/NBCU Photobank

newspapers can be subdivided by ideology; for instance, the *Washington Times* offers more conservative fare than its rival the *Washington Post*.

The ideological fragmentation of the media should give pause to those who believe that mass media are essential to providing the facts to educate the public about policies our local, state, and federal governments consider. If those facts are reported with bias (or worse, not reported at all because of bias), then portions of the public learn only the facts they want to learn, making consensus among the public and, thus, their representatives increasingly difficult.

The terrorist attacks of September 11 caused a temporary shift in the public's attitude toward the media—Americans followed the news more closely and relied heavily on cable network coverage of the attacks and the war on terrorism. Among Americans polled, 69 percent believed that the news media defend America abroad, and the professionalism rating of the news media soared to 73 percent. During this period of extreme stress, however, Americans appeared simply to have united behind their institutions against an unknown threat. By July 2002, less than a year after the attacks, the public's perception and support of the media were essentially back at pre-9/11 levels.

Despite the increasing displeasure that the majority of Americans express about political bias and other shortcomings, traditional media have managed to maintain a reputation as an authoritative source for news in the an ever expanding media market. The nightly news anchors regularly are rated as the most trusted journalists, while tabloid-style journalists such as Geraldo Rivera are ranked at the bottom.[60] A recent survey of Internet users found that 80 percent think the Web versions of the established news organizations such as the *New York Times*, CNN, and the AP Wire Service are credible, while only 10 percent thought the same of blogs and other individual postings.[61] Moreover, most Americans who say they get most of their news from the Internet say that they also rely on at least one traditional form of news media.[62] Web traffic rankings for news sites further demonstrate the strengths of the mainstream media: twenty-four of the top twenty-five most visited news and information sites are produced by established news organizations. The one alternative site making the top twenty-five, the Drudge Report, consists mostly of links to the Web sites of established news sources.[63]

Most important of all is that Americans continue to value the media's watchdog role, with 59 percent believing that press scrutiny keeps political leaders from doing things they should not do.[64] Thus, while public confidence in media organizations has declined and reforms are certainly warranted, Americans have not wavered in their support for a vigorous free press and the role that the media play in a democratic society.

WHAT SHOULD I HAVE LEARNED?

The simple words of the First Amendment, that "Congress shall make no law...abridging the freedom of speech, or of the press," have shaped the American republic as much as or more than any others in the Constitution. With the Constitution's sanction, as interpreted by the Supreme Court over two centuries, today's vigorous and highly competitive news media have emerged. In this chapter we have answered the following questions:

■ **What are the roots of news media in the United States?**

News media, a component of the larger mass media, provide the public with key information about subjects of public interest and play a crucial role in the political process. The news media consist of print, broadcast, and new media. The nation's first newspaper was published in 1690. Until the mid to late 1800s, when independent papers first appeared, newspapers were partisan; that is, they openly supported a particular party. In the twentieth century, first radio in the late 1920s and then television in the late 1940s revolutionized the transmission of political information. The growth of the Internet over the past few decades has fueled the rise of the new media, which consist of online news information from a variety of sources.

■ **What major trends are currently affecting the United States media?**

Trends affecting the modern media include the growth of media conglomerates and an attendant consolidation of media outlets, the increasing use of experts, and narrowcasting in order to capture particular segments of the population. Increasingly, the lines between media types are blurred by technological innovations that continue to transform the way information is produced and distributed, as well as the way that the public perceives the media.

■ **What rules govern the media?**

While the media continue to be governed by institutional norms, the government has gradually loosened restrictions on the media. The Federal Communications Commission (FCC) licenses and regulates broadcasting stations but has been quite willing to grant and renew licenses and has reduced its regulation of licensees. Content regulations have loosened, with the courts using a narrow interpretation of libel. The Telecommunications Act of 1996 further deregulated the communications landscape, and the use of regular press briefings and the rise of embedded journalists show the government's willingness to cooperate with the media.

■ **How do the media cover politics?**

The media cover every aspect of the political process, including the executive, legislative, and judicial branches of government, though the bulk of media attention focuses on the president. Congress, with its 535 members and complex committee system, poses a challenge to the modern media, as does the Supreme Court, with its complex rulings and aversion to media attention. Politicians have developed a symbiotic relationship with the media, both feeding the media a steady supply of news and occasionally being devoured by the latest media feeding frenzy.

■ **How do media influence, media bias, and public confidence shape the issue of media reform?**

By controlling the flow of information, framing issues in a particular manner, and setting the agenda, the media have the potential to exert influence over the public, though generally have far less influence than people believe. While the media do possess biases, a wide variety of news options are available in the United States, providing savvy news consumers an unprecedented amount of information from which to choose. Public opinion regarding the media continues to be largely critical, though Americans continue to give high marks to established news organizations.

Key Terms

affiliates, p. 542
agenda setting, p. 556
blog, p. 545
broadcast media, p. 542
citizen journalism, p. 546
content regulation, p. 549
deep background, p. 552
equal time rule, p. 549
framing, p. 556

mass media, p. 533
media effects, p. 556
muckraking, p. 537
narrowcasting, p. 544
network, p. 542
new media, p. 542
news media, p. 533
New York Times Co. v.
    Sullivan (1964), p. 552

off the record, p. 552
on background, p. 552
on the record, p. 552
press briefing, p. 552
press conference, p. 552
press release, p. 552
print media, p. 542
wire service, p. 542
yellow journalism, p. 536

Researching the Media

In the Library

Baum, Matthew A. *Soft News Goes to War*. Princeton, NJ: Princeton University Press, 2003.

Crouse, Timothy. *The Boys on the Bus*, reprint ed. New York: Random House, 2003.

Entman, Robert M. *Projections of Power: Framing News, Public Opinion, and U.S. Foreign Policy*. Chicago: University of Chicago Press, 2003.

Graber, Doris A. *Mass Media and American Politics*, 8th ed. Washington, DC: CQ Press, 2007.

———. *Processing Politics: Learning from Television in the Internet Age*. Chicago: University of Chicago Press, 2001.

Hamilton, James T.. *All the News That's Fit to Sell*. Princeton, NJ: Princeton University Press, 2004.

Iyengar, Shanto, and Donald R. Kinder. *News That Matters*, reprint ed. Chicago: University of Chicago Press, 1989.

Iyengar, Shanto, and Jenifer A. McGrady. *Media Politics: A Citizen's Guide*. New York: Norton, 2007.

Jamieson, Kathleen Hall, and Paul Waldman. *The Press Effect: Politicians, Journalists, and the Stories That Shape the Political World*. Oxford: Oxford University Press, 2002.

Jones, Jeffrey P. *Entertaining Politics: New Political Television and Civic Culture*. Lanham, MD: Rowman and Littlefield, 2005.

Lichter, S. Robert, and Stephen J. Farnsworth. *The Nightly News Nightmare: Network Television's Coverage of U.S. Presidential Elections, 1988–2000*. Lanham, MD: Rowman and Littlefield, 2002.

McChesney, Robert W. *The Problem of the Media: U.S. Communication Politics in the Twenty-First Century*. New York: Monthly Review, 2004.

Overholser, Geneva, and Kathleen Hall Jamieson, eds. *The Press*. New York: Oxford University Press, 2005.

Rosenstiel, Tom, et al. *We Interrupt This Newscast: How to Improve Local News and Win Ratings, Too*. New York: Cambridge University Press, 2007.

Sabato, Larry J. *Feeding Frenzy: Attack Journalism and American Politics*, updated ed. Baltimore, MD: Lanahan, 2000.

Sabato, Larry J., Mark Stencel, and S. Robert Lichter. *Peepshow: Media and Politics in an Age of Scandal*. Lanham, MD: Rowman and Littlefield, 2001.

Starr, Paul. *The Creation of the Media*. New York: Basic Books, 2004.

On the Web

The Project for Excellence in Journalism studies the performance of the press and offers a weekly analysis of news coverage, as well as an annual report on the state of the media. Go to **www.journalism.org/**.

The Pew Research Center for the People and the Press does national surveys that explore the public's attitudes about the news media and measure the public's use of the Internet and traditional news outlets. Go to **people-press.org**.

The Web site of the Newseum, a museum devoted to the news media and the First Amendment, includes images of the front pages of over a hundred daily newspapers from around the world in their original, unedited form. Go to **www.newseum.org**.

The *Online Journalism Review*, from USC's Annenberg School for Communication, offers commentary, features, and other resources for writers working online. Go to **www.ojr.org/**.

The *Columbia Journalism Review* examines the performance of journalists for newspapers, magazines, radio, television, and the Web, and the forces that affect their performance, through a mix of reporting, analysis, and commentary. Go to **www.cjr.org**.

The *American Journalism Review* covers all aspects of print, television, radio, and online media, examining how the media cover specific stories, the broader coverage trends, ethical dilemmas in the field, and the impact of technology. Go to **www.ajr.org**.

16

Interest Groups

Washington DC, Lobbyist Jack Abramoff looked for two qualities in prospective clients: lots of money and naivete. Abramoff, who struck a plea bargain with Department of Justice investigators on charges of conspiracy, fraud, and tax evasion in 2006, found a perfect client in a number of Indian tribes whom he and his associates reportedly charged approximately $85 million in fees to protect the tribes' gambling interests. They grossly overbilled their clients, who were new to the lobbying scene, and unethically took on Indian clients whose interests clearly opposed those of existing clients. Other Abramoff clients included eLottery, an Internet gambling firm seeking to "kill a bill that would outlaw most online gambling."[1] The company paid Abramoff $2 million, and he used Christian groups to defeat the bill under the pretense that it did not go far enough in preventing gambling on the Internet. Another major client paid Abramoff $9 million in fees to make sure that textile workers in the Mariana Islands, a commonwealth in political union with the United States, would not be covered by U.S. minimum wage laws.

Abramoff's connections in Congress were extensive.[2] He opened his own restaurant near Capitol Hill to provide free food and a place for congressional fund-

raising events. It is estimated that nearly $4.5 million went to lawmakers or their staffers in the form of illegal or highly questionable donations and gifts.

Several members of Congress, including then-Republican House Majority Leader Tom DeLay and a number of prominent Republican consultants and interest-group leaders such as Grover Norquist, head of Americans for Tax Reform, and Ralph Reed, former head of the Christian Coalition, were found by the Senate Committee on Indian Affairs to have engaged in illegal activities. These included extensive anti-gambling lobbying efforts that benefited Abramoff's casino-rich Indian clients.[3] Reed denied knowing that the payments came from gambling interests, but the ongoing revelations of his close ties with Abramoff are believed to have cost him the primary race for Georgia lieutenant governor in July 2006.

While the Abramoff scandal brought renewed debate on the need for lobbying reform and raised public awareness of the often fine line between ethical and unethical—or even illegal—lobbying practices, hiring federal lobbyists has become a must for nearly any business, special interest, or even governmental unit eager to win favor with members of the legislative or executive branch who control the distribution of billions of federal dollars. Since 1998, the number of towns and cities hiring private lobbyists has nearly doubled. This rapid growth in the number of lobbyists, as well as news of their questionable dealings, led Congress in 2007 to pass

■ Scandals related to the interest groups that pressure members of government are not a new development. At left, a political cartoon depicts the broad reach of the Teapot Dome scandal during President Warren G. Harding's administration in the 1920s. At right, a photo of Republicans being hosted at an expensive golf junket in Scotland by lobbyist Jack Abramoff (far left in photo) became emblematic of government corruption before the 2006 elections.

WHAT SHOULD I KNOW ABOUT . . .

- the roots of the American interest group system?
- the development of American interest groups?
- what interest groups do?
- the key attributes of successful interest groups?
- regulating interest groups and lobbyists?

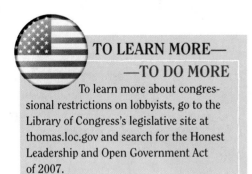

TO LEARN MORE—
—TO DO MORE
To learn more about congressional restrictions on lobbyists, go to the Library of Congress's legislative site at thomas.loc.gov and search for the Honest Leadership and Open Government Act of 2007.

the most extensive lobbying reforms since Watergate. As a result of this law, gone are expensive dinners and drinks, honoraria, and gifts to members of Congress and their staffs.

Lobbying is just one form of interest group politics, yet one that often gives a bad name to interest groups in general. Still, citizen participation in political or civic interest groups is critical to a well-functioning civil society and offers myriad opportunities for political engagement.

The face of interest group politics in the United States is changing as quickly as laws, political consultants, and technology allow. Big business and trade groups are increasing their activities and engagement in the political system at the same time that there is conflicting evidence concerning whether ordinary citizens join political groups. In an influential 1995 essay and later in a 2000 book, political scientist Robert Putnam argued that fewer Americans are joining groups, a phenomenon he labeled "bowling alone."[4] Others have faulted Putnam, concluding that America is in the midst of an "explosion of voluntary groups, activities and charitable donations [that] is transforming our towns and cities."[5] Although bowling leagues, which were once a very common means of bringing people together, have withered, other groups such as volunteer groups, soccer associations, health clubs, and environmental groups are flourishing. Older groups such as the Elks Club and the League of Women Voters, whose membership was tracked by Putnam, are attracting few new members, but this does not mean that people aren't joining groups; they just aren't joining the ones studied by Putnam.

Why is this debate so important? Political scientists believe that involvement in these kinds of community groups and activities enhances the level of **social capital**, "the web of cooperative relationships between citizens that facilitates resolution of collective action problems."[6] The more social capital that exists in a given community, the more citizens are engaged in its governance and well-being, and the more likely they are to work for the collective good.[7] This tendency to form small-scale associations for the public good, or **civic virtue**, as Putnam calls it, creates fertile ground within communities for improved political and economic development.[8] Thus, if Americans truly are joining fewer groups, we might expect the overall quality of government and its provision of services to suffer.

Interest groups are also important because they give the unrepresented or underrepresented an opportunity to have their voices heard, thereby making the government and its policy-making process more representative of diverse populations and perspectives. Additionally, interest groups offer powerful and wealthy interests even greater access to, or influence on, policy makers at all levels of government. To explore the impact of interest groups on policy and the political process, in this chapter we examine the following issues:

social capital
The myriad relationships that individuals enjoy that facilitate the resolution of community problems through collective action.

civic virtue
The tendency to form small-scale associations for the public good.

★ First, we will explore *the roots of the American interest group system*.

★ Second, we will look at *the origins and development of American interest groups*.

★ Third, we will answer the question *what do interest groups do* by looking at the various strategies and tactics used by organized interests.

★ Fourth, we will analyze *what makes an interest group successful*.

★ Finally, we will discuss reform efforts geared toward *regulating interest groups and lobbyists*.

Roots of the American Interest Group System

Interest groups go by various names: special interests, pressure groups, organized interests, nongovernmental organizations (NGOs), political groups, lobby groups, and public interest groups. David B. Truman, one of the first political scientists to study interest groups, defines an organized interest as "any group that, on the basis of one or more shared attitudes, makes certain claims upon other groups in society for the establishment, maintenance, or enhancement of forms of behavior that are implied by shared attitudes."[9] Interest groups are differentiated from political parties largely by the fact that interest groups do not run candidates for office.

Interest group theorists use a variety of theories to explain how interest groups form and how they influence public policy. **Pluralist theory** argues that political power is distributed among a wide array of diverse and competing interest groups. Pluralist theorists such as David B. Truman explain the formation of interest groups through **disturbance theory.** According to this approach, anytime there is a disturbance in a political system, a group will arise. Moreover, one wave of groups will give way to another wave of groups representing a contrary perspective (a countermovement). Thus, Truman would argue, all salient issues will be represented in government. The government, in turn, should provide a forum in which the competing demands of groups and the majority of the U.S. population can be heard and balanced.[10]

Transactions theory arose out of criticisms of the pluralist approach. Transactions theory argues that public policies are the result of narrowly defined exchanges among political actors. Transactions theorists make two main contentions: it is not rational for people to mobilize into groups, and, therefore, the groups that do mobilize will represent elites.

The idea that individuals will not mobilize into groups arises from Mancur Olson's *The Logic of Collective Action.*[11] In this work, Olson assumes that individuals are rational and have perfect information. He uses these assumptions to argue that, especially in the case of collective goods, it makes little sense for individuals to join a group, since they can gain the benefits secured by others at no cost and become "free riders." (The problem of free riders is discussed later in the chapter.)

Olson contends that small groups will be more likely to form. In these groups, social pressures make it more difficult to become free riders. It has been argued that this approach was employed in organizing the American civil rights movement; by breaking the movement into small groups of people's peers, individuals felt pressure to participate that might not have otherwise existed.[12]

Transactionists also argue that the interest group system will be biased in terms of resources, because the relative cost of mobilization is lower for individuals who have greater amounts of time or money available. According to one political scientist, "The flaw in the pluralist heaven is that the heavenly chorus sings with a strong upper-class bias."[13]

More recently, a new wave of political scientists called the neopluralists have evaluated previous theories and data to find a

interest group
An organized group that tries to influence public policy.

pluralist theory
The theory that political power is distributed among a wide array of diverse and competing interest groups.

disturbance theory
The theory that interest groups form in part to counteract the efforts of other groups.

transactions theory
The theory that public policies are the result of narrowly defined exchanges among political actors.

How do special interests develop? Geography often determines the kinds of special interests that are most common in a given region.

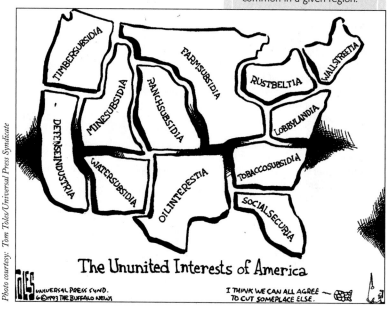

Photo courtesy: Tom Toles/Universal Press Syndicate

The Ununited Interests of America

I THINK WE CAN ALL AGREE — TO CUT SOMEPLACE ELSE.

UNIVERSAL PRESS SYND.
©1993 THE BUFFALO NEWS

population ecology theory
The theory that the life of a political organization is conditional on the density and diversity of the interest group population in a given area.

middle ground. For example, one neopluralist perspective, **population ecology theory,** argues that the formation and life of a political organization is conditional on the density and diversity of the interest group population in a given area. This theory builds on the biological idea that the resources of an ecosystem can only support a certain number of any one species. Growth of these species usually proceeds in an "s" curve, with a slow period of initial growth, followed by a rapid increase in population, and an eventual leveling off when the population has reached its maximum capacity. Population ecology theorists believe that interest group growth follows a similar pattern and is constrained by the relative abundance of resources in a particular environment.[14]

Kinds of Organized Interests

In this book, we use interest group as a generic term to describe the numerous organized groups that try to influence government policy. Thus, interest groups may be public interest groups, business and economic groups, governmental units such as state and local governments, and political action committees (PACs).

With the exception of PACs, most of these groups lobby on behalf of their members. Many also hire D.C.-based lobbying firms to lead or supplement their efforts. (To learn more about a number of prominent interest groups, see Table 16.1.)

public interest group
An organization that seeks a collective good that will not selectively and materially benefit group members.

PUBLIC INTEREST GROUPS Political scientist Jeffrey M. Berry defines **public interest groups** as organizations "that seek a collective good, the achievement of which will not selectively and materially benefit the membership or activists of the organization."[15] For example, many Progressive era groups were created by upper- and middle-class women to solve the varied problems of new immigrants and the poor. Today, civil liberties groups, environmental groups, good government groups, peace

TABLE 16.1 Profiles of Selected Interest Groups

Name (Founded)	Members	PAC	2007–2008 Election Cycle PAC Donations[a]
Public Interest Groups			
AARP (1958)	35 million	no	n/a
Concerned Women for America (1974)	500,000	CWA Legislative Action Committee/PAC	$254,013
League of United Latin American Citizens (LULAC) (1929)	115,000	no	n/a
National Association for the Advancement of Colored People (NAACP) (1909)	500,000	no	n/a
Human Rights Campaign (1980)	600,000	HRC PAC	$1,321,927
Economic Interest Groups			
AFL-CIO (1886)	13 million	AFL-CIO PAC	$1,561,895
American Association for Justice	50,000	AAJ PAC	$5,171,975
National Association of Manufacturers (NAM) (1895)	14,000 companies 350 associations	no	n/a
U.S. Chamber of Commerce (1912)	3 million companies	U.S. Chamber of Commerce PAC	$264,834
Good Government Groups			
Common Cause (1970)	300,000	no	n/a
Public Citizen, Inc. (1971)	160,000	no	n/a
MoveOn.org (1998)	3.3 million	MoveOn PAC	$29,417,213

[a] 2007–2008 data based on FEC reports released October 27, 2008.
Source: http://www.opensecrets.org.

groups, church groups, groups that speak out for those who cannot (such as children, the mentally ill, or animals), and even MoveOn.org are examples of public interest groups.

ECONOMIC INTEREST GROUPS Most groups have some sort of economic agenda, even if it only involves acquiring enough money in donations to pay the telephone bill or to send out the next mailing. **Economic interest groups** are, however, a special type of interest group whose primary purpose is to promote the economic interests of their members. Historically, the three largest categories of economic interest groups were business groups (including trade and professional groups such as the American Medical Association), labor organizations (such as the AFL-CIO), and organizations representing the interests of farmers. The influence of farmers and labor unions is on the decline, however, as big businesses such as Halliburton and Altria (formerly Philip Morris) spend increasingly large amounts contributing to campaigns and hiring lobbyists.

economic interest group
A group with the primary purpose of promoting the financial interests of its members.

Groups that mobilize to protect particular economic interests generally are the most fully and effectively organized of all the types of interest groups.[16] They exist to make profits and to obtain economic benefits for their members. To achieve these goals, however, they often find that they must resort to political means rather than trust the operation of economic markets to produce outcomes favorable for their members.

Thinking Globally

Agricultural Interests in France

In France, less than 5 percent of the population is engaged in agricultural farming, and less than 3 percent of the country's economy is devoted to agriculture. Historically, however, France's National Farmers' Union has been especially powerful and, despite its small size, very adept at resisting limits to agricultural subsidies from the European Union and attempts to open agricultural markets globally.

- What are some of the interest groups in the United States that exercise political influence disproportionate to their size?
- Think of interest groups with which you are familiar in the United States. Would these groups, or similar groups, be active in other parts of the world? Why or why not?

GOVERNMENTAL UNITS State and local governments are becoming strong organized interests as they lobby the federal government or even charitable foundations for money for a vast array of state and local programs. The big intergovernmental associations and state and local governments want to make certain that they get their fair share of federal dollars in the form of block grants or pork-barrel projects. Most states retain lobbyists in Washington, D.C., to advance their interests or to keep them informed about relevant legislation. States seek to influence the amount of money allotted to them in the federal budget, including funds for roads, schools, and anti-poverty programs. In fact, state and local governments may spend a significant proportion of their revenues trying to win federal **earmarks**, monies specifically targeted for programs within a state or specific congressional district to fund basic programs for building roads, schools, enhancing parks or waterways, or other public works projects. (The "Big Seven" intergovernmental associations listed in Table 4.4 also lobby extensively on behalf of their members.)

earmark
Funds that an appropriations bill designates for a particular purpose within a state or congressional district.

POLITICAL ACTION COMMITTEES In 1974, amendments to the Federal Election Campaign Act made it legal for corporations, labor unions, and interest groups to form what were termed **political action committees (PACs)**, which could make contributions to candidates for national elections (see chapter 14 for more on this subject). Technically, a PAC is a political arm of a business, labor, trade, professional, or other interest group legally authorized to raise funds on a voluntary basis from employees or members in order to contribute to a political candidate or party. Unlike interest groups, PACs do not have formal members; they simply have contributors who seek to influence public policy by electing legislators sympathetic to their aims. In contrast, 527 political groups, discussed in chapter 14, have members.

political action committee (PAC)
Federally regulated, officially registered fund-raising committee that represents interest groups in the political process.

The Development of American Interest Groups

Political scientists have long debated how and why interest groups arise, their nature, and their role in a democratic society. Do they contribute to the betterment of society, or are they an evil best controlled by government? From his days in the Virginia Assembly, James Madison knew that factions occurred in all political systems and that the struggle for influence and power among such groups was inevitable in the political process. This knowledge led him and the other Framers to tailor a governmental system of multiple pressure points to check and balance these factions, or what today we call interest groups, in the natural course of the political process. As we discuss in chapter 2, Madison and many of the other Framers were intent on creating a government of many levels—local, state, and national—with the national government consisting of three branches. It was their belief that this division of power would prevent any one individual or group of individuals from becoming too influential. They also believed that decentralizing power would neutralize the effect of special interests, who would not be able to spread their efforts throughout so many different levels of government. Thus, the "mischief of faction" could be lessened. But, as farsighted as they were, the Framers could not have envisioned the vast sums of money or technology that would be available to some interest groups as the nature of these groups evolved over time. (To learn more, see The Living Constitution: First Amendment.)

National Groups Emerge (1830–1889)

Although all kinds of local groups proliferated throughout the colonies and in the new states, it was not until the 1830s, as communications networks improved, that the first national groups emerged. Many of these groups were single-issue groups deeply rooted in the Christian religious revivalism that was sweeping the nation. Concern with humanitarian issues such as temperance (total abstinence from alcoholic beverages), peace, education, slavery, and women's rights led to the founding of numerous associations dedicated to solving these problems. Among the first of these groups was the American Anti-Slavery Society, founded in 1833 by William Lloyd Garrison.

After the Civil War, more groups were founded. For example, the Women's Christian Temperance Union (WCTU) was created in 1874 with the goal of outlawing the sale of liquor. Its members, many of them quite religious, believed that the

What role did abolition play in the development of American interest groups? The American Anti-Slavery Society, one of the earliest American interest groups, was founded by William Lloyd Garrison, publisher of *The Liberator*.

Photo courtesy: Hulton Archive/Getty Images

The Living Constitution

Congress shall make no law respecting...the right of the people peaceably to assemble, and to petition the Government for a redress of grievances.

—FIRST AMENDMENT

This section of the First Amendment prohibits the national government from enacting laws dealing with the right of individuals to join together to make their voices known about their positions on a range of political issues. There was little debate on this clause in the U.S. House of Representatives, and none was recorded in the Senate. James Madison, however, warned of the perils of "discussing and proposing abstract propositions," which this clause was for many years.

Freedom of association, a key concept that allows Americans to organize and join a host of political groups, grew out of a series of cases decided by the Supreme Court in the 1950s and 1960s when many southern states were trying to limit the activities of the National Association for the Advancement of Colored People (NAACP). From the right to assemble and petition the government, along with the freedom of speech, the Supreme Court construed the right of people to come together to support or to protest government actions. First, the Court ruled that states could not compel interest groups to provide their membership lists to state officials. Later, the Court ruled that Alabama could not prohibit the NAACP from urging its members and others to file lawsuits challenging state discriminatory practices. Today, although states and localities can require organized interests to apply for permits to picket or protest, they cannot in any way infringe on their ability to assemble and petition in peaceable ways.

CRITICAL THINKING QUESTIONS

1. Does requiring a government permit infringe upon the right to protest? Under what conditions could a government permit be declined?
2. What is meant by "peaceable" protest? Should these words be strictly interpreted to prohibit physical violence, or could behaviors that are not physical be interpreted as nonpeaceable?

consumption of alcohol was an evil injurious to family life because many men drank away their paychecks, leaving no money to feed or clothe their families. The WCTU's activities took conventional and unconventional forms, including organizing prayer groups, lobbying for prohibition legislation, conducting peaceful marches, and engaging in more violent protests such as the destruction of saloons. The Grange also was formed during the period following the Civil War. The Grange was created as an educational society for farmers to teach them about the latest agricultural developments. Although its charter formally stated that the Grange was not to become involved in politics, in 1876 it formulated a detailed plan to pressure Congress to enact legislation favorable to farmers.

After the Civil War, business interests began to play even larger roles in both state and national politics. A popular saying of the day noted that the Standard Oil Company did everything to the Pennsylvania legislature except refine it. Increasingly large trusts, monopolies, business partnerships, and corporate conglomerations in the oil, steel, and sugar industries became sufficiently powerful to control many representatives in the state and national legislatures.

Perhaps the most effective organized interest of the day was the railroad industry. In a move that couldn't take place today because of its clear impropriety, the Central Pacific Railroad sent its own **lobbyist** to Washington, D.C., in 1861, where he even-

lobbyist
Interest group representative who seeks to influence legislation that will benefit his or her organization or client through political persuasion.

tually became the clerk (staff administrator) of the committees of both houses of Congress that were charged with overseeing regulation of the railroad industry. Subsequently, Congress awarded the Central Pacific Railroad (later called the Southern Pacific) vast grants of lands along its route and large subsidized loans. The railroad company became so powerful that it later went on to have nearly total political control of the California state legislature.

The Progressive Era (1890–1920)

By the 1890s, a profound change had occurred in the nation's political and social outlook. Rapid industrialization, an influx of immigrants, and monopolistic business practices created a host of problems including crime, poverty, squalid and unsafe working conditions, and widespread political corruption. Many Americans began to believe that new measures would be necessary to impose order on this growing chaos and to curb some of the more glaring problems in society. The political and social movement that grew out of these concerns was called the Progressive movement.

Progressive era groups ranged from those rallying for public libraries and kindergartens to those seeking better labor conditions for workers—especially women and children. As discussed in chapter 5, some groups were dedicated to ending racial discrimination, including the NAACP. Groups also were formed to seek woman suffrage.

Not even the Progressives themselves could agree on what the term "progressive" actually meant, but their desire for reform led to an explosion of all types of interest groups, including single-issue, trade, labor, and the first public interest groups. Politically, the movement took the form of the Progressive Party, which sought on many fronts to limit or end the power of the industrialists' near-total control of the steel, oil, railroad, and other key industries.

In response to the pressure applied by Progressive-era groups, the national government began to regulate business. Because businesses had a vested interest in keeping wages low and costs down, more business groups organized to consolidate their strength and to counter Progressive moves. Not only did governments have to mediate Progressive and business demands, but they also had to accommodate the role of organized labor, which often allied itself with Progressive groups against big business.

ORGANIZED LABOR Until the creation of the American Federation of Labor (AFL) in 1886, there was not any real national union activity. The AFL brought skilled workers from several trades together into one stronger national organization for the first time. As the AFL grew in power, many business owners began to press individually or collectively to quash the unions. As business interests pushed states for what are called open shop laws to outlaw unions in their factories, the AFL became increasingly political. It also was forced to react to the success of big businesses' use of legal injunctions to prohibit union organization. In 1914, massive lobbying by the AFL and its members led to passage of the Clayton Act, which labor leader Samuel Gompers hailed as the Magna Carta of the labor movement. This law allowed unions to organize free from prosecution and also guaranteed their right to strike, a powerful weapon against employers.

BUSINESS GROUPS AND TRADE ASSOCIATIONS The National Association of Manufacturers (NAM) was founded in 1895 by manufacturers who had suffered business losses in the economic panic of 1893 and who believed that they were being affected adversely by the growth of organized labor. NAM first became active politically in 1913 when a major tariff bill was under congressional consideration. NAM's tactics were "so insistent and abrasive" and its expenditures of monies so lavish that President Woodrow Wilson was forced to denounce its lobbying tactics as an "unbearable situation."[17] Congress immediately called for an investigation of NAM's activities but found no member of Congress willing to testify that he had ever even encountered a member of NAM (probably because many members of Congress had received illegal contributions and gifts).

The second major business organization came into being in 1912, when the U.S. Chamber of Commerce was created with the assistance of the federal government. NAM, the Chamber of Commerce, and other **trade associations** representing specific industries were effective spokespersons for their member companies. They were unable to defeat passage of the Clayton Act, but organized interests such as cotton manufacturers planned elaborate and successful campaigns to overturn key provisions of the act in the courts.[18] Aside from the Clayton Act, innumerable pieces of pro-business legislation were passed by Congress, whose members continued to insist that they had never been contacted by business groups.

trade association
A group that represents a specific industry.

In 1928, the bubble burst for some business interests. At the Senate's request, the Federal Trade Commission (FTC) undertook a massive investigation of the lobbying tactics of the business community. The FTC's examination of Congress revealed extensive illegal lobbying by yet another group, the National Electric Light Association (NELA). Not only did NELA lavishly entertain members of Congress, but it also went to great expense to educate the public on the virtues of electric lighting. Books and pamphlets were produced and donated to schools and public libraries to sway public opinion. Needy teachers and ministers who were willing to advocate electricity were helped with financial grants. Many considered these tactics unethical and held business in disfavor. These kinds of activities also led the public to view lobbyists in a negative light.

The Rise of the Interest Group State

During the 1960s and 1970s, the Progressive spirit reappeared in the rise of public interest groups. Generally, these groups devoted themselves to representing the interests of African Americans, women, the elderly, the poor, and consumers, or to working on behalf of the environment. Many of their leaders and members had been active in the civil rights and anti–Vietnam War movements of the 1960s. Other groups formed during the Progressive era, such as the American Civil Liberties Union (ACLU) and the NAACP, gained renewed vigor. Many of them had as their patron the liberal Ford Foundation, which helped to bankroll numerous groups, including the Women's Rights Project of the ACLU, the Mexican American Legal Defense and Education Fund, the Puerto Rican Legal Defense and Education Fund, and the Native American Rights Fund (as discussed in chapter 6).[19] The American Association of Retired Persons, now simply called AARP, also came to prominence in this era.

The civil rights and anti-war struggles left many Americans feeling cynical about a government that they believed failed to respond to the will of the majority. They also believed that if citizens banded together, they could make a difference. Thus, two major new public interest groups—Common Cause and Public Citizen—were founded. Common Cause, a good-government group that acts as a watchdog over the federal government, is similar to some of the early Progressive movement's public interest groups. Common Cause effectively has challenged aspects of the congressional seniority system, successfully urged the passage of sweeping campaign financing reforms, and played a major role in the enactment of legislation authorizing federal financing of presidential campaigns. It continues to lobby for accountability in government and for more efficient and responsive governmental structures and practices.

Perhaps more well known than Common Cause is Public Citizen, the collection of groups headed by Ralph Nader (who went on to run as a candidate for president in 1996 and subsequent elections). In 1965, the publication of Nader's *Unsafe at Any Speed* thrust the young lawyer into the limelight. In this book, he charged that the Corvair, a General Motors (GM) car, was unsafe to drive; he produced voluminous evidence of how the car could flip over at average speeds on curved roads. In 1966,

Photo courtesy: Chip Somodevilla/Getty Images

What role does the NRA play in elections? The NRA can be important for mobilizing voters, particularly for Republican candidates. Here, presidential candidate John McCain speaks to NRA leaders at their annual meeting.

he testified about auto safety before Congress and then learned that GM had spied on him in an effort to discredit his work. The $250,000 that GM subsequently paid to Nader in an out-of-court settlement allowed him to establish a litigation center in 1969. The center analyzed the activities of regulatory agencies and concluded that few of them enforced antitrust regulations or cracked down on deceptive advertising practices.

CONSERVATIVE RESPONSE: RELIGIOUS AND IDEOLOGICAL GROUPS During the 1960s and 1970s, various public interest groups grew and achieved success in shaping and defining the public agenda. Conservatives, concerned by the activities of these liberal groups, responded by forming religious and ideological groups that became a potent force in U.S. politics. In 1978, the Reverend Jerry Falwell founded the first major new religious group, the Moral Majority. The Moral Majority was widely credited with assisting in the election of Ronald Reagan as president in 1980 as well as with the defeats of several liberal Democratic senators that same year. Falwell claimed to have sent 3 to 4 million newly registered voters to the polls.[20]

Pat Robertson, a televangelist, formed the Christian Coalition in 1990. Since then, it has grown in power and influence. The Christian Coalition played an important role in the Republicans winning control of the Congress in 1994. In 2008, the group distributed millions of voter guides in churches throughout the United States.

The Christian Coalition also lobbies Congress and the White House. During the Bush administration, the group had the sympathetic ear of the president, who placed a priority on faith-based initiatives. Its influence is likely to be significantly diminished in the Obama administration.

The Christian Coalition is not the only conservative interest group to play an important role in the policy process as well as in elections at the state and national level. The National Rifle Association (NRA), an active opponent of gun control legislation, saw its membership rise in recent years, as well as its importance in Washington, D.C. The NRA and its political action committee spent more than $11 million to help elect John McCain in 2008. And, conservative groups such as Students for Academic Freedom have made their views known in the area of higher education. More recently, students have formed Students for Concealed Weapons on Campus, as discussed in Ideas into Action: Guns on Campus.

BUSINESS GROUPS, CORPORATIONS, AND ASSOCIATIONS Conservative, religious groups were not the only ones organized in the 1970s to advance their views. Many business people, dissatisfied with the work of the National Association of Manufacturers or the U.S. Chamber of Commerce, decided to start new, more politically oriented organizations to advance their political and financial interests in Washington, D.C. The Business Roundtable, for example, was created in 1972. The Roundtable, whose members head about 150 large corporations, is "a fraternity of powerful and prestigious business leaders that tells 'business's side of the story' to legislators, bureaucrats, White House personnel, and other interested public officials."[21] It urges its members to engage in direct lobbying to influence the course of policy formation. Its lobbying

Guns on Campus

Look at the person sitting to the right of you. How would you feel if that person were packing heat? A group of 9,000 students and faculty want to make carrying concealed weapons on campus legal.

Students for Concealed Weapons on Campus works to educate the public about concealed weaponry and to convince state legislatures and school administrations to grant concealment permits to students on campuses across the nation.[a] It gained attention in the wake of the Virginia Tech shootings in 2007 in which thirty-three people were killed by a student gunman on campus. Had students been able to carry weapons legally, the leaders of this new interest group argue, the number of students killed could have been reduced. State legislators in Utah already have passed a law prohibiting gun bans on college campuses.

The Second Amendment of the U.S. Constitution states that "the right of the people to keep and bear Arms, shall not be infringed," yet some Americans argue that the right to bear arms needs some restrictions in today's society, especially in educational settings. The Brady Center to Prevent Gun Violence says that violence on college campuses would increase if concealed weapons were allowed because people between eighteen and twenty-four years of age have the highest rates of drug and alcohol use, mental health problems, and suicide attempts.[b] It argues that even for self-defense purposes, the prevalence of guns on campus would increase fatalities in school shootings because students would be likely to miss their intended targets.

- Would allowing students to carry concealed weapons on campus decrease or increase violence? Why?
- Write a letter to your local state representative and describe why you believe guns should or should not be allowed in your school or university. Be sure to include factual details to support your argument.

NO GUN LEFT BEHIND
The Gun Lobby's Campaign to
Push Guns Into Colleges and Schools

Do guns have a place on college campuses? The Brady Center to Prevent Gun Violence does not think so; this advertisement makes a mockery of the idea.

[a]"About Us," Students for Concealed Weapons on Campus, www.concealedcampus.org/about.htm.
[b]"No Gun Left Behind: The Gun Lobby's Campaign to Push Guns into Colleges and Schools," Brady Center to Prevent Gun Violence.

efforts were instrumental in the Bush administration's decision to not honor the Kyoto Protocol on Climate Change because of its impact on American businesses.

Most large corporations, in addition to having their own governmental affairs departments, employ D.C.-based lobbyists to keep them apprised of legislation that may affect them, or to lobby bureaucrats for government contracts. In the past, large corporations also gave significant sums of soft money to favored politicians or political candidates. While campaign finance reforms (discussed in greater detail in chapter 14) have prohibited such corporate donations, businesses still channel money to favored candidates through political action committees, 527s, and individual donations from employees and their families, as well as through state parties. In the 2008 election, for example, 527 groups, which receive corporate as well as individual donations, contributed almost $200 million to candidates for office.[22]

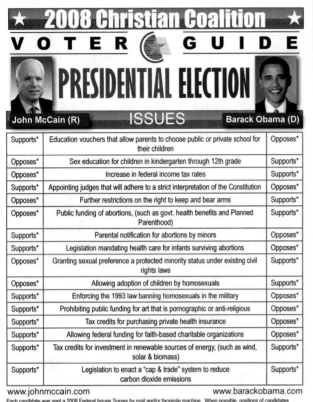

★ **2008 Christian Coalition** ★
V O T E R   G U I D E
PRESIDENTIAL ELECTION

John McCain (R)   ISSUES   Barack Obama (D)

McCain	ISSUES	Obama
Supports*	Education vouchers that allow parents to choose public or private school for their children	Opposes*
Opposes*	Sex education for children in kindergarten through 12th grade	Supports*
Opposes*	Increase in federal income tax rates	Supports*
Supports*	Appointing judges that will adhere to a strict interpretation of the Constitution	Opposes*
Opposes*	Further restrictions on the right to keep and bear arms	Supports*
Opposes*	Public funding of abortions, (such as govt. health benefits and Planned Parenthood)	Supports*
Supports*	Parental notification for abortions by minors	Opposes*
Supports*	Legislation mandating health care for infants surviving abortions	Opposes*
Opposes*	Granting sexual preference a protected minority status under existing civil rights laws	Supports*
Opposes*	Allowing adoption of children by homosexuals	Supports*
Supports*	Enforcing the 1993 law banning homosexuals in the military	Opposes*
Supports*	Prohibiting public funding for art that is pornographic or anti-religious	Opposes*
Supports*	Tax credits for purchasing private health insurance	Opposes*
Supports*	Allowing federal funding for faith-based charitable organizations	Opposes*
Supports*	Tax credits for investment in renewable sources of energy, (such as wind, solar & biomass)	Supports*
Supports*	Legislation to enact a "cap & trade" system to reduce carbon dioxide emissions	Supports*

www.johnmccain.com   www.barackobama.com

Each candidate was sent a 2008 Federal Issues Survey by mail and/or facsimile machine. When possible, positions of candidates on issues were verified or determined using voting records and/or public statements, articles or campaign literature. An asterisk (*) indicates such information was used to determine positions and sources are available on request.

Paid for and authorized by the Christian Coalition; PO Box 37030 - Washington, DC 20013

The Christian Coalition is a pro-family, citizen action organization. This voter guide is provided for educational purposes only and is not to be construed as an endorsement of any candidate or party.

Please visit our web site at www. cc.org

★ **Vote on November 4** ★

Photo courtesy: Christian Coalition of America

How do interest groups influence elections? Voter guides like this one were distributed in conservative churches around the United States as well as at public places and events by the Christian Coalition. Critics charged that the guide distorted the positions of Barack Obama, the Democratic candidate.

These corporate interests also have far-reaching tentacles and ties to lawmakers. A number of congressional spouses as well as sons, daughters, and in-laws, are registered lobbyists. Moreover, as discussed later in the chapter, many lawmakers become lobbyists after leaving office.

ORGANIZED LABOR Membership in labor unions held steady throughout the early and mid-1900s and then skyrocketed toward the end of the Depression. By then, organized labor began to be a potent political force as it was able to turn out its members in support of particular political candidates.

Labor became a stronger force in U.S. politics when the American Federation of Labor (AFL) merged with the Congress of Industrial Organizations (CIO) in 1955. Concentrating its efforts largely on the national level, the new AFL-CIO immediately turned its energies to pressuring the government to protect concessions won from employers at the bargaining table and to other issues of concern to its members, including minimum wage laws, the environment, civil rights, medical insurance, and health care.

More recently, the once fabled political clout of organized labor has been on the wane at the national level. Membership peaked at about 30 percent of the workforce in the late 1940s. Since that time, union membership has plummeted as the nation changed from a land of manufacturing workers and farmers to a nation of white-collar professionals and service workers.

Even worse for the future of the labor movement, at least in the short run, is the split that occurred at the AFL-CIO's 2005 annual meeting, ironically the fiftieth anniversary of the joining of the two unions. Plagued by reduced union membership, and mired in disagreement about how much money to devote to the campaigns of Democrats at a time when Republicans controlled two branches of government, three of the largest member unions plus four additional ones ceded from the AFL-CIO. With the head of the Service Employees International Union (SEIU) noting that the AFL-CIO had grown "pale, male, and stale," the SEIU, the International Brotherhood of Teamsters, and the United Food and Commercial Workers International left to form the Change to Win Coalition.[23]

Thinking Globally

The Solidarity Movement in Poland

On occasion, organized labor activities have helped to bring about major political change. A notable example is the Solidarity movement led by Lech Walesa in Poland during the 1980s. The first independent trade union in Soviet-controlled Eastern Europe, the Solidarity movement encouraged political liberalization in Poland and contributed to the fall of communism in Eastern Europe.

- Where else in the world might an organized labor organization, or any interest group, have the ability to significantly alter governments or their policies?
- Do organized interest groups in the United States have too much power or too little? Explain your answer.

Photo courtesy: Jim West/Zuma Press

Who are the union leaders of today? The Change to Win Coalition was formed in 2005 when seven unions broke away from the AFL-CIO. Here, Andy Stern, president of the Service Employees International Union, (SEIU) speaks with reporters. To his far left is International Brotherhood of Teamsters President James Hoffa.

What Do Interest Groups Do?

Not all interest groups are political, but they may become politically active when their members believe that a government policy threatens or affects group goals. Interest groups also enhance political participation by motivating like-minded individuals to work toward a common goal. Legislators often are much more likely to listen to or be concerned about the interests of a group as opposed to the interests of any one individual.

Just as members of Congress are assumed to represent the interests of their constituents in Washington, D.C., interest groups are assumed to represent the interests of their members to policy makers at all levels of government. In the 1950s, for example, the NAACP was able to articulate the interests of African Americans to national decision makers even though as a group they had little or no electoral clout, especially in the South. Without the efforts of the civil rights groups discussed in chapter 6, it is unlikely that either the courts or Congress would have acted as quickly to make discrimination illegal. By banding together with others who have similar interests, all sorts of individuals—from railroad workers to women to physical therapists to campers to homosexuals to mushroom growers—can advance their collective interests. Getting celebrity support or hiring a lobbyist to advocate those interests in Washington, D.C., or a state capital also increases the likelihood that issues of concern to them will be addressed and acted on favorably.

There is a downside to interest groups, however. Because groups make claims on society, they can increase the cost of public policies. The elderly can push for more costly health care and Social Security programs; people with disabilities, for improved access to public buildings; industry, for tax loopholes; and veterans, for improved benefits. Many Americans believe that interest groups exist simply to advance their own selfish interests, with little regard for the rights of other groups or, more importantly, of people not represented by any organized group.

Whether good or bad, interest groups play an important role in U.S. politics. In addition to enhancing the democratic process by providing increased representation

Comparing Interest Groups

and participation, they increase public awareness about important issues, help frame the public agenda, and often monitor programs to guarantee effective implementation. Most often, they accomplish these things through some sort of lobbying activities as well as participating in elections. But, as the rich and powerful appear to be spending far more than those groups representing poor and working-class interests, there is increasing cause for concern.

Lobbying

lobbying
The activities of a group or organization that seeks to influence legislation and persuade political leaders to support the group's position.

Most interest groups put lobbying at the top of their agendas. **Lobbying** is the process by which interest groups attempt to assert their influence on the policy-making process. The exact origin of the term lobbying is disputed. In mid-seventeenth-century England, there was a room located near the floor of the House of Commons where members of Parliament would congregate and could be approached by their constituents and others who wanted to plead a particular cause. Similarly, in the United States, people often waited outside the chambers of the House and Senate to speak to members of Congress as they emerged. Because they waited in the lobbies to argue their cases, by the nineteenth century they were commonly referred to as lobbyists. Another piece of folklore explains that when Ulysses S. Grant was president, he would frequently walk from the White House to the Willard Hotel on Pennsylvania Avenue just to relax in its comfortable and attractive lobby. Interest group representatives and those seeking favors from Grant would crowd into that lobby and try to press their claims. Soon they were nicknamed lobbyists.

Most politically active groups use lobbying to make their interests heard and understood by those who are in a position to influence or cause change in governmental policies. Depending on the type of group and on the role it is looking to play, lobbying can take many forms. You probably have never thought of the Boy Scouts or Girl Scouts as political. Yet, when Congress began debating the passage of legislation dealing with discrimination in private clubs, representatives of both organizations testified in an attempt to persuade Congress to allow them to remain single-sex organizations.

Can Hollywood celebrities effectively lobby Congress?
Hayden Panettiere, a star on the television show *Heroes*, protests against the inhumane treatment and slaughtering of whales. She has lobbied both Congress and presidential campaigns enthusiastically supporting the cause to "Save the Whales Again."

As Table 16.2 indicates, there are at least twenty-three legal ways for lobbyists and organizations to influence policy at the state and national level. Almost all interest groups lobby by testifying at hearings and contacting legislators. Other groups also provide information that decision makers might not have the time, opportunity, or interest to gather on their own. Of course, information these groups provide is designed to present the group's position in a favorable light, although a good lobbyist for an interest group also will note the downside to proposed legislation. Interest groups also file lawsuits or friend of the court briefs to lobby the courts, and some even engage in protests or demonstrations as a form of lobbying public opinion or decision makers.

Photo courtesy: Carrie Devorah/WENN

LOBBYING CONGRESS Efforts to reform lobbying continue to plague members of Congress, who are the targets of a wide variety of lobbying activities: congressional testimony on behalf of a group, individual letters from interested constituents, campaign contributions, or the outright payment of money for votes. Of course, the last item is illegal, but there are numerous documented instances of money changing hands for votes. Because, as discussed in chapter 7, lobbying plays such

TABLE 16.2 Lobbying Techniques

Technique	State-Based Groups		Washington, D.C.-Based Groups (n = 175)
	Lobbyists (n = 595)	Organizations (n = 301)	
Testifying at legislative hearings	98	99	99
Contacting government officials directly to present point of view	98	97	98
Helping to draft legislation	96	88	85
Alerting state legislators to the effects of a bill on their districts	96	94	75
Having influential constituents contact legislator's office	94	92	80
Consulting with government officials to plan legislative strategy	88	84	85
Attempting to shape implementation of policies	88	85	89
Mounting grassroots lobbying efforts	88	86	80
Helping to draft regulations, rules, or guidelines	84	81	78
Raising new issues and calling attention to previously ignored problems	85	83	84
Engaging in informal contacts with officials	83	81	95
Inspiring letter-writing or telegram campaigns	82	83	84
Entering into coalitions with other groups	79	93	90
Talking to media	73	74	86
Serving on advisory commissions and boards	58	76	76
Making monetary contributions to candidates	—	45	58
Attempting to influence appointment to public office	44	42	53
Doing favors for officials who need assistance	41	36	56
Filing suit or otherwise engaging in litigation	36	40	72
Working on election campaigns	—	29	24
Endorsing candidates	—	24	22
Running advertisements in media about position	18	21	31
Engaging in protests or demonstrations	13	21	20

Source: State-Based Groups: Anthony J. Nownes and Patricia Freeman, "Interest Group Activity in the States," *Journal of Politics* 60 (1998): 92. Washington, D.C.-Based Groups: Kay Lehman Schlozman and John Tierney, "More of the Same: Washington Pressure Group Activity in a Decade of Change," *Journal of Politics* 45 (1983): 358.

an important role in Congress, many effective lobbyists often are former members of that body, former staff aides, former White House officials or Cabinet officers, or other Washington insiders. This type of lobbyist frequently drops in to visit members of Congress or their staff members and often takes them to lunch, to play golf, or to parties.

Lobbying Congress and issue advocacy are skills that many people have developed over the years. In 1869, for example, women gathered in Washington, D.C., for the second annual meeting of the National Woman Suffrage Association and marched to Capitol Hill to hear one of their members (unsuccessfully) ask Congress to pass legislation to enfranchise women under the terms of the Fourteenth Amendment. Practices such as these floor speeches are no longer permitted.

You Are a Lobbyist

Today, lobbyists try to develop close relationships with senators and House members in an effort to enhance their access to the policy-making process. A symbiotic relationship between members of Congress, interest group representatives, and affected bureaucratic agencies often develops. In these iron triangles and issue networks (discussed in chapter 9), congressional representatives and their staff members, who face an exhausting workload and legislation they frequently know little about, often look to lobbyists for information. "Information is the currency on Capitol Hill, not dollars," said one lobbyist.[24] According to one aide: "My boss demands a speech and a statement for the *Congressional Record* for every bill we introduce or co-sponsor—and we have a lot of bills. I just can't do it all myself. The better lobbyists, when they have a proposal they are pushing, bring it to me along with a couple of speeches, a *Record* insert, and a fact sheet."[25]

Not surprisingly, lobbyists work most closely with representatives who share their interests.[26] A lobbyist from the NRA, for example, would be unlikely to try to influence a liberal representative who was on record as strongly in favor of gun control. It is much more effective for a group such as the NRA to provide useful information for

POLITICS NOW

Source: WASHINGTON POST   July 1, 2008   Page A09

Lobbying Congress

The Cold Calls Behind Those Personal Letters to Congress

JEFFREY H. BIRNBAUM

In the past five years, 44 percent of Americans—about 100 million people—have contacted their elected representatives in Washington. Most of them did so at the prompting of a third party—often a lobbying group—according to surveys done for the Congressional Management Foundation.

Which is a major reason that Michele Simmons of Tok, Alaska, and Kiym Gardner of Clarksville, Tenn., have steady, stay-at-home jobs. Simmons and Gardner are among 500 contract workers for Democracy Data & Communications (DDC), an Alexandria company that specializes in lobbying from the grass roots. DDC pays the two women to spend much of their day telephoning people around the country and asking them to sign letters to Congress that press for legislation.

The workers are paid $10 to $15 an hour, depending on their expertise. DDC says lobby groups pay the company $75 to $125 per letter sent, depending on the difficulty of the campaign.

Whether lawmakers know it or not—and some might be disappointed to learn—the practice is not only common but growing. Interest groups, preparing for a new president and the sweeping initiatives he no doubt will launch, are increasingly hiring folks like Simmons and Gardner to build lists of voters-back-home who can be called upon to contact Washington.

The seemingly heartfelt letters they produce are among the most persuasive kinds of communications that Congress receives polls of congressional offices have shown.

Grass-roots recruiters such as Simmons and Gardner act as both salespeople and reporters. They try to persuade the people they call to send a letter on a specific topic and then compose a draft of the missive—subject to the person's approval—based on the stories they hear. The people contacted mail, e-mail or fax the letters to their lawmakers in Washington.

The object, said B. R. McConnon III, chief executive of DDC, "is to find real people with real stories."

Simmons, 49, is, in fact, a former journalist. Gardner, 35, once worked in marketing for NASCAR. Both say they enjoy their jobs because they get to talk to people all day and don't have to commute to work. For Simmons, that could mean a 300-mile trek to Fairbanks.

"I work from 30 to 40 hours a week and I'm free to set my own schedule; that sometimes includes weekend work," Simmons said. "I love it. I love all the people I've had the pleasure to speak with. I've learned a lot. I've worked on issues that range from animal testing to Medicare."

"We have a database of folks to contact who for whatever reason have expressed an interest in the issue of the day," Simmons explained. "I try to describe the issue. If they are interested, then I generally go through a series of questions. At the end, I ask them if they want to have a letter composed based on the information they shared with me."

Simmons said she produces an average of one letter per hour. Gardner gins up between four and eight letters a day, she said. And she is happy for the work. "I live in a small town where there aren't a lot of good-paying jobs," she said.

Still, letters from individuals make up a small fraction of the communications to lawmakers. Many, many more contacts are done by e-mail, through millions of messages generated by interest-group Web sites.

DDC will not say who its clients are. But it must have a lot of them. Last year it had 39 projects of this kind. This year, in anticipation of a busy time for advocates from the grass roots in 2009, its pace is even faster.

Discussion Questions

1. *What role should interest groups play in shaping congressional legislation?*
2. *What legal or ethical problems might the type of lobbying campaigns undertaken by DDC pose for interest groups?*

its supporters and to those who are undecided. Good lobbyists also can encourage members to file amendments to bills favorable to their interests. They also can urge their supporters in Congress to make speeches (often written by the group) and to pressure their colleagues in the chamber. (To learn more about efforts to influence public policy, see Politics Now: Lobbying Congress.)

A lobbyist's effectiveness depends largely on his or her reputation for fair play and provision of accurate information. No member of Congress wants to look uninformed. As one member noted: "It doesn't take very long to figure out which lobbyists are straightforward, and which ones are trying to snow you. The good ones will give you the weak points as well as the strong points of their case. If anyone ever gives me false or misleading information, that's it—I'll never see him again."[27]

Capitol Hill is often a stepping stone to a career as a lobbyist. A 2005 study found that 43 percent of the 198 members of the House and Senate who left office since 1998 became registered lobbyists. Retiring to become a lobbyist was unusual as recently as two decades ago, according to congressional historians.[28] But, over the past decade, House leaders in particular urged many members and their staffers to follow this route. After the 2000 presidential elections, 62 percent of Republicans retiring from office and 15 percent of retiring Democrats joined lobbying firms.[29] After lobbying reforms were passed by Congress in 2007, a number of lawmakers left to avoid falling under more stringent rules, as discussed later in this chapter.

LOBBYING THE EXECUTIVE BRANCH As the executive branch has increasingly concerned itself with shaping legislation, executive branch lobbying efforts have increased in frequency and importance. Groups often target one or more levels of the executive branch because there are so many potential access points, including the president, White House staff, and the numerous levels of the executive branch bureaucracy. Groups try to work closely with the administration to influence policy decisions at their formulation and later implementation stages. As with congressional lobbying, the effectiveness of a group often depends on its ability to provide decision makers with important information and a sense of where the public stands on the issue.

Historically, group representatives have met with presidents or their staff members to urge policy directions. Most presidents also have set up staff positions to provide interest groups or organizations with access to the administration. Many of these offices, such as those dealing with consumer affairs, the environment, minority affairs, or women's issues, are routinely the target of organized interests.

An especially strong link exists between interest groups and regulatory agencies (see chapter 9). Because of the highly technical aspects of much regulatory work, many groups employ Washington attorneys and lobbying firms to deal directly with the agencies. So great is interest group influence in the decision-making process of these agencies that many people charge that the agencies have been captured by the interest groups.

Groups often monitor the implementation of the laws or policies they advocated. The National Women's Law Center, for example, has been instrumental in seeing that Title IX, which was passed by Congress to mandate educational equity for women and girls, be enforced fully. It has successfully sued several colleges and universities that have failed to provide equity in athletic funding for men and women.

LOBBYING THE COURTS The courts, too, have proved a useful target for interest groups.[30] Although you might think that the courts decide cases that affect only the parties involved or that they should be immune from political pressures, interest groups for years have recognized the value of lobbying the courts, especially the Supreme Court, and many political scientists view it as a form of political participation.[31] As shown in Table 16.2, 72 percent of the Washington D.C.-based groups surveyed participated in litigation as a lobbying tool.

Generally, interest group lobbying of the courts can take two forms: direct sponsorship or the filing of *amicus curiae* briefs. When a case a group is interested in but not actually

What role do lobbyists play in Congress? This cartoon presents one popular, although not always correct, view of how legislation gets enacted on Capitol Hill.

Photo courtesy: By permission of Mike Luckovich and Creators Syndicate. Inc.

★ How a bill becomes law in Congress ★

Congressman, here's your bill.

Here's your law.

Special Interest

Mike Luckovich ATLANTA CONSTITUTION ©

sponsoring comes before a court, the organization often will file an *amicus* brief—either alone or with other like-minded groups—to inform the justices of the group's policy preference, generally offered in the guise of legal arguments. Over the years, as the number of both liberal and conservative groups viewing litigation as a useful tactic has increased, so has the number of briefs submitted to the courts. Most major U.S. Supreme Court cases noted in this book have been sponsored by an interest group, or one or both of the parties in the case have been supported by an *amicus curiae* brief. Interest groups also file cases in state supreme courts, but in much lower numbers.

In addition to litigating, interest groups try to influence who is nominated to the federal courts. For example, they play an important role in judicial nominees' Senate confirmation hearings, as discussed in chapter 10. In 1991, for example, 112 groups testified or filed prepared statements for or against the controversial nomination of Clarence Thomas to the U.S. Supreme Court.[32] Although formal interest group activity was more subdued during the 2005 nominations of John G. Roberts Jr. and Samuel A. Alito Jr., groups still spent significant sums of money and other resources advocating for the confirmation or defeat of these nominees.

Litigation and efforts to influence the outcome of judicial nominations to the federal courts are not the only ways that interest groups lobby jurists. It is becoming increasingly more common for interest groups of all persuasions to pay for trips for judges to attend "informational conferences" or simply to interact with judges by paying for club memberships and golf outings. In fact, many commentators criticized the absence of Justice Antonin Scalia from the swearing in of Chief Justice Roberts, because Scalia was on a golf outing at the Ritz Carlton in Bachelor Gulf, Colorado. This outing was part of a legal conference sponsored by the Federalist Society, a conservative group that was very influential in judicial appointments during the Bush administration.[33]

Thinking Globally

Activism in Nigeria

In 2002, hundreds of local women in Nigeria's oil-rich Delta region staged several peaceful but lengthy occupations of oil pipeline stations belonging to Chevron Texaco. After negotiations with the women—who had trapped hundreds of workers—the company agreed to build schools, clinics, and electricity and water systems to end the siege. In 2003, village women occupied a Shell Oil installation in a peaceful demonstration amid surging ethnic violence in the region. Despite its mineral riches, the Delta is one of Nigeria's most impoverished regions with few roads, schools, hospitals, or other public services.

- Nonviolent protest can be a very effective avenue for political change. The women of Nigeria were successful in demanding services their government failed to provide. What are some similar examples in the United States or in other countries?
- Would you be willing to risk imprisonment or other retaliatory measures from the government in order to participate in a public demonstration? How far would you be willing to go to speak out against political injustice? Think about this question from the perspective of individuals living under repressive regimes such as those in Myanmar (Burma), North Korea, and China.

GRASSROOTS LOBBYING As the term implies, grassroots lobbying is a form of interest group activity that prompts individuals to contact their representatives directly in an effort to affect policy.[34] Although it often involves door-to-door informational or petition drives—a tried and true method of lobbying—the term also encompasses more modern forms of communication such as fax and Internet lobbying of lawmakers. As early as the 1830s, women (who could not vote) used petition campaigns to persuade state legislators to enact Married Women's Property Acts that gave women control of their earnings and a greater legal say in the custody of their children. Petitioning has come a long way since then. It is now routine for interest groups to e-mail their members and to provide a direct Web link as well as suggested text that citizens can use to lobby their legislators.

Interest groups regularly try to inspire their members to engage in grassroots activity, hoping that lawmakers will respond to those pressures and the attendant publicity. In essence, the goal of many organizations is to persuade ordinary voters to serve as their advocates. In the world of lobbying, there are few things more useful than a list of committed supporters. Radio talk-show hosts such as Rush Limbaugh try to stir up their listeners by urging them to contact their representatives in Washington, D.C. Other interest groups now run carefully targeted and costly television advertisements pitching one side of an argument. Some

How does Hollywood view unconventional protests by interest groups? In this still from *Sex and the City,* Samantha, one of the movie's main characters, is attacked by a member of an animal rights group offended by Samantha's choice of outerwear.

Photo courtesy: Jayme Oak/starrtrakphoto.com/StarTraks Photo

of these undefined masses, as they join together on the Internet or via text messages, may be mobilized into one or more groups.

PROTESTS AND RADICAL ACTIVISM   An occasional though highly visible tactic used by some groups is protest activity. Although it is much more usual for a group's members to opt for more conventional forms of lobbying or to influence policy through the electoral process, when these forms of pressure-group activities are unsuccessful, some groups (or individuals within groups) resort to more forceful measures to attract attention to their cause. Since the Revolutionary War, violent, illegal protest has been one tactic of organized interests. The Boston Tea Party, for example, involved breaking all sorts of laws, although no one was hurt physically. Other forms of protest, such as Shays's Rebellion, ended in tragedy for some participants. Much more recently, antiwar protestors have been willing to march and risk detention and jail in the United States. And, protesters regularly try to picket or protest meetings of the International Monetary Fund or the World Bank. Political conventions as well as inaugurations also routinely are targeted by protesters.

Some animal rights activists such as People for the Ethical Treatment of Animals (PETA) and some pro-life groups such as Operation Rescue at times rely on illegal protest activities to draw attention to their cause. Members of the Animal Liberation Front, for example, stalked the wife of a pharmaceutical executive, broke into her car, stole her credit cards, and then made over $20,000 in unauthorized charitable donations.[35] Some radical groups post the names of those they believe to be engaging in wrongful activity on the Web, along with their addresses and threats. As a result, some groups have faced federal terrorism charges.

Election Activities

In addition to trying to achieve their goals (or at least draw attention to them) through conventional and unconventional forms of lobbying, many interest groups also become involved more directly in the electoral process. The 2008 Republican and Democratic presidential nominating conventions were the targets of significant organized interest group protests concerning each party's stance on a variety of issues,

SIMULATION

You Are the Leader of Concerned Citizens for World Justice

including the U.S.-led war in Iraq, same-sex marriage, the environment, immigration, and reproductive rights.

Interest Groups and Campaign Finance

CANDIDATE RECRUITMENT AND ENDORSEMENTS Many interest groups claim to be nonpolitical. But, some interest groups recruit, endorse, and/or provide financial or other forms of support for political candidates. EMILY's List (EMILY stands for "Early money is like yeast—it makes the dough rise") was founded to support pro-choice Democratic women candidates, especially during party primary election contests. It now, however, like its Republican counterpart the WISH List (WISH stands for Women in the House and Senate), recruits and trains candidates in addition to contributing to their campaigns. EMILY's List, in 2008 for example, not only provided over $30 million in direct contributions to candidates, it also mobilized volunteers, provided campaign consultants, and paid for some direct media.

Candidate recruitment is often key for attracting women and minority candidates. Just as important are endorsements. Many unions and other organized groups supported Barack Obama and provided much needed volunteers, enthusiasm, and votes.

GETTING OUT THE VOTE Many interest groups believe they can influence public policy by putting like-minded representatives in office. To that end, many groups across the ideological spectrum launch massive get out the vote (GOTV) efforts. These include identifying prospective voters and getting them to the polls on Election Day. Well-financed interest groups such as MoveOn.org and Progress for America often produce issue-oriented ads for newspapers, radio, and television designed to educate the public as well as increase voter interest in election outcomes. Parties and candidates also work to turn out voters, as discussed in chapters 12 and 13.

RATING THE CANDIDATES OR OFFICE HOLDERS Many liberal and conservative ideological groups rate candidates to help their members (and the general public) evaluate the voting records of members of Congress. The American Conservative Union (conservative) and the Americans for Democratic Action (liberal)—two groups at ideological polar extremes—routinely rate candidates and members of Congress based on their votes on key issues. (To learn more, see Analyzing Visuals: Interest Group Ratings of Selected Members of Congress.) These scores help voters know more about their representatives' votes on issues that concern them.

Federal Election Rules, PACs, and the Money Trail

POLITICAL ACTION COMMITTEES As discussed in chapter 14, corporations, labor unions, and interest groups are allowed to form political action committees (PACs). PACs allow these interests to raise money to contribute to political candidates in national elections. Unlike some contributions to interest groups, contributions to PACs are not tax deductible, and PACs generally don't have members who call legislators; instead, PACs have contributors who write checks specifically for the purpose of campaign donations. PAC money plays a significant role in the campaigns of many congressional incumbents, often averaging over half a House candidate's total campaign spending. PACs generally contribute to those who have helped them before and who serve on committees or subcommittees that routinely consider legislation of concern to that group.

What Makes Interest Groups Successful?

Throughout our nation's history, all kinds of interests in society have organized to pressure the government for policy change. Some have been successful, and some have not. Political scientist E. E. Schattschneider once wrote, "Pressure politics is essen-

Analyzing Visuals | Interest Group Ratings of Selected Members of Congress

Interest groups inform their members, as well as the public generally, of the voting records of office holders, helping voters make an informed voting decision. The table displays the 2007 ratings of selected members of Congress by seven interest groups that vary greatly in their ideologies. After reviewing the table, answer the following critical thinking questions:

Member	ACU	ACLU	ADA	AFL-CIO	CoC	LCV	NARAL
Senate							
Mitch McConnell (R-KY)	92	14	10	11	82	7	0
Dianne Feinstein (D–CA)	0	57	90	89	45	87	100
Mel Martinez (R-FL)	80	14	20	16	100	13	0
Charles Schumer (D-NY)	0	71	90	100	55	93	100
House							
John Boehner (R–OH)	100	0	5	4	79	0	0
Sheila Jackson Lee (D–TX)	0	100	100	100	55	90	100
Ileana Ros-Lehtinen (R–FL)	60	33	25	46	90	30	0
Henry Waxman (D–CA)	0	100	90	100	53	95	100

Key
ACU = American Conservative Union
ACLU = American Civil Liberties Union
ADA = Americans for Democratic Action
AFL-CIO = American Federation of Labor–Congress of Industrial Organizations
CC = Christian Coalition
CoC = Chamber of Commerce
LCV = League of Conservation Voters
NARAL = NARAL Pro-Choice America
Members are rated on a scale from 1 to 100, with 1 being the lowest and 100 being the highest support of a particular group's policies.

WHICH members of the Senate would you consider the most liberal? Which groups' ratings did you use to reach your conclusion?

WHICH members of the House would you consider the most conservative? Which groups' ratings did you use to reach your conclusion?

WOULD it be important to know the votes by each representative that each group used to determine their rating? Explain your answer.

tially the politics of small groups. . . . Pressure tactics are not remarkably successful in mobilizing general interests."[36] He was correct; historically, corporate interests often prevail over the concerns of public interest groups such as environmentalists.

All of the groups discussed in this chapter have one thing in common: they all want to shape the public agenda, whether by winning elections, maintaining the status quo, or obtaining favorable legislation or rulings from Congress, executive agencies, or the courts.[37] For powerful groups, simply making sure that certain issues never get discussed may be the goal. In contrast, those opposed to random stops of African American or Middle Eastern drivers win when the issue becomes front-page news and law enforcement officials feel pressured to investigate, if not to stop altogether, the discriminatory practice of racial or ethnic profiling.

Groups often claim credit for winning legislation, court cases, or even elections individually or in coalition with other groups.[38] They also are successful when their

Photo courtesy: *Charles Galley/Getty Images*

Who are interest group leaders? As president of the Children's Defense Fund, Marian Wright Edelman continues to fight against child poverty and for better health care.

leaders become elected officials or policy makers in any of the three branches of the government. For example, Representative Rosa DeLauro (D–CT) was a former political director of EMILY's List. Lynne Cheney, the wife of George W. Bush's vice president, Dick Cheney, is a senior fellow at the conservative American Enterprise Institutute and a former board member of the conservative Independent Women's Forum.

Political scientists have studied several phenomena that contribute in varying degrees—individually and collectively—to particular groups' successes. These include: (1) leaders; (2) patrons and funding; and, (3) a solid membership base.

Leaders

Interest group theorists frequently acknowledge the key role that leaders play in the formation, viability, and success of interest groups while noting that leaders often vary from rank-and-file members on various policies.[39] Without the powerful pen of William Lloyd Garrison in the 1830s, who knows whether the abolition movement would have been as successful? Other notable leaders include Frances Willard of the WCTU, Marian Wright Edelman of the Children's Defense Fund in 1968, and the Reverend Pat Robertson of the Christian Coalition in the 1990s. Most successful groups, especially public interest groups, are led by charismatic individuals who devote most of their energies to the cause.

The role of an interest group leader is similar to that of an entrepreneur in the business world. Leaders of groups must find ways to attract members. As in the marketing of a new product, an interest group leader must offer something attractive to persuade members to join. Potential members of the group must be convinced that the benefits of joining outweigh the costs. Union members, for example, must be persuaded that the cost of their union dues will be offset by the union's winning higher wages for them.

Patrons and Funding

All interest groups require adequate funding to build their memberships as well as to advance their policy objectives. Governments, foundations, and wealthy individuals can serve as **patrons,** providing crucial start-up funds for groups, especially public interest groups.[40] Advertising, litigating, and lobbying are expensive. Without financiers, few public interest groups could survive their initial start-up period. Many interest groups rely on membership dues, direct-mail solicitations, and patrons to remain in business. Charismatic leaders often are especially effective fundraisers and recruiters of new members.

patron
A person who finances a group or individual activity.

Members

Organizations usually are composed of three kinds of members. At the top are a relatively small number of leaders who devote most of their energies to the single group. The second tier of members generally is involved psychologically as well as organizationally. They are the workers of the group—they attend meetings, pay dues, and chair committees to see that things get done. In the bottom tier are the rank and file members who don't actively participate. They pay their dues and call themselves group members, but they do little more. Most group members fall into this last category.

Since the 1960s, survey data have revealed that group membership is drawn primarily from people with higher income and education levels.[41] Individuals who are wealthier can afford to belong to more organizations because they have more money and, often, more leisure time. Money and education also are associated with greater confidence that one's actions will bring results, a further incentive to devote time to organizing or supporting interest groups. These elites often are more involved in politics and hold stronger opinions on many political issues. (To learn more, see Join the Debate: Should There Be Limits on Interest Group Participation?)

People who do belong to groups often belong to more than one. Overlapping memberships often can affect the cohesiveness of a group. Imagine, for example, that you are an officer in the College Republicans. If you call a meeting, people may not attend because they have academic, athletic, or social obligations. Divided loyalties and multiple group memberships frequently affect the success of a group, especially if any one group has too many members who simply fall into the dues-paying category.

Groups vary tremendously in their ability to enroll what are called potential members. (To learn more about group members, see Table 16.3.) According to economist Mancur Olson Jr., all groups provide some **collective good**—that is, something of value, such as money, a tax write-off, a good feeling, or a better environment, that cannot be withheld from a nonmember.[42] If one union member at a factory gets a raise, for example, all other workers at that factory will, too. Therefore, those who don't join or work for the benefit of the group still reap the rewards of the group's activity. The downside of this phenomenon is called the **free rider problem.** As Olson asserts, potential members may be unlikely to join a group because they realize that they will receive many of the benefits the group achieves, regardless of their participation. Not only is it irrational for free riders to join any group, but the bigger the group,

collective good
Something of value that cannot be withheld from a nonmember of a group, for example, a tax write-off or a better environment.

free rider problem
Potential members fail to join a group because they can get the benefit, or collective good, sought by the group without contributing the effort.

TABLE 16.3   Potential Versus Actual Interest Group Members

The goal of most groups is to mobilize all potential members, but as Mancur Olson Jr. points out, the larger the group, the more difficult it is to mobilize. To illustrate the potential versus actual membership phenomenon, here are several examples of groups and their potential memberships.

Population	Group	Number of Potential Members	Number of Actual Members
Governors	National Governors Association (includes territories)	55	55
Political Science Faculty	American Political Science Association	17,000	14,000
Physicians	American Medical Association (AMA)	775,000	250,000
African Americans	National Association for the Advancement of Colored People (NAACP)	37,500,000	500,000
Women	National Organization for Women (NOW)	150,000,000	500,000
Christians	Christian Coalition	207,980,000	350,000

Join the Debate

Should There Be Limits on Interest Group Participation?

OVERVIEW: The First Amendment to the Constitution guarantees the right to freedom of speech, press, association, and the right to "petition the government for a redress of grievances." These are necessary rights in a democracy because they guarantee the right of the people—within the framework of law—to have their voice heard by the government. Grievances can be political or social in nature, and all citizens have the right to petition the government to have their (sometimes narrow) interests or issues addressed. This right includes expressing policy preferences. While political speech and activity as well as the actions of government are regulated by law to prevent the encroachment of undue influence and corruption, the line between appropriate regulation and rights violations may be difficult to discern. Additionally, in order for government to fulfill its functions, it must attempt to balance the claims of diverse competing interests. Because the framework that interest groups and government must operate within is contentious, regulation is necessary. But, when a group lobbies to change government policies, can the government require full disclosure of the group's activities and finances?

Part of the mandate from the Lobbying Disclosure Act of 1995 (LDA) is to facilitate public access to information about lobbying groups as well as about the government's knowledge of their activities. The more recent Honest Leadership and Open Government Act of 2007 has enhanced information about interest group activity by requiring the disclosure of campaign contributions by clients of lobbyists, and by tracking the insertion of earmark provisions in the federal budget by individual members of Congress. The goal is to allow concerned citizens, the media, and watchdog groups to correlate lobbying activities with perceived government response.

The political nature of lobbying activity may mean that interest groups are subject to a higher standard of disclosure and scrutiny. Just as the American people demand transparency in government activity, it seems reasonable that they be provided with information regarding those interest groups monitoring (or supporting) the decisions of government officials. But, what about First Amendment guarantees of free speech and the right to privacy? Could more transparency have the effect of discouraging the expression of concerns and participation in politics? Should interest groups have the same right to privacy as individuals? After all, citizens who contribute less than $200 to campaigns ar e not required to disclose

their influence on the political process. Why should interest groups be denied this standard of privacy?

Arguments IN FAVOR of Regulating Interest Group Activities

- Interest groups are not given a constitutional role to make or influence policy. Though individuals and groups have the right to lobby the government, they have no unrestricted right to do so. Given literally thousands of interests, the government must have some means to prioritize and determine the legitimacy of various groups. For example, should a local 4-H group

the greater the free rider problem. Thus, groups need to provide a variety of other material benefits to convince potential members to join. The American Automobile Association, for example, offers roadside assistance and trip planning services to its members. Similarly, AARP offers a wide range of discount programs to its 35 million members over the age of fifty. Many of those members do not necessarily support all of the group's positions but simply want to take advantage of its discounts.

Several scholars examining interest groups have found that a number of factors help groups overcome the free rider problem. One factor is that members represent-

have the same voice and access to national policy makers as the National Dairy Association?

- Regulation is necessary to ensure the public knows why and in what capacity an interest group is acting. The purpose of federal laws is to ensure accountability in the lobbying process, not to discourage the expression of concerns. The American public needs to know about corruption or misinformation not only coming from the government, but coming from interest groups as well. For instance, the RainbowPUSH Coalition was implicated in lobbying the City of Chicago to keep an after-hours dance club open, even after a fire caused twenty-one deaths. The club owners, RainbowPUSH, and certain Chicago politicians were known to have a business relationship.

- Regulation of interest groups allows the government to level the playing field. Research published by the American Political Science Association (APSA) contends that inequality and unequal access to wealth harms the American democratic process. APSA implies that weathier groups have a larger voice and thus more access to policy makers. Money should not be the only—or even the major—means of influencing public policy. By regulating interest groups, the federal government can help minimize the impact of wealth by letting voters consider the links between interest groups and legislators when they go to the polls.

Arguments AGAINST Regulating Interest Group Activities

- Government regulation of interest groups may stifle political speech. For example, the U.S. Supreme Court upheld the Bipartisan Campaign Reform Act's provision prohibiting groups from issue advertising sixty days prior to a general election. Many scholars and legal experts believe that this is a fundamental violation of political speech rights, as it is now believed that money gives "voice" to the political process—and to deny groups the right to political advertisement is to deny political speech.

- Regulation of groups essentially creates approved speech and politics. By requiring the registration of lobbyists and then regulating their activities, the government is in effect establishing which groups are legitimate and which are not. It is not the government's role to decide the importance of a political group. The government, moreover, should not try to control relationships between politicians and their supporters.

- Government regulation of interest groups is not necessary. In an open, pluralistic society, interest groups are subject to market dynamics. That is, those groups that truly represent broad or important interests will have their views heard over those that do not. Thus, a natural voice is given to those groups deemed by the American people to represent important interests and issues.

Continuing the Debate

1. Is requiring disclosure of group information a violation of the First Amendment and privacy rights? How can this be reconciled with the public's right to know?
2. Does the political nature of lobbyist activity demand a higher level of governmental scrutiny?

To Follow the Debate Online, Go To:

www.opensecrets.org, the Center for Responsive Politics site devoted to resources and information about making lobbying in the United States transparent and regulated. The center is a nonprofit and nonpartisan policy research organization.

www.aclu.org, the site of the American Civil Liberties Union, which has provided testimony to Congress, courts, and regulatory agencies opposing the regulation of lobbyists and their activities. Copies of ACLU statements and testimony are available on their site.

ing other groups or institutions are much more likely than individuals to value efforts to obtain collective goods. Another factor is that once a policy environment appears to threaten existing rights, many individuals come to realize those threats and join groups in exchange for only collective benefits.[43] Moreover, Olson, an economist, fails to consider that many political, Washington, D.C.-based groups count other groups, and not just individuals, as their members. These alliances often are considered carefully by organized interests much in the way some individuals calculate their membership in groups.[44]

These alliances have important implications.[45] Although interest groups do work together in alliances, they also carve out policy niches to differentiate themselves to potential members as well as policy makers. While the National Women's Law Center, for example, vigorously pursues enforcement of Title IX through litigation, the National Organization for Women, although very supportive of Title IX, is more involved in welfare reform as it affects women. Similarly, one study of gay and lesbian groups found that they avoided direct competition by developing different issue niches.[46] Some concentrate on litigation; others lobby for marriage law reform or open inclusion of gays in the military.

Small groups often have an organizational advantage because, for example, in a small group such as the National Governors Association, any individual's share of the collective good may be great enough to make it rational for him or her to join. Patrons, be they large foundations such as the Ford Foundation or individuals such as wealthy financier George Soros, often eliminate the free rider problem for public interest groups.[47] They make the costs of joining minimal because they contribute much of the group's necessary financial support.[48]

Toward Reform: Regulating Interest Groups and Lobbyists

For the first 150 years of our nation's history, federal lobbying practices went unregulated. While the courts remain largely free of lobbying regulations, reforms have altered the state of affairs in Congress and the executive branch. In 1946, in an effort to limit the power of lobbyists, Congress passed the Federal Regulation of Lobbying Act, which required anyone hired to lobby any member of Congress to register and file quarterly financial reports. For years, few lobbyists actually filed these reports and numerous good government groups continued to argue for the strengthening of lobbying laws. Until 1995, however, their efforts were blocked by civil liberties groups such as the ACLU, who argued that registration provisions violate the First Amendment's protections of freedom of speech and of the right of citizens to petition the government.

But, by 1995, public opinion polls began to show that Americans believed the votes of members of Congress were available to the highest bidder. Thus, in late 1995, after nearly fifty years of inaction, Congress passed the first effort to regulate lobbying since the 1946 act. The Lobbying Disclosure Act employed a strict definition of lobbyist (one who devotes at least 20 percent of a client's or employer's time to lobbying activities). It also required lobbyists to: (1) register with the clerk of the House and the secretary of the Senate; (2) report their clients and issues and the agency or house they lobbied; and, (3) estimate the amount they are paid by each client. These reporting requirements made it easier for watchdog groups or the media to monitor lobbying activities. In fact, a comprehensive analysis by the Center for Responsive Politics revealed that by June 2005, 32,890 lobbyists were registered. Nearly $4 million was spent on lobbying for every member of Congress.[49]

After lobbyist Jack Abramoff pleaded guilty to extensive corruption charges in 2006, Congress pledged to reexamine the role of lobbyists in the legislative process. Nevertheless, while legislators said they wanted higher standards set and Democrats complained about "the GOP culture of corruption," no lobbying reform measures were passed in either house prior to the November 2006 election. After the Democrats took control of both houses of Congress in 2007 in the wake of a variety of lobbying scandals, they were able to pass the **Honest Leadership and Open Government Act of 2007.** Among the act's key provisions were a ban on gifts and honoraria to members of Congress and their staffs, tougher disclosure requirements,

Honest Leadership and Open Government Act of 2007
Lobbying reform banning gifts to members of Congress and their staffs, toughening disclosure requirements, and increasing time limits on moving from the federal government to the private sector.

TABLE **16.4**   The Ethics in Government Act

The key provisions of the Ethics in Government Act deal with: (1) financial disclosure, and (2) employment after government service.

1. **Financial disclosure:** The president, vice president, and top-ranking executive employees must file annual public financial disclosure reports that list:
   - The source and amount of all earned income; all income from stocks, bonds, and property; any investments or large debts; the source of a spouse's income, if any.
   - Any position or offices held in any business, labor, or nonprofit organizations.

2. **Employment after government services:** Former executive branch employees may not:
   - Represent anyone before an agency for two years after leaving government service on matters that came within the former employees' sphere or responsibility (even if they were not personally involved in the matter).
   - Represent anyone on any matter before their former agency for one year after leaving it, even if the former employees had no connection with the matter while in the government.

Source: Congressional Quarterly Weekly Report (October 28, 1978): 3121.

and longer time limits on moving from the federal government to the private lobbying sector. Many complained, however that the law did not go far enough. In particular, many commentators were critical of the fact that the ban on gifts applied only to private lobbyists. Thus, state and local agencies and public universities, which spent over $130 million in 2006 to obtain earmarks, are still free to offer tickets for football and basketball games, and provide meals and travel.[50]

Formal lobbying of the executive branch is not governed by the restrictions in the 1995 Lobbying Disclosure Act or the Honest Leadership and Open Government Act. Executive branch employees are, however, constrained by the 1978 Ethics in Government Act. (To learn more, see Table 16.4.) Enacted in the wake of the Watergate scandal, this act attempted to curtail questionable moves by barring members of the executive branch from representing any clients before their agency for one year after leaving governmental service. Thus, someone who worked in air pollution policy for the Environmental Protection Agency and then went to work for the Environmental Defense Fund would have to wait a year before lobbying his or her old agency.

WHAT SHOULD I HAVE LEARNED?

Interest groups lie at the heart of the American social and political system. National groups first emerged in the 1830s. Since that time, the type, nature, sophistication, and tactics of groups have changed dramatically. In this chapter, we have answered the following questions.

■ **What are the roots of the American interest group system?**

An organized interest is a group of people with shared attitudes who make claims on government. Political scientists approach the study of interest groups from a number of theoretical perspectives, including pluralist theory, the transactions approach, and neopluralist approaches such as population ecology theory. Interest groups can be classified in a variety of different ways based on their function and membership.

■ **How did American interest groups develop?**

Interest groups did not begin to emerge in the United States until the 1830s. From 1890 to 1920, the Progressive movement dominated. The 1960s saw the rise of a wide variety of liberal interest groups. During the 1970s and 1980s, legions of conservatives formed new groups to counteract those efforts. Business groups, corporations, and unions established their presence in Washington, D.C.

■ **What do interest groups do?**

Interest groups often fill voids left by the major political parties and give Americans opportunities to make claims, as a group, on government. The most common activity of interest groups is lobbying, which takes many forms. Groups routinely pressure members of Congress and their staffs, the president and the bureaucracy, and the courts; they use a variety of techniques to educate and stimulate the public to pressure key governmental decision makers. Interest groups also attempt to influence the outcome of elections; some run their own candidates for office. Others rate elected officials to inform their members how particular legislators stand on issues of importance to them. Political action committees (PACs), a way for some groups to contribute money to candidates for office, are another method of gaining support from elected officials and ensuring that supportive officials stay in office.

■ **What makes interest groups successful?**

Interest group success can be measured in a variety of ways, including a group's ability to get its issues on the public agenda, winning key pieces of legislation in Congress or executive branch or judicial rulings, or backing successful candidates. Several factors contribute to interest group success, including leaders and patrons, funding, and committed members.

■ **What efforts have been made to regulate and reform interest groups and lobbyists?**

It was not until 1946 that Congress passed any laws regulating federal lobbying. Those laws were largely ineffective and were successfully challenged as violations of the First Amendment. In 1995, Congress passed the Lobbying Disclosure Act that required lobbyists to register with both houses of Congress. By 2007, a rash of scandals resulted in the sweeping reforms of the Honest Leadership and Open Government Act, which dramatically limited what lobbyists can do. The executive branch is regulated by the 1970 Ethics in Government Act.

Key Terms

Researching Interest Groups

In the Library

Baumgartner, Frank, and Beth Leech. *Basic Interests*. Princeton, NJ: Princeton University Press, 1998.

Berry, Jeffrey M., and Clyde Wilcox. *The Interest Group Society*, 4th ed. New York: Longman, 2007.

Cigler, Allan J., and Burdett A. Loomis, eds. *Interest Group Politics*, 7th ed. Washington, DC: CQ Press, 2007.

Grossman, Gene M., and Elhanan Helpman. *Special Interest Politics*. Cambridge, MA: MIT Press, 2001.

Herrnson, Paul S., Ronald G. Shaiko, and Clyde Wilcox, eds. *The Interest Group Connection*, 2nd ed. Washington, DC: CQ Press, 2005.

Kollman, Ken. *Outside Lobbying: Public Opinion and Interest Group Strategies*. Princeton, NJ: Princeton University Press, 1998.

McGlen, Nancy E., et al. *Women, Politics, and American Society*, 4th ed. New York: Longman, 2004.

Nownes, Anthony J. *Total Lobbying: What Lobbyists Want (and How They Try to Get It)*. New York: Cambridge University Press, 2006.

Olson, Mancur, Jr. *The Logic of Collective Action: Public Goods and the Theory of Groups*. Cambridge, MA: Harvard University Press, 1965.

Sirota, David. *Hostile Takeover: How Big Money and Corruption Conquered Our Government—and How We Take It Back*. New York: Crown, 2006.

Truman, David B. *The Governmental Process: Political Interests and Public Opinion*. New York: Knopf, 1951.

On the Web

To see how interest groups grade your political representatives, go to Project Vote Smart at **www.votesmart.org** and click "Interest Group Rating" on the home page.

To learn more about specific interest groups discussed in this chapter, type the name of the group into your browser and ask yourself the following questions as you explore the group's Web site:
- What are this group's stated goals?
- What are the requirements to become a member of the group?
- Does the group provide information that can be used by anyone, even someone not interested in formally joining the group?
- On its Web site, does this group explicitly oppose any other interest groups?

To learn more about lobbying reform efforts, go to Thomas, the legislative information section of the Library of Congress, at **thomas.loc.gov**. Search for the Lobbying Disclosure Act of 1995 and the Honest Leadership and Open Government Act of 2007 in order to find out more about the lobbying restrictions required by this legislation.

17

Domestic Policy

Picture the following scenario: the president is George Bush, the economy is in a downturn, there is turmoil in Iraq, and the issue of health care reform is one of the central issues in an upcoming presidential campaign. While this certainly could be a description of 2008, the scenario is drawn from the events of 1992. Back then, George Bush (the father of George W. Bush) was in the White House, the nation was in an economic recession, and Iraq was recovering from the 1991 Persian Gulf War. In addition, Americans were increasingly worried about the skyrocketing costs of medical care, a growing number of uninsured citizens, and escalating prices for pharmaceuticals. According to public opinion polls, voters placed reform of the health care system at the top of the list of issues the next president should address. How did the country wind up in nearly the same place sixteen years later?

During the 1992 presidential election, Bill Clinton made the issue of health care reform one of the main themes of his campaign to win the White House. Throughout the autumn months of 1992, Clinton regularly condemned President Bush for failing to take action on an emerging national crisis. He promised that under a Clinton administration, there would be major reform of the nation's health care system. After

AMERICAN HEALTH
CHOICES PLAN

HILLARYCLINTON.COM

he prevailed in the election, Clinton quickly sought to fulfill his campaign promise by creating a task force led by his wife, Hillary Rodham Clinton, to provide health care to all Americans. After about a year of preparation, Clinton's health care task force released its proposal to much fanfare, but the plan stalled in Congress under fierce opposition from Republican leaders.[1]

Among the main causes of its demise was a rise in public concern over the impact of the plan on the ability of individuals to choose their own physicians. In order to reach its goal of universal health care coverage, the Clinton reform called for restrictions on individual choices to help control the spiraling costs of health services. Declining public support for the Clinton plan was undoubtedly aided by a series of television ads funded by the health insurance industry that warned Americans they would lose control of their health care under the Clinton proposal. Arguments against the Clinton plan were summed up in a statement by then Republican Senator Bob Dole, who told the *Washington Post*, "More cost. Less choice. More taxes. Less quality. More government control. Less control for you and your family. That's what the president's government-run plan is likely to give you."[2]

Without serious reform efforts throughout the late 1990s and first half of this decade, the health care situation in the nation continued to deteriorate. By the time the presidential election of

■ **The government's role in providing a social safety net has changed markedly over the last century.** Sociologist and progressive reformer Jane Addams, shown at left, provided education and support to Chicago's poor at a time when social services were considered the responsibility of private citizens. While running for the 2008 Democratic presidential nomination, Senator Hillary Clinton, shown at right, unveiled an ambitious health care plan intended to provide all Americans with adequate health coverage.

WHAT SHOULD I KNOW ABOUT . . .

■ the roots of public policy and the policy-making process?

■ the evolution of income security and health care policies in the United States?

■ income security and health care policies today?

■ reform efforts related to energy and environmental policies?

597

2008 rolled around, the problems with health care in America had once again emerged as a central issue. However, all the leading candidates had learned from the failures of the Clinton administration and proposed reforms that recognized the political liabilities of limiting individual choice.

TO LEARN MORE—
—TO DO MORE

To learn more about health care reform efforts in the United States, go to the Kaiser Family Foundation's Web site at www.kaiseredu.org.

Ironically, one of the two Democratic front-runners for the presidential nomination was none other than Hillary Clinton, now a second-term senator from New York. Not surprisingly, it was Senator Clinton who created the most aggressive plan for reforming America's health care system. As a Democratic presidential candidate, Clinton proposed a major reform that promised health insurance for all Americans and control of the skyrocketing costs of medical care. Unlike her plan in the 1990s, the new proposal would provide universal coverage through a more "choice driven" mechanism. Her "American Health Choices Plan" would give families tax credits to help pay for health insurance and require large businesses to help pay for their employees' insurance costs. Clinton's plan would not require small businesses to take part, but it would offer tax credits to encourage them to participate. In unveiling her proposal, Clinton warned that her Republican opponents would "try to equate this plan with government-run health care. Don't let them fool you again." She stressed that her plan would let individuals "keep the doctors you know and trust," and expand "personal choice" while keeping costs down.[3]

Clinton's key Democratic rival, Senator Barack Obama, and the eventual Republican nominee, Senator John McCain, also released health care reform proposals. Like Clinton, Obama and McCain shied away from any measure that would give the appearance of limiting individual choice. Instead, they called for various policies that would use tax incentives and subsidies to allow individuals to gain access to health insurance. They also called for allowing consumers the option of reimporting drugs from other countries to help reduce costs of prescriptions.[4]

While it's clear that health care played a prominent role in the 2008 presidential campaign, it is unclear if the heavy attention will lead to the types of fundamental change proposed by the candidates. After all, in 1992 the nation seemed primed to send a president to Washington who would fix the nation's ailing health care system. A decade and a half later, the nation is still waiting for that reform. The failure to address the nation's health care system has raised questions regarding the policy-making process and efforts to tackle such a mammoth social issue. Has the failure to achieve health care reform been caused by the partisan conflict that so often dominates in Washington, D.C., or is the lack of progress more reflective of the broader difficulties associated with making public policies in a democracy?

Domestic policy is a term that designates a broad and varied range of government programs designed to provide the citizens of a nation with protection from poverty and hunger, to improve their health and physical well-being, to enable transportation, to maintain a healthy and livable environment, and otherwise enable them to lead more secure, satisfying, and productive lives. In a nutshell, domestic policies are intended to enhance quality of life through the establishment of societal conditions that allow citizens to pursue happiness and feel secure. These policies are meant to benefit all segments of society, but they often focus on the less fortunate members who find it more difficult to provide for themselves and their families.

This chapter discusses the policy-making process as well as key domestic policy issues. We will thus explore the following topics:

★ First, we will consider *the roots of public policy: the policy-making process.*

★ Second, we will examine *domestic policy efforts related to income security and health care* through a review of how the government's commitment in these policy areas expanded in the twentieth century.

★ Third, we will provide an overview of *current domestic policy efforts* in the areas of income security and health care.

★ Finally, we will examine reform efforts related to *energy and environmental policies*, including the rise and fall of these areas in terms of the attention of government.

Roots of Public Policy: The Policy-Making Process

While this chapter focuses on domestic policy areas in the United States, we begin with a more general look at the broader process of making government policy. **Public policy** is an intentional course of action followed by government in dealing with some problem or matter of concern.[5] Public policies are thus governmental policies, based on law; they are authoritative and binding on people. Individuals, groups, and even government agencies that do not comply with policies can be penalized through fines, loss of benefits, or even jail terms. The phrase "course of action" implies that policies develop or unfold over time. They involve more than a legislative decision to enact a law or a presidential decision to issue an executive order. Also important is how the law or executive order is carried out. The impact or meaning of a policy depends on whether it is vigorously enforced, enforced only in some instances, or not enforced at all.

public policy
An intentional course of action followed by government in dealing with some problem or matter of concern.

Theories of Public Policy

Political scientists and other social scientists have developed many theories and models to explain the formation of public policies. According to elite theory, the chosen few or elite make the important decisions in society. A proponent of elite theory, political scientist Thomas R. Dye, contends that all societies are divided into elites and masses. The elites have power to make and implement policy, while the masses simply respond to the desires of the elites. Elite theorists believe that an unequal distribution of power in society is normal and inevitable.[6] Elites, however, are not immune from public opinion, nor do they by definition oppress the masses. Dye argues that in complex societies such as the United States, only a tiny minority of people serve as the elites.

Other views of public policy are bureaucratic theory, interest group theory, and pluralist theory. According to bureaucratic theory, all institutions, governmental and nongovernmental, have fallen under the control of a large and ever growing bureaucracy that carries out policy using standardized procedures. This growing complexity of modern organizations has empowered bureaucrats, who become dominant as a consequence of their expertise and competence. Eventually, the bureaucrats wrest power from others, especially elected officials.

According to interest group theory, interest groups—not elites or bureaucrats—control the governmental process. The noted interest group theorist David B. Truman believed that there are so many potential pressure points in the three branches of the federal government, as well as at the state level, that interest groups can step in on any number of competing sides. The government then becomes the equilibrium point in the system as it mediates among competing interests.[7]

Many political scientists subscribe to the pluralist perspective. For example, Robert Dahl argues that political resources in the United States are scattered so widely that no single elite group could ever gain monopoly control over any substantial area of policy.[8] According to political scientist Theodore Lowi, participants in every political controversy get something; thus, each has some impact on how political decisions are made. Lowi contends that governments in the United States rarely say no to any well-organized interest, noting that since all organized interests receive some benefits, the public interest—what is good for the public at large—often tends to lose out in the American system.[9]

A Model of the Policy-Making Process

A popular model used to describe the policy-making process views it as a sequence of stages or functional activities. (This model, depicted in Figure 17.1, can be used to analyze any of the issues discussed in this book.) Public policies do not just happen; rather, they are typically the products of a predictable pattern of events. Models for

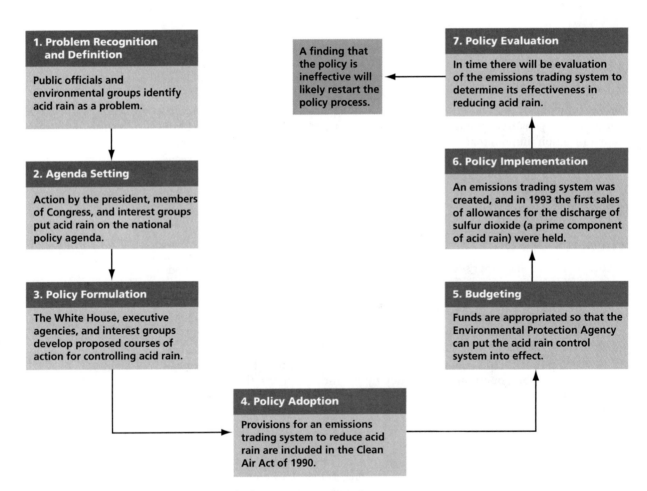

1. Problem Recognition and Definition

Public officials and environmental groups identify acid rain as a problem.

2. Agenda Setting

Action by the president, members of Congress, and interest groups put acid rain on the national policy agenda.

3. Policy Formulation

The White House, executive agencies, and interest groups develop proposed courses of action for controlling acid rain.

4. Policy Adoption

Provisions for an emissions trading system to reduce acid rain are included in the Clean Air Act of 1990.

5. Budgeting

Funds are appropriated so that the Environmental Protection Agency can put the acid rain control system into effect.

6. Policy Implementation

An emissions trading system was created, and in 1993 the first sales of allowances for the discharge of sulfur dioxide (a prime component of acid rain) were held.

7. Policy Evaluation

In time there will be evaluation of the emissions trading system to determine its effectiveness in reducing acid rain.

A finding that the policy is ineffective will likely restart the policy process.

FIGURE **17.1** Stages of the Public Policy Process One of the best ways to understand public policy is to examine the process by which policies are made. While there are many unique characteristics of policy making at the various levels of government, there are commonalities that define the process from which public policies emerge. In the figure, the public policy process is broken down into seven steps. Each step has distinguishing features, but it is important to remember that the steps often merge into one another in a less distinct manner.

analyzing the policy-making process do not always explain *why* public policies take the specific forms that they do, however. That depends on the political struggles over particular policies. Nor do models necessarily tell us *who* dominates or controls the formation of public policy.

Policy making typically can be thought of as a process of sequential steps:

1. **Problem recognition**—identification of an issue that disturbs the people and leads them to call for governmental intervention.

2. **Agenda setting**—government recognition that a problem is worthy of consideration for governmental intervention.

3. **Policy formulation**—identification of alternative approaches to addressing the problems placed on government's agenda.

4. **Policy adoption**—the formal selection of public policies through legislative, executive, judicial, and bureaucratic means.

5. **Budgeting**—the allocation of resources to provide for the proper implementation of public policies.

6. **Policy implementation**—the actual administration or application of public policies to their targets.

7. **Policy evaluation**—the determination of a policy's accomplishments, consequences, or shortcomings.

With this overview in mind, let's now look in more detail at the various stages of the policy process or cycle.

Problem Recognition and Definition

At any given time, there are many conditions that disturb or distress people, such as polluted air and water, the outsourcing of jobs overseas, natural disasters, the rising cost of college tuition, and possible terrorist attacks. All disturbing conditions do not automatically become problems in need of public policy solutions, however. Some of them may be accepted as trivial, inevitable, or beyond the control of government.

For a condition to become a problem, there must be some criterion—a standard or value—that leads people to believe that the condition does not have to be accepted and, further, that it is something with which government can deal effectively and appropriately. For example, natural disasters such as hurricanes are unlikely to be identified as a policy problem because there is little that government can do about them directly. The consequences of hurricanes—the human distress and property destruction that they bring—are another matter. Relief from the devastation of natural disasters can be a focus of government action, and agencies such as the Federal Emergency Management Agency (FEMA) have been set up to reduce these hardships. When these agencies fail to fulfill their roles, as FEMA did in the wake of Hurricane Katrina in 2005, the public requires answers for why government has not done its job.

Perceptions toward government responsibilities also change over time. For example, conditions that were once considered beyond government's responsibility may at a later time be identified as problems because of changes in public outlooks. At one time, care of children was considered the sole prerogative of parents. This perspective began to change in the late 1880s in response to newspaper accounts of child abuse. During the 1960s, a time of social activism and concern about people's rights, all of the state legislatures enacted laws requiring the reporting of child abuse. In 1974, Congress enacted legislation requiring states to create child protection agencies. In 1993, President Bill Clinton signed the National Child Abuse Prevention Act, which established a national database to track child abusers and prevent them from working in childcare centers. In this first decade of the twenty-first century, protection of children is clearly recognized as a public-sector responsibility.

Usually there is not a single, agreed-on definition of a problem. Indeed, political struggle often occurs at this stage because how the problem is defined helps determine what sort of action is appropriate. For example, if we define access to transportation for people with disabilities as a transportation problem, then an acceptable solution is to adapt the regular transportation system or establish other means of transport, such as a special van service. If we define access to transportation as a civil rights problem, however, then people with disabilities are entitled to equal access to the regular transportation system. The civil rights view triumphed with congressional passage of the Americans with Disabilities Act in 1990, which mandated that local and state governments must make transportation accessible to the elderly and to all people with disabilities.

Problems differ not only in their definitions but also in the difficulty of resolving them. For instance, it is more difficult to tackle problems that affect large numbers of people or that require behavioral change than problems that have more focused solutions. In the area of environmental protection, there have been major improvements in surface water quality in the United States since the 1970s.[10] These improvements have been achieved because the solutions were relatively easy to reach through improved sewage treatment plants and stricter wastewater requirements for businesses. No substantial behavioral changes were required of the average U.S. citizen to achieve these accomplishments. In contrast, the issue of global warming stands as a policy problem with no easy solutions. In order to reduce the greenhouse gas emissions that have been linked to climate change, individuals will need to make behavioral adjustments—for example, in the amount of miles they drive and the size and performance of their vehicles. For elected officials eager to show tangible results to their constituents, it makes political sense to work on problems in which improvements can be made quickly and without direct costs to the public.

Note that public policies themselves are frequently viewed as problems or the causes of other problems. Thus, for some people, gun control legislation is a solution to gun violence. To the National Rifle Association (NRA), however, any law that restricts gun ownership is a problem because the NRA views such laws as inappropriately infringing on an individual's constitutional right to keep and bear arms. To social conservatives, legal access to abortion is a problem; for social liberals, laws restricting abortion access fall into the problem category.

Agenda Setting

Once a problem is recognized and defined as such by a significant segment of society, it must be brought to the attention of public officials and it must secure a place on an agenda.

agenda
A set of issues to be discussed or given attention.

systemic agenda
All public issues that are viewed as requiring governmental attention; a discussion agenda.

governmental (institutional) agenda
The changing list of issues to which governments believe they should address themselves.

agenda setting
The constant process of forming the list of issues to be addressed by government.

DEFINING AGENDAS An **agenda** is a set of issues to be discussed or given attention. Every political community—national, state, and local—has a **systemic agenda**. The systemic agenda is essentially a discussion agenda; it comprises "all issues that are commonly perceived by the members of the political community as meriting public attention and as involving matters within the legitimate jurisdiction" of governments.[11] A **governmental** or **institutional agenda** includes only problems to which legislators or other public officials feel obliged to devote active and serious attention. Not all problems that attract the attention of officials are likely to have been widely discussed by the general public, and not all issues on the systemic agenda end up on the institutional agenda.

Problems or issues (an issue emerges when disagreement exists over what should be done about a problem) may move onto an institutional agenda, whether from the systemic agenda or elsewhere, in several ways. The congressional agenda represents issues that demand both legislative attention and official consideration.

GETTING ON THE CONGRESSIONAL AGENDA **Agenda setting** is a competitive process. Congress, for instance, does not have the time or the money to take on all the problems and issues it is called on to handle. Whether because of their influence or skill in developing political support, some people or groups are more successful than others in steering items onto the agenda. Chance plays a small role in agenda setting, except in cases of accidents or natural disasters.

As discussed in chapter 8, the president is an important agenda-setter for Congress. In the State of the Union Address, proposed budget, and special messages, the president presents Congress with a legislative program for its consideration. Much of Congress's time is spent deliberating presidential recommendations, although by no means does Congress always respond as the president might wish. Congress can be recalcitrant even when the president and congressional majorities come from the same party. This scenario was very apparent in 2006 when the Republican-controlled Congress blocked President Bush's plan to allow Dubai Ports World, a company owned by the United Arab Emirates, to take over operations at six major U.S. ports.

Photo courtesy: Chris Kleponis/Reuters

Who affects public policy? Film star Salma Hayek addresses the Senate Judiciary Committee on violence against women.

Citing fears that national security would be threatened, Congress successfully pressured the president to take the deal off the table.[12]

Interest groups are major actors and initiators in the agenda-setting process. Interest groups and their lobbyists frequently ask Congress to legislate on problems of special concern to them. Environmentalists, for instance, call for government action on such issues as global warming, the protection of wetlands, and the reduction of air pollution. Business groups may seek protection against foreign competitors, restrictions on product liability lawsuits, or government financial bailouts.

Problems may secure agenda status because of some crisis, natural disaster, or other extraordinary event. The attacks on the World Trade Center and the Pentagon on September 11, 2001, placed the issue of homeland security at the top of the policy agenda. Some problems and issues draw the attention of the news media and consequently gain agenda status, more salience, or both. The home mortgage crisis in 2008 received significant media attention and corresponding responses from Congress. Similarly, the problem of soaring gas prices, coupled with record oil company profits, grabbed national headlines in 2008,[13] prompting a variety of proposals to lower the cost of gas, such as a temporary removal of the federal gas tax and increased taxes on the profits of oil companies.

Individual private citizens, members of Congress, and other officials acting as policy entrepreneurs may push issues onto the congressional agenda. In the 1960s, Ralph Nader's book *Unsafe at Any Speed* and Rachel Carson's *Silent Spring* brought motor vehicle safety and the misuse of pesticides, respectively, to the attention of Congress and many citizens. Representative Leonor Sullivan (D–MO) worked for a decade to secure the adoption in 1964 of a permanent food stamp program to help the needy. The actors Michael J. Fox, who has Parkinson's disease, and Christopher Reeve, who fought courageously to overcome a severe spinal injury, appeared in front of congressional committees and used their celebrity status to push for greater funding of medical research. Music celebrities Don Henley of the Eagles and Kevin Richardson of the Backstreet Boys testified before Congress on issues ranging from environmental policies to copyright infringement. While books and testimony are themselves important, it is ultimately the media's coverage of the activities that will have the greatest impact on drawing broad public attention to an issue.

Finally, political changes may contribute to agenda setting. The landslide election of Democratic President Lyndon B. Johnson in 1964, along with strong, favorable Democratic majorities in Congress, made possible the enactment of a flood of Great Society legislation. The intent of this legislation was to mitigate domestic problems such as poverty and inadequate medical care for the elderly and needy and to provide education for disadvantaged children. Similarly, the election of Republican President Ronald Reagan, who in his 1981 inaugural address asserted that "Government is not the solution; government is the problem," brought issues concerning the size and activities of government onto national policy agendas. Reagan's administration, however, had only limited success in reducing the size of the government.[14]

Policy Formulation

policy formulation
The crafting of appropriate and acceptable proposed courses of action to ameliorate or resolve public problems.

Policy formulation is the crafting of appropriate and acceptable proposed courses of action to ameliorate or resolve public problems. It has both political and technical components. The political aspect of policy formulation involves determining generally what should be done to reduce acid rain, for example—whether standard setting and enforcement or emissions testing should be used. The technical facet involves correctly stating in specific language what one wants to authorize or accomplish, so as to adequately guide those who must implement policy and to prevent distortion of legislative intent. Political scientist Charles O. Jones suggests that formulation may take different forms.[15]

1. *Routine formulation* is "a repetitive and essentially changeless process of reformulating similar proposals within an issue area that is well established on the government agenda." For instance, the formulation of policy for veterans' benefits represents a standard process of drafting proposals similar to those established in the past.

2. *Analogous formulation* handles new problems by drawing on experience with similar problems in the past. What has been done in the past to cope with the activities of terrorists? What has been done in other states to deal with child abuse or divorce law reform?

3. *Creative formulation* involves attempts to develop new or unprecedented proposals that represent a departure from existing practices and that will better resolve a problem. For example, plans to develop an anti-missile defense system to shoot down incoming missiles represents a departure from previous defense strategies of mutual destruction.

Policy formulation may be undertaken by various players in the policy process: the president, presidential aides, agency officials, specially appointed task forces and commissions, interest groups, private research organizations (or "think tanks"), and legislators and their staffs. The people engaged in formulation are usually looking ahead toward policy adoption. Particular provisions may be included or excluded from a proposal in an attempt to enhance its likelihood of adoption. To the extent that formulators think in this strategic manner, the formulation and adoption stages of the policy process often overlap.

In many cases, elected officials and nongovernmental organizations work as partners in the formulation of public polices. A prime example of these partnerships was the tight relationship between the libertarian Cato Institute and the Bush administration in the construction of the president's Social Security reform efforts.[16]

Policy Adoption

policy adoption
The approval of a policy proposal by the people with the requisite authority, such as a legislature.

Policy adoption is the approval of a policy proposal by the people with requisite authority, such as a legislature or chief executive. This approval gives the policy legal force. Because most public policies in the United States result from legislation, policy adoption frequently requires the building of majority coalitions necessary to secure the enactment of legislation.

In chapter 7, we discuss how power is diffused in Congress and how the legislative process comprises a number of roadblocks or obstacles that a bill must successfully navigate before it becomes law. A majority is needed to clear a bill through each of these obstacles; hence, not one majority but a series of majorities is needed for congressional policy adoption. To secure the needed votes, a bill may be watered down or modified at each of these decision points. Or, the bill may fail to win a majority at one of them and die, at least for the time being.

The adoption of major legislation requires much negotiation, bargaining, and compromise. In some instances, years or even decades may be needed to secure the enactment of legislation on a controversial matter. Congress considered federal aid to public education off and on over several decades before it finally won approval in 1965, for example. At other times, the approval process may move quickly.

The tortuous nature of congressional policy adoption has some important consequences. First, complex legislation may require substantial periods of time in order to pass. Second, the legislation passed is often incremental, making only limited or marginal changes in existing policy. Third, legislation is frequently written in general or ambiguous language, as in the Clean Air Act, which provided amorphous instructions to administrators in the Environmental Protection Agency to set air quality standards that would allow for an "adequate margin of safety" to protect the public health. Phrases such as "adequate margin" are highly subjective and open to a wide range of interpretations. Language such as this may provide considerable discretion to the people who implement the law and also leave them in doubt as to its intended purposes.

Not all policy adoption necessitates formation of majority coalitions. Although a president has many aides and advisers and is bombarded with information and advice, the final decision to veto a bill passed by Congress rests with him or her.

Budgeting

Most policies require money in order to be carried out; some policies, such as those providing income security, essentially involve the transfer of money from taxpayers to the government and back to individual beneficiaries. Funding for most policies and agencies is provided through the budgetary process (discussed in chapter 18). Whether a policy is well funded or poorly funded has a significant effect on its scope, impact, and effectiveness.

Where the Money Goes

A policy can be nullified by a refusal to fund, which was the fate of the Homeownership and Opportunity for People Everywhere (Hope VI) program. In 2006, the Bush administration decided not to seek funds for HOPE VI, a program within the Department of Housing and Urban Development (HUD) that demolished obsolete and severely distressed public housing while introducing community service and self-sufficiency initiatives. President Bush had tried to eliminate HOPE VI twice before by not funding it, but each time Congress directed financial resources to HUD to keep the program alive. However, in 2006, Congress followed the president's lead, and HOPE VI was terminated.[17]

Other policies or programs often suffer from inadequate funding. Thus, the Occupational Safety and Health Administration (OSHA) can afford to inspect annually only a small fraction of the workplaces within its jurisdiction. Similarly, the Department of Housing and Urban Development has funds sufficient to provide rent subsidies only to approximately 20 percent of the eligible low-income families.

The budgetary process also gives the president and the Congress an opportunity to review the government's many policies and programs, to inquire into their administration, to appraise their value and effectiveness, and to exercise some influence on their conduct. Not all of the government's hundreds of programs are fully examined every year. But, over a period of several years, most programs come under scrutiny.

In a given year, most agencies experience only limited or marginal changes in their funding. Still, budgeting is a vital part of the policy process that helps determine the impact and effectiveness of public policies. Having the potential to curb funding can be a powerful tool for congressional committee chairs.

Policy Implementation

policy implementation
The process of carrying out public policy through governmental agencies and the courts.

Policy implementation is the process of carrying out public policies, most of which are implemented by administrative agencies. Some, however, are enforced in other ways. Product liability and product dating are two examples. Product liability laws such as the Food and Drug Act of 1906, the National Traffic and Motor Vehicle Safety Act of 1966, and the Consumer Product Safety Act of 1972 are typically enforced by lawsuits initiated in the courts by injured consumers or their survivors. In contrast, state product-dating laws are implemented more by voluntary compliance when grocers take out-of-date products off their shelves or when consumers choose not to buy food products after the use dates stamped on them expire. The courts also get involved in implementation when they are called on to interpret the meaning of legislation, review the legality of agency rules and actions, and determine whether institutions such as prisons and mental hospitals conform to legal and constitutional standards.

In areas like environmental policy, the courts are regularly asked to determine if government agencies are properly enforcing the nation's laws. For example, a number of state governments filed suit in 2007 against the Environmental Protection Agency (EPA) to get that agency to regulate the emission of greenhouse gases. The Supreme Court found that the EPA was not properly enforcing the provisions of the Clean Air Act of 1990 when it failed to regulate gases that were linked to increasing atmospheric temperatures.[18] (To learn more, see Politics Now: Supreme Court Action on Clean Air.)

Administrative agencies may be authorized to use a number of techniques to implement the public policies within their jurisdictions. These techniques can be categorized as authoritative, incentive, capacity, or hortatory, depending on the behavioral assumptions on which they are based.[19]

1. *Authoritative techniques* for policy implementation rest on the notion that people's actions must be directed or restrained by government in order to prevent or eliminate activities or products that are unsafe, unfair, evil, or immoral. Consumer products must meet certain safety regulations, and radio stations can be fined heavily or have their broadcasting licenses revoked if they broadcast obscenities. Many government agencies have authority to issue rules and set standards to regulate such matters as meat and food processing, the discharge of pollutants into the environment, the healthfulness and safety of workplaces, and the safe operation of commercial airplanes. Compliance with these standards is determined by inspection and monitoring, and penalties may be imposed on people or companies that violate the rules and standards set forth in a particular policy. For example, under Title IX, the federal government can terminate funds to colleges or universities that discriminate against female students. Its detractors sometimes stigmatize this pattern of action as "command and control regulation," although in practice it often involves much education, bargaining, and persuasion in addition to the exercise of authority. In the case of Title IX, for instance, the Department of Education will try to negotiate with a school to bring it into compliance before funding is terminated.

2. *Incentive techniques* for policy implementation encourage people to act in their own best interest by offering payoffs or financial inducements to get them to comply with public policies. Such policies may provide tax deductions to encour-

POLITICS NOW

Source: WASHINGTON POST   April 3, 2007

Supreme Court Action on Clean Air

High Court Faults EPA Inaction on Emissions

ROBERT BARNES AND JULIET EILPERIN

The Supreme Court rebuked the Bush administration yesterday for refusing to regulate greenhouse gas emissions, siding with environmentalists in the Court's first examination of the phenomenon of global warming. The Court ruled 5 to 4 that the Environmental Protection Agency violated the Clean Air Act by improperly declining to regulate new-vehicle emissions standards to control the pollutants that scientists say contribute to global warming.

"EPA has offered no reasoned explanation for its refusal to decide whether greenhouse gases cause or contribute to climate change," Justice John Paul Stevens wrote for the majority. The agency "identifies nothing suggesting that Congress meant to curtail EPA's power to treat greenhouse gases as air pollutants," the opinion continued.

The issue at stake in the case, one of two yesterday that the Court decided in favor of environmentalists, is somewhat narrow. But environmentalists and some lawmakers said it could serve as a turning point, placing new pressure on the Bush administration to address global warming. The Natural Resources Defense Council said in a statement that the ruling "repudiates the Bush administration's do-nothing policy on global warming," undermining the government's refusal to view carbon dioxide as an air pollutant subject to EPA regulation.

The ruling could also lend important authority to efforts by the states either to force the federal government to reduce greenhouse gas emissions or to be allowed to do it themselves. New York is leading an effort to strengthen regulations on power-plant emissions. California has passed a law seeking to cut carbon dioxide emissions from automobiles starting in 2009; its regulations have been adopted by 10 other states and may soon be adopted by Maryland.

The decision in *Commonwealth of Massachusetts et al. v. Environmental Protection Agency* et al. also reinforced the division on the Supreme Court, with its four liberal members in the majority and its four most conservative members dissenting. Justice Anthony M. Kennedy's role as the key justice in this term's 5 to 4 decisions was again on display, as he sided with Stevens, Stephen G. Breyer, Ruth Bader Ginsburg and David H. Souter.

The case dates from 1999, when the International Center for Technology Assessment and other groups petitioned the EPA to set standards for greenhouse gas emissions for new vehicles. Four years later, the EPA declined, saying that it lacked authority to regulate greenhouse gases and that even if it did, it might not choose to because of "numerous areas of scientific uncertainty" about the causes and effects of global warming. Massachusetts, along with other states and cities, took the agency to court.

The Court majority said that the EPA clearly had the authority to regulate the emissions and that its "laundry list" of reasons for not doing so were not based in the law. "We need not and do not reach the question whether on remand EPA must make an endangerment finding.... We hold only that EPA must ground its reasons for actions or inaction in the statute," Stevens wrote.

Chief Justice John G. Roberts Jr. wrote one dissent, which was joined by Justices Samuel A. Alito Jr., Antonin Scalia and Clarence Thomas. He said that global warming may be a "crisis," even "the most pressing environmental problem of our time," but that it is an issue for Congress and the executive branch. He said the Court's majority used "sleight-of-hand" to even grant Massachusetts the standing to sue.

Scalia wrote another dissent, which Roberts and others also joined, saying the EPA had done its duty when it considered the petition and decided not to act. He said the Court "has no business substituting its own desired outcome for the reasoned judgment of the responsible agency."

Discussion Questions

1. *In the* Massachusetts *v.* EPA *(2007) decision, there was significant disagreement among the Supreme Court justices about the role of the courts in requiring the EPA to regulate greenhouse gases. Do you agree with the Court's decision in this case? What is the primary reason you support or oppose this decision?*

2. *The Clean Air Act and its primary amendments were passed before global warming and climate change had become widely accepted scientific views. Should the courts order an agency to interpret older laws to apply to current concerns, or is it the responsibility of Congress to update the laws? Explain your reasoning.*

3. *Should state governments have the ability to use the federal courts to require federal agencies to change the way they interpret acts of Congress? Why or why not?*

age charitable giving or the purchase of alternative fuel vehicles such as hybrid automobiles. Farmers receive subsidies to make their production (or nonproduction) of wheat, cotton, and other goods more profitable. Conversely, sanctions such as high taxes may discourage the purchase and use of such products as tobacco or liquor, and pollution fees may reduce the discharge of pollutants by making this action more costly to businesses.

Photo courtesy: thetruth.com

How does government change the behaviors of citizens? Anti-smoking commercials like those from the Truth.com campaign are excellent examples of hortatory techniques employed by government.

3. *Capacity techniques* provide people with information, education, training, or resources that will enable them to participate in desired activities. The assumption underlying the provision of these techniques is that people have the incentive or desire to do what is right but lack the capacity to act accordingly. Job training may enable able-bodied people to find work, and accurate information on interest rates will enable people to protect themselves against interest-rate gouging. Financial assistance can help the needy acquire better housing and warmer winter coats and perhaps allow them to lead more comfortable lives.

4. *Hortatory techniques* encourage people to comply with policy by appealing to people's "better instincts" in an effort to get them to act in desired ways. In this instance, the policy implementers assume that people decide how to act according to their personal values and beliefs. During the Reagan administration, First Lady Nancy Reagan implored young people to "Just say no" to drugs. Hortatory techniques also include the use of highway signs displaying slogans like "Don't Be a Litterbug" and "Don't Mess with Texas" to discourage littering. Campaigns like "Smokey the Bear's 'Only You Can Prevent Forest Fires'" are meant to encourage compliance with fire and safety regulations in national parks and forests.

Effective administration of public policies depends partly on whether an agency is authorized to use appropriate implementation techniques. Many other factors also come into play, including the clarity and consistency of policies' statutory mandates, adequacy of funding, political support, and the will and skill of agency personnel. Often government will turn to a combination of authoritative, incentive, capacity, and hortatory approaches to reach their goals. For example, public health officials employ all of these tools in their efforts to reduce tobacco use. These techniques include laws prohibiting smoking in public places, taxes on the sales of tobacco products, warning labels on packs of cigarettes, and anti-smoking commercials on television. There is no easy formula that will guarantee successful policy implementation; in practice, many policies only partially achieve their goals.

Policy Evaluation

policy evaluation
The process of determining whether a course of action is achieving its intended goals.

Practitioners of **policy evaluation** seek to determine what a policy is actually accomplishing. They may also try to determine whether a policy is being fairly or efficiently administered. Policy evaluation may be conducted by a variety of players: congressional committees, through investigations and other oversight activities; presidential commissions; administrative agencies themselves; university researchers; private research organizations, such as the Brookings Institution; and the Government Accountability Office (GAO), formerly named the General Accounting Office.

The GAO, created in 1921, is an important evaluator of public policies. Every year, the GAO conducts hundreds of studies of government agencies and programs, either at the request of members of Congress or on its own initiative. The titles of two of its 2008 evaluations convey a notion of the breadth of its work: "Biosurveillance:

Preliminary Observations on Department of Homeland Security's Biosurveillance Initiatives" and "Influenza Pandemic: Federal Agencies Should Continue to Assist States to Address Gaps in Pandemic Planning."

Social scientists and qualified investigators design studies to measure the societal impact of programs and to determine whether these programs are achieving their specified goals or objectives. The national executive departments and agencies often have officials and units responsible for policy evaluation; so do state governments. Evaluation research and studies can stimulate attempts to modify or terminate policies and thus restart the policy process. Legislators and administrators may formulate and advocate amendments designed to correct problems or shortcomings in a policy. In 1988, for example, legislation was adopted to correct weaknesses in the enforcement of the Fair Housing Act of 1968, which banned discrimination in the sale or rental of most housing. Policies are also terminated as a result of the evaluation process; for example, through the Airline Deregulation Act of 1978, Congress eliminated the Civil Aeronautics Board and its program of economic regulation of commercial airlines. This action was taken on the assumption that competition in the marketplace would better protect the interests of airline users. Competition indeed reduced the cost of flying on many popular routes.

The demise of programs is relatively rare, however; more often, a troubled program is modified or allowed to limp along because it provides a popular service. For example, the nation's passenger rail system, Amtrak, remains dependent on government funds. While its northeastern lines are financially self-sufficient, many of Amtrak's longer distance routes are not able to operate without significant government subsidies. Nevertheless, the more rural routes remain popular with legislators in western states, and thus Amtrak continues to receive federal support.[20]

While policy evaluation has become more rigorous, systematic, and objective over the past few decades, judgments by policy makers still are often based on anecdotal and fragmentary evidence rather than on solid facts and thorough analyses. Sometimes a program is judged to be a good program simply because it is politically popular or fits the ideological beliefs of an elected official. Having described the policy-making process on a general level, we now turn our attention to the evolution of domestic policies related to income security and health care.

The Evolution of Income Security and Health Care Policies

Today we take for granted that the federal government plays a major role in providing social services. Yet, most social welfare programs in the United States are largely a product of the twentieth century. In the early history of the country, people did not want or expect the national government to provide for people's welfare beyond some limited assistance to promote public education or to provide for veterans of American wars. (To learn more, see The Living Constitution: Preamble.) When the nation experienced economic downturns, it was widely accepted that everyone should tighten their belts and await economic recovery. Limited help was occasionally available through local governments, but Americans relied heavily on private charity to help the neediest.

This attitude began to change, gradually, in the late nineteenth century, as many farmers and rural Americans sought government help to protect them against falling commodity prices and exploitation by railroads and other corporations. Then, with the very severe economic depression of the mid-1890s, other Americans began to ask the government for help. A group of several hundred unemployed individuals, led by Jacob Coxey of Ohio, marched to Washington, D.C., in 1894 asking for government assistance. While unsuccessful in their effort, "Coxey's Army" reflected an unprecedented

The Evolution of Social Welfare Policy

The Living Constitution

We the People of the United States, in Order to form a more perfect Union, establish Justice, insure domestic Tranquility, provide for the common defence, promote the general Welfare, and Secure the Blessings of Liberty to ourselves and our Posterity, do ordain and establish this Constitution for the United States of America.

PREAMBLE

The Preamble of the U.S. Constitution lets posterity know the purpose and ends of the Constitution, and Supreme Court Justice Joseph Story—who served on the Court from 1812 to 1845, during its formative years—held that the Preamble also provides the "best key to the true interpretation" and spirit of the United States' fundamental law. Though the seemingly austere Preamble is not a source of rights or powers for the federal government, its inclusion in the Constitution was not without comment. Story, an Anti-Federalist, argued that the language of the Preamble could allow for an expansive judicial interpretation of the Constitution, and could do so in such a manner that the federal government would be given the authority of "general and unlimited powers of legislation in all cases."

It is true that the extent and authority of both the federal and state governments have increased, but the Preamble is understood to declare that "the People" are the source of all constitutional authority, and it is they, through constitutional institutions, who determine what constitutes justice and the "general Welfare." Constitutional government, it may be said, should strive to secure the well-being and happiness of all citizens, and it is to this end that social policy in the United States is directed.

The federal government is the only American government with the authority and means to ensure that social policy is fairly applied across the states, and it does faithfully attempt to pursue social policy that reflects the prevailing sentiments of the American people. For example, in 1996, social welfare in the United States was radically transformed to reflect a new understanding of how best to help the unfortunate, and it was done so with the intent to promote the general welfare of all Americans—to balance the interests not only of those whose taxes support the social welfare, but also of those for whom public support is necessary. Thus understood, the Preamble gives expression and guidance to the desires and will of the American people.

CRITICAL THINKING QUESTIONS

1. Does the Preamble's focus on promoting the general welfare of the nation require that the government provide Americans with a basic standard of living no matter what their circumstances may be?
2. Can the language of the Preamble be used to justify expansion of federal health care programs to individuals who do not have health insurance coverage?

new willingness of individuals and groups to ask for help from the federal government to provide assistance in hard times. The severity of the economic depression of the mid-1890s, in fact, led many to reassess their attitude about the government's responsibility to protect Americans from calamity. "In prosperous times, Americans had thought of unemployment as the result of personal failure, affecting primarily the lazy and immoral. . . . In the midst of [the 1890s] depression, such views were harder to maintain, since everyone knew people who were both worthy and unemployed."[21] While attitudes were beginning to change, it would take another, more severe depression for that change to result in government action.

Photo courtesy: Granger Collection

What was Coxey's Army? In 1894, during a severe economic depression, Jacob Coxey led a group of several hundred—known as Coxey's Army—on a march from Ohio to Washington, D.C., in an unsuccessful attempt to push the federal government to provide assistance to the unemployed.

This gradual change in attitude toward government responsibilities also reflected broader social changes in the United States and abroad. As U.S. society became more urban and industrial, self-sufficiency declined and people became more interdependent and reliant on a vast system of production, distribution, and exchange. The ostentation of the very wealthy and the suffering of the many on the bottom rung of the social ladder created fears of an economic revolution if the gap between rich and poor was not reduced. Some industrialized European countries, where class-consciousness ran stronger, established new social welfare programs around this time, with those governments assuming more of a direct responsibility for the well-being of their people. The Great Depression of the 1930s reinforced the notion that hard work alone would not provide economic security for everyone, and it showed that state governments and private charities lacked adequate resources to alleviate economic want and distress. Beginning with the Social Security Act of 1935, which we will describe below, a variety of national programs aimed at providing economic security have emerged.

Income Security

The economic turmoil known as the Great Depression produced massive shock waves throughout American society. To many, only the Civil War was more socially destructive and disruptive to the United States than the Great Depression.[22] Although there had been earlier signs of business trouble, the start of this long and steep economic decline is commonly associated with the great stock market crash of October 1929. Unlike previous economic panics, there seemed to be no bottom to the market sell-off. By 1933, the value of stock on the New York Stock Exchange was less than a fifth of what it had been at its peak in 1929. As might be expected, the decline in the stock market coincided with a more general collapse in the American economy. At the

Photo courtesy: Bettmann/CORBIS

What policy initiatives came about during the Great Depression? The Great Depression, beginning in late 1929 and continuing throughout the 1930s, dramatically pointed out to average Americans the need for a broad social safety net and gave rise to a host of income, health, and finance legislation.

depth of the Great Depression in 1933, the gross national product (GNP) had declined by 25 percent and unemployment reached almost 25 percent, a dramatic increase from the 3 percent level of unemployment in 1929.[23] In some communities that relied on hard-hit industries such as farming or tourism, unemployment reached well over 50 percent.

As a consequence of the Great Depression, social and economic thinking began to change far more intensely and broadly than it had even in the 1890s. Prior to 1929, most modern economic theorists had focused on the value of limited government and a "hands-off" economic policy for government to follow. After 1929, and the collapse of confidence in the private sector, the idea that government could and should be used as a positive influence in society gained widespread approval.[24]

With the election of Franklin D. Roosevelt as president in 1932, the federal government began to play a more active role in addressing hardships and turmoil growing out of the Great Depression. An immediate challenge facing the Roosevelt administration was massive unemployment. The problems of unemployment were viewed as having a corrosive effect on the economic well-being and moral character of American citizens. In Roosevelt's words, an array of programs to put people back to work would "eliminate the threat that enforced idleness brings to spiritual and moral stability."[25]

To address the issue of unemployment, Roosevelt issued an executive order in November 1933 that created the Civil Works Administration (CWA). The intent of the CWA was to put people to work as quickly as possible for the stated goal of building public works projects. Within a month of its start, CWA had hired 2.6 million people; at its peak in January 1934, it employed more than 4 million workers. Wages averaged about $15 a week, a sum that was approximately two and one-half times the typical relief payment given through the Federal Emergency Relief Administration (FERA). While the CWA assisted in building moral and economic capital, critics claimed that it was too political and rife with corruption. In response to such criticisms, Roosevelt ordered the CWA disbanded in 1934.

In 1935, the notion of federal works programs was revived in the form of the Works Progress Administration (WPA). The WPA paid a wage of about $55 a month, about twice the amount of a direct relief payment, yet below what would be available in the private sector. Such a wage would reward work over the dole but would not discourage individuals from seeking market-based employment. A number of concrete accomplishments were attained through the WPA. About 30 percent of the unemployed were absorbed; the WPA also constructed or improved more than 20,000 playgrounds, schools, hospitals, and airfields.[26] These jobs programs did not become permanent, but they established the notion that, in extreme circumstances, the government might become the employer of last resort.

A more permanent and important legacy of the New Deal was the creation of Social Security. The intent of Social Security was to go beyond the various "emergency" programs such as the WPA and provide at least a minimum of economic security for all Americans. Due to the nature of this commitment, passage of the **Social Security Act** in 1935 represented the beginning of a permanent welfare state in America and a dedication to the ideal of greater equity.[27] The act consisted of three major components: (1) old-age insurance (what we now call Social Security); (2) public assis-

Social Security Act
A 1935 law that established old-age insurance (Social Security) and assistance for the needy, children, and others, and unemployment insurance.

Photo courtesy: AP/Wide World Photos

What was the New Deal? Franklin D. Roosevelt's New Deal expanded the role of the federal government in profound ways, including the establishment of Social Security in 1935.

tance for the needy, aged, blind, and families with dependent children (later, people with disabilities were added); and, (3) unemployment insurance and compensation.

The core of the Social Security Act was the creation of a compulsory old-age insurance program funded equally by employer and employee contributions. The act imposed a payroll tax, collected from the employer, equal to 1 percent from both employee and employer starting in 1937. Payroll taxes were to rise a point a year up to 3 percent from both employer and employee, and the payroll tax was applied to the first $3,000 of income. The law originally exempted many categories of workers, including government employees, farm workers, domestic service workers, and casual labor. At the age of sixty-five, workers would receive payments that were based on their lifelong earnings. In 1940, the maximum old-age pension was $85 a month. It was believed that funding Social Security through payroll deductions would ensure its survival, because once average workers contributed their own money to the program, they would view it as a "sacred trust" rather than a form of welfare.[28] Critics of Social Security branded it as "creeping socialism" and something that would lead to an unwanted expansion of government.

The Social Security Act also addressed the issue of unemployment, requiring employers to pay 3 percent of a worker's salary into an insurance fund. If workers became unemployed, they could draw from this fund for a given period of time. During the time laid-off workers drew from the insurance fund, they were required to seek other jobs. This component of the Social Security Act served two basic purposes: on the individual level, it provided income to laid-off workers, expanding the social safety net; on the broader economic level, it acted as an automatic stabilizer, increasing the amount of money in the nation's economy when financial resources were scarce.

Social Security is credited with replacing a piecemeal collection of local programs with a national system. This national system was widely praised but also was perceived to contain two basic flaws: the payroll tax was regressive (the tax fell disproportionately on lower-income contributors), and some workers were excluded from the program. Over the next decades, Social Security was expanded to include a much greater percentage of American workers. The program also became one of the most successful and popular government programs. In the 1930s, poverty rates were highest among the elderly. Today, seniors have the lowest rate of poverty among any age group in the United States.

Health Care

Governments in the United States have long been active in the health care field. Local governments began to establish public health departments in the first half of the nineteenth century, and state health departments followed in the second half. Discoveries related to the causes of diseases and human ailments in the late nineteenth and early twentieth centuries led to significant advances in improving public health. Public sanitation and clean-water programs, pasteurization of milk, immunization programs, and other activities greatly reduced the incidence of infectious and communicable diseases. Public health policies have also been highly effective in reducing the incidence of infectious diseases such as measles, infantile paralysis (poliomyelitis), and smallpox. The increase in American life expectancy from forty-seven in 1900 to over seventy-eight in 2008 is tightly linked to public health programs.

Beginning in 1798 with the establishment of the National Marine Service (NMS) for "the relief of sick and disabled seamen," which was the forerunner of the Public Health Service, the national government has provided health care for some segments of the population. Repeated efforts have been made to expand health care coverage to all Americans, as discussed in the opening vignette. A plan for national health insurance in the 1930s was one of the first universal plans to fail.

National health insurance was considered at the time Social Security legislation was passed. Because of the strong opposition of the American Medical Association (AMA), which was the dominant force in American medicine at the time, health insurance was omitted from the Social Security Act. It was feared that addressing this social need would jeopardize adoption of other important elements of the program. Health insurance remained on the back burner for many years.

The AMA and its allies typically were distrustful of government intervention in their affairs and fearful that regulations would limit their discretion as well as their earnings. In particular, they feared that the intrusion of government into the health care field could limit physician charges, confine the amount of time approved for specific types of hospital visits, and place a lid on charges for prescription drugs. Members of the health care industry viewed these outcomes unfavorably. More generally, conservatives opposed the expansion of government power and contended that such extensions could be harmful to the ideal of individual liberty.

Liberal political leaders did not lose interest in national health insurance, however. In 1958, a bill was introduced in Congress that covered the hospital costs of elderly people receiving Social Security. The AMA again weighed in against this proposal, but by focusing on the aged, the proponents of health insurance changed the terms of the struggle. Strong support developed for providing medical assistance to the elderly, and in 1960 Congress passed legislation benefiting the needy aged. This provision, however, did not satisfy liberals and other supporters of a broader program. The issue was resolved by the 1964 elections, which produced sufficient votes in Congress to enact Medicare and Medicaid, programs that sharply increased access to health care for both the elderly (in the case of Medicare) and the poor (in the case of Medicaid).

The national government's role in health care expanded dramatically with the enactment of these two programs. The share of health care expenditures financed by public spending rose from under 25 percent in 1960 to almost 40 percent in 1970. During this time, public expenditures on health care as a percent of total gross domestic product (GDP) rose by more than 100 percent, from 1.3 percent to 2.7 percent. Total expenditures rose from 5.3 percent of GDP in 1960 to 7.4 percent in 1970.[29]

Income Security and Health Care Policies Today

Income security and health care remain two key domestic policy areas that involve citizens, interest groups, and government. Both areas encompass many complex policies and programs. Although all levels of government (national, state, and local) are involved with the development and implementation of income security and health care policy, we emphasize the national government's role.

Welfare Reform

Income Security Programs

Income security programs protect people against loss of income because of retirement, disability, unemployment, or death or absence of the family breadwinner. Although cases of total deprivation are now rare, many people are unable to provide a minimally decent standard of living for themselves and their families. They are poor in a relative if not an absolute sense. In 2008, the poverty threshold for a four-person family unit was $21,200.[30]

Income security programs fall into two general categories. Social insurance programs are **non-means-based programs** that provide cash assistance to qualified beneficiaries. **Means-tested programs** require that people must have incomes below specified levels to be eligible for benefits (see Table 17.1). Benefits of means-tested programs may come either as cash or in-kind benefits, such as food stamps.

non-means-based program
Program such as Social Security where benefits are provided irrespective of the income or means of recipients.

means-tested program
Income security program intended to assist those whose incomes fall below a designated level.

SOCIAL INSURANCE: NON-MEANS-BASED PROGRAMS   Social insurance programs operate in a manner somewhat similar to private automobile or life insurance. Contributions are made by or on behalf of the prospective beneficiaries, their employers, or both. When a person becomes eligible for benefits, the monies are paid as a matter of right, regardless of the person's wealth or unearned income (for example, from dividends and interest payments).

Old Age, Survivors, and Disability Insurance As mentioned earlier, this program began as old-age insurance, providing benefits only to retired workers. Its coverage was extended to survivors of covered workers in 1939 and to the permanently disabled in 1956. Customarily called Social Security, it is not, as many people believe, a pension program that collects contributions from workers, invests them, and then returns them with interest to beneficiaries. Instead, the current workers pay taxes that directly go toward providing benefits for retirees. In 2008, an employee tax of 7.65 percent was levied on the

TABLE **17.1** Recipients of Social Insurance Programs, 2006

Program Population	Number of Recipients (millions)	Percentage of U.S.
Non-Means-Tested[a]		
Social Security (OASDI)	49.1	16.4
Medicare (only hospital insurance)	43.6	14.4
Veterans' Disability Benefits	2.9	0.96
Unemployment Benefits	3.2	1.1
Means-Tested		
Medicaid	52.4	18.0
Supplemental Security Income	7.2	2.4
Temporary Assistance for Needy Families	4.7	1.6
Food Stamps	27.6	9.1

[a] "Means-tested" refers to the requirement of demonstrated financial need.
Sources: Social Security Administration, www.ssa.gov; Department of Health and Human Services, acf.dhhs.gov; Food Research Action Center, www.frac.org; Department of Veterans' Affairs, www.va.gov/vetdata/; Bureau of Labor Statistics, www.bls.gov/cps.

first $102,000 of wages or salaries and placed into the Social Security Trust Fund. An equal tax was levied on employers. Nearly all employees and most of the self-employed (who pay a 15.3 percent tax) are now covered by Social Security. People earning less than $102,000 pay a greater share of their income into the Social Security Fund, since wages or salaries above that amount are not subject to the Social Security tax. The Social Security tax therefore is considered a regressive tax because it captures larger proportions of incomes from lower- and middle-income individuals than from high-wage earners.

People born before 1938 are eligible to receive full retirement benefits at age sixty-five. The full retirement age gradually rises until it reaches sixty-seven for persons born in 1960 or later. Individuals can opt to receive reduced benefits as early as age sixty-two. In November 2007, the average monthly Social Security benefit for retired workers was $1,053.70, with the maximum monthly benefit set at $2,116. Social Security is the primary source of income for many retirees and keeps them from living in poverty. However, eligible people are entitled to Social Security benefits regardless of how much *unearned* income (for example, dividends and interest payments) they also receive. Beginning with a change in 2004, Social Security recipients between the age of sixty-two and sixty-four had one dollar withheld from their earnings for every two dollars earned after a specific amount of earnings was reached. For recipients age sixty-five, one dollar was withheld for every three dollars earned after the threshold was reached. Social Security recipients older than sixty-five were allowed to earn an unlimited amount of money without any reduction of Social Security benefits.[31]

The trustees of the Social Security Trust Fund predicted in 2006 that, starting in about 2010, Social Security Fund expenditures would begin to increase rapidly as the Baby Boom generation (roughly speaking, those born in the two decades immediately following World War II) reached retirement age. It was estimated that by 2017, payments would exceed revenues collected. Viewing costs and revenues as a proportion of taxable payrolls (to correct for the value of the dollar over time), one can see that projected revenues remain relatively constant over time, while costs are projected to rise substantially. (To learn more about social security costs and revenues, see Figure 17.2.) Aside from the retirement of Baby Boomers, other factors pressuring the fund include increased life expectancies and low fertility rates. In other words, Americans are living longer and having fewer children who as workers will contribute to the Social Security Fund.

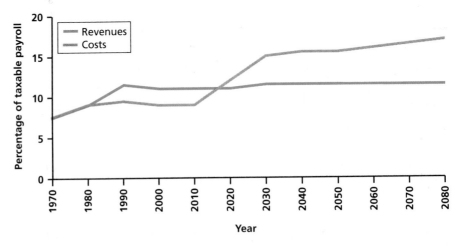

FIGURE 17.2 Social Security Costs and Revenues, 1970–2080 (as percentage of taxable payroll)

Source: Social Security Administration, *Status of the Social Security and Medicare Programs, Summary of the 2004 Annual Reports,* www.ssa.gov.

After George W. Bush was elected in 2000, he promoted his vision of privatizing Social Security through investments in stocks and bonds, and he created a President's Commission to Strengthen Social Security. This panel consisted of sixteen members, with Daniel Patrick Moynihan, the former Democratic senator from New York, and Richard Parsons, co-chief operating officer of AOL Time Warner, serving as co-chairs. By the end of 2001, the panel disappointed proponents of privatization with their set of recommendations. The panel provided three options: (1) allowing workers to invest up to 2 percentage points of their payroll tax in personal accounts; (2) allowing workers to invest up to 4 percentage points of their payroll tax in personal accounts, to a maximum of $1,000 per year; and, (3) allowing workers to invest an additional 1 percent of their earnings in a personal account. Proponents of privatization had hoped for a single recommendation. Congress ignored the recommendations, no doubt influenced by the slump in the stock market and unpopular panel observations. The panel noted they believed that ultimately benefits would have to be cut or more money would have to be assigned to the program.

Should government help people care for their families? Many working-age Americans struggle to make ends meet when taking care of children and elderly parents becomes a full-time job.

Despite controlling both houses of Congress and the presidency after the 2004 elections, Republicans were unable to achieve any substantial reform of Social Security. This may be explained by continued public skepticism regarding the president's plan. According to a 2005 poll by the Pew Research Center for the People and the Press, only about four in ten Americans supported the concept of individualized accounts as part of the Social Security system.[32] Given the central role that these accounts played in Bush's reform efforts, it was not a surprise that his plan was unable to gather the necessary support in Congress. Simply put, many Republican legislators could not risk aligning themselves with the president because of the possibility of a backlash at the polls. In fact, Democratic candidates used President Bush's support for Social Security privatization against their Republican opponents with some success in the 2006 midterm elections. Their takeover of both houses of Congress in 2007 and the 2008 financial meltdown meant an end—for the time-being, at least—to Republican efforts to significantly reform or privatize the program.

Unemployment Insurance As mentioned earlier, unemployment insurance is financed by a payroll tax paid by employers. The program pays benefits to workers who are covered by the government plan and are unemployed through no fault of their own. The Social Security Act provided that if a state set up a comparable program and levied a payroll tax for its support, most of the federal tax would be forgiven (that is, not collected). The states were thus accorded a choice: either set up and administer an acceptable unemployment program, or let the national government handle the matter. Within a short time, all states had their own programs.

Unemployment insurance covers employers of four or more people, but not part-time or occasional workers. Benefits are paid to unemployed workers who have neither been fired for personal faults nor quit their jobs, and who are willing and able to accept suitable employment. State unemployment programs differ considerably in levels of benefits, length of benefit payment, and eligibility for benefits. For example, in 2008, average weekly benefit payments ranged from $404 in Hawaii and $388 in Massachusetts to $179 in Mississippi.[33] In general, less generous programs exist in southern states, where labor unions are less powerful. Nationwide, only about half of the people who are counted as unemployed at any given time are receiving benefits.

In June 2008, the unemployment rate stood at 5.5 percent. (To learn more, see Analyzing Visuals: Unemployment Rates by State.) But, there are considerable

Analyzing Visuals   Unemployment Rates by State

This map shows the rates of unemployment across the United States in the summer of 2008. Based on your analysis of this map and your understanding of the chapter discussion, answer the following critical thinking questions:

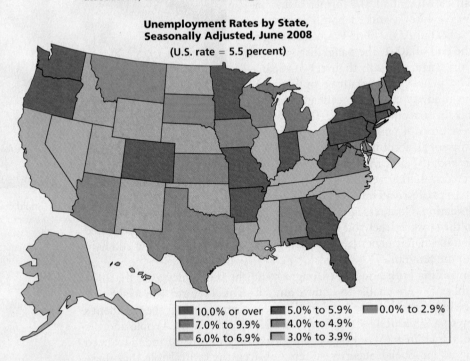

Unemployment Rates by State, Seasonally Adjusted, June 2008
(U.S. rate = 5.5 percent)

- 10.0% or over
- 7.0% to 9.9%
- 6.0% to 6.9%
- 5.0% to 5.9%
- 4.0% to 4.9%
- 3.0% to 3.9%
- 0.0% to 2.9%

WHICH states are suffering from the highest levels of unemployment, and why do you think that is so?

WHY do unemployment rates vary substantially from state to state?

DO you detect any similarities among states with the lowest rates of unemployment?

DO you think the unemployment rate played a role in the 2008 presidential elections?

Source: Bureau of Labor Statistics, Local Area Unemployment Statistics, www.bls.gov/web/laumstrk.htm.

differences across the nation. In Utah and Wyoming, unemployment rates were slightly above 3 percent, while levels of unemployment in Michigan and Rhode Island were over 7 percent. Unemployment rates also vary considerably across races and by age. For example, levels of unemployment for African American males are approximately twice that of whites, with unemployment rates of 15 percent or greater common among young African American males.[34]

SOCIAL INSURANCE: MEANS-TESTED PROGRAMS Means-tested income security programs are intended to help the needy; that is, individuals or families whose incomes fall below specified levels, such as a percentage of the official poverty line. Included in the means-tested categories are the Supplemental Security Income (SSI), Temporary Assistance for Needy Families (TANF), and food stamp programs (see Table 17.1).

Supplemental Security Income This program began under the Social Security Act as a grant-in-aid program to help the needy aged or blind. Grants were financed jointly by the national and state governments, but the states played a major role in determining standards of eligibility and benefit levels. In 1950, Congress extended coverage to needy people who were permanently and totally disabled.

With the support of the Nixon administration, Congress reconfigured the grant programs into the Supplemental Security Income (SSI) program in 1974. Primary funding for SSI is provided by the national government, which prescribes uniform benefit levels throughout the nation. To be eligible, beneficiaries can own only a limited amount of possessions. In 2008, monthly payments were about $477 for an individual and $720 for a married couple.[35] The states may choose to supplement the federal benefits, and forty-eight states do.

For years, this program generated little controversy, as modest benefits go to people who obviously cannot provide for themselves. However, there was a growing perception among conservatives as well as Democratic President Bill Clinton that many social welfare programs were flawed. In 1996, access to SSI and other programs was limited by legislation. Under George W. Bush's administration, funding for SSI has remained fairly stable, with about $38 billion directed to the program in fiscal year 2008.[36]

Family and Child Support In 1950, Aid to Families with Dependent Children (AFDC), the predecessor to the Temporary Assistance for Needy Families (TANF) program, was broadened to include not only dependent children without fathers but also mothers themselves or other adults with whom dependent children were living. The AFDC rolls expanded greatly since 1960 because of the increasing numbers of children born to unwed mothers, the growing divorce rate, and the migration of poor people to cities, where they are more likely to apply for and be provided with benefits.

Because of its clientele, the AFDC program was the focus of much controversy. Critics who pointed to the rising number of recipients claimed that it encouraged promiscuity, out-of-wedlock births, and dependency that resulted in a permanent class of welfare families. To restrict the availability of aid, to ferret out fraud and abuse, and to hold down cost, public officials sought to reform the program. These efforts eventually led to major legislative changes.

In 1988, during President Ronald Reagan's second term, Congress passed legislation to reform AFDC. Titled the Family and Child Support Act, the law sought to move people off welfare and into productive jobs. Each state operated a Job Opportunities and Basic Skills (JOBS) program to provide education, training, and job experience for members of welfare families. Most adult welfare recipients were

Photo courtesy: James Nubile/Image Works

What is workfare? Workfare is a welfare strategy that gives adults the opportunity to learn skills that can lead to employment. Here, one workfare recipient tends to children at his day-care-center job.

enrolled, with the states providing childcare and other services necessary to facilitate participation. The national and state governments shared funding for JOBS, which was successful in helping people gain employment and in reducing public assistance payments. Some analysts, however, questioned whether job training programs for welfare mothers significantly increased the income of mothers or enhanced the well-being of their children.[37]

States were required by the Family and Child Support Act to participate in the AFDC-UP program, which provided benefits for two-parent families in which the principal wage earner was unemployed. A workfare provision included at the insistence of the Reagan administration required one parent in a recipient family to work at least sixteen hours weekly. Other provisions of the act called for stronger enforcement of court orders for child support payments and greater efforts to establish paternity for children born out of wedlock.

The Family and Child Support Act represented significant reform of the welfare system. Because its provisions were phased in, it was not fully implemented until the early 1990s.[38] By 1992, some 500,000 persons were participating in the act's education and training programs, a number that exceeded the required level of participation.[39] Some states, however, had difficulty providing welfare recipients with sufficient job and training opportunities.[40]

Conservatives generally believe that the poor should do more to help themselves. Liberals, on the other hand, generally support income security programs; they believe that poverty results more from social causes than from personal shortcomings. But, in the 1990s, even some liberals questioned the effectiveness of income security programs and began to call for reforms that would help the poor become more self-sufficient. Accepting the need for reform, President Bill Clinton promised to "end welfare as we know it." The Republican majority in Congress was also anxious to reform welfare policies and supported the president's efforts.

In what was hailed as the biggest shift in social policy since the Great Depression, a new welfare bill, the Personal Responsibility and Work Opportunity Reconciliation Act (PRWORA) of 1996, created the Temporary Assistance for Needy Families (TANF) program to replace AFDC. The shift from AFDC to TANF was meant to foster a new philosophy of work rather than welfare dependency. The most fundamental change enacted in the new law was the switch in funding for welfare from an open-ended matching program to a block grant to the states. PRWORA also gave states more flexibility in reforming their welfare programs toward work-oriented goals.

Significant features of the welfare plan included: (1) a requirement for single mothers with a child over five years of age to work within two years of receiving benefits; (2) a provision that unmarried mothers under the age of eighteen were required to live with an adult and attend school in order to receive welfare benefits; (3) a five-year lifetime limit for aid from block grants; (4) a requirement that mothers must provide information about a child's father in order to receive full welfare payments; (5) cutting off food stamps and Supplemental Security Income for legal immigrants; (6) cutting off cash welfare benefits and food stamps for convicted drug felons; and, (7) limiting food stamps to three months in a three-year period for persons eighteen to fifty years old who are not raising children and not working.[41]

The TANF program established guidelines for states to follow. For example, the federal legislation requires states to have a specific proportion of TANF recipients participating in work activities. (Single mothers head most families covered by TANF.) Work activities are broadly defined and can include private-sector employment, subsidized public-sector employment, job readiness assistance, community service, childcare services, education, and other activities. Benefits and conditions differ from state to state, however, with some states providing more generous cash benefits and having fewer eligibility requirements.

In 2002, the Bush administration released a detailed plan for TANF reauthorization. The plan proposed to strengthen work rules to ensure that all welfare families were engaged in meaningful activities that would lead to self-sufficiency. These meaningful activities included not only work but also allowed "individuals participating in substance abuse treatment, rehabilitative services, and work-related training" to qualify for TANF benefits.[42] The administration proposed increasing the proportion of TANF families that would have to participate in work activities and increasing the number of hours of required work.[43] Between 2002 and 2006, Congress passed a number of extensions to keep the TANF program in operation, with President Bush signing a reauthorization in February 2006. This reauthorization did not address the issue of increased work hours but did strengthen enforcement of child support provisions.[44]

Earned Income Tax Credit Program Designed to help the working poor, this program was created in 1975 at the insistence of Senator Russell Long (D–LA). It helps the working poor by subsidizing their wages, and it also provides an incentive for people to go to work. Drawing extensive support from both Democrats and Republicans in Congress, the Earned Income Tax Credit (EITC) is frequently described as being "pro-work and pro-family." The EITC results in a net cash rebate for many low-income taxpayers who pay no federal income tax.

The intent of the EITC was to enhance the value of working and encourage families to move from welfare to work. Advocates also claimed that the program would enhance spending, which would in turn stimulate the economy. In addition to this stimulus, supporters of the EITC had two other objectives: (1) to increase work incentives among the welfare population; and, (2) to refund indirectly part or all of the Social Security taxes paid by workers with low incomes. In theory, the EITC would serve to ease the regressive nature of the Social Security payroll tax.[45]

To claim the EITC on tax returns, a person must have earned income during the year. During 2008, the earned income had to be less than $12,880 if there were no qualifying children, $33,995 with one qualifying child, and $38,646 with more than one qualifying child. In 2006, nearly 23 million families filing federal income tax returns (roughly one tax return in six) claimed the federal EITC. The success of the federal EITC in reducing poverty has led twenty-four states to enact state Earned Income Tax Credits.[46]

Food Stamp Program The initial food stamp program (1939–1943) was primarily an effort to expand domestic markets for farm commodities. Food stamps provided the poor with the ability to purchase more food, thus increasing the demand for American agricultural produce. Attempts to reestablish the program during the Eisenhower administration failed, but in 1961, a $381,000 pilot program began under the Kennedy administration. It was made permanent in 1964 and extended nationwide in 1974. Although strongly opposed by Republicans in Congress, Democrats put together a majority coalition when urban members agreed to support a wheat and cotton price support program wanted by rural and southern Democrats in return for their support of food stamps. In the beginning, recipients had to pay cash for food stamps, but this practice ceased in 1977. Benefiting low-income families, the program has helped to combat hunger and reduce malnutrition.

While the food stamp program remains an essential element of the government's social welfare program, its phenomenal growth in the 1970s and 1980s led to calls for reining it in by the mid-1990s. Evidence of fraudulent practices by some food stamp recipients and local businesses in several communities also led to greater skepticism about its worthiness. Nonetheless, food stamps continue to play an important part in the government's welfare program. Food stamps went to more than 26 million beneficiaries in 2007 at a cost of $33 billion. The average participant received $95 worth of stamps per month.[47] The national government operates several other food programs for the needy. These programs include a special nutritional program for women, infants, and children (WIC); a school breakfast and lunch program; and an emergency food assistance program.

THE EFFECTIVENESS OF INCOME SECURITY PROGRAMS   Many of the income security programs, including Social Security, Supplemental Security Income, and food stamps, are **entitlement programs**. That is, Congress sets eligibility criteria—such as age, income level, or unemployment—and those who meet the criteria are legally "entitled" to receive benefits. Unlike such programs as public housing, military construction, and space exploration, spending for entitlement programs is mandatory. Year after year, funds *must* be provided for them unless the laws creating the programs are changed. This feature of entitlement programs has made it difficult to control spending for them.

Income security programs have not eliminated poverty and economic dependency, but they have improved the lives of large numbers of people. Millions of elderly people in the United States would be living below the poverty line were it not for Social Security. Increasing food and gasoline prices in 2008 are likely to lead to renewed debates about the best way for national, state, and local governments to help struggling Americans.

entitlement program
Income security program to which all those meeting eligibility criteria are entitled.

Health Care

Currently, many millions of people receive medical care through the medical branches of the armed forces, the hospitals and medical programs of the Department of Veterans' Affairs, and the Indian Health Service. The government spent $69 billion in 2007 for health and human services and estimated that it would spend $71 billion in the 2009 fiscal year for health and human services, the construction and operation of facilities, and the salaries of doctors and other medical personnel.[48]

The national government finances most medical research, primarily through the National Institutes of Health (NIH). The National Cancer Institute; the National Heart, Lung, and Blood Institute; the National Institute of Allergy and Infectious Diseases; and the other NIH institutes and centers spend more than $10 billion annually on biomedical research. NIH scientists and scientists at universities, medical schools, and other research facilities receiving NIH research grants conduct the research. Most Americans accept and support extensive government spending on medical research. Congress, in fact, often appropriates more money for medical research than the president recommends.

The United States spends significant sums of money on public health, a larger proportion of its gross domestic product than most other industrialized democracies. Much of the increase in funding for health care has gone to the Medicare and Medicaid programs. Reasons for growth in medical spending include the public's increased expectations, increased demand for services, advances in health care technology, the perception of health care as a right, and the third-party payment system.[49] In many ways the issue of soaring health care costs underlies most of the current problems affecting the American health care system and limits the range of alternatives available to government officials.

A quick review of the increase in health care costs over the past fifteen years helps to demonstrate the magnitude of the problem. Per capita spending on health care in the United States increased by 123 percent in the fourteen-year period between 1990 and 2004. But, per capita income in America increased by only 59 percent during the same time frame, meaning that individual financial resources grew at less than half the rate of the cost of health care. Behind this dramatic increase in health care costs are a number of important factors. First, more people are living

Comparing Health Systems

Comparing Social Welfare Systems

Who receives medical care directly from the federal government? Millions of Americans, including Iraq War veterans, receive health care services from government agencies such as the Department of Veterans Affairs.

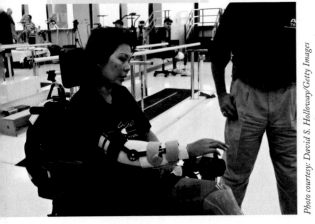

Photo courtesy: David S. Holloway/Getty Images

longer and are requiring costly and extensive care in their declining years. Second, the range and sophistication of diagnostic practices and therapeutic treatments, which are often quite expensive, have increased. Third, the expansion of private health insurance, along with Medicare and Medicaid, has reduced the direct costs of health care to most people and increased the demand for services. More people, in short, can afford care. They may also be less aware of the costs of care. Fourth, the costs of health care have also increased because of its higher quality and because labor costs have outpaced productivity in the provision of hospital care.[50] Fifth, U.S. health care focuses less on preventing illnesses and more on curing them, a more costly approach.

While all areas of health care experienced significant increases in cost since 1990, there were areas within the broader health field that underwent the sharpest spike in prices. Figure 17.3 demonstrates that prescription drug costs increased at rates even greater than those for physicians and hospital stays through 2005, thus increasing the pressure for the federal government to provide some prescription drug benefits as part of Medicare. Because government health care programs such as Medicare and Medicaid are directly affected by soaring prices, policy makers have been challenged to keep these programs fully funded. In 2008, national expenditures for both the Medicare and Medicaid programs were $661 billion. Projected increases for Medicare and Medicaid are expected to grow between 2008 and 2013 at a faster pace than other key areas of the federal budget. (To learn more about the rising cost of entitlement programs, see Table 17.2).

In the next sections, we explore these two key federal health care programs in greater detail, as well as the impact of government-sponsored health care programs on public health.

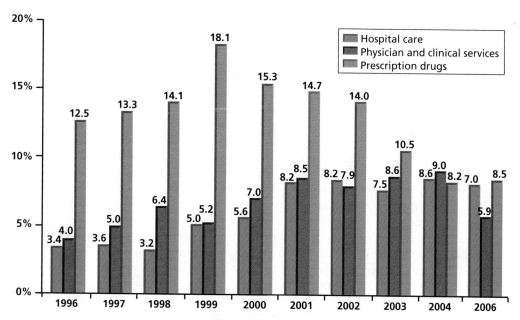

FIGURE **17.3** Increases in U.S. Health Care Spending, 1996–2006 One of the greatest challenges facing health care in the United States is the tremendous growth in the cost of medical services. Since the mid-1990s, health care costs have increased at rates far exceeding national rates of inflation. Prescription drugs, the area of health care with the greatest increases, experienced double-digit growth in costs for much of the past decade. While the cost increases for prescription drugs have come down to the level of other health care services such as physicians and hospitals, overall health care costs continue to increase at very high rates.

Source: Kaiser Family Foundation, "Trends and Indicators in the Changing Health Care Marketplace," www.kff.org.

TABLE **17.2** The Rising Cost of Entitlement and Other Programs

	Outlays (in billions of dollars)		
	2007	2013 estimate	% change
Means-tested entitlements[a]	$367	$504	29%
Social Security	581	842	56%
Defense	549	568	4%
Nondefense discretionary	493	495	–1%

[a] Includes Medicaid, food stamps, Supplemental Security Income, child nutrition programs, earned income tax credits, Temporary Assistance to Needy Families, and other programs.

Source: United States Budget, Fiscal Year 2007, Historical Tables, www.gpoaccess.gov/usbudget/fy09/hist.html, Section 8, Outlays by Budget Enforcement Act Category, April 29, 2008.

Medicare
The federal program established in the Lyndon B. Johnson administration that provides medical care to elderly Social Security recipients.

MEDICARE **Medicare**, which covers persons receiving Social Security benefits, is administered by the Center for Medicare and Medicaid Services in the Department of Health and Human Services. Medicare coverage has two components, Parts A and B. Benefits under Part A come to all Americans automatically at age sixty-five, when they qualify for Social Security. It covers hospitalization, some skilled nursing care, and home health services. Individuals have to pay about $700 in medical bills before they are eligible for Part A benefits. Medicare is financed by a payroll tax of 1.45 percent paid by both employees and employers on the total amount of one's wages or salary.

Part B, which is optional, covers payment for physicians' services, outpatient and diagnostic services, X-rays, and some other items not covered by Part A. Excluded from coverage are eyeglasses, hearing aids, and dentures. This portion of the Medicare program is financed partly by monthly payments from beneficiaries and partly by general tax revenues.

In 2003, President Bush signed into law the Medicare Prescription Drug Improvement and Modernization Act, which since January 2006 provides some prescription drug coverage for seniors who opt to participate. Participants pay a monthly premium of approximately $35; after a $250 annual deductible, they have 75 percent of their prescription costs paid for. For those whose annual prescription drug costs exceed $5,100, the new program pays 95 percent of prescription costs over that amount. There are some odd gaps in the prescription drug coverage, however. Many congressional Democrats found the bill too weak in helping the average senior and claimed its primary beneficiaries would be the pharmaceutical and insurance industries. But, even some Democrats voted for its final passage, as they agreed with the leaders of the American Association of Retired Persons (AARP) that it was time to do something, and this seemed the only plan with a chance to pass.[51]

The addition of the prescription drug benefit troubled many conservatives because of the added costs it is projected to impose on a system that, whatever its merits, is extraordinarily expensive. The actual costs of this new program were understated during the congressional debate, and that leads many to wonder how the federal budget can withstand the additional pressure. Attempts to limit or cap expenditures for the program have had only marginal effects. With millions of Baby Boomers set to retire in the next fifteen years, the system will be under even greater strain.

Medicaid
An expansion of Medicare, this program subsidizes medical care for the poor.

MEDICAID Enacted into law at the same time as Medicare, the **Medicaid** program provides comprehensive health care, including hospitalization, physician services, prescription drugs, and long-term nursing-home care (unlike Medicare) to all who qualify as needy under TANF and SSI. In 1986, Congress extended Medicaid coverage to pregnant women and children in low-income families whose total earnings were less than 133 percent of the official poverty level. The states were also accorded the option of extending coverage to all pregnant women and to all children under one year of age in families with incomes below 185 percent of the poverty level. By 1993, twenty-nine states had chosen to provide this coverage. In 2008, Medicaid served over 58 million people at a cost of $204 billion.[52] Nursing facility services, in-patient general hospital services, home health services, and prescription drugs represented major categories of spending within the Medicaid program.

Medicaid is financed by the national and state governments. The national government pays 50 to 79 percent of Medicaid costs, based on average per capita income, which awards more financial support to poor than to wealthy states. Each state is responsible for the administration of its own program and sets specific standards of eligibility and benefit levels for Medicaid recipients within the boundaries set by national guidelines. In some states, nearly all needy people are covered by Medicaid, while in others, only about one-third of the needy are protected. Some states also award coverage to the "medically indigent," that is, to people who do not qualify for welfare but for whom large medical expenses would constitute a severe financial burden.

While the average amount paid for by the states varies, the portion of state budgets going to Medicaid is similar—ever upward. If Medicaid expenditures continue to grow at their present rate, the proportion of funding that is available for other programs will be reduced.

PUBLIC HEALTH In addition to funding large portions of the nation's health care costs, government plays a major role in managing the growth of both infectious and chronic disease. From AIDS to obesity, public policy makers have attempted to use government power to fight threats to the nation's health. Among the tools employed by government are immunizations, education, advertisements, and regulations. For many contagious diseases such as polio, measles, and chickenpox, the government requires young children to be immunized if they are to be enrolled in day care, preschool, or elementary school. Public health officials also use vaccines in the adult population to manage the spread of diseases such as influenza (the flu). While not requiring citizens to receive flu shots, the government recommends that high-risk groups (infants, senior citizens) receive immunizations and also subsidizes vaccines for low-income populations.

The process of getting a nation immunized against a disease may be more difficult than it seems. The case of the avian (bird) flu helps demonstrate these difficulties. The emergence of this particularly deadly strain of influenza in 2003 put pressure on public health officials to prepare the United States for a possible pandemic. This preparation is extremely challenging for public health officials because the flu strain may quickly mutate, thus making current vaccines incapable of blocking the spread of the virus. For diseases such as AIDS, which is at present incurable and for which no vaccines have been developed, public health officials expend much of their energy attempting to educate the public and thereby alter behaviors that put individuals at risk for becoming infected with AIDS or spreading it to others.

As with many facets of public policy, the deep-seated attachment of Americans to personal liberty limits the types of tools government can employ. The case of obesity illustrates this point. Widely accepted as the second biggest threat to the health of Americans (behind only tobacco), obesity poses a difficult challenge for public health officials. With almost 60 million Americans defined as obese by the Centers for Disease Control and Prevention (CDC), public health officials are expecting an increase in the prevalence of obesity-related illnesses such as heart disease and diabetes.[53] In combating this

Thinking Globally

Health Care Policy

All industrialized nations provide some kind of publicly funded health care. In Canada, universal health care is provided by private practitioners with partial or total government funding. In Finland, Spain, Israel, and Cuba, the government operates health care facilities and employs health care professionals. In the United States, the Veterans' Health Administration and the medical departments of the U.S. Army, Navy, and Air Force are examples of health care systems funded and operated by the federal government.

- The United States does not offer publicly funded universal health care. Should it adopt such a program? Why or why not?
- What are the pros and cons of a health care system where the government operates the facilities and hires the health care providers?
- What countries are most likely to adopt publicly funded universal health care coverage? What characteristics do these countries have in common?

emerging public health threat, the U.S. government is very constrained in the types of tools it can use. Trying to limit the food intake of Americans is a very difficult task because of the personal nature of the activity. It is hard to imagine government attempting to ban certain foods as they have narcotics. Instead, policy makers have attacked obesity through channels that do not directly threaten individual choice. Of the 140 obesity-related bills that came before state legislatures in 2003, most dealt with bettering public understanding of the nutritional value of food or reducing access to fast food and soft drinks within the public school systems. A few bills included increased taxes on soda and junk food, but no bill directly limited the sales of unhealthy food to the general public.[54]

Public opinion polls indicate that most people are satisfied with the quality of health care services provided by physicians and hospitals, but a substantial majority express dissatisfaction over the costs and accessibility of health care.[55] There is, as a consequence, a strong belief in the need to improve the nation's health care system, but some substantial hindrances block easy reform in this area. Most notably, the desire of individuals to maintain control over their health care decisions limits the policy solutions to which government can turn.

Toward Reform: Energy and Environmental Policy

Energy and environmental policies in the United States are prone to cycles that contain dramatic shifts over time. During some eras, these policies remain dormant, barely noticeable within the broader sphere of public policy; at other times, the issues become the dominant players in the political realm. As the first decade of the new millennium has unfurled, energy and environmental issues have made their way out of a period of dormancy and have become dominant players in contemporary domestic politics. Before looking at the current prominence of these concerns in the United States, it is important to examine the cycles that energy policies have undergone during the past fifty years.

In the late 1950s and early 1960s, America was in the midst of one of the most robust economic periods in national history. The nation was prospering, with vibrant manufacturing and transportation sectors that were being bolstered by access to cheap fossil fuels. With the nation's abundant coal supplies and relatively unfettered access to oil, the need for government efforts in the area of energy policy was not very strong. In essence, the issue of energy was largely absent from the government agenda because energy was not seen as much of a problem for the United States.[56] However, the effects of intensive energy use on the nation's environment were becoming more obvious to the nation as a whole. From heavy smog in major cities to thick clouds of smoke in industrial towns, Americans had begun to take notice of deteriorating environmental conditions that were related to its industrial might.

The Foundations of Energy Policy

By the early 1970s, America had grown increasingly dependent on oil from foreign sources. In particular, oil from Middle Eastern nations such as Saudi Arabia and Iran had become a steadily growing share of the nation's energy sources. While foreign oil remained cheap and abundant, there was little demand for the federal government to invest itself in major energy initiatives. But, in 1973, the need for action in the area of energy became all too obvious to the American public, and the energy problem was abruptly thrust onto the government's agenda. On October 17, 1973, the members of the Organization of Arab Petroleum Exporting Countries (OAPEC) announced an

Photo courtesy: Bill Pierce/Time & Life Pictures/Getty Images

What does an energy crisis look like? After the OPEC oil embargo in 1973, soaring gas prices and shrinking supplies led to a rationing of gas in the United States and long lines at the gas pumps. Today, with the cost of oil and gas at high levels, people are looking for ways to be less reliant on this politically volatile, nonrenewable resource.

embargo of oil shipments to any nation that supported Israel during its war with Egypt and Syria; this included the United States.[57] The embargo was compounded when the larger Organization of Petroleum Exporting Countries (OPEC) decided to raise oil prices throughout the world.[58] The cumulative impact of these actions was a dramatic increase in the cost of oil in the United States, with a gallon of gasoline increasing from 38 cents to 55 cents between May 1973 and May 1974.[59] Soaring prices and shrinking supplies led to the first rationing of gas in the United States since the end of World War II and thrust energy to the front of the government agenda.

Policy makers confronted the energy problem with a number of general approaches. First, the federal government created a series of policies that were designed to reduce consumption of petroleum in the United States. The federal government established a national speed limit of 55 miles per hour in order to increase fuel efficiency, and Congress set an earlier date for the start of daylight savings time in an attempt to reduce demand for electricity.[60]

As another component of its conservation approach, the federal government initiated Corporate Average Fuel Efficiency (CAFE) standards in 1975 as a means of improving the gas mileage of automobiles in the United States. Under CAFE, automakers were required to meet average fuel efficiency standards for the fleet of cars that they sold in the United States. For example, General Motors was required to have the automobiles it sold domestically average 18 miles per gallon (MPG) in 1978. This meant GM could sell a large sedan that got 12 MPG if it also sold a smaller car that got 24 MPG. Besides adopting energy conservation measures, the federal government also turned its attention to increasing the availability of energy for the nation. In order to minimize the short-term impact of oil disruptions, Congress established the Strategic Petroleum Reserve in 1975 as part of the Energy Policy and Conservation Act. The Strategic Petroleum Reserve holds about two months of inventory that can be accessed under a presidential order.

With policy initiatives mounting and the complexity of energy policy growing, President Jimmy Carter called for the establishment of a Cabinet-level department that would be devoted to the administration and implementation of energy policy. In 1977, Congress followed up on the president's proposal and established the Department of Energy (DOE).[61] When the DOE was activated on October 1, 1977, a dozen federal programs related to energy were brought under the control of Secretary of Energy James R. Schlesinger. In addition to assuming power over existing federal energy programs, the DOE was handed an array of new programs when Congress adopted the wide-ranging National Energy Act of 1978 (NEA). This comprehensive federal law included a variety of components related to both energy conservation and the expansion of energy sources.

A key component of the 1978 NEA was the Energy Tax Act, which harnessed the government's tax powers as an energy policy tool. Under this legislation, the federal government gave tax breaks to individuals and companies that used alternative energy sources such as solar or geothermal power. Conversely, the Energy Tax Act also penalized inefficient use of energy by establishing a "gas-guzzler tax" on cars that did not reach a minimum MPG threshold. While the purpose of the gas-guzzler tax was to reduce the public demand for such vehicles, the law did not make the impact originally anticipated. This is because it did not apply to vehicles over 6,000 pounds. What was originally considered an exemption for businesses that needed vans and trucks to do their work turned out to be a way around the gas-guzzler tax for business owners, who could purchase or lease sport utility vehicles (SUVs) like the mammoth Hummer to conduct everyday business activities.

Thinking Globally

Fuel Taxes in Europe

For decades, European countries have imposed high taxes on fuel to encourage conservation and fuel-efficient technologies while funding public transportation. In Great Britain, the Netherlands, and Scandinavia, the taxes on gas are more than twice as much as the underlying cost of the fuel. The United States has long been reluctant to follow the European model, and maintaining relatively inexpensive gas has been an important goal of both Democrats and Republicans.

- Should the United States impose higher taxes on fuel consumption? Why or why not? How would such taxes affect you and your family?
- Other than taxation, what other policies might the United States implement to encourage greater fuel conservation?
- The United States and China are the world's largest oil consumers and the biggest producers of greenhouse gases. Economists expect China to double its oil consumption over the next ten years. How might the United States and China work together to lower fuel usage and reduce pollution?

The Foundations of Environmental Policy

As America was being forced to confront energy as a national concern in the 1970s, the issue of the environment was also moving into a prominent role in the national discourse. Americans' growing concerns about environmental conditions led to the first Earth Day in 1970, when millions of the nation's citizenry took part in marches and rallies demanding greater government action to protect the environment. This public pressure had a tremendous impact on the intergovernmental relations between the states and national government, ushering in the "environmental decade" of the 1970s.

With strong public support for increased environmental protection efforts by the federal government, both the Congress and President Richard M. Nixon started the decade with an incredible flurry of legislative and executive initiatives. First, in 1970, Nixon signed into law the National Environmental Policy Act (NEPA), which required the completion of environmental impact statements by federal agencies when a government project was proposed. To help facilitate the oversight of NEPA and other environmental protection efforts, Nixon created the Environmental Protection Agency (EPA) by executive order in December 1970. The EPA assembled many federal environmental programs under one independent executive branch agency, with the agency administrator reporting directly to the president.

Congress followed up its efforts with NEPA by passing the most significant piece of environmental legislation in American history. Under the **Clean Air Act of 1970**, Congress established national primary and secondary ambient air quality standards for six air pollutants. The primary standards were for the protection of human health, while the secondary standards were to protect nonhealth values such as crops, buildings, lakes, and forests.

Clean Air Act of 1970
The law that established the primary standards for air quality in the United States. A revised version was passed in 1990.

In 1972, Congress followed up the Clean Air Act with the Clean Water Act (CWA). With nearly unanimous support among members of Congress, the law established an overly optimistic goal of making all American surface water "swimable and fishable by 1985." Despite significant progress in addressing some of the most egregious sources of water pollution, the problem of water pollution—as well as the uneasy relationship between federal and state control of clean water policies—continues.

Federal policy initiatives grew throughout the 1970s with the passage of legislation such as the Safe Drinking Water Act (1974), which established national standards for drinking water quality; the Resource Conservation and Recovery Act (1976), which eliminated the existence of unsanitary town dumps; and the Comprehensive Environmental Response, Compensation, and Liability Act (Superfund), which was designed to clean up many of the nations hazardous waste sites. However, the arrival of the 1980s would bring a major change to the standing of environmental policy within American politics.

The Hibernation of Energy and Environmental Policies

As the 1970s ended, so did the prominent role that energy and environmental policies held on the government's agenda. This reduced profile for energy initiatives was brought about by a confluence of political and economic factors during the 1980s. With Ronald Reagan's election in 1980, federal involvement in energy policy changed. As a champion of smaller government and deregulation, President Reagan was anxious to reduce the national scope and intensity of federal energy efforts. In accepting the Republican nomination for president, Reagan foreshadowed his approach to energy policy by stating "America must get to work producing more energy. The Republican program for solving economic problems is based on growth and productivity; the [Carter] administration seems to believe the American people would rather see more regulation, taxes, and controls than more energy."

Reagan took both real and symbolic steps to reduce government intervention in the area of energy. Among the real steps was Reagan's 1981 National Energy Policy Plan, which ended the price and allocation controls on crude oil and petroleum products that had been established in the 1970s. Reagan also did not seek to renew tax breaks for alternative energy purchases or maintain government financial support for many alternative fuel research projects. While balking at government support for alternative fuels, the president did call for increased research into finding cleaner ways to use the nation's gigantic coal reserves.[62] Symbolically, Reagan ordered the removal of the solar water-heating panels that President Jimmy Carter had placed on top of the White House, sending a clear message about the ideological differences in the administrations.

Although Reagan's approach to governing helps explain the dearth of energy initiatives during the 1980s, the availability and price of petroleum was at least equally responsible for taking the energy issue off of government's radar screen. After spiraling upward during the 1970s, oil and gasoline prices stabilized during the 1980s. There were no major disruptions in supply, and the public outcry for action on energy issues largely dissipated. Despite the increased dependence on foreign sources of petroleum, Americans were no longer feeling the day-to day pain that they experienced in the previous decade.

During the George Bush and Bill Clinton administrations of the late 1980s and 1990s, energy and environmental policies were not major national priorities. With a few notable exceptions, such as the Clean Air Act of 1990 and the Energy Policy Act of 1992, the national government did not aggressively tackle environmental and energy issues as it had done in the 1970s.

Energy and Environmental Policies Return to Prominence

As with the election of Ronald Reagan in 1980, George W. Bush's victory in 2000 played a significant role in shaping government efforts in energy policy. Only two weeks after being sworn into office, President Bush announced the formation of the National Energy Policy Development Group (NEPDG), which was to be chaired by Vice President Dick Cheney. In forming the group, Bush indicated that the area of energy policy needed greater attention and planning than had been given in the past, and he charged the committee with developing a plan to guide his administration on energy matters.

Almost from its start, however, the NEPDG was surrounded by controversy, primarily related to the secrecy surrounding the group's deliberations and members. Vice President Cheney claimed that the committee needed high levels of confidentiality in order to adequately address difficult issues and refused to share much detail on the work of the group. This secrecy led to a number of Democratic members of Congress demanding access to the committee's work, but their legal challenge was thrown out of federal court.[63]

The NEPDG's work led to the development of Bush's national energy policy in May 2001, which put forth 105 recommendations, some requiring congressional action and others capable of being implemented through regulatory action. Among the cornerstones of the Bush energy policy were plans to allow drilling in Alaska's Arctic National Wildlife Refuge, relaxing rules for the placement of new electrical transmission lines, research into reprocessing nuclear fuel, and greater funding and support for clean coal initiatives.[64]

Within months after the release of Bush's energy plan, the nation suffered the terrorist attacks of September 11, 2001. After 9/11, the issue of energy began to evolve much more as an issue of national security than it had in the past. As American troops headed to war in Iraq, the impact of the national dependence on oil became more apparent to the country than ever before.[65] Demands for new measures to make the nation more energy independent grew, and Congress began to more aggressively assemble a legislative response to the country's energy needs. (To learn more about current efforts to conserve energy, see Ideas into Action: Conduct a Personal Energy Audit.)

These calls for more comprehensive energy policy were also being fueled by the increasing concern regarding **global warming**, an issue related to climate change. Since the 1980s, scientists have warned that the burning of fossil fuels contributes to increased levels of greenhouse gases in the atmosphere, which in turn lead to higher global temperatures. These higher temperatures have a number of significant impacts on the planet, such as melting polar ice, increasing sea levels, prolonged droughts, more intense storms, major habitat destruction, and species extinction. These scientific concerns have spurred international action to manage the problem of global warming. Most of the world's industrial nations ratified the Kyoto Protocol in 1997, which committed them to reducing greenhouse gas emissions. Despite support from the Clinton administration, the United States did not ratify the agreement. President George W. Bush steadfastly refused to join with other nations by signing the treaty, citing the damaging effects of the protocol on the U.S. economy.

In the absence of major federal activity to control global warming, the state governments have taken the lead. Since 2000, many states have put together comprehensive policies to reduce greenhouse gases. For example, in November 2004, the governors of Washington, Oregon, and California agreed to a series of detailed recommendations to reduce global warming pollution.[66] In 2007, a number of states went to the Supreme Court to force the EPA to adopt regulations that would limit the emission of greenhouse gases.

While the states have been more active than the federal government in addressing global warming, Congress did pass significant energy legislation in 2007. With the Democrats controlling both the House and the Senate for the first time in years, many

global warming
The increase in global temperatures due to carbon emissions from burning fossil fuels such as coal and oil.

You Are an Environmental Activist

Conduct a Personal Energy Audit

The issue of energy has become a dominant concern for Americans as gas and electricity prices have soared and the threat of global warming continues to grow. These economic and environmental concerns have led government, businesses, and individuals to pay much more attention to the amount of energy they consume. And, they have helped push new conservation efforts forward throughout the United States. For example, the U.S. Postal Service conducted an extensive review of its energy use when faced with rising gas prices. With a fleet of over 200,000 vehicles, the Postal Service is particularly affected by increasing costs at the pump. For every 1-cent increase in the price of a gallon of gas, the Postal Service must pay an extra $8 million to keep its carriers on the road.

Through its energy audit, the Postal Service identified a number of areas where savings could be achieved. For example, planning postal routes to reduce left turns and U-turns decreases fuel consumption and therefore saves on energy costs. In addition, having carriers travel by foot or bikes in many places reduces energy costs without adding significant delays to the delivery of the mail.

Individuals don't consume energy on the same scale as the U.S. Postal Service, but most Americans have felt the impact of increased energy costs. The average American spends about one out of every five dollars on energy costs. Thus, it's a good time to take an inventory of your personal energy use.

Consider the following questions:
- How does the place where you live affect your energy use? How far do you need to travel to buy groceries, get to work or school, and entertain yourself? Do you live in a part of the country where air conditioning or heating oil costs place a burden on your budget? Are your appliances energy efficient?
- How many miles do you travel by car each year? What type of gas mileage does the vehicle you drive achieve? Do forms of mass transportation exist in your area that you could use rather than a car?
- Visit the Web site for your state government to find out if you are eligible for energy-related tax rebates. Can you identify government policies or programs in your state that can provide you with assistance in saving energy? How might you better use government assistance to reduce your energy consumption?

energy initiatives are back in play on Capitol Hill. Congress eventually passed the Energy Independence and Security Act of 2007, which raised fuel efficiency standards for automobiles, ordered a massive increase in the use of biofuels such as ethanol, and initiated phasing out sales of incandescent light bulbs in the United States.[67]

Alternative Energy Policy Goes Mainstream

With the price of gas spiking above $4 a gallon and the cost of home heating increasing each year, Americans have become much more interested in the availability of alternative energy sources. From solar panels to electric cars, once exotic technologies have become much more sought after by everyday citizens. However, energy usage statistics remind us that fossil fuels still dominate the energy field in the United States. According to the Department of Energy, only 7 percent of all energy used in America comes from renewable sources.[68] In 2007, coal and oil provided almost two-thirds of the nation's energy consumption. With such disparities in usage levels between renewable and nonrenewable sources, it will take significant efforts to move alternative fuels into the mainstream. It appears that such efforts may increasingly come from governments at all levels in the United States.

Over the past decades, many state governments in the United States have begun to adopt Renewable Portfolio Standards (RPS) that require set portions of electricity to be generated from alternative sources. In 2008, over half the states in the nation had RPS standards, with many more considering such policies. For example, California has mandated that the percentage of renewable energy sales increase by at least 1 percent per year to reach at least 20 percent by 2010 and 33 percent by the end of 2020.[69] States

Join the Debate

The Increasing Use of Ethanol

OVERVIEW: The drive to decrease U.S. reliance on oil has promoted the use of a number of alternative sources of energy, such as wind, solar power, and—especially for engines in cars, airplanes, and other vehicles—ethanol. Ethanol fuel can be processed relatively easily from common crops, such as sugar cane, soybeans, and corn. The United States, which is the largest producer of ethanol in the world, relies heavily on corn. Brazil, the second largest producer, uses sugar cane and is considered to be the world's first sustainable biofuels economy.

The process to get the starch necessary for producing ethanol uses only the kernels from corn plants, and then only about 50 percent of those kernels. The conversion of sugar cane is almost six times more efficient than the rate for corn. Other crops, such as switchgrass, promise to be even better, more efficient sources of ethanol than either corn or sugar cane.

While engines can be run entirely on ethanol, it is most common in the United States to mix ethanol with petroleum, with the former constituting 10 percent of the total. Brazil uses a 25 percent ethanol blend. As of January 2008, Missouri, Minnesota, and Hawaii require that only ethanol blends be sold in their states. If engines are tuned properly for ethanol use, it is possible to get higher fuel efficiency (miles per gallon) with higher percentages of ethanol in the blends. The advantages cited for using corn and other plants to produce combustible fuel for vehicles include not only the potential for higher fuel efficiency, but reliance on a renewable source of energy and less air pollution than one gets from use of petroleum-based gasoline.

The conversion of corn and sugar cane to ethanol, of course, means using an important source of food to create a renewable supply of fuel. During 2007 and 2008, global food prices rose sharply and in some cases prompted riots and emergency assistance. The average international price of corn tripled between 2005 and 2008, a trend that many experts agree stems in part from increased demands for corn to be used to make ethanol. Riots by people unable to afford the corn tortillas that make up a key portion of their diet occurred in Mexico in 2007. In 2008, riots by poor people whose food prices had doubled within one month occurred in Somalia.

Surging food prices have a number of causes. One of these is the diversion of crops from food to fuel, a trend that is sometimes encouraged by government subsidies and tax breaks. Other causes included crops destroyed by storms, increases in demand for food from countries like China and India, and rising oil prices, which increase the prices of fertilizer and the costs of operating farm machinery.

Arguments IN FAVOR of Increasing the Use of Ethanol

- It is essential for the U.S. economy and security that we decrease reliance on petroleum and develop alternative sources of energy such as ethanol. International conflict and domestic unrest in oil-producing countries has prompted dramatic increases in the price of oil. Given our dependence on oil and petroleum products, we are very vulnerable to fluctuations in the available supply of oil. Ethanol produced from common crops like corn, soybeans and sugar cane takes advantage of our agricultural capacities and provides us with an independent, renewable source of energy. Most automobiles can use ethanol blends immediately; with relatively minor modifications, vehicles in the near future can use even more ethanol and less petroleum.

- Especially with properly tuned engines, ethanol is cleaner and more fuel efficient than conventional gasoline. Ethanol has a higher octane rating than petroleum-based gasoline. This provides the potential for more miles per gallon than vehicles are currently getting. The lower amounts of fuel needed to operate an engine means less air pollution. In addition, ethanol emits cleaner exhaust than gasoline and will help address concerns about global warming and toxins in the air.

- An increase in the demand for corn, soybeans, and other crops used in making ethanol will boost the economies of agricultural areas and small towns. Farmers have struggled and sought federal

have also used their fiscal powers to increase the adoption of alternative energy technologies. For example, Maine offers its residents up to a $7,000 tax rebate on residential photovoltaic system installations and $1,250 on solar thermal water heaters.

Since 2000, many American cities have become more aggressive in promoting renewable energy use. Austin, Texas, is among a number of cities that allow utility customers to purchase electricity from wind power. When city residents opt in to

subsidies and other assistance since the early twentieth century. Small towns in agricultural areas have languished, many of them losing population. Heavier reliance on ethanol will not only help farmers but will prompt the establishment of processing plants and support services in nearby towns.

Arguments AGAINST Increasing the Use of Ethanol

- **Government intervention through grants, subsidies, and tax credits distorts markets and artificially makes ethanol an attractive source of energy.** Public policies, even when well intentioned, can encourage bad solutions. Alternative sources of energy should withstand the tests of costs and benefits, rather than be a response to political pressures. Corn, in particular, is not a good source of biofuel. Most of the corn plant is not used, and the energy costs of transporting and processing the plants outweigh any gains in the qualities of the fuel that is produced. In 2007, corn ethanol subsidies totaled over $11 billion, and ethanol made the United States only 1.1 percent more energy independent and reduced greenhouse gases produced in the United States by only 0.2 percent.

- **More crops for ethanol come at the cost of a decrease in food supplies and an increase in food prices.** As would be predicted by laws of supply and demand, prices go up with declines in supply. Increases in population and increases in the purchasing power of people in countries like China and India are adding to the demand for food. Food

Photo courtesy: Scott Olson/Getty Images

Should the government invest more in ethanol production? Ethanol has become a popular form of alternative energy, but its increased use has raised numerous concerns.

production, however, cannot increase with more and more acres being devoted to crops that are used for ethanol. The results are the shortages and price increases that have characterized 2007 and 2008.

- **A focus on ethanol diverts attention from the real need, which is conservation.** Presenting ethanol as the solution to the energy crisis deludes Americans and keeps them from the more important quest of reducing their use of energy. The real issues are fuel efficiency for vehicles and excessive use of individual cars. The federal government has lacked the will to force automobile and truck manufacturers to use existing and developing technology to increase fuel efficiency. Investment in rapid mass transit systems will do more to reduce reliance on petroleum and other sources of energy than promoting ways to allow Americans to continue their current patterns of fuel consumption.

Continuing the Debate

1. Should governments adopt public policies designed to encourage the production and use of ethanol?
2. How can government help to ensure an adequate food supply while developing alternative and renewable sources of energy?

To Follow the Debate Online, Go To:

www.ethanol.org, where the American Coalition for Ethanol provides information about ethanol and suggestions for how groups and individuals might influence policy makers to promote its use.

www.e85fuel.com, the site of the National Ethanol Vehicle Coalition, an advocacy group for increased use of ethanol. It is particularly focused on the goal of establishing a requirement that all motor fuel contain at least 15 percent ethanol.

www.energyjustice.net/ethanol for arguments against reliance on ethanol and links to industries that advocate ethanol use.

Austin's "Green Choice" program, the city purchases power from a Texas wind generation facility.[70] The Portland, Oregon, city council created a renewable fuel standard in 2006 that requires 5 percent of all diesel fuel to come from biodiesel sources and gasoline sold in the city to contain at least 10 percent ethanol. The goal of this policy is to create demand for renewable transportation fuels.[71] (To learn more about controversies surrounding ethanol, see Join the Debate: The Increasing Use of Ethanol.)

WHAT SHOULD I HAVE LEARNED?

This chapter examined the policy-making process and key domestic policy issues related to income security, health care, energy, and the environment. The questions we have sought to address are:

■ **What is the policy-making process?**

The policy-making process can be viewed as a sequence of functional activities beginning with the identification and definition of public problems. Once identified, problems must get on the governmental agenda. Other stages of the process include policy formulation, policy adoption, budgeting for policies, policy implementation, and the evaluation of policy.

■ **How did income security and health care policies evolve?**

The origins of income security and health care policy can be traced back to early social welfare initiatives in the nation's history. Only after the Great Depression, however, was a public-sector role in the delivery of social services broadly accepted. Programs initiated in the Great Depression became a model for greater public-sector responsibilities in the areas of income security and health care.

■ **What are the key aspects of current income security and health care policies in the United States?**

Governments at all levels are involved in income security and health care policies. Most income security programs generally take two forms: non-means-based programs and means-tested programs, which indicate that all people who meet eligibility criteria are automatically entitled to receive benefits. Governments in the United States have a long history of involvement in the health of Americans. Most state and local governments have health departments, and the U.S. government has several public health and medical research divisions. Medicare and Medicaid are the two most prominent national programs. As the cost of health care has risen, however, new demands have been made to restrain the rate of growth in costs.

■ **How have energy and environmental policies evolved in the United States?**

As energy sources have become more limited and environmental problems have magnified, government efforts in these policy fields have expanded. Before the 1970s, there was very limited activity on the part of government to establish policies related to energy and environmental protection matters. While the arrival of energy shortages and expanding pollution problems propelled these policy areas into the forefront of government's agenda in the 1970s, their prominence at the federal level has fluctuated greatly. During recent years, skyrocketing energy prices and increasing concerns about global warming and other aspects of climate change have placed these issues once again at the center of American politics.

Key Terms

agenda, p. 602
agenda setting, p. 602
Clean Air Act of 1970, p. 628
entitlement program, p. 622
global warming, p. 630
governmental (institutional)
    agenda, p. 602

means-tested program, p. 615
Medicaid, p. 624
Medicare, p. 624
non-means-based program, p. 615
policy adoption, p. 604
policy evaluation, p. 608
policy formulation, p. 604

policy implementation, p. 606
public policy, p. 599
Social Security Act, p. 612
systemic agenda, p. 602

Researching Domestic Policy

In the Library

Brooks, Robin, and Assaf Razin. *Social Security Reform: Financial and Political Issues in International Perspective*. Cambridge: Cambridge University Press, 2005.

Feldstein, Paul. *Health Policy Issues: An Economic Perspective on Health Reform*, 3rd ed. Chicago: Health Administration Press, 2002.

Gilens, Martin. *Why Americans Hate Welfare: Race, Media, and the Politics of Antipoverty Policy*. Chicago: University of Chicago Press, 2001.

Handler, Joel. *The Poverty of Welfare Reform*. New Haven, CT: Yale University Press, 1995.

Isaacs, Stephen, and James Knickman, eds. *To Improve Health and Health Care*. Vol. 8. San Francisco: Jossey-Bass, 2005.

Kotlikoff, Laurence J., and Scott Burns. *The Coming Generational Storm: What You Need to Know About America's Economic Future*. Cambridge, MA: MIT Press, 2004.

Kraft, Michael. *Environmental Policy and Politics*. New York: Prentice Hall, 2006.

Lindbloom, Charles E., and Edward J. Woodhouse. *The Policy-Making Process*, 3rd ed. Englewood Cliffs, NJ: Prentice Hall, 1993.

Longest, Beaufort B. *Health Policymaking in the United States*, 3rd ed. Chicago: Health Administration Press, 2002.

Oberlander, Jonathan. *The Political Life of Medicare*. Chicago: University of Chicago Press, 2003.

Rabe, Barry G. *Statehouse and Greenhouse: The Emerging Politics of American Climate Change Policy*. Washington, DC: Brookings Institution, 2004.

Rich, Robert, and William White. *Health Policy, Federalism, and the American States*. Washington, DC: Urban Institute, 1996.

Ristinen, Robert P., and Jack P. Kraushaar. *Energy and the Environment*. Hoboken, NJ: Wiley, 2005.

Rushefsky, Mark, and Kant Patel. *Politics, Power, and Policy Making: The Case of Health Care Reform in the 1990s*. Armonk, NY: M. E. Sharpe, 1998.

Sherraden, Michael. *Inclusion in the American Dream: Assets Poverty and Public Policy*. Oxford: Oxford University Press, 2005.

Skocpol, Theda. *The Missing Middle: Working Families and the Future of American Social Policy*. New York: Norton, 2000.

Weil, Alan, and Kenneth Finegold, eds. *Welfare Reform: The Next Act*. Washington, DC: Urban Institute, 2002.

Wilson, Steven F. *Learning on the Job: When Business Takes on Public Schools*. Cambridge: Cambridge University Press, 2006.

Wilson, William J. *The Bridge over the Racial Divide: Rising Inequality and Coalition Politics*. Berkeley: University of California Press, 1999.

On the Web

To understand how public policies are prioritized and analyzed, go to **www.ncpa.org**.

To see an overview of the legislative process for public policy, go to **www.house.gov**.

To understand how public policy laws are made, go to **thomas.loc.gov/home/thomas.html**.

To learn more about how public policies are budgeted, go to **www.cbpp.org**.

To learn about the research institutes and organizations that evaluate policies, go to **www.aei.org** and **www.brookings.org**.

To learn more about the most current Social Security benefits and statistics, go to **www.ssa.gov**.

To learn more about current welfare provisions, go to **www.progress.org**.

For other health care policy initiatives and consumer health information, go to **www.nih.gov**.

To learn more about energy policy in the United States, go to **www.doe.gov**.

To learn more about major environmental policies, go to **www.epa.gov**.

18 Economic Policy

The role of the government in managing prosperity and regulating the economy has long been a subject of debate among scholars and policy makers. The current economic downturn has brought these debates into the homes of most American citizens. The mortgage and banking crisis, higher energy and food prices, and job insecurity have all contributed to concerns over the state of the economy and the role of the government in providing economic security for its citizens. There has also been growing concern over foreign competition and free trade policies as the economies of China and India rapidly expand. While protectionist pressures have increased across the political spectrum, the American government has by and large remained committed to the principles of free trade.[1]

In early 2008, President George W. Bush reiterated that free trade and investment advance America's national security and economic interests. He also stated that the share of exports in the national economy was rising and that American jobs supported by exports pay wages 13 to 18 percent higher than the national average.[2]

Public opinion, however, has not been as supportive of free trade. In a November–December 2007 survey, 44 percent of respondents reported that free trade hurts the economy, while only 27 percent reported that it helps the economy.[3]

With the economic downturn of 2008, concerns over the US economy have grown. In February 2008, the Bush administration, along with Congress, announced a $168 billion fiscal stimulus package to provide Americans with tax relief to help boost consumer demand and alleviate economic hardship. In July 2008, the Federal Reserve Bank governors forecast a 1 to 1.6 percent growth of the economy in 2008, while their April 2008 outlook projected a 0.3 to 1.2 percent growth.[4] By October 2008, however, following the financial meltdown and the resulting announcement and Congressional ratification of a $700 billion federal rescue plan (more often than not referred to as a financial bailout plan or "blank check" by its deriders), the Fed's growth forecasts had become more dismal. An October 2008 International Monetary Fund (IMF) report stated that the "US economic downturn may well become more severe and could evolve into a recession."[5] The September 2008 official unemployment rate was 6.1 percent, while the annual inflation rate from August 2007–August 2008 stood at

■ **What is the proper role of government in the economy?** At left, union members protest against the North American Free Trade Agreement in 1993. At right, Secretary of the Treasury Henry Paulson discusses the 2008 financial rescue plan with reporters.

WHAT SHOULD I KNOW ABOUT . . .

- the roots of government involvement in the economy?
- the tools available to stabilize the economy?
- the economic cost of the war in Iraq?
- the subprime mortgage crisis and the policy responses to it?

5.4 percent.[6] The economy lost 159,000 jobs in September 2008 alone.[7] As US stocks sunk to a 5-year low, Federal Reserve Chair Ben Bernanke stated that the US was tackling a financial crisis of "historic dimensions." In a desperate effort to ease the credit crunch and stimulate the economy, the Fed, in coordination with European and Japanese policy makers, cut rates to 1.5 percent in October 2008. The rate had been 5.25 percent just a year before.

Crises at investment and commercial banks such as Bear Sterns, Lehman Brothers, Merrill Lynch, Wachovia, and Washington Mutual, as well as insurance giant AIG, raised panic across global markets. Banks in other nations, such as Iceland, were taken over by governments or forced to merge at rock bottom prices. The IMF estimated that the 2008 credit crisis would cost up to $1.4 trillion in global financial losses.[8] Voters in America headed to the polls in November 2008 amidst growing uncertainty over the fate of their jobs, savings and homes.

The fiscal stimulation package and the financial rescue package demonstrate the important role of the government in management of the overall economy. The point of contention among economists, politicians, and citizens, however, remains the scope and intensity of government involvement in the economy.

TO LEARN MORE— —TO DO MORE To learn more about the way the Federal Reserve Board has attempted to fight against recession, go to the Board of Governors of the Federal Reserve System at federalreserve.com.

In a global economy, should a national government protect its workers or industries against foreign competition? Against market failures? How sensitive should government economic policies be to issues relating to inequality? More broadly, what should the role of the federal government be in the nation's economic affairs? The last question has been asked, in different ways, ever since the nation began.

There continues to be a lively debate over the proper role of the government in the economy. Those favoring limited government participation are pitted against others who believe the government is responsible for managing the economy through policy. In this chapter, we consider those viewpoints as we describe the policies the government uses to achieve its economic goals.

In this chapter, we will examine the following:

★ First, we will take a historical look at *the roots of government involvement in the economy*.

★ Second, we will examine the government's role in *stabilizing the economy*, sometimes called "macroeconomic regulation."

★ Third, we will look at the *economic cost of the war in Iraq*.

★ Finally, we will examine the *mortgage crisis in the United States and the government's proposed reforms* to respond to it.

The Living Constitution

The Congress shall have power to lay and collect taxes on incomes, from whatever source derived, without apportionment among the several States, and without regard to any census or enumeration.

SIXTEENTH AMENDMENT

Ratified on February 3, 1913, the Sixteenth Amendment modified the Article I prohibition against levying a "direct tax" on individual property, unless the tax in question addresses the rule of apportionment as set forth in Article I, sections 2 and 9. This amendment was yet another revision made to the Constitution in response to a U.S. Supreme Court decision, namely the 1895 *Pollock* v. *Farmers' Loan & Trust Co.*—a judgment in which a divided Court held that Congress could not tax incomes uniformly throughout the United States.

The authority to tax is one of the fundamental rights inherent in legitimate government, and it is the hallmark of good and just governance to tax citizens fairly and equitably. The Constitution gives the House of Representatives sole authority to originate revenue bills, since the Framers believed the House, as the institution that directly represents the people, should determine how taxes should be raised and apportioned. Indeed, during the ratification debates, concern was expressed in regard to the Senate's ability to amend revenue bills as being a potential means for unjust taxation, since the Senate would not directly represent the people in its political capacity.

As the nineteenth century drew to a close, the Supreme Court became aware that in the new industrial age, the *Pollock* decision could threaten national solvency. As a result, the Court began to redefine "direct taxation" so as to help the federal government adapt to the new era. For example, the Court held in 1911 that corporate income could be taxed as an "excise measured by income." And, in its first appraisal of the newly ratified Sixteenth Amendment, the Court began to view income taxes as a form of indirect taxation. The Sixteenth Amendment has thus guaranteed the federal government a consistent and continuous revenue stream, and it is up to the Congress and the president to ensure fair taxation for all Americans.

CRITICAL THINKING QUESTIONS

1. While the Sixteenth Amendment's authorization of the federal income tax has helped to increase the national government's powers, the federal tax system is often criticized in terms of its fairness. Are there alternatives to the current federal income tax system that would be fairer for the American people?

2. There have been calls to amend the Constitution in order to establish a fairer and simpler federal tax system. Should the Constitution be used to create the specific rules of the tax system, or should Congress be responsible for constructing the taxes employed by the federal government?

Roots of Government Involvement in the Economy

During the nation's first century, the states were responsible for managing economic affairs. The national government defined its economic role narrowly, although it did collect tariffs (taxes on imported goods), fund public improvements, and encourage private development. (See The Living Constitution: Sixteenth Amendment.) Congress became active in setting economic policy and

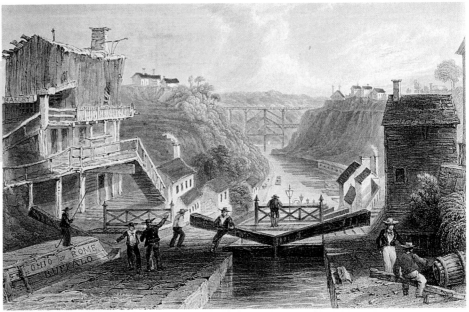

How do public works projects affect economic prosperity? Public works projects such as construction of the Erie Canal spurred settlement and building throughout the state of New York.

Photo courtesy: Bettmann/CORBIS

enacting economic regulation only after people realized that the states alone could not solve the problems affecting the economy.

The Nineteenth Century

Although the U.S. economic system is a mixed free-enterprise system characterized by the private ownership of property, private enterprise, and marketplace competition, the national government has long played an important role in fostering economic development through its policies on taxes, tariffs, the use of public lands, and the creation of a national bank (see chapter 3). For much of the nineteenth century, however, national regulatory programs were few and were restricted to such tasks as steamboat inspection and the regulation of trade with American Indian tribes.

In contrast, the state governments were quite active in promoting and regulating private economic activity. They constructed such public works as the Erie Canal, built roads, and subsidized railroads to encourage trade within and among the states; they also carried on many licensing, inspection, and regulatory programs. For example, the states issued licenses to certify public school teachers and other professionals and established building inspection programs to protect the public interest.

Following the Civil War, the United States entered a period of rapid economic growth. The rise of industrial capitalism brought about the creation of large-scale manufacturing enterprises. Many people began working in factories for wages and crowded into large cities. New problems resulted from industrialization: industrial accidents and disease, labor–management conflict, unemployment, and the emergence of huge corporations that could exploit workers and consumers. Another problem was the hardship that resulted from downturns in the business cycle, which became more severe in the new industrial society. **Business cycles** involve fluctuations between growth and recession, or periods of "boom and bust," and are an inherent part of modern capitalist economies. During recessions, people lose their jobs and income, and the economy experiences a low or even negative growth rate.

Disturbed by the problems resulting from industrialization, many people turned to government for help. Because the states, with their limited jurisdictions, appeared inadequate to cope with industrial problems, the national government was called on to control these new forces. Businesses and conservatives who had welcomed govern-

business cycles
Fluctuations between expansion and recession that are a part of modern capitalist economies.

ment intervention to aid economic development in the early decades of the nineteenth century, however, now proclaimed their faith in **laissez-faire**. Based on Adam Smith's *The Wealth of Nations* (published in 1776), the doctrine of laissez-faire holds that active governmental involvement in the economy is wrong and that the role of government should be limited to the maintenance of order and justice, the conduct of foreign affairs, and the provision of necessary public works such as roads or lighthouses, which are not profitable for private persons to provide. Beyond that, individuals should be left free to pursue their self-interest. Market-based competition and the laws of supply and demand, according to this view, will control individual behavior and ensure that self-interest does not get out of hand. Furthermore, reliance on market forces, instead of government, will deliver the greatest amount of welfare for the greatest amount of people in society.

While opposed to regulation of their activities, businesses did not shun other forms of government intervention in the economy. They strongly supported tariffs that provided protection from foreign competitors. Other favored policies included the giveaway of public lands, subsidies for railroad construction, and the use of armed force to put down strikes. Essentially, what businesses and their supporters considered laissez-faire was an economic system and a set of government policies that would encourage business profits.[9]

The first major government effort to regulate business was caused by growing concern over the power of the railroads. After nearly two decades of pressure from farmers, owners of small businesses, and reformers in the cities, Congress adopted the Interstate Commerce Act in 1887 to regulate the railroad industry. Enforced by the new Interstate Commerce Commission (ICC), the act required that railroad rates should be "just and reasonable."[10] The act also prohibited such practices as pooling (rate agreements), rate discrimination, and charging more for a short haul than for a long haul of goods.

Three years later, Congress dealt with the problem of "trusts," the name given to large-scale, monopolistic businesses that dominated many industries, including oil, sugar, whiskey, salt, and meatpacking. The Sherman Anti-Trust Act of 1890 prohibits all restraints of trade, including price-fixing, bid-rigging, and market allocation agreements. It also prohibits all monopolization or attempts to monopolize, including domination of a market by one company or a few companies. The act was to be

laissez-faire
A French term meaning "to allow to do, to leave alone." It is a hands-off governmental policy that is based on the belief that government involvement in the economy is wrong.

Photo courtesy: Bettmann/CORBIS

What was public sentiment toward big business in the late 1800s? Here, a political cartoonist depicts the perception that the U.S. government was dominated by various trusts in the nineteenth century.

enforced by the Anti-Trust Division of the Department of Justice, which was empowered to sue violators in the federal courts.

The Interstate Commerce Act and the Sherman Anti-Trust Act marked a break from the past and were the key legislative responses of the national government to the new industrialization. The Sherman Anti-Trust Act has been invoked in recent times, as in the Department of Justice lawsuit against the computer software giant Microsoft during the Clinton administration.

During the nineteenth century, government influence grew in the field of agriculture, the largest sector of the economy at that time. The year 1862 was significant: it saw the establishment of the Department of Agriculture, which gained Cabinet status in 1889; the adoption of the Homestead Act, which gave 160 acres of public land in the West free to people willing to live on the land and improve it; and passage of the Morrill Land Grant Act, which subsidized the establishment of state colleges ("land grant schools"). Subsequent legislation set up agricultural experiment stations and established programs to deal with such farm problems as pesticides, commodity standards, and the rail shipment of livestock.

The Progressive Era

The Progressive movement drew much of its support from the middle class and sought to reform America's political, economic, and social systems. There was a desire to bring corporate power under the control of government and make it more responsive to democratic ends. Progressive administrations under presidents Theodore Roosevelt and Woodrow Wilson established or strengthened regulatory programs to protect consumers and to control railroads, business, and banking.

The Pure Food and Drug Act and the Meat Inspection Act, both enacted in 1906, marked the beginning of consumer protection as a major responsibility of the national government. These laws prohibited adulteration and mislabeling of food and drugs and set sanitary standards for the food industry.

To control banking and regulate business, Congress passed three acts. The Federal Reserve Act (1913) created the Federal Reserve System to regulate the national banking system and to provide for flexibility in the money supply in order to better meet commercial needs and combat financial panics. Passage of the Federal Trade Commission (FTC) Act and Clayton Act of 1914 strengthened anti-trust policy. The FTC Act created the Federal Trade Commission and authorized it to prevent "unfair methods of competition," including price discrimination, exclusive dealing contracts, and corporate mergers that lessened competition. These statutes, like the Sherman Anti-Trust Act, sought to prevent businesses from forming monopolies or trusts.

Throughout the nineteenth century, the national government was able to raise the revenue it needed by levying protective tariffs and a few excise taxes, such as those on alcoholic beverages. These additional revenues allowed for generous government pensions for Union veterans of the Civil War and ample spending on internal infrastructure improvements.

As the national government's functions expanded in the late nineteenth and early twentieth century, fiscal constraints forced public officials to focus on the income tax as a way to raise money. In 1895, the Supreme Court held that the income tax was a direct tax, which, according to the U.S. Constitution, had to be allocated among the states in proportion to their population.[11] This ruling made the income tax a political and administrative impossibility. Consequently, the Sixteenth Amendment to the Constitution was adopted in 1913. The Sixteenth Amendment authorized the national government "to lay and collect taxes on incomes, from whatever source derived" without being apportioned among the states. Personal and corporate income taxes have since become the national government's major source of general revenues. Income taxes and particularly the tax burden have also been a source of continued political controversy.

The Great Depression and the New Deal

America's entry into World War I brought the Progressive era to an end. During the 1920s, in the Republican administrations of Presidents Warren G. Harding, Calvin Coolidge, and Herbert Hoover, the federal government reduced its role in restricting private business activities.[12] The economy grew at a rapid pace, and many Americans assumed that the resulting prosperity would last forever. But, "forever" came to an end in October 1929, when the stock market collapsed and the catastrophic worldwide economic decline known as the Great Depression set in. Although the Depression was worldwide in scope, the United States was especially hard hit. All sectors of the economy suffered, and no economic group or social class was spared, although some fared better than others.

The initial response of the Hoover administration was to declare that the economy was fundamentally sound, a claim few believed. Investors, businesspeople, and others lost confidence in the economy. Prices dropped, production declined, and unemployment rose. According to Bureau of Labor Statistics estimates, about one-fourth of the civilian workforce was unemployed in 1933.[13] Many other people worked only part-time or at jobs below their skill levels. The economic distress produced by the Great Depression, which lasted for a decade, was unparalleled before or since that time.

Calling for a "New Deal" for the American people, Franklin D. Roosevelt overwhelmed Herbert Hoover and the Republican Party in the 1932 presidential election. Roosevelt favored strong government action to relieve economic distress and to reform the capitalist economic system while preserving its basic features.

The Depression and the New Deal marked a major turning point in U.S. history in general and in U.S. economic history in particular. During the 1930s, the laissez-faire state was replaced with an **interventionist state**, in which the government began to play an active and extensive role in guiding and regulating the private economy. Until the 1930s, the national government's role in the economy was consistent with a broad interpretation of laissez-faire doctrine in that the government mostly provided a framework of rules within which the economy was left alone to operate. The New Deal, however, established the national government as a major regulator of private businesses, as a provider of Social Security (see chapter 17), and as ultimately responsible for maintaining a stable economy.

While the New Deal was not (and is not) without critics, most people today accept the notion that the government should play a role in the economy. The New Deal brought about a number of reforms in almost every area, including finance, agriculture, labor, and industry.

FINANCIAL REFORMS The first actions of the New Deal were directed at reviving and reforming the nation's financial system. Because of bad investments and poor management, many banks failed in the early 1930s. To restore confidence in the banks, Roosevelt declared a bank holiday the day after he was inaugurated, closing all of the nation's banks. On the basis of emergency legislation passed by Congress, only financially sound banks were permitted to reopen. Many unsound banks were closed for good and their depositors paid off.

Major New Deal banking laws included the Glass-Steagall Act (1933). The Glass-Steagall Act required the separation of commercial and investment banking and set up the Federal Deposit Insurance Corporation (FDIC) to insure bank deposits, originally for $5,000 per account. Legislation was also passed to control abuses in the stock markets. The Securities Act (1933) required that prospective investors be given full and accurate information about the stocks or securities being offered to them. The Securities Exchange Act (1934) created the Securities and Exchange Commission (SEC), an independent regulatory commission. The SEC was authorized to regulate the stock exchanges, enforce the Securities Act, and reduce the number of stocks bought on margin (that is, with borrowed money).

TIMELINE

Growth of the Budget and Federal Spending

interventionist state
Alternative to the laissez-faire state; the government takes an active role in guiding and managing the private economy.

More Oklahomans reach Calif. via the cotton fields of Ariz.

Photo courtesy: Bettmann/CORBIS

How did farm families cope during the Dust Bowl? Many Oklahomans, known as Okies, fled their drought-stricken, dust-engulfed farms for California and other states during the Great Depression.

Farm Subsidies

Making Economic Policy

AGRICULTURE The economic condition of U.S. agriculture, which had been weak even during the prosperous 1920s, became much worse during the Depression. The Agricultural Adjustment Act (AAA) of 1933 sought to boost farm income by restricting agriculture production in order to bring it into better balance with demand. Farmers who reduced their crop production in line with the program were eligible to receive cash payments and other benefits. In 1936, however, the Supreme Court held the AAA unconstitutional on the grounds that the national government lacked authority to regulate farming through any of its powers set out in Article I, section 8.[14] Congress quickly replaced the AAA with the Soil Conservation and Domestic Allotment Act, which paid farmers for taking land out of crop production and devoting it to soil conservation purposes. The crops taken out of production generally were those whose prices the AAA had been designed to increase. This plan did not work very well to increase farm income.

In 1938, Congress adopted the second Agricultural Adjustment Act. The second AAA provided subsidies to farmers raising crops such as corn, cotton, and wheat who grew no more than their allotted acreage. Direct payments and commodity loans were also available from the government to participating farmers. The Supreme Court upheld the constitutionality of the second AAA, finding it an appropriate exercise of Congress's power to regulate interstate commerce.[15] The overall effect of the New Deal agricultural legislation was to protect farmers through extensive government intervention. Some saw this as a needed reform, while others thought it was wasteful and promoted inefficient agricultural choices.

LABOR Anti-labor public officials and public policies had long handicapped organized labor in its relationships with management. The fortunes of labor unions, which were strong supporters of the New Deal, improved significantly in 1935 when Congress passed the National Labor Relations Act. Better known as the Wagner Act after its sponsor, Senator Robert Wagner (D–NY), this statute guaranteed workers' rights to organize and bargain collectively through unions of their own choosing. The act prohibited a series of "unfair labor practices," such as discriminating against employees because of their union activities. The National Labor Relations Board (NLRB) was created to carry out the act and to conduct elections to determine which union, if any, employees wanted to represent them. Unions prospered under the protection provided by the Wagner Act.

The last major piece of New Deal economic legislation passed by Congress was the Fair Labor Standards Act (FLSA) of 1938. Intended to protect the interests of low-paid workers, the law set twenty-five cents per hour and forty-four hours per week as initial minimum standards. Within a few years, wages rose to forty cents per hour, and hours declined to forty per week. The act also banned child labor. The FLSA did not cover all employees, however; it exempted farm workers, domestic workers, and fishermen, for example.

INDUSTRY REGULATIONS During the New Deal, Congress established new or expanded regulatory programs for several industries. The Federal Communications

Commission (FCC), created in 1934 to replace the old Federal Radio Commission, was given extensive jurisdiction over the radio, telephone, and telegraph industries. The Civil Aeronautics Board (CAB) was put in place in 1938 to regulate the commercial aviation industry. The Motor Carrier Act of 1935 put the trucking industry under the jurisdiction of the Interstate Commerce Commission (ICC). Like railroad regulation, the regulation of industries such as trucking and commercial aviation extended to such matters as entry into the business, routes of service, and rates. To a substantial extent, government regulation, as a protector of the public interest, replaced competition in these industries. Supporters of these programs believed they were necessary to prevent destructive or excessive competition. Critics warned that limiting competition resulted in users having to pay more for the services.

THE LEGACY OF THE NEW DEAL ERA   Just as World War I brought down the curtain on the Progressive era, the outbreak of World War II diverted Americans' attention from domestic reform and brought an end to the New Deal era. Many of the New Deal programs, however, became permanent parts of the American public policy landscape. Moreover, the New Deal established the legitimacy and viability of national governmental intervention in the economy. Passive government was replaced with activist government.

The Social Regulation Era

Economists and political scientists frequently distinguish between economic regulation and social regulation. **Economic regulation** focuses on such matters as control of entry into a business, prices or rates businesses charge, and service routes or areas. Economic regulation is usually tailored to the conditions of particular industries, such as railroads or stock exchanges. In contrast, **social regulation** sets standards for the quality and safety of products and the conditions under which goods are produced and services rendered. Social regulation strives to protect and enhance the quality of life.

economic regulation
Government regulation of business practices, industry rates, routes, or areas serviced by particular industries.

social regulation
Government regulation of the quality and safety of products as well as the conditions under which goods and services are produced.

Most of the regulatory programs established through the 1950s fell into the category of economic regulation. From the mid-1960s to the mid-1970s, however, the national government passed social regulatory legislation affecting consumer protection, health and safety, and environmental protection. Congress based this legislation on its commerce clause authority.

This legislation set up several major new regulatory agencies to implement these new social regulations. These agencies include the Consumer Product Safety Commission, the Occupational Safety and Health Administration (OSHA), the Environmental Protection Agency (EPA), the Mining Enforcement and Safety Administration, and the National Transportation Safety Administration (see chapter 9).

The social regulatory statutes took various forms. Some had specific targets and goals, such as the Egg Product Inspection Act and the Lead-Based Paint Poison Prevention Act. Others were loaded with specific standards, deadlines, and instructions for the administering agency. Examples are the Clean Air Act of 1970 (see chapter 17) and the Employee Retirement Income Security Act of 1974 (intended to protect workers' pensions provided by private employers). Other statutes conferred broad substantive discretion on the implementing agency. Thus, the Occupational Safety and Health Act guarantees workers a safe and healthful workplace, but it contains no health and safety standards with which workplaces must comply. These standards are set through rule-making proceedings conducted by the Occupational Safety and Health Administration, which also has responsibility for their enforcement.

As a consequence of this flood of social regulation, many industries that previously had limited dealings with government found they now had to comply with government regulation in the conduct of their operations. For example, the automobile industry, which previously had been lightly touched by anti-trust, labor relations, and

Basic is when a car goes a long way on a little gas.

One of the reasons the Model A was so good was that it gave generous gas mileage. No doubt economy has a lot to do with Pinto's popularity, too. And this year all those extra miles per gallon come with a number of improvements. They're all good reasons why the closer you look, the better we look.

A bigger engine than last year's: First and foremost is a little bigger 2000cc 4-cylinder overhead cam engine as standard. It's been developed for good gas mileage. And for those of you who want even a bit more pep, there's an optional 2300cc engine.

Refined front and rear suspension: We've refined the suspension both front and rear with a new package specifically developed for the '74 model.

(Shown here: 1974 Pinto Sedan, with optional whitewall tires, accent group, and deluxe bumper group.)

Better brakes: Standard front disc brakes for '74 give you efficient and fade resistant braking, and little pedal effort.

Other basics: Still standard for '74 is rack-and-pinion steering, a 4-speed fully synchronized transmission, a body welded into one solid piece of steel, steel guard rails in the doors, and steel reinforcements in the roof.

See the Pinto at your Ford Dealer's: 2-door sedan, 3-door Runabout, and the popular Pinto Wagon. With improved basics for 1974.

When you get back to basics, you get back to Ford.

FORD PINTO
FORD DIVISION *Ford*

Photo courtesy: Gaslight Archives

Why is government regulation needed? The Ford Pinto was manufactured for years despite internal company studies revealing that it had serious safety flaws.

deregulation
A reduction in market controls (such as price fixing, subsidies, or controls on who can enter the field) in favor of market-based competition.

other general statutes, found that its products were now affected by motor vehicle emissions standards and federally mandated safety standards.

Why the surge of social regulation? There are four major reasons.[16] First, the late 1960s and early 1970s were a time of social activism; the consumer and environmental movements were at the peak of their influence. Public interest groups such as the Consumers Union, Common Cause, the Environmental Defense Fund, the Sierra Club, and Ralph Nader's numerous organizations were effective voices for consumer, environmental, and other programs (see chapter 16). Strong support also came from organized labor.

Second, the public had become much more aware of the dangers to health, safety, and the environment associated with various modern products. There was, noted one observer, "a level of public consciousness about environmental, consumer, and occupational hazards that appears to be of a different order of magnitude from public outrage over such issues during both the Progressive era and the New Deal."[17]

Third, members of Congress saw the advocacy of social regulation as a way to gain visibility and national prominence and thus to enhance their election prospects. Senator Edmund Muskie (D–ME), for example, took the lead on environmental issues, while Senator Warren Magnuson (D–WA) successfully pushed for a number of consumer protection laws.

Fourth, the presidents in office during most of this period—the Democrat Lyndon B. Johnson and the Republican Richard M. Nixon—each gave support to the social regulation movement. For them, it was good politics to be in favor of health, safety, and environmental legislation. In most instances, the direct costs to the government of this legislation were minimal.

Deregulation

Beginning in the 1950s and 1960s, economists, political scientists, and journalists began to point out defects in some economic regulatory programs and promoted deregulation of the economy.[18] **Deregulation** is the reduction in market controls (such as price fixing, subsidies, or controls on who can enter the field) in favor of market-based competition. Advocates of deregulation contended that regulation often encouraged lack of competition and monopolistic exploitation, discrimination in services, and inefficiency in operation of regulated industries. For instance, regulatory standards meant that no new major commercial airline was permitted to enter the industry after the Civil Aeronautics Board (CAB) began to regulate the industry in 1938. Consequently, consumers paid higher prices for airfares and had fewer choices than they would in a more competitive market. Critics contended that regulatory commissions like the CAB and the Interstate Commerce Commission were more responsive to the interests of the regulated firms than to the public interest.

For some time, there were no changes in economic regulation despite these criticisms. In the mid-1970s, however, President Gerald R. Ford, seeing regulation as one cause of the high inflation that existed at the time, decided to make deregulation a major objective of his administration. Deregulation was also a high priority for Ford's successor, President Jimmy Carter, and legislation that deregulated commercial airlines, railroads, motor carriers, and financial institutions was enacted during Carter's term as president. All successive presidents have maintained an active deregulatory agenda, though the effects of deregulation have been mixed, as illustrated by the airline, communication, and agricultural sectors.

The Airline Deregulation Act of 1978 completely eliminated economic regulation of commercial airlines over several years. Although many new passenger carriers flocked into the industry when barriers to entry were first removed, they were unable to compete successfully with the existing major airlines. Consequently, there are now fewer major carriers than under the regulatory regime, although new airlines continue to emerge. Competition has lowered some passenger rates, but there is disagreement as to the extent to which passengers have benefited. For example, since enactment of the Airline Deregulation Act, small communities across the United States have been losing service as airlines make major cuts in their routes, despite government subsidies to help maintain service.[19]

As the government removed or modified long-standing regulations in other industries, there was public disagreement over who benefited the most. The landmark Telecommunications Act of 1996 deregulated the radio industry, allowing companies to own an unlimited number of stations nationwide. Deregulation strengthened the position of efficient companies and drove the less efficient into bankruptcy. However, the resulting industry consolidation also resulted in fewer individual owners, less minority ownership, and less diversity of content.

Politicians and citizens alike have expressed concern about concentrated corporate ownership of the media. As Representative Maurice Hinchey (D–NY) wrote in February 2006, "Over the past three decades the number of major U.S. media companies fell by more than half; most of the survivors are controlled by fewer than ten huge media conglomerates."[20] Corporate corruption has also raised concerns about such powerful conglomerates.

In agriculture, too, deregulation has had an impact. In the 1980s and 1990s, agricultural price support programs came under increasing attack from conservatives, who claimed that such government price supports promote inefficiency. Republicans, who took control of Congress in 1995, sought to phase out crop supports as part of the effort to curb federal spending. In 1996, Congress passed a landmark agriculture bill with the aim of phasing out crop subsidies by the year 2002 and making prices more dependent upon the workings of the free market. By 1997, however, Congress was moving away from the intent of the bill, appropriating significant sums of money to rescue farmers from bad weather, crop disease, and falling commodity prices. The 2002 farm bill actually increased agricultural subsidies by 70 percent as part of a ten-year, $180 billion package. The political pressure coming from large-scale farms and agribusinesses was obvious. According to one analyst, "Nearly three-quarters of these funds will go to the wealthiest 10 percent of farmers—most of whom earn more than $250,000 per year."[21]

Price supports and tariffs are other targets of those who favor deregulation in the agricultural sector. In 2005, the U.S. government spent approximately $21 billion in price supports for agricultural products. U.S. Trade Representative Rob Portman proposed reducing that figure to $12 billion, provided the European Union (EU), Japan, and other nations

Can regulations have unintended effects? Major U.S. airlines experienced massive flight cancellations when federal regulators stepped up scrutiny of aircraft inspections after years of more lenient enforcement. How can airlines balance the need for safety without disrupting the flow of business?

Photo courtesy: Justin Sullivan/Getty Images

Photo courtesy: Time Life Pictures/Getty Images

Who was John Maynard Keynes? British economist John Maynard Keynes led a revolution in economics, arguing that government deficit spending during economic downturns could stimulate spending and lead to recovery.

economic stability
A situation in which there is economic growth, rising national income, high employment, and steadiness in the general level of prices.

inflation
A rise in the general price levels of an economy.

recession
A short-term decline in the economy that occurs as investment sags, production falls off, and unemployment increases.

also lowered trade barriers. The United States, the EU, and many poorer nations have kept farm tariffs at an average of 40 percent, which is significantly higher than the approximately 5 percent average tariffs levied on manufactured goods.[22] As U.S. Trade Representative Susan Schwab noted in September 2006, "we are willing to do more in terms of cutting our agricultural support, but we could only do so in response to more market access." She also remarked that the United States had signaled its flexibility.[23] It remains to be seen whether the government can deregulate the agriculture sector effectively in spite of powerful political pressure to distort market prices through subsidies and tariff protection. In the domestic market, the Bush administration failed to convince Congress to reduce subsidies to big farms in the debate leading up to the passage of the April 2008 farm bill.

In spite of the mixed record, economic deregulation has remained a top policy priority among American politicians. The same cannot be said of deregulation efforts in the social sphere. Strong support continues for social regulation to protect consumers, workers, and the environment. Moreover, in some areas in which economic deregulation occurred, there have been calls to "reregulate." This has occurred in the airline industry because of concern about safety and industry domination by a small number of companies. As discussed later in the chapter, the subprime mortgage crisis that developed in 2007 brought new calls for reregulation in the mortgage sector.

Stabilizing the Economy

Until the early 1930s, the prevailing view in the United States was that government intervention in the economy could disrupt natural economic laws but could not improve them. The massive scale and the persistence of the Great Depression challenged that notion, as the economic doctrine promoted by the English economist John Maynard Keynes gained more traction. In his *General Theory of Employment, Interests, and Money* (1936), Keynes argued that deficit spending by a government could supplement the total or aggregate demand for goods and services, especially during recessions. The government's intervention in the economy rose with the New Deal and World War II. The economy expanded, production rose, and unemployment fell to less than 2 percent. But the budget deficit grew. The government had essentially assumed responsibility for economic stability.

Economic stability is a condition in which there is economic growth, a rising national income, high employment, and a steadiness in the general level of prices. Conversely, economic instability involves either inflation or recession. **Inflation** occurs when there is too much demand for the available supply of goods and services, with the consequence that general price levels rise as buyers compete for the available supply. Prices may also rise if large corporations and unions have sufficient economic power to push prices and wages above competitive levels. A **recession** is marked by a decline in the economy. Investment sags, production falls off, and unemployment increases.

The government manages the economy through monetary and fiscal policies. Monetary policies influence the economy through changes in the money supply, while fiscal policies influence the behavior of consumers and businesses through government spending and taxing decisions. The economic slowdown of late 2007 and early 2008 resulted in an active use of monetary and fiscal policy tools to help the economy rebound. Stories in the media focused on a series of interest rate cuts and a fiscal stimulus package designed to avert a recession. The following section explains how the government uses these policy tools for macroeconomic management and stabilization.

Monetary Policy: Controlling the Money Supply

The government conducts **monetary policy** by managing the nation's money supply and influencing interest rates. In an industrialized economy, all those making exchanges—consumers, businesses, and government—use money. That is, prices of goods and services are set in **money** units (dollars), and the amount of money in circulation influences the quantity of goods and services demanded, the number of workers hired, the decisions to build factories, and so on. Money is more than just the currency and coin in our pockets: it includes balances in our checkbooks, deposits in bank accounts, and the value of other assets.

The Federal Reserve System is responsible for changing the money supply. As it makes these changes, it attempts to promote economic stability. The **Board of Governors** has responsibility for the formation and implementation of monetary policy because of its ability to control the credit-creating and lending activities of the nation's banks. When individuals and corporations deposit their money in financial institutions such as commercial banks (which accept deposits and make loans) and savings and loan associations, these deposits serve as the basis for loans to borrowers. In effect, the loaning of money creates new deposits or financial liabilities—new money that did not previously exist. But, we are getting ahead of our story. First, we'll look at the Federal Reserve System and its authority.

THE FEDERAL RESERVE SYSTEM   Created in 1913 to adjust the money supply to the needs of agriculture, commerce, and industry, the Federal Reserve System comprises the Federal Reserve Board (FRB—formally, the Board of Governors of the Federal Reserve System; informally, "the Fed"), the Federal Open Market Committee (FOMC), the twelve Federal Reserve Banks in regions throughout the country, and other member banks.[24] (To learn more about the organization of the Federal Reserve System, see Figure 18.1.)

The president appoints (subject to Senate confirmation) the seven members of the Board of Governors, who serve fourteen-year, overlapping terms. The president can remove a member for stated causes, but this has never occurred. The president designates one board member to serve as chair for a four-year term, which runs from the midpoint of one presidential term to the midpoint of the next to ensure economic stability during a change of administrations. The current chair, Ben Bernanke, was sworn in on February 1, 2006. Prior to this appointment, he served as chair of President George W. Bush's Council of Economic Advisers. Formally, the FRB has much independence from the executive branch, ostensibly so that monetary policy will not be influenced by political considerations. Defenders of the FRB's independent position assert that monetary policy is too important, complex, and technical to be under the day-to-day control of elected public officials, who might be inclined to make inflationary monetary decisions to advance their own short-term political interests (such as being reelected).

Bernanke's prior position at the White House may raise some skeptical eyebrows regarding the Fed's independence from the current administration. It should be noted, however, that his predecessor at the Fed, Alan Greenspan, served during Republican and Democratic administrations for almost two decades. Greenspan, like Bernanke, had also served as a chair of the Council of Economic Advisers (under President Gerald R. Ford). It is expected that Bernanke, like Greenspan before him, will pursue monetary policies that foster low-inflation along with macroeconomic growth over the long term, and that he will withstand political pressure from the White House and Congress.

monetary policy
A form of government regulation in which the nation's money supply and interest rates are controlled.

money
A system of exchange for goods and services that includes currency, coins, and bank deposits.

Board of Governors
In the Federal Reserve System, a seven-member board that sets member banks' reserve requirements, controls the discount rate, and makes other economic decisions.

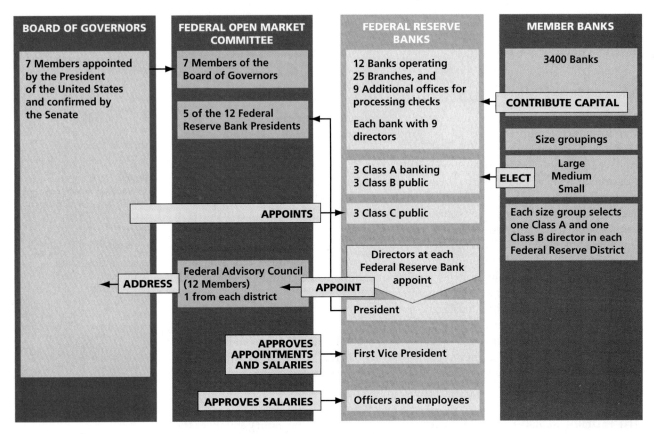

FIGURE 18.1 The Federal Reserve System

Source: Board of Governors of the Federal Reserve System.

At the base of the Federal Reserve System are the twelve Federal Reserve Banks. These are "bankers' banks"; they are formally owned by the Federal Reserve System member banks in each region, and they do not do business with the public.

Monetary authority is allocated to the FRB, the Federal Reserve Bank boards of directors, and the FOMC. In actuality, however, all three are dominated by the FRB and its chair. Public officials and the financial community pay great attention to the utterances of the Fed's chair for clues to the future course of monetary policy. The primary monetary policy tools are the setting of reserve requirements for member banks, control of the discount rate, and open market operations.

Reserve requirements set by the Federal Reserve designate the portion of the banks' deposits that most banks must retain as backing for their loans. The reserves determine how much or how little banks can lend to businesses and consumers. For example, if the FRB changed the reserve requirements and allowed banks to keep $10 on hand rather than $15 for every $100 in deposits that it held, it would free up some additional money for loans. The **discount rate** is the rate of interest at which the Federal Reserve Board lends money to member banks. Lowering the discount rate would encourage local member banks to increase their borrowing from the Fed and extend more loans at lower rates. This would expand economic activity, since when rates are lower, more people should be able to qualify for large purchases by taking out car loans or housing mortgages. As a consequence of cheaper interest rates, more large durable goods (such as houses and cars) should be produced and sold.

In **open market operations**, the FRB buys and sells government securities in the open market. The Federal Open Market Committee meets periodically to decide on purchases or sale of government securities to member banks. When member banks

reserve requirements
Government requirements that a portion of member banks' deposits must be retained to back loans made.

discount rate
The rate of interest at which member banks can borrow money from their regional Federal Reserve Bank.

open market operations
The buying and selling of government securities by the Federal Reserve Bank in the securities market.

How important is the chair of the Federal Reserve to the nation's economic well-being? Ben Bernanke, center, after President George W. Bush announced his nomination to replace Federal Reserve Board Chair Alan Greenspan, at left.

buy long-term government bonds, they make dollar payments to the Fed and reduce the amount of money available for loans. Fed purchases of securities from member banks in essence give the banks an added supply of money. This action increases the availability of loans and should decrease interest rates. Decreases in interest rates stimulate economic activity.

The FRB can also use "moral suasion" to influence the actions of banks and other members of the financial community by suggestion, exhortation, and informal agreement. Because of its commanding position as a monetary policy maker, the media, economists, and market observers pay attention to verbal signals about economic trends and conditions emitted by the FRB and its chair.

How the FRB uses these tools depends in part on its views of the state of the economy. If inflation appears to be the problem, then the Fed would likely restrict or tighten the money supply. If a recession with rising unemployment appears to threaten the economy, then the FRB would probably act to loosen or expand the money supply in order to stimulate the economy.

As mentioned at the beginning of this chapter, the recent economic slowdown led the Fed to lower interest rates at a rapid rate. The Fed's February 2008 report to Congress notes that, in response to the mortgage and financial market turbulence, it engaged in large open market operations and discount rate reductions to increase liquidity in the markets.[25] The Fed announced that in March 2008, it would inject about $200 billion into the U.S. banking system by offering banks low-interest, one-month loans to ease the tightening credit conditions. The Fed would lend another $100 billion through its open market operations to a few dozen major investment banks, who could secure these loans by mortgage-backed

Thinking Globally

Economic Freedom

We can learn how hospitable a country is to business by looking at the rankings of countries on the Economic Freedom of the World index prepared by the Economic Freedom network (www.freetheworld .com). Hong Kong has the highest rating for economic freedom, followed by Singapore. Nations with the least economic freedom include Zimbabwe, Myanmar (Burma), and Venezuela.

- According to the authors of the index, economic freedom is defined by personal choice, voluntary exchange, freedom to compete, and security of privately owned property. What other factors might help to define economic freedom around the world?
- Canada, Great Britain, and the United States all scored an 8.1 (out of 10) on the 2007 economic freedom index. Estonia, a former Soviet republic, scored an 8.0. Is it surprising that a formerly communist-controlled country ranks so closely to long-standing democracies in terms of its business climate? Why or why not?

securities issued by government-sponsored mortgage companies like Freddie Mac and Fannie Mae. The Fed sent clear signals that it is willing to inject larger sums of money, should the need arise, for mortgage lending and for the financial system as a whole to stave off a recession.[26] Heated political debates continue over whether big business or the public at large benefits from the Fed's monetary policy responses to the economic slowdown.

THE FRB AND THE EXECUTIVE AND LEGISLATIVE BRANCHES   Although the public generally holds the president responsible for maintaining a healthy economy, he does not really possess adequate constitutional or legal authority to meet this obligation. The president shares responsibility for fiscal policy with Congress, and Congress authorizes the FRB to make monetary policy. In terms of pressing the Fed to adjust its monetary policy, presidential power is, at its best, "the power to persuade." There are many formal and informal contacts between the White House and the FRB, however, to discuss monetary policy. During formal meetings, the FRB chair can convey some of his views on the economy to the administration. The result is that the president customarily accepts the monetary policy made by the FRB, even if it is not precisely what he would prefer.[27]

Fiscal Policy: Taxing and Spending

fiscal policy
Federal government policies on taxes, spending, and debt management, intended to promote the nation's macroeconomic goals, particularly with respect to employment, price stability, and growth.

Fiscal policy is the deliberate use of the national government's taxing and spending policies to influence the overall operation of the economy and maintain economic stability. The president and Congress formulate fiscal policy and conduct it through the federal budget process. The powerful instruments of fiscal policy are budget surpluses and deficits. These are achieved by manipulating the overall or "aggregate" levels of revenue and expenditures.

According to the Keynesian theory behind fiscal policy, there is a level of total or aggregate spending at which the economy will operate at full employment. Total spending is the sum of consumer spending, private investment spending, and government spending. If consumer and business spending does not create demand sufficient to cause the economy to operate at full employment, then the government should make up the shortfall by increasing spending in excess of revenues. This was essentially what Keynes recommended for the national government during the Great Depression. If inflation is the problem confronting policy makers, then government can reduce demand for goods and services by reducing its expenditures and running a budget surplus.[28]

One type of fiscal policy is discretionary fiscal policy, which involves deliberate decisions by the president and Congress to run budget surpluses or deficits. This can be done by increasing or decreasing spending while holding taxes constant, by increasing or cutting taxes while holding spending stable, or by some combination of changes in taxing and spending. (To learn more about how taxes affect you individually, see Ideas into Action: Discovering Your Tax Burden.)

The first significant application of fiscal policy theory occurred in 1964. President John F. Kennedy, a Democrat committed to getting the country "moving again," brought Keynesian economists to Washington as his economic advisers. These advisers believed that increased government spending, even at the expense of an increase in the budget deficit, was needed to stimulate the economy in order to achieve full employment. Many conservatives opposed budget deficits as bad public policy. President Kennedy's advisers decided that many conservatives and members of the business community would find deficits more palatable, or less objectionable, if they were achieved by cutting taxes rather than by increasing government spending. Furthermore, a tax cut, they reasoned, would increase private-sector spending on goods and services.

Ideas Into Action

Discovering Your Tax Burden

It's no secret that Americans complain about paying taxes. But, while few Americans relish filing a tax return, fewer still actually track the total tax burden placed on them by federal, state, and local governments. Income taxes, sales taxes, property taxes, municipal taxes, and wage taxes all contribute revenue that governments use to provide services for their citizens. The number and type of taxes that affect Americans vary dramatically, depending on where they live.

If you live in New Hampshire, for example, you don't pay any sales taxes, but you do pay some of the highest property taxes in the country. Drivers in San Francisco pay the highest taxes in the nation to fill up their gas tanks. In Chicago, smokers pay more taxes than any other Americans for engaging in that particular vice.

Identify the types of taxes that are levied in your state and municipality. Then, consider the following questions:

- At the Tax Foundation site **www.taxfoundation.org**, examine the data on taxes in your state and municipality. What taxes are placed on individuals in your municipality? How many of those taxes did you pay last year? What is the total amount of taxes that you paid last year, including income taxes, property taxes, excise taxes, and sales taxes?

- What benefits and services do you receive for the taxes that you pay? Consider local and state services (e.g., garbage collection, police and fire protection, education) and federal services (e.g., health care and income security). Do you believe that the benefits of government are worth the financial impact of the taxes you pay? Why or why not?

- To learn more about debates related to tax policy, go to the following Web sites:

  www.taxpolicycenter.org, a joint effort sponsored by the Urban Institute and Brookings Institution.

  www.taxfoundation.org, the site of a tax research organization based in Washington, D.C.

  www.atr.org, site of Americans for Tax Reform, a conservative, anti-tax lobbying organization.

  www.americanprogress.org, site of the Center for American Progress, a liberal think tank.

The result was the adoption of the Revenue Act of 1964, which reduced personal and corporate income tax rates. This variant of fiscal policy, which was more acceptable to business, has been labeled "commercial Keynesianism." The tax-cut stimulus contributed to the expansion of the economy through the remainder of the 1960s and reduced the unemployment rate to less than 4 percent, its lowest peacetime rate and what many people then considered to be full employment.[29] President Reagan in 1981 and President George W. Bush in 2001 and 2003 pushed tax cuts through Congress in part to stimulate a faltering economy.

There remains a serious partisan division over tax politics. By and large, Republicans have remained steadfast supporters of tax cuts, while Democrats have remained committed to tax revenues as the means of funding government programs. In September 1999, President Bill Clinton vetoed a $792 billion tax-cut proposal backed by Republicans because he considered it "wrong for Medicare, wrong for Social Security, wrong for education and wrong for the economy."[30] In May 2006, President George W. Bush was pressing for action on stalled legislation that would ensure a 15 percent tax rate on dividends and capital gains through 2010. In his words, "tax increase would be disastrous for business, disastrous for families, and disastrous for the economy."[31] Democrats argued that the proposed tax legislation overwhelmingly benefited wealthy investors and not the middle class. Partisan divisions notwithstanding, a Democratic-led Congress approved President Bush's $168 billion economic stimulus package in February 2008 in response to the economic downturn. The measure provided rebate checks to low- and middle-income citizens and tax breaks to businesses for investment on new equipment. It also made more mortgages available through government-sponsored mortgage-financing companies.

Join the Debate

Economic Stimulus Payments

OVERVIEW: In April and May 2008, the U.S. government sent checks to individual taxpayers in an attempt to stimulate the economy and keep it from going into a long and harsh recession. The economy was steadily declining. Workers were losing their jobs. Spending—except on food and gasoline—was going down. Families were not able to make mortgage payments and were losing their homes. These factors lowered demand for more goods, which meant businesses cut back production, leading to more workers laid off, which meant less consumer spending and more foreclosures. In an attempt to stop the cycle, Congress and President George W. Bush agreed to fund a $168 billion package that included the checks to taxpayers, some tax incentives for business investments, and increased guarantees to lenders of home mortgages.

The purpose of the 2008 stimulus payments was to encourage lower- and middle-income people to spend money. The checks went to those who filed a tax return for 2007 and earned at least $3,000 if single and $6,000 if filing jointly as a married couple. Most who received a check got $600, or $1,200 if filing jointly. If someone earned more than $75,000 ($150,000 if married) in 2007, the check was for increasingly reduced amounts ($30 less for each $1,000 above $75,000), and the wealthy got nothing. Each dependent child generated an additional $300 payment.

The political calculus for sending money back to taxpayers seemed clear. Symbolically, policy makers were signaling that they were concerned and doing something to improve the economy generally and the fate of individuals specifically. This stimulus package, in contrast to some previous tax cuts, targeted benefits for the majority of wage earners instead of the rich.

What was less clear was the economic calculus. How far would a $600 check go in stimulating growth in jobs and businesses? Especially given higher food and fuel prices, would consumers be able to buy a new car or kitchen appliance? Was $600 going to be enough to keep someone from defaulting on a home mortgage? Would people use their check to pay off some of their credit card debt instead of buying something new?

The Congressional Budget Office reviewed the history of previous programs similar to the 2008 payment approach. They found that consumers spent only 12 to 24 percent of the money they received in 1975 and 20 to 40 percent in 2001. The intended impact on the economy, in other words, was modest, but there was some effect. The CBO testimony prompted some legislators to propose even more targeted relief through extending eligibility for unemployment compensation for those laid off from their jobs and through expanding the food stamp program. The majority of representatives and senators rejected these proposals though the global financial crisis that began in late 2008 put all options back on the table.

Arguments IN FAVOR of Economic Stimulus Payments

- **The government can and should act to keep an economic downturn from turning into a long and harsh recession. By making it possible**

The design of the stimulus package did not please all parties. The Democratic-leaning Economic Policy Institute and the nonpartisan Congressional Budget Office both favored direct aid to low-income families through unemployment benefit and food stamps as more effective ways to stimulate the economy. Republicans were adamantly against unemployment benefits.[32] It is clear that fiscal policy as a tool for government regulation of the economy elicits partisan disagreements. (To learn more about debates related to government stimulus plans, see Join the Debate: Economic Stimulus Payments.)

The latest use of monetary and fiscal policy tools tests the economic policy makers' ability to smooth out business cycles and revive business and customer confidence.

for people to spend more money, the demand for goods will increase and thus spark growth in jobs and the economy. When a cycle of layoffs and lower spending has begun, government action can halt that dynamic. Stimulus payments not only help workers, businesses, and investors but also yield increased tax revenues that may more than offset the costs of the stimulus package.

■ **Economic stimulus efforts directed to low- and middle-income families are effective.** Stimulus payments sent to low- and middle-income taxpayers are likely to be spent immediately. An uptick in consumer spending is exactly what is needed to avoid further economic downturn.

■ **The stimulus payments send an important message to consumers, businesses, and investors.** Adopting a stimulus program allows Congress and the president to reassure citizens that the health of the economy is a concern and that it is being addressed. To do nothing erodes confidence and contributes to a continued decline in the economy.

Arguments AGAINST Economic Stimulus Payments

■ **It is a mistake for government to interfere with market forces.**

Economic woes require economic adjustments, not government intervention. A downturn in the economy is due to a variety of factors, like foreign competition, unsound lending practices, and labor and production inefficiencies. The artificial injection of spending money by the government diverts attention from the real problems.

■ **An indebted government is in no position to indebt itself further with stimulus spending.** Deficit spending—spending more money than is available—is irresponsible and passes on to future generations the burdens and challenges posed by a large and growing debt. With the national debt over $9.3 trillion in 2008, the economic stimulus package may have made political sense but could not be justified economically.

■ **Stimulus payments are more likely to be spent on rising food and fuel costs and on credit card debt than on purchases that stimulate the economy.** Low- and middle-income families will use their $600 stimulus check to pay for food or gasoline or some other basic necessity rather than for a new purchase. The government can help distressed individuals more directly by extending unemployment compensation or providing food stamp supplements. If the objective

is to help businesses, significant measures to adjust to foreign competition or solve other problems would be the better course.

Continuing the Debate

1. Should the government try to stimulate economic activity by sending people a check? Does this approach divert attention from the real reasons for an economic downturn? Explain your answers.

2. Is it likely that $600 or $1,200 checks will be spent on new purchases that will spark economic growth, or is it more likely that the money will be used for other purposes? Are there more effective approaches to halting a downturn? Explain.

To Follow the Debate Online, Go To:

www.cbo.gov, where the Congressional Budget Office has a series of studies and reports on economic stimulus proposals.

www.brookings.edu, for Brookings Institution reports and testimony supporting the 2008 economic stimulus legislation of the federal government.

www.epi.org, the Web site of the Economic Policy Institute, a nonpartisan, nonprofit organization that raised concerns about the 2008 stimulus package.

Policy makers and experts continue to debate the degree and effectiveness of government regulation of the economy during times of economic prosperity and downturns.

The Effects of Globalization

Before we turn to how the budgetary process works, it is important to consider another context for fiscal policy: the international economy. Advances in transportation, communication, and technology have strengthened the link between the United States and the rest of the world. International affairs influence business decisions of American companies that wish to reduce labor costs as well as expand their markets.

Comparing Economic Policy

Free trade has, on balance, had a beneficial impact on the U.S. economy because the competition created by free trade limits price increases on American goods and services, thereby benefiting consumers. In addition, free trade expands the market for high-quality American products that are in demand in the global economy. By 1999, the U.S. economy was enjoying more than eight years of uninterrupted growth, the third longest expansion in the nation's history. Reflecting this growth, the stock market soared by more than 300 percent between 1990 and 1999. Many believed that the higher stock prices were driven by lower labor costs and the relocation of manufacturing to low-wage nations. Lower labor costs can expand profits, which drive stock prices higher.

The 2001 recession did not immediately dampen the enthusiasm for economic globalization. Between July 2000 and January 2004, however, the manufacturing sector lost 3 million jobs. This trend cannot be explained exclusively by globalization and international trade. Productivity gains in the manufacturing sector, a shift in U.S. consumer demand away from manufactured goods, the rising U.S. trade deficit, and the outsourcing of manufacturing jobs help explain the loss of jobs over the past decades.[33] It is overseas competition, however, that is the frequent target of labor unions and politicians who favor protectionism over free trade. **Protectionism** is governmental intervention to set up barriers to international trade, such as tariffs or restrictions on the quantity of imports, in order to protect domestic industry from foreign competition. (To learn one commentator's opinion about the globalization debate, see Politics Now: Is Globalization to Blame for America's Economic Woes?)

Labor unions in the United States are among the strongest critics of free trade. Union leaders warn that free trade with nations such as China or Mexico means that American workers must compete against workers in nations where wages are low, where human rights violations exist, and where environmental restrictions are ineffective or nonexistent. They argue that opening up production to large infusions of new workers drives down wages in the higher-cost nation while improving wages in the lower-cost countries. Union leaders have also stressed the need to restrict "dumping" low-priced foreign goods onto American markets and the need to open other nations to more American goods.

Loss of real, or inflation-adjusted, income has become a serious concern in the United States. In September 1997, the hourly minimum wage was raised from $4.75 to $5.15. It was increased to $5.85 in July 2007 and $6.55 in July 2008. The minimum wage was slated to increase to $7.25 in July 2009. Yet, inflation since 1997 has devalued the wages of many. One analysis estimates a 4 percent loss of real median American household income from 2000 to 2004, in spite of economic expansion in the years of 2002, 2003, and 2004. The same analysis posited that only the top 5 percent of households gained in real income in the 2003–2004 fiscal year, while 5.4 million more Americans fell into poverty between 2000 and 2004.[34] Figure 18.2 shows the growth of the minimum wage since its creation. According to one study, the inflation-adjusted average hourly wage for production workers rose by 75 percent between 1949 and 1979. The same wage rate increased by only 2 percent between 1979 and 2005.[35] According to the Congressional Budget Office, the share of national income of the wealthiest quintile of households increased from 45.4 percent in 1979 to 54.1 percent in 2005. Over the same period, the share of the bottom quintile dropped from 5.8 percent to 4.1 percent.

A number of analysts have warned of globalization's impact on income distribution. Globalization appears to further segment the market into economic winners and losers. During the 1990s, Fortune 500 companies achieved huge gains, yet many of those gains appeared to come at the expense of smaller businesses and workers. In 1999, analysts found that the average real after-tax income of the middle 60 percent of Americans was lower than it was in 1977.[36] In 1990, the income of American CEOs

protectionism
Governmental intervention to set up barriers to international trade, such as tariffs or restrictions on the quantity of imports, in order to protect domestic industry from foreign competition.

POLITICS NOW

Source: NEW YORK TIMES   May 2, 2008

Is Globalization to Blame for America's Economic Woes?

The Cognitive Age

DAVID BROOKS

If you go into a good library, you will find thousands of books on globalization. Some will laud it. Some will warn about its dangers. But they'll agree that globalization is the chief process driving our age. Our lives are being transformed by the increasing movement of goods, people and capital across borders.

The globalization paradigm has led, in the political arena, to a certain historical narrative: There were once nation-states like the U.S. and the European powers, whose economies could be secured within borders. But now capital flows freely. Technology has leveled the playing field. Competition is global and fierce.

New dynamos like India and China threaten American dominance thanks to their cheap labor and manipulated currencies. Now, everything is made abroad. American manufacturing is in decline. The rest of the economy is threatened.

Hillary Clinton summarized the narrative this week: "They came for the steel companies and nobody said anything. They came for the auto companies and nobody said anything. They came for the office companies, people who did white-collar service jobs, and no one said anything. And they came for the professional jobs that could be outsourced, and nobody said anything."

The globalization paradigm has turned out to be very convenient for politicians. It allows them to blame foreigners for economic woes. It allows them to pretend that by rewriting trade deals, they can assuage economic anxiety. It allows them to treat economic and social change as a great mercantilist competition, with various teams competing for global supremacy, and with politicians starring as the commanding generals.

But there's a problem with the way the globalization paradigm has evolved. It doesn't really explain most of what is happening in the world.

Globalization is real and important. It's just not the central force driving economic change. Some Americans have seen their jobs shipped overseas, but global competition has accounted for a small share of job creation and destruction over the past few decades. Capital does indeed flow around the world. But as Pankaj Ghemawat of the Harvard Business School has observed, 90 percent of fixed investment around the world is domestic. Companies open plants overseas, but that's mainly so their production facilities can be close to local markets.

Nor is the globalization paradigm even accurate when applied to manufacturing. Instead of fleeing to Asia, U.S. manufacturing output is up over recent decades. As Thomas Duesterberg of Manufacturers Alliance/MAPI, a research firm, has pointed out, the U.S.'s share of global manufacturing output has actually increased slightly since 1980.

The chief force reshaping manufacturing is technological change (hastened by competition with other companies in Canada, Germany or down the street). Thanks to innovation, manufacturing productivity has doubled over two decades. Employers now require fewer but more highly skilled workers. Technological change affects China just as it does the Americas. William Overholt of the RAND Corporation has noted that between 1994 and 2004 the Chinese shed 25 million manufacturing jobs, 10 times more than the U.S.

The central process driving this is not globalization. It's the skills revolution. We're moving into a more demanding cognitive age. In order to thrive, people are compelled to become better at absorbing, processing and combining information. This is happening in localized and globalized sectors, and it would be happening even if you tore up every free trade deal ever inked.

The globalization paradigm emphasizes the fact that information can now travel 15,000 miles in an instant. But the most important part of information's journey is the last few inches—the space between a person's eyes or ears and the various regions of the brain. Does the individual have the capacity to understand the information? Does he or she have the training to exploit it? Are there cultural assumptions that distort the way it is perceived?

The globalization paradigm leads people to see economic development as a form of foreign policy, as a grand competition between nations and civilizations. These abstractions, called "the Chinese" or "the Indians," are doing this or that. But the cognitive age paradigm emphasizes psychology, culture and pedagogy—the specific processes that foster learning. It emphasizes that different societies are being stressed in similar ways by increased demands on human capital. If you understand that you are living at the beginning of a cognitive age, you're focusing on the real source of prosperity and understand that your anxiety is not being caused by a foreigner.

It's not that globalization and the skills revolution are contradictory processes. But which paradigm you embrace determines which facts and remedies you emphasize. Politicians, especially Democratic ones, have fallen in love with the globalization paradigm. It's time to move beyond it.

Discussion Questions

1. *Should the United States revert to protectionist policies to save American jobs? Explain your reasoning.*

2. *What is the role of investments in education in the midst of a "skills revolution?"*

3. *How does columnist David Brooks, a conservative, differentiate the cognitive age paradigm from the globalization paradigm? Do you agree with his assumptions and arguments? Why or why not?*

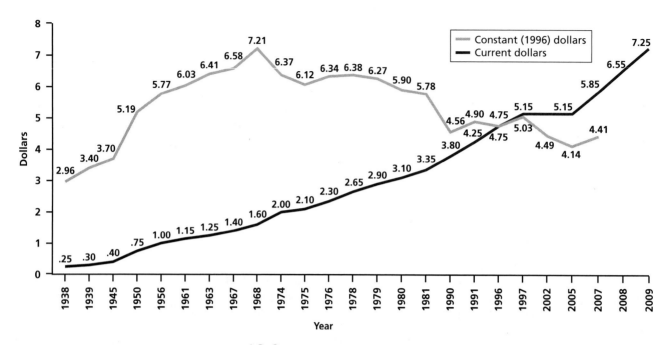

FIGURE 18.2 **Growth in the Minimum Wage over Time** The minimum wage rose from 25 cents an hour in 1938 to $5.85 in 2007. Once inflation is considered, however, workers earned their highest minimum wages in the 1960s and 1970s.

was 107 times higher than that of the average worker; in 2005, it was 411 times more.[37] In general, economists do not share the protectionist views expressed by unions and some politicians. A member of President Bush's Council of Economic Advisers stated in January 2006: "There are many here in Washington and elsewhere who are calling for more barriers to international commerce. These calls for protectionism are at odds with the evidence that decades of trade liberalization have played an important role in helping raise average U.S. living standards. American companies that are globally engaged—through exporting, importing, and foreign direct investment—tend to be the most-productive, highest-paying companies in the United States."[38]

The increased interdependence of economies in an age of globalization suggests that U.S. economic fortunes are more intensively tied to global economic factors. The world GDP share of a group of ten East Asian and South Asian economies (the Asia-10) increased from under 25 percent to 36 percent from 1985 to 2005. At the same time, the U.S. share dropped from about 22 percent to 20 percent, while the European Union's share fell from 24 percent to 19 percent.[39]

Emerging economies like China, India, and Brazil are continuing to post robust growth rates, driven by strong domestic demand and fiscal solvency. Oil-rich countries are also posting large surpluses. The United States, on the other hand, has been running persistent current account deficits. Foreigners held over $14 trillion in U.S. assets in mid-2007. This figure was greater than

Thinking Globally

China's Industrialization

China's emergence as a major economic power has not been without cost. Rapid and unregulated industrialization has created unprecedented environmental degradation. Pollution has made cancer China's leading cause of death. Yet, China has declined to use the kind of tax policies and market-oriented incentives for conservation that have worked well in Japan and many European countries. Severe water shortages have turned farmland into desert, many citizens lack access to safe drinking water, and much of the coastline is so swamped by algal red tides that large sections of the ocean no longer sustain marine life.

- Is it possible for a large country such as China to maintain strong economic growth while improving its environmental track record? If not, why not? If so, how?
- What types of government policies work best to regulate unwanted outcomes, such as pollution, food contamination, and unsafe consumer products? Do the types of effective policies depend on the type of government in place? Why or why not?

the U.S. **gross domestic product (GDP)**,—the GDP is the total market value of all goods and services produced during a year. A significant portion of America's deficit is financed by foreign states. Foreigners, primarily central banks and government investment funds, held over $2.6 trillion in U.S. Treasury securities in 2008.[40] These holdings increased from 13 percent of the total in 1988 to about 27 percent in 2008.[41] The growing influence of sovereign wealth funds—the investment arms of states with huge surpluses—on the U.S. economy is obvious and worrying for those concerned with relative loss of economic dominance and sovereignty. The alarming Fall 2008 economic crisis that began in the U.S. credit markets and spread swiftly throughout the globe raised a different perspective on the greater economic interdependence that has resulted from globalization: when a large economy like that of the United States suffers a major shock, the fallout will have a severe impact on the global economy.

gross domestic product (GDP)
The total market value of all goods and services produced in a country during a year.

The Budget Process

The primary purpose of the federal budget is funding government programs, but manipulating the budget can also be used as part of fiscal policy to stabilize the economy and to counteract fluctuations. Because federal budget planning begins roughly a year and a half before the beginning of the fiscal year in which it takes effect, its immediate influence on the economy is limited. Once a budget is adopted, it takes time to implement the provisions. Because of the difficulty in predicting the future, the budget is not a precise instrument for manipulating the economy. Furthermore, the budget process is complex and disjointed.

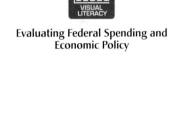

Evaluating Federal Spending and Economic Policy

HOW THE FEDERAL GOVERNMENT RAISES AND SPENDS MONEY The federal government raises money from a variety of sources, with individual income taxes and social insurance and retirement receipts representing over 80 percent of the funds received. (To learn more, see Figure 18.3.) Social insurance and retirement receipts include Social Security, hospital insurance, and other taxes. Between 1991 and 2001, individual income taxes rose from 44.3 percent of total receipts to 49.9 percent. By calendar year 2007, due primarily to tax cuts supported by the Bush administration, individual income taxes accounted for 45.3 percent of total federal government income.[42]

Most government spending is directed toward national defense and human resources. Defense spending consists primarily of maintaining the U.S. armed forces and developing the weapons the military needs. Human resources include the spending categories of health, income security, and Social Security. The human resources share of total outlays grew significantly from its 1991 share of 52.1 percent to 63 percent in calendar year 2006. The projected outlays for 2008 stood at 63.1 percent.[43]

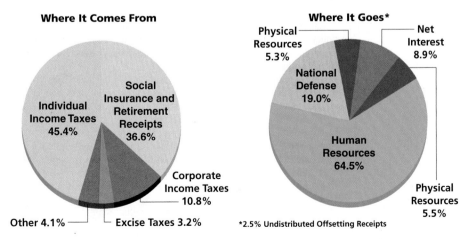

FIGURE **18.3** Receipts and Outlays of the Federal Government

Source: United States Budget, Fiscal Year 2006, www.gpoaccess.gov.

CONGRESS AND THE BUDGET PROCESS   The Budget and Accounting Act of 1921 gave the president authority to prepare an annual budget and submit it to Congress for approval. A staff agency now called the Office of Management and Budget (OMB) was created to assist the president and handle the details of budget preparation (see also chapter 8). The budget runs for a single fiscal year, beginning on October 1 of one calendar year and running through September 30 of the following calendar year. The fiscal year takes its name from the calendar year in which it ends; thus the time period from October 1, 2008, through September 30, 2009, is designated fiscal year (FY) 2009.

The president sends a budget proposal to Congress in January or February of each year. (To learn more, see Table 18.1.) Work on the budget within the executive branch will have begun nine or ten months earlier, however. Acting in accordance with presidential decisions on the general structure of the budget, the OMB provides the various departments and agencies with instructions and guidance on presidential priorities to help them in preparing their budget requests. The departments and agencies then proceed to develop their detailed funding requests. The OMB reconciles the discrepancies between presidential and agency preferences, but it should be remembered that the OMB's mission is to defend the presidential budgetary agenda.[44]

Article I of the Constitution provides that "no money shall be drawn from the Treasury, but in consequence of appropriations made by law." Congress and its legislative committees (such as those on resources, education and educational opportunities, and national security) may authorize spending on programs, but it is Congress and the appropriations committees in each chamber that actually provide the funding needed to carry out these programs. The appropriations committees often deny some, and once in a while all, of the funding authorized by the legislative committees. Consequently, the legislative committees sometimes have resorted to backdoor spending—authorizing agencies to borrow money from the Treasury or creating entitlement programs that make funding mandatory in order to circumvent the appropriations committees.[45]

To give itself more control over the budget process, Congress initiated and enacted the Budget and Impoundment Control Act of 1974. The act establishes a budget process that includes setting overall levels of revenues and expenditures, the size of the budget surplus or deficit, and priorities among different "functional" areas (for example, national defense, transportation, agriculture, foreign aid, and health). The House and Senate established new budget committees to perform these tasks and authorized

TABLE 18.1 The Federal Budget Process

First Monday in February	Congress receives the president's budget.
February 15	Congressional Budget Office (CBO) reports to the budget committees on fiscal policy and budget priorities, including an analysis of the president's budget.
February 25	Congressional committees submit views and estimates on spending to the budget committees.
April 1	Budget committees report concurrent resolution on the budget, which sets a total for budget outlays, an estimate of expenditures for major budget categories, and the recommended level of revenues. This resolution acts as an agenda for the remainder of the budget process.
April 15	Congress completes action on concurrent resolution on the budget.
May 15	Annual appropriations bills may be considered in the House.
June 10	House Appropriations Committee completes action on regular appropriations bills.
June 15	Congress completes action on reconciliation legislation, bringing budget totals into conformity with established ceilings.
June 30	House completes action on all appropriations bills.
October 1	The new fiscal year begins.

Source: Adapted from Howard E. Shuman, *Politics and the Budget*, 3rd ed. © 1992. Reprinted by permission of Prentice Hall, Inc., Upper Saddle River, NJ.

the Congressional Budget Office (CBO), a professional staff of technical experts, to assist the budget committees and to provide members of Congress with their own source of budgetary information so they would be more independent of the OMB.

Typically, budget committees hold hearings on the president's proposed budget and set targets for overall revenue and spending and a ceiling for individual categories of spending. Other committees evaluate requests by various agencies. In most years, reconciliation legislation is necessary to ensure that targets are met. Changes in existing law can be proposed in reconciliation bills. Changes can be proposed in tax rates or benefit levels of entitlement programs. The growth of entitlement spending is a major source of concern to policy makers. As shown in Figure 18.4, growth in spending for entitlements has far exceeded growth in discretionary programs.

Legislative action on all appropriations bills is supposed to be completed by October 1, the start of the fiscal year. It is rare, however, for Congress to pass all appropriations bills by this date. For programs still unfunded at the start of the fiscal year, Congress can pass a continuing resolution, which authorizes agencies to continue operating on the basis of last year's appropriation until approval of their new budget. This procedure can cause some uncertainty in agency operations. When the president and Congress cannot agree, some programs may be shut down until the terms for a continuing resolution are worked out.

MAJOR BUDGET CONFLICTS   Conflict often develops between Congress and the president over the details of the budget and its overall dimensions, such as the size of the deficit, the balance between military and domestic spending, and international agreements affecting domestic economics. Uncertainty also arises over the political feasibility of funding very specific initiatives. Throughout the 1980s, there was conflict between the Democrats in Congress, who favored more domestic spending and less military spending, and President Ronald Reagan and his administration, who favored less domestic spending and more spending on defense. In 1993, the Clinton

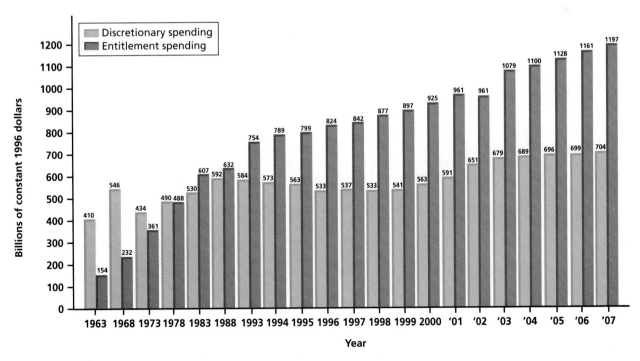

FIGURE 18.4 Entitlements and Discretionary Spending, 1963–2007 (in billions of 1996 dollars)

Source: United States Budget, Fiscal Year 2007, www.gpo.gov.

administration touched off a partisan political struggle in Congress with its budget deficit reduction plan because it included tax increases.

The 1993 struggle between Congress and President Clinton, however, was a love fest compared to the 1995–1996 stalemate. Under the leadership of House Speaker Newt Gingrich, the first Republican congressional majority in forty years devised a plan to balance the budget in seven years. While President Clinton also professed a desire to eliminate annual deficits, he and Congress clashed over which programs to cut to balance the budget. In 1995, 1996, and 1999, Clinton vetoed appropriations bills that he believed cut social programs too severely.

You Are the President and Need to
Get a Tax Cut Passed

BUDGET INITIATIVES OF THE GEORGE W. BUSH ADMINISTRATION   Significant budget changes were adopted when George W. Bush signed the Economic Growth and Tax Relief Reconciliation Act of 2001. While the bill passed the Republican-controlled Congress by a healthy margin, it was not universally embraced. Critics claimed the bill would squander budget surpluses, represented a giveaway to the rich, and would starve the government of needed funds. Supporters viewed it as a reasonable response to high rates of taxation. The bill lowered income tax rates across the board, expanded deductions, and provided taxpayers with rebates in the summer and early fall of 2001.

In 2003, the American economy remained stagnant, and President Bush won congressional approval for another round of income tax cuts. The short-term goal of these cuts was to stimulate the economy by providing taxpayers with more of their own money to spend. Tax withholdings were lowered in the summer of 2003 to reflect the lower rates, and rebate checks were sent to most taxpayers with dependent children. The short-term effect of these cuts was considerable: the GDP rose as consumer spending increased, and the economy continued to expand. By 2007, however, a slowing economy resulted in rate cuts and a fiscal stimulus package that included another round of tax rebate checks mailed to taxpayers in 2008.

The tax rebate checks of 2001, 2003, and 2008 represent examples of how changes in legislation and public policy impact our lives. Many Americans no doubt were happy to get money back from the government. The long-term impact of the cuts, however, remains murky. Deficit hawks argue that these cuts, coupled with the high cost of military operations in Iraq and Afghanistan, will likely cause deficits to soar in the next few years. Other critics charge that these cuts "have conferred the most benefits, by far, on the highest-income households—those least in need of additional resources—at a time when [wealth] already is exceptionally concentrated at the top of the income spectrum."[46] But, congressional Republicans and many conservatives hail these cuts as indicative of a philosophical desire to limit government and stimulate the economy.

In February 2008, President Bush unveiled a $3.1 trillion budget that again increased defense spending to fight the "war on terror." He also vowed to protect his promised tax cuts. The president proposed to save $196 billion over a five-year period in government health programs like Medicare and Medicaid, and to eliminate or sharply scale back 151 "wasted or bloated" programs, including forty-seven educational programs. The budget proposal called for a $515 billion discretionary budget for the Department of Defense and $70 billion for emergency war funding, and it estimated a $409 billion deficit.[47] But, Senate Majority Leader Harry Reid (D–NV]] considered the budget "fiscally irresponsible and highly deceptive, hiding the costs of the war in Iraq while increasing our skyrocketing debt."[48]

The Budget Deficit and the Debt

Large annual budget deficits and a rapidly growing national debt (the sum of annual budget deficits) characterized government finance from the early 1980s through the early 1990s. Several factors contributed to this situation: a severe recession in the early 1980s, the large tax cut enacted in 1981, sharply increased spending for national defense during the 1980s, and continuously expanding spending on such entitlement programs as Social Security, Medicare, and Medicaid.[49] The annual **federal budget deficit**, or the amount by which federal expenditure exceeds federal revenue, which rarely exceeded $60 billion before 1980 and usually was much less than that, averaged $150 billion during the 1980s. These dollar figures have increased in part because of inflation. One way to account for inflation when comparing budget deficits is to express the deficits as a percentage of the U.S. GDP (the total market value of all goods and services produced in the United States during a year). During the 1960s, the budget deficit typically was less than 1 percent of GDP, whereas the deficit rose to between 3 percent and 5 percent of GDP during the 1980s. So, the expected 2008 budget deficit of 2.9 percent of the GDP is not a historic high.

federal budget deficit
The amount by which federal expenditure exceeds federal revenue.

Yearly deficits, however, help to increase total debt. The national debt tripled during the 1980s. By 1996, the national debt was nearly $5 trillion. In May 2008, the national debt stood at an astounding $9.35 trillion, and interest payments on the debt constituted a serious budget expense. In 2007, the government paid $430 billion in interest on the national debt.

While deficits have long been recognized for their potentially negative impact on economies, acceptance of Keynesian economic perspectives since the 1930s has led some economists to justify federal deficits as a means of stimulating economic growth in periods of decline. In contrast to state governments, the federal government (because of its size and macroeconomic responsibilities) legitimizes deficit spending. It is believed that such spending is needed from time to time to stimulate economic recovery and keep vital social and defense-related expenses intact. Deficits are justified in times of recession; however, they are criticized if they are viewed as "structural" or built into the economy even in times of prosperity.

DEFICIT REDUCTION LEGISLATION   Budget surpluses from 1998 to 2002 resulted from several key congressional acts: the Gramm-Rudman-Hollings Act of 1985, the Budget Enforcement Act of 1990, and the Omnibus Budget Reconciliation Act of 1993. The most significant of these was the Gramm-Rudman-Hollings Act, named after its three Senate sponsors: Phil Gramm (R–TX), Warren Rudman (R–NH), and Ernest Hollings (D–SC). The initial deficit reduction effort represented in the Gramm-Rudman-Hollings Act was not very successful in reducing budget deficits, but it represented an early attack on the deficit and paved the way for other initiatives.

The Budget Enforcement Act of 1990 represented another attempt to bring expenditures into line with revenues. The act set limits on discretionary spending and created a "pay as you go" procedure, requiring that increases in spending be offset by decreases in other appropriations so there would be no increase in the deficit. The Omnibus Budget Reconciliation Act of 1993 incorporated a mix of tax increases and entitlement reductions. Under the provisions of this act, the top income tax rate was increased and those with very high incomes were assessed a surcharge. There were increases in corporate taxes and increases in the tax that high-income Social Security recipients would pay. To reduce the growth of entitlements, the Reconciliation Act placed limits on the Medicare program.[50]

Following the Clinton budget and the Reconciliation Act of 1993, significant declines in the deficit were attained. Total income tax receipts rose nearly 25 percent from 1992 to 1995, despite predictions by some economists that higher taxes enacted in the 1993 act would actually produce less revenue. After peaking at $290 billion in 1992, deficits declined to $22 billion in 1997 and turned into a surplus in 1998, 1999, and 2000. The 1998 budget surplus of $69 billion was the first reported surplus since 1969, and by 2000, the surplus had grown to $236 billion.[51] (To learn more, see Analyzing Visuals: Projecting Federal Budget Deficits.)

Analyzing Visuals | Projecting Federal Budget Deficits

This bar graph shows the Office of Management and Budget's budget deficit projections through the year 2012. A budget surplus is projected only in the year 2012. Look at the graph and answer the following questions:

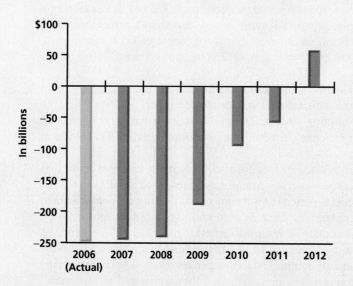

WHAT events could significantly alter the projected deficits on the graph? What might affect the projected deficit in 2012?

SHOULD Americans be concerned about the high deficits that the CBO predicts over the next several years?

WHAT impact does a budget deficit have on the American economy?

Source: Office of Management and Budget, www.whitehouse.gov/omb/budget/; www.washingtonpost.com/wp-srv/politics/interactives/budget08/deficit.html.

BUDGET SURPLUS AND RENEWED DEFICITS   The budget surplus that emerged in 1998 was a testament to a variety of factors. The growing economy prompted substantial revenue growth and a slowing of recession-impacted entitlements. The slowdown in military spending, an aggressive monetary policy, and legislation enacted by Congress also contributed to the new budget environment. The years of budget surpluses, however, would not endure, and by fiscal year 2003, deficits reappeared at $375 billion. The Bush administration acknowledged the budget deficit would be over $500 billion in 2004 but argued that, sparked by tax cuts, economic growth would return and the deficits would disappear within a decade. Critics were not so sure. Tom Daschle, then Democratic minority leader of the U.S. Senate, warned: "Unless we get back on the right track soon, these record deficits could undercut growth and job creation for decades to come." While cautioning against overly alarmist fears, then Federal Reserve Chair Alan Greenspan also warned that the return of large deficits represents "a significant obstacle to long-term stability."[52] Current Federal Reserve Chair Ben Bernanke voiced concern as well that the rising budget deficit would put future living standards at risk.[53]

In February 2006, President Bush signed the Deficit Reduction Act of 2005, which aims to reduce direct spending by the government by $40 billion between 2006 and 2010. This includes a reduction in Medicare spending by $5 billion over the five-year period. The Congressional Budget Office estimated that the budget deficit for 2008 will be $396 billion, including President Bush's request for additional funding for military operations in Iraq and Afghanistan.[54] The Bush administration estimated the 2008 budget deficit at $410 billion, up from $163 billion in 2007.[55] The Office of Management and Budget projects deficits until 2011.[56]

Balancing Military and Domestic Expenditures: Funding the War in Iraq

Wars place a tremendous burden on the economy. The federal government financed the costs of World War II by issuing war bonds and borrowing from financial institutions. Higher taxes helped finance the Korean War. The inflation-adjusted cost of the Vietnam War is estimated at $549 billion.[57] It is thus hardly a surprise that Americans are concerned about the economic costs of the Iraq War, especially in the wake of its declining support and the financial crisis that begin in late 2008.

When the Bush administration went to war with Iraq in 2003, it initially estimated the conflict to cost just $50 to $60 billion. Administration officials suggested that Iraqi oil revenues would pay for the country's postwar reconstruction. In 2008, five years into the war, America's economic slowdown and the upcoming presidential election raised renewed questions about military expenditures in Iraq and Afghanistan. A Congressional Budget Office report estimated that a cumulative total of $752 billion will have been spent to finance combat operations in Iraq, Afghanistan, and elsewhere in 2001–2008. An additional $40 billion has been spent on diplomatic activities and foreign aid over the same time period.[58]

In one study, Nobel laureate economist Joseph Stiglitz of Columbia University and Harvard Professor Linda Bilmes estimate that the costs of the war in Iraq and Afghanistan through the year 2017 could exceed $1.7 to $2.7 trillion.[59] The

Photo courtesy: Mark Wilson/Getty Images

What economic benefits do veterans deserve? Senator Jim Webb (D–VA) announces the passage of a new GI Bill giving comprehensive education benefits to veterans of the conflicts in Iraq and Afghanistan. President Bush and Republican presidential nominee John McCain opposed it based on cost and concerns that many service members instead of reenlisting would leave the military to take advantage of the benefits. But, the CBO estimates that any troop reductions would be offset by new recruits lured by more generous benefits.

Stiglitz-Bilmes study takes into account the costs of combat operations, replenishing military equipment, increasing Department of Defense costs, and taking care of veterans. Stiglitz and Bilmes estimate at least $300 billion in future health care costs for wounded troops. They also estimate that the interest paid on the money borrowed for the wars will add $866 billion to the total cost.[60]

While the CBO estimates remain well below those of Stiglitz and Bilmes, it is apparent that the economic cost of the wars in Iraq and Afghanistan place serious pressures on the government's budget. As support for the war in Iraq wanes, there is growing public concern over the justification of spending such large sums of money, especially in a time of economic distress. As one observer noted, it is time to engage in nation-building at home. America needs to invest in its competitive edge by investing in education, health, and infrastructure.[61] A congressional study by the Joint Economic Committee found that the sums spent on the Iraq War *each day* could enroll an additional 58,000 children in Head Start or give Pell grants to 153,000 students to attend college.[62]

Toward Reform: The Subprime Mortgage Crisis and Regulation

As noted previously, the issue of government regulation or deregulation is a highly contested one. Government leaders in recent decades have celebrated the notion of deregulation. But, problems in the subprime mortgage market followed by a severe financial crisis resulted in greater governmental involvement and oversight in critical sectors of the economy. Many Americans have been affected by the effects of the mortgage crisis as home values dropped and as 1.8 million subprime mortgages reset at higher rates.[63] The surge in home foreclosures and its larger impact on financial markets and the economy as a whole brought "subprime" loans into the vocabulary of most Americans.

The subprime mortgage crisis is not the product of a single administration's blunders. The roots of this crisis may well go back to when President Bill Clinton and the Republican-led Congress repealed the Depression-era Glass-Steagall Act, which had mandated a separation of investment and lending banking. The repeal allowed large commercial lenders such as Citigroup to underwrite and trade in mortgage-backed securities.

After the September 11, 2001, terrorist attacks, interest rates were cut in order to stimulate the economy. The rate reductions made money cheap for creditors, who were able to lend out the money for a sizeable profit margin. These cuts combined with a trend by lenders that began in the early 1990s to offer an array of subprime mortgage loans (loans at higher interest rates than the prime rate). These lenders employed less stringent approval guidelines for borrowers than lenders offering traditional thirty-year, fixed-rate mortgages. Many of the new subprime mortgage loans appealed to people with low credit scores—high-risk candidates for home ownership. Some mortgage brokers engaged in deceptive lending practices, steering borrowers into loans that offered only short-term financial savings while providing higher commissions for the broker and higher profits for the lender.

Between 1994 and 2005, the annual value of subprime loans grew from $35 billion to over $600 billion, raising the subprime share of the total mortgage market from 5 percent to 20 percent. Subprime loans included adjustable rate mortgages, which were offered without any down payment requirements or with low "teaser" rates that were raised after a two or three years.[64] Many of these loans were tenable as long as home values based on a boom in real estate continued to rise, creating more equity for homeowners. This was the case between 2000 and 2006, when housing prices rose nearly 40 percent. The real estate bubble, however, did not last. By the end of 2006, the real estate boom had turned to a slump. New housing starts in 2007 fell by 25 percent, double the drop in 2006.[65] Some analysts predicted an additional 25 percent decline in home prices over the next two or three years, beginning in 2008.

According to the Mortgage Bankers Association, subprime adjustable rate mortgages, which accounted for 6.8 percent of all outstanding home loans, were 43 percent of the loans involved in foreclosures in the first three quarters of 2007.[66] In 2007, U.S. home foreclosures hit a record high, and mortgage delinquency was at its highest rate since 1985. Homeowner equity, the amount of a home's value owned outright by the homeowner, sank to its lowest level since 1945.[67]

The severity of the mortgage crisis resulted in government intervention in the economy. But, Democrats and Republicans disagreed on the scope and intensity of government intervention needed to ameliorate the crisis. As late as May 2007, Fed Chair Ben Bernanke warned Congress against too much government intrusion in the subprime mortgage market. While acknowledging the need for combating abusive lending practices and for ensuring effective disclosures to consumers, Bernanke warned against suppressing responsible lending and eliminating refinancing opportunities for subprime borrowers. He praised, like his predecessor Alan Greenspan, subprime loan products as positive innovations in the credit markets that allowed millions of Americans to own homes. He also noted that homeownership increased due to the expansion of secondary markets where mortgage loans were packaged and sold to investors.[68]

By December 2007, however, the crisis had prompted former Fed Chair Alan Greenspan to suggest that public money should be used to help struggling homeowners. In the same month, the Bush administration announced that it had brokered a deal with the mortgage industry to freeze interest rates for five years on certain subprime mortgages.[69] Apart from interest rate cuts, the Fed lent $160 billion to banks in December 2007 to ease the credit crunch related to the subprime meltdown.[70]

Amid growing signs of cooperation between Democrats and Republicans in Congress and between Congress and the White House, the Senate Banking Committee and the House Financial Services Committee began working on bills that would allow the Federal Housing Administration to insure between $300 billion and $400 billion of additional mortgages to help avert foreclosures.[71] Congress also began working on new mortgage standards that would require mortgage companies to demonstrate that borrowers could afford such loans. The new standards would also require lenders to disclose hidden fees and would prohibit misleading advertisements. The plan was criticized by the industry's most influential actors who all filed complaints stating that such regulation, at a time of tight credit, would make mortgages even more expensive by necessitating additional paperwork and potentially exposing lenders to lawsuits.[72]

In September 2008, U.S. Treasury Secretary Henry Paulson announced that the government was taking mortgage giants Freddie Mac and Fannie Mae into temporary public ownership to stave off their collapse. The Federal Housing Authority stepped in to run these troubled mortgage giants that had lent or underwritten about $5.3 trillion of the total $12 trillion of outstanding mortgage debts in the United States.

By late September, the mortgage crisis had grown in to a full-blown financial crisis. The Bush Administration proposed a $700 billion federal bailout package.[73] The plan was intended to reassure the financial markets by providing $700 billion to allow the government to buy up the bad mortgage-backed securities—also referred to as toxic loans—that were purchased by financial and investment giants. Some analysts argued that the government might be able to make a profit by reselling these securities, once they regained their value, but many Americans were vehemently opposed to what they viewed as a "blank check" to save Wall Street in the wake of rampant greed and record profits.

The first version of the bailout plan failed to gather enough votes in the House of Representatives from Republicans and some left-leaning Democrats, forcing frenzied rounds of House and Senate negotiation. Efforts were made to make the plan more palatable to politicians up for reelection and facing constituents who were overwhelmingly opposed to using taxpayer funds for bailing out Wall Street. President Bush, members of his administration, and congressional leaders sought to present the financial bailout plan as an economic rescue plan. They emphasized the extent to which financial collapse on Wall Street and virtually frozen credit markets would affect the ability of those on Main Street to do business, refinance their homes, or buy a car. A modified version of the Administration's initial bailout plan that provided enhanced oversight of the Treasury Department's use of the $700 billion, an option to use the money to buy equity stakes in faltering banks, some protection to those in danger of losing their homes, and a variety of tax cuts and incentives was passed after a second vote in the House in early October 2008.

WHAT SHOULD I HAVE LEARNED?

The nature and role of the government in the economy, especially the national government, have changed significantly since the nation's founding. In analyzing these developments, this chapter answered the following questions:

■ **What are the roots of government involvement in the economy?**

Efforts by the national government to regulate the economy began with anti-monopoly legislation. Under President Franklin D. Roosevelt, the interventionist state replaced the laissez-faire state. After World War II, many areas of economic policy were settled. Full employment, employee–employer relations, and social regulation became new concerns of government. Even before social regulation began to ebb, economic deregulation, which involves reducing market controls, emerged as an attractive political issue.

■ **What tools does government use to stabilize the economy?**

The national government continues to shape monetary policy by regulating the nation's money supply and interest rates. Monetary policy is controlled by the Federal Reserve System's Board of Governors. Fiscal policy, which involves the deliberate use of the national government's taxing and spending policies, is another tool of the national government and involves the president and Congress setting the national budget. Although the budget is initially suggested by the president, Congress has constitutional authority over the process.

■ **What is the impact of the Iraq War on the economy?**

America's military operations in Iraq since 2003 have placed a significant burden on the U.S. economy. The costs of war in Iraq and Afghanistan include not only combat operations but also replenishing military equipment, covering related Department of Defense expenses, and taking care of veterans. With support for the war in Iraq waning and the economy experiencing a serious downturn, the economic cost of the war may have significant political repercussions.

■ **What are the roots of the subprime mortgage crisis and why are policy reform efforts so contentious?**

The subprime mortgage crisis resulted from inadequate governmental oversight in the financial sector. Deregulation of the financial sector dates back to 1999 when President Bill Clinton and the Republican-led Congress repealed the Depression-era Glass-Steagall Act, which had mandated a separation of investment and lending banking. The subprime mortgage crisis elicited various attempts at reregulation. Such measures faced significant opposition from the financial sector until the credit crisis and ensuing bank and stock market crises of late 2008 necessitated broad emergency measures by the U.S. government, the Federal Reserve, and the governments of nations around the globe to stabilize the U.S. and global economies.

Key Terms

Board of Governors, p. 649
business cycles, p. 640
deregulation, p. 646
discount rate, p. 650
economic regulation, p. 645
economic stability, p. 648
federal budget deficit, p. 663

fiscal policy, p. 652
gross domestic product (GDP), p. 659
inflation, p. 648
interventionist state, p. 643
laissez-faire, p. 641
monetary policy, p. 649

money, p. 649
open market operations, p. 650
protectionism, p. 656
recession, p. 648
reserve requirements, p. 650
social regulation, p. 645

Researching Economic Policy

In the Library

Bitner, Richard. *Greed, Fraud, and Ignorance: A Subprime Insider's Look at the Mortgage Collapse.* Colleyville, TX: LTV Media, 2008.

Chernow, Ron. *Alexander Hamilton.* New York: Penguin, 2004.

Derthick, Martha, and Paul J. Quirk. *The Politics of Deregulation.* Washington, DC: Brookings Institution, 1985.

Fleckenstein, William, and Fred Sheehan. *Greenspan's Bubbles: The Age of Ignorance at the Federal Reserve.* New York: McGraw Hill, 2008.

Greider, William. *One World, Ready or Not: The Manic Logic of Global Capitalism.* New York: Simon and Schuster, 1997.

Iley, Richard A., and Mervyn K. Lewis. *Untangling the U.S. Deficit: Evaluating Causes, Cures and Global Imbalances.* Northampton, MA: Edward Elgar, 2007.

Keech, William. *Economic Politics: The Costs of Democracy.* Cambridge: Cambridge University Press, 1995.

Kettl, Donald F. *Deficit Politics: Public Budgeting in Its Institutional and Historical Context.* New York: Macmillan, 1992.

Krugman, Paul. *The Great Unraveling: Losing Our Way in the New Century.* New York: Norton, 2003.

Phillips, Kevin. *Wealth and Democracy: A Political History of the American Rich.* New York: Broadway, 2002.

Rubin, Robert E., with Jacob Weisberg. *In an Uncertain World: Tough Choices from Wall Street to Washington.* New York: Random House, 2003.

Schiller, Robert. *Irrational Exuberance.* Princeton, NJ: Princeton University Press, 2000.

Stiglitz, Joseph, and Linda Bilmes. *The Three Trillion Dollar War: the True Cost of the Iraq Conflict.* New York: Norton, 2008.

Thurmaier, Kurt M., and Katherine G. Willoughby. *Policy and Politics in State Budgeting.* Armonk, NY: M. E. Sharpe, 2001.

Tonelson, Alan. *The Race to the Bottom: Why a Worldwide Worker Surplus and Uncontrolled Free Trade Are Sinking American Living Standards.* Boulder, CO: Westview, 2002.

On the Web

To learn about the government bureau for economic analysis, go to **www.bea.doc.gov.**

To compare various business cycle indicators, go to **www.tcb-indicators.org.**

To access the most current labor and wages data for your state or region, go to **www.bls.gov/ncs/.**

To learn about current economic policy, go to **www.nber.org.**

To learn more about regulation of financial markets via the Federal Reserve Board, go to **www.federalreserve.gov.**

To learn about current fiscal policy, go to **www.gpoaccess.gov/usbudget/index.html.**

To compare the current fiscal budget with budgets from prior years, go to **www.whitehouse.gov/omb.**

To compare the federal budget with the national debt, go to **www.gpoaccess.gov/usbudget/fy06/index.html.**

Foreign and Defense Policy

The war on terrorism declared by President George W. Bush after the September 11, 2001, attacks on the United States has been a multifaceted, global undertaking that includes military action overseas, increased security measures at home, cooperation among domestic and international intelligence agencies, diplomacy, and the prevention of terrorists' access to weapons of mass destruction. It involves domestic strategies, such as efforts to improve homeland security, as well as international activities, such as the promotion of democracy abroad, military strikes against terrorist organizations and the states that sponsor them, and diplomatic initiatives designed to thwart the spread of religious extremism and nuclear proliferation. In the context of the war on terrorism, the division of U.S. policies into "foreign affairs" and "domestic affairs" is somewhat artificial.

After the events of 9/11, striking the appropriate balance between foreign and domestic affairs so that American interests and objectives are achieved and the American public is protected remains a continuing challenge for the president and

Hon. Alberto Gonzales

others involved in the foreign and defense policy process. For example, three days after the 9/11 attacks, President Bush authorized the National Security Administration (NSA) to eavesdrop on telephone calls and e-mails between American citizens and foreigners suspected of terrorist ties without first seeking a court warrant. The NSA's Terrorist Surveillance Program continued until January 2007, when the White House resumed seeking surveillance warrants from the Federal Intelligence Surveillance Court. When it was disclosed, the NSA's spying program created a great deal of controversy because the 1978 Foreign Intelligence Surveillance Act (FISA) requires the special intelligence court to approve any interception of communications involving U.S. citizens. The program generated debate in Congress over the legality of President Bush's decision to order the NSA to conduct warrantless surveillance of Americans' communications. The Department of Justice, however, argued that the president's constitutional role as commander in chief provides adequate justification for his authorization of such a program. Critics argue that the program violates U.S. law, that the president is unnecessarily extending the reach of the federal government, and that the NSA's limited resources should be targeted at more precise threats to national security.

The debate intensified in the wake of revelations of a much larger data-mining project designed to track the domestic phone records of millions of ordinary U.S. citizens and analyze them for

■ What is the appropriate scope of the government's power to combat threats to national security? At left, a WWII-era poster warns Americans of the potentially deadly consequences of talking about military deployments or troop movements publicly. At right, then Attorney General Alberto Gonzales testifies before Congress about the Bush Administration's controversial domestic eavesdropping program.

WHAT SHOULD I KNOW ABOUT . . .

- the roots of U.S. foreign and defense policy?
- the United States as a world power?
- foreign and defense policy decision making?
- twenty-first-century challenges in foreign and defense policy?
- unilateralism, multilateralism, and foreign policy reform?

signs that Americans are communicating with suspected terrorists. In a White House press briefing on May 11, 2006, President Bush strongly defended his administration's surveillance and monitoring efforts: "We're not mining or trolling through the personal lives of millions of innocent Americans," he stated. "Our efforts are focused on links to al-Qaeda and their known affiliates."[1]

TO LEARN MORE—
—TO DO MORE
To learn more about the history and mission of the National Security Agency, visit the agency's Web site at www.nsa.gov/about/index.cfm.

In August 2007, Congress passed a temporary law that expanded the president's power to monitor communications passing through the United States that involve suspected terrorists. This law expired in February 2008 and efforts to revise the FISA law hinged on a variety of hotly debated issues, including the level of oversight over domestic surveillance that should be exercised and whether to grant retroactive immunity to private telecommunications companies that participated in the NSA's earlier warrantless spying programs.

In the summer of 2008, Congress reached an agreement on the issue and passed the FISA Amendments Act. On July 10, 2008, President Bush signed the bill into law. Important provisions of the law include protections for telecommunications companies from lawsuits for past or future cooperation with the intelligence community and language that allows federal law enforcement agencies to conduct surveillance of any person for up to one week (an increase from the previous forty-eight hours) without a warrant as long as the FISA court is notified. The American Civil Liberties Union (ACLU) has filed a lawsuit challenging the law (*Amnesty et al v. McConnell*) as a violation of free speech and privacy under the First and Fourth Amendments to the Constitution.

Current domestic surveillance programs blur the distinction between domestic and foreign policies and raise complicated constitutional questions about the reach of the federal government in the context of combating terrorism. Domestic issues, such as the privacy rights of ordinary Americans, have become part of the discussion of how best to pursue a defense policy that will thwart terrorism here and abroad. The Bush administration's war on terrorism dramatically changed how the United States conducts foreign and defense policy, ushering in a period of unprecedented unilateral military action abroad, aggressive detention practices for those suspected of terrorist activities, and controversial spying programs at home.

Following the end of the Cold War (1947–1991), U.S. foreign policy began a period of transition. Many wondered what role the United States would play in a world with only one remaining superpower. Most hoped that the world would be a safer place in the new millennium. After September 11, 2001, however, Americans recognized a new and deadly threat: terrorism. Many citizens wondered how the United States, with its superior military resources, could have fallen prey to a devastating series of terrorist attacks on a single fateful day.

To explore the most important elements of U.S. foreign and defense policy, we will examine the following issues in this chapter:

★ First, we will trace *the roots of U.S. foreign and defense policy* in the years before the United States became a world power.

★ Second, we will detail U.S. policy during and after the Cold War, examining *the United States as a world power.*

★ Third, we will study *foreign and defense policy decision making* and the role of the executive branch, Congress, and other groups in foreign policy making.

★ Fourth, we will examine *twenty-first-century challenges* in foreign and defense policy.

★ Finally, we will evaluate the choice between *unilateralism and multilateralism* in the context of U.S. foreign policy making.

Roots of U.S. Foreign and Defense Policy

Like social and economic policy, U.S. foreign and defense policy has evolved. Today, the United States is a powerful and influential presence on the world stage. It was not always this way. When the United States was founded, it was a weak country on the margins of world affairs, with an uncertain future.

Even so, the United States was fortunate. Separated from Europe and Asia by vast oceans, it had abundant resources and industrious people. The United States often stood apart from world engagements, following a policy of **isolationism,** that is, avoiding participation in foreign affairs. However, isolationism was rarely absolute. Even in its early years, the United States engaged in foreign affairs, and it was always a trading nation. Another consistent hallmark of U.S. policy was **unilateralism,** that is, acting without consulting others. **Moralism** was also central to U.S. self-image in foreign policy, with most Americans believing their country had higher moral standards than European and other countries. Many Americans were also proud of their **pragmatism**—their ability to find ways to take advantage of a situation. Thus, when European nations went to war, Americans sold goods to both sides and profited handsomely. When opportunities to acquire more land arose, Americans aggressively pursued them.

To understand how and why the United States emphasized isolationism, unilateralism, moralism, and pragmatism, we must examine the roots of U.S. foreign policy from the Constitution until the beginning of World War II.

isolationism
A national policy of avoiding participation in foreign affairs.

unilateralism
A national policy of acting without consulting others.

moralism
The policy of emphasizing morality in foreign affairs.

pragmatism
The policy of taking advantage of a situation for national gain.

The Constitution

When the Framers of the U.S. Constitution met in Philadelphia in 1789 to write a new governing document for the thirteen states, they wanted a stronger national government to keep the United States out of European affairs and to keep Europe out of American affairs. As a result, the power to formulate and implement foreign policy was given to the national government rather than the states. In addition, many foreign and military powers not enumerated in the Constitution are generally accorded to the national government. (To learn more about these powers, see The Living Constitution.)

The Framers of the Constitution divided authority for many foreign and military policy functions between the president and Congress. The Framers named the president commander in chief of the armed forces but gave Congress power to fund the army and navy and to declare war. The president has authority to negotiate and sign treaties, but treaties only take effect after the Senate ratifies them by a two-thirds majority. Similarly, the president appoints ambassadors and other key foreign and military affairs officials, but the Senate grants advice and consent on the appointments.

This division of responsibility for foreign and military policy stood in marked contrast to the way the European powers of the eighteenth century made foreign policy. In Great Britain and France, the ability to formulate and implement foreign policy resided almost exclusively with the ruling monarch and his or her advisers.

The Living Constitution

To provide for calling forth the Militia to execute the Laws of the Union, suppress Insurrections and repel Invasions;

To provide for organizing, arming, and disciplining, the Militia, and for governing such Part of them as may be employed in the Service of the United States, reserving to the States respectively, the Appointment of the Officers, and the Authority of training the Militia according to the discipline proscribed by Congress;

ARTICLE I, SECTION 8

With the Constitution's Article I militia clauses, a significant defect of the Articles of Confederation was corrected. A fundamental weakness of the earlier document was that it did not grant the central U.S. government adequate means for national defense, and this defect was understood to hamper the Revolutionary War effort. In the view of the Framers, a government without the force to administer its laws or to defend its citizens was either a weak government or no government at all, and these clauses consequently give the federal government authority to call up the state militias in times of national emergency or distress. The clauses address the understanding that military training, proficiency, and organization should be uniform across state and national forces so as to ensure effectiveness and efficiency in military operations.

Despite the fact that the militia clauses passed the convention, many Anti-Federalists were concerned that the federal government could call together the state militias for unjust ends. They held the position that state governments should control their militias in order to prevent any perfidy on the part of the federal government. To this end, the states were given authority to name militia officers and train their forces. During the War of 1812—to the consternation of President James Madison—two state governments withheld their militias, because they believed it was the purview of the state to set the terms for the use of its guards. The Supreme Court has since held that, except for constitutional prohibitions, the Congress has "unlimited" authority over the state militias. The National Defense Act of 1916 mandated the use of the term "National Guard" and gave the president the authority to mobilize the National Guard during times of national emergency or war.

Throughout U.S. history, the National Guard has proved effective and essential in defending the United States. With the extensive use of the National Guard to assist American efforts in Iraq and in the struggle against terrorism, its role has expanded. The militia clauses ensure the unity, effectiveness, and strength of the United States military not only during wartime, but also during other national emergencies.

CRITICAL THINKING QUESTIONS

1. According to the Constitution, the president is the commander in chief of the armed forces. But, Congress has the power to organize the military, fund it, and call it to duty. How does this division of authority work in practice?
2. Should individual states retain the right to withhold National Guard troops if the state government does not approve of the way in which the president intends to use them?

The Early History of U.S. Foreign and Defense Policy

Following the creation of the Constitution, the United States delved gingerly into foreign affairs. As the United States took its place among the family of nations, it remained hesitant about engaging with other countries. George Washington emphasized this in his 1796 Farewell Address, his final address as president, when he asserted that it was the United States' "true policy to steer clear of permanent alliances with any portion of the foreign world." Washington, however, was not an isolationist. While he believed that U.S. democracy and security depended on remaining apart from Europe, he accepted the need for trade—and trade the United States did. Throughout the late eighteenth and nineteenth centuries, American ships plied the world's sea lanes, bringing large profits to U.S. merchants.

Trade led to conflicts. In the 1790s, the United States fought an undeclared naval war with France because France was seizing U.S. ships trading with France's enemies. Shortly thereafter, the United States fought the Barbary Wars against North African Barbary states, which since the 1780s had captured American and other ships, holding sailors for ransom.

In the early 1800s, the British naval practice of impressment, that is, stopping ships to seize suspected deserters of the Royal Navy who were working as merchant sailors, angered the American public. Despite U.S. protests, Great Britain refused to end the practice. Thus, in 1807, Congress passed the **Embargo Act,** which prevented U.S. ships from leaving for foreign ports without the approval of the federal government. President Thomas Jefferson believed that European states, embroiled in the continuing Napoleonic Wars, depended so much on U.S.-provided supplies and raw materials that Great Britain would stop impressment. Jefferson was wrong. U.S. exports fell, the economy suffered, and inflation soared. U.S.-British relations continued to deteriorate, fueled by impressments and by U.S. designs on Canada. These conditions led to the War of 1812 between the United States and Great Britain. Peace talks began even before the first battles were fought, but the war ended only after Great Britain decided to concentrate on defeating Napoleon. The 1814 Treaty of Ghent ended the war, with Great Britain and the United States accepting prewar borders and treaty obligations.

In 1815, Napoleon was defeated, and Europe was at peace for the first time in almost two decades. Europeans celebrated, but the United States feared that European powers, especially France in Latin America and Russia in Alaska and the Northwest, would try to expand their control in the Western Hemisphere. To prevent these actions, President James Monroe in 1823 declared "the American continents, by the free and independent condition which they have assumed and maintain, are henceforth not to be considered as subjects for future colonization by any European power." This declaration became known as the **Monroe Doctrine.** In reality, the Monroe

Embargo Act
Passed by Congress in 1807 to prevent U.S. ships from leaving U.S. ports for foreign ports without the approval of the federal government.

Monroe Doctrine
President James Monroe's 1823 pledge that the United States would oppose attempts by European states to extend their political control into the Western Hemisphere.

Photo courtesy: Allan Cox/Architect of the U.S. Capitol

How did the War of 1812 affect the residents of Washington, D.C.?
During the War of 1812, the British set fire to many buildings in Washington, D.C., including the U.S. Capitol and the White House. Both buildings were repaired and refurbished shortly after the war.

Doctrine was a preference more than a policy, since the United States had little capability to enforce it. However, Great Britain also wanted to keep other European powers out of the Americas. The Royal Navy thus protected British interests and promoted U.S. preferences.

The United States as an Emerging Power

Throughout most of the nineteenth century, the United States gained territory, developed economically, and began to emerge as a world power. This process centered on three areas: trade policy and commerce, continental expansion and manifest destiny, and during the last half of the century, interests beyond the Western Hemisphere.

tariffs
Taxes on imports used to raise government revenue and to protect infant industries.

TRADE POLICY AND COMMERCE As early as 1791, Alexander Hamilton in his *Report on Manufactures* urged Congress to protect domestic industries from foreign competition. However, Hamilton's advice was often ignored as the U.S. government relied on the principles of trade reciprocity and most favored nation (MFN) status. Reciprocity meant that the United States would treat foreign traders in the same way that foreign countries treated U.S. traders, and MFN status meant that U.S. exports would face the lowest **tariffs,** or taxes on imports, offered to any other country.

For most of the early years of the United States' existence, this worked well. However, at the end of the Napoleonic Wars, global peace meant increased competition, and the United States adopted protectionist tariffs designed to keep the home market for domestic producers, as Hamilton had suggested years before. Congress passed the first protectionist tariff in 1816.

Over the next eight years, Congress adopted the "American System" of trade protection by adding increasingly higher tariffs. Tariffs often were 20 to 30 percent of the value of an import, sometimes as high as 100 percent.[2] High protectionist tariffs were the American norm well into the twentieth century. While high tariffs protected the U.S. market for American producers, they also cut off foreign markets for American producers as foreign countries retaliated with their own high tariffs.

manifest destiny
Theory that the United States was divinely mandated to expand across North America to the Pacific Ocean.

CONTINENTAL EXPANSION AND MANIFEST DESTINY In 1800, the United States consisted of the original thirteen states and a few others that had just joined the union. During the nineteenth century, the United States acquired immense quantities of land in various ways. It took land from Native Americans in wars against the Creek, Seminole, Sioux, Comanche, Apache, and other tribes. It bought territory from the French, Spanish, and Russians. It fought the 1846 Mexican War, acquiring a large expanse of Mexican territory in the American Southwest and California. By the end of the century, the United States stretched from the Atlantic to the Pacific.

Some called this expansion **manifest destiny,** believing the United States had a divinely mandated obligation to expand across North America to the Pacific and "overspread the continent allotted by Providence for the free development of our multiplying millions."[3] Manifest destiny permitted Americans to rationalize expansion as legitimate and moral. Even though most Americans criticized the overseas expansionism of others as colonialism, most did not consider U.S. expansion in North America as colonialism because the acquired territory was connected to the United States.

INTERESTS BEYOND THE WESTERN HEMISPHERE The United States did not limit its economic ambitions to North America. By the mid-nineteenth century, the United States concluded a commercial treaty with China, limited Europe's ability to restrict U.S. trade with China, and opened Japan to Western trade. U.S. trade with China and Japan expanded as clipper ships plied the sea lanes in record time between Asia and the United States. The U.S. Civil War reduced American trade in the Pacific for a time, but soon the United States was once again trading with Asian nations. As American economic interests in the Pacific expanded, so did U.S. interest in acquiring Pacific islands to support expansion. Thus, in the 1890s, the United States acquired the Hawaiian Islands, Midway Island, Wake Island, and part of Samoa.

The 1898 Spanish-American War, fought between the United States and Spain over Spanish policies and presence in Cuba, made the world take note of the United States as a rising power. The United States won an easy victory, in the process acquiring Puerto Rico, the Philippines, Guam, and for a few years, Cuba. Not only had the United States defeated an established European power, albeit one in decline, but it also acquired heavily populated overseas territory. The United States had clearly become a colonial power.

This did not sit well with all Americans. Throughout most of the post–Civil War era, Americans did not agree on the U.S. role in world affairs. Both major political parties were generally against colonialism but divided on free trade and whether to intervene overseas. Disagreement became even more heated in 1899 when Filipinos revolted against U.S. rule. The United States sent nearly 200,000 troops to the Philippines over the next three years. When fighting finally ended in 1903, tens of thousands of Filipinos had died, along with five thousand Americans. The costs of empire were considerable.

Photo courtesy: Bettmann/CORBIS

How did the Roosevelt Corollary affect American foreign policy? In this political cartoon, President Theodore Roosevelt is shown policing Panama carrying the "big stick" of military intervention that the Roosevelt Corollary proposed.

The Roosevelt Corollary

In 1903, President Theodore Roosevelt sent a naval squadron to Panama to help it win independence from Colombia. The following year, the United States initiated construction of the Panama Canal, which opened in 1914. The canal helped trade and enabled the U.S. Navy to move ships quickly from the Atlantic to the Pacific and back again. Roosevelt's legacy also included the **Roosevelt Corollary** to the Monroe Doctrine, which advocated a more interventionist posture for the United States in policing world affairs.

Under the Roosevelt Corollary, the United States intervened in the Caribbean and Latin America many times as Roosevelt and subsequent U.S. presidents sent U.S. troops into Cuba, the Dominican Republic, Haiti, Nicaragua, Panama, Mexico, and elsewhere. During this era, many Latin Americans came to regard the United States as "the Colossus of the North," intervening in Latin American affairs whenever it wanted.

Roosevelt Corollary
Concept developed by President Theodore Roosevelt early in the twentieth century that it was the U.S. responsibility to assure stability in Latin America and the Caribbean.

World War I

When World War I broke out in Europe in 1914, the United States at first remained neutral. It was a European war, according to most Americans, and no U.S. interests were involved. In addition, the United States was largely a nation of European immigrants, and Americans were deeply divided about whom to support. It thus made sense for both foreign policy and domestic political reasons to stay out of the war. Indeed, when President Woodrow Wilson ran for a second term in 1916, he used the slogan "He kept us out of war" to win reelection.

Nevertheless, several events, especially Germany's policy of unrestricted submarine warfare, under which German subs sank U.S. ships carrying cargo to Great Britain and France, caused immense problems in U.S.-German relations. Finally, declaring that the United States was fighting "a war to end all wars," Wilson in 1917 led the nation into the conflict. American troops and supplies began to arrive just when the human and material resources of the United States' main allies, Great Britain and France, were nearly exhausted. Even though the United States entered the war late, its armed forces and economic assistance swung the tide of victory to the Allies' side.

After World War I, Wilson put great faith in **collective security** to maintain the peace. To Wilson, collective security was based on the premise that if one country attacked another, then other countries in the international community should all unite against the attacking country. Countries would thus ensure their security collaboratively.

At the Paris Peace Conference following the war, Wilson was instrumental in creating a new international organization, the **League of Nations,** to implement col-

collective security
The concept that peace would be secured if all countries collectively opposed any country that invaded another.

League of Nations
Created in the peace treaty that ended World War I, it was an international governmental organization dedicated to preserving peace.

lective security. However, he failed to build support for the League in the United States. A Democratic president with a Senate controlled by Republicans, Wilson failed to include GOP senators among the U.S. delegates to the peace conference. Besides partisan reasons, many senators believed that U.S. membership in the League of Nations would fly in the face of traditional U.S. isolationism and unilateralism. The Senate thus refused to give the necessary two-thirds vote to ratify the Treaty of Versailles, which formalized the terms of the end of the war, and the United States never joined the League.

The Interwar Years

Following rejection of the Treaty of Versailles, most Americans thought that U.S. interests were best served by isolationism and unilateralism. Nonetheless, new U.S. industries sought more raw materials from foreign countries and American businesses sought new markets overseas. During the 1920s, the United States became the world's leading source of credit and goods as the American economy prospered.

As Europeans rebuilt their economies, they presented a challenge to U.S. industry. Consequently, the Republican-controlled Congress during the 1920s raised tariffs to protect U.S. industry from foreign competition. In 1930, Congress passed the extremely high Smoot-Hawley Tariff, and other countries responded by raising their tariffs. The impact that higher tariffs had on world trade, in conjunction with the Great Depression, was dramatic. By 1932, trade dropped to about one-third its former level.[4]

As the Great Depression of the 1930s worsened, some Americans concluded that isolationism and unilateralism were wrong. They argued that the Depression was worse than it may have been because of the decline in trade brought about by high tariffs. Some believed that the economic turmoil was contributing to the rise of leaders in Germany, Japan, and Italy who were bent on world domination. Some also argued that without the United States, the League of Nations had proven incapable of preserving peace.

The United States and the rest of the world did little to oppose German, Japanese, and Italian aggression in the 1930s, and the world slid toward war. Congress was particularly isolationist, passing Neutrality Acts to keep the United States from becoming involved in foreign conflicts. President Franklin D. Roosevelt occasionally warned against this mentality, but he also knew that the American people and Congress were unwilling to get pulled into another world war without a more direct threat to America itself.

The United States as a World Power

Any doubt about whether the world was headed toward war disappeared on September 1, 1939, when Nazi Germany invaded Poland. Great Britain and France immediately declared war on Germany, and World War II began. In the United States, strong isolationist sentiment persisted. The country remained formally neutral even though it tilted more and more toward Great Britain. Despite the tilt, the United States stayed out of the war for over two years after it had begun in Europe. This changed on December 7, 1941, when Japan bombed **Pearl Harbor,** a U.S. naval base in Hawaii. The next day, the United States declared war on Japan. A few days later, Germany and Italy declared war on the United States, and the United States responded in kind. The United States was then fully engaged in a global war, participating in the Grand Alliance of the United States, Great Britain, the Soviet Union, and several other nations against the Axis powers of Japan, Germany, and Italy.

This global conflict transformed the United States' role in the world. Before World War II, the United States was an essentially isolationist country with a sizeable power base that it rarely used. By the end of the war, the United States was the leader of the most powerful military coalition that the world had ever seen. What is more, the United States had the only major economy in the world that had not been deci-

Pearl Harbor
Naval base in Hawaii attacked by Japan on December 7, 1941, initiating U.S. entry into World War II.

The Evolution of Foreign Policy

Photo courtesy: National Archives and Records Administration

How has the development of nuclear weapons affected foreign policy? During much of the Cold War, the United States and the Soviet Union carried on testing of nuclear weapons. The rapid expansion of nuclear arsenals resulted in a stalemate position known as mutually assured destruction (MAD), whereby a first strike by either superpower would result in a devastating counterstrike.

mated by war. These realities forced the United States to reassess the principles that had guided its foreign and military policy for the previous century and a half.

World War II and Its Aftermath: 1941–1947

After the United States entered World War II, it took a phenomenal industrial and military mobilization to secure victory. The war transformed American society, cost tens of billions of dollars, and cost the lives of more than 400,000 members of the American armed forces. The war ended in Europe on May 8, 1945 (V-E Day), with the Allies bruised but victorious. The war against Japan ended after the United States dropped two atomic bombs on Japan, one on Hiroshima on August 6, 1945, and the other on Nagasaki three days later. On August 15, Japan surrendered, and the Allies celebrated V-J Day and the end to World War II. The birth of the nuclear age made it all the more important for the victorious powers to find a way to keep the peace.

One way to do this, many believed, was to create an improved version of the League of Nations, this time with the participation of all of the world's great powers, including the United States. Thus, even before the war ended, the United States and fifty-one of its allies met in San Francisco to create the **United Nations (UN),** whose purpose was to guarantee the security of member states when attacked and to promote economic, physical, and social well-being around the world. Successful operations of the UN depended on the postwar cooperation of the "Big Three" of the Grand Alliance (the United States, Britain, and the Soviet Union) as well as China and France, which had the five permanent seats on the new UN Security Council. The UN, an **international governmental organization (IGO),** was created by its member states to achieve the international purposes that they designate.[5]

Believing that the collapse of international trade in the 1930s created conditions that led to the rise of dictators and the beginning of World War II, the victorious powers also created new international economic organizations to encourage trade. Meeting in Bretton Woods, New Hampshire, before the war ended, the victorious powers finalized the **Bretton Woods Agreement.**[6] This agreement established the **International Monetary Fund (IMF)** to stabilize exchange rates among major currencies and set their value in terms of the dollar and gold, and the International Bank for Reconstruction and Development, also called the **World Bank,** tasked to help the world recover economically from the destruction of World War II. The IMF and the World Bank continue to operate today.

The U.S. intention to participate in these institutions indicated a shift in U.S. attitudes regarding isolationism and unilateralism. To participate in these institutions, the United States had to be less isolationist and less unilateralist than before the war.

United Nations (UN)
An international governmental organization created shortly before the end of World War II to guarantee the security of nations and to promote global economic, physical, and social well-being.

international governmental organization (IGO)
An organization created by the governments of at least two and often many countries that operates internationally with the objectives of achieving the purposes that the member countries agree upon.

Bretton Woods Agreement
International financial agreement signed shortly before the end of World War II that created the World Bank and the International Monetary Fund.

International Monetary Fund (IMF)
International governmental organization created shortly before the end of World War II to stabilize international financial relations through fixed monetary exchange rates.

World Bank
International governmental organization created shortly before the end of World War II to provide loans for large economic development projects.

multilateralism
The U.S. foreign policy that actions should be taken in cooperation with other states after consultation.

Gradually, then, the country moved toward internationalism and **multilateralism**—a belief that foreign and military policy actions should be taken in cooperation with other states.

The Cold War and Containment: 1947–1960

Although the United States and the Soviet Union were allies during World War II, cooperation between them was strained. After the war, the situation deteriorated as the Soviets imposed communist governments in Eastern Europe and supported revolutionary movements and left-wing political parties throughout the world. Many Americans concluded that the Soviet Union was bent on dominating the world. How should the United States respond?

Truman Doctrine
U.S. policy initiated in 1947 of providing economic assistance and military aid to countries fighting against communist revolutions or political pressure.

This question was answered early in 1947 when both Greece and Turkey were threatened with communist takeover. President Harry S Truman addressed Congress, presenting the **Truman Doctrine:** "I believe that it must be the policy of the United States to support peoples who are resisting attempted subjugation by armed minorities or by outside pressures."[7] Under the Truman Doctrine, the United States provided economic and military aid to Greece and Turkey. A few weeks later, U.S. Secretary of State George Marshall proposed that the United States provide economic assistance to France, Germany, Great Britain, and other European states struggling to rebuild their economies. Congress supported the idea. In its first year of operation (1948–1949), the **Marshall Plan** provided more than $6 billion to European states to rebuild.[8] The Marshall Plan provided the basis for European economic recovery, which prevented communist parties from winning elections throughout Western Europe.

Marshall Plan
European Recovery Program, named after Secretary of State George C. Marshall, of extensive U.S. aid to Western Europe after World War II.

containment
Strategy to oppose expansion of Soviet power, particularly in Western Europe and East Asia, with military power, economic assistance, and political influence.

The Truman Doctrine and the Marshall Plan were the linchpins of the strategy of **containment.** As postulated by diplomat George Kennan, who like many Americans believed that the Soviet Union wanted to dominate the world, the United States would apply "counterforce" wherever the Soviet Union applied pressure.

North Atlantic Treaty Organization (NATO)
The first peacetime military treaty the United States joined, NATO is a regional political and military organization created in 1950.

Containment had other key elements. In 1949, the United States and eleven other countries signed the North Atlantic Treaty, which stated that all signatories considered an attack against one an attack against all.[9] The following year, treaty members created the **North Atlantic Treaty Organization (NATO),** a defense alliance to implement the treaty. Figure 19.1 depicts the strategic alliances of NATO and the Warsaw Pact, a defensive group the Soviets established with their Eastern European satellite countries to counter NATO.

In 1950, North Korea invaded South Korea. Taken by surprise, the United States sent troops under UN auspices to defend South Korea. Fighting dragged on indecisively until the warring parties reached a truce in 1953, dividing Korea almost exactly where it had been divided before North Korea's invasion. It remains divided today, with U.S. troops deployed along the border to protect South Korea.

Starting in the 1950s, much of the U.S. military strategy was based on nuclear weapons and deterrence. Deterrence was the theory that, if a potential enemy wanted to attack but knew that it would in turn be attacked, it would not attack. During the 1950s and 1960s, as the United States and the Soviet Union developed large nuclear arsenals, a new version of deterrence developed called mutual assured destruction (MAD). Under MAD, both the United States and the Soviet Union were deterred from launching a nuclear attack because each knew that if they attacked first, the other would still have enough nuclear weapons remaining to destroy the attacker as a functioning society. U.S. President Dwight D. Eisenhower and Soviet President Nikita Khrushchev held summit meetings in the 1950s to address their differences, but tensions often flared between the two superpowers.

Throughout the 1950s and into the 1960s, the world was largely divided into two camps, one led by the United States and the other by the Soviet Union. Containment was the core U.S. foreign and military policy during the Cold War, and most Americans accepted that containment required the United States to adopt pragmatic poli-

FIGURE 19.1 Cold War Alliances in Europe In 1949, the United States sponsored the creation of the North Atlantic Treaty Organization (NATO), an alliance of Western European nations, the United States, and Canada. Greece and Turkey were formally admitted to NATO membership in 1952, West Germany in 1955, and Spain in 1982. In response to the creation of NATO, the Soviet Union and seven other communist countries established a rival alliance, the Warsaw Pact, in 1949.

cies such as supporting authoritarian governments that opposed communism. While some Americans called for the return of isolationism, most Americans supported the country's more internationalist role in global affairs.

Containment, Cuba, and Vietnam: 1961–1969

When John F. Kennedy became president in 1961, he brought a sense of optimism and activism to the United States that captivated many Americans. "Ask not what your country can do for you," Kennedy urged Americans in his inaugural address, "but what you can do for your country."[10]

Containing the Soviet Union while at the same time establishing cordial relations with it to lessen the peril of nuclear war was high on President Kennedy's foreign and military policy agenda. Thus, in 1961, Kennedy met Khrushchev in Vienna, Austria. The meeting did not go well. Both leaders returned to their respective countries and increased military spending. In 1962, the Soviet Union began to deploy intermediate-range ballistic missiles in Cuba, only ninety miles from Florida, leading to the **Cuban Missile Crisis**.[11] The United States reacted strongly, placing a naval blockade around Cuba and warning the Soviet Union to withdraw the missiles or suffer the consequences. After several days during which the world was closer to nuclear war than it had ever been, Khrushchev backed down and withdrew the missiles. The world breathed a sigh of relief.

Cuban Missile Crisis
The 1962 confrontation that nearly escalated into war between the United States and the Soviet Union over Soviet deployment of medium-range ballistic missiles in Cuba.

Photo courtesy: Bachman/Image Works

What are the lessons of the Vietnam War? Many Americans visit the Vietnam War Memorial in Washington, D.C., to grieve for and honor those in the U.S. military who gave their lives during the conflict in Southeast Asia.

SIMULATION

You Are President John F. Kennedy

Vietnam War
Between 1965 and 1973, the United States deployed up to 500,000 troops to Vietnam to try to prevent North Vietnam from taking over South Vietnam; the effort failed and was extremely divisive within the United States.

The Cuban Missile Crisis led to a period of improved U.S.-Soviet relations. During the crisis, the United States and the Soviet Union had marched to the edge of nuclear war, and neither liked what they had seen. Thus, in 1963, the two nations concluded a partial nuclear test ban treaty and installed a "hot line" between Washington and Moscow to allow the leaders of the two countries to talk directly during crises.

The Cuban Missile Crisis confirmed the majority of Americans' belief that the Soviet Union was an expansionist power. Most Americans believed that containment was the correct strategy, and that the United States remained the moral defender of liberty and justice, acting pragmatically but always with restraint to prevent communist expansion. Few questioned the morality of containment, the necessity for pragmatism, or the need for internationalism and American-led multilateralism.

Then came the **Vietnam War.**[12] The United States sought to contain communism from spreading from North Vietnam into South Vietnam starting in the 1950s, but it was in the mid-1960s that U.S. bombing and ground operations began, and they escalated quickly. While many in South Vietnam were grateful for U.S. assistance, others were actively supporting the communists. The United States became embroiled in a civil war in which it was difficult to determine friend from foe. Eventually, the U.S. presence in Vietnam grew to more than 500,000 troops, 58,000 of whom were killed. As deaths mounted and costs grew, many Americans asked questions they had rarely asked before. Was the United States on the side of justice in Vietnam, or had it only replaced France there as a colonial power? How much killing and how great a cost would the United States bear to prevent the expansion of communism? Was communism still the enemy it had been? Increasingly, U.S. citizens became less persuaded that their mission in Vietnam was moral or that communism was universally dangerous. By the end of the 1960s, Americans were not as sure of their moral superiority as they had been, nor were they sure that containment was the proper strategy on which to base their foreign and military policy. President Lyndon B. Johnson, who had presided over the massive U.S. military escalation in Vietnam, became so unpopular by 1968 that he chose not to run for reelection.

Détente and Human Rights: 1969–1981

When Richard M. Nixon was inaugurated as president in 1969, he declared it was time to move from "an era of confrontation" to "an era of negotiation" in relations with the Soviet Union.[13] Recognizing that nuclear war would destroy life as it existed, searching for a way to exit Vietnam, and trying to improve East–West relations without conceding international leadership or renouncing containment, Nixon undertook policies that began this transformation. The improvement in U.S.-Soviet relations was called **détente.**[14]

The changed nature of U.S.-Soviet relations brought about by détente was best illustrated by the frequency of summit meetings. From 1972 to 1979, American and Soviet leaders met six times, but détente was more than summitry. It also included increased trade, arms control agreements, and cultural exchanges. Détente improved East–West

détente
The relaxation of tensions between the United States and the Soviet Union that occurred during the 1970s.

relations in Europe as well. For example, the heads of government of almost every nation in Europe and North America attended a meeting in Helsinki, Finland, in 1975.

When Jimmy Carter became president in 1977, he intended to pursue détente. However, he rejected Nixon's foreign policy cynicism that had emphasized pragmatism to the virtual exclusion of moralism. Carter instead emphasized **human rights,** that is, the protection of people's basic freedoms and needs. This found a sympathetic ear among many Americans. Once again, they believed, the United States would emphasize morality in foreign policy. Some Americans wondered, however, if Carter's emphasis on human rights was misdirected and was weakening the United States.[15]

Concern about American weakness grew in 1979 when radical Iranians, with the support of Iran's fundamentalist Islamic government, overran the U.S. embassy in Tehran and held the embassy staff captive. The Iranian hostage crisis eroded Carter's support in the United States. For over a year, the country was powerless to win the hostages' release. A failed rescue attempt added to American humiliation. (The hostages were not released until the day that Carter left office in 1981.)

Détente finally died in 1979 when the Soviet Union invaded Afghanistan. Described by Carter in his 1980 State of the Union Address as "the most serious threat to peace since the Second World War,"[16] the Soviet invasion led to an immediate increase in U.S. defense spending.

human rights
The belief that human beings have inalienable rights such as freedom of speech and freedom of religion.

Containment Revisited and Renewed: 1981–1989

The tense U.S.-Soviet relations during Jimmy Carter's last year as president became confrontational during President Ronald Reagan's first term in office. Reagan accelerated the U.S. arms buildup and, in response to Soviet influence in developing countries, initiated an activist foreign policy that included the invasion of Grenada, a pro-Soviet island nation in the Caribbean, and support for the Contras, an insurgency attempting to overthrow the pro-Soviet Sandinista government in Nicaragua in Central America. In addition, Reagan emphasized morality in American foreign policy and pushed to create an open international economic system.[17]

By 1984, however, relations between the United States and the Soviet Union were beginning to improve. The two countries upgraded their hotlines and agreed to expand arms-control talks. Most importantly, the rhetoric from both capitals deescalated. What happened? First, the 1984 U.S. presidential election constrained U.S. rhetoric. Although most Americans supported the arms buildup, they were concerned about confrontation with the Soviets. In response, Reagan moderated his statements. Second, U.S. foreign and military policy initiatives had an impact on Moscow as, in addition to its arms buildup, the United States implemented the **Reagan Doctrine,** under which the United States provided arms to anti-Soviet movements fighting pro-Soviet governments in Afghanistan, Angola, Mozambique, and Nicaragua. These programs increased the cost of Soviet involvement there and led Soviet leaders to rethink their foreign policy. Finally, the Soviet Union had serious internal problems. Its economy was performing poorly and it had a leadership crisis, with three Soviet leaders dying between 1982 and 1985. These problems had to be addressed. To do this, the Soviet Union needed a less confrontational relationship with the United States.

Reagan Doctrine
Policy that the United States would provide military assistance to anti-communist groups fighting against pro-Soviet governments.

Photo courtesy: Tannen Murray/Image Works

How important is the role of diplomacy to successful U.S. foreign policy?
After several tense years in U.S.-Soviet relations, the emergence of Mikhail Gorbachev as Soviet premier in 1985 led to the adoption of stunning reforms in the Soviet Union and a series of increasingly friendly summit meetings between Gorbachev and U.S. President Ronald Reagan.

Recognizing this, Soviet President Mikhail Gorbachev worked with Reagan to improve relations after Gorbachev became the Soviet leader in 1985. Even before Gorbachev's reforms took hold, Gorbachev and Reagan laid the groundwork for a transformation in relations.[18] At the third of five summit meetings, the two leaders signed an agreement to destroy all intermediate-range nuclear weapons. Gorbachev introduced "perestroika"—reforms in domestic, foreign, and military policies that transformed the Soviet Union and U.S.-Soviet relations. Although the reforms were intended to address the serious problems that the Soviet Union faced, they eventually led to the end of the Cold War and the demise of the Soviet Union.[19]

Searching for a New International Order: 1989–2001

George Bush, vice president during President Reagan's two terms, assumed the presidency in 1989 pledging to continue Reagan's foreign policy directions. However, the pace and scope of change in Eastern Europe and the Soviet Union raised questions about the entire direction of U.S. foreign policy. The first question came from Eastern Europe. In 1989, the people of many Eastern European states revolted against their governments. During previous rebellions, Soviet troops stationed in Eastern Europe subdued the rebellions. This time, Gorbachev ordered Soviet troops to remain in their barracks. The rebellions continued, and in every communist country in Eastern Europe, the government fell.

The United States was not quite sure how to respond. At first, Bush proceeded cautiously. As it became clear that the revolutions were irreversible, the United States and other democratic states helped the new noncommunist Eastern European states try to establish democratic political and free market economic systems. Remarkably, in a matter of months, the so-called "Iron Curtain" in Europe had collapsed, with almost no serious bloodshed.

The 1990 Iraqi invasion of Kuwait produced a new challenge. The Bush administration believed that the invasion threatened vital U.S. interests, and the United Nations passed a resolution authorizing the use of force to expel Iraq from Kuwait. Shortly after Congress voted to support the use of military force against Iraq, the Persian Gulf War began in January 1991. In an attack called Operation Desert Storm, U.S. and allied forces defeated Iraq in a matter of weeks. The objective—expelling Iraq from Kuwait—had been achieved with few U.S. casualties.[20] The conduct of Operation Desert Storm reflected the principles of the **Powell Doctrine** articulated by Colin Powell, President Bush's chair of the Joint Chiefs of Staff.

Meanwhile, startling events were unfolding in the Soviet Union. Under Gorbachev, the Soviet Union posed less and less of a threat as the United States and Soviet Union forged an increasingly close relationship. Weakened by a failed coup attempt against Gorbachev in the summer of 1991, its economy in shambles, and torn by internal dissent and the desires of nationalities for independence, the Soviet Union collapsed.[21] The Cold War was over, as was the need for containment. Once again Americans asked questions: What would U.S. strategy now be? With the Cold War over, should the United States cut defense spending, and if so, how much? How much aid should the United States send to its former enemy to help it survive its collapse? What criteria would guide decisions about where and when to employ U.S. forces abroad in a world with only one remaining superpower?

These were the complex questions Bill Clinton faced when he assumed the presidency in 1993. Defining the American role in this world presented a challenge. Clinton's agenda centered on implementing engagement and enlargement, shaping new international economic relationships, deciding when U.S. armed forces should be used overseas, and puzzling over what role the United States should play in the post–Cold War world. **Engagement** meant that the United States would not retreat into isolationism as it did after World War I and for a short time after World War II. Engagement implied that the United States relied on negotiations and cooperation rather than confrontation and conflict, although it would use force when necessary. **Enlargement** meant that the United States would promote democracy, open markets, and other Western political, economic,

Powell Doctrine
The Powell Doctrine advocates an all-or-nothing approach to military intervention. Among other criteria, it emphasizes the use of overwhelming force to ensure a quick and decisive victory, and the adoption of an exit strategy prior to any intervention.

engagement
Policy implemented during the Clinton administration that the United States would remain actively involved in foreign affairs.

enlargement
Policy implemented during the Clinton administration that the United States would actively promote the expansion of democracy and free markets throughout the world.

and social values. In practice, engagement and enlargement led to the implementation of the Partnership for Peace program with former communist states in Eastern Europe and the former Soviet Union and the expansion of NATO.

Deciding when to use U.S. armed forces overseas is a vexing problem. As we have seen, from the end of World War II to the collapse of the Soviet Union, U.S. military intervention was usually tied to containing communism. With the Soviet Union gone, this easy benchmark for deciding when to intervene no longer existed. The administration faced different types of crises in countries in Africa, Eastern Europe, Asia, the Middle East, and the Caribbean and intervened militarily in a number of those countries, but no pattern related to the use of U.S. military force overseas became evident. In some cases the U.S. response was largely humanitarian, other situations dictated peacekeeping or peace enforcement efforts, and still others involved combat activities.

International economic issues were another focus of Clinton's activities. He guided the **North American Free Trade Agreement (NAFTA)** into law, establishing the free flow of goods among Canada, Mexico, and the United States. The United States under Clinton also played an important role in initiating two other major free trade areas: the Free Trade Area of the Americas and the Asia-Pacific Economic Cooperation agreement, as well as creating the **World Trade Organization (WTO)**, charged with overseeing world trade, judging trade disputes, and lowering tariffs.[22]

The War on Terrorism: 2001 to the Present

During his first months as president, George W. Bush (a son of former President George Bush) conducted an active foreign policy. Relations with Latin America, Europe, Russia, and China all loomed large on the new president's agenda, as did security, international economics, immigration, drugs, and the environment. However, suddenly and unexpectedly, the Bush administration's foreign and defense priorities became clearly focused.

On September 11, 2001, members of **al-Qaeda**, a terrorist network founded and funded by Muslim fundamentalist Osama bin Laden, hijacked four jetliners, flying two into the twin towers of New York's World Trade Center. The impact destroyed the towers and killed almost 3,000 people. Another hijacked plane slammed into the Pentagon, killing 189 individuals. The fourth plane headed toward Washington, D.C., but crashed into a field in Pennsylvania after passengers charged the hijackers and forced them to lose control of the plane.[23]

After the 9/11 attacks, President Bush, declaring a **war on terrorism**, organized a coalition of nations to combat the threat posed by terrorist groups such as al-Qaeda. He also demanded that Afghanistan's **Taliban** government, which had provided safe haven for bin Laden and al-Qaeda's terrorist training camps, turn bin Laden over to the United States. When the Taliban

North American Free Trade Agreement (NAFTA)
Agreement that promotes free movement of goods and services among Canada, Mexico, and the United States.

World Trade Organization (WTO)
International governmental organization created in 1995 that manages multilateral negotiations to reduce barriers to trade and settle trade disputes.

al-Qaeda
Worldwide terrorist organization led by Osama bin Laden; responsible for numerous terrorist attacks against U.S. interests, including 9/11 attacks against the World Trade Center and the Pentagon.

war on terrorism
Initiated by George W. Bush after the September 11, 2001, attacks to weed out terrorist operatives throughout the world, using diplomacy, military means, improved homeland security, stricter banking laws, and other means.

Taliban
Fundamentalist Islamic government of Afghanistan that provided terrorist training bases for al-Qaeda.

Photo courtesy: Thomas Nillson/Getty Images

How did the September 11 terrorist attacks affect Americans and American policies? The south tower of the World Trade Center collapses September 11, 2001, after it was struck by a hijacked airplane. The north tower, also struck by a hijacked plane, collapsed shortly after. The attacks caused enormous loss of life and resulted in the creation of the Department of Homeland Security, as well as the passage of a host of controversial laws intended to protect the United States from terrorist threats.

Timeline: Major Acts of Terrorism Affecting the United States, 1990 - Present

January 15, 1990 U.S. embassy bombing—Attack in Lima, Peru, by local revolutionaries.

June 26, 1996 Khobar Towers bombing—Truck bomb explodes outside of the U.S. military's Khobar Towers housing facility in Khobar, Saudi Arabia. Twenty killed and over 300 injured.

September 11, 2001 9/11 terrorist attacks—Planes hijacked by members of al-Qaeda destroy the World Trade Center in New York City and damage the Pentagon in Washington, D.C. A fourth hijacked airplane crashes in Pennsylvania. Nearly 3,000 dead and thousands more injured. The deadliest terrorist attack on U.S. soil in the nation's history.

April 14, 1993 Assassination attempt— Attempted assassination of former President George Bush by Iraqi intelligence during a visit to Kuwait.

October 12, 2000 U.S.S. Cole attack—Attack on the destroyer U.S.S. Cole in Aden, Yemen. A small boat loaded with explosives rams the destroyer.

February 26, 1993 World Trade Center bombing in New York City—Car bomb explodes in an underground garage; six killed and over a thousand injured. Khaled Shaikh Mohammed and more than six others are charged with planning and financing the attack.

August 7, 1998 U.S. embassy bombings—Attacks on embassies in East Africa including Nairobi, Kenya and Dar es Salaam, Tanzania.

April 19, 1995 Oklahoma City bombing—Bombing of the Alfred P. Murrah Federal Building in Oklahoma City, Oklahoma, by anti-government extremists Timothy McVeigh and Terry Nichols. 168 people killed; over 800 injured. The deadliest terrorist attack on U.S. soil until the 9/11 attacks.

refused, the Bush administration launched Operation Enduring Freedom against al-Qaeda and the Taliban regime in October 2001. The military operation included air strikes against Taliban and al-Qaeda targets and support for the Northern Alliance, an Afghani opposition force battling Taliban control. By the end of 2001, the Taliban were overthrown and the United States was committed to peace enforcement in Afghanistan and assistance with the transition to a democratic government.

The terrorist attacks of September 11, 2001, had a profound impact on U.S. foreign policy. (To learn more about acts of terrorism affecting the United States, see the Timeline.) Despite its superpower status and nuclear superiority, the United States appeared vulnerable in a way it had not previously. President Bush responded by inaugurating a global campaign against terrorists and their supporters. Like other presidents before him, George W. Bush was putting his distinctive stamp on how the

December 6, 2004 U.S. consulate bombing—Attack on U.S. Consulate in Jeddah, Saudi Arabia.

March 20, 2002
U.S. embassy bombing—Car bombing at a shopping center near the U.S. Embassy in Lima, Peru, three days before an official visit by President George W. Bush.

July 7, 2005
London bombings—Bombs explode on a double-decker bus and three London Underground trains, killing 56 people and injuring over 700, on the first day of the 31st G-8 Conference. Attacks are the first suicide bombings in Western Europe.

October-November 2001 Anthrax attacks—Anthrax spores mailed to several television networks in New York and to the offices of two Democratic senators in Washington, D.C. Five people die and 17 are sickened. FBI implicates American biodefense scientist, but questions linger after the scientist commits suicide in 2008.

September 13, 2006 U.S. embassy attack—Gunmen attack security guards outside the U.S. Embassy in Damascus, Syria.

2005- 2009
Attacks in Iraq, Afghanistan, Pakistan—Numerous attacks on U.S. contractors and armed forces in Iraq, Pakistan, and Afghanistan; kidnapping and executions of journalists, military personnel, and private contractors.

July 30, 2004
U.S. embassy bombing—Attack on U.S. Embassy in Uzbekistan.

country should address threats to national security. Bush and his foreign policy team concluded that a more ambitious, "muscular" posture was needed to fight threats to U.S. interests. Instead of relying on the reactive strategies of deterrence and containment or the strategies of enlargement and engagement that had characterized the Clinton Administration's approach to foreign policy, the Bush administration advocated a proactive doctrine of preemptive military action, commonly referred to as the **Bush Doctrine.**

When the United States launched its war against Saddam Hussein's regime in Iraq in March 2003, it signaled the implementation of the Bush Doctrine. In past conflicts of this magnitude, the United States had intervened militarily in response to a direct attack (such as Pearl Harbor), or to defend other countries that had been invaded (such as South Korea or Kuwait). The 2003 U.S.-led invasion of Iraq was part

Bush Doctrine
Policy advocated by President George W. Bush of using preemptive military action against a perceived threat to U.S. interests.

Join the Debate

Should the United States Pull Out of the United Nations?

OVERVIEW: The United Nations came into existence in 1945 in the wake of two world wars and the desire of most nations for an international organization dedicated to pursuing global justice, peace, and human rights. To back up its mandate, the United States and the United Nations have usually worked together to help maintain relative global security. For example, UN member nations helped defend South Korea from invasion by North Korea, provided a blueprint to help mediate peace in the Middle East, and voted for sanctions against South Africa to help end racial apartheid. The UN has also helped millions living in famine and aided countless refugees fleeing war and natural disasters by providing food, shelter, clothing, and medical relief.

Since the end of the Cold War, the United States and the United Nations have developed competing and sometimes antagonistic views with regard to the UN's mandate and global role. In 1992, for example, the UN released a bold initiative—the Agenda for Peace—to recast the UN's peacekeeping role. The move was viewed by some U.S. policy makers as giving the UN control over U.S. military and foreign policy resources and it received a great deal of criticism in Congress.

Furthermore, due to disagreements with the United States over a variety of issues, including its military and foreign policy role in the Middle East, its refusal to ratify the Kyoto climate change treaty, and its opposition to a treaty to abolish land mines, the UN voted the United States off the UN Human Rights Commission in 2001. This action infuriated the Bush administration, because countries that engage in human rights violations, such as Sudan, Libya,

and Cuba, retained their seats on the commission. The United States walked out of the UN conference on racism in 2001 because it objected to criticisms of Israel in a draft of the conference's final declaration. The strain between the Bush administration and the United Nations increased even more in 2003 when the UN Security Council refused to sanction military action against Iraq.

On the other hand, the UN also faced criticism for a major financial scandal involving its Oil for Food program, which had been created during Saddam Hussein's regime in order to give the Iraqi people humanitarian aid while sanctions against Hussein's government were in place. A son of the U.N. Secretary General at the time was implicated in this scandal. Nearly $1 billion disappeared into hidden bank accounts and fake corporations, and the U.S. Congress launched an investigation into where the money went.

Arguments IN FAVOR of the United States Pulling Out of the United Nations

- It is difficult for the United Nations to act, and even when it does, it is incapable of enforcing its own resolutions. In 2006, Iran made public its intention to develop nuclear weapons, but the UN could not forge a consensus regarding how to respond. China and Russia balked at imposing sanctions on Iran, creating an impasse within the Security Council. When the UN has passed resolutions on Israel, Palestine, Iraq, and Darfur, there has been no significant implementation. When the United States attacked and occupied Iraq in 2003, it claimed that it was in part enforcing UN resolutions that the UN itself was incapable or unwilling to enforce. Getting the global community to act with one voice can be extremely

weapons of mass destruction (WMDs)
Biological, chemical, and nuclear weapons, which present a sizeable threat to U.S. security.

of a new strategy that sought to promote American security through preemptive military strikes against potentially dangerous nations. Based on faulty intelligence information that suggested the Hussein regime was developing **weapons of mass destruction (WMDs)**—nuclear, chemical, or biological weapons—and believing that Iraq was a safe harbor and potential breeding ground for terrorists, the U.S. government chose to act even though the UN Security Council refused to endorse the recourse to war, and even without the support of key allies such as France and Ger-

difficult, given the diverse interests of the countries that are represented on the Security Council and within the larger UN body.

■ **The United States is not accountable to international organizations when pursuing its own interests.** The United States and the United Nations have divergent interests and understandings of international law and diplomacy. Placing members of the American armed forces under UN command cedes control to an organization that may not always act in the best interests of the United States. The United States must maintain its ability to act in whatever way it sees fit to defend its interests at home and abroad.

■ **Adhering to UN resolutions results in giving up American sovereignty.** Some supporters of U.S. withdrawal from the United Nations believe the UN is attempting to create a "world government" and that to accede to UN mandates and resolutions is to relinquish U.S. sovereignty and U.S. control over its own citizens. Many see the UN as one more instance of the international community trying to institute international government.

Arguments AGAINST the United States Pulling Out of the United Nations

■ **The UN engages in peacekeeping and nation building when the United States will not.** The UN is currently engaged in about fifteen peacekeeping operations, with more than 72,000 uniformed personnel from member nations in places such as Lebanon, Haiti, and Sudan. The UN can provide peacekeeping support when the United States is either unable or unwilling, thus preventing humanitarian disaster and conflict. This is an essential function if global security and stability are to be maintained.

■ **The United States must lead by example.** Because the United States has a unique world military and economic position, it can use its various strengths and principles to promote global peace and justice. Why should other nations respond to UN resolutions and decrees when the United States does not? By acceding to UN requests, the United States can set an example for other nations to follow, and this may help facilitate other nations' compliance with UN wishes to ensure global security. Instead of attempting to form and maintain coalitions to support various actions, the United States can provide leadership and work within the United Nations.

■ **International institutions provide global stability and promote peaceful conflict resolution.** Since the establishment of the United Nations, there have been no worldwide wars. The UN was able to provide security for South Korea and it acts as an international forum for conflict mediation. Though imperfect, the UN affords a medium in which human rights policy is debated and developed and international security and stability discussed. For example, the UN has taken on the cause of disarmament and elimination of weapons of mass destruction and thereby provides legitimacy in this policy domain, whereas the United States cannot. Because the United States is a world power, its membership in the UN gives the organization credibility and validity.

Continuing the Debate

1. Does adhering to UN mandates mean giving up national sovereignty? Explain.
2. What can be done to reconcile U.S. and UN interests? Do the United States and the United Nations have similar interests?
3. Is the United States better off acting unilaterally rather than trying to achieve agreement within the United Nations?

To Follow the Debate Online, Go To:

www.unausa.org, the Web site for the United Nations Association of the United States of America, a nonprofit, nonpartisan organization that seeks to provide effective leadership by the United States in the United Nations.

www.eagleforum.org, the Web site of the Eagle Forum, a conservative advocacy group that opposes continued membership and participation of the United States in the United Nations.

many. The failure of the United States to win approval from the Security Council for the 2003 invasion of Iraq led to vigorous debate at home and abroad, and U.S. actions created hard feelings among many of America's traditional allies. (To learn more about the relations between the United States and its allies, see Join the Debate: Should the United States Pull Out of the United Nations?)

The overthrow of Saddam Hussein's government in the spring of 2003 was relatively quick. The U.S.-led bombing campaign destroyed much of the military and governmental infrastructure in Iraq within days. The Iraqi armed forces seemed helpless and disorganized. Within weeks, U.S. and other allied forces entered Hussein's palaces, tore down statues of the dictator around the country, and began to create a post-Saddam government in Iraq. American forces ultimately captured Saddam Hussein himself on December 13, 2003.

Over time, coalition forces failed to find evidence of an active nuclear weapons program in Iraq—the original justification provided by the Bush administration for a preemptive military strike. As evidence of WMDs failed to materialize, the Bush administration changed its justification for war, arguing that Saddam Hussein posed a severe danger to the world because of his long history of brutality, and emphasizing the goal of promoting democracy in the Middle East through his removal from power.

In the months after President Bush declared an end to major combat, soldiers from the United States and its allies found themselves under attack from mortar fire, roadside bombings, and suicide missions by various insurgents. As the American military presence in Iraq continued, war deaths and injuries mounted. By the end of 2006, more than 2,900 U.S. service men and women had lost their lives in Iraq and more than 22,000 had been injured.[24]

A positive development, however, was the January 2005 election in which the Iraqi people chose representatives for a 275-member national assembly. The election marked an important step in the process of turning over control of the country from the U.S.-led coalition to the Iraqis themselves. But hopes for an end to the growing civil unrest and a withdrawal of U.S. troops declined. On August 14, 2005, the *Washington Post* quoted a dismal assessment of the situation in Iraq from an anonymous U.S. senior official: "the United States no longer expects to see a model new democracy, a self-supporting oil industry, or a society in which the majority of people are free from serious security or economic challenges. . . . What we expected to achieve was never realistic given the timetable or what unfolded on the ground."[25] Throughout 2006, Iraqi insurgents and foreign terrorists continued their attacks against the U.S.-led coalition forces, and increasing sectarian violence led many observers to characterize the chaos in Iraq as a civil war among Sunni, Shi'ite, and Kurdish factions.

When Democrats gained control of both houses of Congress in the 2006 midterm elections, their success was in part attributed to public dissatisfaction with the situation in Iraq. Secretary of Defense Donald Rumsfeld's resignation after the elections and his replacement with Robert M. Gates, a less polarizing figure, suggested the administration intended to adjust its policy on Iraq in response to rising violence there and waning public support.

In early 2007, President Bush announced an American troop surge designed to reduce sectarian violence in Iraq and enable the Iraqi government to make political progress. Escalating violence in Baghdad, however, along with other tensions, made it almost impossible for the Iraqi government to achieve results. By the end of 2007, General David H. Petraeus, the top military official in Iraq, reported a significant decline in suicide attacks and civilian casualties; yet 2007 remained the deadliest year for U.S. troops. By mid-2008, more than 4,000 U.S. military personnel and Department of Defense civilians had died in Iraq, and 30,000 had been reported wounded.

The September 11 terrorist attacks gave the United States two overarching foreign and defense policy priorities: defense of the homeland and pursuing the global war on terrorism. Few Americans disagree with these priorities, but disagreements and controversies continue regarding the means to these ends and the effectiveness of government policies. (To learn more about terrorism responses on campus, see Ideas into Action: The Impact of the War on Terrorism on American Campuses.) Moreover, other foreign

The Impact of the War on Terrorism on American Campuses

American campuses have become part of a national strategy to improve homeland security. Even though most of the 9/11 hijackers were on tourist or work visas, two were in the United States on student visas. Concern over terrorists on student visas increased more when, several months after the attacks, the Immigration and Naturalization Service (INS) admitted it had processed a pre-9/11 visa application from one of the hijackers and granted a student visa to him even after he had conducted one of the attacks and died. In March 2003, the INS came under the Department of Homeland Security (DHS) as the U.S. Citizenship and Immigration Services (USCIS).

The most notable impact on campuses of the efforts to improve security was the implementation of the Student and Exchange Visitor Information System (SEVIS) required by the USA Patriot Act of 2001. SEVIS is a Web-based registration and tracking system operated by the DHS to monitor nearly 1 million international students and their dependents. Last year Immigration and Customs Enforcement officers investigated 3,129 students not complying with visa rules and made 1,108 arrests.

Experts say the computer-based system has improved national security by giving the DHS faster and more reliable information on the whereabouts and activities of foreign students. But, the system has also significantly increased the burden of accountability on universities and international students. Universities and colleges must report the comings and goings of every international student and visiting foreign professor. In April 2008, the DHS announced that it would double the fees paid by international students—from $100 to $200—to help cover the costs of SEVIS.

- Is it fair to require colleges and universities to track their international students and visitors? Should the federal government pay college administrators for such a task, or is such a process the financial responsibility of the colleges and universities that accept foreign students into their programs?
- Do you agree with the decision by the Department of Homeland Security to double the fees associated with studying in the United States to support the costs of maintaining the SEVIS system?
- Is the SEVIS system a violation of privacy for international students and their dependents?
- To learn more about the Student and Exchange Visitor Program, visit www.ice.gov/sevis/.
- What kind of impact is SEVIS having at your college or university? Do you know how many international students are currently enrolled at your institution?
- If you were to study abroad, would your host country track your academic progress and whereabouts?

Sources: U.S. House of Representatives, Committee on Science, "Dealing with Students and Scholars in an Age of Terrorism: Visa Backlogs and Tracking Systems," March 26, 2003; Homeland Security Presidential Directive 2, October 2001; Lynn Franey and Samuel Siringi, "Post-Sept 11 Requirements Put Squeeze on Colleges," *Kansas City Star* (April 27, 2008).

and defense policy issues, such as the threat of a nuclear-armed Iran, increased extremist violence in Afghanistan, the security of Pakistan's nuclear arsenal, and the humanitarian crisis in Sudan, have also captured the public's attention.

Having discussed the history of U.S. foreign policy during the twentieth century and the new direction of foreign policy during the presidency of George W. Bush, we turn to how foreign policy is made and the major players involved.

Foreign and Defense Policy Decision Making

The executive branch is the most powerful branch of government in the formulation and implementation of U.S. foreign and defense policy. Congress also influences and shapes policy, as do the military-industrial complex, the news media, and the public.

The Executive Branch

The executive branch is the locus for creating and implementing U.S. foreign and defense policy; within the executive branch, the president is the most important individual. Among executive departments, the Department of State is primarily responsible for diplomatic activity and the Department of Defense for military policy. Other executive agencies, such as the National Security Council, the Joint Chiefs of Staff, and the Central Intelligence Agency provide additional resources for the president. The relatively new Department of Homeland Security has a role to play in foreign and defense policy making as well.

THE PRESIDENT The president is preeminent in foreign and defense policy for several reasons. The president alone is in charge of all executive-branch resources. The president has greater access to and control over information, and the president alone can act with little fear that his actions will be countermanded.

American presidents have often used their authority to order U.S. armed forces to engage in actions without seeking approval from others. Ronald Reagan ordered air strikes against Libya and the invasion of Grenada; George Bush ordered the invasion of Panama; and Bill Clinton ordered cruise missile attacks against Afghanistan, Iraq, and Sudan. Although these presidents informed congressional leaders of their intended actions, they made the decisions and undertook the actions on their own authority. For far more extensive and serious military commitments—such as the 1991 Persian Gulf War and the 2003 U.S.-led invasion of Iraq—the president sought and received congressional approval in advance.

The president has exclusive sources of information—Department of State diplomats, military attaches working for the Department of Defense, CIA agents, and technical means of gathering information, such as satellites—that others do not have. Private citizens, companies, interest groups, Congress, and the media cannot match the president's information resources.

THE DEPARTMENTS OF STATE AND DEFENSE The Departments of State and Defense have responsibility for implementing U.S. diplomatic and military policy respectively. The **Department of State** employs more than 30,000 people who gather information on foreign political, economic, social, and military situations; represent the United States in negotiations and international organizations; staff U.S. embassies and consulates in more than 180 countries, and manage numerous international assistance programs.

Funding for foreign affairs programs directed by the Department of State was approximately $30 billion in 2008, including funding for economic development, disease prevention, nuclear nonproliferation, anti-terrorism, the Peace Corps, and global peacekeeping capabilities.

The **Department of Defense** contributes to policy formulation and provides the forces to undertake military operations. Under the secretary of defense and other appointed civilian officials, the Department of Defense directs U.S. forces from the Pentagon, a complex across the Potomac River from Washington, D.C. With thousands of civilian employees and millions of active-duty, National Guard, and reserve military personnel, the Department of Defense is among the most influential executive departments.

Within the Department of Defense, the **Joint Chiefs of Staff** is an important advisory body to the president, the secretary of defense, and the National Security Council. The Joint Chiefs of Staff provides a link between senior civilian leadership in the Department of Defense and the professional military, and the office often assists with the coordination of the various branches of the armed forces.

The Department of Defense is also home to some of the nation's most sophisticated intelligence organizations, including the **National Security Agency (NSA),**

You Are the President of the United States

Evaluating Defense Spending

Department of State
Chief executive-branch department responsible for formulation and implementation of U.S. foreign policy.

Department of Defense
Chief executive-branch department responsible for formulation and implementation of U.S. military policy.

Joint Chiefs of Staff
Advisory body to the president that includes the army chief of staff, the air force chief of staff, the chief of naval operations, and the marine commandant.

National Security Agency (NSA)
Intelligence agency primarily responsible for gathering intelligence from electronic and nonelectronic sources and for breaking foreign information transmission codes.

which gathers intelligence from electronic and other sources and undertakes code breaking; the **Central Intelligence Agency (CIA),** which collects and analyzes information necessary to meet national security requirements; and the **National Security Council (NSC),** which advises the president on foreign and military affairs. The CIA is the best-known intelligence agency, but it is only one of many government organizations engaged in intelligence work within the Department of Defense. The Departments of State, Homeland Security, Treasury, and Energy also maintain intelligence units. The CIA is an independent agency and its head, the director of central intelligence, reports directly to the president. The Intelligence Reform and Terrorism Prevention Act of 2004 established a director of national intelligence who oversees the entire intelligence community. After the 9/11 terrorist attacks, the CIA and the rest of the intelligence community were criticized for failing to identify clues that could have prevented the attacks and for relying too heavily on electronic means of gathering intelligence and not heavily enough on human sources. Controversy over faulty intelligence about Iraq, the agency's serious lack of human intelligence sources in a number of trouble spots, and its connection to secret prisons and controversial interrogation techniques generated a great deal of criticism on Capitol Hill and among the public.[26] (To learn more about controversial private security firms in Iraq, see Politics Now: Blackwater.)

Central Intelligence Agency (CIA)
Executive agency responsible for collection and analysis of information and intelligence about foreign countries and events.

National Security Council (NSC)
Executive agency responsible for advising the president about foreign and defense policy and events.

The National Security Council was set up to institutionalize the system by which the U.S. government integrates foreign and military policy and to coordinate U.S. activities on a range of foreign policy and defense issues. Former NSC advisers include Henry Kissinger, Colin Powell, and Condoleezza Rice. The NSC includes the president, the vice president, the secretaries of state and defense, the chair of the Joint Chiefs of Staff, and the director of the CIA.

The NSC staff is relatively small when compared with the large bureaucracies of the Departments of State or Defense. The NSC is located in the west wing of the White House and provides advice on foreign and military affairs directly to the president. As an advisory body, it is closely connected to the president and is shielded from media scrutiny more than other agencies in the executive bureaucracy.

Thinking Globally
Military Spending

According to the Center for Arms Control and Non-Proliferation, the United States accounts for 48 percent of the world's total military spending. The nations of Europe, combined, reflect the second highest amount spent—20 percent, less than half the U.S. total. China's spending accounts for 8 percent of the total, while Russia's military spending now represents a mere 5 percent of the global total, despite its former military strength during the Cold War.

- Are you surprised in any way by these figures? Why or why not?
- Does the war on terrorism justify comparatively high military spending? Explain your answer.

THE DEPARTMENT OF HOMELAND SECURITY Following the 9/11 terrorist attacks on the United States, the Office of Homeland Security was created by executive order and tasked to coordinate the executive branch's efforts to "detect, prepare for, prevent, protect against, respond to, and recover from terrorist attacks against the United States." Legislation in late 2002 converted this office into the Cabinet-level **Department of Homeland Security (DHS).** This was the largest reorganization of the federal government since the creation of the Department of Defense in 1947. The homeland security reorganization brought the functions of twenty-two existing agencies, approximately thirty newly created agencies or offices, and 180,000 employees under a single department. The mission of the department is to protect the American public from future acts of terror by engaging in activities designed to thwart terrorist activities and respond to any future crises.

Department of Homeland Security
Cabinet department created after the 9/11 attacks to coordinate domestic U.S. security efforts against terrorism.

The department is the locus for federal, state, and local homeland security coordination. Staff members work with state, local, and private-sector partners to identify threats, determine vulnerabilities, and target resources. The department includes the Transportation Security Administration (TSA), the organization responsible for aviation security; the Federal Emergency Management Agency (FEMA), the primary federal disaster relief organization; Customs and Border Protection; the Coast Guard; the Secret Service; and immigration services and enforcement.

Immigration

POLITICS NOW

Source: WASHINGTON POST   December 24, 2007

Private Security Firms in Iraq

Warnings Unheeded on Guards in Iraq

STEVE FAINARU

The U.S. government disregarded numerous warnings over the past two years about the risks of using Blackwater Worldwide and other private security firms in Iraq, expanding their presence even after a series of shooting incidents showed that the firms were operating with little regulation or oversight, according to government officials, private security firms and documents.

The warnings were conveyed in letters and memorandums from defense and legal experts and in high-level discussions between U.S. and Iraqi officials. They reflected growing concern about the lack of control over the tens of thousands of private guards in Iraq, the largest private security force ever employed by the United States in wartime.

Neither the Pentagon nor the State Department took substantive action to regulate private security companies until Blackwater guards opened fire Sept. 16, 2007, at a Baghdad traffic circle, killing 17 Iraqi civilians and provoking protests over the role of security contractors in Iraq.

"Why is it they couldn't see this coming?" said Christopher Beese, chief administrative officer for ArmorGroup International, a British security firm with extensive operations in Iraq. "That amazes me. Somebody—it could have been military officers, it could have been State—anybody could have waved a flag and said, 'Stop, this is not good news for us.'"

Private security firms rushed into Iraq after the March 2003 invasion. The U.S. military, which entered the country with 130,000 troops, needed additional manpower to protect supply convoys, military installations and diplomats. Last year, the Pentagon estimated that 20,000 hired guns worked in Iraq; the Government Accountability Office estimated 48,000.

On Feb. 7, 2006, Blackwater guards allegedly killed three Kurdish civilians outside the northern city of Kirkuk. The incident was one of several shootings that caused friction between the U.S. and Iraqi governments. On Christmas Eve 2006, a Blackwater employee killed the bodyguard of an Iraqi vice president in the Green Zone. Six weeks later, a Blackwater sniper killed three security guards for the state-run media network. On May 24, a Blackwater team shot and killed a civilian driver outside the Interior Ministry gates, sparking an armed standoff between the Blackwater guards and Iraqi security forces in downtown Baghdad.

By June 6, concerns about Blackwater had reached Iraq's National Intelligence Committee, which included senior Iraqi and U.S. intelligence officials. Maj. Gen. Hussein Kamal, who heads the Interior Ministry's intelligence directorate, called on U.S. authorities to crack down on private security companies.

U.S. military officials told Kamal that Blackwater was under State Department authority and outside their control, according to notes of the meeting. The matter was dropped.

"We set this thing up for failure from the beginning," said T.X. Hammes, a retired Marine colonel who advised the new Iraqi army from January to March 2004. "We're just sorting it out now," Hammes said. "I still think, from a pure counterinsurgency standpoint, armed contractors are an inherently bad idea, because you cannot control the quality, you cannot control the action on the ground, but you're held responsible for everything they do."

U.S. officials argue that security contractors save money and free up troops for more urgent tasks, such as fighting insurgents. "Certainly there have been moments of frustration where people here have said, 'Maybe we should just take over the whole operation, even if it stretches our forces more,'" Pentagon spokesman Geoff Morell said. "But the reality is that we think our resources are better utilized taking it to the bad guys than guarding warehouses and escorting convoys."

The State Department investigated previous Blackwater shootings and found

no indication of wrongdoing, according to a senior official involved in security matters. He said the U.S. Embassy discussed any concerns the Iraqi government had about the company's conduct. "I'm not aware of the significant warnings," said the official, who spoke on condition of anonymity because of ongoing investigations related to the Sept. 16 shooting.

But the laws governing security contractors still have not been clarified. On Sept. 30, 2006, Congress passed a provision aimed at giving the military authority over all contractors in Iraq, including Blackwater. But the provision has not been implemented by the Pentagon. The 15-month delay "has led to much confusion over who will be covered . . . and has called into question whether the Department plans to utilize this provision," Sen. Lindsey O. Graham (R-S.C.) and Sen. John F. Kerry (D-Mass.), who sponsored the provision, wrote in a letter to Defense Secretary Robert M. Gates shortly after the Sept. 16 incident.

The Pentagon is studying whether the provision can withstand legal scrutiny, Pentagon spokesman Bryan Whitman said.

Discussion Questions

1. *In previous wars, the Department of Defense prohibited private security contractors from participating in combat. This policy was revised in 2005. Should private security forces be involved in combat situations? Why or why not? What role, if any, should private security firms play in military operations?*

2. *What degree of oversight should the Pentagon exercise over private security forces hired by the Department of Defense? How can the Pentagon effectively regulate the actions of private security personnel?*

3. *Should private security personnel be held legally accountable to the country in which they operate? Or, should they operate with legal immunity? Explain your reasoning.*

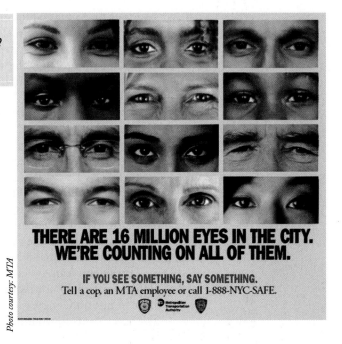

Are Americans safer now than they were before the September 11 terrorist attacks? This poster is part of a security campaign by the Metropolitan Transit Authority of New York State.

Photo courtesy: MTA

Since its creation, the Department of Homeland Security has been the subject of a great deal of criticism. The National Commission on Terrorist Attacks upon the United States—more commonly known as the **9/11 Commission**—was critical of government preparedness; their 2004 report advised a number of corrective measures. In 2005, the 9/11 Public Discourse Project, the successor to the 9/11 Commission, issued a scathing report concerning the nation's efforts to prevent terrorists attacks, citing a need for greater aviation security, including passenger and cargo screening, better incentives for intelligence information sharing, and improved communication capabilities among first responder groups. According to a member of the U.S. House Homeland Security Committee, "Hurricane Katrina showed that we cannot even prepare for a disaster we know is coming, much less a sudden attack. From chemical plants to subways, ports, and the border, we have failed to take the steps needed to close security gaps."[27] In March 2008, DHS adopted the National Response Framework, a new plan for coordinating federal, state, and local emergency resources in the event of a natural or human-made disaster. The plan has yet to be tested.

9/11 Commission
National Commission on Terrorist Attacks upon the United States; this bipartisan, independent group was authorized by Congress and President Bush in 2002 to study the circumstances surrounding the September 11 terrorist attacks, including preparedness and the immediate response. Its 2004 report includes recommendations designed to guard against future attacks.

Congress

The U.S. Constitution gave Congress fewer responsibilities in foreign and defense policy than the president; nevertheless, the legislative branch plays an important role in the policy process. Most would agree that Congress is the second most important actor in shaping American foreign and defense policy.[28] Congress influences foreign and defense policy through its congressional leadership, oversight, approval of treaties and appointments, appropriations, and the War Powers Act.

CONGRESSIONAL LEADERSHIP Normally the president proposes a foreign policy and Congress accepts, modifies, or rejects it. However, even though it rarely uses it, Congress has the power to develop and implement policy. For example, when the Soviet Union in 1957 launched *Sputnik*, the world's first artificial satellite, even though President Eisenhower did not consider it a threat to U.S. security, some members of Congress did. Thus, a Senate armed services subcommittee held hearings on the threat posed by the Soviet space program. Concluding there was a threat, Congress created the National Aeronautics and Space Administration (NASA) to run a U.S. space program, and the National Defense Education Act to provide funding for science and foreign-language education. Although they were civilian programs, they were closely connected to defense.

CONGRESSIONAL OVERSIGHT Congress oversees foreign and defense policy in many ways. We describe below the role of Congress in appointments, appropriations, and the War Powers Act. Congress's other oversight powers include the ability to conduct hearings on foreign and defense policy and to have the president and CIA inform congressional committees about covert operations.

From World War II until the late 1960s, Congress deferred to the president and the military on foreign and defense issues and rarely exercised its oversight responsibilities outside appropriations. The Vietnam War changed this. As questions emerged about U.S. policy toward Vietnam, Congress questioned executive leadership in other areas of foreign and military policy as well. This expanded oversight is now the norm. For example, in 2005 and 2006, the Senate Foreign Relations Committee questioned Bush administration officials and military leaders about growing sectarian violence in Iraq and the NSA's domestic spying program.

TREATIES AND EXECUTIVE AGREEMENTS The Constitution gives the Senate explicit power to approve treaties, but the Senate has rejected treaties only twenty times in U.S. history.[29] The Senate's power to approve treaties is important, however. Presidents want to avoid the embarrassment of Senate rejection of a treaty, the delay of a filibuster, or senatorial refusal to consider a treaty.

Presidents can avoid the treaty process by using executive agreements, which unlike treaties do not require Senate approval. Prior to 1972, the president did not have to inform Congress of the text of these accords. Normally presidents use executive agreements for routine business matters, but executive agreements have also been used for more substantial policy commitments. The expansion of the U.S. role in world affairs after World War II, the increase in the number of independent countries, and the growing complexity of global relations explains why presidents have used executive agreements more frequently over time.

APPOINTMENTS Although the Constitution gives the president the power to appoint ambassadors and others involved in foreign and defense policy, it gives the Senate the responsibility to provide advice and consent on these appointments. Frequently, important appointees to these foreign and defense policy posts have close connections to Congress.

Individual senators have the ability to derail a nomination. Senators can put a hold on the confirmation process to express concern about issues or a specific appointee. For example, in 2005, President Bush nominated John R. Bolton to serve as the U.S. ambassador to the United Nations. Bolton, a former State Department official, has close ties to the Bush family and pursued aggressive tactics against the 2000 presidential vote recount in Florida. His nomination as ambassador to the UN caused a prolonged filibuster by Senate Democrats, who opposed Bolton for a number of reasons, including his skepticism of the United Nations, his opposition to the International Criminal Court, and his harsh management tactics. Ultimately President Bush installed Bolton as ambassador via a congressional recess appointment that lasted until a new Congress convened in January 2007.

APPROPRIATIONS Congress has a key role in shaping foreign and defense policy through its power to appropriate funds, and it influences when and where the United States fights through its control of the budget. While the power to go to war is shared by the executive and legislative branches of government, the power to appropriate funds belongs to the legislature alone. (To learn more about U.S. defense spending since 1940, see Figure 19.2). Congress has been careful about using this power. For example, in 1974 Congress dramatically cut funding for the Vietnam War, helping to force an end to America's involvement in the war. In 1982, Congress used its appropriation power to limit U.S. involvement in Nicaragua, where the Reagan administration had been providing military aid to the Contras, a guerrilla group fighting the Sandinistas, the governing faction, who were receiving aid from Cuba and the Soviet Union.

When Democrats took control of both houses of Congress following the 2006 election, many predicted the new majority would use the power of the purse to limit

You Are the New Appointed Ambassador to the Country of Dalmatia

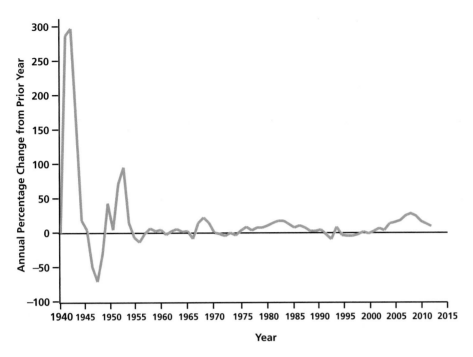

FIGURE 19.2 U.S. Defense Spending, 1940–2012 The figure shows the percentage change from the prior year in the amount of current dollars spent on U.S. defense (data for 2007–2012 are estimated). As the figure illustrates, nothing in modern American history compares to the increase in spending after the United States entered World War II in 1941. Other significant increases in defense spending were related to the Cold War in the early 1950s and the Vietnam War in the 1960s. President George W. Bush's defense increases to fight the war on terrorism after 2001 are the highest since the end of the Cold War in the 1980s.

Source: Harold W. Stanley and Richard G. Niemi, eds., *Vital Statistics on American Politics, 2007–2008* (Washington, DC: CQ Press, 2008). Reprinted by permission.

U.S. involvement in Iraq. However, Democratic legislators were divided. Some wanted to halt funding for the war immediately, while others preferred allocating money for activities such as reconstruction, setting up international security forces, and the ultimate withdrawal of U.S. troops. In 2007, Congress passed a funding bill for operations in Afghanistan and Iraq that required the president to begin the withdrawal of troops if certain benchmarks of progress were not met by specified dates. The president vetoed the bill. Several attempts were made by legislators in 2007 and 2008 to pass provisions designed to curtail funding for operations in Iraq unless the president agreed to some kind of troop withdrawal timetable. All failed to generate sufficient support.

THE WAR POWERS ACT Frustrated with its inability to influence policy on Vietnam, a war that deeply divided the nation, Congress passed the **War Powers Act** in 1973 to try to prevent future interventions overseas without specific congressional approval. Under the act, the president is required to consult with Congress before deploying American troops into hostile situations. Under certain conditions, the president is required to report to Congress within forty-eight hours of the deployment. A presidential report can trigger a sixty-day clock that requires congressional approval for any continued military involvement past the sixty-day window. If Congress does not give explicit approval within sixty days, the president then has thirty days to withdraw the troops. Under the act, the president could respond to an emergency such as rescuing endangered Americans but could not engage in a prolonged struggle without congressional approval.

The War Powers Act is controversial and has not been an effective restraint on presidential military adventurism. When first passed, President Nixon vetoed it, but

War Powers Act
Passed by Congress in 1973; the president is limited in the deployment of troops overseas to a sixty-day period in peacetime (which can be extended for an extra thirty days to permit withdrawal) unless Congress explicitly gives its approval for a longer period.

Congress overrode the president's veto. Nixon then claimed the act was unconstitutional, but such a claim has yet to be formally tested. Only President Ford has reported military activity so as to trigger the War Powers Act's sixty-day clock. Subsequent presidents, including President George W. Bush, have reported military activities to Congress but have failed to do so in a way that triggers the provisions of the act. The fundamental weakness of the War Powers Act is the requirement that the president, not Congress, start the sixty-day clock for congressional approval. In 2008, the National War Powers Commission, led by former Secretaries of State James A. Baker III and Warren Christopher, unanimously concluded after a year of study that the war powers legislation should be replaced. They proposed a new law, the War Powers Consultation Act, which would require the president to consult with Congress before ordering a combat operation that was expected to last more than one week. Following consultation with the president, Congress would be required to vote on whether to approve the action within thirty days.

The Military-Industrial Complex

Before World War II, the United States during peacetime maintained a small military force and required few weapons and supplies. This changed after World War II as the United States became a global superpower with major responsibilities, a large military, and the capability to go to war at a moment's notice. Consequently, a close relationship developed between the Department of Defense and the industries that provided the immense quantities of weapons and supplies. This close relationship also created the danger that the military and defense industries would acquire, because of their shared interests, influence over foreign and military policy.

President Eisenhower, a former general who commanded Allied forces during World War II, warned in his 1961 farewell address that the United States had developed a **military-industrial complex** that included the military and defense industries. This complex, Eisenhower feared, could become an increasingly dominant factor in U.S. politics with "potential for the disastrous rise of misplaced power."[30]

The military-industrial complex has the potential to acquire power for several reasons. First, it has economic clout. During the Cold War, as much as 7 percent of the U.S. gross national product was spent on defense. Second, it has access to technical expertise and political information. Third, the military and defense industries share many interests. For example, both benefited economically when tensions between the United States and the Soviet Union increased. Fourth, personal and professional relationships between the military and defense industries are close, with many newly retired military officers going to work for defense industries. Finally, the military and defense industry officials work closely with legislators and their staffs. Planned or unplanned, undue influence can accompany close working relations. In 2005, for example, it became known that a number of defense contractors had paid Representative Randy "Duke" Cunningham (R–CA) in order to obtain lucrative defense and intelligence contracts from the federal government. The scandal generated interest in lobbying reform (see chapter 16) and new questions about the extent of the defense industry's influence on the legislative process. For his role in the scandal, Cunningham was sentenced to more than eight years in prison in 2006, the longest jail sentence ever given to a member of Congress.[31]

The News Media

News media reports provide the public with valuable information on government actions and policy initiatives related to foreign and defense policy. As discussed in greater depth in chapter 15, the media influence the course of foreign policy but do not determine it.

From World War II to the Vietnam War, the press tended to support the president in foreign and defense policy. As a rule, editors assumed that government statements

military-industrial complex
The grouping of the U.S. armed forces and defense industries.

Analyzing Visuals | Abu Ghraib Prisoner Abuse

Photos of American soldiers demeaning, taunting, and torturing Iraqi detainees in Abu Ghraib prison in Iraq shocked the world when they were published in 2004. Acts of torture violate the Geneva conventions of warfare, to which the United States is a signatory. The resulting scandal led to investigations by both Congress and the Pentagon and a series of trials against the alleged abusers, most of whom were young, lower-level soldiers. Nine army reservists were convicted of abusing detainees; eight received prison sentences. Pentagon officials maintain that the abuse at Abu Ghraib was the product of rogue soldiers who chose to break the rules. Those involved argue they were ordered to use aggressive interrogation techniques by CIA interrogators and personnel higher up in the chain of command. Reports about the use of waterboarding, an interrogation technique widely viewed as torture, generated renewed debate about what is and isn't torture and the treatment of suspected terrorists in U.S. custody. Examine the photograph and consider the following questions:

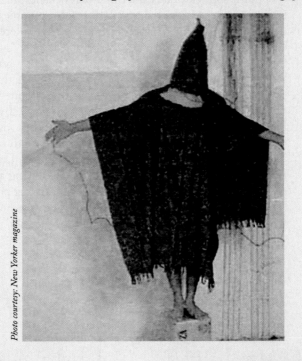

Photo courtesy: New Yorker magazine

WHAT has been the impact—nationally and internationally—of the use of torture on suspected terrorists by the United States?

ARE there instances in which you would condone torture of an enemy? Why or why not?

DOES the use of torture by the United States jeopardize the safety of American troops? Why or why not?

---

were true and printed them as fact. In the mid-1960s, this changed as U.S. involvement in Vietnam grew and reporters based in Vietnam realized that the daily military briefings at times were untrue. This led many journalists to investigate government statements rather than merely repeating them as fact. Some observers complain that since Vietnam and the Watergate scandal during Richard M. Nixon's presidency, the news media have become too intent on investigating and challenging the government, but others argue that freedom of the press is a crucial, constitutionally protected right in the United States and that investigative reporting is critical for a full accounting of government activities. In 2004, the media broke the news about abuse of prisoners at Iraq's Abu Ghraib prison by U.S. military personnel, launching a public outcry and government investigations. (To learn more, see Analyzing Visuals: Abu Ghraib Prisoner Abuse.)

The Public

The American public affects foreign and defense policy through expressions of public opinion, elections, and public action. Dimensions of public opinion on issues of foreign and defense policy identified by scholars and analysts include militarism/non-militarism, isolationism/internationalism, and unilateralism/multilateralism. These dimension tend to fragment public opinion toward most foreign and defense policies, resulting in a core group of people in opposition to nearly every policy. As a result, it is difficult to achieve widespread popular support for any given initiative.

As a rule, the American public is more interested in domestic affairs than foreign and defense policy. (To learn more about historical trends in public opinion, see Figure 19.3.) Nevertheless, public opinion is often on the president's mind when creating or implementing foreign or defense policy. Public opinion rarely determines what an administration does, but it often influences the emphasis that an administration places on a foreign or defense initiative.

In the United States and other democracies, foreign policy or defense crises generally increase presidential popularity, but sometimes the increase is temporary. President George W. Bush's approval ratings skyrocketed from 51 percent to 86 percent shortly after September 11, 2001—the largest "rally effect" ever reported by the Gallup polling organization. Bush's popularity remained high during the war in Afghanistan, fell somewhat at the beginning of the war in Iraq in 2003, and then declined significantly as the war dragged on despite the president's "Mission Accomplished" event on an aircraft carrier in May 2003. By 2008, Bush's job approval rating had slipped to 30 percent or lower in some polls, due in large part to the conflict in Iraq and the federal government's poor response to Hurricane Katrina.

In addition to expressions of public opinion, U.S. citizens exercise electoral control on presidential power every fourth year during a presidential election. Voters can express their approval or disapproval of an existing policy with their vote, but they can send no clear message for preferred alternatives. For example, in 1952, Eisenhower was elected on a vague promise to end the Korean War. With such a vague promise,

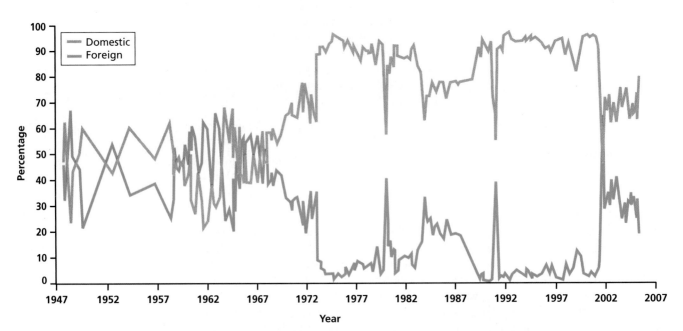

FIGURE 19.3 The Most Important Problem: Domestic or Foreign, 1947–2007

Note: Typical question: "What do you think is the most important problem facing this country today?"

Source: Harold W. Stanley and Richard G. Niemi, eds., *Vital Statistics on American Politics, 2007–2008* (Washington, DC: CQ Press, 2008). Reprinted by permission.

he was as free to end the war by using nuclear weapons as he was to end it by negotiating a truce. He chose the latter.

Public action sometimes shapes foreign and defense policy, as in the widespread resistance to the draft during the Vietnam War. Growing public opposition to the war over time made it difficult to draft soldiers and reach the personnel levels that the military desired. Opposition to the draft also helped move the United States toward an all-volunteer military.

Citizens may also influence U.S. policy through activism, especially when they join or work with **nongovernmental organizations (NGOs),** international organizations that seek a set of objectives but are not formally connected to a government. Amnesty International, for example, monitors human rights violations worldwide and seeks to galvanize world opinion to influence the behaviors of offending governments.

nongovernmental organization (NGO)
An organization that is not tied to a government.

Twenty-First-Century Challenges

As the international community has grown more interconnected over time, forging U.S. foreign and defense policies that both protect American interests and benefit those outside our borders has become more consequential and increasingly challenging. How can the United States best support democracy abroad? What can the United States do to promote peace between Israelis and Palestinians? What is the best way to deter states like Iran from developing nuclear capabilities? What policies are appropriate for relations with increasingly powerful states such as China?

COMPARATIVE

Comparing Foreign and Security Policy

Promoting Democracy in the Middle East

Promoting democracy in the Middle East is a difficult task that can have unexpected consequences. In a surprising outcome, the Islamic resistance movement Hamas won a decisive victory in Palestinian elections in early 2006. Long identified as a terrorist organization by the United States and the European Union because of its commitment to the destruction of Israel, Hamas gained control of the majority of seats in a democratically elected parliament. The United States has refused to do business with a Hamas-controlled government unless it renounces violence and agrees to recognize Israel as a legitimate nation.

Though Saddam Hussein's government in Iraq was easily toppled in 2003, the situation there is far less secure than initially predicted by the Bush administration. Many Iraqis, even those glad to be free of Hussein's tyrannical rule, are troubled by the lawlessness unleashed by Hussein's overthrow. Many resent the U.S. occupation but remain skeptical of the democratically elected government's effectiveness should the United States withdraw its troops. While some parts of Iraq are successfully rebuilding and remain relatively calm, the overall situation remains enormously volatile. Oil pipelines are routinely sabotaged, Iraqi police forces often come under attack, and Iraqis face great uncertainty about the future. The United States has begun turning over control of security to Iraqi forces, but whether the Iraqi government has the capacity to control sectarian violence in the absence of a U.S. presence is an open question.

Iraq remains an unfinished piece of business, as does Afghanistan, which is under assault from reorganized Taliban militias. Additionally, since the U.S. overthrow of the Taliban regime in Afghanistan in 2001, opium production

What role should former U.S. presidents play in crafting American foreign policy? During a controversial April 2008 visit to the Middle East, former president and Nobel Peace Prize winner Jimmy Carter attends a wreath-laying ceremony at Palestinian leader Yasser Arafat's grave. Carter's diplomatic efforts were criticized by the Bush Administration and the Israeli government.

Photo courtesy: Thaer Ganaim/Office of the Palestinian President/Getty Images

has surged.[32] Today, Afghanistan is the world's largest producer of opium. According to the IMF, drug revenue accounts for roughly 75 percent of the country's economy and opium trafficking has contributed to government corruption at all levels.

It is unclear how long the United States will need to provide aid or station troops, or how many more Americans will die in the struggle to make Iraq and Afghanistan democratic havens in the Muslim world. The United States is unlikely to attempt such a sustained preemptive strike again, given the high cost in lives and dollars of long-term military operations without international help.

Transnational Threats to Peace

Terrorist organizations are an ever evolving threat that is not easily contained or defeated with traditional military activities. Operating as nonstate actors, terrorists "blur the line between civilians and the military" and "confound war plans and diplomatic practices based upon enemies with fixed territory and political sovereignty."[33] Some groups, such as al-Qaeda, possess sophisticated economic, political, and military resources and are actively seeking to obtain weapons of mass destruction—nuclear, chemical, or biological weapons. Meeting these threats is a key element of the war on terrorism, which the Bush administration repeatedly cautioned will be both long and costly.

Because of its reliance on computers, the United States is vulnerable to information warfare: attacks on information systems. These threats have led officials to warn about the danger of an "electronic Pearl Harbor" in which information warfare could bring some sectors of the United States to a halt. Indeed, computers and Web sites used by the U.S. government as well as businesses such as CNN, Home Depot, and Amazon.com often have come under attack from individual hackers.

How serious is the threat of information warfare? Government studies have highlighted the vulnerabilities of U.S. infrastructures, including communications and telephones, banking, power grids, water systems, fuel supply networks, and other systems that rely on computers.[34] Indeed, in a 1997 war game, government hackers penetrated computers on military bases, gained access to computers on a navy cruiser, could have closed down the U.S. electric power grid, and positioned themselves to disable the emergency 911 network.[35]

Toward Reform: Choosing Between Unilateralism and Multilateralism

Between the end of World War II and the demise of the Soviet Union, U.S. military intervention overseas usually was tied to the containment of communism. But, the demise of the Soviet Union and the end of the Cold War eliminated this easy benchmark for deciding when to intervene. All U.S. presidents must deal with the complex problem of when to use the U.S. military overseas and whether to act unilaterally or to seek international cooperation.

The events of September 11, 2001, produced a consensus among Americans about the importance of a strong homeland defense and an effective prosecution of the war on terrorism. Nevertheless, the Bush administration's support of preemptive military action generated debate about how to address the future scope of U.S. involvement in world affairs. Since the United States is economically and militarily the most powerful country in the world, why should it limit its foreign and defense actions to only those with which other countries and international organizations like NATO and the UN agree? The easy response is that the United States should always act to protect its national interests, aligning its actions and policies with the UN and

Economic Sanctions and Cuba

other international and nongovernmental organizations when possible, but not allowing those institutions to constrain U.S. actions and policies. On another level, the challenge revolves around the issue of what kind of world the United States wants to have develop. Should it be one where might determines right, or one where mutual agreement determines the course of action?

Proponents of the unilateralist approach argue that when American interests collide with those of the international community, the United States must be willing to engage in unilateral action in order to protect vital national interests—regardless of the level of opposition to those activities by other countries. Unilateralism provides the president with a great deal more flexibility in crafting and executing foreign policy than does a multilateral approach and is certainly an important option during times of a national emergency.

Multilateralism requires a commitment to a process of give-and-take with regard to international consensus building and awareness that the United States will not always be able to dictate the rules of play. Critics of the George W. Bush administration's unilateralist tendencies point to the frightening precedent of launching preemptive wars, and question the morality of invading another country based solely on what it *might* do. They argue that preemptive military action in Iraq generated instability in the region, created greater hostilities with both our allies and adversaries, and did little to dampen the nuclear ambitions of Iran and North Korea. During his second administration, Bush moved away from unilateralism, making diplomatic overtures to Iran and emphasized a multilateral approach in dealing with North Korea.

Beyond the war on terrorism, the same quandaries confront U.S. policy makers after the 9/11 attacks that they struggled with before. Should the United States intervene overseas to stop human rights violations? Should the United States intervene overseas to overthrow dictatorial governments or support democratic governments?

Deciding whether unilateralism or multilateralism will predominate is largely a political issue. Polls in 2007 and 2008 show that roughly half of Americans believe the United States will be safer if it confronts countries that promote terrorism or harbor terrorists; the other half believe America should generally stay out of other countries' affairs. Despite the divide, a clear majority wants the United States to play a major role in solving international problems.[36]

Throughout this chapter, we have seen cases where the United States acted only in the presence of international support and agreement, and other cases, most notably the war in Iraq, where the United States chose to undertake military action despite the opposition of key allies. The challenge is to make U.S. interests and the interests of the global community coincide, and when this is impossible, to promote U.S. interests without damaging the United States' status in the global community.

In the twenty-first century, the United States remains the world's only superpower, but it is vulnerable to terrorist attack even as it confronts other foreign and defense policy challenges. How the United States manages homeland defense, the war on terrorism, and appropriate responses to future international crises is the greatest challenge for twenty-first-century U.S. policy makers.

Photo courtesy: Sgt. Matthew Roe/Bloomberg News/Landov

What kind of commitment should the U.S. make to Iraq in the coming years? General David Petraeus, left, U.S. Commander in Iraq, and Senator John McCain (R-AZ), second from left, walk through a marketplace in Baghdad in 2007 with armed escorts. McCain supported the effectiveness of U.S. military actions in Iraq as a presidential candidate in 2008.

Thinking Globally

The International Criminal Court

The United States, India, and China have declined membership in the International Criminal Court (ICC)—a UN-established institution with jurisdiction over crimes against humanity, war crimes, and genocide. More than one hundred nations have joined the ICC, including the European Union nations, Canada, and most of Latin America.

- Can a multilateral institution such as the ICC function effectively without the support of powerful nations such as the United States and China? Why or why not?
- Should the United States join the ICC? What arguments can you make in favor of membership and what arguments support continued nonparticipation?

WHAT SHOULD I HAVE LEARNED?

Foreign and defense policy are important functions of the U.S. government. This chapter stressed the evolution of foreign and defense policy over time, the role of public and private agencies, and the challenges that American policy makers face in the twenty-first century. In examining these issues, this chapter answered the following questions:

■ **What are the roots of U.S. foreign and defense policy?**

From the earliest days, isolationism, unilateralism, moralism, and pragmatism were central elements of U.S. foreign and defense policy. Foreign and defense policy played a minor role in American politics for most of the nation's first century. As U.S. economic interests expanded, the United States intervened more and more overseas, especially in Latin America. After a delayed entry into World War I, America retreated into isolation but was unable to avoid World War II.

■ **What is the United States' role as a world power?**

After World War II, foreign and defense policy often dominated the American political agenda, and defense spending became one of the biggest items in the national budget. Foreign and defense policy became major concerns, especially issues such as U.S.-Soviet relations, nuclear weapons, and the Vietnam War. Despite debate, an underlying consensus existed that American policy should focus on containing the Soviet Union. After the Soviet Union collapsed, no immediate consensus emerged on the direction of U.S. foreign policy. The terrorist attacks that took place on September 11, 2001, caused the United States to focus much of its energy on a war against terrorism.

■ **What is the process of foreign and defense policy decision making?**

Balances found in other parts of the U.S. political system are generally absent in foreign and defense policy. The executive branch of government dominates foreign and defense policy, with the Departments of State and Defense being particularly important. Within the executive branch, the president is preeminent. Until the War Powers Act, few constraints were placed on presidential prerogatives in foreign and defense policy. Presidential power experienced a post-9/11 resurgence as concerns about national security often eclipsed executive accountability and the protection of civil liberties. Institutions outside the executive also play a role in U.S. foreign and defense policy. These include Congress, the military-industrial complex, the news media, and the public.

■ **What challenges confront the United States in the twenty-first century?**

The United States faces major challenges in foreign and defense policy during the twenty-first century, especially homeland defense and the global war on terrorism. Other challenges include promoting democratic values globally and addressing transnational threats to peace. How well the United States succeeds in meeting these challenges will go a long way toward determining how the country fares in the twenty-first century.

■ **How should America strike a balance between unilateralism and multilateralism?**

Since its creation, the United States has considered itself an exceptional nation. The conduct of American foreign policy is rooted in the belief that the United States represents a role model for the rest of the world and that its values and ideals are universal and worthy of emulation. All recent presidents have pursued the exportation of democracy as a central component of America's foreign policy. The multilateralist approach emphasizes international consensus and multinational implementation of solutions to world problems. A unilateralist approach relies on *American* solutions to international problems, even if these are at odds with international norms.

Key Terms

al-Qaeda, p. 685
Bretton Woods Agreement, p. 679
Bush Doctrine, p. 687
Central Intelligence Agency
    (CIA), p. 693
collective security, p. 677
containment, p. 680
Cuban Missile Crisis, p. 681
Department of Defense, p. 692
Department of Homeland Security, p. 693
Department of State, p. 692
détente, p. 682
Embargo Act, p. 675
engagement, p. 684
enlargement, p. 684
human rights, p. 683
international governmental
    organization (IGO), p. 679
International Monetary Fund
    (IMF), p. 679

isolationism, p. 673
Joint Chiefs of Staff, p. 692
League of Nations, p. 677
manifest destiny, p. 676
Marshall Plan, p. 680
military-industrial complex, p. 698
Monroe Doctrine, p. 675
moralism, p. 673
multilateralism, p. 680
National Security Agency
    (NSA), p. 692
National Security Council
    (NSC), p. 693
9/11 Commission, p. 695
nongovernmental organization
    (NGO), p. 701
North American Free Trade
    Agreement (NAFTA), p. 685
North Atlantic Treaty Organization
    (NATO), p. 680

Pearl Harbor, p. 678
Powell Doctrine, p. 684
pragmatism, p. 673
Reagan Doctrine, p. 683
Roosevelt Corollary, p. 677
Taliban, p. 685
tariffs, p. 676
Truman Doctrine, p. 680
unilateralism, p. 673
United Nations, p. 679
Vietnam War, p. 682
war on terrorism, p. 685
War Powers Act, p. 697
weapons of mass destruction
    (WMDs), p. 688
World Bank, p. 679
World Trade Organization
    (WTO), p. 685

Researching Foreign and Defense Policy

In the Library

Allison, Graham F., and Philip Zelikow. *Essence of Decision: Explaining the Cuban Missile Crisis*, 2nd ed. New York: Pearson, 1999.

Ambrose, Stephen, and Douglas Brinkley (contributor). *Rise to Globalism: American Foreign Policy Since 1938*, 8th ed. New York: Penguin, 1997.

Axelrod, Alan. *American Treaties and Alliances.* Washington, DC: CQ Press, 2000.

Bacevich, Andrew J. *American Empire: The Realities and Consequences of U.S. Diplomacy.* Cambridge, MA: Harvard University Press, 2002.

Boot, Max. *The Savage Wars of Peace: Small Wars and the Rise of American Power.* New York: Basic Books, 2002.

Byman, Daniel, and Matthew C. Waxman. *The Dynamics of Coercion: American Foreign Policy and the Limits of Military Might.* Cambridge: Cambridge University Press, 2002.

Clarke, Richard A. *Against All Enemies: Inside America's War on Terror.* New York: Free Press, 2004.

Ervin, Clark Kent. *Open Target: Where America Is Vulnerable to Attack.* New York: Palgrave Macmillan, 2006.

Forsythe, David P., Patrice C. McMahon, and Andrew Wedeman. *American Foreign Policy in a Globalized World.* New York: Routledge, 2006.

Goldstein, Joshua S. *International Relations*, 6th ed. New York: Longman, 2008.

Halberstam, David. *War in a Time of Peace: Bush, Clinton, and the Generals.* New York: Scribner's, 2001.

Hook, Steven W. *U.S. Foreign Policy: The Paradox of World Power.* Washington, DC: CQ Press, 2005.

Howard, Russell D., James J. F. Forest, and Joanne C. Moore. *Homeland Security and Terrorism: Readings and Interpretations.* New York: McGraw-Hill, 2006.

Johnson, Loch K. *Seven Sins of American Foreign Policy.* New York: Longman, 2007.

Kennan, George F. *American Diplomacy, 1900–1950.* Chicago: University of Chicago Press, 1951.

Lowenthal, Mark M. *Intelligence: From Secrets to Policy*, 2nd ed. Washington, DC: CQ Press, 2003.

Nye, Joseph S., Jr. *The Paradox of American Power: Why the World's Only Superpower Can't Go It Alone.* New York: Oxford University Press, 2002.

Papp, Daniel S. *The Impact of September 11 on Contemporary International Relations.* New York: Longman, 2003.

Talbott, Strobe, and Nayan Chanda, eds. *The Age of Terror: America and the World After September 11.* New York: Basic Books, 2002.

On the Web

To learn more about the reach and worldwide involvement of the United Nations, go to **www.unsystem.org**.

To learn more about the Department of Defense and U.S. military operations around the globe, go to **www.defenselink.mil**.

To learn more about the State Department, go to **www.state.gov**.

To learn more about the CIA and the larger intelligence community, go to **www.cia.gov**.

To learn about the specific workings of the IMF and World Bank, go to **www.imf.org, www.worldbank.org**.

To learn more about strategic security, nuclear nonproliferation, and weapons of mass destruction, among other national security issues, visit the Federation of American Scientists at **www.fas.org**.

The Declaration of Independence

In Congress, July 4, 1776

The Unanimous Declaration of the Thirteen United States of America

When in the Course of human events it becomes necessary for one people to dissolve the political bands which have connected them with another, and to assume, among the powers of the earth, the separate and equal station to which the Laws of Nature and of Nature's God entitle them, a decent respect to the opinions of mankind requires that they should declare the causes which impel them to the separation.

We hold these truths to be self-evident, that all men are created equal, that they are endowed by their Creator with certain unalienable Rights, that among these are Life, Liberty and the pursuit of Happiness. That to secure these rights, Governments are instituted among Men, deriving their just powers from the consent of the governed. That whenever any Form of Government becomes destructive of these ends, it is the Right of the People to alter or to abolish it, and to institute new Government, laying its foundation on such principles and organizing its powers in such form, as to them shall seem most likely to effect their Safety and Happiness. Prudence, indeed, will dictate that Governments long established should not be changed for light and transient causes; and accordingly all experience hath shewn that mankind are more disposed to suffer, while evils are sufferable, than to right themselves by abolishing the forms to which they are accustomed. But when a long train of abuses and usurpations, pursuing invariably the same Object evinces a design to reduce them under absolute Despotism, it is their right, it is their duty, to throw off such Government, and to provide new Guards for their future security. —Such has been the patient sufferance of these Colonies; and such is now the necessity which constrains them to alter their former Systems of Government. The history of the present King of Great Britain is a history of repeated injuries and usurpations, all having in direct object the establishment of an absolute Tyranny over these States. To prove this, let Facts be submitted to a candid world.

He has refused his Assent to Laws, the most wholesome and necessary for the public good.

He has forbidden his Governors to pass Laws of immediate and pressing importance, unless suspended in their operation till his Assent should be obtained; and when so suspended, he has utterly neglected to attend to them.

He has refused to pass other Laws for the accommodation of large districts of people, unless those people would relinquish the right of Representation in the Legislature, a right inestimable to them and formidable to tyrants only.

He has called together legislative bodies at places unusual, uncomfortable, and distant from the depository of their Public Records, for the sole purpose of fatiguing them into compliance with his measures.

He has dissolved Representative Houses repeatedly, for opposing with manly firmness his invasions on the rights of the people.

He has refused for a long time, after such dissolutions, to cause others to be elected; whereby the Legislative Powers, incapable of Annihilation, have returned to the People at large for their exercise, the State remaining in the mean time exposed to all the dangers of invasion from without, and convulsions within.

He has endeavored to prevent the population of these States; for that purpose obstructing the Laws of Naturalization of Foreigners; refusing to pass others to encourage their migration hither, and raising the conditions of new Appropriations of Lands.

He has obstructed the Administration of Justice, by refusing his Assent to Laws for establishing Judiciary powers.

He has made Judges dependent on his Will alone, for the tenure of their offices, and the amount and payment of their salaries.

He has erected a multitude of New Offices, and sent hither swarms of Officers to harass our people, and eat out their substance.

He has kept among us, in times of peace, Standing Armies without the Consent of our legislatures.

He has affected to render the Military independent of and superior to the Civil power.

He has combined with others to subject us to a jurisdiction foreign to our constitution, and unacknowledged by our laws, giving his Assent to their Acts of pretended Legislation:

For quartering large bodies of armed troops among us:

For protecting them, by a mock Trial, from punishment for any Murders which they should commit on the Inhabitants of these States:

For cutting off our Trade with all parts of the world:

For imposing Taxes on us without our Consent:

For depriving us in many cases, of the benefits of Trial by Jury:

For transporting us beyond Seas to be tried for pretended offences:

For abolishing the free System of English Laws in a neighboring Province, establishing therein an Arbitrary government, and enlarging its Boundaries so as to render it at once an example and fit instrument for introducing the same absolute rule into these Colonies:

For taking away our Charters, abolishing our most valuable Laws, and altering fundamentally the Forms of our Governments:

For suspending our own Legislatures, and declaring themselves invested with power to legislate for us in all cases whatsoever.

He has abdicated Government here, by declaring us out of his Protection and waging War against us.

He has plundered our seas, ravaged our Coasts, burnt out towns, and destroyed the lives of our people.

He is at this time transporting large Armies of foreign Mercenaries to compleat the works of death, desolation and tyranny, already begun with circumstances of Cruelty and perfidy scarcely paralleled in the most barbarous ages, and totally unworthy the Head of a civilized nation.

He has constrained our fellow Citizens taken Captive on the high Seas to bear Arms against their Country, to become the executioners of their friends and Brethren, or to fall themselves by their Hands.

He has excited domestic insurrections amongst us, and has endeavored to bring on the inhabitants of our frontiers, the merciless Indian Savages, whose known rule of warfare, is an undistinguished destruction of all ages, sexes and conditions.

In every stage of these Oppressions We have Petitioned for Redress in the most humble terms: Our repeated Petitions have been answered only by repeated injury: A Prince, whose character is thus marked by every act which may define a Tyrant, is unfit to be the ruler of a free people.

Nor have We been wanting in attention to our British brethren. We have warned them from time to time of attempts by their legislature to extend an unwarrantable jurisdiction over us. We have reminded them of the circumstances of our emigration and settlement here. We have appealed to their native justice and magnanimity; and we have conjured them by the ties of our common kindred to disavow these usurpations, which would inevitably interrupt our connections and correspondence. They too have been deaf to the voice of justice and consanguinity. We must, therefore, acquiesce in the necessity, which denounces our Separation, and hold them, as we hold the rest of mankind, Enemies in War, in Peace Friends.

We, therefore, the Representatives of the United States of America, in General Congress, Assembled, appealing to the Supreme Judge of the world for the rectitude of our intentions, do, in the Name, and by Authority of the good People of these Colonies, solemnly publish and declare, That these United Colonies are, and of Right ought to be Free and Independent States; that they are Absolved from all Allegiance to the British Crown, and that all political connection between them and the State of Great Britain, is and ought to be totally dissolved: and that as Free and Independent States, they have full power to levy War, conclude Peace, contract Alliances, establish Commerce, and to do all other Acts and Things which Independent States may of right do. And for the support of this Declaration, with a firm reliance on the protection of Divine Providence, we mutually pledge to each other our Lives, our Fortunes and our sacred Honor.

JOHN HANCOCK

NEW HAMPSHIRE
Josiah Bartlett
William Whipple
Matthew Thornton

MASSACHUSETTS BAY
Samuel Adams
John Adams
Robert Treat Paine
Elbridge Gerry

RHODE ISLAND
Stephen Hopkins
William Ellery

CONNECTICUT
Roger Sherman
Samuel Huntington
William Williams
Oliver Wolcott

NEW YORK
William Floyd
Philip Livingston
Francis Lewis
Lewis Morris

NEW JERSEY
Richard Stockton

John Witherspoon
Francis Hopkinson
John Hart
Abraham Clark

PENNSYLVANIA
Robert Morris
Benjamin Rush
Benjamin Franklin
John Morton
George Clymer
James Smith
George Taylor
James Wilson
George Ross

DELAWARE
Caesar Rodney
George Read
Thomas McKean

MARYLAND
Samuel Chase
William Paca
Thomas Stone
Charles Carroll

VIRGINIA
George Wythe

Richard Henry Lee
Thomas Jefferson
Benjamin Harrison
Thomas Nelson, Jr.
Francis Lightfoot Lee
Carter Braxton

NORTH CAROLINA
William Hooper
Joseph Hewes
John Penn

SOUTH CAROLINA
Edward Rutledge
Thomas Heyward, Jr.
Thomas Lynch, Jr.
Arthur Middleton

GEORGIA
Button Gwinnett
Lyman Hall
George Walton

Federalist No. 10

November 22, 1787

James Madison

To the People of the State of New York.

Among the numerous advantages promised by a well constructed Union, none deserves to be more accurately developed than its tendency to break and control the violence of faction. The friend of popular governments, never finds himself so much alarmed for their character and fate, as when he contemplates their propensity to this dangerous vice. He will not fail therefore to set a due value on any plan which, without violating the principles to which he is attached, provides a proper cure for it. The instability, injustice and confusion introduced into the public councils, have in truth been the mortal diseases under which popular governments have every where perished; as they continue to be the favorite and fruitful topics from which the adversaries to liberty derive their most specious declamations. The valuable improvements made by the American Constitutions on the popular models, both ancient and modern, cannot certainly be too much admired; but it would be an unwarrantable partiality, to contend that they have as effectually obviated the danger on this side as was wished and expected. Complaints are every where heard from our most considerate and virtuous citizens, equally the friends of public and private faith, and of public and personal liberty; that our governments are too unstable; that the public good is disregarded in the conflicts of rival parties; and that measures are too often decided, not according to the rules of justice, and the rights of the minor party; but by the superior force of an interested and over-bearing majority. However anxiously we may wish that these complaints had no foundation, the evidence of known facts will not permit us to deny that they are in some degree true. It will be found indeed, on a candid review of our situation, that some of the distresses under which we labor, have been erroneously charged on the operation of our governments; but it will be found, at the same time, that other causes will not alone account for many of our heaviest misfortunes; and particularly, for that prevailing and increasing distrust of public engagements, and alarm for private rights, which are echoed from one end of the continent to the other. These must be chiefly, if not wholly, effects of the unsteadiness and injustice, with which a factious spirit has tainted our public administrations.

By a faction I understand a number of citizens, whether amounting to a majority or minority of the whole, who are united and actuated by some common impulse of passion, or of interest, adverse to the rights of other citizens, or to the permanent and aggregate interests of the community.

There are two methods of curing the mischiefs of faction: the one, by removing its causes; the other, by controlling its effects.

There are again two methods of removing the causes of faction: the one by destroying the liberty which is essential to its existence; the other, by giving to every citizen the same opinions, the same passions, and the same interests.

It could never be more truly said than of the first remedy, that it is worse than the diease. Liberty is to faction, what air is to fire, an aliment without which it instantly expires. But it could not be a less folly to abolish liberty, which is essential to political life, because it nourishes faction, than it would be to wish the annihilation of air, which is essential to animal life, because it imparts to fire its destructive agency.

The second expedient is as impracticable, as the first would be unwise. As long as the reason of man continues fallible, and he is at liberty to exercise it, different opinions will be formed. As long as the connection subsists between his reason and his self-love, his opinions and his passions will have a reciprocal influence on each other; and the former will be objects to which the latter will attach themselves. The diversity in the faculties of men from which the rights of property originate, is not less an insuperable obstacle to a uniformity of interests. The protection of these faculties is the first object of Government. From the protection of different and unequal faculties of acquiring property, the possession of different degrees and kinds of property immediately results: and from the influence of these on the sentiments and views of the respective proprietors, ensues a division of the society into different interests and parties.

The latent causes of faction are thus sown in the nature of man; and we see them everywhere brought into different degrees of activity, according to the different circumstances of civil society. A zeal for different opinions concerning religion, concerning Government and many other points, as well of speculation as of practice; an attachment to different leaders ambitiously contending for pre-eminence and power; or to persons of other descriptions whose fortunes have been interesting to the human passions, have in turn divided mankind into parties, inflamed them with mutual animosity, and rendered them much more disposed to vex and oppress each other, than to cooperate for their common good. So strong is this propensity of mankind to fall into mutual animosities, that where no substantial occasion presents itself, the most frivolous and fanciful distinctions have been sufficient to kindle their unfriendly passions, and excite their most violent conflicts. But the most common and durable source of factions, has been the various and unequal distribution of property. Those who hold, and those who are without property, have ever formed distinct interests in society. Those who are creditors, and those who are debtors, fall under a like discrimination. A landed interest, a manufacturing interest, a mercantile interest, a monied interest, with many lesser interests, grow up of necessity in civilized nations, and divide them into different classes, actuated by different sentiments and views. The regulation of these various and interfering interests forms the principal task of modern Legislation, and involves the spirit of party and faction in the necessary and ordinary operations of Government.

No man is allowed to be a judge in his own cause; because his interest would certainly bias his judgment, and, not improbably, corrupt his integrity. With equal, nay with greater reason, a body of men, are unfit to be both judges and parties, at the same time; yet, what are many of the most important acts of legislation, but so many judicial determinations, not indeed concerning the rights of single persons, but concerning the rights of large bodies of citizens, and what are the different classes of legislators, but advocates and parties to the causes which they determine? Is a law proposed concerning private debts? It is a question to which the creditors are parties on one side, and the debtors on the other. Justice ought to hold the balance between them. Yet the parties are and must be themselves the judges; and the most numerous party, or, in other words, the most powerful faction must be expected to prevail. Shall domestic manufactures be encouraged, and in what degree, by restrictions on foreign manufactures? are questions which would be differently decided by the landed and the manufacturing classes; and probably by neither, with a sole regard to justice and the public good. The apportionment of taxes on the various descriptions of property, is an act which seems to require the most exact impartiality; yet, there is perhaps no legislative act in which greater opportunity and temptation are given to a predominant party, to trample on the rules of justice. Every shilling with which they over-burden the inferior number, is a shilling saved to their own pockets.

It is in vain to say, that enlightened statesmen will be able to adjust these clashing interests, and render them all subservient to the public good. Enlightened statesmen will not always be at the helm: Nor, in many cases, can such an adjustment be made at all, without taking into view indirect and remote considerations, which will rarely prevail over the immediate interest which one party may find in disregarding the rights of another, or the good of the whole.

The inference to which we are brought, is, that the *causes* of faction cannot be removed; and that relief is only to be sought in the means of controlling its *effects*.

If a faction consists of less than a majority, relief is supplied by the republican principle, which enables the majority to defeat its sinister views by regular vote: It may clog the administration, it may convulse the society; but it will be unable to execute and mask its violence under the forms of the Constitution. When a majority is included in a faction, the form of popular government on the other hand enables it to sacrifice to its ruling passion or interest, both the public good and the rights of other citizens. To secure the public good, and private rights, against the danger of such a faction, and at the same time to preserve the spirit and the form of popular government, is then the great object to which our enquiries are directed: Let me add that it is the great desideratum, by which alone this form of government can be rescued from the opprobrium under which it has so long labored, and be recommended to the esteem and adoption of mankind.

By what means is this object attainable? Evidently by one of two only. Either the existence of the same passion or interest in a majority at the same time, must be prevented; or the majority, having such co-existent passion or interest, must be rendered, by their number and local situation, unable to concert and carry into effect schemes of oppression. If the impulse and the opportunity be suffered to coincide, we well know that neither moral nor religious motives can be relied on as an adequate control. They are not found to be such on the injustice and violence of individuals, and lose their efficacy in proportion to the number combined together; that is, in proportion as their efficacy becomes needful.

From this view of the subject, it may be concluded, that a pure Democracy, by which I mean, a Society, consisting of a small number of citizens, who assemble and administer the Government in person, can admit of no cure for the mischiefs of faction. A common passion or interest will, in almost every case, be felt by a majority of the whole; a communication and concert results from the form of Government itself; and there is nothing to check the inducements to sacrifice the weaker party, or an obnoxious individual. Hence it is, that such Democracies have ever been spectacles of turbulence and contention; have ever been found incompatible with personal security, or the rights of property; and have in general been as short in their lives, as they have been violent in their deaths. Theoretic politicians, who have patronized this species of Government, have erroneously supposed, that by reducing mankind to a perfect equality in their political rights, they would, at the same time, be perfectly equalized and assimilated in their possessions, their opinions, and their passions.

A republic, by which I mean a government in which the scheme of representation takes place, opens a different prospect, and promises the cure for which we are seeking. Let us examine the points in which it varies from pure democracy, and we shall comprehend both the nature of the cure and the efficacy which it must derive from the union.

The two great points of difference, between a democracy and a republic, are, first, the delegation of the government, in the latter, to a small number of citizens, elected by the rest; secondly, the greater number of citizens, and greater sphere of country, over which the latter may be extended.

The effect of the first difference is, on the one hand, to refine and enlarge the public views, by passing them through the medium of a chosen body of citizens, whose wisdom may best discern the true interest of their country, and whose patriotism and love of justice, will be least likely to sacrifice it to temporary or partial considerations. Under such a regulation, it may well happen, that the public voice, pronounced by the representatives of the people, will be more consonant to the public good, than if pronounced by the people themselves, convened for the purpose. On the other hand the effect may be inverted. Men of factious tempers, of local prejudices, or of sinister designs, may by intrigue, by corruption, or by other means, first obtain the suffrages, and then betray the interest of the people. The question resulting is, whether small or extensive republics are most favorable to the election of proper guardians of the public weal, and it is clearly decided in favor of the latter by two obvious considerations.

In the first place, it is to be remarked that, however small the republic may be, the representatives must be raised to a certain number, in order to guard against the cabals of a few; and that however large it may be, they must be limited to a certain number, in order to guard against the confusion of a multitude. Hence, the number of representatives in the two cases not being in proportion to that of the constituents, and being proportionally greatest in the small republic, it follows, that if the proportion of fit characters be not less in the large than in the small republic, the former will present a greater option, and consequently a greater probability of a fit choice.

In the next place, as each Representative will be chosen by a greater number of citizens in the large than in the small Republic, it will be more difficult for unworthy candidates to practise with success the vicious arts, by which elections are too often carried; and the suffrages of the people being more free, will be more likely to center on men who possess the most attractive merit, and the most diffusive and established characters.

It must be confessed, that in this, as in most other cases, there is a mean, on both sides of which inconveniences will be found to lie. By enlarging too much the number of electors, you render the representatives too little acquainted with all their local circumstances and lesser interests; as by reducing it too much, you render him unduly attached to these, and too little fit to comprehend and pursue great and national objects. The Federal Constitution forms a happy combination in this respect; the great and aggregate interests being referred to the national, the local and particular, to the state legislatures.

The other point of difference is, the greater number of citizens and extent of territory which may be brought within the compass of Republican, than of Democratic Government; and it is this circumstance principally which renders factious combinations less to be dreaded in the former, than in the latter. The smaller the society, the fewer probably will be the distinct parties and interests composing it; the fewer the distinct parties and interests, the more frequently will a majority be found of the same party; and the smaller the number of individuals composing a majority, and the smaller the compass within which they are placed, the more easily will they concert and execute their plans of oppression. Extend the sphere, and you take in a greater variety of parties and interests; you make it less probable that a majority of the whole will have a common motive to invade the rights of other citizens; or if such a common motive exists, it will be more difficult for all who feel it to discover their own strength, and to act in unison with each other. Besides other impediments, it may be remarked, that where there is a consciousness of unjust or dishonorable purposes, communication is always checked by distrust, in proportion to the number whose concurrence is necessary.

Hence it clearly appears, that the same advantage, which a Republic has over a Democracy, in controlling the effects of faction, is enjoyed by a large over a small Republic—is enjoyed by the Union over the States composing it. Does this advantage consist in the substitution of Representatives, whose enlightened views and virtuous sentiments render them superior to local prejudices, and to schemes of injustice? It will not be denied, that the Representation of the Union will be most likely to possess these requisite endowments. Does it consist in the greater security afforded by a greater variety of parties, against the event of any one party being able to outnumber and oppress the rest? In an equal degree does the increased variety of parties, comprised within the Union, increase this security? Does it, in fine, consist in the greater obstacles opposed to the concert and accomplishment of the secret wishes of an unjust and interested majority? Here, again, the extent of the Union gives it the most palpable advantage.

The influence of factious leaders may kindle a flame within their particular States, but will be unable to spread a general conflagration through the other States: a religious sect, may degenerate into a political faction in a part of the Confederacy but the variety of sects dispersed over the entire face of it, must secure the national Councils against any danger from that source: a rage for paper money, for an abolition of debts, for an equal division of property, or for any other improper or wicked project, will be less apt to pervade the whole body of the Union, than a particular member of it; in the same proportion as such a malady is more likely to taint a particular county or district, than an entire State.

In the extent and proper structure of the Union, therefore, we behold a Republican remedy for the diseases most incident to Republican Government. And according to the degree of pleasure and pride, we feel in being Republicans, ought to be our zeal in cherishing the spirit, and supporting the character of Federalists.

PUBLIUS

Federalist No. 51

To the People of the State of New York.

February 6, 1788

James Madison

To what expedient then shall we finally resort for maintaining in practice the necessary partition of power among the several departments, as laid down in the constitution? The only answer that can be given is, that as all these exterior provisions are found to be inadequate, the defect must be supplied, by so contriving the interior structure of the government, as that its several constituent parts may, by their mutual relations, be the means of keeping each other in their proper places. Without presuming to undertake a full development of this important idea, I will hazard a few general observations, which may perhaps place it in a clearer light, and enable us to form a more correct judgment of the principles and structure of the government planned by the convention.

In order to lay a due foundation for that separate and distinct exercise of the different powers of government, which to a certain extent, is admitted on all hands to be essential to the preservation of liberty, it is evident that each department should have a will of its own; and consequently should be so constituted, that the members of each should have as little agency as possible in the appointment of the members of the others. Were this principle rigorously adhered to, it would require that all the appointments for the supreme executive, legislative, and judiciary magistracies, should be drawn from the same fountain of authority, the people, through channels, having no communication whatever with one another. Perhaps such a plan of constructing the several departments would be less difficult in practice than it may in contemplation appear. Some difficulties however, and some additional expense, would attend the execution of it. Some deviations therefore from the principle must be admitted. In the constitution of the judiciary department in particular, it might be inexpedient to insist rigorously on the principle; first, because peculiar qualifications being essential in the members, the primary consideration ought to be to select that mode of choice, which best secures these qualifications; secondly, because the permanent tenure by which the appointments are held in that department, must soon destroy all sense of dependence on the authority conferring them.

It is equally evident that the members of each department should be as little dependent as possible on those of the others, for the emoluments annexed to their offices. Were the executive magistrate, or the judges, not independent of the legislature in this particular, their independence in every other would be merely nominal.

But the great security against a gradual concentration of the several powers in the same department, consists in giving to those who administer each department, the necessary constitutional means, and personal motives, to resist encroachments of the others. The provision for defense must in this, as in all other cases, be made commensurate to the danger of attack. Ambition must be made to counteract ambition. The interest of the man must be connected with the constitutional right of the place. It may be a reflection on human nature, that such devices should be necessary to control the abuses of government. But what is government itself but the greatest of all reflections on human nature? If men were angels, no government would be necessary. If angels were to govern men, neither external nor internal controls on government would be necessary. In framing a government which is to be administered by men over men, the great difficulty lies in this: You must first enable the government to control the governed; and in the next place, oblige it to control itself. A dependence on the people is no doubt the primary control on the government; but experience has taught mankind the necessity of auxiliary precautions.

This policy of supplying by opposite and rival interests, the defect of better motives, might be traced through the whole system of human affairs, private as well as public. We see it particularly displayed in all the subordinate distributions of power; where the constant aim is to divide and arrange the several offices in such a manner as that each may be a check on the other; that the private interest of every individual, may be a sentinel over the public rights. These inventions of prudence cannot be less requisite in the distribution of the supreme powers of the state.

But it is not possible to give to each department an equal power of self defense. In republican government the legislative authority, necessarily, predominates. The remedy for this inconveniency is, to divide the legislature into different branches; and to render them by different modes of election, and different principles of action, as little connected with each other, as the nature of their common functions, and their common dependence on the society, will admit. It may even be necessary to guard against dangerous encroachments by still further precautions. As the weight of the legislative authority requires that it should be thus divided, the weakness of the executive may require, on the other hand, that it should be fortified. An absolute negative, on the legislature, appears at first view to be the natural defense with which the executive magistrate should be armed. But perhaps it would be neither altogether safe, nor alone sufficient. On ordinary occasions, it might not be exerted with the requisite firmness; and on extraordinary occasions, it might be prefidiously abused. May not this defect of an absolute negative be supplied, by some qualified connection between this weaker department, and the weaker branch of the stronger department, by which the latter may be led to support the constitutional rights of the former, without being too much detached from the rights of its own department? If the principles on which these observations are founded be just, as I persuade myself they are, and they be applied as a criterion, to the several state constitutions, and to the federal constitution, it will be found, that if the latter does not perfectly correspond with them, the former are infinitely less able to bear such a test.

There are moreover two considerations particularly applicable to the federal system of America, which place that system in a very interesting point of view.

First. In a single republic, all the power surrendered by the people, is submitted to the administration of a single government; and usurpations are guarded against by a division of the government into distinct and separate departments. In the compound republic of America, the power surrendered by the people, is first divided between two distinct governments, and then the portion allotted to each, subdivided among distinct and separate departments. Hence a double security arises to the rights of the people. The different governments will control each other; at the same time that each will be controlled by itself.

Second. It is of great importance in a republic, not only to guard the society against the oppression of its rulers; but to guard one part of the society against the injustice of the other part. Different interests necessarily exist in different classes of citizens. If a majority be united by a common interest, the rights of the minority will be insecure. There are but two methods of providing against this evil: The one by creating a will in the community independent of the majority, that is, of the society itself, the other by comprehending in the society so many separate descriptions of citizens, as will render an unjust combination of a majority of the whole, very improbable, if not impracticable. The first method prevails in all governments possessing an hereditary or self appointed authority. This at best is but a precarious security; because a power independent of the society may as well espouse the unjust views of the major, as the rightful interests, of the minor party, and may possibly be turned against both parties. The second method will be exemplified in the federal republic of the United States. While all authority in it will be derived from and dependent on the society, the society itself will be broken into so many parts, interests and classes of citizens, that the rights of individuals or of the minority, will be in little danger from interested combinations of the majority. In a free government, the security for civil rights must be the same as for religious rights. It consists in the one case in the multiplicity of interests, and in the other, in the multiplicity of sects. The degree of security in both cases will depend on the number of interests and sects; and this may be presumed to depend on the extent of country and number of people comprehended under the same government. This view of the subject must particularly recommend a proper federal system to all the sincere and considerate friends of republican government: Since it shows that in exact proportion as the territory of the union may be formed into more circumscribed confederacies or states, oppressive combinations of a majority will be facilitated, the best security under the republican form, for the rights of every class of citizens, will be diminished; and consequently, the stability and independence of some member of the government, the only other security, must be proportionally increased. Justice is the end of government. It is the end of civil society. It ever has been, and ever will be pursued, until it be obtained, or until liberty be lost in the pursuit. In a society under the forms of which the stronger faction can readily unite and oppress the weaker, anarchy may as truly be said to reign, as in a state of nature where the weaker individual is not secured against the violence of the stronger: And as in the latter state even the stronger individuals are prompted by the uncertainty of their condition, to submit to a government which may protect the weak as well as themselves: So in the former state, will the more powerful factions or parties be gradually induced by a like motive, to wish for a government which will protect all parties, the weaker as well as the more powerful. It can be little doubted, that if the state of Rhode Island was separated from the confederacy, and left to itself, the insecurity of rights under the popular form of government within such narrow limits, would be displayed by such reiterated oppressions of factious majorities, that some power altogether independent of the people would soon be called for by the voice of the very factions whose misrule had proved the necessity of it. In the extended republic of the United States, and among the great variety of interests, parties and sects which it embraces, a coalition of a majority of the whole society could seldom take place on any other principles than those of justice and the general good; and there being thus less danger to a minor from the will of the major party, there must be less pretext also, to provide for the security of the former, by introducing into the government a will not dependent on the latter; or in other words, a will independent of the society itself. It is no less certain than it is important, notwithstanding the contrary opinions which have been entertained, that the larger the society, provided it lie within a practicable sphere, the more duly capable it will be of self government. And happily for the *republican cause*, the practicable sphere may be carried to a very great extent, by a judicious modification and mixture of the *federal principle*.

PUBLIUS

Presidents, Congresses, and Chief Justices: 1789–2009

Term	President and Vice President	Party of President	Congress	Majority Party		Chief Justice of the United States
				House	Senate	
1789–1797	**George Washington** John Adams	None	1st 2nd 3rd 4th	(N/A) (N/A) (N/A) (N/A)	(N/A) (N/A) (N/A) (N/A)	John Jay (1789–1795) John Rutledge (1795) Oliver Ellsworth (1796–1800)
1797–1801	**John Adams** Thomas Jefferson	Federalist	5th 6th	(N/A) Fed	(N/A) Fed	Oliver Ellsworth (1796–1800) John Marshall (1801–1835)
1801–1809	**Thomas Jefferson** Aaron Burr (1801–1805) George Clinton (1805–1809)	Democratic-Republican	7th 8th 9th 10th	Dem-Rep Dem-Rep Dem-Rep Dem-Rep	Dem-Rep Dem-Rep Dem-Rep Dem-Rep	John Marshall (1801–1835)
1809–1817	**James Madison** George Clinton (1809–1812)[a] Elbridge Gerry (1813–1814)[a]	Democratic-Republican	11th 12th 13th 14th	Dem-Rep Dem-Rep Dem-Rep Dem-Rep	Dem-Rep Dem-Rep Dem-Rep Dem-Rep	John Marshall (1801–1835)
1817–1825	**James Monroe** Daniel D. Tompkins	Democratic-Republican	15th 16th 17th 18th	Dem-Rep Dem-Rep Dem-Rep Dem-Rep	Dem-Rep Dem-Rep Dem-Rep Dem-Rep	John Marshall (1801–1835)
1825–1829	**John Quincy Adams** John C. Calhoun	National-Republican	19th 20th	Nat'l Rep Dem	Nat'l Rep Dem	John Marshall (1801–1835)
1829–1837	**Andrew Jackson** John C. Calhoun (1829–1832)[c] Martin Van Buren (1833–1837)	Democratic	21st 22nd 23rd 24th	Dem Dem Dem Dem	Dem Dem Dem Dem	John Marshall (1801–1835) Roger B. Taney (1836–1864)
1837–1841	**Martin Van Buren** Richard M. Johnson	Democratic	25th 26th	Dem Dem	Dem Dem	Roger B. Taney (1836–1864)
1841	**William H. Harrison**[a] John Tyler (1841)	Whig				Roger B. Taney (1836–1864)
1841–1845	**John Tyler** (VP vacant)	Whig	27th 28th	Whig Dem	Whig Whig	Roger B. Taney (1836–1864)
1845–1849	**James K. Polk** George M. Dallas	Democratic	29th 30th	Dem Whig	Dem Dem	Roger B. Taney (1836–1864)
1849–1850	**Zachary Taylor**[a] Millard Fillmore	Whig	31st	Dem	Dem	Roger B. Taney (1836–1864)
1850–1853	**Millard Fillmore** (VP vacant)	Whig	32nd	Dem	Dem	Roger B. Taney (1836–1864)

Term	President and Vice President	Party of President	Congress	Majority Party House	Majority Party Senate	Chief Justice of the United States
1853–1857	**Franklin Pierce** William R. D. King (1853)[a]	Democratic	33rd 34th	Dem Rep	Dem Dem	Roger B. Taney (1836–1864)
1857–1861	**James Buchanan** John C. Breckinridge	Democratic	35th 36th	Dem Rep	Dem Dem	Roger B. Taney (1836–1864)
1861–1865	**Abraham Lincoln**[a] Hannibal Hamlin (1861–1865) Andrew Johnson (1865)	Republican	37th 38th	Rep Rep	Rep Rep	Roger B. Taney (1836–1864) Salmon P. Chase (1864–1873)
1865–1869	**Andrew Johnson** (VP vacant)	Republican	39th 40th	Union Rep	Union Rep	Salmon P. Chase (1864–1873)
1869–1877	**Ulysses S. Grant** Schuyler Colfax (1869–1873) Henry Wilson (1873–1875)[a]	Republican	41st 42nd 43rd 44th	Rep Rep Rep Dem	Rep Rep Rep Rep	Salmon P. Chase (1864–1873) Morrison R. Waite (1874–1888)
1877–1881	**Rutherford B. Hayes** William A. Wheeler	Republican	45th 46th	Dem Dem	Rep Dem	Morrison R. Waite (1874–1888)
1881	**James A. Garfield**[a] Chester A. Arthur	Republican	47th	Rep	Rep	Morrison R. Waite (1874–1888)
1881–1885	**Chester A. Arthur** (VP vacant)	Republican	48th	Dem	Rep	Morrison R. Waite (1874–1888)
1885–1889	**Grover Cleveland** Thomas A. Hendricks (1885)[a]	Democratic	49th 50th	Dem Dem	Rep Rep	Morrison R. Waite (1874–1888) Melville W. Fuller (1888–1910)
1889–1893	**Benjamin Harrison** Levi P. Morton	Republican	51st 52nd	Rep Dem	Rep Rep	Melville W. Fuller (1888–1910)
1893–1897	**Grover Cleveland** Adlai E. Stevenson	Democratic	53rd 54th	Dem Rep	Dem Rep	Melville W. Fuller (1888–1910)
1897–1901	**William McKinley**[a] Garret A. Hobart (1897–1899)[a] Theodore Roosevelt (1901)	Republican	55th 56th	Rep Rep	Rep Rep	Melville W. Fuller (1888–1910)
1901–1909	**Theodore Roosevelt** (VP vacant, 1901–1905) Charles W. Fairbanks (1905–1909)	Republican	57th 58th 59th 60th	Rep Rep Rep Rep	Rep Rep Rep Rep	Melville W. Fuller (1888–1910)
1909–1913	**William Howard Taft** James S. Sherman (1909–1912)[a]	Republican	61st 62nd	Rep Dem	Rep Rep	Melville W. Fuller (1888–1910) Edward D. White (1910–1921)
1913–1921	**Woodrow Wilson** Thomas R. Marshall	Democratic	63rd 64th 65th 66th	Dem Dem Dem Rep	Dem Dem Dem Rep	Edward D. White (1910–1921)
1921–1923	**Warren G. Harding**[a] Calvin Coolidge	Republican	67th	Rep	Rep	William Howard Taft (1921–1930)
1923–1929	**Calvin Coolidge** (VP vacant, 1923–1925) Charles G. Dawes (1925–1929)	Republican	68th 69th 70th	Rep Rep Rep	Rep Rep Rep	William Howard Taft (1921–1930)
1929–1933	**Herbert Hoover** Charles Curtis	Republican	71st 72nd	Rep Dem	Rep Rep	William Howard Taft (1921–1930) Charles Evans Hughes (1930–1941)

Term	President and Vice President	Party of President	Congress	Majority Party		Chief Justice of the United States
				House	Senate	
1933–1945	**Franklin D. Roosevelt**[a] John Nance Garner (1933–1941) Henry A. Wallace (1941–1945) Harry S Truman (1945)	Democratic	73rd 74th 75th 76th 77th 78th	Dem Dem Dem Dem Dem Dem	Dem Dem Dem Dem Dem Dem	Charles Evans Hughes (1930–1941) Harlan F. Stone (1941–1946)
1945–1953	**Harry S Truman** (VP vacant, 1945–1949) Alben W. Barkley (1949–1953)	Democratic	79th 80th 81st 82nd	Dem Rep Dem Dem	Dem Rep Dem Dem	Harlan F. Stone (1941–1946) Frederick M. Vinson (1946–1953)
1953–1961	**Dwight D. Eisenhower** Richard M. Nixon	Republican	83rd 84th 85th 86th	Rep Dem Dem Dem	Rep Dem Dem Dem	Frederick M. Vinson (1946–1953) Earl Warren (1953–1969)
1961–1963	**John F. Kennedy**[a] Lyndon B. Johnson (1961–1963)	Democratic	87th	Dem	Dem	Earl Warren (1953–1969)
1963–1969	**Lyndon B. Johnson** (VP vacant, 1963–1965) Hubert H. Humphrey (1965–1969)	Democratic	88th 89th 90th	Dem Dem Dem	Dem Dem Dem	Earl Warren (1953–1969)
1969–1974	**Richard M. Nixon**[b] Spiro Agnew (1969–1973)[c] Gerald R. Ford (1973–1974)[d]	Republican	91st 92nd	Dem Dem	Dem Dem	Earl Warren (1953–1969) Warren E. Burger (1969–1986)
1974–1977	**Gerald R. Ford** Nelson A. Rockefeller[d]	Republican	93rd 94th	Dem Dem	Dem Dem	Warren E. Burger (1969–1986)
1977–1981	**Jimmy Carter** Walter Mondale	Democratic	95th 96th	Dem Dem	Dem Dem	Warren E. Burger (1969–1986)
1981–1989	**Ronald Reagan** George Bush	Republican	97th 98th 99th 100th	Dem Dem Dem Dem	Rep Rep Rep Dem	Warren E. Burger (1969–1986) William H. Rehnquist (1986–2005)
1989–1993	**George Bush** Dan Quayle	Republican	101st 102nd	Dem Dem	Dem Dem	William H. Rehnquist (1986–2005)
1993–2001	**Bill Clinton** Al Gore	Democratic	103rd 104th 105th 106th	Dem Rep Rep Rep	Dem Rep Rep Rep	William H. Rehnquist (1986–2005)
2001–2009	**George W. Bush** Dick Cheney	Republican	107th 108th 109th 110th	Rep Rep Rep Dem	Dem Rep Rep Dem	William H. Rehnquist (1986–2005) John G. Roberts Jr. (2005–)
2009–2013	**Barack Obama** Joe Biden	Democratic	111th	Dem	Dem	John G. Roberts Jr.

[a]Died in office.
[b]Resigned from the presidency.
[c]Resigned from the vice presidency.
[d]Appointed vice president.

Selected Supreme Court Cases

- *Agostini v. Felton (1997):* The Court agreed to permit public school teachers to go into parochial schools during school hours to provide remedial education to disadvantaged students because it was not an excessive entanglement of church and state.

- *Ashcroft v. Free Speech Coalition (2002):* The Court ruled that the Child Online Protection Act of 1998 was unconstitutional because it was too vague in its reliance on "community standards" to define what is harmful to minors.

- *Atkins v. Virginia (2002):* Execution of the mentally retarded is prohibited by the Eighth Amendment's cruel and unusual punishment clause.

- *Avery v. Midland (1968):* The Court declared that the one-person, one-vote standard applied to counties as well as congressional and state legislative districts.

- *Ayotte v. Planned Parenthood of Northern New England (2006):* A New Hampshire abortion law that did not provide an exception for the woman's health was unconstitutional.

- *Baker v. Carr (1962):* Watershed case establishing the principle of one person, one vote, which requires that each legislative district within a state have the same number of eligible voters so that representation is equitably based on population.

- *Barron v. Baltimore (1833):* Decision that limited the application of the Bill of Rights to the actions of Congress alone.

- *Batson v. Kentucky (1986):* Peremptory challenges cannot be used to exclude all people of a given race (in this case, African Americans) from a jury pool.

- *Benton v. Maryland (1969):* Incorporated the Fifth Amendment's double jeopardy clause.

- *Board of Regents v. Southworth (2000):* Unanimous ruling from the Supreme Court which stated that public universities could charge students a mandatory activities fee that could be used to facilitate extracurricular student political speech so long as the programs are neutral in their application.

- *Boerne v. Flores (1997):* The Court ruled that Congress could not force the Religious Freedom Restoration act upon the state governments.

- *Bowers v. Hardwick (1986):* Unsuccessful attempt to challenge Georgia's sodomy law. The case was overturned by *Lawrence* v. *Texas* in 2003.

- *Bradwell v. Illinois (1873):* In this case, a woman argued that Illinois's refusal to allow her to practice law despite the fact that she had passed the bar violated her citizenship rights under the privileges and immunities clause of the Fourteenth Amendment; the justices denied her claim.

- *Bragdon v. Abbott (1998):* The Court ruled that individuals infected with HIV but not sick enough to qualify as having AIDS were protected from discrimination by the 1990 Americans with Disabilities Act (ADA).

- *Brandenburg v. Ohio (1969):* The Court fashioned the direct incitement test for deciding whether certain kinds of speech could be regulated by the government. This test holds that advocacy of illegal action is protected by the First Amendment unless imminent action is intended and likely to occur.

- *Brown v. Board of Education (1954):* Supreme Court decision holding that school segregation is inherently unconstitutional because it violates the Fourteenth Amendment's guarantee of equal protection; marked the end of legal segregation in the United States.

- *Brown v. Board of Education II (1955):* Follow-up to *Brown* v. *Board of Education*, this case laid out the process for school desegregation and established the concept of dismantling segregationist systems "with all deliberate speed."

- *Brown University v. Cohen (1997):* Landmark Title IX case that put all colleges and universities on notice that discrimination against women would not be tolerated, even when, as in the case of Brown University, the university had tremendously expanded sports opportunities for women.

- *Buckley v. Valeo (1976):* The Court ruled that money spent by an individual or political committee in support or opposition of a candidate (but independent of the candidate's campaign) was a form of symbolic speech, and therefore could not be limited under the First Amendment.

- *Bush v. Gore (2000):* Controversial 2000 election case that made the final decision on the Florida recounts, and thus determined the result of the 2000 election.

- *Cantwell v. Connecticut (1940):* The case in which the Supreme Court incorporated the freedom of religion, ruling that the freedom to believe is absolute, but the freedom to act is subject to the regulation of society.

- *Chandler v. Miller (1997):* The Supreme Court refused to allow Georgia to require all candidates for state office to pass a urinalysis thirty days before qualifying for nomination or election, concluding that this law violated the search and seizure clause.

- *Chaplinsky v. New Hampshire (1942):* Established the Supreme Court's rationale for distinguishing between protected and unprotected speech.

- *Chicago, B&Q R.R. Co. v. Chicago (1897):* Incorporated the Fifth Amendment's just compensation clause.

- *Chisholm v. Georgia (1793):* The Court interpreted its jurisdiction under Article III, section 2, of the Constitution to include the right to hear suits brought by a citizen of one state against another state.

- *City of Cleburne v. Cleburne Living Center (1985):* Established that zoning restrictions against group homes for the retarded have a rational basis.

- *Civil Rights Cases (1883):* Name attached to five cases brought under the Civil Rights Act of 1875. In 1883, the Supreme Court decided that discrimination in a variety of public accommodations, including theaters, hotels, and railroads, could not be prohibited by the act because it was private and not state discrimination.

- *Clinton v. City of New York (1998):* The Court ruled that the line-item veto was unconstitutional because it gave powers to the president denied him by the U.S. Constitution.

- *Clinton v. Jones (1997):* The Court refused to reverse a lower court's decision that allowed Paula Jones's civil case against President Bill Clinton to proceed.

- *Cohens v. Virginia (1821):* The Court defined its jurisdiction to include the right to review all state criminal cases; additionally, this case built on *Martin* v. *Hunter's Lessee*, clarifying the Court's power to declare state laws unconstitutional.

- ***Colorado Republican Federal Campaign Committee v. Federal Election Commission (1996):*** The Supreme Court extended its ruling in *Buckley* v. *Valeo* to also include political parties.

- *Cooper v. Aaron (1958):* Case wherein the Court broke with tradition and issued a unanimous decision against the Little Rock School Board, ruling that the district's evasive schemes to avoid the *Brown II* decision were illegal.

- *Craig v. Boren (1976):* The Court ruled that keeping drunk drivers off the roads may be an important governmental objective, but allowing women aged eighteen to twenty-one to drink alcoholic beverages while prohibiting men of the same age from drinking is not substantially related to that goal.

- *Cruzan by Cruzan v. Director, Missouri Department of Health (1990):* The Court rejected any attempt to extend the right to privacy into the area of assisted suicide. However, the Court did note that individuals could terminate medical treatment if they were able to express, or had done so in writing, their desire to have medical treatment terminated in the event they became incompetent.

- *DeJonge v. Oregon (1937):* Incorporated the First Amendment's right to freedom of assembly.

- *Doe v. Bolton (1973):* In combination with *Roe* v. *Wade*, established a woman's right to an abortion.

- *Dred Scott v. Sandford (1857):* Concluded that the U.S. Congress lacked the constitutional authority to bar slavery in the territories; this decision narrowed the scope of national power while it enhanced that of the states. This case marks the first time since *Marbury* v. *Madison* that the Supreme Court found an act of Congress unconstitutional.

- *Duncan v. Louisiana (1968):* Incorporated the Sixth Amendment's trial by jury clause.

- *Engel v. Vitale (1962):* The Court ruled that the recitation in public classrooms of a non-denominational prayer was unconstitutional and a violation of the establishment clause.

- *Fletcher v. Peck (1810):* The Court ruled that state legislatures could not make laws that voided contracts or grants made by earlier legislative action.

- *Furman v. Georgia (1972):* The Supreme Court used this case to end capital punishment, at least in the short run. (The case was overturned by *Gregg* v. *Georgia* in 1976.)

- *Garcia v. San Antonio Metropolitan Transport Authority (1985):* In this case, the court ruled that Congress has the broad power to impose its will on state and local governments, even in areas that have traditionally been left to state and local discretion.

- *Georgia v. Randolph (2006):* The Court ruled that both residents of a home must consent to a search before that search is regarded as constitutional.

- *Gibbons v. Ogden (1824):* The Court upheld broad congressional power over interstate commerce.

- *Gideon v. Wainwright (1963):* Granted indigents the right to counsel.

- *Gitlow v. New York (1925):* Incorporated the free speech clause of the First Amendment, ruling that the states were not completely free to limit forms of political expression.

- *Gonzales v. O Centro Espirita Beneficente União do Vegetal (2006):* Under the Religious Freedom Restoration Act, the government has to make an exception to the Controlled Substances Act for a substance used in religious services.

- *Gonzales v. Oregon (2006):* Held that the Justice Department does not have the authority to block physician assisted suicides.

- *Gonzales v. Raich (2005):* Upheld power of Congress to ban and prosecute the possession and use of marijuana for medical purposes, even in states that permitted it.

- *Gratz v. Bollinger (2003):* The Court struck down the University of Michigan's undergraduate point system, which gave minority applicants twenty automatic points simply because they were minorities.

- *Gray v. Sanders (1963):* The Court held that voting by unit systems is unconstitutional.

- *Gregg v. Georgia (1976):* Overturning *Furman* v. *Georgia*, the case ruled that Georgia's rewritten death penalty statute is constitutional.

- *Griswold v. Connecticut (1965):* Supreme Court case that established the Constitution's implied right to privacy.

- *Grutter v. Bollinger (2003):* The Court voted to uphold the constitutionality of the University of Michigan law school's affirmative action policy, which gave preference to minority students.

- *Hamdan v. Rumsfeld (2006):* The Court ruled that detainees in the war on terrorism were entitled to the protections of the Geneva Convention and the procedural rights of the Uniform Code of Military Justice, since Congress had not approved of President George W. Bush's system of military tribunals. Congress passed the Military Commissions Act in 2006 to address the Court's ruling in *Hamdan*.

- *Hamdi et al v. Rumsfeld (2004):* The government does not have the authority to detain a U.S. citizen charged as an enemy combatant in the war on terrorism without providing basic due process protections under the Fifth Amendment.
- *Harris v. Forklift Systems (1993):* The Court ruled that a federal civil rights law created a "broad rule of workplace equality."
- *Hill v. McDonough (2006):* Challenging the form of execution prescribed in a defendant's sentence is not a proper use of a *habeas corpus* petition.
- *House v. Bell (2006):* A Tennessee death-row inmate who had otherwise exhausted his federal appeals was provided an exception due to the availability of DNA evidence suggesting his innocence; the case recognized the potential exculpatory power of DNA evidence.
- *Hoyt v. Florida (1961):* The Court ruled that an all-male jury did not violate a woman's rights under the Fourteenth Amendment.
- *Hudson v. Michigan (2006):* Evidence obtained in violation of the "knock and announce" rule is not subject to the restrictions of the exclusionary rule.
- *Hunt v. Cromartie (1999, 2001):* Continuation of redistricting litigation begun with *Shaw* v. *Reno* (1993). The Court reversed district court conclusions that the North Carolina legislature had used race-driven criteria in violation of the equal protection clause to redraw district lines.
- *Immigration and Naturalization Service v. Chadha (1983):* The Court ruled that the legislative veto as it was used in many circumstances was unconstitutional because it violated the separation of powers principle.
- *J.E.B. v. Alabama (1994):* The use of peremptory challenges to exclude jurors of a particular gender is unconstitutional.
- *Kelo v. New London (2004):* The Court ruled that government could take private property and then sell it to private developers so long as that property was slated for economic development that would benefit the surrounding community.
- *Klopfer v. North Carolina (1967):* Incorporated the Sixth Amendment's right to a speedy trial.
- *Korematsu v. U.S. (1944):* In this case, the Court ruled that the internment of Japanese Americans during World War II was not unconstitutional.
- *Lawrence v. Texas (2003):* The Court reversed its 1986 ruling in *Bowers* v. *Hardwick* by finding a Texas statute that banned sodomy to be unconstitutional.
- *League of United Latin American Citizens et al. v. Perry (2006):* Part of the 2004 Texas redistricting plan violated the Voting Rights Act because it deprived Hispanic citizens of the right to elect a representative of their choosing.
- *Lemon v. Kurtzman (1971):* The Court determined that direct government assistance to religious schools is unconstitutional. In the majority opinion, the Court created what has become known as the "Lemon Test" for deciding if a law is in violation of the establishment clause.
- *Lynch v. Donnelly (1984):* In a defeat for the ACLU, the Court held that a city's inclusion of a crèche in its annual Christmas display in a private park did not violate the establishment clause.
- *Malloy v. Hogan (1964):* Incorporated the Fifth Amendment's self-incrimination clause.
- *Mapp v. Ohio (1961):* Incorporated a portion of the Fourth Amendment by establishing that illegally obtained evidence cannot be used at trial.
- *Marbury v. Madison (1803):* Case in which the Court first asserted the power of judicial review in finding that a congressional statute extending the Court's original jurisdiction was unconstitutional.
- *Martin v. Hunter's Lessee (1816):* The Court's power of judicial review in regard to state law was clarified in this case.
- *Maryland v. Craig (1990):* The confrontation clause of the Sixth Amendment does not guarantee defendants an absolute right to come face to face with their accusers.

- *Ex parte McCardle (1869):* Post–Civil War case that reinforced Congress's power to determine the jurisdiction of the Supreme Court.
- *McCleskey v. Kemp (1987):* The Court ruled that the imposition of the death penalty did not violate the equal protection clause.
- *McCleskey v. Zant (1991):* On this appeal of the 1987 *McCleskey* case, the Court produced new standards designed to make it much more difficult for death-row inmates to file repeated appeals.
- *McConnell v. FEC (2003):* Generally speaking, the Bipartisan Campaign Finance Reform Act of 2002 does not violate the First Amendment.
- *McCreary County v. ACLU of Kentucky (2005):* The Court ruled that the display of the Ten Commandments in public schools and courthouses violated the establishment clause.
- *McCulloch v. Maryland (1819):* The Court upheld the power of the national government and denied the right of a state to tax the bank. The Court's broad interpretation of the necessary and proper clause paved the way for later rulings upholding expansive federal powers.
- *Miller v. California (1973):* Case wherein the Supreme Court began to formulate rules designed to make it easier for states to regulate obscene materials and to return to communities a greater role in determining what is obscene.
- *Minor v. Happersett (1875):* The Supreme Court once again examined the privileges and immunities clause of the Fourteenth Amendment, ruling that voting was not a privilege of citizenship.
- *Miranda v. Arizona (1966):* The Fifth Amendment requires that individuals arrested for a crime must be advised of their right to remain silent and to have counsel present.
- *Morrison v. U.S. (2000):* The Court ruled that Congress has no authority under the commerce clause to enact a provision of the Violence Against Women Act providing a federal remedy to victims of gender-motivated violence.
- *Muller v. Oregon (1908):* Case that ruled Oregon's law barring women from working more than ten hours a day was constitutional; also an attempt to define women's unique status as mothers to justify their differential treatment.
- *Near v. Minnesota (1931):* By ruling that a state law violated the freedom of the press, the Supreme Court incorporated the free press provision of the First Amendment.
- *Nebraska Press Association v. Stuart (1976):* Prior restraint case; the Court ruled that a trial judge could not prohibit the publication or broadcast of information about a murder trial.
- *Nevada Department of Human Resources v. Hibbs (2003):* The court upheld the ability of state employees to sue under the Family and Medical Leave Act.
- *New York Times Co. v. Sullivan (1964):* Supreme Court ruling that simply publishing a defamatory falsehood is not enough to justify a libel judgment. "Actual malice" must be proved to support a finding of libel against a public figure.
- *New York Times Co. v. U.S. (1971):* Also called the Pentagon Papers case; the Supreme Court ruled that any attempt by the government to prevent expression carried "a heavy presumption" against its constitutionality.
- *NLRB v. Jones and Laughlin Steel Co. (1937):* Case that upheld the National Labor Relations Act of 1935, marking a turning point in the Court's ideology toward the programs of President Franklin D. Roosevelt's New Deal.
- *In re Oliver (1948):* Incorporated the Sixth Amendment's right to a public trial.
- *Palko v. Connecticut (1937):* Set the Court's rationale of selective incorporation, a judicial doctrine whereby most but not all of the protections found in the Bill of Rights are made applicable to the states via the Fourteenth Amendment.
- *Parker v. Gladden (1966):* Incorporated the Sixth Amendment's right to an impartial trial.
- *Planned Parenthood v. Casey (1992):* This case was an unsuccessful attempt to challenge Pennsylvania's restrictive abortion regulations.

- *Plessy v. Ferguson (1896): Plessy* challenged a Louisiana statute requiring that railroads provide separate accommodations for blacks and whites. The Court found that separate but equal accommodations did not violate the equal protection clause of the Fourteenth Amendment.

- *Pointer v. Texas (1965):* Incorporated the Sixth Amendment's right to confrontation of witnesses.

- *Printz v. U.S. (1997):* The Court found that Congress lacks the authority to compel state officers to execute federal laws, specifically relating to background checks on handgun purchasers.

- *Quilici v. Village of Morton Grove (1983):* The Supreme Court refused to review a lower court's ruling upholding the constitutionality of a local ordinance banning handguns against a Second Amendment challenge.

- *R.A.V. v. City of St. Paul (1992):* The Court concluded that St. Paul, Minnesota's Bias-Motivated Crime Ordinance violated the First Amendment because it regulated speech based on the content of the speech.

- *Reed v. Reed (1971):* Turned the tide in terms of constitutional litigation, ruling that the equal protection clause of the Fourteenth Amendment prohibited unreasonable classifications based on sex.

- *Regents of the University of California v. Bakke (1978):* A sharply divided Court concluded that the university's rejection of Bakke as a student had been illegal because the use of strict affirmative action quotas was inappropriate.

- *Reno v. American Civil Liberties Union (1997):* The Court ruled that the 1996 Communications Decency Act prohibiting transfer of obscene or indecent materials over the Internet to minors violated the First Amendment because it was too vague and overbroad.

- *Reynolds v. Sims (1964):* The Court decided that every person should have an equally weighted vote in electing governmental representatives.

- *Robinson v. California (1962):* Incorporated the Eighth Amendment's right to freedom from cruel and unusual punishment.

- *Roe v. Wade (1973):* The Supreme Court found that a woman's right to an abortion was protected by the right to privacy that could be implied from specific guarantees found in the Bill of Rights and the Fourteenth Amendment.

- *Romer v. Evans (1996):* A Colorado constitutional amendment precluding any legislative, executive, or judicial action at any state or local level designed to bar discrimination based on sexual preference was ruled not rational or reasonable.

- *Rompilla v. Beard (2005):* Counsel must make a reasonable effort to examine information pertaining to the case they are trying.

- *Roper v. Simmons (2005):* Execution of minors violates the Eighth Amendment's prohibition on cruel and unusual punishment.

- *Roth v. U.S. (1957):* The Court held that in order to be obscene, material must be "utterly without redeeming social value."

- *Santa Fe Independent School District v. Doe (2000):* The Court ruled that student-led, student-initiated prayer at high school football games violated the establishment clause.

- *Schenck v. U.S. (1919):* Case in which the Supreme Court interpreted the First Amendment to allow Congress to restrict speech that is "of such a nature as to create a clear and present danger that will bring about the substantive evils that Congress has a right to prevent."

- *Seminole Tribe v. Florida (1996):* Congress cannot impose a duty on states forcing them to negotiate with Indian tribes; the state's sovereign immunity protects it from a congressional directive about how to do business.

- *Shaw v. Reno (1993):* First in a series of redistricting cases in which the North Carolina legislature's reapportionment of congressional districts based on the 1990 Census was contested because the plan included an irregularly shaped district in which race seemed to be a dominant consideration. The Court ruled that districts created with race as the dominant consideration violated the equal protection clause of the Fourteenth Amendment.

- *In re Sindram (1991):* The Court chastised Michael Sindram for filing his petition *in forma pauperis* to require the Maryland courts to expedite his request to expunge a $35 speeding ticket from his record.

- *The Slaughterhouse Cases (1873):* The Court upheld Louisiana's right to create a monopoly on the operation of slaughterhouses, despite the Butcher's Benevolent Association's claim that this action deprived its members of their livelihood and the privileges and immunities granted by the Fourteenth Amendment.

- *Smith v. Massachusetts (2005):* Double jeopardy clause prohibits judges from reconsidering verdicts reached earlier in a trial, even in light of new evidence.

- *South Dakota v. Dole (1987):* The Court ruled that it was permissible for the federal government to require states that wanted transportation funds to pass laws setting twenty-one as the legal drinking age.

- *Stenberg v. Carhart (2000):* The Court ruled that a Nebraska "partial birth" abortion statute was unconstitutionally vague and unenforceable, calling into question the laws of twenty-nine other states.

- *Stromberg v. California (1931):* The Court overturned the conviction of a director of a Communist youth camp under a state statute prohibiting the display of a red flag.

- *Swann v. Charlotte-Mecklenberg School District (1971):* The Supreme Court ruled that all vestiges of *de jure* discrimination must be eliminated at once.

- *Tennessee v. Lane (2004):* Upheld application of the Americans with Disabilities Act to state courthouses.

- *Texas v. Johnson (1989):* The Court overturned the conviction of a Texas man found guilty of setting fire to an American flag.

- *Thornburg v. Gingles (1986):* At-large election of state legislators violates the Voting Rights Act because it dilutes the voting strength of African Americans.

- *Tinker v. Des Moines Independent School District (1969):* Upheld student's rights to express themselves by wearing black armbands symbolizing protest of the Vietnam War.

- *Tory v. Cochran (2005):* Prohibiting defamation of an individual after that person's death is an overly broad exercise of prior restraint.

- *U.S. v. Curtiss-Wright Export Corporation (1936):* The Court upheld the rights of Congress to grant the president authority to act in foreign affairs and to allow the president to prohibit arms shipments to participants in foreign wars.

- *U.S. v. Grubbs (2006):* A warrant does not need to describe the reason for its existence, only the person and things to be seized.

- *U.S. v. Lopez (1995):* The Court invalidated a section of the Gun Free School Zones Act, ruling that regulating guns did not fall within the scope of the commerce clause, and therefore was not within the powers of the federal government. Only states have the authority to ban guns in school zones.

- *U.S. v. Miller (1939):* The last time the Supreme Court addressed the constitutionality of the Second Amendment; ruled that the amendment was only intended to protect a citizen's right to own ordinary militia weapons.

- *U.S. v. Nixon (1974):* In a case involving President Richard M. Nixon's refusal to turn over tape recordings of his conversations, the Court ruled that executive privilege does not grant the president an absolute right to secure all presidential documents.

- *U.S. v. Patane (2004):* Physical evidence obtained in un-Mirandized voluntary statements is admissible in court.

- *U.S. Term Limits v. Thornton (1995):* The Supreme Court ruled that states do not have the authority to enact term limits for federal elected officials.

- *Washington v. Glucksberg (1997):* A state ban on physician assisted suicide does not violate the Fourteenth Amendment's due process clause.

- *Washington v. Texas (1967):* Incorporated the Sixth Amendment's right to a compulsory trial.
- *Webster v. Reproductive Health Services (1989):* In upholding several restrictive abortion regulations, the Court opened the door for state governments to enact new restrictions on abortion.
- *Weeks v. U.S. (1914):* Case wherein the Supreme Court adopted the exclusionary rule, which bars the use of illegally obtained evidence at trial.
- *Westberry v. Sanders (1964):* Established the principal of one person, one vote for congressional districts.
- *Wolf v. Colorado (1949):* The Court ruled that illegally obtained evidence did not necessarily have to be eliminated from use during trial.
- *Youngstown Sheet & Tube Co. v. Sawyer (1952):* The Court invalidated President Harry S Truman's seizure of the nation's steel mills.
- *Zelman v. Simmons-Harris (2002):* The Court concluded that governments can give money to parents to allow them to send their children to private or religious schools.

Glossary

administrative adjudication: A quasi-judicial process in which a bureaucratic agency settles disputes between two parties in a manner similar to the way courts resolve disputes.

administrative discretion: The ability of bureaucrats to make choices concerning the best way to implement congressional intentions.

Administrative Procedures Act: A statute containing Texas's rule-making process.

advisory referendum: A process in which voters cast nonbinding ballots on an issue or proposal.

affiliates: Local television stations that carry the programming of a national network.

affirmative action: Policies designed to give special attention or compensatory treatment to members of a previously disadvantaged group.

agenda: A set of issues to be discussed or given attention.

agenda setting: The constant process of forming the list of issues to be addressed by government.

agriculture commissioner: The elected state official in charge of regulating and promoting agriculture.

the Alamo: A San Antonio mission that was defended by Texans during their war for independence.

al-Qaeda: Worldwide terrorist organization led by Osama bin Laden, responsible for numerous attacks against U.S. interests, including 9/11 attacks against the World Trade Center and the Pentagon.

American Creed: A set of ideas that provide a national identity, limit government, and structure politics in America.

American dream: An American ideal of a happy, sucessful life, which often includes wealth, a house, a better life for one's children, and, for some, the ability to grow up to be president.

amicus curiae: "Friend of the court"; a third party to a lawsuit who files a legal brief for the purpose of raising additional points of view in an attempt to influence a court's decision.

Anglos: Non-Hispanic whites.

annexation: Enlargement of a city's corporate limits by incorporating surrounding territory into the city.

Anti-Federalists: Those who favored strong state governments and a weak national government; opposed the ratification of the U.S. Constitution.

appellate courts: Courts that generally review only findings of law made by lower courts.

appellate jurisdiction: The power vested in an appellate court to review and/or revise the decision of a lower court.

application for discretionary review: Request for Texas Court of Criminal Appeals review, which is granted if four judges agree.

apportionment: The process of allotting congressional seats to each state following the decennial census according to the state's proportion of the population.

Articles of Confederation: The compact among the thirteen original states that was the basis of their government. Written in 1776, the Articles were not ratified by all the states until 1781.

at-large-by-place: An election system in which all positions on the council or governing body are filled by city-wide elections, with each position designated as a seat, and candidates must choose which place to run for.

attorney general: The elected official who is the chief counsel for the state of Texas.

authoritarian system: A system of government that bases its rule on force rather than consent of the governed.

B

balanced budget: A budget in which the legislature balances expenditures with expected revenues, with no deficit.

ballot measure: An election option such as the initiative or referendum that enables voters to enact public policy.

bicameral legislature: A legislature divided into two houses; the U.S. Congress and the state legislatures are bicameral except Nebraska, which is unicameral.

bicameral Texas legislature: The legislature has two bodies, a House of Representatives and a Senate.

biennial legislature: A legislative body that meets in regular session only once in a two-year period.

bill: A proposed law.

bill of attainder: A law declaring an act illegal without a judicial trial.

Bill of Rights: The first ten amendments to the U.S. Constitution, which largely guarantee specific rights and liberties.

Black Codes: Laws denying most legal rights to newly freed slaves; passed by southern states following the Civil War.

block grant: Broad grant with few strings attached; given to states by the federal government for specified activities, such as secondary education or health services.

blog: A Web log; Web-based journal entries that provide an editorial and news outlet for citizens.

Bretton Woods Agreement: International financial agreement signed shortly before the end of World War II that created the World Bank and the International Monetary Fund.

brief: A document containing the legal written arguments in a case filed with a court by a party prior to a hearing or trial.

broadcast media: Television, radio, cable, and satellite services.

Brown v. Board of Education (1954): U.S. Supreme Court decision holding that school segregation is inherently unconstitutional because it violates the Fourteenth Amendment's guarantee of equal protection; marked the end of legal segregation in the United States.

budget execution authority: The authority to move money from one program to another program or from one agency to another agency.

bureaucracy: A set of complex hierarchical departments, agencies, commissions, and their staffs that exist to help a chief executive officer carry out his or her duties. Bureaucracies may be private organizations or governmental units.

Bush Doctrine: Policy advocated by President George W. Bush of using preemptive military action against a perceived threat to U.S. interests.

business cycles: Fluctuations between expansion and recession that are a part of modern capitalist economies.

C

Cabinet: The formal body of presidential advisers who head the fifteen executive departments. Presidents often add others to this body of formal advisers.

campaign consultant: The private-sector professionals and firms who sell to a candidate the technologies, services, and strategies required to get that candidate elected.

campaign manager: The individual who travels with the candidate and coordinates the many different aspects of the campaign.

candidate-centered politics: Politics that focuses directly on the candidates, their issues, and character rather than party affiliation.

candidate debate: Forum in which political candidates face each other to discuss their platforms, records, and character.

captured agency: A government regulatory agency that consistently makes decisions favorable to the private interests that it regulates.

Carter Doctrine: Policy announced after the 1979 Soviet invasion of Afghanistan that the Persian Gulf area was a vital U.S. interest and the United States would fight to maintain access to it.

categorical grant: Grant for which Congress appropriates funds for a specific purpose.

Central Intelligence Agency: Executive agency responsible for collection and analysis of information and intelligence about foreign countries and events.

charter school: Public school sanctioned by a specific agreement that allows the program to operate outside the usual rules and regulations.

checks and balances: A governmental structure that gives each of the three branches of government some degree of oversight and control over the actions of the others.

chief budget officer: The governor, who is charged with preparing the state budget proposal for the legislature.

chief executive officer: The governor, as the top official of the executive branch of Texas state government.

chief of state: The governor in his or her role as the official head representing the state of Texas in its relationships with the national government, other states, and foreign dignitaries.

citizen: Member of the political community to whom certain rights and obligations are attached.

city commission: A form of city government in which elected members serve on the legislative body and also serve as head administrators of city programs.

civic virtue: The tendency to form small-scale associations for the public good.

civil law: Codes of behavior related to business and contractual relationships between groups and individuals.

civil liberties: The personal guarantees and freedoms that the federal government cannot abridge by law, constitution, or judicial interpretation.

civil rights: The government-protected rights of individuals against arbitrary or discriminatory treatment by governments or individuals based on categories such as race, sex, national origin, age, religion, or sexual orientation.

Civil Rights Act of 1964: Legislation passed by Congress to outlaw segregation in public facilities and racial discrimination in employment, education, and voting; created the Equal Employment Opportunity Commission.

Civil Rights Cases (1883): Name attached to five cases brought under the Civil Rights Act of 1875. In 1883, the Supreme Court decided that discrimination in a variety of public accommodations, including theaters, hotels, and railroads, could not be prohibited by the act because it was private, not state, discrimination.

civil service laws: These acts removed the staffing of the bureaucracy from political parties and created a professional bureaucracy filled through competition.

civil service system: The system created by civil service laws by which many appointments to the federal bureaucracy are made.

civil society: Society created when citizens are allowed to organize and express their views publicly as they engage in an open debate about public policy.

clear and present danger test: Test articulated by the Supreme Court in *Schenck v. U.S.* (1919) to draw the line between protected and unprotected speech; the Court looks to see "whether the words used . . ." could "create a clear and present danger that they will bring about substantive evils" that Congress seeks "to prevent."

clemency: The governor's authority to reduce the length of a person's prison sentence.

closed primary: A primary election in which only a party's registered voters are eligible to vote.

cloture: Mechanism requiring sixty senators to vote to cut off debate.

coalition: A group made up of interests or organizations that join forces for the purpose of electing public officials.

cockroach: A member of a constitutional convention who opposes any changes in the current constitution.

collective good: Something of value that cannot be withheld from a nonmember of a group, for example, a tax write-off or a better environment.

collective security: The concept that peace would be secured if all countries collectively opposed any country that invaded another.

commander in chief: The governor in his or her role as head of the state militia.

commissioners court: The legislative body of a county in Texas.

committee: A subunit of the legislature, appointed to work on designated subjects.

Committees of Correspondence: Organizations in each of the American colonies created to keep colonists abreast of developments with the British; served as powerful molders of public opinion against the British.

communications director: The person who develops the overall media strategy for the candidate, blending the free press coverage with the paid TV, radio, and mail media.

comprehensive revision: Constitutional revision through the adoption of a new constitution.

comptroller of public accounts: The elected official who is the state's tax collector.

concurrent powers: Authority possessed by both the state and national governments that may be exercised concurrently as long as that power is not exclusively within the scope of national power or in conflict with national law.

concurrent resolution: A legislative document intended to express the will of both chambers of the legislature, even though it does not possess the authority of law.

confederation: Type of government where the national government derives its powers from the states; a league of independent states.

conference committee: Joint committee created to iron out differences between Senate and House versions of a specific piece of legislation.

congressional review: A process whereby Congress can nullify agency regulations by a joint resolution of legislative disapproval.

conservative: One thought to believe that a government is best that governs least and that big government can only infringe on individual, personal, and economic rights.

constitution: A document establishing the structure, functions, and limitations of a government.

constitutional amendment: A change, addition, or deletion to a constitution.

constitutional county court: Constitutionally mandated court for criminal and civil matters.

constitutional courts: Federal courts specifically created by the U.S. Constitution or by Congress pursuant to its authority in Article III.

Constitutional Revision Commission: Group established to research and draft a constitution for a constitutional convention.

constitutionalism: Limits placed on government through a written document.

containment: Strategy to oppose expansion of Soviet power, particularly in Western Europe and East Asia, with military power, economic assistance, and political influence.

content regulation: Governmental attempts to regulate the electronic media.

contrast ad: Ad that compares the records and proposals of the candidates, with a bias toward the sponsor.

conventional political participation: Political participation that attempts to influence the political process through well-accepted, often moderate forms of persuasion, such as writing letters to government officials, making political contributions, and voting.

cooperative federalism: The relationship between the national and state governments that began with the New Deal.

council–manager: A form of city government in which the city council and mayor hire a professional manager to run the city.

county attorney: Elected official serving as the legal officer for county government and also as a criminal prosecutor.

county auditor: Official appointed by a district judge to audit county finances.

county chairperson: Party leader in a county.

county clerk: Elected official who serves as the clerk for the commissioners court and for county records.

county commissioner: Elected official who serves on the county legislative body, the commissioners court.

county convention: County party meeting to select delegates and adopt resolutions.

county court at law: Statutory county court to relieve county judge of judicial duties.

county executive committee: Precinct chairpersons in a county that assist the county chairpersons.

county judge: Elected official who is the chief administrative officer of county government, serves on the commissioners court, and may also have some judicial functions.

county tax assessor-collector: Elected official who collects taxes for the county (and perhaps for other local governments).

county treasurer: Elected official who serves as the money manager for county government.

court of appeals: Intermediate appellate court for criminal and civil appeals.

criminal district attorney: Elected official who prosecutes criminal cases.

criminal law: Codes of behavior related to the protection of property and individual safety.

critical election: An election that signals a party realignment through voter polarization around new issues.

crossover voting: Participation in the primary of a party with which the voter is not affiliated.

Cuban Missile Crisis: The 1962 confrontation that nearly escalated into war between the United States and Soviet Union over Soviet deployment of medium-range ballistic missiles in Cuba.

cumulative voting: A method of voting in which voters have a number of votes equal to the number of seats being filled, and voters may cast their votes all for one candidate or split them among candidates in various combinations.

D

de facto **discrimination:** Racial discrimination that results from practice (such as housing patterns or other social factors) rather than the law.

de jure **discrimination:** Racial segregation that is a direct result of law or official policy.

dealignment: A general decline in partisan identification and loyalty in the electorate.

debt: The total outstanding amount the government owes as a result of borrowing in the past.

Declaration of Independence: Document drafted by Thomas Jefferson in 1776 that proclaimed the right of the American colonies to separate from Great Britain.

deep background: Information provided to a journalist that will not be attributed to any source.

deficit spending: Government spending in the current budget cycle that exceeds government revenue.

delegate: Role played by elected representatives who vote the way their constituents would want them to, regardless of their own opinions.

democracy: A system of government that gives power to the people, whether directly or through elected representatives.

Department of Defense: Chief executive-branch department responsible for formulation and implementation of U.S. military policy.

Department of Homeland Security: Cabinet department created after the 9/11 attacks to coordinate domestic U.S. security efforts against terrorism.

Department of State: Chief executive-branch department responsible for formulation and implementation of U.S. foreign policy.

departments: Major administrative units with responsibility for a broad area of government operations. Departmental status usually indicates a permanent national interest in a particular governmental function, such as defense, commerce, or agriculture.

deregulation: A reduction in market controls (such as price fixing, subsidies, or controls on who can enter a field) in favor of market-based competition.

détente: The relaxation of tensions between the United States and the Soviet Union that occurred during the 1970s.

direct democracy: A system of government in which members of the polity meet to discuss all policy decisions and then agree to abide by majority rule.

direct incitement test: A test articulated by the Supreme Court in *Brandenberg v. Ohio* (1969) that holds that advocacy of illegal action is protected by the First Amendment unless imminent lawless action is intended and likely to occur.

direct mailer: A professional who supervises a political campaign's direct-mail fund-raising strategies.

direct primary: The selection of party candidates through the ballots of qualified voters rather than at party nomination conventions.

discharge petition: Petition that gives a majority of the House of Representatives the authority to bring an issue to the floor in the face of committee inaction.

discount rate: The rate of interest at which member banks can borrow money from their regional Federal Reserve Bank.

district attorney (DA): Elected official who prosecutes criminal cases.

district clerk: Elected official who is responsible for keeping the records for the district court.

district court: Court of general jurisdiction for serious crimes and high-dollar civil cases.

disturbance theory: Political scientist David B. Truman's theory that interest groups form in part to counteract the efforts of other groups.

divided government: The political condition in which different political parties control the White House and Congress.

domestic dependent nation: A type of sovereignty that makes an Indian tribe in the United States outside the authority of state governments but reliant on the federal government for the definition of tribal authority.

double jeopardy clause: Part of the Fifth Amendment that protects individuals from being tried twice for the same offense.

dual federalism: The belief that having separate and equally powerful levels of government is the best arrangement.

due process clause: Clause contained in the Fifth and Fourteenth Amendments. Over the years, it has been construed to guarantee to individuals a variety of rights ranging from economic liberty to criminal procedural rights to protection from arbitrary governmental action.

due process rights: Procedural guarantees provided by the Fourth, Fifth, Sixth, and Eighth Amendments for those accused of crimes.

E

earmark: Funds that an appropriations bill designates for a particular purpose within a state or congressional district.

economic interest group: A group with the primary purpose of promoting the financial interests of its members.

economic regulation: Government regulation of business practices, industry rates, routes, or areas serviced by particular industries.

economic stability: A situation in which there is economic growth, rising national income, high employment, and steadiness in the general level of prices.

Eighth Amendment: Part of the Bill of Rights that states: "Excessive bail shall not be required, nor excessive fines imposed, nor cruel and unusual punishments inflicted."

elector: Member of the Electoral College chosen by methods determined in each state.

Electoral College: Representatives of each state who cast the final ballots that actually elect a president.

electorate: Citizens eligible to vote.

Embargo Act: Passed by Congress in 1807 to prevent U.S. ships from leaving U.S. ports for foreign ports without the approval of the federal government.

engagement: Policy implemented during the Clinton administration that the United States would remain actively involved in foreign affairs.

engrossed bill: A bill that has been given final approval on third reading in one chamber of the legislature.

enlargement: Policy implemented during the Clinton administration that the United States would actively promote the expansion of democracy and free markets throughout the world.

enrolled bill: A bill that has been given final approval in both chambers of the legislature and is sent to the governor.

entitlement program: Income security program to which all those meeting eligibility criteria are entitled.

enumerated powers: Seventeen specific powers granted to Congress under Article I, section 8, of the U.S. Constitution; these powers include taxation, coinage of money, regulation of commerce, and the authority to provide for a national defense.

Equal Employment Opportunity Commission: Federal agency created to enforce the Civil Rights Act of 1964, which forbids discrimination on the basis of race, creed, national origin, religion, or sex in hiring, promotion, or firing.

equal protection clause: Section of the Fourteenth Amendment that guarantees that all citizens receive "equal protection of the laws."

Equal Rights Amendment: Proposed amendment that would bar discrimination against women by federal or state governments.

equal time rule: The rule that requires broadcast stations to sell air time equally to all candidates in a political campaign if they choose to sell it to any.

equality: The belief that all individuals should be treated similarly, regardless of socio-economic status.

establishment clause: The first clause in the First Amendment; it prohibits the national government from establishing a national religion.

***ex post facto* law:** Law passed after the fact, thereby making previously legal activity illegal and subject to current penalty; prohibited by the U.S. Constitution.

exclusionary rule: Judicially created rule that prohibits police from using illegally seized evidence at trial.

executive agreement: Formal government agreement entered into by the president that does not require the advice and consent of the U.S. Senate.

executive commissioner of health and human services commission: The official appointed by the governor to oversee the state's multi-agency health and human service programs.

Executive Office of the President (EOP): Establishment created in 1939 to help the president oversee the executive branch bureaucracy.

executive order: Rule or regulation issued by the president that has the effect of law. All executive orders must be published in the *Federal Register*.

executive privilege: An implied presidential power that allows the president to refuse to disclose information regarding confidential conversations or national security to Congress or the judiciary.

exit polls: Polls conducted at selected polling places on Election Day.

extradition clause: Part of Article IV that requires states to extradite, or return, criminals to states where they have been convicted or are to stand trial.

extraterritorial jurisdiction (ETJ): The area outside a city's boundaries over which the city may exercise limited control.

F

fairness doctrine: Rule in effect from 1949 to 1985 requiring broadcasters to cover events adequately and to present contrasting views on important public issues.

federal budget deficit: The amount by which federal expenditure exceeds federal revenue.

Federal Employees Political Activities Act: 1993 liberalization of the Hatch Act. Federal employees are now allowed to run for office in nonpartisan elections and to contribute money to campaigns in partisan elections.

Federal Reserve Board: A seven-member board that sets member banks' reserve requirements, controls the discount rate, and makes other economic decisions.

federal system: System of government where the national government and state governments share some powers, derive all authority from the people, and the powers of the national government are specified in a constitution.

The Federalist Papers: A series of eighty-five political papers written by John Jay, Alexander Hamilton, and James Madison in support of ratification of the U.S. Constitution.

Federalists: Those who favored a stronger national government and supported the proposed U.S. Constitution; later became the first U.S. political party.

Fifteenth Amendment: One of the three Civil War amendments; specifically enfranchised newly freed male slaves.

Fifth Amendment: Part of the Bill of Rights that imposes a number of restrictions on the federal government with respect to the rights of persons suspected of committing a crime. It provides for indictment by a grand jury, protection against self-incrimination, and prevents the national government from denying a person life, liberty, or property without the due process of law. It also prevents the national government from taking property without fair compensation.

fighting words: Words that, "by their very utterance inflict injury or tend to incite an immediate breach of peace." Fighting words are not subject to the restrictions of the First Amendment.

filibuster: A formal way of halting action on a bill by means of long speeches or unlimited debate in the Senate.

finance chair: A professional who coordinates the fund-raising efforts for the campaign.

First Amendment: Part of the Bill of Rights that imposes a number of restrictions on the federal government with respect to the civil liberties of the people, including freedom of religion, speech, press, assembly, and petition.

First Continental Congress: Meeting held in Philadelphia from September 5 to October 26, 1774, in which fifty-six delegates (from every colony except Georgia) adopted a resolution in opposition to the Coercive Acts.

first reading: The Texas Constitution requires three readings of a bill by the legislature; first reading is when the bill is introduced, its caption is read aloud, and it is referred to committee.

fiscal policy: Federal government policies on taxes, spending, and debt management, intended to promote the nation's macro-economic goals, particularly with respect to employment, price stability, and growth.

527 political committees: Nonprofit and unregulated interest groups that focus on specific causes or policy positions and attempt to influence voters.

Fourteenth Amendment: One of the three Civil War amendments; guarantees equal protection and due process of the laws to all U.S. citizens.

Fourth Amendment: Part of the Bill of Rights that reads: "The right of the people to be secure in their persons, houses, papers, and effects, against unreasonable searches and seizures, shall not be violated, and no Warrants shall issue, but upon probable cause, supported by Oath or affirmation, and particularly describing the place to be searched, and the persons or things to the seized."

framing: The process by which a news organization defines a political issue and consequently affects opinion about the issues.

free exercise clause: The second clause of the First Amendment. It prohibits the U.S. government from interfering with a citizen's right to practice his or her religion.

free media: Coverage of a candidate's campaign by the news media.

free rider problem: Potential members fail to join a group because they can get the benefit, or collective good, sought by the group without contributing to the effort.

frontier era: The period when Texas constituted a border between American civilization and an area inhabited by a hostile, indigenous population.

front-loading: The tendency of states to choose an early date on the primary calendar.

full faith and credit clause: Section of Article IV of the Constitution that ensures judicial decrees and contracts made in one state will be binding and enforceable in any other state.

full-time equivalent (FTE): A unit of measurement for number of employees.

fundamental freedoms: Those rights defined by the Court to be essential to order, liberty, and justice.

G

General Agreement on Tariffs and Trade: Devised shortly after World War II as an interim agreement until a World Trade Organization could be created to help lower tariffs and increase trade.

general election: Election in which voters decide which candidates will actually fill elective public offices.

general election campaign: That part of a political campaign aimed at winning a general election.

general-law cities: Cities with fewer than 5,000 residents, governed by a general state law rather than by a locally adopted charter.

general ordinance-making authority: The legal right to adopt ordinances covering a wide array of subject areas, authority that cities have but counties do not.

germane: Related to the topic.

gerrymandering: The legislative process through which the majority party in each statehouse tries to assure that the maximum number of representatives from its political party can be elected to Congress through the redrawing of legislative districts.

get out the vote (GOTV): A push at the end of a political campaign to encourage supporters to go to the polls.

Gibbons v. Ogden **(1824):** The Court upheld broad congressional power over interstate commerce. The Court's broad interpretation of the Constitution's commerce clause paved the way for later rulings upholding expansive federal powers.

global warming: The increase in global temperatures that results from carbon emissions from burning fossil fuels such as oil and coal.

good government: A term used for policies that open up agencies to public participation and scrutiny and that minimize conflicts of interest.

government: The formal vehicles through which policies are made and affairs of state are conducted.

government corporation: Business established by Congress to perform functions that can be provided by private businesses (such as the U.S. Postal Service).

governmental (institutional) agenda: The changing list of issues to which governments believe they should address themselves.

governmental party: The office holders and candidates who run under a political party's banner.

governor: Chief elected executive in state government.

governor's message: Message that the governor delivers to the legislature, pronouncing policy goals, budget priorities, and authorizations for the legislature to act.

grandfather clause: Voting qualification provision in many Southern states that allowed only those whose grandfathers had voted before Reconstruction to vote unless they passed a wealth or literacy test.

Great Compromise: A decision made during the Constitutional Convention to give each state the same number of representatives in the Senate regardless of size; representation in the House was determined by population.

gross domestic product (GDP): The total market value of all goods and services produced in a country during a year.

H

hard money: Legally specified and limited contributions that are clearly regulated by the Federal Election Campaign Act and by the Federal Election Commission.

Hatch Act: Law enacted in 1939 to prohibit civil servants from taking activist roles in partisan campaigns. This act prohibited federal employees from making political contributions, working for a particular party, or campaigning for a particular candidate.

hold: A tactic by which a senator asks to be informed before a particular bill is brought to the floor. This stops the bill from coming to the floor until the hold is removed.

home rule: The right and authority of a local government to govern itself, rather than have the state govern it.

human rights: The belief that human beings have inalienable rights such as freedom of speech and freedom of religion.

I

ideology: A set or system of beliefs that shapes the thinking of individual and how they view the world.

impeach: A vote by the House to formally accuse a government official of official wrongdoing.

impeachment: The power delegated to the House of Representatives in the Constitution to charge the president, vice president, or other "civil officers," including federal judges, with "Treason, Bribery, or other High Crimes and Misdemeanors." This is the first step in the constitutional process of removing such government officials from office.

implementation: The process by which a law or policy is put into operation by the bureaucracy.

implied powers: Powers derived from the enumerated powers and the necessary and proper clause. These powers are not stated specifically but are considered to be reasonably implied through the exercise of delegated powers.

impressment: The British practice in the early eighteenth century of stopping ships at sea to seize sailors suspected of having deserted the Royal Navy.

incorporation doctrine: An interpretation of the Constitution that holds that the due process clause of the Fourteenth Amendment requires that state and local governments also guarantee those rights.

incumbency: The holding of an office.

independent executive agency: Governmental unit that closely resembles a Cabinet department but has a narrower area of responsibility (such as the Central Intelligence Agency) and is not part of any Cabinet department.

independent regulatory commission: An agency created by Congress that is generally concerned with a specific aspect of the economy.

indirect (representative) democracy: A system of government that gives citizens the opportunity to vote for representatives who will work on their behalf.

individualism: The belief that each person should act in accordance with his or her own conscience.

inflation: A rise in the general price levels of an economy.

inherent powers: Powers that belong to the national government simply because it is a sovereign state.

initiative: A process that allows citizens to propose legislation and submit it to the state electorate for popular vote.

inoculation ad: Advertising that attempts to counteract an anticipated attack from the opposition before the attack is launched.

insurance commissioner: The official appointed by the governor to direct the Department of Insurance and regulate the insurance industry.

intent calendar: The Senate calendar listing bills on which the author or sponsor has given notice of intent to move to suspend the regular order of business in order that the Senate may consider them.

interagency councils: Working groups created to facilitate coordination of policy making and implementation across a host of governmental agencies.

interest group: An organized group that tries to influence public policy.

international governmental organization (IGO): An organization created by the governments of at least two and often many countries that operates internationally with the objectives of achieving the purposes that the member countries agree on.

International Monetary Fund: International governmental organization created shortly before the end of World War II to stabilize international financial relations through fixed monetary exchange rates.

Internet team: Campaign staff that uses Web-based resources to communicate with voters, raise funds, organize volunteers, and plan events.

interstate compacts: Contracts between states that carry the force of law; generally now used as a tool to address multistate policy concerns.

interventionist state: Alternative to the laissez-faire state; the government takes an active role in guiding and managing the private economy.

iron triangles: The relatively stable relationships and patterns of interaction that occur among an agency, interest groups, and congressional committees or subcommittees.

isolationism: A national policy of avoiding participation in foreign affairs.

issue networks: The loose and informal relationships that exist among a large number of actors who work in broad policy areas.

issue-oriented politics: Politics that focuses on specific issues rather than on party, candidate, or other loyalties.

J

Jim Crow laws: Laws enacted by southern states that discriminated against blacks by creating "whites only" schools, theaters, hotels, and other public accommodations.

Joint Chiefs of Staff: Advisory body to the president that includes chief of staff of the army, chief of staff of the air force, chief of naval operations, and marine commandant.

joint committee: Includes members from both houses of Congress, conducts investigations or special studies.

joint resolution: A legislative document that either proposes an amendment to the Texas Constitution or ratifies an amendment to the U.S. Constitution.

judicial activism: A philosophy of judicial decision making that argues judges should use their power broadly to further justice, especially in the areas of equality and personal liberty.

judicial implementation: Refers to how and whether judicial decisions are translated into actual public policies affecting more than the immediate parties to a lawsuit.

judicial restraint: A philosophy of judicial decision making that argues courts should allow the decisions of other branches of government to stand, even when they offend a judge's own sense of principles.

judicial review: Power of the courts to review acts of other branches of government and the states.

Judiciary Act of 1789: Established the basic three-tiered structure of the federal court system.

jurisdiction: Authority vested in a particular court to hear and decide the issues in any particular case.

justice of the peace court: Local county court for minor crimes and civil suits.

L

laissez-faire: A French term literally meaning "to allow to do, to leave alone." It is a hands-off governmental policy that is based on the belief that government involvement in the economy is wrong.

land commissioner: The elected official responsible for managing and leasing the state's property, including oil, gas, and mineral interests.

League of Nations: Created in the peace treaty that ended World War I, it was an international governmental organization dedicated to preserving peace.

Legislative Budget Board (LBB): A joint legislative committee (with a large staff) that prepares the state budget and conducts evaluations of agencies' programs.

Legislative Council: A joint legislative committee (with a large staff) that provides legal advice, bill drafting, copyediting and printing, policy research, and program evaluation services for members of the legislature.

legislative courts: Courts established by Congress for specialized purposes, such as the Court of Military Appeals.

legislative party caucus: An organization of legislators who are all of the same party, and which is formally allied with a political party.

legislative process: The process the legislature follows in considering and enacting legislation.

libel: False written statements or written statements tending to call someone's reputation into disrepute.

liberal: One considered to favor extensive governmental involvement in the economy and the provision of social services and to take an activist role in protecting the rights of women, the elderly, minorities, and the environment.

liberal constitution: Constitution that incorporates the basic structure of government and allows the legislature to provide the details through statutes.

libertarian: One who favors a free market economy and no governmental interference in personal liberties.

liberty: The belief that government should not infringe upon a person's individual rights.

line-item veto: The authority of a chief executive to delete part of a bill passed by the legislature that involves taxing or spending. The legislature may override a veto, usually with a two-thirds majority of each chamber.

lobbying: The activities of a group or organization that seeks to influence legislation and persuade political leaders to support the group's position.

lobbyist: Interest group representative who seeks to influence legislation that will benefit his or her organization through political persuasion.

local election: Election conducted by local governments to elect officials.

Local Government Code: The Texas statutory code containing state laws about local governments.

logrolling: Vote trading; voting yea to support a colleague's bill in return for a promise of future support.

M

machine: A party organization that recruits its members with tangible incentives and is characterized by a high degree of control over member activity.

majority leader: The elected leader of the party controlling the most seats in the House of Representatives or the Senate; is second in authority to the Speaker of the House and in the Senate is regarded as its most powerful member.

majority party: The political party in each house of Congress with the most members.

majority rule: The central premise of direct democracy in which only policies that collectively garner the support of a majority of voters will be made into law.

manager: A professional executive hired by a city council or county board to manage daily operations and to recommend policy changes.

mandate: A command, indicated by an electorate's votes, for the elected officials to carry out their platforms.

manifest destiny: Theory that the United States was divinely mandated to expand across North America to the Pacific Ocean.

***Marbury* v. *Madison* (1803):** Supreme Court first asserted the power of judicial review in finding that the congressional statute extending the Court's original jurisdiction was unconstitutional.

margin of error: A measure of the accuracy of a public opinion poll.

markup: A process in which legislative committee members offer changes to a bill before it goes to the floor in either house for a vote.

Marshall Plan: European Recovery Program, named after Secretary of State George C. Marshall, of extensive U.S. aid to Western Europe after World War II.

mass media: The entire array of organizations through which information is collected and disseminated to the general public.

matching funds: Donations to presidential campaigns from the federal government that are determined by the amount of private funds a qualifying candidate raises.

***McCulloch* v. *Maryland* (1819):** The Supreme Court upheld the power of the national government and denied the right of a state to tax the bank. The Court's broad interpretation of the necessary and proper clause paved the way for later rulings upholding expansive federal powers.

means-tested program: Income security program intended to assist those whose incomes fall below a designated level.

media consultant: A professional who produces political candidates' television, radio, and print advertisements.

media effects: The influence of news sources on public opinion.

Medicaid: An expansion of Medicare, this program subsidizes medical care for the poor.

Medicare: The federal program established in the Lyndon B. Johnson administration that provides medical care to elderly Social Security recipients.

mercantilism: An economic theory designed to increase a nation's wealth through the development of commercial industry and a favorable balance of trade.

merit system: The system by which federal civil service jobs are classified into grades or levels, to which appointments are made on the basis of performance on competitive examinations.

midterm election: Election that takes place in the middle of a presidential term.

military-industrial complex: The grouping of the U.S. armed forces and defense industries.

minority leader: The elected leader of the party with the second highest number of elected representatives in the House of Representatives or the Senate.

minority party: The political party in each house of Congress with the second most members.

***Miranda* rights:** Statements that must be made by the police informing a suspect of his or her constitutional rights protected by the Fifth Amendment, including the right to an attorney provided by the court if the suspect cannot afford one.

***Miranda* v. *Arizona* (1966):** A landmark Supreme Court ruling that held the Fifth Amendment requires that individuals arrested for a crime must be advised of their right to remain silent and to have counsel present.

monarchy: A form of government in which power is vested in hereditary kings and queens who govern in the interests of all.

monetary policy: A form of government regulation in which the nation's money supply and interest rates are controlled.

money: A system of exchange for goods and services that includes currency, coins, and bank deposits.

Monroe Doctrine: President James Monroe's 1823 pledge that the United States would oppose attempts by European states to extend their political control into the Western Hemisphere.

moralism: The policy of emphasizing morality in foreign affairs.

muckraking: A form of journalism, in vogue in the early twentieth century, concerned with reforming government and business conduct.

multilateralism: The U.S. foreign policy that actions should be taken in cooperation with other states after consultation.

municipal corporation: A city.

municipal court: City court with limited criminal jurisdiction.

N

narrowcasting: Targeting media programming at specific populations within society.

national convention: A party conclave (meeting) held in the presidential election year for the purposes of nominating a presidential and vice presidential ticket and adopting a platform.

national party platform: A statement of the general and specific philosophy and policy goals of a political party, usually promulgated at the national convention.

National Security Agency (NSA): Intelligence agency responsible for gathering intelligence from electronic and other sources and for code breaking.

National Security Council (NSC): Executive agency responsible for advising the president about foreign and defense policy and events.

natural law: A doctrine that society should be governed by certain ethical principles that are part of nature and, as such, can be understood by reason.

necessary and proper clause: The final paragraph of Article I, section 8, of the U.S. Constitution, which gives Congress the authority to pass all laws "necessary and proper" to carry out the enumerated powers specified in the Constitution; also called the elastic clause.

negative ad: Advertising on behalf of a candidate that attacks the opponent's platform or character.

network: An association of broadcast stations (radio or television) that share programming through a financial arrangement.

New Deal: The name given to the program of "Relief, Recovery, Reform" begun by President Franklin D. Roosevelt in 1933 to bring the United States out of the Great Depression.

New Federalism: Federal/state relationship proposed by Reagan administration during the 1980s; hallmark is returning administrative powers to the state governments.

New Jersey Plan: A framework for the Constitution proposed by a group of small states; its key points were a one-house legislature with one vote for each state, the establishment of the acts of Congress as the "supreme law" of the land, and a supreme judiciary with limited power.

new media: Technologies such as the Internet that blur the line between media sources and create new opportunities for the dissemination of news and other information.

***New York Times Co.* v. *Sullivan* (1964):** The Supreme Court concluded that "actual malice" must be proved to support a finding of libel against a public figure.

news media: Media providing the public with new information about subjects of public interest.

9/11 Commission: The National Commission on Terrorist Attacks upon the United States; a bipartisan, independent group authorized by Congress and President Bush in 2002 to study the circumstances surrounding the September 11, 2001, terrorist attacks, including preparedness and response. Its 2004 report includes recommendations for guarding against future attacks.

Nineteenth Amendment: Amendment to the Constitution that guaranteed women the right to vote.

Ninth Amendment: Part of the Bill of Rights that reads "The enumeration in the Constitution, of certain rights, shall not be construed to deny or disparage others retained by the people."

Nixon Doctrine: The policy implemented at the end of the Vietnam War that the United States would provide arms and military equipment to countries but not do the fighting for them.

nomination campaign: That part of a political campaign aimed at winning a primary election.

nongovernmental organization (NGO): An organization that is not tied to a government.

non-means-based program: Program such as Social Security where benefits are provided irrespective of the income or means of recipients.

nonparty legislative caucus: An organization of legislators that is based on some attribute other than party affiliation.

North American Free Trade Agreement (NAFTA): Agreement that promotes free movement of goods and services among Canada, Mexico, and the United States.

North Atlantic Treaty Organization (NATO): The first peacetime military treaty the United States joined, NATO is a regional political and military organization created in 1950.

O

off the record: Information provided to a journalist that will not be released to the public.

Office of Management and Budget (OMB): The office that prepares the president's annual budget proposal, reviews the budget and programs of the executive departments, supplies economic forecasts, and conducts detailed analyses of proposed bills and agency rules.

oligarchy: A form of government in which the right to participate is conditioned on the possession of wealth, social status, military position, or achievement.

on background: Information provided to a journalist that will not be attributed to a named source.

on the record: Information provided to a journalist that can be released and attributed by name to the source.

open market operations: The buying and selling of government securities by the Federal Reserve Bank in the securities market.

open primary: A primary in which party members, independents, and sometimes members of the other party are allowed to vote.

organizational party: The workers and activists who staff the party's formal organization.

original jurisdiction: The jurisdiction of courts that hear a case first, usually in a trial. Courts determine the facts of a case under their original jurisdiction.

overrepresentation and underrepresentation: Higher and lower numbers, respectively, than would be expected from a group in comparison with that group's numbers in the general population.

oversight: Congressional review of the activities of an agency, department, or office.

P

paid media: Political advertisements purchased for a candidate's campaign.

pardon: The authority of a government to cancel someone's conviction of a crime by a court and to eliminate all sanctions and punishments resulting from conviction.

party caucus or conference: A formal gathering of all party members.

party identification: A citizen's personal affinity for a political party, usually expressed by his or her tendency to vote for the candidates of that party.

party in the electorate: The voters who consider themselves allied or associated with the party.

party realignment: A shifting of party coalition groupings in the electorate that remains in place for several elections.

patron: Person who finances a group or individual activity.

patronage: Jobs, grants, or other special favors that are given as rewards to friends and political allies for their support.

Pearl Harbor: Naval base in Hawaii attacked by Japan on December 7, 1941, initiating U.S. entry into World War II.

Pendleton Act: Reform measure that created the Civil Service Commission to administer a partial merit system. The act classified the federal service by grades, to which appointments were made based on the results of a competitive examination. It made it illegal for federal political appointees to be required to contribute to a particular political party.

per diem: Legislators' per day allowance covering room and board expenses while on state business.

permanent party organization: Party organization that operates throughout the year, performing the party's functions.

personal liberty: A key characteristic of U.S. democracy. Initially meaning freedom from governmental interference, today it includes demands for freedom to engage in a variety of practices free from governmental discrimination.

petition for review: Request for Texas Supreme Court review, which is granted if four justices agree.

piecemeal revision: Constitutional revision through constitutional amendments that add or delete items.

Plessy v. Ferguson **(1896):** Plessy challenged a Louisiana statute requiring that railroads provide separate accommodations for blacks and whites. The Court found that separate but equal accommodations did not violate the equal protection clause of the Fourteenth Amendment.

plural executive: An executive branch in which power and policy implementation are divided among several executive agencies rather than centralized under one person; the governor does not get to appoint most agency heads.

pocket veto: If Congress adjourns during the ten days the president has to consider a bill passed by both houses of Congress, without the president's signature, the bill is considered vetoed.

policy adoption: The approval of a policy proposal by the people with the requisite authority, such as a legislature.

policy evaluation: The process of determining whether a course of action is achieving its intended goals.

policy formulation: The crafting of appropriate and acceptable proposed courses of action to ameliorate or resolve public problems.

policy implementation: The process of carrying out public policy through governmental agencies and the courts.

political action committee (PAC): Federally mandated, officially registered fund-raising committee that represents interest groups in the political process.

political culture: Commonly shared attitudes, beliefs, and core values about how government should operate.

political equality: The principle that all citizens should participate equally in government; implied by the phrase "one person, one vote."

political ideology: The coherent set of values and beliefs about the purpose and scope of government held by groups and individuals.

political party: A group of office holders, candidates, activists, and voters who identify with a group label and seek to elect to public office individuals who run under that label.

political socialization: The process through which individuals acquire their political beliefs and values.

politico: Role played by elected representatives who act as trustees or as delegates, depending on the issue.

politics: The study of who gets what, when, and how—or how policy decisions are made.

poll tax: Tax levied in many southern states and localities that had to be paid before an eligible voter could cast a ballot.

pollster: A professional who takes public opinion surveys that guide political campaigns.

popular consent: The idea that governments must draw their powers from the consent of the governed.

popular sovereignty: The notion that the ultimate authority in society rests with the people.

populists: People who support the promotion of equality and of traditional values and behaviors.

pork: Legislation that allows representatives to bring home the bacon to their districts in the form of public works programs, military bases, or other programs designed to benefit their districts directly.

positive ad: Advertising on behalf of a candidate that stresses the candidate's qualifications, family, and issue positions, without reference to the opponent.

Powell Doctrine: An all-or-nothing approach to military intervention advocated by Colin Powell: use overwhelming force for quick, decisive victory, and have an exit strategy before any intervention.

pragmatism: The policy of taking advantage of a situation for national gain.

precedent: Prior judicial decision that serves as a rule for settling subsequent cases of a similar nature.

precinct chairperson: Party leader in a voting precinct.

precinct convention: Precinct party meeting to select delegates and adopt resolutions.

preemption: A concept derived from the Constitution's supremacy clause that allows the national government to override or preempt state or local actions in certain areas.

president of the Texas Senate: The lieutenant governor of Texas, serving in his constitutional role as presiding officer of the Senate.

president pro tempore: The official chair of the Senate; usually the most senior member of the majority party.

press briefing: A relatively restricted session between a press secretary or aide and the press.

press conference: An unrestricted session between an elected official and the press.

press release: A document offering an official comment or position.

press secretary: The individual charged with interacting and communicating with journalists on a daily basis.

primary election: Election in which voters decide which of the candidates within a party will represent the party in the general election.

print media: The traditional form of mass media, comprising newspapers, magazines, newsletters, and journals.

prior restraint: Constitutional doctrine that prevents the government from prohibiting speech or publication before the fact; generally held to be in violation of the First Amendment.

privileges and immunities clause: Part of Article IV of the Constitution guaranteeing that the citizens of each state are afforded the same rights as citizens of all other states.

proportional representation: A voting system that apportions legislative seats according to the percentage of the vote won by a particular political party.

prospective judgment: A voter's evaluation of a candidate based on what he or she pledges to do about an issue if elected.

pro-tempore (pro-tem): A legislator who serves temporarily as legislative leader in the absence of the Senate president or House Speaker.

public counsels: Officials appointed by the governor to represent the public before regulatory agencies.

public funds: Donations from the general tax revenues to the campaigns of qualifying presidential candidates.

public interest group: An organization that seeks a collective good that will not selectively and materially benefit the members of the group.

public opinion: What the public thinks about a particular issue or set of issues at any point in time.

public opinion polls: Interviews or surveys with samples of citizens that are used to estimate the feelings and beliefs of the entire population.

public policy: An intentional course of action followed by government in dealing with some problem or matter of concern.

Public Utility Commission: A full-time, three-member paid commission appointed by the governor to regulate public utilities in Texas.

push polls: "Polls" taken for the purpose of providing information on an opponent that would lead respondents to vote against that candidate.

Q

quasi-judicial: Partly judicial; authorized to conduct hearings and issue rulings.

quorum: The minimum number required to conduct business (as in a legislative body).

R

raiding: An organized attempt by voters of one party to influence the primary results of the other party.

Railroad Commission: A full-time, three-member paid commission elected by the people to regulate oil and gas and some transportation entities.

random sampling: A method of poll selection that gives each person in a group the same chance of being selected.

Reagan Doctrine: Policy that the United States would provide military assistance to anti-communist groups fighting against pro-Soviet governments.

reapportionment: The reallocation of the number of seats in the House of Representatives after each decennial census.

recall: A process in which voters can petition for a vote to remove office holders between elections.

recession: A short-term decline in the economy that occurs as investment sags, production falls off, and unemployment increases.

redistrict: Redraw election-district boundaries.

redistricting: The redrawing of congressional districts to reflect population changes or for political advantage.

referendum: An election whereby the state legislature submits proposed legislation to the state's voters for approval.

regional primary: A proposed system in which the country would be divided into five or six geographic areas and all states in each region would hold their presidential primary elections on the same day.

regular session: The biennial 140-day session of the Texas legislature, beginning in January of odd-numbered years.

regulations: Rules that govern the operation of a particular government program that have the force of law.

republic: A government rooted in the consent of the governed; a representative or indirect democracy.

reservation land: Land designated in a treaty that is under the authority of an Indian nation and is exempt from most state laws and taxes.

reserve (or police) powers: Powers reserved to the states by the Tenth Amendment that lie at the foundation of a state's right to legislate for the public health and welfare of its citizens.

reserve requirements: Government requirements that a portion of member banks' deposits must be retained to back loans made.

retrospective judgment: A voter's evaluation of the performance of the party in power.

revisionist: A member of a constitutional convention who will not accept less than a total revision of the current constitution.

revolving door: An exchange of personnel between private interests and public regulators.

right to privacy: The right to be let alone; a judicially created doctrine encompassing an individual's decision to use birth control or secure an abortion.

Roe v. Wade (1973): The Supreme Court found that a woman's right to an abortion was protected by the right to privacy that could be implied from specific guarantees found in the Bill of Rights applied to the states through the Fourteenth Amendment.

Roosevelt Corollary: Concept developed by President Theodore Roosevelt early in the twentieth century that it was the U.S. responsibility to assure stability in Latin America and the Caribbean.

rule making: A quasi-legislative administrative process that has the characteristics of a legislative act.

Rule of Four: At least four justices of the Supreme Court must vote to consider a case before it can be heard.

runoff primary: A second primary election between the two candidates receiving the greatest number of votes in the first primary.

S

sampling error or margin of error: A measure of the accuracy of a public opinion poll.

Second Continental Congress: Meeting that convened in Philadelphia on May 10, 1775, at which it was decided that an army should be raised and George Washington of Virginia was named commander in chief.

second reading: The Texas Constitution requires three readings of a bill by the legislature; the second reading is when debate and consideration of amendments occur before the whole chamber.

secular realignment: The gradual rearrangement of party coalitions, based more on demographic shifts than on shocks to the political system.

select (or special) committee: Temporary committee appointed for specific purpose, such as conducting a special investigation or study.

selective incorporation: A judicial doctrine whereby most but not all of the protections found in the Bill of Rights are made applicable to the states via the Fourteenth Amendment.

Senate two-thirds rule: The rule in the Texas Senate requiring that every bill win a vote of two-thirds of the senators present to suspend the Senate's regular order of business, so that the bill may be considered.

senatorial courtesy: Process by which presidents, when selecting district court judges, defer to senators of their own party who represent the state where the vacancy occurs; also the process by which a governor, when selecting an appointee, defers to the state senator in whose district the nominee resides.

seniority: Time of continuous service on a committee.

separation of powers: A way of dividing power among three branches of government in which members of the House of Representatives, members of the Senate, the president, and the federal courts are selected by and responsible to different constituencies.

Seventeenth Amendment: Made senators directly elected by the people; removed their selection from state legislatures.

Sharpstown scandal: The legislative scandal of 1969–1972, which resulted in a bribery conviction of the House Speaker and others and set the stage for the 1973 reform session.

Shays's Rebellion: A 1786 rebellion in which an army of 1,500 disgruntled and angry farmers led by Daniel Shays marched to Springfield, Massachusetts, and forcibly restrained the state court from foreclosing mortgages on their farms.

sheriff: Elected official who serves as the chief law enforcement officer in a county.

simple resolution: A legislative document proposing an action that affects only the one chamber in which it is being considered, such as a resolution to adopt House rules or to commend a citizen.

single-member district: An election system for legislative bodies in which each legislator runs from and represents a single district, rather than the entire geographic area encompassed by the government.

Sixteenth Amendment: Authorized Congress to enact a national income tax.

Sixth Amendment: Part of the Bill of Rights that sets out the basic requirements of procedural due process for federal courts to follow in criminal trials. These include speedy and public trials, impartial juries, trials in the state where crime was committed, notice of the charges, the right to confront and obtain favorable witnesses, and the right to counsel.

slander: Untrue spoken statements that defame the character of a person.

social capital: The myriad relationships that individuals enjoy that facilitate the resolution of community problems through collective action.

social conservative: One who believes that traditional moral teachings should be supported and furthered by the government.

social contract: An agreement between the people and their government signifying their consent to be governed.

social contract theory: The belief that people are free and equal by God-given right and that this in turn requires that all people give their consent to be governed; espoused by John Locke and influential in the writing of the Declaration of Independence.

social regulation: Government regulation of the quality and safety of products as well as the conditions under which goods and services are produced.

Social Security Act: A 1935 law that established old-age insurance (Social Security) and assistance for the needy, children, and others, and unemployment insurance.

social welfare policy: Government programs designed to improve quality of life.

soft money: The virtually unregulated money funneled by individuals and political committees through state and local parties.

solicitor general: The fourth-ranking member of the Department of Justice; responsible for handling all appeals on behalf of the U.S. government to the Supreme Court.

sovereign immunity: The right of a state to be free from lawsuit unless it gives permission to the suit. Under the Eleventh Amendment, all states are considered sovereign.

Spanish-American War: Brief 1898 war against Spain because of Spanish policies and presence in Cuba and U.S. desire to attain overseas territory.

Speaker of the House: The only officer of the House of Representatives specifically mentioned in the Constitution; elected at the beginning of each new Congress by the entire House; traditionally a member of the majority party.

Speaker of the Texas House: The state representative who is elected by his or her fellow representatives to be the official leader of the House.

Speaker's lieutenants: House members who make up the Speaker's team, assisting the Speaker in leading the House, either informally, or in a role as a committee chair or other institutional leader.

Speaker's race: The campaign to determine who shall be the Speaker of the Texas House for a given biennium.

Speaker's team: The leadership team in the House, consisting of the Speaker and his or her most trusted allies among the members, most of whom the Speaker appoints to chair House committees.

special election: Election held at a time other than general or primary elections.

special (called) session: A Texas legislative session of up to thirty days, called by the governor, during an interim between regular sessions.

spoils system: The firing of public-office holders of a defeated political party and their replacement with loyalists of the newly elected party.

spot ad: Television advertising on behalf of a candidate that is broadcast in sixty-, thirty-, or ten-second duration.

staggered terms: Terms of office for members of boards and commissions that begin and end at different times, so that a governor is not usually able to gain control of a majority of the body for a long time.

Stamp Act Congress: Meeting of representatives of nine of the thirteen colonies held in New York City in 1765, during which representatives drafted a document to send to the king listing how their rights had been violated.

standing committee: Committee to which proposed bills are referred.

stare decisis: In court rulings, a reliance on past decisions or precedents to formulate decisions in new cases.

State Board of Education: The fifteen-member elected body that sets some education policy for the state and has limited authority to oversee the Texas Education Agency and local school districts.

state convention: Party meeting held to adopt the party's platform, elect the party's executive committee and state chairperson, and in a presidential election year, elect delegates to the national convention and choose presidential electors.

state executive committee: Sixty-two-member party committee that makes decisions for the party between state conventions.

state party chairperson: Party leader for the state.

state senatorial district convention: Party meeting held when a county is a part of more than one senatorial district.

statutory constitution: Constitution that incorporates detailed provisions in order to limit the powers of government.

stratified sampling: A variation of random sampling; Census data are used to divide a country into four sampling regions. Sets of counties and standard metropolitan statistical areas are then randomly selected in proportion to the total national population.

straw polls: Unscientific surveys used to gauge public opinion on a variety of issues and policies.

strict constructionist: An approach to constitutional interpretation that emphasizes the Framers' original intentions.

strict scrutiny: A heightened standard of review used by the Supreme Court to determine the constitutional validity of a challenged practice.

strong mayor–council: A form of city government in which the mayor has strong powers to run the city by hiring, managing, and firing staff and controlling executive departments; the mayor also serves on the council.

substantive due process: Judicial interpretation of the Fifth and Fourteenth Amendments' due process clause that protects citizens from arbitrary or unjust laws.

succession: The constitutional declaration that the lieutenant governor succeeds to the governorship if there is a vacancy.

suffrage movement: The drive for voting rights for women that took place in the United States from 1890 to 1920.

sunset law: A law that sets a date for a program or regulation to expire unless reauthorized by the legislature.

superdelegate: Delegate slot to the Democratic Party's national convention that is reserved for an elected party official.

supremacy clause: Portion of Article VI of the U.S. Constitution mandating that national law is supreme to (that is, supercedes) all other laws passed by the states or by any other subdivision of government.

suspect classification: Category or class, such as race, that triggers the highest standard of scrutiny from the Supreme Court.

symbolic speech: Symbols, signs, and other methods of expression generally also considered to be protected by the First Amendment.

systemic agenda: All public issues that are viewed as requiring governmental attention; a discussion agenda.

T

Taliban: Fundamentalist Islamic government of Afghanistan that provided terrorist training bases for al-Qaeda.

tariffs: Taxes on imports used to raise government revenue and to protect infant industries.

Tejanos: Native Texans of Mexican descent.

temporary party organization: Party organization that exists for a limited time and includes several levels of conventions.

Tenth Amendment: Part of the Bill of Rights that reiterates powers not delegated to the national government are reserved to the states or to the people.

term limits: Restrictions that exist in some states about how long an individual may serve in state or local elected offices.

Texan Creed: A set of ideas—primarily individualism and liberty—that shape Texas politics and government.

Texas Association of Counties: Professional association and lobbying arm for county governments.

Texas Commission on Environmental Quality: As of 2002, the new name for the Texas Natural Resource Conservation Commission.

Texas Court of Criminal Appeals: Court of last resort in criminal cases.

Texas Education Agency: The state agency that oversees local school districts and disburses state funds to districts.

Texas Municipal League: Professional association and lobbying arm for city governments.

Texas Rangers: A mounted militia formed to provide order on the frontier.

Texas secretary of state: The state official appointed by the governor to be the keeper of the state's records, such as state laws, election data and filings, public notifications, and corporate charters.

Texas Supreme Court: Court of last resort in civil and juvenile cases.

think tank: Institutional collection of policy-oriented researchers and academics who are sources of policy ideas.

third reading: The Texas Constitution requires three readings of a bill by the legislature; third reading is the final reading in a chamber, unless the bill returns from the other chamber with amendments.

Thirteenth Amendment: One of the three Civil War amendments; specifically bans slavery in the United States.

Three-Fifths Compromise: Agreement reached at the Constitutional Convention stipulating that each slave was to be counted as three-fifths of a person for purposes of determining population for representation in the U.S. House of Representatives.

ticket-split: To vote for candidates of different parties for various offices in the same election.

Title IX: Provision of the Educational Amendments of 1972 that bars educational institutions receiving federal funds from discriminating against female students.

totalitarianism: A form of government in which power resides in a leader who rules according to self-interest and without regard for individual rights and liberties.

tracking polls: Continuous surveys that enable a campaign to chart its daily rise or fall in support.

trade association: A group that represents a specific industry.

trial courts: Courts of original jurisdiction where a case begins.

trial de novo: New trial, necessary for an appeal from a court that is not a court of record.

Truman Doctrine: U.S. policy initiated in 1947 of providing economic assistance and military aid to countries fighting against communist revolutions or political pressure.

trustee: Role played by elected representatives who listen to constituents' opinions and then use their best judgment to make final decisions.

turnout: The proportion of the voting-age public that votes.

Twenty-Fifth Amendment: Adopted in 1967 to establish procedures for filling vacancies in the office of president and vice president as well as providing for procedures to deal with the disability of a president.

Twenty-Second Amendment: Adopted in 1951, prevents a president from serving more than two terms or more than ten years if he came to office via the death or impeachment of his predecessor.

U

unconventional political participation: Political participation that attempts to influence the political process through unusual or extreme measures, such as protests, boycotts, and picketing.

unfunded mandates: National laws that direct states or local governments to comply with the federal rules or regulations (such as clean air or water standards) but contain no federal funding to defray the cost of meeting these requirements.

unilateralism: A national policy of acting without consulting others.

unitary system: System of government where the local and regional governments derive all authority from a strong national government.

unit rule: A traditional party practice under which the majority of a state delegation can force the minority to vote for its candidate.

United Nations (UN): An international governmental organization created shortly before the end of World War II to guarantee the security of nations and to promote global economic, physical, and social well-being.

U.S. v. Nixon (1974): Key Supreme Court ruling on power of the president, finding that there is no absolute constitutional executive privilege to allow a president to refuse to comply with a court order to produce information needed in a criminal trial.

V

veto: The formal, constitutional authority of the chief executive to reject bills passed by both houses of the legislative body, thus preventing their becoming law without further legislative action.

veto power: The formal, constitutional authority of the president to reject bills passed by both houses of Congress, thus preventing their becoming law without further congressional action.

Vietnam War: Between 1965 and 1973, the United States deployed up to 500,000 troops to Vietnam to try to prevent North Vietnam from taking over South Vietnam; the effort failed and was extremely divisive within the United States.

Virginia Plan: The first general plan for the Constitution, proposed by James Madison and Edmund Randolph. Its key points were a bicameral legislature, an executive chosen by the legislature, and a judiciary also named by the legislature.

voter canvass: The process by which a campaign gets in touch with individual voters, either by door-to-door solicitation or by telephone.

W

war on terrorism: Initiated by President George W. Bush after the 9/11 attacks to weed out terrorist operatives throughout the world, using diplomacy, military means, improved homeland security, stricter banking laws, and other means.

War Powers Act: Passed by Congress in 1973; the president is limited in the deployment of troops overseas to a sixty-day period in peacetime (which can be extended for an extra thirty days to permit withdrawal) unless Congress explicitly gives its approval for a longer period.

weak mayor–council: A form of city government in which the mayor has no more power than any other member of the council.

weapons of mass destruction: Biological, chemical, and nuclear weapons, which present a sizeable threat to U.S. security.

whip: One of several representatives who keep close contact with all members and take nose counts on key votes, prepare summaries of bills, and in general act as communications links within the party.

winner-take-all system: An electoral system in which the party that receives at least one more vote than any other party wins the election.

wire service: An electronic delivery of news gathered by the news service's correspondents and sent to all member news media organizations.

World Bank: International governmental organization created shortly before the end of World War II to provide loans for large economic development projects.

World Trade Organization: International governmental organization created in 1995 that manages multilateral negotiations to reduce barriers to trade and settle trade disputes.

writ of certiorari: A request for the Court to order up the records from a lower court to review the case.

writ of habeas corpus: A court order in which a judge requires authorities to prove that a prisoner is being held lawfully and that allows the prisoner to be freed if the judge is not persuaded by the government's case. *Habeas corpus* rights imply that prisoners have a right to know what charges are being made against them.

Y

yellow journalism: A form of newspaper publishing in vogue in the late nineteenth century that featured pictures, comics, color, and sensationalized, oversimplified news coverage.

Juicio administrativo (administrative adjudication): Un proceso cuasi-judicial en el cual una agencia del gobierno (burocracia) da resolución a un conflicto entre dos partes. El proceso es similar a la resolución de un juez en una corte del sistema judicial.

Discrecionalidad administrativa (administrative discretion): La flexibilidad que posee un burócrata de interpretar e implementar las leyes del Congreso de acuerdo a su propio juicio con respecto a lo que el Congreso quiso decir.

Ley de Procesos Administrativos (administrative procedures act): Estatuto que contiene los procesos normativos del Estado de Texas.

Referéndum (advisory referendum): Proceso mediante el cual la ciudadanía vota directamente por o en contra de una iniciativa, aunque el resultado del proceso no tiene el peso de ley.

Filiales (affiliates): Estaciones de televisión locales que llevan programación de una red televisiva nacional.

Acción afirmativa (affirmative action): El conjunto de políticas públicas diseñadas para dar atención especial o trato preferencial a los miembros de un grupo previamente discriminado con el fin de recompensarlo por dicha discriminación.

Agenda (agenda): Una lista de ítems a discutir durante una reunión o junta.

La formación de la agenda (agenda setting): El proceso mediante el cual se conforma la lista de temas a tratar en cualquier reunión gubernamental.

Comisionado de Agricultura (agricultural commisssioner): El funcionario de un estado electo para hacerse cargo de regular y promover la industria agrícola.

El Álamo (the Alamo): Una misión religiosa en San Antonio que fue defendida por los texanos durante la guerra por la independencia del estado.

al-Qaeda (al-Qaeda): Organización mundial terrorista dirigida por Osama bin Laden y responsable de numerosos ataques terroristas en contra de los intereses de los Estados Unidos, incluyendo los ataques a las Torres Gemelas en Nueva York y al Pentágono en Washington el 11 de Septiembre.

El credo americano (american creed): El conjunto de ideas que dan identidad nacional, imponen límites al gobierno, y contribuyen a estructurar los canales por los cuales fluye el quehacer político de los Estados Unidos.

El sueño americano (american dream): El ideal americano de una vida feliz y exitosa que a menudo incluye una vida de riqueza, la propiedad de una casa, una mejor existencia para sus hijos e hijas, y, para algunos, la posibilidad de poder llegar a ser presidente.

Amicus Curiaem (amicus curiae): Latín: "Amigo de la corte." Consiste en un memorando de una persona o grupo ajeno a un conflicto judicial diseñado para añadir a un caso, ya sea en pro o en contra de algo o alguien, y de esta manera influir en la dictaminación de la corte.

Anglos (Anglos): Personas de raza "blanca" no Hispanos.

Anexión (annexation): Ampliación de los límites de una ciudad o pueblo incorporando territorios o poblados circundantes.

Los anti-Federalistas (Anti-Federalists): Un grupo político activo en los comienzos de los Estados Unidos que prefería una concentración de poderes y facultades en los gobiernos estatales y un gobierno nacional débil; este grupo se opuso a la ratificación de la constitución de los Estados Unidos porque, según ellos, concentraba demasiados poderes y facultades en el gobierno federal.

Cortes de apelación (appellate courts): Las cortes superiores que revisan y reafirman o anulan las dictaminaciones o veredictos de las cortes de distrito.

Jurisdicción de apelación (appellate jurisdiction): La facultad depositada en las cortes de apelaciones de revisar y reafirmar o cancelar las dictaminaciones o veredictos de las cortes de distrito.

Petición de revisión discrecional (application for discretionary review): La petición de que la Corte de Apelaciones Criminales de Texas revise la dictaminación o el veredicto de una corte inferior, aunque se requiere que cuatro jueces así lo convengan.

aporcionamiento (apportionment): El proceso mediante el cual se determina cuantos diputados le corresponden a un estado según el censo decenal de población.

Los Artículos de la Confederación (articles of confederation): El pacto entre los trece estados originales de los Estados Unidos y que constituía la base de su gobierno. Aunque los artículos fueron escritos en 1776, éstos no fueron ratificados por todos los trece estados hasta 1781.

"En general y por lugar" (at-large-by-place): Un sistema electoral en el cual todos puestos del cabildo o cualquier otro cuerpo de gobierno se eligen en una elección general y luego a cada puesto se le llama "una curul" y cada persona debe elegir por qué distrito se quiere lanzar.

Procurador de Justicia (attorney general): El funcionario electo para servir como el abogado del Estado de Texas.

Un sistema autoritario (authoritarian system): Un sistema de gobierno que se apoya en el uso de la fuerza para mantenerse en el poder, y no en el consentimiento de los gobernados.

Presupuesto equilibrado (balanced budget): Un presupuesto que contiene gastos sólo por el monto de impuestos que se espera recabar, o sea sin déficit.

Iniciativa electoral (ballot measure): Una medida de orden público (por ejemplo, una ley o normatividad sobre algo) que el gobierno pone ante los electores para que sean éstos mediante su voto directo los que decidan a favor o en contra de la misma.

Legislatura bicameral (bicameral legislature): Una legislatura que se divide en dos cámaras; en los Estados Unidos la legislatura es bicameral porque tiene un Senado y una Cámara de Representantes. Todas las legislaturas estatales también son bicamerales, excepto Nebraska, que es unicameral.

La legislatura bicameral en Texas (bicamenral Texas legislature): La legislatura del Estado de Texas tiene dos cámaras, una cámara de representantes y un senado.

Legislatura bienal (biennial legislature): Un cuerpo legislativo que se reúne en la sesión ordinaria solamente una vez cada dos años.

Proyecto de ley (bill): Una propuesta de ley ante una legislatura o congreso.

Revocación (bill of attainder): Una ley que declara algo ilegal sin la necesidad de un proceso judicial.

Declaración de Derechos y Garantías Individuales (Bill of Rights): Se le llama así a las primeras diez enmiendas a la constitución de los Estados Unidos, que contienen los derechos y garantías de los ciudadanos.

Los códigos negros (Black Codes): Leyes que negaban derechos y garantías ciudadanos a los esclavos recientemente emancipados; estos códigos fueron aprobados principalmente en los estados del sur después de la guerra civil.

Partida presupuestal (block grant): Un monto de dinero otorgado generalmente sin muchas condicionantes; estos fondos son generalmente concedidos a los estados por el gobierno federal con designaciones generales, tales como la educación o los servicios médicos.

Blog (blog): Un registro hecho en una página de Internet, generalmente por un usuario; funciona a manera de diario, página editorial, comentario, reflexión, etc., que les permite a los ciudadanos expresarse libremente sobre eventos, noticias, candidatos, etc.

El Acuerdo de Bretton Woods (Bretton Woods Agreement): El acuerdo financiero internacional concluido y firmado poco antes del fin de la Segunda Guerra Mundial, el cual creó el Banco Mundial y el Fondo Monetario Internacional, y estableció el orden financiero mundial de la postguerra.

Expediente (brief): Un documento que contiene los argumentos legales de un caso ante una corte hechos por una de las partes antes de la audiencia o juicio.

Medios electrónicos de difusión masiva (broadcast media): Televisión, radio, cable, y transmisiones satelitales.

Brown v. Board of Education (1954): La dictaminación de la Suprema Corte de Justicia en la cual se señala que la segregación de las razas es intrínsecamente anticonstitucional porque viola las garantías de la 14ª enmienda a la constitución de los Estados Unidos que requiere un trato igualitario para todos; esta dictaminación marcó el fin de la segregación racial en los Estados Unidos.

Autoridad presupuestaria (budget execution authority): La autoridad de transferir fondos públicos de un programa a otro de una agencia gubernamental a otra.

La burocracia (bureaucracy): El sistema de agencias, departamentos, comisiones, y personal gubernamentales organizados de manera jerárquica y cuyo propósito es auxiliar a los líderes políticos a cumplir con sus obligaciones mediante la ejecución de las leyes y programas del gobierno. Las burocracias pueden también ser privadas, ya que muchas grandes compañías tienen sus propias burocracias.

La Doctrina Bush (Bush Doctrine): La política oficial de los Estados Unidos, emitida por el presidente George W. Bush, de reservarse el derecho de atacar militarmente a un país u organización de manera anticipatoria o preventiva cuando se perciba que éste o ésta representa una amenaza futura para los intereses de los Estados Unidos.

El ciclo comercial o de negocios (business cycle): Las fluctuaciones o altibajos naturales que se dan entre la expansión y la recesión (aceleración y desaceleración) de una economía y que se presume son un componente natural del capitalismo moderno.

El gabinete (Cabinet): El cuerpo de los colaboradores presidenciales, cada uno de los cuales dirige uno de los quince departamentos ejecutivos o secretarías de la burocracia de los Estados Unidos. Los presidentes a menudo integran a otras personas a este cuerpo de consejeros formales, a veces mediante la creación de nuevas secretarías.

Asesor de campaña (campaign consultant): Llámase así al profesional que trabaja para una firma del sector privado que ofrece a un candidato sus tecnologías, servicios, y estrategias para la campaña política mediante la cual éste busca ser electo a un puesto público.

Coordinador de campaña (campaign manager): La persona que coordina los muchos y diversos aspectos de la campaña de un candidato; éste generalmente viaja junto con el candidato a dondequiera que éste vaya.

Campañas centradas en el candidato (candidate-centered politics): Una campaña política que se centra directamente sobre el candidato, los temas que éste maneja, y su carácter y personalidad, más que sobre su partido político.

Debate de los candidatos (candidate debate): Foro público en el cual los candidatos se reúnen para discutir sus plataformas, ideas, programas, y características personales.

Agencia gubernamental "capturada" (captured agency): Una agencia del gobierno que constantemente toma decisiones favorables a los intereses privados de aquellas personas u organizaciones que se supone debe regular y vigilar.

Doctrina Carter (Carter Doctrine): La política oficial de los Estados Unidos, formulada por el Presidente Jimmy Carter después de la invasión soviética de Afganistán en 1979, que predica que el área del golfo pérsico es vital para los intereses de los Estados Unidos y éste país debe estar dispuesto a todo para mantener el libre acceso al golfo.

Una partida categórica (categorical grant): Una partida o bolsa gubernamental que el congreso crea para un propósito muy específico.

Agencia Central de Inteligencia (Central Intelligence Agency): Agencia gubernamental de los Estados Unidos responsable de la colección y análisis de la información e inteligencia sobre otros países y acontecimientos del escenario mundial.

Escuela particular (charter school): Una escuela pública creada mediante un acuerdo específico que le permite que funcione fuera de las reglas y normatividades generalmente aplicadas a las escuelas públicas regulares.

Pesos y contrapesos o Equilibrio de poderes (checks and balances): Un concepto político de organización gubernamental que da a cada uno de los tres poderes del gobierno una cierta autoridad de contrapeso o supervisión y control sobre las acciones de los otros dos poderes.

Oficial de Hacienda (chief budget officer): Término para designar al gobernador que se encarga de la elaboración del presupuesto del estado para que luego la legislatura lo discuta y apruebe.

Jefe del Ejecutivo (chief executive officer): El gobernador del estado, a quien se le considera como el funcionario máximo del poder ejecutivo del Estado de Texas.

Jefe de Estado (chief of state): El gobernador en su papel como la cabeza oficial que representa al Estado de Texas en sus relaciones con el gobierno nacional, con otros estados, y con dignatarios extranjeros.

Ciudadano(a) (citizen): Miembro de la comunidad política quien posee ciertos derechos y obligaciones para con la comunidad.

Comisión Municipal (city commission): Una forma de gobierno local en la cual se elige a los miembros del cuerpo legislativo o cabildo y, al mismo tiempo, cada uno de éstos sirve también como administrador de una dependencia del gobierno municipal.

Virtud cívica (civic virtue): La inclinación de los ciudadanos de una comunidad a constituir asociaciones para promover el interés público.

Derecho civil (civil law): El conjunto de códigos que regula la conducta de grupos e individuos con respecto a sus negocios y otras relaciones contractuales.

Las libertades civiles (civil liberties): Las garantías de acción libre de las personas que el gobierno no puede coartar ni restringir mediante leyes o normas, cambios a la constitución, o interpretaciones del poder judicial.

Los derechos civiles (civil rights): Las garantías de protección contra la discriminación basada en la raza, el sexo, el origen nacional, la edad, la religión, o la orientación sexual, que poseen los individuos y que el gobierno debe garantizar.

Ley de los derechos civiles de 1964 (Civil Rights Act *of* 1964): Legislación aprobada por el Congreso en 1964 con el motivo de prohibir la segregación de las razas en instalaciones públicas y vedar la discriminación racial en el empleo, la educación, y el voto; esta misma ley creó la Comisión para la Oportunidad de Igualdad en el Empleo.

Los casos de los derechos civiles (1883) (*Civil Rights Cases* of 1883): Nombre único que se le da a cinco casos interpuestos ante la corte por violaciones a la legislación sobre los derechos civiles de 1875. En 1883, la Suprema Corte de Justicia dictaminó, lamentablemente, que la discriminación en instalaciones tales como los teatros, los hoteles, y los ferrocarriles, no se podía prohibir puesto que estas instalaciones eran de índole privada y no pública.

Leyes de la función pública o del servicio civil (civil service laws): Estas leyes eliminaron la posibilidad de que los políticos repartieran los puestos públicos a sus partidarios o a sus aliados como botín político; estas leyes crearon el servicio civil de carrera, mediante el cual se instituyó una burocracia profesionalizada, cuyo criterio para la promoción y el ascenso era el mérito y la competencia y no el favoritismo.

Servicio Civil de Carrera (civil service system): El sistema creado por las leyes de función pública o del servicio civil de carrera, que regula y norma la designación, promoción, y ascenso de los burócratas federales.

Sociedad civil (civil society): El tipo de sociedad que surge como producto de las libertades de asamblea, prensa, y expresión que ejercen los ciudadanos al llevar a cabo un debate abierto sobre las política públicas del país.

Prueba del "peligro claro y presente" (clear and present danger test): Prueba establecida por la Suprema Corte de Justicia en el caso *Schenck* vs. Los Estados Unidos (1919) para definir aquellas expresiones protegidas por la constitución y la leyes y aquellas no sancionadas por éstas; el criterio que indicó la Suprema Corte considera si "las palabras utilizadas . . ." pudieran "crear un peligro claro y presente de tal manera que provoquen un mal sustancial" que el congreso desea "evitar."

Clemencia (clemency): La autoridad que tiene el gobernador de reducir la duración de la sentencia de un prisionero.

Elección interna "cerrada" (closed primary): Una elección interna de un partido político en la cual solamente las personas registradas para votar bajo ese partido político pueden participar.

Voto para poner fin a un debate (Cloture): Un mecanismo que requiere el voto de tres quintas partes de los senadores para poner fin a un debate en el Senado.

Coalición (coalition): Un grupo compuesto de intereses, personas u organizaciones que se juntan con el fin de elegir a políticos de su preferencia.

Una cucaracha (cockroach): Un asistente a una convención constitucional que se opone a cualquier cambio en la constitución vigente.

Un bien colectivo (collective good): Un beneficio público, el cual es un logro de un grupo de menor tamaño y del cual no se puede privar a nadie, ni siquiera a aquellos que no contribuyeron a lograrlo; dos ejemplos de un bien colectivo son un recorte de impuestos o programas medioambientalistas que redundan en un aire o agua más limpio.

Seguridad colectiva (collective security): El concepto que predica que la paz se puede lograr si todos los países se opusieran colectivamente a cualquier país que agrediera a otro.

Comandante-en-Jefe (commander-in-chief): El gobernador(a) en su papel como cabeza de la milicia de un estado.

Corte de los Comisionados (commissioners court): El cuerpo legislativo de un condado en el Estado de Texas.

Comisión (committee): Una subunidad de la legislatura que trata los proyectos de ley sobre un tema específico.

Comisiones de Correspondencia (Committees of Correspondence): Organizaciones que surgieron en cada uno de las trece colonias americanas creadas para mantener a colonos al corriente de lo que sucedía con la corona británica; estas comisiones fueron importantes formadoras de opinión pública en contra de la corona británica.

Director de Prensa y Difusión (communications director): La persona que desarrolla la estrategia global de un candidato en los medios de comunicación masiva, utilizando a la vez la cobertura gratuita con los comerciales pagados en radio, televisión, y el correo electrónico.

Revisión total (comprehensive revision): Término que significa la adopción de una nueva constitución en vez de simplemente hacerle cambios a la que ya existe.

Recaudador de impuestos (comptroller of public accounts): Es un funcionario electo cuya función es recaudar los impuestos en un estado.

Facultad compartida (concurrent powers): Un poder o facultad compartida por el gobierno de un estado y el gobierno federal y que ambos pueden ejercer simultáneamente mientras dicho poder o facultad no sea exclusivo del gobierno nacional o contradiga las leyes de la federación.

Resolución conjunta (concurrent resolution): Un documento legislativo que expresa la voluntad de ambas cámaras legislativas simultáneamente pero que no necesita la firma del presidente porque no es ley.

Confederación (confederation): Tipo de gobierno donde el gobierno central no es autónomo sino que deriva sus facultades de los estados que lo componen; una liga de estados independientes entre sí.

Comisión de reconciliación legislativa (conference committee): Dícese de una comisión mixta compuesta de senadores y diputados cuya función es reconciliar las dos distintas versiones de un proyecto de ley aprobado por el Senado y otro aprobado por la Cámara de Diputados hasta lograr la redacción de un documento exáctamente igual.

Revisión del congreso (congressional review): Un proceso mediante el cual el congreso pueda dejar nula una normatividad emitida por una agenciagubernamental a través de una resolución conjunta; esto equivale a una anulación legislativa.

Un conservador (conservative): Una persona que cree que el mejor gobierno es el que gobierna menos (es decir es un gobierno mínimalista) y que un gobierno grande no puede más que vulnerar los derechos personales y económicos del individuo.

Constitución (constitution): Documento que establece la estructura, las funciones, y los límites de un gobierno.

Enmienda constitucional (constitutional amendment): Un cambio, adición, o derogación a una constitución.

Corte constitucional de un condado (constitutional county court): Una corte designada por mandato constitucional como el foro oficial para desahogar material penal y civil.

Cortes constitucionales (constitutional courts): Todas las cortes federales de los Estados Unidos creadas de acuerdo al Artículo 3º de la constitución o creadas por el congreso conforme a las facultades otorgadas a éste en el mismo Artículo 3º.

Comisión constitucional de revisión (Constitutional Revision Commission): Un grupo que se establece para que investigue y redacte el borrador de una constitución; este documento sirve como base de los debates en una convención constitucional.

Constitucionalismo (constitutionalism): Lo límites impuestos a un gobierno a través de un documento escrito.

Contención (containment): Estrategia de los Estados Unidos durante la Guerra Fría para resistir la expansión del poder soviético, particularmente en Europa occidental y Asia del este, mediante el uso de la fuerza militar, los incentivos económicos, y la influencia política.

Normatividad de contenidos (content regulation): Los intentos del gobierno por regular los medios de comunicación electrónicos.

Publicidad de contraste (contrast ad): Un pieza publicitaria que compara la experiencia y el historial de los candidatos así como su ofertas política con un sesgo hacia el que lo patrocina.

Participación política convencional (conventional political participation): Es aquella participación política que intenta influir sobre el proceso político a través de formas de tácticas de persuasión, tales como el escribir cartas a los oficiales de gobierno, el contribuir fondos a campañas políticas, y el salir a votar.

Federalismo cooperativo (cooperative federalism): La relación entre el gobierno federal y los gobiernos del estado que inició a partir del Nuevo Trato (New Deal).

Cabildo-Administrador (council-manager): Una forma de gobierno local en la cual el cabildo y el alcalde de una ciudad emplean a un(a) administrador(a) profesional para encargarse del funcionamiento diario de la ciudad.

Abogado del condado (county attorney): Un oficial electo por un condado que funge como el representante legal del condado y al mismo tiempo como el fiscal del mismo condado.

Auditor del condado (county auditor): Un funcionario designado por el juez de distrito para fiscalizar las finanzas del condado.

Líder del condado (county chairperson): Líder de un partido político a nivel condado.

Oficial del condado (county clerk): Un funcionario electo que funge como secretario del gobierno del condado y que es responsable de de los registros y archivos del condado.

Comisionado del condado (county commissioner): Un funcionario electo que forma parte del cuerpo legislativo de un condado; al cuerpo legislativo de un condado se le llama la corte de comisionados.

Convención del condado (county convention): Una reunión de los miembros de un partido político a nivel de un condado con el propósito de elegir delegados y adoptar resoluciones.

Corte del condado (county court at law): La corte de un condado creada por un estatuto legal y diseñada para auxiliar al juez del condado en el desempeño de sus deberes judiciales.

Comité ejecutivo del condado (county executive committee): Los jefes de las secciones de un partido político en un condado que ayudan a los jefes del partido político en sus labores políticas en el condado.

Juez del condado (county judge): Se le llama así al funcionario electo pero que funge no como juez sino como presidente del cuerpo administrativo del gobierno del condado, al cual se le llama la corte del condado; el juez del condado puede o no tener también algunas funciones judiciales.

Recaudador de impuestos del condado (county tax assessor-collector): Un funcionario electo cuya función es hacer cumplir las leyes impositivas y recaudar los impuestos del condado (tarea que a veces desempeña también para otros gobiernos locales).

Tesorero del condado (county treasurer): Un funcionario electo que se encarga de la administración de los recursos financieros del gobierno del condado.

Tribunal de apelaciones (court of appeals): Es la corte inmediata superior ante la cual se interponen apelaciones en materia de derecho penal y civil.

Fiscal del Distrito (criminal district attorney): Es un funcionario electo que procesa los casos penales, fungiendo como parte acusadora.

Derecho penal (criminal law): El conjunto de códigos que regulan la conducta humana con el motivo de proteger la propiedad y la seguridad de los habitantes.

Elección crítica (critical election): Una elección que representa un cambio de preferencias partidistas del electorado de un partido a otro debido al surgimiento de nuevos temas que polarizan a los votantes y los hacen cambiar de partido.

Votación cruzada (crossover voting): Una elección interna de un partido político donde votan personas no afiliadas a ese partido político.

La crisis de los misiles de Cuba (Cuban Missile Crisis): La confrontación ocurrida en octubre de 1962 entre los Estados Unidos y la Unión Soviética después de que los soviéticos desplegaron misiles balísticos de mediano alcance en Cuba.

Votación acumulativa (cumulative voting): Un método de votación en el cual cada votante tienen un número de votos iguales al número de los puestos de elección popular en juego y en el cual los votantes pueden otorgar todos sus votos a un solo candidato o repartirlos entre varios candidatos en diversas combinaciones de su preferencia.

Discriminación *de facto* (*de facto* discrimination): Un tipo de discriminación racial que surge de las prácticas cotidianas de una sociedad (tal como ciertos patrones discriminatorios en la distribución de beneficios sociales, etc.) pero que no tiene sustento en la ley misma.

Discriminación *de jure* (*de jure* discrimination): Un tipo de discriminación que surge como resultado directo de la legislación o de las políticas públicas de un Estado.

Realineación electoral (dealignment): Un declive general en la identificación y la lealtad partidistas en el electorado en contra de un partido político y a favor de otro.

Deuda (debt): La cantidad total que debe un gobierno como resultado de lo que ha pedido prestado en el pasado.

La declaración de la independencia (Declaration of Independence): El documento redactado por Thomas Jefferson en 1776 que proclamaba el derecho de las colonias americanas de separarse de la Gran Bretaña.

Historia profunda (deep background): La información que proporciona alguien a un periodista bajo condición de que el periodista no revele sus fuentes ni de dónde la obtuvo.

Gasto deficitario (deficit spending): El gasto del gobierno en el ciclo presupuestal vigente que excede los ingresos totales del gobierno.

Delegado (delegate): Una persona electa por un grupo para ir a votar por ellos de la manera que determinen los miembros del grupo, independientemente de los deseos, opiniones, o preferencias personales del delegado.

Democracia (democracy): Un sistema de gobierno que deriva su autoridad del pueblo y que le rinde cuentas al pueblo, ya sea directamente o a través de sus representantes electos.

Departamento de la Defensa (Department of Defense): Departamento o secretaría del ejecutivo responsable de la formulación e implementación de las políticas públicas militares.

Departamento de Seguridad Nacional (Department of National Security): Departamento o secretaría del ejecutivo, creado después de que los ataques terroristas del 11 de Septiembre de 2001 para coordinar los esfuerzos gubernamentales de los Estados Unidos en contra del terrorismo.

Departamento de Estado (Department of State): Departamento o secretaría del ejecutivo responsable de la formulación e implementación de la política exterior de los Estados Unidos.

Departamentos o Secretarías (departments): Unidades burocráticas integrales que tienen la responsabilidad administrar un área amplia de las operaciones del gobierno. El hecho de que el Estado cree un nuevo departamento o secretaría es generalmente un indicador de la existencia de un interés nacional permanente en esa área; algunos ejemplos son la defensa nacional, el comercio, o la agricultura, entre otras.

Desregulación o liberalización (deregulation): Una reducción en los controles del mercado (tales como los subsidios o controles del precio en quién puede incorporar un campo) a favor de la competición basada en el mercado.

Détente (Détente): Término que se utiliza para referirse a la distensión (relajación de tensiones) entre los Estados Unidos y la Unión Soviética que ocurrió en los años 70.

Democracia directa (direct democracy): Un sistema de gobierno en el cual miembros de la comunidad se reúnen para discutir entre ellos todas las decisiones sobre las políticas públicas para luego votar; este tipo de democracia supone que la comunidad está dispuesta a seguir la voluntad de la mayoría.

Prueba de la provocación directa (direct incitement test): Un criterio articulado por la Suprema Corte de Justicia en el caso *Brandenburg* vs. *Ohio* (1969) y que predica que el incitar directamente a la violencia o a la rebelión no es un delito sino que es parte de la libertad de expresión garantizada por la primera enmienda a la constitución, a menos que el llamado provoque un delito al momento o inmediatamente después.

Estratega de correos (direct mailer): Un profesional que supervisa las estrategias de recaudación financiera de una campaña que utilizan el correo directo.

Elección interna directa (direct primary): La selección de un candidato de un partido político a través del voto de los simpatizantes y militantes de éste en vez de una selección en una convención del partido.

Petición para sesión plena o de descarga (discharge petition): Solicitud de la mayoría de la Cámara de Diputados para que se discuta un asunto ante el pleno debido a la falta de acción dentro de la comisión pertinente.

Tasa de descuento (discount rate): El tipo de interés que se otorga a los bancos que son miembros o que están registrados con el Banco Central en su región cuando éstos piden dinero prestado de la reservas federales.

Fiscal de distrito (DA or District Attorney): Funcionario electo que representa al gobierno ante la corte en todos los casos penales.

Secretario de distrito (district clerk): Funcionario electo responsable de mantener los archivos de la corte de distrito.

Corte de distrito (district court): Corte que posee la jurisdicción sobre delitos serios y demandas civiles donde está en juego un valor monetario relativamente alto.

Teoría del disturbio (disturbance theory): Teoría inventada por el politólogo David B. Truman que predica que muchos grupos de la sociedad civil o de intereses se forman en parte para hacerle frente a las acciones de otros grupos.

Gobierno dividido (divided government): Una condición política del sistema gubernamental en la cual un partido político controla el poder ejecutivo y otro el congreso.

Nación dependiente (domestic dependent nation): Un tipo de soberanía que coloca a una tribu india de los Estados Unidos fuera de la autoridad del gobierno del estado pero dependiente del gobierno federal en la forma en que se estructura la autoridad política dentro de la tribu.

Excepción de cosa juzgada (double jeopardy clause): Cláusula que se encuentra en la quinta enmienda a la constitución y que protege a los ciudadanos de ser enjuiciados dos veces por el mismo delito.

Federalismo dual (dual federalism): La idea de que tener varios niveles de gobierno totalmente separados pero con facultades y poderes similares redunda en un mejor gobierno.

Derecho procesal (due process clause): Un conjunto de cláusulas contenidas en las enmiendas quinta y catorceava de la constitución de los Estados Unidos y que se han interpretado a lo largo de los años como cláusulas que garantizan a los individuos una variedad de derechos que van desde la libertad económica hasta las protecciones del acusado de un delito en la corte así como de las acciones arbitrarias del gobierno.

Garantías del derecho procesal (due process rights): Las protecciones y resguardos de los que goza el individuo acusado de un delito y que se mencionnan en las enmiendas cuarta, quinta, sexta, y octava de la constitución de los Estados Unidos.

Partida exclusiva (earmark): Fondos dedicados dentro de un presupuesto, los cuales se señalan para un propósito o proyecto muy específico en un estado o un distrito electoral.

Grupo de intereses económicos (economic interest group): Un grupo que se forma u organiza con el propósito de promover los intereses financieros de sus miembros.

Regulación de la economía (economic regulation): Reglamentos emitidos por el gobierno que norman las prácticas comerciales, las tarifas, las rutas operativas, y las áreas de ejercicio de una industria.

Estabilidad económica (economic stability): Una situación en la cual existen a la vez un crecimiento económico constante, salarios al alza, bajo desempleo, y mínima inflación en general.

Octava enmienda (Eighth Amendment): Parte de la Declaración de los Derechos y Garantías Individuales de la constitución que dice que a nadie se le impondrán una fianza excesiva, ni multas desproporcionadas, ni serán los castigos crueles e inusuales.

Elector (elector): Miembro del Colegio Electoral (cuerpo que elige al presidente de los Estados Unidos) y que se selecciona por distintos métodos en cada estado del país.

Colegio Electoral (Electoral College): El cuerpo de representantes de cada estado que eligen (realmente) al presidente de los Estados Unidos.

Electorado (electorate): El conjunto de ciudadanos que pueden votar.

Ley del embargo (Embargo Act): Ley aprobada por el Congreso de los Estados Unidos en 1807 para prevenir que cualquier embarcación del país se hiciera a la mar con dirección a puertos extranjeros sin la aprobación previa del gobierno federal.

Engagement (engagement): Doctrina formulada por el Presidente Bill Clinton que predicaba que los Estados Unidos deberían ser mucho más proactivos en su política exterior con miras a transformar al mundo.

Proyecto de ley absorto (engrossed bill): Un proyecto de ley al que se le ha dado la aprobación final después de la tercera lectura en en la legislatura.

Enlargement o Engrandecimiento (enlargement): Doctrina formalada por la administración de Bill Clinton que predicaba que los Estados Unidos deberían promover activamente a través de su política exterior la expansión de la democracia y del libre mercado en todo el mundo.

Proyecto de ley inscrito (enrolled bill): Un proyecto de ley que ha ya aprobado por las dos cámara de una legislatura y que se ha enviado ya al gobernador para su firma y proclamación en ley.

Programa social (entitlement program): Programa de seguridad social a cuyos beneficios tienen derecho todos aquellos que demuestren un cierto nivel de necesidad.

Facultades enumeradas (enumerated powers): Las diecisiete cláusulas que especifican los poderes del congreso en el Artículo I, Sección 8, de la constitución de los Estados Unidos; estas facultades incluyen el gravar impuestos, la impresión de la moneda nacional, la regulación del comercio, y la autoridad de velar por la defensa nacional.

Comisión de Oportunidades para la Igualdad del Empleo (Equal Employment Opportunity Commission): Agencia federal creada para hacer cumplir la ley de los derechos civiles de 1964 y que prohíbe la discriminación en base a la raza, el credo, el origen nacional, la religión, o el género cuando se emplea, asciende, o despide a un empleado.

Cláusula de protección igualitaria (equal protection clause): Sección de la catorceava enmienda de la constitución que especifica que todos los ciudadanos deben recibir la "protección igualitaria de las leyes," es decir, todos los ciudadanos deben ser tratados como iguales ante la ley.

La enmienda de los derechos igualitarios (Equal Rights Amendment): Enmienda a la constitución de los Estados Unidos que hubiera eliminado (si hubiera sido aprobada) la discriminación contra la mujer por los gobiernos estatales o el gobierno federal.

La regla de igual tiempo (equal time rule): La norma legal que requiere que las estaciones de televisión y radio vendan el tiempo aire a todos los demás candidatos por igual (mismos espacios, precios, etc.) si deciden vendérselo a uno.

Igualdad (equality): La creencia que todos los seres humanos deben ser tratados de la misma manera, sin importar su estado socioeconómico.

Cláusula del establecimiento (establishment clause): Parte de la primera enmienda de la constitución de los Estados Unidos que prohíbe que el gobierno nacional sancione a una religión en particular o establezca una religión nacional.

Ley *ex post facto* (*ex post facto* law): Dícese de una ley aprobada por el congreso después de un hecho o evento y que impondría en teoría castigos retroactivos a un actividad antes legal; la aprobación de leyes *ex post facto* está prohibida por la constitución de los Estados Unidos.

Regla de exclusión (exclusionary rule): Una norma judicial que prohíbe a la policía utilizar en un juicio evidencia obtenida de manera ilegal.

Acuerdo ejecutivo (executive agreement): Un acuerdo internacional formal del gobierno federal pactado por el presidente y que no requiere del consentimiento o aprobación del Senado de los Estados Unidos.

Comisionado Ejecutivo de la Comisión de Salud y Servicios Humanos (executive commissioner of the health and human services commission): El funcionario designado por el gobernador para dirigir a todas las agencias gubernamentales encargadas de proveer los servicios de salud y seguridad social del estado.

Oficina Ejecutiva del Presidente (EOP or Executive Office of the President)): Agencia creada en 1939 para auxiliar al presidente a dirigir a la burocracia federal.

Decreto ejecutivo (executive order): Una regla o normatividad pública emitida por el presidente y que tiene el mismo efecto que una ley. Todos los decretos ejecutivos deben publicarse en *El Diario de la Federación*.

Privilegio del ejecutivo (executive privilege): Una facultad presidencial que le permite al jefe del poder ejecutivo rehusarse a compartir cierta información con el congreso o el poder judicial si éste la considera confidencial o si estimara que su divulgación pone en riesgo la seguridad nacional.

Encuestas de salida (exit polls): Encuestas conducidas en ciertos lugares afuera de las casillas electorales con el fin de recabar datos sobre la elección.

Cláusula de extradición (extradition clause): Parte del Artículo IV de la constitución que requiere que los estados extraditen o devuelvan a un sospechoso al estado donde se le busca para ser enjuiciado o de donde haya escapado.

Jurisdicción extraterritorial (ETJ or extraterritorial jurisdiction): El área fuera del fundo legal de una ciudad en la cual el gobierno municipal puede ejercer ciertas facultades limitadas.

Doctrina de la imparcialidad (fairness doctrine): Norma gubernamental que tuvo efecto entre 1949 y 1985 y que requería a los locutores, periodistas, directores de noticias, etc., dar cobertura adecuada a un evento, candidato, o tema, y presentar todas las opiniones, en pro y en contra, por igual.

Déficit presupuestario federal (federal budget deficit): La diferencia entre el gasto federal (más) y la recaudación tributaria total del gobierno (menos).

Ley sobre las actividades políticas de los empleados federales (Federal Employees Political Activities Act): Ley aprobada en 1993 que relajó las restricciones sobre las actividades políticas de los empleados federales que imponía la llamada Ley Hatch. A través de esta nueva ley, se les permite ahora a los empleados federales lanzarse a un puesto público en elecciones no partidistas y contribuir financieramente a una campaña electoral, aunque sea partidista.

Banco de la reserva federal o Banco Central (Federal Reserve Board): El banco del gobierno federal que cuenta con siete miembros en su comité ejecutivo y cuya función es establecer los requisitos alrededor de las reservas monetarias de los bancos y fijar la tasa interbancaria, entre otras decisiones financieras.

Sistema federal (federal system): Un sistema de gobierno en el cual los estados y la federación comparten ciertos poderes y facultades, pero siempre derivan toda su autoridad del pueblo; las facultades del gobierno federal, sin embargo, están claramente especificadas en la constitución de los Estados Unidos, recayendo todas las demás en los estados y el pueblo.

Los Ensayos Federalistas (The Federalist Papers): Una serie de ochenta y cinco ensayos de naturaleza política escritos por John Jay, Alexander Hamilton, y James Madison, que presentaban los principales argumentos a favor de la ratificación de la constitución de los Estados Unidos.

Los Federalistas (Federalists): Aquellas figuras políticas que, en los primeros años de los Estados Unidos, favorecían un gobierno federal fuerte y apoyaban y promovían la ratificación de la constitución del país; este grupo se convertiría más tarde en el primer partido político del país.

Décimaquinta enmienda (Fifteenth Amendment): Una de las tres enmiendas a la constitución aprobada durante de la guerra civil; otorgaba derechos cívicos y políticos específicos a los esclavos varones recientemente emancipados.

Quinta enmienda (Fifth Amendment): Parte de la Declaración de los Derechos y Garantías Individuales que impone restricciones al gobierno federal con respecto a los derechos de los acusados de un delito. Otorga el derecho a un gran jurado; a la protección en contra de la autoincriminación; y prohibe al gobierno federal que le niegue a una persona la vida, la libertad, o lo prive de su propiedad sin haber seguido estríctamente el derecho procesal. Prohibe también al gobierno la expropiación o nacionalización de una propiedad privada sin debida compensación.

Palabras agresivas (fighting words): Palabras que "ante el mero hecho de ser pronunciadas causan una injuria o alteran el orden público." Tales palabras no están sujetas a las restricciones que impone la primera enmienda.

Filibuster (filibuster): Una manera formal de obstruir cualquier acción sobre un projecto de ley por medio de interminables discursos, debates, o discusiones ilimitadas en el Senado. Un filibuster es posible gracias a que en el Senado no se impone un límite de tiempo a ningún senador durante el debate y discusión de un proyecto de ley.

Oficial de finanzas (finance chair): Un profesional que coordina los esfuerzos para la recaudación de fondos de una campaña política.

Primera enmienda (First Amendment): La primera parte de la Declaración de los Derechos y Garantías Individuales que impone un número de restricciones al gobierno federal con respecto a las libertades civiles del pueblo, garantizando así la libertad de expresión, la libertad de prensa, la libertad de asamblea, la libertad de religión, y la libertad de petición.

Primer congreso continental (First Continental Congress): Reunión celebrada en Filadelfia entre el 5 de septiembre y el 26 de octubre de 1774, en el cual cincuenta y seis delegados (de todas las colonia excepto Georgia) adoptaron una resolución en oposición a la Ley de Coacción.

Primera lectura (first reading): La constitución de Texas requiere que a un proyecto de ley se le den tres lecturas en el pleno de la legislatura; la primera lectura tiene como propósito presentar el proyecto de ley, anunciar su título, y enviarlo a la comisión pertinente.

Política fiscal (fiscal policy): El conjunto de políticas públicas del gobierno federal que tienen que ver con los impuestos, el gasto, y la deuda, y cuyo propósito es dar forma a las metas macroeconómicas del país con respecto al empleo, la estabilidad de los precios, y el crecimiento económico.

Comités políticos 527 (527 political committees): Grupos de intereses no lucrativos y no regulados que enfocan sus campañas mediáticas a favor o en contra de las posiciones específicas de un candidato o partido y que buscan así influir en los votantes.

Catorceava enmienda (Fourteenth Amendment): Una de las tres enmiendas de la Guerra Civil; ésta garantiza la protección igualitaria y los derechos procesales de la constitución a todos los ciudadanos.

Cuarta enmienda (Fourth Amendment): Parte de la Declaración de los Derechos y Garantías Individuales que reza que: "El derecho del pueblo a la seguridad en su persona, domicilio, papeles, y posesiones, en contra de cateos y confiscaciones excesivos, no podrá ser violado, y no se autorizarán órdenes de cateo excepto bajo causa justificada y apoyada por un juramento o afirmación, y deberá describir específicamente el lugar a ser cateado, y las personas que han de ser arrestadas o las cosas que han de ser confiscadas."

Enmarcación (framing): Técnica mediante la cual un medio de comunicación define el giro que se le va a dar a la noticia y por lo tanto puede afectar de manera profunda la opinión pública.

Cláusula del libre ejercicio religioso (free exercise clause): La segunda parte de la primera enmienda que prohíbe al gobierno de los Estados Unidos interferir con la libertad de un ciudadano a practicar su religión.

Cobertura gratuita (free media): Dícese de aquella cobertura mediática que se le da a una campaña política en virtud de que es noticia.

Problema del pez rémora o del zángano (free rider problem): Dícese de aquellos posibles miembros de un grupo que deciden no unirse a éste porque pueden conseguir los mismos beneficios o disfrutar de un bien colectivo logrado por el grupo sin tener que invertir o contribuir su propio esfuerzo para la obtención del beneficio.

La era de la frontera (frontier era): El período histórico en el que Texas era un territorio fronterizo entre los Estados Unidos y las zonas del suroeste del país habitadas por los mexicanos y las tribus indias.

Cargarse al frente (front-loading): La tendencia de los estados a organizar las elecciones presidenciales internas de los partidos cada vez más temprano en el calendario de elecciones con el propósito de influir más directamente en quien va a ser el candidato.

Cláusula de la entera fe y crédito (full faith and credit clause): Sección del artículo IV de la constitución que obliga a los gobiernos de los estados a dar reconocimiento legal a los decretos judiciales y los contratos hechos en un estado dentro de su propio territorio. También se le llama la cláusula de la reciprocidad.

Equivalencia de tiempo completo (FTE or full-time equivalent): Unidad de medida mediante la cual se determina el número de empleados.

Libertades básicas (fundamental freedoms): Dícese de aquellos derechos especificados por la corte como esenciales para el orden, la libertad, y la justicia.

Acuerdo General sobre Tarifas y Comercio (General Agreement on Tariffs and Trade): Convenio establecido poco después la Segunda Guerra Mundial de manera temporal hasta que se pudiese crear una organización mundial de comercio; tenía como propósito crear un régimen comercial que ayudara a bajar o eliminar las tarifas arancelarias y aumentar el comercio internacional.

Elección general (general election): Elección en la cual los votantes deciden qué candidatos ocuparán los puestos públicos mediante su sufragio; se contrapone a las elecciones internas de los partidos políticos en las cuales se eligen a los candidatos.

Campaña electoral general (general election campaign): La parte de una campaña política que tiene como objetivo ganar la elección general.

Ciudades de leyes generales (general law cities): Poblados con menos de 5,000 habitantes gobernados por las leyes generales del estado y no por un cabildo y sus propios estatutos locales.

Autoridad para constituir estatutos propios (general ordinance-making authority): El derecho legal de las ciudades de adoptar sus propios estatutos municipales en una amplia gama de asuntos públicos; esta autoridad la poseen las ciudades pero no los condados.

Vinculado (germane): Que está relacionado a un cierto asunto.

Gerrymandering (gerrymandering): El proceso legislativo mediante el cual el partido de la mayoría en cada legislatura estatal intenta asegurar para sí el número máximo de diputados en el congreso federal a través de la manipulación demográfico-geográfica de los distritos federales en el estado.

Movilización del voto (GOTV or get-out-the-vote): El esfuerzo que hacen los partidos políticos por sacar a los electores a las urnas el día de las elecciones.

Gibbons v. Ogden **(1824):** Caso de la Suprema Corte en el cual los magistrados sostuvieron que el congreso federal tiene amplios poderes y facultades en la regulación del comercio interestatal. La interpretación de la constitución tan ampliamente a favor del gobierno federal sirvió para que a partir de entonces el gobierno federal se adjudicara todo tipo de poderes y facultades antes reservadas solamente a los gobiernos de los estados.

Calentamiento global (global warming): El aumento en las temperaturas de las regiones del planeta que resulta de las emisiones de monóxido de carbono producto del uso de combustibles como el petróleo y el carbón.

El buen gobierno (good government): El conjunto de políticas que abren las burocracias a la participación y al escrutinio del público y que reducen al mínimo los conflictos de intereses.

Gobierno (government): La institución en la cual se elaboran las políticas públicas y se conducen los asuntos del estado.

Empresa paraestatal (government corporation): Un negocio establecido por el Congreso para realizar ciertas funciones económicas que se pueden también proporcionar por empresas privadas (tales como el servicio postal en los Estados Unidos).

Agenda (institucional) gubernamental (governmental (institutional) agenda): La lista que asuntos a tratar en un momento dado a la cual un gobierno cree que debe abocarse.

Partido del gobierno (governmental party): El conjunto de funcionarios y candidatos de un partido político que ocupan los puestos del gobierno en su mayoría.

Gobernador (governor): La persona electa que ocupa el puesto de jefe de gobierno en un estado.

Mensaje del gobernador (governor's message): Mensaje que el gobernador entrega a la legislatura y que anuncia los objetivos de sus políticas públicas, las prioridades de su presupuesto, y las acciones que recomienda a la legislatura.

Cláusula de abuelo (grandfather clause): Una disposición que se utilizaba en muchos estados del sur que le permitía votar solamente a aquellas personas cuyos abuelos habían tenido el derecho a votar antes de La Reconstrucción a menos que pudiesen pasar una prueba de "riqueza" o de alfabetismo.

Gran Acuerdo (Great Compromise): Una decisión que se tomó durante la convención constitucional de otorgar a cada estado el mismo número de representantes en el Senado sin importar su tamaño y de otorgar a cada estado un número de representantes en la Cámara de Diputados de acuerdo al tamaño de su población.

Producto interno bruto o PIB (Gross Domestic Product or GDP): El valor comercial total de todas las mercancías y servicios producidos en un país durante un año.

Dinero duro (hard money): Aquellas contribuciones monetarias a las campañas políticas especificadas, limitadas, y reguladas claramente por La Ley Federal de Campañas Electorales y por la Comisión Federal Electoral.

La ley Hatch (Hatch Act): Ley decretada en 1939 que prohibía a los funcionarios públicos el activismo electoral en campañas políticas. La ley les prohibía a los empleados federales el contribuir dinero a campañas políticas, hacer trabajo electoral por un partido político o hacer campaña a favor de un candidato en particular.

Postergación (hold): Una táctica mediante la cual un senador pide ser informado antes de que un proyecto de ley llegue al pleno, táctica que demora o bloquea indefinidamente la llegada del proyecto de ley al pleno de la cámara.

Gobierno autónomo (home rule): El derecho y la autoridad de una comunidad local de gobernarse a sí misma, sin la interferencia del gobierno del estado.

Los derechos humanos (human rights): La creencia de que todos los seres humanos tienen derechos inalienables, tales como la libertad de expresión y la libertad de religión.

Ideología (ideology): Un sistema de creencias que conforma el pensamiento de una persona y de cómo ve el mundo.

Enjuiciar políticamente (impeach): Un voto de la cámara de diputados mediante el cual se acusa formalmente a un político o juez del gobierno haber cometido un delito oficial.

Juicio político (impeachment): La facultad delegada a la cámara de diputados por la constitución de acusar formalmente al presidente, vicepresidente, u otros "oficiales civiles," incluyendo a jueces federales, de "traición, soborno, y otros crímenes y delitos serios." Éste es el primer paso en el proceso constitucional para quitar a un oficial del gobierno de su puesto.

Implementación (implementation): El proceso mediante el cual una ley o una política pública se pone en operación por la burocracia.

Facultades o poderes implícitos (implied powers): Las facultades del congreso que se deducen de la dieciochoava cláusula de la Sección 8 del Artículo I de la constitución, a la cual se le conoce como la "cláusula de lo necesario y apropiado" porque le otorga al congreso el poder de hacer lo que sea "necesario y apropiado" para hacer cumplir la constitución. Estos poderes no se indican específicamente en la cláusula sino se consideran facultades implícitas.

Impresión (impressment): La práctica británica en el Siglo XVIII de detener a los barcos en altamar para aprender a aquellos marineros sospechosos de haber desertado de la Real Fuerza Naval.

Doctrina de la incorporación (incorporation doctrine): Interpretación de la constitución que sostiene que aquella cláusula que forma parte del derecho procesal contenida en la catorceava enmienda a la constitución exige que los estados y los gobiernos locales también están obligados a otorgar todas las garantías y derechos individuales.

Vigencia o "en turno" o incumbencia (incumbency): Dícese de la condición del funcionario que ocupa un puesto público en un momento dado.

Agencia ejecutiva autónoma (independent executive agency): Una unidad gubernamental que se asemeja a un departamento o secretaría del gobierno federal pero que tiene un área de responsabilidad más estrecha (tal como la Agencia Central de Inteligencia o CIA) y que no es parte del gabinete del presidente.

Comisión reguladora independiente (independent regulatory commission): Una agencia creada por el Congreso que se encarga de regular un aspecto específico de la economía o la vida social o política del país.

Democracia (representativa) indirecta (indirect (representative) democracy): Un sistema de gobierno que da a los ciudadanos la oportunidad de elegir, mediante el sufragio, a quienes han de fungir como sus representantes dentro el gobierno y que han de trabajar a favor del pueblo.

Individualismo (individualism): La creencia que cada persona debe actuar de acuerdo a su propia conciencia.

Inflación (inflation): Un aumento generalizado de los precios en una economía.

Poderes o facultades inherentes (inherent powers): Poderes que le pertenecen a un gobierno nacional simplemente por el hecho de ser un estado soberano.

Iniciativa (initiative): Un proceso que les permite a los ciudadanos proponer legislación y presentarla directamente al electorado para que sea éste el que la apruebe o desapruebe.

Anuncio de inoculación (inoculation ad): Publicidad o anuncio que tiene como objeto neutralizar el efecto de un ataque que prepara la oposición, antes de que ésta lo ejecute.

Comisionado para la Regulación de la Industria de Seguros (insurance commissioner): Un funcionario designado por el gobernador para dirigir el Departamento de Seguros, cuyo objeto es regular la industria de seguros, ya sea automovilísticos, médico, de vida, de propiedad, etc.

Calendario de intenciones (intent calendar): El calendario del Senado que enumera los proyectos de ley e indica que sus autores o patrocinadores han dado notificación de que desean suspender las reglas generales para que el proyecto de ley pase inmediatamente al pleno del Senado.

Consejos interburocráticos (interagency councils): Grupos de trabajo creados para facilitar la coordinación de la formulación y la implementación de políticas públicas cuando éstas requieren de la cooperación de varias agencias gubernamentales.

Grupo de intereses (interest group): Un grupo organizado que intenta influir en las políticas públicas que afectan a sus miembros.

Organización gubernamental internacional o OGI (international governmental organization or IGO): Una organización creada por los gobiernos de por lo menos dos y a menudo muchos países que funciona internacionalmente con el objeto de lograr los propósitos comunes de los países miembros.

Fondo Monetario Internacional (International Monetary Fund): Organización gubernamental internacional creada poco antes del fin de la Segunda Guerra Mundial para estabilizar las relaciones financieras internacionales a través de tasas monetarias fijas.

Equipo Internet (Internet team): Personal de una campaña política que utiliza la Internet para comunicarse con los votantes, recabar fondos, organizar a los voluntarios, y planear eventos de campaña.

Pactos interestatales (interstate compacts): Contratos entre dos estados que tienen la fuerza de una ley; generalmente se utiliza como una herramienta para tratar asuntos políticos que conciernen a varios estados.

Estado intervencionista (interventionist state): Alternativa al estado del liberalismo comercial en la cual el gobierno toma un papel activo en la guía y el manejo de la economía del país.

Triángulos de hierro (iron triangles): Las relaciones y los patrones de interacción relativamente estables entre las agencia gubernamentales, los grupos de intereses, y las comisiones o subcomisiones del congreso.

Aislacionismo (isolationism): Una política nacional que consiste en evitar la participación en asuntos internacionales.

Redes temáticas (issue networks): Las relaciones informales que existen entre una gran cantidad de actores que trabajan en una área de la política pública.

Política unitemática: La política que se centra en un tema específico más que en un partido, un candidato, u otras lealtades.

Leyes Jim Crow (Jim Crow Laws): Leyes decretadas por los estados del sur de los Estados Unidos que discriminaban contra las personas de raza negra mediante la creación de escuelas, teatros, hoteles, y otras instalaciones públicas para "blancos solamente."

Jefes de Personal en Conjunto (Joint Chiefs of Staff): Organismo consultivo del presidente que incluye al jefe de personal del ejército, al jefe de personal de la fuerza aérea, al jefe de operaciones navales, y al comandante de la marina.

Comisión conjunta (joint committee): Comisión que incluye a miembros de ambas cámaras del congreso y conduce investigaciones o estudios especiales.

Resolución conjunta (joint resolution): Un documento legislativo que propone una enmienda a la constitución de Texas o que ratifica una enmienda a la constitución de los Estados Unidos.

Activismo judicial (judicial activism): Una filosofía judicial que sustenta que los jueces debe utilizar sus facultades ampliamente para hacer justicia, especialmente en las áreas de la igualdad y de la libertad personal.

Implementación judicial (judicial implementation): Un concepto que se refiere al tema de la implementación de políticas públicas derivadas de un veredicto en una corte y que van más allá de las partes de un juicio.

Restricción judicial (judicial restraint): Una filosofía judicial que sostiene que las cortes deben respetar las decisiones de los otros poderes del gobierno, aún cuando éstas ofenden los principios de los jueces.

Revisión judicial (judicial review): La facultad de las cortes de revisar y modificar las decisiones de los otros poderes del gobierno federal y de los estados.

Ley judicial de 1789 (Judicial Act of 1789): Ley que estableció la estructura del sistema judicial federal como lo conocemos hoy, incluyendo los tres niveles que posee—distrito, apelaciones, y Suprema Corte.

Jurisdicción (jurisdiction): La autoridad que posee una corte de dar audiencias y emitir veredictos en un caso en particular.

Corte de un juez de paz (justice of the peace court): Corte menor de un condado local que tiene jurisdicción en delitos y demandas civiles menores.

Liberalismo o laissez-faire (laissez-faire): Un término francés que significa "dejad hacer." Es una política gubernamental que se basa en la creencia de que el gobierno no debe intervenir en la economía y que toda intervención del gobierno en la economía es equivocada.

Comisionado de la tierra (land commissioner): El funcionario electo responsable de manejar y de arrendar las propiedades del estado, incluyendo las concesiones del petróleo, del gas, y de los recursos minerales.

Liga de las Naciones (League of Nations): Organización internacional intergubernamental creada mediante el tratado de paz que concluyó la Primera Guerra Mundial y cuyo objetivo era la preservación de la paz.

Comité presupuestario legislativo (Legislative Budget Board or LBB): Un comité legislativo conjunto (con un personal numeroso) que prepara el presupuesto estatal y conduce evaluaciones de los programas de las burocracias.

Consejo legislativo (legislative council): Comité legislativo conjunto (con un personal numeroso) que proporciona asesoría jurídica, ayuda a redactar proyectos de ley, edita, e imprime trabajos de investigación sobre políticas públicas y servicios de evaluación de programas para beneficio de los miembros de la legislatura.

Cortes legislativas (legislative courts): Cortes especiales establecidas por el congreso para ciertos propósitos especializados, tales como la corte de corte marcial o la corte militar de apelaciones.

Grupo legislativo de un partido (legislative party caucus): Una organización de legisladores que pertenecen a un mismo partido político, y que se alía formalmente con un partido político.

Proceso legislativo (legislative process): El proceso que sigue una legislatura en la consideración y aprobación de legislación.

Difamación (libel): Declaraciones escritas falsas o declaraciones escritas que ponen la reputación de una persona en desprestigio.

Liberal (liberal): Filosofía política que se manifiesta a favor de una amplia intervención del gobierno en la economía y la creación de programas y servicios sociales y que favorece el activismo en la protección de los derechos de las mujeres, de los ancianos, de las minorías, y del medio ambiente.

Constitución liberal (liberal constitution): Una constitución que conforma la estructura básica de gobierno y luego le permite a la legislatura que ésta elabore los detalles del sistema a través de estatutos.

Libertarian (libertario): Persona que favorece una economía de mercado libre y la no interferencia gubernamental en las libertades individuales.

Libertad (liberty): La creencia que el gobierno no debe infringir los derechos individuales de una persona.

Veto por artículo (line-item veto): La autoridad otorgada a un ejecutivo de anular o suprimir (vetar) sólo aquella parte de un proyecto de ley aprobado por la legislatura y enviado a éste para su firma y proclamación con la cual no está de acuerdo. La legislatura puede eliminar el veto del ejecutivo (total o parcial) pero para eso requiere de dos terceras partes de cada cámara.

Cabildeo (lobbying): Las actividades de un grupo o de una organización que buscan influir sobre una cierta legislación y persuadir a líderes políticos de apoyar la posición del grupo.

Cabildero (lobbyist): Representante de un grupo de intereses (voluntario o contratado) que busca influir mediante la persuasión política sobre una legislación que beneficia a la organización.

Elección local (local election): La elección organizada por funcionarios electorales locales para elegir a funcionarios de los gobiernos locales.

Código de los Gobiernos Locales (Local government code): El código estatutario de Texas que contiene las leyes del estado que rigen a los gobiernos locales.

Reciprocidad legislativa (logrolling): El intercambio de votos; o sea el votar a favor de un proyecto de un colega a cambio de recibir su ayuda en la votación de un proyecto propio en el futuro.

Máquina (machine): Una organización dentro de un partido político que recluta sus miembros mediante el ofrecimiento de incentivos tangibles; una máquina se caracteriza por un alto grado de control de las actividades de los miembros.

Líder de la mayoría (majority leader): El líder de un partido político que controla la mayoría de las curules en la cámara de diputados o en el senado; es generalmente la segunda autoridad del partido, siguiéndole sólo al Presidente de la Càmara de Diputados o del Senado; se le considera una figura de gran poder político dentro de la cámara.

Partido de la mayoría (majority party): El partido político con mayor membresía en cada càmara del congreso.

Gobierno por mayoría (majority rule): La premisa de la democracia directa que reza que solamente las políticas que obtengan la mayoría del voto pueden ser hechas ley.

Administrador o gerente (manager): Un ejecutivo profesional empleado por el cabildo o la corte del condado para manejar las operaciones diarias de la entidad y recomendar cambios en las políticas públicas.

Mandato (mandate): Una orden, votada por los electores, de que los funcionarios electos lleven a cabo sus plataformas.

Destino manifiesto (manifest destiny): Teoría que sostiene que los Estados Unidos fueron escogidos por Dios para expandirse por toda Norteamérica hasta el Océano Pacífico.

Marbury v. Madison **(1803):** Por primera vez en su historia, la Suprema Corte de los Estados Unidos afirmó su poder de revisión judicial, al encontrar que parte del estatuto que creaba al sistema judicial del país era anticonstitucional.

Margen de error (mangin of error): La medida utilizada para medir la veracidad de una encuesta de opinión pública.

Período de revisión (markup): El proceso mediante el cual los miembros de las comisiones legislativas ofrecen modificaciones a un proyecto de ley antes de que éste sea presentado formalmente para someterse al voto de la legislatura.

El Plan Marshall (Marshall Plan): Programa nombrado en honor a su creador, el Secretario de Relaciones Exteriores de los Estados Unidos George C. Marshall (1947-1952). El programa consistía en una serie de préstamos a las naciones Europeas que

habían sido devastadas por la Segunda Guerra Mundial.

Medios de comunicación masiva (mass media): El conjunto de organizaciones con el propósito de recaudar información para luego diseminarla entre el público en general.

Peso por peso (matching funds): Las contribuciones monetarias hechas por el gobierno federal a los candidatos con el propósito de otorgarles a sus campañas un monto financiero igual al monto recaudado por las campañas mismas. Las contribuciones se determinan después de evaluar la cantidad de fondos privados recabados por cada candidato.

McCulloch v. *Maryland* **(1819):** La Suprema Corte de los Estados Unidos dictaminó que la política del gobierno federal de negarle a los gobiernos de los estados el derecho de imponer impuestos estatales a los bancos era constitucional. Con esta interpretación de la constitución, la Suprema Corte abrió la pauta para futuras interpretaciones de igual amplitud que permitirían una expansión de las facultades del gobierno federal.

Programa con prueba socioeconómica (means-tested program): Programa diseñado para ayudar a las personas cuyos ingresos económicos se encuentran por debajo del nivel considerado como la media.

Consultor de medios (media consultant): Un profesional contratado por negocios o campañas políticas con el fin de crear una imagen positiva ante los medios de comunicación (radio, televisión, prensa escrita, etc.).

Efectos de los medios (media effects): La influencia que tienen los medios de comunicación sobre la opinión pública.

Programa de salud pública (medicaid): Programa creado como parte del Seguro de Salud Pública. El programa es subsidiado por el gobierno federal de los Estados Unidos y provee asistencia económica a las personas con bajos recursos económicos para cubrir sus gastos de salud.

Seguro de Salud Pública (medicare): Programa federal mediante el cual se otorga asistencia médica y tratamiento hospitalario a personas mayores de 65 años de edad, aunque la cobertura es sólo parcial.

Mercantilismo (mercantilism): Una teoría económica que sostiene que el objetivo del Estado debe ser incrementar la riqueza monetaria de una nación a través del desarrollo de sus industrias comerciales; esta teoría funciona en la práctica mientras exista un comercio equitativo entre naciones.

Sistema de méritos (merit system): El sistema mediante el cual los empleos en el gobierno federal se clasifican en varios niveles y a cada funcionario público se le asigna un nivel correspondiente a su desempeño y competitividad laboral.

Elección intermedia (midterm election): Elección que ocurre a la mitad de un término presidencial.

Complejo militar-industrial (military-industrial complex): Una coalición de las fuerzas armadas y las fuerzas de seguridad de los Estados Unidos con empresas privadas clientelares con el propósito de sostener los presupuestos federales otorgados a éstas burocracias.

Líder de la minoría (minority leader): El líder del partido con el segundo número más alto de representantes electos en la Cámara de Diputados o en la Cámara de Senadores.

Partido de la minoría (minority party): El partido político con el segundo número más alto de representantes electos en cada cámara del congreso.

Los derechos Miranda (Miranda rights): Declaraciones que debe hacer un oficial al momento de arrestar a un sospechoso. El oficial tiene la obligación de informar al sospechoso de sus derechos constitucionales, los cuales son protegidos por la quinta enmienda de la constitución de los Estados Unidos. Los derechos del sospechoso incluyen el derecho a guardar silencio y el derecho a un abogado (proporcionado por la corte en caso de insolvencia económica).

Miranda vs. *Arizona* **(1966):** La Suprema Corte de los Estados Unidos dictaminó en este caso que cualquier sospechoso arrestado por cualquier delito tiene el derecho constitucional a permanecer en silencio y a tener un consejero legal (un abogado) a su lado en todo momento de proceso judicial. Además se dictaminó que al momento de su arresto, el policía debe informarle al sospechoso todos sus derechos.

Monarquía (monarchy): Una forma de gobierno en la cual el poder se concentra únicamente en los monarcas (de forma hereditaria) que gobiernan supuestamente por el bien común.

Política monetaria (monetary policy): Una forma de regulación o normatividad del gobierno federal mediante la cual se fija la distribución monetaria y las tasas de interés de la nación.

Dinero (money): Un sistema de intercambio de productos y servicios, el cual incluye el uso de algún tipo de moneda, billetes y depósitos bancarios.

Doctrina de Monroe (Monroe doctrine): Doctrina ideada por el presidente James Monroe en 1823. Esta doctrina dictaminaba que los Estados Unidos se opondrían a cualquier tipo de colonización en el hemisferio occidental por parte de las naciones Europeas.

Moralismo (moralism): La inclinación de mezclar la moralidad con la política exterior.

El periodismo de escándalo (muckraking): Una forma de periodismo practicada por primera vez a principios del siglo XX. La idea principal de esta ideología periodista es reformar la cultura gubernamental e industrial atrayendo la atención a hechos o conductas bochornosas.

Multilateralismo (multilateralism): La creencia que los Estados Unidos debe tomar en cuenta las opiniones de otras naciones antes de tomar decisiones en relación a su política exterior

Corporación Municipal (municipal corporation): Término legal utilizado para referirse al gobierno local en alguna ciudad, pueblo, condado, aldea, etc.

Corte municipal (municipal court): Corte de la ciudad con una jurisdicción limitada a sólo ciertos delitos menores.

Periodismo con enfoque local (narrowcasting): El enfocar una programación periodística a cierta audiencia en particular o a grupos específicos dentro de una sociedad.

Convención nacional (national convention): Una reunión casi meramente festiva que realizan los partidos políticos el año en que se llevan a cabo las elecciones presidenciales. El propósito principal de esta reunión de militantes partidistas es dar a conocer a los contendientes oficiales para la presidencia y la vicepresidencia.

Plataforma nacional del partido (national party platform): Una declaración de las metas generales y específicas de un partido, al igual que la filosofía de un partido político, promulgadas generalmente en la convención nacional.

Agencia de seguridad nacional (NSA): Agencia de inteligencia responsable de recabar información de una amplia variedad de fuentes, principalmente fuentes electrónicas por medio de descifrar códigos extranjeros.

Consejo de seguridad nacional (NSC): Agencia ejecutiva responsable de aconsejar al presidente sobre los acontecimientos relevantes a la seguridad nacional y a la política exterior de los Estados Unidos.

Derecho natural (natural law): Una doctrina que promulga que la sociedad debe ser gobernada por ciertos principios morales que forman parte de la naturaleza humana y como tal pueden ser entendidos por la razón.

Cláusula de lo necesario y apropiado (nessesary and proper clause): El párrafo final del Artículo I, Sección 8, de la constitución de los Estados Unidos. Este artículo da al Congreso la autoridad de aprobar todas las leyes que considere "necesarias y apropiadas" para llevar a cabo sus obligaciones de acuerdo a la constitución en la Constitución; también llamada la cláusula elástica.

Publicidad negativa (negative ad): Anuncios en radio, televisión, periódicos o en la Internet diseñados para atacar la plataforma política o el carácter del candidato opositor.

Red (network): Una asociación de las estaciones de difusión masiva (radio o televisión) que comparten su programación por medio de un arreglo financiero.

Nuevo Trato (New Deal): El nombre dado al programa de "recuperación y reforma" comenzada por Presidente Franklin D. Roosevelt en 1933 para sacar a los Estados Unidos de la Gran Depresión.

Nuevo federalismo (new federalism): Iniciativa que tiene que ver con la relación entre la federación y los estados propuesta por la administración de Ronald Reagan durante los años 80s. Esta iniciativa devolvió facultades administrativas a los gobiernos estatales.

Plan de Nueva Jersey (New Jersey Plan): Estructura de representación parlamentaria propuesta ante la asamblea constituyente de los Estados Unidos por un grupo de estados pequeños. Esta propuesta consistía en otorgar un voto a cada estado dentro de la legislatura federal, en hacer de las leyes aprobadas por el congreso la "ley suprema" de la nación, y en crear un poder judicial supremo con poderes limitados.

Nuevos medios de comunicación (new media): Nuevas tecnologías como la Internet que borran la línea divisoria entre los medios de comunicación tradicionales y los modernos y que crean nuevas oportunidades para la creación y diseminación de información.

New York Times Co. vs. *Sullivan* (1964): Caso en el que la Suprema Corte de los Estados Unidos dictaminó que alguien que acuso a otra persona de difamación, pero especialmente las figuras públicas como los artistas, etc., debe demostrar que hubo "malicia" o "dolo."

Medios de comunicación (news media): Medios de comunicación que proveen al público información noticiosa sobre temas de interés público.

Comisión 9/11 (9/11 Commission): La Comisión Nacional que se encargó de evaluar y calificar los acontecimientos terroristas del 11 de Septiembre en los Estados Unidos. La Comisión fue un grupo autorizado por el congreso y el Presidente George W. Bush en el 2002 para estudiar las circunstancias alrededor de los ataques terroristas del 11 de Septiembre del 2001, examinar la respuesta oficial del gobierno estadounidense, y dar recomendaciones sobre cómo prevenir y enfrentar futuros ataques terroristas.

Diecinueveava enmienda (nintheenth amendment): Enmienda a la constitución de los Estados Unidos que garantizó a las mujeres el derecho al voto.

Novena enmienda (ninth amendment): Parte de Declaración de los Derechos y Garantías Individuales que reza que "No por el hecho de que la Constitución enumera ciertos derechos ha de entenderse que niega o menosprecia otros que retiene el pueblo."

Doctrina Nixon (Nixon doctrine): Política ejecutiva ejercida al final de la guerra de Vietnam que predicaba que los Estados Unidos proporcionarían el armamento y el equipo militar a países que desearan continuar la guerra contra el comunismo, sin intervención directa de las fuerzas armadas de Estados Unidos.

Campaña de postulación o nominación (nomination campaign): Aquella parte de una campaña política que tiene como objetivo el ganar la elección interna o primaria de un partido político.

Organización no gubernamental (NGO): Una organización que no forma parte de un gobierno.

Programa no sujeto a pruebas socioeconómicas (non-means-based program): Programas, como el Programa del Seguro Social, en el cual los beneficios sociales que se proporcionan a una persona no están correlacionados al ingreso de ésta.

Asociación legislativa no partidista (nonparty legislative caucus): Una organización de legisladores que se basa en una cierta característica o interés común entre sus miembros y no en la afiliación partidista de éstos.

Acuerdo de Libre Comercio de Norteamérica (NAFTA): Acuerdo que promueve la libre circulación de mercancías y de servicios entre Canadá, México, y los Estados Unidos.

Organización del Tratado de Atlántico Norte (OTAN): El primer tratado militar realizado durante un período de paz en el cual los Estados Unidos se unió a otros países en una organización internacional (la OTAN) creada en 1949 con fines políticos y militares.

Extraoficialmente (off the record): Información proporcionada a un periodista bajo la condición de que no sea hecha pública.

Oficina del Manejo del Presupuesto (OMB): La oficina que prepara el presupuesto anual del presidente al igual el presupuesto de los departamentos ejecutivos, que provee pronósticos económicos, y que conduce análisis detallados de las cuentas públicas.

Oligarquía (oligarchy): Una forma de gobierno en la cual el derecho de participar en el gobierno se limita a un grupo de personas que poseen una cierta riqueza, un cierto estatus social, una posición militar, etc.

Información de trasfondo (on background): La información proporcionada a un periodista que puede ser atribuida públicamente a su fuente.

Oficialmente (on the record): Información proporcionada a un periodista que puede ser hecha pública y ser atribuida a su fuente, incluso citando el nombre de ésta.

Operaciones de mercado abierto (open market operations): La compra y venta de bonos del gobierno por el Banco de la Reserva Federal en los mercados financieros.

Elección interna o primaria abierta (open primary): Una elección interna de un partido político (para elegir candidatos) en la cual se permite que votantes no partidistas y a veces miembros de partidos opuestos puedan votar.

Partido organizacional (organizational party): Los trabajadores y activistas que sirven de personal a la organización formal del partido.

Jurisdicción original (original jurisdiction): La prerrogativa que posee una corte de aceptar o rechazar un caso antes de que éste proceda a otra corte. Las cortes de jurisdicción original determinan los hechos y datos esenciales de un dado caso mientras éste esté bajo su consideración.

Sobrerrepresentación y subrepresentación (overrepresentation and under-representation): Se dice de una situación en la cual los números de representantes de un grupo social en un cuerpo son más altos o más bajos, respectivamente, que los números de ese grupo en la población en general.

Vigilancia (oversight): Actividades de vigilancia y fiscalización por parte del congreso con respecto a las actividades de una agencia, un departamento, o una oficina de la burocracia.

Medios pagados (paid media): Anuncios propagandísticos comprados por la campaña política de un candidato.

Perdón o indulto (pardon): La facultad de un gobierno (generalmente del poder ejecutivo) de anular un veredicto emitido por una corte y de eliminar todas las sanciones y castigos que de ese veredicto se deriven.

Conferencia o junta del partido (party caucus or conference): Reunión formal de todos los miembros de un partido.

Identificación partidista (party identification): Afinidad personal de un ciudadano para con un partido político, expresada generalmente por su tendencia a votar por los candidatos de ese partido.

Partido en el electorado (party in electorate): Los votantes que se consideran parte de un partido político.

Realineación partidista (party realignment): El cambio generalizado en las preferencias partidistas en el electorado de un país que no varía mucho de una elección a otra sino que es más o menos permanente y cambia sólo con otra realineación partidista.

Patrocinador (patron): Persona que financia a un grupo o una actividad.

Patrocinio (patronage): Trabajos, concesiones, u otros favores especiales que se dan como recompensas a los amigos y a los aliados políticos a cambio de su apoyo.

Pearl Harbor (Pearl Harbor): Base naval en Hawaii, la cual fue atacada por Japón el 7 de diciembre de 1941, forzando la entrada de los Estados Unidos a la Segunda Guerra Mundial.

Ley Pendleton (Pendleton Act): Reforma que creó la Comisión de la Función Pública para administrar un sistema burocrático basado en el mérito individual. Esta ley clasificó todos los puestos federales en niveles, los cuales sirven para asignar los puestos públicos sólo a personas que demuestren su preparación y competencia para ocupar tal puesto mediante un examen. Esta misma ley penalizó que se obligara a aquellas personas nombradas a cualquier puesto público por un político a contribuir a un partido en particular.

Per diem (per diem): Viáticos, basados en el costo diario de vida, dados a un legislador o a un burócrata por cada día en el cual se encuentren viajando por algún asunto oficial.

Organización permanente del partido (permanent party organization): Organización del partido que funciona todo el año haciendo el trabajo necesario para mantener el partido.

Libertad personal (personal liberty): Una característica clave de la democracia de los Estados Unidos. Al principio, la libertad personal significaba el estar libre de cualquier interferencia gubernamental, pero hoy incluye una variedad de prácticas francas de cualquier discriminación por parte del gobierno.

Petición para la revisión (petition for review): Petición de reconsideración de una decisión tomada por una corte inferior hecha ante la Suprema Corte de Texas; esta la petición se concede si cuatro de los magistrados de la Suprema Corte de Texas votan a favor de reconsiderar la decisión.

Revisión fragmentaria (piecemeal revision): Cambios a la constitución llevados a cabo mediante enmiendas pequeñas a la misma constitución que agregan, abrogan, o modifican partes de ésta.

Plessy vs. *Ferguson* **(1896):** Plessy desafió un estatuto del Estado de Louisiana que requería que los ferrocarriles proporcionaran carros separados para los negros y para los blancos. La Suprema Corte dictaminó en este caso que la política "separados, aunque iguales" no violaba la cláusula de protección igualitaria bajo la enmienda catorce.

Ejecutivo plural (plural executive): Un tipo de poder ejecutivo en el cual las facultades de un gobierno se dividen entre varias agencias ejecutivas, cada una con su titular autónomo e independiente, en lugar de quedar todas bajo una sola persona. En este tipo de poder ejecutivo, el gobernador no nombra a la mayoría de los miembros del gabinete.

Veto de bolsillo (pocket veto): Situación en la cual un proyecto de ley se considera permanentemente vetado si el presidente no firma ni rechaza el proyecto de ley aprobado por el congreso y éste entra en receso dentro de diez días hábiles.

Adopción de políticas (policy adoption): La aprobación de una política pública por quienes tienen la autoridad de hacerlo, por ejemplo, una legislatura.

Evaluación de políticas (policy evaluation): El proceso de determinar si una política está produciendo los resultados deseados.

Formulación de políticas (policy formulation): El proceso mediante el cual se formulan políticas públicas adecuadas y dirigibles para mejorar o resolver problemas públicos.

Implementación de políticas (policy implementation): El proceso de llevar a cabo las propuestas formuladas para mejorar el bienestar público, proceso realizado por las agencias gubernamentales y las cortes.

Comité de Acción Política (PAC): Comité sancionado por la ley y oficialmente encargado de recaudar fondos para hacer campaña a favor de un candidato; estos fondos generalmente

pertenecen a un grupo y representan sus intereses en el proceso político.

Cultura política (political culture): Actitudes, creencias, y valores comúnmente compartidos con respecto a la manera en que debe funcionar un gobierno.

Igualdad política (political equality): La idea que todos los ciudadanos deben participar igualmente en el gobierno; este principio queda encerrado en la frase "una persona, un voto".

Ideología política (political ideology): Un sistema coherente de valores y de creencias que tienen ciertos individuos con respecto a las funciones y el alcance de un gobierno.

Partido político (political party): Un grupo de funcionarios, candidatos, activistas, y votantes que se identifican con una filosofía y organización política y que quieren elegir a puestos públicos a personas del grupo.

Socialización política (political socialization): El proceso mediante el cual los individuos adquieren sus creencias y valores políticos.

Político (politico): Papel que juegan los representantes electos a puestos públicos quienes actúan como administradores o como delegados (dependiendo del tema) en representación de los votantes.

Política (politics): El estudio del a quién le toca qué, cómo y cuándo o el proceso mediante el cual se toman las decisiones sobre el reparto de los recursos de una sociedad.

Impuesto de casilla (poll tax): Impuesto que se utilizaba en los estados del sur de los Estados Unidos y que debía ser pagado al llegar a la casilla, antes de que un votante pudiera ejercer su derecho al voto.

Encuestador (pollster): Un profesional que mide la opinión pública que sirve como guía a las campañas políticas.

Consentimiento popular (popular consent): La idea que los gobernantes obtienen su autoridad del consentimiento del pueblo.

Soberanía popular (popular sovereignty): La noción de que la autoridad en una sociedad recae en el pueblo.

Populistas (populists): Se dice de aquellos individuos que apoyan la igualdad entre los ciudadanos y promueven valores y conductas tradicionales.

Gordo (pork): Legislación que permite que los miembros del congreso traigan a su distrito o estado el recursos en forma de programas y obras públicas, tales como bases militares; en general, son recursos designados a programas que benefician al distrito o estado de un miembro del congreso directamente.

Anuncio positivo (positive ad): Propaganda de algún candidato que tiene la intención de resaltar las credenciales o las cosas buenas del candidato, su familia, sus valores, sus creencias, o sus propuestas, sin hacer referencia a su contrincante.

Doctrina Powell (Powell doctrine): Doctrina basada en el principio "todo o nada" con respecto a la intervención militar en otro país. Esta doctrina fue inventada por Colin Powell, quien argumentaba que si se iba a utilizar la fuerza militar, ésta debería ser masiva para lograr una victoria rápida, decisiva. La doctrina predica también que toda intervención debe tener una estrategia de salida antes de iniciar la intervención.

Pragmatismo (pragmatism): La política de aprovechar una situación para beneficio nacional.

Precedente (precedent): Decisión judicial previa que sirve como normatividad fundamental para casos subsecuentes de naturaleza similar.

Presidente de casilla (precint chairperson): Líder de un partido en una casilla electoral.

Convención seccional (precint convention): Reunión de los miembros de un partido político en la sección territorial que cubre una casilla electoral con el motivo de seleccionar delegados y adoptar resoluciones.

Ataque preventivo (preemption): Un concepto derivado de la "cláusula de la supremacía" que se encuentra en la constitución (Artículo VI) y que le da al gobierno nacional la prerrogativa de cancelar una decisión de un gobierno local o estatal o de actuar con anticipación a la toma de decisiones de los gobiernos locales o estatales.

Presidente del Senado de Texas (President of the Texas Senate): El vicegobernador de Texas al momento de fungir en su papel constitucional como presidente del senado del estado.

Presidente pro tempore (president pro tempore): El oficial electo que preside sobre el senado de Texas y que es generalmente el miembro con mayor antigüedad del partido que tiene la mayoría de las curules.

Rueda de prensa (press briefing): Una sesión relativamente restringida entre un secretario de prensa o un ayudante de éste y representantes de los medios de comunicación.

Conferencia de prensa (press conference): Una sesión sin restricciones entre un funcionario público y representantes de los medios de comunicación.

Comunicado de prensa (press release): Un documento que ofrece un comentario o una posición oficial y que se hace llegar a los miembros de los medios de comunicación.

Secretario de prensa (press secretary): Titular de las actividades de comunicación oficial de una agencia del gobierno o de un político ante los periodistas y que da los informes oficiales al público en general sobre algún tema.

Elección primaria o interna (primary election): Elección en la cual los votantes deciden cuál de los precandidatos de un partido va a ser el candidato oficial del partido en la elección general.

Medios impresos (print media): La forma tradicional de los medios de comunicación que abarca los periódicos, las revistas, los boletines de noticias, los semanarios, etc.

Censura anticipada (prior restraint): Doctrina constitucional que le permite al gobierno prohibir a los ciudadanos expresar o imprimir sus ideas. A este concepto se le considera generalmente como una violación de la primera enmienda constitucional.

La cláusula de privilegios e inmunidad (privileges and immunities clause): Parte del Artículo IV de la constitución que garantiza que los ciudadanos de cada estado tengan los mismos privilegios e inmunidad que los ciudadanos de los demás estados.

Representación proporcional (proportional representation): Un sistema de votación que reparte las curules legislativas según el porcentaje del voto recibido por cada partido político.

Juicio prospectivo (prospective judgment): Evaluación de un candidato hecha por un votante que se basa en lo que éste promete hacer sobre un tema específico si es electo al puesto público por el cual compite.

Pro-tempore (pro-tempore): Un legislador que sirve temporalmente como líder legislativo ante la ausencia del presidente del senado o del presidente de la cámara de diputados.

Consejos públicos (public counsels): Funcionarios designados por el gobernador para representar al público ante ciertas agencias gubernamentales, principalmente aquellas agencias reguladoras.

Fondos públicos (public funds): Financiación de campañas políticas con impuestos de los contribuyentes que se dan a los candidatos que cumplan con ciertos requisitos.

Grupo de interés público (public interest group): Una organización que busca un bien colectivo que no beneficie a los miembros de la organización sino a todo el público.

Opinión pública (public opinion): Lo que piensa el público en general acerca de un tema o temas en un dado momento.

Encuestas de opinión pública (public opinion polls): Entrevistas hechas a los ciudadanos que se utilizan para medir el sentir de la población con respecto algún tema en particular.

Política pública (public policy): Una acción o programa del gobierno diseñado para hacerle frente a un problema o preocupación de la ciudadanía.

Comisión de servicios públicos (public unity commission): Una comisión de tiempo completo con tres miembros pagados y que es designada por el gobernador para regir los servicios públicos que provee el gobierno de Texas.

Encuestas propaganda (push polls): Una "pregunta" diseñada de tal manera que proporciona un dato negativo del contrincante con el propósito de predisponer al encuestado en contra de éste.

Cuasi-judicial (quasi-judicial): Audiencia semi-judicial; cuerpo autorizado para llevar a cabo audiencias y emitir veredictos.

Quorum (quorum): El número mínimo de miembros requerido para conducir una sesión (como en un cuerpo legislativo).

Redada (raiding): Un movimiento organizado por los votantes de un partido con el fin de influenciar los resultados de una elección interna en otro partido.

Comisión Ferroviaria (Railroad Commission): Una comisión de tiempo completo compuesta de tres miembros electos por el pueblo y a quienes se les paga, cuya misión es regular la industria del petróleo, el gas, y algunas agencias del transporte.

Muestreo al azar (random sampling): Un método para seleccionar de un grupo a un cierto número de encuestados aleatoriamente y en el cual cada miembro del grupo tiene las mismas posibilidades de ser seleccionado.

Doctrina Reagan (Reagan Doctrine): Política exterior que sostenía que los Estados Unidos proporcionarían ayuda militar a los grupos guerrilleros anticomunistas que luchaban contra gobiernos amigos de la Unión Soviética.

Repartición de curules entre los estados (reapportionment): La reasignación del número de curules de la cámara de representantes entre los estados de acuerdo a su población total después de cada censo decenal.

Revocación de mandato (recall): Un proceso electoral en el cual los votantes pueden solicitar que se lleve acabo un voto para quitar a un funcionario electo con el cual están inconformes.

Recesión (recession): Una declive a corto plazo en la economía nacional que ocurre al caer las inversiones y la producción de bienes, lo cual motiva un aumento en el desempleo.

Redistritar (redistrict): El rediseñar los límites de los distritos electorales del congreso.

Redistritación (redistricting): El rediseño de los distritos electorales del congreso con el propósito de ajustarlos a los cambios en la población o para obtener una ventaja política al ganar un mayor número de curules.

Referéndum (referendum): Una elección en la cual la legislatura en un estado hace una propuesta de ley a los votantes del estado para que sean éstos los que directamente la aprueben.

Elección primaria regional (regional primary): Un sistema en el cual el país sería dividido en cinco o seis áreas geográficas y todos los estados en cada región celebrarían sus elecciones primarias presidenciales en un mismo día.

Sesión regular (regular session): La sesión bienal de 140 días de la legislatura de Texas que comienza en enero de los años nones.

Normas burocráticas (regulations): Reglas que crea la burocracia, basadas en la legislación del congreso, y que gobiernan la operación de un programa del gobierno; éstas tienen el mismo peso que la ley.

República (republic): Un gobierno nacido del consentimiento del pueblo gobernado; una democracia representativa o indirecta.

Tierra de reserva (reservation land): Porciones territoriales designadas mediante un tratado como tierras bajo la autoridad de una nación indígena, la cual está exenta de la mayoría de las leyes y de los impuestos del estado en donde se encuentra.

Poderes reservados o policíacos (reserved or police powers): Poderes reservados a los estados por la décima enmienda. Estos poderes o facultades se basan en la idea de que cada estado tiene el derecho de legislar con respecto a la salud pública y al bienestar de sus ciudadanos.

Requisitos de reserva (reserve requirements): Los requisitos que impone el gobierno a los bancos de que una porción de sus depósitos debe quedar guardada para respaldar los préstamos hechos por el mismo banco.

Juicio retrospectivo (retrospective judgment): La evaluación que hace un votante con respecto al desempeño del partido político que ostenta el poder en el momento de una elección.

Revisionista (revisionist): Un miembro de una convención constitucional que no acepta más que una revisión total de la constitución.

Puerta que gira (revolving door): Un intercambio de personal que sucede entre intereses privados y reguladores públicos—o sea entre compañías privadas y agencias gubernamentales.

Derecho a la privacidad (right to privacy): El derecho de permanecer en soledad sin interferencia gubernamental; doctrina judicial que abarca la decisión de una persona de utilizar anticonceptivos o de practicarse un aborto.

Roe v. Wade **(1973):** Caso de la Suprema Corte de los Estados Unidos en el cual se dictaminó que el derecho de una mujer al aborto está protegido por el derecho a la privacidad, el cual está garantizado por la constitución en la enmienda catorceava.

Corolario Roosevelt (Roosevelt Corollary): El concepto desarrollado por el presidente Theodore Roosevelt a principios del Siglo XX. Este concepto promulgaba que los Estados Unidos tenían la obligación de asegurar la estabilidad de América Latina y el Caribe.

Normar (rule making): Un proceso administrativo, burocrático, cuasi-legislativo que tiene las características de un acto legislativo porque hace reglas derivadas de la ley y que tienen el mismo peso que la ley de la que se derivan.

Regla de cuatro (rule of four): Por lo menos cuatro magistrados de la Suprema Corte de los Estados Unidos deben estar de acuerdo antes de que a un caso se le pueda dar una audiencia ante la Corte.

Desempate en elección primaria (runoff primary): Una segunda elección primaria con fines de desempatar la contienda entre los dos precandidatos que recibieron el mayor número de votos en la primera ronda.

Error de muestreo o margen de error (sampling error or margin of error): Una medida de la exactitud de una encuesta de opinión pública.

Segundo Congreso Continental (Second Continental Congress): Junta convocada en Filadelfia el 10 de mayo de 1775 en la cual se decidiría la creación de un ejército y el nombramiento de George Washington de Virginia como el primer comandante en jefe de las fuerzas armadas.

Segunda lectura (second reading): La constitución de Texas requiere que se le den tres lecturas a un proyecto de ley en la legislatura; la segunda lectura es cuando se lleva acabo la discusión y se proponen enmiendas ante el pleno.

Realineación secular (secular realignment): El cambio gradual de las coaliciones que conforman las bases de un partido político, basado más en cambios demográficos que en choques al sistema político.

Comisión selecta o especial (select or special committe): Comisión temporal creada con un propósito específico, tal como conducir una investigación o un estudio especial.

Incorporación selectiva (selective incorporation): Una doctrina judicial en cual se dice que la catorceava enmienda no obliga a los estados a respetar todas las protecciones que otorgan las garantías individuales, sino solamente algunas.

Regla de los dos tercios del senado (Senate two-thirds rule): Regla en el senado de Texas que requiere que cada proyecto de ley obtenga dos tercios del voto de los senadores presentes para poder suspender el orden regular de la sesión y debatir el proyecto.

Cortesía senatorial (senatorial courtesy): Proceso por el cual los presidentes, al seleccionar a jueces de la corte de distrito, difieren a los senadores de su propio partido que representan el estado donde ocurre la vacante; también el proceso por el cual un gobernador, al seleccionar a una persona a quien va a nombrar a un puesto público, difiere al senador estatal del distrito donde el candidato reside.

Antigüedad (seniority): Tiempo de servicio continuo en una comisión.

Separación de poderes (separation of powers): Una manera de dividir el poder para evitar la centralización de éste. En los Estados Unidos el poder del gobierno esta dividido en tres partes: el legislativo (la cámara de representantes y el senado); el ejecutivo (el presidente); y el judicial (los jueves en las cortes federales).

Decimoséptima enmienda (seventeenth amendment): Ordena que los senadores de la república sean electos directamente por el voto popular y no por las legislaturas de los estados.

Escándalo de Sharpstown (Sharpstown Scandal): El escándalo de corrupción de 1969 a 1972 que resultó en un veredicto de culpable de soborno del presidente y de otros miembros de la cámara de diputados; sirvió de base para las reformas de 1973.

Rebelión de Shays (Shays rebellion): Una rebelión en 1786 en la cual un ejército de 1,500 campesinos molestos dirigidos por Daniel Shays marcharon sobre Springfield, Massachusetts. Shays tomó el control de la corte estatal con el propósito de prevenir que sus tierras fueran rematadas por la corte para pagar sus deudas.

Alguacil (sheriff): Funcionario público electo como el principal oficial que aplica la ley a nivel de un condado.

Resolución simple (simple resolution): Un documento legislativo que propone una acción del cuerpo legislativo que le compete solamente a la cámara en la cual se presentó dicho documento; por ejemplo, una resolución para adoptar o modificar las reglas de la cámara o para dar un reconocimiento a un ciudadano.

Distrito uninominal (single member district): Un sistema de elección en el cual cada legislador es electo por y representa a un solo distrito.

Décimosexta enmienda (sixteenth amendment): Enmienda que autorizó al congreso de los Estados Unidos decretar un impuesto sobre el ingreso personal.

Sexta enmienda (sixth amendment): Parte de la Declaración de los Derechos y Garantías Individuales que precisa los requisitos básicos del derecho procesal que las cortes federales deben seguir en cualquier proceso penal. Éstos incluyen el derecho a un juicio expedito y público, a jurados imparciales, a llevar a cabo el juicio en el estado donde el crimen fue cometido, a ser informado de los cargos que se imputan, al derecho de enfrentar al acusador, y a obtener testigos fiables, y a tener un abogado presente en todo momento.

Difamación (slander): Declaraciones habladas de índole falsa que arruinan el carácter público de una persona.

Capital social (social capital): Las innumerables relaciones entre los individuos de una sociedad que facilitan la resolución de los problemas de la comunidad mediante la acción colectiva coordinada.

Conservador social (social conservative): Un individuo que cree que las enseñanzas morales tradicionales se deben apoyar y fomentar desde el gobierno.

Contrato social (social contract): Un acuerdo entre el pueblo y el gobierno en el cual el pueblo da su consentimiento a ser gobernado.

Teoría del Contrato Social (social contract theory): La creencia que las personas son libres e iguales por derecho divino y que se requiere que toda persona dé su consentimiento para ser gobernada; esta teoría fue formulada por John Locke y fue muy influyente en la declaración de la independencia de los Estados Unidos.

Regulación social (social regulation): La regulación del gobierno a la calidad y seguridad de los productos de consumo así como a las condiciones bajo las cuales tales productos se almacenan y producen.

Ley de la Seguridad Social (Social Security Act): Ley aprobada en 1935, la cual estableció el sistema de pensiones (Seguridad Social) y programas de ayuda a los necesitados, a los niños, a los desempleados, etc.

Política de asistencia social (social welfare policy): Los programas del gobierno diseñados para mejorar la calidad de vida en los Estados Unidos.

Dinero suave (soft money): Contribuciones financieras políticas no reguladas por la ley que donan personas o comités políticos a través las oficinas de los partidos locales y estatales.

Abogado General (solicitor general): La cuarta persona en rango dentro del poder judicial; es responsable de dirigir todas las apelaciones a nombre de los Estados Unidos en la Suprema Corte.

Inmunidad soberana (sovereign immunity): El derecho de un gobierno o nación de no ser sometido a los procesos legales de otro país, a menos que éste así lo autorice. Bajo la undécima enmienda, todos los estados se consideran soberanos.

Guerra contra España (Spanish-American War): Guerra en1898 contra España debido a las políticas y a la presencia españolas en Cuba. Los Estados Unidos lograron conquistar varios territorios antes pertenecientes a España.

Presidente de la Cámara de Diputados (Speaker of the House): Es el único oficial de la Cámara de Diputados o Representantes mencionado específicamente en la constitución; es electo al principio de la primera sesión del congreso por todos los miembros de la cámara; tradicionalmente es un miembro del partido de la mayoría.

Presidente de la Cámara de Diputados de Texas (Speaker of the Texas House): El representante o diputado estatal que es electo por sus compañeros para fungir como el líder oficial de la cámara en tu totalidad.

Lugartenientes del Presidente de la Cámara de Diputados (Speaker's lieutenants): Diputados que forman parte del equipo del Presidente de la Cámara de Diputados. Asisten al presidente en el mantenimiento el orden en la cámara formal o informalmente y fungen como presidentes de las comisiones.

Contienda para Presidente de la Cámara de Diputados (Speaker's race): La campaña para determinar quién será el presidente de la Cámara de Diputados de Texas.

Equipo del Presidente de la Cámara de Diputados (Speaker's team): El equipo de liderazgo en la Cámara de Diputados o Representantes. Consiste del Presidente de la Cámara y sus aliados, a los cuales el presidente designa como jefes de las comisiones legislativas.

Elección especial (special election): Una elección realizada a destiempo para llenar un puesto público vacante.

Sesión especial (special session): Una sesión legislativa de Texas de hasta treinta días, convocada por el gobernador, durante el período en el cual la legislatura se encuentra en receso.

Sistema de patrocinio (spoil systems): El despido masivo de servidores públicos en cuanto hay un cambio de partido político en el poder. Éstos son reemplazados por lo general con miembros del nuevo partido en el poder.

Anuncio al momento (spot ad): Anuncio en el cual se da cobertura al nombre de un candidato en televisión por sesenta, treinta, o diez segundos.

Términos escalonados (staggered terms): Períodos de servicio público que no están empatados sino que comienzan y terminan en distintos tiempos, de modo que un gobernador no puede generalmente tener control de una mayoría del cuerpo legislativo durante mucho tiempo porque por lo menos algunos miembros de éste terminan su período de servicio.

Congreso de la Ley de las Estampillas (stamp act congress): Reunión de representantes de nueve de las trece colonias llevada a cabo en la Ciudad de Nueva York en 1765. En esta reunión los representantes redactaron un documento a enviar al Rey de Inglaterra para demostrarle cómo habían sido violados sus derechos.

Comisión Permanente (standing committee): Se refiere a la comisión legislativa a la cual envían un proyecto de ley para su consideración preliminar.

Stare decisis (stare decisis): Término del sistema judicial que se refiera al nivel de confianza que se tiene en una decisión anterior o precedente judicial para que éste sirva de base para formular decisiones en casos nuevos.

Comisión de Educación del Estado (State Board of Education): Comisión que consta de quince miembros electos para fijar la política educativa del estado. La comisión tiene también facultades limitadas de supervisión sobre la Agencia de la Educación de Texas y los distritos escolares del estado.

Convención Estatal (state convention): La reunión de los miembros del partido para adoptar la plataforma de éste y para elegir al comité ejecutivo y al presidente del partido y, en un año donde hay una elección presidencial, para elegir a los delegados a la convención nacional y a quienes serán miembros del Colegio Electoral.

Comité ejecutivo del estado (state executive committee): Comité de un partido político que consta de sesenta y dos miembros, el cual toma las decisiones del partido entre convenciones estatales.

Presidente Estatal de Partido (state party chair person): Líder del partido en el estado.

Convención senatorial de distrito (state senatorial district convention): Reunión del partido cuando un solo condado es parte de dos o más distritos senatoriales.

Constitución estatutaria (statutory constitution): Constitución que incorpora provisiones detalladas para limitar los poderes del gobierno.

Muestreo estratificado (stratified sampling): Una variación del muestreo al azar. En este tipo de muestreo se utilizan los datos del censo nacional para dividir al país en cuatro regiones de muestreo. El siguiente paso es seleccionar aleatoriamente un número de condados y de áreas metropolitanas muestra en proporción a la población nacional total.

Sondeos rápidos (straw polls): Encuestas rápidas y poco científicas que calibran la opinión pública sobre una variedad de temas y de políticas públicas.

Construccionista estricto (strict constructionist): Una filosofía legal que predica que cualquier intento de interpretar o leer la constitucional debe apegarse a las intenciones originales de los fundadores de los Estados Unidos.

Escrutinio estricto (strict scrutiny): Un estándar de indagación y examen utilizado por la Suprema Corte para determinar la validez constitucional de una práctica que se encuentra bajo cuestionamiento.

Alcalde Fuerte y Cabildo (strong mayor-council): Una forma de gobierno local en la cual el alcalde tiene poderes fuertes para gobernar la ciudad, mediante sus facultades sobre el personal y los departamentos del gobierno; en este sistema el alcalde también es miembro activo del cabildo.

Proceso debido sustancial (substantive due process): Interpretación judicial a la quinta y catorceava enmiendas de la constitución en donde se protege a los ciudadanos de leyes arbitrarias o injustas.

Sucesión (succession): La declaración constitucional que dice que el vicegobernador puede asumir la gubernatura si el puesto estuviera vacante.

Movimiento del sufragio (suffrage movement): El movimiento del derecho al voto para las mujeres que ocurrió en los Estados Unidos de 1890 a 1920.

Ley de la Puesta del Sol (sunset law): Ley que fija una fecha para que expire un programa o una regulación a menos que sea reautorizada por la legislatura correspondiente.

Superdelegado (superdelegate): Delegado de la convención nacional del Partido Demócrata que es generalmente un funcionario electo o una figura importante del partido.

Cláusula de la supremacía (supremacy clause): Porción del Artículo VI de la constitución de los Estados Unidos que establece que las leyes federales son la suprema ley de la nación, es decir, son superiores al resto de las leyes aprobadas por los estados o por cualquier otra subdivisión de gobierno.

Clasificación sospechosa (suspect classification): Categoría o clase de individuos, tal como la raza, que inmediatamente provoca un mayor nivel de escrutinio por parte de la Suprema Corte.

Discurso simbólico (symbolic speech): Símbolos, muestras, y otros métodos de expresión generalmente también considerados protegidos por la primera enmienda.

Agenda sistémica (systematic agenda): Todos los temas de interés público que exigen la atención gubernamental; una agenda a discutir.

Taliban (Taliban): El gobierno islámico fundamentalista de Afganistán que proporcionó el entrenamiento a terroristas para al-Qaeda.

Tarifas (tariffs): Impuestos sobre las importaciones destinados a elevar los ingresos del gobierno y a proteger a las industrias nacionales.

Tejano (tejanos): Texanos con orígenes mexicanos.

Organización temporal del partido (temporary party organization): Organización de un partido político que existe por un tiempo limitado e incluye varios niveles de convenciones.

Décima enmienda (tenth amendment): Parte de los derechos y garantías individuales de la constitución que reitera que los poderes no delegados al gobierno nacional ni prohibidos a los estados pertenecen a los estados o al pueblo.

Límites de elección (term limits): Restricciones que existen en algunos estados sobre el número de veces que un individuo puede desempeñar sus servicios en puestos públicos electos.

Credo de Texas (Texas Creed): Un sistema de ideas (basadas principalmente en el individualismo y la libertad) que rigen la política y el gobierno del Estado de Texas.

Asociación de Condados de Tejas (Texas Association of Counties): Asociación profesional y brazo de cabildeo de los gobiernos de los condados del estado.

Comisión Texana sobre la Calidad Ambiental (Texas Commission on the Environment): Nombre que se le dio en el 2002 a la antes Comisión para la Conservación de los Recursos Naturales de Texas.

Corte Suprema de Texas para Casos Criminales (Texas Court of Criminal Appeals): Corte del último recurso en casos tipificados como un delito o crimen grave.

Agencia de Educación de Texas (Texas Education Agency): La agencia del estado que supervisa a los distritos escolares locales y reparte fondos del estado a aquellos que lo necesiten.

Liga Municipal de Texas (Texas Municipal League): Asociación profesional y brazo de cabildeo de los gobiernos locales en Texas.

Guardabosques de Texas (Texas Rangers): Una milicia montada que se formó para proporcionar orden a lo largo de la frontera con México.

Secretario de Estado de Texas (Texas Secretary of State): El funcionario del estado designado por el gobernador para que se encargue de mantener los archivos del estado, por ejemplo, las leyes del estado, las estadísticas referentes a éste, datos y registros sobre las elecciones, las notificaciones públicas, y las cartas corporativas.

Suprema Corte de Texas (Texas Supreme Court): Corte de último recurso en casos civiles y juveniles.

Thinktank (thinktank): Institución que reúne a investigadores y académicos que estudian las políticas públicas de un gobierno, para luego producir ideas y hacer recomendaciones a estos mismos gobiernos.

Tercera lectura (third reading): La constitución de Texas requiere tres lecturas a un proyecto de ley en la legislatura; la tercera lectura es la última lectura en una cámara antes del voto, a menos que el proyecto provenga de la otra cámara con enmiendas.

Decimotercera enmienda (thirteenth amendment): Una de las tres enmiendas aprobadas después de la Guerra Civil; la enmienda prohíbe la esclavitud en los Estados Unidos.

Acuerdo de los Tres-Quintos (Three-fifths Compromise): Acuerdo alcanzado en la convención constituyente que estipulaba que cada esclavo debía ser contado como tres quintos de una persona, con el propósito de determinar la población total para establecer la representación en la Cámara de Diputados de los Estados Unidos.

Voto cruzado (ticket-split): Votar por candidatos de diversos partidos políticos en una misma elección.

Título IX (Title IX): Disposiciones legislativas de 1972 que prohíben que las instituciones educativas reciban fondos federales si discriminan contra estudiantes del sexo femenino en sus programas deportivos.

Totalitarismo (totalitarianismo): Una forma de gobierno en la cual todo el poder recae en un líder que gobierna según su interés propio y sin el respeto para los derechos y garantías individuales.

Encuestas de seguimiento (tracking polls): Encuestas continuas que le permiten a una campaña política monitorear la variación en el apoyo del público en general.

Asociación comercial (trade association): Un grupo u organización que representa a una industria específica.

Cortes (trial courts): Cortes con jurisdicción original, es decir, donde comienza un caso.

Juicio *de novo* (trial *de novo*): Juicio que se vuelve a llevar a cabo, lo cual se hace necesario debido a una apelación interpuesta por una corte que no es la corte donde el juicio se llevó a cabo originalmente.

Doctrina Truman (Truman Doctrine): Política de los Estados Unidos iniciada en 1947 predicada sobre el compromiso de los Estados Unidos de proporcionar ayuda económica y asistencia militar a los países que luchaban contra regímenes comunistas.

Fideicomisario (trustee): Dícese del papel de los representantes del pueblo electos, porque escuchan a los ciudadanos que representan para luego utilizar su mejor juicio y tomar decisiones políticas y legislativas.

Participación electoral (turnout): La porción del electorado en edad de votar y que así lo hizo.

Vigesimoquinta enmienda (twenty-fifth amendment): Enmienda constitucional adoptada en 1967 para establecer las formas de elegir al presidente y al vicepresidente. A su vez la enmienda establece los procedimientos a seguir en caso de que el presidente quede inhabilitado.

Vigesimosegunda enmienda (twenty-second amendment): Enmienda constitucional adoptada en 1951 con el propósito de evitar que un presidente sirva más de dos términos (de cuatro años) o más de diez años si el presidente obtuvo la presidencia por la muerte o el enjuiciamiento político de su predecesor.

Participación política poco convencional (unconventional political participation): Participación política que procura influenciar el proceso político con medidas inusuales o extremas, tales como protestas y boicoteos.

Mandatos sin fondos (unfunded mandates): Leyes nacionales que ordenan a los estados o a los gobiernos locales a seguir reglas o normas federales (tales como estándares limpios del aire o del agua) sin darles también algún financiamiento federal para pagar el costo de satisfacer estos requisitos.

Unilateralismo (unilateralism): Una política nacional que consiste en el actuar sin consultar a otros gobiernos.

Sistema unitario (unitary system): Sistema del gobierno donde los gobiernos locales y regionales derivan se autoridad de un gobierno nacional fuerte.

Regla de unidad (unit rule): Práctica tradicional dentro de un partido político bajo la cual la mayoría de la delegación de un estado puede forzar a la minoría a votar por un candidato.

Naciones Unidas (O.N.U): Organización gubernamental internacional creada poco antes el final de la Segunda Guerra Mundial para garantizar la seguridad de las naciones y promover el bienestar económico, político, y social.

Los Estados Unidos. **vs.** *Nixon* **(1974):** Decisión de la Suprema Corte de los Estados Unidos que dictaminó que no hay existía un "privilegio ejecutivo" constitucional absoluto que le permita al presidente rechazar una orden judicial que le ordena entregar al poder judicial información necesaria en un proceso penal.

Veto (veto): El acto y efecto formal (constitucional) del ejecutivo de rechazar proyectos de ley aprobados por ambas cámaras del cuerpo legislativo.

Poder de veto (veto power): La autoridad formal (constitucional) del ejecutivo de rechazar proyectos de ley aprobados por ambas cámaras del cuerpo legislativo.

Guerra de Vietnam(Vietnam War): Entre 1965 y 1973, los Estados Unidos desplegaron 500,000 tropas a Vietnam para intentar evitar que Vietnam del Norte tomara el control sobre Vietnam del Sur; el esfuerzo falló pero el conflicto causó divisiones importantes y polarizó a la población de los Estados Unidos.

Plan Virginia (Virginia Plan): El primer plan general para la constitución, propuesto por James Madison y Edmund Randolph durante la convención constituyente. Sus puntos dominantes eran una legislatura bicameral, un ejecutivo electo por la legislatura, y un poder judicial también nombrado por la legislatura.

Propaganda política zonificada (voter canvass): El proceso mediante el cual una campaña política se pone en contacto con el electorado, repartiendo volantes informativos entre la población, llamando por teléfono a los electores, o yendo a los domicilio de los votantes.

Guerra contra el Terrorismo (War against Terrorism): Iniciada por presidente George W. Bush después de los ataques del 11 de Septiembre para erradicar el terrorismo en el mundo, utilizando una combinación de diplomacia y fuerza militar. En los Estados Unidos, el presidente propuso cambios al aparato de la seguridad nacional, a leyes de actividades bancarias, y a otros aspectos de la vida nacional con el mismo motivo.

Ley de las Facultades de Guerra (War Powers Act): Ley aprobada por el congreso en 1973; limita al presidente en el despliegue de tropas en ultramar a un período del sesenta días en tiempos de paz (que puede ser extendido hasta treinta días adicionales para permitir su retiro) a menos que el congreso dé explícitamente su aprobación por un período más largo.

Sistema de Alcalde débil y Cabildo Fuerte (weak mayor-council): Una forma de gobierno de una ciudad en la cual el alcalde no tiene ningún poder por encima de los miembros del cabildo.

Armas de la destrucción total (weapons of mass destruction): Armas biológicas, químicas, y nucleares, que presentan una amenaza importante a la seguridad internacional.

Azote o látigo (whip): Uno de varios diputados/senadores que mantienen disciplinados a todos los miembros de su partido político, preparan resúmenes de actividades, y en general actúan como comunicadores dentro de su partido.

Ganador toma-todo (winner take all sysyem): Un sistema electoral en el cual el partido que recibe por lo menos un voto más que cualquier otro partido gana la elección.

Servicio noticioso (wire service): Un servicio de entrega electrónica de noticias recabadas por los corresponsales de una compañía noticiosa, enviadas a todos los medios que compran el servicio.

Banco mundial (World Bank): Organización intergubernamental internacional creada poco antes del fin de la Segunda Guerra Mundial que da los préstamos a las naciones para proyectos para el desarrollo económico.

Organización del comercio mundial (World Trade Organization): Organización intergubernamental internacional creada en 1995 que promueve negociaciones multilaterales para reducir las trabas al comercio internacional y que resuelve conflictos comerciales entre las naciones.

Orden Judicial *certiorari* (writ of certiorari): Una orden de una corte superior que solicita los archivos pertenecientes a un caso juzgado en una corte inferior porque va a revisar el caso en apelación.

Orden Judicial *Habeas Corpus* (writ of habeas corpus): Un orden judicial en el cual un juez requiere que las autoridades demuestren que han detenido a una persona de manera legal; el juez puede liberar al preso si el gobierno no demuestra ante el juez que hay razones para detenerlo. Una orden judicial de habeas corpus implica que los presos tienen ciertos derechos, tales como el saber qué cargos se les están imputando.

Periodismo amarillista (yellow journalism): Una forma de periodismo en boga a finales del Siglo XIX que cubría los acontecimientos con caricaturas, fotos, colores, y palabras muy sensacionalistas y que sobresimplificó la cobertura de noticias.

Notes

Chapter 1

1. Thomas Byrne Edsall, "The Era of Bad Feelings," *Civilization* (March/April 1996): 37.

2. Jack C. Plano and Milton Greenberg, *The American Political Dictionary*, 6th ed. (New York: Holt, Rinehart and Winston, 1982).

3. Frank Michelman, "The Republican Civic Tradition," *Yale Law Journal* 97 (1988): 1503.

4. U.S. Agency for International Development, "Agency Objectives: Civil Society," November 16, 2001.

5. Thomas Carothers, "Democracy Promotion: A Key Focus in a New World Order," *Foreign Affairs* (March/April 2006): 55–68.

6. Pew Forum on Religion and Public Life, "Growing Number of Americans Say Islam Encourages Violence" (July 24, 2003.)

7. FOX News/Opinion Dynamics Poll, February 8–9, 2005.

8. Richard Allen Greene, "Religion and Politics in America," *BBC News* (September 15, 2004); Roper Center iPoll.

9. This discussion draws heavily from Terence Ball and Richard Dagger, *Political Ideologies and the Democratic Ideal*, 5th ed. (New York: Longman, 2004).

10. Ball and Dagger, *Political Ideologies and the Democratic Ideal*, 2.

11. Isaiah Berlin, *The Crooked Timber of Humanity: Chapters in the History of Ideas* (New York: Vintage, 1992), 1.

12. William Safire, *Safire's New Political Dictionary* (New York: Random House, 1993), 144–5.

13. Jack C. Plano and Milton Greenberg, *The American Political Dictionary*, 9th ed. (Fort Worth, TX: Harcourt Brace, 1993), 16.

14. Philip E. Converse, "The Nature of Belief Systems in Mass Publics," in David E. Apter, ed., *Ideology and Discontent* (New York: Free Press, 1964), 206–21.

15. Haya El Nasser, "Immigrants Assimilate Faster," *USA Today* (May 13, 2008): 3A.

16. Susan A. MacManus, *Young v. Old: Generational Combat in the 21st Century* (Boulder, CO: Westview, 1995), 3.

17. Dennis Cauchon, "Who Will Take Care of an Older Population?" *USA Today* (October 25, 2005): 1–2B.

18. Gallup Poll, June 11–14, 2007.

19. Democracy Corps Poll, November 29–December 3, 2007.

20. CBS News Poll, February 27, 2006, www.cbsnews.com/ntdocs/pdf/poll_katrina_022706.pdf.

21. Jeff Duncan, "California Fires Can't Be Compared to Katrina, Officials Say," *Times-Picayune* (October 27, 2007).

22. CNN Poll, March 14–16, 2008.

23. Jon Cohen and Dan Balz, "U.S. Outlook is Worse Since '92, Poll Finds," *Washington Post* (May 13, 2008).

Chapter 2

1. See Richard B. Bernstein with Jerome Agel, *Amending America* (New York: New York Times Books, 1993), 138–40.

2. *Oregon v. Mitchell*, 400 U.S. 112 (1970).

3. Bernstein with Agel, *Amending America*, 139.

4. For an account of the early development of the colonies, see D. W. Meining, *The Shaping of America*, vol. 1: *Atlantic America, 1492–1800* (New Haven, CT: Yale University Press, 1986).

5. For an excellent chronology of the events leading up to the writing of the Declaration of Independence and the colonists' break with Great Britain, see Calvin D. Linton, ed., *The Bicentennial Almanac* (Nashville, TN: Thomas Nelson, 1975).

6. See Garry Wills, *Inventing America: Jefferson's Declaration of Independence* (New York: Random House, 1978). Wills argues that the Declaration was signed solely to secure foreign aid for the ongoing war effort.

7. See Gordon S. Wood, *The Creation of the American Republic, 1776–1787*, reissue ed. (New York: Norton, 1993).

8. For more about the Articles of Confederation, see Merrill Jensen, *The Articles of Confederation* (Madison: University of Wisconsin Press, 1940).

9. Charles A. Beard, *An Economic Interpretation of the Constitution of the United States*, reissue ed. (Mineola, NY: Dover, 2004).

10. Quoted in Richard N. Current et al., *American History: A Survey*, 6th ed. (New York: Knopf, 1983), 170.

11. John Patrick Diggins, "Power and Authority in American History: The Case of Charles A. Beard and His Critics," *American Historical Review* 86 (October 1981): 701–30; Robert Brown, *Charles Beard and the Constitution: A Critical Analysis of "An Economic Interpretation of the Constitution"* (Princeton, NJ: Princeton University Press, 1956).

12. Jackson Turner Main, *The Anti-Federalists: Critics of the Constitution, 1781–1788* (Chapel Hill: University of North Carolina, 2004).

13. Wood, *Creation of the American Republic*.

14. For more on the political nature of compromise at the convention, see Calvin C. Jillson, *Constitution Making: Conflict and Consensus in the Federal Constitution of 1787* (New York: Agathon, 1988).

15. Quoted in Doris Faber and Harold Faber, *We the People* (New York: Charles Scribner's Sons, 1987), 31.

16. Quoted in Current et al., *American History*, 168.

17. Bernard Bailyn, *The Ideological Origins of the American Revolution* (Cambridge, MA: Belknap Press, 1967).

18. *U.S. Term Limits v. Thornton*, 514 U.S. 779 (1995).

19. Richard E. Neustadt, *Presidential Power: The Politics of Leadership from FDR to Carter* (New York: Macmillan, 1980), 26.

20. Quoted in Faber and Faber, *We the People*, 51–52.

21. Federal Republicans favored a republican or representative form of government (do not confuse this term with the modern Republican Party, which came into being in 1854; see chapter 12). Ultimately, the word *federal* referred to the form of government embodied in the new Constitution, and *confederation* referred to a "league of states," as under the Articles, and later was applied in the "Confederacy" of 1861–1865.

22. See Ralph Ketcham, ed., *The Anti-Federalist Papers and the Constitutional Debates* (New York: New American Library, 1986).

23. See Herbert J. Storing, *What the Anti-Federalists Were For* (Chicago: University of Chicago Press, 1981), for a fuller discussion of Anti-Federalist views.

24. See Alan P. Grimes, *Democracy and the Amendments to the Constitution* (Lexington, MA: Lexington, 1978).

25. David E. Kyvig, *Repealing National Prohibition* (Chicago: University of Chicago Press, 1978).

26. See Jane J. Mansbridge, *Why We Lost the ERA* (Chicago: University of Chicago Press, 1986).

27. *Marbury v. Madison*, 5 U.S. 137 (1803).

28. Speech by Attorney General Edwin Meese III before the American Bar Association, July 9, 1985, Washington, DC. See also Antonin Scalia and Amy Gutman, eds. *A Matter of Interpretation: Federal Courts and the Law* (Princeton, NJ: Princeton University Press, 1998).

29. Speech by Associate Justice William J. Brennan Jr. at Georgetown University Text and Teaching Symposium, October 10, 1985, Washington, DC.

30. Mark V. Tushnet, *Taking the Constitution Away from the Courts.* (Princeton, NJ: Princeton University Press, 2000).

31. Bruce Ackerman, *We the People: Foundations* (Cambridge, MA: Belknap Press, 1991).

Chapter 3

1. Evan Thomas, "How Bush Blew It," *Newsweek* (September 19, 2005), http://www.msnbc.msn.com/id/9287434/site/newsweek/page/3/.

2. See Spencer S. Hsu, "Katrina Report Spreads Blame: Homeland Security, Chertoff Singled Out," *Washington Post* (January 12, 2006): A1.

3. Ben Feller, "Bush: Cooperation for Gustav Better than for Katrina," *Associated Press* (September 1, 2008).

4. *Missouri* v. *Holland*, 252 U.S. 416 (1920).

5. John Mountjoy, "Interstate Cooperation: Interstate Compacts Make a Comeback," *Council of State Governments*, available online at http://www.csg.org.

6. *McCulloch* v. *Maryland*, 17 U.S. 316 (1819).

7. *Gibbons* v. *Ogden*, 22 U.S. 1 (1824).

8. *Dred Scott* v. *Sandford*, 60 U.S. 393 (1857).

9. *Plessy* v. *Ferguson*, 163 U.S. 537 (1896).

10. *Panhandle Oil Co.* v. *Knox*, 277 U.S. 218, 223 (1928).

11. *Indian Motorcycle Co.* v. *U.S.*, 238 U.S. 570 (1931).

12. *Pensacola Telegraph* v. *Western Union*, 96 U.S. 1 (1877).

13. *U.S.* v. *E. C. Knight*, 156 U.S. 1 (1895).

14. *Pollock* v. *Farmers Loan and Trust*, 157 U.S. 429 (1895); and *Springer* v. *U.S.*, 102 U.S. 586 (1881).

15. John O. McGinnis, "The State of Federalism," testimony before the Senate Government Affairs Committee, May 5, 1999.

16. *NLRB* v. *Jones and Laughlin Steel Co.*, 301 U.S. 1 (1937).

17. *U.S.* v. *Darby Lumber Co.*, 312 U.S. 100 (1941).

18. *Wickard* v. *Filburn*, 317 U.S. 111 (1942).

19. Morton Grodzins, "Centralization and Decentralization in the American Federal System," in Robert A. Goldwin, ed., *A Nation of States* (Chicago: Rand McNally, 1963), 3–4.

20. Alice M. Rivlin, *Reviving the American Dream* (Washington, DC: Brookings Institution, 1992), 92.

21. Rivlin, *Reviving the American Dream*, 98.

22. Richard P. Nathan et al., *Reagan and the States* (Princeton, NJ: Princeton University Press, 1987), 4.

23. T. R. Reid, "States Feel Less Pinch in Budgets, Services," *Washington Post* (May 9, 2004): A3.

24. Michael Powell, "Art of Politickin'; As the Republican Rivals Get Out in South Carolina, It's Survival of the Folksiest," *Washington Post* (February 19, 2000): C1.

25. Ken Dilanian, "War Costs May Total $2.4 Trillion," *USA Today* (October 24, 2007): 1A.

26. Gene Healy and Timothy Lynch, "Power Surge: The Constitutional Record of George W. Bush," Cato Institute, 2006, 20.

27. Marianne Arneberg, "Cuomo Assails Judicial Hodgepodge," *Newsday* (August 15, 1990); 15.

28. *Webster* v. *Reproductive Health Services*, 492 U.S. 490 (1989).

29. *Stenberg* v. *Carhart*, 530 U.S. 914 (2000).

30. *Ayotte* v. *Planned Parenthood of Northern New England* 546 U.S. 320 (2006).

31. *Gonzales* v. *Carhart*, 550 U.S. _____ (2007).

32. *U.S.* v. *Lopez*, 514 U.S. 549 (1995).

33. *Seminole Tribe* v. *Florida*, 517 U.S. 44 (1996).

34. *Boerne* v. *Flores*, 521 U.S. 507 (1997).

35. *Printz* v. *U.S.*, 521 U.S. 898 (1997).

36. *Florida Prepaid* v. *College Savings Bank*, 527 U.S. 627 (1999).

37. *U.S.* v. *Morrison*, 529 U.S. 598 (2000).

38. *Gonzales* v. *Raich* 545 U.S. 1 (2005).

39. Linda Greenhouse, "The Rehnquist Court and Its Imperiled States' Rights Legacy," *New York Times* (June 12, 2005): A3.

40. Linda Greenhouse, "In a Momentous Term, Justices Remake the Law and the Court," *New York Times* (July 1, 2003): A18.

41. *Nevada Department of Human Resources* v. *Hibbs*, 538 U.S. 72 (2003).

42. *Gonzales* v. *Oregon*, 546 U.S. 243 (2006).

43. *U.S.* v. *Georgia*, 546 U.S. 151 (2006).

Chapter 4

1. Albert L. Sturm, "The Development of American State Constitutions," *Publius* 12 (Winter 1982): 62–68.

2. Albert L. Kohlmeier, *The Old Northwest as the Keystone of the Arch of the American Federal Union* (Bloomington, IN: Principia, 1938), and *Pathways to the Old Northwest* (Indianapolis: Indiana Historical Society, 1988).

3. George E. Mowry, *The Progressive Era, 1900–1920* (Washington, DC: American Historical Association, 1972).

4. John J. Carroll and Arthur English, "Traditions of State Constitution Making," *State and Local Government Review* 23 (Fall 1991): 103–9.

5. Dan Durning, "Governors and Administrative Reform in the 1990s," *State and Local Government Review* 27 (Winter 1995): 36–54.

6. Thad L. Beyle and Robert Dalton, "Appointment Power: Does It Belong to the Governor?" *State Government* 54:1 (1981): 6.

7. Leon W. Blevins, *Texas Government in National Perspective* (Englewood Cliffs, NJ: Prentice Hall, 1987), 169.

8. Michael Berkman and Christoper Reenock, "Incremental Consolidation and Comprehensive Reorganization of American State Executive Branches," *American Journal of Political Science* 48 (October 2004): 796–812.

9. Michael P. McDonald, "A Comparative Analysis of Redistricting Institutions in the U.S.," *State Politics and Policy Quarterly* 4 (Winter 2004): 371–95.

10. Council of State Governments, *The Book of the States, 2008* (Lexington, KY: Council of State Governments, 2008), 47.

11. "Schwarzenegger Wants Part-time Legislature," April 7, 2004, http://sfgate. com.

12. Diana Gordon, "Citizen Legislators—Alive and Well," *State Legislatures* 20 (January 1994): 24–27.

13. Melinda Gann Hall, "State Supreme Courts in American Democracy: Probing the Myths of Judicial Reform," *American Political Science Review* 95 (June 2001), 315–30.

14. Elizabeth R. Gerber, *Stealing the Initiative* (Upper Saddle River, NJ: Prentice Hall, 2001).

15. Patrick McMahon, "Voters Like Recall Idea, but Few Want One," *USA Today* (October 14, 2003): 3A; Andy Bowers, "Can You Recall Your Governor?" *Slate*, July 30, 2003, http://slate.msn.com.

16. Alexis de Tocqueville, *Democracy in America*, ed. Phillips Bradley (New York: Knopf, 1945), 40.

17. *City of Clinton v. Cedar Rapids and Missouri River Railroad Co.* (Iowa, 1868).

18. Steven P. Erie, *Rainbow's End: Irish-Americans and the Dilemmas of Urban Machine Politics, 1840–1985* (Berkeley: University of California Press, 1988); Alfred Steinberg, *The Bosses* (New York: New American Library, 1972); Seymour Mandelbaum, *Boss Tweed's New York* (New York: Wiley, 1955); and Milton Rakove, *Don't Make No Waves—Don't Back No Losers: An Insider's Analysis of the Daley Machine* (Bloomington: Indiana University Press, 1975).

19. Samuel P. Hays, "The Politics of Reform in Municipal Government in the Progressive Era," *Pacific Northwest Quarterly* 55 (October 1964): 157–66.

20. Raymond Wolfinger, "Reputation and Reality in the Study of Community Power," *American Sociological Review* 25 (October 1960): 636–44; Nelson Polsby, *Community Power and Political Theory* (New Haven, CT: Yale University Press, 1963); and Robert E. Agger, Daniel Goldrich, and Bert Swanson, *The Rulers and the Ruled: Political Power and Impotence in American Communities* (New York: Wiley, 1964).

21. Laura R. Woliver, *From Outrage to Action: The Politics of Grass-Roots Dissent* (Urbana: University of Illinois Press, 1993); and Matthew A. Crenson, *Neighborhood Politics* (Cambridge, MA: Harvard University Press, 1983).

22. Jenny Mandel, "Interior Seeks to Settle Indian Trust Fund Disputes for $7 Billion," *Government Executive*, March 29, 2007, www. gov-exec. com/ dailyfed/ 0307/ 032907m1. htm.

23. Center on Budget and Policy Priorities, www.cbpp.org/pubs/povinc. htm.

24. National Governors Association, http://www.nga.org.

25. Dennis Cauchon, "States Getting Budgets Under Control," *USA Today* (November 12, 2003): 3A.

26. Steven Ginsberg and Chris L. Jenkins, "Vote Quiets Anti-Tax Clarion Call in Virginia," *Washington Post* (April 29, 2004): A1.

Chapter 5

1. Paul Duggan, "Lawyer Who Wiped Out D.C. Ban Says It's About Liberties, Not Guns," *Washington Post* (March 18, 2007): A1.

2. *D.C. v. Heller,* 554 U.S. _____ (2008).

3. The absence of a bill of rights led Mason to refuse to sign the proposed Constitution, noting that he "would sooner chop off his right hand than put it to the Constitution as it now stands." Quoted in Eric Black, *Our Constitution: The Myth That Binds Us* (Boulder, CO: Westview, 1988), 75.

4. Quoted in Jack N. Rakove, "Madison Won Passage of the Bill of Rights but Remained a Skeptic," *Public Affairs Report* (March 1991): 6.

5. *Barron v. Baltimore.* 32 U.S. 243 (1833).

6. *Allgeyer v. Louisiana.* 165 U.S. 578 (1897).

7. *Gitlow v. New York*, 268 U.S. 652 (1925).

8. *Near v. Minnesota*, 283 U.S. 697 (1931). For more about *Near*, see Fred W. Friendly, *Minnesota Rag: The Dramatic Story of the Landmark Case That Gave New Meaning to Freedom of the Press* (New York: Random House, 1981).

9. *Palko v. Connecticut*, 302 U.S. 319 (1937).

10. Continental Congress to the People of Great Britain, October 21, 1774, in Philip Kurland and Ralph Lerner, eds., *The Founders' Constitution*, vol. 5 (Chicago: University of Chicago Press, 1987), 61.

11. *Reynolds v. U.S.*, 98 U.S. 145 (1879).

12. *Cantwell v. Connecticut*, 310 U.S. 296 (1940).

13. *Zobrest v. Catalina Foothills School District*, 506 U.S. 813 (1992).

14. *Engel v. Vitale*, 370 U.S. 421 (1962).

15. *Lemon v. Kurtzman*, 403 U.S. 602 (1971).

16. *Widmar v. Vincent*, 454 U.S. 263 (1981).

17. *Board of Education v. Mergens*, 496 U.S. 226 (1990).

18. *Lamb's Chapel v. Center Moriches Union Free School District*, 508 U.S. 384 (1993).

19. *Rosenberger v. University of Virginia*, 515 U.S. 819 (1995).

20. *Mitchell v. Helms*, 530 U.S. 793 (2000).

21. *Zelman v. Simmons-Harris*, 536 U.S. 639 (2002).

22. *Lee v. Weisman*, 505 U.S. 577 (1992).

23. *McCreary County v. ACLU of Kentucky*, 545 U.S. 844 (2005).

24. *Church of the Lukumi Babalu Aye v. Hialeah*, 508 U.S. 525 (1993).

25. *Employment Division, Dept. of Human Resources of Oregon v. Smith*, 494 U.S. 872 (1990).

26. *Boerne v. Flores*, 521 U.S. 507 (1997).

27. *Gonzales v. O Centro Espirita Beneficente União do Vegetal*, 546 U.S. 418 (2006).

28. *U.S. v. Seeger*, 380 U.S. 163 (1965).

29. *Cruz v. Beto*, 405 U.S. 319 (1972).

30. *O'Lone v. Shabazz*, 482 U.S. 342 (1987).

31. Tony Mauro, "Stern's Raunch Is Better than Silence," *USA Today* (May 12, 2004): 13A.

32. David M. O'Brien, *Constitutional Law and Politics*, vol. 2: *Civil Rights and Civil Liberties* (New York: Norton, 1991), 345.

33. See Frederick Siebert, *The Rights and Privileges of the Press* (New York Appleton-Century, 1934), 886, 931–40.

34. *Schenck v. U.S.*, 249 U.S. 47 (1919).

35. *Brandenburg v. Ohio*, 395 U.S. 444 (1969).

36. *New York Times Co. v. U.S.*, 403 U.S. 713 (1971).

37. *Nebraska Press Association v. Stuart*, 427 U.S. 539 (1976).

38. *Tory v. Cochran*, 544 U.S. 734 (2005).

39. *Abrams v. U.S.*, 250 U.S. 616 (1919).

40. *Stromberg v. California*, 283 U.S. 359 (1931).

41. *Tinker v. Des Moines Independent Community School District*, 393 U.S. 503 (1969).

42. Harry Kalven Jr., *Negro and the First Amendment* (Chicago: University of Chicago Press, 1966).

43. Henry Louis Gates Jr., "Why Civil Liberties Pose No Threat to Civil Rights," *New Republic* (September 20, 1993).

44. *R.A.V. v. City of St. Paul*, 505 U.S. 377 (1992).

45. *Virginia v. Black*, 538 U.S. 343 (2003).

46. *Chaplinsky v. New Hampshire*, 315 U.S. 568 (1942).

47. *New York Times Co. v. Sullivan*, 376 U.S. 254 (1964).

48. *Chaplinsky v. New Hampshire*, 315 U.S. 568 (1942).

49. *Coben v. California*, 403 U.S. 15 (1971).

50. *Regina v. Hicklin*, L.R. 2 Q.B. 360 (1868).

51. *Roth v. U.S.*, 354 U.S. 476 (1957).

52. *Miller v. California*, 413 U.S. 15 (1973).

53. *Barnes v. Glen Theater*, 501 U.S. 560 (1991).

54. *Reno v. American Civil Liberties Union*, 521 U.S. 844 (1997); David G. Savage, "Ban on 'Virtual' Child Porn Is Upset by Court," *Los Angeles Times* (April 17, 2002): A1; *Ashcroft v. American Civil Liberties Union*, 542 U.S. 656 (2004).

55. *U.S. v. Williams* 553 U.S. *TK* (2008).

56. *DeJonge v. Oregon*, 229 U.S. 353 (1937).

57. *Barron* v. *Baltimore*, 32 U.S. 243 (1833).

58. *Dred Scott* v. *Sandford*, 60 U.S. 393 (1857).

59. *U.S.* v. *Miller*, 307 U.S. 174 (1939).

60. *D.C.* v. *Heller*, 554 U.S. 554 _____ (2008).

61. *Stein* v. *New York*, 346 U.S. 156 (1953).

62. *Wilson* v. *Arkansas*, 514 U.S. 927 (1995).

63. *Hudson* v. *Michigan*, 547 U.S. 586 (2006).

64. *U.S.* v. *Sokolov*, 490 U.S. 1 (1989).

65. *U.S.* v. *Matlock*, 415 U.S. 164 (1974).

66. *Georgia* v. *Randolph*, 547 U.S. 103 (2006).

67. *Johnson* v. *U.S.*, 333 U.S. 10 (1948).

68. *Winston* v. *Lee*, 470 U.S. 753 (1985).

69. *South Dakota* v. *Neville*, 459 U.S. 553 (1983).

70. *Michigan* v. *Tyler*, 436 U.S. 499 (1978).

71. *Hester* v. *U.S.*, 265 U.S. 57 (1924).

72. *Kyllo* v. *U.S.*, 533 U.S. 27 (2001).

73. David G. Savage, "Court Says No to Home Snooping," *Los Angeles Times* (June 12, 2001): A1.

74. *Carroll* v. *U.S.*, 267 U.S. 132 (1925).

75. *U.S.* v. *Arvizu*, 534 U.S. 266 (2002).

76. *Skinner* v. *Railway Labor Executives' Association*, 489 U.S. 602 (1989).

77. *Vernonia School District* v. *Acton*, 515 U.S. 646 (1995).

78. *Board of Education of Independent School District No. 92 of Pottawatomie County* v. *Earls*, 536 U.S. 822 (2002).

79. John Wefing, "Employer Drug Testing: Disparate Judicial and Legislative Responses," *Albany Law Review* 63 (2000): 799–801.

80. *Ferguson* v. *City of Charleston*, 532 U.S. 67 (2001).

81. *Counselman* v. *Hitchcock*, 142 U.S. 547 (1892).

82. *Brown* v. *Mississippi*, 297 U.S. 278 (1936).

83. *Lynum* v. *Illinois*, 372 U.S. 528 (1963).

84. *Rhode Island* v. *Innis*, 446 U.S. 291 (1980).

85. *U.S.* v. *Patane*, 542 U.S. 630 (2004).

86. *Weeks* v. *U.S.*, 232 U.S. 383 (1914).

87. *Mapp* v. *Ohio*, 367 U.S. 643 (1961).

88. *Stone* v. *Powell*, 428 U.S. 465 (1976).

89. *U.S.* v. *Grubbs*, 547 U.S. 90 (2006).

90. *Johnson* v. *Zerbst*, 304 U.S. 458 (1938).

91. *Powell* v. *Alabama*, 287 U.S. 45 (1932).

92. *Gideon* v. *Wainwright*, 372 U.S. 335 (1963).

93. *Argersinger* v. *Hamlin*, 407 U.S. 25 (1972).

94. *Rothgery* v. *Gillespie County*, 554 _____ (2008).

95. *Strauder* v. *West Virginia*, 100 U.S. 303 (1880).

96. *Taylor* v. *Louisiana*, 419 U.S. 522 (1975).

97. *Batson* v. *Kentucky*, 476 U.S. 79 (1986).

98. *J.E.B.* v. *Alabama*, 511 U.S. 127 (1994).

99. *Maryland* v. *Craig*, 497 U.S. 836 (1990).

100. *Hallinger* v. *Davis*, 146 U.S. 314 (1892).

101. *O'Neil* v. *Vermont*, 144 U.S. 323 (1892).

102. See Michael Meltsnet, *Cruel and Unusual: The Supreme Court and Capital Punishment* (New York: Random House, 1973).

103. *Furman* v. *Georgia*, 408 U.S. 238 (1972).

104. *Gregg* v. *Georgia*, 428 U.S. 153 (1976).

105. *McCleskey* v. *Kemp*, 481 U.S. 279 (1987).

106. *McCleskey* v. *Zant*, 499 U.S. 467 (1991).

107. *Atkins* v. *Virginia*, 536 U.S. 304 (2002).

108. *Roper* v. *Simmons*, 543 U.S. 551 (2005).

109. *House* v. *Bell*, 547 U.S. 518 (2006).

110. *Hill* v. *McDonough*, 547 U.S. 573 (2006).

111. *Baze* v. *Rees*, 553 U.S. TK (2008).

112. *Olmstead* v. *U.S.*, 277 U.S. 438 (1928).

113. *Griswold* v. *Connecticut*, 381 U.S. 481 (1965).

114. *Eisenstadt* v. *Baird*, 410 U.S. 113 (1972).

115. *Roe* v. *Wade*, 410 U.S. 113 (1973).

116. *Beal* v. *Doe*, 432 U.S. 438 (1977); and *Harris* v. *McRae*, 448 U.S. 297 (1980).

117. *Webster* v. *Reproductive Health Services*, 492 U.S. 490 (1989).

118. *Planned Parenthood of Southeastern Pennsylvania* v. *Casey*, 502 U.S. 1056 (1992).

119. Karen O'Connor, *No Neutral Ground: Abortion Politics in an Age of Absolutes* (Boulder, CO: Westview, 1996).

120. "House Sends Partial Birth Abortion Bill to Clinton," *Politics USA* (March 28, 1996): 1.

121. *Stenberg* v. *Carhart*, 530 U.S. 914 (2000).

122. *Bowers* v. *Hardwick*, 478 U.S. 186 (1986).

123. *Lawrence* v. *Texas*, 539 U.S. 558 (2003).

124. *Cruzan* v. *Director, Missouri Dept. of Health*, 497 U.S. 261 (1990).

125. *Vacco* v. *Quill*, 521 U.S. 793 (1997).

126. Office of the Attorney General, Memorandum for Asa Hutchinson, Administrator, the Drug Enforcement Administration, November 6, 2001.

127. *Oregon* v. *Ashcroft*, 192 F. Supp. 2d 1077 (2002); and Kim Murphy, "U.S. Cannot Block Oregon Suicide Law, Judge Rules," *Los Angeles Times* (April 18, 2002): A1.

128. Attorney General's petition for a writ of *certiorari*, *Gonzales* v. *Oregon*, 2005.

129. *Gonzales* v. *Oregon* 546 U.S. 243 (2006).

130. Jennifer Levin, "Alternative Reality About Public, War," *Associated Press* (May 29, 2007).

131. "Surveillance Under the USA Patriot Act," American Civil Liberties Union, April 3, 2003.

132. *Rasul* v. *Bush*, 542 U.S. 466 (2004).

133. *Boumediene* v. *Bush* 553 U.S. _____ (2008).

134. *Hamdan* v. *Rumsfeld*, 548 U.S. 557 (2006).

135. Shane Scott, David Johnston, and James Risen, "Secret U.S. Endorsement of Severe Interrogations," *New York Times* (October 7, 2007): A1.

136. Scott, Johnston, and Risen, "Secret U.S. Endorsement of Severe Interrogations."

Chapter 6

1. Dan Eggen, "Civil Rights Focus Shift Roils Staff at Justice," *Washington Post* (December 13, 2005): A1.

2. Adam Zagorin, "Why Were These U.S. Attorneys Fired?" *Time* (March 7, 2007).

3. Eggen, "Civil Rights Focus Shift Roils Staff at Justice."

4. Dan Eggen, "Politics Alleged in Voting Cases," *Washington Post* (January 23, 2006): A1.

5. David E. Rosenbaum et al., "New Twist in Texas Districting Dispute," *New York Times* (December 3, 2005).

6. *League of United Latin American Citizens* v. *Perry*, 547 U.S. 399 (2006).

7. *Civil Rights Cases*, 109 U.S. 3 (1883).

8. *Plessy* v. *Ferguson*, 163 U.S. 537 (1896).

9. Jack Greenberg, *Judicial Process and Social Change: Constitutional Litigation* (St. Paul, MN: West, 1976), 583–86.

10. Juan Williams, *Eyes on the Prize: America's Civil Rights Years, 1954–1965* (New York: Penguin, 1987), 10.

11. *Williams* v. *Mississippi*, 170 U.S. 213 (1898); *Cummins* v. *Richmond County Board of Education*, 175 U.S. 528 (1899).

12. *Bailey* v. *Alabama*, 211 U.S. 452 (1908).

13. *Muller* v. *Oregon*, 208 U.S. 412 (1908).

14. *Missouri ex rel. Gaines* v. *Canada*, 305 U.S. 337 (1938).

15. Richard Kluger, *Simple Justice* (New York: Vintage, 1975), 268.

16. *Sweatt* v. *Painter*, 339 U.S. 629 (1950); and *McLaurin* v. *Oklahoma*, 339 U.S. 637 (1950).

17. *Sweatt* v. *Painter*, 339 U.S. 629 (1950).

18. *Brown* v. *Board of Education*, 347 U.S. 483 (1954).

19. But see Gerald Rosenberg, *The Hollow Hope: Can Courts Bring About Social Change?* (Chicago: University of Chicago Press, 1991).

20. Quoted in Williams, *Eyes on the Prize*, 10.

21. *Brown* v. *Board of Education II*, 349 U.S. 294 (1955).

22. Quoted in Williams, *Eyes on the Prize*, 37.

23. *Cooper* v. *Aaron*, 358 U.S. 1 (1958).

24. *Heart of Atlanta Motel* v. *U.S.*, 379 U.S. 241 (1964).

25. *Swann* v. *Charlotte-Mecklenburg School District*, 402 U.S. 1 (1971).

26. *Freeman* v. *Pitts*, 498 U.S. 1081 (1992); *Missouri* v. *Jenkins*, 515 U.S. 70 (1995).

27. *Parents Involved in Community Schools* v. *Seattle School District*, 551 U.S. _____ (2007).

28. *Griggs* v. *Duke Power Co.*, 401 U.S. 424 (1971).

29. Jo Freeman, *The Politics of Women's Liberation* (New York: Longman, 1975), 57.

30. *Hoyt* v. *Florida*, 368 U.S. 57 (1961).

31. Betty Friedan, *The Feminine Mystique* (New York: Dell, 1963).

32. *Korematsu* v. *U.S.*, 323 U.S. 214 (1944). This is the only case involving race-based distinctions applying the strict scrutiny standard where the Court has upheld the restrictive law.

33. *Reed* v. *Reed*, 404 U.S. 71 (1971).

34. *Craig* v. *Boren*, 429 U.S. 190 (1976).

35. *Mississippi University for Women* v. *Hogan*, 458 U.S. 718 (1982).

36. *Craig* v. *Boren*, 429 U.S. 190 (1976).

37. *Orr* v. *Orr*, 440 U.S. 268 (1979).

38. *J.E.B.* v. *Alabama ex rel. TB*, 440 U.S. 268 (1979).

39. *U.S.* v. *Virginia*, 518 U.S. 515 (1996).

40. *Nguyen* v. *INS*, 533 U.S. 53 (2001).

41. *Rostker* v. *Goldberg*, 453 U.S. 57 (1981).

42. *Michael M.* v. *Superior Court of Sonoma County*, 450 U.S. 464 (1981).

43. *Rostker* v. *Goldberg*, 453 U.S. 57 (1981).

44. *U.S.* v. *Virginia*, 518 U.S. 515 (1996).

45. *Meritor Savings Bank* v. *Vinson*, 477 U.S. 57 (1986).

46. *Oncale* v. *Sundowner Offshore Services, Inc.*, 523 U.S. 75 (1998).

47. *Hishon* v. *King & Spalding*, 467 U.S. 69 (1984).

48. *Johnson* v. *Transportation Agency*, 480 U.S. 616 (1987).

49. *Davis* v. *Monroe Country Board of Education*, 526 U.S. 629 (1999).

50. Joyce Gelb and Marian Lief Palley, *Women and Public Policies* (Charlottesville: University of Virginia Press, 1996).

51. *Jackson* v. *Birmingham Board of Education*, 544 U.S. 167 (2005).

52. *Hernandez* v. *Texas*, 347 U.S. 475 (1954).

53. *White* v. *Register*, 412 U.S. 755 (1973).

54. *San Antonio Independent School District* v. *Rodriguez*, 411 U.S. 1 (1973).

55. *Edgewood Independent School District* v. *Kirby*, 777 SW 2d 391 (1989).

56. "MALDEF Pleased with Settlement of California Public Schols Inequity Case, *Williams* v. *California*," August 13, 2004.

57. ennard Strickland, "Native Americans," in Kermit Hall, ed., *The Oxford Companion to the Supreme Court of the United States* (New York: Oxford University Press, 1992), 557.

58. Louis Sahagun, "Tribes Fear Backlash to Prosperity," *Los Angeles Times* (May 3, 2004): B1.

59. *Employment Division of the Oregon Department of Human Resources* v. *Smith*, 494 U.S. 872 (1990).

60. *Boerne* v. *Flores*, 521 U.S. 507 (1997).

61. Dee Brown, *Bury My Heart at Wounded Knee* (New York: Holt, Rinehart and Winston, 1971).

62. *Cobell* v. *Norton*, 204 F3d 1081 (2001). For more on the Indian trust, see http://www.indiantrust.com/overview.cfm.

63. Richard Luscombe, "Tribes Go on Legal Warpath," *The Observer* (April 25, 2004): 20.

64. Michael McNutt, "Group Supports Indians in Office," *Daily Oklahoman* (May 15, 2006).

65. Al Kamen, "DOE Trips on Security Blanket," *Washington Post* (May 25, 2001): A1.

66. Roger Daniels, *Asian America: Chinese and Japanese in the United States Since 1850* (Seattle: University of Washington Press, 1988).

67. *Yick Wo* v. *Hopkins*, 118 U.S. 356 (1886).

68. *Ozawa* v. *U.S.*, 260 U.S. 178 (1922).

69. Andrew L. Aoki, and Don T. Nakanishi, "Asian Pacific Americans and the New Minority Politics," *PS: Political Science and Politics* 34 (2001): 606.

70. *Korematsu* v. *U.S.*, 323 U.S. 214 (1944).

71. Diane Helene Miller, *Freedom to Differ: The Shaping of the Gay and Lesbian Struggle for Civil Rights* (New York: New York University Press, 1998).

72. Sarah Brewer, David Kaib, and Karen O'Connor, "Sex and the Supreme Court: Gays, Lesbians, and Justice," in Craig A. Rimmerman, Kenneth D. Wald, and Clyde Wilcox, eds., *The Politics of Gay Rights* (Chicago: University of Chicago Press, 2000).

73. Evan Gerstmann, *The Constitutional Underclass: Gays, Lesbians, and the Failure of Class-Based Equal Protection* (Chicago: University of Chicago Press, 1999).

74. Deborah Ensor, "Gay Veterans Working for Change," *San Diego Union* (April 13, 2002): B1.

75. John White, "'Don't Ask' Costs More than Expected," *Washington Post* (February 14, 2006): A4.

76. *Romer* v. *Evans*, 517 U.S. 620 (1996).

77. *Lawrence* v. *Texas*, 539 U.S. 558 (2003).

78. Joan Biskupic, "Court's Opinion on Gay Rights Reflects Trends," *USA Today* (July 18, 2003): 2A.

79. David Pfeiffer, "Overview of the Disability Movement: History, Legislative Record and Political Implications," *Policy Studies Journal* (Winter 1993): 724–42; and "Understanding Disability Policy," *Policy Studies Journal* (Spring 1996): 157–74.

80. Joan Biskupic, "Supreme Court Limits Meaning of Disability," *Washington Post* (June 23, 1999): A1.

81. *Sutton v. United Air Lines, Inc.*, 527 U.S. 471 (1999).

82. *Tennessee v. Lane*, 541 U.S. 509 (2004).

83. American Association of People with Disabilities, www.aapd-dc.org.

84. *Regents of the University of California v. Bakke*, 438 U.S. 265 (1978).

85. *Johnson v. Santa Clara County*, 480 U.S. 616 (1987).

86. Ruth Marcus, "Hill Coalition Aims to Counter Court in Job Bias," *Washington Post* (February 8, 1990): A10.

87. *Adarand Constructors v. Pena*, 515 U.S. 200 (1995).

88. Cert. denied, *Texas v. Hopwood*, 518 U.S. 1033 (1996). See also Terrance Scurz, "UT Minority Enrollment Tested by Suit: Fate of Affirmative Action in Education is at Issue," *Dallas Morning News* (October 14, 1995).

89. *Grutter v. Bollinger*, 539 U.S. 306 (2003).

90. *Gratz v. Bollinger*, 539 U.S. 306 (2003).

91. *Grutter v. Bollinger*, 539 U.S. 306 (2003).

92. Victoria Colliver, "Class Action Considered in Wal-Mart Suit," *San Francisco Chronicle* (September 25, 2003): B1.

93. *Ledbetter v. Goodyear Tire and Rubber Co.*, 550 U.S. _____ (2007).

94. "Wal-Mart's Immigrant Labor Problem," *Tampa Tribune* (November 14, 2003): 10.

Chapter 7

1. For an outstanding account of Pelosi's campaign for the whip post, see Juliet Eilperin, "The Making of Madam Whip: Fear and Loathing—and Horse Trading—The Race for the House's No. 2 Democrat," *Washington Post* (January 6, 2002): W27.

2. "Mother of All Whips," *Pittsburgh Post-Gazette* (February 9, 2002): A11.

3. Steven S. Smith and Eric D. Lawrence, "Party Control of Congress in the Republican Congress," in Lawrence C. Dodd and Bruce I. Oppenheimer, eds., *Congress Reconsidered*, 6th ed. (Washington, DC: CQ Press, 1997), 163–4. For more on the role of parties in the organization of Congress, see Forrest Maltzman, *Competing Principals: Committees, Parties, and the Organization of Congress* (Ann Arbor: University of Michigan Press, 1997); and Marc J. Hetherington and William J. Keefe, *Parties, Politics, and Public Policy in America*, 10th ed. (Washington, DC: CQ Press, 2006).

4. "What Is the Democratic Caucus?" http://dcaucusweb.house.gov/about/what_is.asp.

5. Barbara Hinckley, *Stability and Change in Congress*, 3rd ed. (New York: Harper and Row, 1983), 166.

6. Katharine Seelye, "Congressional Memo: New Speaker, New Style, Old Problem," *New York Times* (March 12, 1999): A18.

7. Charles Babington, "Pelosi Seeks House Minority 'Bill of Rights,' Hastert Dismisses Democrats' Complaint, Saying GOP Record Is Better than Foes," *Washington Post* (June 24, 2004): A23.

8. Barbara Sinclair, "The Struggle over Representation and Law-making in Congress: Leadership Reforms in the 1990s," in James A. Thurber and Roger H. Davidson, eds., *Remaking Congress: Change and Stability in the 1990s* (Washington, DC: CQ Press, 1995), 105.

9. David R. Mayhew, "Supermajority Rule in the U.S. Senate" *PS: Political Science and Politics* 36 (January 2003): 31–36.

10. Woodrow Wilson, *Congressional Government: A Study in American Government* (New York: Meridian Books, 1956; originally published in 1885), 79.

11. Roger H. Davidson, "Congressional Committees in the New Reform Era: From Combat to the Contract," in Thurber and Davidson, *Remaking Congress*, 28.

12. For more about committees, see E. Scott Adler, *Why Congressional Reforms Fail: Reelection and the House Committee System* (Chicago: University of Chicago Press, 2002); Thomas Mann and Norman Ornstein, *The Broken Branch* (New York: Oxford University Press, 2006), 34–45; and Paul J. Quirk, "Deliberation and Decision Making," in Paul J. Quirk and Sarah A. Binder, eds., *Institutions of Democracy: The Legislative Branch* (New York: Oxford University Press, 2005), 330–42.

13. Christopher Deering and Steven S. Smith, *Committees in Congress*, 3rd ed. (Washington, DC: CQ Press, 1997).

14. Woodrow Wilson, *Congressional Government* (New York: Houghton Mifflin, 1885).

15. Kenneth A. Shepsle, *The Giant Jigsaw Puzzle: Democratic Committee Assignments in the Modern House* (Chicago: University of Chicago Press, 1978).

16. Tim Groseclose and Charles Stewart III, "The Value of Committee Seats in the House, 1947–91," *American Journal of Political Science* 42 (April 1998): 453–74.

17. Charles S. Bullock III, "House Careerists: Changing Patterns of Longevity and Attrition," *American Political Science Review* 66 (December 1972): 1295–1300.

18. Richard F. Fenno Jr., "U.S. House Members in Their Constituencies: An Exploration," *American Political Science Review* 71 (September 1977): 883–917.

19. Richard F. Fenno Jr., *Home Style: House Members in Their Districts* (Boston: Little, Brown, 1978), 32; Schneider, Judy et al. *Congressional Deskbook 2005–2007: 109th Congress.* Alexandria, VA: The Capital Net.

20. Hedrick Smith, *The Power Game* (New York: Ballantine Books, 1989), 108.

21. Gary W. Cox and Jonathan N. Katz, "Why Did the Incumbency Advantage in U.S. House Elections Grow?" *American Journal of Political Science* 40 (May 1996): 478–97; Kenneth N. Bickers and Robert M. Stein, "The Electoral Dynamics of the Federal Pork Barrel," *American Journal of Political Science* 40 (November 1996): 1300–26; and Diana Evans, *Greasing the Wheels: Using Pork Barrel Projects to Build Majority Coalitions in Congress* (New York: Cambridge University Press, 2004).

22. Marjorie Randon Hershey, "Congressional Elections," in Gerald M. Pomper et al., *The Election of 1992: Reports and Interpretations* (Chatham, NJ: Chatham House, 1993), 159.

23. Alan I. Abramowitz, "Incumbency, Congressional Spending, and the Decline of Competition in House Elections," *Journal of Politics* 53 (February 1991): 34–56.

24. Mildred L. Amer, "Membership of the 110th Congress: A Profile." Congressional Research Service (December 15, 2006).

25. "Congress Has Wealth to Weather Economic Downturn." (March 13, 2008), www.opensecrets.org/2006/03/congress-has-wealth-to-weather.html.

26. Amer, "Membership of the 110th Congress."

27. Warren E. Miller and Donald Stokes, "Constituency Influence in Congress," *American Political Science Review* 57 (March 1963): 45–57.

28. Public Opinion Online, Accession Number 0363310, Question Number 054, June 14–18, 2000, Lexis-Nexis RPOLL.

29. Nancy E. McGlen et al., *Women, Politics and American Society*, 4th ed. (New York: Longman, 2004).

30. Cindy Simon Rosenthal, *Women Transforming Congress* (Norman: University of Oklahoma Press, 2003); Karen O'Connor, ed., *Women and Congress: Winning, Running, and Ruling* (Binghamton, NY: Haworth 2003); and Susan J. Carroll, ed., *The Impact of Women in Public Office* (Bloomington: Indiana University Press, 2002).

31. Michele L. Swers, *The Difference Women Make* (Chicago: University of Chicago Press, 2002).

32. *Congressional Quarterly Weekly Report* (January 6, 2001).

33. David E. Price, "Reflections on *Congressional Government* at 120 and Congress at 216," Speech delivered at the Woodrow Wilson International Center for Scholars, November 14, 2005.

34. Norman Ornstein, "GOP Moderates Can Impact Policy—If They Dare," *Roll Call* (February 12, 2003).

35. Byron York, "Bored by Estrada? Owen May Be a Reprise," *The Hill* (March 19, 2003): 43.

36. Price, "Reflections on *Congressional Government* at 120 and Congress at 216."

37. See L. Martin Overby, "The Senate and Justice Thomas: A Note on Ideology, Race, and Constituent Pressures," *Congress and the Presidency* 21 (Autumn 1994): 131–6.

38. John W. Kingdon, *Congressmen's Voting Decisions*, 3rd ed. (Ann Arbor: University of Michigan Press. 1989).

39. Kingdon, *Congressmen's Voting Decisions*. See also Lee Sigelman, Paul J. Wahlbeck, and Emmett H. Buell Jr., "Vote Choice and the Preference for Divided Government: Lessons of 1992," *American Journal of Political Science* 41 (July 1997): 879–94.

40. Ken Kollman, "Inviting Friends to Lobby: Interest Groups, Ideological Bias, and Congressional Committees," *American Journal of Political Science* 41 (April 1997): 519–44. See also Marie Hojnacki and David C. Kimball, "Organized Interests and the Decision of Whom to Lobby in Congress," *American Political Science Review* 92 (December 1998): 775–90.

41. Robert Beirsack, Paul Herrnson, and Clyde Wilcox, *After the Revolution: PACs, Lobbies, and the Republican Congress* (Boston: Allyn and Bacon, 1999).

42. Barbara S. Romzck and Jennifer A. Utter, "Congressional Legislative Staff: Political Professionals or Clerks?" *American Journal of Political Science* 41 (October 1997): 1251–79; Susan Webb Hammond, "Recent Research on Legislative Staffs," *Legislative Studies Quarterly* (November 1996): 543–76; and Michael T. Heaney, "Brokering Health Policy: Coalitions, Parties, and Interest Group Influence," *Journal of Health Politics, Policy, and Law* 31 (October 2006): 887–944.

43. Keith Krehbiel, "Cosponsors and Wafflers from A to Z," *American Journal of Political Science* 39 (November 1995): 906–23.

44. Don Phillips, "Biden Stalls Transportation Picks," *Washington Post* (March 28, 2002): A4.

45. David E. Sanger, "Rounding Out a Clear Clinton Legacy," *New York Times* (May 25, 2000): A1.

46. Sanger, "Rounding Out," A1, A10.

47. Eric Schmitt, "How a Hard-Driving GOP Gave Clinton a Trade Victory," *New York Times* (May 26, 2000): A1.

48. John Burgess, "A Winning Combination: Money, Message, and Clout," *Washington Post* (May 25, 2000): A4.

49. David E. Rosenbaum, "With Smiles and Cell Phones, a Last-Minute Assault on the Undecided," *New York Times* (May 25, 2000): A11.

50. Schmitt, "How a Hard-Driving."

51. Schmitt, "How a Hard-Driving."

52. Sanger, "Rounding Out," A1, A10.

53. Andrew Beadle, "Up Against a Wall? Election-Year Politics and a New Trade Dispute Pose a Challenge to Otherwise Strong Relations Between the US and China," *Journal of Commerce* (April 5, 2004): 24.

54. Paul Blustein, "U.S. Takes Parts of Fight with China to WTO," *Washington Post* (March 31, 2006): D5.

55. Dan Eggen and Peter Baker, "A Defiant Stance in Jefferson Probe," *Washington Post* (May 27, 2006): A1, A10.

56. William F. West, "Oversight Subcommittees in the House of Representatives, *Congress and the Presidency* 25 (Autumn 1998): 147–60.

57. Price, "Reflections on *Congressional Government* at 120 and Congress at 216," 10.

58. Mann and Ornstein, *The Broken Branch*, 1–22.

59. This discussion draws heavily on Steven J. Balla, "Legislative Organization and Congressional Review," Paper delivered at the 1999 meeting of the Midwest Political Science Association.

60. Cindy Skrzycki, "Reforms' Knockout Act, Kept Out of the Ring," *Washington Post* (April 18, 2006). D1.

61. *Wall Street Journal* (April 13, 1973): 10.

62. Note from Senator Jay Rockefeller to Vice President Dick Cheney, July 13, 2003. Reprinted in Charles Babington and Dafna Linzer, "Senator Sounded Alarm in '03" *Washington Post* (December 20, 2005): A10.

63. Quoted in Stewart M. Powell, "Lee Fight Signals Tougher Battles Ahead on Nomination," *Commercial Appeal* (December 21, 1997): A15.

Chapter 8

1. "Two Hundred Years of Presidential Funerals," *Washington Post* (June 10, 2004): C14.

2. "The Fold: Presidential Funerals; Farewell to the Chiefs," *Newsday* (June 9, 2004): A38.

3. Gail Russell Chaddock, "The Rise of Mourning in America," *Christian Science Monitor* (June 11, 2004): 1.

4. Richard E. Neustadt, *Presidential Power and the Modern Presidency* (New York: Free Press, 1991).

5. Edward S. Corwin, *The President: Office and Powers, 1787–1957*, 4th ed. (New York: New York University Press, 1957), 5.

6. Quoted in Corwin, *The President*, 11.

7. Winston Solberg, *The Federal Convention and the Formation of the Union of the American States* (Indianapolis, IN: Bobbs-Merrill, 1958), 235.

8. Reynolds Holding, "Executive Privilege Showdown," *Time Magazine* (March 21, 2007).

9. Benjamin I. Page and Mark P. Petracca, *The American Presidency* (New York: McGraw-Hill, 1983), 262.

10. Page and Petracca, *The American Presidency*, 268.

11. Jim Lobe, "Bush 'Unsigns' War Crimes Treaty," AlterNet.com, May 6, 2002. See also Lincoln P. Bloomfield Jr., "The U.S. Government and the International Criminal Court," Remarks to the Parliamentarians for Global Action, Consultative Assembly of Parliamentarians for the International Criminal Court and the Rule of Laws, Address delivered at the United Nations, New York, September 12, 2003.

12. Quoted in Solberg, *The Federal Convention*, 91.

13. *Clinton v. City of New York*, 524 U.S. 417 (1998).

14. "War Powers: Resolution Grants Bush Power He Needs," *Rocky Mountain News* (September 15, 2001): B6.

15. *Public Papers of the Presidents* (1963), 889.

16. Quoted in Neustadt, *Presidential Power*, 9.

17. Quoted in Paul F. Boller Jr., *Presidential Anecdotes* (New York: Penguin Books, 1981), 78.

18. Lyn Ragsdale and John Theis III, "The Institutionalization of the American Presidency, 1924–1992," *American Journal of Political Science* 41 (October 1997): 1280–1318.

19. Quoted in Page and Petracca, *The American Presidency*, 57.

20. Alfred Steinberg, *The First Ten: The Founding Presidents and Their Administrations* (New York: Doubleday, 1967), 59.

21. Samuel Kernell, *Going Public: New Strategies of Presidential Leadership*, 4th ed. (Washington, DC: CQ Press, 2006), 3.

22. Jeffrey Cohen, "Presidential Rhetoric and the Public Agenda," *American Journal of Political Science* 39 (February 1995): 87–107.

23. Neustadt, *Presidential Power*, 1–10.

24. George Reedy, *The Twilight of the Presidency* (New York: New American Library 1971), 38–39.

25. Kernell, *Going Public*.

26. Dan Balz, "Strange Bedfellows: How Television and Presidential Candidates Changed American Politics," *Washington Monthly* (July 1993).

27. William E. Gibson, "Job Approval Ratings Steady: Personal Credibility Takes a Hit," *News and Observer* (August 19, 1998): A16.

28. Quoted in Peter Baker, "In an Election Year, GOP Wary of Following Bush," *Washington Post* (March 10, 2006): A6.

29. See Louis Fisher, *Constitutional Conflicts Between Congress and the President*, 7th ed. (Lawrence: University Press of Kansas, 2007).

30. Franklin D. Roosevelt, Press Conference, July 23, 1937.

31. Lyndon B. Johnson, *The Vantage Point* (New York: Holt, Rinehart and Winston, 1971), 448.

32. Morris Fiorina, *Divided Government*, Longman Classics (New York: Longman, 2002); and David R. Mayhew, *Divided We Govern: Party Control, Lawmaking, and Investigations, 1946–2002*, 2nd ed. (New Haven, CT: Yale University Press, 2005).

33. See Lance LeLoup and Steven Shull, *The President and Congress: Collaboration and Conflict in National Policymaking* (Boston: Allyn and Bacon, 1999).

34. See Cary Covington, J. Mark Wrighton, and Rhonda Kinney, "A 'Presidency-Augmented' Model of Presidential Success on House Roll Call Votes," *American Journal of Political Science* 39 (November 1995): 1001–24; and Wayne P. Steger, "Presidential Policy Initiation and the Politics of Agenda Control," *Congress and the Presidency* 24 (Spring 1997): 102–14.

35. Quoted in Thomas E. Cronin, *The State of the Presidency*, 2nd ed. (Boston: Little, Brown, 1980), 169.

36. Robert A. Caro, *Master of the Senate: The Years of Lyndon Johnson* (New York: Knopf, 2002).

37. Paul C. Light, *The President's Agenda: Domestic Policy Choice from Kennedy to Carter* (Baltimore, MD: Johns Hopkins University Press, 1983).

38. *Youngstown Sheet and Tube v. Sawyer*, 343 U.S. 579 (1952).

39. Mary Leonard, "Bush Begins Talks on Human Cloning," *Boston Globe* (January 17, 2002): A6.

40. "Resisting Secrecy," *Plain Dealer* (April 30, 2002): B8.

41. Richard Reeves, "Writing History to Executive Order," *New York Times* (November 16, 2001): A25.

Chapter 9

1. Gardiner Harris, "Bush Plan Shows U.S. Is Not Ready for Deadly Flu," *New York Times* (October 8, 2005).

2. Anita Manning and David Jackson, "Bird Flu Plan Lacks a Key Detail," *USA Today* (May 4, 2006): 2A.

3. Harris, "Bush Plan Shows U.S. Is Not Ready for Deadly Flu."

4. Harris, "Bush Plan Shows U.S. Is Not Ready for Deadly Flu."

5. Stephen Barr, "Users Mostly Rate Agencies Favorably," *Washington Post* (April 13, 2000): A29.

6. Harold D. Lasswell, *Politics: Who Gets What, When and How* (New York: McGraw-Hill, 1938).

7. Quoted in Robert C. Caldwell, *James A. Garfield* (Hamden, CT: Archon Books, 1965).

8. David Osborne and Ted Gaebler, *Reinventing Government* (Reading, MA: Addison-Wesley, 1992), 20–21.

9. Office of Personnel Management, *The Fact Book*, http://www.opm.gov/feddata/factbook/2005/factbook2005.pdf.

10. Barbara Slavin, "State Department Having Staffing Trouble," *USA Today* (December 2005): 10A.

11. Paul Weinstein Jr. and Marc Dunkelman, "Blackwater May Be Tip of the Iceberg," *Baltimore Sun* (October 12, 2007): 15A.

12. "Blackwater Boss Grilled over Iraq," BBC News (October 2, 2007).

13. Weinstein and Dunkelman, "Blackwater."

14. Stephen Barr, "Some Trainees Voice Frustration with Presidential Management Intern Program," *Washington Post* (November 26, 2001): B2.

15. Kenneth J. Cooper, "U.S. May Repay Loans for College," *Washington Post* (December 13, 2001): A45.

16. "A Century of Government Growth," *Washington Post* (January 3, 2000): A17. On the difficulty of counting the exact number of government agencies, see David Nachmias and David H. Rosenbloom, *Bureaucratic Government: U.S.A.* (New York: St. Martin's Press, 1980).

17. The classic work on regulatory commissions is Marver Bernstein, *Regulating Business by Independent Commission* (Princeton, NJ: Princeton University Press, 1955).

18. *Humphrey's Executor v. U.S.*, 295 U.S. 602 (1935).

19. H. H. Gerth and C. Wright Mills, *From Max Weber* (New York: Oxford University Press, 1958).

20. Karen DeYoung, "Saudis Detail Steps on Charities; Kingdom Seeks to Quell Record on Terrorist Financing," *Washington Post* (December 3, 2002): A1.

21. "Interagency Coordination Efforts Hampered by the Lack of a National Communication Strategy" GAO-05-323 Report.

22. Michael Lipsky, *Street-Level Bureaucracy: Dilemmas of the Individual in Public Services* (New York: Russell Sage Foundation, 1980).

23. Cornelius M. Kerwin, *Rulemaking: How Government Agencies Write Law and Make Policy*, 2nd ed. (Washington, DC: CQ Press, 1999), xv.

24. Jack C. Plano and Milton Greenberg, *The American Political Dictionary*, 6th ed. (New York: Holt, Rinehart and Winston, 1982), 236.

25. Stephen Barr, "For IRS, a Deadline to Draft a Smile," *Washington Post* (January 31, 1999): H1.

26. FOX News, Opinion Dynamics Poll, May 20, 2003, Lexis-Nexis RPOLL.

27. Quoted in Arthur Schlesinger Jr., *A Thousand Days* (Greenwich, CT: Fawcett Books, 1967), 377.

28. Thomas V. DiBacco, "Veep Gore Reinventing Government—Again!" *USA Today* (September 9, 1993): 13A.

29. George A. Krause, "Presidential Use of Executive Orders, 1953–1994," *American Politics Quarterly* 25 (October 1997): 458–81.

30. Irene Murphy, *Public Policy on the Status of Women* (Lexington, MA: Lexington Books, 1974).

31. "By Any Other Name: Whatever FEMA Is Ultimately Called, It's Still an Agency in Need of Profound Reform," *Washington Post* (May 10, 2006): A24.

32. Mathew McCubbins and Thomas Schwartz, "Congressional Oversight Overlooked: Police Patrols Versus Fire Alarms," *American Journal of Political Science* 28 (1987): 165–79.

33. Rosemary O'Leary, *Environmental Change: Federal Courts and the EPA* (Philadelphia: Temple University Press, 1993).

34. Wendy Hansen, Renee Johnson, and Isaac Unah, "Specialized Courts, Bureaucratic Agencies, and the Politics of U.S. Trade Policy," *American Journal of Political Science* 39 (August 1995): 529–57.

Chapter 10

1. Linda Greenhouse, "In Steps Big and Small. Supreme Court Moved Right," *New York Times* (July 1 2007): A1.

2. Linda Greenhouse. "On Court That Defied Labeling, Kennedy Made Boldest Mark," *New York Times* (June 29, 2008): A1.

3. Greenhouse, "In Steps Big and Small."

4. Bernard Schwartz, *The Law in America* (New York: American Heritage, 1974), 48.

5. Julius Goebel Jr., *History of the Supreme Court of the United States, vol. 1: Antecedents and Beginnings to 1801* (New York Macmillan, 1971), 206.

6. *Marbury v. Madison*, 5 U.S. 137 (1803).

7. *Martin v. Hunter's Lessee*, 14 U.S. 304 (1816).

8. Quoted in Goebel, *History of the Supreme Court*, 280.

9. *Chisholm v. Georgia*, 2 U.S. 419 (1793).

10. *Fletcher v. Peck*, 10 U.S. 87 (1810); *Martin v. Hunter's Lessee*, 14 U.S. 304 (1816); *Cohens v. Virginia*, 19 U.S. 264 (1821).

11. *McCulloch v. Maryland*, 17 U.S. 316 (1819).

12. *Marbury v. Madison*, 5 U.S. 137 (1803).

13. *Marbury v. Madison*, 5 U.S. 137 (1803).

14. This discussion draws heavily on Jack C. Plano and Milton Greenberg, *The American Political Dictionary*, 10th ed. (Fort Worth, TX: Harcourt Brace, 1996), 247.

15. *Strauder v. West Virginia*, 100 U.S. 303 (1888).

16. *Duren v. Missouri*, 439 U.S. 357 (1979).

17. *Batson v. Kentucky*, 476 U.S. 79 (1986) (African Americans), and *J. E. B. v. Alabama*, 511 U.S. 127 (1994) (women).

18. David W. Neubauer, *Judicial Process: Law, Courts, and Politics* (Pacific Grove, CA: Brooks/Cole, 1991), 57.

19. Cases involving citizens from different states can be filed in state or federal court.

20. Sheldon Goldman and Elliot E. Slotnick, "Clinton's First Term Judiciary: Many Bridges to Cross," *Judicature* (May/June 1997): 254–55.

21. Neil Lewis, "Deal Ends Impasse over Judicial Nominees," *New York Times* (May 19, 2004): A19.

22. Dan Balz and Amy Goldstein, "Filibuster Showdown Looms in Senate: Democrats Prepare for Next Court Pick," *Washington Post* (September 28, 2005): A4.

23. Quoted in Nina Totenberg, "Will Judges Be Chosen Rationally?" *Judicature* (August/September 1976): 93.

24. Quoted in Judge Irving R. Kaufman, "Charting a Judicial Pedigree," *New York Times* (January 24, 1981): A23.

25. Quoted in Lawrence Baum, *The Supreme Court*, 3rd ed. (Washington, DC: CQ Press, 1989), 108.

26. See Barbara A. Perry, *A Representative Supreme Court? The Impact of Race, Religion, and Gender on Appointments* (New York: Greenwood, 1991).

27. Clarence Thomas was raised a Catholic but attended an Episcopalian church at the time of his appointment, having been barred from Catholic sacraments because of his remarriage. He again, however, is attending Roman Catholic services.

28. Amy Goldstein, "Bush Set to Curb ABA's Role in Court Appointments," *Washington Post* (March 18, 2001): A2.

29. Subsequent revelations about Brandeis's secret financial payments to Frankfurter to allow him to handle cases of social interest to Brandeis (while Brandeis was on the Court and couldn't handle them himself) raise questions about the fitness of both Frankfurter and Brandeis for the bench. Still, no information about Frankfurter's legal arrangements with Brandeis was unearthed during the committee's investigations or Frankfurter's testimony.

30. John Brigham, *The Cult of the Court* (Philadelphia: Temple University Press, 1987).

31. Stephen L. Wasby, *The Supreme Court in the Federal Judicial System*, 4th ed. (Chicago: Nelson-Hall, 1988), 194.

32. Wasby, *The Supreme Court in the Federal Judicial System*, 194.

33. Wasby, *The Supreme Court in the Federal Judicial System*, 199. Much of this change occurred as the result of an increase in state criminal cases, of which nearly 100 percent concerned constitutional questions.

34. Justice Stevens chooses not to join this pool. According to one former clerk, "He wanted an independent review," but Stevens examines only about 20 percent of the petitions, leaving the rest to his clerks. Tony Mauro, "Ginsburg Plunges into the Cert Pool," *Legal Times* (September 6, 1993): 8.

35. Paul Wahlbeck, James F. Spriggs II, and Lee Sigelman, "Ghostwriters on the Court? A Stylistic Analysis of U.S. Supreme Court Opinion Drafts," *American Politics Research 30* (March 2002): 166–92. Wahlbeck, Spriggs, and Sigelman note that "between 1969 and 1972—the period during which the justices each became entitled to a third law clerk . . . the number of opinions increased by about 50 percent and the number of words tripled."

36. Richard A. Posner, *The Federal Courts: Crisis and Reform* (Cambridge, MA: Harvard University Press, 1985), 114.

37. Todd C. Peppers, *Courtiers of the Marble Palace: The Rise and Influence of the Supreme Court Law Clerk* (Palo Alto, CA: Stanford University Press, 2006).

38. Edward Lazarus, *Closed Chambers: The First Eyewitness Account of the Epic Struggles Inside the Supreme Court* (New York: Random House, 1998).

39. "Retired Chief Justice Warren Attacks Freund Study Group's Composition and Proposal," *American Bar Association Journal 59* (July 1973): 728.

40. Kathleen Werdegar, "The Solicitor General and Administrative Due Process," *George Washington Law Review* (1967–1968): 482.

41. Rebecca Mae Salokar, *The Solicitor General: The Politics of Law* (Philadelphia: Temple University Press, 1992), 3.

42. Quoted in Elder Witt, *A Different Justice: Reagan and the Supreme Court* (Washington, DC: CQ Press, 1986), 133.

43. See, for example, Lawrence Baum, *The Supreme Court*, 4th ed. (Washington, DC: CQ Press, 1992), 106.

44. Richard C. Cortner, *The Supreme Court and Civil Liberties* (Palo Alto, CA: Mayfield, 1975), vi.

45. *Brown v. Board of Education*, 347 U.S. 483 (1954); *Planned Parenthood of Southeastern Pennsylvania v. Casey*, 585 U.S. 833 (1992); *Grutter v. Bollinger*, 539 U.S. 306 (2003).

46. Gregory A. Caldeira and John R. Wright, "*Amicus Curiae* Before the Supreme Court: Who Participates, When and How Much?" *Journal of Politics 52* (August 1990): 803.

47. See also John R. Hermann, "American Indians in Court: The Burger and Rehnquist Years," Ph.D. dissertation, Emory University, 1996.

48. *U.S. v. Nixon*, 418 U.S. 683 (1974).

49. Linda Greenhouse, "With O'Connor Retirement and a New Chief Justice Comes an Awareness of Change," *New York Times* (January 28, 2006): A10.

50. *Clinton v. James*, 520 U.S. 681 (1997).

51. *Atkins v. Virginia*, 536 U.S. 304 (2002).

52. Donald L. Horowitz, *The Courts and Social Policy* (Washington, DC: Brookings Institution, 1977), 538.

53. *Brown v. Board of Education*, 347 U.S. 483 (1954).

54. *Webster v. Reproductive Health Services*, 492 U.S. 490 (1989).

55. See, for example, Tracey E. George and Lee Epstein, "On the Nature of Supreme Court Decision Making," *American Political Science Re-*

view 86 (1992): 323–37; Melinda Gann Hall and Paul Brace, "Justices' Responses to Case Facts: An Interactive Model," *American Politics Quarterly* (April 1996): 237–61; Lawrence Baum, *The Puzzle of Judicial Behavior* (Ann Arbor: University of Michigan Press, 1997); and Gregory N. Flemming, David B. Holmes, and Susan Gluck Mezey, "An Integrated Model of Privacy Decision Making in State Supreme Courts," *American Politics Quarterly* 26 (January 1998): 35–58.

56. Lee Epstein and Jeffrey A. Segal, "Changing Room: The Court's Dynamics Have a Way of Altering a Justice's Approach to the Law," *Washington Post* (November 20, 2005): B1.

57. Jeffrey A. Segal and Harold J. Spaeth, *The Supreme Court and the Attitudinal Model Revisited* (New York: Cambridge University Press, 2002).

58. Gerard Gryski, Eleanor C. Main, and William Dixon, "Models of State High Court Decision Making in Sex Discrimination Cases," *Journal of Politics* 48 (1986): 143–55; and C. Neal Tate and Roger Handberg, "Time Binding and Theory Building in Personal Attribute Models of Supreme Court Voting Behavior, 1916–1988," *American Political Science Review* 35 (1991): 460–80.

59. Donald R. Songer and Sue Davis, "The Impact of Party and Region on Voting Decisions in the U.S. Courts of Appeals, 1955–86," *Western Political Quarterly* 43 (1990): 830–44.

60. H.W. Perry, *Deciding to Decide: Agenda Setting in the United States Supreme Court* (Cambridge, MA: Harvard University Press, 1991); and Gregory A. Caldeira, John R. Wright, and Christopher Zorn, "Strategic Voting and Gatekeeping in the Supreme Court," *Journal of Law, Economics, and Organization* 15 (1999): 549–72.

61. Forrest Maltzman and Paul J. Walhbeck, "May It Please the Chief? Opinion Assignments in the Rehnquist Court," *American Journal of Political Science* 40 (1996): 421–43.

62. James F. Spriggs, Forrest Maltzman, and Paul J. Wahlbeck, "Bargaining on the U.S. Supreme Court: Justices' Responses to Majority Opinion Drafts," *Journal of Politics* 61 (1999): 485–506.

63. Kevin T. McGuire and James A. Stimson, "The Least Dangerous Branch Revisited: New Evidence on Supreme Court Responsiveness to Public Preferences," *Journal of Politics* 66 (2004): 1018–35.

64. Charles M. Cameron, Donald R. Songer, and Jeffrey A. Segal, "Strategic Auditing in a Political Hierarchy: An Informational Model of the Supreme Court's Certiorari Decisions," *American Political Science Review* 94 (2000): 101–16.

65. Pablo T. Spiller and Rafael Gely, "Congressional Control or Judicial Independence: The Determinants of U.S. Supreme Court Labor-Relations Decisions, 1949–1988," *RAND Journal of Economics* 23 (1992): 463–92.

66. Timothy R. Johnson and Andrew D. Martin, "The Public's Conditional Response to Supreme Court Decisions," *American Political Science Review* 92 (June 1998): 299–309.

67. *Korematsu* v. *U.S.*, 323 U.S. 214 (1944).

68. *Youngstown Sheet & Tube Co.* v. *Sawyer*, 343 U.S. 579 (1952). The Supreme Court ruled that President Truman's seizure and operation of U.S. steel mills in the face of a strike threat were unconstitutional, because the Constitution implied no such broad executive power. See Alan Westin, *Anatomy of a Constitutional Law Case* (New York: Macmillan, 1958); and Maeva Marcus, *Truman and the Steel Seizure Case* (New York: Columbia University Press, 1977).

69. *U.S.* v. *Nixon*, 418 U.S. 683 (1974).

70. Gallup Poll, June 1–4, 2006, Lexis–Nexis RPOLL.

71. *Boumediene* v. *Bush*, 553 U.S._____ (2008).

72. *Ashcroft* v. *Free Speech Coalition*, 535 U.S. 234 (2002).

73. *U.S.* v. *Williams*, 553 U.S._____ (2008).

74. "Supreme Court Cases Overruled by Subsequent Decision," U.S. Government Printing Office. Accessed online at http://www.gpoaccess.gov/constitution/pdf/con041.pdf.

75. See, for example, *Colegrove* v. *Green*, 328 U.S. 549 (1946).

76. *Baker* v. *Carr*, 369 U.S. 186 (1962).

77. Charles Johnson and Bradley C. Canon, *Judicial Policies: Implementation and Impact*, 2nd ed. (Washington, DC: CQ Press, 1998), ch. 1.

78. *Reynolds* v. *Sims*, 377 U.S. 533 (1964).

79. *Hunt* v. *Cromartie*, 546 U.S. 541 (1999).

80. *Mississippi University for Women* v. *Hogan*, 458 U.S. 718 (1982).

Chapter 11

1. Richard Dawson et al., *Political Socialization*, 2nd ed. (Boston: Little, Brown, 1977), 33.

2. Robert D. Hess and David Easton, "The Child's Changing Image of the President," *Public Opinion Quarterly* 14 (Winter 1960): 632–42; and Fred I. Greenstein, *Children and Politics* (New Haven, CT: Yale University Press, 1965).

3. Laura Pappano, "Potential War Poses Threat to Teachers," *Boston Globe* (March 9, 2003): B9.

4. James Simon and Bruce D. Merrill, "Political Socialization in the Classroom Revisited: The Kids Voting Program," *Social Science Journal* 35 (1998): 29–42.

5. Simon and Merrill, "Political Socialization in the Classroom Revisited."

6. Harold W. Stanley and Richard G. Niemi, *Vital Statistics on American Politics, 2007–2008* (Washington, DC: CQ Press, 2008).

7. *Statistical Abstract of the United States, 1997* (Washington, DC: Government Printing Office, 1997), 1011.

8. Pew Project for Excellence in Journalism 2008.

9. Gallup Poll, December 6–9, 2007.

10. USA Today and CNN/Gallup Tracking Poll, USAToday.com.

11. Edward S. Greenberg, "The Political Socialization of Black Children," in Edward S. Greenberg, ed., *Political Socialization* (New York: Atherton Press, 1970), 131.

12. Susan Page and Maria Puente, "Views of Whites, Blacks Differ Starkly on Disaster," *USA Today* (September 13, 2005): A1, A2.

13. Elaine J. Hall and Myra Marx Ferree, "Race Differences in Abortion Attitudes," *Public Opinion Quarterly* 50 (Summer 1986): 193–207; and Jon Hurwitz and Mark Peffley, "Public Perceptions of Race and Crime: The Role of Racial Stereotypes," *American Journal of Political Science* 41 (April 1997): 375–401.

14. Elaine S. Povich, "Courting Hispanics: Group's Votes Could Shift House Control," *Newsday* (April 21, 2002): A4.

15. Karen M. Kaufmann and John Petrocik, "The Changing Politics of American Men: Understanding Sources of the Gender Gap," *American Journal of Political Science* 43 (July 1999): 864–87.

16. Margaret Trevor, "Political Socialization, Party Identification, and the Gender Gap," *Public Opinion Quarterly* 63 (Spring 1999): 62–89.

17. Alexandra Marks, "Gender Gap Narrows over Kosovo," *Christian Science Monitor* (April 30, 1999): 1.

18. Pew Research Center for People and the Press, 2002.

19. Susan A. MacManus, *Young v. Old: Generational Combat in the 21st Century* (Boulder, CO: Westview, 1995).

20. Pew Forum on Religion and Public Life, "U.S. Religious Landscape Survey," http://www.pewforum.org.

21. CNN Exit Polls, www.cnn.com/election/2008/results/polls.

22. Alan M. Winkler, "Public Opinion," in Jack Greene, ed., *The Encyclopedia of American Political History* (New York: Charles Scribner's Sons, 1988), 1038.

23. Quoted in *Public Opinion Quarterly* 29 (Winter 1965–1966): 547.

24. *Literary Digest* 125 (November 14, 1936): 1.

25. Robert S. Erikson, Norman Luttbeg, and Kent Tedin, *American Public Opinion: Its Origin, Contents, and Impact* (New York: Wiley, 1980), 28.

26. Diane J. Heith, "Staffing the White House Public Opinion Apparatus 1969–1988," *Public Opinion Quarterly* 62 (Summer 1998): 165.

27. Francis J. Connolly and Charley Manning, "What 'Push Polling' Is and What It Isn't," *Boston Globe* (August 16, 2001): A21.

28. Suzanne Soule, "Will They Engage? Political Knowledge, Participation and Attitudes of Generations X and Y," paper prepared for the 2001 German and American Conference, 6.

29. Soule, "Will They Engage?" quoting Richard G. Niemi and Jane Junn, *Civic Education* (New Haven, CT: Yale University Press, 1998).

30. Quoted in Everett Carll Ladd, "Fiskin's 'Deliberative Poll' Is Flawed Science and Dubious Democracy," *Public Perspective* (December/January 1996): 41.

31. "Don't Know Much About…" *Christian Science Monitor* (May 16, 2002): 8.

32. "Don't Know Much About History, Geography…" *Pittsburgh Post-Gazette* (January 22, 2003): E2; Laurence D. Cohen, "Geography for Dummies," *Hartford Courant* (December 8, 2002): C3.

33. "Gender Gap in Political Knowledge Persists in 2004, National Annenberg Election Survey Shows," http://www.nacs.org.

34. V. O. Key Jr., *The Responsible Electorate: Rationality in Presidential Voting, 1936–1960* (Cambridge, MA: Belknap Press of Harvard University, 1966).

35. Richard Nodeau et al., "Elite Economic Forecasts, Economic News, Mass Economic Judgements and Presidential Approval," *Journal of Politics* 61 (February 1999): 109–35.

36. Michael Towle, Review of *Presidential Responsiveness and Public Policy-making: The Public and the Policies* by Jeffrey E. Cohen, *Journal of Politics* 61 (February 1999): 230–2.

37. John E. Mueller, *War, Presidents, and Public Opinion* (New York: Wiley, 1973), 69.

38. Roderick P. Hart, *The Sound of Leadership: Presidential Communication in the Modern Age* (Chicago: University of Chicago Press, 1987).

39. See, for example, Benjamin Page and Robert Shapiro, "Effects of Public Opinion on Policy," *American Political Science Review* 57 (March 1983): 175–90; Alan D. Monroe, "Public Opinion and Public Policy, 1980–1993," *Public Opinion Quarterly* 62 (Spring 1998): 6–28; and Kathleen M. McGraw, Samuel Best, and Richard Timpone, "'What They Say or What They Do?' The Impact of Elite Explanation and Policy Outcomes on Public Opinion," *American Journal of Political Science* 39 (February 1995): 53–74.

40. Benjamin Ginsberg, *The Captive Public* (New York: Basic Books, 1986), ch. 4.

41. "George Gallup Is Dead at 82," *New York Times* (July 28, 1984): A1.

42. Herbert Asher, *Polling and the Public: What Every Citizen Should Know* (Washington, DC: CQ Press, 1988), 109.

Chapter 12

1. John F. Bibby, "Party Networks: National-State Integration, Allied Groups, and Issue Activists," in John C. Green and Daniel M. Shea, eds., *The State of the Parties: The Changing Role of Contemporary American Parties*, 3rd ed. (Lanham, MD: Rowman and Littlefield, 1999).

2. This conception of a political party was originally put forth by V. O. Key Jr. in *Politics, Parties, and Pressure Groups* (New York: Crowell, 1958).

3. John H. Aldrich, *Why Parties? The Origin and Transformation of Party Politics in America* (Chicago: University of Chicago Press, 1995).

4. By contrast, Great Britain did not develop truly national, broad-based parties until the 1870s.

5. See *Historical Statistics of the United States: Colonial Times to 1970*, part 2, series Y-27-28 (Washington, DC: Government Printing Office, 1975), based on unpublished data prepared by Walter Dean Burnham. See also Harold W. Stanley and Richard G. Niemi, *Vital Statistics on American Politics 2005–2006* (Washington, DC: CQ Press, 2006), for contemporary turnout figures.

6. U.S. Census Bureau, Population Profile of the United States: 2000 (Internet release), available from http://www.census.gov/population/pop-profile/2000/profile2000.pdf.

7. On the subject of party realignment, see Walter Dean Burnham, *Critical Elections and the Mainsprings of American Politics* (New York: Norton, 1970); Kristi Andersen, *The Creation of a Democratic Majority* (Chicago: University of Chicago Press, 1979); and John R. Petrocik, "Realignment: New Party Coalitions and the Nationalization of the South," *Journal of Politics* 49 (May 1987): 347–75.

8. See Burnham, *Critical Elections and the Mainsprings of American Politics*, for a defense of realignment theory.

9. For a perspective on reconsidering the relevance and validity of critical realignments, see David Mayhew, *Electoral Realignments* (New Haven, CT: Yale University Press, 2004).

10. Morris P. Fiorina, *Retrospective Voting in American National Elections* (New Haven, CT: Yale University Press, 1981); and Charles H. Franklin and John E. Jackson, "The Dynamics of Party Identification," *American Political Science Review* 77 (1983): 957–73.

11. See, for example, V. O. Key Jr., "A Theory of Critical Elections," *Journal of Politics* 17 (February 1955): 3–18.

12. See Everett Carll Ladd, "The Brittle Mandate: Electoral Dealignment and the 1980 Presidential Election," *Political Science Quarterly* 96 (1981): 1–25.

13. Everett Carll Ladd, "Like Waiting for Godot: The Uselessness of 'Realignment' for Understanding Change in Contemporary American Politics," in Byron Shafer, ed., *The End of Realignment? Interpreting American Electoral Eras* (Madison: University of Wisconsin Press, 1991).

14. For a discussion of secular realignment in the South, see Jeffrey M. Stonecash, "Class and Party: Secular Realignment and the Survival of Democrats Outside the South," *Political Research Quarterly* 53:4 (2000): 731–52.

15. M. V. Hood, Quentin Kidd, and Irwin L. Morris, "Of Byrds and Bumpers: Using Democratic Senators to Analyze Political Change in the South, 1960–1995," *American Journal of Political Science* 43 (April 1999): 465–87.

16. For a discussion of the disruptive effects of polarization, see David R. Jones, "Party Polarization and Legislative Gridlock," *Political Research Quarterly* 54 (2001): 125–41.

17. Earl Black and Merle Black, *The Rise of Southern Republicans* (Cambridge, MA: Harvard University Press, 2002).

18. Morris P. Fiorina, *Culture War? The Myth of a Polarized America*, 2nd ed. (New York: Pearson Longman, 2006).

19. For a discussion of how the Bush campaign's 2004 efforts to increase turnout paid off in Florida, see Abby Goodnough, "Bush Secured Victory by Veering from Beaten Path," *New York Times* (November 7, 2004).

20. See David E. Price, *Bringing Back the Parties* (Washington, DC: CQ Press, 1984), 284–8.

21. Anthony Downs, *An Economic Theory of Democracy* (New York: Harper's, 1957); Joseph A Schlesinger, *Political Parties and the Winning of Office* (Ann Arbor, MI: University of Michigan Press, 1994).

22. Arend Lijphart, *Patterns of Democracy: Government Forms and Performance in Thirty-Six Countries* (New Haven, CT: Yale University Press, 1996), chapter 8.

23. Christian Collet and Martin P. Wattenberg, "Strategically Unambitious: Minor Party and Independent Candidates in the 1996 Congressional Elections," in John C. Green and Daniel M. Shea, eds., *The*

State of the Parties: The Changing Role of Contemporary American Parties, 3rd ed. (Lanham, MD: Rowman and Littlefield, 1999).

24. Marc J. Hetherington, "The Effect of Political Trust on the Presidential Vote, 1968–1992," *American Political Science Review* 93 (1999): 311–26.

25. John Clifford Green, Paul S. Herrnson, and John C. Green, eds., *Responsible Partisanship: The Evolution of American Political Parties Since the 1950s* (Lawrence: University Press of Kansas, 2003).

26. Cornelius P. Cotter, James L. Gibson, John F. Bibby, and Robert J. Huckshorn, *Party Organizations in American Politics* (Pittsburgh: University of Pittsburgh Press, 1989).

27. Bibby, "Party Networks."

28. Raymond J. La Raja, "State and Local Political Parties," in Michael J. Mablin, ed., *The Election After Reform: Money, Politics, and the Bipartisan Campaign Reform Act* (Lanham, MD: Rowman and Littlefield, 2006); and http://www.pewtrusts.org/uploadedFiles/wwwpewtrustsorg/Reports/Improving_elections/IMSP_Shifting_Gears_0905.pdf.

29. Mark Leibovich, "Howard Dean: He Still Has the Power," *Washington Post* (January 18, 2005).

30. Although Republicans for the House maintained their fund-raising edge in 2006, the 31 Democratic candidates for the Senate raised an average of $8.6 million, while their 33 Republican counterparts raised an average $6.7 million. [Update for 2008 to come] See Opensecrets.org.

31. Catharine Richert, "Party Unity: United We Stand Opposed," *CQ Weekly* (January 14, 2008): 143.

32. Sidney M. Milkis, *The President and the Parties: The Transformation of the American Party System Since the New Deal* (New York: Oxford University Press, 1993).

33. Steven Schier, "Bush Is Parliamentary, Not Bipartisan," *The Hill* (July 12, 2005).

34. See S. Sidney Ulmer, "The Political Party Variable on the Michigan Supreme Court," *Journal of Public Law* 11 (1962): 352–62; Stuart Nagel, "Political Party Affiliation and Judges' Decisions," *American Political Science Review* 55 (1961): 843–50; David W. Adamany, "The Party Variable in Judges' Voting: Conceptual Notes and a Case Study," *American Political Science Review* 63 (1969): 57–73; Sheldon Goldman, "Voting Behavior on the United States Courts of Appeals, 1961–1964," *American Political Science Review* 60 (1966): 374–83; and Robert A. Carp and C. K. Rowland, *Policymaking and Politics in the Federal District Courts* (Knoxville: University of Tennessee Press, 1983).

35. Randall D. Lloyd, "Separating Partisanship from Party in Judicial Research: Reapportionment in the U.S. District Courts," *American Political Science Review* 89 (June 1995): 413–20.

36. The Farmer-Labor Party did survive in a sense; having endured a series of defeats, it merged in 1944 with the Democrats, and Minnesota's Democratic candidates still officially bear the standard of the Democratic-Farmer-Labor (DFL) Party. At about the same time, also having suffered severe electoral reversals, the Progressives stopped nominating candidates in Wisconsin. The party's members either returned to the Republican Party, from which the Progressives had split early in the century, or became Democrats.

37. Sarah M. Morehouse, "Legislatures and Political Parties," *State Government* 59 (1986): 19–24.

38. See Steven E. Finkel and Howard A. Scarrow, "Party Identification and Party Enrollment: The Difference and the Consequence," *Journal of Politics* 47 (May 1985): 620–42.

39. Black and Black, *The Rise of Southern Republicans*.

40. Karen M. Kaufmann and John R. Petrocik, "The Changing Politics of American Men: Understanding the Sources of the Gender Gap," *American Journal of Political Science* 43 (July 1999): 864–87.

41. Michael Dawson, *Behind the Mule: Race and Class in African-American Politics* (Princeton, NJ: Princeton University Press, 1994); and Louis Bolce, Gerald DeMaio, and Douglas Muzzio, "Blacks and the Republican Party: The 20 Percent Solution," *Political Science Quarterly* 107 (Spring 1992): 63–79.

42. Abby Goodnough, "Hispanic Vote in Florida: Neither a Bloc nor a Lock," *New York Times* (October 17, 2004).

43. For a look at how supporting restricting immigration has imperiled California Republicans' appeal to Hispanic voters, see Shaun Bowler, Stephen P. Nicholson, and Gary M. Segura, "Earthquakes and Aftershocks: Race, Direct Democracy, and Partisan Change," *American Journal of Political Science* 50:1 (2006): 146–59.

44. William H. Flanigan and Nancy H. Zingale, *Political Behavior of the American Electorate*, 11th ed. (Washington, DC: CQ Press, 2006).

45. Flanigan and Zingale, *Political Behavior of the American Electorate*, 2006.

46. The presidential election of 1960 may be an extreme case, but John F. Kennedy's massive support among Catholics and Richard M. Nixon's less substantial but still impressive backing by Protestants demonstrates the polarization that religion could once produce. See Philip E. Converse, "Religion and Politics: The 1960 Election," in Angus Campbell et al., *Elections and the Political Order* (New York: Wiley, 1966), 96–124.

47. The Pew Forum on Religion and Public Life, U.S. Religious Landscape Survey, February 2008.

48. Flanigan and Zingale, *Political Behavior of the American Electorate*, 2006.

49. For a discussion of recent trends in party strength, see Morris P. Fiorina, "Parties and Partisanship: A 40-Year Retrospective," *Political Behavior* 24 (2002): 93–115.

50. Bruce E. Keith et al., *The Myth of the Independent Voter* (Berkeley: University of California Press, 1992).

51. Elmer E. Schattschneider, *Party Government* (New York: Farrar and Rinehart, 1942).

Chapter 13

1. William A. Galston, "Civic Education and Political Participation," *Political Science and Politics* 37 (2004): 263–6.

2. Steven J. Rosenstone and John Mark Hanson, *Mobilization, Participation, and Democracy in America* (New York: Macmillan, 1993).

3. U.S. Census Bureau, "Voting and Registration in the Election of November 2004," http://www.census.gov/prod/2006pubs/p20-556.pdf.

4. See, for example, Laura Stoker and M. Kent Jennings, "Life-Cycle Transitions and Political Participation: The Case of Marriage," *American Political Science Review* 89 (1995): 421–36; and Paul R. Abramson, John H. Aldrich, and David W. Rohde, *Change and Continuity in the 1996 Elections* (Washington, DC: CQ Press, 1998).

5. Thomas M. Guterbock and Bruce London, "Race, Political Orientation, and Participation: An Empirical Test of Four Competing Theories," *American Sociological Review* 48 (1983): 439–53.

6. Carol A. Cassel, "Hispanic Turnout: Estimates from Validated Voting Data," *Political Science Quarterly* 55 (June 2002): 391–408.

7. See http://www.census.gov/Press-Release/www/releases/archives/voting/004986.html.

8. League of United Latin American Citizens, http://www.lulac.org.

9. Sidney Verba, Kay Lehman Schlozman, and Henry E. Brady, *Voice and Equality: Civic Voluntarism in American Politics* (New York: Belknap, 1996). Data on relationship between religious service attendance and voting were calculated by the authors obtained from the Pew Research Center's study *Political Landscape More Favor-*

able to Democrats: Trends in Political Values and Core Attitudes, 1987–2007, March 22, 2007.

10. Joseph Graf, *Small Donors and Online Giving: A Study of Donors to the 2004 Presidential Campaigns* (Washington, DC: Institute for Politics, Democracy, and the Internet, 2006).

11. Benjamin Highton, "Easy Registration and Voter Turnout," *Journal of Politics* 59 (1997): 565–75.

12. Stephen Knack and J. White, "Election-Day Registration and Turnout Inequality," *Political Behavior* 22 (March 2000): 29–44.

13. J. Eric Oliver, "The Effects of Eligibility Restrictions and Party Activity on Absentee Voting and Overall Turnout," *American Journal of Political Science* 40 (May 1996): 498–513.

14. International Institute for Democracy and Electoral Assistance, "Global Database," http://www.idea.int/vt/survey/voter_turnout_pop2.cfm.

15. Marg N. Franklin and Wolfgang P. Hirczy, "Separated Powers, Divided Government, and Turnout in U.S. Presidential Elections," *American Journal of Political Science* 42 (January 1998): 316–26.

16. Rosenstone and Hansen, *Mobilization, Participation, and Democracy in America.*

17. "Voters Win with Election Day Registration," A Demos Policy Brief, Winter 2008, http://www.demos.org/pubs/Voters%20Win.pdf. For a summary of voter registration laws and requirements for all states, see http://usgovinfo.about.com/blvrbystate.htm.

18. Benjamin Highton and Raymond E. Wolfinger, "Estimating the Effects of the National Voter Registration Act of 1993," *Political Behavior* 20:2 (1998), 79–104.

19. Arend Lijphart, "Unequal Participation: Democracy's Unsolved Dilemma," *American Political Science Review* 91 (March 1997): 1–14.

20. Gary C. Jacobson, *The Politics of Congressional Elections*, 7th ed. (New York: Longman, 2008).

21. Harold W. Stanley and Richard G. Niemi, *Vital Statistics on American Politics 2007–2008* (Washington, DC: CQ Press, 2007).

22. Morris P. Fiorina, *Divided Government* (Boston: Allyn and Bacon, 1996); Kyle E. Saunders, Alan I. Abramowitz, and Jonathan Williamson, "A New Kind of Balancing Act: Electoral Uncertainty and Ticket-Splitting in the 1996 and 2000 Elections," *Political Research Quarterly* 58 (March 2005): 69–78.

23. Martin P. Wattenberg, *The Decline of American Political Parties, 1952–1996* (Cambridge, MA: Harvard University Press, 1998).

24. Cable News Network, 2008 election results, http://www.cnn.com/ELECTION/2008/.

25. Henry Cisneros, "Winning the Crucial Hispanic Vote in 2000," *Campaigns and Elections* (August 1, 1999.)

26. Paula McClain and James Stewart, *"Can We All Get Along?": Racial and Ethnic Minorities in American Politics*, 4th ed. (Boulder, CO: Westview, 2005); Pei-te Lien, *The Politics of Asian Americans: Diversity and Community* (New York: Routledge, 2004).

27. Cable News Network, 2008 election results, http://www.cnn.com/ELECTION/2008/.

28. See http://www.cnn.com/ELECTION/2008/.

29. Kathleen A. Dolan, *Voting for Women: How the Public Evaluates Women Candidates* (Boulder, CO: Westview, 2004).

30. John C. Green, *The Faith Factor: How Religion Influences American Elections* (Westport, CT: Praeger, 2007).

31. Warren E. Miller and J. Merrill Shanks, *The New American Voter* (Cambridge, MA: Harvard University Press, 1996), 270.

32. Voter News Service Exit Poll, http://www.cnn.com/ELECTION/2004/.

33. Cable News Network, 2008 election results, http://www.cnn.com/ELECTION/2008/.

34. Michael S. Lewis-Beck and Mary Stegmaier, "Economic Determinants of Electoral Outcomes," *Annual Review of Political Science* 3 (2000): 183–219.

35. Paul Allen Beck, *Party Politics in America*, 8th ed. (New York: Longman, 1998); David Adamany, "Cross-over Voting and the Democratic Party's Reform Rules," *American Political Science Review* 70 (1976): 536–41; Ronald Hedlund and Meredith W. Watts, "The Wisconsin Open Primary: 1968 to 1984," *American Politics Quarterly* 14 (1986): 55–74; and Gary D. Wekkin, "The Conceptualization and Measurement of Crossover Voting," *Western Political Quarterly* 41 (1988): 105–14.

36. Gary D. Wekken, "Why Crossover Voters Are Not 'Mischievous' Voters," *American Politics Quarterly* 19 (1991): 229–47; and Todd L. Cherry and Stephan Kroll, "Crashing the Party: An Experimental Investigation of Strategic Voting in Primary Elections," *Public Choice* 114 (2003): 387–420.

37. Of these ten states, South Dakota is the only state outside the South to hold a runoff primary. A runoff is held only if no candidate receives at least 35 percent of the vote, however. See "Statutory Election Information of the Several States," *The Green Papers*, http://www.thegreenpapers.com/slg/sei.phtml?format=sta.

38. Shaun Bowler, Todd Donovan, and Caroline Tolbert, eds., *Citizens as Legislators: Direct Democracy in the United States* (Columbus: Ohio State University Press, 1998).

39. For a more in-depth discussion of initiative, referendum, and recall voting, see Larry J. Sabato, Howard R. Ernst, and Bruce Larson, *Dangerous Democracy? The Battle over Ballot Initiatives in America* (Lanham, MD: Rowman and Littlefield, 2001); and David S. Broder *Democracy Derailed: Initiative Campaigns and the Power of Money* (New York: Harcourt, 2000).

40. Howard R. Ernst, "The Historical Role of Narrow-Material Interests in Initiative Politics," in Larry J. Sabato, Howard R. Ernst, and Bruce Larson, eds., *Dangerous Democracy? The Battle over Ballot Initiatives in America* (Lanham, MD: Rowman and Littlefield, 2001).

41. Elaine Ciulla Kamarck and Kenneth M. Goldstein, "The Rules Matter: Post-Reform Presidential Nominating Politics," in L. Sandy Maisel, *The Parties Respond: Changes in American Parties and Campaigns* (Boulder, CO: Westview, 1994), 174.

42. Paul R. Abramson, John H. Aldrich, Phil Paolino, and David W. Rohde, "'Sophisticated' Voting in the 1998 Presidential Primaries," *American Political Science Review* 86 (March 1992): 55–69.

43. R. Michael Alvarez and Jonathan Nagler, "Economics, Issues, and the Perot Candidacy: Voter Choice in the 1992 Presidential Election," *American Journal of Political Science* 39 (1995): 714–44.

44. U.S. Census Bureau, Census 2000 and earlier censuses.

45. For more information, visit the Center for Voting and Democracy's page on "Faithless Electors": http://www.fairvote.org/e_college/faithless.htm.

46. George Serra, "What's in It for Me? The Impact of Congressional Casework on Incumbent Evaluation," *American Politics Quarterly* 22 (1994): 403–20.

47. Glenn R. Parker and Suzanne L. Parker, "Correlates and Effects of Attention to District by U.S. House Members," *Legislative Studies Quarterly* 10 (May 1985): 223–42.

48. Jamie L. Carson, "Strategy, Selection, and Candidate Competition in U.S. House and Senate Elections," *Journal of Politics* 67 (2005): 1–28.

49. Gary W. Cox and Jonathan N. Katz, "Why Did the Incumbency Advantage in U.S. House Elections Grow?" *American Journal of Political Science* 40 (May 1996): 478–97.

50. Jonathan Krasno, *Challengers, Competition, and Reelection: Comparing Senate and House Elections* (New Haven, CT: Yale University Press, 1994).

51. "How to Rig an Election," *Economist* (April 25, 2002).

52. Matthew Mosk and Lori Montgomery, "Md. Court Spurns Assembly Map: Glendening Plan Ruled Unconstitutional; Judges to Redraw Lines," *Washington Post* (June 12, 2002).

53. *Wesberry* v. *Sanders*, 376 U.S. 1 (1964).

54. *Thornburg* v. *Gingles*, 478 U.S. 30 (1986).

55. *Shaw* v. *Reno*, 113 S.Ct. 2816 (1993).

56. In *Davis* v. *Bandemer*, 478 U.S. 109 (1986), the Court found that gerrymandering was not a political question but was unable to determine a standard by which to judge constitutionality.

57. *League of United Latin American Citizens et al.* v. *Perry*, No. 05-204 (2006).

58. Sunhil Ahuja et al., "Modern Congressional Election Theory Meets the 1992 House Elections," *Political Research Quarterly* 47 (1994): 909–21; and Paul S. Herrnson, *Congressional Elections: Campaigning at Home and in Washington*, 2nd ed. (Washington, DC: CQ Press, 1998).

59. Gary C. Jacobson and Michael A. Dimock, "Checking Out: The Effects of Bank Overdrafts on the 1992 House Elections," *American Journal of Political Science* 38 (1994): 601–24; and Herrnson, *Congressional Elections*.

60. For an example of how this could have worked in 2008, see the National Association of Secretaries of State, "Fact Sheet: 2008 Calendar and the NASS Rotating Regional Presidential Primaries Plan," March 5, 2008.

61. MIT News Office, " MIT, Caltech Join Forces to Develop Reliable, Uniform US Voting Machine," December 14, 2000.

Chapter 14

1. Patrick J. Kenney and Tom W. Rice, "The Psychology of Political Momentum," *Political Research Quarterly* 47 (December 1994): 923–38.

2. See "Candidates and Nominations," in Paul S. Herrnson, *Congressional Elections: Campaigning at Home and in Washington*, 4th ed. (Washington, DC: CQ Press, 2004), 35–68.

3. Dennis W. Johnson, *No Place for Amateurs: How Political Consultants Are Reshaping American Democracy* (New York: Routledge, 2001).

4. Five liberal Democratic U.S. senators, including George McGovern of South Dakota, were defeated in this way in 1980, for example.

5. Girish Gulati, Marion Just, and Ann Crigler, "News Coverage of Political Campaigns," in Lynda Kaid, ed., *The Handbook of Political Communication Research* (New York: Lawrence Erlbaum, 2004).

6. Diana C. Mutz, "Effects of Horse-Race Coverage on Campaign Coffers: Strategic Contributing in Presidential Primaries," *Journal of Politics* 57 (November 1995): 1015–42.

7. See "Media, Old and New," in Johnson, *No Place for Amateurs*, 115–47.

8. See http://www.opensecrets.org.

9. "What an Election Costs," Canadian Broadcasting Corporation, March 17, 2004.

10. *McConnell* v. *Federal Election Commission*, 540 U.S. 93 (2003).

11. *Federal Election Commission* v. *Wisconsin Right to Life, Inc.*, 551 U.S. _____ (2007).

12. Joseph E. Cantor, *Campaign Finance: An Overview* (Washington, DC: Congressional Research Service, March 29, 2007).

13. See http://www.opensecrets.org.

14. See "The Internet Campaign," in Herrnson, *Congressional Elections*.

15. Steven T. Engel and David J. Jackson, "Wielding the Stick Instead of Its Carrot: Labor PAC Punishment of Pro-NAFTA Democrats," *Political Research Quarterly* 51 (September 1998): 813–28.

16. Janet M. Box-Steffensmeier and J. Tobin Grant, "All in a Day's Work: The Financial Rewards of Legislative Effectiveness," *Legislative Studies Quarterly* 24 (November 1999): 511–23.

17. Frank Sorauf, *Inside Campaign Finance: Myths and Realities* (New Haven, CT: Yale University Press, 1992), chapter 6.

18. Richard A. Smith, "Interest Group Influence in the U.S. Congress,"

Legislative Studies Quarterly 20 (1995): 89–139. See also Christopher Magee, "Do Political Action Committees Give Money to Candidates for Electoral or Influence Motives?" *Public Choice* 112 (2004): 373–99.

19. Richard L. Hall and Frank W. Wayman, "Buying Time: Moneyed Interests and the Mobilization of Bias in Congressional Committees," *American Political Science Review* 84 (1990): 797–820.

20. See http://www.opensecrets.org.

21. Herrnson, *Congressional Elections*, 133.

22. Amy Keller, "Helping Each Other Out: Members Dip into Campaign Funds for Fellow Candidates," *Roll Call* (June 15, 1998): 1.

23. For member contribution activity at the state level, see Jay K. Dow, "Campaign Contributions and Intercandidate Transfers in the California Assembly," *Social Science Quarterly* 75 (1994): 867–80. For member contribution activity at the congressional level, see Bruce A. Larson, "Ambition and Money in the U.S. House of Representatives: Analyzing Campaign Contributions from Incumbents' Leadership PACs and Reelection Committees" (Ph.D. dissertation, University of Virginia, 1998). For a briefer account, see Paul S. Herrnson, "Money and Motives: Spending in House Elections," in Lawrence C. Dodd and Bruce I. Oppenheimer, eds., *Congress Reconsidered*, 6th ed. (Washington, DC: CQ Press, 1997).

24. Federal Election Commission, http://www.fec.gov.

25. Larson, "Ambition and Money in the U.S. House of Representatives."

26. *Buckley* v. *Valeo*, 424 U.S. 1 (1976).

27. Jeffrey Milyo and Thomas Groseclose, "The Electoral Effects of Incumbent Wealth," *Journal of Law and Economics* 42 (1999): 699–722.

28. Trevor Potter, "Issue Advocacy and Express Advocacy," in Anthony Corrado et al., eds., *Campaign Finance Reform: A Sourcebook* (Washington, DC: Brookings Institution, 1997).

29. Federal Election Commission Release, "Party Financial Activity Summarized," December 14, 2004, http://www.fec.gov.

30. Michael Janofsky, "Advocacy Groups Spent Record Amount on 2004 Election," *New York Times* (December 17, 2004).

31. See Internal Revenue Service, *Publication 557: Tax-Exempt Status for Your Organization*, revised March 2005.

Chapter 15

1. Marc Lynch, *Voices of the New Arab Public: Iraq, Al Jazeera, and Middle East Politics Today* (New York: Columbia University Press, 2006); Mohamed Zayani, ed., *The Al-Jazeera Phenomenon* (Boulder, CO: Paradigm, 2005). On April 17, 2008, *The National*, an English-language daily based in Abu Dhabi, added its voice to the expanding free press in the Middle East.

2. See Mitchell Stephens, *A History of News: From the Drum to the Satellite* (New York: Viking, 1989).

3. For a delightful rendition of this episode, see Shelley Ross, *Fall from Grace* (New York: Ballantine, 1988), chapter 12.

4. Richard L. Rubin, *Press, Party, and Presidency* (New York: Norton, 1981), 38–39.

5. Stephen Bates, *If No News, Send Rumors* (New York: St. Martin's, 1989), 185.

6. See Doris A. Graber, *Mass Media and American Politics*, 3rd ed. (Washington, DC: CQ Press, 1989), 12; and Thomas C. Leonard, *The Power of the Press: The Birth of American Political Reporting* (New York: Oxford University Press, 1986), chapter 7.

7. Darrell M. West, *The Rise and Fall of the Media Establishment* (Boston: Bedford/St. Martin's, 2001).

8. Pew Research Center for the People and the Press, "Cable and Internet Loom Large in Fragmented Political News Universe: Perceptions of Partisan Bias Seen as Growing, Especially by Democrats,"

January 11, 2004.

9. Pew Research Center, "Cable and Internet Loom Large."

10. J. D. Power and Associates report, "Although Cable Continues to Lose Market Share to Satellite Providers, Cable Subscribers Are Switching to Digital Service at a Rapid Pace," http://www.jdpower.com.

11. Annenberg National Election Study, 2004, http://www.annenberg-publicpolicycenter.org.

12. Pew Research Center for the People and the Press, "Internet News Audience Highly Critical of News Organizations—Views of Press Values and Performance: 1985–2007," August 9, 2007.

13. Pew Research Center for the People and the Press, "Maturing Internet News Audience—Broader Than Deep: Online Papers Modestly Boost Newspaper Readership," July 30, 2006.

14. Darrell West, *Digital Government: Technology and Public Sector Performance* (Princeton, NJ: Princeton University Press, 2005).

15. Robert J. Klotz, The *Politics of Internet Communication* (Lanham, MD: Rowman and Littlefield, 2004).

16. Cass R. Sunstein, *Republic.com 2.0* (Princeton, NJ: Princeton University Press, 2007); and Anthony G. Wilhelm, *Digital Nation* (Cambridge, MA: MIT Press, 2004).

17. Project for Excellence in Journalism, *State of the News Media 2006: An Annual Report on American Journalism*, March 2006, http://www.stateofthenewsmedia.com/2006/.

18. David Barstow, "Message Machine: Behind Military Analysts, the Pentagon's Hidden Hand," *New York Times* (April 20, 2008).

19. Donald L. Jorand and Benjamin I. Page, "Shaping Foreign Policy Opinions: The Role of TV News," *Journal of Conflict Resolution* 36 (June 1992): 227–41.

20. Pew Research Center, "Maturing Internet News Audience."

21. Sunstein, *Republic.com 2.0.*

22. Clive Thompson, "Blogs to Riches: The Haves and Have-Nots of the Blogging Boom," *New York Magazine* (February 13, 2006); Project for Excellence in Journalism, *State of the News Media 2008: An Annual Report on American Journalism*, March 2008, http://www.stateofthenewsmedia.com/2008/.

23. See, for example, Steve Outing, "The 11 Layers of Citizen Journalism," *Poynteronline*, June 13, 2005, http://www.poynter.org; Tom Grubusuch, "'Potemkin Village' Redux," *Online Journalism Review*, November 19, 2006, http://www.ojr.org; and Kim Hart, "For Local News Site, Model Just Didn't Click," *Washington Post* (January 15, 2007), D07.

24. Vanessa Hua, "Korean Online Newspaper Enlists Army of 'Citizen Reporters,'" *San Francisco Chronicle* (September 18, 2005).

25. Project for Excellence in Journalism, *State of the News Media 2008.*

26. See, for example, Bryan Bender, "The War in Close-Up," *Boston Globe* (May 4, 2006): A1; Vauhini Vara, "News Sites Solicit Articles Straight from Readers," *Wall Street Journal Online*, April 11, 2005; Geoffrey A. Fowler, "'Citizen Journalists' Evade Blackout on Myanmar News," *Wall Street Journal* (September 28, 2007): A1.

27. Christopher Stern, "FCC Chairman's Star a Little Dimmer," *Washington Post* (July 25, 2003): E01, http://www.washingtonpost.com.

28. Mark K. Miller. "On Hold: Rankings Change Little as Regulatory Uncertainty Keeps Station Trading in Neutral," *Broadcasting and Cable* (April, 19, 2004): 50.

29. Frank Ahrens, "Divided FCC Enacts Rules on Media Ownership," *Washington Post* (December 19, 2007): D01; Stephen Labaton, "F.C.C. Reshapes Rules Limiting Media Industry," *New York Times* (December 19, 2007): A1.

30. *RTNDA* v. *FCC*, 229 F3d 269 (DC Cir. 2000).

31. Tim Wu, "Network Neutrality, Broadband Discrimination," *Colorado Journal of Telecommunications and High Technology Law* 2 (2003). For additional arguments in support of Internet neu-

trality, see Save the Internet, http://www.savetheinternet.com.

32. Testimony of J. Gregory Sidak before the United States Senate Committee on Commerce, Science, and Transportation, *Net Neutrality*, February 7, 2006; Bret Swanson, "Let There Be Bandwidth," *Wall Street Journal* (March 7, 2006). For additional arguments opposing net neutrality, see U.S. Internet Industry Association, http://www.usiia.org.

33. See Adam Liptak, "Verizon Blocks Messages of Abortion Rights Group," *New York Times* (September 27, 2007): A1; Cecilia Kang, "Comcast Defends Rolse as Internet Traffic Cop," *Washington Post* (February 13, 2008): D01; and David Weinberger, "Beyond Net Neutrality," *Boston Globe* (February 28, 2008): A11.

34. *New York Times Co.* v. *U.S.*, 403 U.S. 713 (1971).

35. Jillian Harrison, "Embedded Journalism Limited in Perspective, Tufts U. Professors Say," *University Wire*, April 15, 2003.

36. U.S. Senate press gallery and U.S. House of Representatives radio-television correspondents' gallery.

37. List of White House correspondents, http://www.washingtonpost.com/wp-srv/politics/administration/whbriefing/correspondents.html.

38. *New York Times Co.* v. *Sullivan*, 376 U.S. 254 (1964). See also Steven Pressman, "Libel Law: Finding the Right Balance," *Editorial Research Reports* 2 (August 18, 1989): 462–71.

39. *Curtis Publishing Co.* v. *Butts*, 388 U.S. 130 (1967); *Associated Press* v. *Walker*, 388 U.S. 130 (1967).

40. Thomas Patterson, *Out of Order* (New York: Vintage, 1994).

41. John R. Zaller, "Monica Lewinsky's Contribution to Political Science," *PS: Political Science and Politics* 31 (June 1998): 182–9.

42. Lori Robertson, "In Control," *American Journalism Review* (February/March 2005).

43. Harold W. Stanley and Richard G. Niemi, *Vital Statistics on American Politics*, 4th ed. (Washington, DC: CQ Press, 1994), 28.

44. John R. Hibbing and Elizabeth Theiss-Morse, *Congress as Public Enemy: Political Attitudes Toward American Political Institutions* (New York: Cambridge University Press, 1995).

45. Karen Aho, "Broadcasters Want Access, but Will They Deliver Serious Coverage?" *Columbia Journalism Review* 5 (September/October 2003), http://www.cjr.org.

46. Larry Bartels, "Messages Received: The Political Impact of Media Exposure," *American Political Science Review* 87 (June 1993): 267–85.

47. Benjamin I. Page, Robert Y. Shapiro, and Glenn R. Dempsey, "What Moves Public Opinion?" *American Political Science Review* 81 (March 1987): 23–44.

48. Shanto Iyengar and Donald R. Kinder, *News That Matters*, reprint ed. (Chicago: University of Chicago Press, 1989).

49. Thomas E. Nelson, Rosalee A. Clawson, and Zoe M. Oxley, "Media Framing of a Civil Liberties Conflict and Its Effect on Tolerance," *American Political Science Review* 92 (September 1997): 567–83.

50. Marc Hetherington, "The Media's Role in Forming Voters' National Economic Evaluations in 1992," *American Journal of Political Science* 40 (May 1996): 372–95.

51. David Domke, David P. Fan, Dhavan V. Shah, and Mark D. Watts, "The Politics of Conservative Elites and the 'Liberal Media' Argument," *Journal of Communication* 49 (Fall 1999): 35–58.

52. American Society of Newspaper Editors, *The Changing Face of the Newsroom* (Washington, DC: ASNE, 1989), 33; William Schneider and I. A. Lewis, "Views on the News," *Public Opinion* 8 (August/September 1985): 6–11, 58–59; and S. Robert Lichter, Stanley Rothman, and Linda S. Lichter, *The Media Elite* (Bethesda, MD: Adler and Adler, 1986).

53. Pew Research Center for the People and the Press, "The Web: Alarming, Appealing and a Challenge to Journalistic Values," March 17, 2008.

54. Martin Gilens and Craig Hertzman. "Corporate Ownership and News Bias: Newspaper Coverage of the 1996 Telecommunication Act," *Journal of Politics* 62 (May 2000), 369–86.

55. Eric Alterman, *What Liberal Media? The Truth About Bias and the News* (New York: Basic Books, 2003).

56. See http://www.stateofthenewsmedia.org/2004/narrative_overview_audience.asp?media=1.

57. Girish Gulati, Marion Just, and Ann Crigler, "News Coverage of Political Campaigns," in Lynda Kaid, ed., *The Handbook of Political Communication Research* (New York: Lawrence Erlbaum, 2004).

58. Project for Excellence in Journalism, "Candidates and the Primaries of 2008: What Were the Media Master Narratives?" May 25, 2008, http://www.journalism.org/node/11266.

59. Pew Research Center for the People and the Press, "Public More Critical of Press, but Goodwill Persists, June 26, 2005."

60. Pew Research Center for the People and the Press, "News Media's Improved Image Proves Short-Lived," August 4, 2002.

61. Center for the Digital Future, USC Annenberg School, *Annual Internet Survey*, January 2008, http://www.digitalcenter.org/pdf/2008-Digital-Future-Report-Final-Release.pdf.

62. Pew Research Center, "Maturing Internet News Audience—Broader Than Deep."

63. For the most current Web traffic rankings organized by category, see http://www.alexa.com.

64. Pew Research Center, "News Media's Improved Image Proves Short-Lived."

Chapter 16

1. Karen Tumulty, "The Man Who Brought Down Washington," *Time* (January 16, 2006): 30–44.

2. Susan Schmidt, James V. Garamaldi, and R. Jeffrey Smith, "Investigating Abramoff—Special Report," *Washington Post*, http://www.washingtonpost.com.

3. Philip Shenon, "Senate Report Lists Lobbyist's Payments to Ex-Leader of Christian Coalition," *New York Times* (June 23, 2006): B2.

4. Robert D. Putnam, "Bowling Alone: America's Declining Social Capital," *Journal of Democracy* 6 (1995): 650–65; and Putnam, *Bowling Alone: The Collapse and Revival of American Community* (New York: Simon and Schuster, 2000).

5. Everett Carll Ladd, quoted in Richard Morin, "Who Says We're Not Joiners," *Washington Post* (May 2, 1999): B5.

6. John Brehm and Wendy Rahn, "Individual-Level Evidence for the Causes and Consequences of Social Capital," *American Journal of Political Science* 41 (July 1997): 999.

7. Mark Schneider et al., "Institutional Arrangements and the Creation of Social Capital: The Effects of Public School Choice," *American Political Science Review* 91 (March 1997): 82–93.

8. Nicholas Lemann, "Kicking in Groups," *Atlantic Monthly* (April 1996), NEXIS.

9. David B. Truman, *The Governmental Process: Political Interests and Public Opinion* (New York: Knopf, 1951), 33.

10. Truman, *The Governmental Process*, ch. 16.

11. Mancur Olson, *The Logic of Collective Action* (Cambridge, MA: Harvard University Press, 1965).

12. Dennis Chong, *Collective Action and the Civil Rights Movement* (Chicago: University of Chicago Press, 1990).

13. E. E. Schattschneider, *The Semisovereign People* (New York: Holt Rinehart, and Winston, 1960), 35.

14. David Lowery and Virginia Gray, "The Population Ecology of Gucci Gulch or the Natural Regulation of Interest Group Numbers in the American States," *American Journal of Political Science* 39 (February 1995): 1–29.

15. Jeffrey M. Berry, *Lobbying for the People: The Political Behavior of Public Interest Groups* (Princeton, NJ: Princeton University Press, 1977), 7.

16. Berry, *Lobbying for the People*, 7.

17. Quoted in Grant McConnell, "Lobbies and Pressure Groups," in Jack Greene, ed., *Encyclopedia of American Political History*, vol. 2 (New York: Macmillan, 1984), 768.

18. Lee Epstein, *Conservatives in Court* (Knoxville: University of Tennessee Press, 1985).

19. Jack L. Walker, "The Origins and Maintenance of Interest Groups in America," *American Political Science Review* 77 (June 1983): 390–406.

20. Peter Steinfels, "Moral Majority to Dissolve: Says Mission Accomplished," *New York Times* (June 12, 1989): A14.

21. David Mahood, *Interest Groups Participation in America: A New Intensity* (Englewood Cliffs, NJ: Prentice Hall, 1990), 23.

22. Political Moneyline, http://www.tray.com.

23. Chris Kutalik, "What Does the AFL-CIO Split Mean?" *Labor Notes* (September 2005): http://www.labornotes.org.

24. Michael Wines, "For New Lobbyists, It's What They Know," *New York Times* (November 3, 1993): B14.

25. Quoted in Kay Lehman Schlozman and John T. Tiemey, *Organized Interests and American Democracy* (New York: Harper and Row, 1986), 85.

26. Ken Kollman, "Inviting Friends to Lobby: Interest Groups, Ideological Bias, and Congressional Committees," *American Journal of Political Science* 41 (April 1997): 519–44.

27. Quoted in Norman J. Ornstein and Shirley Elder, *Interest Groups, Lobbying and Policy Making* (Washington, DC: CQ Press, 1978), 77.

28. Jeffrey H. Birnbaum, "Hill a Steppingstone to K Street for Some," *Washington Post* (July 27, 2005): A19.

29. Birnbaum, "Hill a Steppingstone to K Street for Some."

30. Some political scientists speak of "iron rectangles," reflecting the growing importance of a fourth party, the courts, in the lobbying process.

31. Clement E. Vose, "Litigation as a Form of Pressure Group Activity," *Annals* 319 (September 1958): 20–31.

32. Karen O'Connor, "Lobbying the Justices or Lobbying for Justice?" in Paul Herrnson, Ronald G. Shaiko, and Clyde Wilcox, eds., *The Interest Group Connection*, 2nd ed., (Washington, DC: CQ Press, 2005), 267–88.

33. Brian Ross, "Supreme Court Ethics Problem?" *Nightline*, ABC News, January 23, 2006.

34. Robert A. Goldberg, *Grassroots Resistance: Social Movements in Twentieth Century America* (Belmont, CA: Wadsworth, 1991).

35. Michelle Garcia, "Animal Rights Activists Step Up Attacks in N.Y.," *Washington Post* (May 9, 2005): A3.

36. Schattschneider, *The Semisovereign People*.

37. Ken Kollman, *Outside Lobbyists: Public Opinion and Interest Group Strategies* (Princeton, NJ: Princeton University Press, 1998); and Karen O'Connor, *Women's Organizations' Use of the Courts* (Lexington, MA: 1980).

38. Marie Hojnacki, "Interest Groups' Decisions to Join Alliances or Work Alone," *American Journal of Political Science* 41 (January 1997): 61–87.

39. Lee Ann Banaszak, *Why Movements Succeed or Fail: Opportunity, Culture, and the Struggle for Woman Suffrage* (Princeton, NJ: Princeton University Press, 1996); Frank R. Baumgartner and Beth L. Leech, *Basic Interests: The Importance of Groups in Politics and in Political Science* (Princeton, NJ: Princeton University Press, 1990); Nancy E. McGlen et al., *Women, Politics, and American So-*

ciety, 4th ed. (New York: Longman, 2004); Robert H. Salisbury, "An Exchange Theory of Interest Groups," *Midwest Journal of Political Science* 13 (1969): 1–32; Jack Walker, *Mobilizing Interest Groups in America: Patrons, Professions, and Social Movements* (Ann Arbor: University of Michigan Press, 1991).

40. Walker, *Mobilizing Interest Groups in America*.

41. Schattschneider, *The Semi Sovereign People*, 35.

42. Mancur Olson Jr., *The Logic of Collective Action: Public Goods and the Theory of Groups* (Cambridge, MA: Harvard University Press, 1965).

43. David C. King and Jack L. Walker, "The Provision of Benefits by Interest Groups in the United States," *Journal of Politics* 54 (May 1992): 394.

44. Hojnacki, "Interest Groups' Decisions."

45. William Browne, "Organized Interests and Their Issue Niches: A Search for Pluralism in a Policy Domain," *Journal of Politics* 52 (May 1990): 477.

46. Donald P. Haider-Markel, "Interest Group Survival: Shared Interests Versus Competition for Resources," *Journal of Politics* 59 (August 1997): 903–12.

47. Leslie Wayne, "And for His Next Feat, Billionaire Sets Sights on Bush," *New York Times* (May 31, 2004): A14.

48. Walker, "The Origins and Maintenance of Interest Groups," 390–406.

49. Center for Responsive Politics, http://www.opensecrets.org.

50. Richard Simons, "Bush Signs Bill to Tighten Lobbying Rules," *Los Angeles Times* (September 15, 2007): A13.

Chapter 17

1. Robert Pear, "Health Care Plan Isn't Cast in Stone," *New York Times* (January 22, 1994).

2. Ann Devroy, "President Insists Congress Enact Reforms in Welfare, Health Care," *Washington Post* (January 26, 1994): A1.

3. Perry Bacon Jr. and Ann Kornblut, "Clinton Presents Plan for Universal Coverage," *Washington Post* (September 18, 2007): A1.

4. Kaiser Family Foundation, "2008 Presidential Candidate Health Care Proposals: Side by Side Summary," www.health08.org/sidebyside.cfm.

5. James E. Anderson, *Public Policymaking: An Introduction*, 2nd ed. (Boston: Houghton Mifflin, 1994), 5. This discussion draws on Anderson's study.

6. Thomas R. Dye, *Who's Running America?* (Englewood Cliffs, NJ: Prentice Hall, 1976).

7. David B. Truman, *The Governmental Process* (New York: Knopf, 1951).

8. Robert Dahl. *Who Governs?* (New Haven, CT: Yale University Press, 1961).

9. Theodore J. Lowi, *The End of Liberalism* (New York: Norton, 1979).

10. Environmental Protection Agency, "Overview of the National Water Program," www.epa.gov.

11. Roger W. Cobb and Charles D. Elder, *Participation in American Politics: The Dynamics of Agenda-Building*, 2nd ed. (Baltimore, MD: Johns Hopkins University Press, 1983), 85.

12. Linda Feldmann and Gail Russell Chaddock, "Why the Dubai Deal Collapsed," *Christian Science Monitor* (March 10, 2006).

13. John M. Broder, "Democrats Divided over Gas Tax Break," *New York Times* (April 29, 2008).

14. Charles O. Jones, ed., *The Reagan Legacy: Promise and Performance* (Chatham, NJ: Chatham House, 1988).

15. Charles O. Jones, *An Introduction to the Study of Public Policy*, 3rd ed. (Monterey, CA: Brooks/Cole, 1984), 87–89.

16. Donald Lambro, "Social Security Reform Mulled," *Washington Times* (December 2, 2004), www.washingtontimes.com.

17. Judy Sarasohn, "Bush's '06 Budget Would Scrap or Reduce 154 Programs," *Washington Post* (February 22, 2005): A13.

18. Robert Barnes and Juliet Eilperin, "High Court Faults EPA Inaction on Emissions," *Washington Post* (April 3, 2007): A01.

19. This discussion draws on Anne Schneider and Helen Ingram, "Behavioral Assumptions of Policy Tools," *Journal of Politics* 52 (May 1990): 510–29.

20. Government Accountability Office, "Amtrak Management: Systematic Problems Require Actions to Improve Efficiency, Effectiveness, and Accountability," GAO-06-145, April 2005, www.gao.gov.

21. Robert Divine et al., *America Past and Present*, 5th ed. (New York: Longman, 1999), 456.

22. Jeffrey Cohen, *Politics and Economic Policy in the United States*, 2nd ed. (Boston: Houghton Mifflin, 2000), 49.

23. Cohen, *Politics and Economic Policy in the United States*.

24. Thomas Lynch, *Public Budgeting in America*, 4th ed. (Englewood Cliffs, NJ: Prentice Hall, 1995), 24.

25. Ronald Edsforth, *The New Deal: America's Response to the Great Depression* (Oxford: Blackwell, 2000), 137.

26. Robert McElvaine, *The Great Depression: America 1929–1941* (New York: Times Books, 1984), 265.

27. Edsforth, *The New Deal*, 231.

28. McElvaine, *The Great Depression*, 257.

29. Robert Rich and William White, "Health Care Policy and the American States: Issues of Federalism," in Rich and White, eds., *Health Policy, Federalism, and the American States* (Washington, DC: Urban Institute Press, 1996), 20.

30. Department of Health and Human Services, aspe.hhs.gov.

31. Fact Sheet, Social Security, www.ssa.gov.

32. Pew Research Center for the People and the Press, "Survey Finds Bush Failing in Social Security Reform," March 3, 2005.

33. Economic Policy Institute, "State Unemployment Insurance Policies as of June 2004," www.epinet.org.

34. Bureau of Labor Statistics, "Employment Situation Summary," www.bls.gov.

35. Social Security Administration, ssa-custhelp.ssa.gov.

36. Budget of the United States Government, Fiscal Year 2007, Historical Tables, Section 11, Outlays for Payments, www.whitehouse.gov/omb/budget/fy2007/pdf/hist.pdf.

37. H. Carl McCall, "New York State's Job Training and Job Creation Programs: Prospects for Welfare Reform," Controllers Report, November 21, 1996.

38. *BNA Daily Labor Report* (March 16, 1994).

39. *Congressional Quarterly Weekly Report* 50 (March 28, 1992): 809–10.

40. Christopher Conte, "A Special News Report on People and Their Jobs in Offices, Fields, and Factories," *Wall Street Journal* (March 9, 1993): A1.

41. Steven G. Koven, Mack C. Shelley II, and Bert E. Swanson, *American Public Policy: The Contemporary Agenda* (Boston: Houghton Mifflin, 1998), 271.

42. The White House, "Working Toward Independence," news release, February 2002, www.whitehouse.gov.

43. Nanette Relave, "TANF Reauthorization and Work Requirements," *Reauthorization Resource*, February 2002, www.welfareinfo.org.

44. Department of Health and Human Services, "Welfare Reform Reauthorized," February 8, 2006, www.hhs.gov.

45. Colin Campbell and William Pierce, *The Earned Income Credit* (Washington, DC: American Enterprise Institute, 1980).

46. Center on Budget and Policy Priorities, *The Earned Income Tax Credit: Boosting Employment, Aiding the Working Poor*, www.cbpp.org.

47. Department of Agriculture, "Food Stamp Program Annual Summary," March 24, 2006, www.fns.usda.gov.

48. "Fiscal Year 2006: Mid-Session Review Budget of the U.S. Government," July 13, 2005, www.whitehouse.gov/omb/budget/fy2006/pdf/06msr.pdf.

49. Mark Rushefsky and Kant Patel, *Politics, Power, and Policy Making: The Case of Health Care Reform in the 1990s* (Armonk, NY: M. E. Sharpe, 1998), 27.

50. Henry J. Aaron, *Serious and Unstable Condition: Financing America's Health Care* (Washington, DC: Brookings Institution, 1991), ch. 2.

51. John F. Dickerson, "Can We Afford All This?" *Time* (December 8, 2004), 48–51; Edward Walsh and Bill Brubaker, "Drug Benefits Impact Detailed," *Washington Post* (December 8, 2003): A10.

52. Congressional Budget Office, "Medicaid: Federal Outlays in Billions of Dollars," 2005, www.house.gov

53. Centers for Disease Control and Prevention, Obesity Home Page, www.cdc.gov/nccdphp/dnpa/obesity/.

54. Ceci Connolly, "Public Policy Targeting Obesity," *Washington Post* (August 10, 2003): A1.

55. Marilyn Werber Serafina, "Medicrunch," *National Journal* 27 (July 29, 1995): 1937.

56. Richard H. K. Vistor, *Energy Policy in America Since 1945: A Study of Business-Government Relations* (Cambridge: Cambridge University Press, 1987).

57. Vito Stagliano, *A Policy of Discontent: The Making of a National Energy Strategy* (Tulsa, OK: Pennwell, 2001).

58. Energy Information Administration, Department of Energy, "25th Anniversary of the 1973 Oil Embargo," 1998, www.eia.doe.gov/emeu/25opec/anniversary.html.

59. Energy Information Administration, Department of Energy, www.eia.doe.gov/oil_gas/petroleum/data_publications/wrgp/mogas_history.html.

60. Department of Energy, Energy Timeline 1971–1980, www.energy.gov/about/timeline1971–1980.htm.

61. Charles O. Jones and Randall Strahan, "The Effect of Energy Politics on Congressional and Executive Organizations in the 1970s," *Legislative Studies Quarterly* 10 (May 1985): 151–79.

62. Ronald Reagan, Statement on the National Energy Policy Plan Transmitted to Congress, October 4, 1983, www.presidency.ucsb.edu/ws/index.php?pid=40588.

63. Carol D. Leonnig and Jim VandeHei, "Cheney Wins Court Ruling on Energy Panel Records," *Washington Post* (May 11, 2005): A01.

64. National Energy Policy Development Group, National Energy Policy Plan, www.whitehouse.gov/energy/2001/index.html.

65. Jan H. Kalicki and David L. Goldwyn, *Energy and Security: Toward a New Foreign Policy Strategy* (Baltimore, MD: Johns Hopkins University Press, 2005).

66. Barry G. Rabe, *Statehouse and Greenhouse: The Emerging Politics of American Climate Change Policy* (Washington, DC: Brookings Institution, 2004).

67. Steven Mufson, "House Sends President an Energy Bill to Sign," *Washington Post* (December 19, 2007): A01.

68. Energy Information Administration, Department of Energy, "Renewable Energy Fact Sheet," www.eia.doe.gov/neic/infosheets/renewableenergy.html.

69. California Energy Commission, "Renewable Portfolio Standard," www.energy.ca.gov/portfolio/index.html.

70. Austin Energy, " Green Choice Program," www.austinenergy.com.

71. City of Portland, Oregon, www.portlandonline.com; Oregon Office of Sustainable Development, "Clean Energy Economic Development."

Chapter 18

1. "Bush: Outsourcing Painful, but Remedy Is Worse," edition.cnn.com.

2. The White House, www.whitehouse.gov/news/releases/2008/02/20080226-4.html.

3. *LA Times*/Bloomberg poll, pollingreport.com/trade.htm.

4. http://www.bloomberg.com/apps/news?pid=20601087&sid=aCDlHroUxpSQ&refer=home accessed on October 7, 2008.

5. http://www.abc.net.au/news/stories/2008/10/03/2381245.htm accessed on October 7, 2008

6. http://www.bls.gov/news.release/empsit.nr0.htm; and http://www.bls.gov/news.release/cpi.nr0.htm accessed on October 7, 2008.

7. http://news.bbc.co.uk/2/hi/americas/7652112.stm accessed on October 7, 2008.

8. http://news.bbc.co.uk/2/hi/business/7656741.stm accessed on October 7, 2008.

9. Howard R. Smith, *Government and Business* (New York: Ronald, 1958), 99.

10. After 108 years of operation, the ICC expired at the end of 1995 as part of the effort by congressional Republicans to reduce federal regulations and allow market forces more freedom in which to operate.

11. *Pollack* v. *Farmers' Loan and Trust Co.*, 158 U.S. 429 (1895).

12. This discussion of the New Deal draws on Louis M. Hacker and Helene S. Zahler, *The United States in the Twentieth Century* (New York: Appleton-Century-Crofts, 1952); and William E. Leuchtenberg, *Franklin D. Roosevelt and the New Deal* (New York: Harper and Row, 1963).

13. Department of Labor, www.dol.gov/asp/programs/history/chapter5.htm.

14. *U.S.* v. *Butler*, 297 U.S. 1 (1936).

15. *Wickard* v. *Filburn*, 317 U.S. 111 (1942).

16. Larry Gerston, Cynthia Fraleigh, and Robert Schwab, *The Deregulated Society* (Pacific Grove, CA: Brooks/Cole, 1988), 32–34.

17. David Vogel, "The 'New' Social Regulation in Historical and Comparative Perspective," in Thomas K. McCraw, ed., *Regulation in Perspective* (Cambridge, MA: Harvard University Press, 1981), 160.

18. A leading study is Martha Derthick and Paul J. Quirk, *The Politics of Deregulation* (Washington, DC: Brookings Institution, 1985).

19. Micheline Maynard, "Airlines' Cuts Making Cities No-Fly Zones," *New York Times* (May 21, 2008), www.nytimes.com.

20. Maurice Hinchey, "More Media Owners," *Nation* (February 6, 2006), www.thenation.com.

21. Sara Fitzjerald, "Liberalizing Agriculture: Why the U.S. Should Look to New Zealand and Australia," www.heritage.org.

22. "Farmings Front and Center at the Talks: Negotiators Slog Away in the Advance of WTO Meeting," *USA Today* (November 11, 2005), www.usatoday.com.

23. For Susan Schwab remarks, see www.iht.com/articles/2006/09/10/business/trade.php.

24. About 38 percent of the nation's commercial banks are members of the Federal Reserve System. See www.richmondfed.org.

25. Federal Reserve Board, Report to the Congress, www.federalreserve.gov/boarddocs/hh/2008/february/0208mpr_part1.htm.

26. Andrews, "Employment Falls for Second Month."

27. This is the conclusion reached by John T. Woolley, *Monetary Politics: The Federal Reserve and the Politics of Monetary Policy* (New York: Cambridge University Press, 1984).

28. James E. Anderson, David W. Brady, Charles S. Bullock III, and Joseph Stewart Jr., *Public Policy and Politics in America*, 2nd ed. (Monterey: Brooks/Cole, 1984), 38–40.

29. James D. Savage, *Balanced Budgets and American Politics* (Ithaca, NY: Cornell University Press, 1988), 176–9.

30. "Clinton Vetoes Tax Bill; Republicans Vow to Press for Cuts," September 23, 1999, www.cnn.com.

31. "Bush Makes Case for Extending Cuts," May 4, 2006, www.cbsnews.com.

32. Maura Reynolds, "Congress OKs $168-Billion Stimulus Package," www.latimes.com.

33. Congressional Budget Office, "What Accounts for the Decline in Manufacturing Employment?" *Economic and Budget Issue Brief* (February 18, 2004), www.cbo.gov.

34. "Economy Up, People Down: Declining Earnings Undercut Income Growth," August 31, 2005, www.epi.org.

35. "By the Numbers," Inequality.org, www.demos.org/inequality/numbers.cfm.

36. Kevin Phillips, *Wealth and Democracy: A Political History of the American Rich* (New York: Broadway, 2002), 111, 412.

37. "By the Numbers," Inequality.org.

38. Matthew Slaughter, "The Economic Outlook," www.whitehouse.gov.

39. Department of the Treasury, www.treas.gov/tic/mfh.txt.

40. Kenneth Rogoff, "Foreign Holdings of U.S. Debt: Is Our Economy Vulnerable?" *Brookings* (June 26, 2007), www.brookings.edu.

41. Kimberly Amadeo, "The U.S. National Debt and How It Got So Big," *About.com*, useconomy.about.com/od/fiscalpolicy/p/US_Debt.htm.

42. Congressional Budget Office, "Revenues, Outlays, Deficits, Surpluses, and Debt Held by the Public, 1968 to 2007," cbo.gov/budget/data/historical.xls.

43. "Historical Tables," Budget of the United States Government for Fiscal Year 2008, www.whitehouse.gov/omb/budget/fy2008/pdf/hist.pdf.

44. This discussion on budgeting draws on James E. Anderson, *Public Policymaking: An Introduction*, 2nd ed. (Boston: Houghton Mifflin, 1994), ch. 5.

45. Donald F. Kettl, *Deficit Politics: Public Budgeting in Its Institutional and Historical Context* (New York: Macmillan, 1993).

46. Isaac Shapiro and Joel Friedman, "Tax Returns: A Comprehensive Assessment of the Bush Administration's Record on Cutting Taxes," Center on Budget and Policy Priorities, April 23, 2004, www.cbpp.org.

47. "Brief Analysis: President Bush's FY 2009 Budget," U.S. Senate, Budget Committee Majority, February 5, 2008.

48. David Stout, "Bush Sends Congress $3 Trillion Budget," *Washinton Post* (February 4, 2008).

49. Paul E. Peterson, "The New Politics of Deficits," in John E. Chubb and Paul E. Peterson, eds., *The New Direction in American Politics* (Washington, DC: Brookings Institution, 1985), ch. 13.

50. Aaron Wildavsky and Naomi Caiden, *The New Politics of the Budgetary Process*, 4th ed. (New York: Addison Wesley Longman, 2001): 146–8.

51. "The Budget Surplus and Fiscal Discipline," Budget of the U.S. Government for Fiscal Year 2002, www.whitehouse.gov/omb/budget/fy2002/guide04.html.

52. Edmund Andrews, "Federal Deficit Alarm Sounded," *San Francisco Chronicle* (May 7, 2004): C1–2.

53. "Bernanke Voices U.S. Deficit Fears," BBC, March 15, 2006, news.bbc.co.uk.

54. Congressional Budget Office, "Monthly Budget Review Fiscal Year 2008," March 2008, www.cbo.gov.

55. Reuters, March 6, 2008, www.reuters.com/article/economicNews/idUSN0626239720080306.

56. "The Federal Budget: The Deficit," *Washington Post* (February 5, 2007), www.washingtonpost.com.

57. Jonathan Weissman, "Projected Iraq War Costs Soar," *Washington Post* (April 27, 2006), www.washingtonpost.com.

58. Congressional Budget Office, "Analysis of the Growth in Funding for Operations in Iraq, Afghanistan, and Elsewhere in the War on Terrorism," February 11, 2008, www.cbo.gov/ftpdocs/89xx/doc8971/02–11-WarCosts_Letter.pdf.

59. Joseph Stiglitz and Linda Bilmes, *The Three Trillion Dollar War: The True Cost of the Iraq Conflict* (New York: Norton, 2008).

60. Joseph Stiglitz and Linda Bilmes, "The Iraq War Will Cost Us $3 Trillion, and Much More," *Washington Post* (March 9, 2008), www.washingtonpost.com.

61. Thomas Friedman, "Who Will Tell the People?" *New York Times* (May 4, 2008), www.nytimes.com.

62. Nicholas Kristof, "Iraq, $5,000 per second?" *New York Times* (March 23, 2008), www.nytimes.com.

63. Associated Press, "Paulson: Mortgage Aid Expansion Possible," www.msnbc.msn.com/id/223011892.

64. Economic Policy Institute, Briefing Paper 197, February 28, 2008, 4.

65. Mortgage Bankers Association, "Sharp Decline in Housing and Mortgage Activity Expected Again This Year," February 15, 2008, www.mbaa.org/NewsandMedia/PressCenter/60107.htm.

66. Mortgage Bankers Association, "Delinquencies and Foreclosures Increase in Latest MBA National Delinquency Survey," December 6, 2007, www.mbaa.org/NewsandMedia/PressCenter/58758.htm.

67. Edmund Andrews and Vikas Bajaj, "Home Starts Up on One-Time Event, Still Weak," Reuters, July 17, 2008.

68. Les Christie, "Bernanke: Go Slow on Subprime Regulation," May 17, 2007, http://money.cnn.com.

69. "Paulson Rules Out Bailout for Mortgage Crisis," December 17, 2007, www.msnbc.msn.com.

70. "Bush and Fed Step Torward Mortgage a Rescue," *New York Times* (March 5, 2008).

71. David Herszenhorn and Vikas Bajaj, "A Bipartisan Bid on Mortgage Aid Is Gaining Speed," *New York Times* (April 2, 2008).

72. "Stephen Labaton, "Loan Industry Fighting Rules on Mortgages," *New York Times* (April 28, 2008).

73. http://www.guardian.co.uk/business/2008/sep/07/freddiemacfanniemae accessed on October 8, 2008.

Chapter 19

1. "President Bush Discusses NSA Surveillance Program," White House press briefing, May 11, 2006, http://www.whitehouse.gov.

2. Alfred E. Eckes Jr., *Opening America's Market: U.S. Foreign Trade Policy Since 1776* (Chapel Hill: University of North Carolina Press, 1995).

3. John L. O'Sullivan, writing in 1845, quoted in Julius W. Pratt, "The Ideology of American Expansion," in Avery Craven, ed., *Essays in Honor of William E. Dodd* (Chicago: University of Chicago Press, 1935), 343–4.

4. Charles P. Kindleberger, *The World in Depression, 1929–1939* Berkeley: University of California Press, 1986).

5. For a good description of the UN and its early years, see Ruth B. Russell, *A History of the United Nations Charter: The Role of the United States, 1940–1945* (Washington, DC: Brookings Institution, 1958).

6. See W. M. Scammell, *The International Economy Since 1945* (New York: St. Martin's, 1980); and Richard N. Gardner, *Sterling-Dollar Diplomacy in Current Perspective: The Origins and Prospects of Our International Economic Order* (New York: Columbia University Press, 1980).

7. Harry S Truman, speech before a joint session of Congress, March 12, 1947.

8. Corrected for inflation, this was over $100 billion in 2004.

9. The North Atlantic Treaty's original signatory states were Belgium, Canada, Denmark, France, Great Britain, Iceland, Italy, Luxembourg, the Netherlands, Norway, Portugal, and the United States. As of 2008, NATO had twenty-six members.

10. John F. Kennedy, inaugural address, January 20, 1961, Public Papers of the Presidents of the United States (Washington, DC: Government Printing Office).

11. See Graham Allison, *Essence of Decision: Explaining the Cuban Missile Crisis* (Boston: Little, Brown, 1971).

12. For a discussion of U.S., Soviet, and Chinese views of the Vietnam War, see Daniel S. Papp, *Vietnam: The View from Moscow, Beijing, Washington* (Jefferson, NC: McFarland, 1981).

13. Richard M. Nixon, inaugural address, January 20, 1969, Public Papers of the Presidents of the United States (Washington, DC: Government Printing Office).

14. Michael Froman, *The Development of the Idea of Détente* (New York: St. Martin's, 1982).

15. R. C. Schroeder, "Human Rights Policy," *CQ Research Reports* 1 (1979), CQ Researcher Online, http://library.cqpress.com.

16. Jimmy Carter, State of the Union Address, January 21, 1980, Public Papers of the Presidents of the United States (Washington, DC: Government Printing Office).

17. See Colin S. Gray, "Strategic Forces," in Joseph Kruzel, ed., *1986–1987 American Defense Annual* (Lexington, MA: Lexington Books, 1986). For a discussion of Reagan's early international economic policies, see Jeffrey E. Garten, "Gunboat Economics," *Foreign Affairs* 63 (1985): 538–99.

18. See Stephen E. Ambrose, *Rise to Globalism: American Foreign Policy Since 1938*, 8th revised ed. (New York: Penguin, 1998); Steven W. Hook and John Spanier, *American Foreign Policy Since World War II*, 15th ed. (Washington, DC: CQ Press, 2000); Richard Mandelbaum and Strobe Talbott, *Reagan and Gorbachev* (New York: Vintage, 1987); and Richard A. Melanson, *American Foreign Policy Since the Vietnam War*, 3rd ed. (Armonk, NY: M. E. Sharpe, 2000).

19. Karen Brutents and Larisa Galperin, "Origins of the New Thinking," *Russian Social Science Review* 47:1 (2006): 73–102; David Laibman, "The Soviet Demise: Revisionist Betrayal, Structural Defect, or Authoritarian Distortion?" *Science and Society* 69:4 (2005): 594–606; and John Muelle, "What Was the Cold War About? Evidence from Its Ending," *Political Science Quarterly* 119:4 (2004/2005): 609–31.

20. For good discussions of the events that led to the decline and fall of the Soviet Union, see William Head and Earl H. Tilford Jr., *The Eagle in the Desert: Looking Back on U.S. Involvement in the Persian Gulf War* (Westport, CT: Praeger, 1996).

21. See Geoffrey Hosking, *The Awakening of the Soviet Union* (Cambridge, MA: Harvard University Press, 1990); David Remnick, *Lenin's Tomb: The Last Days of the Soviet Empire* (New York: Random House, 1993); and Jeffrey T. Checkel, *Ideas and International Political Change: Soviet/Russian Behavior and the End of the Cold War* (New Haven, CT: Yale University Press, 1997).

22. Jeffrey J. Schott, *The WTO After Seattle* (Washington, DC: Institute for International Economics, 2000); and Bhagirath L. Das, *World Trade Organization: A Guide to New Frameworks for International Trade* (New York: St. Martin's, 2000).

23. See Daniel S. Papp, *The Impact of September 11 on Contemporary International Relations* (New York: Pearson, 2003).

24. The U.S. Department of Defense provides figures for confirmed U.S. military deaths and other casualties but does not maintain records of Iraqi military or civilian casualties. Information concerning Iraqi deaths is compiled largely from various news reports. During 2006 alone, it is estimated that 5,000–10,000 Iraqi police and military and 15,000–20,000 civilians lost their lives.

25. Robin Wright and Ellen Knickmeyer, "U.S. Lowers Sights on What Can Be Achieved in Iraq," *Washington Post* (August 14, 2005): A1.

26. U.S. Senate, Select Committee on Intelligence, Report of the Select Committee on Intelligence on the U.S. Intelligence Community's Prewar Intelligence Assessments on Iraq (Washington, DC: Government Printing Office, 2004); Josh Meyer and Greg Miller, "The Prisoner Problem," *Los Angeles Times* (September 7, 2006): A1; and David Stout, "Senate Panel Defies Bush on Detainee Bill," *New York Times* (September 14, 2006): A10.

27. Representative Bennie Thompson (D–MS), quoted in a prepared statement given December 5, 2005, before the U.S. House of Representatives, Committee on Homeland Security.

28. James M. Lindsay, "Congress, Foreign Policy, and the New Institutionalism," *International Studies Quarterly* 38 (June 1994): 281–304.

29. *Congress A to Z*, 4th ed. (Washington, DC: CQ Press, 2003).

30. For Eisenhower's thoughts on the subject, see Dwight D. Eisenhower, *The White House Years* (Garden City, NY: Doubleday, 1963–1965).

31. Roxana Tiron, "Cunningham Sentenced to Eight Years, Four Months," *The Hill* (March 3, 2006).

32. Testimony of U.S. Ambassador Maureen Quinn, Afghanistan coordinator at the Department of State; Mary Beth Long, deputy assistant secretary of defense for counter-narcotics; and Michael A. Braun, chief of operations for the Drug Enforcement Administration before the U.S. House of Representatives Committee on International Relations, March 17, 2005.

33. Steven W. Hook, *U.S. Foreign Policy: The Paradox of World Power* (Washington, DC: CQ Press, 2005), 319.

34. President's Commission on Critical Infrastructure Protection, *Critical Foundations: Protecting America's Infrastructures* (Washington, DC: Government Printing Office, 1997).

35. John Christensen, "Bracing for Guerrilla Warfare in Cyberspace," CNN Interactive, April 6, 1999; and Kenneth H. Bacon, Department of Defense news briefing, April 16, 1998.

36. This information is sourced from several 2007 and 2008 polls conducted by Gallup, CBS, and CNN. All are available at PollingReport.com.

Chapter 1: The Political Landscape

MULTIPLE-CHOICE QUESTIONS

1. According to traditional democratic theory, all of the following are characteristics of an ideal democracy EXCEPT
   - (A) freedom of speech.
   - (B) a bill of rights.
   - (C) equality of voting.
   - (D) citizens have collective control over the government's policy agenda.
   - (E) government extends rights to everyone who is subject to its laws.

2. The following functions are shared by all governments EXCEPT
   - (A) maintaining a national defense.
   - (B) ensuring social equality.
   - (C) preserving order.
   - (D) providing public services.
   - (E) socializing the young.

3. Which of the following concepts is fundamental to democracies?
   - (A) economic equality.
   - (B) tyranny of the majority.
   - (C) majority rule with minority rights.
   - (D) bicameralism.
   - (E) seniority.

4. On which of the following indicators of democratic health does American democracy do poorly?
   - (A) political equality.
   - (B) majority rule.
   - (C) minority rights.
   - (D) voter turnout.
   - (E) freedom of speech.

5. Linkage institutions are mechanisms through which citizens can influence the policy agenda. All of the following are linkage institutions EXCEPT
   - (A) the Constitution.
   - (B) political parties.
   - (C) interest groups.
   - (D) the media.
   - (E) elections.

6. Liberals are likely to support all of the following EXCEPT
   - (A) freedom of choice in abortions.
   - (B) government regulation.
   - (C) increased taxes on the rich.
   - (D) social welfare programs.
   - (E) prayer in schools.

7. How are older Americans different from younger Americans?
   - I. Older Americans are more likely to vote.
   - II. Older Americans are more conservative.
   - III. Older Americans are more supportive of investing Social Security funds in the stock market.
   - IV. Older Americans are more likely to favor spending money on national defense.
   - (A) III only.
   - (B) I and II only.
   - (C) I, II, and III only.
   - (D) II, III, and IV only.
   - (E) I, II, and IV only.

8. The United States is expected to have a minority majority population by 2050. What does this mean?
   - (A) Hispanic Americans will outnumber African Americans.
   - (B) Female conservatives will outnumber male conservatives.
   - (C) Asian Americans will outnumber Hispanic Americans.
   - (D) Voters under the age of thirty will outnumber senior citizens.
   - (E) The minority populations will outnumber the Caucasian population.

FREE-RESPONSE QUESTION

1. Democracy is a key feature in the U.S. political system. Democracy is instilled and maintained through a set of values referred to as political culture. Many scholars believe that in spite of this shared culture, the United States is experiencing a culture war.
   - a) Identify and describe three aspects of American political culture.
   - b) Define "culture war" and identify one issue that is divisive to the American people.

Chapter 2: The Constitution

MULTIPLE-CHOICE QUESTIONS

1. Which of the following institutions was specifically outlined in the Constitution?
   - (A) the Federal Reserve System.
   - (B) the Cabinet.
   - (C) federal district courts.
   - (D) the Electoral College.
   - (E) the Department of State.

2. The Seventeenth Amendment changed the nature of senatorial elections by
   - (A) prohibiting PACs from contributing to senatorial campaigns.
   - (B) establishing a group of electors from each state to nominate senators.
   - (C) permitting senatorial debates to be aired on television.
   - (D) scheduling senatorial elections to be held every two years.
   - (E) requiring senators to be elected directly by the public.

3. Which of the following statements accurately describe the system of checks and balances?
   I. The system of checks and balances limits tyranny of the majority because one institution cannot gain total power over the others.
   II. The power to veto bills allows the president to check Congress.
   III. The system of checks and balances grew out of a long political tradition but is not defined by the Constitution.
   IV. Congress checks the power of the judicial branch by nominating Supreme Court justices.
   (A) I only.
   (B) III only.
   (C) I and II only.
   (D) III and IV only.
   (E) I, II, and III only.

4. Which of the following statements best summarizes the Supreme Court's decision regarding flag burning?
   (A) Flag burning is an unconstitutional desecration of a venerated object.
   (B) Laws that prohibit flag burning infringe on citizens' freedom of speech.
   (C) A democratic society can restrict flag burning if there is clear majority sentiment against the practice.
   (D) The government has an obligation to protect revered symbols and icons of American democracy.
   (E) Only Congress has the authority to prohibit flag burning; states cannot prohibit the practice.

5. Which of the following concepts guided both the Articles of Confederation and the Constitution?
   (A) the exclusionary rule.
   (B) limited government.
   (C) checks and balances.
   (D) state supremacy.
   (E) direct democracy.

6. The Bill of Rights was added to the Constitution to
   (A) clarify the Supreme Court's power of judicial review.
   (B) ensure equal voting rights.
   (C) protect individual liberties.
   (D) define all powers reserved for the federal and state governments.
   (E) prevent the supremacy of one faction of government over another.

7. Which of the following statements are true about the Declaration of Independence?
   I. The Declaration contains important statements about the philosophy that undergird American government.
   II. The bulk of the Declaration is a list of grievances against King George III.
   III. The Declaration outlines the basic institutions and processes of American government.
   IV. The Declaration implores the Netherlands to aid the colonies in their revolt against the British Empire and the "merciless Indian savages."

(A) I only.
(B) IV only.
(C) I and II only.
(D) II and IV only.
(E) I, II, and III only.

8. The Three-Fifths Compromise at the Constitutional Convention
   (A) allowed cloture to be invoked, ending a filibuster in the Senate, with the support of 60 senators.
   (B) prescribed the proportion of states required to ratify a constitutional amendment.
   (C) provided a formula by which slaves would be counted for apportioning the House of Representatives.
   (D) established the percentage of votes necessary for electors to be chosen under the original provisions of the Electoral College system.
   (E) established the percentage of members of the House required to pass a bill raising revenue.

9. Which of the following arguments did the Anti-Federalists make against ratifying the Constitution?
   (A) It entrusted too much power in the king of England.
   (B) It prohibited political parties.
   (C) It made the states too powerful.
   (D) It neglected to protect important liberties.
   (E) It destroyed the mercantile class.

10. In which of the following ways does the Constitution protect the rights of individuals?
    (A) It gives Congress the power to impeach the president.
    (B) It invests the president with the powers of commander in chief.
    (C) It prevents Congress from passing bills of attainder.
    (D) It allows states to collect taxes.
    (E) It divides government into the national and state levels.

FREE-RESPONSE QUESTIONS

1. The Constitution has been amended over time to reflect changes in the American political system. No issue has received more attention among these amendments than that of voting rights.
   a) Describe three amendments that had an impact on voting rights.
   b) Describe how each amendment has changed the nature of the electorate.

2. The Declaration of Independence states *"Governments are instituted among men, deriving their just powers from the consent of the governed."*
   a) Describe one way in which this ideal of government was implemented into a state constitution during the Revolutionary period.
   b) Describe one way in which this ideal of government was neglected in a state constitution during the Revolutionary period.
   c) Describe one way in which this ideal of government was implemented into the U.S. Constitution in 1787.
   d) Describe one way in which this ideal of government was neglected in the U.S. Constitution in 1787.

Chapter 3: Federalism

MULTIPLE-CHOICE QUESTIONS

1. Both the national and state governments have the power to
   (A) coin money.
   (B) tax.
   (C) establish post offices.
   (D) declare war.
   (E) conduct foreign relations.

2. The elastic clause gives Congress the authority to
   (A) overrule the president's veto.
   (B) pass laws necessary to carry out its enumerated powers.
   (C) overturn state laws.
   (D) check the power of the Supreme Court by approving the president's nominees for justices.
   (E) dismiss members of the federal judiciary for making unpopular decisions.

3. Which of the following statements about federalism is true?
   (A) Power is concentrated in a central government that oversees policy making and the enforcement of laws.
   (B) Power is shared among state governments in such a way that all states have identical laws.
   (C) Power is divided among levels of government.
   (D) Power is relegated primarily to local governments.
   (E) Power is vested mostly in state governments.

4. In a confederation,
   (A) power is divided between a central government and regional governments.
   (B) the sovereignty within a nation is held entirely by the central government.
   (C) sovereignty is shared at the national, state, and local levels.
   (D) power is held at the regional level, with the central government exercising only such influence as the regional governments give it.
   (E) regional governments hold sovereignty regarding domestic policy while the national government holds sovereignty in national security policy.

5. The full faith and credit clause would require all of the following EXCEPT
   (A) that a marriage performed in Las Vegas is valid in other states.
   (B) that a driver's license is valid in other states.
   (C) that a divorced parent pay child support even if his or her children reside in another state.
   (D) that a birth certificate issued by any state must be recognized by other states.
   (E) that something against the law in one state is against the law in all other states.

6. What is the difference between block grants and categorical grants?
   (A) Block grants are given by the federal government to the states. Categorical grants are given by the states to the federal government.
   (B) States have greater flexibility over how to use block grants.
   (C) Block grants are always smaller than categorical grants.
   (D) States prefer categorical grants to block grants because they come with fewer strings attached.
   (E) Categorical grants are prohibited by the constitutional requirement that each state receives block grants according to its population.

7. A resident of New Mexico is threatened by an angry mob while visiting relatives in Texas. The local police must provide the New Mexican with the same protection it provides the Texas relatives. This is an example of
   (A) the Tenth Amendment.
   (B) the supremacy clause.
   (C) the rights of the accused.
   (D) the privileges and immunities clause.
   (E) dual federalism.

8. When there is a dispute about whether an issue falls under the jurisdiction of the federal or a state government,
   (A) the president decides and issues an executive order.
   (B) a court rules on the matter.
   (C) Congress votes to determine who has the authority.
   (D) the state legislatures must decide whether to overrule the federal government.
   (E) the issue falls to the jurisdiction of local governments.

9. "Dual federalism" refers to the fact that
   (A) the Constitution provides two layers of government in the nation: the national and the state.
   (B) there are two major forms of aid from the national governments to the states: categorical and block grants.
   (C) both the national and state governments can levy taxes on citizens.
   (D) there are two distinct eras in American history: the era before cooperative federalism and the era since the development of federalism.
   (E) there is a distinct line between policies surrounding public education and private education in the states.

10. Which of the following statements accurately describe public participation in a federal system?
    I. Multilevel elections allow voters to influence more government bodies.
    II. Concerned citizens may join both state and national political groups to try to influence policy making.
    III. People are more likely to participate in state-level politics because state governments are always more responsive.
    IV. Political parties offer voters more choice among candidates.
    (A) I only.
    (B) III only.
    (C) I and II only.
    (D) I, II, and III only.
    (E) II, III, and IV only.

FREE-RESPONSE QUESTIONS

1. The federal system in the United States was intended to divide power between the federal government and state governments. Since the creation of the federal system, however, power has tended to gravitate from the states to the federal government.
   a) Explain how TWO of the following have shifted power to the federal government:
      * *McCulloch v. Maryland.*
      * federal grants to states.
      * the civil rights movement.
   b) Explain how ONE of the following Supreme Court cases from the Rehnquist Court reverted power back to the states from the federal government.
      * *United States* v. *Lopez.*
      * *United States* v. *Morrison.*
      * *Printz* v. *United States.*

2. Several parts of the Constitution have important implications for federalism.
   a) Describe the relevance of these for federalism:
      * supremacy clause
      * Tenth Amendment
      * necessary and proper, or "elastic," clause
   b) Explain how federalism has affected federal/state relations in ONE of the following areas:
      * environmental policy
      * international relations
      * elections

Chapter 4: State and Local Government

MULTIPLE-CHOICE QUESTIONS

1. Which of the following powers is given to most state governors but not the president of the United States?
   (A) the line-item veto.
   (B) assigning members to legislative committees.
   (C) determining the budget.
   (D) issuing pardons.
   (E) declaring laws unconstitutional.

2. Which of the following statements about state constitutions is accurate?
   (A) All state constitutions contain a bill of rights.
   (B) All state constitutions give executive power to a governor and legislative power to a bicameral legislature.
   (C) Most state constitutions are shorter than the U.S. Constitution.
   (D) State constitutions typically provide fewer details about specific policies than does the U.S. Constitution.
   (E) State constitutions supersede the U.S. Constitution.

3. Which of the following best summarizes the most common method states use to amend their constitutions?
   (A) The state senate proposes amendments which must be ratified by the state house of representatives.
   (B) The state house of representatives proposes amendments which must be ratified by the state senate.
   (C) The state legislature proposes amendments which must be ratified by the voters.
   (D) The voters propose amendments which must be ratified by the state legislature.
   (E) The governor proposes amendments which must be ratified by the state legislature.

4. Which of the following best describes gubernatorial elections?
   (A) Gubernatorial campaigns are candidate centered.
   (B) Gubernatorial campaigns are party centered.
   (C) The winner of gubernatorial elections is heavily influenced by the coattail effect.
   (D) Gubernatorial races are seldom at the top of the ticket.
   (E) Governors are usually elected during presidential election years.

5. The recent trend toward legislative professionalism in state government includes
   I. increasing legislators' salaries.
   II. reducing the influence of interest groups.
   III. lengthening legislative sessions.
   IV. reducing the power of the state executive branch.
   V. limiting the number of professional staff members employed by the legislature.
   (A) I and III only.
   (B) II and V only.
   (C) II, IV, and V only.
   (D) I, II, III, and IV only.
   (E) I, III, IV, and V only.

6. The increase in the number of governments in the United States is mostly attributable to the growth in what type of government?
   (A) county.
   (B) municipal.
   (C) township.
   (D) school district.
   (E) special district.

7. What was the impact of the U.S. Supreme Court's decision in *Baker* v. *Carr*?
   (A) All states had to have an equal number of state house districts.
   (B) State senate districts had to be the same size as state house districts.
   (C) Rural interests began to dominate urban interests in state legislatures.
   (D) The influence of rural interests in state legislatures declined.
   (E) States could not discriminate on the basis of race in local and state elections.

8. Which of the following best describes how most state laws are created?
   (A) The governor proposes bills that become law once ratified by both houses of the legislature.
   (B) Both houses of the legislature pass identical versions of a bill and the governor signs it.

(C) Both houses of the legislature pass identical versions of a bill that becomes law when the state supreme court determines that is does not violate the state constitution.

(D) The state house of representatives passes a bill which must then be approved by the U.S. Congress.

(E) The state legislature passes a bill which must then be ratified by the state's voters in the next general election.

9. Which of the following are common methods for selecting state judges?
   I. Partisan elections.
   II. Nonpartisan elections.
   III. Appointment.
   IV. Appointment followed by retention elections.
   (A) I and IV only.
   (B) II and III only.
   (C) I, III, and IV only.
   (D) II, III, and IV only.
   (E) I, II, III, and IV.

10. All of the following are forms of direct democracy EXCEPT
    (A) town meetings.
    (B) line-item vetoes.
    (C) recall elections.
    (D) initiatives.
    (E) referenda.

FREE-RESPONSE QUESTIONS

1. Presidents and governors serve as leaders of their respective governments. Describe two formal legislative powers that can make governors more effective legislative leaders than presidents. Describe two nonformal abilities that presidents and governors need in order to be effective leaders.

2. While the Constitution only allows individual citizens to vote directly for three offices (one representative and two senators), states are able to give their citizens a much more active voice. Identify and describe TWO ways in which a state has broader power of the electorate, either through direct policy making or through elective offices.

Chapter 5: Civil Liberties

MULTIPLE-CHOICE QUESTIONS

1. In which of the following cases did the Supreme Court enforce the use of the exclusionary rule in state trials?
   (A) *Near* v. *Minnesota*.
   (B) *Miranda* v. *Arizona*.
   (C) *Miller* v. *California*.
   (D) *Mapp* v. *Ohio*.
   (E) *Gregg* v. *Georgia*.

2. *Roth* v. *United States* is a Supreme Court case that addresses the
   (A) Sixth Amendment rights of defendants.
   (B) definition of obscenity.
   (C) right of free speech.
   (D) definition of probable cause.
   (E) right to privacy.

3. Which of the following statements accurately describe the exercise of religious freedom in public schools and universities?
   I. A nondenominational prayer required in schools is constitutional and does not violate the First Amendment.
   II. Schools must allow student religious groups to meet if other student groups are permitted to do so.
   III. Federal funding may be used by religious schools to construct buildings and acquire educational supplies.
   IV. States can forbid all types of prayer in school.
   V. The separation of church and state is clearly stated in the elastic clause of the Constitution.
   (A) I and IV only.
   (B) II and V only.
   (C) II and III only.
   (D) II, III, and IV only.
   (E) III, IV, and V only.

4. In *Engel* v. *Vitale* (1962), the Supreme Court ruled that
   (A) the reciting of a state-required prayer in public school constitutes an impermissible establishment of religion under the First Amendment.
   (B) the Gideon society could distribute Bibles in public schools under the free exercise clause of the First Amendment.
   (C) the eminent domain clause of the Fifth Amendment prevents government from taking religious property for public purposes.
   (D) public school children may wear crosses as necklaces as a permissible mode of symbolic speech under the First Amendment.
   (E) the Second Amendment "right to bear arms" does not apply in religious facilities.

5. Under reasonable time, place, and manner restrictions, all of the following are protected under the First Amendment EXCEPT
   (A) picketing.
   (B) libel.
   (C) flag burning.
   (D) political demonstrations.
   (E) criticizing government officials.

6. The Supreme Court has regularly cited the due process clause of the Fourteenth Amendment to
   (A) extend the protection of the Bill of Rights to be binding on the states.
   (B) assert its power of judicial review.
   (C) allow the executive branch to infringe on civil liberties.
   (D) ensure the right to bear arms.
   (E) impose limitations on the exercise of defendants' rights.

7. In which of the following cases did the Supreme Court rule that the death penalty is not a form of cruel and unusual punishment?
   (A) *Gregg* v. *Georgia.*
   (B) *Gideon* v. *Wainwright.*
   (C) *Barron* v. *Baltimore.*
   (D) *Engel* v. *Vitale.*
   (E) *Gitlow* v. *New York.*

8. Which of the following generalizations about the Supreme Court's stance on abortion is true?
   (A) In *Roe* v. *Wade*, the Supreme Court ruled that abortions infringe on the constitutional rights of the unborn.
   (B) The Supreme Court is usually conservative and therefore favors the right to life in all situations unless the mother's health is at risk.
   (C) The Supreme Court has always been distinctly pro-choice and has struck down state laws that attempted to interfere with the performing of abortions.
   (D) The Supreme Court permitted the right to an abortion in certain circumstances in *Roe* v. *Wade*, but it has since upheld several restrictions on abortions.
   (E) The Supreme Court has consistently upheld a woman's right to an abortion, even if she is in her third trimester or if she is a minor.

9. Under reasonable time, place, and manner restrictions, the right to assemble extends to groups in all of the following situations EXCEPT
   (A) a hate group such as the Ku Klux Klan holding a rally.
   (B) right-to-life advocates blocking access to abortion clinics.
   (C) an antiwar demonstration that threatens to harm the morale of American troops.

(D) a religious group holding a public prayer meeting.
(E) a labor union starting a picket line.

10. The right of government to keep a newspaper from publishing information that would be harmful to the morale of troops deployed in a military conflict
   (A) would be denied as "prior restraint."
   (B) would be allowed under the "no quartering of soldiers" provision of the Third Amendment.
   (C) would be denied as entailing a "clear and present danger."
   (D) would be allowed as denying "seditious speech."
   (E) would be allowed under the USA Patriot Act.

FREE-RESPONSE QUESTIONS
1. Many Supreme Court cases concern the First Amendment.
   a) Identify and describe two provisions in the First Amendment which pertain to the issue of religion.
   b) Choose ONE of the following Supreme Court cases.
      • *Lemon* v. *Kurtzman*
      • *Engel* v. *Vitale*
      • *Employment Division* v. *Smith*
   c) For the case you chose above, identify which part of the First Amendment pertains to this case.
   d) For the case you chose in (b), describe the ruling the Supreme Court made in this case.

2. The Patriot Act was passed after the terrorist attacks of September 11, 2001.
   a) Describe the Patriot Act.
   b) Identify and describe a provision in the Bill of Rights that the Patriot Act affects.
   c) Explain how the Patriot Act might limit the application of the provision in the Bill of Rights identified in (b).

Chapter 6: Civil Rights

MULTIPLE-CHOICE QUESTIONS
1. The Civil Rights Act did all of the following EXCEPT
   (A) create the Equal Employment Opportunity Commission.
   (B) deny federal funding to businesses and schools that practiced racial discrimination.
   (C) prevent racial discrimination in housing.
   (D) prohibit racial discrimination in hotels, in restaurants, and on public transportation.
   (E) outlaw job discrimination.

2. Which of the following generalizations accurately describe the advancement of civil rights in the twentieth century?
   I. The Fourteenth Amendment served as the foundation on which the Supreme Court based many of its decisions regarding civil rights.
   II. The national government has opted to pursue civil rights at the expense of limited government.
   III. The Supreme Court typically finds that racial classifications are unconstitutional.

IV. The Supreme Court has outlawed all laws that classify citizens by race, gender, sexual orientation, ethnicity, and disability.
   (A) II only.
   (B) IV only.
   (C) I and II only.
   (D) III and IV only.
   (E) I, II, and III only.

3. The Equal Rights Amendment did not become part of the Constitution because
   (A) it was not ratified by enough states.
   (B) the Senate voted against it after the House had passed it.
   (C) the women's rights movement has focused primarily on preserving protectionist laws.
   (D) the Supreme Court found it unconstitutional.
   (E) feminists decried it for neglecting to take a firm position on women's rights.

4. Opponents of affirmative action claim that it
   (A) violates the First Amendment guarantee of free speech.
   (B) fails to sufficiently compensate minorities for past discrimination.

(C) encourages reverse discrimination.

(D) excuses the federal government from having to enforce civil rights.

(E) favors certain minority groups over other minority groups.

5. Which of the following statements accurately describes the relationship between *Plessy* v. *Ferguson* and *Brown* v. *Board of Education*?

(A) *Plessy* reinforced the advancement of civil rights begun by the Supreme Court in *Brown*.

(B) The Supreme Court overturned its decision in *Plessy* with its *Brown* ruling.

(C) Both *Plessy* and *Brown* extended voting rights to disenfranchised African Americans in the South.

(D) Both *Plessy* and *Brown* made desegregation in public schools compulsory.

(E) The Supreme Court extended the precedent established in *Plessy* with its *Brown* decision.

6. Which of the following groups has focused on ensuring civil rights for Hispanic Americans and Latinos?

(A) MALDEF.

(B) AIM.

(C) NAACP.

(D) EEOC.

(E) ADA.

7. Where is the guarantee of "equal protection of the laws" found?

(A) in the Bill of Rights.

(B) in the Supreme Court's decision in *Korematsu* v. *United States*.

(C) in the Supreme Court's decision in *Brown* v. *Board of Education*.

(D) in the Fourteenth Amendment.

(E) in the preamble to the Constitution.

8. In which of the following cases did the Supreme Court first declare gender discrimination unconstitutional?

(A) *Faragher* v. *City of Boca Raton*.

(B) *Reed* v. *Reed*.

(C) *Stanton* v. *Stanton*.

(D) *Craig* v. *Boren*.

(E) *Dothard* v. *Rawlinson*.

9. All of the following were methods used by southern states to reduce the electoral voice of African Americans EXCEPT

(A) tests about the Constitution.

(B) white primaries.

(C) literacy tests.

(D) poll taxes.

(E) the Fifteenth Amendment.

10. In the case of *California* v. *Bakke*, the Supreme Court ruled that

(A) Japanese Americans could be placed in camps during World War II.

(B) migrant workers were entitled to compensation in case of injury through unemployment insurance.

(C) affirmative action admissions to a medical school could cause "reverse discrimination."

(D) women were entitled to equal pay for equal work.

(E) the "white primary" was unconstitutional.

FREE-RESPONSE QUESTIONS

1. Civil rights has been an issue that has affected the United States since the founding. All branches of government have been involved in the civil rights arena.

a) Do TWO of the following:

• Identify and describe one Supreme Court case in the twentieth century that affected civil rights.

• Identify and describe one law passed by Congress in the twentieth century that affected civil rights.

• Identify and describe one presidential action in the twentieth century that affected civil rights.

b) Identify ONE nongovernmental institution that has helped advance civil rights, and describe the actions it has taken.

2. The civil rights movement of the 1950s and 1960s was successful in part due to strong individual leadership. Choose TWO of the following:

• Earl Warren

• Martin Luther King Jr.

• Lyndon Johnson

For each person you have chosen,

a) Identify and describe one specific action through which each of these two individuals helped advance civil rights for African Americans.

b) Describe the opposition each of the two individuals faced while trying to advance civil rights for African Americans.

Chapter 7: Congress

MULTIPLE-CHOICE QUESTIONS

1. Conference committees

(A) register bills to be introduced on the floor and schedule debate.

(B) handle proposed legislation that deals with more than one area of policy.

(C) work out compromises between House and Senate versions of bills.

(D) combine members of both the House and Senate to consider overlapping policy areas.

(E) educate the public about the a\ctivities of Congress.

2. According to Table 7.5 on p. 251, incumbents have all of the following advantages over their challengers EXCEPT

(A) incumbents spend more money than do challengers.

(B) incumbents can brag about federal spending projects in their districts.

(C) incumbents can increase visibility among their constituents by using the franking privilege.

(D) incumbents provide casework for their constituents.

(E) challengers have a clean political record, and incumbents do not.

3. In which of the following ways does Congress conduct legislative oversight?

I. Appointing conference committees to investigate the actions of the bureaucracy.

II. Determining the federal budget.

III. Holding hearings to question agency officials.

IV. Inspecting government offices.

(A) I and III only.

(B) II and III only.

(C) III and IV only.

(D) I, II, and III only.

(E) I, III, and IV only.

4. Which of the following statements accurately describe legislative committees?

I. Committees are in session only when preparing bills to be introduced onto the floor.

II. Junior members of Congress have few opportunities to sit on committees.

III. The Speaker of the House has a great deal of influence in appointing committee chairs.

IV. Conference committees are composed of senators whose task is to amend bills that are in danger of being killed in Congress.

(A) III only.

(B) I and III only.

(C) II and III only.

(D) I, II, and IV only.

(E) I, III, and V only.

5. A senator can often prevent the Senate from voting on the bill being debated on the Senate floor by

(A) conducting oversight.

(B) filibustering.

(C) introducing another bill.

(D) holding hearings.

(E) logrolling.

6. On a bill with high visibility, members of Congress are most likely to vote

(A) along party lines.

(B) according to their personal ideology.

(C) in a presidential coalition.

(D) in keeping with the needs of their constituency.

(E) according to the pressures of lobbyists.

7. Which of the following can be seen as an advantage of divided government?

(A) Divided government creates clear lines of accountability for policy failures and successes.

(B) Political parties are better able to enact their policy platforms.

(C) Divided government encourages compromise between the parties.

(D) The president maintains the upper hand in negotiations with Congress.

(E) Increased voter turnout.

8. After a House committee reviews a bill and writes its report, the bill typically goes to the

(A) Senate.

(B) House appropriate subcommittee.

(C) president.

(D) House floor for debate.

(E) House Rules Committee.

9. Which of the following is a difference between the House and Senate?

(A) Power is more decentralized in the Senate.

(B) The filibuster is more common in the House than in the Senate.

(C) The Senate allows twice as much time as the House does for debate on a bill.

(D) Members of the House have large constituencies.

(E) The legislative process starts in the House; the Senate can only debate bills once the House has passed them.

10. Which of the following statements about congressional parties is accurate?

(A) The majority party controls all of the seats on a majority of the committees.

(B) Both political parties have became more extreme and more homogenous.

(C) Both political parties have moderated, taking policy positions closer to the median voter.

(D) The House operates on a nonpartisan basis while the Senate is heavily partisan.

(E) Political parties are much weaker and disjointed than they were thirty years ago.

FREE-RESPONSE QUESTIONS

1. Congress is organized in such a way that its leaders have important roles.

a) Describe how the Speaker of the House of Representatives is selected and describe that position's power.

b) Discuss how the president of the Senate is selected and describe that position's power.

c) Explain how the powers of the two positions reflect the differences in the two houses of Congress.

d) Identify another leader, other than the Speaker of the House or the president of the Senate, and describe that position's power.

2. Sometimes one party has control of Congress and the presidency. This gives the majority party advantages in Congress, yet passing legislation is still difficult.

a) Describe the legislative advantages of the majority party in Congress with respect to both committee structure and leadership.

b) Explain why, even with single-party control, passing legislation is difficult. Use two examples to support your explanation.

Chapter 8: The Presidency

MULTIPLE-CHOICE QUESTIONS

1. A bill that is vetoed by the president
   (A) goes to a conference committee for revision.
   (B) must be rewritten by the representative who authored it.
   (C) will never become law.
   (D) goes to a federal court for approval of the veto.
   (E) can become law if Congress overrides the veto.

2. Which of the following statements accurately describe a step in the process of removing a president from office?
   I. The accused president is tried by the Senate.
   II. The chief justice of the Supreme Court decides if the president is guilty of the crime with which he is charged.
   III. The House of Representatives votes to impeach the president.
   IV. A two-thirds vote in the Senate is required to remove the president from office.
   V. A conference committee holds hearings to consider public opinion of the president's performance.
   (A) I and II only.
   (B) I and IV only.
   (C) I, III, and IV only.
   (D) II, III, and V only.
   (E) III, IV, and V only.

3. The War Powers Act checks the president's power by
   (A) prohibiting him from issuing executive agreements that engage the country in war.
   (B) increasing the power of Congress to control the military budget.
   (C) preventing him from sending troops into crisis situations without congressional approval.
   (D) mandating that Congress approve the president's decision to use weapons of mass destruction.
   (E) requiring troops to be withdrawn in sixty days unless Congress declares war or issues an extension.

4. Presidents attempt to influence policy making in all of the following ways EXCEPT by
   (A) appealing directly to the public for support.
   (B) proposing legislation in congressional committees.
   (C) offering favors such as backing during reelection.
   (D) exchanging support for policies with representatives.
   (E) building coalitions among party members.

5. Which of the following tasks falls to the vice president?
   (A) leading Cabinet meetings.
   (B) presiding over the Senate.
   (C) commanding the military.
   (D) determining the federal budget.
   (E) overseeing congressional elections.

6. Which of the following factors is the greatest influence on a citizen's approval of the president?
   (A) the citizen's party affiliation.
   (B) the president's success in working with Congress.
   (C) the citizen's state of residence.
   (D) the president's success in diplomacy.
   (E) the president's understanding of the Constitution.

7. Which of the following statements about the presidential veto is true?
   (A) Presidents frequently veto legislation.
   (B) Congress rarely overrides a veto.
   (C) The pocket veto has been declared unconstitutional by the Supreme Court.
   (D) Presidents can use a line-item veto to reject only part of a bill.
   (E) Presidents are more likely to veto Supreme Court decisions than congressional legislation.

8. All of the following are powers of the president EXCEPT
   (A) conducting diplomatic relations.
   (B) granting pardons.
   (C) dismissing Supreme Court justices.
   (D) negotiating treaties.
   (E) appointing top-level administrators to serve in the bureaucracy.

9. As set forth in the Constitution, the order of presidential succession is the vice president, then the
   (A) Speaker of the House.
   (B) secretary of state.
   (C) Senate majority leader.
   (D) attorney general.
   (E) chief justice of the Supreme Court.

10. Which of the following presidential appointments requires Senate confirmation?
    (A) press secretary.
    (B) chief of staff.
    (C) White House counsel.
    (D) Council of Economic Advisors.
    (E) secretary of state.

FREE-RESPONSE QUESTIONS

1. The president has to make instant decisions regarding war making.
   a) Identify a military power of the legislative branch and a military power of the executive branch.
   b) Describe how the Wars Powers Act (1973) tried to curtail the president's power in foreign affairs
   c) Describe one action taken by a president involving foreign affairs since the passage of the Wars Powers Resolution, and explain Congress's reaction to it.

2. Along with the roles assigned to the president by the Constitution, the president also serves as leader of his political party.
   a) Explain TWO ways the president's role as party leader can make him a more effective legislative leader.
   b) Explain TWO reasons president's do not exercise more authority over members of Congress.

Chapter 9: The Executive Branch and the Federal Bureaucracy

MULTIPLE-CHOICE QUESTIONS

1. Which of the following statements accurately describes the size of the federal bureaucracy?
   (A) Homeland Security is the largest department in the bureaucracy.
   (B) The State Department is the largest department in the bureaucracy.
   (C) The size of the federal bureaucracy has remained relatively stable in recent years.
   (D) The size of the federal bureaucracy has doubled since the September 11, 2001, terrorist attacks.
   (E) The percentage of the workforce employed by the federal government has increased slightly in recent years.

2. Most federal bureaucrats are hired in which of the following ways?
   (A) They are awarded positions by the political party in power.
   (B) They take an examination to prove their qualifications.
   (C) They are appointed to a position by the president.
   (D) They work in the legislative branch and then move to the bureaucracy.
   (E) They get their positions in exchange for campaign contributions.

3. The role of the bureaucracy is to
   (A) implement policies.
   (B) maintain order.
   (C) promote the general welfare.
   (D) secure the blessings of liberty to ourselves and our posterity.
   (E) ensure domestic tranquility.

4. Which of the following reasons accurately describe why it may be difficult for the bureaucracy to implement laws passed by Congress?
   I. Laws are often written in terms of broad policy goals.
   II. Laws are often unclear about the details of a policy.
   III. Congress frequently fails to give the bureaucracy enough money to effectively implement policies.
   IV. Bureaucracies often lack the necessary authority to meet their responsibilities.
   (A) I and II only.
   (B) II and IV only.
   (C) I, II, and IV only.
   (D) II, III, and IV only.
   (E) I, II, III, and IV.

5. Which of the following is a government corporation?
   (A) the Department of the Interior.
   (B) the Food and Drug Administration.
   (C) the Bureau of Engraving.
   (D) General Motors.
   (E) Amtrak.

6. The president exercises his influence over the federal bureaucracy in which of the following ways?
   (A) hiring interest groups to influence certain agencies.
   (B) appointing administrators sympathetic to the president's policy agenda.
   (C) creating new Cabinet-level agencies.
   (D) frequently removing administrators from office.
   (E) having federal judges disband ineffective agencies.

7. Which of the following is the most likely effect of administrative discretion?
   (A) Administrative discretion is a major contributor to skyrocketing implementation costs.
   (B) Laws are implemented in ways that are consistent with bureaucrats' personal preferences.
   (C) High job turnover results from poorly crafted public policies.
   (D) Fewer bureaucrats gain necessary job skills because administrative discretion encourages laziness.
   (E) Administrative discretion results in poorly crafted public policies.

8. The Department of Homeland Security was created to address which of the following concerns?
   (A) the free-rider problem.
   (B) administrative discretion.
   (C) the proliferation of constituency service and casework.
   (D) fragmentation of responsibility among various bureaucracies.
   (E) standard operating procedures.

9. A citizen would best express his or her concern about airport safety in which of the following ways?
   (A) filing a complaint with the National Transportation Safety Board.
   (B) voting for a new secretary of the Department of Transportation.
   (C) abstaining from voting in the next congressional election.
   (D) writing a letter to the Supreme Court.
   (E) hiring someone to inspect aircraft manufacturing plants.

10. The Pendleton Civil Service Act is significant because
   (A) it instituted an affirmative action policy for hiring and promoting federal bureaucrats.
   (B) it created the federal civil service and prescribed that the hiring of civil servants be based on merit.
   (C) it gave the president more control over federal agencies.
   (D) it reduced the number of federal civil servants working outside of Washington, D.C.
   (E) it established clear boundaries between state and federal bureaucracies.

FREE-RESPONSE QUESTIONS

1. Iron triangles, or subgovernments, often form around a specific policy area to shape and administer relevant policies. Select ONE of the following policy areas and complete the tasks below.
   • agriculture
   • the environment
   • product safety
   • oil

a) Identify the participants in the iron triangle.
b) Describe something each participant would receive from each of the other participants in the triangle.

2. In the first half of U.S. history, bureaucracies tended to act in a client-oriented role. However, since the early 1900s, the bureaucracy has become more of a regulator.

a) Identify TWO agencies that serve in a regulatory capacity, and give an example of a regulation they have made.
b) Describe ONE complaint made about the federal bureaucracy acting in the role of a regulator.

Chapter 10: The Judiciary

MULTIPLE-CHOICE QUESTIONS

1. A plaintiff cannot bring suit unless he or she has fulfilled which of the following requirements?
   (A) paid bail.
   (B) filed an *amicus curiae* brief.
   (C) appealed the case.
   (D) hired a public defender.
   (E) established standing to sue.

2. Which of the following statements are true about the cases on the Supreme Court's docket?
   I. The Supreme Court tries to hear every case that is appealed to it.
   II. Cases pertaining to civil liberties are more likely to be placed on the docket.
   III. The U.S. solicitor general decides which cases the Supreme Court will hear.
   IV. The Supreme Court has original jurisdiction in cases involving civil disputes among residents of a particular state.
   (A) II only.
   (B) IV only.
   (C) I and II only.
   (D) II and III only.
   (E) III and IV only.

3. Courts with appellate jurisdiction focus their attention on which aspect of a case?
   (A) the facts presented by both parties in the original case.
   (B) the *amicus curiae* briefs registered with the court.
   (C) the backgrounds of the jury members in the original case.
   (D) the legal issues involved in the original case.
   (E) the testimonies of both sides given before the Supreme Court.

4. Congress influences the ideology of the Supreme Court by
   (A) passing laws to limit judicial review and prohibit judicial activism.
   (B) issuing recommendations on pending cases through the Senate Judiciary Committee.
   (C) approving or rejecting the president's nomination of Supreme Court justices.
   (D) choosing which cases the Supreme Court will hear.
   (E) nominating justices for the president's approval.

5. All of the following statements accurately describe the federal court system EXCEPT
   (A) very few federal cases actually go to trial.
   (B) federal courts only handle cases involving federal laws.
   (C) all federal judges must be nominated by the president and confirmed by the Senate.

   (D) lower courts are expected adhere to the precedents set by higher courts.
   (E) some federal courts have original jurisdiction, whereas others have appellate jurisdiction.

6. Approximately 90 percent of criminal cases in the United States
   (A) are cases in which the defendants' rights have been abused by law enforcement officials.
   (B) are appealed to the Supreme Court.
   (C) involve First Amendment rights.
   (D) are closed to the public during the trial.
   (E) are resolved by plea bargaining and do not go to trial.

7. Which of the following is the most frequent outcome of a case on the Supreme Court's docket?
   (A) It significantly alters current policies.
   (B) The justices vote unanimously.
   (C) It reverses the decision of the lower court.
   (D) It overrules the Court's own precedent.
   (E) The lower court's decision stands.

8. The decision of a federal court is most likely determined by
   (A) the argument put forth by the prosecution.
   (B) the argument put forth by the defense.
   (C) precedents set in similar cases.
   (D) which law school the judge attended.
   (E) briefs submitted by the federal government.

9. Which of the following methods is an interest group most likely to use to influence the federal judiciary?
   (A) running advertisements endorsing a Supreme Court nominee.
   (B) giving campaign contributions to prospective federal judges.
   (C) filing *amicus curiae* briefs.
   (D) contributing money to the Federal Judiciary Retirement Fund.
   (E) recruiting candidates to run against disliked federal judges.

10. What is the significance of the Supreme Court's decision in *Marbury* v. *Madison*?
    (A) It articulated the doctrine of *habeas corpus*.
    (B) It established the Supreme Court's power to exercise judicial review.
    (C) It limited the influence and authority of the Supreme Court.
    (D) It established the doctrine of implied powers.
    (E) It established the principle of equal protection of the laws as the cornerstone for expanding civil rights.

FREE-RESPONSE QUESTIONS

1. Define *plea-bargaining*. Why do prosecutors agree to use this method rather than a full trial? Why do defendants agree to use this method rather than a full trial?

2. Many of the writers of the Constitution believed that the federal Judiciary would be the weakest of the three branches of government. Today, however, many consider the Supreme Court the most powerful of the three branches. This is due mainly to the use of judicial review and the theory of judicial activism.

a) Define "judicial review" and describe a case in which judicial review was used.
b) Describe "judicial activism."
c) Describe TWO reasons the federal courts can be considered undemocratic.
d) Explain ONE way in which one of the other branches of the federal government can rein in the power of the federal courts.

Chapter 11: Political Socialization and Public Opinion

MULTIPLE-CHOICE QUESTIONS

1. All of the following influence the formation of an individual's political beliefs EXCEPT
   (A) schooling.
   (B) the family.
   (C) religion.
   (D) the mass media.
   (E) the month in which the individual was born.

2. How are older Americans different from younger Americans?
   I. Older Americans are more likely to vote.
   II. Older Americans are more conservative.
   III. Older Americans are more supportive of investing Social Security funds in the stock market.
   IV. Older Americans are more likely to favor spending money on national defense.
   (A) III only.
   (B) I and II only.
   (C) I, II, and III only.
   (D) II, III, and IV only.
   (E) I, II, and IV only.

3. Which of the following are liberals most likely to endorse?
   (A) military intervention.
   (B) tax cuts.
   (C) free-market solutions to public policy problems.
   (D) increased spending on the poor.
   (E) increased defense spending.

4. According to the gender gap theory, women are more likely to
   (A) vote for a Democratic candidate.
   (B) support military spending.
   (C) vote for an independent candidate.
   (D) disapprove of increased social spending.
   (E) vote for a Republican candidate.

5. The United States is expected to have a minority majority population by 2050. What does this mean?
   (A) Hispanic Americans will outnumber African Americans.
   (B) Female conservatives will outnumber male conservatives.
   (C) Asian Americans will outnumber Hispanic Americans.
   (D) Voters under the age of thirty will outnumber senior citizens.
   (E) The minority populations will outnumber the Caucasian population.

6. Which of the following statements about sound bites is accurate?
   (A) The news media have had to narrow their scope of coverage because they have only a limited amount of material to broadcast.
   (B) The news media have tended to report longer and longer sound bites because that decreases the amount of time they must spend researching and reporting stories.
   (C) The complexity of most sound bites is not fully understood by the general public.
   (D) The media's tendency to focus on sound bites allows politicians to avoid an in-depth discussion of issues.
   (E) Politicians avoid using sound bites because they make a politician sound trite.

7. The failure of the *Literary Digest* poll occurred because
   (A) the sample was too small to predict the outcome of the election.
   (B) the questions on the survey were not phrased to obtain accurate results.
   (C) mail surveys rarely can be representative of the population.
   (D) the survey oversampled voters with high incomes.
   (E) computer technology of the day was inadequate to process the data accurately.

8. Sampling error refers to
   (A) the pollster making mistakes in selecting a sample.
   (B) the sample not being representative of the population.
   (C) coding mistakes that mean that responses are not accurately reported.
   (D) the level of confidence in the findings of a public opinion poll.
   (E) using a nonrandom procedure for drawing a sample of the population.

9. Which of the following is the most common form of political participation in the United States?
   (A) expressing one's ideas in a public opinion poll.
   (B) participating in a mass demonstration.
   (C) voting in a presidential election.
   (D) contacting a public official regarding a public issue.
   (E) joining an interest group for the purpose of influencing legislation.

10. The "gender gap" refers to the idea that women
    (A) are denied equal protection of the law in economic matters in the United States.
    (B) cannot take combat roles in the military.
    (C) are more likely to vote for Democrats than are men.
    (D) are proportionally underrepresented among members of Congress.
    (E) live on average longer than men, affecting their Social Security costs.

FREE-RESPONSE QUESTIONS

1. Political socialization is a major process for developing public opinions.
   a) Define political socialization.
   b) Explain how two of the following agents affect political socialization.

   • mass media
   • school
   • religion

   c) Explain why the family is considered to have the greatest influence on political socialization.

2. One of the most consistent ways that Americans learn about public opinion is through polling.
   a) Describe the advantage of a random sample for public opinion polling over a nonrandom sample.
   b) Describe one advantage and one disadvantage of telephone surveys compared t person-to-person interviewing.
   c) Describe what public opinion polls tell us about levels of political information that Americans have.
   d) Describe what public opinion polls tell us about political attitudes held by Americans.

Chapter 12: Political Parties

MULTIPLE-CHOICE QUESTIONS

1. According to Table 12.2 on p. 436, members of which group are most likely to be Democrats?
   (A) Jews.
   (B) Catholics.
   (C) Protestant Evangelicals.
   (D) Women.
   (E) Those under thirty years old.

2. Which of the following best explains why the United States has a two-party system?
   (A) The Constitution mandates a two-party system.
   (B) Federal laws mandate a two-party system.
   (C) In every state except California, state laws mandate a two-party system.
   (D) Seats in Congress are awarded on a winner-take-all basis.
   (E) Seats in Congress are awarded according to the principles of proportional representation.

3. Which of the following statements are generally true of third parties?
   I. Third-party officeholders threaten the political standing of the United States in the eyes of other nations.
   II. Third parties expand the political agenda.
   III. Third parties rarely gain enough support in the electorate to win.
   IV. Third-party success may indicate popular discontent.
   (A) I only.
   (B) III only.
   (C) II and III only.
   (D) I and IV only.
   (E) II, III, and IV only.

4. Political parties play an important role in democracy because they
   (A) guarantee voters radically different choices of policy outcomes.
   (B) offer politicians unique identities.
   (C) connect the public with policy-making institutions.
   (D) contribute to a centralized federal government.
   (E) control each of the three branches of government.

5. The process that parties use to nominate their candidate for the presidency is called
   (A) a critical election.
   (B) a national convention.
   (C) an open primary.
   (D) a closed primary.
   (E) a national committee.

6. When were local party organizations strongest?
   (A) when party machines controlled large cities.
   (B) during the New Deal coalition.
   (C) during a realignment.
   (D) during a dealignment.
   (E) immediately after a presidential election.

7. Which of the following statements accurately describe critical elections?
   I. Critical elections are often associated with significant political or social events.
   II. After a critical election, the previously existing minority party usually collapses and a new party forms.
   III. A critical election ensures that the previously existing majority party will maintain its position of power.
   IV. Critical elections usually signal the beginning of a new political era.
   (A) II only.
   (B) IV only.
   (C) I and IV only.
   (D) II and III only.
   (E) I, II, and IV only.

8. All of the following were part of the New Deal coalition EXCEPT
   (A) urbanites.
   (B) bankers.
   (C) labor unions.
   (D) Southerners.
   (D) Jews.

9. In addition to officially nominating a party's candidate for the presidency, national conventions perform which of the following tasks?
    (A) select the new chairs of the party's national committee.
    (B) raise funds for the general election.
    (C) determine the party's platform.
    (D) elect delegates to the next convention.
    (E) organize new party coalitions in Congress.

10. All of the following are criticisms raised against the nomination system EXCEPT
    (A) few citizens are permitted to participate in the nomination process.
    (B) too much weight is placed on early primaries in unrepresentative states.
    (C) the campaign process is too long.
    (D) it discourages many qualified politicians from running.
    (E) the media have too much power to shape the presidential campaigns.

FREE-RESPONSE QUESTIONS

1. The Republican Party has had fewer members than the Democratic Party in every election since 1952. Yet, Republicans have been able to win the presidency in nine out of fourteen elections. Explain THREE reasons for Republican success in winning the presidency while having fewer members than the Democratic Party.

2. Political parties are linkage institutions in American politics, helping convert public preferences into governmental action.
    a) Describe THREE ways in which parties serve as linkage institutions.
    b) Explain one reason political parties have been weakening since the 1960s.

Chapter 13: Voting and Elections

MULTIPLE-CHOICE QUESTIONS

1. The electoral votes of most states are allocated by which of the following methods?
    (A) Each party's candidate receives electoral votes based on his or her percentage of the state's popular vote.
    (B) Each elector chooses the candidate he or she thinks is best suited to represent the needs of the state.
    (C) The winner of the popular election in the state receives 75 percent of the state's electoral votes and the loser receives 25 percent.
    (D) All of the state's electors cast their votes for whichever candidate won the state's popular vote.
    (E) The loser in the popular election receives one electoral vote and the winner receives the rest of the state's electoral votes.

2. Issue voting requires all of the following conditions EXCEPT
    (A) the person must be familiar with each candidate's policy positions.
    (B) the person must have developed a pattern of policy voting over several elections.
    (C) the person must know his or her own position on policy issues.
    (D) the person must vote for the candidate whose policy positions coincide with his or her own preferences.
    (E) the person must be able to determine policy differences among the candidates.

3. Suffrage is most likely to be denied to a citizen who is
    (A) African American.
    (B) disabled.
    (C) eighteen years old.
    (D) a convicted felon.
    (E) a pauper.

4. Who is most likely to engage in ticket splitting?
    (A) nonvoters.
    (B) primary election voters.

(C) Democrats.
(D) Republicans.
(E) independents.

5. Which of the following statements help to explain why voter turnout is lower in the United States than in most other democracies?
    I. Citizens in other democracies vote more often and therefore have developed stronger voting habits.
    II. Citizens in most other democracies are required by law to vote.
    III. Citizens in most other democracies are not required to register to vote.
    IV. Citizens in other democracies face starker differences between the viable political parties.
    (A) I and II only.
    (B) I and III only.
    (C) II and III only.
    (D) II and IV only.
    (E) III and IV only.

6. Which of the following is a reason young Americans are typically the least politically active?
    (A) They have little political experience.
    (B) They spend too much time watching television news.
    (C) They have been socialized through their formal education to distrust the government.
    (D) They pay higher taxes than older Americans, making them especially cynical.
    (E) Young voters are more mobile than older voters, but most states require that citizens live at the same address for a full year before they are allowed to participate.

7. Which of the following statements about young voters is accurate?
    (A) Young voters are more likely to support third-party candidates.
    (B) Young citizens are more likely to vote than older citizens.

(C) Young voters typically vote through the mail.
(D) Young citizens do not need to register to vote if they live with at least one parent.
(E) Young voters typically vote for president but do not vote for congressional seats.

8. The Motor Voter Act was intended to
(A) expand suffrage to minorities.
(B) lower the voting age.
(C) redistribute states' electoral votes.
(D) increase voter registration.
(E) raise the voting age.

9. How are Oregon's elections different from most other elections in the United State?
(A) All Oregon elections are nonpartisan.
(B) All Oregon elections are conducted through the mail.
(C) Oregon revokes the driver's license of nonvoters.
(D) Oregon allows citizens to vote at sixteen years old.
(E) Election Day in Oregon is a state holiday and only emergency or essential employees are allowed to work.

FREE-RESPONSE QUESTIONS

1. The Electoral College, not the voters, elects the president in the United States.
   a) Describe ONE way in which the Electoral College system affects the way in which presidential candidates campaign. Give an example.
   b) Describe ONE way in which the Electoral College is undemocratic. Give an example.
   c) Explain ONE reason the Electoral College is not abolished.

2. During presidential primaries, some states receive more attention than others.
   a) Why do Iowa and New Hampshire usually receive more media attention than other states?
   b) How could the system of nominating candidates be changed to decrease the importance of Iowa and New Hampshire?
   c) What obstacles keep the changes from taking place that you mentioned in (b)?

Chapter 14: The Campaign Process

MULTIPLE-CHOICE QUESTIONS

1. The Federal Election Campaign Act established all of the following EXCEPT
(A) a fund to partially fund presidential campaigns.
(B) rules for the disclosure of all campaign financing and spending information.
(C) limits on personal contributions to presidential and congressional candidates.
(D) a fund for public donations to congressional campaigns.
(E) the Federal Election Commission to regulate campaign financing.

2. Which of the following is true concerning the use of PACs in political campaigns?
(A) The Constitution requires businesses to finance campaigns.
(B) Businesses can channel an unlimited amount of money through a PAC to a given candidate.
(C) The president officially established PACs in a 1974 executive order.
(D) PACs must be registered with and monitored by the FEC.
(E) The Supreme Court has struck down all efforts to regulate campaign finance.

3. Which of the following factors contributes most to the cost of a presidential campaign?
(A) direct-mail campaigns.
(B) television advertising.
(C) hiring a campaign coordinator.
(D) soliciting donations via the Internet.
(E) printing posters and campaign paraphernalia.

4. Presidential campaigns in the United States differ from most European campaigns in which of the following ways?
(A) American campaigns cost candidates less in personal contributions.
(B) Candidates in other countries are not allowed to appear on television.
(C) Campaigns in the United States are geared toward a general election.
(D) American campaigns are much longer than other campaigns.
(E) Candidates in the United States are selected by party elites.

5. Media coverage of campaigns tends to focus on
(A) foreign and military policy.
(B) social and environmental policy.
(C) candidate biographies and background.
(D) campaign strategies and the horse race.
(E) accusations of media bias and wrongdoing.

6. The main loophole to the McCain-Feingold legislation is
(A) 527s.
(B) soft money.
(C) hard money.
(D) bundling.
(E) *Buckley* v. *Valeo*.

7. Federal matching funds are available to
(A) governors.
(B) members of the House.
(C) senators.
(D) presidential candidates.
(E) judges.

FREE-RESPONSE QUESTIONS

1. The United States holds some of the longest and most expensive political campaigns in the world. To finance their campaigns, candidates rely heavily on contributions from the following:
   • PACs
   • soft money

- matching funds
- individual contributions

a) Define each of the above sources of campaign contributions.

b) Choose TWO of these sources and describe the positive impact that each has on political campaigns.

c) Choose TWO of these sources and describe the negative impact that each has on political campaigns.

d) Choose TWO of these sources and describe TWO legal restrictions that have been placed on them.

Chapter 15: The Media

MULTIPLE-CHOICE QUESTIONS

1. Which of the following is a consequence of investigative journalism?
   (A) more stringent requirements for becoming a journalist.
   (B) increased news coverage of scandals.
   (C) a better informed citizenry.
   (D) increased reliance of television news.
   (E) a more in-depth understanding of political issues by typical Americans.

2. Who is most likely to receive media coverage?
   (A) Congress.
   (B) the House of Representatives.
   (C) the Senate.
   (D) the president.
   (E) the Supreme Court.

3. Which of the following statements about journalists is accurate?
   (A) Journalists consider themselves more liberal than does the general public.
   (B) Journalists have a liberal bias in their coverage of politics.
   (C) Journalists have a conservative bias in their coverage of politics.
   (D) Journalists have a Democratic bias in their coverage of politics.
   (E) Journalists have a Republican bias in their coverage of politics.

4. Which of the following statements are true about the media's agenda-setting effect?
   I. The agenda-setting effect influences the criteria by which citizens evaluate political leaders.
   II. The agenda-setting effect is particularly strong among uninformed citizens.
   III. The agenda-setting effect is the media's direct impact on how Americans vote.
   IV. The agenda-setting effect rewards investigative journalism.
   (A) I and II only.
   (B) III and IV only.
   (C) I, II, and III only.
   (D) I, III, and IV only.
   (E) II, III, and IV only.

5. What is one foreseeable political consequence of narrowcasting?
   (A) The print media will appeal to a greater percentage of the public.

   (B) Politicians will have more freedom to act according to their own agenda because they will be able to avoid the public eye.
   (C) Journalists will be forced to concentrate more on political issues than on politicians.
   (D) The gap between the political elite and the politically uninformed majority will increase.
   (E) The public will become more informed about politics.

6. What is the primary objective of the American media?
   (A) enriching democracy.
   (B) informing the public.
   (C) accurately depicting public policy debates.
   (D) providing a means for the government to communicate with the people.
   (E) making a profit.

7. A journalist who regularly reports on predictions about interest rates would probably be on which of the following beats?
   (A) White House.
   (B) Senate Appropriations Committee.
   (C) Department of the Interior.
   (D) Congress.
   (E) Federal Reserve Board.

8. If a political candidate wanted to deliver his or her message to the most politically informed Americans in the electorate, through which medium would the candidate be most likely to reach them?
   (A) television.
   (B) radio.
   (C) mass mailings.
   (D) newspapers.
   (E) the Internet.

9. The Federal Communications Commission (FCC) is which of the following?
   (A) an arm of Congress devoted to communications issues.
   (B) a special interest group.
   (C) the federal judiciary.
   (D) an independent regulatory agency.
   (E) a White House agency.

10. Which of the following have been decreasing over the years?
    (A) news outlets.
    (B) press conferences.
    (C) State of the Union Addresses.
    (D) media events.
    (E) trial balloons.

FREE-RESPONSE QUESTIONS

1. In the past twenty years, the media in the United States have undergone a transformation from "broadcasting" to "narrowcasting."
   a) Explain the difference between broadcasting and narrowcasting.
   b) Describe how narrowcasting affects bias in the media.
   c) Describe how narrowcasting can affect the media's ability to influence public opinion.

2. The independent media in American politics can both hurt candidates' chances for getting elected to office as well as help candidates' chances at getting elected to office.
   a) Identify and describe TWO ways the media may hurt the chances of a candidate for office.
   b) Identify and describe TWO ways candidates can use the media to help their campaigns

Chapter 16: Interest Groups

MULTIPLE-CHOICE QUESTIONS

1. Smaller interest groups often meet with more success because
   (A) they have highly developed methods of fundraising.
   (B) their members have a great incentive to actively pursue their collective good.
   (C) they make large campaign contributions.
   (D) they have more resources with which to mobilize the public.
   (E) they pursue only less politicized issues.

2. Citizens concerned about a proposal to redistribute federal funding to public schools would form which of the following groups?
   (A) public interest group.
   (B) economic interest group.
   (C) consumer interest group.
   (D) elite interest group.
   (E) class action group.

3. Lawmakers often rely on lobbyists for all of the following reasons EXCEPT
   (A) to come up with new policy ideas that they can introduce in Congress.
   (B) for advice on strategies to advance or prevent a piece of legislation.
   (C) for money that can legally supplement a lawmaker's salary.
   (D) to encourage group members to vote for them during reelection.
   (E) for expertise on a certain issue.

4. Iron triangles are composed of
   (A) a Cabinet department, a legislative committee, and a federal judge.
   (B) a corporate board, an interest group, and the Speaker of the House.
   (C) a PAC, an interest group, and a congressional candidate.
   (D) an interest group, a legislative committee, and a federal agency.
   (E) a local civic group, a state legislator, and a federal department.

5. Proponents of the pluralist theory argue that power is nearly evenly distributed among interest groups because
   (A) the public participates equally in different types of interest groups.
   (B) all interest groups receive the same amount of federal funds.
   (C) each policy area is assigned a limited number of related interest groups.
   (D) interest groups each get the same attention from politicians.
   (E) competition prevents any one group from becoming more influential.

6. Which of the following statements accurately describe methods that interest groups employ to influence policy making?
   I. Class action lawsuits allow interest groups to sue in the name of a larger section of the public.
   II. Interest groups meet with judges about cases that affect their policy area.
   III. Interest groups make more PAC contributions to incumbents rather than challengers.
   IV. Lobbyists provide policy expertise to lawmakers.
   V. Interest groups pay committee members to introduce favorable legislation.
   (A) III only.
   (B) I and IV only.
   (C) II and V only.
   (D) I, III, and IV only.
   (E) II, IV, and V only.

7. Interest groups differ from political parties in which of the following ways?
   (A) Interest groups link the public to the political process.
   (B) Interest groups pursue general policy goals in the political arena.
   (C) Interest groups try to shape specific policy goals.
   (D) Interest groups are not allowed to play any part in political campaigns.
   (E) Interest groups unite politicians with the same political ideology.

8. Which of the following causes would most likely be taken up by a single-issue group?
   (A) abortion.
   (B) corporate taxation.
   (C) international trade.
   (D) workers' rights.
   (E) social justice.

9. Interest groups do all of the following except
   (A) link the public to the political process.

(B) nominate candidates for elective office.
(C) try to shape specific policy goals.
(D) play a part in political campaigns.
(E) unite politicians with the same political ideology.

10. Which of the following interest groups is known to be the largest in membership size?
(A) National Rifle Association (NRA).
(B) League of Conservative Voters.
(C) Christian Coalition.
(D) American Association of Retired Persons (AARP).
(E) National Association for the Advancement of Colored People (NAACP).

FREE-RESPONSE QUESTIONS

1. Interest groups play an important role in the American political system, helping the concerns of the electorate with policy makers. Choose ONE interest group from the following list:
   • National Association for the Advancement of Colored People (NAACP)
   • Health Insurance Association of America (HIAA)
   • National Rifle Association (NRA)
   • National Education Association (NEA)

For the group you selected, complete the following tasks:
   a) Identify a government institution to which this group would appeal to pursue its policy interests.
   b) Identify TWO resources that the group has at its disposal, and explain how it uses these resources to influence policy making.

2. The United States has a pluralistic governmental system, in which people have multiple points of access to the government. Interest groups serve an important function, connecting citizens with their government.
   a) Differentiate between an interest group and a political party.
   b) Choose TWO topics from the following list, and identify a specific interest group that is concerned with each.
   • environmental interests
   • economic interests
   • equality interests
   • public interests
   c) Choose ONE of the groups you picked in (b), and describe one method the group has used to influence policy making.

Chapter 17: Domestic Policy

MULTIPLE-CHOICE QUESTIONS

1. The federal government spends the most money on social welfare programs that benefit
(A) African Americans.
(B) Hispanics.
(C) those whose income is below the official poverty line.
(D) the unemployed.
(E) the elderly.

2. Who benefits from the Earned Income Tax Credit?
(A) the unemployed.
(B) the working poor.
(C) all employees.
(D) all employers.
(E) the self-employed.

3. Which of the following best describes income distribution in the United States in recent decades.
(A) Most Americans belong to the middle class because income is distributed fairly equally.
(B) A rising tide lifts all boats.
(C) The United States has narrower extremes of income than do European countries.
(D) From each according to his ability, to each according to his need.
(E) The rich get richer, and the poor get poorer.

4. Which of the following factors is expected to put a financial strain on Social Security?
(A) People are retiring earlier.
(B) The cost of living is stagnant.
(C) The number of retirees is growing.
(D) Revenue is expected to exceed expenditures by 2010.
(E) Rising unemployment will drain the program's income.

5. What change to Social Security did President George W. Bush propose?
(A) Turning over the entire Social Security system to a private corporation that would invest in the stock market.
(B) Raising taxes on current workers to pay for current retirees.
(C) Raising taxes on current workers to build up the Social Security Trust Fund to pay for future retirees.
(D) Devolving Social Security to the states and giving each state a block grant to cover 90 percent of the cost.
(E) Allowing workers to invent part of their Social Security taxes into a private investment account.

6. The cost of health care in the United States is very high for all of the following reasons EXCEPT
(A) modern medicine can treat more illnesses.
(B) malpractice suits lead to higher insurance rates.
(C) Americans often lack incentive to keep costs low because they do not directly pay the bill.
(D) more people are getting sick than ever before.
(E) new medical technologies are expensive.

7. The biggest portion of total health care costs in the United States is paid for by
(A) individuals.
(B) employers.
(C) doctors and hospitals.
(D) insurance companies.
(E) national, state, and local governments.

8. Which of the following statements accurately describes coal?
   I. Coal is a dirtier fuel than oil.
   II. Coal is a more abundant natural resource in the United States than oil.

III. More of the energy America uses comes from coal than from oil.
IV. Coal contributes to global warming.
V. America imports more coal than oil.
(A) I and III only.
(B) II and V only.
(C) II, IV, and V only.
(D) I, II, III, and IV only.
(E) I, II, IV, and V only.

9. Which of the following statements about the American health care system is accurate?
(A) The health care system is run by the federal government instead of state and local governments.
(B) All Americans receive the same quality health care.
(C) The health care system covers more people at a lower per capita cost than in other democracies.
(D) American doctors are required to treat all patients regardless of their ability to pay.
(E) The health care system costs more and covers a smaller percentage of the population than in other democracies.

10. Which of the following is a benefit of multiple use policies that allow mining, logging, and grazing interests to use public lands at very low costs?
(A) The federal government maximizes revenue.
(B) Mining, logging, and grazing improve the overall health of the environment by creating clearings and meadows for wildlife.
(C) Mining, logging, and grazing bring people to public lands that would otherwise receive few visitors.
(D) The multiple use policy promotes jobs in otherwise depressed areas.

(E) The multiple use policy increases America's dependence on imported natural resources.

FREE-RESPONSE QUESTIONS
1. Social welfare in the United States consists of two kinds of policy: entitlement programs and means-tested programs.
a) Define "entitlement program" and identify one such program.
b) Define "means-tested program" and identify one such program.
c) Explain the changes that ONE of the following presidents has brought to a means-tested program.
• Ronald Reagan
• Bill Clinton
• George W. Bush

2. Environmental policies have been an increasingly important topic in American politics. Three major areas of concern are
• pollution
• wilderness preservation
• global warming

Select ONE of the environmental concerns listed above, and respond to the following:
a) Identify and describe specific legislation that has been passed by the federal government to deal with the concern you selected.
b) Evaluate the effectiveness of the legislation you identified in (a).
c) Explain one reason some groups oppose the policy you identified in (a).

Chapter 18: Economic Policy

MULTIPLE-CHOICE QUESTIONS
1. According to Keynesian economic theory, increasing government spending
(A) threatens the economy by raising the federal deficit.
(B) stimulates the economy by creating demand among consumers.
(C) does little to curb unemployment.
(D) creates a supply among consumers and encourages them to save.
(E) prevents the Federal Reserve System from managing banks.

2. All of the following factors indicate that the United States has a mixed economy EXCEPT
(A) the federal government determines monetary policy.
(B) the Justice Department can sue monopolistic companies.
(C) Congress sets tariffs on imported goods.
(D) the federal government owns the means of production.
(E) there is a federal minimum age requirement for employment.

3. Which of the following is one reason Republican presidents usually focus their attention on controlling inflation?
(A) Controlling inflation is a bigger concern to investors than is unemployment.

(B) They hope to attract the votes of middle- and lower-class Americans.
(C) They endorse Keynesian economics.
(D) Controlling inflation keeps people from buying too much.
(E) They want to avoid having to solve the problem of high unemployment.

4. Some believe that inflation occurs when there is too much money in circulation. To overcome this problem, the government could do which of the following?
(A) decrease loan rates to make them more available to the public.
(B) increase the amount of credit available to the public.
(C) decrease the amount of money in banks, thus raising loan rates and discouraging people from borrowing.
(D) limit the number of bonds sold to the public to discourage people from buying.
(E) increase the amount of money in banks to help people borrow money.

5. Which of the following individuals were proponents of supply-side economics?
I. John Maynard Keynes
II. Franklin D. Roosevelt

III. Ronald Reagan
IV. George W. Bush
(A) I only.
(B) III only.
(C) I and II only.
(D) III and IV only.
(E) I, III, and IV only.

6. Which of the following government institutions has the greatest impact on the economy?
   (A) Senate Economic Committee.
   (B) Federal Reserve Board.
   (C) Office of Management and Budget.
   (D) Council of Economic Advisors.
   (E) House Allocations Committee.

7. Antitrust policies are designed to prevent
   (A) a company from having a monopoly over a specific good or service.
   (B) the expansion of large multinational corporations.
   (C) the government from interfering in international business transactions.
   (D) the spread of dot-com businesses into traditional economic spheres.
   (E) the Federal Reserve Board from gaining too much power over economic policy.

8. The government could exercise fiscal policy in which of the following ways?
   (A) increasing agricultural subsidies.
   (B) buying bonds from banks.
   (C) selling bonds to banks.
   (D) establishing the federal funds rate.
   (E) setting the interest rate banks charge each other for overnight loans.

9. Which of the following statements about the Federal Reserve Board is accurate?
   (A) Its members are elected directly by the public.
   (B) Its members serve at the discretion of the president, meaning the president can dismiss them at any time.

(C) It is part of the judicial branch, but its members are appointed by the legislative branch.
(D) Democrats and Republicans are prohibited from serving on the Federal Reserve Board.
(E) Its members are appointed for fourteen-year terms to remain isolated from politics.

10. All of the following are steps in the budgetary process EXCEPT
   (A) the Congressional Budget Office works closely with the president to finalize the budget that he will propose to Congress.
   (B) the House Ways and Means Committee and the Senate Finance Committee work together to write the tax codes.
   (C) the Office of Management and Budget reviews and assesses the budget proposals submitted by each agency.
   (D) Congress passes a budget resolution to set a cap on expenditures for the fiscal year.
   (E) the Appropriations Committee decides how to divide federal resources among the departments and agencies

FREE-RESPONSE QUESTIONS

1. Define "global economy." Describe one aspect of the global economy that is helpful to the economy of the United States and one aspect of the global economy that is detrimental to the economy of the United States.

2. The federal government and its agencies have several tools for trying to control the economy. Two of the primary tools are monetary and fiscal policy.
   a) Describe ONE way monetary policy is used to control the economy.
   b) Describe ONE way fiscal policy is used to try to control the economy.
   c) Describe TWO reasons the federal government and its agencies are not always successful in their attempts to control the economy.

Chapter 19: Foreign and Defense Policy

MULTIPLE-CHOICE QUESTIONS

1. Which of the following institutions would be most likely to press for international environmental regulations?
   (A) multinational corporations.
   (B) NATO.
   (C) Congress.
   (D) nongovernmental organizations.
   (E) the Joint Chiefs of Staff.

2. Which of the following best explains why the United States got involved in the Vietnam War?
   (A) NATO membership required the United States to treat a war against one member country as a war against all.
   (B) UN membership required the United SKtates to treat a war against one member country as a war against all.

(C) The United States was committed to the isolationism doctrine.
(D) The United States was committed to the doctrine of containment.
(E) The United States was committed to the Monroe Doctrine.

3. Economic sanctions typically are the least effective when
   (A) they are unilateral.
   (B) the economy of the targeted nation is weak.
   (C) the nation imposing sanctions is not part of NATO.
   (D) the oil market is doing well.
   (E) they are proposed by human rights groups.

4. Congress influences foreign policy by
   I. declaring war.
   II. ratifying treaties.

III. appropriating money for foreign and military policies.
IV. commanding the armed forces.
 V. confirming ambassadors.
(A) I and IV only.
(B) II and V only.
(C) III, IV, and V only.
(D) I, II, III, and V only.
(E) I, III, IV, and V only.

5. Which of the following statements best explains why defense spending decreased in the 1990s?
(A) Most resources were channeled into increasing the standing army, which costs less to maintain than military equipment does.
(B) Weapons could be produced more cheaply as a result of new technology.
(C) The United States succeeded in containing all world threats.
(D) The United States decided to scrap its nuclear program and focus on conventional weapons, which are better suited to fight terrorism.
(E) East–West tensions lessened with the end of the Cold War.

6. All of the following are characteristic of foreign policy during the Cold War EXCEPT
(A) increased military spending.
(B) an end to détente.
(C) the arms race.
(D) isolationism.
(E) the rise of the military-industrial complex.

7. President George W. Bush's foreign policy tenets included all of the following EXCEPT
(A) preemptive strikes against terrorists.
(B) prevention of developing threats against American interests.
(C) unilateralism if necessary.
(D) U.S. military preeminence.
(E) elimination of the military-industrial complex.

8. Which of the following bureaucratic institutions is primarily responsible for coordinating American intelligence activities abroad?
(A) Department of Defense.
(B) Federal Bureau of Investigation.
(C) Federal Communications Commission.
(D) Central Intelligence Agency.
(E) State Department.

9. Which of the following was a major consequence of the Vietnam War?
(A) The United States failed to stop the spread of communism throughout Asia.
(B) The Cold War came to an end, leaving the United States as the sole superpower.
(C) NATO was created to protect the United States and Western nations from the threat of communism.
(D) The United States abandoned the doctrine of détente as the cornerstone of its foreign policy.
(E) American citizens lost faith in the government after being lied to about the war.

10. American foreign policy is conducted mostly by the
(A) Senate Foreign Relations Committee.
(B) president and executive branch.
(C) National Security Agency.
(D) Joint Chiefs of Staff.
(E) House Foreign Affairs Committee.

FREE-RESPONSE QUESTIONS

1. In the post–World War II era, the United States has been involved in two extended global conflicts: the Cold War and the war on terrorism.
a) Identify ONE armed conflict the United States was involved in during the Cold War, and describe the rationale for this conflict.
b) Identify ONE armed conflict the United States was involved in during the war on terrorism, and describe the rationale for this conflict.
c) For either (a) or (b) above, explain the arguments used against U.S. involvement in this conflict.

2. The president is responsible for leading the nation in foreign policy, as commander in chief, and in war making.
a) Identify and describe TWO constitutional powers the president has in foreign policy making or as commander in chief.
b) Identify and describe ONE nonconstitutional power the president has in foreign policy making or as commander in chief.
c) Describe TWO limits on the president's foreign policy powers or powers as commander in chief.

AP* Test Prep Answers and Explanations

Chapter 1: The Political Landscape

MULTIPLE-CHOICE QUESTIONS

1. **(B) is correct.** Although a bill of rights often reinforces a democracy, it is not necessarily indicative of a democracy. The essential elements of a democracy can be specified in a constitution. The Bill of Rights does protect the freedoms guaranteed under this democratic form of government, but it does not itself establish a democracy.

2. **(B) is correct.** All governments share certain functions, such as maintaining a national defense, preserving order, providing public services, and socializing the young. All governments also collect taxes. Ensuring social equality, however, is not typically a function of government. While some governments may try to reduce social inequality, very few attempt to eliminate it. Democratic governments attempt to ensure political equality but not social or economic equality.

3. **(C) is correct.** A democracy must listen to the will of the people, as expressed by a majority of its citizens. At the same time, democracies must ensure that the rights of the minority are respected. Thus, democracies operate under majority rule but protect minority rights.

4. **(D) is correct.** When compared with other democracies, voter turnout in the United States is very low. American democracy does reasonably well at ensuring majority rule with minority rights. Political equality, or "one person, one vote," is a hallmark of American democracy. The First Amendment guarantees freedom of speech, another essential element of democracy.

5. **(A) is correct.** The Constitution establishes and limits the powers of government. It is not considered a linkage institution because it is not a mechanism for citizens to influence the policy agenda. Linkage institutions include parties, interest groups, the media, and elections—each of which enables citizens to affect the policy agenda.

6. **(E) is correct.** Liberals tend to favor government regulation of the economy but tend to oppose some examples of government regulation on "moral issues." As a result, liberals would favor freedom of choice in abortion, but they would not favor prayers in public schools.

7. **(E) is correct.** Because older Americans are more conservative than younger counterparts, they are more likely to favor greater military spending. However, older Americans are less likely to favor investing Social Security funds in the stock market. These differences are important because senior citizens are more likely to vote than younger Americans, suggesting that government policies may be disproportionately tilted toward older Americans and away from younger Americans.

8. **(E) is correct.** A minority majority population means that more than half the U.S. population would be composed of minority group members rather than Caucasians. Hispanic Americans have become the largest minority group, recently surpassing African Americans. If the percentages continue to change at the same rate, the United States will reach a minority majority sometime in the middle of the twenty-first century.

FREE-RESPONSE QUESTION

This question has an 8 point rubric: 3 three points for identifying aspects of the American political culture, 3 three points for describing the aspects of political culture, and 1 point each for defining and describing the culture war. This response has 3 three points for identifying the three aspects in the first sentence. It is also a good habit to underline your main points when writing for the Advanced Placement U.S. Government Exam. This will help ensure that the reader will find and award you your points.

1. Three major aspects of American political culture are *liberty, individualism, and populism.* Americans belief in *liberty* is their desire to live freely with minimum interference from the government. Examples can be seen in the Declaration of Independence or the Civil War, fought to free the slaves. *Individualism*, another aspect of political culture, is the belief that people should succeed or fail based on their own merits and efforts. Americans have always resented a privileged class, and prefer the self-made man. A sign that *populism* is important to the American political culture is the fact that both Democrats and Republicans try to claim that they are on the side of the ordinary people. Both parties say that they are the ones who help the voice of the people to be heard.

The student receives 1 point for the description of liberty. The examples given would not be needed to earn the point. The examples on their own, without the description given in the preceding sentence, would not be enough to earn the point.

The student stumbles into an answer here, but "the voice of the people being heard" is enough of a definition to earn the point.

Again, the student earns the point in the first sentence. The second sentence does not detract from this, but it is not needed to earn the point.

Stating that there are two opposing groups and using any wording which indicates the strong dislike, mistrust, hatred between the two groups is enough to award a point for the definition of "culture war." 1 point.

The student need only name the issue to receive the 8th point. Although the student names several issues, all of which are acceptable, only 1 point is awarded.

In spite of having a common political culture, many people believe that the United States is in the midst of a culture war. A *culture war* is where Americans divide into two camps, liberal Democrats and conservative Republicans. The two camps see each other not just as political opponents, but as fools or scoundrels whose election could mean the downfall of our nation. *Abortion, gun rights, and gay marriage are all examples* of issues that are part of the culture war in the United States.

Chapter 2: The Constitution

MULTIPLE-CHOICE QUESTIONS

1. **(D) is correct.** All but one of the answer choices evolved out of interpretations of the Constitution. Bear in mind that the Constitution is really only a blueprint for government—it lays out only the basic structure and powers of the three branches and defines the powers of the federal and state governments. Most governmental bodies have resulted from particular needs neither specified nor denied in the Constitution. However, the Framers of the Constitution did create the Electoral College to choose the president as a means of keeping government out of the hands of the poor and uneducated majority.

2. **(E) is correct.** The Seventeenth Amendment allows voters to directly elect their own senators. Previously, as stated in Article I of the Constitution, senators were selected by state legislatures. This was another way the Framers attempted to distance government from the populace.

3. **(C) is correct.** Madison devised the system of checks and balances primarily to prevent any one branch, if it came under the control of a majority faction, from dominating the whole government. Thus, checks and balances help prevent tyranny of the majority. These checks include the ability of the president to veto laws passed by Congress and the president's authority to nominate Supreme Court justices. The system is clearly defined in the first three articles of the Constitution; it is not merely a part of the unwritten body of tradition that has evolved.

4. **(B) is correct.** While Americans generally disdain flag burning, the Supreme Court has determined that the Constitution protects the practice as an exercise of free speech. Therefore, the Texas law against "desecration of a venerated object" was unconstitutional. This means that neither Congress nor the states can pass laws that prohibit flag burning because it is a protected form of political expression.

5. **(B) is correct.** The authors of the Articles of Confederation were so determined to minimize the power of the federal government that ultimately they created one that was not politically or economically viable. The challenge they faced in writing the Constitution was to create a more centralized government without risking giving it too much power. The concept of limited government is therefore the correct answer.

6. **(C) is correct.** Recall the debate surrounding the ratification of the Constitution: Anti-Federalists feared that it favored the elite over the majority, whose individual freedoms were not sufficiently addressed. The promise of a bill of rights was necessary to win over those states that hesitated to vote for adoption of the Constitution. Think also about what rights are guaranteed by the first ten amendments: free speech, freedom of religion, freedom to petition, protection against unlawful searches and seizures, and the right to a trial by jury. All of these address personal liberty and assert the basic natural rights of citizens.

7. **(C) is correct.** While the bulk of the Declaration of Independence is a list of grievance against King George, it is also a political and philosophical treatise about American political beliefs. The basic institutions and processes of government, however, are outlined in the Constitution, not the Declaration.

8. **(C) is correct.** Although all of the options could provide for a three-fifths ratio, only the treatment of slaves was specified in the Constitution. As a result, the others, though they may be correct (as in the case of invoking cloture), do not stem from the Constitution.

9. **(D) is correct.** Anti-Federalists feared that the Constitution did not give significant protection to individual liberties, such as freedom of speech and freedom of the press. They were concerned that such omissions indicated that citizens would not retain these liberties under the Constitution. To alleviate these concerns, the Federalists agreed that the first order of business under the new government would be the addition of a bill of rights to the Constitution to ensure that these fundamental liberties were protected. The Constitution did not give any powers to the king of England, weakened the authority of the states, and was silent about political parties. The Anti-Federalists also feared that the Constitution was a class-based document that would increase the power of the mercantile class.

10. **(C) is correct.** The Constitution prohibits Congress from infringing on individual rights by passing bills of attainder. Every citizen is entitled to the right of due process by law—no one may be found guilty without first being tried. This idea of justice forms the cornerstone of the American judiciary system.

FREE RESPONSE QUESTIONS

Identifies an amendment that had an impact on voting rights. 1 point.

1. These amendments would serve as appropriate examples for this question:
   - Fifteenth Amendment (1870): extended voting rights to freed slaves (male) after the Civil War
   - Nineteenth Amendment (1920): gave women the right to vote
   - Twenty-Third Amendment (1961): granted residents of Washington, D.C., the right to vote
   - Twenty-Fourth Amendment (1964): prohibited states from using poll taxes or tests to prevent citizens from voting
   - Twenty-Sixth Amendment (1971): changed the minimum voting age from twenty-one to eighteen

   The Constitution largely left voting rights up to the states, which generally granted voting rights only to free males. Over time, amendments such as the Fifteenth, Nineteenth, and Twenty-Fourth have been added to the Constitution to extend voting rights to all Americans.

Describes how the Fifteenth Amendment changed the nature of the electorate. 1 point.

   The Civil War ended slavery in the South, but it would take government intervention to ensure that newly freed slaves would be treated as citizens. Southern states held out against the Fourteenth Amendment, which extended citizenship to freed slaves, so it became necessary to add a new amendment, the Fifteenth, which would specifically allow these disenfranchised Americans to vote. For the first time, African Americans were able to vote legally and to hold public office. The Fifteenth Amendment was not wholly successful, but it did act as a first step toward righting to wrongs of slavery.

Identifies an amendment that had an impact on voting rights. 1 point. Describes how the Twenty-Fourth Amendment changed the nature of the electorate. 1 point.

   It took 100 years and another amendment for the Fifteenth Amendment to be fully realized. Southern states sidestepped the Fifteenth Amendment by imposing poll taxes on voters. Most freed slaves were poor, so these measures prevented them from voting. The civil rights movement of the 1960s brought to light such injustices. The Twenty-fourth Amendment was passed to prohibit southern states from using the poll tax to prevent African Americans from voting. Today people of all races are able to vote without the imposition of any tax.

Identifies an amendment that had an impact on voting rights. 1 point. Describes of the Nineteenth Amendment changed the nature of the electorate. 1 point. This response identifies three valid amendments and offers adequate descriptions of how they changed the nature of the electorate. Total score on question, 6 of 6 points.

   American women, too, were denied the right to vote for more than a century. The Nineteenth Amendment extended the vote to them. Since then, not only have women been able to serve as senators, representatives, mayors, and governors, but also women's issues have found a place in the political arena. Politicians, to win the votes of half the electorate, now address such issues as abortion, family leave, and equal opportunity in the workplace. The Nineteenth Amendment, therefore, both doubled the number of eligible voters and changed the political landscape of the United States.

Expanding voting rights in New York would earn the student 1 point in this 4 point rubric. Again, remember to underline your main points. Labeling your answers (a, b, c, d) will also help the reader to quickly find and award your points.

Limiting the vote to white males is worth a point.

Although the House members are elected by the people, the president is elected by the Electoral College, and senators were originally elected by state legislatures. Because of these two errors, no point would be awarded for part c.

The appointment, not the election, of federal judges would qualify for a point in (d). Total score on this question, 3 out of 4.

2. Americans like to have a say in their government. Before the Constitution was written, however, this was not always the case. Although the state and national governments did give considerable voice to the American people, there were several instances where the people were shortchanged on democracy.
   a) During the Revolutionary period, the state of *New York expanded voting rights*, allowing farmers of moderate means to vote, not just wealthy landowners. This would be an example of governing by consent.
   b) Most states *only allowed white males to vote*. This was not very democratic since women, Native Americans, and blacks were barred from having any say in elections.
   c) Under the Constitution, people could elect the *president, senators, and members of the House of Representatives*. This was a very democratic notion.
   d) Under the Constitution, *the people did not elect federal judges*. Rather, they received lifetime appointments.

Chapter 3: Federalism

MULTIPLE-CHOICE QUESTIONS

1. **(B) is correct.** The federal government has sole authority to conduct foreign relations, establish post offices, coin money, and declare war. The only listed power that is shared by both the national and state governments is the power to tax. This is why citizens pay a variety of state, local, and federal taxes.

2. **(B) is correct.** This clause in Article I of the Constitution gives Congress the authority to "make all laws which shall be necessary and proper for carrying into execution the

foregoing Powers, and all other Powers vested by [the] Constitution." That is, it gives Congress implied powers beyond those specifically listed in the Constitution. The elastic clause allows flexibility for the federal government to change and adapt over time.

3. **(C) is correct.** This question simply asks you to identify the basic premise of federalism, which is that the government is divided between various levels of government. In the United States, government is divided into local, state, and national levels.

4. **(D) is correct.** Under the Articles of Confederation, the state governments held the final power while the national government had only such powers as the thirteen regional (or state) governments gave it. The other definitions provided as options describe different arrangements of power.

5. **(E) is correct.** The full faith and credit clause requires that a state's public acts, records, and civil judicial proceedings be recognized in all other states. These include driver's licenses, birth and death certificates, and marriage licenses. However, each state passes its own laws, which might be different from another state's law on the same topic. For example, each state sets its own speed limits, which do not automatically apply elsewhere.

6. **(B) is correct.** The federal government often encourages states to assist with federal policy priorities through grants. Categorical grants often come with strings attached. One of the most common requirements is that the state must follow specific federal regulations to receive the money. Block grants, however, have fewer strings attached and allow greater discretion to a state to decide how to spend the money. It is no surprise, then, that states much prefer block grants to categorical grants.

7. **(D) is correct.** The privileges and immunities clause gives residents of any state equal protection under the law, no matter what state they happen to be in. This clause serves to unite the states by extending equal national citizenship regardless of state lines.

8. **(B) is correct.** It is the role of the courts to settle disputes between the federal and state levels of government. A court, through its interpretation of the Constitution, determines whether a particular issue falls under the scope of the federal or state level of government. This is one reason the court system has grown more extensive over the course of American history.

9. **(A) is correct.** Dual federalism is used to describe the original view of the relationship between the levels of government as clearly separated, or layered. The other four responses also refer to contrasts between two things, but not to dual federalism.

10. **(C) is correct.** In a federal system, the electorate chooses local, state, and national representatives. This gives them the potential to influence government at each level. Similarly, a government divided into levels offers more points of access for political groups; a citizen concerned about gun control can join either a state or a national advocate group, or both. State governments are not necessarily more responsive. Even if political parties do offer more choice, they are not exclusive to a federal system—many unitary governments have multiparty systems.

FREE RESPONSE QUESTIONS

Notice the student does not give any introduction in the answer. None is needed. In the AP Government exam, points are awarded for content, not style. This response correctly explains how the *McCulloch* case and the federal grant system have given the federal government more power. 2 points.

1. a) *McCulloch v. Maryland*. In this case, the state of Maryland tried to place a tax on a federal bank located in Baltimore. The Supreme Court ruled that national laws are supreme to state laws. Therefore, states cannot set up laws that go against national laws. This helped make the federal government more powerful.

   The federal grant system has also increased the power of the federal government. The federal government will give money to states for different projects, such as the building of highways. The states, however, are required to abide by the conditions of aid that the federal government puts on these grants, such as speed limits.

In section (b), the student both describes the case and explains how it has shifted power from the federal government back to the states. 2 points. Total score, 4 out of 4.

   b) *United States v. Lopez*. The Supreme Court ruled that a federal law outlawing guns in a school zone was unconstitutional. Guns, the Court ruled, had nothing to do with commerce. This gave more power to the states to create their own laws about guns.

   Printz v. United States. In this case, the Court struck down a federal mandate that states conduct a background check on people who want to purchase a handgun. Again, this gave more power to the states to create their own laws regulating guns.

This paragraph sets the stage and is a good introductory paragraph but earns no points.

2. The Founding Fathers had a difficult task. They had to concentrate power more than it had been concentrated under the Articles of Confederation, and they had to make sure power was not too concentrated. One of the ways they dealt with this issue was with federalism—the division of power between levels of government. Some powers were put in the national government, some in state governments, and some shared by both.

This paragraph provides an excellent description of the supremacy clause and its relevance for federalism. 1 point.

   The supremacy clause is the part of the Constitution that the framers put in at the end that says that the Constitution, the laws made by the national government that do not violate the Constitution, and treaties made by the national government override conflicting state laws. By this provision, the framers sought to solve one of the major problems of the Articles—the lack of power for the national government.

This paragraph describes the Tenth Amendment and its relevance for federalism. 1 point.

This paragraph gives an explanation of the impact of international relations (the Cold War) on federalism (control over education) for 1 point. Total score on this question; 4 of 4.

The Tenth Amendment is the part of the Constitution that attempts to reserve to the states powers not given to the national government nor denied to the states. In essence, the states have powers of their own, but the states and the national government continue to argue over exactly what these are.

During the 1950s and 60s, the United States became very fearful that the Soviets had surpassed us in military technology. The launching of Sputnik made the federal government much more concerned with education in the United States. Up until this time, education had been primarily in the hands of the state governments. But with the passage of the National Defense Education Act, federal aid started pouring into schools to build up their math and science departments. Federal money still goes into the schools, but now with more strings attached. This gives the federal government more control over what had been a state institution.

Chapter 4: State and Local Government

MULTIPLE-CHOICE QUESTIONS

1. **(A) is correct.** The line-item veto is a powerful tool that forty-two governors have. With it, governors often have the final say in the budget because they can simply remove parts of it with which they disagree. State legislatures often accept the governor's final version of the legislation since they seldom have the votes to override it.

2. **(A) is correct.** State constitutions are subordinate to the U.S. Constitution. They are also different from the U.S. Constitution in that they are typically longer and include many details about specific public policies. Each state has a different constitution and therefore a different way of organizing the state's government. For example, Nebraska's constitution establishes a unicameral legislature, but the other forty-nine states have bicameral legislatures. One similarity between the state constitutions and the U.S. Constitution is that all of these documents contain a bill of rights.

3. **(C) is correct.** While the specific process for amending a state constitution varies from state to state, the most common method is for state legislatures to propose amendments which must then be approved by voters in the next general election. In some states, the legislature must propose the amendment in two consecutive sessions.

4. **(A) is correct.** Many states have moved their gubernatorial elections from presidential election years so that the governor's race will be at the top of the ticket. Thus, gubernatorial elections are determined less by party (and coattail) influences and more by the characteristics of the candidates.

5. **(A) is correct.** In recent years, state legislatures have undergone reforms to make them more efficient and effective. These reforms are known collectively as legislative professionalism and include longer sessions, better pay for legislators, and an increase in the number of staff members who assist legislators.

6. **(E) is correct.** Between 1962 and 2007, the number of special districts increased 49 percent, while the number of other types of government often shrank.

7. **(D) is correct.** *Baker* v. *Carr* established the principle of "one person, one vote" and required that states draw their House districts so that each had equal population. Prior to this decision, a state's House districts varied considerably in size, with rural districts being heavily overrepresented in the legislature. After *Baker* v. *Carr*, states redrew their district lines, increasing the influence of urban areas so that representation matched their population; this decreased the influence of rural areas.

8. **(B) is correct.** Most lawmaking at the state level is parallel to lawmaking at the federal level. Both houses of the state legislature must pass identical versions of the same bill, which then becomes law when the governor signs it. The other procedures for making state laws are relatively rare but include a legislative override of the governor's veto, citizen initiatives, and citizen referenda.

9. **(E) is correct.** States vary considerably in how judges are selected, and all of the methods mentioned are common. Judges are appointed in thirteen states, compete in partisan elections in eleven states, compete in nonpartisan elections in nineteen states, and are appointed but must sit for retention elections in seventeen states.

10. **(B) is correct.** Direct democracy occurs when citizens play a direct role in politics and policy making. States can be outlets for direct democracy in many different ways. Initiatives and referenda allow citizens to have a direct influence on public policies. Recall elections allow citizens to end an elected official's term early. Town meetings are still used in some parts of New England to create local laws. While many state governors have line-item veto authority, it is not an example of direct democracy.

FREE RESPONSE QUESTIONS

The student distinguishes between the power of a gubernatorial veto and a presidential veto to earn 1 point here.

The line-item veto is a second legislative power. The description earns the student a 2nd point in this section.

Building public support, coupled with the examples, is good for 1 point.

1. One power that makes many governors stronger than presidents is the veto. Although both governors and presidents have the power to veto, it is usually more difficult for a state legislature to override a governor's veto than it is for Congress to override the president's. The line-item veto is a power that many governors have that the president does not. The line-item-veto allows a governor to strike a specific clause from legislation. This was designed to allow governors to remove wasteful spending from bills. Congress gave President Clinton the power of the line-item-veto, but the Supreme Court ruled it unconstitutional.

Both presidents and governors need to build public support if their programs are going to be successful. When the public is not backing a plan by a governor or a president, it is much less likely that they will receive legislative support. For example, when George W. Bush tried to reform Social Security, it was not received well by the public and went nowhere with Congress. Likewise, when Governor Schwarzenegger failed to get the California voters to pass a package of reform legislative propositions, he had a much more difficult time getting the state legislature to support his programs.

An executive need for media skills is worth a 2nd point. Total score for this question, 4 of 4 points.

Creating a good media image goes hand-in-hand with building public support for presidents and governors. From a press conference, when an executive must answer sometimes difficult questions from reporters, to a media event, where the executive's mere presence becomes newsworthy, executives need good skills in dealing with the press.

The question on democracy in the states was prefaced with a comparison to the federal government. Legislators are also elected at the federal level (representatives, senators), and therefore this response would not warrant any points. The student would have been better to write about either the initiative process, the referendum, or the recall. No points for the first section.

The election of judges is allowed at the state but not the national level. 2 points earned here: 1 for the identification and 1 for the explanation. Total score, 2 of 4 points.

2. Many states have direct election of their legislature. This gives the people a stronger say in the laws that are made. If the states legislature passes an unpopular bill, or continues to raise taxes, they can be voted out of office. This would be one way in which states have given the people a greater say in elections.

Other states have allowed for the election of judges. While all federal judges are appointed for life, some states allow the people to vote for a judge like they would for any other elected office. Some argue that elected judges may feel pressured to decide cases in a way that would please their constituency, but little evidence has been found to support this argument.

Chapter 5: Civil Liberties

MULTIPLE-CHOICE QUESTIONS

1. **(D) is correct.** In *Mapp* v. *Ohio*, the Supreme Court extended the protection of the Fourteenth Amendment to defendants in state trials. Specifically, as in federal cases, state courts must adhere to the exclusionary rule: prosecutors cannot use evidence acquired through unreasonable search and seizure to convict a person.

2. **(C) is correct.** In *Roth*, the Court ruled that obscenity is not protected under the Constitution as a form of free speech.

3. **(C) is correct.** The Supreme Court ruled that student religious groups should have the same right to assemble as any other extracurricular group and, in *Lemon* v. *Kurtzman*, that parochial schools may receive federal funding as long as they use it for educational rather than religious purposes. Of course, it is always permissible for students to pray silently in school.

4. **(A) is correct.** The *Engel* decision was based on the establishment clause of the Constitution. The other four possible answers have to do with religion but do not address the issues raised in *Engel* v. *Vitale*.

5. **(B) is correct.** Only libel is not protected by the First Amendment, because it represents an intentional misconstruing of the truth. However, libel is difficult to prove in court since the plaintiff must present evidence of malicious intent. Furthermore, the negative attention generated by a libel suit often dissuades public officials from pursuing claims.

6. **(A) is correct.** Throughout the twentieth century, the Supreme Court gradually extended the protection of the Bill of Rights to citizens of the states. It has done so by citing the due process clause of the Fourteenth Amendment. Previously, the Supreme Court had ruled that the Bill of Rights did not apply to the states. Now, citizens can be assured that state, local, and national governments cannot infringe on most of the protections guaranteed by the Bill of Rights.

7. **(A) is correct.** In the 1976 case of *Gregg* v. *Georgia*, the Supreme Court dismissed Gregg's argument that the death

penalty constitutes cruel and unusual punishment. The Court allowed capital punishment, citing it as "an extreme sanction, suitable to the most extreme of crimes." This case set the precedent for excluding the death penalty from the definition of cruel and unusual punishment.

8. **(D) is correct.** In *Roe* v. *Wade*, the Supreme Court allowed abortion in the first trimester, and it allowed abortion in the second trimester with some state regulation. However, the Court has also upheld several state laws that limit abortion rights, such as parental notification laws.

9. **(B) is correct.** The right to assemble is protected by the First Amendment; even a hate group may convene as

long as it is not endorsing or performing any crime against an individual. However, according to a 1994 Supreme Court decision, right-to-life advocates who block access to an abortion clinic violate the right of women to enter the clinic. This decision was then endorsed by Congress, which passed the Freedom of Access to Clinic Entrances Act. Thus, governments can pass laws that ensure access to abortion clinics, such as laws that restrict protestors from a specified buffer zone around abortion clinics.

10. **(A) is correct.** Under the First Amendment, banning of prior restraint of publication is a very strong rule.

FREE RESPONSE QUESTIONS

There are no points to be found in this section. Introductions are not needed in the free response section of the AP Government Exam.

1. Freedom of religion holds a special place in the hearts and minds of the American people. From the Pilgrims sailing to America to escape the Church of England and worship freely to the Mormons crossing the desert pulling handcarts to establish a new community in Utah, Americans yearn for religious freedom. That is one reason religion is mentioned in the First Amendment. The Founding Fathers wanted everyone to know how important it was. Today, we take these freedoms for granted. But it was only through the hard-fought battles of the Revolutionary War that America truly became a free nation.

The writer gets 2 points for identifying the establishment clause and the free exercise clause. The writer also gets 2 points for the description of the establishment clause and free exercise clause. The paragraph, however, could have been shortened considerably.

The First Amendment has two parts that pertain to religion. One is called the establishment clause, which states that there cannot be a national church, one supported by tax money or endorsed by the federal government. The Founders didn't want what they had in England, where the Anglican Church was the official state church. We had many churches in the United States: Congregationalists in New England, Lutherans, Catholics, Quakers in the Middle Colonies, the Anglican Church and Baptist Churches in the South. How could they even have decided on one state church? The free exercise clause stated that the federal government couldn't keep people from practicing their religion as they saw fit. Now this doesn't mean that we can do anything. No human sacrifices or multiple marriages. But the government cannot stop you from being a Catholic or a Jew.

One point for linking the establishment clause to the Lemon case.

One point for describing the Court's ruling in Lemon. The total score is 6 of 6, but the writer could have made a much more concise answer.

The Supreme Court hears cases on religion all the time. One such case was Lemon v. Kurtzman. This case had to do with states giving money to private religious schools. Some people complained that it went against the establishment clause. The Supreme Court disagreed. It said a state can give money to a religious school as long as it's not for religious purposes and doesn't get the government too involved in religion. The Court also said the money could not help advance the religion.

All in all, the Founders did a pretty good job of setting up the First Amendment, which still protects our freedoms today.

2. In the aftermath of the terrorist attacks on the World Trace Center on September 11, 2001, Congress passed a law called the USA Patriot Act that was designed to give law enforcement agencies more power to investigate and arrest terrorists. Congress thought that under the crisis circumstances that existed, it was reasonable to give those expanded investigation powers even if it meant that some of the protections of the Fourth Amendment would be compromised. The significance of the Patriot Act was that civil libertarians thought that it provided a dangerous compromise for average citizens who might be investigated.

The Fourth Amendment requires that if people are to be investigated, it must be with a valid search warrant signed by a judge and based on probable cause. This Amendment was meant to keep people safe from investigations and is based on the idea that people are innocent until proven guilty.

This paragraph fails to point out how the Patriot Act might compromise the Fourth Amendment.

Some people believe that the Patriot Act compromises the Fourth Amendment too much. Critics of the Act fear that it will infringe on some citizens' basic rights of privacy.

Chapter 6: Civil Rights

MULTIPLE-CHOICE QUESTIONS

1. **(C) is correct.** The Open Housing Act of 1968 eliminated housing discrimination. Since housing is not a form of public accommodation, the Civil Rights Act did not address this form of discrimination. It did, however, prohibit many other types of discrimination.

2. **(E) is correct.** The Supreme Court has developed different standards to determine if classification systems are permissible. For example, the Supreme Court considers classification based on race to be *inherently suspect* and therefore usually impermissible. Classification based on gender, however, is considered under an intermediate standard. Other classification systems (e.g., disability, age, sexual orientation) may be considered reasonable only for achieving a legitimate government goal. The Fourteenth Amendment is regularly cited in civil rights cases, and the preference for limited government has been ignored in the pursuit of civil rights. Thus, only answers I, II, and III are correct.

3. **(A) is correct.** The Equal Rights Amendment was first introduced in Congress in 1923 and finally passed both houses in 1972. It was not ratified by enough states, however, to become part of the Constitution. Some opposition to the amendment was based on the view that it was an attack on the family.

4. **(C) is correct.** Some critics of affirmative action see it as a mechanism of reverse discrimination. One such example is the case of *Regents of the University of California* v. *Bakke*, in which the Supreme Court found the university's quotas for enrolling minorities unconstitutional. Allan Bakke was denied enrollment in favor of a minority applicant to fulfill the university's quota.

5. **(B) is correct.** In *Plessy* v. *Ferguson*, the Supreme Court judged segregation to be constitutional as long as races were allowed facilities of equal quality. More than fifty years later, the Warren Court struck down segregation in its *Brown* v. *Board of Education* ruling, therefore overturning the Court's earlier ruling in *Plessy*.

6. **(A) is correct.** The Mexican American Legal Defense and Education Fund (MALDEF) has a long history of fighting for the civil rights of Hispanic Americans. The American Indian Movement (AIM) and the National Association for the Advancement of Colored People (NAACP) have fought for the rights of Native Americans and African Americans, respectively. While the Equal Employment Opportunity Commission (EEOC) may help to ensure equal job opportunities for Hispanic Americans, this is not necessarily their focus. The Americans with Disabilities Act (ADA) protects the civil rights of disabled Americans and does not specifically address Hispanic Americans.

7. **(D) is correct.** Nowhere does the Constitution or the Bill of Rights endorse equality for all citizens. Rather, the requirement for "equal protection of the laws" can be found in the Fourteenth Amendment, which was passed in the wake of the Civil War. In many cases, the Fourteenth Amendment has been the foundation for important advancements in civil rights.

8. **(B) is correct.** The Supreme Court first ruled against gender discrimination in the case of *Reed* v. *Reed*. It struck down an Idaho law that granted men automatic preference over women in determining which parent would be administrator of a daughter's estate. The court ruled that gender cannot be used as the sole qualification for determining the winner of such a case.

9. **(E) is correct.** The Fifteenth Amendment guaranteed African Americans the right to vote. Despite this written guarantee, southern states employed various instruments to prevent or diminish the ability of African Americans to meaningfully participate in elections. Literacy tests, often about the national or state constitution, were administered in such a way as to prevent African Americans from passing. Poll taxes fell disproportionately on African Americans. White primaries excluded African Americans from the main election for determining officeholders, as the winner of the primary was virtually assured of victory in the general election.

10. **(C) is correct.** In the case of *Regents of the University of California* v. *Bakke*, the Supreme Court found the university's quotas for enrolling minorities unconstitutional. Allan Bakke was denied enrollment in favor of a minority applicant to fulfill the university's quota, an unconstitutional "reverse discrimination."

FREE RESPONSE QUESTIONS

The identification of the Supreme Court is worth 1 point. The description that follows is worth the 2nd point.

The identification of Congress is worth 1 point. The description that follows is worth a 2nd point.

1. The civil rights era from 1954 to 1968 brought about great changes in the rights of African Americans in the United States. The federal government was involved at several levels.

   The Supreme Court ruled in the case of *Brown* v. *Board of Education* that the equal protection clause of the Fourteenth Amendment required that schools could no longer be segregated. The next year, the Court said that schools needed to be desegregated "with all deliberate speed."

   Congress and the president got into the act as well. The Congress passed two very important bills in 1964 and 1965. The Civil Rights Act of 1964 was a broad, sweeping bill that made private businesses serve black Americans in the same way that they served others. The next year, Congress expanded voting rights through the passage of the Voting Rights Act of 1965.

The identification of churches is worth 1 point. The description that follows is worth a 2nd point. Total score on this question, 6 of 6.

Churches were also important in the civil rights movement. Martin Luther King Jr. headed up the Southern Christian Leadership Conference, which was instrumental in helping organize boycotts, marches, and petition drives throughout the South in the 1950s and 60s.

2. a) *Earl Warren* took over as Chief Justice of the U.S. Supreme Court when the case of *Brown* v. *Board of Education* was being discussed. Warren helped the Court reach a unanimous decision to end the federal policy of segregation.

The writer identifies and describes an action by Warren and Johnson (1 point each). The description, although brief, is adequate. 1 point each.

Lyndon Johnson took over as President when Kennedy was assassinated. Johnson was able to get the *Civil Rights Act of 1964* through Congress. The act struck down discrimination in the workplace and public accommodations such as hotels.

The examples of the crisis at Central High and Thurmond's filibuster are two good examples of the opposition these leaders faced, although it was actually Eisenhower, and not Warren, who had to handle the Little Rock situation. Score is 6 of 6 points.

b) Although the Brown case required that public schools desegregate their student population, few did so either quickly or willingly. *Central High School in Little Rock*, Arkansas, for example, went so far as to have the National Guard surround the school to keep black students from attending. And while the Civil Rights Act of 1964 brought about swift changes to ensuring civil rights for blacks, President Johnson had to work very hard to get the bill through a hostile Senate where Southerners such as Strom Thurmond tried to black its passage with a filibuster.

Chapter 7: Congress

MULTIPLE-CHOICE QUESTIONS

1. **(C) is correct.** Conference committees are composed of House and Senate members who seek a compromise when the House and Senate pass different versions of the same bill. After the conference committee reaches a compromise, the bill returns to the House and Senate, where it must be passed without amendments before it is sent to the president.

2. **(E) is correct.** Challengers do not necessarily have a clean record just because they are new to the potential governmental position. Many challengers have held other posts, and ones who have not would have no record at all. Furthermore, incumbents, just because they have already served in Congress, do not necessarily have a poor record. In fact, it is to their advantage to demonstrate to the public their record of service to the constituency.

3. **(B) is correct.** Standing committees conduct legislative oversight primarily by holding hearings in which they question bureaucrats. Each committee conducts oversight of the federal departments that fall within its policy area. The budgets of these departments are controlled by Congress, a strong form of oversight.

4. **(C) is correct.** The Speaker has a great deal of influence in the House, guiding the party leaders in assigning positions on House committees. Congressional committees have other duties besides referring bills to the floor, including oversight and numerous legislative tasks.

5. **(B) is correct.** In the Senate, there is no limit to debate over a piece of legislation. A senator who has the floor is free to talk for as long as he or she wishes. The senator may attempt to stall by talking a bill to death. This tactic, called a filibuster, prevents senators from calling for a vote. The Senate may simply adjourn without voting.

6. **(D) is correct.** A number of different factors may influence a representative's vote on a bill concerned with a highly publicized issue. With reelection in mind, members of Congress would *most likely* vote as their constituency would want them to on high-profile issues. On issues that receive less public visibility, members are more likely to vote in accordance with their personal ideology.

7. **(C) is correct.** Divided government occurs when the party controlling the presidency does not control both houses of Congress. Under divided government, it is nearly impossible for one party to enact its legislative agenda. The parties must reach a compromise in order to get things done. Such compromises help to prevent extreme public policies and force the parties to reach a mutually agreeable solution.

8. **(E) is correct.** After a bill has been reviewed by a committee in the House, it is not yet ready to be debated on the floor of the House. Most bills must first be submitted to the House Rules Committee (revenue, budget, and appropriations bills are the exceptions). The Rules Committee sets a limited time for debate and may set rules for amending the bill. This gives the House Rules Committee a significant degree of influence over proposed legislation.

9. **(A) is correct.** Power in the Senate is more decentralized than in the House. The House is headed by the Speaker, who exerts considerable influence over the legislative process. In the Senate, the filibuster gives individual senators considerable power, resulting in a more decentralized chamber. Only the Senate provides for unlimited debate and therefore enables the filibuster.

10. **(B) is correct.** In recent years, congressional parties have strengthened. Congressional Democrats have become more consistently liberal and congressional Republicans have become more consistently conservative, while the distance between the political parties has increased.

FREE RESPONSE QUESTIONS

1. The leaders in the two chambers of Congress are very important and they are selected in different ways.

   In the House of Representatives, the leader is the Speaker of the House and he is elected by the members of the House. Because one party has the majority, in fact the Speaker is always selected in an election in that party. When the whole House votes, all members of the majority party vote for their candidate for Speaker, ensuring his election. For example, when the Republican Party had a majority in the House of Representatives, that party met in caucus to agree to support Dennis Hastert for the Speaker position, and when the whole House voted, he won election.

   Once elected, the Speaker is a very powerful leader. He presides over the House and therefore can help control debate. He plays a major role in making assignments to standing committees. Because of these powers, the Speaker is the most powerful member of the House.

   In the Senate, things are quite different. The president of the Senate is the vice president of the United States. He is elected to the office by the Electoral College and not by the members of the Senate. Traditionally, the president of the Senate serves mostly a symbolic role in leadership. His only real power comes in voting when there is a tie in the Senate.

   The Senate is smaller than the House of Representatives, with only 100 members compared to the 435 in the House. Because of the sizes of the two houses, leaders play a different role. In the House, the Speaker is a very important leader because committees are more important in the House and rules of debate are much stricter. In the Senate, there is more of a debating society, and the leader is much less important. Often, amendments are made to bills during floor debate in the Senate and the leader is not important. All the leader does is recognize the speakers. He cannot control debate as the Speaker can in the House.

   In the House of Representative, each party has a Whip. The job of the party Whip is to make sure the party members vote with the party on important issues. Although they have no constitutional function in the Congress, their ability to influence important positions within the party makes them a powerful force.

Describes how the Speaker is chosen. 1 point.

Describes the powers of the Speaker. 1 point.

Describes how the president of the Senate is chosen. 1 point.

Describes the powers of the president of the Senate. 1 point.

Explains chamber leadership differences. 2 points.

Identifies and describes a third congressional office. 2 points. Total score on response, 8 of 8.

2. The majority party in Congress has numerous advantages in the legislative process. All chairs of the committees come from the majority party. Committees all have more members of the majority party on them. The chair of the committee can decide to hold a vote on moving a piece of legislation to the next stage and is usually successful since he or she has more members from his or her party in the committee. The majority party also selects the Speaker of the House, who chairs the Rules Committee, schedules legislation, oversees the rules for the legislation, and oversees the debate on the legislation.

   Even when one party controls both the White House and the Congress, passing legislation is still difficult. There are many things that can stop legislation from passing. First, there is no guarantee of party discipline. One defecting member of a political party has the potential to slow the legislation. Often members within a party will disagree significantly during the markup process. One committee chair can also essentially hold a piece of legislation hostage in committee. Finally, in the Senate there are maneuvers that give the minority party power, such as filibustering. All a minority party senator has to do is declare their intent to filibuster, and then there is a requirement that 60 votes cut off the filibuster. If the majority party does not have 60 in the Senate, passing any legislation will be difficult.

Chapter 8: The Presidency

MULTIPLE-CHOICE QUESTIONS

1. **(E) is correct.** While a presidential veto usually effectively kills proposed legislation, Congress can override the veto and has done so in about 4 percent of the vetoes. The Constitution gives the president the power to veto as a means to check Congress, and it gives Congress the power to override a veto as a means of checking the president. Veto overrides, however, require a supermajority of each chamber.

2. **(C) is correct.** As sanctioned by the Constitution, the process of removing a president from office is as follows: (1) the House votes to impeach the president, (2) the Senate carries out the impeachment trial, over which the chief justice of the Supreme Court presides, and (3) the Senate must have a two-thirds vote to convict and remove the president. Statements I, III, and IV describe these steps.

3. **(E) is correct.** The War Powers Act maintains a president's ability to act quickly and decisively by sending troops to a troubled spot, but it prevents him from sidestepping Congress's power to declare war by requiring that those troops be withdrawn after sixty days. Congress is, by virtue of its size, a slow institution. The time limit gives Congress time to debate and declare war if it chooses to. If it does not, the president must withdraw the troops.

4. **(B) is correct.** If the answer does not leap out at you, try eliminating those ways that you know presidents *do* try to influence policy decisions. They do appeal directly to the electorate through public appearances or televised addresses. They also offer to support the legislation of a representative in exchange for that representative's vote, and they do work closely with party leaders in Congress to build coalitions. There is also an understanding between presidents and Congress that representatives who support the president's agenda receive small favors. While presidents often do push their own proposals through Congress, they cannot introduce a bill themselves—they must find a member of Congress to endorse it for them. This enforces the separation of powers set forth in the Constitution.

5. **(B) is correct.** The vice president has few official responsibilities, other than presiding over the Senate and assuming the presidency if there is a vacancy. Commanding the military and heading the Cabinet are duties that fall to the president, creating the federal budget falls to the Congress, and running congressional elections belongs to the states.

6. **(A) is correct.** A citizen's approval of the president is often derived from party affiliation. A president most likely acts in keeping with the platform that was approved by members of the party. By relying on party identification, a person is able to make a judgment about the president, even if he or she is not well informed about the president's performance. Historically, those who identify with the president's party give the president approval more than 40 percentage points higher than do those who identify with the opposition party.

7. **(B) is correct.** Recent presidents have vetoed an average of thirty-five bills in each term. However, it is fairly unusual for Congress to override a president's veto. Fewer than 5 percent of vetoed bills are overridden, largely because it is difficult to achieve a two-thirds vote in both houses of Congress.

8. **(C) is correct.** Presidents can nominate justices, but they cannot remove them from their seats on the Supreme Court. Once justices have been nominated by the president and approved by Congress, they hold their positions for life. The Constitution specifies that justices have no term limit. Justices can be impeached, but this has happened only once.

9. **(A) is correct.** The Constitution authorizes the vice president to take over the office of the presidency if the president dies, resigns, is impeached, or is otherwise unable to perform his duties. If the vice president is also unable to serve for any of these reasons, the Speaker of the House assumes the presidency until the next election.

10. **(E) is correct.** Because the secretary of state is a member of the president's cabinet, a nominee for the position must be confirmed by the Senate. The National Security Council, the chief of staff, the White House counsel, and the Council of Economic Advisors are part of the president's personal staff of advisers and are not required to be approved by the Senate.

FREE RESPONSE QUESTIONS

1. The Founding Fathers had intended to make the president stronger in foreign affairs than Congress. But in keeping with the ideals of checks and balances, they also gave some power over foreign relations to Congress. One power the president has over foreign relations is to dispatch troops. As commander in chief, the president can order the military to strike at America's enemies or defend America's interest overseas. But the President cannot declare war. Only Congress can declare war.

   Following a long conflict in Vietnam, which was never a declared war, Congress decided to rein in the power of the president as commander in chief. The War Powers Act, passed in 1973, required the president to consult with Congress before dispatching troops. Once the troops were deployed, the president had to seek congressional approval for these actions within 30 days.

   Since the passage of the War Powers Act, there have been numerous military actions ordered by presidents without congressional approval. George Bush I ordered Operation Shield and Operation Desert Storm to remove the Iraqis from Kuwait. American troops were stationed in Saudi Arabia for months before Congress finally gave official sanction to the action.

Explains one power the president has. 1 point.

Explains one power Congress has. 1 point.

Explains the War Powers Act. 1 point.

Describes an action taken by the president since the passage of this act and Congress's reaction. 2 points. Total score on this question, 5 of 5 points.

2. a) The presidency is considered the highest office in the land. The presidency is the only office that is elected by all Americans. One role the president plays in politics is that of party leader. The president is able to use the position of party leader to become a more effective national leader in two ways. First, a popular president can help *members of their own party get re-elected*. A president can campaign in a congressman's district and help them get more votes. In exchange for this, presidents can expect the congressman to sup-

Presidential coattails are one way to earn support.

While a veto is a powerful tool used by presidents, it is not specific to their role as party leader, and therefore not worth a point.

All politics are local. If their constituents do not vote to reelect them, it doesn't matter if the president is mad at them.

port the president's legislative program. Second, presidents can veto to *strike down bills* they do not support, giving them a strong hand in making Congress pass legislation of which they approve.

b) While president do have some tools to try to keep their party in line, helping them pass laws, congressmen do not always listen to the president. *First,* congressmen do not owe their office to the president; it is their constituents that elect them to the House or Senate. If a congressman has to choose between upsetting the president or upsetting their constituency in an election year, they would rather upset the president. *Second,* a president's ability to help a congressmen get re-elected is no guaranteed. In mid-term elections, the president's party often loses seats. Or if a president is unpopular, a congressman may actually avoid being linked to the president.

Only the more popular presidents are able to use coattails. Lame duck presidents often have a difficult time campaigning on behalf of their fellow party members. Total score on question, 3 of 4 points.

Chapter 9: The Executive Branch and the Federal Bureaucracy

MULTIPLE-CHOICE QUESTIONS

1. **(C) is correct.** Despite the common misconception, the federal bureaucracy actually has *not* grown. In fact, the American population has grown and the social responsibilities of the government have increased without the size of the federal bureaucracy changing much. State and local bureaucracies, however, have grown considerably.

2. **(B) is correct.** Civil service is based on the merit system. Applicants must take an exam, and those individuals in the highest scoring group are hired. Most bureaucratic positions are filled this way, though the president does appoint some people to high-level positions.

3. **(A) is correct.** Bureaucracies are essentially implementers of policies crafted by Congress, the president, and sometimes the courts.

4. **(E) is correct.** Bureaucracies are often faced with daunting tasks. They are expected to implement policies that frequently lack important details. They may be tasked with achieving an important goal but given neither the authority nor the money to do so effectively. Thus, it is not surprising that Americans are frequently frustrated with the bureaucracy, even though many of the problems are beyond their control.

5. **(E) is correct.** Government corporations perform tasks that could be done by private enterprise and charge fees for their services. Amtrak is such a government corporation. The Department of the Interior is a Cabinet-level department, the Food and Drug Administration is an independent regulatory commission, the Bureau of Engraving is an independent executive agency, and General Motors is a private business.

6. **(B) is correct.** Each new president has the task and the privilege of filling countless bureaucratic posts. He therefore solicits individuals who not only are well qualified but also are likely to endorse the president's policy proposals and work to advance his agenda. The constitutional system of checks and balances, however, requires that all appointees be confirmed by Congress.

7. **(B) is correct.** Administrative discretion is the ability of bureaucrats to select among several viable alternatives when implementing policies crafted by Congress. Because such policies are frequently vague, administrative discretion can be considerable. This freedom to mold policy outcomes allows bureaucrats to select courses of action that are most consistent with their personal policy beliefs.

8. **(D) is correct.** Responsibility for a single policy area is often split between various federal bureaucracies. The fragmentation can lead to overlap and inefficiency. The Department of Homeland Security was created after the 9/11 terrorist attacks revealed weaknesses caused by the fragmentation of authority over domestic security among forty-six federal agencies.

9. **(A) is correct.** One of the ways federal agencies assess the effectiveness of their policy implementation is by gauging public reaction. Citizens' complaints also help agencies enforce regulations and prosecute violators.

10. **(B) is correct.** The Pendleton Civil Service Act of 1883 created the federal civil service system. Hiring and promotions in this system are based on the merit system. With regard to hiring, applicants must take an exam, and those individuals in the highest scoring group are hired. Most federal bureaucratic positions are filled this way, though the president does appoint some people to high-level positions.

1. Iron triangles often form among an interest group, a federal agency, and a legislative committee or subcommittee to shape policies in a particular policy arena. One example of an iron triangle that deals with environmental issues might include an interest group such as Greenpeace, the Environmental Protection Agency, and the Senate Environment and Public Works Committee or one of its subcommittees.

> Correctly identifies all three participants in an iron triangle. 3 points.

For example, suppose hundreds of residents near a few different power plants have developed chronic asthma from the plants' emissions. They may take their case to the EPA and seek assistance from Greenpeace, which has the resources to draw attention to their cause. Greenpeace brings the issue into the political arena by demanding tighter federal regulation of plant emissions. It issues many reports to the EPA showing a link between the chemicals emitted by the plants and the illnesses of the residents. The EPA may also become involved if citizens register their complaints directly with the agency. As a result of these claims, the EPA may send inspectors to test the air quality in the neighborhoods around each plant. The EPA, with the help of Greenpeace, has gathered enough information to prompt the need for new regulations. However, suppose federal law prohibits the EPA from making certain industry changes to power plants. The EPA and Greenpeace then must enlist the help of a sympathetic committee, such as the Senate Environment and Public Works Committee.

> The agency receives information from the interest group. 1 point.

The interest group now lobbies the committee—it provides information about the effects of plant emissions and pledges support for committee members in the next congressional election. The EPA also appeals to the committee and can argue that it had already done its best to shoulder the complaints of the public, thereby shielding committee members from angry voters. The committee, to appease the voters and Greenpeace, may revise the law to allow further regulation by the EPA. Alternatively, it may increase the budget of the EPA so that the agency can develop some kind of solution on its own.

> Congressional committee members receive information and campaign support from the interest group. 1 point.

> Congressional committee members receive help with constituents' complaints from the agency. 1 point.

> The interest group receives legislation it desires from the congressional committee. 1 point.

> The agency receives additional funding from the congressional committee. 1 point.

Either way, each member of the iron triangle benefits. The interest group has succeeded in influencing policy. The agency, with the help of Greenpeace's resources, has done its job of enforcing regulations or may have increased its budget to do so. The members of the committee are allowed to remain out of the fray; voters are not likely to take out their anger on the committee members at the polls, and the committee is absolved of most of the responsibility of resolving the issue by handing the practicalities over to the EPA. Finally, by working together, these three participants have solidified their relationship with each other in case another issue arises.

> This response identifies the participants in an environmental iron triangle and describes how the iron triangle forms during various steps of the policy process. The student successfully applies a theoretical concept to a real-world situation to demonstrate a knowledge of iron triangles and the way they operate in politics. The only link missing is an explicit expression of something the interest group might receive from the agency. Total score on question, 8 of 9 points.

2. a) The Securities and Exchange Commission is responsible for regulating the sales of stocks. The SEC makes sure that the stock market is operating fairly. One requirement the SEC has made is for companies selling stocks to submit a report every 3 months showing how well they are doing economically. The Environmental Protection Agency regulates the amount of pollution that is in the air. If a locality, such as Los Angeles, is allowing too much pollution, the EPA can fine the city (usually by withholding federal highway funds).

> The writer both identifies an agency and gives an example. 2 points.

> Another identification and example. 2 points.

b) One major complaint about the bureaucracy acting as a regulator is the cost. Many small businesses cannot afford to meet all the provisions established by an agency of an act like the Americans with Disabilities Act. When an agency comes in and insists they replace all their desks to make them wheelchair accessible, some small businesses cannot afford it and simply shut down.

> The writer correctly explains a complaint. Total score on question, 5 of 5.

Chapter 10: The Judiciary

MULTIPLE-CHOICE QUESTIONS

1. **(E) is correct.** A plaintiff must have sufficient standing to sue. This means that he or she has a legitimate personal stake in the case. It must be evident that the plaintiff has suffered as a result of another person's actions or of a government action. A citizen cannot simply bring a suit against a law with which he or she disagrees.

2. **(A) is correct.** The Supreme Court justices select the cases they will hear, not the solicitor general. However, very few

appeals are chosen. Cases involving civil liberties are more likely to draw the attention of the Supreme Court.

3. **(D) is correct.** Courts with appellate jurisdiction do not become directly involved with the facts of a case. Rather, they review how a case was handled in a lower court—how the ruling was decided and whether or not that ruling appropriately applied the law to the case.

4. **(C) is correct.** The Constitution authorizes Congress to confirm the president's nominees for federal judgeships as part of the system of checks and balances. The Senate Judiciary Committee is fairly active in this role; about one-fifth of the nominees have been denied a position on the bench.

5. **(B) is correct.** Federal courts sometimes interpret state laws. In some cases, the Supreme Court must decide if a state law violates the Constitution. Federal courts also have jurisdiction over "diversity of citizenship" cases in which the litigants reside in different states; federal judges weigh the appropriate state laws.

5. **(E) is correct.** Most criminal cases are resolved through plea bargaining. The prosecutor and the defendant's attorney work out a deal in which the defendant receives a lighter sentence for pleading guilty. This saves the public considerable money by minimizing court costs while guaranteeing a conviction.

7. **(E) is correct.** Most Supreme Court rulings uphold the decision made by the lower court. This is the principle of *stare decisis*, meaning "let the decision stand."

8. **(C) is correct.** Most court rulings are based on precedents set by previous cases that addressed a similar issue. Judges are not required to rule by precedent, but precedents do serve as a guide and help to make the law more uniform.

9. **(C) is correct.** While state judges may be elected, all federal judges are appointed. Therefore, interest groups cannot influence elections for federal judges. It would also be illegal for interest groups to contribute money to a federal judge's retirement account. While interest groups do sometimes run advertisements in support or opposition to a Supreme Court appointee or a high-profile case (such as abortion), this is very rare. It is very common, however, for interest groups to file *amicus curiae* briefs in which they try to persuade the Supreme Court to decide a case a certain way.

10. **(B) is correct.** Under Chief Justice John Marshall, the Supreme Court used *Marbury* v. *Madison* to establish the principle of judicial review. Judicial review allows the Supreme Court to determine if laws passed by Congress are consistent with the Constitution. By extension, this principle also allows the Supreme Court to determine if executive branch actions are constitutional.

FREE RESPONSE QUESTIONS

> This sentence correctly describes a plea bargain for 1 point.

> The cost and time are two major considerations. 1 point earned.

> The hope of lesser jail time for a defendant is correct for the 3rd point. Total score on question, 3 of 3.

> Defines judicial review. 1 point.

> Gives an example of a case involving judicial review. 1 point.

> Defines judicial activism. 1 point.

> Gives an example of a case involving judicial activism. 1 point.

> Describes two ways in which federal judges could be considered undemocratic. 2 points.

> Explains how a president could contain the power of the courts. 1 point. Total score on question, 7 of 7.

1. In the United States justice system, plea bargains are commonly used. A plea bargain occurs when a person charged with a crime agrees to plead guilty to a lesser crime, or fewer crimes, in exchange for a lighter sentence. Prosecutors agree to plea bargains because it speeds up the process of incarcerating a criminal. It is also much less expensive than going to trial, which could takes months to complete and cost thousands of dollars. Defendants often prefer to plea bargain because it will help them to spend less time in jail. Sometimes a plea bargain will involve no jail time at all.

2. a) *Judicial Review* is when a federal court rules on the constitutionality of a law or governmental action. When the Taney Court ruled in the *Dred Scott* case that slaves were property and could therefore be taken into free territories, they were using judicial review.

b) *Judicial activism* is the belief that judges should not be bound by a strict interpretation of the Constitution. Instead, judges must be willing to make decisions to meet the pressing needs of society, or to make a just decision that may not be found in the Constitution. The case of *Brown v. Board of Education* would be one such example. In this case, the Warren Court struck down segregation laws, not based on a provision of the Constitution, but because they said it was wrong and detrimental to treat black children differently than white children.

c) Judges are *appointed to federal courts, not elected*. This is not very democratic. It would be more democratic to have the judges elected, but then that might influence the way in which they decided cases. Also, federal judges are *mainly from prestigious, expensive law schools*. This is elitism, which is also undemocratic.

d) The president can restrain the courts by the *type of person they appoint* to serve as judges. Of course, there is no guarantee that the person the president appoints is going to act in the manner the president predicted they would. But a candidate who appears to be a strict constructionist is more likely to act this way than a person who everyone knows is liberal.

Chapter 11: Political Socialization and Public Opinion

MULTIPLE-CHOICE QUESTIONS

1. **(E) is correct.** People learn about government and form their beliefs primarily through their family, what they are taught in school, and what they see and hear on television. Factors such as a religious upbringing can also influence a person's political ideology. However, the month in which a person was born has no bearing on his or her political beliefs.

2. **(E) is correct.** Because older Americans are more conservative than younger counterparts, they are also more likely to favor greater military spending. However, older Americans are less likely to favor investing Social Security funds in the stock market. These differences are important because senior citizens are more likely to vote than younger Americans, suggesting that government policies may be disproportionately tilted toward older Americans and away from younger Americans.

3. **(E) is correct.** Liberals typically have supported increased spending to aid the poor. This may require higher taxes on the wealthy to achieve. Conservatives, however, favor lower taxes, greater defense spending, and greater military intervention around the world.

4. **(A) is correct.** The gender gap theory predicts that women are more likely to vote for a Democratic candidate than a Republican. The gender gap is a significant predictor because women outnumber men in the United States.

5. **(E) is correct.** A minority majority population means that more than half the U.S. population would be composed of minority group members rather than Caucasians. Hispanic Americans have become the largest minority group, recently surpassing African Americans. If the percentages continue to change at the same rate, the United States will reach a minority majority sometime in the middle of the twenty-first century.

6. **(D) is correct.** Sound bites result in very little substantive news coverage and allow candidates to avoid an in-depth discussion of important issues. Why talk about an issue in depth when the media will relegate your words to a simple sound bite?

7. **(D) is correct.** The *Literary Digest Poll* is perhaps the most famous example of the problem of drawing a nonrepresentative sample. By sending surveys only to those with cars and telephones during the depths of the Great Depression, the magazine unwittingly created a sample that was wildly at variance with the population as a whole. Because of that, the poll wrongly predicted that Alf Landon would win the presidency in 1936, but he lost in a landslide.

8. **(D) is correct.** In all sampling, there is a potential that the sample drawn is not perfectly reflective of the population as a whole. In random sampling, the likelihood of such error can be estimated mathematically. The other answers all can cause error as well, but they occur in ways that cannot be estimated and are therefore not "sampling error."

9. **(C) is correct.** There are many effective ways to participate in politics. However, only by voting do more than half of Americans participate in politics. This is not to say that voting is the most significant form of participation—others might be. However, it is the most common form.

10. **(C) is correct.** All of the possible answers refer to differences between men and women. However, in politics, the gender gap only refers to the fact that, since 1980, women have tended to be more supportive of Democrats than have men. This trend is especially strong among unmarried women.

FREE RESPONSE QUESTIONS

Very thorough definition. 1 point.

A good explanation of the role of the family in political socialization. 2 points.

A good explanation of how schools play a role in political socialization. 2 points.

1. Political socialization is the process through which people learn their political values and orientations. It is a process that begins very early in life and continues throughout life. Political socialization is one way that people become loyal to their nation.

   Two of the primary agents of political socialization are family and school. Families have the earliest and perhaps longest-lasting impact on political views. From the very earliest memories, children learn about politics through the discussions about politics that their parents have. Most children learn their parents' political party affiliation at an early age. Usually, children become members of the same party as their parents. This shows how important family is in political socialization.

   School is another important agent of socialization. In school, students learn about American politics and history. Through teaching and learning, American students learn to value the capitalistic economic system and democratic political system enjoyed in America. Through reciting the Pledge of Allegiance and singing patriotic songs, students become patriotic themselves. As a result, one can readily see the importance of school in political socialization.

Of all the factors that will influence an individual's socialization, family is the most controlling variable. There are a couple of reasons for this. First, children tend to be of the same class and ethnic group as their parents. Also, parents are with their children from the time they are born until they first enter the voting booth. Along with all the social values that a parent gives to their child come political values.

Of course, other important agents of socialization include the mass media and people with whom one works. But family and school are perhaps the most important.

> A good explanation of why the family is such an important factor. Total score on question, 4 of 4.

2. A random sample is better than a non-random sample because random people can answer questions better than selected people. Random people can give "real" answers while selected people are members of the elite and don't really know what the people are thinking. As a result, a random sample gives everyone an equal chance of being selected and therefore is more likely to be representative of the population as a whole. With a non-random sample, we cannot estimate how likely the sample is to represent the people.

Telephone surveys are both great and bad. They are great because everyone with a phone can be surveyed. They are bad because people without telephones cannot be surveyed. Surveys tell us that Americans don't know much about politics. They can't answer even simple questions well. For example, in Jay-walking, Jay Leno shows that people are really dumb in answering questions about politics.

> This paragraph almost earns a point for saying that people are not well informed. But the example is not from a survey, and there is no discussion of what polls tell us about attitudes.

Chapter 12: Political Parties

MULTIPLE-CHOICE QUESTIONS

1. **(A) is correct.** While 48 percent of Jews identify themselves as Democrats, fewer than 40 percent of women, Catholics, Protestants, and those under thirty years old are Democrats.

2. **(D) is correct.** Congressional seats are awarded on a winner-take-all basis. This means that a party is not rewarded unless that party wins the election, because only the winner has a say in Congress. Since small parties will almost never have a voice in Congress, they have an incentive to join with other groups in the hopes of forming a majority coalition that will result in their victory. This helps encourage a two-party system. In contrast, if seats are allocated according to proportional representation, parties can have votes in the legislature according to their electoral strength. Under this system, small parties do not have the same incentive to merge with other parties, encouraging a multiparty system. Neither the Constitution nor statutes mandate political parties.

3. **(E) is correct.** While third parties seldom win elections, they nonetheless have an important influence on American politics. Third parties bring new issues into the political arena, and they offer an alternative to voters who are displeased with the two major parties.

4. **(C) is correct.** Political parties are important to democracy because they link the American people with their government. Voters, members of Congress, and even the president may share the same party affiliation. By electing the candidate of their preferred party, voters are able to advance their own policy preferences in the political arena.

5. **(B) is correct.** A political party officially nominates its candidate for the presidency at a national convention. It is attended by party delegates from all fifty states.

6. **(A) is correct.** From the late nineteenth century through the 1930s, local parties were often incredibly powerful in large cities such as New York and Chicago. These cities were controlled by party machines whose bosses used the patronage system to reward people who supported the party. Today, staffing city government is much more professionalized, and local parties have declined significantly.

7. **(C) is correct.** Critical elections reveal fissures in each party's coalition of supporters and result in a realignment of support behind each party. This realignment may propel what used to be the minority party to power, though the coalition forming the new majority party is likely to be different from the party's earlier makeup. Therefore, critical elections usher in a new political era in American politics.

8. **(B) is correct.** The New Deal coalition comprised urbanites, labor unions, Catholics, Jews, the poor, Southerners, and African Americans. Bankers, however, remained with the Republican Party. This successful coalition kept Democrats dominant for decades.

9. **(C) is correct.** National committees meet and decide on the party's official platform for the next four years. The platform is the best available statement of a party's policy positions.

10. **(A) is correct.** While the nomination system has many faults, exclusivity is not one of them. All registered voters can participate in open primaries, and all registered partisans can participate in closed parties. Under the current nomination system, the door is wide open to participation by ordinary citizens, and about one-fourth of Americans weigh in with their candidate preferences. The days of candidates being selected by a small group of political elites are long over.

FREE RESPONSE QUESTIONS

1. Since 1952, there have always been more self-proclaimed Democrats in the United States than Republicans. Yet the Democrats find it much harder to win presidential elections. There are three reasons for this. First, independent voters, who make up almost 40 percent of all voters today, tend to vote Republican in presidential elections. This is one reason both Democratic and Republican candidates tend to drift toward the center in the general election.

> The role of independent voters is important in Presidential elections. 1 point.

Second, third-party candidates can have an impact on elections. In 1968 and 1972, George Wallace pulled votes away from the Democratic Party, allowing Republican Richard Nixon to win both times. In 2000, Ralph Nader pulled enough votes away from Al Gore to allow Bush to become president. Of course, the knife cuts both ways. Ross Perot running as a third-party candidate caused George Bush I to lose his election to Democrat Bill Clinton. Still, it is Democrats who are hurt more often by third-party candidates than Republicans.

> A strong explanation of the role of third-party candidates. 1 point.

Finally, Republicans tend to vote more than do Democrats. A 10 percent lead in self-identified voters doesn't help the Democrats if that 10 percent doesn't go to the polls and cast their votes.

> Not much discussion here, but enough to earn a 3rd point. Total score, 3 of 3.

2. a) Three ways in which political parties serve as linkage institutions are:
   1) *running campaigns:* political parties poll voters to find out what issues the people are concerned about and then organize the campaign to highlight their candidate's stance on these issues.
   2) *recruiting candidates:* parties choose candidates whose views they believe are in line with the public's. A candidate whose stand on issues is seen as too extreme is not likely to get nominated by one of the major parties.
   3) *Parties coordinate policy making.* Political leaders in the House and Senate work to make sure their party members vote in support of party issues.

> Remember, you do not need an essay response on the AP Gov exam. Bullet point responses are acceptable. In this response, the student does a good job of describing two ways in which parties serve as linkage institutions. Coordinating policy-making is not clearly connected to a party's role as a linkage institution, and therefore does not earn a point. 2 of 3 points awarded in part (a).

b) Political parties are not as strong today as they were 50 years ago in part *because of television.* Television allows candidates to access the people directly, without the help of their party. Arnold Schwarzenegger of California has a much more liberal stance on issues than the Republican Party in that state. Zell Miller, a Democrat, spoke at the Republican National Convention in 2004. Both men retained their offices, in spite of tweaking their parties noses, because they can directly access the voters.

> Identifying television as a cause of the weakening of political parties is good, but it does not earn a point without an explanation.

> A good explanation of how television has weakened parties. The examples that follow ensure the earning of the point. Total score for this response, 3 of 4.

Chapter 13: Voting and Elections

MULTIPLE-CHOICE QUESTIONS

1. **(D) is correct.** Most states award their electoral votes in a "winner-take-all" system. Whichever candidate wins the popular vote in the state receives all of that state's electoral votes.

2. **(B) is correct.** While many people who vote according to issue preferences probably have developed certain voting habits over the course of several elections, this is not necessarily a requirement for choosing candidates in this manner. Well-informed first-time voters could also vote according to those issues on which they agree with a particular candidate.

3. **(D) is correct.** Suffrage, or the right to vote, has gradually expanded in the United States. Laws or constitutional amendments have extended suffrage to those who do not own property, women, African Americans, Native Americans, and those at least eighteen years old. However, suffrage can be denied to those in prison and even those who have completed their sentences. Thus, a convicted felon would be the person most likely to be denied suffrage.

4. **(E) is correct.** Ticket splitting is voting for one party for one office and for another party for other offices. Independents are most likely to engage in ticket splitting. Nonvoters do not engage in ticket splitting because they do not vote. Primary election voters are given a slate of candidates who all belong to the party running the primary (except in the relatively rare blanket primaries).

5. **(E) is correct.** In most other democracies, governments take the effort to register citizens to vote. In the United States, however, this is an individual's responsibility and a prerequisite for voting. This works to lower voter turnout.

In addition, the differences between the Democratic candidate and the Republican candidate are likely to be smaller than the differences between the various candidates in multiparty European democracies. This also works to lower American turnout compared with other democracies. However, American voters are asked to vote more frequently; this leads to voter fatigue, not the development of good voting habits. Finally, only a handful of democracies require their citizens to vote.

6. **(A) is correct.** Young people do not vote primarily because they have not had enough experience to develop political awareness and form their beliefs about government. In school, students are taught the virtues of a federal government, not distrust of it.

7. **(A) is correct.** Young voters are less likely to have strong attachments to political parties, partly because they have less experience with political parties. Without partisan attachments, young voters are more likely to support independent or third-party candidates. One of the biggest distinctions about young citizens, however, is that they are much less likely to vote than older Americans.

8. **(D) is correct.** The Motor Voter Act allows people to register to vote when they get or renew a driver's license. This increases voter registration by making it easier for people to register. However, while more people have registered, voter turnout has not been significantly affected by the Motor Voter Act.

9. **(B) is correct.** Oregon has been conducting elections by mail since 1998, when voters passed a referendum to eliminate polling places and conduct all elections through the United States Postal Service.

FREE RESPONSE QUESTIONS

The writer could have argued the reverse as well, that candidates will focus more on states where they are competitive. The example of Bush in California (or Kerry in Texas) is good for another point.

Losing the popular election and still being elected president is worth 1 point. The example of Bush in 2000 is worth another point. Although Clinton did not receive a majority of popular votes in either of his elections, he still had more popular votes than any of his competitors. This example would not have been awarded a point. Fortunately, the student had already earned 2 points for this section.

Small states supporting the Electoral College is worth the 3rd point. In fact, the student could have simply extended the argument that amending the Constitution is a difficult enough barrier to keep the system from being changed. Total score, 5 of 5.

This one sentence is enough information to earn 1 point. The examples that follow are not required, but they do help reinforce the point.

The question only asks for one change. In giving two, the student ensures that if one of the answers is deemed unacceptable for some reason, he or she may still earn the point for (b).

A weak explanation, but enough to earn a point. The student would have been safer to explain why the parties are fearful of upsetting Iowa and New Hampshire. Total score on this question, 3 of 3.

1. a) Since most states have a winner-take-all system, candidates *will not focus on states where they are not likely to win.* For example, George W. Bush did not campaign much in California in either 2000 or 2004 because he was so far behind in the polls.

b) The Electoral College is undemocratic because a candidate *could lose the popular vote and still be elected* president if they have a majority of electoral votes. George W. Bush was able to do this in 2000. Likewise, Bill Clinton was able to win the presidency twice without every having won a majority of popular votes.

c) The reason that the Electoral College system has not changed is that it is in the Constitution. And to change the Constitution, it would take three-quarters of the states to approve the change. *Small states, which are over represented in the Electoral College system, are unlikely to vote to change this system.*

2. Iowa and New Hampshire receive more media attention than any other state because they are the first two contests in the process of nominating candidates for the presidency. If a candidate does well in these two states, they can use that momentum to start winning the bigger primaries and caucuses that follow. Jimmy Carter in 1976 and Barack Obama in 2008 were both able to use upset wins in Iowa as momentum to capture the Democratic nomination. Rudy Giuliani, once considered a frontrunner for the Republican nomination in 2008, ignored Iowa and New Hampshire and concentrated instead on Florida. By the time the Florida nomination came around, he was so out of the news cycle, he failed miserably and soon had to abandon his campaign.

The influence of Iowa and New Hampshire could be lessened if other states held earlier primaries. The parties could lessen the influence of Iowa and New Hampshire if they would assign the dates for primaries and caucuses rather than allowing the states to decide their own dates (with some restrictions).

The parties themselves are fearful of upsetting Iowa or New Hampshire, and losing their votes. Therefore, the parties discourage other states from moving their primaries earlier. This is what happened to Florida and Michigan. They moved their primaries earlier and were punished by the Democratic National Committee (but not by the Republicans).

Chapter 14: The Campaign Process

MULTIPLE-CHOICE QUESTIONS

1. **(D) is correct.** All of the other choices were established. Not surprisingly, members of Congress were reluctant to provide any funds to the campaigns of their future opponents.

2. **(D) is correct.** For a business to make contributions through a PAC, it must register the PAC with the Federal Election Commission (FEC). The PAC then must report on all of its activities and spending so that the FEC can closely monitor it to ensure that it is not making illegal contributions directly to candidates.

3. **(B) is correct.** Television time is expensive and consumes more than half of the budget for a presidential or senatorial campaign. Most candidates apparently believe that their policy positions are a crucial part of their campaign, and they are willing to pay substantial sums to communicate them to voters.

4. **(D) is correct.** The United States often receives criticism for its long campaign season. In most European countries, for example, campaigns last only a few months. As a result, European campaigns are also less expensive than American campaigns.

5. **(D) is correct.** The media tend to focus on campaign strategies and the horse race rather than a discussion of the issues. Thus, the media are more likely to report on which candidate is ahead in the polls rather than the candidates' differences on important policy issues. A study by the Project for Excellence in Journalism found that that 63 percent of news stories dealt with the horse race and campaign strategies; only 32 percent dealt with the substance of the campaign, including issues, policies, and the candidates' backgrounds.

6. **(A) is correct.** 527 groups are able to advertise for an issue and thus enable some to thwart the goal of the McCain-Feingold legislation.

7. **(D) is correct.** Federal matching funds are available for presidential candidates who meet certain rules.

FREE RESPONSE QUESTIONS

1. Today's political campaigns are long, drawn-out media extravaganzas that cost millions of dollars. To reach voters, candidates must spend large sums of money on television advertising, travel, and a professional campaign staff. The difficulties of financing such an event and the ways these difficulties are overcome ultimately infringe on the practice of democracy.

To run for office, a candidate must have hundreds of thousands of dollars at his or her disposal. This money is necessary to buy a candidate exposure—it allows the candidate to convey his or her political beliefs to the public through television and even just to maintain a constant presence in the minds of the public. The more money you can spend, the more visible you will be, and ultimately the more successful you'll be in the race. Any candidates who cannot afford to spend such large sums on campaigning are instantly at a disadvantage. Some qualified people interested in running are not able to because of the impossibility of acquiring such funds. In a true democracy, anyone with political knowledge and experience should be able to run for office. However, very few Americans can, thus putting wealthy people and incumbents at a distinct advantage. Furthermore, third-party candidates who represent the middle and lower classes or who have innovative new ideas are not able to spread their message and compete against wealthier politicians. The cost of campaigns therefore limits political participation and discourages the introduction of innovative policies from different sectors of the electorate.

Expensive campaigns also act as a deterrent to democracy because they often allow businesses to gain a foothold in the political arena. Candidates are able to finance their campaigns only with the help of soft money and PACs. Soft money is all the donations to a party for its general use, most of which goes indirectly to campaigning, and PACs are funding vehicles established by businesses to channel money into campaigns. Candidates, then, receive a great deal of campaign support indirectly from businesses, to which they are somewhat beholden when they reach office. Campaigns therefore allow business interests to play a role in the election process. Rather than being elected by the will of the people and taking office with their needs in mind, politicians shape the political agenda around the needs of those businesses, which helped them get to Capitol Hill.

In an effort to curb abuses in campaign funding, Congress has set up regulations for how they operate. PACs must register with the Federal Election Commission if they contribute more than $1,000 to candidates. The McCain-Feingold bill worked to get rid of

None of this is applicable to the question. Be sure to keep your answer focused on the specifics of the question.

This phrase defines. 1 point.

This phrase defines PACs somewhat. 1 point.

Within the context, the reader is able to infer that the student sees this as a negative impact of PACs on campaigns. 1 point.

The student briefly describes two regulations, good for 2 points.

This response presents an interesting argument, which, unfortunately, addresses only part of the question. Two sources of campaign funding go totally undefined, and without definitions, it is impossible to describe either a positive or a negative impact. 5 of 10 points.

soft money altogether in 2002. This regulation, however, has only seemed to push the money in a new direction, 527 groups.

By enacting campaign finance reforms that limit soft money and PAC donations, campaigns might become more democratic. Moreover, if all candidates were guaranteed the same amount of money with which to run their campaigns and free, equal airtime, as is done in many other countries, all people who wanted to run for office would have a fair chance, and businesses would not be able to influence politics so easily.

Chapter 15: The Media

MULTIPLE-CHOICE QUESTIONS

1. **(B) is correct.** Investigative journalism often seeks to root out political scandal. Scandals are more likely to achieve higher ratings than, say, an in-depth analysis of an issue. Scandals therefore receive more air time.

2. **(D) is correct.** The president is the most likely politician to be featured in the media. This is because it is easier to focus on one person than on the 535 members of Congress. As a result, presidents have been able to gain significant political power through public opinion.

3. **(A) is correct.** In polls, 40 percent of journalists indicated that they leaned to the left, while only 25 percent of the general public indicated that they were liberals. Studies show, however, that most news stories contain no systematic ideological or partisan bias.

4. **(C) is correct.** Research on media effects has largely determined that the media have no direct effect on citizens' political attitudes. However, the media may have an indirect effect on attitudes by influencing the importance Americans assign to a particular policy issue. That is, the media do not influence what Americans think, but they influence what Americans think about. The agenda-setting effect is strongest for citizens who are informed about politics and who trust the media. The agenda-setting effect is not directly related to investigative journalism.

5. **(D) is correct.** People who choose to watch news stations like CNN and C-SPAN will have direct access to congressional proceedings and in-depth political analysis. They will gain more political knowledge than was ever available to the public before. However, the majority of Americans will choose to watch other specialized stations instead and will become even less politically knowledgeable.

6. **(E) is correct.** The main objective of the American media is to make a profit. While the media may also strive to accurately portray news events and inform the public, these are all secondary to making money. In other countries, the public may own the major networks; in the United States, most major media outlets are private businesses.

7. **(E) is correct.** Journalists typically stick to one beat and become familiar with that policy area. A journalist covering interest rates would most likely get his or her information from the spokespeople for the Federal Reserve Board, which helps regulate the economy by influencing interest rates.

8. **(D) is correct.** Studies have shown that newspaper readers possess the most political knowledge and usually are the more active members of the electorate. The print media generally analyze issues in greater depth than do the other media, which instead tend to rely on sound bites and other visual information.

9. **(D) is correct.** The Federal Communications Commission is an independent regulatory agency.

10. **(B) is correct.** Presidents are holding fewer regularly scheduled press conferences.

FREE RESPONSE QUESTIONS

Response gives a strong definition of broadcasting and narrowcasting. Major points are underlined to help the reader easily find the points, with examples given to further support the response. 2 points earned.

A good description of the media bias and, again, good examples in case the reader does not consider the description strong enough. 1 point earned.

1. a) Broadcasting dominated the electronic media from the 1950s through the 1980s when there were only three major networks: NBC, ABC, CBS. In order to attract as many viewers as possible, *these stations would air stories with broad interest.* They did not want to appear too liberal or too conservative for fear of losing voters. With the rise of cable television, stations now looked to attract a niche audience. This is sometimes done with entertainment programming (e.g., ESPN, the Cooking Network) or with news programs. Rather than having a news program that is written to cover all spectrums of viewers, from liberal to conservative, narrowcasting will have some shows slanted with a conservative bias (such as Fox News) and some shows slanted liberal (such as CNN).

b) To attract a conservative audience, Fox News will give a more conservative view on the news. For example, a story about illegal immigration is more likely to talk about violent crime rates among Latinos than the contributions Latinos make to the U.S. economy. *Narrowcasting tends to make the news stories either more conservative or more liberal.*

A clear explanation of the impact of bias. The explanation is not needed to earn the point but again serves as a safety net in case the reader is unsure the answer is worthy of a point. 1 point earned. Total score, 4 of 4.

c) *Narrowcasting causes the media to reinforce the views people already have on an issue.* With people choosing to only hear their own side of an argument repeated over and over on the news, the American people have become more extreme.

2. The media may hurt candidates running for office through investigative journalism or allowing negative advertising to be run. Through investigative journalism, reporters will search for scandals and negative information about a candidate in order to receive higher ratings for their news programs. Such reporting can tarnish the reputation of a candidate and hurt his chances at being elected. Additionally, with the rise of the Internet, many scandals involving political figures have originated on Web sites only to later be picked up by the mainstream media. Negative advertisements may also be run against a candidate. Media outlets may choose to run such advertisements. Even though there is an expectation that the candidate has the right to respond, such negative advertisements often either drive down voter turnout or have a negative impact on the candidate.

On the other hand, having access to the media greatly helps candidates. Candidates can stage media events, leak trial balloons, make direct appearances on television, go on debates, or use sound bites to promote their campaigns. Media events occur when a candidate for office stages an event to draw positive attention to him or herself, such as appearing at a school or charity event. This event is covered in the media as a news story and provides attention to the candidate without the candidate having to spend any money on the campaign. Trial balloons occur when a candidate leaks information to a reporter hoping that the story will get into the mainstream media in order to gauge public opinion of a campaign event. For example, a presidential candidate may leak information about his choice for vice president and then take polls to see if this choice helps the campaign or not.

Chapter 16: Interest Groups

MULTIPLE-CHOICE QUESTIONS

1. **(B) is correct.** In a small interest group, members' share of a collective good is large enough that they are more likely to participate actively to maintain the group's success. In contrast, the success of a large group is divided among many more people and might be less apparent to them. Therefore, large groups are more likely to suffer from the free-rider problem.

2. **(A) is correct.** Public education is an issue that affects all Americans, not just those who are members of an interest group. An interest group that focuses on public education would therefore be a public interest group. Any successes achieved by the group would benefit the public as a whole.

3. **(C) is correct.** Lobbyists are forbidden by law from contributing any money directly to lawmakers for any reason. They must establish a PAC to make campaign contributions, and this money, in theory, can be used only for general party purposes; it cannot go to a specific candidate. All interest group donations, moreover, are monitored by the Federal Election Commission.

4. **(D) is correct.** An iron triangle, or subgovernment, is composed of an interest group, the federal agency, and the legislative committee that all handle a specific policy. They work closely together to create policies in the given policy area that benefits those involved.

5. **(E) is correct.** Pluralists believe that interest groups have about the same amount of power because they must compete with each other for influence. If, for example, one

group increases its efforts to reach politicians, other groups will quickly follow suit to catch up and will therefore balance the system again.

6. **(D) is correct.** Interest groups frequently file class action lawsuits in an attempt to reverse policy decisions. They also solidify their relationships with members of Congress by channeling the bulk of their campaign contributions to incumbents. Interest groups also share their policy expertise with lawmakers when they believe it will encourage lawmakers to pass favorable legislation. It is illegal for interest groups to pay for legislative favors and unethical for judges to meet with interest group representatives.

7. **(C) is correct.** Interest groups concentrate most of their efforts on shaping policy during the political process. They maintain frequent contact with lawmakers while Congress is in session. Political parties, on the other hand, try to shape the policy agenda by having their candidates elected to office. They therefore apply their efforts mostly to campaigns.

8. **(A) is correct.** Single-issue groups have a narrow focus. Members of single-issue groups usually have incredibly strong feelings about the issue that concerns them. Such issues often appeal to their emotions. Abortion is one such issue.

9. **(B) is correct.** Interest groups do not run candidates but attempt to influence policy makers.

10. **(D) is correct.** The AARP is the largest interest group in the United States.

FREE RESPONSE QUESTIONS

Chooses one group from list.

Identifies an institution to which the NAACP would appeal. 1 point.

This sentence hints at a resource, but a more direct statement would ensure the point.

This is a clear statement identifying a resource of the NAACP. 1 point.

This section, in conjunction with the discussion of concentrating on certain congressional committees in the previous paragraph, constitutes an explanation of how the NAACP would use the resource of black population to influence policy making. 1 point.

This is a somewhat rambling discussion of the NAACP, a target to which it would appeal, a resource at its disposal, and how that resource might be used. No second resource is identified. Total score on question, 3 of 5 points.

The student correctly defines political parties.

The explanation for interest groups, coupled with the definition of a political party, is enough to earn a point in part (a).

The student correctly identifies the NAACP and the AFL-CIO for the 2 identification points in part (b).

The use of courts has been one of the strongest methods of the NAACP. Total score on this question, 4 of 4.

1. The National Association for the Advancement of Colored People has been an influential interest group since the early twentieth century, when it formed to fight for the rights of African Americans. It has become a powerful and prestigious interest group.

This group works with the Department of Justice to make sure civil rights are enforced, but otherwise it pursues its interests primarily in the legislative arena. It is most likely to win the attention and cooperation of members of Congress whose constituencies include a high percentage of African Americans. It would also be most likely to concentrate its efforts on a few key committees in the House and Senate that handle urban housing, education, and labor policy. For example, the NAACP might lobby members of the Senate Labor and Human Resources Committee about the minimum wage or the House Education and the Workforce Committee about after-school programs in low-income school districts. With the help of the NAACP, in fact, Congress passed the Civil Rights Act of 1964, the Voting Rights Act of 1965, and the Fair Housing Act of 1968. These legislative victories also demonstrate the success of the NAACP in pursuing its interests and representing a major group of Americans.

The most powerful resource of the NAACP is the body of people whom it represents, African Americans. They are one of the largest minority groups in the United States and, when organized under the NAACP, have had significant political successes. However, only about half of all African Americans vote. To encourage African Americans to exercise this right and thus wield their power, the NAACP has initiated voter registration and education efforts. If voter turnout were higher among this portion of the electorate, more African Americans might be elected to influential governmental positions to work directly for the group. They would also gain political clout because politicians, to win their votes, would have to pay attention to their concerns. An interest group is, in part, as powerful as its members are vocal.

2. a) Political parties and interest groups both play important roles in the American political system. *Parties* work to control the government by getting their members elected to office. Once in office, these politicians can help make the laws that their party favors. *Interest groups*, on the other hand, do not nominate people to run for office. They may support a candidate who is running, but they do not run their own candidate. Instead, interest groups put pressure on the government (both elected officials and non elected officials) to try to get their agenda put into action. For example, the NRA doesn't nominate anyone to run for office, but they strongly endorse candidate who are pro-gun. The NRA may also bring cases before the courts to try to protect gun rights.

b) The *NAACP* would be a group interested in equality interests. The *AFL-CIO* would be an interest group concerned with economic interests.

c) The *NAACP has successfully challenged segregation in the court system*. In the case of *Brown v. Board of Education*, the NAACP was able to have the Supreme Court rule that segregation was unconstitutional.

Chapter 17: Domestic Policy

MULTIPLE-CHOICE QUESTIONS

1. **(E) is correct.** The most expensive social welfare programs are Social Security and Medicare, both of which primarily benefit the elderly. Programs for the poor account for only 17 percent of social welfare spending.

2. **(B) is correct.** Instead of paying taxes, the working poor receive money from the government through a program called the Earned Income Tax Credit. This program distributes $20 billion to poor families.

3. **(E) is correct.** In recent decades, income inequality has continued to grow. Thus, the adage that the rich get richer and the poor get poorer accurately describes income distribution in the United States in recent decades. Income distribution in European democracies is more equal than in the United States.

4. **(C) is correct.** Because the number of retirees is growing, Social Security cannot remain solvent without cutting benefits or earning additional revenue, either through tax

increases or cuts in other government programs. Of course, none of these solutions is politically palatable. Social Security also faces financial challenges associated with the increasing cost of medical care.

5. **(E) is correct.** President George W. Bush proposed changing the Social Security program to allow current workers to invest part of their Social Security contributions into a personal investment account that might contain stocks or bonds. However, the pay-as-you-go nature of Social Security means that the transition costs for such a program would actually hasten Social Security's bankruptcy. A slumping stock market also reminded Americans of the pitfalls of investing in the stock market. Thus, Bush was unable to marshal enough support for his proposal.

6. **(D) is correct.** More people are undergoing medical treatment because more types of illnesses can be treated today, but people are not actually getting sick in greater numbers. Yet, cutting-edge medical treatments are extremely expensive. In addition, patients have little incentive to seek out less expensive treatments because they often are not paying the bill themselves. Instead, the government and insurance companies pick up the bulk of the tab.

7. **(E) is correct.** Despite the common misconception that the American health care system is entirely privatized, the government is actually the greatest financial contributor. It funds nearly 50 percent of health care, while insurance companies pay about 30 percent, and individuals pay about 20 percent.

8. **(D) is correct.** Coal is America's most plentiful resource but also its dirtiest and a contributor to global warming. Although the United States has significant coal deposits, it relies more heavily on oil for its energy. Because domestic supplies of oil are insufficient to meet demand, the U.S. is a net importer of oil.

9. **(E) is correct.** Most other democracies have nationalized health care systems in which everyone has equal access to health care at virtually no cost, while still spending a smaller percentage of their gross domestic product than the United States. Many Americans lack insurance, either through the government or their employer, and cannot afford to buy insurance or pay for medical treatment.

10. **(D) is correct.** Environmental groups often spar with "wise use" advocates who believe that public lands should be managed so as to allow conservation and recreation along with economic uses such as grazing, mining, and logging. In the West, these industries are often the lifeblood of communities that would otherwise have very little economic opportunity.

FREE RESPONSE QUESTIONS

A very brief answer, but it both defines entitlement and gives an example. 2 points.

Again short, but on target. A definition and an example. 2 points.

Strongly supported by Republicans, Clinton brought about more welfare reform than the far more conservative Reagan was able to. Correct response, 1 point. Total score, 5 of 5.

The student gives a specific act (the Clean Air Act) and gives a strong and specific explanation of it. 2 points earned.

A simple explanation, but enough to earn a point.

The student gives two example. Either would suffice. Only one was necessary to earn the point. Total score, 4 of 4.

1. a) Entitlement programs are government run programs that pay money out to *individuals who qualify, regardless of any neediness. Social Security* is an entitlement program.

b) Means tested programs are programs that *give aid only to those people who qualify,* such as those living below the poverty line. *Food stamps* would be a means tested program.

c) Clinton wanted to change the means tested programs of Johnson's Great Society. Clinton moved the nation from welfare to what he called "workfare." Limits were put on how much money the federal government would give to the states for their welfare programs. Individuals were also limited as to how much they were able to collect from welfare and how long they were able to stay on welfare.

2. From the time the first smokestacks began to rise around Pittsburgh, America has been pumping pollutants into the air. In 1970, Congress passed the *Clean Air Act* in an effort to cut back on this environmental problem. The Clean Air Act required fuels *(especially gasoline) to produce fewer pollutants.* This act also required *manufacturers to cut back on the amount of particle waste* that they released into the air.

The Clean Air Act has been weakened over the years. But air *pollution levels are lower today because of it.* The smog in LA is still the worst in the nation, but it is better than what it had been in the 1960s before the Clean Air Act.

Automakers and manufacturers have both found problems with the Clean Air Act. Automakers do not like the increased expense of making a cleaner burning engine and have fought Congress over this bill for years. Manufacturers likewise do not like the increased cost of filtering their smokestacks and argue it makes them less competitive with foreign industries that do not have such regulations.

Chapter 18: Economic Policy

MULTIPLE-CHOICE QUESTIONS

1. **(B) is correct.** Keynesian economic theory endorses an active government because government spending creates demand among consumers. Government spending can create jobs for the unemployed and help businesses expand.

2. **(D) is correct.** In a communist system, the government owns the means of production; in a pure capitalist system, the government plays no part at all in the economy. The United States has a mixed economy that falls between these two extremes. The private sector is large, but the government has established many measures to regulate and influence it.

3. **(A) is correct.** Republican presidents focus on keeping inflation down because this helps the investor class, which is worried that inflation will erode their savings. Democrats, however, are more concerned with the interests of the working class and thus focus on minimizing unemployment.

4. **(C) is correct.** The Federal Reserve Board controls how much money is issued from the Federal Reserve Bank to all other banks. When it limits those available funds, banks are forced to offer loans at higher rates. This discourages people from applying for loans, which are one cause of the overcirculation of money.

5. **(D) is correct.** According to supply-side economics, government policies should stimulate the economy by increasing the supply of goods and services. Both Ronald Reagan and George W. Bush were strong advocates for supply-side economic policies. In contrast, economist John Maynard Keynes argued that government policies should stimulate the economy by influencing the demand for goods. Thus, to pull the United States out of the Great Depression, Franklin D. Roosevelt advocated massive government spending programs.

6. **(B) is correct.** The Federal Reserve Board has the most direct influence over the economy because it controls the money supply. It is also able to act quickly and decisively because it is a relatively nonpartisan government institution. Some even claim that the chair of the Federal Reserve Board is the second most powerful politician in the country.

7. **(A) is correct.** Antitrust laws were developed at the turn of the twentieth century to check the power of such business magnates as John D. Rockefeller. These laws prevent any one company from monopolizing a particular market.

8. **(A) is correct.** The government exercises fiscal policies through its taxing, spending, and borrowing policies. Increasing agricultural subsidies is a form of government spending. On the other hand, monetary policy is the government's effort to influence the money supply. All of the other response options are forms of monetary policy.

9. **(E) is correct.** Long terms for members of the Federal Reserve Board allow them greater independence. They do not have to appeal to anyone to be reelected, and they do not necessarily have to please the president or Congress once they have been guaranteed a fourteen-year post.

10. **(A) is correct.** The president works closely with the Office of Management and Budget, an executive office, to formulate his budget proposal. The Congressional Budget Office works with congressional committees to review and amend the president's proposal. The tax codes determine how much money the government has to spend, a necessary first step in budgeting.

FREE RESPONSE QUESTIONS

1. Once, the fight in the United States over the economy was between Thomas Jefferson's view of small farmers and Alexander Hamilton's view of an industrial giant protected by high tariffs. Neither man's visions would accurately portray the modern economy of the United States. Today we live in a global economy. One in which we trade freely with other nations, where industries and corporations are no longer bound by geographical and political borders. "Japanese" cars are made in California and Tennessee; McDonalds are open in China and Russia. NAFTA allows the United States, Mexico, and Canada to trade freely, with no tariffs at all between these nations. With growing technology, even jobs can be exported with having to move people around. An X-ray taken at a local hospital is often sent to India to be looked at.

> Definition of global economy, good for 1 point.

The global economy has had both positive and negative effects on the United States. On the positive side, Americans can buy many items at a lower price. Many household goods from shoes to televisions are now sold for much lower prices than they were twenty years ago. With low labor costs in places like China and Indonesia, imported goods are

> An example of a positive impact of the global economy on the United States. 1 point.

An example of a negative impact of the global economy on the United States. 1 point. Total score on this essay, 3 of 3 points.

Correct explanation of monetary policy. 1 point.

1 point for an explanation of how monetary policy can be used.

A correct description of fiscal policy. 1 point.

Taxing and spending are the two main tools of fiscal policy. 1 point.

An explanation of one difficulty in trying to control the economy. 1 point.

A 2nd point earned for this example. Total score on this questions, 6 of 6.

much more affordable. But on the negative side, there is a question of product safety. Last year, there was found to be a high level of lead in many products made in China. These goods had not been properly inspected, and the factories where they were made would not have been allowed to open in the United States due to safety issues. There are also moral questions involved in this global economy. Is it right to pay a company for a product made by political prisoners?

For better or worse, the global economy is here to stay.

2. a) *Monetary policy* is when the government (the Federal Reserve) tries to control the economy by controlling the availability of money. One way monetarism works is through *interest rates*. The Fed can raise interest rates to discourage people from barrowing money, or lower them to encourage barrowing. This will then affect the availability of money.

b) *Fiscal policy* is when the government tries to control the economy through taxing and spending. *Low taxes and high spending* will stimulate the economy (but also drive a nation into debt). High taxes and low spending will slow the economy.

c) One reason it is so difficult for the government to control the economy is that the *budget is made months ahead of time*. Say the government is trying to stimulate the economy by spending more money. Six months later, when the spending takes place, the economy might have already recovered. *Another reason the government has a difficult time controlling the economy is that government spending only accounts for about 20 percent of the economy*. The other 80 percent is the private sector, which may be taking the opposite actions of the government. For example, if the government gives tax breaks to stimulate the economy, but businesses increase their prices, the tax breaks won't have much of an impact.

Chapter 19: Foreign and Defense Policy

MULTIPLE-CHOICE QUESTIONS

1. **(D) is correct.** Nongovernmental organizations such as Greenpeace and Amnesty International form to advance particular causes across nations.

2. **(D) is correct.** U.S. membership in NATO and the UN did not impel the United States to war. The Vietnam War was fundamentally about the U.S. desire to contain the spread of communism. The United States had abandoned isolationism (and the Monroe Doctrine) after World War II.

3. **(A) is correct.** Sanctions brought by only one country against another are doomed to failure because the sanctioned country can simply divert its trade elsewhere. When the United States imposed a grain embargo on the Soviet Union for invading Afghanistan, the Soviets simply bought grain from other countries; only U.S. farmers were hurt by the embargo. Sanctions are thus effective only when a group of countries agrees to impose trade restrictions on a country together.

4. **(D) is correct.** Congressional foreign policy powers include declaring war, ratifying treaties, and confirming ambassadors. Perhaps most importantly, Congress has the power of the purse, which means it controls how much money will be appropriated for foreign and military policies. While Congress raises, organizes, and funds the military, the Constitution specifically states that the president will be commander in chief of the armed forces.

5. **(E) is correct.** The end of the Cold War opened the door for lower spending for national defense. However, defense spending increased once again after the terrorist attacks of 9/11 to provide improved homeland security and to fight the war on terrorism.

6. **(B) is correct.** Isolationism is the doctrine that the United States should stay out of military conflicts in other countries. Isolationism was a central part of American foreign policy prior to World War II. The Cold War is notable for the doctrine of containment, not isolationism.

7. **(E) is correct.** George W. Bush pursued an aggressive foreign policy doctrine to counter terrorism. The Bush doctrine relied on preemptive attacks against terrorists and was later expanded to preemptive attacks against developing threats. The aggressiveness is evident in Bush's belief in unilateralism and American military preeminence. The military-industrial complex refers to the close relationship between the U.S. military and private defense contractors; it would not make sense for Bush to eliminate their close relationship.

8. **(D) is correct.** Although the CIA has a somewhat glorified image of conducting espionage and covert operations, it actually collects most of its data from legitimate sources, such as foreign governmental reports. This information is then used to help make foreign policy decisions.

9. **(E) is correct.** The Vietnam War had a great impact on American attitudes toward government. Americans came to realize that the federal government is capable of lying when it suits the interests of those in power. It also reminded Americans that the United States is not invincible.

10. **(B) is correct.** The president is the chief initiator of foreign policy in the United States. Presidents are aided in foreign policy decision making by several executive branch agencies, including the State Department, the Department of Defense, the National Security Council, and the Central Intelligence Agency.

FREE RESPONSE QUESTIONS

The Korean War would be a correct identification. 1 point.

Containment would count as a rationale for the Korean War. 1 point.

The War in Iraq is part of the war on terrorism. 1 point.

is not easy, but the student's explanation of the continuing conflict is worth a point.

Another point awarded for this description of an argument against the War in Iraq. Total score on this question, 5 of 5.

1. a) A conflict the United States was involved in during the Cold War was the Korean War. The United States became involved in Korea as part of Truman's containment policy. Truman believed the United States needed to keep communism from spreading past its current borders, and that meant keeping communists in North Korea out of South Korea.

b) The War in Iraq would be a conflict the United States was involved in during the war on terrorism. The causes of the War in Iraq are a bit confusing. President Bush said it was to remove any weapons of mass destruction, but few have been found since the invasion. The continuing American military presence in Iraq, however, is considered the frontline for fighting terrorist organizations, according to many.

c) Those who oppose the War in Iraq argue that using force in the Middle East simply creates more terrorists rather than lessening their numbers. They would argue that the United States would be better off fighting the causes of terrorism rather than the already developed terrorists.

One constitutional power is identified and described. 2 points.

A second constitutional power is identified and described. 2 points.

Student correctly identifies and explains one non-constitutional power of the president. 1 point.

2. The Constitution gives the president a great amount of power when it comes to foreign policy. One power the president has is to appoint ambassadors. An ambassador represents the United States to another nation. If the president wants to work to improve America's relations with another nation, the president might send a more diplomatic ambassador. If the president feels he must take a hard-line stance, an ambassador with a different set of skills might be needed. The president can also send the military to strike at an enemy. Reagan used this power to strike at terrorists in Libya. Bush I invaded Panama. Clinton attacked terrorist bases in Afghanistan. Bush II launched invasions of Afghanistan and Iraq.

Along with his constitutional powers, the president can also use non-constitutional powers in conducting foreign affairs. Executive agreements allow the president to make pacts with the leaders of other nations. These agreements do not need congressional approval and therefore are often used instead of treaties.

Two limits on the president's powers are described here. 2 points. Total score on the question, 7 of 7 points.

But there are limits to a president's powers. Presidents cannot declare war. Only Congress is able to do this. The president is also reliant upon Congress to fund military actions. In theory, if the president were acting in a manner that Congress did not like, (such as the invasion of a small nation) they could stop the action simply by stopping the flow of money. This is unlikely to occur, however. Congress does not want to be seen as unsupportive of our troops when they are in harm's way.